Nineteenth-Century
Literature Criticism

Archive Volume

Guide to Gale Literary Criticism Series

When you need to review criticism of literary works, these are the Gale series to use:

If the author's death date is: **You should turn to:**

After Dec. 31, 1959
(or author is still living)

CONTEMPORARY LITERARY CRITICISM

for example: Jorge Luis Borges, Anthony Burgess,
William Faulkner, Mary Gordon,
Ernest Hemingway, Iris Murdoch

1900 through 1959

TWENTIETH-CENTURY LITERARY CRITICISM

for example: Willa Cather, F. Scott Fitzgerald,
Henry James, Mark Twain, Virginia Woolf

1800 through 1899

NINETEENTH-CENTURY LITERATURE CRITICISM

for example: Fedor Dostoevski, Nathaniel Hawthorne,
George Sand, William Wordsworth

1400 through 1799

LITERATURE CRITICISM FROM 1400 TO 1800
(excluding Shakespeare)

for example: Anne Bradstreet, Daniel Defoe,
Alexander Pope, François Rabelais,
Jonathan Swift, Phillis Wheatley

SHAKESPEAREAN CRITICISM

Shakespeare's plays and poetry

Antiquity through 1399

CLASSICAL AND MEDIEVAL LITERATURE CRITICISM

for example: Dante, Homer, Plato, Sophocles, Vergil,
the Beowulf Poet

Gale also publishes related criticism series:

CHILDREN'S LITERATURE REVIEW

This series covers authors of all eras who write for the preschool
through high school audience.

SHORT STORY CRITICISM

This series covers the major short fiction writers of all nationalities
and periods of literary history.

ISSN 0732-1864

Volume 20

Nineteenth-Century Literature Criticism

Archive Volume

Excerpts from Criticism of Various
Topics in Nineteenth-Century Literature,
including Literary and Critical Movements,
Prominent Themes and Genres, Anniversary
Celebrations, and Surveys of National Literatures

Janet Mullane
Robert Thomas Wilson
Editors

Robin DuBlanc
Associate Editor

Gale Research Inc. • Book Tower • Detroit, Michigan 48226

STAFF

Janet Mullane, Robert Thomas Wilson, *Editors*

Robin DuBlanc, *Associate Editor*

Rachel Carlson, *Senior Assistant Editor*

Grace Jeromski, Ronald S. Nixon, *Assistant Editors*

Cherie D. Abbey, Sheila Fitzgerald, Paula Kepos,
Jelena Krstovic, Marie Lazzari, Thomas Ligotti, Emily B. Tennyson, *Contributing Editors*
Denise Michlewicz Broderick, Melissa Reiff Hug, Debra A. Wells, *Contributing Assistant Editors*

Jeanne A. Gough, *Permissions & Production Manager*
Lizbeth A. Purdy, *Production Supervisor*
Cathy Beranek, Christine A. Galbraith, Suzanne Powers, Kristine E. Tipton,
Lee Ann Welsh, *Editorial Assistants*
Linda Marcella Pugliese, *Manuscript Coordinator*
Maureen A. Puhl, *Senior Manuscript Assistant*
Donna Craft, Jennifer E. Gale, *Manuscript Assistants*

Victoria B. Cariappa, *Research Supervisor*
Maureen R. Richards, *Research Coordinator*
Mary D. Wise, *Senior Research Assistant*
Joyce E. Doyle, Kevin B. Hillstrom, Karen O. Kaus, Eric Priehs,
Filomena Sgambati, Laura B. Standley, *Research Assistants*

Janice M. Mach, *Text Permissions Supervisor*
Kathy Grell, Mabel E. Gurney, *Permissions Coordinators*
Josephine M. Keene, *Senior Permissions Assistant*
H. Diane Cooper, Anita L. Ransom, Kimberly F. Smilay, *Permissions Assistants*
Melissa A. Brantley, Denise M. Singleton,
Sharon D. Valentine, Lisa M. Wimmer, *Permissions Clerks*

Patricia A. Seefelt, *Picture Permissions Supervisor*
Margaret A. Chamberlain, *Picture Permissions Coordinator*
Pamela A. Hayes, Lillian Tyus, *Permissions Clerks*

Library of Congress Catalog Card Number 81-6943
ISBN 0-8103-5820-4
ISSN 0732-1864

Computerized photocomposition by
Typographics, Incorporated
Kansas City, Missouri

Printed in the United States of America

Contents

Preface

The study of literature embraces many disciplines, including history, sociology, psychology, and philosophy. To thoroughly comprehend a literary work, it is often necessary to understand the history and culture of the author's nation, the literary movements the author belonged to or disdained, the political passions and social concerns of the author's era, and the themes common to the literature of the author's nation. Thus, to gain a fuller perspective on an author, a student often needs to examine many social, historical, and literary factors.

Many schools reflect the necessity for such a broad view of literature by including historical and thematic surveys in their curricula. In these courses, themes that recur throughout many works of literature are examined, the literary tempers of various historical eras are assessed, and literary and critical movements are defined. Increasingly, comparative literature courses and thematic surveys of foreign literature are being offered by colleges and universities, introducing students to the most significant literature of many nations. In order to provide important information on the variety of topics encountered by the general reader or student of literature, *Nineteenth-Century Literature Criticism (NCLC)* is extending its scope by creating the *NCLC* Archive volumes. Once a year, *NCLC* will devote an entire volume to criticism of literary topics that cannot be addressed by our regular format.

Scope of the Series

NCLC is designed to serve as an introduction to the authors of the nineteenth century and to the most significant commentators on these authors. Since a vast amount of relevant critical material confronts the student, *NCLC* presents significant passages from the most important published criticism to aid students in the location and selection of critical commentary.

Standard volumes of *NCLC* comprise surveys of the careers of ten to fifteen authors who represent a variety of nationalities and genres. The authors selected include the most important writers of the era, as well as lesser-known figures whose significant contributions to literary history are important to the study of nineteenth-century literature. Each author entry represents a historical overview of the critical response to the author's work: early criticism is presented to indicate initial reactions, later selections represent any rise or decline in the author's reputation, and current analyses provide students with a modern perspective. Every attempt is made to identify and include excerpts from seminal essays on each author's work.

Scope of the Archive Volumes

The *NCLC* Archive volumes will enhance the usefulness of the series by examining literary topics that cannot be covered under the author approach used in the rest of the series. Such topics will include literary and critical movements, significant genres, important themes and subjects in nineteenth-century literature, literary reaction to political and historical events, prominent literary anniversaries, and discussions of foreign literatures often overlooked by English-speaking readers. For example, the first *NCLC* Archive volume will examine the principal issues in the study of American slave narratives, a group of writings that flourished during the period prior to the Civil War and that has had a profound impact on literature by many twentieth-century black Americans; the development and characteristics of the *Bildungsroman,* the most important German contribution to the novel genre; the origins, distinguishing features, and influence of French Symbolism, a late nineteenth-century literary movement that is frequently recognized as the source of the modern artistic temper as characterized by formal experimentation and alienation from society; the relationship between opium use and literary creativity during the nineteenth century, a subject that remains of interest from a literary perspective as well as from historical, sociological, and medical points of view; the genesis and aesthetics of the Pre-Raphaelite Movement, which shaped much of the literature and art of Victorian England; and finally, the methodology of the Russian Civic Critics, a small but significant group of literary commentators of the mid-nineteenth century who are often credited with initiating the precepts of socialist realism, today the official doctrine of Soviet art.

The subjects of Archive entries are chosen for their usefulness and timeliness; the length of each entry is determined by the importance of the topic and the amount of criticism available in English. Topics considered in *NCLC* Archive volumes are restricted as much as possible to the period 1800 to 1899, and only literary movements and subjects that had their greatest influence during this period are discussed. In some cases this means that we will include discussion of authors who are covered in *Twentieth-Century Literary Criticism (TCLC)* or in *Literature Criticism from 1400 to 1800 (LC 1400-1800)*. For example, many of the writers associated with the French Symbolist movement lived into the era covered by the *TCLC* series, which studies authors who died between 1900 and 1959, yet the movement was born, had its greatest influence, and came to a close in the period covered by *NCLC*. To ensure a complete discussion of French Symbolism, the editors have included criticism of all important authors associated with the movement, regardless of death dates. However, we have duplicated no criticism from *TCLC*.

Organization of the Book

This Archive volume includes excerpted criticism on six topics. Each subject consists of the following elements:

- The *introduction* briefly defines the subject of the entry and provides social and historical information important to an understanding of the criticism.

- The *criticism* is arranged thematically. Entries commonly begin with general surveys of the subject or essays providing historical or background information, followed by essays that develop particular aspects of the topic. For example, the entry devoted to French Symbolism begins with a section of essays that discuss the development of the movement and its distinguishing features. This is followed by sections devoted to descriptions of Symbolist principles by members of the movement; contemporary appraisals of the movement; the influences that gave rise to the movement; the relationship between Symbolism and Decadence; analyses of Symbolist dramas and Symbolist prose; and the decline of the movement and its influence on twentieth-century writers. Each section has a separate title heading and is identified with a page number in the table of contents for easy reader access.

  The critic's name is given at the beginning of each piece of criticism; when an unsigned essay is later attributed to a critic, the critic's name appears in brackets at the beginning of the excerpt and in the bibliographic citation. Anonymous essays are headed by the title of the journal in which they appeared. Publication information (such as publisher names and book prices) and parenthetical numerical references (such as footnotes or page and line references to specific editions of works) have been deleted at the editor's discretion to provide smoother reading of the text.

- Critical essays are prefaced by *explanatory notes* providing the reader with information about both the critic and the criticism that follows. Included are the critic's reputation, individual approach to literary criticism, and particular expertise in the subject under discussion. Also noted are the relative importance of a work of criticism, the scope of the excerpt, and the growth of critical controversy or changes in critical trends regarding the subject. In some cases, these notes include cross references to related criticism in the entry.

- A complete *bibliographical citation* designed to facilitate the location of the original essay or book follows each piece of criticism.

- *Illustrations* throughout the entry include portraits of the authors under discussion, important manuscript pages, letters, magazine covers, book illustrations, and reproductions of artwork associated with the topic.

- The *additional bibliography* appearing at the end of each subject entry suggests further reading on the topic, in some cases including essays for which the editors could not obtain reprint rights. Where appropriate, the bibliography is divided into two categories: Primary Sources, which lists important creative works discussed in the entry that are available in English, and Secondary Sources, which directs readers to additional criticism on the subject.

An appendix lists the sources from which material in each volume has been reprinted. It does not, however, list every book or periodical consulted in the preparation of a volume.

Cumulative Indexes

Each volume in the *NCLC* series includes a cumulative index listing all the authors who have appeared in the following Gale series: *Contemporary Literary Criticism, Twentieth-Century Literary Criticism, Nineteenth-Century Literature Criticism, Literature Criticism from 1400 to 1800, Classical and Medieval Literature Criticism,* and *Short Story Criticism.* Archive entries devoted to a single author will be listed in this index. Also included are cross-references to the

Gale series *Children's Literature Review, Authors in the News, Contemporary Authors, Contemporary Authors Autobiography Series, Dictionary of Literary Biography, Concise Dictionary of American Literary Biography, Something about the Author, Something about the Author Autobiography Series,* and *Yesterday's Authors of Books for Children.* This index, which lists birth and death dates when available, will be particularly valuable for those authors who are identified with a certain period but whose death dates cause them to be placed in another, or for those authors whose careers span two periods. For example, Feodor Dostoevski is found in *NCLC,* yet Leo Tolstoy, another major nineteenth-century Russian novelist, is found in *TCLC.*

Each *NCLC* Archive volume also includes a cumulative nationality index listing all authors who have appeared in regular *NCLC* volumes. Authors are listed by nationality, followed by the volume numbers in which they appeared.

Subsequent Archive volumes will cumulate a subject index derived from the table of contents to provide users with easy access to the topics covered in the Archive volumes. Titles discussed in the Archive entries will not be included in the *NCLC* cumulative title index.

Acknowledgments

No work of this scope can be accomplished without the cooperation of many people. The editors especially wish to thank the copyright holders of the excerpted criticism included in this volume, the permissions managers of many book and magazine publishing companies for assisting us in securing reprint rights, and Anthony Bogucki for assistance with copyright research. We are also grateful to the staffs of the Detroit Public Library, the Library of Congress, the University of Michigan Library, and the Wayne State University Library for making their resources available to us.

Suggestions are Welcome

In response to various suggestions, several features have been added to *NCLC* since the series began, including: explanatory notes to excerpted criticism that provide important information regarding critics and their work; a cumulative author index listing authors in all Gale literary criticism series; entries devoted to criticism on a single work by a major author; and more extensive illustrations.

The editors welcome additional comments and suggestions for expanding the coverage and enhancing the usefulness of the series.

Authors to Be Featured in Upcoming Volumes

Thomas Carlyle (Scottish philosopher, historian, essayist, and critic)—Carlyle was a central figure of the Victorian age in England and Scotland. Known to his contemporaries as the "sage of Chelsea," he was a satirical and trenchant commentator on the social, spiritual, and political issues of the day. His unique, hard-hitting prose style, which has both infuriated and impressed critics from the nineteenth century to the present, suits the iconoclasm and moralistic fervor of such important and controversial works as *Sartor Resartus, Latter-Day Pamphlets,* and *The French Revolution.*

Emily Dickinson (American poet)—Dickinson is considered one of the greatest and most original American poets. Her numerous short lyrics on the subjects of nature, love, death, and immortality include some of the best-loved poems in the English language.

Feodor Mikhailovich Dostoevski (Russian novelist, short story writer, and journalist)—Considered one of the most outstanding and influential writers of modern literature, Dostoevski is renowned for his acute psychological insight, profound philosophical acumen, and brilliant prose style. In his works, Dostoevski sought to reconcile the spiritual and the physical through his tormented heroes, characters capable of both the highest virtue and the lowest degradation. *NCLC* will devote an entire entry to Dostoevski's great political novel *The Possessed,* which is admired for its striking portrait of the central character, Nikolay Stavrogin, who is possessed by the life-denying forces of nihilism.

Johann Wolfgang von Goethe (German poet, novelist, dramatist, short story and novella writer, essayist, and critic)— Often judged Germany's greatest writer, Goethe was a shaping force in the major literary movements of the late eighteenth and early nineteenth centuries. His first novel, *The Sorrows of Young Werther,* which recounts the despair and eventual suicide of a young artist in love with another man's wife, epitomizes the *Sturm und Drang* movement. This intensely emotional work created a sensation throughout Europe and will be the subject of an entire entry in *NCLC.*

Victor Marie Hugo (French novelist, poet, dramatist, and critic)—Hugo is regarded as one of the leaders of the Romantic movement in French literature. Although he is renowned in his own country primarily for his poetry, he is chiefly known outside France for the novels *Les misérables* and *The Hunchback of Notre Dame.* Criticism of the latter work will form a complete entry in *NCLC.*

Giacomo Leopardi (Italian poet and essayist)—Considered the greatest Italian poet since Dante, Leopardi was influential in formulating Italian Romanticism. His lyric poems, noted for their haunting beauty and intense despair, suggest the illusory nature of human happiness.

John Henry Newman (English theologian and writer)—An influential theologian, Newman was a key figure in the Oxford movement, whose adherents advocated the independence of the Church of England from the state and sought to establish a doctrinal basis for Anglicanism in the Church's evolution from Catholicism. Newman's subsequent conversion to Roman Catholicism inspired his best-known work, *Apologia pro vita sua,* an eloquent spiritual autobiography tracing the development of his beliefs.

Thomas Love Peacock (English novelist, poet, and critic)—Peacock is best remembered for his series of novels satirizing intellectual and artistic thought in England during the first half of the nineteenth century. Considered unique in both form and content, Peacock's novels are especially noted for their erudite, classical style, comic characters, and elements of romance.

Stendhal (French novelist, novella writer, autobiographer, and critic)—Stendhal played an important role in the development of the modern psychological novel. In works that combine elements of both realism and romanticism, Stendhal produced subtle analyses of characters alienated from, yet intimately connected with, their society.

William Makepeace Thackeray (English novelist, essayist, short story, fairy tale, and sketch writer)—Best known for his satiric sketches and novels of upper- and middle-class English life, Thackeray is credited with introducing greater realism and a simpler style to the English novel. While *Vanity Fair* is generally accounted his greatest book, many critics consider *The History of Henry Esmond, Esq.,* a historical novel in autobiographical form, Thackeray's most carefully executed and elegantly written work. *NCLC* will devote an entire entry to *Henry Esmond,* described by Edgar T. Harden as "a work of tantalizing complexity."

Henry David Thoreau (American essayist, poet, and translator)—The most representative and influential of the New England Transcendentalists, Thoreau embodies the spirit of American individualism. The supremacy of the individual conscience over the authority of the state is the theme of his essay "Civil Disobedience," in which Thoreau advocates nonviolent dissent as a moral response to immoral laws. "The most famous essay in American literature," according to Michael Meyer, "Civil Disobedience" will be the subject of an entire *NCLC* entry.

Additional Authors to Appear
in Future Volumes

About, Edmond François 1828-1885
Aguilo I. Fuster, Maria 1825-1897
Aksakov, Konstantin 1817-1860
Aleardi, Aleardo 1812-1878
Alecsandri, Vasile 1821-1890
Alencar, José 1829-1877
Alfieri, Vittorio 1749-1803
Allingham, William 1824-1889
Almquist, Carl Jonas Love 1793-1866
Alorne, Leonor de Almeida 1750-1839
Alsop, Richard 1761-1815
Altimirano, Ignacio Manuel 1834-1893
Alvarenga, Manuel Inacio da Silva
    1749-1814
Alvares de Azevedo, Manuel Antonio
    1831-1852
Anzengruber, Ludwig 1839-1889
Arany, Janos 1817-1882
Arène, Paul 1843-1896
Aribau, Bonaventura Carlos 1798-1862
Arjona de Cubas, Manuel Maria de
    1771-1820
Arnault, Antoine Vincent 1766-1834
Arneth, Alfred von 1819-1897
Arnim, Bettina von 1785-1859
Arriaza y Superviela, Juan Bautista
    1770-1837
Asbjörnsen, Peter Christen 1812-1885
Ascasubi, Hilario 1807-1875
Atterbom, Per Daniel Amadeus
    1790-1855
Aubanel, Theodore 1829-1886
Auerbach, Berthold 1812-1882
Augier, Guillaume V.E. 1820-1889
Azeglio, Massimo D' 1798-1866
Azevedo, Guilherme de 1839-1882
Bakin (pseud. of Takizawa Okikani)
    1767-1848
Bakunin, Mikhail Aleksandrovich
    1814-1876
Baratynski, Jewgenij Abramovich
    1800-1844
Barnes, William 1801-1886
Batyushkov, Konstantin 1778-1855
Beattie, James 1735-1803
Becquer, Gustavo Adolfo 1836-1870
Bentham, Jeremy 1748-1832
Béranger, Jean-Pierre de 1780-1857
Berchet, Giovanni 1783-1851
Berzsenyi, Daniel 1776-1836
Black, William 1841-1898
Blair, Hugh 1718-1800
Blicher, Steen Steensen 1782-1848
Bocage, Manuel Maria Barbosa du
    1765-1805

Boratynsky, Yevgeny 1800-1844
Borel, Petrus 1809-1859
Boreman, Yokutiel 1825-1890
Borne, Ludwig 1786-1837
Botev, Hristo 1778-1842
Brinckman, John 1814-1870
Brown, Charles Brockden 1777-1810
Büchner, Georg 1813-1837
Campbell, James Edwin 1867-1895
Castelo Branco, Camilo 1825-1890
Castro Alves, Antonio de 1847-1871
Chivers, Thomas Holly 1807?-1858
Claudius, Matthias 1740-1815
Clough, Arthur Hugh 1819-1861
Cobbett, William 1762-1835
Colenso, John William 1814-1883
Coleridge, Hartley 1796-1849
Collett, Camilla 1813-1895
Comte, Auguste 1798-1857
Conrad, Robert T. 1810-1858
Conscience, Hendrik 1812-1883
Cooke, Philip Pendleton 1816-1850
Corbière, Edouard 1845-1875
Crabbe, George 1754-1832
Cruz E Sousa, João da 1861-1898
Desbordes-Valmore, Marceline
    1786-1859
Deschamps, Emile 1791-1871
Deus, Joao de 1830-1896
Dinis, Julio 1839-1871
Dinsmoor, Robert 1757-1836
Du Maurier, George 1834-1896
Eminescy, Mihai 1850-1889
Engels, Friedrich 1820-1895
Espronceda, José 1808-1842
Ettinger, Solomon 1799-1855
Euchel, Issac 1756-1804
Ferguson, Samuel 1810-1886
Fernández de Lizardi, José Joaquín
    1776-1827
Fernández de Moratín, Leandro
    1760-1828
Fet, Afanasy 1820-1892
Feuillet, Octave 1821-1890
Fontane, Theodor 1819-1898
Freiligrath, Hermann Ferdinand
    1810-1876
Freytag, Gustav 1816-1895
Ganivet, Angel 1865-1898
Garrett, Almeida 1799-1854
Garshin, Vsevolod Mikhaylovich
    1855-1888
Gezelle, Guido 1830-1899
Ghalib, Asadullah Khan 1797-1869
Goldschmidt, Meir Aaron 1819-1887

Goncalves Dias, Antonio 1823-1864
Griboyedov, Aleksander Sergeyevich
    1795-1829
Grigor'yev, Appolon Aleksandrovich
    1822-1864
Groth, Klaus 1819-1899
Grun, Anastasius (pseud. of Anton
    Alexander Graf von Auersperg)
    1806-1876
Guerrazzi, Francesco Domenico
    1804-1873
Gutierrez Najera, Manuel 1859-1895
Gutzkow, Karl Ferdinand 1811-1878
Ha-Kohen, Shalom 1772-1845
Halleck, Fitz-Greene 1790-1867
Harris, George Washington 1814-1869
Hayne, Paul Hamilton 1830-1886
Hazlitt, William 1778-1830
Hebbel, Christian Friedrich 1813-1863
Hebel, Johann Peter 1760-1826
Hegel, Georg Wilhelm Friedrich
    1770-1831
Heiberg, Johann Ludvig 1813-1863
Herculano, Alexandre 1810-1866
Hertz, Henrik 1798-1870
Herwegh, Georg 1817-1875
Hoffman, Charles Fenno 1806-1884
Hooper, Johnson Jones 1815-1863
Horton, George Moses 1798-1880
Howitt, William 1792-1879
Hughes, Thomas 1822-1896
Imlay, Gilbert 1754?-1828?
Irwin, Thomas Caulfield 1823-1892
Isaacs, Jorge 1837-1895
Jacobsen, Jens Peter 1847-1885
Jippensha, Ikku 1765-1831
Kant, Immanuel 1724-1804
Karr, Jean Baptiste Alphonse
    1808-1890
Keble, John 1792-1866
Khomyakov, Alexey S. 1804-1860
Kierkegaard, Soren 1813-1855
Kinglake, Alexander W. 1809-1891
Kingsley, Charles 1819-1875
Kivi, Alexis 1834-1872
Koltsov, Alexey Vasilyevich 1809-1842
Kotzebue, August von 1761-1819
Kraszewski, Josef Ignacy 1812-1887
Kreutzwald, Friedrich Reinhold
    1803-1882
Krochmal, Nahman 1785-1840
Krudener, Valeria Barbara Julia de
    Wietinghoff 1766-1824
Lampman, Archibald 1861-1899
Lebensohn, Micah Joseph 1828-1852

Leconte de Lisle, Charles-Marie-René 1818-1894
Leontyev, Konstantin 1831-1891
Leskov, Nikolai 1831-1895
Lever, Charles James 1806-1872
Levisohn, Solomon 1789-1822
Lewes, George Henry 1817-1878
Leyden, John 1775-1811
Lobensohn, Micah Gregory 1775-1810
Longstreet, Augustus Baldwin 1790-1870
López de Ayola y Herrera, Adelardo 1819-1871
Lover, Samuel 1797-1868
Luzzato, Samuel David 1800-1865
Macedo, Joaquim Manuel de 1820-1882
Macha, Karel Hynek 1810-1836
Mackenzie, Henry 1745-1831
Malmon, Solomon 1754-1800
Mangan, James Clarence 1803-1849
Manzoni, Alessandro 1785-1873
Marii, Jose 1853-1895
Markovic, Svetozar 1846-1875
Martínez de La Rosa, Francisco 1787-1862
Mathews, Cornelius 1817-1889
McCulloch, Thomas 1776-1843
Merriman, Brian 1747-1805
Meyer, Conrad Ferdinand 1825-1898
Montgomery, James 1771-1854
Morton, Sarah Wentworth 1759-1846
Müller, Friedrich 1749-1825
Murger, Henri 1822-1861
Neruda, Jan 1834-1891
Nestroy, Johann 1801-1862
Niccolini, Giambattista 1782-1861
Nievo, Ippolito 1831-1861
Obradovic, Dositej 1742-1811
Oehlenschlager, Adam 1779-1850
O'Neddy, Philothee (pseud. of Theophile Dondey) 1811-1875

O'Shaughnessy, Arthur William Edgar 1844-1881
Ostrovsky, Alexander 1823-1886
Paine, Thomas 1737-1809
Perk, Jacques 1859-1881
Pisemsky, Alexey F. 1820-1881
Pompeia, Raul D'Avila 1863-1895
Popovic, Jovan Sterija 1806-1856
Praed, Winthrop Mackworth 1802-1839
Prati, Giovanni 1814-1884
Preseren, France 1800-1849
Pringle, Thomas 1789-1834
Procter, Adelaide Ann 1825-1864
Procter, Bryan Waller 1787-1874
Pye, Henry James 1745-1813
Quental, Antero Tarquinio de 1842-1891
Quinet, Edgar 1803-1875
Quintana, Manuel José 1772-1857
Radishchev, Aleksander 1749-1802
Raftery, Anthony 1784-1835
Raimund, Ferdinand 1790-1836
Reid, Mayne 1818-1883
Renan, Ernest 1823-1892
Reuter, Fritz 1810-1874
Rogers, Samuel 1763-1855
Ruckert, Friedrich 1788-1866
Runeberg, Johan 1804-1877
Rydberg, Viktor 1828-1895
Saavedra y Ramírez de Boquedano, Angel de 1791-1865
Sacher-Mosoch, Leopold von 1836-1895
Satanov, Isaac 1732-1805
Schiller, Johann Friedrich von 1759-1805
Schlegel, Karl 1772-1829
Senoa, August 1838-1881
Shulman, Kalman 1819-1899
Sigourney, Lydia Howard Huntley 1791-1856

Silva, Jose Asuncion 1865-1896
Slaveykov, Petko 1828-1895
Smith, Richard Penn 1799-1854
Smolenskin, Peretz 1842-1885
Stagnelius, Erik Johan 1793-1823
Staring, Antonie Christiaan Wynand 1767-1840
Stifter, Adalbert 1805-1868
Stone, John Augustus 1801-1834
Taunay, Alfredo d'Ecragnole 1843-1899
Taylor, Bayard 1825-1878
Tennyson, Alfred, Lord 1809-1892
Terry, Lucy (Lucy Terry Prince) 1730-1821
Thompson, Daniel Pierce 1795-1868
Thompson, Samuel 1766-1816
Tiedge, Christoph August 1752-1841
Timrod, Henry 1828-1867
Tommaseo, Nicolo 1802-1874
Tompa, Mihaly 1817-1888
Topelius, Zachris 1818-1898
Turgenev, Ivan 1818-1883
Tyutchev, Fedor I. 1803-1873
Uhland, Ludvig 1787-1862
Valaoritis, Aristotelis 1824-1879
Valles, Jules 1832-1885
Verde, Cesario 1855-1886
Villaverde, Cirilio 1812-1894
Vinje, Aasmund Olavsson 1818-1870
Vorosmarty, Mihaly 1800-1855
Weisse, Christian Felix 1726-1804
Welhaven, Johan S. 1807-1873
Werner, Zacharius 1768-1823
Wescott, Edward Noyes 1846-1898
Wessely, Nattali Herz 1725-1805
Woolson, Constance Fenimore 1840-1894
Zhukovsky, Vasily 1783-1852

American Slave Narratives

INTRODUCTION

American slave narratives are autobiographical accounts by black Americans describing their experiences in slavery and often their flight from servitude in the South to freedom in the North. While such narratives appeared in the United States as early as 1703 and as late as 1944, critics agree that the genre flourished from the beginning of the abolitionist movement in 1831 to the end of the Civil War in 1865. During this period slave narratives emerged as the key documents in the antislavery cause. As firsthand accounts of enslavement, these narratives exposed the brutality of the chattel system and demonstrated the dignity of black men and women at a time when their very humanity was often questioned by whites. Widely distributed and extremely popular in the antebellum period, slave narratives subsequently lost currency among readers and scholars, who repudiated their historical authenticity and literary worth. A reevaluation beginning in the 1940s, however, affirmed the slave narratives' primacy as historical documents and brought them attention in other disciplines. Currently, slave narratives are acknowledged as a rich source for such fields as anthropology, sociology, folklore, linguistics, economics, and political science. In addition, the slave narrative is now recognized as a distinctive and important literary genre and is the subject of increasing attention from literary critics and scholars.

Critics suggest that the American slave narrative grew out of the tradition of Indian captivity narratives—American settlers' accounts of their abduction by Indians—which were popular from about 1680 to 1760. The first narrative of a slave's life in America appeared in the transcript of a fugitive slave's trial, *Adam Negro's Tryall,* printed in Boston in 1703. Many eighteenth-century slave narrators were Africans, and their stories, including works by Olaudah Equiano and James Gronniosaw, highlight the vivid adventures that befell them after leaving their homelands. At the same time, the narrators imbued these writings with a pious religiosity that led them to accept servitude as God's will, a burden to be borne as an act of faith. These eighteenth-century narrators described the degradation attached to slavery, but overt political protest generally did not enter the narratives until the 1830s. From that time until the end of the Civil War, abolitionists—who were usually white Northerners—encouraged ex-slaves to record their stories and sponsored their publication and distribution. Printed as full-length books, broadsides, pamphlets, and journal articles and letters, the narratives were often "told-to" accounts transcribed by white abolitionists who to varying degrees edited or embellished the texts. After 1865 over sixty book-length narratives appeared, notably those of Booker T. Washington and George Washington Carver, but they lacked the political and popular impact of those appearing before 1865. The largest single group of slave narratives collected were the 2,194 oral histories of elderly ex-slaves gathered in the South from 1936 to 1938 under the federal government's Work Projects Administration. Generally disregarded in literary studies because they were spoken rather than written, these interviews are credited with sparking the reassessment of American slave narratives in the twentieth century. Taking into account both the oral and written versions,

An antislavery emblem that was painted on teacups and embroidered on items sold to raise money for abolitionism.

scholars estimate there are more than 6,000 slave narratives extant.

Critics cite many reasons for the popularity of slave narratives in the antebellum period. Slavery was the most explosive issue of the day, and readers, particularly in the North, were eager to learn more about it. The narratives generally share several characteristics that appealed to popular audiences: a simple, forthright style; vivid characters; and striking, dramatic incidents, particularly daring escapes, such as that by Henry Box Brown, who packed himself into a small crate and was shipped north to waiting abolitionists. Also important in drawing readers, according to critics, was the relatively graphic presentation of violence, brutality, and sexual assault in slave life. Offered to provoke moral outrage, such material also satisfied readers' appetite for sensationalism. At the same time, the narrators' accounts of the struggle to attain freedom and selfhood were underscored by a righteous tone and religious purpose that fulfilled the nineteenth-century demand for moral intent in literature. Because a primary goal of the slave narratives was to obtain the sympathy of white Americans, slave narrators were led to adopt conventional literary values, techniques, and language. A major question facing students of the narratives is to what extent white sponsors imposed their own voices and styles on narrators. A number of narratives, particularly certain "told-to'' accounts by illiterate authors, bear strong marks of their ''editors.'' However, the finest of the slave narratives—such as Frederick Douglass's acknowledged masterpiece, *Narrative of the Life of Frederick Douglass*—maintain a high level of authorial control. Critics stress that the slave narrators' primary defense against the impositions of white narrators was to subvert white literary forms and language through ironic humor and other devices. In fact, a number of critics consider masked intent and deception to be the salient characteristics of slave narratives. Since the most recent burgeoning of black American literature in the 1960s, many scholars have begun to trace the influence of slave narratives on such twentieth-century authors as Charles Chesnutt, Langston Hughes, Richard Wright, Ralph Ellison, James Baldwin, and Alice Walker.

The following entry presents a range of materials and topics pertinent to the study of American slave narratives: the historical and social background that gave rise to the genre; overviews examining literary, historical, and social issues surrounding slave narratives; representative contemporary responses; essays probing a wide array of literary concerns, including language, theme, and technique; inquiries into the narratives' worth as historical documents; eighteenth-century antecedents to the slave narratives of the antebellum period; and the slave narratives' crucial role in the development of subsequent black American literature.

HISTORICAL AND SOCIAL BACKGROUND

MARION WILSON STARLING

[*Starling's* The Slave Narrative: Its Place in American History *is considered the first thorough study of the genre. Originally presented as the author's Ph.D thesis in 1946, the work, while widely regarded as seminal, was not published until 1981. In the following excerpt from the book, Starling describes historical and social conditions in the United States from colonial times until the Civil War that gave rise to the slave narrative. Among the subjects discussed are early attitudes toward slavery, slave insurrections, the first literary depictions of American slavery, and the role of the steam printing press in the development of the abolitionist movement, which led, in turn, to the proliferation of slave narratives in the antebellum period.*]

The autobiographical record of George Washington Carver, published in 1944, is the last of more than six thousand extant narratives of American Negro slaves, the first of which was published nearly two and a half centuries ago, the narrative of one Adam, ''servant of John Saffin, Esquire,'' printed in Boston in 1703. . . . [These] narratives make up an interesting supplement to the literature of the institution of slavery in America, a literature recognized as having special significance as ''a summary of the literature of the world on the subject.'' The group furnishes a continuous record of that institution, from the time that slavery first achieved a definite place in the American scheme until long after the decree to eradicate the system had been officially uttered.

Before 1865, the history of the slave narrative ebbs and flows in the same general rhythm as the history of the antislavery crusade in America. It begins in the wake of the humanitarian efforts of Judge Samuel Sewall of Boston, the publication of whose *Selling of Joseph* in 1701 launched the literature of abolitionism in this country. In the course of the eighteenth

century it eddies about for a time, in company with narratives of the picaresque type. Except for this digression, occasioned by recognition of a resemblance between the career of the swashbuckling slave out for adventure and the then popular ''rake's progress'' literature, the slave narrative is apparently dependent upon antislavery sympathies for its progress.

At the end of the eighteenth century, in England and then in America, it achieves its first literary significance as a vehicle of propaganda in the English abolitionists' campaign, one of the earliest manifestations of the wave of Romanticism sweeping Europe. Its boom years come with the rise of abolitionism in New England, from the 1830s to the 1860s when, as one critic points out, ''the strange anomaly of Negro bondage in the first democratic state became the motive force of a humanitarian protest which may be called the second wave of the romantic movement in the social realm, and which gathered intensity second only to the original agitation for human rights in the eighteenth century.'' By the late 1840s, the slave narrative has become such a popular feature of the antislavery crusade that one contemporary critic, calling attention to its ''very wide influence on public opinion,'' claimed that it represented ''a new department to the literature of civilization,'' which America had the ''mournful honor of adding'' [see excerpt by Ephraim Peabody below]. Another critic, writing in the early 1850s, complained that the ''whole literary atmosphere has become tainted'' with ''those literary nigritudes— little tadpoles of the press . . . which run to editions of hundreds of thousands'' [see excerpt below from *Graham's Magazine*].

After the romantic fanfare that hoisted the literature of the slave into the public eye had died down, however, the slave narrative that was such a fascinating part of the antislavery program of the 1850s, revealing ''the index of [the slaves'] inner life, and of their habits of thought,'' all but vanished from common knowledge. Slave narrative volumes trickled occasionally from the press, passing unnoticed into the vast waters of post-Civil War turmoil. The coming of the scholars' crusade in the middle 1920s, with its goal of formulating a ''usable past,'' brought attention to some twenty slave narratives rediscovered in uncatalogued library deposits, secondhand stalls, or attics. Enlisting the aid of federal subsidies, social historians in the 1930s started projects for collecting slave narratives from the lips of ex-slaves while there was yet time. Interest in the slave narrative gained a place in the 1940s.

Antislavery sentiment manifested itself as early as 1646, when, by order of the Massachusetts General Court, a group of slaves unlawfully brought from Africa was returned to that country at its expense, accompanied by a letter expressing the indignation of the court at the infringement on Massachusetts' laws to end ''bond slaveryie, villinage or captivitie amongst us.'' By 1776 it was an integral part of the spirit of the time throughout the country. The colonists, with Jefferson of Virginia as their scribe, expressed in blistering terms their condemnation of King George III for forcing continuation of the slave trade on them to his profit. The paragraph was struck from the original draft of the Declaration of Independence in deference to the wishes of some rice and indigo growers in South Carolina and Georgia and some owners of slave ships in New England. The discarded clause is a valuable record of the current attitude toward the slavery system, stating, in part:

> Determined to keep open market where men should
> be bought and sold, he has prostituted his negative
> for suppressing every attempt to prohibit or restrain
> this execrable commerce; and that this assemblage

of horrors might want no fact of distinguished die, he is now exciting those very people to rise in arms among us, and to purchase that liberty of which he has deprived them by murdering the people on whom he has also obtruded them: thus paying off former crimes committed against the liberties of one people, with crimes which he urges them to commit against the lives of another.

Slavery was felt to be both an unnatural evil and a nuisance by the eighteenth-century American. Sincere sympathy for the oppressed condition of the slave did not prevent the kind of reaction to the slaves as human creatures that we find in the following candid statement from such an avowed champion of the rights of the enslaved Negro as the Quaker John Woolman:

> The blacks seem far from being our kinsfolks; and did we find an agreeable disposition, and sound understanding, in some of them, which appeared as a good foundation for a true friendship between us, the disgrace arising from an open friendship with a person of so vile a stock, in the common esteem, would naturally tend to hinder it. They have neither honors, riches, outward magnificence, nor power; their dress coarse, and often ragged; their employ drudgery, and much in the dirt: they have little or nothing at command, but must wait upon and work for others, to obtain the necessaries of life; so that, in their present situation, there is not so much to engage the friendship, or move the affection of selfish men.

Benjamin Franklin, while agreeing with Woolman as to the injustice to the slave of the conditions of slavery, and while interested in cooperating with the plans of Benjamin Lay and Anthony Benezet for the abolition of the system, was also personally prejudiced against the Negro as a member of a society of which he was a part. He would not employ a member of that race in his home or his business; and he issued what is probably the first expression of color prejudice in American letters, in a pamphlet entitled *Observations concerning the Increase of Mankind,* which he published in 1755 and which concludes with the following query:

> The number of purely white people in the world is proportionately very small. . . . I could wish their numbers were increased. And while we are, as I may call it, *scouring* our planet, by clearing America of woods, and so making this side of our globe reflect a bright light to the eyes of inhabitants in Mars or Venus, why should we in the sight of superior beings, darken its people? Why increase the sons of Africa, by planting them in America, where we have so fair an opportunity, by excluding all blacks and tawneys, of increasing the lovely white and red? But perhaps I am partial to the complexion of my Country, for such partiality is natural to mankind.

The slave narratives of the eighteenth century all reveal the slaves' awareness of a social prejudice against the slave as a Negro, quite apart from his economic disadvantage at being a slave. What the slaves most frequently wanted to do about it was to get away from the America where even a kindly saint like Woolman and a cosmopolite like Franklin did not welcome him. (pp. 1-3)

Whatever the evil to the slave of the slavery system, however, there were slaves who considered slavery a blessing rather than a curse, because it had been the means of introducing them to the Christian religion. Thus Phillis Wheatley writes, in her panegyric "On Being Brought from Africa to America":

> 'Twas mercy brought me from my *Pagan* land,
> Taught my benighted soul to understand
> That there's a God, that there's a *Savior* too:
> Once I redemption neither sought nor knew.

> Some view our sable race with scornful eye,
> "Their color is a diabolic die".
> Remember, *Christians, Negros,* black as *Cain,*
> May be refin'd, and join th'angelic train.

A like depth of gratitude to the institution of slavery for having brought him to Christ is to be found in the autobiographical portions of the writings of Phillis Wheatley's contemporary, the slave Jupiter Hammon, of the estate of John Lloyd of Queens Village, Long Island. (p. 5)

Slave insurrections, the existence of which is indicated in the clause struck from the original draft of the Declaration of Independence as quoted above, were more prevalent from the time of the American Revolution on than has been known until very recently. An authority lists forty-seven slave revolts between the generally known slave plot of 1741 in New York City and the next generally known slave revolt, the Gabriel plot in Henrico County, Virginia, in 1800—including two in Massachusetts, two in New York, five in New Jersey, five in North Carolina, five in Louisiana, six in Georgia, nine in Virginia, and thirteen in South Carolina. Twenty-four of the insurrections occurred between 1774 and 1799. In September, 1774, John Adams' wife, Abigail, wrote him of the slave plot discovered among the slaves of Boston and the surrounding region, expressing a sentiment held by many persons, in her closing remark: "I wish most sincerely there was not a slave in the province; it always appeared a most iniquitous scheme to me to fight ourselves for what we are daily robbing and plundering from those who have as good a right to freedom as we have." During the period of the American Revolution, there were hundreds of manumissions of slaves by owners who either shared Mrs. Adams's views, or were fearful of slave revolts; also, thousands of slaves seized the opportunity afforded by the commotion attending the revolutionary activity among the colonists, to obtain their freedom by flight and by enlistment in the opposing armies.

It was a period, of course, of worldwide outburst of revolutionary activity. The cry of "Liberty, Fraternity, Equality" of the French revolutionists impressed the American Negroes still enslaved after the American Revolution ended, as representing precisely those things they were deprived of, despite the humanitarian avowals of the Declaration of Independence. Thus anarchic slave projects began to acquire formidable proportions in the newly united states, especially after the revolt of the slave in San Domingo. This revolt, which began in 1791 and brought panic to Southern slaveholders as it strode on through fourteen years of heroic determination to the victorious culmination of an independent Negro republic, became an important subject of conversation in the North and the South and caused an exodus of hundreds of slaveholders from their plantations into cities like Richmond, Norfolk, and Charleston.

The slave insurrections were labor uprisings. From the time of the slave Adam on up through the slave narratives, there are echoes of slave discontent over labor without compensation. Operating as "a commercial system of exploitation" during nine-tenths of the years of its existence and throughout approximately nine-tenths of the area it covered, American slavery was subject to the cycles of prosperity alternating with depression characteristic of any system of private gain dependent upon a world market. Therefore, in times of depression and panic, the slaves were the chief sufferers. Their already meager rations of food and clothing dropped to subhuman standards; slave families were separated as bankrupt slaveholders sold or leased thousands of slaves to other slaveholders; inhuman methods were employed to goad the slaves to maximum production at minimum expense to the owners. The frightful slave insurrection of 1741 in New York City occurred during the severe winter of 1740-41, when suffering among the poor of the city, generally, and among the slaves especially, was acute. Likewise, the severe economic depression of the years 1791-1802, 1810-16, 1821-31, 1835-40, and 1854-56 spanned the years of the most serious slave insurrections, of which one authority itemizes a "minimum list" of two hundred ten reported revolts. Inspirited by such additional factors as the revolutionary philosophy prevalent from the 1770s on through the eighteenth century, or the rapid growth and spread of the equalitarian Methodist religion from 1785, or stirring debates in Congress in 1784 and 1808 and 1820 and 1832-60 over slavery—no amount of counsel from comfortably fixed, mellowly aging Jupiter Hammons could dissuade slavery-maddened young desperadoes from making periodical assaults upon the system. The insurrectionists felt they had nothing to lose, in the first place, unless it be that heaven they had been told about but more or less doubted. Where flight from the system was possible, they fled, by the tens of thousands, to the Dutch, the Indians, the Mexicans, the British armies, the Canadians, the French, the Northern states, the British Isles. Where their masters were willing, thousands of slaves hired themselves out nights or engaged in incredibly ingenious projects for earning money, and bought their freedom from their masters, the prices asked varying from about one hundred and fifty to six thousand dollars, with six hundred dollars as the average amount set. But there were thousands of slaves who could not brook the idea of paying for a freedom that they were learning to believe was the birthright of every man; thousands who thought the dogged labor of a Venture Smith or a Lunceford Lane, working days for the master and nights to earn money to pay the master for themselves, was idiotic. Therefore, they uprose—an estimated fifty thousand at one time in 1800. In that "most important year" in the history of the American Negro slave revolts, Nat Turner and John Brown were born, Denmark Vesey bought his freedom, and the Gabriel conspiracy took place.

The notion that slavery in the North was radically different from slavery in the South seems to have begun with the enthusiastic reception given Crevecoeur's *Letters from an American Farmer,* which that enterprising Frenchman, sometime resident of frontier sections of Pennsylvania and upper New York State and onetime visitor to South Carolina, published in London in 1782, the literary market at that time being very much interested in works having the "common man" and the "noble savage" formula. No earlier record can be found stereotyping slavery above and below the Mason-Dixon line, whereas from that year onward Crevecoeur's sharp differentiation between the nature of slavery "in the Northern provinces" and in the South is to be found repeatedly: the happy condition of the slaves in the former region is contrasted with the barbarous treatment of the slaves in the latter. In the excruciating climax of "Letter XI," his description of the slave suspended in a cage on a plantation near Charleston, South Carolina, to be pecked to death by birds and devoured by insects, became a classic in Europe, after its adoption by the Romanticist Herder for the first of five *Neger-Idyllen,* with the title "Die Frucht am Baume," as part of Herder's *Briefe zu Beförderung der Humanität.* Heralded as "the gospel of humanitarianism," Herder's work spread propaganda for the doctrines of tolerance and humanitarianism through the Europe of the Age of Romanticism. Crevecoeur's picture was later borrowed, via Herder, by Kolb, Kotzebue, and Zameo. The recent discovery that the birdcage story had appeared in French literature as early

as the 1750s casts doubt upon Crevecoeur's having had the actual experience he reports in "Letter XI," especially in view of the fact that the already celebrated story did not appear in the French edition of the book and was withdrawn from subsequent English editions. But it is not necessary to discredit Crevecoeur's having had a firsthand acquaintance with somewhat similar conditions in and around Charleston because of this discovery that the motif for his dramatic climax was borrowed from a known source. The slave narratives include dozens of equally barbarous though not equally picturesque episodes, and it is possible therefore that Crevecoeur decided to substitute the birdcage motif for some revelation of a slaveholder's brutality that he had witnessed that was quite as atrocious but not so effective as literary material. Certainly his description of conditions on a large plantation has an authentic ring when compared with hundreds of other descriptions of large plantations. But whether Crevecoeur was reporting a bonafide experience or not, the generalization that proceeded from his story stuck. Henceforth, the best-known concept on the Continent for Southern slavery was the birdcage episode, accepted as the norm of slave experiences below the Mason-Dixon line, in contradistinction to a purportedly humane state of affairs for the slave above that line.

Contemporary records both corroborate and refute Crevecoeur's label of "happy" for the condition of slaves in the North. Since the majority of the slave establishments in the North consisted of fewer than a dozen slaves, the deplorable degradation characteristic of slave life on plantations, with hundreds or even thousands of slaves, very seldom occurred in the North. The slave narrators Abraham Johnstone, Robert Voorhis, Thomas Cooper, George White, and William Grimes tell of their dread of being sold to plantations farther south than Delaware or Maryland. As early as the 1780s, the stories of the hardships and inhuman cruelties that increased with the size of the plantation had struck the slave on the smaller, Northern farms with horror as he listened to fugitive slaves fortunate enough to escape to the North, where they changed their names and quickly settled down as laborers or craftsmen, although they were always in danger of recapture by their owners. Gronniosaw and Venture Smith, however, in their narratives of slave life in New York and Connecticut in the 1770s and 1780s, provide evidence of exploitation of slave labor by greedy slaveholders that shows that the real basis for a difference between the characteristics of slavery in the North and the South was the number of slave laborers owned and the slave labor expected. Slaveholders who really wanted to make a profit out of such labor, whether in the South or the North, had to engage in or at least countenance drastic methods to force the slaves to produce. Although no slave narratives draw so barbarous a picture of slave life in New England as Timothy Dwight in Part Two of his long poem, *Greenfield Hill,* published in 1792, Dwight gives the title "State of Negro Slavery in Connecticut" to his argument preceding the section, and being an intelligent citizen of Connecticut himself, he must have thought that he knew what he was doing.

One critic of Dwight's treatment of slavery in *Greenfield Hill* stresses the onset of sentimentalism at this time in antislavery literary productions, under the influence of the sentimentalism of European writers. If by "European" he means particularly the English Denham's *Cooper Hill* and the Irish Goldsmith's *Deserted Village,* he is probably right as to literary models. But it is well to remember that the immediate source of inspiration for Dwight's poem was irritation at the reports of European travelers about the United States; that his underlying theme was his "much-lov'd native land"; and that his stated purpose was to contribute both to the amusement of his countrymen and to "their improvement in manners, and in economic, political, and moral sentiments." In his implied comparison of Connecticut's "Fair Verna" and Ireland's "Sweet Auburn," Dwight links the plight of the Connecticut slave and the Irish peasant, the "uncur'd gangrene of the reasoning mind" of the first poem fitting into the "to hastn'ning ills a prey" of the second. (pp. 6-9)

How freely antislavery literature circulated in the state of Virginia we know from the large collection of antislavery pamphlets gathered and annotated by George Washington. The antislavery section of Jefferson's *Notes on Virginia,* emphasizing the evil effect of slavery upon the character of the slaveholding class, was published first in 1784 and passed through seven editions. Judge St. George Tucker, professor of law at William and Mary College, brought out in the late 1790s a thoughtful analysis of the problem of maintaining a system of slavery in a modern world, entitled *A Dissertation on Slavery, with a Proposal for the Gradual Abolition of It in the State of Virginia.* From the 1770s to the end of the eighteenth century, Thomas Jefferson's opposition to slavery and to the slave trade as inimical to the concepts of individual freedom and economic independence had dominated the thought of the South's leading state. But the expanding interests of the slaveholders slowly displaced Jefferson's philosophy in the Southern mind. His agitation for insertion of a clause in the Ordinance of 1784 that would have excluded slavery after 1800 from the entire region from which came Kentucky, Tennessee, Alabama, and Mississippi brought the tantalizing result of defeat by a single vote. Commenting on the defeat, the disheartened Jefferson wrote: "Thus we see the fate of millions unborn hanging on the tongue of one man, and Heaven was silent in that awful moment." Abolition societies had sprung up in the 1780s and 1790s in many cities of the South as well as in the North, meeting annually by representation in the American Convention of Delegates from Abolition Societies, but the increasing danger from slave revolts and increasing dependence upon slave labor in the newly developed cotton culture brought the South gradually to repudiation of Jeffersonian equalitarian doctrines. That Jefferson himself lost interest in continuing the campaign to free the slaveholder of the evil of irresponsible power, as well as his victim, the slave, we may infer from the fact that he found it feasible, in 1814, to apologize for his "reluctance to lead a crusade for emancipation."

Meanwhile, the recurrence of slave rebellions was turning the South into a "huge fortress in which prisoners were held, at hard labor, for life," as far as about one-third of its inhabitants was concerned. By law, all men who were not Negroes became part of a standing army throughout the South after 1800. Militia companies and volunteer military units abounded, patrol duty was demanded of all white men, overseers were armed on the plantations, and guards and standing armies were to be found in all Southern cities. Fear that slaves congregated in common centers would promote further insurrections discouraged the development of industrial centers. Maryland, Kentucky, and Tennessee passed laws between 1796 and 1801 making manumission of slaves easier; but the great plantation oligarchs of eastern Virginia, North Carolina, South Carolina, Georgia, and Louisiana never seriously considered the elimination of slavery. With the phenomenal upturn in financial prospects caused by the sudden spurt in profits from the production of cotton and sugar, by 1805 it was certain to the Southerners that al-

though slavery was a dangerous and unnatural system, it was to be encouraged and fostered rather than abolished.

With slavery disappearing in the North, which lacked such economic complications as the lure of cotton and sugar culture in the South, a tendency to criticize the South began to develop. Cognizance of this tendency can be noted in Jefferson's warning to Governor Monroe of Virginia to proceed as humanely as possible in sentencing the insurrectionists in the thwarted Gabriel plot, with the explanation that the "other states and the world at large will forever condemn us if we indulge a principle of revenge, or go one step beyond absolute necessity—they cannot lose sight of the rights of the two parties, and the object of the unsuccessful one." Therefore sentences of execution were reduced to the thirty-five key slaves in the plot, ten condemned slaves being reprieved and banished before the date set. (pp. 11-12)

There were more than a hundred abolition societies in the South of the 1820s, earnestly laboring in the cause of the slave and ranging in scope from one group's avowed purpose of preventing cruelty to animals to projected plans for the gradual or immediate emancipation of the slaves. Elihu Embree established the country's first abolitionist newspaper in Jonesborough, Tennessee, in April of 1820. Entitled *The Emancipator,* it was a straightforward little sheet, issued from April to October of that year, which presented stories and excerpts from speeches designed to enlist sympathizers with the cause of emancipation. In the winter of 1821-22 a second abolitionist paper appeared in the little town of Mount Pleasant, Ohio, the place in which the founder of *The Genius of Universal Emancipation,* Benjamin Lundy, happened to be at the time. A few months later Lundy found it advisable to move his paper to the "more sympathetic climate" of Jonesborough, where it became a quiet "feeder" for Southern abolition societies, bringing to their attention numerous stories of the effect of slavery upon all members of a slave society, and advocating plans of gradual emancipation. In 1825 Lundy moved his paper to Baltimore, from which city it continued to be published until the end of 1830, when he made the decision to move *The Genius of Universal Emancipation* to Washington—a decision that was indirectly responsible for the most dramatic turn in the tide of antislavery sentiment in America's history.

The Southerners were "extremely, perhaps excessively sensitive" on the subject of slavery, as one enthusiast for developing the art of human relations observed in a thoughtful discussion of the matter in 1823. Recalling the fact that slavery had been established in the country as a national rather than as a sectional practice, and that New England ship merchants had shared with British slave traders the odium of importing the African to America for that purpose, one Samuel Miller of Princeton tried to discourage the growing tendency among Northerners to indulge in "contemptuous or acrimonious language" when speaking of Southern slaveholders. In an address delivered before the Synod of New Jersey, in New-Ark, he asserted that the slaveholders "freely acknowledge the deplorable character of the evil, as it exists among themselves," "lament it," "mourn over it," and give evidence of a desire to "apply some adequate remedy to the acknowledged calamity." Miller advocated promotion of a national effort to bring about gradual emancipation of the slaves, the interim period to be devoted to training the slaves intellectually and morally and building up a trust fund through systematic saving of a portion of the profit from the slave's labor, so that at the time of emancipation he could enter upon life as a freedman with a sum of money sufficient to give him a fair start. (pp. 15-16)

It was not by way of inspiration from reasoned addresses and indefatigable efforts for the adoption of gradual emancipation plans that slavery was destined to be scotched, however, but rather by way of one of the most recent of the industrial inventions revolutionizing the western world, the harnessing of steam to the printing press, which led immediately to the production of journals for the masses. Whereas before the middle 1820s newspapers had been organs of the professional and mercantile classes for the most part, at a subscription cost of from five to eight dollars a year, by 1828 the number of periodicals had more than doubled, the "penny newspaper" began to appear on the city street corner, and the American public launched its campaign for government support and direction of schooling throughout the North and West. The result was that, within a single generation, the ability to read and write passed from the hands of a well-educated few, into the possession of the "most numerous reading public the world has ever known," according to one historian, who adds:

> In the United States, Tom, Dick, and Harry in the thirties and forties hurried to express in print their whole gamut of yearnings, doubts, hopes, and fears, their adventures in intellectual discovery, their remedies for social ills, their preachments against wickedness. It was the most abundant outpouring the nation had ever known and a documentary revelation of the many-sided American mind such as exists for no earlier epoch.

The interests of the masses expanded. The plain people began to take a more active part in intellectual matters, and hundreds of periodicals came into being to satisfy the new curiosities of the semiliterate masses. According to Lowell, "Every possible form of intellectual and physical dyspepsia brought forth its gospel." There were approximately seventy-five labor weeklies, more than thirty temperance journals, and a quantity of religious, scientific, technical, propagandist, professional, agricultural, and juvenile periodicals, in addition to a small group of belletristic magazines. It was by way of this new era for journalism that the crusade that brought the slavery question into the homes and consciousness of the American people was to be waged.

Garrison was the bombshell discovery of the mild-mannered abolitionist editor, Benjamin Lundy, who met him in an editor's office in Bennington, Vermont, in the course of a walking tour which had commenced in Philadelphia for the purpose of soliciting funds for *The Genius of Universal Emancipation*. This was in 1829. Garrison was twenty-three at the time and editor of the *Bennington Journal of the Times*. He had held this position since 1827, and his editorship was marked for intrepid espousal of the cause of the oppressed, with strong leanings toward reform movements. His career as an editor had begun in his home town of Newburyport, Massachusetts, at the age of twenty, with the *Newburyport Free Press*, at the end of a struggling boyhood during which he had helped his widowed mother by working in a Newburyport printer's office and had acquired an education on the side. Garrison had never been South, never had come into contact with slavery, when the itinerant Lundy met the young enthusiast for the rights of the common man, and tapped the dynamite in his being with the revelation that there were in the United States more than two million human beings who, along with their children after them, were denied their natural rights by being held as slaves for life. In a flash, Garrison's whole purpose for living changed, and when Lundy returned to Baltimore, Garrison went with him as associate editor of his abolitionist paper. (pp. 17-18)

For a little while Garrison gave at least lip service to the policy of gradual emancipation upon which Lundy had founded his paper. But by September of 1829 he could no longer hold back his conviction that immediate emancipation was the only possible aim for the abolitionist. In an article under his name appearing in a September issue of the *Genius,* he therefore recanted what he had said in favor of gradual emancipation in the course of an address he had made in Baltimore on July 4 of that year. Each editor wrote under his own name from that point on. Whatever the immediate cause for dissolving the partnership the following year, the irreconcilable difference in attitude toward the position of the slaveholder in the slavery controversy was reason enough for Lundy and Garrison to have agreed to disagree at any moment at all.

Boston was a last-minute choice of a place of publication for the journal that Garrison planned to start, after his breakup with Lundy. Washington had been his earlier choice, because the upper South seemed the logical place for headquarters of any abolitionist campaign. It is a little curious that no words have been devoted to speculation about how much of the tragedy of sectional misunderstanding might have been avoided had Lundy not suddenly decided to move his paper from Baltimore to Washington, causing Garrison to alter his plans and take his paper up to Boston, thinking that the one abolitionist paper would be enough for Washington and gallantly giving up the field to his senior. *The Liberator* in Washington would undoubtedly have got Garrison into difficulties, but it would not have been an innovation there.

In an address, "To the Public," on the first page of the first issue of *The Liberator*, January 1, 1831, Garrison contrasted the interest in abolitionism in the South with the state of apathy existing in the North. The proposals he had issued the preceding August concerning the publication of *The Liberator* in Washington had been hailed in some Southern sections but were "palsied by public indifference" in Northern parts. This reception had influenced Garrison in the final decision to take his paper to a Northern city, as it was more needed by the North than by the South, he had come to believe. His own words here are important:

> During my recent tour for the purpose of exciting the minds of people by a series of discourses on the subject of slavery, every place that I visited gave fresh evidence of the fact, that a greater revolution in public sentiment was to be effected in the free states—and particularly in New England—than at the South. I found contempt more bitter, opposition more active, detraction more relentless, prejudice more stubborn, and apathy more frozen than among slave owners themselves. Of course there were individual exceptions to the contrary.

Garrison deserves a gifted biographer. So much calumny was heaped upon his name by Northern politicians, merchants, bankers, and socialites as well as by the "solid South" that there may be some like the little old lady who interrupted a lecturer on World War I by jumping up from her seat and exclaiming: "I do not *want* the facts! I *know* the Germans started the war!" The facts reveal, none the less, that Garrison's only sin was his quixotism. He singlehandedly fastened the romantic movement to the institution of slavery. Uninhibited by a knowledge of complicating factors involved in the slavery problem, he was able to cut straight through to the core, the outrage to a group of two million human beings. The result was a growing reversal in the popular attitude toward the slave above the Mason-Dixon line, which spread slowly through the five hundred subscribers to *The Liberator* by the end of 1831, who grew in number to 2300 by 1834. Through other anti-slavery journals founded in the 1830s, the audience increased to 1,095,000 different subscribers to the eleven antislavery periodicals established by the end of 1836. Probably completely unaware that advertisements for runaway slaves owned by eighteenth-century New Englanders had repeatedly appeared in Boston papers from the time of the founding of the *Boston News Letter* in 1704 until emancipation in the 1790s, Garrison thought there had been nothing before in the history of humankind so barbarous as the advertisements for runaway slaves that he was finding in the Southern newspapers of the day. A "master of the shears," Garrison would clip an advertisement, copy it in *The Liberator,* indicate its source, and then attack it in terms of the romanticist's emphasis upon the worth of the common man.

> (Commenting upon an announcement of a slave arrested at Palmyra on the charge of stealing) What has she stolen! Why—hem—haw—*she has stolen herself:* SHE IS A RUNAWAY SLAVE. What a horrible sin! And this is the PROOF that slaveholders would ABOLISH slavery if they COULD, but would not manumit a slave on any condition; and if he steals HIMSELF, would pursue him to the ends of the earth, at any expense. This is the *abstract* abolishment of *abstract* slavery. What *abstract,* nay, what *practical* nonsense!
>
> (pp. 18-20)

The fugitive slave Frederick Douglass tells in his narrative of the abrupt change in the attitude of the slave toward his own social condition that was effected by Garrison and his followers. Previously a fugitive slave or an ex-slave had carefully concealed the fact, because "a colored man was deemed a fool who confessed himself a runaway slave, not only because of the danger to which he had exposed himself of being retaken, but because it was a confession of a very *low* origin!" But under the aegis of the Garrisonians, the stigma hitherto attached to the slave condition was supplanted by open-armed welcome as man and brother in some of the most genuinely cultured homes in the land. (p. 20)

The chief weapons used by the abolitionists were the journal, the convention, and the Bible. Offshoots from the Garrisonian stem later chose to include political tactics as part of their equipment, notably James Birney and Gerrit Smith. In the harmonious exhilaration of the early 1830s, however, there was general agreement with Garrison's design of arousing the wrath of the people against the gangrenous evil in existence in the South. With romantic zeal and unreadiness, the Garrisonians lent their imaginations and talents to the gravest problem of the age, which they pounced upon excitedly as their own special job. William Ellery Channing joined Mrs. Child and Edmund Quincy as chief literary aides; Sumner and Gerrit Smith joined John Quincy Adams and Wendell Phillips on the antislavery platform. By 1836, the writings appeared in a dozen antislavery journals at once, and the speeches, often magnificent things, reminiscent of the days of Cicero or of Archbishop Laud, were slathered across the yard-square pages of *The Liberator* as from an endless vat of inspiration, with Garrison wielding the giant ladle. Antislavery societies sprang up all over the North, with headquarters in Boston, New York, and Philadelphia, in which centers quarterly, semiannual, and annual conventions were held beginning in 1833. Gradually the doctrines of the abolitionist leaders began to permeate the masses, helped immeasurably by the publicity given the antislavery journals by irate Southerners "replying" by way of the general

press. Although the churches remained aloof from the controversy, for the most part, the common man reading his Bible aloud at night in the bosom of his family found the verses which the abolitionists were advertising in their crusade, on almost every page of his best-loved chapters. By the time that the fugitive slaves had begun to arrive more or less openly, contributing their speeches to the antislavery meetings and their narratives to the antislavery journals, the interest of the great Northern middle class had been secured. (p. 24)

Fortunately, the slaves knew that they now had somewhere to flee, and they fled. After 1835, there was no need for a Northern editor to toy imaginatively with advertisements of runaway slaves cut from Southern newspapers. The slaves themselves began to arrive, to tell of the terrors from which they had escaped. The figure of the fugitive slave, panting in a swamp, with the slave holder brandishing a whip and surrounded by bloodhounds close upon his heels, became so popular as a symbol that dinner plates were made with the scene for a center motif; the handles of silverware were embossed with the story; the ladies of one Massachusetts town embroidered a bed quilt for Garrison of squares covered with drawings and inscriptions "illustrating the cause;" and the fad even extended to the embellishment of transparent window blinds. . . . (p. 29)

Escape from slavery by means of flight soon became the purpose of many thousands of slaves, in many cases taking the place of the slave's former dream of emancipation, which changing laws in the Southern States rendered a virtual impossibility by the early 1840s. Although about one-half of the separately published slave narratives of this period tell of their author's escape from slavery as young, unmarried men, the overwhelming majority of the total narratives of the period tell of the flight of whole families, of fathers going ahead on reconnoitering trips and braving incredible dangers, including probable death if caught, in their return trips to take their families to some "place" they had found for them. Sometimes a whole plantation would cooperate to conceal the preparations for flight of certain individual slaves for whom life at the hands of the master or overseer was, for different reasons, even less bearable than usual. The record of slaves who refused succor to fugitive slaves is very meagre. A slave asked for help by a pitifully hungry, haunted-looking fugitive would give all he had, even when discovery meant certain flagellation, and his own food allotment barely provided him with the strength needed to keep up with his "task work." The few slaves who betrayed their fellow slaves out of jealousy of their scheme or hope of ingratiating themselves with their masters seem abnormally few, considering the proportionate distribution of such natures in ordinary society. It is possible that there were more of them than the narratives record, but if there were their memory must have been erased by more potent factors.

The antislavery journals teemed with accounts of the slave flights, each of which, like Tolstoi's generalization concerning the unhappy family, had a pattern distinctively its own. There was the slave who, sold from his wife and children, to be sent from Virginia to Louisiana, was successful in escaping from the slave gang, found his way to his family by traveling nights and enduring remarkable privations for concealment in the daytime, hid himself near his family in order to steal one after another of them under cover of night until all were under his care, and then fled with them all to the North. One gigantic black slave battered his way through many trials in his escape with his wife and four children from a plantation near Savannah, Georgia, to the promised freedom of Canada. One slave couple got as far as Indiana from Missouri with their thirteen-month-old baby when they were caught by the pursuers, who shot the baby dead in the mother's arms while the father grappled with them, finally killing the one who had killed the child but having to leave its dead body and flee with the mother, reaching safety, at length, in Canada. (pp. 30-1)

A new interest in clipping advertisements from the Southern newspapers began to engage abolitionist editors as the amount of rewards offered by frantic slaveholders for the recovery of their decamped property began to soar to exciting heights. A reward of fifteen hundred dollars, for example, was offered in the advertisement for the eleven fugitive slaves described in the following excerpt from a Wheeling, Virginia, journal:

> Ran away on Monday night, 23rd instant, from near Wheeling, four large Negro men; named Brace, Andrew, Jack, and Charles; two women, Ginny and Lucy; four boys, George, William, Ben, and Frank; and one little girl, Eliza. Brace and Andrew are both stout and hearty young Negroes, twenty-one or twenty-two years old. Brace is square built, about five feet eight inches high, with two front teeth broken off. Andy is rather spare and rough-boned, about five feet eleven inches high, with large white eyes, one little finger off (about half). Both of these boys have thick lips, and are remarkably dull and awkward in appearance and manners; and the property of Alexander Mitchell. Jack and Charles, aged about thirty-five years. Jack is near six feet high, stout, and rough made, with a stern and determined countenance. Ginny and Lucy, aged from thirty to thirty-three years, both of short and square make, both quite black and thick-lipped, Lucy with front teeth out. Charles is about five feet nine or ten inches high, of light, keen, and sprightly form. The boy George is fourteen years old, bow-legged and stammers when talking; William and Ben about twelve years old; William is lame with a bad sore on his hip from a fall; Frank is about eight years old; the little girl Eliza is younger. The last nine Negroes are the property of Andrew Mitchell and Susan Mitchell. These Negroes have good clothes of various kinds; the small boys generally wore linsey roundabouts and hair caps. Andy, Brace, Jack, Ginny, and Lucy are brothers and sisters, with strong family likeness; there is no doubt but this family will keep together. . . . It is thought . . . that they are headed for Canada.

Theodore Weld conceived the idea of massing such advertisements as the above together, adding to the excerpts already printed in *The Liberator* hundreds of others that he found in the Southern newspapers, and publishing the material as a book, under the title *American Slavery as It is: The Testimony of a Thousand Witnesses, as Taken from Southern Papers*. This book, notwithstanding the fact that its data can be verified as having actually come from the pages of the Southern press, from the *Richmond Enquirer* to the *New Orleans Picayune*, infuriated the Southerner against the "lying" abolitionists with their "viper's brains." It had a prodigious sale, at two dollars a copy, the profits from the sale being dedicated to the relief of fugitive slaves. It was the handbook of the antislavery movement from that time until Emancipation and became such a favorite with Harriet Stowe that she is said to have kept the book in her work basket by day and to have slept with it under her pillow by night.

When the fugitive slave reached the North, he was encouraged to tell of his life as a slave at hundreds of antislavery meetings arranged for the purpose. A behind-the-scenes view of the abolitionists' management of these recitals is given in one of the slave narratives:

> I was generally introduced as a "chattel,"—a "thing"—a piece of Southern property—the chairman assuring the audience that *it* could speak. . . . During the first three or four months my speeches were almost exclusively made up of narrations of my own personal experience as a slave. "Let us have the facts," said the people. . . . "Give us the facts," said Collins; "we will take care of the philosophy."
>
> (pp. 31-2)

[William Wells Brown's narrative,] published at the Boston office of the American Anti-Slavery Society in July, 1847, was in its fourth American edition by June, 1849, eight thousand copies having been sold in the first year and a half of its appearance. By July of 1849, the ten thousandth had been sold. In the same year, the narrative was published in London by Charles Gilpin, with a sale of eleven thousand copies before the end of 1849. Gilpin reprinted the narrative each year until 1852. The London publisher Bennett brought it out in a slightly revised edition in 1853, and the book continued to be reprinted throughout the 1850s. When one remembers Gladstone's estimation in a speech before Parliament in 1852 that not more than about five percent of the new books published in England had a sale of more than five hundred copies, the figures of sale for Brown's narrative take on significance. More important still, his narrative is but one of ten slave narratives published or reprinted in England between 1835 and 1863 that "made" the five-hundred-copies-and-over group. The popularity of the book-length slave narrative was exciting publishers on both sides of the Atlantic Ocean.

Eight of the ten American Negro slave narratives listed in the *British Catalog of Books, 1835-1863* were narratives of fugitive slaves: Brown's *Narrative of William Wells Brown, a Fugitive Slave, Written by Himself*; Frederick Douglass' *Narrative of the Life of Frederick Douglass, an American Slave, Written by Himself*, originally published in Boston in 1845, and also his second version of his autobiography, *My Bondage and My Freedom*, five thousand copies of which were sold within two days of its publication in New York and Auburn in 1855; Josiah Henson's *The Life of Josiah Henson, Formerly a Slave, Now an Inhabitant of Canada, as Narrated by Himself to Samuel Eliot*, published first in Boston in 1849 and then in London by Gilpin; James W. C. Pennington's *The Fugitive Blacksmith; or, Events in the History of James W. C. Pennington, Pastor of a Presbyterian Church, New York, Formerly a Slave in the State of Maryland, United States*, published first in London by Gilpin, in 1849; Moses Roper's *A Narrative of Moses Roper's Adventures and Escape from American Slavery* published first in London in 1837; Austin Steward's *Twenty-Two Years a Slave and Forty Years a Freeman*, published first in Rochester, New York, in 1857; William Craft's *Running a Thousand Miles for Freedom; or, The Escape of William and Ellen Craft from Slavery*, published in London by Tweedie, in 1860; and Samuel Ringgold Ward's *Autobiography of a Fugitive Negro*, published in London by J. Snow, in 1855. The other two slave narratives included the manumitted South Carolinian slave Zamba's *Life and Adventures of Zamba, an African Negro King, and His Experiences of Slavery in South Carolina*, published first in London by Smith and Elder in 1847; and the kidnapped Solomon Northup's *Twelve Years a Slave, Narrative of Solomon Northup, a Citizen of New York, Kidnapped in Washington City in 1841 and Rescued in January, 1853, from a Cotton Plantation near Red River, in Louisiana*, which was published simultaneously in Buffalo, New York, and London in 1853.

Although the *Life of William Grimes, the Runaway Slave, Written by Himself* was published separately in book form in New York as early as 1825, the vogue of the fugitive slave narrative did not set in until the second half of the 1830s, when the Northern abolitionists' curiosity concerning the doings of the slaveholders had risen to the highest pitch. Some two dozen narratives in addition to the eight above listed make up the roster of narratives by popular fugitive slaves. (pp. 35-7)

The immense popularity of the narratives, in the opinion of [Ephraim Peabody], was owing both to the Northerner's curiosity concerning the South and to a "sense of justice" that predisposed men to "hear the testimony given by those who have suffered, and who have had few among their own number to describe their sufferings." He referred to the eight thousand copies of William Wells Brown's narrative already sold; said of Douglass' narrrative that by 1849, "in this country alone," it had passed through seven editions and was at that time out of print; and reported of the fugitive slave narratives in general that they were "scattered through the whole of the North." (p. 37)

The fugitive slaves and their narratives undoubtedly did much to key the country up to the Act of Emancipation of 1863. Writing of the important part they played in the crusade to achieve that goal, a contemporary declared:

> Even now, when it is all over, the flesh creeps, and the blood curdles in the veins, at the account of the dreadful cruelties practised on the slaves in many parts of the South. I would advise no one to read such histories today unless his nerves are very well strung. What was it then when the stories were told by the fugitives themselves? What was it when the cries of the sufferers were going up every hour? When the slaveholders were adding new territory to defile with blood? Under such conditions you could hardly expect from those who knew these facts, moderate language and soft words. The antislavery men were like a cannon ball which flies straight to its mark and shatters everything in its way. They were terribly in earnest, and, like Luther, every one of their words was half a battle.

England joined the New Englanders in honoring the fugitives Roper, Douglass, Bibb, Pennington, William Wells Brown, Henry Box Brown, John Anderson, Henson, Ward, the Crafts, and many others. Between twenty and thirty thousand slaves had fled from the South from the 1830s to the 1840s; at the Fugitive Slaves Convention, over which the ex-fugitive slave Frederick Douglass presided at Casenovia, Canada, in 1855, it was estimated that the number of fugitives then resident in Canada alone was fifty thousand. Except in Canada, where the fugitives settled down into more or less normal pursuits to earn their livelihood, lecturing seemed to be the chief means of subsistence that came into the fugitive's mind, whether or not he had ever heard a lecture in his life before. Hoping to stem a tide that could only lead to distressing conditions, William Wells Brown sent a message by way of *The Liberator* in 1851 to slaves planning to come to England:

> Too many of our fugitive brethren are of opinion that because they can tell, by the fireside, the wrongs they have suffered in the prison house of slavery, that they are prepared to take the field as lecturers. And this being the fact, there are numbers here [London], who have set themselves up as lecturers, and

> who are, in fact, little less than beggars. . . . I would say to our fugitive brethren, if you don't want to become beggars, don't come to England.

The warning was timely, as the spectacular triumphs abroad of Brown, Douglass, Pennington, Ward, and, later, Henson, had filled with luckless aspirations the minds of thousands with lesser endowments.

The publicity and the opportunities given a few hundred of the thousands of slaves who fled from slavery from the 1830s to the 1860s greatly furthered the abolitionists' program, demonstrating the fact that many slaves were not only normally capable of behaving like human beings, but were even demonstrably superior to average men, especially in consideration of the fact that they had grown to manhood before even the barest rudiments of an education were available to them. The role of these slaves was a curious one, however, combining the features of stunt performers, star witnesses, and charity patients. The embarrassment to traveling Southerners caused by the overt attention paid slave lecturers in New England, on the high seas, all over the British Isles, and even at the Peace Conference at Paris engendered a hatred of the slave in some quarters where it had not existed earlier. Also, to the abolitionist, the slave was likely to be viewed more as a specimen with propagandist value than as an ordinary human being. (pp. 38-40)

It was to . . . [the dedicated New England abolitionists] that the slave narrator owed his opportunities in the most important period of the history of his literary efforts. The Act of Emancipation ended that heyday. There was to be no romantically "repentant Republic" at his feet. Nor was the tone of the American Negro's story to change appreciably. Between the *Narrative of the Life of Frederick Douglass, an American Slave, Written by Himself,* published in 1845, and Richard Wright's *Black Boy,* published in 1945, there are curious similarities, considering the hundred years' distance in time. Repetition of the popularity of autobiographies of American Negroes in general recalls a recent critic's observation that the literary crusade today is "not unlike that conducted by abolitionist writers in the period between 1830 and 1860." Johnson's *Along This Way* (1933), Langston Hughes's *The Big Sea* (1940), DuBois's *Dusk of Dawn* (1940), and Redding's *No Day of Triumph* (1942) are enjoying with *Black Boy* a popularity that shows that America is again interested in the subjective record of the Negro within its bounds. (p. 49)

Marion Wilson Starling, in her The Slave Narrative: Its Place in American History, *G. K. Hall & Co., 1981, 363 p.*

INTRODUCTORY OVERVIEWS

GILBERT OSOFSKY

[Osofsky delineates the central concerns presented in slave narratives and asserts their value as a true record of life under the chattel system.]

The slave narratives are tales of bondage and freedom written or told by former slaves. There are many thousands of such narratives if one includes the stories of fugitives collected by antislavery advocates and published in the abolitionist press, or those gathered for publication in nineteenth- and twentieth-century documentary accounts. Brief descriptions of slavery from the mouths of those who lived it appear in many nineteenth-century books, such as William Still's *The Underground Rail Road* (1883), Levi Coffin's *Reminiscences* (1876), Benjamin Drew's *North-Side View of Slavery* (1856), Lydia Maria Child's *Isaac T. Hopper: A True Life* (1854), Wilson Armistead's *A Tribute for the Negro* (1848). The WPA slave-narrative collection in the Library of Congress runs to seventeen volumes. Perhaps most remarkable of this extensive literature are the four-score full-length autobiographies of slaves published before the Civil War. These books are the main focus of this essay.

A literature so diffuse obviously varies widely in style, purpose, and competence. Some books are works of enduring value from a literary as well as "protest" perspective. The autobiographies of Frederick Douglass, Henry Bibb, and Solomon Northup fuse imaginative style with keenness of insight. They are penetrating and self-critical, superior autobiography by any standards. The quality of mind and spirit of their authors is apparent.

Because the best narratives reflect the imaginative minds of the most gifted and rebellious slaves, their value as reliable sources for the study of slavery has been questioned. To doubt the relevancy of autobiographies written by exceptional slaves, however, is a specious argument in its inception. The great slave narrative, like all great autobiography, is the work of the especially perceptive viewer and writer. In describing his personal life, the sensitive and creative writer touches a deeper reality that transcends his individuality. Frederick Douglass, for example, was certainly an exceptional man, but his autobiography has much to teach us about the slaves around him, his friends and enemies on the plantation and in the city, and many other typical aspects of American slavery. Douglass is gibingly critical of the weaknesses of many of his fellow slaves. He derides those who adopted the master's code of behavior, those who fought for the baubles and goodies used as rewards and bribes, and those who dissipated their energy in wild sports and drinking bouts during holidays. Douglass presents a many-sided depiction of the slave experience—his is no papier-mâché book or antislavery tract. The historians who fail to use such a book or the narratives of a Bibb, a Brown, a Northup, or a Samuel Ringgold Ward because they are "exceptional" men might as well argue that Claude Brown and Eldridge Cleaver are unsuitable commentators on today's ghetto. To exclude the "exceptional" is to eliminate all strong autobiography as a distortion of the events of its time. Yet it is these writers whose books are most likely to interpret reality with insight and clarity.

The majority of slave narratives, like most autobiographies, are more parochial and weaker in literary quality. Many are confused. A blatant illustration is the rambling memoir of that delightful character William Grimes ("Old Grimes"), who escaped from Georgia, settled in New Haven, and became a handyman and general factotum to students at Yale. In his poorly organized tales, ends of stories precede beginnings, detailed descriptions of many jobs (horse trader, barber, gambler, waiter, laborer, pimp, grocer) and of his legal difficulties are presented in confusing bits and pieces, and at one juncture an unexplained wife arrives on the scene.

Volumes compiled to raise money in the North for the purchase of relatives in slavery, such as the autobiographies of Lunsford Lane and Noah Davis, were written hurriedly and hawked from door to door. As their books demonstrate, these authors were men of unusual ability and integrity, but they had little time

for leisurely reminiscing or training in literary style. Lane, for example, worked around the clock to raise money for the food and freedom of his family. He simultaneously sold tobacco, pipes, and lumber, ran a hauling service, and labored as a domestic. Another author of a narrative, Davis, was a slave shoemaker and preacher who learned letters by copying customers' names from the shoes he repaired and passages from the New Testament. Their life stories abound with accounts of their own response to slavery and the experiences of others. The very shortcomings of their books as literature in part testify to their authenticity as historical sources. The style of their books is a product of their schooling.

A number of slave narratives are of such doubtful validity that they may be shelved at the start. When the authenticity of a "memoir," *The Narrative of James Williams* (1838), dictated by one black man to the Quaker poet John Greenleaf Whittier, was questioned, Williams was nowhere to be found. The book was withdrawn from publication. Williams seems to have been a free Negro who culled stories from neighbors and invented others for a little ready cash. The antislavery press is full of warnings against such bogus fugitives. Two other books, *The Slave: Or the Memoirs of Archie Moore* (1836) and *The Autobiography of a Female Slave* (1856), were works of antislavery fiction. The first was written by the American historian Richard Hildreth; the second was composed by Mattie Griffith, the white daughter of a Kentucky slaveholder. Such potential hoaxes led to careful investigation of the stories fugitives wrote for publication. Narrators were subjected to detailed questioning by committees of knowledgeable people; letters were written to former masters and neighbors for corroboration. A tale so seemingly improbable as the life of Henry Bibb led to an extensive correspondence with white Southerners, all of whom verified Bibb's account—the improbable was the real. Solomon Northup's fantastic experiences were verified by a basketful of legal documents.

Because few slaves were literate enough to write their names, much less their autobiographies, and were thus forced to rely on amanuenses, usually abolitionists, scholars have rightly wondered where the slave's experience began and that of the antislavery recorder left off. Some have maintained that the typical slave narrative is so doctored that all are suspect as sources. Ulrich B. Phillips, for example, believed that most narratives "were issued with so much abolitionist editing that as a class their authenticity is doubtful."

We should be wary of such sweeping generalizations that assign the majority of surviving books to the trash heap. Phillips cited the reminiscences of Josiah Henson as a prime instance of an unreliable slave narrative. My own analysis indicates that in the early editions it is an honest autobiography. Henson became a leader among the fugitives in Canada and received widespread coverage in the antislavery press. Many abrasive news stories resulted from his serious break with the Garrisonian abolitionists on the question of emigration to Canada but none questioned the authenticity of his autobiography. . . . No scholarly or social purpose is served by assuming such narratives, *a priori*, to be unreliable sources.

The most obviously false accounts readily give themselves away. The Preface to the life of the militant black abolitionist and fugitive slave J. W. Loguen, for example, relates how the author who recorded Loguen's experiences invented transitional incidents to tie together what seemed to him a disjointed account. He gave an appearance of coherence to his story and destroyed its credibility in the process. Elleanor Eldridge's

A slave couple in their quarters.

amanuensis, after the manner of third-rate contemporary fiction, spiced her book with imaginary and gushy romances. Innumerable paragraphs exhort the reader to sympathize with the trials of the lowly as they would with the meanderings of kings and queens. In other lurid tales of suffering and woe and torture, cruelty after shocking cruelty appears with such deadening regularity that one easily recognizes the presence of a morality play, not the record of a human life. What the nineteenth century called ''shame-shame'' is pervasive in many narratives. (pp. 9-14)

Nevertheless, the simple stories of slave life in most narratives, with their unembroidered descriptions of plantation activities, camp meetings in the woods, and many other aspects of daily routine, are striking in the consistency of themes that appear among individuals who lived on widely separated plantations, in different states, and in different decades. A coherent pattern of slave life emerges in these diverse testimonies, yet most of our present historical accounts of slavery exclude or underestimate the significance of these themes. Our histories have been written primarily from the surviving manuscript records of slaveholders and therefore tend to reflect the concerns and biases of the master caste. The witnesses who wrote or dictated

narratives must be heeded if a balanced account of the history of slavery in the United States is to be written.

To understand the narrative literature it is important to keep in mind the relative ease of *occasional* escape from the plantation. The narratives are replete with stories of slaves who ran off to hide in woods and swamps, thereby escaping slavery for at least some portion of their lives. The frequency of such stories in slave autobiographies makes clear that running away was a common means of black protest and rebellion against slavery.

Repeatedly slaves speak of leaving in fear of sale or transportation to the Deep South, or as a means of protest against unusually brutal and unjustified physical punishment, or in an attempt to find friends, husbands, wives, children, and parents who were sold to a new master or sent to a different section of the country. It was not only possible for slaves to escape and hide out for long periods of time, but the more skillful could also remain away almost as long as they chose. All the narrators are wise in the ways of nature, knowledgeable in animal lore and in techniques for foraging and living off the land. They often arranged to contact friends and family on the plantation to supply them with food on secret visits. (pp. 14-15)

One of the most illustrious slaves in American history, Nat Turner, took to the woods after his revolt collapsed and devised ingenious ways of avoiding capture. He burrowed into the earth, skillfully camouflaged his hideout with materials gathered in the forest, found ways to round up food, and emerged only at night. Though the entire slave South was on the lookout for him, Turner lived in this way—comfortably, he said—for about eight weeks. He was finally discovered by accident when a hunting dog strayed into his hideaway for a piece of meat. If Nat Turner could remain hidden for so long with an army of searchers on his trail, less valuable prey had an even better chance to go undetected.

The relative ease of occasional escape *within* the plantation South must be contrasted with the difficulty of escape to freedom in the North. Narrators tell us that most slaves on plantations lacked a sense of geography and a knowledge of the outside world. Even a man as inquisitive as Frederick Douglass admitted that there was a time in his life when he hadn't heard of the North; he learned about the abolitionists only by accident. One of John Brown's admirers and followers, James Redpath, who interviewed numbers of slaves, expressed amazement at their lack of geographical knowledge. Redpath met slaves who had never heard of Europe, did not know their own states, and could not tell him the terminus of the railroad that ran by their own locality. (pp. 16-17)

Many narrators blame such ignorance on practiced deceit by their masters; they argued that the master caste consciously exploited slave ignorance and gullibility for its own advantage. There is abundant evidence in the narratives to demonstrate at least the partial truth of that charge. One slave asked his master who abolitionists were, and was told that they rounded up slaves for sale in Deep South markets. One of Harriet Tubman's major tasks during the Civil War was to counsel plantation blacks that it was safe to board Northern gunboats. Numbers of slaves had been encouraged to believe that Yankees were cannibals who looked upon them as tasty morsels. . . . Leonard Black said derisively that " 'Slaves are taught ignorance as we teach our children knowledge."

In the deepest sense the entire South was a prison house, and all white men, solely because of their skin color, were prison keepers. By law and custom every white was permitted to stop any black along the road and ask him to present his pass or freedom papers or explain why he was away from the plantation. To collect the reward on a fugitive or perhaps claim the person of a slave whose master could not be located must have been enticing bait for the poor whites who patrolled the Southern countryside. A good catch not only seemed a fulfillment of one's communal responsibility but also might mean instant wealth. The most thrilling passages of slave autobiographies deal with strategies fugitives used for handling or avoiding such confrontations with whites. (pp. 18-19)

Further, slaves had to avoid "guards," both black and white. Most slaves and free blacks in the narratives were willing to assist fugitives, but certain black Judases sabotaged the escape plans of many. Henry Bibb's schemes were exposed at least four times by black traitors; the escape plans of Leonard Black, Frederick Douglass, and John Little were revealed by fellow Negroes, Black's by his closest friend. Little was betrayed by a free black who received a ten-dollar reward for his service. James Adams of Virginia said he feared to tell even his father and mother of his plans to leave. (p. 19)

This barrier to escape poses a limitation of the use of slave narratives as sources. Most though not all of the books were written by men and women who were closest to free territory and who escaped from the Border States, not the Deep South: few escaped permanently from plantations in Louisiana, Mississippi, and Alabama. Solomon Northup, Henry Watson, Peter Still, and Henry Bibb all describe parts of their lives spent in the heartland of the cotton-producing South, but these accounts are not typical. It is unfortunate for comparative purposes that we have so few descriptions of slavery as slaves saw it in the Deep South. The efficient slave control that choked off routes of escape also blocked history's access to full understanding of black bondage in America.

Successful fugitives passed through chinks in the wall of the closed society. It was an article of lore, repeated in most slave autobiographies, that the best time to plan a permanent escape was on a Saturday night or during some holiday when slaves were on the move on visits and fugitives were, therefore, least likely to be detected. Even to conceive the possibility of escape under these conditions required a special quality of mind: imagination, independence, cunning, daring, and a sense of self-pride. It required a strategic appearance of obedience to their masters, like seeming most satisfied at the moment they were most discontented. . . . It called for the use of subtle psychological weapons. It demanded all the shrewdness and practiced deceit one finds in such abundance in the rich folklore of Old John, the symbolic slave hero who mastered the art of tricking "Ole Massa," of fooling him, of "puttin' him on."

The narratives permit a measure of access to the privacy of the mind of a slave and the conversations that took place in the slave cabin. No adequate analysis can be made of the much debated question of the impact of slavery on the personalities of bondsmen without hearing the stories slaves told one another when their owners were not around. As such they are crucial evidence of the ideas that passed through a slave's consciousness, his mind, if not his mouth. Such stories, crammed with aggressive humor—and wit is one of mankind's most useful aggressive tools—reveal the difficulty of enslaving a man's mind as one has enslaved his body. Lewis Clarke, a slave who recorded much of this inside humor, said he would not vouch for the truth of many anecdotes, but they were tales "slaves delight to tell each other." Many of the tales are surely apocryphal in a technical sense—they probably refer to things slaves wished to say as well as to the things they said.

Some slaves undoubtedly felt loyalty and affection for their owners, but the stories of fugitives describe even this relationship as one of ambivalence. Slaves often held two overlapping attitudes: a willingness to accept life with an owner who treated them fairly, an *entente cordiale* rather than a feeling of serious devotion; and a private sense of irreverence for many of their master's ideas. This irreverence was the subject of much slave humor.

Peter Randolph, one of sixty-six slaves emancipated on the death of their owner, told a story he had overheard on his plantation in Virginia. The following conversation is said to have occurred between the slave Pompey and his master, as the slaveowner prepared to fight a duel:

Pompey, how do I look?

O, massa, mighty.

What do you mean "mighty," Pompey?

Why, massa, you look noble.

What do you mean by "noble"?

Why, sar, you just look like one *lion*.

Why, Pompey, where have you ever seen a lion?

I see one down in yonder field the other day, massa.

Pompey, you foolish fellow, that was a *jackass*.

Was it, massa? Well you look just like him.

It is quite unlikely that this confrontation took place as Pompey remembered it, but it is not unreasonable to assume that he wished it had, or thought of saying such things, or told other slaves like Randolph that he had replied in this manner. That the slaves told such stories to one another is a clue to their state of mind—and there are numbers of similar examples in the narrative literature.

Lewis Clarke of Kentucky recalled meeting two slaves sent out to dig a grave for their departed owner and recounted their conversation at the gravesite:

> Two slaves were sent out to dig a grave for old master. They dug it very deep. As I passed by I asked Jess and Bob what in the world they dug it so deep for. It was down six or seven feet. I told them there would be a fuss about it, and they had better fill it up some. Jess said it suited him exactly. Bob said he would not fill it up; he wanted to get the old man as near *home* as possible. When we got a stone to put on his grave, we hauled the largest we could find, so as to fasten him down as strong as possible.
>
> (pp. 20-2)

The ultimate in irreverences was the occasional letter fugitives sent to former masters after they had successfully "taken the long walk." (p. 23)

Milton Clarke taunted his owner with a note from Oberlin telling him not to worry too much about his ex-slave or the loss of the two hundred dollars a year Clarke paid him for the right to hire his own time (find self-employment): "he had found by experience he had wit enough to take care of himself, and he thought the care of his master was not worth the two hundred dollars a year which he had been paying for it, for four years; that, on the whole, if his master would be quiet and contented, he thought he should do very well."

A considerable portion of most slave narratives deals with the methods of escape. The narrative literature probably acquired some of its popularity in the 1840's and 1850's because of the excitement of these tales. The melodrama and romance of the escape—the elements that Harriet Beecher Stowe skillfully weaves into *Uncle Tom's Cabin*—are less significant, however, than the evidence of the demands of courage and imagination required for execution of a successful escape plan. Such shrewdness and guile were characteristic of slave response in other less dramatic aspects of the plantation experience. For many slaves deception was a socially useful weapon of survival.

A number of the most impressive stories of practiced deceit deal with stealing food. As Eugene D. Genovese has shown in his brilliant analysis of the plantation economy, it was difficult to supply bondsmen with a nutritionally balanced diet that would satisfy the body needs of hard-working laborers. Slaves who were hungry, therefore, stole food; others undoubtedly also found thieving satisfying as a form of aggression and revenge. Inventiveness was necessary if one was to avoid detection. Aunt Peggy, for example, was an artist at stealing little pigs. One day the "Philistines were upon her" as she was boiling her catch in a large kettle. Peggy put a door on the kettle, seated her daughter on the door, covered the young

girl with a heavy quilt, and told the inquisitive overseer the child had a heavy cold and was taking a steam bath. (pp. 24-5)

Cunning and intelligence had to be concealed. Numbers of slaves who appeared *too intelligent* were sometimes difficult to sell: they were assumed to be troublesome. A man as perceptive and enterprising as Lunsford Lane devoted as much effort to hiding his abilities as he did to raising money to buy his family out of slavery. Lane always wore shabby clothing and looked very poor, as he hid every penny he earned. He told no one but his wife how much money he had saved. (p. 25)

Fugitive slaves honed the art of pretense into a sharp-edged tool of self-defense. There are innumerable stories of women who pretended to be men and men who made wigs of horses' manes to dress as women, or wore false beards. An amazing use of disguises permitted William and Ellen Craft to get to Boston, and their story became familiar throughout the North. Numbers of light-skinned slaves passed for whites, some audaciously stopping at the best restaurants and hotels to exchange gossip on the price of land, cotton, and slaves. A man like Douglass simply pretended to be free and got away with it. (p. 28)

Ingenuity, deception, courage, and aggressive humor also pervade the stories of slave religious attitudes and behavior. Some of the most impressive passages in the autobiographies deal with the slave's quest for meaningful spiritual guidance.

Many fugitives were men of piety and unbending social standards. Lunsford Lane's father, Edward, was noted as "a man of prayer," and his son as well. Lunsford read scripture with regularity, attended church as often as he could, and was Puritanical in personal behavior. Noah Davis, William Troy, R. S. W. Savrick, Alexander Hemsley, Dan Josiah Lockhart, Daniel West, Eli Johnson, and Josiah Henson were slave preachers, "professors," "exhorters." (p. 30)

Many narrators went to school to become clergymen after they acquired their freedom: J. W. C. Pennington, Peter Randolph, J. W. Loguen, Josiah Henson, Noah Davis, Samuel Ringgold Ward. Perhaps the most well-known fugitive of his generation, Anthony Burns, is a perfect case in point. The attempt to free Burns after he escaped to Boston in 1854 and the subsequent battle to return him to slavery electrified the North. Burns, as a slave, was a devout man, a Baptist preacher who tried "to lead his fellow-servants to a knowledge of the Redeemer." When Burns acquired his freedom he delivered a speech in the Reverend Dr. Pennington's church in New York City in which he described how Christ came to him as a young boy. "Until my tenth year I did not care what came of me," he said, "but soon after I began to hear about a North, and to feel the necessity for freedom of soul and body." (pp. 30-1)

It is essential that this sense of piety among slaves be separated as a concept from the attitudes bondsmen expressed toward the kind of religious fare they often received on the plantation. For centuries slaves had been admonished to put to memory and soul those portions of the sacred books which advised servants to be especially obedient to their masters. Henry Watson paraphrased the typical sermon he heard at Vicksburg (before Grant):

> Suppose you do not deserve it, or at least do not deserve so much punishment for the fault you committed, you perhaps have escaped a great many more, and are at last paid for all. Or, suppose you are quite innocent of what is laid to your charge, and suffer wrongfully in that particular thing; is it not possible

you may have done some other bad thing which was never discovered, and that Almighty God, who saw you doing it would not let you escape without punishment some time or another? And ought you not in such a case to give glory to him, and be thankful that he would rather punish you in this world for your wickedness than destroy your soul for it in the next? But, suppose that this even was not the case,—a case hardly to be imagined; and that you have by no means, known or unknown, deserved the correction you have received, there is this great comfort in it, that if you bear it patiently and leave your cause in the hands of God, he will reward you for it in heaven; and this punishment you suffer unjustly here, shall turn to your exceeding great glory hereafter.

(pp. 31-2)

The narrators tell us some slaves accepted such gospel, but they also say considerable numbers of bondsmen thought such preaching was hypocritical perversion of holy scripture. White preachers were described by one slave as men with "God in the face, and the devil in the heart." Independently of one another, and from different sections of the South, many slave narrators also recorded these sermons in order to mock them. Andrew Jackson, Harriet Jacobs, John Thompson, Frederick Douglass, Peter Randolph, Lunsford Lane, and Solomon Northup, independent of one another, ridiculed the supposedly devout preacher and slaveholder as hypocrites. In his earliest years as an antislavery lecturer Frederick Douglass convulsed Northern audiences by derisively mimicking sermons he had listened to: "Oh, consider the wonderful goodness of God! Look at your hard, horny hands, your strong muscular frames, and see how mercifully he has adapted you to the duties you are to fulfill!. . . while to your masters who have slender frames and long delicate fingers, he has given brilliant intellects, that they may do the thinking while you do the working." (p. 33)

[Many] slaves, repulsed by indigestible spiritual admonitions to embrace their suffering, sought guidance elsewhere. Some confined their religion to their private lives and transformed it into an institution which the master caste might notice, or poke fun at, or bring visitors to see, or try to stifle—but which flourished nonetheless. In place of listless sermons black preachers offered slave congregations soul-shaking and personally satisfying spiritual messages. The gospel, as preached in the more formal slaveowner-dominant Christian services, "was so mixed with slavery," a freedman suggested, "that the people could see no beauty in it, and feel no reverence for it." Nancy Howard said she prayed for her owners because they didn't know how to read scripture right. (p. 34)

The narrators describe a variety of masterful tactics improvised by slaves to satisfy their spiritual hunger, to release their emotional energy, to experience the "whole gospel," the "free gospel." On one Louisiana plantation slaves would attend the standard service in the morning and then assemble in one another's cabins in the afternoon for an all-black gathering, with a black pastor. Most of the stories that have come down to us refer to slipping away at night and holding meetings in the secrecy of the woods. (pp. 34-5)

It was important to keep these prayer meetings concealed. Often women would wet down old quilts and rags to prevent sound from carrying in the distance, and hang them on trees and bushes to create the atmosphere of a room. Behind these drapes, slaves would huddle to pray and sing. At some meetings, the slaves lay prostrate with their faces close to the ground, "so that no sound could escape to warn the master or the overseer." (p. 35)

Elements of the demonic and superstitious fused with slave religion. Witches, as in African and European folklore, were said to ride people at night, and entered into the stories slaves told one another. Slaves had faith in dreams and messages from the Lord. The archetype of such conviction was Harriet Tubman, who lived only partially in the world of her present and mostly in some trancelike contact with what she conceived as the eternal verities. The writer who recorded her autobiography mentions dozens of dreams revealing Harriet Tubman's prescience. . . . (p. 37)

Harriet Tubman's faith in the spiritual guidance of dreams was shared by even the most sophisticated and worldly of the narrators. Douglass, Bibb, Lewis Clarke, Josiah Henson, and Peter Still visited local wise men, conjurers, and healers when especially troublesome personal or sexual problems needed resolving. (Bibb's use of the toad as a love charm parallels similar rites of Afro-Brazilian sexual magic.) They also had faith in dream interpretation. . . . (pp. 37-8)

[In his book *Slavery* Stanley Elkins] suggests that slaves found models of behavior and authority, "significant others," in the master caste. The narrators say the models were more likely to be other slaves. Many plantations had some powerful black slave whose courage others respected, whose overwhelming physical presence coupled with a sense of self-esteem was admired by the other slaves. Slave preachers and storytellers and local healers skilled in root medicine or capable of interpreting one's dreams, were also admired: men like Lunsford Lane, who was so adept at healing through herbs and roots that fellow blacks called him "Doctor," or the fugitive Harry Thomas, who practiced medicine in Canada, and Alfred T. Jones, who opened an apothecary shop. If even a modicum of truth resides in the abundant folklore of slavery collected since the end of the Civil War, there must have been thousands of such individuals on the plantations.

One must also include as models the slave drivers, and the many patriarchs and matriarchs, the older Uncles and Aunties, who appear throughout slave autobiographies. Slaves generally felt deference and respect for the aged on the plantation, a reverence similar to that found among many African tribal groups. The older person stands symbolically between this world and the next—to do injury to him is to tempt the wrath of the shades; to respect him is partially to assure a gracious welcome for yourself in the nether world. (p. 38)

To fail to see these many social types, these black "significant others," is to blind oneself to the facts of the slavery experience. The most crucial problems of a man's life were resolved by fellow slaves of special gifts. The slave narrators leave no record of slaves' counseling with their masters about their deepest hopes. To satisfy the mind and body, as well as the spirit, it was necessary to turn elsewhere.

These are the most striking central themes of the narratives, but they are far from the only ones. Every subtle and banal aspect of the slave regime is somewhere touched upon and illuminated by these autobiographies. Music, dancing, and laughter are discussed as means to lighten the burdens of a toiling life. Northup said he couldn't survive without his blessed fiddle: "Had it not been for my beloved violin, I scarcely can conceive how I could have endured the long years of bondage. Often, at midnight, when sleep had fled . . . and my soul disturbed and troubled with the contemplation of my fate, it would sing me a song of peace." Douglass, too, played the violin, and others played banjoes, drums, and other instruments. (p. 39)

Numerous slaves talk of their perpetual war to prevent debasement. The powerful, the self-willed, those whose spirits could not be broken and who sometimes repulsed physically all attempts to whip them, presented the ultimate challenge to the mystique of the all-powerful master caste. The more the pressure of debasement was applied to some, the more rebellious they became. This is especially evident in the common stories fugitives tell of learning to read and write. Austin Steward vowed to teach himself letters after his master destroyed his spelling book and whipped him for having it. Peter Still maneuvered his way into a Sabbath school in Lexington despite his owner's opposition to "getting learning." Northup, who knew how to write, contrived a pen from old duck feathers and ink from the bark of a maple tree. (p. 40)

This struggle over letters must be seen within the broader context of the strategic and psychic importance of controlling learning. Slaveowners certainly hesitated to foster education for such obvious reasons as preventing bondsmen from writing passes and freedom papers. A subconscious and more meaningful question in control of language is also at stake. Through the ages, in the most widely divergent cultures, the right to proscribe letters or command a man's name is understood as the power to subordinate—the "word" has quasi-magical, mystical connotations. The right to control it is the power to order reality, to subjugate man himself. Conquerors and conquered have both understood this truth. (pp. 40-1)

Strikingly similar experiences took place in slavery. The concept is evident in stories slaves tell of their sense of loss in not knowing their birth dates. To deprive one of such vital information is to cloud his sense of self. One also finds it among former slaves who insist on selecting their own names as free men. Douglass and Wells Brown permit their family names to be changed at will, but both refuse to relinquish their given names. For them "Frederick" and "William" signified their sense of being, their manhood. (pp. 41-2)

This relation of selfhood to learning also helps explain a major trend of Reconstruction social history. Yankee teachers sent South to build school houses in the 1860's and 1870's were greeted enthusiastically by the freedmen. Makeshift schools were jammed with pupils. It was common to note the awe with which youngsters regarded the mastery of penmanship, or to comment on the similar attitude of older folk. . . . Slaves spoke of the "wonderful power" in letters, the "mysteries of literature," and the rewards that flowed from control of the written word. One observer thought they envisioned education as a "sort of talisman." These slaves hungered not only for knowledge but also for a sense of self. By crowding the schoolhouses they were laying claim to their manhood as well as to their McGuffey's Readers.

Many other suggestive themes in these books call for further investigation on the part of scholars: the many class- and color-conscious hatreds that divided slaves among themselves; the discussion of slavery's debasement of their *masters* and corruption of whites generally; the pattern of use and abuse of black women as field hands and as sexual partners; the role of the white mistress on the plantations. The image of blessed, genteel, white Southern femininity must find some place for the woman who tried to kill Moses Roper because he looked too like her husband, or for the ladies the Clarke brothers referred to as she-wolves, screech owls, and she-bears.

A further consideration of major importance is the length of time slaves remained with a single owner or on one plantation.

It is the exceptional fugitive who lived on one place all his life. On the contrary, it was typical to have three, five, and sometimes more masters in the course of one's servitude. It is not necessary to posit evil intent on the part of the master caste to understand this. Families weren't destroyed capriciously. But the slave autobiographies explain that the disruptions were caused most often by indebtedness—and subsequent forced sales—and secondly by divisions of estates upon death. Some of the most hectic sections of the narratives deal with attempts of husbands and fathers to keep their families intact in the face of these realities. If the disruption so evident on the plantations that fugitives describe was typical of the entire slave South, it is certainly necessary to modify the image of a relatively stable plantation experience for most bondsmen.

The narratives are essential sources for the study of slavery for all these reasons. One can understand more clearly now why they were a popular literature more than a century ago. (pp. 42-3)

> *Gilbert Osofsky, "Introduction: Puttin' On Ole Massa, The Significance of Slave Narratives," in* Puttin' On Ole Massa: The Slave Narratives of Henry Bibb, William Wells Brown, and Solomon Northup, *edited by Gilbert Osofsky, Harper & Row, Publishers, 1969, pp. 9-44.*

VERNON LOGGINS

[*Loggins's* The Negro Author: His Development in America to 1900, *acknowledged as a significant early survey of black American fiction, is regarded as a ground-breaking study of the slave narrative. Critics credit Loggins with presenting crucial bibliographical data on the narratives, which provided a basis for the work of all subsequent scholars. In the following excerpt from his book, Loggins gives a detailed biographical and literary-historical overview of slave narrators and their works during the period when the genre flourished.*]

The period of intense abolition agitation saw the full flowering of Negro biography. . . . [The] form had by 1840 become something of a distinct, if humble, type in American literature. After that year it was extravagantly cultivated. Not only the anti-slavery public, but the whole world, it seems, was eager to hear the life story of any Negro who had escaped from slavery or who had done anything else extraordinary. Genuine autobiographical accounts, such as those of Douglass, Brown, Ward, and Pennington, appeared as pamphlets, as serials in newspapers, and as full volumes. Other narratives were represented as dictated, and still others were written by able hands as pure biographies. In the mass of such writing truth was undoubtedly of secondary importance. There came a number of purely fictitious biographies, which, like the *Memoirs of Archy Moore*, were originally thrust upon the public as genuine. Without a single exception, the Negro biographies written before 1865 have been long out of print, and are today comparatively unknown. But they are in themselves of interest, and in the Negro literature of the greatest importance. And as an influence over the kind of American fiction which was in the middle of the nineteenth century perhaps the most widely read, that represented by such a work as Harriet Beecher Stowe's *Uncle Tom's Cabin*, they have been too much disregarded by critics.

Among the lesser Negro leaders of the period who published narratives of their lives no one was more outstanding in his experiences and in his achievements than Henry Bibb. He was one whom Whittier referred to as an example of what the more intelligent blacks in America could accomplish. When Harriet Beecher Stowe was preparing to write *Uncle Tom's Cabin* as a serial for the *National Era,* she thought of him as one who might give her information regarding the intimate customs of slaves on cotton plantations. After he had settled permanently in Canada, he was an acknowledged leader among his people, editing for a time a newspaper called the *Voice of Freedom.* His autobiography, published in 1849, was made up of details which he as an antislavery agent had recounted on lecture tours in the East and in the West, where he spoke mainly to farmers at meetings held in "log cabins and schoolhouses."

The book appeared as *Narrative of the Life and Adventures of Henry Bibb, Written by Himself.* The author of the introduction, Lucius C. Matlock, to whom the task of editing the manuscript was entrusted, claimed that "the work of preparation for the press was that of orthography and punctuation merely, an arrangement of the chapters and a table of contents—little more than falls to the lot of publishers generally." That which distinguishes the *Narrative,* that which no doubt aroused Mrs. Stowe's interest in Bibb, is the elaborate portrayal of the actual life of slaves in the South. Bibb's experiences as a bondman carried him from Kentucky to New Orleans, thence to the borders of the Red River country, and finally to Missouri. Conscious that he was more white than black, possessed of a belligerent disposition, and awake to the abuses of slavery, he related his impressions with vividness and allowed them to argue for themselves. Suggestive of the material which makes up the body of his *Narrative* are the descriptions of the superstitions among the Negroes of the South. He speaks of receiving from a "conjurer" an antidote against "being struck by any one."

> After I had paid him his charge, he told me to go to the cow-pen after night, and get some fresh cow manure, and mix it with red pepper and white people's hair, all to be put into a pot over the fire, and scorched until it could be ground into a snuff.

Another "conjurer" seeks to aid him in winning the affections of any girl whom he might desire.

> After I had paid him, he told me to get a bull frog, and take a certain bone out of the frog, dry it, and when I got a chance I must step up to any girl whom I wished to make love me, and scratch her somewhere on her naked skin with this bone, and she would be certain to love me, and would follow me in spite of herself; no matter who she might be engaged to, nor who she might be walking with.

He tries the scheme on a girl with whom he is in love, but wins nothing but the fire of her anger. He meets with a similar distressing experience when he pulls a lock of hair from his sweetheart's head, intending to gain her everlasting devotion by wearing the lock in his shoe. Built up with such details, Bibb's *Narrative* has interest. The style might easily have been his own. The passages quoted illustrate the consistent homeliness of the idiom and the faultiness of the grammar.

Mrs. Stowe probably never met Henry Bibb, for he was already definitely settled in Canada when she made her inquiries regarding him. But while she was engaged in the composition of *Uncle Tom's Cabin,* she did very likely interview Josiah Henson, another lesser Negro leader of the period. And she undoubtedly built up in a measure her portrait of Uncle Tom from impressions which she received from reading Henson's first autobiography, which was published in 1849 as *The Life of Josiah Henson, Formerly a Slave, Now an Inhabitant of Canada, as Narrated by Himself.* It is a pamphlet of seventy-six pages, the anonymous editor of which asserted that it was composed from Henson's dictation, that it was read to him for verification, and that "the substance of it, therefore, the facts, the reflections, and very often the words, are his; and little more than the structure of the sentences belongs to another." At the time of the publication of the *Life* Henson was, according to his own statement, sixty years of age. He blunderingly tells the story of his forty years of slavery, during which time he served as a farm laborer in Maryland and as a superintendent of a plantation in Kentucky. There is considerable comment on his piety, on his success as a Methodist preacher, and on his view, long maintained, that it was a sin to get out of slavery by deception. He becomes more interesting when he tells of his conversion from this view, after, as he claimed, he had been cheated by his unscrupulous master out of the sum of money which he had accumulated to pay for his manumission and had escaped being sold in the New Orleans slave market by the merest chance. His easy flight to Canada, where he states that he arrived in October, 1830, is described in detail; and the account ends with a brief summary of his experiences as a Canadian agent of the Underground Railroad.

Although the *Life* seems to have attracted little attention in antislavery circles, it at least led to Mrs. Stowe's interest in Henson. Shortly before the publication of *Uncle Tom's Cabin* was begun, when Henson was in England acting as the self-appointed representative of a Negro colony in Dawn, Canada, he was publicly accused of being an impostor. But after he was popularly identified with Mrs. Stowe's hero, his honesty was apparently never questioned. Since he was everywhere known as the real Uncle Tom, the publication of his autobiography became a profitable pursuit for him. In 1858 came *Truth Stranger than Fiction: Father Henson's Story of His Own Life,* a volume of more than two hundred pages, supposedly written by Henson himself. It was provided with an introduction by Mrs. Stowe, in which she declared, "Among all the singular and ineresting records to which the institution of American slavery has given rise, we know of none more striking, more characteristic and instructive, than that of Josiah Henson." The book shows too much that Henson was trying to live up to the ideal of the fictional hero whose creation he had helped to inspire. If the Uncle Tom of Mrs. Stowe's novel had ever gone to England as a free man and had visited the Archbishop of Canterbury, he might have spoken of the occasion as Henson claimed he experienced it in 1851.

> The Archbishop expressed the strongest interest in me, and after about an hour's conversation he inquired, "At what university, sir, did you graduate?" "I graduated, your grace," said I in reply, "at the university of adversity." "The university of adversity," said he, looking up in astonishment; "where is that?" "It is my lot, your grace," said I, "to be born a slave, and to pass my boyhood and all the former part of my life as a slave. I never entered a school, never read the Bible in my youth, and received all my training under the most adverse circumstances. This is what I mean by graduating in the university of adversity." "I understand you, sir," said he. "But is it possible that you are not a scholar?" "I am not," said I. "But I should never have suspected that you were not a liberally educated man. I have heard many negroes talk, but never have seen one that could use such language as you."

In 1876 Henson paid a final visit to England, and another version of his life was published in London in that year as *An Autobiography of Josiah Henson (Mrs. Harriet Beecher Stowe's "Uncle Tom"), from 1789-1876.* An enlarged edition, in which it was claimed that one hundred thousand copies of the book had been sold, was issued in 1878. No one of the versions of Henson's life supports Mrs. Stowe's declaration regarding his interest and singularity. If there is anything which makes him unique in Negro literature, it is the success with which he exploited his identification with her hero.

Josiah Henson said of two other characters in *Uncle Tom's Cabin,* "The white slaves, George Harris, and his wife, Eliza, were my particular friends." About Eliza there might be some doubt, but Henson could easily have known the man who was chief model for George Harris. He was Lewis Clarke, whom Mrs. Stowe knew personally, and with whose autobiography, *Narrative of the Sufferings of Lewis Clarke, during a Captivity of More than Twenty-Five Years among the Algerines of Kentucky* (1845), she was familiar. However, the Clarke revealed in the *Narrative* is too bitter and ungoverned a hater to have found a true portrayal from the Christian and womanly pen of Mrs. Stowe. His calling the slaveholders of Kentucky by the name of Algerines suggests the mood of his book. One of the early sentences is, "The night in which I was born, I have been told, was dark and terrible, black as the night for which Job prayed, when he besought the clouds to pitch their tent round about the place of his birth; and my life of slavery was but too exactly prefigured by the stormy elements that hovered over the first hour of my being." From the beginning to the end of the book he is tempestuous, unrelenting in his turbulent abuse of slaveholders, especially those among them who happened to be of the female sex.

> Of all the animals on this earth, I am most afraid of a real mad, passionate, raving, slave-holding woman!

When Clarke escaped from slavery in 1841, he, according to his *Narrative,* did so by passing as a white man. He claimed that his father was a native of Scotland, and his temperament certainly seems to be more Celtic than Negro. Of all the biographical accounts attributed to fugitives his is probably the strongest in revengeful hatred. He is far removed in character from Mrs. Stowe's gentlemanly George Harris. It is easily believable that the blunt style of Clarke's *Narrative* is what it was represented as being, a faithful record of his own dictation.

The year following his flight to freedom Lewis Clarke began his long career as an antislavery agent, during which he seems to have done little more than relate his story to audiences and sell his book. Two of his brothers, Milton and Cyrus, also succeeded in breaking away from slavery and also engaged in abolition work. In 1846, Lewis' *Narrative* was reprinted along with a parallel account of Milton's life, the joint autobiography being entitled *Narratives of the Sufferings of Lewis and Milton Clarke, Sons of a Soldier of the Revolution, during a Captivity of More than Twenty Years among the Slave-Holders of Kentucky, One of the So Called Christian States of North America; Dictated by Themselves.* Milton's story is similar to Lewis', but he seems not to have been such a bellicose hater.

If one acquainted with the history of the Negro's past in America were called upon to name the most spectacular and picturesque person whom the race has produced, one would probably think first of Sojourner Truth. She could neither read nor write; but the *Narrative of Sojourner Truth, Northern Slave,* published in 1850 as the work of an anonymous biographer, contains so many quotations attributed to her that she is entitled to a place among the makers of slave narratives. A reprint of the work, issued five years later, was provided with one of Mrs. Stowe's brief prefaces, mainly a plea to the public to buy the little volume and thus aid an African woman confronting

old age. Even though this was in 1855, Sojourner Truth characteristically lived on until 1883, long enough for the 1850 *Narrative* to be enlarged into another anonymous biography, *Narrative of Sojourner Truth, a Bondswoman of Olden Time,* published in 1875 and reissued in augmented editions in 1883 and 1884. As early as 1835, when the only name Sojourner Truth had was Isabella, she had been made much of in W. L. Stone's *Matthias and His Impostures* and in G. Vale's reply to that work, *Fanaticism; Its Sources and Influence, Illustrated by the Simple Narrative of Isabella.* Stone, apparently because of his deep hatred of the Matthias cult, considered her the most wicked of the wicked, and accused her of having murdered one man by serving him poisoned blackberries and of having attempted to get rid of an entire family in the same fashion. Vale cleared her of these charges, and pictured her as ignorant, illiterate, and superstitious, possessed with a type of mind that became an easy prey to the extravagant delusions of Matthias. In all of her antislavery and reform work she was to remain a religious fanatic; it was her wild African mysticism that made her such an interesting and bizarre figure.

As we are told in each version of her *Narrative,* she was born a slave in the state of New York near the end of the eighteenth century. Her original master was a Dutch farmer. Through some sort of legal complication which she herself could not exactly explain, she, according to her own statement, did not become free until 1828, one year after all the slaves in the state of New York were supposed to be emancipated. Her main troubles in slavery, including frequent beatings, were due, she said, to the fact that she got into the hands of an English-speaking master and had great difficulty in learning to make herself understood in his language. After her liberation, she came to New York, joined the Methodists and then the followers of Matthias, left the city "because of its wickedness" after she awoke to the realization "that Matthias was mad," and, under the picturesque name of Sojourner Truth, began the series of ramblings which were to last the rest of her life and which were to carry her over the entire North before the end of the Civil War and into the South after the abolition of slavery. She lectured in her homely manner for immediate emancipation and for woman suffrage, and worked at manual labor when she needed what she called "the where-withal to pay tribute to Caesar." Her association with Matthias' group possibly inculcated in her the desire to join some sort of social and religious community. At one time she considered Amos Bronson Alcott's colony at Fruitlands, and when her *Narrative* was originally published, she was living as a member of the Northampton Association.

Sojourner Truth is best explained by her own sayings. Her 1850 *Narrative* is one of the most interesting of all the Negro biographies published before 1865 because the unparalleled creature whom it treats is given free rein to show up her true mettle. No passage is more indicative of her character than that dealing with the supposed kidnapping of her son by an Alabama slaveholder. She makes the Southerner a monster, the murderer of his wife.

> He knocked her down with his fist, jumped on her with his knees, broke her collar-bone, and tore out her wind-pipe!

To get her child from the clutches of such a man, she turns to God.

> Oh, God, you know how much I am distressed, for I have told you again and again. Now, God, help me to get my son. If you were in trouble, as I am, and

> I could help you, as you can me, think I wouldn't
> do it? . . . Oh, God, you know I have no money, but
> you can make the people do for me. I will never give
> you peace till you do, God.

When she did get her son returned to her, God was given all
the credit for her success.

> Oh, my God! I know'd I'd have him again. I was
> sure God would help me to get him. Why, I felt *so
> tall within*—I felt as if *the power of a nation* was
> with me.

"The power of a nation" was with her again when she felt it
her duty to quiet a crowd of boisterous young men who were
trying to break up a "camp meeting" which she was attending.

> Shall I run away and hide from the Devil? Me, a
> servant of the living God? Have I not faith enough
> to go out and quell that mob, when it is written,
> "One shall chase a thousand and put ten thousand
> to flight?" I know there are not one thousand here;
> and I know I am a servant of the living God. I'll go
> to the rescue, and the Lord shall go with me and
> protect me. . . . Oh, I felt as if I had three hearts!
> and that they were so large my body could hardly
> hold them!

She approaches the mob with a song, apparently of her own
composition, beginning:

> It was early in the morning—it was early in the morning,
> 　Just at the break of day—
> When he rose—when he rose—when he rose,
> 　And went to heaven on a cloud.

She sings and harangues, and finally the young men promise
to go away after she has given them one more hymn. "Amen!
it is sealed!" she says, and begins another song:

> I bless the Lord I've got my seal—to-day and to-day—
> To slay Goliath in the field—to-day and to-day;
> The good old way is a righteous way,
> I mean to take the kingdom in the good old way.

Made up of such pictures, the *Narrative of Sojourner Truth,
Northern Slave,* was an extraordinary contribution to anti-slavery literature.

Different from most American Negroes who have in any measure served as leaders for their race, Sojourner Truth was no
imitator of Anglo-Saxon character and ways. Like the remote
southern plantation Negro, she was her true self, an African
child of nature living on American soil. The *Narrative* shows
her healthy, strong as a man, unafraid, optimistic, singing and
preaching with bounding joy, profoundly emotional, and infinitely religious. (pp. 212-22)

A few other Negroes of the period who are accredited with
having written accounts of their lives or who became the subjects of biographies belong to the class of minor leaders. Austin
Steward, at one time "president" of Wilberforce Colony in
Canada, published in 1857 what on the surface seems to be an
authentic autobiography, *Twenty-Two Years a Slave, and Forty
Years a Freeman.* Daniel H. Peterson, who claimed that he
was owned in his childhood by a Maryland relative of President
Tyler, became a preacher of some prominence and published
in 1854 *The Looking-Glass,* probably his own work. Although
it is characterized as a "narrative," it is less an account of
Peterson's life than an alluring description of Liberia as the
proper home for unhappy American blacks. Peterson had spent
some time in Africa, and gives his impressions as a "true
report." Perhaps no Negro biography offers more interesting

pictures of southern plantation life than Peter Randolph's *Sketches
of Slave Life, or, Illustrations of the Peculiar Institution,* a
second edition of which was published at Boston in 1855.
Randolph had been emancipated by his Virginia master, had
settled in Boston, and, if he produced the *Sketches of Slave
Life* without too much aid from an editor, had learned how to
write lively and concrete description. Lunsford Lane, whom a
writer in the *Liberator,* possibly William Lloyd Garrison himself, characterized as a "modest, intelligent man, and very
prepossessing in his appearance," evoked considerable sympathy from abolition circles in the early forties. His peculiar
situation was described in *The Narrative of Lunsford Lane,
Formerly of Raleigh, N. C.,* published in Boston in 1842. He
had spent thirty-two years of his life in slavery, serving as
"waiter and messenger" to governors of the state of North
Carolina. In1835, he bought himself out of bondage, but was
not allowed to remain in his native city. He appealed to northern
Abolitionists, and sufficient funds, including a contribution of
thirty dollars from Gerrit Smith, were raised to enable him to
purchase his wife and children. He came with his family to
Boston, told his story on the abolition platform, saw his *Narrative* through a number of editions, and in 1863 was made
the subject of a full-length and pleasingly written biography,
Lunsford Lane: or, Another Helper from North Carolina, the
work of William G. Hawkins. No claim was made that Lane
was himself the author of the original *Narrative;* but he was
named as the publisher and as the holder of the copyright, and
the simple style might, it seems, have been his own. The
straightforwardness of the pamphlet is very different from the
dull tediousness of Israel Campbell's *Bond and Free,* the one
other autobiography supposedly by a Negro leader which should
be mentioned. The book, a long and incoherent survey of the
life of a preacher so pious that he thought it a sin for a Negro
to run away from slavery, was published in Philadelphia in
1861. He was then residing in Canada, and claimed that he
wrote the book in order to secure money to ransom three of
his children who were still slaves in Kentucky. The attempt at
fictional effects, especially the use of conversation, does not
suggest too strongly that Campbell was really the author.

The narratives published between 1840 and 1865 of Negroes
who apparently did nothing else deserving public notice except
to get out of slavery run into the hundreds. Many are no more
than thumb-nail sketches, such as one finds in Benjamin Drew's
The Refugee: or, The Narratives of Fugitive Slaves in Canada
(1856). The book contains about four hundred pages of brief
"life stories," which Drew claimed he had gathered in the
course of a tour in Canada West. He said: "While his infor-
mants talked, the author wrote: nor are there in the whole
volume a dozen verbal alterations which were not made at the
moment of writing, while in haste to make the pen become a
tongue for the dumb." The antislavery newspapers abound in
such cameo biographies, most of them told in the first person
as true records of the words of the fugitives. Adequately representative of the whole mass is a single one, "Narrative of
James Curry, a Fugitive Slave," which appeared in the *Liberator* for January 10, 1840. The story, even then growing
old, of a slave's hardships and adventurous flight to freedom,
it was prefaced with the following note:

> There are, there can be, no narratives of more ab-
> sorbing interest, than those of runaway slaves from
> this land of republican tyranny. The one which oc-
> cupies so large a portion of our present number is
> recited in a very artless manner, and will repay a
> careful perusal. It is a real case, and no fiction, as
> written down from the lips of the self-emancipated

bondman by a talented female, who will accept our thanks for the favor she has done us in communicating it for publication in the *Liberator*.

Narratives of similar *genre* came in a flood of pamphlets, and some assumed the proportions of sizable volumes. Most of them are monotonous, full of repetition, badly written, and roughly printed. But a few are readable. The *Narrative of Henry Box Brown* (1849) relates Brown's unique experience in winning his way to freedom by submitting to be "sent by express" from Richmond to Philadelphia "packed in a box three feet long and two feet wide." The story of his romantic escape provided enough publicity to make him a lecturer on the abolition platform, and inspired some lover of the minstrel song, "Uncle Ned," to compose a ballad, one stanza of which is:

> Brown laid down the shovel and the hoe,
>   Down in the box he did go;
> No more slave work for Henry Box Brown,
>   In the box by express he did go.

Perhaps no two slaves in their flight for freedom ever thrilled the world so much as did William and Ellen Craft, a young couple married according to the rites of slavery. Ellen was so fair that she could pass as white, and William was black. During the Christmas holidays of 1848 they left Macon, Georgia, where they were bound to different masters, she disguised in man's clothes as a young planter, and he as the accompanying servant. The ruse succeeded, and the two reached the safety of the Underground Railroad at Philadelphia. They became heroes, about whom speeches were made and poems were written. According to one report President Polk declared after the passage of the Fugitive Slave Law that he would employ military force for their capture. But they fled to England, where they were put to school in an institution founded by Lady Byron for the benefit of children of rural districts. The story of the Crafts was ideal for a "narrative," but it seems not to have been told in book form until it appeared in London in 1860 as *Running a Thousand Miles for Freedom*. The *Narrative of the Life of Moses Gandy* (1844) has an interest in that it was penned by George Thompson, the celebrated English Abolitionist, who claimed in the preface that he "carefully abstained from casting a single reflection or animadversion" of his own. Linda Brent's story, *Incidents in the Life of a Slave Girl* (1861), is fairly readable, probably because of the "editing" of Lydia Maria Child. But of all the narratives of this class the least dull perhaps is the work of an anonymous biographer, whose unusual subject matter is suggested by the full title of his book, *Twelve Years a Slave; Narrative of Solomon Northup, a Citizen of New York, Kidnapped in Washington City in 1841, and Rescued in 1853, from a Cotton Plantation near the Red River in Louisiana*. The book, published in 1853, does not seem too long, even though it contains more than three hundred pages. A perusal of it makes one realize that the narratives of fugitives would have been more effective if they had been written as pure biographies and not as "dictated" or "edited" autobiographies. The absurd style in which the "dictated" autobiography might be written is apparent in the opening of L. A. Chamerovzow's rendering of *Slave Life in Georgia: A Narrative of the Life, Sufferings, and Escape of John Brown* (1855):

> My name is John Brown. How I came to take it, I will explain in due time. When I was in slavery, I was called Fed. Why I was so named, I cannot tell.

Such unrealistic expression is a distinguishing mark of a typical "dictated" autobiography, the category in which the majority of the narratives of obscure fugitives belong.

The publication of the life stories of Negroes was not confined to accounts of fugitives. In 1849, there appeared in Philadelphia the *Religious Experience and Journal of Mrs. Jarena Lee*, "revised and corrected from the original manuscript, written by herself." Her distinction was that she defied the regulations and in spite of her sex became a preacher in the African Methodist Episcopal Church. *A Narrative of the Life of Noah Davis: Written by Himself at the Age of Fifty-Four* was published in Baltimore about 1859. Davis had been a slave and published his book in order to "raise sufficient means to free his last two children from slavery." But, possibly because he was living in Baltimore and wished to sell his *Narrative* there, slavery is scarcely referred to in it. Davis presents himself as a meek and gentle soul, interested in no topic in the world besides religion. We can probably accept as really of Negro authorship *An Autobiography, with Details of a Visit to England* (1862), by Jeremiah Asher, a Baptist preacher who had charge of colored congregations in Providence and Philadelphia. With ample internal evidence indicating actual Negro authorship is *A Narrative of the Life and Travels of Mrs. Nancy Prince, Written by Herself*, the first edition of which was published in 1850. It is a naïve description of the impressions received by an American Negro woman during a sojourn of several years in Russia, where she claimed her husband was a servant in the Czar's household. It contains also an account of a visit to Jamaica. Several years before the publication of the *Narrative* Mrs. Prince had lectured in New England on the "manners and customs of Russia." And she was the author of at least one open letter, published in the *Liberator* for September 17, 1841.

A final group of the biographies of the period includes those which were published as authentic fact accounts, but which were in reality pure works of fiction created by white writers. It is impossible to draw the line between the true and the fictional in even the most honest of the biographies. The deception which could be resorted to in the name of antislavery propaganda has been shown in the discussion of *A Narrative of the Life and Adventures of Charles Ball*, reprinted in its original form as late as 1853, and brought out with slight changes in 1858 as *Fifty Years in Chains*. The occasional unscrupulousness of even such an organization as the American Anti-Slavery Society is seen in the fact that the spurious *Narrative of James Williams*, which it had suppressed in 1838, was in 1841 advertised as again for sale among its publications. A Negro known as James Williams and not the amanuensis, John G. Whittier, was responsible for its misrepresentation. But it is not likely that any Negro whatsoever had anything to do with the *Life and Opinions of Julius Melbourn*, published at Syracuse in 1847 and reissued in an enlarged edition in 1851. The parts of the book ascribed to Melbourn and the parts designated as contributed by the editor, Jabez D. Hammond, are dangerously alike in style. Melbourn is presented as a cultivated free mulatto who lived in Raleigh, North Carolina, from his birth in 1790 until he took up his residence in England in 1835. The account of his life throughout bears the face of fiction. Yet its truthfulness as actual autobiography was apparently unquestioned at the time the book was published.

The *Autobiography of a Female Slave* (1857) is still rated as a genuine "slave narrative" by those, it must be assumed, who have only looked at the title and have never read the book. How it could have been accepted as a true history by the *Liberator* in 1857 is difficult to determine. For the account is a pale tale of blacks and mulattoes parading as the creatures of sentimental romance. The author was Mattie Griffiths, a young Kentucky woman, who, according to Lydia Maria Child, turned Abolitionist after she had read the speeches of Charles Sumner, freed her slaves, and refused to accede to the wishes of her relatives to deny publicly that she had written the *Autobiography of a Female Slave*. Even more excitingly fictional than the first work of its *genre*, Aphra Behn's *Oronooko*, is *The Life and Adventures of Zamba, an African Negro King; and His Experiences of Slavery in South Carolina*, published in London in 1847 as "written" by Zamba and "corrected and arranged" by Peter Neilson. The pictures of slavery which it presents are possibly true to fact; but the stereotyped adventure plot taxes the reader's credulity beyond all reason. Kate E. R. Pickard, for a time engaged as a teacher in a school in Tuscumbia, Alabama, published in 1856 a lengthy book founded no doubt on actual events, but worked up into a stirring tale of action. It was called *The Kidnapped and the Ransomed, Being the Personal Recollections of Peter Still and His Wife "Vina," after 40 Years of Slavery*. The appropriateness of Peter Still's story for fictional treatment is conveniently suggested by Kate E. R. Pickard's own summary:

> Kidnapped, in his early childhood, from the doorsteps of his home in New Jersey; more than forty years a slave in Kentucky and Alabama; his unsuccessful appeal to the great Henry Clay; his liberation through the generosity of a Jew; his restoration to his mother by the slightest threads of memory; the yearning of his heart for his loved ones; the heroic but disastrous attempt of Conklin to bring his wife and children to him—wherever these incidents of his life were detailed they seldom failed to draw from the hand of the listener some contribution towards the exorbitant sum demanded for the liberation of his family.

Seth Conklin, a sort of Benjamin Lundy of the fifties, is the principal figure in the most thrilling episode in the story; and, perhaps to give verisimilitude to the effect of the whole, a biographical sketch of Conklin, the work of William Howard Furness, is tacked on at the end.

The final, and perhaps the most significant, statement which should be made regarding the biographies of obscure Negroes, whether real or imagined, is that they were commercially successful. That they provided antislavery propaganda must not be ignored. But that they sold rapidly is a surer reason for their great abundance. (pp. 224-32)

> Vernon Loggins, "Biography, Poetry, and Miscellaneous Writings, 1840-1865," in his The Negro Author: His Development in America to 1900, *1931*. Reprint by Kennikat Press, Inc., 1964, pp. 212-51.

FRANCES SMITH FOSTER

[*Smith Foster surveys the cultural matrix of the slave narratives, stressing the narrators' obligation to present themselves and American society in a manner inoffensive to their white audience.*]

Slave narratives are the personal accounts by black slaves and exslaves of their experiences in slavery and of their efforts to obtain freedom. Written after the physical escape had been accomplished and the narrators were manumitted or fugitive slaves, these narratives were retrospective endeavors which helped the narrators define, even create, their identities as they attempted to relate the patterns and implications of their slavery experiences. More important, the narratives soon became the attempts of black slaves and exslaves to alter and, eventually,

to abolish an institution which was increasingly vital to the continued prosperity of their white audience.

Though some are aesthetically superb and rank with the best literature, the slave narratives were not created for a limited audience of refined and cultivated sensibilities. On the other hand, they bear only limited resemblance to authentic black folk literature. Although some commercialization is apparent in the latter part of their development, slave narratives maintain integrity and do not come under the category of "mass culture." The authors of slave narratives usually wrote in a simple, direct style with a realistic eye upon the needs and expectations of a variety of readers. They attempted to urge the various elements of society to realize their collective need to eliminate injustices and to work for a unity of peace and understanding.

The narrators sought to inform their readers of the inhuman and immoral characteristics of slavery. They tried to communicate with an audience with which they did not share cultural or moral concerns—an audience, in fact, which was increasingly certain that real and significant differences between whites and blacks necessitated vigilance lest there develop undue social and intellectual intercourse between them. At the same time, this audience was increasingly aware that blacks were the foundation of what could well be the most profoundly important institution in America. Thus the narrators could expect a certain amount of interest in their experiences and attitudes, but they could not assume sympathy for their beliefs. The narrators hoped to persuade their readers to accept not only the autobiographical truth of their message, but also the necessity for every individual's working against the institution of slavery. They had to do this without raising suspicions that they were advocating social equality or seriously challenging theories of racial superiority. Thus slave narratives were didactic writings, created as a response to the specific needs of a specific society. As a genre, the slave narratives were influenced by their social ambience, and they were adapted to the changes of expectations, assumptions, and needs within that environment.

The earliest slave narratives vary only slightly from other personal narratives of their time. Like the others, they tell of geographical explorations, oceanic adventures, and encounters with Indians. They, too, place a great emphasis upon the religious implications of the narrator's experiences. Like other personal narratives, the slave narratives chronicle incidents in an individual's experience, and they provide the reader with insights into an individual's mind as well as into the structure and working of that individual's society. In the slave narratives, as in other autobiographical literature, the authors are keenly interested in the clues provided by the narrated experiences about their identities and about the ultimate significance of their lives. They investigate the process of their spiritual and emotional development and try to assess the effects of social and familial relationships upon the ways in which they see themselves. Statements and arguments about philosophical, political, and religious beliefs are interspersed throughout their stories of physical bondage and escape.

Their combination of autobiographical and social concerns is perhaps one of the secrets of the early popularity of slave narratives. The colonists favored art that was relevant to their particular circumstances to such an extent that, according to James D. Hart, "Books were often judged by the amount of help they furnished the reader in his quest for worldly advancement." Slave narratives, like other personal narratives, were especially popular because they illustrated religious and political truths while relating interesting and exciting true-to-life adventures.

Although they were, in the beginning, simply a variation of the personal narrative tradition in American literature, slave narratives soon emerged as a distinct genre recognizable by its form, content, and relation to the cultural matrix. As the sociohistorical experiences of the narrators became more obviously different from those of their audience, their writings reflected this change.

Race was the most crucial factor in the development of the slave narratives because in the United States the slaves' experiences of bondage and freedom were a product of race. It is doubtful that American slavery began as a result of racial prejudice. Winthrop Jordan, in fact, declares it was merely a coincidence: ''At the start of English settlement in America, no one had in mind to establish the institution of Negro slavery. Yet in less than a century the foundations of a peculiar institution had been laid.'' Regardless of intentions, however, by the end of the seventeenth century a system of racial slavery heretofore unknown to the English world had evolved. This peculiar institution framed the relationship between the black narrator and a virtually all-white readership. As the differences in experiences between the races became more institutionalized, the differences between the perceptions and values of the races increased. The communication process had to respond to these differences, and the response accordingly helped to shape and to inform slave narratives.

The search for spiritual identity in the slave narratives was complicated by the desire to use incidents in the narrator's life as examples of the experiences of many others like him. As a result, the slave narrator increasingly focused upon the effects of a dehumanizing environment upon his race rather than upon his own individuality. In most cases the desire to recognize oneself and to be recognized as a unique individual had to counter the desire to be a symbol, and it created the tension that is a basic quality of slave narratives.

The problem of distinguishing between the individual self and the community self and the desire to present the symbolic nature of one's personal experiences while maintaining one's own inimitability is traditional for autobiographical writers. For the slave narrator the question is complicated by his status as a black man in the United States. When white writers realize a dichotomy between their individual perceptions and the expectations of society, they must weigh one legitimate role against another. Egoism confronts socialization. The tension is internalized because the white writer is a member of the society that he is addressing. Slave narrators were not recognized as members of the same society as their audience. The slave narrator was an alien whose assertions of common humanity and civil rights conflicted with some basic beliefs of that society that he was addressing. The differences between personal and group preferences must be dealt with in that context. (pp. 3-6)

The black, who in the ante-bellum society attempted to define himself and to assess the factors which had made him as he was, found that the process of communicating this knowledge to a group which had doubts about his human status and which was guilty of his enslavement was fraught with special problems. He had to overcome the incredulity of persons whose surprise that a black could write overshadowed any attempt to understand or to consider what he was writing about. He had to convince his readers to accept the validity of his knowledge and conclusions, which in many instances profoundly contra-

An advertisement for a slave auction in New Orleans.

dicted their own. Furthermore, if he was to obtain their sympathy and aid, he had to do this in a manner which did not threaten or embarrass his readers.

For some narrators the difficulty of these tasks was compounded because they not only had to affirm for their readers the validity of their perceptions, but they also had to reaffirm that validity for themselves. This need was a direct result of the cultural matrix within which the black narrators existed. In a white society that questions and ultimately denies the humanity of blacks, it is difficult for blacks to take their humanness for granted. In such an environment most narrators needed continually to defend their own humanity to their readers and to themselves. As racist attitudes created an increasingly dehumanizing atmosphere for black narrators, their narratives reflected their intensified struggles to affirm their humanness.

Comparisons between the slave narratives by Africans and those by Afro-Americans reveal the effects of racism upon the attitudes of the narrators and the issues addressed in their writings. The narrators who began their lives in Africa maintained a strong sense of who they were and what they should be about throughout their enslavement. In their writings ''our manners,'' ''our buildings,'' and ''our lives'' are the bases for information, comparisons, and judgments.

In describing his introduction to white civilization, Olaudah Equiano often makes comparisons such as the following:

> I was astonished at the wisdom of the white people in all that I saw; but was amazed at their not sacrificing, or making any offerings, and eating with unwashed hands, and touching the dead. I likewise could not help remarking the particular slenderness of their women, which I did not at first like; and I thought they were not so modest and shame-faced as the African women.

Equiano's appreciation for some features of European civilization and astonishment at the barbarity of other aspects indicate the existence of some external set of values by which he can judge such factors. For many years he entertained the idea of returning home "and thought if I could get home what wonders I should have to tell."

Such tendencies to compare cultures did not seemingly diminish with time. After sixty years in American slavery, Venture Smith still considered himself an African in exile and evaluated incidents in terms of his own country. After relating an incident when he was cheated out of some money, he says:

> Such a processing as this committed on a defenseless stranger, almost worn out in the hard service of the world, without any foundation in reason or justice, whatever it may be called in a Christian land, would in my native country have been branded as a crime equal to highway robbery. But Captain Hart was a *white gentleman,* and I a *poor African,* therefore it was *all right, and good enough for the black dog.*

In contrast, a major concern of the Afro-American slave was to discover and preserve proof of his right to disagree with whites, for the Afro-American was born into a denial of human respect. Henry Bibb explains:

> I was born May 1815, of a slave mother . . . and was claimed as the property of David White Esq. . . . I was *flogged up;* for where I should have received moral, mental, and religious instruction, I received stripes without number, the object of which was to degrade and keep me in subordination. I can truly say, that I drank deeply of the bitter cup of suffering and woe. I have been dragged down to the lowest depths of human degradation and wretchedness, by Slaveholders.

The Afro-American narrator had no direct experience in any other society and often knew no more of his own personal history than the season of his birth or the appearance of his mother. His predicament was more completely one of exclusion from the only society he knew than of introduction to a new and hostile one. He often emphasized that he was a native of this country and, in fact, related to some of its oldest or most prominent citizens. His confrontation was not with contrasting values of an alien society but with alien ideas concerning his place in society. His comparisons were between his freedom as a child and his bondage as an adult, between his role as slave and the roles of whites as masters. Insofar as might makes right, his recognition of personal impotence threatened his acceptance of the validity of his perceptions. His comparisons were supported by references to differences between the ideals which Christianity and the American society extol and the failures of slaveholders to live up to these values. Hence the Afro-American narrator is likely to evoke the Bible as his authority and to compare his bondage with that of the children of Israel.

The narratives of Afro-American slaves also indicate there were differences between African and Afro-American slaves. Charles Ball implies racial differences when he tells of his grandfather's "great contempt for his fellow slaves, they being, as he said, a mean and vulgar race, quite beneath his rank, and the dignity of his former station." To Ball, a black born in U.S. slavery, his grandfather held "strange and peculiar notions of religion." Among other things, the old African maintained that

> the religion of the country was altogether false, and indeed, no religion at all; being the mere invention of priests and crafty men, who hoped thereby to profit through the ignorance and credulity of the multitude. In support of this opinion, he maintained that there could only be one true standard of faith, which was the case of his country.

Apparently, Africans were more successful in rejecting psychological and physical enslavement than Afro-Americans. (pp. 9-12)

J. W. C. Pennington maintains the Afro-American slave was in a defenseless state because slavery eliminated a viable Afro-American culture. "To estimate the sad state of a slave child," he says, "you must look at it as a helpless human being thrown upon the world without the benefit of its natural guardians. It is thrown into the world without a social circle to flee to for hope, shelter, comfort, or instruction." Pennington makes it clear that it is not simply a deprived childhood that he laments when he says,

> Whatever may be the ill or favoured condition of the slave in the matter of mere personal treatment, it is the chattel relation that robs him of his manhood, and transfers his ownership in himself to another. It is this that transfers the proprietorship of his wife and children to another. It is this that throws his family history into utter confusion, and leaves him without a single record to which he may appeal in vindication of his character, or honour. . . .

> Suppose insult, reproach, or slander should render it necessary for him to appeal to the history of his family in vindication of his character, where will he find that history? He goes to his native state, to his native country, to his native town; but nowhere does he find any record of himself *as a man.*

For the Afro-American narrator, life is a series of attempts to discover and proclaim his validity in spite of his perceived defects. The Afro-American's narratives most often end with a commitment to continue the struggle for recognition, "to contend," as Henry Bibb declares, "for the natural equality of the human family, without regard to color, which is but fading *matter,* while *mind* makes the man."

The evolution of slave narratives began more from social reality or historical imperative than from literary consciousness. The peculiar nature of their situation and their intent made compromise mandatory for slave narrators. The nature of these compromises determined the form and content of the narratives.

It was vital to the slave narrators that they maintain in their works a close relationship with the reality of the Afro-American experience. It was also necessary that they avoid unnecessarily antagonizing their audience. Yet, as the experiences of black slaves in the United States became more distinct from those of any other group, their writings had to reflect these changes; and, as slavery became more brutal, its depictions had to become more brutal also. The narrator's fidelity to the reality of the American slave experience was at the risk of offending many Americans who, regardless of their humanitarian beliefs, were, after all, members of the society being criticized. Moreover, the narratives ran the risk of alienating segments of people because the accounts of slavery presented an unsavory view of the South in particular and the United States in general. This made the narratives potentially offensive to American nationalists, though popular with those in the North who encouraged regionalism and with those in England who still smarted over the result of the War of Independence.

This dilemma is illustrated in Ephraim Peabody's mixed review, "Narratives of Fugitive Slaves" [see excerpt below]. His enthusiasm is obvious when he says:

> We place these volumes without hesitation among the most remarkable productions of the age—remarkable as being pictures of slavery by the slave, remarkable as disclosing under a new light the mixed elements of American civilization, and not less remarkable as a vivid exhibition of the force and working of the native love of freedom in the individual mind.

The praise is tempered with caution, however, when, in the midst of what is intended as a highly sympathetic review, he complains that "these books give the impression that the Slave States constitute one vast prison house, of which all the whites without exception are the mere keepers, with no interest in the slaves further than they can be made subservient to the pleasure or profit of their owners. But this is far from the case." He advises slave narrators to give what he considers *"more balanced views of slavery."* He further warns that he will not condone any "censorious, loose, and violent treatment" of slavery because it would antagonize antislavery southerners and northerners having personal ties to the South who would otherwise help the movement.

Slave narrators, especially those of the nineteenth century, were in a difficult situation. They wished to contradict the masters' version of slavery by presenting the black slave's views, and they wanted to do this with an audience and with supporters who were more closely related by culture and vested interests to the masters than to the slaves. Their narratives show great efforts to appease without neutralizing their position. It became almost axiomatic that for every two or three bad experiences related, one good experience must be recounted.

The manner in which comparisons between the United States and Britain were handled shows how this was done. Slave narrators considered Britain a more enlightened and hospitable country than the United States. Such bias could easily be interpreted as anti-Americanism and as such would seriously impede any attempts by blacks to change any American institution. The narrators had to develop a compromise that would allow them to gain American sympathizers without sacrificing their strong appreciation for the antislavery positions of other countries. Their decision to ignore as foci of attacks sources of slavery such as racism, discrimination, and economics and to concentrate upon the weakness of the institution was one compromise because this reduced the number of persons in the United States who were obviously being criticized and focused discussions of Britain's merits upon one area: slavery. (pp. 12-15)

There was, however, sufficient nationalism in the United States to require diplomacy. Equiano does not condemn the entire New World. He describes Robert King, his master in the West Indies, as a Quaker from Philadelphia who "possessed a most amiable disposition and temper, and was very charitable and humane." The problem, as Equiano presents it, is that there

were very few masters like King, and those persons were not capable of protecting their slaves from exploitation by the majority of inhabitants in that area.

When Parliament abolished slavery in Britain and all British colonies in 1833, the pro-British flavor of the narratives became even more pronounced. When the Compromise of 1850 allowed the expansion of slavery into the territories and made fugitive slaves unsafe in any area of the United States, slave narratives began to display anti-American tendencies. It is not uncommon to find narratives in which the writers' displeasure is directed not only against slaveholders but against the U.S. government as well. Their bitterness is obvious when Ellen and William Craft report they "thought it best, at any sacrifice, to leave the mock-free Republic, and come to a country where we and our dear little ones can be truly free."

In order to minimize the antagonism which could result from such declarations, the narrators usually tried to explain their repatriation as unavoidable. The Crafts concede:

> We shall always cherish the deepest feelings of gratitude to the Vigilance Committee of Boston (upon which were many of the leading abolitionists), and also to our numerous friends, for the very kind and noble manner in which they assisted us to preserve our liberties and to escape from Boston, as it were, like Lot from Sodom. . . . Oh! may God bless the thousands of unflinching disinterested abolitionists of America, who are labouring through evil as well as through good report, to cleanse their country's escutcheon from the foul and destructive blot of slavery, and to restore to every bondman his God-given rights.

Others, such as Lewis Clarke, indicate the lengths to which they went to avoid repatriation and the depths of their desires to remain in the areas of their births. Clarke went first to Cincinnati, then to Cleveland, but in both places he was not safe. Finally, he moved to Canada. His relief at being free is mixed with sorrow for, as he explains:

> A strange sky was over me, a new earth under me, strange voices all around; even the animals were such as I had never seen. A flock of prairie-hens and some black geese were altogether new to me. I was entirely alone; no human being, that I had ever seen before, where I could speak to him or he to me.
>
> And could I make that country ever seem like *home?*

Clarke, when he admits that he would have preferred remaining in Kentucky, tries to assuage not only any ideas of un-Americanism but also the fears of northerners that hoards of exslaves would migrate north if slavery were abolished:

> Some people are very much afraid all the slaves will run up north, if they are ever free. But I can assure them that they will run *back* again, if they do. If I could have been assured of my freedom in Kentucky, then, I would have given anything in the world for the prospect of spending my life among my old acquaintances where I first saw the sky, and the sun rise and go down.

The slave narrators' ability to praise Britain for its antislavery attitudes without appearing to be anti-American may even have been a factor in their popularity in the United States, for, in spite of their strong nationalism, many Americans still deferred to Great Britain as a model for cultural and social living. At any rate, the exslaves' willingness to include positive images of Americans prevented pro-British biases from being a significant obstacle to the narratives' success when published in the United States.

The initial stages in the evolution of the slave narratives are directly related to the changes in the institution of slavery. The first writings were autobiographical narratives of the authors' lives and experiences as slaves. The narratives included descriptions of the structure and practices of slavery. As slavery became more inhumane, the narratives began to expose its abuses and to agitate for the abolition of the slave trade. Finally, they began to defend blacks as legitimate and respectable members of the human race and to focus upon the perniciousness of a system which pretended otherwise. They began to demand the immediate elimination of all forms of slavery. During this process, the basic concerns of the narratives became increasingly compatible with those of antislavery societies.

This is one reason for the fact that the majority of the nineteenth-century narratives were published in cities which were centers of antislavery action: Boston, Philadelphia, New York, and London. Some narratives, such as Frederick Douglass's and William Wells Brown's, were actually printed in the offices of abolitionist societies. It became increasingly common for narrators to acknowledge their friends' suggestions that they relate their slave experiences to support antislavery movements. Two prefatory statements, one written in 1789 and the second in 1848, illustrate not only the changing emphasis of slave narrators but also their stylistic evolution from philosophic arguments to outright propaganda. (pp. 15-18)

Slave narratives, however, were not supported by abolitionists only. There are four major reasons for their widespread popularity. Some writers, such as James Gronniosaw and Olaudah Equiano, emphasized their conversions and other religious experiences. Consequently, their works were also useful for the religious and moral education and persuasion of their readers. Others, like Frederick Douglass and William Wells Brown, included discussions of the social and political relevance of their experiences. They enjoyed an especially good market during the pre-Civil War period, for they provided details about the life-styles and attitudes of southern whites and blacks for many who simply wanted to know more about the South.

A third reason for the popularity of many slave narratives was that under the label of education, scenes of violence and cruelty were presented which not only could awaken moral outrage against slavery but at the same time did satisfy the public's appetite for sensationalism. In the introductory essay to *Four Fugitive Slave Narratives,* Robin Winks states the argument thus: "The fugitive slave narratives were the pious pornography of their day, replete with horrific tales of whippings, sexual assaults, and explicit brutality, presumably dehumanized and fit for Nice Nellies to read precisely because they dealt with black, not white, men."

The fourth reason for the popularity of slave narratives is a result of the first three. As it became financially advantageous to print slave narratives, publishers encouraged sales through various promotional techniques. An interesting example is the case of *Slavery in the United States: A Narrative of the Life and Adventures of Charles Ball, a Black Man, Who Lived Forty Years in Maryland, South Carolina, and Georgia as a Slave.* First published in Lewiston, Pennsylvania, in 1836, it was moderately successful and, in fact, was reissued in New York, Pittsburgh, and London. Twenty-two years later, when the popularity of slave narratives was at its all-time high, Ball's narrative was, as John Nelson describes it, "seized upon, con-

densed slightly, bound in a fiery red cover, with great wavering gilt letters staring out at the reader, and handed out to an eager public under the astonishing title *Fifty Years in Chains.*" With the eager assistance of the commercial publishers, the slave narratives in the nineteenth century became the equivalent of the twentieth-century Westerns. (pp. 20-1)

> *Frances Smith Foster, in her* Witnessing Slavery: The Development of Ante-bellum Slave Narratives, *Greenwood Press, 1979, 182 p.*

CONTEMPORARY RESPONSES

EPHRAIM PEABODY

[*Peabody was a prominent Unitarian minister in Boston and the author of several minor religious works. His review of five slave narratives, excerpted below, is widely regarded as one of the most perceptive and fair-minded assessments of the genre to appear in the nineteenth century. Peabody here acknowledges the importance of regarding slavery from the point of view of the slave, a stance that many historians and critics rejected well into the twentieth century. He also praises the narratives as literary works and outlines the horrors of slavery as described in them.*]

America has the mournful honor of adding a new department to the literature of civilization,—the autobiographies of escaped slaves. . . . We place these volumes [slave narratives of Henry Watson, Lewis and Milton Clarke, William W. Brown, Frederick Douglass, and Josiah Henson] without hesitation among the most remarkable productions of the age,—remarkable as being pictures of slavery by the slave, remarkable as disclosing under a new light the mixed elements of American civilization, and not less remarkable as a vivid exhibition of the force and working of the native love of freedom in the individual mind.

There are those who fear lest the elements of poetry and romance should fade out of the tame and monotonous social life of modern times. There is no danger of it while there are any slaves left to seek for freedom, and to tell the story of their efforts to obtain it. There is that in the lives of men who have sufficient force of mind and heart to enable them to struggle up from hopeless bondage to the position of freemen, beside which the ordinary characters of romance are dull and tame. They encounter a whole *Iliad* of woes, not in plundering and enslaving others, but in recovering for themselves those rights of which they have been deprived from birth. Or if the *Iliad* should be thought not to present a parallel case, we know not where one who wished to write a modern *Odyssey* could find a better subject than in the adventures of a fugitive slave. What a combination of qualities and deeds and sufferings most fitted to attract human sympathy in each particular case!

A man born and bred a slave becomes so possessed by the idea of liberty, that neither fear, nor the habit of obedience, nor the hopelessness of deliverance, can stifle the irrepressible desire to be free. It grows, silently,—for he dares not utter it even to his companions,—year by year, until at length, whatever the consequences, he must obey this secret, ever-urging instinct of his soul. He has heard that far to the North there is a region where, could he but reach it, he would be free. He cannot read, he dares not ask questions, but he treasures up every floating hint as to the direction; he hoards up the chance money he receives, for the needs of the journey which is never out of his thoughts; as the time approaches, he hesitates on the brink of his dread enterprise, for he hears of the failure of others who have made similar attempts, and the penalties of failure are worse than death. But the unslumbering passion will not let him rest. (pp. 61-2)

One of the many unanswerable arguments which show how unfounded the assertion is that the blacks are naturally incompetent to bear the responsibilities of freedom, is derived from the fact, that in so many of them there exists this intense longing to possess it,—a sense of its value which all the appliances of slavery have not been able to crush out. Most men at the North have seen numbers of fugitive slaves. In a single town of New England with which we are acquainted, there are more than two hundred, and there cannot be less than thousands scattered through the different cities and villages; and they constitute, to say the least, as orderly, intelligent, and useful a portion of the population as the great body of foreign immigrants.

These biographies of fugitive slaves are calculated to exert a very wide influence on public opinion. We have always been familiar with slavery, as seen from the side of the master. These narratives show how it looks as seen from the side of the slave. They contain the *victim's* account of the working of this great institution. When one escapes from the South, and finds an opportunity of speaking and has the power to speak, it is certain that he will have attentive listeners. Not only curiosity, but a sense of justice, predisposes men to hear the testimony given by those who have suffered, and who have had few among their own number to describe their sufferings. The extent of the influence such lives must exert may be judged of, when we learn the immense circulation which has been secured for them. Of Brown's *Narrative,* first published in 1847, not less than eight thousand copies have been already sold. Douglass's *Life,* first published in 1845, has in this country alone passed through seven editions, and is, we are told, now out of print. They are scattered over the whole of the North, and all theoretical arguments for or against slavery are feeble, compared with these accounts by living men of what they personally endured when under its dominion.

These narratives are for many reasons worthy of attention. The statements they contain may be partial and prejudiced, but are not likely to be more so than are the estimates formed of slavery by those who profit from its continuance. At any rate, in forming a just judgment of this institution, it is quite as important to know what it is to Henson the slave, as what it is to McDuffie the master.

These narratives, however, do not give a full and complete view of the whole subject. There is one point of great moment, which they tend to make us forget, intead of bringing it forward into the light. We refer to the position of the antislavery men of the South. These books give the impression that the Slave States constitute one vast prisonhouse, of which all the whites without exception are the mere keepers, with no interest in the slaves further than they can be made subservient to the pleasure or profit of their owners. But this is far from being the case. It may not be, certainly it is not, a common feeling, but there is nowhere a more settled and bitter destination of slavery than is sometimes met with at the South. And, strange as it may seem, so entangled is the whole subject, so complicated are the relations and powers of the several States and of the Union, that, though the slave may find the most sympathy personally at the North, our main hope of the abolition of slavery as an institution depends on the efforts of the enemies of slavery at the South. (pp. 63-5)

These narratives, without any such intention on the part of the writers, reveal incidentally, but very vividly, some of the necessary evils of this mournful institution. The white children, in great part, grow up uneducated; for schools cannot be sustained in the country by the scattered population which alone slavery allows. In early years, they are exposed to acquiring the habit of indulging the domineering and selfish passions towards those weaker than themselves. Great numbers of men, ashamed to work, spend much of their time in gambling and horse-racing, and in unending talks about street-fights and party politics. The profits of their plantations depend on the large amount of work which they can extract from the slave, and on the small amount of food and clothing on which he can be made to live. Thus, without those checks which exist between the free laborer and his employer, there is a perpetual temptation to harshness and cruelty; and there never yet was a continuous influence of this kind brought to bear on a man, which did not finally reveal itself in the character. In addition to this, so far as the white males are concerned, there is another evil which can never be passed over when slavery is spoken of,—the temptation to licentiousness. The work *marriage* among the slaves has no legal, and scarcely a moral meaning. And the result of their relations with the whites is seen written ineffaceably in the variable color of the slave population. The horror of amalgamation at the South must be a qualified one. There is far less of it than at the North. A single fact is sufficient to answer all opposing arguments or assertions. In passing through the streets of New Orleans, among the first ten children you meet, there will probably be five different colors. At the South the prejudice is not against color, but against the blacks ceasing to be a servile class.

In reading these narratives, we are forcibly struck with the peculiar hardships to which the female slave is subjected. All that should in a civilized land be her protection makes her lot doubly accursed. She suffers all that the male suffers, and in addition miseries peculiar to herself. Her condition is hopeless. There are few females who, even if they could resolve to leave their children behind them, can ever hope to escape from bondage. The bearing of children, except for a very brief period, does not exempt them from labor in the fields, and this under the perpetual terror of the overseer's lash. If they possess any attractiveness of person, they are too often exposed to the danger of becoming doubly victims, first, to the corrupting urgencies of the white males around them, and then to the jealous dislike of the females. And in addition to all, the children whom they have borne in misery are liable to be taken from them, and sold away from their knowledge into hopeless bondage. Doubtless these evils do not appear on every plantation; but exposure to them is incident to slavery, is a part of the institution, and cannot be separated from it. And these narratives show how easily exposure passes into horrible reality.

In reading these little volumes, there is another evil of American slavery whose horrors are constantly brought before the mind. We refer to the internal slave trade. If we leave out of view the physical horrors of the Middle Passage, we believe that this internal slave trade is a system more accursed, more deserving of execration, the cause of more suffering, than the direct trade from Africa. It is a horrible phantom, making miserable the whole slave population of the South. They who are never made the victims of this traffic, who live and die on the same plantation, know that, at any moment,—sometimes from the selfishness of avaricious masters, sometimes from the misfortunes or death of the kind-hearted,—they are liable to be sold to the slave-dealer who will bid highest, and sent to some other region, under circumstances which, to their ignorant imaginations, seem worse than the reality proves. When added to all other deprivations and sufferings, this horrible fear, weighing incessantly on the thoughts of millions of men and women, is itself an evil of terrible magnitude.

But a still more important consideration is to be kept in mind. The blacks of the South are no longer such as their fathers were when brought from the shores of Africa. They have ceased to be savages. In its worse or better forms, all of them have caught some tincture of civilization. The better class of slaves are more civilized, have less of the brutal about them, than the lower class of whites. With increasing civilization, there is a development of the affections, of the moral sensibilities, and of that forethought also which makes men more apprehensive of future evil. They have learned to place the same estimate on kindred and domestic bonds as their masters; and they have intelligence enough to understand the nature of those advantages which they never must look on except as blessings from whose enjoyment thay are to be for ever excluded. The very improvement, which is sometimes put forward as one of the compensations of their lot, has made them sensitive to forms of suffering from which their forefathers were protected by their more brutal condition. The coffle of slaves torn from their families, which the slave-driver conducts by slow and weary stages from Virginia to the sugar-houses of the South, is, to the eye of reason, a more mournful spectacle than the barracoons on the coast of Africa. The wretched beings subjected to this doom are not less dragged away from all to which they are most attached, and carried, powerless victims, to a region and a fate which they most of all dread, but they are capable of a more clinging and paralyzing fear, and feel with infinitely more keenness everything that tears and wounds the affections. Every truth of religion which has dawned on their minds, every domestic bond they have learned to value, every idea and sentiment of a better kind which they have insensibly derived from intercourse with a better instructed race around them, only makes them more sensitive to the lot to which they are doomed. Common humanity demands that, if this traffic—"without mercy and without natural affection"—is to go on, the slaves should be kept as near the condition of brutes as possible. Ignorance, brutality, and callousness to every claim of the affections, if suffering only is to be thought of, constitute a boon for the slave, by putting him into a state of moral insensibility, scarcely less blessed than the state induced by that medical discovery of the present time which promises so to alleviate the physical pains of man.

Is there exaggeration in this? We wish we could believe there was; but there is not. A perpetual fear haunts the slaves, as the fear of ghosts haunts superstitious children, with the mournful difference that the slaves' apprehensions are well founded. This dread of being torn from their families, of being sold to they know not whom, and of being sent to the cotton and sugar plantations of the Southwest, is seen running through and giving a dark coloring to all the narratives before us. In fact, the slaves are not merely liable to be thus sold, but the threat of it serves as an instrument of the police to make them submissive and industrious. It is held up constantly as a punishment for the refractory and disobedient; and that it may be more effective, every circumstance which can make it alarming to the slave's imagination is kept before him. But in trying to avoid this peril, it does not do for him to show too many of the qualities of a self-supporting manhood. The slave's path is a Mahomet's bridge. His virtues may be as dangerous to himself as his vices. If a slave is restless, intelligent, and enterprising,

the master is tempted to sell him to the South, lest he should escape to freedom and the North. And no matter what the master's feelings or wishes, if he becomes poor, or dies, his slaves are always exposed, even if they be not actually subjected, to this doom. (pp. 71-4)

Ephraim Peabody, "Narratives of Fugitive Slaves,"
in The Christian Examiner and Religious Miscellany,
Vol. XLVII, July, 1849, pp. 61-93.

GRAHAM'S MAGAZINE

[*The following excerpt from a review of* Uncle Tom's Cabin *by Harriet Beecher Stowe includes a notorious negative response to all forms of antislavery literature. Vehemently denouncing "niggerism" in literature, the anonymous critic asserts that accounts of slavery are not written to win justice for the slave, but are merely commercial ventures calculated to exploit readers' taste for sensationalism.*]

That sudden popularity and success are not always evidences of merit to be relied upon, Barnum has taught us with the Woolly Horse, Tom Thumb, and his Mermaid. Locke's moon hoax, if we remember, was for a while the rage, and deceived astronomers royal and republican; and the whole French people, in a frenzy of patriotic devotion to Napoleon I., have shown the world the "pink and model of an emperor," in a very scurvy fellow. And in the sudden hurrah which bursts from the throats of the many over the "Cabin literature," we feel no certainty that Milton, Shakespeare, Byron, Wordsworth, Scott, and Cooper, are in any imminent danger of being burned by the hands of the common hangman, to the tantaralara of an African dance. The truth is, nothing has a slower growth than *truth*—nothing is, for a time, more fertile and luxuriant than error. A popular rage for any thing is a pretty good test of its worthlessness, and when the book presses are occupied with prurient French novels, sanctified dissertations upon negro carousals, and puritanical eulogies of blasphemous psalm-singing, almost to the exclusion of the Bible and healthy and robust works, we need scarcely stop to prove that the devil is having a pretty good time of it among the sons of mean—or that such taste is false and damnable.

Our female agitators have abandoned Bloomers in despair, and are just now bestride a new hobby—an intense love of black folks, *in fashionable novels!* Flannel ceases to be cut into garments for the children of Africa, but they are most intolerably drenched with ink—on the principle, we suppose, of "like to like." If woe, expressed in big capital letters, had the power of tears, we should be in danger of a second deluge on Chestnut street some fine morning; but this sort of grief, even when illustrated with very sorry engravings, is intended to deplete the pocket—so you need not get out your handkerchief, dear madam! but open your pocket-book to its widest capacity. Sambo is a pretty good golddigger, just now—work him who will; and those who

> Would not have a slave to till their ground,

use him pretty severely in the press-room.

We have a regular incursion of the blacks. The shelves of booksellers groan under the weight of Sambo's woes, done up in covers! What a dose we have had and are having! The population of readers has gone a wool-gathering! Our "Helots of the West" are apparently at a premium with the publishers just now; and we have Northern folks as anxious to make money of them, as the Southrons can be, for their lives. A plague of all black faces! We hate this niggerism, and hope it may be done away with. We cannot tolerate negro slavery of this sort—we are abolitionists on this question! If we are threatened with any more negro stories—here goes! We will call our retainers together and arm them; we will raise the *slogan* of Montrose; we will "gather a band" of our contributors (some tall fellows among them!—Herbert, who describes a battle so well, would fight one, "like four," as the French say!) and go into the South to put down negrodom! "Graham" could do this—just as easily as Abraham long ago armed about 318 of his "trained servants," and pursued the enemy unto Dan. Besides, he might have the assistance of a garrison along with his army! Well, we hope we shall not be provoked. It is all very well for the South to talk of the negro excitements, and to take things to heart. If they had to read all those negro-books that overflow us, North of Mason and Dixon's line, *then,* indeed, we should despair of them. We don't want, therefore, to hear any more complaints from Georgia or Carolina. 'Tis we, the readers of the North, who are aggrieved by these blasts and counter-blasts, and none have a better right to be angry, and talk of nullification than we have.

In the name of the Prophet—not the bookseller's profit!—let us have done with this woolly-headed literature. . . . (p. 209)

We have thought over this subject very deliberately, and we do not find—even under the inspiration of these novels, which run to editions of hundreds of thousands—that we are a whit more convinced, than by the very sober prose of Greeley and Doctor Bailey, that "the question is all on one side." Say what we will, we commenced living together—North and South—under some very express and many implied contracts, and no fine hairsplitting in morals can make that act an honest one which is a clear evasion, if not an open violation, of the agreement. If the South have combustible materials about them, and we undertook not to damage their property by firing it at midnight, we have no right to be letting off fire-crackers all around the house in the day time, for the amusement of young Jonathans in breeches or petticoats. The South may very properly say to us—"Look you, sir, you undertook to attend to the Northern end of the farm, we have no fancy here for the exploits of jugglery—you may beat even the Chinese in throwing unsheathed knives about our heads, but you had better be at home attending to business. If your time is not fully occupied in the field or workshop—go out into the lanes and alleys of your cities—feed the hungry, clothe the naked, and attempt to reclaim the abandoned and the outcast. You will find work for your hands, good sir, and meek madam; ample and urgent! We will take care of Sambo and Dinah; and come when you will, you will find them clothed and fed somewhere on the plantation. If they are sick, they shall be nursed, and, if possible, cured. You will not find one of them dying under the hedge, their very bones rotting from disease or starvation!"

Ah! Brother of the North, what becomes of scores of laborers with *you,* whose sweat and sinews have enriched some gigantic capitalist at the cost of health and hope? When age comes upon him, or he is laid upon a bed of fever and languishing, fierce and prolonged, are his comforts attended to—his expenses paid? Unless you are greatly belied, you give "the laborer his *hire;*" but you give him no more. The sickly workman—is he not speedily cast adrift? Able-bodied men can be had, even with you, for dollars. The hollow cough of a consumptive operative is not music in factories, or the history of every year's toil is a lie! You do not, it is true, "sell" your hand—you have long ago taken the pith from his bones—the warmth from his blood:

no! you do *not* sell him, neither could you a slave in the same condition; but you abandon him to want, wretchedness, and death. He may be a *man*—a *free* man, if you like; but could you do worse were he a dog? Go home, brother! each system has its evils; and, with each other's help, we shall cure them by and bye—but it will be by something else than *talk*! There will have to be some very earnest work, and some very manly sacrifices on *both* sides before that day. But it will come!

We have taken up the "Cabin literature" for the purpose of saying frankly what we think of the whole business—for it is a *business,* and nothing more. We have spoken temperately and critically of the books, indignantly and perhaps warmly of the spirit which pervades them, and we say by way of emphasis, that we despise the whole concern—the spirit which dictated them is false. They are altogether speculations in patriotism—a question of dollars and cents, not of slavery or liberty. The whole literary atmosphere has become tainted with them—they are corrupt altogether and abominable. Many of the persons who are urging on this negro crusade into the domain of letters, have palms with an infernal itch for gold. They would fire the whole republic if they could but rake the gems and precious stones from the ashes. They care nothing for principle, honor or right, and though anxious to be regarded as martyrs, their chief concern is about the *stakes.* He would be an explorer worthy of all honor who could stumble upon a truth which they would not sacrifice for shillings.

For the present we are done with this subject. We hope we are done with it forever.

In the meanwhile, let us see the amiable publishers and writers and most valorous moralists, who are hurling stones at their brothers of the South, do a little something, from the great wealth thus achieved, for the *free negroes of the North.* Many of these bold reformers control influential presses, but we do not see Sambo educated by them to set their type, carry their papers, drive their presses, or keep their books. Cuffy is not in the editorial room with paste and scissors—no! he is in the street, lounging upon the cellar-door, in rags and degraded. If he could read, he would be astonished at the sympathy which that dapper little gentleman who has just past bestows—in type—upon his race. But we would advise Cuff not to presume upon his knowledge. We don't believe he could get a dollar out of his friend to save his soul—kicks we imagine would be more plentiful than coppers, and, unless Cuffy has a taste for oratory, he is not likely to get even a civil word from his white brother—and that only at an agitation meeting, where subscribers are to be picked up, and pretty Quaker girls, in youthful innocence, take poetry for Gospel. (pp. 214-15)

"Black Letters; or Uncle Tom-Foolery in Literature," in Graham's Magazine, *Vol. XLII, No. 2, February, 1853, pp. 209-15.*

LITERARY CONCERNS: LANGUAGE, THEME, AND TECHNIQUE

STEPHEN BUTTERFIELD

[*Butterfield analyzes language in the slave narratives, surveying such techniques as understatement, irony, indignation, and biblical prose. He also examines how the slave narrators adapted nineteenth-century white rhetoric to their own uses.*]

Slave-narrative rhetoric stems largely from the writer's Christian perspective and involvement in abolitionist politics. Sermons, direct contact with the facts of slavery, and the religious culture of Afro-America compose the main black influences on the choice of language. The white influences came from the Bible and other Christian literature, editorials in abolitionist newspapers, Websterian and Garrisonian oratory, the expectations of the white reading public, and the antithetical prose style inherited from eighteenth-century England. Some of the stylistic devices of this period have all but disappeared; others have ripened into modes of expression that are now characteristic of black political writing. The concrete diction, ironic humor, understatement, polemics, and epithet that we recognize in contemporary black essayists all appear first in the slave narrative. Although black writers in the slavery period wrote according to the standards of English and American whites and imitated the style of their white models, at the same time they initiated traditions that were developed and refined by their descendants into something distinctly "black."

There are some exceptions to the rule that diction and syntax were derived from white models. Occasionally we find idioms that sound as if they might be derived from the speech of the narrator's own background:

> I got into a fair way of buying myself again (Grandy).

> . . . when he was present, it was cut and slash—knock down and drag out (W. W. Brown).

Henry Bibb, who at one point was sold to Indians, describes an Indian dance as though he were speaking aloud:

> Their dress for the dance was most generally a great bunch of bird feathers, coon tails, or something of the kind stuck in their heads, and a great many shells tied about their legs to rattle while dancing. Their manner of dancing is taking hold of each others hands and forming a ring around the large fire in the centre, and go stomping around it until they would get drunk or their heads would get to swimming, and then they would go off and drink, and another set come on. . . .

Some authors also go out of their way to imitate dialect when they reconstruct the speech of their characters:

> Say, brudder, way you come from, and which side you goin day wid dat ar little don up buckra? (Craft and Craft).

> Jake, I is gwine to wip you today, as I did dem toder boys.

Although the syntax of slave narratives is usually formal and periodic, it is possible to find paragraphs of loose, rhythmic prose, where the order of clauses approximates modern usage. We are most likely to encounter them in minor works which are otherwise uninteresting as literature, such as the autobiography of James Mars:

> They hitched up the parson's team, put on board what few things he had and his family, in the still of a dark night, for it was very dark, and started for Norfolk, and on the way we run afoul of a man's woodpile, for it was so dark he could not see the road.

> . . . The beguilers were both, I do not say preachers, but they were both deceivers, and he talked so smooth to mother that he beguiled her.

Here the clauses, arranged in simple order of subject and verb, are linked together by "and" and "for"; the tense of "run" in the first quotation is colloquial; there is very little subordination and no attempt to build expectation through the use of antitheses or items arranged in a progressive series. Key words in the narrative are repeated to create mood ("in the still of a dark night . . . for it was very dark . . . so dark, etc."). Just as in oral dialogue, the author interrupts himself in midsentence to qualify the thought and relies on repetition and emphasis to amplify material rather than additional images or complexity of phrasing.

What helps to account for this simplicity and looseness of syntax is that the *Life of James Mars* appeared several years after the peak of the slave narrative period, and was written for his own family; it was not part of a political movement, and the writer therefore was under no sense of obligation to impress white readers or sway public opinion.

The language of more typical slave narratives, though far from idiomatic and colloquial, is close to the material facts of experience. The slave narrator's political role requires the use of description, detail, and concrete language. He is called upon, as part of his activity in the antislavery movement, to supply first-hand information about slavery from the victim's point of view. What it was like to pick cotton and tobacco, how often and for what offenses the slaves were whipped, their standard of living, the duties expected of them, what took place during a slave auction—these and others were questions which might be in the mind of a reader unfamiliar with the slave system, and to which the slave narrative gave specific answers.

> At noon the cart appeared with our breakfast. It was in large trays, and was set on the ground. There was bread, of which a piece was cut off for each person; then there was small hominy boiled, that is, Indian-corn, ground in the hand-mill, and besides this two herrings for each of the men and women, and one for each of the children. Our drink was the water in the ditches, whatever might be its state . . . (Grandy). . . .

There is in many narratives a preoccupation, amounting at times almost to an obsession, with the whips, paddles, spiked collars, chains, gags, cowhides, and cages used to control the slaves. We see the South as a vast torture chamber, the memories of the instruments of torture sealed indelibly into the narrator's brain, as though this tireless enumeration of the objects of horror were a rite of exorcism.

> The whip had a short wooden stock, braided over with leather, and was loaded at the butt. The lash was three feet long, or thereabouts, and made of rawhide strands.

> . . . Winding the lash around his hand, and taking hold of the small end of the stock, he walked up to me, and with a malignant look, ordered me to strip (Northup).

> He tied Sarah up and whipped her, until the flesh so cleaved from the bone, that it might easily have been scraped off with the hand; while the blood stood in puddles under her feet (Thompson). . . .

The effect is to drive home to the reader what kind of social system he supports every time he pays taxes, goes to the polls, and sings the national anthem; but perhaps, too, by thus confronting his memories, the writer lays them to rest with the realization that, having endured everything, there is nothing further to be feared, nothing to lose but his chains, and that he can never be intimidated by white power again.

The concrete detail of men familiar with specific work is also used for purposes other than giving information about slavery.

Thompson describes his experiences aboard a whaling vessel in the same manner:

> The harpoon is sharp, and barbed at one end, so that when it has once entered the animal, it is difficult to draw it out again, and has attached to its other end a pole, two inches thick and five feet long. Attached to this is a line 75 or 100 fathoms in length, which is coiled into the bow of the boat.

Passages such as these are not notably more concrete than white writing of the same period, as one can easily demonstrate by opening to any page in *Moby Dick*. But there is a difference of emphasis and context that distinguishes the white from the black. Compare Melville and Thompson on the same subject:

> Thus the whale-line folds the whole boat in its complicated coils, twisting and writhing around it in almost every direction. All the oarsmen are involved in its perilous contortions; so that to the timid eye of the landsmen they seem as Indian jugglers, with the deadliest snakes sportively festooning their limbs.

Melville's language is symbolic and weighted with ambiguous moral meanings: the rope is a snake, a traditional Christian symbol of evil, but "complicated . . . twisting and writhing around . . . in almost every direction." It involves "all the oarsmen," including those who had nothing to do with coiling it in the tub. And the crew live with it and by it as a necessary tool of their livelihood, only peripherally aware that it can kill them. Indeed, more than peripheral awareness of this fact would make them less efficient as oarsmen and increase the danger.

Thompson also makes the imagery of a whaling voyage carry moral and allegorical meanings, as is evident from the sermon at the end of his narrative. But in his and most of the other slave narratives, the language is a direct consequence of a political purpose. It is the political objective, the role of the book as a weapon in a class, race, and cultural struggle, that more than anything else distinguishes the concreteness of these black writers from that of Melville. For them there can be nothing morally ambiguous about the need to resist and abolish slavery, and there is little ambiguity about the reason for their suffering. Although they look at the issues from a Christian perspective, they do not see oppression in terms of a symbol structure that transforms evil into a metaphysical necessity. For to do so would be to locate the source of evil outside the master-slave relationship and thus cut the ideological ground from under the abolitionist movement.

It is true that the literary disadvantage of such a heavy concentration on political involvement may be to reduce experience to a single dimension, to iron the complexity out of language and turn it into a vehicle for reporting data that will be of service to the cause. But the best writers in the history of black autobiography are able to share the same political involvement of the mediocre ones without being noticeably crippled by a monotonous style or a one-dimensional outlook. Their close grasp of the material facts of human social relationships, their ability to bring power and clarity of thought to political issues and to connect personal conflict, frustration, and quest for identity with the large streams of mass movements in human history, are precisely the greatest strengths of Frederick Douglass, W.E.B. Du Bois, J. Saunders Redding, Richard Wright, and George Jackson as authors. These qualities are what we miss in all but a few white Americans; they appear first in black literature with the attempt of the slave narrative to describe the master-slave relationship in the most persuasive and explicit of terms.

In addition, the slave narrator's rendering of concrete experience leads naturally to the use of understatement. The facts which he gives are so overwhelming in their barbarity and so convincing as a case against slavery that his political conclusion is an anticlimax. Anything he can say is bound to understate the point; it is an inevitable rhetorical method. This, for example, is Wells Brown's description of the taming of Randall, a slave who had laid his overseer's posse "prostrate on the ground" rather than allow himself to be whipped, but who was finally captured with the aid of pistols and clubs:

> He was then taken to the barn, and tied to a beam. Cook gave him over one hundred lashes with a heavy cowhide, had him washed with salt and water, and left him tied during the day. The next day he was untied and taken to a blacksmith's shop, and had a ball and chain attached to his leg. He was compelled to labor in the field, and perform the same amount of work that the other hands did.

The account concludes: "When his master returned home, he was much pleased to find that Randall had been subdued in his absence."

Wells Brown is one of the best sources, other than Douglass, for examples of understatement and the use of experience alone to state the antislavery case. Elsewhere in his narrative he tells of seeing a slave jump into the water from a steamboat to avoid being punished for stealing meat. Despite his cries and pleadings, the pursuers strike him with pike-poles until he drowns. After hauling the corpse on board with a hook, they accuse him of "playing possum" and kick the body to make him get up. The men leave when there is no response, and the captain says after them, "you have killed this nigger; now take him off my boat." The body is then dragged ashore, left for the night, and picked up by the trash cart the next morning. Brown's only comment is: "During the whole time, I did not see more than six or seven persons around it, who, from their manner, evidently regarded it as no uncommon occurrence."

The most effective understatement by Wells Brown concludes his description of a case where a woman had jumped off his boat. The large room on the lower deck contained "men and women, promiscuously—all chained two and two," and a "strict watch" kept on them; for, he continues, echoing the cautionary language that might be used by a trader toward the sentries, "cases have occurred in which slaves have got off their chains, and made their escape at landing-places, while the boats were taking in wood." It is not until the final line that the true restraint of his tone is revealed:

> with all our care, we lost one woman who had been taken from her husband and children, and having no desire to live without them, in the agony of her soul jumped overboard, and drowned herself. She was not chained.

In the image of release from chains, Brown is making use of a grimly ironic motif that is common in slave literature: death brings freedom. When a slave dies he is "free at last." But the cautionary echoes add an especially subtle undertone: the trader would see her death as a loss of capital, a consequence of failing to make sure the woman was properly chained like the others. Brown returns to this simpleminded, yet coldly factual explanation, after having shown her jump to be the last resort of a free human spirit. In effect, he mimics the slaveholder's attitude ("see what happens when you don't keep chains on them") and then leaves it stripped for exposure by a significant silence.

Irony and shifts in tone between satire and rage are more explicit. As might be expected, these methods suit especially well the temperament of the more militant authors, such as Ward and Douglass, but one also finds examples in the narratives of Grandy, Thompson, Northup, Wells Brown, and William and Ellen Craft.

> While we were lying there by the jail, two vessels came from Eastern Shore, Virginia, laden with cattle and colored people. The cattle were lowing for their calves, and the men and women were crying for their husbands, wives, and children (Grandy).

> But when I thought of slavery with its Democratic whips—its Republican chains—its evangelical bloodhounds, and its religious slaveholders—when I thought of all this paraphernalia of American Democracy and Religion behind me . . . I was encouraged to press forward . . . (ibid.).

> The very amiable, pious-hearted Mr. Theophilus Freeman, partner or consignee of James H. Burch, and keeper of the slave pen in New-Orleans, was out among his animals early in the morning. With an occasional kick of the older men and women, and many a sharp crack of the whip about the ears of the younger slaves, it was not long before they were all astir, and wide awake (Northup).

The irony in these three passages indicates the major sources of ironic and satirical perception in the slave narrative: the contradictions between the official rhetoric of the American Promise and the actual treatment of black people, and between the theory that slaves were chattel goods and the fact that they were human beings. Underlying both contradictions are the larger ones between master and slave, pro- and antislavery religion, and the economic systems of North and South. The slave's location in society where the contradictions were sharpest naturally inclines him toward the use of a literary method whose essence is contradiction.

INDICTMENT

> Commonwealth of Virginia,   } In the Circuit Court, the
> Norfolk County, ss.   } Grand Jurors impannelled

> and sworn to inquire of offences committed in the body of the said County on their oath present, that Margaret Douglass, being an evil disposed person, not having the fear of God before her eyes, but moved and instigated by the devil, wickedly, maliciously, and feloniously, on the fourth day of July, in the year of our Lord one thousand eight hundred and fifty-four, at Norfolk, in said County, did teach a certain black girl named Kate to read in the Bible, to the great displeasure of Almighty God, to the pernicious example of others in like case offending, contrary to the form of the statute in such case made and provided, and against the peace and dignity of the Commonwealth of Virginia.

>   Victor Vagabond, Prosecuting Attorney

> (Craft and Craft. The passage is probably based on an actual conviction of a white woman in Virginia for this crime.)

In this parody of legal language and institutions by William and Ellen Craft, the irony is based on four contradictions: (1) between the religious ideals given lip service by whites and those permitted to blacks; (2) between the theoretical purpose of law, which is "the peace and dignity of the Commonwealth of Virginia," and the actual purpose of the Indictment, which is the forcible suppression of a subject class; (3) between the

traditions of the American Revolution invoked by the date of the "crime" and supposedly represented by the state, and the way that institution reacts when a black person behaves in the same traditions; and (4) between the subject and the pompous officialisms of the language.

The Crafts in fact are extremely good at parody. At one point in their journey, on board a steamer from Savannah to Charleston, the captain advises Ellen, who is disguised as William's master, to watch her "boy" like a hawk when they get to the North.

> Before my master could speak, a rough slave dealer, who was sitting opposite, with both elbows on the table, and with a large piece of broiled fowl in his fingers, shook his head with emphasis, and in a deep Yankee tone, forced through his crowded mouth the words, "Sound doctrine, captain, very sound." He then dropped the chicken into the plate, leant back, placed his thumbs in the armholes of his fancy waistcoat, and continued, "I would not take a nigger to the North under no consideration. I have had a deal to do with niggers in my time, but I never saw one who ever had his heel upon free soil that was worth a d——n. Now stranger," addressing my master, "if you have made up your mind to sell that ere nigger, I am your man; just mention your price, and if it isn't out of the way, I will pay for him on this board with hard silver dollars" (Craft and Craft).

The details of the slave trader's mannerisms are close in spirit to the quasi-surrealist caricatures of Ralph Ellison. He speaks with his mouth full of chicken, in a deep *Yankee* tone; the involvement of Yankees in the slave trade, and the fact that they often made the most brutal, savage, despicable racists in the business, is an irony remarked in several of the slave narratives, as well as in *Uncle Tom's Cabin*. The trader puts his elbows on the table, shaking his head, placing his presumably greasy thumbs in his waistcoat, showing off his expertise on the subject of "niggers" to a fugitive slave, and offering to buy her husband in "hard silver dollars" as evidence, we suppose, of his honesty, plain dealing, and sterling dependability in business affairs. The perception that sees the world in terms of irony and caricature is shaped by having to live with oppression, hypocrisy, contradiction, and double identity as daily conditions of existence. (pp. 32-42)

Samuel Ward parodies the ideology of slavery, not by means of caricature, but by pretending to argue the slaveholder's point of view. His comments on the sale of his mother, which synthesize the tones of irony and outrage, must be quoted at length to reflect their roots in abolitionist oratory. Just prior to this passage, his father has been whipped, and his mother is to be punished somehow for defending him.

> Besides, if so trifling a thing as the *mere marriage relation* were to interfere with the supreme proprietor's right of a master over his slave, next we should hear that slavery must give way before marriage! Moreover, if a negress may be allowed free speech, touching the flogging of a negro, simply because that negro happened to be her husband, how long would it be before some such claim would be urged in behalf of some other member of a negro family, in unpleasant circumstances? Would this be endurable in a republican civilized community, A.D. 1819? By no means. It would sap the very foundation of slavery—it would be like "the letting out of water": for let the principle be once established that the negress Anne Ward may speak as she pleases about the flagellation of her husband, the negro William Ward, as

Former slaves honoring Abraham Lincoln and celebrating the Emancipation Proclamation.

a matter of right, and like some alarming and death-dealing infection it would spread from plantation to plantation, until property in husbands and wives would not be worth the having. No, no: marriage must succumb to slavery, slavery must reign supreme over every right and every institution, however venerable or sacred; *ergo,* this free-speaking Anne Ward must be made to feel the greater rigors of the domestic institution. Should she be flogged? That was questionable. She never had been whipped, except, perhaps, by her parents; she was now three-and-thirty years old—rather late for the commencement of training; she weighed 184 lbs. avoir-dupoise; she was strong enough to whip an ordinary-sized man; she had as much strength of *will* as of mind; and what did not diminish the awkwardness of the case was, she gave most unmistakeable evidence of "rather tall resistance," in case of an attack. Well, then, it were wise not to risk this; but one most convenient course was left to them, and that course they could take with perfect safety to themselves, without yielding one hair's breadth of the rights and powers of slavery, but establishing them—they could sell her, and sell her they would: she was their property, and like any other stock she *could* be sold, and like any other unruly stock she *should* be brought to the market. . . .

However, this [her] sickly boy, if practicable, must be raised for the auction mart. Now, to sell his mother *immediately,* depriving him of her tender care, might endanger his life, and, what was all-important in his life, his saleability. Were it not better to risk a little from the freedom of this woman's tongue, than to jeopardize the sale of this *article*? Who knows but, judging from the pedigree, it may prove to be a prime lot—rising six feet in length, and weighing two hundred and twenty pounds, more or less, some day? To ask these questions was to answer them; there was no resisting the force of such valuable and logical consideration. Therefore the sale was delayed; the young animal was to run awhile longer with his—(I accommodate myself to the ideas and facts of slavery, and use a corresponding nomenclature)—dam (Ward).

Ward's use of animal nomenclature and age and weight statistics to parody the idea that slaves were chattel goods recalls Swift's method in *A Modest Proposal:*

> It is true, a child just dropped from its dam may be supported by her milk for a solar year, with little other nourishment. . . .

The best feature of Ward's irony is that every single reason he pretends to espouse in defense of selling his mother is, from

31

the slaveholder's point of view, valid. It would indeed "sap the very foundation of slavery" if Anne Ward were allowed to assert her identity as a human being with family loyalties in place of her legal definition as an article of property. The contradiction between master and slave is completely antagonistic; the interests of one cannot be asserted without suppressing the interests of the other. The effect of the ironic mask is consequently to denounce the whole institution rather than any single injustice. It is made clear in the content, as well as the tone, that slavery is the chief target, for the woman is sold in order to defend the rights and powers of the system.

The tone of the passage is that of the impassioned orator, speaking directly to an audience of whom he asks rhetorical questions and then gives answers. Certain words and phrases seem intended to carry the weight of the additional anger, sarcasm, pause, and innuendo that could be supplied by a speaker's voice: for example, the underscoring of *"could," "should," "article," "immediately," "mere marriage relation,"* the repetition of "no, no," "slavery," "sell her," and the name "Anne Ward," and the understatement of "rather tall resistance." Ward builds up expectations in the reader, too, by means of progressive clauses: "Well then, it were wise not to risk this; but one most convenient course was left to them, and that course they could take with perfect safety to themselves. . . ." The expectations are then satisfied by concluding with the crowning injustice, contradiction, or irony of the incident. The writer demonstrates by his ability to parody the oppressor that he is the real master of the situation; he comprehends the oppressor's ideas, and exposes their flimsiness and hypocrisy to the ridicule of his audience; he is utterly free of the oppressor's image of himself, and throws it back in his face with a sardonic laugh. The response which this tone demands from the reader is not pity, but respect.

The slave experience affects the style of the narrative, then, by impelling it in the direction of precise description, detailed rendering of work gangs, plantation conditions, and atrocities, understatement, irony, parody, and indignation. The use of parody provides still another analogue to the response of the colonialized "native," who parodies the mannerisms, ideology, culture, and self-righteous ignorance of the white colonizer. The slave narrator may be different from the "native" in that his parody appropriates the best traditions of the master culture for his own use; Ward, for example, upholds the Western concepts of marriage, republicanism, free speech, government by the consent of the governed, and the right of revolution. His appeal is for full acceptance as a Westerner and American. (pp. 43-6)

In speaking of the "white influence" on the slave narratives, . . . we must qualify repeatedly the nature and source of the influence. Some of it came directly from the slave's reading of white literature or exposure to white speeches and sermons; much more came from white materials *as assimilated* by Afro-American social life: Christian imagery drawn from black church and revival meetings, language rhythms from the speech of Negro preachers, religious and political symbols and slogans that had special meanings in a black context. As in the case of white American values, the slave narrator refits white styles to a purpose and identity derived from black experience.

The Christian impact on slave narrative language was conveyed through the prose of the King James Bible, John Bunyan's *Pilgrim's Progress*, the *Journal* of John Woolman and perhaps other Quaker writing, the traditional Christian symbols of cross, lance, cup, ark, flood, chariot, golden city, wounds of Christ,

etc., interpreted anew by black history and eloquence, and the oratorical cadences of revivals and sermons. It is common in most of the narratives to run across passages like these:

> Little did Mr. Adams know, when he was uttering that speech, that he was "opening the eyes of the blind"; that he was breaking the iron bands from the limbs of one poor slave, and setting the captive free. But bread cast upon the waters, will be found and gathered after many days (Thompson).

> Malinda was to me an affectionate wife. She was with me in the darkest hours of adversity. She was with me in sorrow, and joy, in fasting and feasting, in trial and persecution, in sickness and health, in sunshine and in shade (Bibb).

> I was a starving fugitive, without home or friends— a reward offered for my person in the public papers— pursued by cruel manhunters, and no claim upon him to whose door I went . . . he took me in, and gave me of his food, and shared with me his own garments (Pennington).

(pp. 47-8)

These passages echo the rhetoric of Bible and preachment. In the quotation from Henry Bibb, paraphrasing a marriage service to describe his wife would serve to remind the reader indirectly of the sacredness of the marriage relation, whether black or white, and thus help to move the emotions in condemnation of the master's disregard for slave marriages.

Other passages use both this rhetoric and the tradition of the sermon to build carefully, by means of an architecture of periodic and parallel clauses, toward effects that approximate the African song of praise:

> For about three weeks the storm raged most furiously, the wind became a hurricane, the waves rolled and dashed mountain high, sweeping our boats from their hangings, and dashing them in pieces; while the sun was hid by dark and portentious clouds.

> All hands looked upon the captain as their deliverer, while he stood looking at the clouds, seemingly with deprecating vengeance. But it was the work of our God, whom the winds obey, and to whom the sea does homage. Well might the Scripture say, "He has his ways in the whirlwinds, and his paths are known to the mighty deep." He looks, and the fearfully threatening clouds hide their deformed faces; He speaks, and the winds are hushed in profound silence; He commands, and the lofty billows lowly bow their heads (Thompson).

The Scriptural allusions dominate the atmosphere of the writing, but the final sentence, in which each clause repeats and amplifies the form of the previous, may be a lingering breath of Africa. God has an African immediacy and presence in nature; his attributes are listed as parts of the storm. He walks before the eyes of the listener, like the God of James Weldon Johnson's poem, "The Creation." The parallel lines, a method extending all the way up to the speeches of Martin Luther King, occur also in the work of many contemporary African poets.

In their use of Christian rhetoric, the slave narratives parallel the development of colonial and early federal autobiographies, journals, and diaries by William Bradford, Samuel Sewall, Cotton Mather, Jonathan Edwards, John Woolman, and many other whites less well known. There is a similar alternation between lofty cadence and ordinary detail, and the same tendency in each group to slip into the language of Scripture and read religious significance into any casual incident. The *Narrative* of Noah Davis, for example, occasionally gives us something of the flavor of "Sinners in the Hands of an Angry God":

> As I sat on the shoe-bench, I picked up a bunch of bristles, and selecting one of the smallest, I began to wonder, if God could see an object so small as that. No sooner had this inquiry arose in my heart, than it appeared to me, that the Lord could not only see the bristle, but that He beheld me, as plainly as I saw the little object in my hand; and not only so, but that God was then looking through me, just as I would hold up a tumbler of clear water to the sun and look through it.

Elsewhere we find strains of the religious mysticism of Edwards' *Personal Narratives* and Woolman's *Journal:*

> I felt such a love and peace flowing in my soul, that I could not sit longer; I sprang to my feet, and cried out, "Glory to God!" (Davis).

> About two rods from Uncle Harry's house I fell upon my knees . . . with hands uplifted to high heaven. . . . I received a spiritual answer of approval; a voice like thunder seeming to enter my soul, saying, I am your God and am with you; though the whole world be against you, I am more than the world; though wicked men hunt you, trust in me, for I am the Rock of your Defence (Thompson).

The influence of Woolman, in fact, was probably direct. The *Journal,* first published in 1794, enjoyed wide circulation as both a spiritual odyssey and an antislavery tract. Woolman himself was instrumental in persuading the Quakers to take a stand against slavery and his essays, particularly "Some Considerations on the Keeping of Negroes," were part of the arsenal of abolitionist literature (if one may use so military a term for the gentle and pacifistic Woolman) which many of the slave narrators would have encountered in their efforts to get an education. Woolman was well known to the prominent abolitionists of the early nineteenth century, among them Channing, Whittier, and Phillips. Woolman's mystical experiences are unmistakeably like Thompson's, and, again like Thompson, he ends his *Journal* with a sea voyage that supplies metaphors and context for a sermon. Pennington, who was sheltered and taught by Quakers as a hungry, illiterate fugitive, would certainly have been given the *Journal* to whet his appetite for learning; and, as a final note of evidence for a direct relationship between the white narrative and the black, both Pennington and Thompson seem to have structured their autobiographies like Woolman's. There were scores of less renowned Quaker spiritual journals that followed the same pattern: the subject feels divine intimations in childhood, passes through a phase of youthful frivolities, repents of them in a series of acute spiritual conflicts, is converted to Quakerism, surrenders his will to the inner light, and experiences a call to the ministry. Thompson, though far from saintly and pacifistic in tone, was clearly affected by this pattern, and Pennington differs from it only in the overlay of another, equally standard pattern—the flight to freedom.

One other parallel with the slave narratives, and possible source of influence on them, were the narratives of white prisoners of war held by the British during the Revolution. These included, among quite a large number, *A Narrative of the Capture and Treatment of John Dodge, by the English at Detroit; The Old Jersey Captive, or, a Narrative of the Captivity of Thomas Andros;* and *A Narrative of Colonel Ethan Allen's Captivity.* The accounts of Allen and Andros were popular: first appearing in 1779 and 1781, respectively, they had been widely distributed and were still on the scene when the slave narrators began arriving with empty stomachs, hungry minds, and determined purpose in the major cities of the North. Ethan Allen's narrative came out again in 1846, though it had gone through several previous editions, and Andros' *Old Jersey Captive* was reprinted in Boston in 1833. The Revolutionary War prison narratives are full of descriptions of tortures, misery, and oppression no less compelling than the whippings and maimings related by the slaves. Like the slave narrators, Andros appeals to Christian piety and makes ironic references to the enemy's institutions. One might well speculate that some of the slave narrators were inspired in their accounts by the discovery of a prison narrative; their appeals to the ideas of the Revolution as just cause for the rebellion of slaves certainly attempt to include themselves under the same blanket of public sympathy that covered the resistance of the colonials to the British. If prison narratives were enlisting a patriotic response from the white readership, the fugitive slaves would have every reason, and impulsion, to demand a hearing for their suffering on the same terms.

The parallel between the white autobiographies and the slave narratives shows yet again that the values of the black writers not only mirror, but magnify and intensify those of the white cultural mainstream. The slave narratives speak like a conscience to the ghosts of Mather, Edwards, Andros, and Allen, in their own language. They are echoing the same religion, the same Biblical texts, the same spirit of freedom, even the same experiences, but in a way that, by implication, mocks and denounces the dismal failure of white America's Christianity to live up to the hopes and ideals of those early autobiographies. For it is to defend them against this Christianity that the slaves are calling on the Christian God. Only in the *Journal* of Woolman does the religion of the white culture seem whole and clean enough to merit the respect and acceptance of the blacks. (pp. 49-52)

The Crafts twice allude to *Pilgrim's Progress* as a source of metaphor to express their flight from slavery. The South is their "City of Destruction," the free states, and finally England, the "Great City." Hawthorne, in "The Celestial Railroad" and the chapter, "The Flight of Two Owls" in *The House of Seven Gables,* parodies Bunyan but with no connection to slavery. By applying Bunyan's work to a contemporary context with life-and-death issues, the Crafts were breathing new life into it, giving it an unexpected range and dimension that Hawthorne did not know it could possess. The image of a journey through suffering and trial, surrounded by devil-inspired obstacles, to the "Great City," expresses succinctly how the slave narrators generally conceived of their escapes. In this they were building on Negro Christian folk motives as well as on Bunyan, for there were any number of songs with Biblical images ("Twelve Gates to the City," "Crossing Over Jordan," "Let My People Go") that expressed the same theme to black listeners. It was a supremely ironic commentary on the white Protestant culture for which *Pilgrim's Progress* was bedside and fireside reading that this literary badge of their righteousness should have inspired faith, hope, and the courage to resist in their black victims. It was the courage to resist that Bunyan gave to the religious dissenters of England who migrated to America to escape persecution, and two centuries later he was being used as a weapon against their descendants.

In the Christianity of the early black writer one finds total rejection of proslavery religion and total certainty that God is on the side of the oppressed. A day of reckoning will come, when God, the same God who holds Edwards' sinners over the pit as one holds a spider or some loathsome insect over the fire, will deal with the sins of the slaveholder in the same manner. There is often the suggestion that the instrument God has chosen for this task is the rebellious black slave. (p. 53)

The most fascinating, and, in a way, most terrible parallel between the Puritan autobiography and the slave narrative—terrible because of what it reveals about American culture and because of the way in which it strips the distractions of civilization from the man and throws him back entirely on his own spiritual resources—is the religious mysticism inspired in each by the wilderness and by the loneliness and introspection man feels while confronting it. To Mather, the wilderness was a catalyst for all the complex attitudes that made up the intellectual superstructure of Puritanism: the interpretation of the struggle to found their society as a dramatic battle between God and the Devil, their hatred for the heathen Indian, contempt, fear, and racism toward black people, sexual repression, the sense of God's direct presence and intervention in human affairs, belief in witchcraft, and the search for signs of God's will in the phenomena of nature. In New England folk traditions, the ''black man'' wandered freely through the heathen forest, presiding over the black mass, bedevilling churches and settlements with Indian attacks and spectral visitations, and organizing covens of witches. By the time of Edwards, the forest has been Christianized enough to inspire visions of the Son of God, and in Bryant is a microcosm of God Himself.

The historical and literary counterpoint of this tradition is to be found in the apocalyptic visions of Nat Turner in the back woods of Virginia:

> . . . and shortly afterwards, while laboring in the field, I discovered drops of blood on the corn as though it were dew from heaven . . . and I then found on the leaves in the woods hieroglyphic characters, and numbers, with the forms of men in different attitudes, portrayed in blood. . . . I heard a loud noise in the heavens, and the Spirit instantly appeared to me and said the Serpent was loosened, and Christ had laid down the yoke he had borne for the sins of men, and that I should take it on and fight against the Serpent, for the time was fast approaching when the first should be last and the last should be first. . . . And on the appearance of the sign . . . I should arise and prepare myself, and slay my enemies with their own weapons.

Here is the most explicit example of any of the slave narratives of Christian rhetoric and imagery which is adapted to the needs of the slave. The materials of the white master's culture have been mobilized to strike him down. When this passage is juxtaposed with Cotton Mather's *Wonders of the Invisible World,* the effect is something like insight into the crazy wheels of America's race history. Both works superimpose religion on nature, both reinforce their values with signs and symbols from the wilderness, which they have no difficulty finding once the need for them has created the mental set. It should be granted that both works, too, may have as their basis the experience of being ''touched'' by the Holy Spirit, plunged directly into unmitigated confrontation with the self and its true relationship to other people and things—a confrontation which proves unendurable to Mather and from which he must shield himself by making the wilderness into an object of terror. For Mather, ''heathen,'' ''black man,'' ''devil,'' ''serpent,'' libido, the ''inner light,'' and any evidence of Puritan mendacity are all

in the same category, to be suppressed with the assistance of God and the gallows. For Nat Turner, the wilderness remains a source of inspiration. Turner may also be acting in the African tradition of the direct, personal relationship with God which we have already seen in Thompson's praise song to the storm at sea. Nat's bloody deeds are no more appealing than Mather's, in themselves, but this very fact lends them a tragic/triumphant grandeur; he has been chosen to focus the evil of slavery and send it boiling back onto the slaveholder's head, and as the bearer of a yoke of evil, he cannot remain untainted. But it is the white man who is the serpent; the blood of Christ is transposed into a symbol and a call for insurrection. Asked by Gray if he felt that he was wrong, Turner replies ''Was not Christ crucified?'' The wilderness has returned him to society as a messenger of war, the state of war being the essence of the slave system, the bitter truth which he publishes with axe and gun. As the black man is last, so shall he be first.

It must be considered that the white man Thomas Gray was the ghost writer of Nat Turner's *Confessions,* but in this case there does not seem to have been much difference between white influence and actual white authorship. The rhetoric and imagery seems to differ from that of other Christian-influenced slave writing only in its degree of militancy and intensity of purpose. What gives power to the imagery is the living culture of prayer meeting and revival from which it is derived.

The best instance of sermon rhetoric used for artistic purposes occurs in the *Life of John Thompson.* Chapter nineteen of that book is an extended allegorical comparison between the voyage of a whaling ship, from which Thompson had recently returned, and ''the passage of a Christian from earth to glory.'' In the exactness of image, the management of sound and cadence, and the control of the overall narrative and metaphor, it is a piece that compares with Father Mapple's Sermon in *Moby Dick.*

Thompson expands the imagery of a flight or journey to encompass his struggle to build a Christian identity. In doing so, he is wholly consistent with the approach of the other Christian slave narrators, in particular Ward, Davis, Pennington, and the Crafts. What makes Thompson's work unusual is the elaborate care he has taken to explore all of its aesthetic dimensions.

> While at sea and learning the uses of the various nautical instruments, I also studied their spiritual application.

He has placed the chapter at the climax of his autobiography; it opens with the phrase, ''while at sea,'' which, in context, should be read as a description of his spiritual state, and closes with the words, ''secure an everlasting rest at the right hand of God.'' In between is the voyage of the Christian from sin to salvation.

The helm of the ship is conscience, the rudder is understanding, the masts are judgment and reason; the sails are the affections, and ''education stands in the place of carving and gilding.'' If the sails are overloaded, there is danger of foundering. ''Pride represents too taut rigging,'' and falsehood or ''assumed professions'' are false colors. At its first launching, the ship was ''dashed on the rocks of presumption'' but repaired by the Owner at the cost of His ''only begotten and well beloved son.'' The planks and timbers, on the conversion of the individual, are cemented, bolted, and caulked by Faith, Love, and eternal Truth. The soul ''receives sailing orders from the inspired oracles'' and is wafted toward the port of endless rest by the Holy Ghost. There are similar spiritual equivalents for storms, clear and rocky coasts, sunlight, and calm. The whole complex performance is given life by the music of the language:

> Every piece is hewn by the law in the work of conviction; every faculty purged from sin and guilt by the great atonement, received by faith in Christ Jesus; every plank bent by the fire of divine love, all fitted to their places by the invincible energy of sovereign grace, and the structure is completed according to the model prepared in the council of peace, and published in the gospel, which divine illumination is made visible to the mental eye, through which it is received into the heart, and leaves its impress there. . . .
>
> If faith is not genuine and enduring; if those principles typified by the planks and timbers of a ship, be rotten or unsound at heart, not consistent with each other, and not shaped so as to lie compactly; or if each is not well secured by bolts of the endurable metal of eternal truth from the mine of divine revelation; if all is not carefully caulked with the powerful cement of unfailing love and redeeming blood; in a word, if Christ is not the sole foundation, and his righteousness the grand security, then on the slightest trial, the seams open, the vessel bilges, and every soul on board is lost. . . .
>
> How carefully then should we accompany our prayers with watching, heedfully marking every changeful appearance of the sky. How eagerly should we seize the first favorable moment, when the long wished for opportunity of sailing was in our power. . . . Nor must the fairest gale entice us to sea without the heavenly pilot; for without thee, blessed Jesus, we can do nothing; to thee we must turn in every difficulty, and upon thee call in every time of danger. We dare trust no other at the helm, because no other can safely steer us past the rocks and quicksands. How kind thy promise, to be with us when passing through deep and dangerous waters. How gracious thy word which engages never to leave nor forsake us. . . .

Assigning specific allegorical equivalents to all the details of the metaphor is a method very much in the general tradition of Christian writing, where the intention is to teach an attitude toward life. The structure of the sermon is an elaborate conceit. Within that structure, the language creates its effects in the manner of a free-form poem: by the repetition of words and syntax, the use of parallel clauses, the rhythm of stressed syllables, and the shifts between moral meaning and image.

The first half of the first sentence, for example, has three parallel subjects, each beginning with the word "every" ("Évery píece is héwn by the láw . . . évery fáculty púrged from sín and guílt . . . évery plánk bént by the fíre of divíne lóve. . . ."). Each clause ends on a stressed syllable, like the stop at the end of a line of poetry; the cadence varies between iambic and anapestic, like that of speech, with the images receiving the heavier stress. The second half of that sentence, following the conjunction "and," links the three parallel clauses under a single governing idea: the "módel prepáred in the coúncil of peáce, and públished in the góspel, whích divíne illūminátion is máde vísible to the méntal éye. . . ." Here again, the cadence tends to be metrical (the phrase up to the first comma has four anapestic feet, with a weak syllable missing from the first), and the consonants are strongly alliterative.

The second paragraph is a well-executed, periodic *tour de force,* with a conclusion powerful enough to satisfy the expectations built up by the five parallel "if" clauses that precede it. The second and third clauses translate the first into images;

the fourth translates the image into an additional concept, that is, redemption through the love of Christ; and the fifth summarizes and climaxes the first four by juxtaposing the Christian's ultimate hope (salvation through Christ) and his ultimate fear (the loss of the soul). The image of the ship is maintained throughout, with the thought shuttling back and forth between the two terms of the metaphor to reinforce each term with the other. The "ship of death" archetype, submerged but always present, takes on the insistent force of deep ocean swell; coming as it does at the end of a factual account of whaling, during which the reader familiar with Milton, Melville, and Lawrence gazes out the porthole of Thompson's journalism and wonders if the author knew he was floating on a sea of symbolism, the effect when the poem begins is like being led suddenly for a walk on the waves.

There may be a third term for the metaphor, a trade wind of antislavery meaning that would make Thompson's sermon a magnificent compression of politics, religion, and poetry. He would not have found a more knowledgeable, sophisticated, or responsive audience than the congregations of New Bedford's three or four black churches, for whom the use of whaling images to convey antislavery material was probably a time-honored tradition. In 1859, of the 25,000 native American seamen, more than half were Negroes, and 2,900 of them served in the whale fishery. New Bedford was also a haven for fugitive slaves. One new arrival was shipped North in a box by sea; and, according to a brother in his church, "the first time he came into church I thought he would set it on fire. I tell you he *blowed* there!" Whales were also compared to slavery itself in the *Abolitionist,* a journal of the New England Anti-Slavery Society: "We found the Leviathan weltering in the sea of popularity. . . . We have fixed the harpoon, and the monster begins to blow and bellow. We are now pulling upon the line, and we shall soon, we trust, come to lancing." And by 1863 the metaphor had become popular enough for Lincoln to use it as he signed the Emancipation Proclamation. [In a footnote Butterfield states: Lincoln's exact wording was "we are like whalers who have been on a long chase. We have at last got the harpoon into the monster, but we must now look how we steer, or with one flop of his tail he will send us all into eternity." The same metaphor perhaps casts a shadow over Walt Whitman's famous poem, "O Captain, My Captain."] Thompson's voyage of the soul toward everlasting rest, then, may also imply a symbolic hunt for the Leviathan of slavery and a flight on the sea from the slave-catching hunters. He may be inspiring his listeners with the theme that flight from the master is worthless unless the fugitive is also running *toward* something, i.e. submission to the eternal God. A relationship this intimate between poetry, reality, and audience is coveted in vain by most contemporary poets.

After sounding the maximum danger of the journey ("the seams open, the vessel bilges, and every soul on board is lost"), the sermon moves smoothly into a reference to prayer as a safeguard, and then, with no break in continuity, becomes itself a prayer. The last paragraph has the same structure as the first two: parallel clauses and repeated words and syntax patterns, the content of which builds steadily toward some sort of climax: "How carefully. . . . How eagerly. . . . How kind. . . . How gracious." The climax in this case is the prayer to Christ. The handling of words within sentences also shows an accomplished control over language: "we dare trust no other at the helm, because no other can safely steer us. . . ." "No other" is used the first time as an object, the second as a subject, giving a sense of variety within a rhythmic pattern. And the repetitions of "every" as part of a prepositional phrase are echoes of the repeated "everys" of the first paragraph, where they were part of the subject.

All in all, this chapter is the highest level of art touched by Christian rhetoric anywhere in the slave narratives, although Thompson's autobiography taken as a whole is not the best work. The sermon is an example of a black writer taking traditional Christian forms and giving them a blood transfusion through his own experience as a fugitive and wanderer.

In Pennington there is a good description of an abandoned and dilapidated plantation which does essentially the same thing: it realizes a traditional Christian theme through black experience, and constructs a response to and defense against the cultural oppression of slavery.

> To see the once fine smooth gravel walks, overgrown with grass—the redundances of the shrubbery neglected—the once finely painted picket fences, rusted and fallen down—a fine garden in splendid ruins—the loftly ceiling of the mansion thickly curtained with cobwebs—the spacious apartments abandoned, while the only music heard within as a substitute for the voices of family glee that once filled it, was the crying cricket and cockroaches! Ignorant slave as I was at that time, I could but pause for a moment, and recur in silent horror to the fact that, a strange reverse of fortune, had lately driven from that proud mansion, a large and once opulent family. What advantage was it now to the members of that family, that the father and head had for near half a century stood high in the counsels of the state, and had the benefit of the unrequited toil of hundreds of his fellowmen, when they were already grappling with the annoyances of that poverty, which he had entailed upon others.

Pennington's message is the vanity of earthly things, and the house itself a *memento mori* which reminds the reader to lay up his treasures in heaven; but it is specifically slavery that the writer attacks as an earthly vanity; the Christian point of view has been adapted to the needs of political struggle against a specific object, and, as in the case of Thompson, affects the language by transforming it into sermon oratory. The first sentence is a series of parallel clauses with repetition of key words, and the subordination of the final clauses in the last sentence brings out the irony in the material: the first has become last, the despoiler of others is himself despoiled.

A brief comparison with the house of Usher illustrates that we are dealing with a characteristic "black" way of handling material. For all its cracked face, dank tarn, and brilliantly rendered miasma of decay, Usher's house is deliberately removed from history and society, a separate world in itself. The house of Pennington's description has connections to the past and present; it is both a product and an object lesson of time, a lesson that applies in the world beyond the author's private imagination. The language is rooted in the soil of the politics and religion practiced by black abolitionists.

The features of style we have noted appear in many varied contexts wherever elevation of tone is called for, and sometimes where it is inappropriate: parallel clauses, repeated words placed in different positions in the sentence, rolling periods with a metrical cadence that build to a climax, antithesis, formal and sometimes pompous and melodramatic diction in the manner of the time, and images designed to play on the emotions; all these methods are used also for non-Christian content, or occur almost as a matter of habit or mannerism. In the following

sentence by Henry Bibb, the main appeal is in the sound. The oratorical tone is not applied to any specific object and so seems inept and merely sentimental:

> I was struggling against a thousand obstacles which had clustered around my mind to bind my wounded spirit still in the dark prison of mental degradation.

Elsewhere he plans his effects with more skill:

> I have often suffered from the sting of the cruel slave driver's lash on my quivering flesh—I have suffered from corporeal punishment in its various forms—I have mingled my sorrows with those that were bereaved by the ungodly soul drivers—and I also know what it is to shed the sympathetic tear at the grave of a departed friend; but all this is but a mere trifle compared with my sufferings from then to the end of six months subsequent.

Here the parallel clauses are cumulative in their effect, arranged in order of ascending importance.

The same style and method of arrangement occurs in this passage from Solomon Northup:

> He fears he will be caught lagging through the day; he fears to approach the gin-house with his basketload of cotton at night; he fears, when he lies down, that he will oversleep himself in the morning. Such is a true, faithful, unexaggerated picture and description of the slave's daily life . . . on the shores of Bayou Boeuf.

The styles of Webster and Garrison were among the immediate literary models from which this rhetoric is derived. Turning to Webster's *Plymouth Oration*, for example, we find similar techniques and cadences:

> No sculptured marble, no enduring monument, no honorable inscription, no ever-burning taper that would drive away the darkness of the tomb, can soften our sense of the reality of death, and hallow to our feelings the ground that is to cover us, like the consciousness that we shall sleep, dust to dust, with the objects of our affections.

Indeed, as F. O. Matthiessen points out, oratory was the dominant literary tradition of the period. Emerson, Thoreau, and Whitman all show the influence of the oration, and the most popular medium of political communication was public address. The slave narratives, as instruments in a political struggle, would be especially open to this influence and would receive it from a vast number of immediate sources. Webster's cadences can be heard in Garrison and Thoreau as well as in Thompson and Pennington; and Garrison most directly affects the style of Frederick Douglass, as the latter's mentor and first exposure to abolitionist literature in the years following his escape.

The dignity achieved by an elevated tone can also be accounted among the many reasons why slaves would take Webster, Garrison, and John Q. Adams as stylistic models. In the popular white fiction of the period, the black writer was perpetually confronted with assaults on that dignity in the form of the Jupiters, Dinahs, Pompeys, Sambos, Catos, Mingos, and other stereotypes ranging in character from loyal dogs to libidinous black savages, who clown, simper, drink, steal, and gabble their way through the pages of William Gilmore Simms, A. J. Knott, and John S. Robb. Some of the most vicious anti-Negro portraits, although he was not popular, appear in the stories of Edgar Allan Poe. The "negro" of white fiction usually spoke a dialect that was intended to demean his intelligence. The slave writer's choice of formal diction and polished periods was a key element in the construction of his human identity, for it countered these parodies with the most effective weapon available: the ability to command, and parody, the master's voice. The best slave narrators, in fact, beat the Negrophobic writers at their own game, by alternating at will between parody and credible representation, whereas the master's blindness placed credible representation of anything black beyond his reach.

The greatest problem of the slave narrative, solved in Thompson and Douglass, was how to assimilate the magic of the enemy's language into a new identity entirely under the slave's control. Thompson achieves a solution, as we have seen, by synthesizing religious rhetoric, African poetic survivals, and his personal background in the whaling industry, using as a catalyst for these diverse elements the great historical movement of black life in the nineteenth century—the flight to freedom. (pp. 54-64)

> *Stephen Butterfield, "The Shape of Flame: Language and the Slave Experience" and "The White Influence," in his* Black Autobiography in America, *University of Massachusetts Press, 1974, pp. 32-46, 47-64.*

RAYMOND HEDIN

[*Hedin examines the picaresque tradition in slave narrative literature and explores its evolution from the earliest eighteenth-century accounts through the nineteenth century. The critic intends to highlight the picaresque as an instance of how the slave narrators used "the written word and existing literary traditions not to imitate 'Ole Massa' but to subvert him."*]

Did [black American] culture begin in slavery's negation of African culture, so that the black American can only be understood by reference to an identity he has lost and knows he no longer has? Or did it begin in some creative interplay between cultures, so that the black American is truly an Afro-American, not deprived of culture but endowed through his painful experience with a rich amalgam of his old and new worlds? The relatively negative explanations of these origins, from Ulrich Phillips down through Stanley Elkins and beyond, have grown out of a relatively bleak sense of the black American's current state, just as the more positive interpretations of the 1960s and 1970s . . . owe a good deal to a different view of black Americans today.

Most studies of black American culture have concentrated on its oral aspects—folk tale, music, religion—because they have seemed most distinctive. But the question of the origin of *written* expression among black Americans is equally interesting and complex. Is there in fact a black American literary culture at all? Or has the history of words written by blacks in this country been simply a history of operating on alien ground, of imitating—willingly or not—the forms, techniques, even attitudes of an overwhelmingly dominant "white" literary tradition? Those who propose the latter view, such as Addison Gayle, often go on to call for a distinctively "black esthetic" to remedy the situation; their sense of a negative literary history among blacks grows out of their conviction that literary independence is still to be achieved, or at best is just beginning. In *The Way of the New World*, his full-length study of the black American novel, Gayle asserts that, at least up to the present day, the written word has been corrupted for black writers by

the extent to which it has a long history of being used to keep blacks in their place:

> Whether the vehicle for the dissemination of such images was poetry, prose, or fiction, the [written] word was used to distort truth to an alarming and dangerous degree. In part, this was due to the inability of the black writer to retaliate in kind, to use the weapons of the oppressor in his own defense. Stripped of his language, the symbols, images, and metaphors which had sustained him in the faraway home, he was forced, like a man come naked into the world, to measure himself by yardsticks fashioned by others and to face the wilderness without the msot elemental of defenses—the capacity to utilize language to define his own experiences.

Much of what Gayle says would be hard to dispute. But he does the black American literary tradition a disservice by not taking it back to its real origins, the slave narrative, the first distinctive literary form that black Americans produced. The slave narrative itself was a heavily influenced form, to be sure. In order to have their desired effect of discrediting slavery and of moving their readers to abolish it, the ex-slaves who wrote narratives of their former lives needed to use arguments the predominantly white audience would find compelling and to shift their emphasis as readers shifted pre-occupations. Thus began a history of writing not so much for themselves as for the larger society. Further, they had to contend with northern editors, who suppressed certain unmentionables and no doubt suggested appropriate lines of thought. But to be influenced is not necessarily to be usurped. Most of the ex-slaves wrote their narratives relatively unaided, so far as we can tell. To use arguments suitable to one's particular audience is the mark of a skillful writer, not of a toady. And, most importantly, the slave narrator was much more than a passive assimilator of another culture's literary traditions. It is true that the nature of the slave narrator's audience in the three decades leading up to the Civil War—the slave narrative's peak period—did not allow him to make use of images and tales from his African past. But in his cunning, strategic manipulation of already existing arguments and narrative modes, the slave narrator demonstrated that, far from being deprived of his old trickster skills, he had simply found new territory in which to use them. I offer the following thoughts on the slave narrator's relationship to and use of the picaresque tradition to suggest that he was able to find ways to use the written word and existing literary traditions not to imitate "Ole Massa" but to subvert him.

It is important to remember that throughout the eighteenth century American slave narratives were free of outside influence; pressures and corresponding strategies came later. The first slave narrative, *Adam Negro's Tryall*, was published in 1703, two years after the first abolitionist pamphlet in America, Samuel Sewall's *The Selling of Joseph*. As this conjunction suggests, the slave narrative in this country was related from the beginning to the anti-slavery movement. But that movement was not so well-defined nor intense in the eighteenth century as it would become. For that reason, because slavery had not yet settled into an established "life," in Ulrich Phillips' terms, and because a higher percentage of narrators in this early period came directly from Africa and had not yet modified their style to fit their new status, the eighteenth-century narratives varied in voice and emphasis. They include, for instance, Briton Hammon (1760), who survives pirates and cannibals, shipwrecks and incarcerations in a series of adventures after he escapes from his master; Arthur (1768), an unrepentant criminal who began his career at age fourteen and was executed at age twenty-one; John Marrant (1785), who makes no mention of race and very little of slavery as he wanders in the wilderness, converting Indians; Gustavus Vassa (1789), as much an adventurer, traveller, and proto-capitalist as he was an anti-slavery agitator; and Venture (1798), who became a Bunyanesque legend among both black and white more for his reputed six-foot girth and feats of strength than for anything he said or did about slavery.

These narratives suggest the traditional picaresque in a number of ways, but the resemblance resulted more from a natural fit of the picaresque mode with the slaves' own experience than from a need the narrators felt to shape the description of their lives for a literary purpose. The slaves who became narrators in this period led surprisingly autonomous, or at least semi-autonomous, lives. Like the picaro, they were often adventurous, not just in the act of escape (as later narrators would be) but throughout their lives. Confronted by a hard world without institutions to offer them shelter—not even a plantation in many cases—some of them converted to Christianity. Most of them hardened themselves and acted as individualistically and asocially as circumstances would allow. In short, their narratives were picaresque because their lives were picaresque. Neither were they burdened, if that is the right word, by overriding social purposes. Though anti-slavery elements appear in them, they do not dominate. The narrators seem to feel free to follow their interests or observations wherever they lead. It seems not to dawn on them to focus narratives entirely on the slavery issue, perhaps because slavery had not defined them either in their rather mobile lives nor in their own minds.

A few generations later, by the 1820s and 1830s, however, most slave narratives came to be written by men and women who had been born slaves, of slave parents, on established farms and plantations. For them the conditions of slavery had become physically and psychologically unavoidable in ways not true for eighteenth-century narrators. Thus, when they wrote, they were inclined to direct their energies toward one overriding goal, the destruction of an institution that surrounded and influenced every area of their lives. The range of observation, like the choice of narrative mode, now became weighted; both had to be appropriate to the purpose of discrediting slavery.

The slave narrators now began to write under a form of purpose not felt before. There is no reason to believe that this pressure of purpose was primarily external, from abolitionist sponsors; for the ex-slave had his own stake in finding ways to write that would serve the cause of abolition. But the social and political context of the slavery debate did go a long way toward establishing what indeed was appropriate. And, because that context became increasingly moralistic, the slave narrators had to fall in step. (pp. 630-34)

"I *will* be as harsh as truth, and as uncompromising as justice," Garrison wrote in the opening issue of the *Liberator* on New Year's Day in 1831; and although Garrison's was by no means the only voice of note, abolitionist rhetoric tended increasingly to follow his absolutist lead. In the 1830s and 1840s, slavery became not just a crime but a sin, "a *national* sin," an evil "offending the heavens with its atrocity." And as slavery became, in Frederick Douglass's words, "one of those monsters of darkness to whom the light of truth is death," any argument that blurred the distinction between the forces of light and the forces of darkness stood outside the pale.

While slave narrators tended ever the more to write anti-slavery documents, the guidelines within which their narratives might

be acceptable to that end also became increasingly clear. In the moral rather than the political sense, they must show "no compromise with slavery, no union with slaveholders." It was no accident that Garrison concluded his preface to the 1845 *Narrative of the Life of Frederick Douglass* with this "religious and political motto," as he put it.

The mandate of clear-cut morality exerted several effects on slave narratives of the period. One was to move the narrators toward emphasizing that slavery was an impersonal *system*, and that the system was an unmitigated evil because it worked by a corrupt, internal logic regardless of the particular moral state of a given slaveowner as person. Douglass makes it clear that even morally good whites became corrupted by the mere act of becoming slaveowners. When the benign and gentle Sophia Auld unwittingly drank "the fatal poison of irresponsible power" by marrying a slaveowner and therefore became one herself, her "cheerful eye, under the influence of slavery, soon became red with rage . . . and that angelic face gave place to that of a demon." J.W.C. Pennington's 1849 narrative explicitly articulates the underlying logic of slavery: "Talk not then about kind and christian masters. They are not masters of the system. The system is master of them. . . ." The slave-owners, writes Solomon Northup in 1853, "cannot withstand the influence of habit and associations that surround them." Hence the slave narrators maintain a subtle and compassionate stance as well as an absolute moral distinction; it is not that they see evil everywhere, it is that the system produces evil everywhere.

But the need to maintain a moral dichotomy involved the narrator's depiction of the slave as well as of slavery. The effect was to eliminate the out-and-out rogue as an acceptable narrator. The individualistic, self-concerned, partly asocial adventurers who glided rather lightly through some of the eighteenth-century narratives were much less evident once the absolutism of the anti-slavery cause began to demand that the victims of slavery be as righteous as the cause of freedom itself. But—and herein lies the dilemma—the picaro could not disappear entirely because the survival techniques of the picaro were becoming even more important to the slave than they had been before. During the 1830s, southern prickliness in reaction to the abolitionist onslaught, together with an intensified fear of rebellion engendered by Nat Turner's 1831 revolt, accelerated the tightening of formal and informal slave codes throughout the South. As a result, slaves had even fewer rights and less legal recourse than before. The new restrictions intensified their sense of being victims in a pervasive *system;* it had the corresponding effect, as Marion Starling points out, of driving increasing numbers of them to flight. The escape became more prominent in slave narratives, often comprising an entire work. Escape of necessity involved the slave in a good deal of cunning, deceit, and even violence. Thus actions traditionally defined as questionable if not immoral increased in the narratives at precisely the same time when the slaves' devotion to morality became essential to the purity of the anti-slavery argument. The earlier, natural fit of the slave narrative with the picaresque now became an uneasy fit, and the narrator had to find strategies for turning to his own advantage the tradition that he was, in a sense, trapped in.

The dilemma now of the slave narrator—to keep himself clearly on the side of morality while depicting actions often hardly moral at all—was complicated by the arguments that southern apologists began to advance during the 1830s to support the notion that slavery was a positive good. It was then, as George

Fredrickson has shown, that previously tacit racist assumptions were articulated as formal racist ideology. The pro-slavery argument took to asserting openly that blacks were subhuman, biologically inferior, hence naturally and rightly subordinate to whites. (pp. 634-36)

The theory that blacks were subhuman had northern adherents, even among some abolitionists, who simply denied that it justified enslavement. Both emotionally and geographically, however, this argument cut two ways: what was set forth originally to salve the slaveowner's conscience ended up evoking fear in both North and South that brutish slaves, once released, might have neither the capacity nor inclination to keep their pent-up energies within ethical restraints. The violence of the Santo Domingo rebellion and of Nat Turner's revolt did not go unnoticed. (p. 637)

In such a context, the escape sections of slave narratives became crucial. They revealed how slaves really acted once they were out from under the "civilizing" restraints of the plantation for the first time. Much was at stake; for if freedom were thought to mean the unleashing of an id-dominated beast, a moral primitive, then the cause of freedom would lose support. The slave narrator had not only to defend his morality but his humanity (read "rationality"), all the while describing how he lied, stole, and even fought and killed his way to freedom.

All of this helps explain the consistent, self-conscious attempts of slave narrators at this time to purify the picaro, to bring within the pale what they dared not consign to outer darkness. The narrators are acutely aware of even minor offences—the plucking of chickens, the taking of the master's money, the telling of lies and the wearing of disguises. The main tactic they adopt is to deflect responsibility back onto slavery itself. The view of slavery as a pervasive system provided them a standpoint from which to argue that there was no other recourse within such a system. As Henry Bibb writes, "the only weapon of self-defence that I could use successfully, was that of deception. It is useless for a poor helpless slave, to resist a white man in a slaveholding State." Bibb proves a master at subverting the logic of slavery in matters of morality. Accused of stealing a jackass, he defends himself with a fine picaresque rationale:

> But I well knew that I was regarded as property, and so was the ass; and I thought if one piece of property took off another, there could be no law violated in the act; no more sin committed in this than if one jackass had rode off another.

A more common defense, if less whimsical, was to argue that the corrupting effects of the system were as unavoidable for the slave as they were the master. "Slavery," writes William Wells Brown in full awareness of the issue, "makes its victims lying and mean; for which vices it afterwards reproaches them, and uses them as arguments to prove that they deserve no better fate." The slave narrators likewise turn the argument around, using slave "immorality" as further evidence against the absurdity and immorality of the slavery system and in support of abolition. It is not that slaves are beasts, they suggest: slavery bestializes. "The dark night of slavery closed in upon me," Frederick Douglass writes, "and behold a man transformed into a brute!" In a reversal of image as well as argument, the slavery system becomes the monster. (pp. 637-38)

The same issues of morality and humanity arose in the narrators' depiction of violence done during escapes; and here too they found ways to turn the issues around. Since violence is both the most conventionally immoral of actions and the most unsettling to readers anxious about the nature of the unchained slave, the narrators are careful how they describe it. With an eye toward decorum and morals, they nearly always present violent acts as defensive, unavoidable, and necessary to their escape, much as they defend less serious misdeeds. But in reply to charges that they are mere brutes, they work skillfully to show that even their most violent actions rested upon ineluctable, rational choice. For, though the admission that slaves have been bestialized into violence by slavery might serve to condemn slavery, it could not reassure readers who feared that freedom might bring carnage.

Pennington provides a representative example of the narrator determined to preserve morals and rationality. He is emphatic in asserting that no malice or vengefulness motivated what violence his escape necessitated:

> If you ask me whether I had expected before I left home, to gain my liberty by shedding men's blood, or breaking their limbs? I answer, no! and as evidence of this, I had provided no weapon whatever; not so much as a penknife—it never once entered my mind.

But when violence does loom ahead, he shows himself responding thoughtfully, not instinctively:

> We had a hill to rise, and during the ascent he gained on me. Once more I thought of self-defence. I am trying to escape peaceably, but this man is determined that I shall not.

> My case was now desperate; and I took this desperate thought: "I will run him a little farther from his coadjutor; I will then suddenly catch a stone, and wound him in the breast." This was my fixed purpose.

The quoting of his own thoughts during the crisis is shrewd; the point is not just that violence was rational under the circumstances but that Pennington thought tactically. Danger activates in him combat strategy, not rage. (p. 639)

By the time of [Solomon] Northup's narrative (1853) and even before, slave narrators had hit upon an obvious argument to justify even violence. They drew on the precedent of the American Revolution. The slave Andrew Jackson, for instance, explicitly appeals to a rationale for resistance that his namesake would have been proud of:

> Some may think I did wrong in this, and I am very sure it was very hazardous, for the penalty is very severe upon slaves who strike a white man, but I was after a prize, for which I was willing to risk my life. And I doubt not, any one who reads this, would have done the same. And if it was right for the revolutionary patriots to fight for liberty, it was right for me, and it is right for any other slave to do the same. And were I now a slave, I would risk my life for freedom. "Give me liberty or give me death," would be my deliberate conclusion.

A shift toward more political awareness in the slave narratives naturally coincided with the general abolitionist shift during the 1840s and 1850s toward political in place of primarily religious arguments. Nat Turner's claim in 1831 that "my wisdom came from God" gave place in the following decades to the assertion of many slave narrators that their wisdom rested upon the Declaration of Independence, the American Revolution, and the European revolutions of 1848. Some scholars have suggested that every such political argument in the narratives must therefore be seen as the work of northern editors, not as the exslaves' own ideas. The question may always remain moot unless unknown galley sheets come to light. But there is no inherent reason why many of the narrators should not have known enough about American history and its ironies by the time they wrote to make such arguments themselves. Once they escaped, after all, education became a first priority. Moreover, the narrators did not abandon their emphasis on rational morality in favor of political argumentation, though many abolitionists did. They reinforced one with the other. What American could argue against Jackson's suggestion that "Give me liberty or give me death" was both a "deliberate conclusion" and moral? Or against Pennington's analogy between the desire of slaves for freedom and the desires of "our white brethren" in Europe who have been justifiably "reaching out their hands to grasp more freedom . . . so tenacious are they of their own liberties"? With that context established in the public mind, Northup, for instance, could afford to assert the morality of his violent resistance so long as he took care to demonstrate its necessity and his rationality throughout.

In fact, in beginning to suggest that previously unpleasant forms of resistance were not merely the unfortunate result of slavery's corrupting power, but were, by analogy to just revolutions, a positive good, the slave narrators carried to its ultimate conclusion the logic of their earlier concern with morality. If the cause of freedom had initially imposed on them an absolute morality, that was because freedom came to be seen as an absolute good by both abolitionists and slaves, a conclusion the dawn of literary romanticism did nothing to undercut. In consequence of that conviction, to obtain freedom became not just a right but a duty, the highest duty in fact, to which every other consideration became subordinate. Many male narrators, for instance, describe the pain of leaving their families behind in order to escape as a pain they can bear only because the *duty* to escape bondage is even stronger. Hence taking to the road came to seem less a picaro's antiromantic wandering and more the romantic fulfillment of a hero's quest, a quest with social, moral, and ideal justification. And the morality of the road, questionable were it only self-interested, became noble. The slave narrator turned himself from a picaro into a romantic and a revolutionary hero.

Such developments were of course neither simple nor universal. Many a slave narrator remained hesitant and defensive about morality and violence. But overall, the inherent logic of the slaves' stance turned the tone of the slave narrative around. In the long run they stood the imposed requirement of absolute morality on its head, using it to validate actions it had originally seemed to bring into question; the restrictions of mores were transcended by the mandates of a higher morality. The picaro became "justified."

A prime example of how confident and effective the justified picaresque could be in these contexts appears in the 1860 narrative, *Running a Thousand Miles for Freedom,* in which William and Ellen Craft detail their escape from slavery twelve years earlier. There are striking similarities between the rationale offered for their actions and the arguments used by the American colonies against Britain to justify the Revolution. Writing on the eve of the Civil War, the Crafts take pains in their opening chapter to convey "some idea of the legal as well as the social tyranny from which we fled." After quoting verbatim from the laws of Louisiana, South Carolina, and Georgia which rendered slaves utterly defenseless, they go on to assert that "the practical working of slavery is worse than the odious laws by which it is governed." Hence one context for their narrative is the conviction that there is no recourse for the slave

within the tightening system of slavery; the other is their awareness of the Revolution and what it demanded under similar circumstances:

> Having heard while in Slavery that "God made of one blood all nations of men," and also that the American Declaration of Independence says, that "We hold these truths to be self-evident, that all men are created equal; that they are endowed by their Creator with certain inalienable rights; that among these are life, liberty, and the pursuit of happiness"; we could not understand by what right we were held as "chattels." Therefore, we felt perfectly justified in undertaking the dangerous and exciting task of "running a thousand miles" in order to obtain those rights which are so vividly set forth in the Declaration.

Flight and its techniques, whatever they need be, therefore, have the strongest sanction imaginable. A bit of initial reluctance is useful, but at this late date the Crafts are uneasy only about tactics; they are perfectly confident of their ethics:

> My wife had no ambition whatever to assume this disguise, and would not have done so had it been possible to have obtained our liberty by more simple means; but we knew it was not customary in the South for ladies to travel with male servants; and therefore, notwithstanding my wife's fair complexion, it would have been a very difficult task for her to have come off as a free white lady, with me as her slave; in fact, her not being able to write would have made this quite impossible.

The rest of the narrative combines complete ethical confidence with the pleasures of deceit that such justification permits. If eighteenth-century slave narrators wrote before apology was required, the Crafts now write when it is no longer necessary. The light-skinned Ellen disguises herself as an aristocratic, male slave owner, William poses as her loyal slave, and together they bluff their way from Macon, Georgia to Philadelphia. They are nervous throughout the adventure, but in the writing of the narrative they revel openly in the dramatic ironies their ruse makes possible. ("The gentleman said my master could obtain the very best advice in Philadelphia. Which turned out to be quite correct. . . ." When a train conductor asks William if he would like to be free, he replies, "Yes, sir, but I shall never run away from such a good master as I have at present.")

But the irony of the narrative extends beyond the local, for the Crafts predicate their escape on the accuracy of their hard-won sense of southern society. They know all too well the kinds of deference granted southern "gentlemen," the latitude of behavior allowed them; and they exploit that knowledge fully, manipulating southern manners with great skill in order to escape the system of slavery on which those manners were built. When Ellen feigns deafness to avoid being recognized by a Mr. Cray, an old friend of her master, Cray defers to her (his) state, saying "I shall not trouble that fellow any more," and retreats to a respectful distance. Later, when Ellen's bandaged hand does not prevent an official from demanding that she register her name, southern chivalry prevents her illiteracy—and their ruse—from being detected:

> Just then the young military officer with whom my master travelled and conversed on the steamer from Savannah stepped in, somewhat the worse for brandy; he shook hands with my master, and pretended to know all about him. He said, "I know his kin (friends) like a book"; and as the officer was known in

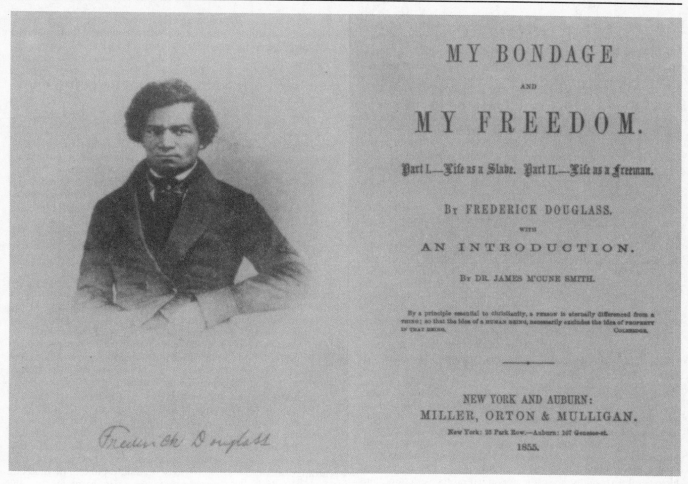

The title page and frontispiece to Frederick Douglass's second autobiography, a revised and updated companion to his masterpiece, Narrative of the Life of Frederick Douglass, an American Slave, Written by Himself.

Charleston, and was going to stop there with friends, the recognition was very much in my master's favor.

Instances such as these abound and make it clear that the "representative" role thrust on slave narrators in the decades preceding the Civil War now serves less to restrict the Crafts' narrative than to broaden the significance of their triumph. It is as if everything slavery taught the slave about the nature of the master and his world now rose up to mock those masters and that world. And by playing skillfully not only on their knowledge of the master but on the master's assumptions about the slave, the Crafts reveal a good deal about the strategies of survival that slaves drew on within slavery as well as in the act of escaping it. By using William's extreme loyalty to his "master" to allay suspicions that he might escape, the Crafts deliberately and self-consciously exploit the "Sambo" behavior, the identification with the master, that has since become subject of much debate. The Crafts reveal in full splendor just how cunning such behavior could be, just how scornful of "Massa" the man behind the mask of docility could be.

With the Crafts, then, the slave narrative picaresque has come full circle, from an unselfconscious, individualistic mode to a defensive strategy to a positive weapon. Eighteenth-century narrators in many ways assimilated, genuinely "put on" the

behavior and ethic of the slaveowner's world to survive in that world, and even to thrive in it. Now the Crafts "put on" the master himself—and his loyal slave—but ironically and as a ruse, from the base of ethical security from which they can not only escape the world of the slaveowner but satirize that world and heap scorn on it. The picaresque has led to the nonfictional novel of manners. The nineteenth-century slave narrator who began by working within limits ended up learning how to transcend those limits by making them serve his ends. Both the necessity of accepting limits and the ability to transcend them were constant elements in slave culture; they would prove to be among the most interesting and long-lasting legacies of the slave narrative to the post-emancipation black writer. (pp. 640-45)

Raymond Hedin, "The American Slave Narrative: The Justification of the Picaro," in American Literature, Vol. 53, No. 4, January, 1982, pp. 630-45.

ROBERT B. STEPTO

[*Stepto thoroughly analyzes the issue of authorial control in the slave narratives. Examining the "authenticating devices" used by four slave narrators or their sponsors, the critic identifies four categories of narratives, ranging from a basic account with the least authorial control to a "generic" document, which exhibits a great deal of authorial control and approaches the artistic level of history, fiction, and autobiography.*]

The strident, moral voice of the former slave recounting, exposing, appealing, apostrophizing, and above all *remembering* his ordeal in bondage is the single most impressive feature of a slave narrative. This voice is striking because of what it relates, but even more so because the slave's acquisition of that voice is quite possibly his only permanent achievement once he escapes and casts himself upon a new and larger landscape. In their most elementary form, slave narratives are full of other voices which are frequently just as responsible for articulating a narrative's tale and strategy. These other voices may belong to various "characters" in the "story," but mainly they appear in the appended documents written by slaveholders and abolitionists alike. These documents—and voices—may not always be smoothly integrated with the former slave's tale, but they are nevertheless parts of the narrative. Their primary function is, of course, to authenticate the former slave's account; in doing so, they are at least partially responsible for the narrative's acceptance as historical evidence. However, in literary terms, the documents collectively create something close to a dialogue—of forms as well as voices—which suggests that, in its primal state or first phase, the slave narrative is an *eclectic narrative* form. A "first phase" slave narrative that illustrates these points rather well is Henry Bibb's *Narrative of the Life and Adventures of Henry Bibb, an American Slave* (1849).

When the various forms (letters, prefaces, guarantees, tales) and their accompanying voices become integrated in the slave narrative text, we are presented with another type of basic narrative which I call an *integrated narrative*. This type of narrative represents the second phase of slave narrative narration; it usually yields a more sophisticated text, wherein most of the literary and rhetorical functions previously performed by several texts and voices (the appended prefaces, letters, and documents as well as the tale) are now rendered by a loosely unified single text and voice. In this second phase, the authenticating documents "come alive" in the former slave's tale as speech and even action; and the former slave—often while assuming a deferential posture toward his white friends, editors, and guarantors—carries much of the burden of introducing and authenticating his own tale. In short, as my remarks on Solomon Northup's *Twelve Years a Slave* (1854) will suggest, a "second phase" narrative is a more sophisticated narrative because the former slave's voice is responsible for much more than recounting the tale.

Because an integrated or second-phase narrative is less a collection of texts and more a unified narrative, we may say that, in terms of narration, the integrated narrative is in the process of becoming—irrespective of authorial intent—a generic narrative, by which I mean a narrative of discernible genre such as history, fiction, essay, or autobiography. This process is no simple "gourd vine" activity: an integrated narrative does not become a generic narrative overnight, and indeed, there are no assurances that in becoming a new type of narrative it is transformed automatically into a distinctive generic text. What we discover, then, is a third phase to slave narration wherein two developments may occur: the integrated narrative (phase II) may be dominated either by its tale or by its authenticating strategies. In the first instance, as we see in Frederick Douglass's *Narrative of the Life of Frederick Douglass, an American Slave, Written by Himself* (1845), the narrative and moral energies of the former slave's voice and tale so resolutely dominate

the narrative's authenticating machinery (voices, documents, rhetorical strategies) that the narrative becomes, in thrust and purpose, far more metaphorical then rhetorical. When the integrated narrative becomes, in this way, a figurative account of action, landscape, and heroic self-transformation, it is so close generally to history, fiction, and autobiography that I term it a *generic narrative*.

In the second instance, as we see in William Wells Brown's *Narrative of the Life and Escape of William Wells Brown* (1852; appended to his novel, *Clotel, or The President's Daughter*), the authenticating machinery either remains as important as the tale or actually becomes, usually for some purpose residing outside the text, the dominant and motivating feature of the narrative. Since this is also a sophisticated narrative phase, figurative presentations of action, landscape, and self may also occur; however, such developments are rare and always ancillary to the central thrust of the text. When the authenticating machinery dominates in this fashion, the integrated narrative becomes an *authenticating narrative*.

As these remarks suggest, one reason for investigating the phases of slave narrative narration is to gain a clearer view of how some slave narrative types become generic narratives, and how, in turn, generic narratives—once formed, shaped, and set in motion by certain distinctly Afro-American cultural imperatives—have roots in the slave narratives. . . . Moreover, it bears on our ability to distinguish between narrative modes and forms, and to describe what we see. When a historian or literary critic calls a slave narrative an autobiography, for example, what he or she sees most likely is a first-person narrative that possesses literary features to distinguish it from ordinary documents providing historical and sociological data. But a slave narrative is *not* necessarily an autobiography. We need to observe the finer shades between the more easily discernible categories of narration, and we must discover whether these stops arrange themselves in progressive, contrapuntal, or dialectic fashion—or if they possess any arrangement at all. As the scheme described above . . . suggests, I believe there are at least four identifiable modes of narration within the slave narratives, and that all four have a direct bearing on the development of subsequent Afro-American narrative forms.

PHASE I: ECLECTIC NARRATIVE

Henry Bibb's *Narrative of the Life and Adventures of Henry Bibb, an American Slave*, begins with several introductory documents offering, collectively, what may be the most elaborate guarantee of authenticity found in the slave narrative canon. What is most revealing—in terms of eclectic narrative form, authenticating strategy, and race rituals along the color line—is the segregation of Bibb's own "Author's Preface" from the white-authored texts of the "Introduction." Bibb's "Author's Preface" is further removed from the preceding introductory texts by the fact that he does not address or acknowledge what has gone before. There is no exchange, no verbal bond, between the two major units of introductory material; this reflects not only the quality of Bibb's relations with his benefactors, but also his relatively modest degree of control over the text and event of the narrative itself.

The "Introduction" is basically a frame created by Bibb's publisher, Lucius Matlack, for the presentation of guarantees composed mostly by abolitionists in Detroit (where, in freedom, Bibb chose to reside). Yet Matlack, as the publisher, also has his own authenticating duties to perform. He assures the reader that while he did indeed "examine" and "prepare"

Bibb's manuscript, "The work of preparation . . . was that of orthography and punctuation merely, an arrangement of the chapters, and a table of contents—little more than falls to the lot of publishers generally." When Matlack tackles the issue of the tale's veracity, he mutes his own voice and offers instead those of various "authentic" documents gathered by the abolitionists. These gentlemen, all members of the Detroit Liberty Association, appear most sympathetic to Bibb, especially since he has spoken before their assemblies and lived an exemplary Christian life in their midst. To aid him—and their cause—they have interrogated Bibb (to which he submitted with "praiseworthy spirit") and have solicited letters from slaveholders, jailors, and Bibb's acquaintances, so that the truth of his tale might be established. No fewer than six of these letters plus the conclusion of the Association's report, all substantiating Bibb's story, appear in the "Introduction"; and, as if to "guarantee the guarantee," a note certifying the "friendly recommendation" of the abolitionists and verifying Bibb's "correct deportment" (composed, quite significantly, by a Detroit *judge*) is appended as well.

The elaborate authenticating strategy contained in Matlack's "Introduction" is typical of those found in the first-phase or eclectic narrative. The publisher or editor, far more than the former slave, assembles and manipulates the authenticating machinery, and seems to act on the premise that there is a direct correlation between the quantity of documents or texts assembled and the readership's acceptance of the narrative as a whole. I would like to suggest that Matlack's "Introduction" also constitutes a literary presentation of race rituals and cultural conditions, and that, as such, it functions as a kind of metaphor in the narrative.

To be sure, Matlack displays typical nineteenth-century American enthusiasm and superficiality when he writes of the literary merits of slave narratives: "Gushing fountains of poetic thought have started from beneath the rod of violence, that will long continue to slake the feverish thirst of humanity outraged, until swelling to a flood it shall rush with wasting violence over the ill-gotten heritage of the oppressor." However, the thrust of his "Introduction" is to guarantee the truth of a tale and, by extension, the *existence* of a man calling himself Henry Bibb. In his own aforementioned remarks regarding the preparation of Bibb's text for publication, Matlack appears to address the issue of the author's—Bibb's—credibility. However, the issue is really the audience's—white America's—credulity: their acceptance not so much of the former slave's escape and newfound freedom, but of his literacy. Many race rituals are enacted here, not the least of which is Matlack's "conversation" with white America across the text and figurative body of a silent former slave. The point we may glean from them all is that, insofar as Bibb must depend on his publisher to be an intermediary between his text and his audience, he relinquishes control of the narrative—which is, after all, the vehicle for the account of how he obtained his voice in freedom.

While we are impressed by the efforts of the Detroit Liberty Association's members to conduct an investigation of Bibb's tale, issue a report, and lend their names to the guarantee, we are still far more overwhelmed by the examples of the cultural disease with which they wrestle than by their desire to find a cure. That disease is, of course, cultural myopia, the badge and sore bestowed upon every nation mindlessly heedful of race ritual instead of morality: Henry Bibb is alive and well in Detroit, but by what miraculous stroke will he, as a man, be able to cast his shadow on this soil? The effort in the

narrative's "Introduction" to prove that Bibb exists, and hence has a tale, goes far to explain why a prevailing metaphor in Afro-American letters is, in varying configurations, one of invisibility and translucence. Indirectly, and undoubtedly on a subconscious level, Matlack and the abolitionists confront the issue of Bibb's inability "to cast his shadow." But even in their case we may ask: Are they bolstering a cause, comforting a former slave, or recognizing a man?

The letters from the slaveholders and jailors Bibb knew while in bondage must not be overlooked here, for they help illuminate the history of the disease we are diagnosing. The letter from Silas Gatewood, whose father once owned Bibb, is designed solely to portray Bibb as "a notorious liar . . . and a rogue." Placed within the compendium of documents assembled by the abolitionists, the letter completes, through its nearly hysterical denunciation of Bibb, the "Introduction's" portrait of America at war with itself. The debate over Bibb's character, and, by extension, his right to a personal history bound to that of white Americans, is really nothing less than a literary omen of the Civil War. In this regard, the segregation of Bibb's "Author's Preface" from the introductory compendium of documents is, even more than his silence within the compendium, indicative of how the former slave's voice was kept muted and distant while the nation debated questions of slavery and the Negro's humanity.

Bibb's "Preface" reveals two features to his thinking, each of which helps us see how the former slave approached the task of composing a narrative. In answer to his own rhetorical question as to why he wrote the narrative, he replies, "in no place have I given orally the detail of my narrative; and some of the most interesting events of my life have never reached the public ear." This is not extraordinary except in that it reminds us of the oral techniques and traditions that lay behind most of the written narratives. The former slave's accomplishment of a written narrative should by no means be minimized, but we must also recognize the extent to which the abolitionist lecture circuit, whether in Michigan, Maine, or New York, gave former slaves an opportunity to structure, to embellish, and above all to polish an oral version of their tale—and to do so before the very audiences who would soon purchase hundreds, if not thousands, of copies of the written account. The former slave, not altogether unlike the semi-literate black preacher whose sermons were (and are) masterpieces of oral composition and rhetorical strategy, often had a fairly well developed version of his or her tale either memorized or (more likely) sufficiently *patterned* for effective presentation, even before the question of written composition was entertained. Certainly such was the case for Bibb, and this reminds us not to be too narrow when we call the basic slave narrative an eclectic narrative form. Oral as well as written forms are part of the eclectic whole.

The second revealing feature of Bibb's "Preface" returns us to a point on which his publisher, Matlack, began. Bibb appears extremely aware of the issue of his authorship when he writes:

> The reader will remember that I make no pretension to literature; for I can truly say, that I have been educated in the school of adversity, whips, and chains. Experience and observation have been my principal teachers, with the exception of three weeks schooling which I have had the good fortune to receive since my escape from the "grave yard of the mind," or the dark prison of human bondage.

That Bibb had only three weeks of formal schooling is astonishing; however, I am intrigued even more by the two metaphors for slavery with which he concludes. While both obviously suggest confinement—one of the mind, the other of his body—it seems significant that Bibb did not choose between the two (for reasons of style, if no other). Both images are offered *after* the act of writing his tale, possibly because Bibb is so terribly aware of both. His body is now free, his mind limber, his voice resonant; together they and his tale, if not his narrative, are his own.

On a certain level, we must study Matlack's "Introduction," with all its documents and guarantees, and Bibb's "Author's Preface" as a medley of voices, rather than as a loose conglomerate of discrete and even segregated texts. Together, both in what they do and do not say, these statements reflect the passions, politics, interpersonal relations, race rituals, and uses of language of a cross-section of America in the 1840's. But on another level, we must hold fast to what we have discovered regarding how Bibb's removal from the primary authenticating documents and strategy (that is, from the "Introduction") weakens his control of the narrative and, in my view, relegates him to a posture of partial literacy. Bibb's tale proves that he has acquired a voice, but his narrative shows that his voice does not yet control the imaginative forms which his personal history assumes in print.

In the Bibb narrative, the various texts within the "Introduction" guarantee Bibb and his tale; Bibb sustains this strategy of guarantee late in his tale by quoting letters and proclamations by many of the same figures who provided documents for the "Introduction." As we will discover in Solomon Northup's narrative, this use of authenticating documents within the text of the tale indicates the direction of more sophisticated slave narrative texts. Indeed, the question of whether the authenticating documents and strategies have been integrated into the central text (usually the tale) of the slave narrative is a major criterion by which we may judge author and narrative alike. The inclusion and manipulation of peripheral documents and voices suggests a remarkable level of literacy and self-assurance on the part of the former slave, and the reduction of many texts and strategies into one reflects a search, irrespective of authorial intent, for a more sophisticated written narrative form. Here, then, is a point of departure from which we may study the development of pregeneric narratives into generic and other sophisticated narrative types.

PHASE II: INTEGRATED NARRATIVE

While I am not prepared to classify Solomon Northup's *Twelve Years a Slave* (1854) as an autobiography, it is certainly a more sophisticated text than Henry Bibb's, principally because its most important authenticating document is integrated into the tale as a voice and character. *Twelve Years a Slave* is, however, an integrated narrative unsure of itself. Ultimately, its authenticating strategy depends as much upon an appended set of authenticating texts as upon integrated documents and voices.

In comparison to the Bibb "Introduction," the Northup introductory materials appear purposely short and undeveloped. Northup's editor and amanuensis, a Mr. David Wilson, offers a one-page "Preface," not a full-blown "Introduction," and Northup's own introductory words are placed in the first chapter of his tale, rather than in a discrete entry written expressly for that purpose. Wilson's "Preface" is, predictably, an authenticating document, formulaically acknowledging whatever "faults of style and of expression" the narrative may contain while assuring the reader that he, the editor and a white man, is convinced of Northup's strict adherence to the truth. Nor-

thup's own contributions, like Bibb's, are not so much authenticating as they are reflective of what a slave may have been forced to consider while committing his tale to print.

Northup's first entry is simply and profoundly his signature—his proof of literacy writ large, with a bold, clear hand. It appears beneath a pen-and-ink frontispiece portrait entitled "Solomon in His Plantation Suit." His subsequent entries quite self-consciously place his narrative amid the antislavery literature of the era, in particular, with Harriet Beecher Stowe's *Uncle Tom's Cabin* (1852) and *Key to Uncle Tom's Cabin* (1853). If one wonders why Northup neither establishes his experience among those of other kidnapped and enslaved blacks nor positions his narrative with other narratives, the answer is provided in part by his dedicatory page. There, after quoting a passage from *Key to Uncle Tom's Cabin* which, in effect, verifies his account of slavery because it is said to "form a striking parallel" to Uncle Tom's, Northup respectfully dedicates his narrative to Miss Stowe, remarking that his tale affords "another *Key to Uncle Tom's Cabin.*"

This is no conventional dedication; it tells us much about the requisite act of authentication. While the Bibb narrative is authenticated by documents provided by the Detroit Liberty Association, the Northup narrative begins the process of authentication by assuming kinship with a popular antislavery novel. Audience, and the former slave's relationship to that audience, are the key issues here: authentication is, apparently, a rhetorical strategy designed not only for verification purposes, but also for the task of initiating and insuring a readership. No matter how efficacious it undoubtedly was for Northup (or his editor) to ride Miss Stowe's coattails and share in her immense notoriety, one cannot help wondering about the profound implications involved in authenticating personal history by binding it to historical fiction. In its way, this strategy says as much about a former slave's inability to confirm his existence and "cast his shadow" as does the more conventional strategy observed in the Bibb narrative. Apparently, a novel may authenticate a personal history, especially when the personal history is that of a former slave.

While not expressing the issue in these terms, Northup seems to have thought about the dilemma of authentication and that of slave narratives competing with fictions of both the pro- and anti-slavery variety. He writes:

> Since my return to liberty, I have not failed to perceive the increasing interest throughout the Northern states, in regard to the subject of Slavery. Works of fiction, professing to portray its features in their more pleasing as well as more repugnant aspects, have been circulated to an extent unprecedented, and, as I understand, have created a fruitful topic of comment and discussion.
>
> I can speak of Slavery only so far as it came under my own observation—only so far as I have known and experienced it in my own person. My object is, to give a candid and truthful statement of facts: to repeat the story of my life, without exaggeration, leaving it for others to determine, whether even the pages of fiction present a picture of more cruel wrong or a severer bondage.

Clearly, Northup felt that the authenticity of his tale would not be taken for granted, and that, on a certain peculiar but familiar level enforced by rituals along the color line, his narrative would be viewed as a fiction competing with other fictions. However, in this passage Northup also inaugurates a counterstrategy. His reference to his own observation of slavery may be a just and subtle dig at the "armchair sociologists" of North and South alike, who wrote of the slavery question amid the comforts of their libraries and verandas. But more important, in terms of plot as well as point of view, the remark establishes Northup's authorial posture as a "participant-observer" in the truest and (given his bondage) most regrettable sense of the phrase. In these terms, then, Northup contributes personally to the authentication of *Twelve Years a Slave:* he challenges the authenticity of the popular slavery fictions and their power of authenticating his own personal history by first exploiting the bond between them and his tale and then assuming the posture of an authenticator. One needn't delve far into the annals of American race relations for proof that Northup's rhetorical strategy is but a paradigm for the classic manipulation of the master by the slave.

As the first chapter of *Twelve Years a Slave* unfolds, Northup tells of his family's history and circumstances. His father, Mintus Northup, was a slave in Rhode Island and in Rensselaer County, New York, before gaining his freedom in 1803 upon the death of his master. Mintus quickly amassed property and gained suffrage; he came to expect the freedoms that accompany self-willed mobility and self-initiated employment, and gave his son, Solomon, the extraordinary advantage of being born a free man. As a result, Solomon writes of gaining "an education surpassing that ordinarily bestowed upon children in our condition," and he recollects leisure hours "employed over my books, or playing the violin." Solomon describes employment (such as lumber-rafting on Lake Champlain) that was not only profitable but also, in a way associated with the romance of the frontier, adventurous and even manly. When Solomon Northup married Anne Hampton on Christmas Day of 1829, they did not jump over a broomstick, as was the (reported) lot of most enslaved black Americans; rather, the two were married by a magistrate of the neighborhood, Timothy Eddy, Esq. Furthermore, their first home was neither a hovel nor a hut but the "Fort House," a residence "lately occupied by Captain Lathrop" and used in 1777 by General Burgoyne.

This saga of Solomon's heritage is full of interest, and it has its rhetorical and strategical properties as well. Northup has begun to establish his authorial posture removed from the condition of the black masses in slavery—a move which, as we have indicated, is as integral to the authenticating strategy as to the plot of his tale. In addition to portraying circumstances far more pleasant and fulfilling than those which he suffers in slavery, Northup's family history also yields some indication of his relations with whites in the district, especially the white Northups. Of course, these indications also advance both the plot and the authenticating strategy. One notes, for example, that while Mintus Northup did indeed migrate from the site of his enslavement once he was free, he retained the Northup surname and labored for a relative of his former master. Amid his new prosperity and mobility, Mintus maintained fairly amicable ties with his past; apparently this set the tone for relations between Northups, black and white. One should be wary of depicting New York north of Albany as an ideal or integrated area in the early 1800's, but the black Northups had bonds with whites—perhaps blood ties. To the end Solomon depends on these bonds for his escape from slavery and for the implicit verification of his tale.

In the first chapter of *Twelve Years a Slave,* Henry B. Northup, Esq., is mentioned only briefly as a relative of Mintus Northup's former master; in the context of Solomon's family history, he is but a looming branch of the (white) Northup family tree. However, as the tale concludes, Henry Northup becomes a voice and character in the narrative. He requests various legal documents essential to nullifying Solomon's sale into bondage; he inquires into Solomon's whereabouts in Bayou Boeuf, Louisiana; he presents the facts before lawyers, sheriffs, and Solomon's master, Edwin Epps; he pleads Solomon's case against his abductors before a District of Columbia court of law; and, most important, after the twelve years of assault on Solomon's sense of identity, Henry Northup utters, to Solomon's profound thanksgiving, Solomon's given name—not his slave name. In this way Henry Northup enters the narrative, and whatever linguistic authentication of the tale Solomon inaugurated by assuming the rather objective posture of the participant-observer-authenticator is concluded and confirmed, not by appended letter, but by Henry Northup's presence.

This strategy of authentication functions hand in hand with the narrative's strategy of reform. Like the carpenter, Bass, who jeopardizes his own safety by personally mailing Solomon's appeals for help to New York, Henry Northup embodies the spirit of reform in the narrative. In terms of reform strategy, Henry Northup and Bass—who, as a Canadian, represents a variation on the archetype of deliverance in Canada—are not only saviors but also models whose example might enlist other whites in the reform cause. Certainly abolitionists near and far could identify with these men, and that was important. Slave narratives were often most successful when they were as subtly pro-abolition as they were overtly antislavery—a consideration which could only have exacerbated the former slave's already sizeable problems with telling his tale in such a way that he, and not his editors or guarantors, controlled it.

But Henry Northup is a different kind of savior from Bass: he is an American descended from slaveowners, and he shares his surname with the kidnapped Solomon. Furthermore, his posture as a family friend is inextricably bound to his position in the tale as a lawyer. At the end of *Twelve Years a Slave,* Henry Northup appears in Louisiana as an embodiment of the law, as well as of Solomon Northup's past (in all its racial complexity) come to reclaim him. In this way, Solomon's *tale* assumes the properties of an integrated narrative—the authenticating texts (here, the words and actions of Henry Northup) are integrated into the former slave's tale. But in what follows after the tale, we see that Solomon's *narrative* ultimately retrogresses to the old strategies of a phase-one eclectic narrative. Whereas the Bibb narrative begins with a discrete set of authenticating texts, the Northup narrative ends with such a set— an "Appendix."

The Northup Appendix contains three types of documents. First comes the New York state law, passed May 14, 1840, employed by Henry Northup and others to reclaim Solomon Northup from bondage in Louisiana. There follows a petition to the Governor of New York from Solomon's wife, Ann Northup, replete with legal language that persists in terming her a "memorialist." The remaining documents are letters, mostly from the black Northups' white neighbors, authenticating Solomon's claim that he is a free Negro. Despite our initial disappointment upon finding such an orthodox authenticating strategy appended to what had heretofore been a refreshingly sophisticated slave narrative (the narrative does not need the Appendix to fulfill its form), the Appendix does have its points of interest. Taken as a whole, it portrays the unfolding of a law; the New York law with which it begins precipitates the texts that follow, notably, in chronological order. On one level, then, Northup's Appendix is, far more than Bibb's Introduction, a story in epistolary form that authenticates not only his tale but also those voices within the tale, such as Henry Northup's. On another level, however, the Appendix becomes a further dimension to the reform strategy subsumed within the narrative. Just as Bass and Henry Northup posture as model reformers, the narrative's Appendix functions as a primer, complete with illustrative documents, on how to use the law to retrieve kidnapped free Negroes. Thus, the Appendix, as much as the tale itself, can be seen (quite correctly) as an elaborate rhetorical strategy against the Fugitive Slave Law of 1850.

In the end, the Northup narrative reverts to primitive authenticating techniques, but that does not diminish the sophistication and achievement of the tale within the narrative. We must now ask: To what end does the immersion of authenticating documents and strategies within the texture of Northup's tale occur? Furthermore, is this goal literary or extraliterary? In answering these questions we come a little closer, I think, to an opinion on whether narratives like Northup's may be autobiographies.

Northup's conscious or unconscious integration and subsequent manipulation of authenticating voices advances his tale's plot and most certainly advances his narrative's validation and reform strategies. However, it does little to develop what Albert Stone has called a literary strategy of self-presentation [see Additional Bibliography]. The narrative renders an extraordinary experience, but not a remarkable self. The two need not be exclusive, as Frederick Douglass's 1845 *Narrative* illustrates, but in the Northup book they appear to be distinct entities, principally because of the eye or "I" shaping and controlling the narration. Northup's eye and "I" are not so much introspective as they are inquisitive; even while in the pit of slavery in Louisiana, Northup takes time to inform us of various farming methods and of how they differ from practices in the North. Of course, this remarkable objective posture results directly from Northup assuming the role of a participant-observer for authentication purposes. But it all has a terrible price. Northup's tale is neither the history nor a metaphor for the history of his life; and because this is so, his tale cannot be called autobiographical.

PHASE IIIA: GENERIC NARRATIVE

In the first two phases of slave narrative narration we observe the former slave's ultimate lack of control over his own narrative, occasioned primarily by the demands of audience and authentication. This dilemma is not unique to the authors of these narratives; indeed, many modern black writers still do not control their personal history once it assumes literary form. For this reason, Frederick Douglass's *Narrative of the Life of Frederick Douglass, an American Slave, Written by Himself* (1845) seems all the more a remarkable literary achievement. Because it contains several segregated narrative texts—a preface, a prefatory letter, the tale, an appendix—it appears to be, in terms of the narrative phases, a rather primitive slave narrative. But each ancillary text is drawn to the tale by some sort of extraordinary gravitational pull or magnetic attraction. There is, in short, a dynamic energy between the tale and each supporting text that we do not discover in the Bibb or Northup narratives, save perhaps in the relationship between Solomon Northup and his guarantor-become-character, Henry Northup. The Douglass narrative is an integrated narrative of a very special order. The integrating process does, in a small way, pursue the conventional path found in Northup's narrative,

creating characters out of authenticating texts (William Lloyd Garrison silently enters Douglass's tale at the very end); however, its new and major thrust is the creation of that aforementioned energy which binds the supporting texts to the tale, while at the same time removing them from participation in the narrative's rhetorical and authenticating strategies. Douglass's tale dominates the narrative because it alone authenticates the narrative.

The introductory texts to the tale are two in number: a "Preface" by William Lloyd Garrison, the famous abolitionist and editor of *The Liberator;* and a "Letter from Wendell Phillips, Esq.," who was equally well known as an abolitionist, crusading lawyer, and judge. In theory, each of these introductory documents should be classic guarantees written almost exclusively for a white reading public, concerned primarily and ritualistically with the white validation of a newfound black voice, and removed from the tale in such ways that the guarantee and tale view silently and surreptitiously for control of the narrative as a whole. But these entries are not fashioned that way. To be sure, Garrison offers a conventional guarantee when he writes, "Mr. Douglass has very properly chosen to write his own Narrative, in his own style, and according to the best of his ability, rather than to employ some one else. It is, therefore, entirely his own production; and . . . it is, in my judgment, highly creditable to his head and heart." And Phillips, while addressing Douglass, most certainly offers a guarantee to "another" audience as well:

> Every one who has heard you speak has felt, and, I am confident, every one who read your book will feel, persuaded that you give them a fair specimen of the whole truth. No one-sided portrait,—no wholesale complaints,—but strict justice done, whenever individual kindliness has neutralized, for a moment, the deadly system with which it was strangely allied.

But these passages dominate neither the tone nor the substance of their respective texts.

Garrison is far more interested in writing history (specifically, that of the 1841 Nantucket Anti-Slavery Convention, and the launching of Douglass's career as a lecture agent for various antislavery societies) and recording his own place in it. His declaration, "I shall never forget his [Douglass's] first speech at the convention," is followed within a paragraph by, "*I rose, and declared that Patrick Henry, of revolutionary fame, never made a speech more eloquent in the cause of liberty . . . I reminded the audience of the peril which surrounded this self-emancipated young man . . . I appealed to them,* whether they would ever allow him to be carried back into slavery,—law or no law, constitution or no constitution" (italics added). His "Preface" ends, not with a reference to Douglass or his tale, but with an apostrophe very much like one he would use to exhort and arouse an antislavery assembly. With the following cry Garrison hardly guarantees Douglass's tale, but enters and reenacts his own abolitionist career instead:

> Reader! are you with the man-stealers in sympathy and purpose, or on the side of their down-trodden victims? If with the former, then you are the foe of God and man. If with the latter, what are you prepared to do and dare in their behalf? Be faithful, be vigilant, be untiring in your efforts to break every yoke, and let the oppressed go free. Come what may— cost what may—inscribe on the banner which you unfurl to the breeze, as your religious and political motto—"NO COMPROMISE WITH SLAVERY! NO UNION WITH SLAVEHOLDERS!"

In the light of this closure, and (no matter how hard we try to ignore it) the friction that developed between Garrison and Douglass in later years, we might be tempted to see Garrison's "Preface" at war with Douglass's tale for authorial control of the narrative as a whole. Certainly there is a tension, but that tension is stunted by Garrison's enthusiasm for Douglass's tale. Garrison writes:

> This *Narrative* contains many affecting incidents, many *passages* of great eloquence and power; but I think the most thrilling one of them all is the *description* Douglass gives of his feelings, as he stood soliloquizing respecting his fate, and the chances of his one day being a free man. . . . Who can read that *passage,* and be insensible to its pathos and sublimity? [Italics added.]

Here Garrison does, probably subconsciously, an unusual and extraordinary thing—he becomes the first guarantor we have seen in this study who not only directs the reader to the tale, but also acknowledges the tale's singular rhetorical power. Garrison enters the tale by being at the Nantucket convention with Douglass in 1841 (the same year Solomon Northup was kidnapped) and by, in effect, authenticating the impact, rather than the facts, of the tale. He fashions his own apostrophe, but finally he remains a member of Douglass's audience far more than he assumes the posture of a competing or superior voice. In this way Garrison's "Preface" stands outside Douglass's tale but is steadfastly bound to it.

Such is the case for Wendell Phillips's "Letter" as well. As I have indicated, it contains passages which seem addressed to credulous readers in need of a "visible" authority's guarantee, but by and large the "Letter" is directed to Frederick Douglass alone. It opens with "My Dear Friend," and there are many extraliterary reasons for wondering initially if the friend is actually Frederick. Shortly thereafter, however, Phillips declares, "I am glad the time has come when the 'lions write history,'" and it becomes clear that he both addresses Douglass and writes in response to the tale. These features, plus Phillips's specific references to how Douglass acquired his "A B C" and learned "where the 'white sails' of the Chesapeake were bound," serve to integrate Phillips's "Letter" into Douglass's tale.

Above all, we must understand in what terms the "Letter" is a cultural and linguistic event. Like the Garrison document, it presents its author as a member of Douglass's audience; but the act of letter-writing, of correspondence, implies a moral and linguistic parity between a white guarantor and black author which we haven't seen before—and which we do not always see in American literary history *after* 1845. The tone and posture initiated in Garrison's "Preface" are completed and confirmed in Phillips's "Letter"; while these documents are integrated into Douglass's tale, they remain segregated outside the tale in the all-important sense that they yield Douglass sufficient narrative and rhetorical space in which to render personal history in—and as—a literary form.

What marks Douglass's narration and control of his tale is his extraordinary ability to pursue several types of writing with ease and with a degree of simultaneity. The principal types of writing we discover in the tale are: syncretic phrasing, introspective analysis, internalized documentation, and participant observation. Of course, each of these types has its accompanying authorial posture, the result being that even the telling of the tale (as distinct from the content of the tale) yields a portrait of a complex individual marvelously facile with the tones, shapes, and dimensions of his voice.

Douglass's syncretic phrasing is often discussed; the passage most widely quoted is probably, "My feet have been so cracked with the frost, that the pen with which I am writing might be laid in the gashes." The remarkable clarity of this language needs no commentary, but what one admires as well is Douglass's ability to conjoin past and present, and to do so with images that not only stand for different periods in his personal history but also, in their fusion, speak of his evolution from slavery to freedom. The pen, symbolizing the quest for literacy fulfilled, actually measures the wounds of the past, and this measuring process becomes a metaphor in and of itself for the artful composition of travail transcended. While I admire this passage, I find even more intriguing the syncretic phrases that pursue a kind of acrid punning upon the names of Douglass's oppressors. A minor example appears early in the tale, when Douglass deftly sums up an overseer's character by writing, "Mr. Severe was rightly named: he was a cruel man." Here Douglass is content with "glossing" the name; but late in the tale, just before attempting to escape in 1835, he takes another oppressor's name and does not so much gloss it or play with it as *work upon* it—to such an extent that, riddled with irony, it is devoid of its original meaning: "At the close of the year 1834, Mr. Freeland again hired me of my master, for the year 1835. But, by this time, I began to want to live *upon free land* as well as *with Freeland;* and I was no longer content, therefore, to live with him or any other slaveholder." Of course, this is effective writing—far more effective than what is found in the average slave narrative. But my point is that Douglass seems to fashion these passages for both his readership and himself. Each example of his increasing facility and wit with language charts his ever-shortening path to literacy; thus, in their way, Douglass's syncretic phrases reveal his emerging comprehension of freedom and literacy, and are another introspective tool by which he may mark the progress of his personal history.

But the celebrated passages of introspective analysis are even more pithy and direct. In these, Douglass fashions language as finely honed and balanced as an aphorism or Popean couplet, and thereby orders his personal history with neat, distinct, and credible moments of transition. When Mr. Auld forbids Mrs. Auld from teaching Douglass the alphabet, for example, Douglass relates, "From that moment, I understood the pathway from slavery to freedom. . . . Whilst I was saddened by the thought of losing the aid of my kind mistress, I was gladdened by the invaluable instruction which, by the merest accident, I gained from my master." The clarity of Douglass's revelation is as unmistakable as it was remarkable. As rhetoric, the passage is successful because its nearly extravagant beginning is finally rendered quite acceptable by the masterly balance and internal rhyming of "saddened" and "gladdened," which is persuasive because it is pleasant and because it offers the illusion of a reasoned conclusion.

Balance is an important feature to two other equally celebrated passages which open and close Douglass's telling of his relations with Mr. Covey, an odd (because he *worked* in the fields alongside the slaves) but vicious overseer. At the beginning of the episode, in which Douglass finally fights back and draws Covey's blood, he writes: "You have seen how a man was made a slave; you shall see how a slave was made a man." And at the end of the episode, to bring matters linguistically as well as narratively full circle, Douglass declares:

"I now resolved that, however long I might remain a slave in form, the day has passed forever when I could be a slave in fact. I did not hesitate to let it be known of me, that the white man who expected to succeed in whipping, must also succeed in killing me."

The sheer poetry of these statements is not lost on us, nor is the reason why the poetry was created in the first place. One might suppose that in another age Douglass's determination and rage would take a more effusive expression, but I cannot imagine that to be the case. In the first place, his linguistic model is obviously scriptural; and in the second, his goal, as Albert Stone has argued, is the presentation of a *"historical self,"* not the record of temporary hysteria.

This latter point, to refer back to the Northup narrative, is one of the prime distinctions between Solomon Northup and Frederick Douglass—one which ultimately persuades me that Douglass is about the business of discovering how personal history may be transformed into autobiography, while Northup is not. Both narratives contain episodes in which the author finally stands up to and soundly beats his overseer, but while Douglass performs this task and reflects upon its place in his history, Northup resorts to effusion:

> As I stood there, feelings of unutterable agony over-whelmed me. I was conscious that I had subjected myself to unimaginable punishment. The reaction that followed my extreme ebullition of anger produced the most painful sensations of regret. An unfriended, helpless slave—what could I *do*, what could I *say*, to justify, in the remotest manner, the heinous act I had committed . . . I tried to pray . . . but emotion choked my utterance, and I could only bow my head upon my hands and weep.

Passages such as these may finally link certain slave narratives with the popular sentimental literary forms of the nineteenth century, but Douglass's passages of introspective analysis create fresh space for themselves in the American literary canon.

Internal documentation in Douglass's tale is unusual in that, instead of reproducing letters and other documents written by white guarantors within the tale or transforming guarantees into characters, Douglass internalizes documents which, like the syncretic and introspective passages, order his personal history. Again a comparison of Douglass and Northup is useful, because while both authors present documents having only a secondary function in the authenticating process, their goals (and, perhaps one might say, their ambitions) seem quite different.

Northup, for example, documents slave songs in two major passages: first in the text of the tale, and then in a segregated text serving as a musical interlude between the tale and the Appendix. His discussion of the songs within the tale is one dimensional, by which I mean it merely reflects his limited comprehension and appreciation of the songs at a given moment in his life. Rather than establishing Northup within the slave community, remarks like "those unmeaning songs, composed rather for [their] adaptation to a certain tune or measure, than for the purpose of expressing any distinct idea" or "equally nonsensical, but full of melody" serve only to reinforce his displacement as a participant-observer. One might have assumed that Northup (who was, after all, kidnapped into slavery partly because of his musicianship) found music a bond between him and his enslaved brethren, and in passages such as these would relinquish or soften his objective posture. But apparently the demands of audience and authentication precluded such a shift.

In contrast, Douglass's discussion of slave songs begins with phrases such as "wild songs" and "unmeaning jargon" but concludes, quite typically for him, with a study of how he grew to "hear" the songs and how that hearing affords yet another illumination of his path from slavery to freedom:

> I did not, when a slave, understand the deep meaning of those rude and apparently incoherent songs. I was myself within the circle; so that I neither saw nor heard as those without might see and hear. They told a tale of woe which was then altogether beyond my feeble comprehension. . . . Every tone was a testimony against slavery, and a prayer to God for deliverance from chains. The hearing of those wild notes always depressed my spirit, and filled me with ineffable sadness. I have frequently found myself in tears while hearing them. The mere recurrence to those songs, even now, afflicts me; and while I am writing these lines, an expression of feeling has already found its way down my cheek.

The tears of the past and present interflow. Douglass not only documents his saga of enslavement but also, with typical recourse to syncretic phrasing and introspective analysis, advances his presentation of self.

Douglass's other internalized documents are employed with comparable efficiency, as we see in the episode where he attempts an escape in 1835. There the document reproduced is the pass or "protection" Douglass wrote for himself and his compatriots in the escape plan:

> This is to certify that I, the undersigned, have given the bearer, my servant, full liberty to go to Baltimore, and spend the Easter holidays. Written with mine own hand, &c., 1835.
>
> William Hamilton,
> Near St. Michael's, in Talbot county, Maryland.

The protection exhibits Douglass's increasingly refined sense of how to manipulate language—he has indeed come a long way from that day when Mr. Auld halted his A B C lessons. But even more impressive, I believe, is the act of reproducing the document itself. We know from the tale that each slave managed to destroy his pass when the scheme was thwarted; Douglass is reproducing his language from memory, and there is no reason to doubt a single jot of his recollection. He can draw so easily from the wellsprings of memory because the protection is not a mere scrap of memorabilia, but a veritable roadsign on his path to freedom and literacy. In this sense, his protection assumes a place in Afro-American letters as an antedating trope for such documents as "The Voodoo of Hell's Half Acre" in Richard Wright's *Black Boy*, and the tale framed by the prologue and epilogue in Ralph Ellison's *Invisible Man*.

All of the types of narrative discourse discussed thus far reveal features of Douglass's particular posture as a participant-observer narrator, a posture that is as introspective as Solomon Northup's is inquisitive. But the syncretic phrases, introspective studies, and internalized documents only exhibit Douglass as a teller and doer, and part of the great effect of his tale depends upon what he does *not* tell, what he refuses to reenact in print. Late in the tale, at the beginning of the eleventh chapter, Douglass writes:

> I now come to that part of my life during which I planned, and finally succeeded in making, my escape from slavery. But before narrating any of the peculiar circumstances, I deem it proper to make known my intention not to state all the facts connected with the transaction . . . I deeply regret the necessity that im-

pels me to suppress any thing of importance connected with my experience in slavery. It would afford
me great pleasure indeed, as well as materially add
to the interest of my narrative, were I at liberty to
gratify a curiosity, which I know exists. . . . But I
must deprive myself of this pleasure, and the curious
gratification which such a statement would afford. I
would allow myself to suffer under the greatest im-
putations which evil-minded men might suggest, rather
than exculpate myself, and thereby run the hazard of
closing the slightest avenue by which a brother slave
might clear himself of the chains and fetters of slavery.

John Blassingame has argued, in *The Slave Community* (1972),
that one way to test a slave narrative's authenticity is by gauging
how much space the narrator gives to relating his escape, as
opposed to describing the conditions of his capitivity. If the
adventure, excitement, and perils of the escape seem to be the
raison d'être for the narrative's composition, then the narrative
is quite possibly an exceedingly adulterated slave's tale or a
bald fiction. The theory does not always work perfectly: Henry
"Box" Brown's narrative and that of William and Ellen Craft
are predominantly recollections of extraordinary escapes; yet,
as far as we can tell, these are authentic tales. But Blassingame's theory nevertheless has great merit, and I have often
wondered to what extent it derives from the example of Douglass's tale and from his fulminations against those authors who
unwittingly excavate the Underground Railroad and expose it
to the morally thin mid-nineteenth-century American air.
Douglass's tale is spectacularly free from suspicion because
he never divulges a detail of his escape to New York. (That
information is given ten years later, in *My Bondage and My
Freedom* and other statements.) This marvelously rhetorical
omission or silence both sophisticates and authenticates his
posture as a participant-observer narrator. When a narrator
wrests this kind of preeminent authorial control from the ancillary voices in the narrative, we may say that he controls the
presentation of his personal history, and that his tale is becoming autobiographical. In this light, then, Douglass's last few
sentences of the tale take on special meaning:

But, while attending an anti-slavery convention at
Nantucket, on the 11th of August, 1841, I felt strongly
moved to speak. . . . It was a severe cross, and I took
it up reluctantly. The truth was, I felt myself a slave,
and the idea of speaking to white people weighed me
down. I spoke but a few moments, when I felt a
degree of freedom, and said what I desired with considerable ease. From that time until now, I have been
engaged in pleading the case of my brethren—with
what success, and what devotion, I leave those acquainted with my labors to decide.

With these words, the *narrative,* as Albert Stone has remarked,
comes full circle. We are returned not to the beginning of the
tale, but to Garrison's prefatory remarks on the convention and
Douglass's first public address. This return may be pleasing
in terms of the sense of symmetry it affords, but it is also a
remarkable feat of rhetorical strategy: having traveled with
Douglass through his account of his life, we arrive in Nantucket
in 1841 to hear him speak. We become, along with Mr. Garrison, his audience. The final effect is that Douglass reinforces
his posture as an articulate hero, while supplanting Garrison
as the definitive historian of his past.

Even more important, I think, is Douglass's final image of a
slave shedding his last fetter and becoming a man by first
finding his voice and then, as surely as light follows dawn,
speaking "with considerable ease." In one brilliant stroke, the

quest for freedom and literacy, implied from the start even by
the narrative's title, is resolutely consummated.

The final text of the narrative, the Appendix, differs from the
one attached to the Northup narrative. It is not a series of letters
and legal documents, but a discourse by Douglass on *his* view
of Christianity and Christian practice, as opposed to what he
exposed in his tale to be the bankrupt, immoral faith of slaveholders. As rhetorical strategy, the discourse is effective because it lends weight and substance to what passes for a conventional complaint of slave narrators, and because Douglass's
exhibition of faith can only enhance his already considerable
posture as an articulate hero. But more specifically, the discourse is most efficacious because at its heart lies a vitriolic
poem written by a northern Methodist minister that Douglass
introduces by writing: "I conclude these remarks by copying
the following portrait of the religion of the south, (which is,
by communion and fellowship, the religion of the north,) which
I soberly affirm is 'true to life,' and without caricature or the
slightest exaggeration." The poem is strong and imbued with
considerable irony, but what we must appreciate here is the
effect of the white Northerner's poem conjoined with Douglass's *authentication* of the poem. The tables are clearly reversed: Douglass has not only controlled his personal history,
but also fulfilled the prophecy suggested by his implicit authentication of Garrison's "Preface" by explicitly authenticating what is conventionally a white Northerner's validating
text. Douglass's narrative thus offers what is unquestionably
our best portrait in Afro-American letters of the requisite act
of assuming authorial control. An author can go no further than
Douglass did without himself writing all the texts constituting
the narrative.

PHASE IIIB: AUTHENTICATING NARRATIVE

In an authenticating narrative, represented here by William
Wells Brown's *Narrative of the Life and Escape of William
Wells Brown* (not to be confused with Brown's 1847 volume,
*Narrative of William Wells Brown, a Fugitive Slave, Written
by Himself),* the narrator exhibits considerable control of his
narrative by becoming an editor of disparate texts for authentication purposes, far more than for the goal of recounting
personal history. The texts Brown displays include passages
from his speeches and other writings, but for the most part
they are testimonials from antislavery groups in both America
and England, excerpts from reviews of his travel book, *Three
Years in Europe* (1852), selections from antislavery verse, and,
quite significantly, letters to Brown's benefactors from his
last master in slavery, Mr. Enoch Price of St. Louis. Brown's
control of his narrative is comparable to Douglass's, but while
Douglass gains control by improving upon the narrative failures
of authors like Henry Bibb, Brown's control represents a refinement of the authenticating strategies used by publishers
like Bibb's Lucius Matlack, who edited and deployed authenticating documents very much like those gathered by Brown.
In this way, Brown's narrative is not so much a tale of personal
history as it is a conceit upon the authorial mode of the white
guarantor. Control and authentication are achieved, but at the
enormous price of abandoning the quest to present personal
history in and as literary form.

Brown's "Preface," written notably by himself and not by a
white guarantor, is peculiar in that it introduces both his narrative and the text authenticated by the narrative, *Clotel; or,
The President's Daughter.* By and large, the tone of the "Preface" is sophisticated and generally that of a self-assured writer.
Unlike Bibb or Northup, Brown does not skirmish with other

authenticators for authorial control of the text, nor is he anxious about competition from other literary quarters of the antislavery ranks. He scans briefly the history of slavery in North America and reasons, with the British (with whom he resides after passage of the 1850 Fugitive Slave Law), that they who controlled the American colonies when slavery was introduced should feel ''a lively interest in its abolition.'' All this is done without resort to conventional apologia or the confession of verbal deficiencies; Brown is humble not so much in his rhetoric as in his goal: ''If the incidents set forth in the following pages should add anything new to the information already given to the public through similar publications, and should thereby aid in bringing British influence to bear upon American slavery, the main object for which this work was written will have been accomplished.'' That Brown introduces a personal narrative and a somewhat fictive narrative *(Clotel)* with language and intentions commonly reserved for works of history and journalism constitutes his first admission of being motivated by extraliterary concerns. His second admission emerges from his persistent use of the term ''memoir.'' In contrast to a confession or autobiography, a memoir refers specifically to an author's recollections of his public life, far more than to his rendering of personal history as literary form or metaphor. This former kind of portrait is, of course, excactly what Brown gives us in his narrative.

The narrative is, as I have indicated, bereft of authorship. Brown rarely renders in fresh language those incidents of which he has written elsewhere; he simply quotes himself. His posture as the editor and not the author of his tale disallows any true expression of intimacy with his personal past. This feature is reinforced by certain objectifying and distancing qualities created by third-person narration. Brown's 1847 narrative begins, ''I was born in Lexington, Ky. The man who stole me as soon as I was born, recorded the births of all the infants which he claimed to be born his property, in a book which he kept for that purpose. . . .'' Thus, it inaugurates the kind of personal voice and hardboiled prose which is Brown's contribution to early Afro-American letters. In contrast, the opening of the 1852 narrative is flat, without pith or strength: ''William Wells Brown, the subject of this narrative, was born a slave in Lexington, Kentucky, not far from the residence of the late Hon. Henry Clay.'' These words do not constitute effective writing, but that is not Brown's goal. The goal is, rather, authentication, and the seemingly superfluous aside about Henry Clay—which in another narrative might very well generate the first ironic thrust against America's moral blindness—appears for the exclusive purpose of validation. In this way Brown commences an authentication strategy which he will pursue throughout the tale.

The tale or memoir is eclectic in its collection of disparate texts; however, very few of the collected texts merit discussion. I will simply list their types to suggest both their variety and their usefulness to Brown:

1. The scrap of verse, usually effusive, always saccharine, culled from antislavery poets known and unknown. The verse expresses high sentiment and deep emotion when the text requires it, engages the popular reading public, and suggests erudition and sensitivity.

2. Quotations from Brown's speeches at famous institutions like Exeter Hall and from ''addresses'' bestowed on him after such speeches. These advance the memoir, embellish Brown's résumé, and authenticate his claim that he was where he said he was.

3. Quotations from Brown's travel book, *Three Years in Europe*, and from the book's reviews. The passages of personal history advance the memoir and validate ''The energy of the man,'' as well as call attention to the book. The reviews call further attention to the book, and authenticate Brown's literacy and good character.

4. Testimonies and testimonials from various abolitionist groups in the United States and England, white and colored. These texts profess the success of Brown's labors as a lecturing agent, ''commend him to the hospitality and encouragement of all true friends of humanity,'' and, upon his departure for England, provide him with what Douglass would have termed a ''protection'' for his travels. These are, in short, recommending letters attached to Brown's résumé validating his character and the fact that he is a fugitive slave.

5. Two letters from a former master, Enoch Price of St. Louis, dated before and after the Fugitive Slave Law was passed in 1850.

The Enoch Price letters are undoubtedly the most interesting documents in Brown's compendium, and he makes good narrative use of them. While the other assembled documents merely serve the authenticating strategy, Price's letters, in their portrait of a slaveholder ironically invoking the dictates of fair play while vainly attempting to exact a bargain price for Brown from his benefactors, actually tell us something about Brown's circumstances. Despite the lionizing illustrated by the other documents, Brown is still not a free man. He is most aware of this, and for this reason the narrative concludes, not with another encomium, but with the second of Price's letters once again requesting payment—payment for lost property, payment for papers that will set Brown free. All Brown can do under the circumstances is refuse to acknowledge Price's supposed right to payment, and order his present condition by controlling not so much his tale, which is his past, as the authentication of himself, which is his present and possibly his future. As the editor of his résumé—his present circumstance—Brown must acknowledge slavery's looming presence in his life, but he can also attempt to bury it beneath a mountain of antislavery rhetoric and self-authenticating documentation. Through the act of self-authentication Brown may contextualize slavery and thereby control it. In these terms, then, the heroic proportions to Brown's editorial act of including and manipulating Enoch Price's letters become manifest.

Brown's personal narrative most certainly authenticates himself, but how does it also authenticate *Clotel?* The answer takes us back to Brown's ''Preface,'' where he outlines the extraliterary goals of both narratives, and forward to the concluding chapter of *Clotel,* where he writes:

> My narrative has now come to a close. I may be asked, and no doubt shall, Are the various incidents and scenes related founded in truth? I answer, Yes. I have personally participated in many of those scenes. Some of the narratives I have derived from other sources; many from the lips of those who, like myself, have run away from the land of bondage. . . . To Mrs. Child, of New York, I am indebted for part of a short story. American Abolitionist journals are another source from whence some of the characters appearing in my narrative are taken. All these combined have made up my story.

Brown's personal narrative functions, then, as a successful rhetorical device, authenticating his *access* to the incidents, characters, scenes, and tales which collectively make up *Clotel.*

A slave family posing in front of their living quarters.

In the end, we witness a dynamic interplay between the two narratives, established by the need of each for resolution and authentication within the other. Since *Clotel* is not fully formed as either a fiction or a slave narrative, it requires completion of some sort, and finds this when it is transformed into a fairly effective antislavery device through linkage with its prefatory authenticating text. Since Brown's personal narrative is not fully formed as either an autobiography or a slave narrative, it requires fulfillment as a literary form through intimacy with a larger, more developed but related text. *Clotel* is no more a novel than Brown's preceding personal narrative is autobiography, but together they represent a roughly hewn literary tool which is, despite its defects, a sophisticated departure from the primary phases of slave narration and authentication.

Brown's personal narrative is hardly an aesthetic work, but that is because Brown had other goals in mind. He is willing to forsake the goal of presenting personal history in literary form in order to promote his books and projects like the Manual Labor School for fugitive slaves in Canada, to authenticate *Clotel,* and to authenticate himself while on British soil. He is willing to abandon the goals of true authorship and to assume instead the duties of an editor in order to gain some measure of control over the present, as opposed to illuminating the past. Brown's narrative is present and future oriented: most of his anecdotes from the past are offered as testimony to the energy and character he will bring to bear on future tasks. In short,

just as Douglass inaugurates the autobiographical mode in Afro-American letters, Brown establishes what curiously turns out to be the equally common mode of the authenticating narrative. (pp. 3-31)

Robert B. Stepto, "I Rose and Found My Voice: Narration, Authentication, and Authorial Control in Four Slave Narratives," in his From Behind the Veil: A Study of Afro-American Narrative, *University of Illinois Press, 1979, pp. 3-31.*

KEITH BYERMAN

[*Byerman explores deception in situation, language, and theme as an integral aspect of the slave narratives.*]

Authors of slave narratives faced a peculiar set of problems in designing their stories. First, the existence of a narrative meant that much of the inherent drama was removed; for the story to be told at all, the escape attempt, which was the climax of the action, must have been successful. Further, if the narrative served in part to point out the inhumanity of slavery to a northern audience, then the narrator had to explain his own civilized action, including his moralizing tale. How had he managed to avoid the brutalizing effects of the system and to adopt so successfully the values of his audience? And finally, the language of the narrative had to negotiate between the conventions accepted by northern readers and the linguistic practices of southern blacks. Too much convention might raise doubts about the authenticity of the story, while a style too reflective of black speech and thought would alienate that audience. The argument of this essay is that one important method of addressing these hazards was the use of black folk materials. Moreover, these materials were not merely adornments but essential parts of the thematic and stylistic fabric of the narratives.

The folkloric element in Afro-American literature has drawn increasing attention from critics. The analysis of such material generally focuses on such important twentieth-century figures as Zora Neale Hurston, Jean Toomer, and Ralph Ellison, and is usually thematic in nature. Folk material in the slave narratives has been most frequently observed by historians, and they generally are concerned with the historical reality such material reflects. In some cases, literary critics have explicitly denied the relevance of folklore to the narratives; one commentator even writes that "slave narratives tend to diminish the cultural value of Afro-American folktales and songs."

Such views do not sufficiently take into account a key aspect of the narratives: the use of deceit and the trickster motif as thematic, stylistic, and structural elements in many of the narratives. In most cases, the narrative can only exist because the narrator has managed, through masking, forgery, or lying, to reach a place of relative security from the power of slaveholders. While several of the narrators expressly denounce their own deception as immoral, it can be shown that the denunciations are themselves masks adopted to suit the audience. Moreover, the publication of such authenticating documents as letters to and from former masters serves to validate the truth of the narrative, and also echoes the taunts of Brer Rabbit when he has triumphed over his foes. This aspect of the narratives, then, far from being a secondary motif, is central to the design of the stories; the selves created by the narrators and the ultimate meanings of the narratives are dictated by such folk material.

Lawrence Levine, in *Black Culture and Black Consciousness*, has distinguished between animal tales, in which the weak use cleverness to replace the strong in positions of power, and the human or John-the-slave tales, in which motherwit is used to gain some immediate, short-term benefit such as food or money. In a few cases, freedom itself is the reward for clever behavior. The function of such tales, whether animal or human, is to provide psychological sustenance to slaves:

> But in terms of the values they [the tales] inculcated, the models of action they held up for emulation, the disrespect and even contempt they taught concerning the strong, the psychic barriers they created against the inculcation of many of the white world's values, it would be difficult to maintain that they should be viewed primarily as a means of control. What the tales gave to the masters with one hand they more than took back with the other. They encouraged trickery and guile; they stimulated the search for ways out of the system; they inbred a contempt for the powerful and an admiration for the perseverance and even the wisdom of the undermen; they constituted an intragroup lore which must have intensified feelings of distance from the world of the slaveholder.

The need for such a powerful alternative becomes clear when one examines the nature of the white world that the narratives describe. Though the narrators call it a system, it is the arbitrary, fluid, unsystematic nature of the slaveholder's world that is emphasized. For example, while cruelty is stressed repeatedly, it is the inconsistent application of deception and violence that makes life in the South so harsh. In such a world, the definition of trickster behavior becomes relative, especially when masters are capable of conscious deceit. Moses Grandy must buy himself three times because of the dishonesty of his master; Josiah Henson has his purchase price changed; Austin Steward's master tried kidnapping free blacks in order to regain his fortune. Frederick Douglass explains how Mr. Covey achieved his effectiveness as a slave breaker largely by seeming to be in several places at once. William Craft repeats a story of greed and deceit that he has heard: a master, who had lived with a black woman for several years and treated her as his wife, suddenly died, leaving no known white heirs and no will. The woman and her children, having no owner, assumed themselves to be free.

> But, poor creatures, they were soon sadly undeceived. A villain residing at a distance, hearing of the circumstances, came forward and swore that he was a relative of the deceased; and as this man bore, or assumed, Mr. Slator's name, the case was brought before one of those horrible tribunals, presided over by a second Judge Jeffreys, and calling itself a court of justice, but before whom no colored person, nor an abolitionist, was ever known to get his full rights.

> A verdict was given in favor of the plaintiff, whom the better portion of the community thought had willfully conspired to cheat the family.

The result of the decision is that the wife is deprived of her money and her children are sold to other slaveholders. One beautiful daughter, rather than accept a life of concubinage, commits suicide.

As important as these incidents are to the design of the narratives, conscious deception on the part of masters is not foregrounded nearly as much as moral dishonesty, which need not be conscious. Masters and mistresses whose outward characters are flawless are shown to be capable of behavior inconsistent with their putative moral values. Harriet Jacobs, an attractive young woman, is faced with the threat of rape by her otherwise moral master:

> He told me I was his property; that I must be subject to his will in all things. My soul revolted against the mean tyranny. But where could I turn for protection? No matter whether the slave girl be black as ebony or as fair as her mistress. In either case, there is no shadow of law to protect her from insult, from violence, or even from death; all these are inflicted by fiends who bear the shape of men.

One strategy of the narrators is to declare that their experience is of the mildest and most moral form of slavery. One of the ironies repeated in the narratives is the direct correlation between religious devotion and immoral behavior. Douglass is the most articulate in arguing that the deeper the faith, the greater the mistreatment:

> Another advantage I gained in my new master was, he made no pretensions to, or profession of, religion; and this, in my opinion, was truly a great advantage. I assert most unhesitatingly, that the religion of the south is a mere covering for the most horrid crimes,—a justifier of the most appalling barbarity,—a sanctifier of the most hateful frauds,—and a dark shelter under which the darkest, foulest, grossest, and most infernal deeds of slaveholders find the strongest protection. Were I to be again reduced to the chains of slavery, next to that enslavement, I should regard being the slave of a religious master the greatest calamity that could befall me. For all slaveholders with whom I have ever met, religious slaveholders are the worst.

Consistently, the narratives portray devout masters who beat, rape, and sell their slaves. Some of the most bitter irony is reserved for these figures. While such behavior is frequently seen as individual hypocrisy, it is most often explained as an inherent product of the system. In a society of distorted relationships, religion is necessarily one of the casualties.

Indeed, systemic disorder is apparent in every aspect of southern life. Economic misfortunes, such as a depressed cotton market, may necessitate the breaking up of slave families. Punishment is often unrelated to crime. Henry Bibb tells of the bruises left on his infant child after it was beaten by a mistress irritated by its crying. Josiah Henson is permanently crippled when an overseer from another farm believes himself to have been bumped by Henson during a drunken party.

A major sign of the disordered and self-deceiving world of the masters is the uncertain paternity of many narrators. Frequently, the comment is made that they or those they know are virtually identical to the white children with whom they play. The only physical difference is color. But this obvious resemblance must never be acknowledged. Everyone, both black and white, must not see what they cannot help seeing. The situation complicates life for everyone: masters, to the extent that they allow paternal feelings to meliorate the treatment of their darker children, risk losing some control over slaves; mistresses, unable to charge their husbands with infidelity, can only vent their frustration and anger on the innocent victims of such liaisons, but must never acknowledge the reason for such mistreatment; the children of this illicit intercourse, who have the clearest family backgrounds among slaves, are the ones least able to certify this aspect of their identity. Thus, in a region with a reputation for a conservative, highly-structured social order, the narrators present a world in which such basic securities as fidelity, family, and identity are problematical.

Given a morally ambiguous world among masters, it is hardly surprising that the narrators find deceit to be an important part of their own lives. A rigid set of moral convictions is actually more deleterious than flexibility in such matters. Not to steal may mean that the family will suffer physically; open assertion of one's manhood or one's paternity could lead to flogging or death; loyalty to the white family reinforces the system of enslavement. And, as Frederick Douglass points out, frankness about one's means of escape only aids and abets the slave-holders. But even under such circumstances, where moral values are so nearly inverted, the narrators take care to justify their deceptions. Their dishonest behavior is not random; it always has good, immediate cause. Repeatedly they state that open, honest, straightforward behavior has been tried without success; deceit serves as a last resort in the pursuit of morally good ends.

On the most concrete level, theft is frequently accepted as the means of acquiring the necessities of life. What raises the stealing above the level of petty crime, besides its physical necessity, is the recurrent, rather sophistic argument that such behavior cannot be theft since a slave, being property, cannot actually steal other property from his master. Josiah Henson, as a superintendent over fellow slaves, got more work out of them than white overseers. When his efforts and those of the others were not recognized, "one of the means I took to gain the good-will of my fellow sufferers, was by taking from him some things he did not give, in part payment of my extra labor." Such verbal and logical manipulation in defense of behavior that a northern audience would interpret as criminal suggests a trickster sensibility at work.

Another kind of manipulation involves the use of folk practices to achieve some control over the arbitrary behavior of whites. Both Henry Bibb and Frederick Douglass describe their efforts to avoid beatings by carrying roots said to have magical powers. While both note that this belief is ineffectual and based on ignorance and superstition, Bibb's recollection suggests that the ineffectiveness actually resulted from his own arrogance, while Douglass observes that he was never beaten again. Their accounts appease the audience's disesteem for superstition, while still leaving open a possible means of controlling masters.

On a more abstract level, deceit became crucial in the realization of literacy and freedom, which Robert Stepto has defined as primary and interrelated concerns of black literature. Repeatedly, narrators describe the subterfuges necessary to the acquisition of reading and writing skills. Given the general prohibition against teaching slaves, devious methods had to be employed to acquire even the rudiments of an education. Frederick Douglass pretended to more knowledge than he had in order to trick boys on the street into teaching him additional letters and simple words. After Austin Steward buys a spelling book:

> Every spare moment I could find was devoted to that employment. . . . But here Slavery showed its cloven foot in all its hideous deformity. It finally reached the ears of my master that I was learning to read; and then, if he saw me with a book or a paper in my hand, oh, how he would swear at me, sending me off in a hurry, about some employment. Still I persevered, but was more careful about being seen making any attempt to learn to read.

Such comment reveals a man who is self-determining; neither his values or his behavior is dictated by the master. He will not allow threats to affect the pursuit of education; he simply

becomes more covert in that pursuit. Possible discovery and punishment are simply contingencies to be anticipated. They have no bearing on the goal itself. Deceit as a means to a self-determined and culturally-valued end carries with it no moral opprobrium. Given the conditions of Steward's enslavement, the implication is that both the education and the deceit are valorized by an Afro-American, not a southern white, culture.

The escape, the most dramatic episode in the narratives, is also the one that required the greatest deception. In fact, most of the suspense arises from doubt as to the probable success of this climactic deception. In many cases, the escapes involve simple techniques of deceit. In order to get to Ohio, William Wells Brown pretends to hate the idea of going to a free state. William Green takes the first successful step in his escape by hiding in the home of the community's cruelest master, rightly assuming that he would never be sought for in such a place. James Pennington, faced with the necessity to lie to prevent capture, reflects that "the facts in this case are my private property. These men have no more right to them than a highway robber has to my purse." He then invents a story of his own smallpox infection to prevent the discovery of the truth.

Other narratives recount more elaborate patterns of deception. In the stories of Harriet Jacobs and William and Ellen Craft, the initial cunning of the scheme is enriched with adaptations to changing circumstances. In both cases there is a continuous threat of exposure and punishment. While they go far beyond the rather simple pattern of the trickster tales, they do so as elaborations of the basic elements of disguise, verbal play, and exploitation of the weaknesses of the strong. For instance, the Crafts manipulate color prejudice by disguising Ellen as a young master, knowing that such a figure would not be challenged if seen in the company of a dark-skinned man. They anticipate the difficulty of her illiteracy by contriving a sling for her right arm. Problems of possible recognition, of hotel registration, and of reading are all solved by more and more complete adoption of the role of invalid master.

The escape of Harriet Jacobs is effected not by running a thousand miles in disguise, but rather by staying where she is and only seeming to be safely in the North. By writing letters that are carried to and posted from New York and Boston, she convinces her master that she has escaped and thus is in a position to negotiate her own and her children's absolute freedom. Moreover, her apparent situation ameliorates her actual one by focusing the search for her elsewhere. Her real escape is secondary to this initial drama of pretense.

The most complex treatment of escape is that offered by Frederick Douglass. This complexity comes not through the telling but precisely through his refusal to tell how he gets to the North. To tell would be to place some persons who aid slaves in embarrassing and perhaps dangerous circumstances. More important, "such a statement would most undoubtedly induce greater vigilance on the part of slaveholders than has existed heretofore among them; which would, of course, be the means of guarding a door whereby some dear brother bondman might escape his galling chains." But the concern here is not merely practical; Douglass's secret knowledge is the source of black magical effects on the slaveholder:

> I would leave him to imagine himself surrounded by myriads of invisible tormentors, ever ready to snatch from his infernal grasp his trembling prey. Let him be left to feel his way in the dark; let darkness commensurate with his crime hover over him; and let him feel that at every step he takes, in pursuit of the flying

> bondman, he is runnning the frightful risk of having
> his hot brains dashed out by an invisible agency.

Such a statement goes far beyond the overt purposes of the narrative and in fact may ultimately subvert them. The obvious function of the antebellum narratives was to contribute to the abolitionist cause. And, as Frances Foster has pointed out, that goal requires a consideration of the values of the northern audience. Those values comprise religious piety, moral conventions (such as honesty, frankness, and chastity), political democracy, rationality, some racial bias, and economic individualism. As Foster has explained, the narratives accommodated themselves to these prevailing values.

But accommodation does not necessarily imply that the narrators give unconditional support to such conventions. In fact, the structures and styles of the narratives suggest that the accommodation is a form of masking, and that the narrators' values are much closer to those of Afro-American culture. The evasiveness of Douglass's story offers such an alternative view. The escape passage is preceded by an argument against those who openly and moralistically operate the Underground Railroad, and is followed by a recitation of such facts of his escape as he considers to be publishable. Between these rather conventionally presented parts of the story comes what amounts to a conjuration. Douglass calls up the forces of darkness and seeks to cast a spell on the slaveholder. His appeal to dark and invisible forces is clearly at odds with the highly rational style of most of the narrative. The implication here is that the language of logical and moral argument is not sufficient to the task of defeating the evil forces of slavery. A different appeal, in a different language, must be brought to bear in the struggle. That appeal is based on the very folk beliefs which Douglass himself had dismissed as superstition.

Such eruptions occur frequently in the texts. William Green, in the midst of a recitation of his story in standard English, suddenly and briefly shifts into a colloquial style:

> I told him I was not a going to stay there night and
> day too, and he might sell me, for I did not want to
> stay with him no how . . . I jumps at him and snatches
> the whip from him; he aims another blow at me. I
> caught him by the collar and threw him upon the
> ground; and down upon the ground we had it; he and
> I, blow for blow, kick for kick, there we fought until
> almost out of breath. . . . When I had wallowed him
> in the dirt to my heart's content I let him go.

Understandably, Green finds "correct" usage insufficient to the demands of this particular moment in the narrative. But the implication is that the more conventional style of the larger narrative is a linguistic posture adopted to accommodate the white audience.

Stylistic duplicity can also be found in the recurring use of irony in virtually all the narratives, for irony is the linguistic equivalent of trickster behavior. As such it is found even in otherwise straightforward narratives like that of Solomon Northup. Having been kidnapped by slave-traders, he and others are led toward the boats taking them to the deep South. "So we passed, hand-cuffed and in silence, through the streets of Washington—through the Capital of a nation, whose theory of government, we are told, rests on the foundation of man's inalienable right to life, LIBERTY, and the pursuit of happiness! Hail! Columbia, happy land, indeed!" Similarly, Samuel Ringgold Ward, reflecting on the escape of his parents, speaks of the slave-holders' possible reaction: "What was the precise sensation produced by the departure of my parents, in the minds

of their owners—how they bore it, how submissively they spoke of it, how thoughtfully they followed us with their best wishes, and so forth, I have no means of knowing: information on the questionable topics was never conveyed to us in any definite, systematic form." Verbal play of a more subtle form than the sarcasm of Northup and Ward can be seen in William Craft's narration. The disguising of his wife as a white slaveholder is the source of assorted ironic comments on their relationship and the perceptions of others. The most sustained is the consistent use of masculine pronouns to refer to Ellen in disguise.

Such linguistic irony is part of a larger pattern of situational irony: the very existence of slavery created in the South cultural contradictions that the narratives develop at length. The most common is the discrepancy between religious piety and practice. Virtually all narrators present this distance as an irony of the culture and not merely a matter of hypocrisy.

Similarly, Frederick Douglass plays with the efforts of slaveholders to deprive blacks of education:

> The very decided manner with which he spoke, and
> strove to impress his wife with the evil consequences
> of giving me instruction, served to convince me that
> he was deeply sensible of the truths he was uttering.
> It gave me the best assurance that I might rely with
> the utmost confidence on the results which, he said,
> would flow from teaching me to read. What he most
> dreaded, that I most desired. What he most loved,
> that I most hated. That which to him was a great
> evil, to be carefully shunned, was to me a great good
> to be diligently sought; and the argument which he
> so warmly urged, against my learning to read, only
> served to inspire me with a desire and determination
> to learn. In learning to read, I owe almost as much
> to the bitter opposition of my master, as to the kindly
> aid of my mistress. I acknowledge the benefit of both.

The dramatic tone is significant here. Douglass would have acquired an education in any case; what he calls attention to is his control over the situation. He has mastered the master by turning an admonition into its very opposite. The slave gains a secret knowledge that will enable him to end his slavery. In recalling that moment, he delights in the trick he has played. In true trickster fashion, the weak character has used the flaw of the strong to gain superiority.

A more bitter irony occurs when the narrators discuss slaves. The narrators, or those writing authenticating or introductory prefaces, indicate directly or by implication that the experience described is of slavery in its mildest form. Harriet Jacobs states that she was not aware of being a slave until she was six years old, while William Wells Brown, Austin Steward, J.W.C. Pennington, and James Mars view their respective geographic areas as having reputations for benevolent slave systems. Having established this idea, various demonstrations are made of the cruel, dehumanizing character of slave life in these areas. Thus Pennington:

> The mildest form of slavery, if there be such a form,
> looking at the chattel principle as the definition of
> slavery, is comparatively the worst form; for it not
> only keeps the slave in the most unpleasant apprehension,
> like a prisoner in chains awaiting his trial;
> but it actually, in a great majority of cases, where
> kind masters do exist, trains him under the most
> favorable circumstances the system admits of, and
> then plunges him into the worst of which it is capable.

Often the narrators, rather than making such a general observation, will lead into or follow the "mildest form" statement with a story of brutal beating or of slave breeding. Samuel Ward, after describing the rather flexible conditions of his parents' lives as slaves, next tells of mistreatment and threatened sale. The only thing that prevented sale and separation was the illness of the child Samuel:

> Now to sell his mother *immediately*, depriving him of her tender care, might endanger his life, and, what was all-important in his life, his saleability. . . . What depths of anxiety must my mother have endured! How must the reality of his condition have weighed down the fond heart of my father concerning their child! Could they pray for his continued illness? No; they were parents. Could they petition God for his health? Then they must soon be parted forever from each other and from him, were that prayer answered.

Similar conundrums face the narrators in this system, which they go to some trouble to define as having the family at the center of the social order. Thus, while these narrators momentarily assent to traditional southern depictions of the peculiar institution, they do so only more firmly to establish the heinous nature of the system. If they are the products of slavery in its mildest form, then the harsher forms must be beyond comprehension.

The most significant irony, all things considered, is that essentially duplicitous behavior and language are used to make a moral argument to a moralistic audience. The narrators frequently address this very question. Henry Bibb argues the need for deceit as a protective measure. "In fact, the only weapon of self defense that I could use successfully, was that of deception." Later, he elaborates on subterfuge:

> I had no disposition to steal a horse from any man. But I ask, if a white man had been captured by the Cherokee Indians and carried away from his family for life into slavery, and could see a chance to escape and get back to his family; should the Indians pursue him with a determination to take him back or take his life, would it be a crime for the poor fugitive, whose life, liberty and future happiness were all at stake, to mount any man's horse by the way side, and ride him without asking any questions, to effect his escape? Or who would not do the same thing to rescue a wife, child, father, or mother? Such an act committed by a white man under the same circumstances would not only be pronounced proper, but praiseworthy; and if he neglected to avail himself of such a means of escape he would be pronounced a fool.

Such a statement can only be made in the framework of a relative rather than an absolute moral system. Conditions dictate behavior, which is judged against a standard of reasonableness. Bibb claims that *not* being dishonest in such a situation would be the truly irresponsible action. Moreover, the analogy he makes with whites and Indians, while superficially logical, begs certain questions. The comparison presupposes that blacks and whites are equal in reason and in moral intelligence. It also assumes that slave-catchers are the equivalents of "wild" Indians. Neither assumption would be automatically granted by Bibb's audience. His argument pushes past those points as though they had no special significance. In the very act of justifying deceit, the narrator again engages in it.

A more serious case, because more central to the narrative, is the problem Harriet Jacobs confronts in dealing with her own sexual behavior. In order to avoid becoming the concubine of her master, Harriet chooses to take another white man as her sexual partner. She hopes that this will lead to her sale and eventual freedom; moreover, by this method, she will gain a measure of revenge against a master who she feels has robbed her of happiness through his obscene threats. Such behavior on her part is, she realizes, totally unacceptable to her audience. (William Craft presents a more conventional view when he tells the story of a slave girl who committed suicide rather than allow herself to be violated.) Jacobs confesses the immorality of her behavior, but claims that the reader who has not experienced such conditions cannot understand them: "You never exhausted your ingenuity in avoiding the snares, and eluding the power of a hated tyrant; you never shuddered at the sound of his footsteps, and trembled within hearing of his voice." She then dismisses the moral issue with the same relativism as Bibb: "Still, in looking back, calmly, on the events of my life, I feel that the slave woman ought not to be judged by the same standard as others." In the interpretations of Bibb and Jacobs, though there is a universal morality, extreme social conditions limit its applicability, and, in addition, the desire for life, freedom, and integrity supercedes any narrow judgment of behavior. Such a view is more in line with the description Lawrence Levine provides of Afro-American cultural values than with the conventions of antebellum America.

J.W.C. Pennington makes the strongest case against his own deception by overtly denouncing it. He cannot accept the view that his refusal to reveal the identity of his owner and his fabricated story of smallpox can satisfactorily be justified by the necessities of the moment. Deception is absolutely unacceptable to him: "The history of that day has never ceased to inspire me with a deeper hatred of slavery; I never recur to it but with the most intense horror at a system which can put a man not only in peril of liberty, limb, and life itself, but which may even send him in haste to the bar of God with a lie upon his lips." Moreover, he does not believe that deceit is effective: "If you ask me whether I now really believe that I gained my liberty by those lies? I answer, No! I now believe I should be free, had I told the truth; but, at that moment, I could not see any other way to baffle my enemies, and escape their clutches."

The trouble with this argument is that it is not supported by the narrative itself. The truth of the events of the story do not provide evidence of Pennington's morality. Freedom *was* gained through deception. But to admit as much would be to invalidate the ethical persona the author is trying to create for his audience. The narrative seems to have a power of its own that defies its creator: to change the story would be to lie, but to record only the events opens up unacceptable possible meanings, including the advisability of lying. Pennington evades this dilemma through misdirection:

> Whatever my readers may think, therefore, of the history of events of the day, do not admire in it the fabrications. . . . *See* how human bloodhounds gratuitously chase, catch, and tempt him to shed blood and lie; how when he would do good, evil is thrust upon him.

He imposes a rigid interpretation, precisely because he fears that the reader will admire his fabrications. He would make the slave an absolute victim, because to do otherwise would be to reveal himself as a trickster.

Some narratives suggest in their language thorough adoption of the conventions of the audience. The styles are those of nineteenth-century popular literature: sentimental, sensational yet moralistic, often elaborate and even labored. William Hayden anticipates the return of his parent: "My mind was racked with intense anguish—my heart throbbed violently, and I very often found my cheeks bathed with tears, emanating from the vast solicitude which I felt; yea, deeply felt, on account of her whom, by the laws of nature and of God I was called upon to term—*mother*." Numerous episodes of separation and reuniting use similarly elevated language, which owes more to the authors' reading than to direct articulation of experience. William Craft, in like manner, says of an abolitionist poem he uses, "I cannot give a more correct description of the scene, when she was called from her brother to the stand, than will be found in the following lines. . . ." As a further example, William Green quotes a rather abstract passage from an anti-slavery speech by Horace Mann and declares it "a true definition of American Slavery."

In each case, the narrator relies on the language of his audience to relate an experience about which he has more direct knowledge than they do. The style foregrounds itself when it is used in such a manner. The narrator calls attention to his acquisition of certain linguistic conventions and converts his story into the acceptable patterns of his readers. But this display by its very nature implies a manipulation of language for the author's own purposes. It suggests the adoption of a verbal mask that not only tells the audience what it wants to hear, but does so in the sometimes stilted style that it is most comfortable reading. Thus, just as John the Slave of the folktales would tell the master what he thought the white man wanted to know without actually revealing his own aims, so the slave narrators tell the northern audience what they want to hear.

The motives for so much duplicity (whether conscious or not is finally inconsequential) are easily understood in the unequal relationships of the former slaves with their masters, but the reasons for deceiving the readers of the narratives are more obscure. After all, a major purpose of these works was to attract allies in a great moral cause. But there existed an ambivalence toward this audience. They were whites and thus not entirely different in their attitudes from the southern masters. Repeatedly, narrators point out that they had learned to distrust all whites, and various episodes, especially those dealing with escape, tend to verify the wisdom of this feeling, even in the North. Henry Bibb was betrayed by supposed friends after reaching Cincinnati, and Solomon Northup, though a free man living in New York, was kidnapped and taken to Louisiana. Moreover, once safely in the North, the fugitives experienced difficulties in employment and racial attitudes. Much of William Grimes's narrative is given over to legal difficulties he encountered in New Haven; because he is black, Frederick Douglass has trouble finding work as a caulker in Massachusetts shipyards; Harriet Jacobs fears that her daughter might be reenslaved, even though she is living in a wealthy home on Long Island. The North fails to live up to its reputation as the promised land.

Thus, one problem is that the very people who have repeatedly disappointed the narrators must be appealed to. Openly complaining about one's present life would alienate those needed for the more important campaign. And so the emphasis is placed on the inhumanity of southern life, and as a further attraction, on those qualities that make the narrator seem most like his audience. Any flaws in that persona are shown to result from the evil effects of slavery.

But to identify or even appear to identify completely with the audience is of course to devalue one's experience of slave culture. The history recorded in the narratives then becomes purely negative; it is proof only of the dehumanizing effects of slavery. But that system somehow produced those who were intelligent, assertive, and freedom-loving enough to escape it and to write their own stories. The source of those strengths lay behind them in the South, not in the North that they come to as adults. These same resilient qualities are shown to be necessary in the qualified freedom of the "free" states. Masking and careful asessment of those in power are as necessary as they were in slavery. To refute such abilities completely would be to repudiate a sense of the world that had been acquired with great suffering and sacrifice. But to claim them openly would be to give away the game. And so one subtly valorizes those characteristics of the folk culture that made freedom and the story of that freedom possible.

Logically, then, the narratives show the traditional triumph of the trickster. Through whatever means necessary, the narrators gain control over their experiences. In recording the successful escape from slavery, they contradict the claims of slave-holders about a harmonious system. In the process of telling, they create selves who are themselves refutations of the claims of black inferiority. The construction of intelligible, effective, coherent narratives put the lie to the arguments of both southerners and northerners that blacks were inherently incapable of civilization. By making trickery such an important part of the story, they demonstrate both the weakness of southern whites and the strength of black life. By telling the story of their experience within a linguistic pattern that they undercut in various ways, they manipulate the northern audience into a certain way of thinking despite the racial and moral prejudices of that audience. Like Brer Rabbit and John the Slave, they do what they have to in order to gain their ends, but, unlike those wily but selfish tricksters, the creators of the slave narratives engage in deceit so as to enhance basic moral values. (pp. 70-80)

Keith Byerman, "We Wear the Mask: Deceit as Theme and Style in Slave Narratives," in The Art of Slave Narrative: Original Essays in Criticism and Theory, *edited by John Sekora and Darwin T. Turner, Western Illinois University, 1982, pp. 70-82.*

MELVIN DIXON

[*Dixon discusses religious conversion and the escape into nature as central themes in the slave narratives. The critic stresses the importance of defining Afro-American Christianity as a fusion of traditional African religion and American Christianity.*]

That Christianity is easily recognizable in the language of the [slave] songs and narratives has led many critics to emphasize the spiritual docility and otherworldliness of slave thought. However, a deeper study of the dual aspects of culture contact and acculturation between European and African belief structures reveals that slaves needed a language and a flexible vocabulary more for communication than for belief. Thus it is more realistic to examine how Christianity was "the nearest available, least suspect, and most stimulative system for expressing their concepts of freedom, justice, right and aspiration." In the literature, that Christian imagery becomes "an arsenal of pointed darts, a storehouse of images, a means of making shrewd observations." [In a footnote Dixon identifies the source of these quotes as "The Social Implications of the Negro Spiritual," by John Lovell, Jr., in *The Social Implications of Early Negro Music in the United States,* Bernard Katz, editor].

Revolutionary sentiments, plans for escape, and insurrection were often couched in the religious imagery which was the slave community's weapon against despair and moral degradation. This literature contained ideas that reached the masses of slaves primarily through the ''church'' within the slave community and the men and women preached, testified, and told God all their troubles.

Using the Bible as a storehouse of myth and history that could be appropriated for religious syncretism and a practical philosophy based on historical immediacy, the slave community identified with the children of Israel; but they did not stop there. Slaves knew that deliverance would come, as proven by their African assurance of intimacy and immortality with the Supreme Being, and by the wider implications of the biblical past. Both systems of belief helped the slave know that he could actively participate in deliverance and judgment by joining God's army, singing with a sword in his hand, or walking in Jerusalem just like John. The slave was sure he was experiencing all of history: the past, present and future. Moses very often came to slaves in the person of Harriet Tubman and other ex-slaves who went back into Egypt, heard the children ''yowlin','' and led them to the promised land in the North. Historical immediacy created and sustained through the oral tradition that healing moment of deliverance and salvation:

> O Mary don' you weep don' you moan
> Pharaoh's army got drownded.

Upon the rock that was traditional African religion as well as American Christianity, the slave community built a church. Out of religious syncretism and an oral literature they established an active contemporary apocalypse in the realm of their own daily experiences. The historical moment for the slave was never abstract, but imminent. The time for deliverance and witness was now. The complexity of the religious experience, as well as the complexity of the day-to-day social experience in the slave quarters, centered in a conversion-like initiation, became further testing grounds for individual and corporate faith in the possibility of freedom. And as the slave lived, he would reckon with time, community, and his own life journey. (pp. 300-01)

Slavery had brought black men and women face to face with the extreme fact of their wretchedness as individuals. Conversion to an inner cult, an in-group morality, provided the very real awareness that individual loneliness and despair could be resolved in group solidarity. The conversion experience emphasized a person's recognition of his own need for deliverance from sin and bondage into a holy alliance with God as the avenging deity. . . . Conversion also provided for socioreligious mobility and status within the slave community. Conversion also confirmed an African orientation of personal duty on both a ritualistic and humanistic level. Ritual, duty, and creative expression all served as outlets for individual expression without disturbing communal solidarity. Song and personal testimony, as forms of an oral lierature, allowed for individual interpretation while they ''continually drew [the slave] back into the communal presence and permitted him the comfort of basking in the warmth of the shared assumptions of those around him.'' Conversion to these shared assumptions provided a basis for self-esteem, new values, and an important defense against degradation. (p. 301)

Conversion as rebirth or transformation was a central event in the slave's recorded life. In this way it gave individuals an outline of personal history and made them aware of their part in the larger history of the racial group. In fact, by achieving a personal witness (a personal historical sense or vision in which man is the essential binder of time and space), individual men and women could participate in the larger history and further regenerate themselves by attaining freedom and salvation. Testimonies in the narratives speak directly to this transformation and regeneration. . . . (pp. 302-03)

When slaves came to write their formal autobiographies they emphasized a conversion-like model of personal experience and testimony to construct their own ''witness'' to the horrors of slavery and the regenerative joy of freedom. The conversion experience helped to organize the individual life and unite it with time and the eternal presence of God. As one slave testified to this historical pattern:

> The soul that trusts in God need never stumble nor fall, because God being all wise and seeing and knowing all things, having looked down through time before time, foresaw every creeping thing and poured out His spirit on the earth. The earth brought forth her fruits in due season. In the very beginning every race and every creature was in the mind of God and we are here, not ahead of time, not behind time, but just on time. It was time that brought us here and time will carry us away.

The use of historical and religious language and symbol is seen most clearly in the escape episode in slave narratives. The nearby woods or the wilderness into which the fugitive escapes becomes the testing ground of his faith in God and in himself:

> If you want to find Jesus, go in de wilderness
> Go in de wilderness, go in de wilderness
> Mournin' brudder, go in de wilderness
> To wait upon de Lord.

The scenes of self-revelation and the experience of grace and a final rebirth become as characteristic to the narratives as they are to the songs. What is developed from this imagery, shared between oral and written modes, is a literature of struggle and fulfillment. The thematic transformation in the text parallels the transformation in its creators. The change is from chattel status, unholiness, and damnation in the hell which was slavery to the integrity of being a man and a saved child of God now walking the paved streets of a heavenly city, the promised North. The slave has been delivered. Conversion was the correlative for a subjective synthesis of history; earning freedom through escape (or insurrection) was heroic action.

That religion and freedom went hand in hand is evidenced by the entire experience of the fugitive slave. Often poorly equipped for long journeys and with few geographic aids, he was alone with only God to help him endure the wilderness. Often leaders of fugitive parties were ministers themselves. One preacher, a Methodist, tried to persuade John Thompson to join his band of runaways. Thompson was unwilling to escape with them, and only several months later did he attempt his escape alone, once he was assured of God's presence. Thompson described the occasion and method of that first fugitive group and his own skepticism:

> The Methodist preacher . . . urged me very strongly to accompany them, saying that he had full confidence in the surety of the promises of God . . . he believed he was able to carry him safely to the land of freedom, and accordingly he was determined to go. Still I was afraid to risk myself on such uncertain promises; I dared not trust an unseen God.

> On the night on which they intended to start. . . they knelt in prayer to the great God of Heaven and Earth,

invoking Him to guard them . . . and go with them
to their journey's end.

Most often the slave's idea of freedom was a consequence of his recognition of his slave status. He needed little outside influence to convince him of the advantages of freedom. Even as far south as Louisiana and in as isolated a region as Bayou Boeuf to which Solomon Northup was kidnapped, the idea of freedom was a regular topic among the slaves, as Northup writes:

> They understand the privileges and exemptions that belong to it—that it would bestow upon them the fruits of their own labor, and that it would secure to them the enjoyment of domestic happiness. They do not fail to observe the difference between their own condition and the meanest white man's and to realize the injustice of the laws.

Thus, freedom, an essential aspect of human development, was a value within the slave community which also outlined a socio-religious mobility for its attainment. The mobility established in the slave's conversion experience became the philosophical model for further initiation into free status and identity.

The first step in this mobility on the personal level involved a recognition of one's wretchedness as a slave, a realization that one is different and deprived. "I was born a slave," wrote Harriet Jacobs, "but I never knew it till six years of happy childhood had passed away . . . When I was six years old, my mother died, and then, for the first time, I learned by the talk around me, that I was a slave." (pp. 303-05)

The moment of self-discovery has been one of the more dramatic turning points in the personal history of every black American. The moment called for new tactics or behavior that would help the individual come to grips with his feelings of difference and alienation from the society at large. William Du Bois once wrote of his own experience that:

> Then it dawned upon me with a certain suddenness that I was different from the others; or like, mayhap in heart and life and longing, but shut out from their world by a vast veil. I had therefore no desire to tear down that veil, to creep through; I held all beyond it in common contempt, and lived above it in a region of blue sky and great wandering shadows.

That crucial self-discovery, which can happen suddenly and by accident, is nonetheless the beginning of a collective consciousness and group identity. As poet Margaret Walker once wrote in her more contemporary account, it was a bitter hour "when we discovered we / were black and poor and small and different and / nobody cared and nobody / wondered and nobody understood."

By the force of this personal alienation the individual began to see himself as a member of an oppressed group. Within the group experience, perhaps because of it, the individual resolved to remedy the situation for himself and the others who were joined to him by the extreme pressures of racial oppression. The slave could openly rebel or secretly escape. He could also accommodate himself to the subservient role slavery defined for him, as no doubt some slaves did. Whatever action the slave finally took was considered not the end of experience, but the beginning of a long confrontation from which he hoped to wrench his freedom.

Black religion told the slave where to seek liberation: "Jesus call you, go in the wilderness." (pp. 305-06)

[Slaves] often secreted themselves in the woods, even if only to meditate on their condition. In the wilderness of nature, freedom was revealed as a man's right in the natural harmony of God's created world. Henry Bibb meditated in the woods and wrote: "I thought of the fishes of the water, the fowls of the air, the wild beasts of the forest, all appeared to be free to go where they pleased, and I was an unhappy slave." Nature furnished the slave with examples of freedom and the harmony of all life with God just as his African religious tradition continued to inform him. In the new American environment, the harmony of the natural world was easily given religious significance. Natural imagery was analogous to freedom and revealed a point of contact between man and God. The slave resolved to seek that contact and unity in the wilderness. Frederick Douglass once described this communion: "I was in the wood, buried in its somber gloom and hushed in its solemn silence, hidden from all human eyes, shut in with nature and with nature's God, and absent from all human contrivances. Here was a good place to pray, to pray for help, for deliverance."

From the slave's point of view, the life pilgrimage of man was possible only through a renewed contract with nature, and by so doing he could effect a new covenant with God. This qualification of the life experience is evident in the ordinary day-to-day struggle of the slave in the hot fields and dramatized vividly in the plight of the fugitive. In nature the slave found a guide for the fulfillment of his identity; once he saw himself as a wretched slave, then too, even as he saw himself as a child of God, for the power of God as reflected in the world around him was strong enough to deliver him from slavery. This was one basic element of the slave's belief pattern, and he responded accordingly when Jesus called him into the woods. Thus the slave felt himself converted to the community of believers and to the mission of freedom. (p. 307)

Often the fugitives' only companion was God, and they believed that it was He alone who could deliver man from the death and hell experience of slavery and escape. One recalls John Thompson's reluctance to escape with the Methodist preacher because he doubted an unseen God. But because membership in the community of believers, in God's army, required an unconditional faith in God's power and willingness to deliver his children, Thompson had to be converted. He had to hear God's voice and believe. When saved from a dangerous situation, Thompson began to believe in God's presence and then, started his life pilgrimage toward the salvation and freedom slaves felt was theirs to achieve. Thompson's personal witness united him to his community and to the cause of freedom that he now has the strength and guidance to seek alone:

> I knew it was the hand of God, working in my behalf; it was his voice warning me to escape from the danger towards which I was hastening. Who would not praise such a God? Great is the Lord, and greatly to be praised.
>
> I felt renewed confidence and faith, for I believed that God was in my favor, and now was the time to test the matter . . . I fell upon my knees, and with hands uplifted to high heaven, related all the late circumstances to the Great King, saying that the whole world was against me without cause, besought his protection, and solemnly promised to serve him all the days of my life. I received a spiritual answer of approval; a voice like thunder seeming to enter my soul, saying, I am your God and am with you; though the world be against you, I am more than the world; though wicked men hunt you, trust in me, for I am the Rock of your Defense.

Had my pursuers then been near, they must have heard me, for I praised God at the top of my voice. I was determined to take him at his word, and risk the consequences.

I retired to my hiding place in the woods.

(pp. 309-10)

Slaves believed that God moved through nature to help the fugitive. Moreover, through nature, God made his presence known by presenting obstacles and avenues for deliverance during the fugitive's journey. Most often the same natural force, such as a wide river, was both obstacle *and* aid. The dual quality of nature in the slave's thought makes it more crucial for man to take an active part in seeking deliverance, for he must be capable of identifying the voice as he did through his conversion experience and those good people who share in God's word: the children of God, the *true* believers. These barriers become an important test of man's faith in the power of God to make possible the freedom and salvation the slave seeks. Again, man must earn his freedom.

When Henry Bibb attempted escape alone, nature was his guide: "I walked with bold courage, trusting in the arm of Omnipotence; guided by the unchangeable North Star by night, and inspired by an elevated thought that I was fleeing from a land of slavery and oppression, bidding farewell to handcuffs, whips, thumbscrews and chains." Once having gained freedom for himself, he returned to rescue his wife and child. Caught again in slave territory, he felt he had to renew his covenant with God; he "passed the night in prayer to our Heavenly Father, asking that He would open to me even the smallest chance for escape."

In the woods following their escape, Bibb and his wife and child encounter nature at its harshest level:

So we started off with our child that night, and made our way down to Red River swamps among the buzzing insects and wild beasts of the forest. We wandered about in the wilderness for eight or ten days. . . . Our food was parched corn . . . most of the time we were lost. We wanted to cross the Red River but could find no conveyance to cross it. I recollect one day of finding a crooked tree which bent over the river. . . . When we crossed over on the tree . . . we found that we were on an island surrounded by water on either side. We made our bed that night in a pile of dry leaves. . . . We were much rest-broken, wearied from hunger and travelling through briers, swamps and cane breaks. . . .

Then Bibb encountered the wolves who lived there and who came howling out of the night close to them:

The wolves kept howling. . . . I thought that the hour of death for us was at hand . . . for there was no way for our escape. My little family were looking up to me for protection, but I could afford them none. . . . *I was offering up my prayers to that God who never forsakes those in the hour of danger who trust in him. . . .* I was surrounded by those wolves. But it seemed to be the will of a merciful providence that our lives should not be destroyed by them. I rushed forth with my bowie knife in hand. . . . I made one desperate charge at them . . . making a loud yell at the top of my voice that caused them to retreat and scatter which was equivalent to a victory on our part. *Our prayers were answered,* and our lives were spared through the night. (Emphasis mine.)

Through prayer Bibb was able to unite himself to the greater force of God and thus renew his own life force. However, his escape with his family had further complications and eventually they were recaptured. Once again Bibb escaped alone and began a new life in free territory without them. This last escape found Bibb secreted aboard a ship which conveyed him out of the waters of slavery and trial and into the promised North:

When the boat struck the mouth of the river Ohio, and I had once more the pleasure of looking on that lovely stream, my heart leaped up for joy at the glorious prospect that I should again be free. Every revolution of the mighty steam-engine seemed to bring me nearer and nearer the "promised land."

Henry Bibb's narrative is characteristic of the many slave autobiographies in which the protagonist confronts and is confronted by the challenge of survival and deliverance from the wilderness. Man, here, endures the test of the wilds in order to reap his reward of freedom, which is a direct result of his alliance with God. In the end he will be delivered on foot or aboard a particular conveyance which will provide a secret cover for his rebirth.

The escape episode in nature or secreted aboard a ship is an experience of the womb, the woods, or a dark cover that will give birth to a new man. Escape, then, is the central transforming episode in the death-rebirth cycle of life as viewed by the slave. By dint of his escape and his hiding, man becomes enlightened about his condition and reborn through his confrontation fighting his own fear, the wolves, the deep water of Jordan or the slave "patrollers." (pp. 311-12)

Henry "Box" Brown made more poignant use of the death-rebirth theme. He nailed himself up in a box and shipped himself to free territory as cargo. During the long journey he experienced the physical effects of dying: "I felt a cold sweat coming over me which seemed to be a warning that death was about to terminate my earthly miseries; but as I feared even that less than slavery, I resolved to submit to the will of God, and, under the influence of that impression, I lifted up my soul in prayer to God, who alone was able to deliver me. My cry was soon heard." When the box arrived at its destination a friend knocked to see if Brown was still alive inside. Brown's rebirth began: "The joy of the friends was very great. When they heard that I was alive they soon managed to break open the box, and then came my resurrection from the grave of slavery. I rose a free man; but I was too weak, by reason of long confinement in that box, to be able to stand, so I immediately swooned away."

By all accounts the God of the fugitive is a God who offers immediate freedom and deliverance to his chosen people. But this deliverance is on the condition of man's trial—man's willingness to be struck dead and achieve enlightenment through his despair, fear and solitude. Man with God conquers Egypt and death so that a freeman can be born.

In their long search for freedom, as in their religion and literature, slaves defined life as a pilgrimage. Just as life for the African was a continual practice of maintaining harmony and force within the ontological hierarchy established between man, the ancestors, and natural phenomena, so too was life for the Afro-American a pilgrimage toward renewed contact with God. The slave narrators preserve the dualism between the African and the Christian components in black religious syncretism, and we find through their emphasis on the escape experience that the narrators and bards gave the wilderness confrontation a central place in recounting the progress of their lives. For the narrators, this crucial moment of escape is also symbolic of the fusion of the two divergent cultural modes: the African and the American. Out of this cultural confrontation and, in some cases, moral entanglement the slave is converted and reconverted to himself, his community, his God. By engaging the wilderness the slave, as fugitive, renews his primal covenant with God through nature and becomes a freeman. From this primary connection with spiritual and natural forces, man derives his creativity, his freedom, and his spiritual redemption. His self and soul are strengthened. (pp. 313-14)

> Melvin Dixon, "Singing Swords: The Literary Legacy of Slavery," in The Slave's Narrative, edited by Charles T. Davis and Henry Louis Gates, Jr., Oxford University Press, 1985, pp. 298-317.

JOANNE M. BRAXTON

[Braxton asserts that the female voice in slave narratives has been unjustly neglected and calls for a reassessment of women's slave narratives as an important source for new themes and archetypes within the established canon. The critic cites Harriet Jacobs's Incidents in the Life of a Slave Girl as equal to Frederick Douglass's Narrative in distinction and significance.]

I believe, with James Olney, that students of autobiography are themselves vicarious autobiographers, and I know that I read every text through my own experience, as well as that of my mother and my grandmothers. As black American women, we are born into a mystic sisterhood, and we live our lives within a magic circle, a realm of shared language, reference, and allusion within the veil of our blackness and our femaleness. We have been as invisible to the dominant culture as rain; we have been knowers, but we have not been known. (p. 379)

The treatment of the slave narrative genre has been one of the most skewed in Afro-American literary criticism. It has been almost always the treatment of the narratives of heroic male slaves, not their wives or sisters. By focusing almost exclusively on the narratives of male slaves, critics have left out half the picture. (p. 380)

The resistance to a gynocritical or gynocentric approach to the slave narrative genre has been dominated by male bias, by linear logic, and by either/or thinking. We have been paralyzed by issues of primacy, and authorship, and by criteria of unity, coherence, completion, and length. Academic systems, which do not value scholarship on black women or reward it, have told us that we are not first, not central, not major, not authentic. The suggestion has been that neither the lives of black women nor the study of our narratives and autobiographies have been legitimate.

I want to supplement the either/or thinking that has limited the consideration of evidence surrounding the narratives of women, and the inclusion of such works in the slave narrative genre. Instead of asking "Is it first? Is it major? Is it central? Does it conform to established criteria?" this study asks, "How would the inclusion of works by women change the shape of the genre?"

To begin with, the inclusion of works by women would push the origin of the slave narrative genre back by two years, and root it more firmly in American soil, for the genre begins, not with The Interesting Narrative of Olaudah Equiano, or Gustavus Vassa, the African, published in London in 1789, but with the narrative of a slave woman entitled "Belinda, or the

Cruelty of Men Whose Faces Were Like the Moon," published in the United States in 1787, a narrative of a few pages which would be considered too short by conventional standards. [In a footnote Braxton states: A woman called "Belinda" wrote "The Cruelty of Men Whose Faces Were Like the Moon: the Petition of an African Slave to the Legislature of Massachusetts." The title of the text suggests an awareness of racial and sexual oppression that is both race and sex specific. Belinda speaks to the cruelty of men, white men, whose moon-like faces symbolize strangeness, spiritual barrenness and death.]

Traditionally, the 1845 Narrative of the Life of Frederick Douglass, An American Slave, Written by Himself, has been viewed as the central text in the genre, and based on this narrative, critic Robert Stepto has defined the primary Afro-American archetype as that of the articulate hero who discovers the "bonds among freedom, literacy, and struggle." Once again, the narrative experience of the articulate and rationally enlightened female slave has not been part of the definition. Stepto, in his otherwise brilliant work on the Narrative of Frederick Douglass, An American Slave, Written by Himself (1845), makes no attempt to define a corresponding female archetype; I propose that we consider as a counterpart to the articulate hero the archetype of the outraged mother. She appears repeatedly in Afro-American history and literary tradition, and she is fully represented in Harriet "Linda Brent" Jacobs' Incidents in the Life of a Slave Girl: Written by Herself (1861). (pp. 380-82)

When viewed from a gynocritical or gynocentric perspective, Incidents arrives at the very heart and root of Afra-American autobiographical writing. Although other works appear earlier, this full-length work by an Afra-American writing about her experiences as a slave woman is indeed rare. Yet despite its rarity, Incidents speaks for many lives; it is in many respects a representative document.

Incidents is descended both from the autobiographical tradition of the heroic male slaves and a line of American women's writings that attacks racial oppression and sexual exploitation. It combines the narrative pattern of the slave narrative genre with the conventional literary forms and stylistic devices of the 19th century domestic novel in an attempt to transform the so-called "cult of true womanhood" and to persuade the women of the north to take a public stand against slavery, the most political issue of the day. The twin themes of abolition and feminism are interwoven in Jacobs' text.

Like Harriet Beecher Stowe's hybrid, Uncle Tom's Cabin, Incidents focuses on the power relationships of masters and slaves and the ways in which (slave) women learn to manage the invasive sexuality of (white) men. Unlike Stowe, who demonstrates her anxiety about the authorship of Uncle Tom's Cabin by saying that God wrote it, the author of Incidents claims responsibility for every word, and yet she publishes under the pseudonym "Linda Brent."

Although I had read the critical literature on women's autobiography, it was Incidents that taught me that the silences and gaps in the narrative of women's lives are sometimes more significant than the filled spaces. "Linda Brent" obscures the names of persons and places mentioned in the text, and although she denies any need for secrecy on her own part, she writes that she deemed it "kind and considerate toward others to pursue this course." Thus she speaks as a disguised woman, whose identity remains partly obscured. A virtual "madwoman in the attic," Linda leads a veiled and unconventional life. Her dilemma is that of life under slavery as a beautiful, desirable female slave, object of desire as well as profit.

Linda adheres to a system of black and female cultural values that motivate her actions and inform the structure of this text. First of all, the author's stated purpose is to "arouse the woman of the North to a realizing sense of the condition of two millions of women at the South." If the white women of the North know the true conditions of the slave women of the South, then they cannot fail to answer Jacobs' call to moral action.

In order to balance our understanding of the slave narrative genre, we need first to read those narratives written by women (and to read them closely), and secondly to expand the range of terms used in writing about those narratives. An analysis of the imagery, thematic content, uses of language, and patterns of narrative movement in *Incidents in the Life of A Slave Girl* moves us closer to a characterization of the behavior of the outraged mother and to a more balanced understanding of the slave narrative genre.

As one who is small and relatively powerless in the face of her oppression, the outraged mother makes use of wit and intelligence to overwhelm and defeat a more powerful foe. In her aspect as trickster, "Linda" employs defensive verbal postures as well as various forms of disguise and concealment to outwit and escape Dr. Flint, the archetypal patriarchal rapist slavemaster:

1. She must conceal her quest for literacy and her ability to read in order to prevent the master from slipping her foul notes in an attempt to seduce her.

2. She must conceal her love for a free black man she eventually sends away for his own good, as well as the identity of the white man who becomes the father of her children and who eventually betrays her.

3. She conceals her pregnancy from everyone.

4. She must conceal her plans to run away, working hard and attempting to appear contented during the time she formulates these plans.

5. When Linda "runs away," she is disguised as a man and taken to the Snaky Swamp, a location she finds more hospitable than landed slave culture.

6. She is then concealed in the home of a neighboring white woman (a slaveholder sympathetic to her plight), and, finally, in a crawl space in her grandmother's house for seven years.

7. While concealed in her grandmother's house, Linda deceives the master by writing letters a friend mails from New York. When Flint takes off to New York to look for the fugitive, she is practically in his own back yard.

8. Linda is taken to the North in disguise, and even after she arrives there, she must conceal her identity with a veil, which she only removes when her freedom is purchased by a group of Northern white women. Through quick-thinking, the use of sass and invective, and a series of deceptions, Linda finally realizes freedom for herself and her children.

"Sass" is a word of West African derivation associated with the female aspect of the trickster figure. The OED attributes the origin of "sass" to the "sassy tree," the powerfully poisonous Erythophloeum quineense (Cynometra Manni). A decoction of the bark of this tree was used in West Africa as an ordeal poison in the trial of accused witches, women spoken of as being wives of Exu, the trickster god. (pp. 383-86)

Webster's Third International Dictionary defines "sass" as talking impudently or disrespectfully to an elder or a superior, or as talking back. Throughout the text, Linda uses "sass" as a weapon of self-defense whenever she is under sexual attack by the master; she returns a portion of the poison he has offered her. In one instance Dr. Flint demands: "Do you know that I have a right to do as I like with you,—that I can kill you, if I please?" Negotiating for respect, Linda replies: "You have tried to kill me, and I wish you had; but you have no right to do as you like with me." "Sass" is an effective tool that allows "Linda" to preserve her self-esteem and to increase the psychological distance between herself and the master. She uses "sass" the way Frederick Douglass uses his fists and his feet, as a means of expressing her resistance.

It is a distinctive feature of the outraged mother that she sacrifices opportunities to escape without her children; Linda is motivated by an overwhelming concern for them, a concern not apparent in the narratives of the questing male slaves. This concern is shown in chapter titles like "A New Tie to Life," "Another Link to Life," "The Children Sold," "New Destination for the Children," and "The Meeting of Mother and Daughter."

The outraged mother resists her situation not so much on behalf of herself as on behalf of her children. She is part of a continuum; she links the dead, the living, and the unborn. "I knew the doom that awaited my fair baby in slavery, and I determined to save her from it, or perish in the attempt. I went to make this vow at the graves of my poor parents, in the burying ground of the slaves." In the case of Jacobs' narrative, the sense of the continuum of *women's* oppression is also clear.

It is the prospect of her daughter's life under slavery that finally nerves Jacobs to run away. "When they told me my new-born babe was a girl, my heart was heavier than it had ever been before. Slavery is a terrible thing for men; but it is far more terrible for women," Jacobs write. "Superadded to the burden common to all, *they* have wrongs, and sufferings and mortifications peculiarly their own."

Another important difference between this narrative and those of the heroic male slaves is that Linda celebrates the cooperation and collaboration of all the people, black and white, slave and free, who make her freedom possible. She celebrates her liberation and her children's as the fruit of a collective, not individual effort.

The inclusion of *Incidents in the Life of a Slave Girl, Written by Herself* in the slave narrative genre and the autobiographical tradition of black Americans, permits a more balanced view of that genre and that tradition, presenting fresh themes, images, and uses of language. *Incidents* occupies a position as central to that tradition as the 1845 *Narrative of Frederick Douglass*. Only in this perspective does the outraged mother emerge as the archetypal counterpart of the articulate hero.

Further study of all such texts and testimonies by women will allow us to fill out an understanding of that experience and culture which I have designated as Afra-American, and help us correct and expand existing analyses based too exclusively on male models of experience and writing. The study of black women's writing helps us to transform definitions of genre, of archetype, of narrative traditions, and of the African-American experience itself. (pp. 386-87)

Joanne M. Braxton, "Harriet Jacobs' 'Incidents in the Life of a Slave Girl': The Re-Definition of the

REPRESENTATION OF THE BOX,

In which a fellow mortal travelled a long journey, in quest of those rights which the piety and republicanism of this country denied to him, the right to possess.

As long as the temples of humanity contain a single worshipper, whose heart beats in unison with that of the God of the universe; must a religion and a government which could inflict such misery upon a human being, be execrated and fled from, as a bright angel, abhors and flees from the touch of hideous sin.

A drawing of the crate in which Henry Box Brown was shipped from Virginia to Pennsylvania.

Slave Narrative Genre,'' in The Massachusetts Review, Vol. XXVII, No. 2, Summer, 1986, pp. 379-87.

JAMES OLNEY

[*Olney posits that, with the notable exception of Frederick Douglass's work, slave narratives are artless accounts constructed of mere conventions "untransformed and unredeemed." The critic demonstrates through three close textual examples how the sponsors of narratives often determined the narrator's tone and prose style. Because most slave narratives are neither influenced nor ordered by their authors' imaginations, Olney concludes, they do not qualify as literary art. He avers, however, that the narratives set the themes, content, and form of all subsequent black American literature.*]

Anyone who sets about reading a single slave narrative, or even two or three slave narratives, might be forgiven the natural assumption that every such narrative will be, or ought to be, a unique production; for—so would go the unconscious argument—are not slave narratives autobiography, and is not every autobiography the unique tale, uniquely told, of a unique life? If such a reader should proceed to take up another half dozen narratives, however (and there is a great lot of them from which to choose the half dozen), a sense not of uniqueness but of overwhelming *sameness* is almost certain to be the result. And if our reader continues through two or three dozen more slave narratives, still having hardly begun to broach the whole body of material (one estimate puts the number of extant narratives at over six thousand), he is sure to come away dazed by the mere repetitiveness of it all: seldom will he discover anything new or different but only, always more and more of the same. This raises a number of difficult questions both for the student of autobiography and the student of Afro-American literature. Why should the narratives be so cumulative and so invariant, so repetitive and so much alike? Are the slave narratives classifiable under some larger grouping (are they history or literature or autobiography or polemical writing? and what relationship do these larger groupings bear to one another?); or do the narratives represent a mutant development really different in kind from any other mode of writing that might initially seem to relate to them as parent, as sibling, as cousin, or as some other formal relation? What narrative mode, what manner of story-telling, do we find in the slave narratives, and what is the place of memory both in this particular variety of narrative and in autobiography more generally? What is the relationship of the slave narratives to later narrative modes and later thematic complexes of Afro-American writing? The questions are multiple and manifold. I propose to come at them and to offer some tentative answers by first making some observations about autobiography and its special nature as a memorial, creative act; then outlining some of the common themes and nearly invariable conventions of slave narratives: and finally attempting to determine the place of the slave narrative 1) in the spectrum of autobiographical writing, 2) in the history of American literature, and 3) in the making of an Afro-American literary tradition. (pp. 148-49)

[Autobiography] may be understood as a recollective/narrative act in which the writer, from a certain point in his life—the present—, looks back over the events of that life and recounts them in such a way as to show how that past history has led to this present state of being. Exercising memory, in order that he may recollect and narrate, the autobiographer is not a neutral and passive recorder but rather a creative and active shaper. Recollection, or memory, in this way a most creative faculty, goes backward so that narrative, its twin and counterpart, may go forward: memory and narration move along the same line only in reverse directions. Or as in Heraclitus, the way up and the way down, the way back and the way forward, are one and the same. When I say that memory is immensely creative I do not mean that it creates for itself events that never occurred (of course this can happen too, but that is another matter). What I mean instead is that memory creates the *significance* of events in discovering the pattern into which those events fall. And such a pattern, in the kind of autobiography where memory rules, will be a teleological one bringing us, in and through narration, and as it were by an inevitable process, to the end of all past moments which is the present. It is in the interplay of past and present, of present memory reflecting over past experience on its way to becoming present being, that events are lifted out of time to be re-situated not in mere chronological sequence but in patterned significance.

Paul Ricoeur, in a paper on ''Narrative and Hermeneutics,'' makes the point in a slightly different way but in a way that allows us to sort out the place of time and memory both in autobiography in general and in the Afro-American slave narrative in particular. *"Poiesis,"* according to Ricoeur's analysis, "both reflects and resolves the paradox of time"; and he continues: "It reflects it to the extent that the act of emplotment combines in various proportions two temporal dimensions, one chronological and the other non-chronological. The first may be called the episodic dimension. It characterizes the story as made out of events. The second is the configurational dimension, thanks to which the plot construes significant wholes out of scattered events." In autobiography it is memory that, in the recollecting and retelling of events, effects "emplotment"; it is memory that, shaping the past according to the configuration of the present, is responsible for "the configurational dimension" that "construes significant wholes out of scattered events." It is for this reason that in a classic of autobiographical literature like Augustine's *Confessions,* for example, memory is not only the mode but becomes the very subject of the writing. I should imagine, however, that any reader of slave narratives is most immediately struck by the almost complete dominance of "the episodic dimension," the nearly total lack of any "configurational dimension," and the virtual absence of any reference to memory or any sense that memory does anything but make the past facts and events of slavery immediately present to the writer and his reader. (Thus one often gets, "I can see even now. . . . I can still hear . . . ," etc.) There is a very good reason for this, but its being a very good reason does not alter the consequence that the slave narrative, with a very few exceptions, tends to exhibit a highly conventional, rigidly fixed form that bears much the same relationship to autobiography in a full sense as painting by numbers bears to painting as a creative act.

I say there is a good reason for this, and there is: The writer of a slave narrative finds himself in an irresolvably tight bind as a result of the very intention and premise of his narrative, which is to give a picture of "slavery *as it is.*" Thus it is the writer's claim, it *must* be his claim, that he is not emplotting, he is not fictionalizing, and he is not performing any act of *poiesis* (=shaping, making). To give a true picture of slavery as it really is, he must maintain that he exercises a clear-glass, neutral memory that is neither creative nor faulty—indeed, if it were creative it would be *eo ipso* faulty for "creative" would be understood by skeptical readers as a synonym for "lying." Thus the ex-slave narrator is debarred from use of a memory that would make anything of his narrative beyond or other than the purely, merely episodic, and he is denied access, by the very nature and intent of his venture, to the configurational dimension of narrative.

Of the kind of memory central to the act of autobiography as I described it earlier, Ernst Cassirer has written: "Symbolic memory is the process by which man not only repeats his past experience but also reconstructs this experience. Imagination becomes a necessary element of true recollection." In that word "imagination," however, lies the joker for an ex-slave who would write the narrative of his life in slavery. What we find Augustine doing in Book X of the *Confessions*—offering up a disquisition on memory that makes both memory itself and the narrative that it surrounds fully symbolic—would be inconceivable in a slave narrative. Of course ex-slaves do exercise memory in their narratives, but they never talk about it as Augustine does, as Rousseau does, as Wordsworth does, as Thoreau does, as Henry James does, as a hundred other autobiographers (not to say novelists like Proust) do. Ex-slaves *cannot* talk about it because of the premises according to which they write, one of those premises being that there is nothing

doubtful or mysterious about memory: on the contrary, it is assumed to be a clear, unfailing record of events sharp and distinct that need only be transformed into descriptive language to become the sequential narrative of a life in slavery. In the same way, the ex-slave writing his narrative cannot afford to put the present in conjunction with the past (again with very rare but significant exceptions to be mentioned later) for fear that in so doing he will appear, from the present, to be reshaping and so distorting and falsifying the past. As a result, the slave narrative is most often a nonmemorial description fitted to a pre-formed mold, a mold with regular depressions here and equally regular prominences there—virtually obligatory figures, scenes, turns of phrase, observances, and authentications—that carry over from narrative to narrative and give to them as a group the species character that we designate by the phrase "slave narrative." (pp. 149-51)

The conventions for slave narratives were so early and so firmly established that one can imagine a sort of master outline drawn from the great narratives and guiding the lesser ones. Such an outline would look something like this:

A. An engraved portrait, signed by the narrator.

B. A title page that includes the claim, as an integral part of the title, "Written by Himself" (or some close variant: "Written from a statement of Facts Made by Himself"; or "Written by a Friend, as Related to Him by Brother Jones"; etc.).

C. A handful of testimonials and/or one or more prefaces or introductions written either by a white abolitionist friend of the narrator (William Lloyd Garrison, Wendell Phillips) or by a white amanuensis/editor/author actually responsible for the text (John Greenleaf Whittier, David Wilson, Louis Alexis Chamerovzow), in the course of which preface the reader is told that the narrative is a "plain, unvarnished tale" and that naught "has been set down in malice, nothing exaggerated, nothing drawn from the imagination"—indeed, the tale, it is claimed, understates the horrors of slavery.

D. A poetic epigraph, by preference from William Cowper.

E. The actual narrative:

1. a first sentence beginning, "I was born . . . ," then specifying a place but not a date of birth;

2. a sketchy account of parentage, often involving a white father;

3. description of a cruel master, mistress, or overseer, details of first observed whipping and numerous subsequent whippings, with women very frequently the victims;

4. an account of one extraordinarily strong, hardworking slave—often "pure African"—who, because there is no reason for it, refuses to be whipped;

5. record of the barriers raised against slave literacy and the overwhelming difficulties encountered in learning to read and write;

6. descriptions of a "Christian" slaveholder (often of one such dying in terror) and the accompanying claim that "Christian" slaveholders are invariably worse than those professing no religion;

7. description of the amounts and kinds of food and clothing given to slaves, the work required of them, the pattern of a day, a week, a year;

8. account of a slave auction, of families being separated and destroyed, of distraught mothers clinging to their children as they are torn from them, of slave coffles being driven South;

9. description of patrols, of failed attempt(s) to escape, of pursuit by men and dogs;

10. description of successful attempt(s) to escape, lying by during the day, travelling by night guided by the North Star, reception in a free state by Quakers who offer a lavish breakfast and much genial thee/thou conversation;

11. taking of a new last name (frequently one suggested by a white abolitionist) to accord with new social identity as a free man, but retention of first name as a mark of continuity of individual identity;

12. reflections on slavery.

F. An appendix or appendices composed of documentary material—bills of sale, details of purchase from slavery, newspaper items—, further reflections on slavery, sermons, antislavery speeches, poems, appeals to the reader for funds and moral support in the battle against slavery.

About this "Master Plan for Slave Narratives" (the irony of the phrasing being neither unintentional nor insignificant) two observations should be made: First, that it not only describes rather loosely a great many lesser narratives but that it also describes quite closely the greatest of them all, *Narrative of the Life of Frederick Douglass, An American Slave, Written by Himself*, which paradoxically transcends the slave narrative mode while being at the same time its fullest, most exact representative; second, that what is being recounted in the narratives is nearly always the realities of the institution of slavery, almost never the intellectual, emotional, moral growth of the narrator (here, as often, Douglass succeeds in being an exception without ceasing to be the best example: he goes beyond the single intention of describing slavery, but he also describes it more exactly and more convincingly than anyone else). The lives in the narratives are never, or almost never, there for themselves and for their own intrinsic, unique interest but nearly always in their capacity as illustrations of what slavery is really like. Thus in one sense the narrative lives of the ex-slaves were as much possessed and used by the abolitionists as their actual lives had been by slaveholders. This is why John Brown's story is titled *Slave Life in Georgia* and only subtitled "A Narrative of the Life, Sufferings, and Escape of John Brown, A Fugitive Slave," and it is why Charles Ball's story (which reads like historical fiction based on very extensive research) is called *Slavery in the United States,* with the somewhat extended subtitle "A Narrative of the Life and Adventures of Charles Ball, A Black Man, who lived forty years in Maryland, South Carolina and Georgia, as a slave, under various masters, and was one year in the navy with Commodore Barney, during the late war. Containing an account of the manners and usages of the planters and slaveholders of the South—a description of the condition and treatment of the slaves, with observations upon the state of morals amongst the cotton planters, and the perils and sufferings of a fugitive slave, who twice escaped from the cotton country." The central focus of these two, as of nearly all the narratives, is slavery, an institution and an external reality, rather than a particular and individual life as it is known internally and subjectively. This means that unlike autobiography in general the narratives are all trained on one and the same objective reality, they have a coherent and defined audience, they have behind them and guiding them an organized group of "sponsors," and they are possessed of very specific motives, intentions, and uses understood by narrators, sponsors, and audience alike: to reveal the truth of slavery and so to bring about its abolition. How, then, could the narratives be anything but very much like one another?

Several of the conventions of slave-narrative writing established by this triangular relationship of narrator, audience, and sponsors and the logic that dictates development of those conventions will bear and will reward closer scrutiny. The conventions I have in mind are both thematic and formal and they tend to turn up as often in the paraphernalia surrounding the narratives as in the narratives themselves. I have already remarked on the extra-textual letters so commonly associated with slave narratives and have suggested that they have a different logic about them from the logic that allows or impels Franklin to include similarly alien documents in his autobiography; the same is true of the signed engraved portraits or photographs so frequently to be found as frontispieces in slave narratives. The portrait and the signature (which one might well find in other nineteenth-century autobiographical documents but with different motivation), like the prefatory and appended letters, the titular tag "Written by Himself," and the standard opening "I was born," are intended to attest to the real existence of a narrator, the sense being that the status of the narrative will be continually called into doubt, and so it cannot even begin, until the narrator's real existence is firmly established. Of course the argument of the slave narratives is that the events narrated are factual and truthful and that they all really happened to the narrator, but this is a second-stage argument; prior to the claim of truthfulness is the simple, existential claim: "I exist.""Photographs, portraits, signatures, authenticating letters all make the same claim: "This man exists." Only then can the narrative begin. And how do most of them actually begin? They begin with the existential claim repeated. "I was born" are the first words of Moses Roper's *Narrative,* and they are likewise the first words of the narratives of Henry Bibb and Harriet Jacobs, of Henry Box Brown and William Wells Brown, of Frederick Douglass and John Thompson, of Samuel Ringgold Ward and James W.C. Pennington, of Austin Steward and James Roberts, of William Green and William Grimes, of Levin Tilmon and Peter Randolph, of Louis Hughes and Lewis Clarke, of John Andrew Jackson and Thomas H. Jones, of Lewis Charlton and Noah Davis, of James Williams and William Parker and William and Ellen Craft (where the opening assertion is varied only to the extent of saying, "My wife and myself were born").

We can see the necessity for this first and most basic assertion on the part of the ex-slave in the contrary situation of an autobiographer like Benjamin Franklin. While any reader was free to doubt the motives of Franklin's memoir, no one could doubt his existence, and so Franklin begins not with any claims or proofs that he was born and now really exists but with an explanation of why he has chosen to write such a document as the one in hand. With the ex-slave, however, it was his existence and his identity, not his reasons for writing, that were called into question: if the former could be established the latter would be obvious and the same from one narrative to another. Franklin cites four motives for writing his book (to satisfy descendants' curiosity; to offer an example to others; to provide himself the pleasure of reliving events in the telling; to satisfy his own vanity), and while one can find narratives by ex-slaves that might have in them something of each of these motives— James Mars, for example, displays in part the first of the motives, Douglass in part the second, Josiah Henson in part the third, and Samuel Ringgold Ward in part the fourth—the truth is that behind every slave narrative that is in any way characteristic or representative there is the one same persistent and dominant motivation, which is determined by the interplay of narrator, sponsors, and audience and which itself determines the narrative in theme, content, and form. The theme is the reality of slavery and the necessity of abolishing it; the content is a series of events and descriptions that will make the reader see and feel the realities of slavery; and the form is a chronological, episodic narrative beginning with an assertion of existence and surrounded by various testimonial evidences for that assertion.

In the title and subtitle of John Brown's narrative cited earlier—*Slave Life in Georgia: A Narrative of the Life, Sufferings, and Escape of John Brown, A Fugitive Slave*—we see that the theme promises to be treated on two levels, as it were titular and subtitular: the social or institutional and the personal or individual. What typically happens in the actual narratives, especially the best known and most reliable of them, is that the social theme, the reality of slavery and the necessity of abolishing it, trifurcates on the personal level to become subthemes of literacy, identity, and freedom which, though not obviously and at first sight closely related matters, nevertheless lead into one another in such a way that they end up being altogether interdependent and virtually indistinguishable as thematic strands. Here, as so often, Douglass' *Narrative* is at once the best example, the exceptional case, and the supreme achievement. The full title of Douglass' book is itself classic: *Narrative of the Life of Frederick Douglass, An American Slave, Written by Himself.* There is much more to the phrase "written by himself," of course, than the mere laconic statement of a fact: it is literally a part of the narrative, becoming an important thematic element in the retelling of the life wherein literacy, identity, and a sense of freedom are all acquired simultaneously and without the first, according to Douglass, the latter two would never have been. The dual fact of literacy and identity ("written" and "himself") reflects back on the terrible irony of the phrase in apposition, "An American Slave": How can both of these—"American" and "Slave"—be true? And this in turn carries us back to the name, "Frederick Douglass," which is written all around the narrative: in the title, on the engraved portrait, and as the last words of the text:

> Sincerely and earnestly hoping that this little book may do something toward throwing light on the American slave system, and hastening the glad day of deliverance to the millions of my brethren in bonds—faithfully relying upon the power of truth, love, and justice, for success in my humble efforts—and solemnly pledging myself anew to the sacred cause,—I subscribe myself,
>
> Frederick Douglass

"I subscribe myself"—I write my self down in letters, I underwrite my identity and my very being, as indeed I have done in and all through the foregoing narrative that has brought me to this place, this moment, this state of being.

The ability to utter his name, and more significantly to utter it in the mysterious characters on a page where it will continue to sound in silence so long as readers continue to construe the characters, is what Douglass' *Narrative* is about, for in that lettered utterance is assertion of identity and in identity is freedom—freedom from slavery, freedom from ignorance, freedom from non-being, freedom even from time. (pp. 152-57)

In narrating the events that produced both change and continuity in his life, Douglass regularly reflects back and forth (and here

he is very much the exception) from the person written about to the person writing, from a narrative of past events to a present narrator grown out of those events. In one marvellously revealing passage describing the cold he suffered from as a child, Douglass says, "My feet have been so cracked with the frost, that the pen with which I am writing might be laid in the gashes." One might be inclined to forget that it is a vastly different person writing from the person written about, but it is a very significant and immensely effective reminder to refer to the writing instrument as a way of realizing the distance between the literate, articulate writer and the illiterate, inarticulate subject of the writing. Douglass could have said that the cold caused lesions in his feet a quarter of an inch across, but in choosing the writing instrument held at the present moment—"the pen with which I am writing"—by one now known to the world as Frederick Douglass, he dramatizes how far removed he is from the boy once called Fred (and other, worse names, of course) with cracks in his feet and with no more use for a pen than for any of the other signs and appendages of the education that he had been denied and that he would finally acquire only with the greatest difficulty but also with the greatest, most telling success, as we feel in the quality of the narrative now flowing from the literal and symbolic pen he holds in his hand. Here we have literacy, identity, and freedom, the omnipresent thematic trio of the most important slave narratives, all conveyed in a single startling image.

There is, however, only one Frederick Douglass among the ex-slaves who told their stories and the story of slavery in a single narrative, and in even the best known, most highly regarded of the other narratives—those, for example, by William Wells Brown, Charles Ball, Henry Bibb, Josiah Henson, Solomon Northup, J.W.C. Pennington, and Moses Roper—all the conventions are observed—conventions of content, theme, form, and style—but they remain just that: conventions untransformed and unredeemed. The first three of these conventional aspects of the narratives are, as I have already suggested, pretty clearly determined by the relationship between the narrator himself and those I have termed the sponsors (as well as the audience) of the narrative. When the abolitionists invited an ex-slave to tell his story of experience in slavery to an anti-slavery convention, and when they subsequently sponsored the appearance of that story in print, they had certain clear expectations, well understood by themselves and well understood by the ex-slave too, about the proper content to be observed, the proper theme to be developed, and the proper form to be followed. Moreover, content, theme, and form discovered early on an appropriate style and that appropriate style was also the personal style displayed by the sponsoring abolitionists in the letters and introductions they provided so generously for the narratives. It is not strange, of course, that the style of an introduction and the style of a narrative should be one and the same in those cases where introduction and narrative were written by the same person—Charles Stearns writing introduction and narrative of Box Brown, for example, or David Wilson writing preface and narrative of Solomon Northup. What is strange, perhaps, and a good deal more interesting, is the instance in which the style of the abolitionist introducer carries over into a narrative that is certified as "Written by Himself," and this latter instance is not nearly so isolated as one might initially suppose. I want to look somewhat closely at three variations on stylistic interchange that I take to represent more or less adequately the spectrum of possible relationships between prefatory style and narrative style, or more generally between sponsor and narrator: Henry Box Brown, where the preface and narrative are both clearly in the manner of Charles Stearns; Solomon Northup, where the enigmatical preface and narrative, although not so clearly as in the case of Box Brown, are nevertheless both in the manner of David Wilson; and Henry Bibb, where the introduction is signed by Lucius C. Matlack and the author's preface by Henry Bibb, and where the narrative is "Written by Himself"—but where also a single style is in control of introduction, author's preface, and narrative alike.

Henry Box Brown's *Narrative*, we are told on the title-page, was

WRITTEN FROM A
STATEMENT OF FACTS MADE BY HIMSELF
WITH REMARKS UPON THE REMEDY FOR SLAVERY

BY CHARLES STEARNS.

Whether it is intentional or not, the order of the elements and the punctuation of this subtitle (with full stops after lines two and three) make it very unclear just what is being claimed about authorship and stylistic responsibility for the narrative. Presumably the "remarks upon the remedy for slavery" are by Charles Stearns (who was also, at 25 Cornhill, Boston, the publisher of the *Narrative*), but this title-page could well leave a reader in doubt about the party responsible for the stylistic manner of the narration. Such doubt will soon be dispelled, however, if the reader proceeds from Charles Stearns' "preface" to Box Brown's "narrative" to Charles Stearns' "remarks upon the remedy for slavery." The preface is a most poetic, most high-flown, most grandiloquent peroration that, once cranked up, carries right over into and through the narrative to issue in the appended remarks which come to an end in a REPRESENTATION OF THE BOX in which Box Brown was transported from Richmond to Philadelphia. Thus from the preface: "Not for the purpose of administering to a prurient desire to 'hear and see some new thing,' nor to gratify any inclination on the part of the hero of the following story to be honored by man, is this simple and touching narrative of the perils of a seeker after the 'boon of liberty,' introduced to the public eye . . . ," etc.—the sentence goes on three times longer than this extract, describing as it proceeds "the horrid sufferings of one as, in a *portable prison*, shut out from the light of heaven, and nearly deprived of its balmy air, he pursued his fearful journey. . . ." (pp. 158-60)

The narrative itself, which is all first person and "the plain narrative of our friend," as the preface says, begins in this manner:

> I am not about to harrow the feelings of my readers by a terrific representation of the untold horrors of that fearful system of oppression, which for thirty-three long years entwined its snaky folds about my soul, as the serpent of South America coils itself around the form of its unfortunate victim. It is not my purpose to descend deeply into the dark and noisome caverns of the hell of slavery, and drag from their frightful abode those lost spirits who haunt the souls of the poor slaves, daily and nightly with their frightful presence, and with the fearful sound of their terrific instruments of torture; for other pens far abler than mine have effectually performed that portion of the labor of an exposer of the enormities of slavery.

Suffice it to say of this piece of fine writing that the pen—than which there were others far abler—was held not by Box Brown but by Charles Stearns and that it could hardly be further removed than it is from the pen held by Frederick Douglass, that pen that could have been laid in the gashes in his feet made by the cold. At one point in his narrative Box Brown is

made to say (after describing how his brother was turned away from a stream with the remark "We do not allow niggers to fish"), "Nothing daunted, however, by this rebuff, my brother went to another place, and was quite successful in his undertaking, obtaining a plentiful supply of the finny tribe." It may be that Box Brown's story was told from "a statement of facts made by himself," but after those facts have been dressed up in the exotic rhetorical garments provided by Charles Stearns there is precious little of Box Brown (other than the representation of the box itself) that remains in the narrative. And indeed for every fact there are pages of self-conscious, self-gratifying, self-congratulatory philosophizing by Charles Stearns, so that if there is any life here at all it is the life of that man expressed in his very own overheated and foolish prose.

David Wilson is a good deal more discreet than Charles Stearns, and the relationship of preface to narrative in *Twelve Years a Slave* is therefore a great deal more questionable, but also more interesting, than in the *Narrative of Henry Box Brown*. Wilson's preface is a page and a half long; Northup's narrative, with a song at the end and three or four appendices, is three hundred thirty pages long. In the preface Wilson says, "Many of the statements contained in the following pages are corroborated by abundant evidence—others rest entirely upon Solomon's assertion. That he has adhered strictly to the truth, the editor, at least, who has had an opportunity of detecting any contradiction or discrepancy in his statements, is well satisfied. He has invariably repeated the same story without deviating in the slightest particular. . . ." Now Northup's narrative is not only a very long one but is filled with a vast amount of circumstantial detail, and hence it strains a reader's credulity somewhat to be told that he "invariably repeated the same story without deviating in the slightest particular." Moreover, since the style of the narrative (as I shall argue in a moment) is demonstrably not Northup's own, we might well suspect a filling in and fleshing out on the part of—perhaps not the "onlie begetter" but at least—the actual author of the narrative. But this is not the most interesting aspect of Wilson's performance in the preface nor the one that will repay closest examination. That comes with the conclusion of the preface which reads as follows:

> It is believed that the following account of his [Northup's] experience on Bayou Bœuf presents a correct picture of Slavery, in all its lights and shadows, as it now exists in that locality. Unbiased, as he conceives, by any prepossessions or prejudices, the only object of the editor has been to give a faithful history of Solomon Northup's life, as he received it from his lips.

> In the accomplishment of that object, he trusts he has succeeded, notwithstanding the numerous faults of style and of expression it may be found to contain.

To sort out, as far as possible, what is being asserted here we would do well to start with the final sentence, which is relatively easy to understand. To acknowledge faults in a publication and to assume responsibility for them is of course a commonplace gesture in prefaces, though why the question of style and expression should be so important in giving "a faithful history" of someone's life "as . . . received . . . from his lips" is not quite clear; presumably the virtues of style and expression are superadded to the faithful history to give it whatever literary merits it may lay claim to, and insofar as these fall short the author feels the need to acknowledge responsibility and apologize. Nevertheless, putting this ambiguity aside, there is no doubt about who is responsible for what in this sentence, which, if I might replace pronouns with names, would read thus: "In the accomplishment of that object, David Wilson trusts that he [David Wilson] has succeeded, notwithstanding the numerous faults of style and of expression [for which David Wilson assumes responsibility] it may be found by the reader to contain." The two preceding sentences, however, are altogether impenetrable both in syntax and in the assertion they are presumably designed to make. Casting the first statement as a passive one ("It is believed . . .") and dangling a participle in the second ("Unbiased . . ."), so that we cannot know in either case to whom the statement should be attached, Wilson succeeds in obscuring entirely the authority being claimed for the narrative. It would take too much space to analyze the syntax, the psychology (one might, however, glance at the familiar use of Northup's given name), and the sense of these affirmations, but I would challenge anyone to diagram the second sentence ("Unbiased . . .") with any assurance at all.

As to the narrative to which these prefatory sentences refer: When we get a sentence like this on describing Northup's going into a swamp—"My midnight intrusion had awakened the feathered tribes [near relatives of the 'finny tribe' of Box Brown/Charles Stearns], which seemed to throng the morass in hundreds of thousands, and their garrulous throats poured forth such multitudinous sounds—there was such a fluttering of wings—such sullen plunges in the water all around me—that I was affrighted and appalled"—when we get such a sentence we may think it pretty fine writing and awfully literary, but the fine writer is clearly David Wilson rather than Solomon Northup. Perhaps a better instance of the white amanuensis/sentimental novelist laying his mannered style over the faithful history as received from Northup's lips is to be found in this description of a Christmas celebration where a huge meal was provided by one slaveholder for slaves from surrounding plantations: "They seat themselves at the rustic table—the males on one side, the females on the other. The two between whom there may have been an exchange of tenderness, invariably manage to sit opposite; for the omnipresent Cupid disdains not to hurl his arrows into the simple hearts of slaves." The entire passage should be consulted to get the full effect of Wilson's stylistic extravagances when he pulls the stops out, but any reader should be forgiven who declines to believe that this last clause, with its reference to "the simple hearts of slaves" and its self-conscious, inverted syntax ("disdains not"), was written by someone who had recently been in slavery for twelve years. "Red," we are told by Wilson's Northup, "is decidedly the favorite color among the enslaved damsels of my acquaintance. If a red ribbon does not encircle the neck, you will be certain to find all the hair of their woolly heads tied up with red strings of one sort or another." In the light of passages like these, David Wilson's apology for "numerous faults of style and of expression" takes on all sorts of interesting new meaning. The rustic table, the omnipresent Cupid, the simple hearts of slaves, and the woolly heads of enslaved damsels, like the finny and feathered tribes, might come from any sentimental novel of the nineteenth century—one, say, by Harriet Beecher Stowe; and so it comes as no great surprise to read on the dedication page the following: "To Harriet Beecher Stowe: Whose Name, Throughout the World, Is Identified with the Great Reform: This Narrative, Affording Another Key to Uncle Tom's Cabin, Is Respectfully Dedicated." While not surprising, given the style of the narrative, this dedication does little to clarify the authority that we are asked to discover in and behind the narrative, and the dedication, like the pervasive style, calls into serious question the status of *Twelve Years a Slave* as autobiography and/or literature.

For Henry Bibb's narrative Lucius C. Matlack supplied an introduction in a mighty poetic vein in which he reflects on the paradox that out of the horrors of slavery have come some beautiful narrative productions. "Gushing fountains of poetic thought, have started from beneath the rod of violence, that will long continue to slake the feverish thirst of humanity outraged, until swelling to a flood it shall rush with wasting violence over the ill-gotten heritage of the oppressor. Startling incidents authenticated, far excelling fiction in their touching pathos, from the pen of self-emancipated slaves, do now exhibit slavery in such revolting aspects, as to secure the execrations of all good men, and become a monument more enduring than marble, in testimony strong as sacred writ against it." The picture Matlack presents of an outraged humanity with a feverish thirst for gushing fountains started up by the rod of violence is a peculiar one and one that seems, psychologically speaking, not very healthy. At any rate, the narrative to which Matlack's observations have immediate reference was, as he says, from the pen of a self-emancipated slave (self-emancipated several times), and it does indeed contain startling incidents with much touching pathos about them; but the really curious thing about Bibb's narrative is that it displays much the same florid, sentimental, declamatory rhetoric as we find in ghostwritten or as-told-to narratives and also in prefaces such as those by Charles Stearns, Louis Alexis Chamerovzow, and Lucius Matlack himself. Consider the account Bibb gives of his courtship and marriage. Having determined by a hundred signs that Malinda loved him even as he loved her—"I could read it by her always giving me the preference of her company; by her pressing invitations to visit even in opposition to her mother's will. I could read it in the language of her bright and sparkling eye, penciled by the unchangable finger of nature, that spake but could not lie"—Bibb decided to speak and so, as he says, "broached the subject of marriage":

> I said, "I never will give my heart nor hand to any girl in marriage, until I first know her sentiments upon the all-important subjects of Religion and Liberty. No matter how well I might love her, nor how great the sacrifice in carrying out these God-given principles. And I here pledge myself from this course never to be shaken while a single pulsation of my heart shall continue to throb for Liberty."

And did his "dear girl" flunk the challenge thus proposed by Bibb? Far from it—if anything she proved more high-minded than Bibb himself.

> With this idea Malinda appeared to be well pleased, and with a smile she looked me in the face and said, "I have long entertained the same views, and this has been one of the greatest reasons why I have not felt inclined to enter the married state while a slave; I have always felt a desire to be free; I have long cherished a hope that I should yet be free, either by purchase or running away. In regard to the subject of Religion, I have always felt that it was a good thing, and something that I would seek for at some future period."

It is all to the good, of course, that no one has ever spoken or could ever speak as Bibb and his beloved are said to have done—no one, that is, outside a bad, sentimental novel of date c. 1849. Though actually written by Bibb, the narrative, for style and tone, might as well have been the product of the pen of Lucius Matlack. But the combination of the sentimental rhetoric of white fiction and white preface-writing with a realistic presentation of the facts of slavery, all parading under the banner of an authentic—and authenticated—personal narrative, produces something that is neither fish nor fowl. A text like Bibb's is committed to two conventional forms, the slave narrative and the novel of sentiment, and caught by both it is unable to transcend either. Nor is the reason far to seek: the sensibility that produced *Uncle Tom's Cabin* was closely allied to the abolitionist sensibility that sponsored the slave narratives and largely determined the form they should take. The master-slave relationship might go underground or it might be turned inside out but it was not easily done away with.

Consider one small but recurrent and telling detail in the relationship of white sponsor to black narrator. John Brown's narrative, we are told by Louis Alexis Chamerovzow, the "Editor" (actually author) of *Slave Life in Georgia,* is "a plain, unvarnished tale of real Slave-life"; Edwin Scrantom, in his letter "recommendatory," writes to Austin Steward of his *Twenty-Two Years a Slave and Forty Years a Freeman,* "Let its plain, unvarnished tale be sent out, and the story of Slavery and its abominations, again be told by one who has felt in his own person its scorpion lash, and the weight of its grinding heel"; the preface writer ("W.M.S") for *Experience of a Slave in South Carolina* calls it "the unvarnished, but ower true tale of John Andrew Jackson, the escaped Carolinian slave"; John Greenleaf Whittier, apparently the dupe of his "ex-slave," says of *The Narrative of James Williams,* "The following pages contain the simple and unvarnished story of an AMERICAN SLAVE"; Robert Hurnard tells us that he was determined to receive and transmit Solomon Bayley's *Narrative* "in his own simple, unvarnished style"; and Harriet Tubman too is given the "unvarnished" honorific by Sarah Bradford in her preface to *Scenes in the Life of Harriet Tubman:* "It is proposed in this little book to give a plain and unvarnished account of some scenes and adventures in the life of a woman who, though one of earth's lowly ones, and of dark-hued skin, has shown an amount of heroism in her character rarely possessed by those of any station in life." The fact that the varnish is laid on very thickly indeed in several of these (Brown, Jackson, and Williams, for example) is perhaps interesting, but it is not the essential point, which is to be found in the repeated use of just this word—"unvarnished"—to describe all these tales. The Oxford English Dictionary will tell us (which we should have surmised anyway) that Othello, another figure of "dark-hued skin" but vastly heroic character, first used the word "unvarnished"—"I will a round unvarnish'd tale deliver / Of my whole course of love"; and that, at least so far as the OED record goes, the word does not turn up again until Burke used it in 1780, some 175 years later ("This is a true, unvarnished, undisguised state of the affair"). I doubt that anyone would imagine that white editors/amanuenses had an obscure passage from Burke in the back of their collective mind—or deep down in that mind—when they repeatedly used this word to characterize the narrative of their ex-slaves. No, it was certainly a Shakespearean hero they were unconsciously evoking, and not just any Shakespearean hero but always Othello, the Noble Moor.

Various narrators of documents "written by himself" apologize for their lack of grace or style or writing ability, and again various narrators say that theirs are simple, factual, realistic presentations; but no ex-slave that I have found who writes his own story calls it an "unvarnished" tale: the phrase is specific to white editors, amanuenses, writers, and authenticators. Moreover, to turn the matter around, when an ex-slave makes an allusion to Shakespeare (which is naturally a very infrequent occurrence) to suggest something about his situation or imply something of his character, the allusion is never to Othello. Frederick Douglass, for example, describing all the imagined horrors that might overtake him and his fellows should they try to escape, writes: "I say, this picture sometimes appalled us, and made us

> 'rather bear those ills we had,
> Than fly to others, that we knew not of.'"

Thus it was in the light of Hamlet's experience and character that Douglass saw his own, not in the light of Othello's experience and character. Not so William Lloyd Garrison, however, who says in the preface to Douglass' *Narrative,* "I am confident that it is essentially true in all its statements; that nothing has been set down in malice, nothing exaggerated, nothing drawn from the imagination. . . ." We can be sure that it is entirely unconscious, this regular allusion to Othello, but it says much about the psychological relationship of white patron to black narrator that the former should invariably see the latter not as Hamlet, not as Lear, not as Antony, or any other Shakespearean hero but always and only as Othello.

> When you shall these unlucky deeds relate,
> Speak of them as they are. Nothing extenuate,
> Nor set down aught in malice. Then must you speak
> Of one that lov'd not wisely but too well;
> Of one not easily jealous, but, being wrought,
> Perplex'd in the extreme. . . .

The Moor, Shakespeare's or Garrison's, was noble, certainly, but he was also a creature of unreliable character and irrational passion—such, at least, seems to have been the logic of the abolitionists' attitude toward their ex-slave speakers and narrators—and it was just as well for the white sponsor to keep him, if possible, on a pretty short leash. Thus it was that the Garrisonians—though not Garrison himself—were opposed to the idea (and let their opposition be known) that Douglass and William Wells Brown should secure themselves against the Fugitive Slave Law by purchasing their freedom from ex-masters; and because it might harm their cause the Garrisonians attempted also to prevent William Wells Brown from dissolving his marriage. The reaction from the Garrisonians and from Garrison himself when Douglass insisted on going his own way anyhow was both excessive and revealing, suggesting that for them the Moor had ceased to be noble while still, unfortunately, remaining a Moor. *My Bondage and My Freedom,* Garrison wrote, "in its second portion, is reeking with the virus of personal malignity towards Wendell Phillips, myself, and the old organizationists generally, and *full of ingratitude and baseness towards as true and disinterested friends as any man ever yet had upon earth.*" That this simply is not true of *My Bondage and My Freedom* is almost of secondary interest to what the words I have italicized reveal of Garrison's attitude toward his ex-slave and the unconscious psychology of betrayed, outraged proprietorship lying behind it. And when Garrison wrote to his wife that Douglass' conduct "has been impulsive, inconsiderate and highly inconsistent" and to Samuel J. May that Douglass himself was "destitute of every principle of honor, ungrateful to the last degree and malevolent in spirit," the picture is pretty clear: for Garrison, Douglass had become Othello gone wrong, Othello with all his dark-hued skin, his impulsiveness and passion but none of his nobility or heroism.

The relationship of sponsor to narrator did not much affect Douglass' own *Narrative:* he was capable of writing his story without asking the Garrisonians' leave or requiring their guidance. But Douglass was an extraordinary man and an altogether exceptional writer, and other narratives by ex-slaves, even those entirely "Written by Himself," scarcely rise above the level of the preformed, imposed and accepted conventional. Of the narratives that Charles Nichols judges to have been written without the help of an editor—those by "Frederick Douglass, William Wells Brown, James W.C. Pennington, Samuel Ringgold Ward, Austin Steward and perhaps Henry Bibb"—none but Douglass' has any genuine appeal in itself, apart from the testimony it might provide about slavery, or any real claim to literary merit. And when we go beyond this bare handful of narratives to consider those written under immediate abolitionist guidance and control, we find, as we might well expect, even less of individual distinction or distinctiveness as the narrators show themselves more or less content to remain slaves to a prescribed, conventional, and imposed form; or perhaps it would be more precise to say that they were captive to the abolitionist intentions and so the question of their being content or otherwise hardly entered in. Just as the triangular relationship embracing sponsor, audience, and ex-slave made of the latter something other than an entirely free creator in the telling of his life story, so also it made of the narrative produced (always keeping the exceptional case in mind) something other than autobiography in any full sense and something other than literature in any reasonable understanding of that term as an act of creative imagination. An autobiography or a piece of imaginative literature may of course observe certain conventions, but it cannot be only, merely conventional without ceasing to be satisfactory as either autobiography or literature, and that is the case, I should say, with all the slave narratives except the great one by Frederick Douglass.

But here a most interesting paradox arises. While we may say that the slave narratives do not qualify as either autobiography or literature, and while we may argue, against John Bayliss and Gilbert Osofsky and others, and they have no real place in American Literature (just as we might argue, and on the same grounds, against Ellen Moers that *Uncle Tom's Cabin* is *not* a great American novel), yet the undeniable fact is that the Afro-American literary tradition takes its start, in theme certainly but also often in content and form, from the slave narratives. Richard Wright's *Black Boy*, which many readers (myself included) would take to be his supreme achievement as a creative writer, provides the perfect case in point, though a host of others could be adduced that would be nearly as exemplary (Du Bois' various autobiographical works; Johnson's *Autobiography of an Ex-Coloured Man;* Baldwin's autobiographical fiction and essays; Ellison's *Invisible Man;* Gaines' *Autobiography of Miss Jane Pittman;* Maya Angelou's writing; etc.). In effect, Wright looks back to slave narratives at the same time that he projects developments that would occur in Afro-American writing after *Black Boy* (published in 1945). Thematically, *Black Boy* reenacts both the general, objective portrayal of the realities of slavery as an institution (transmuted to what Wright calls "The Ethics of Living Jim Crow" in the little piece that lies behind *Black Boy*) and also the particular, individual complex of literacy-identity-freedom that we find at the thematic center of all of the most important slave narratives. In content and form as well *Black Boy* repeats, *mutatis mutandis,* much of the general plan given earlier in this essay describing the typical slave narrative: Wright, like the ex-slave, after a more or less chronological, episodic account of the conditions of slavery/Jim Crow, including a particularly vivid description of the difficulty or near impossibility—but also the inescapable necessity—of attaining full literacy, tells how he escaped from southern bondage, fleeing toward what he imag-

ined would be freedom, a new identity, and the opportunity to exercise his hard-won literacy in a northern, free-state city. That he did not find exactly what he expected in Chicago and New York changes nothing about *Black Boy* itself: neither did Douglass find everything he anticipated or desired in the North, but that personally unhappy fact in no way affects his *Narrative*. Wright, impelled by a nascent sense of freedom that grew within him in direct proportion to his increasing literacy (particularly in the reading of realistic and naturalistic fiction), fled the world of the South, and abandoned the identity that world had imposed upon him ("I was what the white South called a 'nigger'''), in search of another identity, the identity of a writer, precisely that writer we know as "Richard Wright." "From where in this southern darkness had I caught a sense of freedom?" Wright could discover only one answer to his question: "It had been only through books . . . that I had managed to keep myself alive in a negatively vital way." It was in his ability to construe letters and in the bare possibility of putting his life into writing that Wright "caught a sense of freedom" and knew that he must work out a new identity. "I could submit and live the life of a genial slave," Wright says, "but," he adds, "that was impossible." It was impossible because, like Douglass and other slaves, he had arrived at the crossroads where the three paths of literacy, identity, freedom met, and after such knowledge there was no turning back.

Black Boy resembles slave narratives in many ways but in other ways it is crucially different from its predecessors and ancestors. It is of more than trivial insignificance that Wright's narrative does not begin with "I was born," nor is it under the guidance of any intention or impulse other than its own, and while his book is largely episodic in structure, it is also—precisely by exercise of symbolic memory—"emplotted" and "configurational" in such a way as to construe "significant wholes out of scattered events." Ultimately, Wright freed himself from the South—at least this is what his narrative recounts—and he was also fortunately free, as the ex-slaves generally were not, from abolitionist control and free to exercise that creative memory that was peculiarly his. On the penultimate page of *Black Boy* Wright says, "I was leaving the South to fling myself into the unknown, to meet other situations that would perhaps elicit from me other responses. And if I could meet enough of a different life, then, perhaps, gradually and slowly I might learn who I was, what I might be. I was not leaving the South to forget the South, but so that some day I might understand it, might come to know what its rigors had done to me, to its children. I fled so that the numbness of my defensive living might thaw out and let me feel the pain—years later and far away—of what living in the South had meant." Here Wright not only exercises memory but also talks about it, reflecting on its creative, therapeutic, redemptive, and liberating capacities. In his conclusion Wright harks back to the themes and the form of the slave narratives, and at the same time he anticipates theme and form in a great deal of more recent Afro-American writing, perhaps most notably in *Invisible Man. Black Boy* is like a nexus joining slave narratives of the past to the most fully developed literary creations of the present: through the power of symbolic memory it transforms the earlier narrative mode into what everyone must recognize as imaginative, creative literature, both autobiography and fiction. In their narratives, we might say, the ex-slaves did that which, all unknowingly on their part and only when joined to capacities and possibilities not available to them, led right on to the tradition of Afro-American literature as we know it now. (pp. 160-70)

James Olney, "'I Was Born': Slave Narratives, Their Status as Autobiography and as Literature," in The Slave's Narrative, edited by Charles T. Davis and Henry Louis Gates, Jr., Oxford University Press, 1985, pp. 148-75.

QUESTIONS OF HISTORICAL AUTHENTICITY

WILLIAM W. NICHOLS

[*Nichols discusses the issue of the historical authenticity of the slave narratives, touching briefly upon such topics as irony, the mythology of violence, and the slaves' "use of the mask" in their works.*]

Few of Ulrich B. Phillips's appraisals of Southern history [in his *Life and Labor in the Old South*] have gone unquestioned, but one judgment which he seems to have made almost in passing remains unexamined as a guide for research among the documents of Negro American slavery. Regarding the use of slave narratives as evidence, Phillips said: "Solomon Northup went as a Negro kidnaped into slavery and wrote a vivid account of plantation life from the under side. But ex-slave narratives in general, and those of Charles Ball, Henry Box Brown and Father Henson in particular, were issued with so much abolitionist editing that as a class their authenticity is doubtful." In major works on slavery since Phillips, the only evidence of disagreement with him on this matter is negative: historians have generally chosen to ignore even Solomon Northup's *Twelve Years a Slave,* which had Phillips's approval. Slave narratives have been dismissed, for the most part, as evidence for the writing of Southern history. The extraordinary paradox here is that the widespread agreement with Phillips' dismissal of the narratives has been accompanied by a frequent, almost ritualistic, assertion that "any history of slavery must be written in large part from the standpoint of the slave. . . ."

A dramatic example of the kind of illogic which such contradictory impulses produce is found in Kenneth Stampp's *The Peculiar Institution: Slavery in the Ante-Bellum South.* In the first paragraph of his preface, Stampp affirms the historian's faith that knowledge of the past is important for understanding the present, and he adds: "In this instance I firmly believe that one must know what slavery meant to the Negro and how he reacted to it before one can comprehend his more recent tribulations." Such a statement would seem to commit Stampp firmly to providing testimony from slaves about the nature of their experience, and he does, in fact, make references to at least four slave narratives, though with little apparent conviction regarding their significance. As Phillips did, he relies mainly for evidence upon the records of planters and the reports of travellers in the South. Well into the book, Stampp explains this apparent contradiction: "Since there are few reliable records of what went on in the minds of slaves, one can only infer their thoughts and feelings from their behavior, that of their masters, and the logic of their situation." That would seem to close the case. Because the narratives of slave experience are unreliable, historians are forced to look at slavery through other eyes. But incredibly, Stampp appears to reopen the case in his last paragraph by quoting a slave narrative which maintains that slavery cannot be honestly described by anyone but the slaves.

Scholarly doublethink regarding slave narratives has another convolution, and again Kenneth Stampp's work provides a good example. In 1964 Stampp reviewed . . . Charles H. Nichols's *Many Thousand Gone: The Ex-Slaves' Account of Their Bondage and Freedom,* and after summarizing the book's themes and weaknesses, he concluded: "In my opinion, a well-edited anthology of slave narratives would have been of greater value to the historian than the snippets that were woven together in this rather unsatisfactory volume." If, as Stampp appears to be suggesting here, there are enough reliable narratives to warrant a well-edited anthology, there it becomes difficult to understand why the slaves' thoughts and feelings can only be inferred from "their behavior, that of their masters, and the logic of their situation," as Stampp put it in *The Peculiar Institution.* Furthermore, there seems to be implied in Stampp's final judgment the possibility that even reliable slave narratives should be kept in their place. Historians, he appears to suggest, should not attempt to weave them into the larger fabric of Southern history.

Another measure of the strange treatment accorded slave narratives by important historians can be taken from Stanley Elkins's *Slavery: A Problem in American Institutional and Intellectual Life* (1959). In his introductory essay on the historiography of slavery, Elkins makes liberal allowances for the biases of eyewitness accounts. Of the sometimes conflicting perceptions of slavery by Fanny Kemble, Nehemiah Adams, Sir Charles Lyell, Susan Dabney, and Frederick Law Olmstead, he says, "much is gained and not much lost on the provisional operating principle that they were all telling the truth." But in a footnote to this passage, Elkins briefly discusses slave narratives, and he suggests that a rather different principle should be applied to them: "To this material [the accounts of white travelers and eyewitnesses] should be added whatever is dependable from the reminiscences and narratives of slaves themselves." Elkins does not explain how one is to determine what is dependable, although it seems clear that one cannot, even provisionally, assume the narrators were telling the truth. He continues in the same footnote to mention two narratives which are "particularly convincing" and two which "are heavily edited by abolitionists, though not entirely undependable." After that impressionistic and debatable poll of the hundreds of slave narratives, Elkins turns to the best-known of all ex-slave autobiographers: "Frederick Douglass' *My Bondage and Freedom* . . . is obviously not the work of an ordinary slave, but some of the author's insights into the slave system are valuable."

It would be fruitless to argue with Elkins's assertion that Frederick Douglass was not an ordinary slave. He was unquestionably an extraordinary man. Yet the fact that Elkins bothers to make such an obvious point suggests a link between his treatment of slave narrative and his interpretation of slave psychology. If one is to argue, as Elkin does, that slavery in the American South was successful on a very large scale in infantilizing its victims, then a man like Douglass must be treated emphatically as an exception. Beyond that, the very existence of fugitive slave narratives, unless they can be seen as essentially the products of white abolitionist imaginations, would seem to be evidence against the totally coerced slave personality which Elkins posits. For an ex-slave to look back upon his own past and believe that it represents something worthy of transmission to other men probably requires a significant amount of self-esteem. More importantly, when the slave narratives are given a close reading in the light of Elkins's hypotheses, they may well provide substantive evidence to refute his view of the typical slave as a "Sambo." As I read Solomon Northup's *Twelve Years a Slave,* for instance, the one narrative which both Phillips and Elkins consider reliable, it strongly suggests that, even on plantations in the Deep South, there existed a vital slave culture which might have provided the kind of psychological support, which, Elkins maintains, was not available. (pp. 403-05)

Northup's first hint of a slave culture appears in his descriptions of slave pens in Washington and Richmond. There he found communities of shared emotion, and he reports the frequent exchange of angry autobiographies and reflections on injustice. The fact that many of the men and women in the slave pens had just been separated from friends and families does not seem to have destroyed their willingness to risk new human relationships. Early in his own captivity, while aboard a boat taking him to the South, Northup participated with two other slaves in planning a daring mutiny which they were unable to attempt. Throughout the narrative, in fact, Northup reports secret, rebellious conversations among slaves, discussions which would have meant certain punishment if they had been overheard by members of the planter class. Sometimes the conversations are reminiscent of folk tales in their tough humor and masked resentment. When Northup himself rebelled against the brutality of one of his masters, Tidbeats, and was narrowly saved from hanging, several slaves met afterwards in his cabin to discuss the event. "They gathered around me," Northup says, "asking many questions about the difficulty with Tidbeats in the morning—and the particulars of all the occurrences of the day. Then Rachel came in, and in her simple language, repeated it over again—dwelling emphatically on the kick that sent Tidbeats rolling over on the ground—whereupon there was a general titter throughout the crowd." That general titter probably meant a good deal in the emotional lives of the slaves, and the group's response suggests the possibility that rebellious slaves could become a kind of secret hero to slaves who gave the impression of docility. (p. 406)

I have focussed, perhaps unfairly, on the work of Stampp and Elkins because they have at least said something about slave narratives as historical evidence. In a good many works on slavery the narratives are simply ignored. But my purpose in the brief discussion of Stampp and Elkins has been to suggest a basis for a rather sweeping indictment of historians who have attempted to understand slavery while dismissing the testimony of slaves. I am not a professional historian, but my limited acquaintance with the extensive literature on slavery has convinced me that, however crudely I may have apprehended it, there has been a significant failure in the historiography of slavery. There may be convincing evidence to show that most slave narratives are unreliable, but that evidence has not been published. The very fact that the narratives could be so generally treated as though they had been systematically discredited makes me wonder if scholars have been viscerally reluctant to confront ex-slaves' views of themselves and their past. Whatever the reason, the narratives have unquestionably received cavalier treatment. (p. 407)

It seems inevitable, however, that the slaves' view of slavery will become an integral part of American history before too many years have passed. The editorial process of identifying reliable texts of the narratives has already begun, and Gilbert Osofsky has written a strong defense of narratives as historical evidence [see sexcerpt above]. Furthermore, work being carried on in the related areas of folklore, music history, and anthropology seems destined to force scholars to recognize the

existence of a slave culture that informs the best of the narratives. Thus it may be worthwhile to speculate briefly on the effects slave narratives are likely to have on the writing of Southern history.

My guess is that many of the difficult problems in the historiography of slavery will be untouched by what one has to call the "new evidence." Such matters as profitability, infant mortality, and many issues raised in the comparative treatment of Latin American and North American slavery may not be significantly illuminated by this material. Rather, there will probably be some changing emphases in the treatment of Southern history. The concept of irony in Southern history may receive added emphasis, for example. When one adds to those ironies which C. Vann Woodward has explicated the bitter ironies of slave experience as seen by the ex-slaves, the history of the South becomes a kind of absurd drama that might be closer to the imaginative world of William Faulkner than to much of the history that has been written. Slave narratives are controlled by the ironic vision, a sense of gigantic discrepancies between what men say, what they seem to intend, and what they actually do.

Perhaps the slave narratives will encourage a reappraisal of the significance of violence in the history of the South. Reading

A slave rests from his work on the woodpile.

in slave narratives, I have been struck by similarities between their treatment of violence and Frantz Fanon's theories about the relationships between violence and the self-image of oppressed people. For instance, Frederick Douglass suggests in all three of his autobiographies that the turning point in his life came when he asserted himself violently against Covey, a slave-breaker. In his first autobiography he describes his own response to that event in these religious terms: "I felt as I never felt before. It was glorious resurrection, from the tomb of slavery, to the heaven of freedom." Fanon's imagery is more starkly existential, but he seems to be repeating Douglass' vision of oppression when he says in *The Wretched of the Earth*: "For the native, life can only spring up again out of the rotting corpse of the settler." Such affirmations suggest what I would call a mythology of violence, a view of the self and the world that posits meaning in violent, perhaps even suicidal, self-assertion. That such a mythology did not often become a revolutionary program for slaves in the South may not necessarily cancel altogether its significance in slave culture. And if there is anything at all to this "mythology of violence" in the fantasy life of slaves, then the whole matter of role-playing, the slave's creative use of a mask, will need more study than it has had.

In general, it seems likely that the slaves' views of the South will add complexity to the historical record. Without denying the essential inhumanity of American Negro slavery as an institution, the slave narratives may help us to understand something of the paradox of black American experience. . . . (pp. 408-09)

William W. Nichols, "Slave Narratives: Dismissed Evidence in the Writing of Southern History," in PHYLON: The Atlanta University Review of Race and Culture, *Vol. XXXII, No. 4, fourth quarter (Winter 1971), pp. 403-09.*

FRANCES SMITH FOSTER

[*Smith Foster asserts that in their effort to gain the support of white citizens, slave narrators unwittingly perpetrated such negative black stereotypes as the tragic mulatto and the ineffectual black matriarchal family.*]

Although the nineteenth-century slave narratives were intended to promote the welfare of the American slave by providing real and accurate accounts of his life, they contributed heavily to the development of racial distortions and myths. In their attempts to synthesize art and history, to create general concepts from specific events, and to cater to the demands of less hostile whites in order to gain their help in controlling more hostile whites, the slave narrators perpetrated and perpetuated images and ideas which were not entirely accurate but which gained increased respectability from their inclusion in the slave narratives.

Their focus upon the institution of slavery as the evil and the South as the location of that evil tended to diminish the role of racism, one of the basic reasons for slavery and a trait which existed in the North as well as in the South. In setting the physical axis as South to North and identifying that journey with the thematic movement of chattel to man, sin to salvation, and in ending most narratives with the safe arrival in free territories which offered the promise of just rewards for honest labor, the slave narratives provided additional ammunition for the antisouthern forces without challenging or identifying the racist assumptions which both anti- and prosouthern forces shared. (p. 127)

Of greater importance than the extraneous uses to which the majority of the slave narratives could be directed are the pervasive but basically false and destructive depictions that they reinforced. One of the most dramatic and tantalizing stereotypes which the slave narratives developed was that of the mulatto. The mulatto was a manifestation of the most evil results of slavery. He embodied the defilement of womanhood and the violation of marital sacraments. In addition, he was the living proof that the sins of the father are visited upon his sons. Not only was he a product of evil, but evil was visited upon him because his complexion was a constant reminder of his origins.

The tragic mulatto theme so captivated the antislavery imaginations that many believed the southern black population was predominantly mulatto. This misconception was strengthened by the high percentage of slave narratives by racially mixed authors. The group included some of the best-known and most articulate spokesmen, such as Frederick Douglass, William Wells Brown, and Josiah Henson, as well as Ellen Craft and Moses Roper, who had used their color to effect the most dramatic of escapes. In their narratives, the mulattoes emphasized the commonplaceness of miscegenation as well as the turmoil this caused in family life. Not everyone was misled into believing that dark-complexioned people were a minority in the slave population, but the number of mulattoes who wrote slave narratives encouraged considerable speculation about the impact of racial mixing upon society.

The number of mulatto narrators could be explained as the result of extraordinary pressures upon that group. If mulattoes were, as many narrators have said, singled out for particularly harsh treatment, it would be easy to assume that fewer members of that group could adjust to slavery and consequently that a higher percentage of them would try to escape. Their color, it could be argued, which was a disadvantage in slavery, could be easily used to facilitate their escape, and there are several popular narratives which show how the mulatto protagonist passed for white or Indian as he openly traveled out of slave territory.

This theory is countered by the fact that while a substantial number of narrators were mulattoes, the majority of the writers were not, and relatively few of the mulatto narrators who could pass chose to try that method of escape. Obviously, it was not simply a case of mulatto enslavement being so much more oppressive and the escape avenues being more available that created their substantial representation in the works.

The best reasons can be deduced from facts about the antislavery movement itself. Two basic tenets of the nineteenth-century abolitionists were that slavery prevented normal family relationships and that the kind of absolute authority that slave owners legally possessed over slaves encouraged atrocities. These ideas are easily combined in the concept of miscegenation (which to the abolitionist meant the sexual exploitation of women slaves by white men). Anti-slavery movements often pictured such exploitation as epidemic and as threatening, at least in the South, some of the fundamental institutions of civilization. The mulatto character had great value as a symbol of the sins fostered by slavery. In addition, such characters catered to the predilections of nineteenth-century audiences for sensationalism.

Historians, as well as blacks other than authors of slave narratives, have indicated that the mulatto was not always the tragic and omnipresent figure the slave narratives depict. Fogel and Engleman, for example, provide evidence that in the twenty-three decades of black and white contact in this country between 1620 and 1850, only 7.7 percent of the slave population was mulatto (though by 1860 that figure had risen to 10.4 percent). These figures include the unions between mulatto and black as well as between mulatto or black and white. Though cliometricians such as Fogel and Engleman are often criticised for their quantitatively based views, it is important to note that this percentage is approximately the same as the estimate offered by social historian John Hope Franklin. According to Franklin, "By 1850 there were 246,000 [7.7 percent] mulatto slaves out of a total slave population of 3.2 million. By 1860 there were 411,000 [10.5 percent] mulatto slaves out of a total slave population of 3.9 million." The number seems to have increased extremely rapidly between 1850 and 1860, but this does not necessarily mean a higher percentage of rapes or illicit unions because the children of mulattoes were naturally also counted as mulattoes.

Although many mulattoes were abused because of their heritage, as the slave narratives indicate, still others were given significantly better treatment for the same reason. Such advantages included social prestige and material awards. Franklin reminds us that while some men "felt nothing" for their black children, other men developed "a great fondness for their Negro children and emancipated them and provided for them." Evidence that the "high yellow" individuals were often awarded greater social status among blacks is also abundant.

The emphasis which slave narratives gave to the mulatto and the interest which the readers manifested in that figure were disproportionate; furthermore, the narratives did not challenge assumptions of racial inferiority. The ante-bellum racial attitude held that an increased percentage of Caucasian blood made a more intelligent and aggressive person, one who was less likely to accept enslavement. Based on the proportion of mulatto narrators and the ways in which mulattoes were depicted, the slave narratives did not discourage such ideas.

The greatest disadvantage of the slave narratives' emphasis upon the mulatto was that he became a symbol of the absence of a viable black family structure and in the process contributed to the further degradation of the black woman's image. The designation of a slave as a mulatto meant the union of a white man and a black woman. Although evidence shows that interracial sexual relationships were not confined to that arrangement, social and legal sanctions prevented any possible misinterpretation of that relationship. Slave narratives did not challenge this idea, but presented the slave woman as the unwilling and distraught victim. Emphasis upon the mulatto encouraged, therefore, the popular notion that sexual exploitation was frequent in slave quarters.

Writing in 1843, Stephen S. Foster exemplifies the popular image of slave women when he declares:

> By converting woman into a commodity, to be bought and sold, and used by her claimant as his avarice or lust may dictate, he totally annihilates the marriage institution; and transforms the wife into what he very significantly terms a "BREEDER," and her children into "STOCK."

> This change in woman's condition from a free moral agent to a chattel, places her domestic relations entirely beyond her own control, and makes her a mere instrument for the gratification of another's desires. The master claims her body as his property, and of course employs it for such purposes as best suit his

inclinations—demanding free access to her bed; nor can she resist his demands, but at the peril of her life. Thus is her chastity left entirely unprotected, and she is made the lawful prey of every pale-faced libertine, who may choose to prostitute her!!

As a result of such depictions, the black woman became closely identified with illicit sex. If the "negress" were not a hot-blooded, exotic whore, she was a cringing, terrified victim. Either way she was not pure and thus not a model of womanhood. Moreover, her ability to survive sexual degradation was her downfall. As victim she became the assailant, since her submission to repeated violations was not in line with the values of sentimental heroines who died rather than be abused. Her survival of these ordeals and continued participation in other aspects of slave life seemed to connote, if not outright licentiousness, at least a less sensitive and abused spirit than that of white heroines.

Her portrayal as a victim of rape and an object of barter left little room for other, more positive, images. What may have been advanced as a more positive portrayal turned out to be another negative picture: that of the slave mother, the center of a weak and impermanent family structure, performing both the masculine and feminine roles. The image of the matriarch did not eliminate the lusty, animalistic image or the insensitive and impure one, nor did it help establish the black woman as sister to the white female.

The reasons for the failure of either depiction are understood when the general attitudes of the ante-bellum era toward women are considered. Less fragile than her grandmother seemed to be, the mid-nineteenth-century lady emerged as the superintendent of "the arts, social deportment, and domestic standards." She was considered physically inferior to men, but morally superior. She was pure, sensitive both to the beauties and to the horrors of the world. According to James D. Hart, it was publicly acknowledged that the "leading features of the American woman were domestic fidelity, social cheerfulness, unostentatious hospitality, and moral and religious benevolence." Although a few radicals had called the first Women's Rights Convention in 1848, most women seemed to consider the home as their rightful domain. Hart points out that "anyone outside this sphere was either more or less than a woman." A female slave, with the emphasis upon her physical exploitation and her lack of masculine protection, home, and family, suffered from the contrast.

With the attitude that miscegenation was rampant came the notion that slave marriages were frequent and casual and that children received only intermittent and cursory family support. The stereotype of the slave family as reinforced in the slave narratives was that it was at best a weak and impermanent unit. The image of the matriarch not only prevented unquestioning acceptance of the black woman as woman, but it also provided the stereotype for what kind of family unit could exist under slavery.

The broken-family motif appears even when the protagonist is the legitimate offspring of a slave couple. Narrators emphasize the division of the family by reminders that marriage among slaves was not recognized by law and thus any slave marriage was subject to the will of the master and could be dissolved at any time. They also emphasized the law that slave children belong to the owners of the mothers.

In slave narratives the dominant image of the slave family unit is a fatherless home. Often he has been sold to a distant place.

Sometimes he has been killed or has even run away. Usually, he is identified as the property of a neighboring slaveholder. The father lives in one place, while his wife and children reside on her master's property. (pp. 128-33)

While the mulatto and the ineffective, matriarchal family helped support the concept of the helpless black slave, they did not create it. . . . [The] entire structure of the narratives was based on the image of the lonely wayfarer. The idea of a strong family unit was incompatible with such a foundation. The viability of the slave family had to be denied to increase the pathos of the homeless victim. Such pathos is also encouraged in the romanticized reports of the rare and brief instances of a nuclear family relationship in slave narratives. The narrator's depiction of such families is simplistic and highly idealistic. The narrators imply that loving, harmonious familial relations are the natural impulse of blacks by emphasizing the strong love and devotion among kith and kin. They attribute all problems to slavery, which, they assert, is antithetical to the existence of a viable black family. (p. 135)

Every narrator emphasized the strains that slavery placed upon the family unit and the inevitable division of families that were enslaved. They emphasized those situations, the instances wherein a husband could not protect the chastity of his wife or the parents could neither plan for their children's futures nor protect an infant from harm. (p. 136)

Slave narratives do not mention interfamilial bickering or delinquencies among children. Instead, they focus upon the many individuals who were sold, beaten, or murdered for trying to protect their spouses or children. They describe the heartbreak of persons who chose not to marry or bear children because they would be powerless to protect them. They confess that many ran away rather than be forced to observe the humiliation of their loved ones. The obvious message of the narratives was that the family ties were strong among slaves and that left to themselves, they could work hard and peacefully. A fair summation of their argument would be: Slavery and family, no! Freedom and family, yes!

The extent to which slavery destroys the inherent bond between mother and child is reported by Frederick Douglass. He states that his sole contact with his mother consisted of four or five occasions when, after completing a full day's work, she would walk the twelve miles between plantations to see him. During these brief nocturnal reunions, his mother would lie with him until he slept. When Douglass awoke at dawn, she would have returned to her owner's plantation. He reports that "never having enjoyed, to any considerable extent, her soothing presence, her tender and watchful care, I received the tidings of her death with much the same emotions I should have probably felt at the death of a stranger." (p. 137)

The effect of such comments in the narratives was to maintain that slavery seriously weakened or virtually destroyed the family and social structure of the black, and that it in turn contributed to the dehumanization of the slave. Therein lie the beginnings of the idea of the black matriarchal family and the broken family which Moynihan and others have asserted to this day. What it does not acknowledge is that alternative family structures may have arisen among slaves which, although not apparently of the nuclear mode of white middle-class Americans, could fulfill and satisfy the needs of the slaves in ways which the nuclear model could not.

There is a contradiction in the narrators' presentation of the family structure: They depict heroic struggles of slaves to main-

tain the purity of a family relationship the existence of which was considered impossible. Familial attachments were so great, in fact, that upon obtaining his own freedom, the exslave's next actions were to rescue his relatives and any other victim of bondage. Many fugitives risked their own freedom to return to the slave states in efforts to find and rescue their families. Some were captured several times because they returned to help others. William Craft, Henry Bibb, Noah Davis, Moses Grandy, Lewis Clarke, William Hayden, and Lunsford Lane are a few of the better-known narrators who chronicled their attempts to free their kinsmen. The narratives do not provide plausible sources of such fidelity and strength that would compel so many slaves to protect their loved ones at the risk of being beaten or sold. Nor do they help explain why exslaves would risk their hard-gained freedom and their lives to help others become free if, in fact, slavery had so devastated the black family and its culture.

Recent research makes such a paradox even more interesting, for scholars have presented evidence that not only did slaves have strong family ties, but the family unit was considered an asset by the slaveholders and worth much effort to keep families together. Historians such as Herbert G. Gutman and Eugene Genovese admit that good intentions were not always actualized and more families were separated than the owners may have wished, but their research shows that while the fear of separation was strong, that fear was not usually realized. Scholars also challenge the assumptions that the slave family was an impermanent and ineffective unit. From private correspondence between slaves, personal interviews, census records, and other kinds of public documents many historians are increasingly agreeing with Genovese, who says, "[T]he average plantation slave lived in a family setting, developed strong family ties, and held the nuclear family as the proper social norm."

Not only does he maintain that the nuclear family unit was the most common environment for slaves, but Genovese maintains that the male's role was strong and the relationship within the black family had its bad and good times:

> Both masters and ex-slaves tell us about some plantations on which certain women were not easily or often punished because it was readily understood that, to punish the woman, it would be necessary to kill her man first. These cases were the exception, but they tell us at the start that the man felt a duty to protect his woman. . . . Beyond that, the man of the house did do various things. He trapped and hunted animals to supplement the diet in the quarters, and in his small but important and symbolic way he was a breadwinner. He organized the garden plot and presided over the division of labor with his wife. He disciplined his children—or divided that function with his wife as people in other circumstances do—and generally was the source of authority in the cabin. This relationship within the family was not always idyllic. In many instances, his authority over both wife and children was imposed by force. Masters forbade men to hit their wives and children and whipped them for it; but they did it anyway and often. And there is not much evidence that women readily ran to the master to ask that her husband be whipped for striking her. The evidence on these matters is fragmentary, but it suggests that the men asserted their authority as best they could; the women expected to have to defer to their husbands in certain matters; and that both tried hard to keep the master out of their lives.

Other historians of American slavery, such as George P. Rawick, support the idea that the slaves had a strong family structure, but argue that it was not a nuclear structure. Rawick maintains that the slaves created a family system that was more appropriate and consequently more beneficial than the nuclear family:

> The slave community acted like a generalized extended kinship system in which all adults looked after all children and there was little division between "my children for whom I'm responsible" and "your children for whom you're responsible." . . . There was always some older persons who would, with relative ease, take over the role of absent parents. . . . Indeed, the activity of the slave in creating patterns of family life that were functionally integrative did more than merely prevent the destruction of personality that often occurs when individuals struggle unsuccessfully to attain the unattainable. It was part and parcel, as we shall see, of the social process out of which came black pride, black identity, black culture, the black community, and black rebellion in America.

John Blassingame in *The Slave Community* makes a highly revealing statement, but fails to pursue its implications: "In spite of the fact that probably a majority of the planters tried to prevent family separations in order to maintain plantation discipline, practically all of the black autobiographers were touched by the tragedy." Although Blassingame does not elaborate upon this idea, it is obvious that the slave narrator group included a disproportionate number of mulattoes, and that many of the narrators came from broken homes as well. Although it is possible that slave narrators were not a random sample of the population and consequently gave accounts that were valid for only one segment of the slave population, it is more probable that the traditions of the slave narrative genre determined the selection of details and emphases.

The content, structure, and communicative context of the slave narratives made them create a particular kind of literature, to shape and reveal their realities in ways most beneficial to their needs. That this is so can be seen as much from what was said and how as from what was not said and why. For example, the slave narratives tend to diminish the cultural value of Afro-American folktales and songs. Douglass mentions that singing slaves were not necessarily happy slaves and that their "sorrow songs" were full of meaning to the slaves that were singing them, but does not admit any real significance for him other than "opening his eyes to the overwhelming oppression of slavery in a very transcendental experience." Henry Bibb wryly admits an early faith in conjuration and witchcraft. Several narratives indicate the solace and inspiration of secret worship services. Few deal extensively with these early experiences or acknowldge them as vital influences. Although the majority of Afro-American folktales celebrate the wit and imagination of the weaker individual over the stronger, in the slave narratives the trickster image is subordinated. The dominant figure is the innocent victim, and the emphasis after freedom is upon the attainment of literacy, Christianity, and white middle-class values. This is true in spite of the fact that scholars such as Sterling Stuckey have made a strong case for the existence and strength of a viable black culture. "Slaves," says Stuckey, "were able to fashion a life style and a set of values—an ethos—which prevented them from becoming imprisoned altogether by the definitions which the larger society sought to impose. . . . The process of dehumanization was not so pervasive. . . . A very large number of slaves, guided by this ethos, were able to maintain their essential humanity."

The evidence of other kinds of slave literature and the recorded testimony of hundreds of exslaves also provide evidence of a more complex and positively functional environment than that offered by the nineteenth-century slave narrators. Although the slave narratives are guilty of perpetuating racist illusions and of perpetrating some inaccurate and potentially damaging stereotypes of their own, their ultimate significance is not damaged by this. If one attempts to study them in the context of their time, it becomes apparent why many of these seeming weaknesses exist. These same documents then become even more important for what their "negative" as well as "positive" aspects reveal. What is important is the influence that the slave narrators had upon their society and ultimately upon ours. (pp.138-41)

> *Frances Smith Foster, in her* Witnessing Slavery: The Development of Ante-bellum Slave Narratives, *Greenwood Press, 1979, 182 p.*

ANTECEDENTS: THE EIGHTEENTH-CENTURY SLAVE NARRATIVE

WILLIAM L. ANDREWS

[*In a survey of the eighteenth-century American slave narrative, Andrews stresses how most early narrators subjugated themselves to Christian ideology, which dictated that all of life's adversities, including bondage, were merely tests of faith meant to be borne without complaint. The critic examines the written confessions of condemned black felons as well as works by several African-born narrators, tracing the themes, stylistic devices, and motifs that were to shape the nineteenth-century slave narrative.*]

The opening statement of black autobiography in America is addressed "To The Reader" of *A Narrative of the Uncommon Sufferings and Surprizing Deliverance of Briton Hammon, A Negro Man,—Servant to General Winslow of Marshfield, in New-England* (1760):

> As my Capacities and Condition of Life are very low, it cannot be expected that I should make those Remarks on the Sufferings I have met with, or the kind Providence of a good GOD for my Preservation, as one in a higher Station; but shall leave that to the Reader as he goes along, and so I shall only relate Matters of Fact as they occur to my Mind—

What follows thereafter is a fourteen-page account of Hammon's thirteen-year separation from his master, during which time he was shipwrecked, captured by Florida Indians, imprisoned by the Spanish in Havana, and worked as a cook aboard an English man o' war before being fortuitously and joyfully reunited with General Winslow in London. The exact authorship of this narrative is a matter of dispute, but the sphere of responsibility claimed by the black subject and ostensible narrator of the story is explicitly defined. The persona states in his preliminary address to the reader that he will limit himself to relating "Matters of Fact as they occur to my Mind." The persona's sense of class, if not caste, differences between himself and his reader determines the role he will play in this unprecedented autobiographical enterprise. His job is to relate spontaneously, not reflect intellectually or emotionally on the facts of his unusual career. His reduced "Capacities" and his low "Condition of Life" disqualify him from commenting on the personal effects of his "Sufferings" or the cosmic significance of his ''Preservation.'' His superiors may decide what conclusions to draw from the events of Hammon's telling.

The division of literary labor explicitly stated in Hammon's ''To The Reader'' pervades Afro-American autobiography during the first fifty years of its existence. It was assumed that the black first-person narrator, poorly lettered if literate at all, was too unsophisticated to be much more than an oral data resource. There is no evidence before 1810 that Afro-American slave narrators were involved in the transcription, editing, prefacing, or publication of their life stories. A widely-selling autobiography, *A Narrative of the Most Remarkable Particulars in the Life of James Albert Ukawsaw Gronniosaw, An African Prince* (1770) was ''related by himself'' but ''committed to paper by the elegant pen of a young lady of the town Leominster, for *her own* private satisfaction'' (italics mine). The anonymous amanuenisis-editor of *A Narrative of the Life and Adventures of Venture a Native of Africa* (1798) pledged that he had added ''nothing in substance to what [Smith] related himself.'' However, he acknowledged that he had ''omitted'' ''many other interesting and curious passages of his life'' because of considerations of space and size in the printing of the autobiography. The largest group of slave narratives published during this time, the confessions of condemned black felons, were all dictated to amanuenses who did not need to be told the moral, political, or financial ramifications of their writing. In the lurid *Dying Confession of Pomp, A Negro Man,* broadside publisher Jonathan Plummer promised that he had ''endeavored to preserve the ideas'' of the criminal while takaing ''liberty to arrange the matter in my own way, to word his thoughts more elegantly . . . than he was able to express them.''

One may reconstruct from these statements what appears to have been a standard procedure for the composition and publication of Afro-American autobiographies in the late eighteenth century. The actual subject of the autobiography, the narrator himself, reported the basic ''who-what-and-where'' of his past experience. An amanuensis-editor took down these facts, ''improving'' their diction and style according to his or her own standards of taste and decorum. More importantly, the job of selecting, arranging, and assigning significance to the facts of the narrator's life rested in the hands of the editor. In other words, editors granted blacks the capacity to know about themselves what linguists today term ''brute facts''— ''simple empirical observations recording sense experiences.'' But even the most well-meaning of editorial collaborators arrogated to themselves decisions regarding the institutional frameworks and ethical meanings of these brute facts. It is important for today's readers of dictated slave narratives to remember, as John Searle has pointed out, that aside from ''brute facts'' there are many kinds of facts that do not belong under this rubric because they depend for their meaning on the rules and values of human institutions. Such institutions, be they socio-economic (slavery), moral (the Judeo-Christian ethic), or aesthetic (the myth of life as a spiritual journey), bind many of the facts of human experience in complexly interwoven ''systems of constitutive rules.'' If, as Searle has argued, ''every institutional fact is underlain by a (system of) rule(s) of the form '*X* counts as *Y* in context *C*,''' then the crucial role of the editor-amanuensis in early slave autobiography can be distinguished clearly. It is the editor who decides what ''context *C*'' will be; it is the editor who decides whether and how the brute facts of the slave's narration are to be contextualized and thus how they will be received as ''institutional facts'' by their white readers.

The early Afro-American slave narrative is almost always a variant of what James Olney has called ''autobiography simplex,'' in which ''a single metaphor,'' a ''dominant faculty or function or tendency'' controls the career of the narrator and, by extension, one's interpretation of that career. It is very hard to tell whether this single metaphor emanates from the slave narrator's own perception of his life or whether it is applied to that life, like a kind of overlay, by amanuensis-editors and preface-writers. One may feel confident that the dominant metaphor of black criminal confessions—the black outlaw as recreant and rebel against white paternal authority—did not occur spontaneously to a condemned black felon. But in cases like Hammon's or Gronniosaw's, editors probably solicited these stories *because* they conformed or were conformable to cultural myths and literary traditions with an already established audience appeal, such as Indian captivity or evangelical conversion narratives. When editors recognized affinities between black narrators and Western archetypes like Mr. Christian, the Biblical Joseph, or Job, they stressed these parallels in their prefaces and gave them precedence in their characterizations of the black subjects themselves.

Reading the first fifty years of Afro-American slave narrative is thus something of an exercise in creative hearing. There are so many silences in these autobiographies, so few expressions of personal feelings and ethnic experience that lay outside the structures of discourse that the Judeo-Christian literary and cultural tradition imposed on early slave narratives. Briton Hammon is the first invisible man in Afro-American first-person narrative. If he were not identified as a Negro in the title of his story, one would be hard pressed to find in the narrative any indications of a black man's special perspective on what captivity and deliverance meant in the New World. James Gronniosaw thought early in his slave career that ''every body and every thing despised me because I was black.'' But this important insight into his alien racial situation in the white man's world is never invoked again as a means of explaining a career of almost unrelieved and clearly unjustified misery in England and America. Silences such as these made it possible for amanuensis-editors of early slave narratives to accommodate the stories of their subjects to the organizing and selection principles and the cultural values of popular white autobiographical genres, in particular, the captivity narrative, the conversion account, the criminal confession, the spiritual pilgrimage, and the journal of ministerial labors. Within the boundaries of these genres, black self-portraits were cropped and framed according to the standards of an alien culture. For the most part, then, the intention of early slave narratives was primarily to celebrate the acculturation of the black man into established categories of the white social and literary order. The record of such ritual-like processes was transmitted through a reportorial style that became itself ritualized according to the culturally-sanctioned eulogistic or didactic purposes that each narrative was put to. In the dictated slave narratives, these ritual elements need to be analyzed in order to understand the selection, structuring, and evaluative principles that initially determined the nature and direction of the Afro-American autobiographical tradition. Once the early slave narrator achieved authorial autonomy, the subject of analysis necessarily shifts to the ways in which self-composed autobiographies register individual and at times culture-opposing decisions about the meaning of Afro-American experience and how to express that meaning. Ultimately, the history of Afro-American autobiography from 1760 to 1810 reveals an emerging creative tension between black individual and white cultural perspectives on the identity of the black self and its relationship to white society. Now it is important to recognize some of the terms in which this tension appeared and the kinds of "autobiographical acts" that evolved as indicators and attempted resolutions of that tension.

One of the fundamental moral issues treated in any autobiography is the proper relationship between the individual and the world. In the popular, white autobiographical exempla of the late eighteenth century, the Christian individual was instructed, not surprisingly, that he or she must live in the world but must not be of the world. In America, living within the settlement world was considered a desideratum for survival and a modicum of the amenities of a frontier society. As the Indian captivity narrative proved, the settlement was a realm of order and security, an outpost of moral values in a land of savagery. Outside the white man's sunny clearings lay darkness, chaos, and destruction, to be warded off only by the merciful hand of Providence. This did not mean, of course, that fallen human nature could not find much to tempt it within the gates of the civilized world. In evangelical conversion narratives from England and America, the narrator characterizes his or her unregenerate past as a time of self-indulgence, sensuousness, or irresponsibility, oftentimes exacerbated by the corruptness of society. After conversion these narrators generally feel called to redeem the world through their individual example. Keeping their moral distance from the carnality of the world, spiritual autobiographers count their suffering and alienation from the world as a blessing; their missionary individualism gains strength and self-confidence as it refuses to compromise with the world. However, as the criminal confessions indicate, an excessively uncompromising self, one that became a law unto itself in both a secular and spiritual sense, needed to be restrained and punished by the world. One could not spurn some worldly institutions, such as the home, the church, or the state, without casting oneself in the role of subversive or rebel. To step outside the divinely-sanctioned institutions of the world was, once again, to plunge into the chaos of the unbridled self and savagery. (pp. 6-9)

Most early slave narratives are structured around these same assumptions about the relationship of the individual soul and the world. In Hammon's narrative, the world outside the control of his benevolent master is extremely precarious and oppressive. Once the slave is separated from his master's care and influence, he is rendered defenseless and directionless in the great world. Only God can resurrect him from the Spanish dungeon in Jamaica; only "Divine Goodness" is strong enough to restore the black man, "like one arose from the Dead," to his patron. Let the slave stray outside the known world of stratified white-over-black relationships, Hammon's narrative implies, and he will risk a life in limbo. He will become a type of the lost soul, disconnected from all his society's terms for order, sustained solely by the survival instinct.

Gronniosaw's narrative draws more explicitly on the presumed pathos of the Negro as a lost soul in the sinful world while also giving its readers one of the first portraits of the ex-slave as wretched freeman. Whether enslaved or free, James Gronniosaw is a man in search of a refuge from the world. Ever the alien, even in his African boyhood, young James finds upon conversion to Christianity an initial sense of self-sufficiency. "I felt an unwillingness in myself to have anything more to do with the world, or to mix with society again." Nor would he have had to, but his master, Mr. Freelandhouse, dies not long after James's conversion, leaving him free and patronless. He attaches himself to Mrs. Freelandhouse and other members of her family, but they all die hastily, forcing Gron-

niosaw to have to decide once again what to do with himself. He emigrates to England, in search of "some Christian friends, with whom I hoped to enjoy a little sweet and comfortable society" safe from the wickedness of the world. In subsequent years, the pious freeman finds some succor and much adversity in England, but he professes to have found peace in the hope of "the everlasting glories of the world to come." For now, he is "willing, and even desirous to be counted as nothing, a stranger in the world, and a pilgrim" who waits faithfully for his deliverance from "the evils of this world." To be a nullity in the world is not something just to be accepted but to be desired, for it enables Gronniosaw to claim a greater heavenly identity the less worldly identification he engages in.

In the black criminal confession, the majority of which concern slave-born men, the narrator's first and greatest mistake is his rejection of parental advice and/or his master's supervision in favor of a bid for self-sufficiency in the world. Virtually all these slaves characterize their relationships with their masters as lenient and often morally instructive. Joseph Mountain, criminal extraordinaire, grew up as a house slave in Philadelphia, where he learned reading, writing, and "the sentiments of virtue." But he "neglected" his training, shipped to England (for unstated reasons), and soon went "in quest of amusements" in London. The remainder of his narrative lists in detail the various "species of debauchery" he took up after falling in with a band of gamblers and highwaymen. The average black criminal narrative is the story of a young man whose break with the authority figures in his life is presented as a symbol of his willful contempt for all systems of ordering and restraining the self. The anarchic careers of escaped slaves like Arthur, Edmund Fortis, and Stephen Smith proved the necessity of maintaining the status quo in the social hierarchy and hinted strongly that the Negro who fled outside it would find himself lost in the chaos of his own selfish appetites.

Slave narratives based on the captivity, conversion, and criminal confession models draw much of their emotional appeal from the depiction of the black man as a helpless or wayward figure when placed on his own in the world. He may be able to survive alone, but there is little sense of heroic achievement in the individualism of a Hammon or a Gronniosaw. The restless, rootless lives and ignominious deaths of men like Arthur and Joseph Mountain provide testimony for the widespread colonial belief that the average Afro-American needed support and supervision, if not rigorous control, on his life's voyage between the Scylla of the savage self and the Charybdis of the perverted world. The narratives we have examined so far climax in either rituals of reintegration and domestication for homeless blacks awash in the world or professions of black reconciliation to the white socio-moral order. In either case, the black individual discovers that his felicity coincides with his fate within the instituted structures that white society has erected for him as a bulwark against the world. At the conclusion of the large majority of slave narratives between 1760 and 1810, there is an attempt to turn the tragedy of the lost and desperate Negro into a sort of Christian comedy by showing the wandering protagonist being led providentially home to the protective authority of his master, the state, or his Heavenly Father.

To make the experience of eighteenth-century blacks fit this archetypal myth of unity, division, and reintegration, many concepts crucial to an evaluation of the meaning of a Negro's life had to be defined in very limited ways. The ideas of captivity and deliverance, freedom and necessity, ignorance and enlightenment, salvation and damnation—the thematic sub-structure of most early slave narratives—are generally defined according to the "constitutive rules" of white institutions and culture. As a result, much early black autobiography traffics in ignorance about the actual choices black people had in the Western world and misconceptions about what those choices actually meant to blacks. In the white Indian captivity narrative, escape from the savages meant deliverance from bondage into freedom and community among one's fellows. But when Briton Hammon was released from the Florida Indians who held him, he was not restored to a community. He was subjected to worse savagery from the Spanish authorities in Jamaica who ransomed him only to imprison him for more than four years. White people are not Hammon's fellows; they are with rare exception part of the indifferent and cruel world. At the end of his story, Hammon declares that he has been "freed from a long and dreadful Captivity," that he has been "return'd to my own Native Land," and that the Lord is to be praised for his deliverance. And yet such ritual statements as these in ordinary captivity narratives sound peculiar, if not contradictory, coming from a man of Hammon's race and caste. In what sense was he "freed" if the experience led to his being restored to a previous slave-master? In what sense might a black slave speak of New England as his "Native Land"? The dualistic worldview and racist terms for order that underlie the genre of the captivity narrative do not admit the sorts of specialized semantic questions one might wish to pose to the first Afro-American slave narrator.

These kinds of questions proliferate upon reading a typical black criminal confession too. Drawn up according to the formulae of the time, these accounts never answer satisfactorily the question of why a slave ran away or why a black man became a criminal in the first place. Some blamed "lewd women," others strong drink and Sabbath-breaking, and one admitted that he had always been "naturally too much inclined to vice" to live virtuously. But none traced his sociopathic behavior back to his alien condition in American society or his prior treatment as a slave. The implication of almost all black criminal narratives is that the slave youth was at home in bondage; he became an ingrate when he alienated himself from that familial institution. The attempt of the amanuensis-editors of these narratives is to mold the condemned man's story into an exemplus of the prodigal son. Thus, even though he faces the gallows, the typical criminal narrator professes to have found peace and hope at the end of his miserable career. The punishment handed down by his white surrogate father, the judge in his trial, seems to him fair and necessary as a just "forfeiture" of life to "the injured laws of his country." He gives himself up to his heavenly father's mercy and grace, hoping to be welcomed into "the Paradise of never ending bliss" once he has expiated his sins on the gallows.

Inasmuch as the black criminal confession was usually narrated by escaped slaves or rebellious ex-slaves, it is an obvious literary ancestor of the famous fugitive slave narratives of the mid-nineteenth century. However, nothing in the literature of anti-slavery in America better illustrates the revolution in social attitudes toward the slave than the thematic polarities between eighteenth-century and nineteenth-century fugitive slave narratives. Perhaps the greatest rhetorical achievement of the slave narrative from 1830 to 1865 was its identification of the fugitive with romanticized culture heroes like Moses, Patrick Henry, or even Spartacus. But in the eighteenth-century slave narrative the rebellious slave is treated as a skulker from duty, not a seeker of liberty. The interrogators and amanuenses of these

condemned men were agents, not reformers, of church and state, and the narratives they published aimed at justifying the ways of God and the state to the black man. Even Rev. Richard Allen, who remembered his youth in slavery as "a bitter pill" and who vigorously defended blacks from criminal slander in broadly social contexts, could find nothing to mitigate the awful guilt of John Joyce, murderer of a white woman. In Allen's eyes, the causes of Joyce's deed stemmed from the fact that he, like too many black Philadelphians, had been a "slave of Sin." In two or three decades, abolitionists and some ex-slaves would begin to indict slavery itself as a cause of black transgressions against morality and law. But in the first fifty years of the slave narrative, the slavery of sin received much more condemnation than the sin of slavery.

In the conventional conversion narrative, which is a kind of slave narrative in spiritual terms, the hero is God acting through Christ, not the convert himself or herself. The epigraph from Isaiah 42:16 supplied for Gronniosaw's title page is illustrative: "I will bring the blind by a way that they know not; I will lead them in paths that they have not known; I will make darkness light before them; and crooked things straight. These things will I do unto them, and not forsake them." Gronniosaw's is the story of what various "men of power," the Christian God and His white earthly instruments, did "unto" the black man. The Negro is pictured as the object, not the subject of action. His purpose as narrator is to discover how his experiences "have all been sanctified to me." Believing himself a blessedly alienated pilgrim in the world, he does not examine his adversities to find out how the world works. A spirit in transit finds in his temporal path only "the footsteps of Providence." Thus, Gronniosaw never wonders why, during one snowy winter in Colchester, he had to depend on the charity of four carrots from "a gentleman's gardener" to keep his family alive because he could find no work. He never speculates on what lay behind the "envious and ill natured" reaction of "the inferior people" of Norwich when they saw him and his wife prospering in their town. He simply states that "the inferior peope" "worked under price on purpose to get my business from me; and they succeeded so well that I could scarcely get anything to do, and we became again unfortunate." To Gronniosaw, life is a matter of good or bad fortune overseen by Providence for unseen purposes.

As a structure in which Afro-American experience could be organized and interpreted, therefore, the evangelical conversion narrative proved a mixed blessing for the early slave narrative. In the Scriptures and the conversion narratives that drew on them was expressed a concept of life whose telos was liberation from bondage. If slaves brought to their narratives a "pregeneric myth" of the black quest for freedom and literacy, then the conversion narrative offered a model quest story in which liberation was defined as spiritual enlightenment through which one could transcend, if not escape, the power of the world. Moreover, the publication of conversion narratives about blacks supported humanitarian arguments that, far from being a sub-human brute, the African had a soul as worthy of salvation in God's eyes as the Caucasian's.

Nevertheless, there were serious liabilities in the conversion narrative's concept of liberation when it was applied to the experience of slaves. As Sacvan Bercovitch has stressed, the personal literature of the Puritans, from which the conversion narrative was descended, teaches that "self-examination serves not to liberate but to constrict; selfhood appears as a state to be overcome, obliterated. Thus the conversion model offered the slave narrator an ideal of freedom *from* the self, not *for* the self. In this way the conversion narrative sanctioned and encouraged self-hatred and the rejection of one's past—attitudes that later black autobiographers have identified as special racist nemeses of black people in search of their authentic selves. The conversion narrative's view of the origins and Christian response to the evils of the world also handicapped the early Afro-American autobiographer. Implicitly or explicitly, the narratives of Hammon, Gronniosaw, and Marrant echo George White's faith that despite "adversity, pain, and sickness" the Christian must "rejoice in the wisdom of God, as ordering all events." The miseries of this world will "turn to his advantage," White assured his reader, since "whom the Lord loveth he chasteneth" (Proverbs 3:12). As a result of this conviction, none of the early black narratives of deliverance and conversion questions or, more importantly, analyzes reversals and suffering, whether of natural origin (sickness and accidents) or human (deceptions, fraud, or violence). The evangelical world-view gave the slave narrator no tools for discovering or terms for describing causation on the worldly level. Either his pious outlook had estranged him from any inkling of the racial, social, and economic factors that molded his life into a pattern of struggle, or he found no way of talking about these factors in a narrative form that viewed the world in simplistic Manichean categories. At any rate, not until the mid-nineteenth century would slave narrators speak of the trouble they had seen as an injustice to their humanity to be resisted, not a trial for their faith to be endured. Until slave narratives could break with the evangelical world-view and start assigning culpability to *men* for the evils *they* brought on their peers, the genre could not distinguish itself as an Afro-American literary form.

The first steps in this direction appear in the narratives of three onetime slaves: Pomp, Venture Smith, and George White. None of these men espouses abolitionism *per se* in his life story, but all testify against "the peculiar institution" as they had known it, and all seized their opportunities to escape its pernicious influence. George White was born a slave in Virginia in 1764. At the age of five he was separated from his mother, whom he never saw again. He does not detail the "cruel bondage" that was his for the next twenty-one years until he was freed, but he censures the "vice and immorality" that arose from the "abject slavery" he witnessed in the Old Dominion. In the first two pages of his narrative, White delivered the most unrelenting attack on slavery as a social system that had yet appeared in Afro-American autobiography. Significantly, this was the first American Negro actually to compose and write down his life story himself.

Venture Smith was enslaved both in his native Africa and in Connecticut. He pictures himself abused and betrayed by his masters on both sides of the ocean. Against the arbitrary authority of white men he repeatedly rebelled, either by running away or fighting back. Yet he eventually opted for a socially-sanctioned route to freedom, purchasing himself with money he had saved from a variety of odd jobs hired on his own time. His concluding remark on this phase of his life withholds comment on the morality of slavery as an institution, but it does state his claims against the particular white who exploited him: "Being thirty-six years old, I left Colonel Smith once more for all. I had already been sold three different times, made considerable money with seemingly nothing to derive it from, had been cheated out of a large sum of money, lost much by misfortunes, and paid an enormous sum for my freedom." (pp. 9-14)

Disillusionment with the myth of black acculturation into white society is the explicit theme of Venture Smith's dictated autobiography. If life in slavery subjects the Negro to white treachery and meanness, life as a freeman, Smith discovers, offers him little relief though he may try to play the white man's game even to the point of adopting middle-class values. "I bought nothing which I did not absolutely want," Smith points out in his own defense. "Expensive gatherings of my mates I commonly shunned, and all kinds of luxuries I was perfectly a stranger to." Such Franklinesque self-denial helped Smith accumulate the money with which to buy his enslaved family. But if Smith thought the acquisition of real estate, sailing vessels, capital, and other blacks as slaves would win him respect among whites, he admits at the end of his narrative how mistaken he was. After years of being robbed, cheated, or otherwise outmaneuvered by whites (and some blacks), Smith realizes that, slave or free, the black man can only be an outsider in the white world. Institutions like the courts preserve the supremacy of white power over the upwardly-mobile Negro, as Smith learns when he is shown the futility of resisting a rich white man's suit against him. With the financial power to appeal the matter from court to court, the white man can obtain the verdict he wants regardless of the travesty of justice. For, as Smith observes with trenchant irony, "Captain Hart was a *white gentleman*, and I a *poor African*, therefore it was *all right, and good enough for the black dog.*"

Venture Smith is the first in a long line of black autobiographers to dedicate himself to the American quest for material success, only to find his goal an ever-receding mirage. The ironic revelation that he is still "a black dog" in white society regardless of his money and property leads him to declare at the end of his narrative, "Vanity of vanities, all is vanity." For Venture Smith, prototype of the black bourgeois autobiographer, the falsity of the myth of assimilation and success seems to have been only part of the lesson of his life experience, however. He also realized at the end of his secular quest, without power, community, or religious faith to assuage his sense of alienation and loss, that he could yet find consolation in his love for his wife, his conviction of his own integrity, and above all, his freedom. By recognizing these quasi-existential resources, not the glimmering promises of the American Dream, as fundamental necessities for the black outsider, Smith posited early in the slave narrative tradition a concept of Afro-American fulfillment independent of the myths of integration and success popularized by the predominant culture.

Like Venture Smith, George White was also an ambitious man to whom freedom from slavery was merely the first stage in an extended quest for status and power in the white world. There were key differences between the two men's strategies and careers, however. Smith hoped to "make it" as a black rugged individualist in the rough-and-tumble of American economic life. White opted for status in a white institution as his ticket to the kind of independence and power he desired. Smith's is a story of constant reversals of fortune leading to a largely embittered conclusion. White's *Brief Account* recalls a string of triumphs over considerable odds. After his emancipation from twenty-six years of slavery, White's narration recounts his ecstatic conversion to Christianity and the evolution of his conviction of having been called to the ministry. He applies for an exhorter's license in the New York Methodist Conference, overcoming illiteracy and platform phobia to qualify for it. Convinced later that "God required me to preach his gospel in a more direct manner, than my license as an exhorter permitted me to attempt," White petitions for a preaching license

The title page and frontispiece to the American edition of the narrative of Olaudah Equiano, a noted eighteenth-century African autobiographer.

and endures repeated refusals by his white examiners to admit him to full ministerial status in the Methodist Church. Eventually, however, he wins the Presiding Elder's approval and ordination as a fullfledged preacher in the predominantly white church. The lesson of his experience defies the disillusionment of Venture Smith: "by putting my trust in God," White states, "and obeying his will, under all these trials, infinite goodness has caused all events to turn to my account at last."

This image that White assumed, that of the patient man of faith enduring trials under the guidance of the Lord, is consistent with the formulae of the other narratives of Christian pilgrimage that were published in the names of blacks during this time. White is singular, however, in the direction that his pilgrimage took—towards a specific position within a white institution. This is the first of many slave narrators to depict the quest for freedom as necessitating a physical break with the institution of slavery followed by extensive psychological negotiations with other institutions of white society. From the Methodists, White petitioned for the kind of power and social legitimacy that he felt a black man needed in order to achieve his goals in the white man's world. In exchange, White was willing to

accept the discipline—indeed, the slights and racist resistance—of the institution as the price his individuality had to pay for power and authority.

White had little trouble with his white "brethren" when he applied for a license to exhort. The early Methodist Church in America did not specify exactly what an exhorter's duty was, but it is clear that he occupied the lowest standing in the church's hierarchy, beneath Bishop, Elder, Deacon, and Preacher. It appears that the exhorter's role was limited to para-ministerial duties, such as the leading of Sabbath School classes, prayer meetings, and other informal evangelistic gatherings. A vision from God only a few months after becoming an exhorter heightens White's sense of calling beyond this level of service. His sermon to a licensing committee does not move them, however, nor do his second and third performances in subsequent months. He declares that he accepted these "trials" in "the spirit of Christian fortitude" until his fifth petition for a preaching license in the winter of 1807. Then, when the committee again tells him he ought to remain an exhorter he replies that he cannot be satisfied without "greater liberty than I now enjoy." When asked what sort of "liberty" he feels is denied him as an exhorter, he answers, "liberty to speak from a text." At this point a member of the committee whom White thought was a friend informs him that "It was the devil who was pushing me on to preach" (pp. 24-25). Although hurt by this impugning of his motives, White shows no further resentment of this sort of intimidation, nor does he speculate on its cause. Instead, he says that he put the matter into God's hands and, eventually, saw it work out to his vindicaion and triumph.

The life quest of George White for always "greater liberty" did not allow him to be satisfied with freedom from slavery or just the freedom to operate in the lowest echelon of white institutional life. He wanted "liberty to speak from" and interpret the white man's talismanic text, the Bible. Three years after he gained this liberty, he took the further and unprecedented liberty to speak from the text of his own life, composing and writing his own autobiography in 1810. The title page of the *Brief Account* also bears a quasi-talismanic inscription: *Written by Himself,* White was the first Afro-American slave narrator to author his autobiography autonomously, without literary intermediaries. Like many of the most important Afro-American autobiographies, White's is of the "oratorical" subgenre whose major theme is *"vocation,* the special summons that guided an entire life's work and now its story." *The Brief Account* compels special attention because it conceives of vocation in such archetypal terms for black American culture— "liberty," "speak," "text"—terms that apply prophetically to the black wordsmith in many subsequent guises, not only as a preacher but also as rhetor, writer, creator, and, as they all appeared to the eyes of fearful whites, destroyer. White's preaching and literary ambitions thus threatened institutional and racial hierarchies in two realms of speech action, for the role of black exhorter and slave narrator had been based on the idea that whites had to preside over a Negro's "liberty to speak from a text."

If George White was aware in some sense of the social or literary import of his struggle to become a preacher, he gives no inkling of this in the *Brief Account.* He approaches the reader of his autobiography in the same posture that he used in petitioning the white men who would decide his fitness to preach. As he recounts past humiliations and frustrations at the hands of his white "brethren," he imputes to them no ulterior or base motives. Taking the conventional spiritual autobiographer's approach to the evils of earthly experience, White refuses to complain of unfairness or injustice; it was all simply a series of "trials" of his faith that he had to undergo. By playing the role of persevering Christian stoic, White had won over the suspicious whites who heard him preach. In the same manner, he hoped perhaps to elicit his reader's admiration and trust. The persona that White adopted as both probationary black preacher and autobiographer was, therefore, clearly designed for the primary purpose of winning friends and influencing people. The aspiring ex-slave was a man of great will and determination who had no intention of allowing anyone to stand in the way of his goals in life. Yet his persona masks these features of his character along with any negative feelings he may have had about the way the white Methodists stymied him. Evidently, the black narrator was not ready in 1810 to take his white reader into his confidence concerning the institutional facts of race relations in the Methodist episcopacy. What we are left with is an autobiography that seems in some ways as unselfconscious and incomplete, perhaps as a result of self-censorship, as dictated slave narratives were because of the editing practices of whites. The *Brief Account* of George White suggests that even when the slave narrative gained the

"greater liberty" of autonomous authorship, it still needed a liberating sense of self and social consciousness if it was to do literary justice to the Afro-American mind and experience. Although the Afro-American was a complex bicultural entity, the first fifty years of the slave narrative tradition presented him one-dimensionally in accordance with the character typology of the Western tradition. The dynamics of the relationship of black self and white society were similarly explained in accordance with the simplistic plot formulae of popular white literary genres. In these ways the dialectic of the Afro-American's perspective on the self and the world, the "double-consciousness" and "twoness" that DuBois alludes to in *The Souls of Black Folk,* was channeled in one direction in the early slave narrative—in the direction of black acculturation into an appointed status in white society. In only one case do we find a slave narrator of this era genuinely exploring his bicultural perspective on himself and the world and speaking through a persona designed to come to terms with and express his "twoness." This case is that of Olaudah Equiano.

The most famous black autobiography of the late eighteenth and early nineteenth centuries was published in London in 1789 under the title, *The Interesting Narrative of the Life of Olaudah Equiano, or Gustavus Vassa, the African.* On the strength of its lasting popularity, Equiano's narrative has become a genuine classic, one that a number of literary historians have claimed for Afro-American letters. This is a debatable conclusion, since Equiano's autobiography reveals that he probably spent no more than a total of two years' time in America during his entire life. In 1756 at the age of eleven this son of Ibo nobility arrived in Virginia to work on a plantation, but he was purchased soon thereafter by a British naval officer who took him to England, Holland, and Canada during the next few yeas. In 1763 Equiano found himself in the British West Indies where he worked as an itinerant trader and witnessed many of the horrors of slavery as practiced in those islands. Purchase of his freedom in July, 1766, meant that he could set his course for England, "where my heart had always been." Equiano rarely visited America during the next twenty years, and then only during short stopovers in seaports. During the last decade of his life he devoted himself to anti-slavery work in England, where he was married in 1792 and died in 1797. It was the West Indian model of slavery, over which the British government presided, that spurred him to become the first black autobiographer in English to undertake a detailed analysis and powerful denunciation of slavery. However, as a British subject addressing a British audience, Equiano could identify himself with a far more outspoken anti-slavery movement in England than any black American could find in the new United States. Thus, the facts of Equiano's life and his attitude toward slavery offer grounds to argue that this man's literary compatriots were figures like Ignatius Sancho and Ottabah Cugoano, African-born Englishmen, not the Afro-Americans discussed thus far in this essay.

When read in light of the schematized, one-dimensional Afro-American slave narratives of the late eighteenth and early nineteenth centuries, Equiano's 400-page personal history seems the product of a very different literary mind, one acting on a principle of "greater liberty" far in advance of that which spurred George White forward. More than quadruple the size of any other slave narratives of its era, the *Interesting Narrative* takes special advantage of the idea common to evangelicals and romantics that all incidents of life become meaningful and valuable when viewed from an enlightened and redeemed perspective. With no editor to channel the reconstruction of his past through a single, monolithic point of view, Equiano was left free to explore his life through a bicultural perspective. He brought to the writing of autobiography the memory (improved by research) of an African pastoral way of life that he pictured as the moral superior of the West in every respect except religion. Yet Equiano was no facile nostalgist. He had spent almost thirty-five years being initiated into the wonders and terrors of the European Christian world order, and he could not blink the material and technological superiority of that civilization over the one from which he had been kidnapped. Unable to deny his affinities with either civilization, Equiano created an autobiographical persona that embraced both. Instead of writing a narrative testimonial to the blessings of acculturation, Equiano used his bicultural perspective to write an analysis of the *process* of acculturation, the process by which the African was divested, voluntarily or involuntarily, of his native cultural values and identity and assumed his new role in the white world order. This was an unprecedented undertaking for a slave narrator.

Equiano's identification with his African heritage is made plain in the first chapter of his autobiography. As he characterizes the purity, simplicity, harmony, and justice of the people of his village, he consistently unites himself with them through the use of the first person plural pronoun. His use of present tense in his sketch of tribal life implies that he is not reminiscing about a lost African Eden but is depicting a vital, continuing socio-cultural order. His people are not savages; Equiano cites Western scholars to back up his claim of a "strong analogy" between "the manners and customs of my countrymen and those of the Jews, before they reached the land of promise." To any Bible-studying English reader, this analogy would further identify Africans as God's chosen, but as yet unenlightened, people. A professing Christian, Equiano is one African who has reached "the land of promise" in a spiritual sense. The middle chapters of his narrative distinguish between the slaveocratic Americas and the metaphorical land of promise the African must find.

Equiano's initiation into the terror and outrage of slavery aboard the slaveship *African Snow* and in Barbadoes and Virginia is perhaps the most famous portion of his story. Masterfully, the narrator shifts from the perspective of the mature, cosmopolitan social commentator to the innocent eye of an African boy horrified by his first encounter with murderous white "spirits." At the end of his account of his fearful introduction to the New World, Equiano shifts his narrative tone once again, this time from shocked to outraged innocence, upbraiding his reader; "might not an African ask you—Learned you this from your God, who says unto you, Do unto all men as you would men should do unto you?" While the narrator illustrates his boyhood naiveté about the white man's technology—such as when he places a book to his ear in the hope that it will talk to him—Equiano endows that same innocence with moral superiority, once it has been reinforced by revealed truth such as the Golden Rule. Thus the narrator as "African" shows the reader as "nominal Christian" that the former has overtaken the latter in terms of moral progress and civilization. The major part of the narrative outlines the process by which the African progressed from viewing whites as marvellous and terrible spirits, to thinking them "men superior to us," to judging them finally as a materially advanced, but morally backsliding people. . . . Far from playing the one-dimensional role of African critic of English civilization, Equiano demonstrates to his reader that through his many successes in the West—as trader, adventurer, mariner, missionary, and government bureaucrat—he has be-

come qualified to speak and act as a genuine intermediary between Africa and England. Self-consciously Anglo-African, he concludes his narrative by proposing a solution to the slavery problem that would benefit both Africans and Englishmen. Put simply, he argues that the English should abolish slavery and the slave trade and pour their energies into "the rapid extension of manufactures" within the untapped "African markets." Instead of the morally unprofitable commerce in human beings, let the English devote themselves to their best self-interest, the cultivation of the African in his own land as a free trading partner. Like an English business promoter, Equiano marshalls statistics to prove, for instance:

> If the blacks were permitted to remain in their country, they would double themselves every fifteen years. In proportion to such increase will be the demand for manufactures. Cotton and indigo grow spontaneously in most part of Africa; a consideration this of no small consequence to the manufacturing towns of Great Britain. It opens a most immense, glorious, and happy prospect—the clothing, &c., of a continent ten thousand miles in circumference, and immensely rich in productions of every denomination in return for manufactures.

In such rapturous phrases, Equiano created a westernized Africa in his own image; one in which his black countrymen reached "the land of promise"—spiritual and material salvation—according to the English middle-class model, but without sacrificing their physical or moral autonomy along the way. The bicultural perspective lets Equiano stand at the end of his narrative with one foot in England and the other in Africa, hoping equally that his plan of reconciliation will civilize England morally and Africa materially. Such a reconciliation is possible, one realizes, because the narrative has demonstrated that the persona as Anglo-African has achieved it within himself.

Contrast, by way of conclusion, the achievements of the two African-born, American-trained slave narrators contemporary with Equiano. James Gronniosaw's and Venture Smith's stories are predicated on the assumption that balance and reconciliation between the self and "the world" are impossible. Both men learn that the world is of and for the white man; the black man must either give up or give into the world. Gronniosaw seeks spiritual refuge from the world and gives up hope of affecting it in any meaningful way. Venture Smith retreats from an unjust world into his own inviolable selfhood, similarly hopeless of a black man's self-affirming options in the white world. Neither man's narrative draws on his African origins for values and "terms for order" that could counterbalance the overwhelmingly negative view of black prospects in the white world that both narratives put forward. Both Gronniosaw and Smith present the Afro-American's choice as between the world and the self, between corruption and subjugation in the world or integrity (albeit an isolated and abused one) of the self apart from the world. Equiano, on the other hand, did not see his options in such diametric terms. By defining himself as a bicultural man, he found the means to imagine his relationship to the world in terms that did not require his becoming either totally co-opted by or totally alienated from the Western socio-cultural order. Perhaps because Equiano had grown up outside America's system of black conditioning and acculturation, he escaped the categorical, self-constricting thinking of men like Gronniosaw and Smith. The causes of Equiano's intellectual independence are much less easy to trace, however, than their effects; this man was able to create a persona independent of both extremes of his contemporaries' images of the westernized African. He was not the innocent African as sacrificial lamb

(Gronniosaw), nor was he the outraged African as shorn and dishonored lion (Smith). He was both—and he was neither. He was outsider and insider and somewhere in between, with the self-appointed freedom to move from pole to pole on the axis of African-Western concepts of self. It was this intellectual and aesthetic freedom of the imagination that was Equiano's special triumph as a slave narrator. Concomitantly, the special tragedy of the Afro-American slave narrative contemporaneous with Equiano's is that it could imagine no such fluid and expansive concept of the black self. Instead it remained grounded, until the mid-nineteenth century, in a world of fixed American opposites, of the saved and the damned, of the self and the world, and ultimately, of the white and the black. (pp. 15-22)

> *William L. Andrews, "The First Fifty Years of the Slave Narrative, 1760-1810," in* The Art of Slave Narrative: Original Essays in Criticism and Theory, *edited by John Sekora and Darwin T. Turner, Western Illinois University, 1982, pp. 6-24.*

THE ROLE OF THE SLAVE NARRATIVE IN THE DEVELOPMENT OF SUBSEQUENT BLACK AMERICAN LITERATURE

SIDONIE SMITH

[*Smith discusses how twentieth-century black American autobiographers utilized and adapted prominent themes of the nineteenth-century slave narrative. The critic stresses that while the earlier narratives focused on acquiring legal freedom and an identity, twentieth-century autobiographers address the problem of securing a valid place in a free but still hostile American society.*]

The slave narrative is apparently a narrative of success. But there is also another story implicit, if not actually explicit, within the slave narrative. That story is the story of failure to find real freedom and acceptance within American society, a disturbing sequel to the successful story of the radical break away from southern society. (p. 24)

Granted, the northern black was free of master and overseer, of auction block and arbitrary separation from family. He could even improve his social position in the North. But Solomon Northup's experience clearly dramatizes the illusory nature of the free sanctuary of the North. Born a free slave in New York, he was kidnapped by slavers and sold down South: thirteen years later he finally regained his freedom. Other ex-slaves lived with this lurking threat of recapture. Then in 1850, Congress passed the Fugitive Slave Bill, requiring northerners not only to refuse assistance to escaped slaves but to assist in returning them to the South.

Leon F. Litwack in his study *North of Slavery* discusses extensively the real limitations of black American freedom in the North—political, economic, educational, and religious—and concludes that white supremacy reigned in the North as it did in the South. The community of abolitionists that accepted the slave as an equal was a very small community indeed, and even it argued the feasibility of Negro membership in the movement. Such debates reflected the acknowledgment of differences between the races, so that it was often the abolitionists themselves who perpetuated the projective stereotypes of the Negro. Moreover, practical considerations often clashed with the individual ex-slave's needs for self-improvement, a di-

lemma Douglass dramatizes when he discusses his speaking efforts:

> It was impossible for me to repeat the same old story month after month, and to keep my interest in it. . . . "Tell your story, Frederick," would whisper my then revered friend, William Lloyd Garrison, as I stepped upon the platform. I could not always obey, for I was now reading and thinking. New views of the subject were presented to my mind. It did not entirely satisfy me to *narrate* wrongs; I felt like *denouncing* them. I could not always curb my moral indignation for the perpetrators of slave-holding villainy, long enough for a circumstantial statement of the facts which I felt almost everyone must know. Besides I was growing, and needed room. "People won't believe you ever was a slave, Frederick, if you keep on this way," said Friend Foster.

Even in the North, even in the abolitionist community, the black American met opposition to his quest after self-realization.

And so the ex-slave moved on again. Expatriation became the answer for some. After finding that agents were in Boston to return him South, William Wells Brown fled to England. So did William and Ellen Craft. From England, the Crafts concluded their account with the following indictment: "In short, it is well known in England, if not all over the world, that the Americans, as a people, are notoriously mean and cruel towards all colored persons, whether they are bond or free." (pp. 25-6)

During slavery, the journey toward freedom was a geographical one: change of place was enough. Then when the Civil War brought an end to slavery, "everyplace" in America was to become a symbolic North. Theoretically a free American, the black was about to benefit from all the privileges of that identity; former dreams were to become realities. A change of place would no longer be necessary. For a while, the exhilaration of Reconstruction prolonged the exuberance of the new order; but, ominously, the promise of that new order gave way before the repressive measures of the late nineteenth century. Patterns of disenfranchisement, segregation, and racial subordination became the new way of life: the slave system was merely replaced with the race system. Thus, as the experience of the escaped slave prophesied, freedom was a chimera. The black American, though he was no longer three-fifths of a human being, was only three-fifths of a citizen. Consequently, he found himself plagued by a dual identity and dual reality—the promised reality of full American citizenship and the daily reality of the status of a Negro that belied that promise. The socially determined identity that had plagued him as a slave, imprisoning him in the stereotypes of white America, prevailed, condemning him to invisibility: "One was never told, 'You are a man.' It was always, 'You are a Negro,'" remembers J. Saunders Redding. Still a bastard in his own country, the black continued his quest for freedom; only now it became much more complex, much more ambiguous.

Thus the autobiography of the black American has continued to be a form of slave narrative. The two patterns inherent in the slave narrative, however, tend to separate. On the one hand, there is the story of a successful *break into* the community, a reenactment of America's secular drama of selfhood. This autobiographical tradition reflects, through the story of a social calling, the slave narrative's focus on the achievement of place within northern society. On the other hand, there is the story of the *break away* from the imprisoning community, a reenactment of the sacred quest for selfhood. Hence, this tradition reflects more the initial direction of the slave narrative and the later illusory nature of the achievement of freedom.

In the secular pattern, the autobiographer reviews the events of his life from the vantage point of achieved success, imposing upon them a pattern of movement toward fame: having legitimized himself by becoming a respected member of society— as entertainer, athlete, artist, social leader, political figure— he has achieved a viable form of freedom. Precisely because the autobiographer considers this fulfillment a result of his social calling, he focuses on the achievements of his public self, gleaning the chaotic past experience of his life for those significant moments relevant to his choice of and success in that calling, shaping them into a work whose purpose is to make a statement about how his life led to such an achievement of "place" within society. He may choose several points at which to end: the moment at which he chose his calling or, more likely, the moment of a major success that was particularly meaningful to him as a culmination of his earlier efforts.

Often underlying this structural pattern in American autobiography is the myth of the Horatio Alger hero, a manifestation of the secularization of puritanism first embodied in Benjamin Franklin's *Autobiography*. From a lowly beginning on the fringes of society, the hard-working and virtuous individual rises slowly yet steadily to success and social prominence: self-realization is fulfilled by social arrival. In this traditional myth of American identity, the individual's relationship to society is fluid, and his possibilities are unlimited. For the black American, this pattern becomes especially expressive and often painfully ironic since he begins on the furthest fringe of the social scale (the fluidity of his movement is problematic) and the odds against him are greater (his unlimited possibilities are in fact narrowly limited). In reenacting the successful struggle with his background and his society, he reinforces and reaffirms the "American" side of his dual identity. Freedom becomes synonymous with the ability to participate in the American myth of democratic possibility.

Booker T. Washington was probably the first well-known black Horatio Alger. . . . After achieving such stature and power in American society, Washington was urged by others to write his autobiography. The popularity of *Up From Slavery*, which became a best seller soon after publication, indicated how inspiring his rise to fame had been. (pp. 28-31)

Washington's *Up From Slavery* is central to a discussion of black American autobiography in two ways. First, since Washington is a black Horatio Alger, his narrative is representative of the pattern of autobiography that finds its public and private motivations in the individual's need to reaffirm his successful achievement of place in American society and its corollary sense of freedom. Such autobiographies are narratives of social callings, the stories of public personalities—athletes, entertainers, teachers, political leaders. Their titles alone suggest the meanings of the pattern imposed by the narrators. A large number name the personality whose life narrative is being told: *Lena* (Lena Horne), *The Joe Louis Story, The Archie Moore Story, The Raw Pearl* (Pearl Bailey). That the name has become publicly respected signals success: the name itself symbolizes a viable form of freedom. Another group of titles name the sphere in which public fame has been won: *The Fastest Bicycle Rider in the World* (Marshall W. "Major" Taylor), *Black Wings* (Lieutenant William J. Powell), *Father of the Blues* (W.C. Handy), *Born to Play Ball* (Willie Mays), *Breakthrough to the Big League* (Jackie Robinson). A third group suggests the direction of the personal journey—up, out, away, from the onus of racial handicap: *Movin' On Up* (Mahalia Jackson), *I Always Wanted to Be Somebody* (Althea Gibson), *Victory Over Myself* (Floyd Patterson), *Bursting Bonds* (William Pickens), and *Up From Slavery* itself.

There is, of course, a risk in forcing all these titles, and autobiographies, together as representative of a structural pattern in black American autobiography. In doing so, I do not mean to minimize the importance of the individual achievements nor to question the centrality of this tradition in the black experience. Like the slave narrators before them, these autobiographers have struggled for their freedom against overwhelming odds. Writing about that struggle is certainly a way of assessing the nature and cost of success as well as a way of reaffirming it. These autobiographers too enact a "rite of coherence" upon the chaos of their lives. Their autobiographies are thus characterized by the prototypal motifs already elaborated in the first chapter, for example, the quest after wholeness and authenticity, the moments of disillusionment. Moreover, like the slave narrators before them, these autobiographers, rebels in their own way, are making public and political statements about the ability of the black American to achieve greatness. They are cultural heroes and heroines whose narratives are examples of the possibility of success within American society.

But a cruel irony lies at the center of Washington's "success story." In the end, he achieved his powerful place only through the acrobatics of the mask of Christian invisibility. And so his life story implies the second major pattern in black autobiography, the bleaker vision, which focuses on the self's inability to achieve a "place" in American society. Imprisoned within either black or white society or both, the individual is shackled to the chains of a socially imposed identity. Hence, his life is characterized by profound loneliness and alienation from society or possibly even from self. Finally, unwilling to wear the necessary mask, he becomes a rebel who, like the slave narrator in his first avatar as slave, breaks defiantly with society and its exacting price of self-sacrifice, to search once again for the freedom of authenticity. The conclusion of this second pattern of autobiography is characterized by a symbolic death and/or rebirth—perhaps the geographical flight from an old way of life, or disillusionment, or acceptance and thus transcendence of past experience, or an actual rebirth into a new identity. (pp. 45-8)

The slave narratives define three dominant responses of the black slave to his environment that were to continue after slavery was officially abolished—conciliation, apparent acquiescence facilitated by conscious masking, and rebellion. The young protagonist of Richard Wright's *Black Boy,* growing up in the South in the first decades of the twentieth century, where disenfranchisement, segregation, and racial subordination formed the bases for continued existence, must choose among these alternatives. His impulse is to rebel openly, but to do so is to risk death. Yet he recognizes an even greater risk than death: to accept—or even appear to accept—the self-denial the South demanded of him was to invite psychological suicide. Richard, who finds it impossible to accept or to mask his rebellion against this fate, ultimately chooses open rebellion. Thus, for Wright the autobiographer, warfare—between his essential self and his environment—becomes the basic metaphor for depicting his struggle from childhood innocence to self-awareness.

Although the autobiographies of both Washington and Wright are narratives about southern black American experience, the patterns imposed upon that experience form sharply contrasting portraits of self-expression. Washington traces the journey of the self from alienation into social acceptance and prominence within southern society: Wright traces the movement of the self further and further into alienation from society, black and white, until flight to the North becomes imperative. If Washington is representative of the self finding expression through the mask of Christian love, Wright is the opposite, refusing any mask and thereby finding self-expression only through warfare and violence. If Washington finds self-fulfillment through ostensibly sacrificing his own individual concerns for the sake of the community, Wright defies violently the community that refuses to allow his self-assertion. The violence of the autobiography reflects the violence of the confrontation between the self seeking autonomy and the society that refuses to allow it. Whereas Washington reflects the slave narrator's desire for a future of personal and social betterment, Wright reflects the slave's needs for rebellion. Wright redirects our attention away from hope back toward the violent confrontations so prominent in the slave narrative.

The theme of violent self-expression, in which manhood is predicated on resistance to society and in which the individual's violent self is a product of violence directed to that self by society, is prominent in the slave narrative. Douglass, as we have observed, narrates the incident that became the turning point of his life, the moment in which he chose to fight back rather than suffer degradation at the hands of the overseer Covey. This moment of violent self-assertion precipitated a strong sense of manliness. He was, however, more fortunate than many others: he lived to write about it.

[Ralph] Ellison's *Invisible Man* is itself a kind of critical exploration of the patterns of selfhood in black American autobiography, a fictional slave narrative that recapitulates the various avatars of the black self in his quest after a free identity up to the 1940s and presages the complex developments in black autobiography after that. As a prospective Booker T. Washington, the naive protagonist begins his quest for identity with a scholarship to "Tuskegee." Washington . . . is reincarnated as Dr. Bledsoe, the powerful southern educator who cultivates the mask of humility in order to manipulate others, black and white. Because the naive youth has threatened the equilibrium of Bledsoe's power structure, he is sent running North, a movement that recalls the flight of Richard Wright. Both men run North with the hope of future betterment; Richard, however, unlike Ellison's naif who is coerced into running, does so because he can no longer sacrifice his authentic impulses to the social identity demanded of him. In fact, Richard is no naif; he is only too self-conscious of his imprisoning role. Violence, characteristic of Richard's confrontations with society, erupts again and again in *Invisible Man*, here as in, *Black Boy*, pitting black against black—the boxing match, the Golden Day mayhem, the paint factory explosion, the finally the riot. The intense pressure of the stereotype is immitigable. The resultant destruction, abetted by both black and white society, is of the authentic self: the invisible man is, ultimately, only a black sambo doll controlled by society's strings. For although Ellison's youthful protagonist does realize his dream of becoming another leader when he joins the Brotherhood, he, unlike Dr. Bledsoe who controls in his leadership, is a pawn in the Brotherhood's game of power.

The youth's belief in his visibility is the illusion that is finally and violently destroyed during the destruction of the riot. This disillusion is precisely what befalls Langston Hughes [in his first autobiography, *The Big Sea*,] when he finds that he has merely been a reflection of his white patron's fantasies of the black poet. Moreover, the invisible man's febrile narrative is redolent of that "nausea" that results from Hughes' sudden recognition of invisibility, his physical reaction mirroring his spiritual recoil. The underground sojourn is a figurative image of Hughes' nervous breakdown, a state from which he can review his experience and find some kind of release in the mere recognition of his lack of freedom. The ex-slave could escape this slavery, but the contemporary slave can escape it perhaps only by going underground and escaping American society altogether in a life of expatriation.

And yet, there is another possibility—embodied within Ellison's characterization of Ras the Exhorter, the black nationalist. Although the invisibile man (and Ellison himself) ultimately characterizes Ras as a destructive agent (Ras the Destroyer) who, like Dr. Bledsoe and Lucius Brockway, fights in the end not against the white community but against other blacks, he gives Ras some of the most compelling speeches in the novel. By the time Ellison wrote, the black nationalist movement, manifested in various forms, had already had a long history, stretching back into the nineteenth century and the early twentieth with Marcus Garvey's Back-to-Africa movement. Then in the late 1950s and early 1960s it exploded upon the American scene as the Black Muslim movement. Espousing black pride and solidarity, black nationalism calls for separation from, not assimilation into, the corrupt white community. The authentic black self unites with other black selves to form a new community led by the "black" leader, a militant attacker who rejects the long tradition of emasculated leadership. This is a new and significantly changed version of the black man's traditional attempt to find authentic selfhood in some social role. If Booker T. Washington's *Up From Slavery* chronicles an earlier phase of the black leader's drama of selfhood, *The Autobiography of Malcolm X* chronicles its recent phase, though this phase too has its predecessors in Frederick Douglass' *My Bondage and My Freedom* and W.E.B DuBois' *Dusk of Dawn*.

Ellison's insights in this case are prophetic even though he personally has little sympathy for *any kind* of public identity. Ras's name is symbolic of his public identity as a black nationalist leader; he is an "exhorter" spewing forth his wrath upon the white man. Malcolm Little's "X" is similarly symbolic of his vision of his public identity in American society, and he, like Ras, spews forth wrath. This "X" is not, however, the only name he bears in his autobiography. His first identity is Malcolm Little, alias "nigger," his final, El Hajj Malik El-Shabazz. The story of these names is the story of his life, for here as elsewhere black autobiography focuses on the drama of names and naming. (pp. 79-81)

"Run!"

"Where?"

The first exclamation of Claude Brown's *Manchild in the Promised Land* echoes the slave narrative of more than a century ago. The second summarizes in one word the dilemma that has characterized the contemporary black self's search for the freedom of an authentic identity. William Wells Brown and his contemporaries never had to ask "Where?" when they ran: they knew a "free" self lay to the North. But after emancipation, American society continued to imprison the black in a social identity that forbade legitimate self-assertion. In response, the black self could, like Booker T. Washington, choose to wear a mask and play the role that would insure his acceptance and even prominence, or he could, like Wright and others of the migrant generation—including Claude Brown's own parents—refuse to be enslaved by a social mask and again journey northward to the "promised land" as the slave had earlier.

Because of the great and continuing black migration, the North continued to function as a potential symbol of freedom. However, as the experiences of Langston Hughes, Malcolm X, Horace Cayton, and Brown's parents dramatize, this generation was ultimately a disillusioned one. But what of the next? In his prologue, Brown describes the difference between the generation of migrators and their children. Whereas the older one is disillusioned, the younger is desperate: "To add to their misery, they had little hope of deliverance. For where does one run to when he's already in the promised land?"

Because geographical escape is no longer a viable possibility, the black self is thrown back on its own resources and forced to discover an interior escape route from imprisonment to freedom. Malcolm X and Eldridge Cleaver freed themselves by being reborn into full black manhood, Maya Angelou into full black womanhood. Moreover, Malcolm X and Cleaver channel that recovered manhood into a social identity within the black community. Cayton, on the other hand, discovered the negative possibilities of such a social identity: immersion in a public role ultimately returned him to the chains of nonidentity. However, another possibility emerges: both Cayton and Cleaver recognize the positive possibilities for the self's escape through the act of writing itself. Freedom comes through artistic confrontation. Claude Brown's autobiography embodies this very possibility. . . . (pp. 155-56)

Sidonie Smith, in her Where I'm Bound: Patterns of Slavery and Freedom in Black American Autobiography, *Greenwood Press, 1974, 194 p.*

CHARLES T. DAVIS AND HENRY LOUIS GATES, JR.

[*In the following excerpt from Gates and Davis's introduction to their* The Slave's Narrative, *an anthology of commentary on the genre, they briefly describe the decline of interest in the slave narrative for several decades after the Civil War. In addition, the critics explore the significance of the nineteenth-century slave narrative to subsequent black American literature, using the opposing opinions of Arna Bontemps and Ralph Ellison as the center of the discussion.*]

Once thought to be only a kind of ephemeral, politically motivated writing, the slave narrative continues to command the attention of scholars, a full century after slavery was abolished. Whereas these narratives initially were the province of historians and then literary critics, now they are of importance to anthropologists and folklorists, historians of art and musicologists, sociologists and political scientists, linguists and psychologists, philosophers and legal historians, and economists and theologians. (p. xiv)

It is especially significant that the slave narrative has become the basis of both slave historiography, particularly with Blassingame's 1972 publication of his re-creation of the fabric and texture of life in the slave quarters [*The Slave Community* (see Additional Bibliography)], and of Afro-American literary history, with John Herbert Nelson in 1926 [see Additional Bibliography] and Vernon Loggins in 1931 arguing for the narrative's central role not only in the birth and shape of Afro-American fictional narrative forms, but also in the subsequent developments of black autobiography. In 1966, Arna Bontemps

put the matter well in a statement about black literary ancestry that has influenced Afro-American literary history ever since.

From the narrative came the spirit and vitality and the angle of vision responsible for the most effective prose writing by black American writers from Williams Wells Brown to Charles W. Chesnutt, from W. E. B. Dubois to Richard Wright, Ralph Ellison and James Baldwin. . . . [see Additional Bibliography].

Indeed, from 1760 to the present, almost *half* of the Afro-American literary tradition was created when its authors and their black readers were either slaves or former slaves. Have there ever been more curious origins of a literary tradition? The slave narrative arose as a response to and refutation of claims that blacks *could* not write. (pp. xiv-xv)

Since the status of the slave narrative as history and literature seems self-evident to us, how could the narratives have been "lost" to us for such a dark period, when the apparent "silence" of the slave was drawn upon by a host of commentators as "evidence" of either the total brutal environment of slavery or else of an inherent mental deficiency within the slave? After all, slave narratives were extraordinarily popular texts. Arna Bontemps found their closest analogue in this century to be the Western. I think rather the genre of detective fiction is a more apt formal analogue, since the plots of all the slave narratives turn upon the resolution of a mystery, already resolved in fact by the first-person "detective" narrator. Both forms, moreover, share conventions of realism (verisimilitude), despite the fact that the slave narratives also shared contradictory characteristics with the sentimental novel (florid asides, strident polemics, the melodramatic imagination). (p. xv)

We can achieve an idea of the role that the words of ex-slaves were able to play in the fight against slavery by considering the following comments published between 1845 and 1855. Lucius C. Matlock, in 1845 wrote that

Naturally and necessarily, the enemy of literature, [American slavery] has become the prolific theme of much that is profound in argument, sublime in poetry, and thrilling in narrative. From the soil of slavery itself have sprung forth some of the most brilliant productions, whose logical levers will ultimately upheave and overthrow the system. . . . Startling incidents authenticated, far excelling fiction in their touching pathos, from the pen of self-emancipated slaves, do now exhibit slavery in such revolting aspects, as to secure the execrations of all good men and become a monument more enduring than marble, in testimony strong as sacred writ against it.

In that same year, Wendell Phillips wrote that

I am glad the time has come when the "lions write history." We have been left long enough to gather the character of slaves from the involuntary evidence of the masters. One might, indeed, rest sufficiently satisfied with what, it is evident, must be, in general, the results of such a relation without seeking further to find whether they have followed in every instance.

Ten years later, in a review of Douglass's second slave narrative, *Putnam's Monthly* said that

Our English literature has recorded many an example of genius struggling against adversity,—of the poor Ferguson, for instance, making himself an astronomer, of Burns becoming a poet, of Hugh Miller finding his geology in a stone quarry, and a thousand similar cases—yet none of these are so impressive as the case of solitary slave, in a remote district, surrounded by none but enemies, conceiving the project of his escape, teaching himself to read and write to facilitate it, accomplishing it at last, and subsequently raising himself to a leadership in a great movement on behalf of his brethren.

The curious and direct relation between reading and writing, on one hand, and legal freedom, on the other, was evident to both the slave narrators and to their reviewers. (pp. xvi-xvii)

How could these narratives with such broad readership simply "disappear" for sixty years? One reason was suggested, prophetically, by Frederick Douglass in an editorial he printed in 1856, "Opposing slavery and hating its victims has come to be a very common form of abolitionism." Once legal slavery disappeared, a more subtle form of subjugation, as we know, displaced it in a relation of *de facto* to *de jure*. The concomitant economic, political, and social conspiracy, between 1876 and 1915, most certainly had profound literary ramifications. Within American society, the literary presence of the speaking black subject was replaced by the deafening silence of his absence; essentially as an object, a figure in the fictions of nonblacks, did the black then "exist" in mainstream literature. Blacks, of course, continued to publish poetry, fiction, autobiographies, essays, and letters between 1865 and the turn of the century, but primarily in black periodicals. With the end of slavery, however, the black seems to have lost his great, unique theme until Jim Crow racism and segregation recreated it. The stilling of the black "voice" assumed myriad forms, not the least distressing of which was the effective destruction of black arts and letters existing before 1865. Only with great devotion and diligence have we even begun to restore the fragments of the lost records of the Afro-American mind. And who can estimate what these losses have cost the development of literature and art?

Since the New Negro Renaissance, literary scholars have been wrestling with the question of the influence of the slave narratives on the form of subsequent Afro-American literary works. That the matter is still alive is perhaps best illustrated by the divergent opinions on this question expressed by Ralph Ellison and Arna Bontemps, two Afro-American creative writers and critics whose works are central to the Afro-American canon.

On the one hand, in a 1978 interview with Ishmael Reed, Steve Cannon, and Quincy Troupe, published in *Y'Bird*, Ralph Ellison responded at length to Cannon's question about certain structural similarities between *Invisible Man* and the slave narratives. Ellison's considered response bears repeating:

> Cannon: [*Invisible Man*] reads very much like a slave narrative, doesn't it? Would you say you've borrowed the techniques?

> Ellison: No, that's coincidental. And, frankly, I think too much has been made of the slave narrative, as an influence on contemporary writing. Experience tends to mold itself into certain repetitive patterns, and one of the reasons we exchange experiences is in order to discover the repetitions and coincidences which amount to a common group experience. We tell ourselves our individual stories so as to become aware of our *general* story. I wouldn't have had to read a single slave narrative in order to create the narrative pattern of *Invisible Man*. It emerges from experience and from my own sense of literary form, out of my sense of experience as shaped by history and my familiarity with literature.

Because the Afro-American historical experience incorporates patterns of northern and western migration, Ellison continues,

... the movement from South to North became a basic pattern for my novel. The pattern of movement and the obstacles encountered are so basic to Afro-American experience (and to my own, since my mother took me North briefly during the Twenties, and I came North again in '36), that I had no need of slave narratives to grasp either its significance or its potential for organizing a fictional narrative. I would have used the same device if I had been writing an autobiography.

Invisible Man, of course, is a fictional autobiography of a nameless protagonist, which both embodies and transcends almost two centuries of repeated black narrative strategies. As Robert B. Stepto and James Olney have argued in fine detail [see excerpts above], these strategies were first employed in the slave narrative. Nevertheless, Ellison's perceptive claim—that this pattern of South-to-North migration is "so basic to Afro-American experience"—raises as many questions as it resolves, precisely because historical experience and textual experience reinforce each other in a dialectical relationship so complex that the identification of origins is, at best, rendered problematic.

This is not to say that the Afro-American historical experience can be characterized by vertical migration (or "elevation," the nineteenth-century keyword that "migration" supplanted), simply because this recurs as one of the black textual tradition's repeating tropes. Rather, Olney and Stepto argue that a crucial feature of the structure of *Invisible Man* placed it, at its publication in 1952, at the "end" of a narrative tradition of figuration that had commenced in English in 1760 with Briton Hammon's slave narrative. For the literary critic, this textual fact is what is important to literary history. That Ellison would have "used the same device if I had been writing an autobiography," seems to strengthen the critic's argument, since their histories of narrative ignore certain arbitrary distinctions between "fiction" and "non-fiction." Ellison's final word on the subject inserts "consciousness" as a substitute for intention, which is one reason critics qualify any author's account of their own origins. Ellison concludes:

> All this is not to put down the slave narrative, but to say that it did not influence my novel as a *conscious* functional form. And, don't forget, the main source of any novel is other *novels*; these constitute the culture of the form, and my loyalty to our group does nothing to change that; it's a cultural, literary reality. (Emphasis added)

The key sentence in this exchange is Ellison's observation that "the pattern of movement and the obstacles encountered are so basic to Afro-American experience." It is precisely this pattern of movement that the art of the slave's narrative willed to the black textual tradition, making it possible both for us to transcend the chaos of individual memory, since these collective texts constitute the beginnings of the Afro-American canon, and for the trope itself to inform black novels, which emerged in the nineteenth-century directly from the slave narrative. Arna Bontemps makes this argument for the key place of the narrative in Afro-American literary history: that both fictional and autobiographical forms, as conflated in James Williams' *Narrative* (1836), Harriet Wilson's *Our Nig* (1859), in Richard Wright's *Black Boy* (1945), and in *Invisible Man*, emerge from the ex-slave's tale. Bontemps would concur with Burton's dictum from *The Anatomy of Melancholy* "Our style betrays us." As Bontemps stated in 1966:

> *Consciously* or *unconsciously*, all of [the major black writers] reveal in their writing a debt to the narratives,

a debt that stands in marked contrast to the relatively smaller obligations they owe the more recognized arbiters of fiction or autobiography [see Additional Bibliography]. (Emphasis added)

Ellison reverses Bontemps' claim about the narratives, detail by detail. Perhaps anticipating an Ellisonian revision of this formal relationship between black fictional and non-fictional forms, Bontemps implies that the structural patterns implicit to the slave narrative were simultaneously formal *and* cultural; and, whereas relations of content are readily imitated, borrowed, or derived, relations of form are not only implicitly ideological, but also shared, or "collective," despite the intention or conscious desires of an author. "If not all of them had read slave narratives," Bontemps continues, "they had heard them by word of mouth or read or listened to accounts these had inspired. Thus, when they put pen to paper, what came to light, like emerging words written in invisible ink, were their own versions of bondage and freedom." Bontemps argues that the evidence is to be found in these texts themselves. Where Ellison, curiously, places a priority upon "experience," Bontemps maintains that we know "experience" through our canonical texts, which, taken together, will to the tradition what we might think of as received *textual experience*.

If Bontemps and Ellison serve as convenient emblems of two modes of thinking about the narrative's role in Afro-American literary history, then Theodore Parker's reflections upon the status of American literature at mid-point in the nineteenth century and his opinions of the slave narrative, help us to understand the milieu in which these narratives were written, published, and distributed. Parker was a theologian, a Unitarian clergyman, and a publicist for ideas, whom Perry Miller described as "the man who next only to Emerson . . . was to give shape and meaning to the Transcendental movement in America." In a speech on "The Mercantile Classes" delivered in 1846, Parker laments the sad state of "American" letters:

> Literature, science, and art are mainly in [poor men's] hands, yet are controlled by the prevalent spirit of the nation. . . . In England, the national literature favors the church, the crown, the nobility, the prevailing class. Another literature is rising, but is not yet national, still less canonized. We have no American literature which is permanent. Our scholarly books are only an imitation of a foreign type; they do not reflect our morals, manners, politics, or religion, not even our rivers, mountains, sky. They have not the smell of our ground in their breath.

Parker, to say the least, was not especially pleased with American letters and their identity with the English tradition. Did Parker find any evidence of a truly American discourse?

> The real American literature is found only in newspapers and speeches, perhaps in some novel, hot, passionate, but poor and extemporaneous. That is our national literature. Does that favor man—represent man? Certainly not. All is the reflection of this most powerful class. The truths that are told are for them, and the lies. Therein the prevailing sentiment is getting into the form of thoughts.

Parker's analysis, of course, is "proto-Marxian," embodying as it does the reflection theory of base and superstructure. It is the occasional literature, "poor and extemporaneous," wherein "American" literature dwells.

Three years later, in his major oration on "The American Scholar," Parker at last found an entirely original genre of American Literature:

Yet, there is one portion of our permanent literature, if literature it may be called, which is wholly indigenous and original. The lives of the early martyrs and confessors are purely Christian, so are the legends of saints and other pious men; there was nothing like this in the Hebrew or heathen literature, cause and occasion were alike wanting for it. So we have one series of literary productions that could be written by none but Americans, and only here; I mean the Lives of Fugitive Slaves. But as these are not the work of the men of superior culture they hardly help to pay the scholar's debt. Yet all the original romance of Americans is in them, not in the white man's novel.

Parker was right about the originality, the peculiarly *American* quality, of the slave narratives. But he was wrong about their inherent inability to "pay the scholar's debt"; . . . scholars had only to learn to *read* the narratives for their debt to be paid in full, indeed many times over. As Charles Sumner said in 1852, the fugitive slaves and their narratives "are among the heroes of our age. Romance has no storms of more thrilling interest than theirs. Classical antiquity has preserved no examples of adventurous trial more worthy of renown." Parker's and Sumner's views reveal that the popularity of the narratives in antebellum America most certainly did not reflect any sort of common critical agreement about their nature and status as art. (pp. xvii–xxii)

The slave narrative represents the attempts of blacks to *write themselves into being*. What a curious idea: through the mastery of formal Western languages, the presupposition went, a black person could become a human being by an act of self-creation through the mastery of language. Accused of having no collective history by Hegel in 1813, blacks responded by publishing hundreds of individual histories. As Ellison defined this relationship of the particular to the general, to Steve Cannon, "We tell ourselves our individual stories so as to become aware of our *general* story." (p. xxiii)

[The] narratives of ex-slaves are, for the literary critic, the very generic foundation which most subsequent Afro-American fictional and non-fictional narrative forms extended, refigured, and troped. This is as true of Booker T. Washington's *Up from Slavery* and of *The Autobiography of Malcolm X* as it is of Zora Neale Hurston's *Their Eyes Were Watching God*, Richard Wright's *Black Boy*, and Ralph Ellison's *Invisible Man*. Ishmael Reed's novel, *Flight to Canada*, a formal parody or a structural signification upon the conventions of the slave narrative, makes this implicit literary relationship apparent. As many [literary critics] . . . argue, the Afro-American literary tradition, and especially its canonical texts, rests on the framework built, by fits and starts and for essentially polemical intentions, by the first-person narratives of black ex-slaves. (p. xxxiii)

Charles T. Davis and Henry Louis Gates, Jr., "Introduction: The Language of Slavery," in The Slave's Narrative, *edited by Charles T. Davis and Henry Louis Gates, Jr., Oxford University Press, 1985, pp. xi–xxxiv.*

ADDITIONAL BIBLIOGRAPHY

PRIMARY SOURCES

Asher, Jeremiah. *Incidents in the Life of the Rev. J. Asher.* 1850. Reprint. Freeport, N.Y.: Books for Libraries Press, 1971, 80 p.

Ball, Charles. *Slavery in the United States: A Narrative of the Life and Adventures of Charles Ball, a Black Man.* 1836. Reprint. St. Clair Shores, Mich.: Scholarly Press, 1970, 400 p.

————. *Fifty Years in Chains; or, The Life of an American Slave.* 1859. Reprint. St. Clair Shores, Mich.: Scholarly Press, 1970, 430 p.

Bibb, Henry. *Narrative of the Life and Adventures of Henry Bibb, an American Slave.* 1849. Reprint. Salem, N.H.: Ayer Company Publishers, 1969, 204 p.

Blassingame, John W., ed. *Slave Testimony: Two Centuries of Letters, Speeches, Interviews, and Autobiographies.* Baton Rouge: Louisiana State University Press, 1977, 777 p.

Bontemps, Arna, ed. *Five Black Lives: The Autobiographies of Venture Smith, James Mars, William Grimes, the Rev. G. W. Offley, and James L. Smith.* Middletown, Conn.: Wesleyan University Press, 1971, 240 p.

Brent, Linda [pseudonym of Harriet B. Jacobs]. *Incidents in the Life of a Slave Girl.* Edited by Lydia Maria Child. 1861. Reprint. New York: Harcourt Brace Jovanovich, 1973, 210 p.

Brown, William Wells. *Narrative of William Wells Brown, a Fugitive Slave.* 1847. Reprint. New York: Johnson Reprint Corporation, 1970, 110 p.

Douglass, Frederick. *The Narrative and Selected Writings.* New York: Random House, 1983, 448 p.

————. *Life and Times of Frederick Douglass.* Secaucus, N.J.: Stuart Lyle, 1984, 514 p.

————. *My Bondage and My Freedom.* Edited by William L. Andrews. Urbana: University of Illinois Press, 1988, 496 p.

Drew, Benjamin. *North-Side View of Slavery: The Refugee; or, The Narratives of Fugitive Slaves in Canada.* 1856. Reprint. New York: Johnson Reprint Corporation, 1968, 387 p.

Henson, Josiah. *Father Henson's Story of His Own Life.* New York: Irvington, 1986, 224 p.

Northup, Solomon. *Twelve Years as a Slave.* Edited by Sue Eakin and Joseph Logsdon. Library of Southern Civilization, no. 1. Baton Rouge: Louisiana State University Press, 1968, 274 p.

Pennington, James W. *Fugitive Blacksmith.* 1850. Reprint. Westport, Conn.: Negro Universities Press, 1971, 84 p.

Truth, Sojourner. *Narrative of Sojourner Truth.* 1878. Reprint. New York: Arno Press, 1968, 320 p.

Ward, Samuel Ringgold. *Autobiography of a Fugitive Negro.* 1855. Reprint. New York: Arno Press, 1968, 412 p.

Washington, Booker T. *Up from Slavery.* New York: Penguin, 1986, 336 p.

Wilson, Harriet E. *Our Nig: Sketches from the Life of a Free Black.* Edited by Henry L. Gates. New York: Random House, 1983, 168 p.

SECONDARY SOURCES

Andrews, William L. *To Tell a Free Story: The First Century of Afro-American Autobiography, 1760-1865.* Urbana: University of Illinois Press, 1986, 353 p.
    Explores the theme of freedom in slave narratives and measures the increasing freedom with which narrators told their stories in the first 100 years of the genre's existence.

Bailey, David Thomas. "A Divided Prism: Two Sources of Black Testimony on Slavery." *The Journal of Southern History* XLVI, No. 3 (August 1980): 381-404.
    Considers the historical reliability of two sources of slave testimony: book-length narratives and autobiographies and twentieth-century interviews.

Baker, Houston A., Jr. "Terms for Order: Acculturation, Meaning, and the Early Record of the Journey" and "Autobiographical Acts and the Voice of the Southern Slave." In his *The Journey Back: Issues in Black Literature and Criticism,* pp. 1-26, pp. 27-52. Chicago: University of Chicago Press, 1980.
    Examines, respectively, the eighteenth-century slave narrative and the antebellum slave narrative in relation to the white tradition of autobiography.

————. "Figurations for a New American Literary History: Archaeology, Ideology, and Afro-American Discourse." In his *Blues, Ideology, and Afro-American Literature: A Vernacular Theory,* pp. 15-63. Chicago: University of Chicago Press, 1984.
    Contains a discussion of the narratives of Olaudah Equiano and Frederick Douglass as exemplary instances of literary works that established a basis for Afro-American discourse.

Banes, Ruth A. "Antebellum Slave Narratives as Social History: Self and Community in the Struggle against Slavery." *Journal of American Culture* 5, No. 2 (Summer 1982): 62-70.
    Details how slave narrators adapted such conventions of eighteenth-century autobiography as "the exemplary self" and the parable form to create a mode of social criticism in their narratives.

Bayliss, John F. Introduction to *Black Slave Narratives,* edited by John F. Bayliss, pp. 7-21. New York: The Macmillan Co., 1970.
    An overview of slave narratives offering several approaches to the study of the genre.

Blassingame, John W. *The Slave Community: Plantation Life in the Antebellum South.* New York: Oxford University Press, 1972, 262 p.
    A "composite portrait" of nineteenth-century southern slave life. Blassingame's was one of the first studies to make extensive use of the accounts of slaves, and his book includes a survey of various slave narratives and arguments for their historical reliability.

————. "Black Autobiographies as History and Literature." *The Black Scholar* 5, No. 4 (December 1973-January 1974): 2-9.
    A survey decrying the suppression of slave narratives after the Civil War and asserting their status as an authentic and vital literary genre.

————. "Using the Testimony of Ex-Slaves: Approaches and Problems." *The Journal of Southern History* XLI, No. 4 (November 1975): 473-92.
    A detailed assessment of slave narratives as a viable historical source, including a discussion of the WPA interviews.

Bontemps, Arna. "The Negro Contribution to American Letters." In *The American Negro Reference Book,* edited by John P. Davies, pp. 850-78. Englewood Cliffs, N.J.: Prentice-Hall, 1966.
    A description of post-Civil War slave narratives. Bontemps discusses the connection between these narratives and twentieth-century black American literature.

————. "The Slave Narrative: An American Genre." In *Great Slave Narratives,* edited by Arna Bontemps, pp. vii-xix. Boston: Beacon Press, 1969.
    A noted overview of slave narratives, asserting their crucial role in American history and literature.

Botkin, B. A. "The Slave as His Own Interpreter." *U.S. Library of Congress Quarterly Journal of Current Acquisitions* 2, No. 1 (July-September 1944): 37-63.
    Briefly surveys the establishment and procedures of the WPA project that was initiated to collect oral histories from ex-slaves in the 1930s. Botkin includes excerpts from several of the interviews.

Brignano, Russell C. *Black Americans in Autobiography: An Annotated Bibliography of Autobiographies and Autobiographical Books Written Since the Civil War.* Durham, N.C.: Duke University Press, 1974, 118 p.
    Lists and annotates autobiographical works composed by black Americans from 1865 to 1973. An additional unannotated section provides autobiographical works written before 1865 that have been either printed for the first time or reprinted since 1945.

Cade, John B. "Out of the Mouths of Ex-Slaves." *The Journal of Negro History* XX, No. 3 (July 1935): 294-337.
Compiles information on various aspects of slave life as recorded in the WPA interviews of the 1930s, including information on shelter, clothing, food, the slave's work, and punishment.

Costanzo, Angelo. *Surprizing Narrative: Olaudah Equiano and the Beginnings of Black Autobiography.* Contributions in Afro-American and African Studies, no. 104. New York: Greenwood Press, 1987, 149 p.
A detailed study of early black autobiography focusing on the narrative of Olaudah Equiano, whom Costanzo considers the era's outstanding slave narrator.

Escott, Paul D. *Slavery Remembered: A Record of Twentieth-Century Slave Narratives.* Chapel Hill: University of North Carolina Press, 1979, 221 p.
A comprehensive record of twentieth-century interviews with former slaves, including those conducted at Fisk University in the 1920s in addition to the WPA interviews of the 1930s. Escott presents summaries of the information gathered in the oral histories and provides tables showing the various demographic factors that can be used to gauge the authenticity of the information in the interviews.

Feldstein, Stanley. *Once a Slave: The Slaves' View of Slavery.* New York: William Morrow and Co., 1971, 329 p.
Examines slaves' attitudes toward slavery and describes various aspects of life under the chattel system. Feldstein draws his information solely from slave narratives.

Foster, Frances S. "Briton Hammon's *Narrative*: Some Insights into Beginnings." *CLA Journal* XXI, No. 2 (December 1977): 179-86.
Discusses Briton Hammon's *A Narrative of the Uncommon Sufferings and Surprising Deliverance of Briton Hammon, a Negro Man* as the earliest extant work by a black author in North America.

Gates, Henry-Louis, Jr. "Binary Oppositions in Chapter One of *Narrative of the Life of Frederick Douglass, an American Slave, Written by Himself.*" In *Afro-American Literature: The Reconstruction of Instruction,* edited by Dexter Fisher and Robert B. Stepto, pp. 212-232. New York: Modern Language Association of America, 1979.
Suggests that the slave narrative incorporates traditions of the sentimental novel, the European picaresque, and confessional literature. Gates applies his theory specifically to the first chapter of Frederick Douglass's first autobiography.

Mackethan, Lucinda H. "Huck Finn and the Slave Narratives: Lighting Out as Design." *The Southern Review* 20, No. 2 (April 1984): 247-64.
Compares Mark Twain's novel *The Adventures of Huckleberry Finn* with such slave narratives as those by William Wells Brown and Frederick Douglass. Mackethan suggests that in his work Twain borrowed structure, incident, and language from slave narratives.

Margolies, Edward. "Ante-Bellum Slave Narratives: Their Place In American Literary History." *Studies in Black Literature* 4, No. 3 (Autumn 1973): 1-8.
An overview touching upon such issues as Romanticism in the slave narratives, the narratives' role in the evolution of black American literature, and the rise of plantation novels as a reaction to the narratives.

Minter, David. "Conceptions of the Self in Black Slave Narratives." *American Transcendental Quarterly* 24, Part 2 (Fall 1974): 62-8.
Focuses on the various aspects and conceptions of self portrayed in slave narratives and traces their influence on such later works of black American literature as Ralph Ellison's *Invisible Man* and Richard Wright's *Native Son.*

Nelson, John Herbert. *The Negro Character in American Literature.* College Park, Md.: McGrath Publishing Co., 1926, 146 p.
One of the first literary surveys to accord significance to the slave narratives. The author's commentary on the best-known narratives is today considered dated and lacking in critical acumen.

Nichols, Charles H., Jr. "Slave Narratives and the Plantation Legend." *Phylon* X, No. 3 (Third Quarter 1949): 201-10.
Contrasts the romantic depictions of slave life in such plantation novels as John Pendleton Kennedy's *Swallow Barn* with the brutal ones presented in the slave narratives.

———. "Who Read the Slave Narratives?" *The Phylon Quarterly* XX, No. 2 (Summer 1959): 149-62.
Examines the avid public interest in slave narratives during the antebellum period and provides sales figures for various works.

———. *Many Thousand Gone: The Ex-Slaves' Account of Their Bondage and Freedom.* Bloomington: Indiana University Press, 1963, 229 p.
Provides an overview of slave narratives and depictions of various aspects of slave life from the point of view of the slave narrators. Nichols's work, which was originally presented many years earlier as a doctoral dissertation, is considered one of the important early assessments of the genre.

Rawick, George P. *The American Slave: A Composite Autobiography.* Vol. 1, *From Sundown to Sunup: The Making of the Black Community.* Contributions in Afro-American and African Studies, no. 11. Westport, Conn.: Greenwood Publishing Co., 1972, 208 p.
A sociological study of the formation of black society in the United States. This book is the introductory volume to an eighteen-volume compilation of oral slave narratives.

Stone, Albert E. "Identity and Art in Frederick Douglass's *Narrative.*" *CLA Journal* XVII, No. 2 (December 1973): 192-213.
A discussion of literary artistry in slave narratives that focuses on the *Narrative of the Life of Frederick Douglass, an American Slave, Written by Himself.*

Taves, Ann. "Spiritual Purity and Sexual Shame: Religious Themes in the Writings of Harriet Jacobs." *Church History* 56, No. 1 (March 1987): 59-72.
Explores issues of sexuality and spirituality in *Incidents in the Life of a Slave Girl,* by Harriet Jacobs.

Wesling, Donald. "Writing as Power in the Slave Narrative of the Early Republic." *Michigan Quarterly Review* XXVI, No. 3 (Summer 1987): 459-72.
A deconstructionist view of the slave narratives emphasizing the theme of literacy as an assertion of power.

Williams, Kenny J. "'We Hold These Truths to Be Self-Evident . . .'. The Slave Narrative and the Prose of Freedom." In his *They Also Spoke: An Essay on Negro Literature in America, 1787-1930,* pp. 80-114. Nashville, Tenn.: Townsend Press, 1970.
Traces the American democratic philosophy in the slave narratives and outlines the journey motif common to them. The critic also suggests that the direct and forthright style of the narratives planted the first seeds of the Realism movement in American literature.

Winks, Robin W. Introduction to *Four Fugitive Slave Narratives,* edited by Robin W. Winks, pp. v-xxxiv. Reading, Mass.: Addison-Wesley Publishing Co., 1969.
A brief introduction to narratives by Josiah Henson, William Wells Brown, and Austin Steward and to *The Refugee: A North-Side View of Slavery.* Each of these works is also prefaced by a biographical and critical introduction.

Woodward, C. Vann. "History from Slave Sources." *The American Historical Review* 79, No. 2 (April 1974): 470-81.
Reviews *The American Slave: A Composite Autobiography,* the multi-volume edition of oral slave narratives edited by George P. Rawick (see citation above). Woodward also discusses the slave narratives' historical authenticity and their uses for the historian.

Yellin, Jean Fagan. "Written by Herself: Harriet Jacobs' Slave Narrative." *American Literature* 53, No. 3 (November 1981): 479-86.
Details the discovery of a group of letters that verifies the long-disputed authenticity of Jacobs's *Incidents in the Life of a Slave*

Girl, Written by Herself. The critic points to the book's importance as an early work by a black woman and as an unusually candid treatment of women's sexuality.

Yetman, Norman R. ''The Background of the Slave Narrative Collection.'' *American Quarterly* XIX, No. 3 (Fall 1967): 534-53.
    Documents the waning of interest in the slave narratives after the Civil War, the resurgence of interest during the 1930s, and the social and historical conditions that led to the formation of the WPA's slave narratives project.

————. ''Ex-Slave Interviews and the Historiography of Slavery.'' *American Quarterly* 36, No. 2 (Summer 1984): 181-210.
    Assesses the use of the WPA slave interviews in recent historical scholarship.

The *Bildungsroman* in Nineteenth-Century Literature

INTRODUCTION

Scholars consider the *Bildungsroman,* or apprenticeship novel, the most significant German contribution to the novel genre. Used to describe works that deal with the psychological growth of a central character from adolescence to maturity, the term *Bildungsroman* is most closely associated with a small group of German novels written in the late eighteenth century and the first half of the nineteenth. Although Christoph Martin Wieland's *Geschichte des Agathon* (*The History of Agathon*), which appeared in 1765-66, is often cited as the earliest *Bildungsroman* because it was the first German novel devoted entirely to a protagonist's inner development, Johann Wolfgang von Goethe's *Wilhelm Meisters Lehrjahre* (*Wilhelm Meister's Apprenticeship*), published in 1795-96, is the most famous example of the *Bildungsroman* and is today regarded as the prototype of the genre.

The designation *Bildungsroman* was first used by the critic Karl Morgenstern in lectures presented in the 1820s at the University of Dorpat. Morgenstern specified a twofold purpose for the genre: first, to portray ''the hero's *Bildung* [formation] as it begins and proceeds to a certain level of perfection,'' and second, to foster ''the *Bildung* of the reader to a greater extent than any other type of novel.'' It was not until 1870, however, when the philosopher Wilhelm Dilthey applied the term in his *Des Leben Schleiermacher,* that the concept of the *Bildungsroman* gained wide critical currency. Although some scholars use the term *Bildungsroman* interchangeably with *Erziehungsroman, Zeitroman, Künstlerroman,* and *Entwicklungsroman,* these various types of novels exhibit important differences. The *Erziehungsroman* stresses the role of education in the protagonist's formation; the *Zeitroman* focuses as much on revealing the spirit of the protagonist's era as on his or her personal growth; and the *Künstlerroman* traces the path of a young artist struggling to understand his or her vocation. In distinguishing the *Entwicklungsroman* from the *Bildungsroman,* critics point out that the former is a much more general term denoting any novel whose structure derives from a central character's developing personality.

The typical *Bildungsroman* traces the progress of a young person toward self-understanding and a sense of social responsibility. Usually, the protagonist is a sensitive and gifted young man who encounters numerous problems and makes several false starts before he accomplishes his goals. The focus of the *Bildungsroman* is always on one central character who undergoes an important transformation; further, the scope of the novel is limited as a rule because the protagonist's life before his self-awakening begins and after finding his place in society remains unknown. Structurally, the *Bildungsroman* normally emphasizes dialogue instead of plot development, thereby keeping the reader's attention squarely on the growth of the hero or heroine's character. These features of the *Bildungsroman* are well illustrated by its chief example, *Wilhelm Meister.* When the novel opens, a wealthy, naive young man, unsure about the direction his life should take, has fallen in love with an actress. Learning that she has been unfaithful to him, he decides to go into business despite his avowed love for the

An illustration from Johann Wolfgang von Goethe's Wilhelm Meister's Apprenticeship.

theater. Soon persuaded to support a troupe of actors, his interest in the theater is rekindled and he begins to perform on the stage. Much of the novel deals with the actors' intrigues, Wilhelm's friendships with the various members of the troupe, and his failed love affairs. The novel ends with Wilhelm being dissuaded from a career in the theater, with his marriage, and with his transformation into a responsible adult.

Goethe's novel was emulated by later German authors, but they also departed from the pattern he established. In his *Hyperion; oder, Der Eremit in Griechenland* (*Hyperion; or, The Hermit of Greece*), which appeared in 1797, Friedrich Hölderlin concentrated more on style than on characterization, striving for a kind of verbal perfection that would overshadow *Wilhelm Meister.* Novalis, in his *Heinrich von Ofterdingen* (*Henry of Ofterdingen*), written in 1799, differentiated his *Bildungsroman* from Goethe's by setting the action in the medieval period. One of the most highly regarded *Bildungsromane,* Adalbert Stifter's *Der Nachsommer* (*Indian Summer*), published in 1857, is considered especially original because its outcome is evident and ensured from the very beginning of the novel. In terms of structure, Gottfried Keller expanded the *Bildungsroman* in his *Die grüne Heinrich (Green Henry),* written in 1854, by providing information about both the protagonist's childhood and his later life.

Although the *Bildungsroman* is primarily associated with German novels of the late eighteenth and the nineteenth century, the genre, particularly as exemplified by *Wilhelm Meister,* proved extremely influential. Stressing *Wilhelm Meister*'s importance to its era in Europe, Thomas Mann wrote that it was "an educational and cultural epic so far-reaching, so all-embracing, that a shrewd romantic critic could say that the French Revolution, Fichte's *Wissenschaftslehre (Theory of Science),* and the novel *Wilhelm Meister* were the three great events of the period." Thomas Carlyle was so impressed by the work that he translated it into English in 1824 and imitated it in his *Sartor Resartus.* Other nineteenth-century English authors also produced *Bildungsromane*—Charles Dickens's *Great Expectations,* George Meredith's *The Ordeal of Richard Feverel: A History of Father and Son,* and Charlotte Brontë's *Jane Eyre* are all examples of the genre. Though these novels resemble their German counterparts, scholars have noted that transplanted to England, the form took on some unique characteristics. The English *Bildungsroman* tended to have a more confessional quality, it often involved the protagonist's move from the country to the city, it was more concerned with the theme of religious doubt, and it ended less optimistically than the German variety. In the twentieth century, the *Bildungsroman* has continued to evolve. Mann's *Joseph und seine Brüder (Joseph and His Brothers)* and his *Der Zauberberg (The Magic Mountain),* for example, offer an innovative approach to the *Bildungsroman* through the ironic use of various elements of the tradition. In addition, critics have started to explore the female *Bildungsroman,* which follows the growth of a young woman toward emotional and social maturity, as a variation on the type. While its themes and techniques continue to interest modern readers, lively critical discussion about the scope and characteristics of the *Bildungsroman* persists, attesting to the pervasive influence and enduring relevance of the genre.

GENERAL SURVEYS OF THE *BILDUNGSROMAN* GENRE

MARTIN SWALES

[*A Canadian educator and critic, Swales is the author of* The German Novelle *and* The German "Bildungsroman" from Wieland to Hesse. *In the following excerpt from the latter work, he provides an overview of the history and major traits of the* Bildungsroman *genre. For additional commentary by Swales, see excerpt below.*]

[In his *Wilhelm Meister und seine Brüder: Untersuchungen zum deut schen Bildungsroman,* Jürgen Jacobs] speaks of the Bildungsroman as an "unfulfilled genre." While one knows what Jacobs means—that the Bildungsroman operates with an implied teleology that it only imperfectly fulfills—I believe it is wrong to identify the genre itself with that teleology. In so doing, Jacobs abstracts the notion of genre from its realization in the specific literary work and makes the genre concept something extraliterary. As Monika Schrader so well puts it: "the praxis of the work of art itself—and not literary theory—must be the starting point and basis for the definition of the literary

genre." I want to insist that the genre works *within* individual fictions in that it is a component of the expectation to which the specific novels refer and which they vivify by their creative engagement with it. The degree to which the expectation is or is not fulfilled is not the criterion for participation in the genre construct. As long as the model of the genre is intimated as a sustained and sustaining presence in the work in question, then the genre retains its validity as a structuring principle within the palpable stuff of an individual literary creation. In other words, the notion of a genre must, in my view, operate as a function of the imaginative literature written with reference to that concept; it is not a petrified, extraliterary thing. Even the nonfulfillment of consistently intimated expectation can, paradoxically, represent a validation of the genre by means of its controlled critique. The problematic of the Bildungsroman texts is the *raison d'être* of the genre of which they partake.

The term *Bildungsroman* was first used by Karl Morgenstern in the early 1820s. He defined the genre as follows:

> It will justly bear the name *Bildungsroman* firstly and primarily on account of its thematic material, because it portrays the *Bildung* of the hero in its beginnings and growth to a certain stage of completeness; and also secondly because it is by virtue of this portrayal that it furthers the reader's *Bildung* to a much greater extent than any other kind of novel.

This first usage of the term has only recently come to light. In view of the suggestiveness of Morgenstern's comments it is surprising that the term *Bildungsroman* was used only infrequently until the late nineteenth century, when it was, so to speak, put on the map by Dilthey. Since then, the term has enjoyed great currency. This might lead one to conclude that the term—and with it the essential implications of the genre—only acquires resonance *after* the great line of eighteenth- and nineteenth-century Bildungsromane. But I do not believe this is so. The term may not have gained currency until late, but . . . many of the implications of the genre are commonplaces within nineteenth-century novel theory in Germany. Morgenstern may have coined the term and summarized some of its possible implications, but the kind of novel he was envisaging had been analyzed before, by the critic Friedrich von Blanckenburg in his *Versuch über den Roman (Essay on the Novel)* of 1774. This work of novel theory grew out of Blanckenburg's enthusiasm for a specific work of fiction, Christoph Martin Wieland's *Agathon* (1767), and for the way in which that individual creation is shot through with theoretical implications in that it overtly (and thematically) transforms the traditional novel genre by investing it with a new psychological and intellectual seriousness. The Bildungsroman was born in a remarkable fusion of theory and practice—and with it the German novel came of age. Moreover, as Fritz Martini has shown, Morgenstern's coinage of the term *Bildungsroman* is, like Blanckenburg's treatise, a theoretical response to a particular work of fiction. For Morgenstern, the work which inaugurated the modern novel in all its resonance was Goethe's *Wilhelm Meister's Apprenticeship.*

It is because of this precise historicity of the Bildungsroman genre, expressed in a twofold interlocking of theory and practice, that I intend to use this term, despite the time-lag which afflicts the term itself, in preference to two others with which it has often been felt to be interchangeable: *Erziehungsroman* and *Entwicklungsroman.* I would suggest that the Erziehungsroman is, unlike the Bildungsroman, explicitly (and narrowly) pedagogic in the sense that it is concerned with a certain set of values to be acquired, of lessons to be learned. . . . [The]

Bildungsroman both in theory and in practice is concerned with a much more diffuse—and therefore more general—process by which the individual grows and evolves. The word *Bildung* implies the generality of a culture, the clustering of values by which a man lives, rather than a specifically *educational* attainment. The term *Entwicklungsroman* is much more general, and it is one which carries less emotive and intellectual ballast than does *Bildungsroman.* I would take the former term to embrace any novel having one central figure whose experiences and whose changing self occupy a role of structural primacy within the fiction. *Entwicklungsroman,* then, is a fairly neutral indicator of a certain kind of fictive organization, whereas *Bildungsroman* is a genre term that has both cultural and philosophical resonance.

I want to argue that the Bildungsroman genre was born in specific historical circumstances, that is, within the *Humanitätsideal* of late eighteenth-century Germany. It is a novel form that is animated by a concern for the whole man unfolding organically in all his complexity and richness. *Bildung* becomes, then, a total growth process, a diffused *Werden,* or becoming, involving something more intangible than the acquirement of a finite number of lessons. Such a concern is the expression of a particular kind of bourgeois humanism, one that retains a special (albeit problematic) hold over the German imagination. The centrality of the concept *Bildung,* of the self-realization of the individual in his wholeness, for such figures as Goethe, Schiller, and Wilhelm von Humboldt is well known. The urgency of their concern is a measure of the anguish with which they perceived the growing threat of narrowness and specialization in the society around them. One of the most eloquent statements of that perception comes in a magnificent—and crucial—passage from Schiller's *Letters on the Aesthetic Education of Man:*

> With us, too, the image of the human species is
> projected in magnified form into separate individuals—but as fragments . . . with the result that in order
> to get any idea of the totality of human nature one
> has to go the rounds from individual to individual . . .
> taking from this one his memory, from that one his
> tabulating intelligence, from yet another his mechanical skill, and piece them together into a picture
> of the species. With us it might almost seem as though
> the various faculties appear as separate in practice as
> they are distinguished by the psychologist in theory,
> and we see not merely individuals, but whole classes
> of men, developing but one of their potentialities,
> while of the rest, as in stunted plants, only vestigial
> traces remain. . . . Enjoyment has become divorced
> from labour, the means from the end, the effort from
> the reward. Everlastingly chained to a single little
> fragment of the whole, man himself develops into
> nothing but a fragment. . . . Thus little by little the
> concrete life of the individual is destroyed in order
> that the abstract idea of the whole may drag out its
> sorry existence.

Such concerns were not confined to the great artists. One must also stress that many of the implications of the Bildungsroman have their roots not simply in specifically cultural concerns of the last decades of the eighteenth century, but also in a much broader complex of intellectual currents. Dilthey, in his essay *The Eighteenth Century and the Historical World,* stressed the importance of historicism for the eighteenth century. On one level, this historicism is the espousal of a universal principle in that it upholds a powerful teleological force as the motive power of universal history; on another level (with, say, Herder), it involves a recognition of the specificity of historical

change, a realization that the growth and evolution of man are interlocked with quite particular social and geographical circumstances. These two strands within historicism are, Dilthey argued, a potent legacy to the nineteenth century. They also . . . find their way into the Bildungsroman. Indeed, for much nineteenth-century German thinking, history is the vital domain in which idea and empirical reality, spirit and the contingencies of given social context, interact. The tensions in German historiography from Dilthey onward have been well documented by Carlo Antoni in his important study, *From History to Sociology.* The conflict between the principles of materialistic relativism and of metaphysical self-realization, between, to shift the concepts but not the ground of the debate, *Naturwissenschaften* (natural sciences) and *Geisteswissenschaften* (sciences of the mind, that is, the humanities), is a vital issue in the intellectual life of nineteenth-century Germany, and it is one whose roots extend back to the age in which the Bildungsroman was born. The Bildungsroman, like any novel, is concerned with the *history* of its hero. This history is enacted within the finite realm of social practicality, and it also partakes of the infinite realm of his inwardness, of his human potentiality. Immanuel Kant, in his *Ideas for General History in a Cosmopolitan Sense* (1784), sketched for his readers the general process by which man, in fulfilling his nature, obeys that teleology which is embedded in the species to which he belongs. Kant insisted that the species eventually "works its way up to the condition in which all seeds which nature has planted can be fully developed, and the human species can fulfill its destiny on earth." Here one senses a general, programmatic statement of that *Bildung* whose operation in the life of one individual the Bildungsroman seeks to document. In a fascinating aside Kant at one point asks whether he is truly offering history, given that he is, by definition, talking of that which has not yet been realized: "It is admittedly a surprising, and to all appearances wayward, undertaking to attempt the composition of a *history* according to some idea of how the world ought to evolve if it is to be in accord with certain rational goals. It would seem that such an intention could only produce a novel." It is indeed at the intersection of story (history) and mind (idea) that the Bildungsroman will generate its characteristic import, one which evolves out of an artistically controlled, and frequently unresolved, tension.

The finest discussion of these issues in terms specific to novel fiction is to be found in Blanckenburg's *Essay on the Novel.* His theory emerges as the recognition of a specific literary achievement, the first edition of Wieland's *Agathon.* Blanckenburg's criticism derives its cogency from the fact that Wieland's fiction is overtly *also* a work of novel theory. *Agathon* engages the reader again and again in a debate about the nature of novel fictions—and about their applicability to the case which this novel puts before us. Indeed, it is because *Agathon* is a novel which takes issue with conventional norms of novel writing that it is for Blanckenburg a serious artistic achievement. What Wieland repudiates by implication is the romance which so long-windedly fuses love story and adventure novel: a pair of constant lovers is separated at the beginning of the novel, then go through all manner of episodic adventures, only to be reunited at the end. For Blanckenburg, Wieland's signal achievement resides in his ability to get inside a character, to portray the complex stuff of human potential which, in interaction with the outside world, yields the palpable process of living and changing. Because Wieland's novel shows this process, this *Werden,* it confers artistic—and human—dignity and cohesion on that sequence of adventures through which the hero passes. Moreover, it is this process in all its complexity that matters, on which narrative time, energy, and interest is expended, and not the celebration of any goal which can thereby be attained. Blanckenburg senses the profound resonance of *Agathon,* a resonance which one can gauge from the following entry in Johann Georg Sulzer's *General Theory of the Fine Arts* (Leipzig, 1773-1775). There is, significantly, no entry under *novel,* only the following gloss on the adjective *novelistic:* "Thus one describes whatever in content, tone, or expression bears the characteristics which prevailed in earlier novels—such as fondness for adventures, stiltedness in actions, events, feelings. The natural is more or less the exact opposite of the novelistic." If, then, the German novel comes of age with *Agathon,* it does so by breaking with, or, more accurately, by reshaping and deepening, past norms and by demonstrating an intense and sustained concern for the growth of an individual in all his experiential complexity and potentiality. It would seem, then, that it is precisely this interest in the inner life and processes of the individual which confers poetic seriousness on what was hitherto an improbable narrative of colorful episodic events.

The modern German novel was born—but not without, as it were, a "bad conscience." The novel, it seems, retains that questionable legacy of being largely events, adventures, episodes, and little (or no) human and poetic substance. Looking at subsequent theories of the novel in Germany, one has the impression that the novel, as a genre, stands in constant need of rehabilitation. That rehabilitation and what it entails was expressed with almost monotonous intensity in German novel theory throughout the nineteenth century, and it was nearly always formulated as a concern for the achievement of *poetry* within the novel: the danger with the novel is that it so easily backslides into the condition of *prose.* The paradigmatic statement is to be found in Georg Wilhelm Friedrich Hegel's comments on the novel in his *Aesthetics:*

> This novelistic quality is born when the knightly existence is again taken seriously, is filled out with real substance. The contingency of outward, actual existence has been transformed into the firm, secure order of bourgeois society and the state, so that now the police, the law courts, the army occupy the position of those chimerical goals which the knight used to set himself. Thereby the knightly character of those heroes whose deeds fill recent novels is transformed. They stand as individuals with their subjective goals of love, honor, ambition or with their ideals of improving the world, over against the existing order and prose of reality which from all sides places obstacles in their path. . . . Especially young men are these new knights who have to make their way, and who regard it as a misfortune that there are in any shape or form such things as family, bourgeois society. . . . It is their aim to punch a hole in this order of things, to change the world. . . . These struggles are, however, in the modern world nothing but the apprenticeship, the education of the individual at the hands of the given reality. . . . For the conclusion of such an apprenticeship usually amounts to the hero getting the corners knocked off him. . . . In the last analysis he usually gets his girl and some kind of job, marries and becomes a philistine just like the others.

This is, it seems to me, a crucial passage, not just for the perceptions it offers of the nature of the novel genre, but also for its essential ambivalence. On the one hand, Hegel affirms the seriousness of this kind of novel fiction, a seriousness which derives from its ability to anchor the time-honored epic pattern

in modern bourgeois reality. In this sense, Hegel seems to offer approval of that process by which the world prevails over the hero's dreams, desires, and fantasies to the point where the somewhat fastidious, idealistic young man is licked into shape and taught to affirm society and all it stands for. Yet on the other hand, Hegel also suggests that there is something debased, and debasing, about this process. That the highest wisdom of the novel—and of its latter-day knightly adventurer—should reside in the acquirement of wife, family, and job security seems a sorry reduction of the grand model. The ambivalence is, of course, characteristic of much of Hegel's thinking: on the one hand, contemporary reality is apostrophized as the finest, most rational self-realization of the world spirit in its historical workings; on the other hand, that given reality is but a phase with a built-in impetus toward self-transcendence. The hedging of bets in regard to prosaic bourgeois reality is characteristic not only of Hegel himself, but also . . . of the Bildungsroman genre. And the uncertainty becomes nowhere more apparent, as Hegel perceived, than in the vexed problem of the novel's ending.

In another passage from the *Aesthetics* Hegel makes clear that the original impetus to epic writing was a sense of the magic and poetry of the world. Yet modern society presupposes "a reality already ordered into *prose,* on the basis of which it [the novel] reattains for poetry its lost rights." Hence, Hegel continues, the central conflict in the modern novel is that "between the poetry of the heart and the resisting prose of circumstances." Some kind of reconciliation can, apparently, be effected: the world of prose can be made to lose some of its hard edges and to allow for a validation of the poetry of the heart. And Hegel insists that this area of validation, this room for aesthetic maneuver, must be granted particularly to that artist who is committed to rendering the prose of real life "without himself remaining enmeshed in the realm of the prosaic and the everyday."

The issues Hegel raised, which can be summarized under the heading of "poetic" versus "prosaic" modes of being and of artistic creation, can be traced through the theoretical remarks on the novel made by Friedrich Schleiermacher (1819-1832), Karl Immermann (1826), Arthur Schopenhauer (1851), Karl Gutzkow (1855), Friedrich Theodor Vischer (1857), Otto Ludwig (1860), Friedrich Spielhagen (1874), and Gustav Freytag (1886). They are commonplaces within nineteenth-century novel theory in Germany, and they reflect that unease about the novel genre that informs Wieland's *Agathon* and Blanckenburg's *Essay on the Novel.* This ongoing bad conscience accounts, in my view, for the fact that one specific version of the novel, the Bildungsroman, became the dominant mode for the major narrative talents of German literature. I have no wish to claim that Germans are congenitally incapable of writing novels other than Bildungsromane. On the other hand, the fact remains that most German novel writing of distinction partakes of this genre construct and that the distinction derives from the artistic resonance with which dominant social, intellectual, psychological, and cultural concerns are taken up and explored. It is part of the historicity of the genre that on its first emergence it was hailed as giving respectability to a debased literary mode, as legitimating and redeeming the popular form by marrying the traditional episodic and providential plot with a thoroughgoing concern for the experiential potentiality of the central character. Thomas Mann suggested as much when he wrote that the Bildungsroman is the "sublimation and rendering inward of the novel of adventures."

What precisely is meant here? At the simplest level, one should note that the Bildungsroman is a novel which gives dignity to the creaky mechanics of a providential plot by suggesting that the adventures that befall the hero and the people he meets are significant insofar as they strike an answering chord in him, as they are part of his potentiality. If this is the case, it follows that the characters and experiences are allowed to recur because they are abidingly present in the selfhood of the hero. The Bildungsroman, with its concern for the *Werden* of an individual, is able—in Hegel's and so many theoreticians' terms—to redeem the prosaic facticity of the given social world by relating it to the inner potentialities of the hero. It is a novel form which esteems possibilities as much as actualities; indeed, at times it runs the risk of esteeming actualities only insofar as they are validated and underwritten by the hero's inwardness. It is surely for this reason, for the mediation between "poetic" and "prosaic," that the Bildungsroman became such a central model for novel writing in Germany in the late eighteenth and the nineteenth centuries, and indeed, even into the twentieth.

It is worth noting here that one novel, above all others, was the object of immediate and thoroughgoing critical debate, a debate which marked out the vital issues in such a way as to make that text and its reception almost a paradigm for all that followed. I am thinking, of course, of Goethe's *Wilhelm Meister's Apprenticeship*. . . . [The] reception and discussion to which it gave rise must be documented in any discussion of German novel theory. Two phases of the reception of *Wilhelm Meister* are particularly important: first, the interchange of letters involving Goethe, Schiller, Humboldt, and Christian Gottfried Körner; and second, the Romantic reaction, as exemplified by Friedrich Schlegel and Novalis. It is noteworthy that Goethe himself expressed considerable uncertainty about his own novel. To Johann Peter Eckermann he commented: "People look for a center, and that is hard—and not even good." But at times he was prepared to formulate some kind of overall idea, "that man in spite of all his stupidity and confusions does, guided by some higher hand, yet attain a happy goal."

This unease about the central idea of the novel is the mainspring of the exchange of letters between Goethe and Schiller. Schiller, as Klaus Gille points out in his indispensable book [*Wilhelm Meister im Urteil der Zeitgenossen*], consistently suggested that *Wilhelm Meister* is too tentative in its handling of the underlying idea, an idea which for Schiller was the development (*Bildung*) of the hero toward some state of (aesthetic) wholeness. The correspondence revolves around the tension between what Schiller called his "whim concerning the clearer enunciation of the principal idea," and Goethe's obliqueness in the novel. As Goethe himself admitted to Schiller: "the flaw which you quite rightly notice comes from my innermost nature—from a certain realistic tic." One notes the tact and good humor with which the disagreement was aired. The conciliatory tone derives, I think, not simply from the formal yet cordial relations that prevailed between the two men, but also from the specific object under discussion. Schiller called his concern for a clearer idea a *Grille,* a whim, and Goethe acknowledged the lack of clear-cut idea to be a "flaw" and attributed it to his "realistic tic." Each man, by implication, recognized the other's position as a valid counterweight to his own idiosyncratic preferences ("whim," "tic"). Each response emerges in the debate as but one pole within the necessary interpretative dialectic generated by this, in Goethe's term, "incalculable" novel.

One notes how wonderfully perceptive are Schiller's comments on *Wilhelm Meister*. He was able to be genuinely appreciative of precisely those qualities in the novel which would seem to be the source of his reservations. He observed that Wilhelm "achieves definiteness, without losing his lovely openness to redefinition," and that the "idea of mastery cannot and may not stand as his purpose and goal *before* him [Wilhelm] . . . rather it must stand as leader *behind* him." What Schiller acknowledged in such remarks is the tentativeness of Goethe's novel, a tentativeness born of that "realistic tic" which prevents the novel from becoming the overtly allegorical embodiment of certain "ideal" energies. We are, in other words, concerned with a tentative process, one in which (to use the terms implicit in Kant's *Ideas for General History in a Cosmopolitan Sense*) there is a tension between history and teleology, between actuality and notionality, between pattern constructed after the event and shaping purpose known in advance of its self-realization. The openness, the obliqueness of Goethe's novel is . . . the deepest source of the book's meaning. Its resonant oscillation between idea and reality is enacted in the Goethe-Schiller correspondence, and this gives meaning to Goethe's remark of 1815 about that correspondence, referring to it as "the great achievement which Schiller and I managed: to continue uninterruptedly a common *Bildung* despite our totally divergent directions." Thus the process explored in the novel was apparently continued in the exchange of letters: the divergent directions were the necessary response to the informing dialectic of the novel and to the issues it raised.

One further insight emerges from this correspondence. In November 1796 Schiller wrote to Goethe commenting on the nature of the main character and of his function within the fiction as a whole. In so doing he took up observations made by both Körner and Humboldt. Körner had insisted (and Gille suggests that he was arguing under the impact of Blanckenburg's novel theory) on the primacy of Wilhelm as the harmoniously developing, individual hero, whereas Humboldt had suggested that the novel functioned "completely independently of any particular individuality." Once again, two differing positions adopted vis-à-vis the novel text precisely uncover a significant dialectic. Schiller took up the differing viewpoints and suggested the interlocking of both perceptions within the characterization of Wilhelm. Wilhelm is, in other words, both an individual character with a specific life-history and also a reservoir of human potentiality: "It is, of course, a delicate and awkward aspect of this novel, that, in the figure of Meister, it closes neither with a consistent individuality nor with a consistent ideality, but with a mixture of the two." . . . [As] far as I am aware, the insights contributed by Schiller, Körner, and Humboldt have not been surpassed (indeed, they have seldom been equaled) by modern criticism of the Bildungsroman.

The Romantic reaction to *Wilhelm Meister* is significant in that it involves a restatement and deepening of many of the issues raised by the Goethe-Schiller correspondence. Friedrich Schlegel perceived the great historical significance of the novel, seeing it as one of the "tendencies" (albeit imperfectly fulfilled) of the age. In his *Athenäum* review (1798) he praised the irony of the novel, the way in which Goethe's narrative skill dissolves the weight and seriousness of prosaic facticity through a perspective of ironic detachment. He saw the novel as self-reflective, integrating discursive elements into its narrative flow: the novel is, then, "pure, high poetry" in that it is witty, alert, and agile, a kind of essayism of the spirit. In his later (1808) review of *Wilhelm Meister,* Schlegel repeated his vindication of the novel's poetic essence, but added an acknowledgment of its didactic aim, which derives from the concept of *Bildung* as "a mediator between emotion and reason, . . . which encompasses both.'' Schlegel, then, could cherish the novel for its obliqueness *and* its didacticism, for its irony *and* its high cultural and moral concern. At one level, of course, one can see the change in emphasis as a function of Schlegel's own personal and intellectual development between 1798 and 1808. But at another level, we must recognize that both positions are appropriate to *Wilhelm Meister* and to its responsiveness to different readings.

An oscillation between two responses also characterizes Novalis's comments on *Wilhelm Meister*. Up to about 1800 Novalis's assessment is positive in that he praised the irony, the sheer poetry with which Goethe handled banal and everyday material. But then he changed his evaluation drastically: in a bitter outburst he denounced the novel as ''a *Candide* aimed at poetry,'' as ''utterly prosaic and modern.'' Once again, it must be stressed that Novalis's change of heart was not mere inconsistency on his part. The very terms of his argument make his voice one among many within nineteenth-century novel theory in Germany. And perhaps *Wilhelm Meister* is the archetypal Bildungsroman in the sense that it focuses with paradigmatic energy on a whole number of issues concerning plot, individual development, and the selfhood of the hero, concerning above all else the poetry of the heart (inwardness and potentiality) vis-à-vis the unyielding, prosaic temporality of practical social existence. It is no accident that most nineteenth-century novel theory in Germany seems to be a running commentary on the Bildungsroman and, more specifically, on Goethe's *Wilhelm Meister*.

It has been stressed over and over again that the Bildungsroman is a novel form that is unremittingly concerned with the *Werden* of an individual hero. One needs to ask how this process is intimated narratively and how it embodies the dialectic of ''poetry'' and ''prose.'' The passage already quoted from Hegel is particularly suggestive here. In terms of its portrayal of the hero, the Bildungsroman operates with a tension between a concern for the sheer complexity of individual potentiality on the one hand and a recognition on the other that practical reality—marriage, family, career—is a necessary dimension of the hero's self-realization, albeit one that by definition implies a delimitation, indeed, a constriction, of the self. The tension is that between the *Nebeneinander* (the ''one-alongside-another'') of possible selves within the hero and the *Nacheinander* (the ''one-after-another'') of linear time and practical activity, that is, between potentiality and actuality. This tension is, it seems to me, central to the process of thematic argument of the Bildungsroman. Michael Beddow . . . argues that the genre is essentially an epic of inwardness, one that celebrates the imagination of the hero as the faculty which allows him to transcend the limitations of everyday practicality. In this sense, Beddow argues, the Bildungsroman stresses its own fictionality, stresses that it is a product of the human imagination, and thereby establishes an alternative model to the prevailing social reality. There is, I think, great cogency to Beddow's contention, but I feel that he makes the genre too unproblematic in that he stresses one side of the dialectic I have described, to the obliteration of its other pole. The major novels of the tradition are, it seems to me, not simply allegories of the inner life. Practical reality continues to impinge on the cherished inwardness of the hero, and precisely this process is the source of the irony, the obliqueness, the uncertainty which so many commentators have noticed. It is, moreover, the same process that makes the ''learning from life'' which the hero undergoes such a tentative progression. Over and over again, the novels themselves pose the question of whether the hero has achieved

any kind of worthwhile goal or insight. The notion of organic growth, of a maturing process that somehow eludes even conceptual terms, is a difficult one to pinpoint in terms of unequivocal narrative realization. Perhaps we are essentially concerned with an article of faith that seeks to assert the reconcilability of human wholeness on the one hand and the facts of limited and limiting social experience on the other. This would be characteristic of the late eighteenth century when the genre emerged; but it should not mislead us into seeing comfortable solutions where the novel itself can only offer directions, implications, and intimations of the possible.

Reading the major novels of the tradition (even its eighteenth-century exemplars), one is persistently struck by the pervasive tentativeness of the narrative undertaking. This precariousness, this hedging of bets, issues in an uncertain relationship to lived experience, whereby the linearity of plot on occasion gives way to symbolically patterned recurrence. Many critics have noted the lack of edge, of once-and-for-all finality in the treatment of human action and interaction in the Bildungsroman. Secondary characters are allowed to disappear and reappear in a remarkably providential way; they are rarely ''lost'' because they are relatable to the hero's potentiality. Hence, they are frequently waiting in the wings, available when the hero needs them. Ultimately, many of them may prove to be related to him or to each other. It is, then, characteristic of the Bildungsroman genre that it embodies a skepticism about the law of linear experience. And thereby it tends, in part at least, to call into question that dimension of human self-realization that is activity and actuality, a dimension that is embodied by plot in realistic novel fictions. This *Nacheinander* of linear experience is acknowledged in the Bildungsroman, but with considerable, often discursively formulated, reservations. The *Nacheinander* often emerges, in Robert Musil's phrase, as the ''law of life which, overburdened and dreaming of simplicity, one longs for.'' That law, like its aesthetic correlative, plot, may be an escapist fiction, a cosy dissolving of human complexity into interpretatively unproblematic causality. Musil is, of course, particularly radical in his argumentation. One remembers the famous reflections on character in *The Man Without Qualities,* where it is suggested that character is most truly a reservoir of unrealized potentiality rather than a finite sum of knowable actualities. The inhabitant of a country, we are told, has at least nine characters, dependent upon his profession, nationality, class, sex, and so on. But he also has a tenth character: ''and this is nothing but the passive fantasy of unfilled spaces: it allows the man everything—but with one exception. He cannot take seriously what his at least nine other characters do and what happens to them.'' Thus the essential character of the man would be the inward, unrealized self, the ''player of roles which belong to him as little as do the laws of the country in which he lives.'' In many ways, Musil's conclusions go far beyond those of the major Bildungsroman novelists in that he withdraws, both in philosophical and aesthetic terms, any allegiance to plot, to those specifics through which the self realizes itself in activity. Nonetheless, the questions raised by his novel are also urgent intimations from the Bildungsroman tradition.

It is important to stress, however, that unlike *The Man Without Qualities,* the Bildungsroman texts . . . work with a relationship to plot, to story, which, for all its tentativeness, is retained intact. In one sense, of course, the relatability of the world of external action to the growth and unfolding of the hero's selfhood can imply an insufficient recognition of the chain of cause and effect within practical affairs. That is to say, the Bildungsroman too rarely operates with a precise sense of the moral integrity and otherness of the people with whom the protagonist comes into contact. There can be something rarefied about the Bildungsroman, a sense that the community with which the hero is to be reconciled is not rendered mimetically; rather, it is intimated through the conceptual cohesion of the novelist's fiction, through the writer's collusion with *his* artistic community of notional readers. In other words, it is the *reader* who is initiated into the wholeness and complexity of *Bildung;* the hero and the world through which he moves are only redeemable through the symbolic transformations made possible by an artistic labor of love.

But this is only part of the import generated by the major Bildungsromane. . . . Indeed, these works are remarkable because they do not reach the point of dissolving all relationship to plot, to the *Nacheinander* that is the story. In one sense, they seem to promise just such an obliteration of the flow of resistantly linear experience. Yet, in another sense, they seem unable to break faith with the novel form and to offer an epistemological or aesthetic treatise. The novels themselves remind us that however much the protagonist craves to know only a beneficent reality that will not resist the ''poetry'' of his selfhood, reality, the law of linearity, will not be gainsaid. Indeed, the Bildungsromane suggest that there is an inalienable need in man to have a story, to know himself as part of that linear flow of experience which cannot be halted at will. For it is the story which binds together contingencies into the weighty sequence of a human destiny. As Barbara Hardy has so well put it, the narrative storyline is not just ''an aesthetic invention used by artists to control, manipulate, and order experience, but it is a primary act of mind transferred from life itself. . . . In order really to live, we make up stories about ourselves and others.'' The story, then, becomes the guarantor that one is living. Obliteration of the story may seem to promise the realization of human wholeness, but ultimately it is a wholeness bought at the unacceptable price of stasis, bloodlessness, death. Moreover, as W. B. Gallie reminds us, the story, like human history, is founded in the attempt to deal with contingencies ''by rendering these contingencies acceptable.'' All of this, Gallie reflects, may not be philosophically respectable. But then the novel, like history, is not a philosophical tract.

Compared with the major exemplars of realistic fiction, the plot of the Bildungsroman, of course, always tends to feel somewhat feeble and half-hearted. But in the context of its own narrative implication, the allegiance to story in the Bildungsroman, however tentative, is quite remarkable. And the tentativeness is offset by a gain: the Bildungsroman is able to offer a critique of those cherished human presuppositions explored by Frank Kermode in his study, *The Sense of an Ending.* It allows the novel to concern itself with a definition of experience which precludes any simple sense of finality, of ''over and done with.'' Of course, the notion of a goal still has a place within human affairs. Yet, ultimately, the meaning of the growth process, of the *Werden,* is to be found in the process itself, not in any goal whose attainment it may make possible. The grasping for clarity and losing it, the alternation of certainty of purpose with a sense of the overriding randomness of living, these are seen to be the very stuff of human experience and such meaning and distinction as men are able to attain. The Bildungsroman, then, is written for the sake of the journey, and not for the sake of the happy ending toward which that journey points.

This obliqueness of the German Bildungsroman (a quality Schiller discerned in Goethe's *Wilhelm Meister*) separates the genre from other comparable novel fictions. In his study of the English novel from Dickens to Golding, Jerome H. Buckley persuasively uses the model of the Bildungsroman as his organizing framework. What emerges from his study, however, is that the English novel of adolescence is essentially concerned to find a certain practical accommodation between the hero and the social world around him. Buckley's sketch of the genre could apply to the major German exemplars, except that it fails to allow for the problematic elusiveness of so many of the texts. . . . This is not, of course, to raise objections to Buckley's study, which is concerned with another and very different novel tradition. But it is worth noting that the English fiction he examines offers a far greater allegiance to plot, to actuality, to the linear growth of the hero to some kind of adult clarity, than does the German Bildungsroman. Moreover, the English novel of adolescence (*Great Expectations, The Way of All Flesh, Jude the Obscure, Clayhanger, Portrait of the Artist as a Young Man*) operates with a precisely articulated and documented sense of the specific pressures—societal, institutional, psychological—which militate against the hero's quest for self-fulfillment. Such kinds of resistance are rarely portrayed in the German Bildungsroman with any bite or urgency. The forces which oppose its hero are less susceptible of realistic portrayal for the reason that they tend to be ontologically, rather than socially, based. The resistance ranged against the Bildungsroman hero is not a tyrannical parent, not social or economic sanctions; rather, it is the limitations set to any and every existence within the sphere of outward, practical being (however beneficently organized that sphere may be). At several points in his study of the English Bildungsroman Buckley outlines the relationship of English writers to Goethe's *Wilhelm Meister.* Once again, Goethe's novel provokes a highly revealing critical disagreement. It is praised for its openness, its questioning—and is also condemned for its vagueness and bloodlessness. These are hardly original responses. Once again they allow one to conclude that the lifeblood of *Wilhelm Meister,* and of the genre which it so persuasively embodies, is consistently sustained irresolution.

One final thematic concern of the Bildungsroman should be mentioned here, the nature and the limitations of human consciousness. It is tempting in view of the implied but so rarely realized teleology of so much Bildungsroman narration to define the goal pursued by the hero as that of greater, or more perfect, consciousness. Frequently, however, we find that the novels themselves are much more subtle, even evasive, than this. Often we are shown that consciousness is a function of being and that being (specific existence) is in its turn a function of the characters' embeddedness in a given psychological or social context. It follows, then, that neither ''consciousness'' nor ''activity'' are separate realms which man can choose to enter or leave. Rather, he inhabits both in their interdependence. The major novels within the Bildungsroman tradition recognize this. Where such is not the case, where novels operate with the simple model of an intact, private self that may choose to enter experience or not, then they succumb to what J. P. Stern has criticized as ''the taint of a chimerical freedom— as though somehow it were possible *not* to enter the river of experience that flows all one way.'' But the major achievements of the tradition do, in my view, suggest that the protagonist's capacity for reflection is part of the whole living process in which he is embedded: it neither antedates nor postdates his actual experiences, but is of a piece with them. Hence, intellectual learning never abidingly transcends the limitations of the hero's life and selfhood. To take two obvious examples, it seems to me essential to recognize that in both Goethe's

Wilhelm Meister and Thomas Mann's *The Magic Mountain* the seeming goal or "Grail" of both novels—the admission to the Society of the Tower in one, the snow vision in the other—is, as it were, taken back by the ongoing movement of the plot. In both cases we are concerned with a kind of privileged moment, where the possibility of human wholeness is glimpsed, is even discursively formulated. Yet this wholeness is not simply a set of wise sayings which, once learned, guarantee the inalienable possession of that wholeness they intimate. Rather, that wholeness, if it exists anywhere, informs the very flux of a character's life and experience. Wilhelm Meister finds himself clutching a set of maxims but feeling no wiser than before; Hans Castorp totters back to the sanatorium where he forgets those lessons he has affirmed with such conviction.

The Bildungsroman, both in theory and in practice, is little known outside Germany. This is unfortunate, specifically because many developments within the twentieth-century novel help us to see the Bildungsroman for the unique and challenging fictional mode that it is. (pp. 11-37)

> Martin Swales, "The 'Bildungsroman' as a Genre,"
> in his The German "Bildungsroman" from Wieland
> to Hesse, *Princeton University Press, 1978, pp. 9-37.*

M. M. BAKHTIN

[*A respected twentieth-century Russian essayist, literary theorist, and philosopher of language, Bakhtin is best known for his influence on the Structuralist and Semiotic literary movements. He was a prominent figure in the Russian intellectual circles of the 1920s, joining in the lively debate about Neo-Kantianism, Phenomenology, and the merits of the Formalists versus the sociological critics. In his critical writings, Bakhtin particularly emphasized the concept of discourse (slovo) and advocated the idea that literature must be studied along with its sociological and cultural context. Although many of his works were not published until the 1970s, Bakhtin is now considered an exceptionally acute and original thinker. The following excerpt was intended to have been part of a book on Goethe and the* Bildungsroman. *However, the manuscript and galleys of the book were destroyed during the German invasion of Russia, and only the essay "The 'Bildungsroman'" survives. Here, Bakhtin describes the main characteristics of the genre, asserting that "this type of novel can be designated in the most general sense as the novel of human emergence."*]

There exists a special subcategory of the novel called the "novel of education" (*Erziehungsroman* or *Bildungsroman*). Usually included (in chronological order) are the following major examples of this generic subcategory: Xenophon's *Cyropaedia* (classical), Wolfram von Eschenbach's *Parzival* (Middle Ages), Rabelais' *Gargantua and Pantagruel*, Grimmelshausen's *Simplicissimus* (the Renaissance), Fénelon's *Télémaque* (neoclassicism), Rousseau's *Emile* (since there is a considerable novelistic element in this pedagogical treatise), Wieland's *Agathon*, Wetzel's *Tobias Knout*, Hippel's *Lebensläufe nach aufsteigender Linie*, Goethe's *Wilhelm Meister* (both novels), Jean Paul's *Titan* (and several of his other novels), Dickens' *David Copperfield*, Raabe's *Der Hungerpastor*, Gottfried Keller's *Der grüne Heinrich*, Pontoppidan's *Lucky Peter*, Tolstoy's *Childhood, Adolescence, and Youth*, Goncharov's *An Ordinary Story* and *Oblomov*, Romain Rolland's *Jean-Christophe*, Thomas Mann's *Buddenbrooks* and *Magic Mountain,* and others.

Some scholars, guided by purely compositional principles (the concentration of the whole plot on the process of the hero's education), significantly limit this list (Rabelais, for example,

is excluded). Others, conversely, requiring only the presence of the hero's development and emergence in the novel, considerably expand this list, including such works, for example, as Fielding's *Tom Jones* or Thackeray's *Vanity Fair*.

It is clear even at first glance that this list contains phenomena that are too diverse, from the theoretical and even from the biographical standpoint. Some of the novels are essentially biographical or autobiographical, while others are not; in some of them the organizing basis is the purely pedagogical notion of man's education, while this is not even mentioned in others; some of them are constructed on the strictly chronological plane of the main hero's educational development and have almost no plot at all, while others, conversely, have complex adventuristic plots. Even more significant are the differences in the relationship of these novels to realism, and particularly to real historical time.

All this forces us to sort out in a different way not only this list, but also the entire problem of the so-called *Bildungsroman*.

It is necessary, first of all, to single out specifically the aspect of man's essential *becoming*. The vast majority of novels (and subcategories of novels) know only the image of the *ready-made* hero. All movement in the novel, all events and escapades depicted in it, shift the hero in space, up and down the rungs of the social ladder: from beggar to rich man, from homeless tramp to nobleman. The hero sometimes attains, sometimes only approaches his goal: the bride, the victory, wealth, and so on. Events change his destiny, change his position in life and society, but he himself remains unchanged and adequate to himself.

In the majority of subcategories of the novel, the plot, composition, and entire internal structure of the novel postulate this unchanging nature, this solidity of the hero's image, this static nature of his unity. The hero is a *constant* in the novel's formula and all other quantities—the spatial environment, social position, fortune, in brief, all aspects of the hero's life and destiny—can therefore be *variables*.

The actual content of this constant (the ready-made and unchanging hero) and the actual signs of his unity, permanence, and self-identity can vary immensely, beginning with the identity provided by the empty name of the hero (in certain subcategories of the adventure novel) and ending with a complex character, whose individual aspects are disclosed only gradually, throughout the course of the entire novel. The principle for guiding the selection of essential features and combining and unifying them into the whole of the hero's image can vary. Finally, various compositional methods can be used to reveal this image.

But given all the possible differences in construction, in the image of the hero itself there is neither movement nor emergence. The hero is that immobile and fixed point around which all movement in the novel takes place. The permanence and immobility of the hero are prerequisite to novelistic movement. An analysis of typical novel plots shows that they presuppose a ready-made, unchanging hero; they presuppose the hero's static unity. Movement in the fate and life of this ready-made hero constitutes the content of the plot; but the character of the man himself, his change and emergence do not become the plot. Such is the predominant type in this category of novel.

Along with this predominant, mass type, there is another incomparably rarer type of novel that provides an image of man in the process of becoming. As opposed to a static unity, here one finds a dynamic unity in the hero's image. The hero himself, his character, becomes a variable in the formula of this type of novel. Changes in the hero himself acquire *plot* significance, and thus the entire plot of the novel is reinterpreted and reconstructed. Time is introduced into man, enters into his very image, changing in a fundamental way the significance of all aspects of his destiny and life. This type of novel can be designated in the most general sense as the novel of human *emergence*.

A human being can, however, emerge in quite diverse ways. Everything depends upon the degree of assimilation of real historical time.

In pure adventure time, of course, man's emergence is impossible. . . . But it is quite possible in cyclical time. Thus, in idyllic time one can depict man's path from childhood through youth and maturity to old age, showing all those essential internal changes in a person's nature and views that take place in him as he grows older. Such a sequence of development (emergence) of man is cyclical in nature, repeating itself in each life. Such a cyclical (purely age-oriented) novel had not been created as a pure type, but elements of it were scattered throughout the work of eighteenth-century idyllists and the work of novelists of regionalism and *Heimatskunst* in the nineteenth century. Moreover, in the *humoristic branch* of the *Bildungsroman* (in the narrow sense) represented by Hippel and Jean Paul (to some degree Sterne as well), the idyllic-cyclical ingredient is immensely significant. That ingredient is also in evidence to a greater or lesser degree in other novels of emergence (it is very strong in Tolstoy, and this links him directly to the traditions of the eighteenth century).

Another type of cyclical emergence, which retains a connnection (but not such a close one) with man's age, traces a typically repeating path of man's emergence from youthful idealism and fantasies to mature sobriety and practicality. This path can be complicated in the end by varying degrees of skepticism and resignation. This kind of novel of emergence typically depicts the world and life as *experience*, as a *school*, through which every person must pass and derive one and the same result: one becomes more sober, experiencing some degree of resignation. This type is represented in its purest form in the classical novel of education in the second half of the eighteenth century, and above all in Wieland and Wetzel. To a very real extent, Keller's *Der grüne Heinrich* belongs here as well. Elements of this type are to be found in Hippel, Jean Paul, and, of course, Goethe.

The third type of novel of emergence is the biographical (and autobiographical) type. There is no longer any cyclical quality here. Emergence takes place in biographical time, and it passes through unrepeatable, individual stages. It can be typical, but this is no longer a cyclical typicality. Emergence here is the result of the entire totality of changing life circumstances and events, activity and work. Man's destiny is created and he himself, his character, is created along with it. The emergence of man's life-destiny fuses with the emergence of man himself. Fielding's *Tom Jones* and Dickens's *David Copperfield* are novels of this type.

The fourth type of novel of emergence is the didactic-pedagogical novel. It is based on a specific pedagogical ideal, understood more or less broadly, and depicts the pedagogical process of education in the strict sense of the word. Included in this pure type are such works as Xenophon's *Cyropaedia*, Fénelon's *Télémaque*, and Rousseau's *Emile*. But there are elements of

this type in other subcategories of the novel of emergence as well, including works by Goethe and Rabelais.

The fifth and last type of novel of emergence is the most significant one. In it man's individual emergence is inseparably linked to historical emergence. Man's emergence is accomplished in real historical time, with all of its necessity, its fullness, its future, and its profoundly chronotopic nature. In the four preceding types, man's emergence proceeded against the immobile background of the world, ready-made and basically quite stable. If changes did take place in this world, they were peripheral, in no way affecting its foundations. Man emerged, developed, and changed within one epoch. The world, existing and stable in this existence, required that man adapt to it, that he recognize and submit to the existing laws of life. Man emerged, but the world itself did not. On the contrary, the world was an immobile orientation point for developing man. Man's emergence was his private affair, as it were, and the results of this emergence were also private and biographical in nature. And everything in the world itself remained in its place. In and of itself the conception of the world as an experience, a school, was very productive in the *Bildungsroman*: it presented a different side of the world to man, a side that had previously been foreign to the novel. It led to a radical reinterpretation of the elements of the novel's plot and opened up for the novel new and realistically productive points for viewing the world. But the world, as an experience and as a school, remained the same, fundamentally immobile and ready-made, given. It changed for the one studying in it only during the process of study (in most cases that world turned out to be more impoverished and drier than it had seemed in the beginning).

In such novels as *Gargantua and Pantagruel*, *Simplicissimus*, and *Wilhelm Meister*, however, human emergence is of a different nature. It is no longer man's own private affair. He emerges *along with the world* and he reflects the historical emergence of the world itself. He is no longer within an epoch, but on the border between two epochs, at the transition point from one to the other. This transition is accomplished in him and through him. He is forced to become a new, unprecedented type of human being. What is happening here is precisely the emergence of a new man. The organizing force held by the future is therefore extremely great here—and this is not, of course, the private biographical future, but the historical future. It is as though the very *foundations* of the world are changing, and man must change along with them. Understandably, in such a novel of emergence, problems of reality and man's potential, problems of freedom and necessity, and the problem of creative initiative rise to their full height. The image of the emerging man begins to surmount its private nature (within certain limits, of course) and enters into a completely new, *spatial* sphere of historical existence. Such is the last, realistic type of novel of emergence.

Aspects of this historical emergence of man can be found in almost all important realistic novels, and, consequently, they exist in all works that achieve a significant assimilation of real historical time. (pp. 19-24)

M. M. Bakhtin, "The 'Bildungsroman' and Its Significance in the History of Realism (Toward a Historical Typology of the Novel)," in his Speech Genres and Other Late Essays, *edited by Caryl Emerson and Michael Holquist, translated by Vern W. McGee, University of Texas Press, 1986, pp. 10-59.*

FRANÇOIS JOST

[Jost describes the evolution of the Bildungsroman, *commenting on the ways in which its chief representatives from* Wilhelm Meister *on have shaped and expanded the genre.]*

The death certificate of the Bildungsroman, and even that of the novel, has been so often reproduced in studies on the art of the narrative that the literary world should have ratified the document a long time ago. Instead of mourning the demise of the genre, however, novelists are occupied with the question of how to meet the need of their reading public. An authentic kinship, it is true, between many of those nineteenth- and twentieth-century novels which still are usually called Bildungsromane and their recognized prototype, *Wilhelm Meisters Lehrjahre,* can be established only if one believes in the evolution of the various species rather than in their extinction. Since our social patterns constantly change and since literature will always in some manner reflect the state of society, the notion of a fixed literary form remains an incongruity even though some forms show a surprising longevity. . . . (p. 125)

Goethe's Wilhelm enjoyed the education that an upper-class bourgeois businessman of the second half of the eighteenth century was able and willing to provide for his progeny. He is twenty when he enters the stage of the novel. Advice and support other than financial is barely needed. In his early childhood he had absorbed the entire "Kinderstube-Philosophie" and—anachronistically—the whole "Struwwelpeter-Moral." We are dealing here with a first characteristic of the standard Bildungsroman. In later nineteenth-century specimens, particularly in Great Britain, the protagonist, a boy of five or ten, depends on his family (which sometimes rejects him) and is denied Wilhelm's basic training for a successful career and a carefree existence. One of the reasons for some heroes' final distress or failure in life is to be seen in the parents' neglect of their educational duties.

The classic Bildungsroman is by no means identical with the novel of infancy or childhood. Such a novel may qualify for the label *Erziehungsroman, Erziehung* meaning elementary education with a pedagogue or tutor, a role assumed by the family and by instructors. In the Anglo-Saxon world the word "education" has a much wider acceptance than the word *Erziehung* has in the German *Sprachraum.* It comprises also *Bildung.* English and American university professors are educators: in Germany, an *Erzieher* is a teacher in grade school, or an employee of an *Erziehungsanstalt,* a correctional institution. The German professor has to provide *Bildung,* not *Erziehung.* Formation does not currently have the meaning of *Bildung,* a meaning perfectly rendered by the French *formation* and its philological equivalents in other Romance languages. *Sich bilden* means to give one's mind, one's character, and one's personality their final shape, their final form. The verb *bilden,* the etymological root of Bildungsroman, assumes reflexive implications and the accurate name for our species could be *Selbstbildungsroman.*

Wilhelm is mentally and morally well equipped for the journey he is asked to undertake by his father, who plies a flourishing trade. The reader of the *Lehrjahre,* however, does not learn much about the son's work performed when he is supposed to be on duty. In fact, Wilhelm prefers to explore a broader world than that of business, namely the full spectrum of human life. He does it rather candidly, optimistically—on the whole, the traditional Bildungsroman is *lebensbejahend.* After struggling for his *Bildung,* the protagonist realizes that outsiders seldom reach their goal and that the material and spiritual riches granted by society should elicit his gratitude and soften his possible rancors. (pp. 125-26)

Specific social and poetical circumstances partly explain the birth and growth of the Bildungsroman. At the time *Wilhelm Meister* was first published, namely in 1795-1796, Germany was divided into hundreds of independent states governed by members of ruling dynasties. They witnessed the rise of the bourgeoisie, and the French Revolution had been a stern warning to them. To keep peace and order became the primary duty of every citizen. During the second half of the eighteenth century, the German-speaking part of Europe had outstanding pedagogical innovators like Johann Bernhard Basedow (1724-1790), the great pioneer; he was followed by Joachim Heinrich Campe and Heinrich Pestalozzi, both born in 1746, whose ideals were kept alive by the next generation, by pedagogues like Herbart (1776-1841) and Fröbel (1782-1852). Early education became of paramount importance. Children had to be trained for very precise purposes: they had to become self-disciplined citizens and useful members of an enlightened society governed by enlightened rulers.

The education of adolescents and adults, however, took place in *höheren Bildungsanstalten,* that is, in universities, through contact with a select society and largely through literature, especially the novel. If we look for examples illustrating the axiom that literature is necessarily rooted in society, we may remember Germany's preoccupation with education, especially since the late eighteenth century, and analyze the reasons for the flowering of the Bildungsroman.

Since *Wilhelm Meisters Lehrjahre* remains the paragon of the genre, we have to expound briefly the principles on which it rests. The first of these and by far the most significant one is symbolically expressed in the title. William Master, through his apprenticeship, through his experience, will become master of himself. Apprenticed to the world, he starts out to be an oxymoron—*Lehrling-Meister.* In the course of the novel he finds his own personality and at the end he reaches a degree of self-recognition sufficient for a masterly conduct of life. This principle fits perfectly into the ideals, if not of the *Sturm und Drang* movement, at least into those of European romanticism in general. To seek one's own self, to develop the self according to one's specific nature, amounts to encouraging individualism, an obvious tenet of nineteenth-century Western culture. Two major aspects of romanticism, however, are missing. Goethe wants Meister to bridle his eccentricities in order to fit into his social milieu and to be worthy of it. Although he is happy to escape traditional institutions and temporarily rejects conventional social patterns, his apprenticeship leads to adaptation, not to rebellion. Furthermore, Meister does not express any feelings resembling *Weltschmerz.* He is, on the contrary, invited to replace the sad *memento mori* by a merry *memento vivere, gedenke zu leben!* He educates himself for that world which he is destined to live in.

The time spent in preparing oneself for a happy life should not, moreover, be a time of hardship. The whole journey should be pleasant, not only the arrival in the harbor. This is not to say that Meister's craft succeeds in avoiding every tempest, but it escapes all fatal dangers. Its captain has to face the caprices of the sea, but he sails safely between the whirlpools of Charybdis and the rocks of Scylla. He has illusions and commits mistakes. Thus the whole voyage represents a full human experience: Goethe believes in the basic formative virtues of such a test. The time from puberty to maturity, therefore, the way from inexperience to experience, is not an ordeal, but a challenge, although Meredith's *Ordeal of Richard Feveral* is a good Bildungsroman *anglico modo*. Wisdom, according to Goethe, comes to man through follies and truth through errors. Only errors can cure errors: such is the recipe of autotherapy the novel suggests. No mentor tells Wilhelm that he should renounce one of the careers with which he experiments, that of an actor. He himself discovers that with this profession he would be forced to go through life with a mask. He would have to play the role of others and would not be able to live according to his own nature, which should be the ultimate fulfillment of man's destiny.

Goethe's novel is highly didactic. It is a book of wisdom expounding the maxims governing Wilhelm's behavior. There is hardly an episode which does not express or imply a pedagogical lesson. This fact reveals the author's intention. The plot, the structure of which is very loose, is by no means organized according to Wilhelm's will or initiative. He remains a rather passive hero in so far as he is guided by the educative power of his surroundings. Instead of creating situations, he confronts them. The process of maturation he experiences is comparable to that which a fruit has to undergo. It has to suffer rain and sun and wind, but never decides the weather. Obviously, however, Meister has to react intelligently to the vagaries of his environmental climate.

The history of the variations our species underwent in the course of two centuries must include not only the study of the matter, that is themes and plots, but also the manner, that is, narrative techniques. In his book *Aspects of the Novel* Edward Morgan Forster has a chapter entitled "Flat and Round Characters." The metaphor should be expanded and applied to the novel itself, to the whole cast of characters. Thus one may speak of flat novels, like the picaresque novel, or round novels, like the Bildungsroman, and, to use a new image, of polygonal novels, which might also be called fresco novels. The flat novel contains characters which are basically unrelated, or related only temporarily or by chance. They do not form a homogeneous group of actors. They happen to be in contact with one other, enter on stage and exit according to the author's fantasy. The protagonist is no exception. He remains a static figure, does not undergo any change except that he may, at the end, be more clever in the pursuit of his life of roguery.

The Bildungsroman has one central character and only one, who, during the course of the action, is bound to undergo a profound evolution. He is in the center of the plot, in the center of the circle formed by his antagonists. This situation is essential to the Bildungsroman and suggests that we may classify the genre among the round novels. Indeed, many novels other than the Bildungsromane present similar characteristics, *Werther* for example. We shall have to speak of *Wilhelm Meisters Lehrjahre*, however, the prototype of the genre to be examined. Only Meister's destiny, and by no means that of Marianne and Aurelie, or of Lothario and Serlo, or of Mignon and Felix, captivates our attention. All these characters cruise around Wilhelm in perfectly circular or elliptic orbits.

This is in contrast to our third category of novels, the fresco type. In *War and Peace*, for instance, Tolstoi presents a coherent group of characters who progress while in contact with each other. The image of a concave polygon expresses the idea that interchanges take place between each side and several others. The fate of more than one central personage is at stake; the destiny of all major *dramatis personae* interests the reader, although less than that of the *maxima persona*. Anna Karenina

is certainly that persona in another of Tolstoi's novels; in many ways, however, she is *prima inter pares,* some other figures being almost as fascinating as she is. The action progresses because several characters, either together or in turn, are presented as progressing. Spontaneously one thinks of Laclos's *Les Liaisons dangereuses*.

In the classic Bildungsroman there is only one central character developing among some walkers-on, in the midst of a crowd of quasi-supernumeraries. Furthermore, the classic Bildungsroman has hardly any room for truly epic episodes or breathtaking happenings. . . . The German species is most often structured according to the principles of Rousseau, whom Goethe very much admired. In the preface to *La Nouvelle Héloïse,* written in the form of a dialogue, the imaginary interlocutor, at one point, tells the author that the plot lacks interest. There is not one rascal the good people have to fear, he argues, no surprise, no *coup de théâtre*. Rousseau's answer to the objection hints at one of the new directions the art of the narrative was about to take: "You want ordinary characters and extraordinary events? I believe that I would prefer the opposite." Psychological concerns, which had already been salient in *Clarissa,* and much earlier in *La Princesse de Clèves,* gained new momentum. Surprising happenings, however, like those we witness in these two works, were not obligatory any more in fiction; no astounding situation, no *deus ex machina* had to provide some clue or resolve a suspense in an action otherwise doomed to a dead end. The appearance of the Bildungsroman is a consequence of the birth of the realistic novel in the modern sense of the word. It definitely closes the era of the romance.

An examination of the content—characters and plots—of some major novels listed under the rubric Bildungsroman should lead to a better understanding of the genre. We may forget for the time being the chronology of their publication in order to perceive their common nature more accurately. While they share most overall features, obviously many aspects related to structure and setting vary from one work to the next, just as the author's intention may change from novel to novel. It is a matter of distinguishing essence and existence. A brief comparison of an early and late sample of the genre with *Wilhelm Meister* is intended to illustrate this fact. Fanny Burney's preBildungsroman *Evelina, or the History of a Young Lady's Entrance into the World,* written twenty years before the archetype of the genre, is an epistolary novel. Romain Rolland's *Jean-Christophe* is a straightforward third-person narrative, somehow a post-Bildungsroman in the sense that it was published at a time—at the beginning of the twentieth century—when the concept had been severely undermined by various literary trends and when *Wilhelm Meister*—and its closest family— had lost much of its appeal. Nonetheless, these two works, if contrasted with Goethe's novel, will further our understanding of the philosophy underlying the Bildungsroman.

Evelina is a round novel exactly like *Wilhelm Meister*. Even more than Goethe's hero, however, Fanny Burney's heroine remains the toy of the circumstances into which she is driven against her will or, at least, without her doing. She remains the only focus of the plot, despite the parade of eccentrics, who seem to be offspring of *Humphry Clinker,* and despite the impeccable Lord Orville, who grants the plot a happy end. Nonetheless Evelina is the sole character who develops in the course of her apprenticeship, or, as the subtitle says, in the course of her *Entrance into the World*. Clearly she moves from inexperience to experience, while all the characters she is confronted with remain static: thus Mr. Villars, who plays a significant role in the story, never meets with any of the performers of the plot other than Evelina, his ward.

There is still an essential difference between the two novels resulting from the fact that Fanny Burney describes a lady's apprenticeship, while Goethe's hero is a man. The only goal Evelina seems to strive toward is her happiness, to be achieved by making a wealthy, distinguished gentleman happy. At no point in the novel does the reader feel that Evelina wants to know herself, that she ever suspects life could grant sources of fulfillment other than those derived from the benefits of a Lord's esteem and love and from a Lord's estate. In fact, when she marries Orville at the age of eighteen, she has completed her destiny. Her profession consists of being a useful member of the smallest society: her family, her neighbors, and her relatives. The fine qualities she has acquired in the process of her education curriculum promptly receive, like Pamela's, their supreme and final reward: a perfect husband.

The implications suggested by a novel like *Wilhelm Meister* are different. At the last page Wilhelm shows himself ready for life. In the English novel, the last page is an end; in the German one it is a beginning. For this reason many Bildungsromane with male characters have sequels or correlatives. After *Wilhelm Meisters Lehrjahre*, Goethe describes his hero's *Wanderjahre*. Wieland's *Agathon*—the first version of which precedes *Meister* by thirty years—is followed by *Agathodämon*, Stifter's *Nachsommer* by *Witiko*, Keller's *Der grüne Heinrich* by *Martin Salander*. From the point of view of Eugène Rastignac, *Le Père Goriot* may be considered a kind of Bildungsroman. Balzac has Rastignac come back on stage in many of his *Scènes de la vie parisienne*. Hemingway used a similar procedure. Nick Adams, the hero of *In Our Time*, appears again, under the name of Frederick Henry, in *A Farewell to Arms*. The example of Faulkner's *Go Down, Moses* might also be cited. *Evelina*—the genuine feminine Bildungsroman belongs to a later era—cannot be complemented or expanded by a sequel. Fanny Burney's heroine confronts us with a dilemma. After her marriage to Orville she will either start a life of psychological adventures, in which case her *Bildung* will prove to be an obvious failure, and even more so the novel itself, since, as it stands, it depicts her *Bildung* as an absolute success; or, as the reader must expect, she will always remain a faithful wife. In the latter case she would cease to be a literary theme. In literature the anchor of wedlock tends to be the standard symbol of boredom, an idea Byron expressed in his *Don Juan:*

> Romances paint at full length people's wooings
> But only give a bust of marriages;
> For no one cares for matrimonial cooings,
> There's nothing wrong in a connubial kiss:
> Think you, if Laura had been Petrarch's wife,
> He would have written sonnets all his life?

At first view it seems difficult to detect any common feature between *Evelina* and *Jean-Christophe*. The rapprochement, however, is possible, at least under the aegis of *Wilhelm Meister*. Even if hundreds of pages of Rolland's *roman fleuve*, his *opus magnum*, are devoted to social satire, to philosophical considerations and to the description of life and manners in "la belle époque," one single character only has the readers' full attention from the beginning to the end, for only Jean-Christophe undergoes a significant change: again we are dealing with a round novel. This is not to say that secondary figures, which may appear at different times in the course of the action, remain stationary during the several decades of the hero's apprenticeship. Their psychological development, however, is

interesting only to the extent that it conditions or illustrates Jean-Christophe's own progress.

Romain Rolland's masterpiece poses two problems. The first is related to the *roman de formation* in France. Mainly for political and ethno-psychological reasons—the French are a nation of individualists—the *Lehrjahre* were seldom a model for nineteenth-century French novelists. Fromentin's *Dominique* is a tale concerned with renunciation of love, Alain-Fournier's *Le Grand Meaulnes* is a story of dreams and escapism, and Colette's *Le Blé en herbe* belongs to a sort of apprenticeship novel in which Goethe's pedigree is only vaguely visible. The second problem is inherent to Rolland's work. It is a complete biography of the hero and thereby exceeds by far the traditional frame of the genre which limits itself to the *making* of the hero, while the *being* of a hero is beyond its concerns. Jean-Christophe's entire life, however, is a quest and a search for his identity, a fact that saves Rolland the trouble of writing a sequel.

Jean-Christophe is a Künstlerroman: the protagonist is an artist, a musician. While Wilhelm refuses to become a professional actor, Jean-Christophe pursues his vocation. Hence a new question arises: since the hero of a Bildungsroman, according to Goethe, has to become useful to society, and since artists are often outsiders, one may wonder whether a Künstler may qualify as protagonist of such a novel. He may, in so far as his goal consists of finding his true personality; he may not, if his apprenticeship lacks a social purpose. Novelists have good reasons, however, for having their heroes try their hands and talents at the arts. A painting, a statue, a song is the most personal expression of the self. "Le style est l'homme même": styles are generated only through creative activities. Many German Bildungsromane are to a certain degree Künstlerromane. In English literature the trend started with Disraeli's *Contarini Fleming* and culminated in *A Portrait of the Artist as a Young Man*. In our context, however, the basic common feature the reader of *Jean-Christophe* and of *Wilhelm Meister* identifies spontaneously is the positive attitude toward life exhibited by the main characters, an attitude shared or forecast by *Evelina*. All three heroes are affirmative, self-made personalities.

Occasionally the spirit of the *Lehrjahre* has been faithfully imitated. Free adaptations, however, were by far more frequent than accurate transpositions of new plots to the basic patterns of the original. *Der grüne Heinrich* is an example in point. In its first version Keller has Heinrich leave Zurich for Munich where, at the age of twenty, he wants to study the art of painting. . . . The mysterious, enigmatic, and somehow esoteric "Society of the Tower" in which Wilhelm is involved and where he gets acquainted with Natalie, his "beautiful find," has its counterpart in the family circle of the country castle where Heinrich meets Dortchen Schönfund. From the genological point of view, the change Keller made in his second version is most important. Heinrich's final happiness with Judith now stamps the novel as an authentic Bildungsroman. In the original edition, on the contrary, the reader found a *zypressendunklen Schluss*: grass grew on Green Henry's early grave. Death, Keller realized, tends to weaken, even to invalidate the plot of a true apprenticeship novel, which is a *Schauspiel*, not a *Tragödie*. This statement calls for an explanation. Since the protagonist is a mortal being, he may die at any stage of his terrestrial pilgrimage. However, the novel, *qua* Bildungsroman, is constructed in view of the protagonist's career, success, and triumph over deficiencies and mishaps. If at the end of the *Lehrjahre* death comes for Wilhelm, the critic is faced with a dilemma: either the novel lacks unity of tone and intent, and when writing his first chapter the author had not yet conceived the overall idea of his work; or he wished to surprise his readers with a lugubrious dénouement which would teach this superb lesson: *Bildung* is superfluous, since one's apprenticeship is nothing but a voyage to the shore of the Styx. After a few pages of *Anna Karenina* or of *Madame Bovary* we know that the heroines are doomed to failure; after a few pages of *Wilhelm Meister* we know that the hero is predestinated for a happy life. *Maler Nolten*, published at the close of Goethe's reign, when its author, Eduard Mörike, was twenty-eight, foreshadows Keller's original text, since the novel concludes with the hero's death. Although often compared with *Meister, Nolten*, written during Goethe's later years, represents a pseudo-type of the species, close also to the *Wahlverwandtschaften*. Mörike carefully prepared the reader for the hero's untimely demise.

Stifter's Heinrich, like Keller's, wants to acquire his own *Bildung* at a stage of his life when he is ready to do so. After receiving good instruction in all basic fields of knowledge from a private mentor who supervised the first steps of his intellectual and psychological progress, he chooses to assume himself the responsibility for his future existence. Again, this stage constitutes the core of the novel. And, again, external events invite the reader to draw parallels between *Wilhelm Meisters Lehrjahre*, *Der grüne Heinrich*, and *Der Nachsommer*. The name of Stifter's hero, as we just said, is Heinrich as that of Keller's, and the name of the hero's wife is Natalie, like that of Wilhelm's. A major episode of the plot, actually the crucial one, takes place at the Asperhof, the estate of Freiherr von Risach—reminiscent of Lothario's "Turmgesellschaft," and of the castle of Green Henry's count. Like Wilhelm, who was an actor, like Keller's Heinrich, who was a painter, Stifter's protagonist, after studying natural sciences, geology in particular, is attracted to the arts. In all three cases, however, art is not the goal, but only a means, be it a most significant one, to attain *Bildung*. *Bildung* develops fitness for life and protects the hero from any terminal downfall.

Similar shiftings in emphasis and design, and even more striking ones, took place in the United Kingdom. Thomas Carlyle was born the very year (1795) the novel he was to translate started to be printed. He familiarized England with the new species, but offered no thoroughbred specimen. As far as its content is concerned, *Sartor Resartus* is close to Swift's *A Tale of a Tub*, while some of its formal features, especially in the second book, are reminiscent of *Wilhelm Meister*. Disraeli's *Vivian Grey* and Bulwer Lytton's *Ernest Maltravers* are among the first post-Goethean Bildungsromane in English literature. Although they only marginally qualify, they count among the first English variations of the species.

One reason why Great Britain offers only very few examples of the classical Bildungsroman—and they are rather mediocre *Romane*—has already been explained. *Bildung* (formation) being conceived as a synonym of *Erziehung* (education), the "hero" may begin his novelistic career at any stage of his life. *Lehrjahre*, however, or *Lehrzeit* imply that the *Lehrling* is beyond childhood. This fact does not prevent Goethe from giving occasional flashbacks to happenings that occurred in Wilhelm's early years. Yet on the whole the original Bildungsroman is not the novel of infancy in which the protagonist is pushed on stage in a pram, nor is it the novel of early upbringing. Wilhelm is an adolescent who enjoys the love and care of his parents, a young man who does not want to draw any more on the wisdom and experience of his tutors, who feels the urge to fly out of his nest in order to find, outside the circle of his familiar environment, his personal liberty, his own self. Such circumstances are seldom found in the English novel, while they are quite usual in German literature.

The contemporary Bildungsroman is often far removed from the traditional bourgeois setting. An essential feature of the species, however, is the protagonist's struggle for selfness rather than his display of selfishness. The apprentice's objective is his integration into a certain society which is not necessarily a nation's dominating class. Cesare Pavese's *Il compagno* shows a young guitarist who, apprenticed to the Communist party, earns his diploma as *uomo educato* while serving as a loyal member in a political group. Self-fulfillment, a condition for man's happiness, may be achieved in diverse social strata, and the notion of Bildungsroman may be interpreted on various levels.

So far we were mainly concerned with two aspects of the traditional Bildungsroman; first with the pedagogical, sociological and moral principles underlaying the *Lehrjahre;* then with the achievements of some of Goethe's precursors and followers, who illustrate nuances and divergences between the model and the works usually considered specimens of the genre. Now a third question arises, that of its evolution in more recent times, for the Bildungsroman survives in a social climate widely different from that which presided over Wilhelm's destiny.

The discussion calls for some preliminary remarks about terminology. Although it is or should be generally recognized that the classical Bildungsroman is not a tale of youthful growth, a work similar to or identical with any kind of *Erziehungsroman* or *Entwicklungsroman*, many studies about our species often treat all three terms as synonymous. Thus the meaning of the word Bildungsroman has been expanded to include many of its variants. The most prosperous ones belong to the category encompassing novels of infancy, childhood, and early adolescence. Yet such works may be considered *pre-Bildungsromane* only, since the protagonist is not yet ready for *Bildung*, only for *Erziehung*. German novelists generally assumed their characters to be endowed with all the benefits received from responsible and loving parents, and were treating themes of continuing education, *Selbstbildung*. English authors, on the contrary, especially in the Victorian age, tended to illustrate the inadequacy of extant pedagogical systems: many of their novels, although called Bildungsromane, may be interpreted as critiques of a regime unconcerned about the future of the nation. A continuing education supposes a beginning education. The second half of the English nineteenth century offers only few *Bildungsromane* in the traditional sense of the word. Most of them are centered on the life of outcast or underprivileged children, or of pubescent youths. Their struggles and their fate may certainly provide for the plot of a novel—or for a melodrama. Many protagonists are born into slavery in one way or another. As we learn from history, slavery is the cement of all empire building. In ancient Rome prisoners of war became slaves; in America, chiefly Africans, and in England, countless David Copperfields who had to help construct backstage the modern British Commonwealth. Evidently we are far removed from the classical premises of the Bildungsroman in which the protagonist does not need a slingshot to get rid of some extraneous Goliath, but willpower and self-discipline to free himself from the Philistine within. David Copperfield is not Wilhelm Meister. The former quenches his thirst with milk, the latter with wine.

Not only the age of the heroes, but also mood and tone, pitch and key of the entire works may differ from those discernible in Goethe and his disciples. Many post-*Meister* novels—we are still thinking mainly of English works—depart from the model, in that they are conceived as tragedies. Their point of departure is determined by depressing family conditions and sordid social circumstances, a fact that by no means excludes charm and sentimentality. If the setting is London, at least some chapters of the story call for headings like "triste" or "mestissimo." *Of Human Bondage* starts with this remark: "The day broke gray and dull." Some scenes of *Great Expectations* are as gloomy as the gloomiest in *David Copperfield*. Pip is a victim of child labor, a little orphan whom destiny puts into the open concentration camp of Victorian industrial establishments with a pocket knife, so to speak, as his only weapon. He is as unhappy a child as Cosette in Hugo's *Les Misérables*.

Like Cosette, Pip is an instrument of social criticism. In scores of masterpieces children tell the truth about cultural, religious, and political institutions. Sterne could be considered the modern founder of that genre, although *Tristram Shandy* is not really the best example, since the work is chiefly about somehow individual characters. The prize for that category may go to Günter Grass, though his novel *Die Blechtrommel* is not meant to be a Kindheitsroman or a Bildungsroman. For satirical purposes Oskar Matzerath, an inmate in an asylum, narrates his life from the age of zero minus nine months till the age of thirty. When he was three, however, he ceased to grow: the dwarf is equippd with a noisy tin drum which he beats when he wishes to remind the reader of certain past events—mainly related to Hitler's Germany—or to protest against the world of grown-ups, of people, of *Bildung*.

Clearly the most fertile soil for the variation of the species we are presently dealing with, the novel of childhood and adolescence, was that of Great Britain, where it appealed to scores of writers even before and beyond the Victorian age, and from where it was exported to the United States. The basic elements of what we may call the English Bildungsroman have been most accurately described in the following text:

> A child of sensibility grows up in the country or in a provincial town, where he finds constraints, social and intellectual, placed upon the free imagination. His family, especially his father, proves doggedly hostile to his creative instincts or flights of fancy, antagonistic to his ambitions, and quite impervious to the new ideas he has gained from unprescribed reading. His first schooling, even if not totally inadequate, may be frustrating insofar as it may suggest options not available to him in his present setting. He therefore, sometimes at a quite early age, leaves the repressive atmosphere of home (and also the relative innocence), to make his way independently in the city (in the English novels, usually London). There his real "education" begins, not only his preparation for a career but also—and often more importantly—his direct experience of urban life. The latter involves at least two love affairs or sexual encounters, one debasing, one exalting, and demands that in this respect and others the hero reappraise his values. By the time he has decided, after painful soul-searching, the sort of accommodation to the modern world he can honestly make, he has left his adolescence behind and entered upon his maturity. His initiation complete, he may then visit his old home, to demonstrate by his presence the degree of his success or the wisdom of his choice.

These lines provide an accurate outline of plots found in many English Bildungsromane. Yet we should not forget that in the years *Great Expectations* appeared, Thomas Hughes published two of the most popular English novels related to our genre, *Tom Brown's Schooldays* and its sequel, *Tom Brown at Oxford*: justly forgotten Erziehungsromane which are not quite Bildungsromane, however. They testify to England's worries about education at a time when pedagogical facilities were still mainly reserved for the upper crust of society.

The deep discrepancy between the nineteenth-century British Bildungsroman and the traditional German specimens leads to the conclusion that England possesses a most vital variation of her own, that is, the *Entwicklungsroman*, in which the hero—for whom the author feels free to choose any course of action—may start developing at any age. The word "Bildungsroman," now, is used metaphorically. While Bildung supposes development, not every development implies Bildung. Although the difference between the two terms is less frequently stressed today than it used to be, in literary scholarship the distinction should be maintained. After all, what is literary criticism without some "sens des nuances" and instinct for subtle discriminations? It is possible or probable that world literature offers more examples of the English variation—which is not confined to England—than imitations of the German standard model. The former, therefore, to reverse the chronological order, could be considered the genus and the latter, the Meister type, the species. As a consequence, the current denomination appears to be a synecdoche: the part is put for the whole; the rather precisely defined classic Bildungsroman stands for a class in which practically every novel can be admitted, that of the *Entwicklungsroman*—since there is hardly any novel without *Entwicklung*, development.

In quite a few countries children have also been chosen as protagonists for reasons other than political and social satire or humanitarian commiseration. (pp. 126-38)

The classic Bildungsroman sets a time limit for the hero's formation. During his whole life, it is true, man should heed the advice of the Delphic Oracle: "Know thyself," and, therefore, strive to find himself. Nevertheless, the authentic specimens of the apprenticeship novel do not lead the protagonist beyond the age of his intellectual maturity or beyond the point at which he has acquired a sense of full social responsibility. They are neither novels of late bloomers nor of early suicides.

While the English *Entwicklungsroman* as described before is a legitimate offspring of the Bildungsroman, world literature presents other kinds of progenies. There are numerous novels, often labeled Bildungsromane, which do not at all resemble the standard patterns in overall intent, in form, in mood or plot. They represent perversions of the species, they are monsters—in our context only, to be sure, for their intrinsic value is not the subject of our discussion.

Today *Wilhelm Meisters Lehrjahre* and its German predecessors, such as Wieland's *Agathon*, or its pseudo-models, like *Ardinghello* in which Heinse trains his hero for carnal pleasure, or *Anton Reiser* in which Moritz leads his hero to his final breakdown as a *Künstler*, belong to literary history and criticism rather than to the body of living works. For the study of our species Goethe's work remains a kind of touchstone, but in contemporary literature "Meisterism" in its original form exists no more than does Petrarchism. Yet the concept of a certain love in Western communities is best analyzed in the *Canzoniere*, and the concept of a certain education is best illustrated in *Wilhelm Meister*. Subsequent individual works belonging to either the sonnet or the Bildungsroman should be judged in relation to their respective family traditions and in relation to the achievements of their founding fathers. Many of these works depart widely from their original model. Meaningful comparisons among them are possible only if the critic measures the distance separating each of them from the poles Petrarch and Goethe drove into the ground of their specific literary territories. Just as most Italian poets after Petrarch composed sonnets, most German novelists in Goethe's time and later wrote Bildungsromane: Wackenroder, one of the creators of the *Künstlerroman*, Tieck, whose *William Lovell* was published the very same year as *Wilhelm Meister*, Friedrich Schlegel and Novalis, Jean Paul and Eichendorff. In Germany the genre continued to be cultivated throughout the nineteenth century and was exemplified in the twentieth by major authors: Hesse wrote *Narziss und Goldmund*, Mann, *Der Zauberberg*.

Now we have to turn to some Bildungsromane which may be remarkable novels, though, qua Bildungsromane, they remain monsters. They may bring glory to literature, but only little honor to the species they are wrongly supposed to illustrate. Using Goethe's novel as our compass, we shall examine some of the unusual turns taken by works classified as apprenticeship novels.

A Bildungsroman is not a self-inclusive "spectacle dans un fauteuil." It concludes with an open end which, considering the logics of the plot, is assumed to be a happy one. This is not the case in many specimens of various European literatures, those, especially, which do not provide for a final homecoming or decisive reconciliation with society. In the school of life, this sort of protagonist is often a drop-out; he is not admitted to the commencement exercises where the diplomas of manhood are delivered. In *The Ordeal of Richard Feverel*, for example, Meredith narrates Richard's entire life, from his boyhood to the duel which causes his downfall. His death is followed by that of his beloved Lucy, who promptly joins him in the grave. Does *Sons and Lovers*, to mention another example, belong to the same category? D. H. Lawrence's masterpiece is filled with irreparable tragedies, and even if Paul, after losing everything he loved—Clara, Miriam, and his mother—hopes at the end of the novel to be able to start a new life, he can hardly claim to be the protagonist of a Bildungsroman. The future he envisions is not based on his past; on the contrary, it will be a break with the past: no self-discovery has taken place. Similarly, Ernst, the hero of *The Way of All Flesh*, after a turbulent youth wishes to start a new life for which, however, he has not been specially prepared, a life devoted to literature. In both Lawrence's and Butler's novels a similar psychological problem is treated: on the one hand, the mother-son relationship, and the father-son relationship, on the other hand.

No *Bildungsziel* is apparent either in George Eliot's *The Mill on the Floss*. The novel describes the fate of two children, Maggie and her brother Tom. They seal it dramatically by drowning in the river. In *Jude the Obscure*, Thomas Hardy permits his hero to die a victim of social institutions, marriage and systems of higher education, that is, *Bildungsanstalten* which are satirized on almost every page. The story of *Marius the Epicurian* is set at the time of Marcus Aurelius. After studying all philosophies available to him, Walter Pater's protagonist becomes a Christian and concludes his life as a victim of the plague. This British "fureur de tuer" was not triggered by the *Lehrjahre*. But England, to be sure, also had novels,

like *Pendennis*, in which the hero did finally adjust to society. Pen's last statement might be signed by Wilhelm: "I take the world as it is, and being of it I will not be ashamed of it."

The protagonist of a traditional Bildungsroman is not fatally struck by the events he is supposed to master. Nor does he waste the fruit of his *Bildung*. Above all, some positive results should be seen. *L'Éducation sentimentale*, like the novels just mentioned, ignores the fundamentally teleological character of the sterling species. Flaubert's work hardly reminds the reader of Wilhelm Meister. Frédéric at the last page of the novel is merely older than at the beginning . . . and collects the only reward, melancholy souvenirs, the mediocrity of his character deserves. Every individual has a self; every hero of a Bildungsroman, however, must develop or strive for a better self, which is the object of his quest. Goethe believed that generally man is good, while men might be bad. He shared this view with Rousseau, whose novel *Émile*, almost always considered a mere pedagogical treatise, is an authentic forerunner of the English Bildungsroman, since the protagonist starts his career as an infant. If a man finds himself, he probably finds a good man, and he may serenely face his destiny.

The Bildungsroman or Entwicklungsroman is also a psychological novel. In psychology the time factor is essential. Witiko, Stifter's apprentice, however, should not need sixty years to prepare himself for a happy life, unless he is thinking of the life beyond. He is the dinosaur of the present group, while the hero of Joyce's *Ulysses* remains its ephemera. Obviously the opposite would be true, were we to discuss literary values. But let us pursue our reasoning. Clearly, a day is a day. With the information the reader of *Ulysses* might have gathered from the *Portrait* and *Dubliners*, however, a day may well be worth ten years, the standard time of an apprenticeship plot, the time, also, which Homer's hero needed to prepare himself for a careless, untroubled life with his Penelope. He got his *Bildung* in Troy and at sea. In the broadest sense of the word the Bildungsroman is as old as literature.

In a narrower sense, however, the modern *Ulysses* does not belong to the species. Stephen, it is true, after his final meeting with Bloom, as we are told, finds his self. While the reader of any apprenticeship novel is entitled to peruse the *curriculum vitae* of the protagonist in its entirety, that is, to follow his development step by step in order to judge the hero's progress, his merits and achievements, Joyce, despite the length of the novel, offers only a "comprimé," since the action lasts no longer than eighteen hours. His procedure reminds one of the classical stage in France. No psychological development could exceed the time the earth needs to turn around its axis. During that time a hero, kept prisoner in his palace—including its park—was to accomplish only one action. Joyce's characters, on the contrary, not only move around freely, but are engaged in a variety of adventures. The French playwright Racine and the Irish novelist use the notion of time in a similar way; for the former expects his audience to know the mythological setting of his *Phèdre* just as Joyce assumes the reader of his *Ulysses* to be familiar with his earlier works. As a rule, though, the Bildungsroman stands fully by itself: no extraneous information has to complement the understanding of the characters or the plot.

The feminine Bildungsroman—not necessarily the author, but the protagonist being a woman—is another variation of the species. Given the climate of the present times, no gift of prophecy is needed to suspect that its future prosperity is guaranteed. Yet one fundamental question needs answering first.

A portrait of Johann Wolfgang von Goethe.

Is there a genological difference between a feminine and a masculine Bildungsroman? In the early history of the genre such a distinction must be made. To the critic who admits that *Evelina* is a sort of Bildungsroman the novel necessarily belongs to the species under discussion. He does not justify his opinion with the fact that the author is a lady, but that the protagonist is a lady. He notices that the purpose of the apprenticeship and the goal to be reached in Fanny Burney's work are not those Wilhelm Meister was to achieve. Since the Bildungsroman is teleologically oriented, *Evelina* and the *Lehrjahre* clearly aim at different targets and represent two separate educational ideals. One novel concludes with a happy end, the other, with a happy beginning, Wilhelm having been equipped, in the course of five hundred pages, for a prosperous life. In a society, however, in which role and function of men and women tend to become identical, the feminine and masculine Bildungsromane will become, sooner or later, identical as well.

Evidently any work may show different colors, emit different fragrances, utter different tones according to the sex of its author and its characters. The Bildungsroman is no exception. Today the *differencia specifica* separating the feminine and the masculine variations cannot yet be defined by mere color, fragrance, and tone. There are still more basic divergences to be seen in the circumstances under which the protagonist has to complete his *Bildung* and the means he has to choose in order to reach his goal. These divergences may be summarized in a few words: in a feminine Bildungsroman the heroine has to struggle with a world dominated by masculine power; in the masculine Bildungsroman the hero must in addition wrestle with a world tyrannized by feminine charm. Quite understandably the two variations present other discriminating elements related to sensitiveness and logicalness. The contemporary feminine Bildungsroman has been most adequately defined as the representation of the "crisis occasioned by a woman's awakening in her late twenties or early thirties to the stultification and fragmentation of a personality devoted not to self-fulfillment and awareness, but to a culturally determined, self-sacrificing, and self-effacing existence. This crisis and the resultant struggle for individuality and integration continues to occupy the central thematic position of the feminine Bildungsroman in the mid-seventies."

Yet a feminine Bildungsroman—and a masculine one as well—may belong to the monster category. It may be a mixture of most diverse kinds of novels. Evidently, Gide's *La Symphonie pastorale* is a kind of Bildungsroman. Gertrude is fifteen when she starts her apprenticeship. The narrator of the story, a pastor, is her tutor. He finds her in an isolated farm: she is blind and has been deprived of any elementary education. At the outset of the story we are obviously dealing with an *Erziehungsroman*. The parson teaches her how to speak and succeeds in transforming her into a sociable human being. In the course of her education and her *Bildung*, the clergyman's initial *caritas* changes into *carnalitas*, and when Gertrude, after successful eye surgery, sees and realizes the wickedness of the world, she commits suicide. The novel does not illustrate a personal search for selfhood: *Bildung* is not acquired, but received, and received in vain. Furthermore, the novel is polygonal: the role played by the pastor is as important to the reader as the fate of Gertrude.

In contrast to *La Symphonie pastorale*, there exist authentic feminine Bildungsromane; they are about to occupy a major place on the literary scene. The question concerning the form its variations are to assume remains unanswered, although we can already read outstanding samples, such as Doris Lessing's *Children of Violence*. The symbolism of the heroine's name is patent. Lessing does not narrate the life of some contemplative Mary Rest, but of an active Martha Quest in search of her self, active in the sense that she ceaselessly exposes herself to the formative powers of the world. With that fundamental idea, although not with its structural patterns, the five-volume novel follows the trail staked out by *Wilhelm Meister*. Martha pursues her quest under circumstances and in settings hardly known in Goethe's time. Yet the spirit of the *Lehrjahre* is present, though often to a reduced degree. Such a conclusion may be derived from Simone de Beauvoir's *Mémoires d'une jeune fille rangée* and *La Force de l'âge*. The *Bildungsdrang* exemplified in the two works may be compared in some respects with specific attitudes, with the urge for fulfillment noticed in Erica Jong's *Fear of Flying*.

The literary critic who accepts *Wilhelm Meister* as the prototypical mold of the Bildungsroman may divide the species into three groups. He detects only a few novels *à la mode de* Goethe, while numerous works labeled Bildungsromane crack and break the sacred cast: essential elements of their substance drip and flow through irreparable fissures. In our context, these works of the second group, regardless of their intrinsic value, have been called monsters. There is a third group: most authors of modern Bildungsromane—whether or not they were acquainted with or even inspired by the *Lehrjahre* is irrelevant to the present genological study—shape their plots according to some of Goethe's principles. And yet his mold is beyond repair. Our times have produced authentic *Bildungsromane*, but not all their settings, problems, and characters fit the frame designed and defined by the German master. The feminine Bildungsroman, in particular, provides for a new matrix which, nevertheless, remains a retouched replica of the Goethean mold.

Natural history shows that all species undergo evolutions and will never reappear in their original form. The fittest survive. None of those species, however, remains the fittest forever; competition in nature is keen and changes succeed one another in time. Literature is engaged on a similar path of continued progression, of constant improvement, as optimists would say; the fact remains that, for better or worse, the history of the variations is irreversible. The family tree of the Bildungsroman includes illustrious ancestors, such as *Parzival* and *Euphues*. Yet neither Wolfram nor Lyly will be reborn, for the dynamics of literature are those of a specific society. The sighs of those critics who regret the disaggregation of the good old genres of yesteryear will not slacken the continuous, ineluctable change of all things human. (pp. 138-44)

> *François Jost, "Variations of a Species: The 'Bildungsroman',"* in Symposium, *Vol. XXXVII, No. 2, Summer, 1983, pp. 125-46.*

RANDOLPH P. SHAFFNER

[*Shaffner discusses the various characteristics, types, and definitions of the* Bildungsroman.]

[An] apprenticeship itself, not to a particular art, trade, or calling in a technical sense but rather to life, presupposes both "the idea that living is an art which may be learned" and the belief that a young person can become adept in the art of life by passing through its stages "until at last he becomes a 'Master.'" Susanne Howe credits these two doctrines with having inspired both the name and the story of Goethe's hero, Wilhelm Meister [see excerpt below]. Indeed, the concept of "Wilhelm Lehrling" (William apprentice) ultimately presages a "Wilhelm Meister" (William master). But, this final concern with mastership notwithstanding, the apprenticeship novel restricts its scope to the duration solely of the apprenticeship.

One presupposition of the type entails the key notion of choice. Directing attention to Wilhelm Meister's own words in the novel's concluding statement, François Jost argues that the *Apprenticeship* presents to the reader an individual who, "by his own choice and by his own effort" attains a happiness that he "would not change with anything in life." The notion of choice is a key concept "not only with Goethe, but it appears to a certain degree in every apprenticeship novel" [see excerpt above]. Even when powerful influences would seem to predetermine his choice, the apprentice nonetheless assumes the freedom to pursue his preference.

Serving as a minimal antecedent to the presumptuous notion of mastership, the apprenticeship also presupposes that its candidate must initially embody the potential for, or capability of, becoming a master. He now must incorporate the latent possibility of emerging as, if not a genius, then at the least an exceptional individual.

Hans Castorp expresses in Thomas Mann's *Magic Mountain* a clear awareness of this latent prerequisite. Ironically denying his existence as a "man of genius," he nevertheless affirms his faith in the ascending stages of transsubstantiation or "Steigerung" that characterize his theory of alchemistic-hermetic pedagogy. He reminds Clawdia Chauchat, "But of course matter that is capable of taking those ascending stages by dint of outward pressure must have a little something in itself to start with."

It should be noted that the inherent qualities that render a particular individual capable of ascending these stages toward complete formation do not necessarily constitute in themselves transcendent genius. The supreme goal of culture, as Hermann Weigand suggests, "finds its realization only in so far as it calls into play the totality of man's faculties in his every act of assimilating the sense data of experience." Such a goal, in whatever supreme degree it may find realization, remains nevertheless a human end toward which any human being may aspire. "A man asks himself," Goethe entreats, "to what is he best suited? in order to develop this zealously in himself; he sees himself as apprentice, as journeyman, as assistant, at the latest and with utmost caution as master."

The exceptional individual, in accord with Goethe's description, develops himself zealously for the life that conforms to his exceptional endowments. And occupation notwithstanding, only the individual who would claim adaptability solely to death could fail to qualify for an apprenticeship to life. Each human being carries within himself the potential for development as a unique, and hence exceptional, individual. Whether he aspires to realize his potentialities invites, of course, a vital but separate concern. The apprenticeship novel presupposes only the existence of univeral potentialities in its own apprentice, who, more importantly, demonstrates aspiration as well.

In such an optimistic vein I should cite Weigand's remark pertinent to the basic stance of the apprenticeship novel: "The keynote of the true 'Bildungsroman' is an affirmative attitude toward life as a whole." This attitude constitutes one of the most attractive aspects of the apprenticeship, and it may also account for the essential aspiration noted above.

Turning now to the essential nature of the apprenticeship, the abstract notion of an apprenticeship in isolation can be more clearly concretized through a summary of its distinguishing qualities. (pp. 16-17)

[An] itemized checklist of several distinguishing traits should prove helpful in suggesting concrete potentialities within the apprenticeship novel, as follows:

1. a tendency toward the inner life
2. a striving for "savoir vivre," or knowledge of the world
3. a critical view of the world
4. the presentation of an individual development
5. a variegated description of life and the world
6. an individual's confrontation with his environment
7. a view of life as an evolution
8. the presupposition of a definite attainable goal
9. the presentation of an individual who profits from the lessons of the world
10. a focus on the how and why of the process of development
11. an obligatory acknowledgment of both human and natural influences
12. a self-formation according to internal purpose
13. a consciousness in the attempt to achieve a recognizable typical goal
14. a harmonious cultivation of a multifarious personality
15. the attainment of the goal of formation prior to death

16. a recognition of the goal of formation as open ended

17. an organic development according to inner capacity

18. a presentation of the universal within the process of a particular human life

19. the portrayal of a gradation of successive stages or steps in the course of a human life

20. a striving for organic, ethical, and aesthetic formation accompanied by an attempt to reconcile oneself with reality

21. the view of art solely as a partial means toward the unfolding of personality

22. an archetypal conception of Man as the ultimate goal

23. a special attention to the organization of the process and plot of the novel

To this list of concrete features can be added . . . five presuppositions . . . :

1. the idea that living is an art which the apprentice may learn

2. the belief that a young person can become adept in the art of life and become a master

3. the key notion of choice

4. the prerequisite of potential for development into a master

5. an affirmative attitude toward life as a whole

Several additional qualities that may be seen to augment the above checklists, if only to emphasize that no list should preclude supplementation, entail themes that frequently emerge from critical studies of the apprenticeship novel, for instance:

1. mastery of circumstances

2. self-reliance

3. earnest, purposeful activity as opposed to dilettantism

4. an insatiable yearning and striving for life's meaning

5. a deepening consciousness of human experience

6. a release from bondage to false ideals

7. self-expression

8. a continuous trial-and-error development of the natural gifts incipient in man's essence—in the sense, for example, of Pindar's noted dictum urging, ''Become the one you are.''

Countless other themes apply, of course, but these few recur continually in critical studies of the type.

The recognition that these innate qualities of the apprenticeship novel often exist only in potentiality should forestall their misconstruction as normative prescriptions. But the conversion of these inherent qualities into formal existence has, in fact, set historical precedence in a variety of realized combinations subsequently qualifying as apprenticeship novels. Necessarily, the modified nature of each particular product must be acknowledged as unique, for only by virtue of its power of modification can a novel be said to preserve its individuality, even as it stands under the single and purely functional rubric, in this case, of apprenticeship novel.

If such, then, is the nature of the apprenticeship type, a focus on the phases of development within the type is of concern preliminary to arriving at a reasonably inclusive definition. Howe in ''the barest possible outline'' of the apprenticeship pattern delineates the path that Borcherdt chooses to call the way of cultivation, the ''Bildungsweg'' [see excerpt below]. According to Howe, the adolescent apprentice on the path to self-formation

> sets out on his way through the world, meets with reverses usually due to his own temperament, falls

in with various guides and counsellors, makes many false starts in choosing his friends, his wife, and his life work, and finally adjusts himself in some way to the demands of his time and environment by finding a sphere of action in which he may work effectively.

This pattern, as Howe describes it, exists quiescently in any apprenticeship novel. But the vital issue of self-formation or self-adjustment within the pattern poses a notable problem. If indeed the formation generates itself, then the hero must be termed an active agent of his own development. On the other hand, if his development arises wholly from outer-inducement, then he falls before the charge of a dangerous passivity. Heinrich Keiter and Tony Kellen clearly imply the passivity of such a drifter's struggle within life's briny flood:

> The hero swims midway in the sea of life, frequently in danger of being swallowed up by the waves, often gently wafted by them. So powerful influences not infrequently affect him in his life, force him back, toss him, until he is no longer fully conscious of his intention, or in a totally different way, until he comes at last to a clear insight into his destiny.

The hero of this pattern of apprenticeship surfaces as no hero at all but rather an auspicious recipient of good fortune. When we acknowledge the predominant role played by the sea of influences in determining his path toward cultivation, even the realized goal, as Wilhelm Meister ultimately conceives it, appears gratuitously and adventitiously bestowed.

On the other hand, if sufficient stress is laid on the role of the swimmer in his essentially individual act of swimming, then the notion of formation extends to embrace an active, albeit passive, idea. E. L. Stahl highlights the active nature of the apprentice's role through an analogy that serves to supplant the swimmer in the ocean with the clay in a potter's hand. The apprenticeship novel ''treats man as a creature, on whom the forces of the world have an effect, like the clay that lies in the potter's hand, not [and here is Stahl's essential point] like a purely passive thing allowing itself to be molded, but rather bringing with it into the world very definite active powers, upon which those external forces now act.'' And yet on closer scrutiny the swimmer, better than the clay, would appear as the proper analogy, for it more accurately and graphically conveys the notion of an active strength contributed by the apprentice to his own progress in his apprenticeship.

The idea of definite phases or of a specific sequence of stages in a hero's development exists potentially in every pattern of apprenticeship. Wilhelm Dilthey calls these stages ''Stufen'' or steps. He defines the common pattern of the apprenticeship novel, supported by examples from Goethe to Hölderlin, as the representation of a young man of a definite time who

> enters life in fortunate twilight, searches for kindred souls, encounters friendship and love, . . . falls into conflict with the harsh realities of the world . . . and so grows to maturity through diverse experiences of life, finds himself, and becomes assured of his duty in the world.

According to this delineation of the pattern, the apprentice develops in conformity with a pre-determined sequence of natural laws, that is, in definite stages: ''A regular development is contemplated in the life of the individual; each of its stages has a characteristic value and is at the same time the foundation of a higher stage.'' The discords and conflicts of life, moreover, ''appear as the indispensable gates of passage for the individual on his way toward maturity and harmony.''

Dilthey's conception of the individual's conflicts with harsh reality constituting indispensable phases of transition toward eventual maturity and harmony finds a fellow advocate in Jost. Jost posits an essential world-individual confrontation that effects the hero's transformation: "Always the apprenticeship novel presents a certain free play of antagonistic forces, the world and individuality, the latter, in the course of the confrontation, becoming a personality, a term that implicates a moral character." Jost adds by way of clarification that this transformation, as explained by Goethe, results from cultivation.

Both Dilthey's and Jost's descriptions of the apprenticeship pattern conflict, however, with Borcherdt's. Borcherdt charges that Dilthey limits the concept of the apprenticeship novel to representatives of the type in the time of Goethe. The dual emphasis on "development in precise conformity [with] fixed stages of deployment" and on "direction toward a clearly outlined goal, which is presented as the ideal condition of the complete man," excludes from consideration, not only the novels of Wolfram, Grimmelshausen, and Wieland that preceded the age of Goethe, but also the works of Stifter, Keller, Raabe, Paul Ernst, Kolbenheyer, Hesse, and Mann that followed. Only in the golden age of Goethe, Borcherdt argues, did the concept of culture embrace conjointly both the goal of consummate humanitarianism, "vollendete Humanität," and the path to this goal. An enlargement of the field of vision, however, must necessarily lead to the conclusion "that Dilthey's definition and nomenclature appear too restricted." The novels of the later periods of the nineteenth century, while retaining the development of an individual as the object of fiction, have come to reveal instead "an assimilation of the individual into the community" or at least into an attitude of social consciousness. The goals of these later novels supersede the entirely too confined concept of culture in the period of Goethe as an expression of the personality's self-formation.

In his own alternative description of the apprenticeship's general pattern Borcherdt endeavors to separate the path not only from the goal but also from its artistic expression in phases. The goal or "Bildungsziel" relates to the pattern as a conclusion, an "Abschluß," only incidentally, for it changes "with the developmental phases of the history of ideas and with the particular author's worldview." In general it represents the complete unfolding of all man's natural talents. On the other hand, the path or "Bildungsweg" provides "the fixed line toward the goal and thereby the regularity of the devlepoment." It represents an apprentice's attempt to grasp the universe and thus attain a stage in his personal development. Within this concept of the path of culture as a principle of development, the world does not oppose the individual in a confrontation of I and world, "Ich und Welt," as Dilthey asserts, but rather serves as a school of life, "Schule des Lebens." The path of the individual follows a uniform pattern: "From error to truth, from confusion to clarity, from unconsciousness to consciousness." Truth, clarity, and consciousness constitute the goal; error, confusion, and unawareness, the pattern or path to the goal.

The *Goethe-Handbuch* reinforces Borcherdt's insistence on development as social adjustment, instead of conflict, between the individual and the community. Regarding the goal of the apprenticeship novel the Handbook concludes, "Its theme is the cultivation of the self through the world; in the process of adjustment the hero becomes a microcosm." Conceivably both views, the apprentice's confrontation with the world and his socialization into the world, could be said to coexist as poten-

tialities within the general apprenticeship type. But in any case definite phases of development are seen to occur.

For instance, the artistic expression, the "künstlerische Form" of the apprenticeship pattern, as distinguished by Borcherdt from the pattern itself, normally unfolds in three phases: the years of youth, the "Jugendjahre," which from unawareness evolve toward consciousness; the years of travel, the "Wanderjahre," which comprise love, friendship, crises, and failures; and "the refinement and entrance into a terrestrial stage of paradise." The boundaries that separate the early years from the subsequent years of travel, and the travel years from the final years of refinement, generally come into focus only in retrospect "on the turning points or through reliance on memory." (pp. 17-22)

Whether we see adjustment or conflict as the more common avenue of an apprentice's confrontation with the harsh realities of his environment, Dilthey's description of a regular development through stages, each possessing in itself intrinsic value even as it serves as the basis for a higher stage, remains a constant principle of the apprenticeship pattern. The number of stages depicted within any particular pattern varies, of course, as a matter of modified temporal choice. But the pattern itself is innately potential in the apprenticeship type.

Having established the nature and pattern of the hero's apprenticeship to life, it remains for us to characterize the end toward which that pattern is directed: its goal. Howe's general description of the apprenticeship form as the "novel of all-round development or self-culture" defines the type in terms of the apprentice's objective. Self-culture or self-formation indeed permeates the apprenticeship novel as its primary recurrent theme. But just as Borcherdt has recognized the need to distinguish the path of the apprenticeship from its goal, we cannot afford to overlook two very different natures of the goal itself. A common conception frequently assumes that culture must suffice as its own end. Indeed, the history of this notion extends to the origins of Western thought. The simple Socratic maxim "Know thyself" initially proposed self-formation as a direct objective of the will. The Renaissance version of the same idea found expression in the goal of universal man, "uomo universale," requiring the development of all natural gifts to the highest level of excellence and their fusion into a work of art. The Renaissance insisted almost exclusively on the formation of the personality for its own sake.

The modern period has only altered the Renaissance objective of "uomo universale," substituting "bourgeois" for "universal." Thomas Mann depicts Goethe, himself the last universal man of modern times, as a revolutionary seeking to supplant the goal of the universal man with the modern bourgeois ideal. The bourgeois love of order, its value of personal productivity and practical achievement, and its devotion to professional duties reveal an attitude toward life that postulates as its objective: "being solidly planted in life." This goal formerly was restricted to the ranks of the nobility, who scorned not only the "universal man" with his yearning for the unattainable but also the "bourgeois" devotion to occupation. Mann, however, implies that Goethe, in replacing Renaissance "personality" by bourgeois "occupation," has sought to establish for all men, regardless of class, a new common goal, a new "uomo universale," the modern ideal: "The bourgeois, supra-bourgeois character." Characterizing this modern evolution of the universal out of the bourgeois, Mann summarizes: "the respectable, the bourgeois, as the home of the universally human; world fame as son of the bourgeois; this combination of the beginnings with the most surprising development is no-where so much at home as with us.''

Mary Hatch's interpretation of the apprentice's goal as a bour-geois calling arises immediately from Mann's argument. She proposes essentially to equate "occupation and personality de-velopment.'' Kenneth Rexroth reflects the same restricted view when he praises Goethe rather disparagingly as "the greatest poet of the business ethic,'' indeed "a self-made aristocrat and nobleman of the cloth, the hero of all German Burghers to come after him.''

All three conceptions of the goal—the Socratic "Know thy-self,'' the Renaissance "uomo universale,'' and the modern bourgeois ideal—commonly assume that self-formation, whether defined as self-knowledge, development of the personality, or achievement of the occupational ideal, constitutes a willful objective of the individual.

In the apprenticeship novel, however, we would do well to forestall such an assumption. Ralph Waldo Emerson in his celebrated essay on "Self-reliance'' clearly defines the nature of the proper goal. He draws the image of a ship that voyages in a zigzag line of a hundred tacks so as to establish its average tendency. For his purpose the analogy adequately depicts self-reliance, but it also clarifies the bilateral nature of the goal of an apprenticeship to life. The seemingly countless tacks that represent direct objectives of the apprentice are in retrospect subordinated to their collective drift, which can be seen to represent the indirect and ultimate objective of self-formation. "Bildung'' or culture, therefore, does not comprise a self-contained end.

In this vein Max Scheler emphatically cautions, "Certain goals are reached only when one does *not willingly* intend them.'' His insistence on the separation of volition from assured suc-cess does not preclude determination of purpose, but it does attempt to deny the possibility of self-formation as a direct objective of the will. In a discerning and penetrating address to the Lessing Institute of Berlin in 1925 Scheler forewarned his audience,

> Cultivation is *not* "desiring to make oneself a work of art,'' is *not* self-enamored intending of oneself, be it his beauty, his virtue, his form, or his knowl-edge. It is just the opposite of such intentional self-gratification, whose culmination is dandyism. Man *is* no work of art and *should* be no work of art! In the course of his life *in* the world, *with* the world; in the active conquest of its and his own passions or restraints; in love and deed, be it object related, be it brother related, be it government related; in hard work, which, yielding profits, intensifies, exalts, and expands the *powers and the self* . . ., the development of culture proceeds, occurs, behind the back of mere purpose and of mere will. And only he who will *lose* himself in a noble cause or in some kind of true common interest—unafraid of what may happen to him—will *reclaim himself,* that is, his true self, re-claim it from within the godhead itself and the power and the purity of its breath.

It can be seen, therefore, that the self cannot become the ap-prentice's direct goal, except as it is lost in the unexpected acquisition of a true self, an "echtes Selbst.'' But any objective involving the loss of self consequently negates the will, thus paradoxically denying itself as an objective. We must turn then to the indirect goal of the apprentice, which more appropriately identifies with culture or self-formation, since both it and cul-ture represent by-products of the will turned toward something

other than the self. Indeed, this something else becomes the direct goal of the apprentice.

W. H. Bruford in his article on Goethe's *Wilhelm Meister* further accentuates the indirect nature of an apprentice's ulti-mate goal: "The harmonious personality that the 'uomo univ-ersale' sought in self-cultivation is attained indirectly in work for something which is not the self, for culture, like happiness, comes to those who do not pursue it as an end in itself.'' Goethe expresses the same idea as a loss of self in action on behalf of others; and Roy Pascal follows Goethe's precedent in his own definition of the apprenticeship novel as "the story of the formation of a character up to the moment when he ceases to be self-centered and becomes society-centered, thus beginning to shape his true self'' [see excerpt below].

Recognizing self-formation as an indirect goal, we may turn . . . to the paradox of the hero's passivity. Quoting Goethe, Her-mann Pongs formulates the motto of an indirectly achieved self-cultivation: "Make an agent of yourself!'' Contrasting Goethe's hero with Wieland's Agathon, he notes that "Wil-helm does not actually form himself through culture; instead a kinetic adaptability develops, through which he becomes formed by life itself, owing to continual error throughout.'' Stumbling over endless mistakes, the apprentice confronts the elusive goal of culture less as an active contributor to his own formation than as an active recipient of his being formed by life. But, as Pongs points out, in order not to confuse this active passivity with the unaware passivity of the hero of the novel of development, we need be reminded of the apprentice's consciousness, which emerges as "the modern restriction against the encroachment of the novel of development, as the conscious process of self-cultivation through culture, until the hero arrives at a clear understanding of himself.'' Such a process of self-formation through formation appears initially to constitute a pleonasm unless the objectives of the two separate processes are identified as the indirect and the direct goals, respectively.

Hermann Weigand designates both goals in the masterpieces of Goethe and Mann. The indirect objective in each work is a total integration of human experience, which evolves coinci-dentally from the apprentice's primary focus on conscious ac-tivities. Wilhelm Meister descries his direct goal as "a brilliant career on the stage,'' only to discover years later that he lacks the fundamental qualifications for success. Similarly, Hans Castorp sacrifices all prospects of a practical career to the direct "pursuit of a quixotic passion.'' Weigand concludes that "in each case, the by-product of these strivings, struggles, pursuits, and passions is something infinitely richer than the specific result coveted, altogether regardless of success or failure.'' He identifies this by-product or incidental yield as life-art, "Le-benskunst,'' otherwise known as self-formation.

Although broader in scope than all the direct goals contributing to its latent growth and eventual realization, the indirect goal of self-culture ultimately reveals its own innate limits. It is inherently restricted to the humanitarian concept of man. Ar-guing from the classical notion of formation, which the nine-teenth century partially adopted as a philosophical humanitarian concept of culture, a "humanitätsphilosophische Bildungs-idee,'' Berta Berger claims that in the 1700's God no longer served as the goal of culture. The humanitarian idea of man as the measure of culture superseded the religious idea of cul-ture, the "religiöse Bildungsidee,'' that had envisioned God or Christ as the archetype or model, as, for example, in the Christian concept of culture during the Middle Ages. "God is now no longer,'' Berger remarks with reference to the eighteenth century, ''the archetype or model, but rather man, man who perfects all his individual talents in their totality through contact with his environment.'' The indirect goal, as Keiter and Kellen note in their depiction of the hero of the apprenticeship novel, ''is ultimately always humanitarianism.'' The true apprentice ''has usually already become at the conclusion of his apprenticeship a man.''

Within the limits set by the objective of forming a man, then, the ancient dictum ''Know thyself'' essentially retains its relevance despite this shift in focus from direction to indirection in the individual's goal. Even though indirectly achieved, self-realization remains innately confined to the self. Not even knowledge of the world can encroach on the priority given to self as the ultimate goal. ''More important than the world itself,'' Jost affirms in describing the realized goal of Wilhelm Meister, the apprentice ''recognizes his place in the world; he begins to distinguish, to be able to define this man who is himself.'' To achieve the goal of culture, therefore, is to ''know thyself,'' while ''to understand the world is given to us in addition.'' The gift of understanding the world, an unexpected bonus, accrues from a typical phenomenon that Howe describes as the apprentice's growth into ''an expanding and deepening consciousness of human experience, an increased awareness of living.''

From one perspective the goal of self-realization represents a reach that certainly transcends the humanly limited grasp of its aspirant. Consider, for example, as Jost proposes, the analogue of Dante's Purgatorio, in which the individual who himself is destined ''to become realized must pass through his childhood and his adolescence.'' An individual's purgatory implies in a similar sense an ascent ''toward an ideal, whatever it be,'' which prevails upon the apprentice ''to exalt himself to the stars.'' His ethereal aspiration represents ''the very quintessence of the apprenticeship novel.'' However, the apprentice's purgatory must be seen as no more than ''a catharsis'' that restricts the goal to man himself as the optimum surrogate for God. The Eden created by the catharsis thus remains a singularly human paradise.

From a strictly practical point of view the universal goal of self-cultivation must be viewed as indirect because its attainment cannot be limited to one side of an all-round formation. It entails instead a multivariety of direct goals, each of which participates only obliquely in the general tendency of the self-forming whole. Wagner characterizes such an objective as ''an all-round culture and not the alignment with a narrowly defined result.'' Considered separately from its partial contribution to the whole, any direct alignment with a narrowly circumscribed objective proves inadequate in and of itself. The hero of an apprenticeship novel, as Christine Touaillon suggests, ''should not be reared unilaterally for a limited purpose, but rather formed universally, and the great life forces should contribute to this formation.''

Both inner and outer natures cooperate to assist the apprentice toward his all-encompassing ideal. The limited aims that attract his immediate attention often betray the composition date of the novel in which he appears. The apprenticeship novel, as Touaillon explains, ''shows quite clearly in all of its stages the ideals of the era that produced it.'' In particular she enumerates several of these ideals:

> By turns [the apprenticeship novel] will rear its hero to become a Christian, a blithe spirit, an artist, a harmonious human being, and an inwardly autonomous individual. It is a far-reaching type, having

> within its limits a great deal of room . . . the incidents are inner and outer nature.

Its direct aims may alter with time or even within the particular work of an era, but the indirect goal of a multifarious self-cultivation exists potentially as well as universally in the apprenticeship type as a whole.

The absolute comprehensiveness of this ultimate goal should preclude its misconception as a possible objective of the apprentice himself. As Borcherdt reminds us, the ultimate aim is ''Perfection of all man's talents and powers to a complete whole, to a microcosm as mirror of the macrocosm.'' Such a universal perfection can find its potential realization in an apprentice only as the emergent by-product of his limited perspective and active will. Hermann Weigand, as noted above, regards this goal of culture as the supreme concern of Mann's *Magic Mountain:* here the ideal ''finds its realization only in so far as it calls into play the totality of man's faculties in his every act of assimilating the sense date of experience.'' And this ''Erlebnis,'' this integration of experience, cannot relate directly to the process of culture except as the culminating achievement marking the completion of the process. The apprentice realizes his ultimate goal, the formation of himself, when he at last renounces all conceivable direct aims as not in themselves ultimate or self-contained.

This idea of an indirectly achieved self-formation points up an all important paradox: the innate necessity for striving renders a standstill in the lifetime process of culture impossible. Wagner expressly counsels that any suspension of forward pressure can only signify retrogression in the process:

> Culture is a duty, whose ideal goal can never be attained unless it is constantly pursued. For a standstill here means a step back. Development, culture is a striving forward, a search for knowledge and perfection, which, for those who strive assiduously, always continues like life itself.

This open-ended nature of the goal explains why the conclusions of the various apprenticeship novels considered by Howe in her survey of the type in England are ''as diverse as the personalities and careers of the different authors themselves.'' They vary from marriage to the proper woman and settling on an ancestral estate to a career of public service as a member of Parliament, a doctor, a reformer, or a writer. But even ''when the hero settles down to his vocation, we get no sense of smug completeness. None of them has solved the problem.'' The novel, of course, must end. But though it breaks off, the apprentice persists in striving for his ideal, that is, his most recently adopted direct goal.

Heinrich Meyer attributes the open end of the apprenticeship novel to the limited perspective of the author himself. Out of this natural limitation arises one of the most obvious differences between the apprenticeship novel and the novel of education. For whereas the former ''reflects the present state of an author's self-knowledge and therefore has no clear ending that must result from the antecedents,'' the novel of education ''has'' such an end. Meyer tends to equate the apprenticeship novel with autobiography, but in both types he expresses awareness of the open end.

At this point we are confronted with a further but final paradox, namely, an indirectly attained goal at the conclusion of an open-ended novel. A solution, of course, exists potentially in the cyclic conception of the ending as a beginning. Within this notion the apprenticeship novel emerges not as a standard novel at all but as a forenovel. ''In a sense,'' as Jost depicts it, ''the apprenticeship novel is only a sort of pre-novel, or preamble. Indeed, at the conclusion of the work the hero appears to us armed for life, ready to live his novel.'' He disappears from the book's view, a quiescent master in the art of forming his own life. His human existence, like the shape of the novel that represents his life, is, in M. H. Abrams' estimation, ''circuitous yet open-ended.'' It ''will go on after the novel ends, to a succeeding stage which will incorporate all that he has experienced before.'' Irrespective of his future, however, the apprentice may estimate himself at the novel's end, even as Goethe guardedly concludes, ''at the last moment and with utmost caution as master.'' (pp. 22-7)

> *Randolph P. Shaffner, in his* The Apprenticeship Novel: A Study of the ''Bildungsroman'' as a Regulative Type in Western Literature with a Focus on Three Classic Representatives by Goethe, Maugham, and Mann, *Peter Lang, 1984, 168 p.*

THE *BILDUNGSROMAN* IN GERMANY

GEORG LUKÁCS

[*Lukács, a Hungarian literary critic and philosopher, is acknowledged as a leading proponent of Marxist thought. His development of Marxist ideology was part of a broader system of thought in which he sought to further the values of rationalism (peace and progress), humanism (Socialist politics), and traditionalism (Realist literature) over the countervalues of irrationalism (war), totalitarianism (reactionary politics), and modernism (post-Realist literature). The subjects of his literary criticism are primarily the nineteenth-century Realists—Balzac and Tolstoy—and their twentieth-century counterparts—Gorky and Mann. In his major works, Lukács explicated his belief that ''unless art can be made creatively consonant with history and human needs, it will always offer a counterworld of escape and marvelous waste.'' In the following excerpt from his* The Theory of the Novel, *he posits that the* Bildungsroman *''steers a middle course between abstract idealism . . . and Romanticism.'' Lukács goes on to argue that there are inherent problems in depicting the integration of an individual into society that even an artist as great as Goethe could not surmount.*]

[The theme of *Wilhelm Meister*] is the reconciliation of the problematic individual, guided by his lived experience of the ideal, with concrete social reality. This reconciliation cannot and must not be the result of accommodation or of a harmony existing from the start which would make it a modern humorous novel . . . , except that, whereas in such novels the preexisting harmony is a necessary evil, here it would become the central good. (p. 132)

The type of personality and the structure of the plot are determined by the necessary condition that a reconciliation between interiority and reality, although problematic, is nevertheless possible; that it has to be sought in hard struggles and dangerous adventures, yet is ultimately possible to achieve. For this reason the interiority depicted in such a novel . . . [in] its relation to the transcendent world of ideas is neither subjectively nor objectively very strong; the soul is not purely self-dependent, its world is not a reality which is, or should be, complete in itself and can be opposed to the reality of the outside world as a postulate and a competing power; instead, the soul in such a novel carries within itself, as a sign of its

tenuous, but not yet severed link with the transcendental order, a longing for an earthly home which may correspond to its ideal—an ideal which eludes positive definition but is clear enough in negative terms. Such an interiority represents on the one hand a wider and consequently more adaptable, gentler, more concrete idealism, and, on the other hand, a widening of the soul which seeks fulfilment in action, in effective dealings with reality, and not merely in contemplation. It is an interiority which stands halfway between idealism and Romanticism, and its attempt, within itself, to synthesise and overcome both of them is rejected by both as a compromise.

It follows from this possibility, given by the theme itself, of effecive action in social reality, that the organisation of the outside world into professions, classes, ranks, etc., is of decisive importance for this particular type of personality as the substratum of its social activity. The content and goal of the ideal which animates the personality and determines his actions is to find responses to the innermost demands of his soul in the structures of society. This means, at least as a postulate, that the inherent loneliness of the soul is surmounted; and this in turn presupposes the possibility of human and interior community among men, of understanding and common action in respect of the essential. Such community is not the result of people being naïvely and naturally rooted in a specific social structure, not of any natural solidarity of kinship (as in the ancient epics), nor is it a mystical experience of community, a sudden illumination which rejects the lonely individuality as something ephemeral, static and sinful; it is achieved by personalities, previously lonely and confined within their own selves, adapting and accustoming themselves to one another; it is the fruit of a rich and enriching resignation, the crowning of a process of education, a maturity attained by struggle and effort.

The content of such maturity is an ideal of free humanity which comprehends and affirms the structures of social life as necessary forms of human community, yet, at the same time, only sees them as an occasion for the active expression of the essential life substance—in other words, which takes possession of these structures, not in their rigid political and legal being-for-themselves, but as the necessary instruments of aims which go far beyond them. The heroism of abstract idealism and the pure interiority of Romanticism are therefore admitted as relatively justified, but only as tendencies to be surmounted and integrated in the interiorised order; in themselves and for themselves, they appear as reprehensible and doomed to perdition, as also is philistinism—the acceptance of an outside order, however lacking in idea it may be, simply because it is the given order.

This structure of the relationship between the ideal and the soul relativises the hero's central position, which is merely accidental: the hero is picked out of an unlimited number of men who share his aspirations, and is placed at the centre of the narrative only because his seeking and finding reveal the world's totality most clearly. In the tower where Wilhelm Meister's years of apprenticeship are recorded, those of Jarno and Lothario and others—both members and non-members of the League—are recorded too, and the novel itself contains, in the memories of the Canoness, a close parallel to the story of the hero's education. It is true that in the novel of disillusionment, the central character's position is also often accidental (whereas abstract idealism has to make use of a hero marked out and placed at the centre of events by his loneliness); but this is more a means of exposing the corrupting nature of reality:

where all interiority is bound to come to grief, any individual destiny is merely an episode, and the world consists of an infinite number of such isolated, mutually heterogeneous episodes which have only the fatality of failure in common. Here, however, the philosophical basis of the relativity of the hero's position is the possibility of success of aspirations aimed at a common goal; the individual characters are closely linked together by this community of destiny, whereas in the novel of disillusionment the parallelism of their lives had only to enhance their loneliness.

This is why Goethe in *Wilhelm Meister* steers a middle course between abstract idealism, which concentrates on pure action, and Romanticism, which interiorises action and reduces it to contemplation. Humanism, the fundamental attitude of this type of work, demands a balance between activity and contemplation, between wanting to mould the world and being purely receptive towards it. This form has been called the 'novel of education'—rightly, because its action has to be a conscious, controlled process aimed at a certain goal: the development of qualities in men which would never blossom without the active intervention of other men and circumstances; whilst the goal thus attained is in itself formative and encouraging to others—is itself a means of education.

A story determined by such a goal has a certain calm based on security. But this is not the calm of an a-prioristic world; the will towards education, a will that is conscious and certain of its aim, is what creates the atmosphere of ultimate security. The world of such a novel in itself and for itself is by no means free from danger. In order to demonstrate the risk which everyone runs and which can be escaped by individual salvation but not by a-prioristic redemption, many characters have to perish because of their inability to adapt themselves, whilst others fade away because of their precipitous and unconditional surrender in the face of reality. Ways towards individual salvation do exist, however, and a whole community of men is seen to arrive successfully at the end of them, helping one another, as well as occasionally falling into error during the process. And what has become a reality for many must be at least potentially accessible to all.

The robust sense of security underlying this type of novel arises, then, from the relativation of its central character, which in turn is determined by a belief in the possibility of common destinies and life-formations. As soon as this belief disappears—which, in formal terms, amounts to saying: as soon as the action of the novel is constructed out of the destinies of a lonely person who merely passes through various real or illusory communities but whose fate does not finally flow into them—the form of the work must undergo a substantial change, coming closer to that of the novel of disillusionment, in which loneliness is neither accidental nor the fault of the individual, but signifies that the desire for the essence always leads out of the world of social structures and communities and that a community is possible only at the surface of life and can only be based on compromise. The central character becomes problematic, not because of his so-called 'false tendencies', but just because he wants to realise his deepest interiority in the outside world. The educative element which this type of novel still retains and which distinguishes it sharply from the novel of disillusionment is that the hero's ultimate state of resigned loneliness does not signify the total collapse and defilement of all his ideals but a recognition of the discrepancy between the interiority and the world. The hero actively realises this duality: he accommodates himself to society by resigning himself to

accept its life forms, and by locking inside himself and keeping entirely to himself the interiority which can only be realised inside the soul. His ultimate arrival expresses the present state of the world but is neither a protest against it nor an affirmation of it, only an understanding and experiencing of it which tries to be fair to both sides and which ascribes the soul's inability to fulfil itself in the world not only to the inessential nature of the world but also to the feebleness of the soul.

In most individual examples the dividing line between this post-Goethean type of novel of education and the novel of disillusionment is often fluid. The first version of *Der Grüne Heinrich* shows this perhaps most clearly, whereas the final version stands definitely upon the course required by its form. But the possibility of such indeterminacy (although it can be overcome) reveals the one great danger inherent in this form because of its historico-philosophical base: the danger of a subjectivity which is not exemplary, which has not become a symbol, and which is bound to destroy the epic form. The hero and his destiny then have no more than personal interest and the work as a whole becomes a private memoir of how a certain person succeeded in coming to terms with his world. (The novel of disillusionment counteracts the increased subjectivity of the characters by the crushing, equalising universality of fate.) Such a subjectivity is even more difficult to surmount than that of the impersonal narrative: it endows everything—even if the technique is perfectly objectivised—with the fatal, irrelevant and petty character of the merely private; it remains a mere aspect, making the absence of a totality the more painfully obvious as it constantly claims to create one. The overwhelming majority of modern 'novels of education' have completely failed to avoid this pitfall.

The structure of the characters and destinies in *Wilhelm Meister* determines the structure of the social world around them. Here, too, we have an intermediate situation: the structures of social life are not modelled on a stable and secure transcendent world, nor are they in themselves an order, complete and clearly articulated, which substantiates itself to become its own purpose; such a world would exclude any possibility of the hero's seeking or losing his way. But neither do these structures form an amorphous mass, for then the interiority oriented towards finding an order would always remain homeless and the attainment of the goal would be unthinkable from the start. The social world must therefore be shown as a world of convention, which is partially open to penetration by living meaning.

A new principle of heterogeneity is thereby introduced into the outside world: a hierarchy of the various structures and layers of structures according to their penetrability by meaning. This hierarchy is irrational and incapable of being rationalised; and the meaning, in this particular case, is not objective but is tantamount to the possibility of a personality fulfilling itself in action. Irony here acquires crucial importance as a factor in the creation of the work because no structure in itself and for itself can be said to possess such meaning, nor not to possess it; it is quite impossible to decide from the start whether any structure is thus eligible or not, and only its interaction with the individual can reveal this. The necessary ambiguity is further increased by the fact that in each separate set of interactions it is impossible to tell whether the adequacy or inadequacy of the structure of the individual is due to the individual's success or failure or whether it is a comment on the structure itself. But such an ironic affirmation of reality—for this uncertainty lights up even a reality totally lacking in idea—is, after all, only an intermediate stage: the completion of the process of education must inevitably idealise and romanticise certain parts of reality and abandon others to prose, as being devoid of meaning.

Yet the author must not abandon his ironic attitude, replacing it by unconditional affirmation, even when describing the eventual homecoming. This objectivation of social life is merely the occasion for something which lies outside and beyond it to become visible, fruitful and active, and the earlier ironic homogeneisation of reality, to which the homecoming owes its character of reality—its nature which always remains opaque to subjective views and tendencies, its independent existence vis-à-vis them—cannot be abolished even at the eventual homecoming without endangering the unity of the whole. And so the attained, meaningful and harmonious world is just as real and has the same characteristics of reality as the different degrees of meaninglessness and of partial penetration by meaning which preceded it in the story.

In this ironic tact of the Romantic presentation of reality lies the other great danger inherent in this form of the novel, which only Goethe—and not always he—succeeded in escaping. It is the danger of romanticising reality to a point where it becomes a sphere totally beyond reality or, still more dangerously from the point of view of artistic form-giving, a sphere completely free from problems, for which the forms of the novel are then no longer sufficient. (pp. 132-39)

The surmounting of this danger is not entirely problem-free even in Goethe. Although he places strong emphasis on the merely potential and subjective nature of the penetration of meaning into the social sphere in which the hero finds fulfilment, the notion of community on which the whole edifice is based requires that the social structures should here possess a greater, more objective substantiality and, therefore, a more genuine adequation to the normative subjects, than those spheres which have been overcome.

This objective removal of the fundamental problematic brings the novel closer to the epic; yet it is impossible for a work which began as a novel to end as an epic, and it is likewise impossible, once such overlapping has occurred, to make the work homogeneous again by the renewed use of irony. This is why, in *Wilhelm Meister,* the world of the nobility, which does not belong completely to the novel and so is somewhat fragile, has to be set as a symbol of active life-domination against the marvellously unified atmosphere of the theatre, which is born of the true spirit of the novel form. Certainly, by the nature of the marriages which conclude the novel, the nobility as a social estate is interiorised with the maximum epic and sensuous intensity, so that the objective superiority of a class is transformed to mean a better opportunity for a freer, more generous way of life for anyone possessing the necessary inner potentialities. But in spite of this ironic reservation, a social class is nevertheless raised to a height of substantiality to which it cannot inwardly be equal. Within this class, although confined to a small circle of its members, a universal and all-embracing cultural flowering is supposed to occur, capable of absorbing the most varied individual destinies. In other words, the world thus confined within a single class—the nobility—and based upon it, partakes of the problem-free radiance of the epic.

Not even the supreme artistic tact with which Goethe introduces new problems at this late stage in the novel can alter the immanent consequences of the novel's ending. The world he describes, with its merely relative adequation to essential life,

contains no element that can offer a possibility for the necessary stylisation. This is why Goethe was obliged to introduce the much-criticised fantastic apparatus of the last books of the novel, the mysterious tower, the all-knowing initiates with their providential actions, etc. Goethe makes use here of the methods of the (Romantic) epic. He absolutely needed these methods in order to give sensuous significance and gravity to the ending of the novel, and although he tried to rob them of their epic quality by using them lightly and ironically, thus hoping to transform them into elements of the novel form, he failed. With his creative irony, by means of which he was able everywhere else to give substance to things that were in themselves unworthy of artistic treatment and to control any tendency to go beyond the novel form, he devalued the miraculous by revealing its playful, arbitrary and ultimately inessential character. And he could not prevent it from introducing a disrupting dissonance into the total unity of the whole; the miraculous becomes a mystification without hidden meaning, a strongly emphasised narrative element without real importance, a playful ornament without decorative grace. This was more than a concession to the taste of the period (as many have claimed in apology), and after all it is quite impossible to imagine *Wilhelm Meister* without this miraculous element, however inorganic it may be. An essential formal necessity forced Goethe to use it and its use had to fail only because, given the author's fundamental intention, it was oriented towards a less problematic form than that imposed by its substratum—that is to say, the historical epic.

Again, the author's utopian outlook prevents him from stopping at the mere portrayal of the time-given problematic; he cannot be satisfied with a mere glimpse, a merely subjective experience of an unrealisable meaning; he is forced to posit a purely individual experience, which may, postulatively, have universal validity, as the existent and constitutive meaning of reality. But reality refuses to be forced up to such a level of meaning, and, as with all the decisive problems of great literary forms, no artist's skill is great and masterly enough to bridge the abyss. (pp. 140-43)

Georg Lukács, "'Wilhelm Meister's Years of Apprenticeship' as an Attempted Synthesis," in his The Theory of the Novel: A Historico-Philosophical Essay on the Forms of Great Epic Literature, *translated by Anna Bostock, The M.I.T. Press, 1971, pp. 132-43.*

ROY PASCAL

[*In the following excerpt, Pascal explores how all of Goethe's literary techniques in* Wilhelm Meister *are designed to emphasize and elucidate the theme of personal development, or* Bildung.]

No other German novel has enjoyed anything like the esteem and prestige of *Wilhelm Meisters Lehrjahre;* its influence on the German novel-tradition has remained pervasive and profound. Yet it is a 'problematical composition', as Goethe called it, with faults that are often magnified in its progeny. If we compare it with the novels of Goethe's contemporary, Jane Austen, it is clear that it probes deeper into human fate and shapes situations and characters that were beyond the imagination of the English writer; at the same time it is, in a peculiar sense, far less mature as a work of art than such works as *Emma,* not only in the indefiniteness of its general shape, but also in the imprecision of many characters and events. This immaturity belongs to its whole nature. For while Jane Austen, like all classical novelists, was concerned to show characters choosing between certain moral alternatives within an un-questioned socio-moral reality, the main task for Wilhelm Meister is to discover the validity of this reality and of moral decision altogether. The novel is the story of this discovery.

Intricate psychological processes are involved, and numerous variant attitudes are described. And its deliberate complexity is made more difficult because of the way in which it was written. Goethe did not start out from his conclusions, but came to them during a long period in which the work lay fallow. He wrote what are roughly the first five books in the early Weimar period, between 1777 and 1785, the version that is known as *Wilhelm Meister's Theatrical Mission*. He picked it up again in 1793 and finished it in 1795, rewriting the early books and adding three more. The theme was radically altered, and every reader can detect the change of style between the earlier and later sections. Because of this, it is helpful to discuss first the earlier version.

The theme of the *Mission*, the *Sendung*, can be rapidly summed up. Wilhelm Meister is the son of a prosperous merchant. As a child he is fascinated by his puppet-theatre, later by the real stage. He falls in love with an actress, Mariane, and in revolt against 'the clogging, dragging burgher life' he determines to run away with her and devote himself to the theatre. The shock of discovering her to be untrue to him throws him into a severe illness. Sent on a business-trip, to learn more about the world and trade, he falls in with the members of a disrupted troupe of actors, and rebuilds the troupe round himself, spending some weeks with them acting at a Count's mansion. Ultimately he goes to the town 'H' to join the troupe of a famous director, Serlo, and devotes himself with enthusiasm to the theatre as his profession, with the first object of producing *Hamlet*. The *Sendung* closes with his signing a contract with Serlo; it was to be concluded by the account of the production of *Hamlet*, and probably the establishment of a National Theatre. Wilhelm realises his mission; what was potentially within him comes at the end to fulfilment.

His object is more complex than it appears. Partly it is as an actor and producer that he finds fulfilment for his own inherent taste and talent for the theatre. But he is also something of a writer, a 'Dichter', and the theme of theatre often merges in that of poetry, about which he rhapsodises to Werner, his prosaic brother-in-law. The poet finds meaning in the world, 'he lives the dream of the world as a man awake' . . . 'hence the poet is at one and the same time the teacher, prophet and friend of Gods and men', and Wilhelm admits to his ambition, his feeling of being 'called' to be a poet. This theme fades out of the story, but of course it gives substance to Wilhelm's devotion to art, even as a mere executant.

Wilhelm's mission is, however, not only a matter of subjective impulse; it embraces the 'sublime purpose' of creating a National Theatre. Viëtor rightly stresses the great moral importance of this apparently merely artistic intention. In a Germany split up by political, religious, and social divisions, the theatre was one of the main agencies of cultural and moral education, the only place where the intellectual leaders could meet the German public. Wilhelm and his actor friends are always discussing, we are told, 'the great influence of the theatre on the cultural development of a nation and the world'. In this sense, the *Sendung* is the story of the 'education' of Germany, rather than that of Wilhelm Meister, who, since he discovers that his first intimations were 'right', is not educated, but educates. Goethe is actually referring to contemporary theatrical devel-

opments, for Serlo is the great actor-producer Schröder, and 'H' is Hamburg where Schröder made his reputation.

The development of Wilhelm's own personality is less well worked out than the creation of a National Theatre. Wilhelm is not one with the actors, who are embroiled in their petty jealousies, anxieties, interests; nor is he a practical man like Serlo. We are interested in him because of his idealism, his poetic sensitiveness, his candour, his human kindliness and goodness. He holds the actors together, helps them and shelters them, and tries to give them a deeper appreciation of their calling and their plays. But we do not see how he himself profits and develops through his art, though this theme is suggested from time to time. His discovery of Shakespeare is a turning-point in his artistic life, and the discussion and production of *Hamlet* is the culmination of the novel; but it is something more which is tantalisingly left fragmentary. On reading Shakespeare, Wilhelm says, he learns immeasurably about mankind, but also 'these few glances I have taken at Shakespeare's world incite me more than anything else to make swifter progress in the real world and to mingle in the tide of fates'. Jarno, the nobleman to whom he is speaking, encourages him to quit the trivial society he is in, and Wilhelm appreciates his advice, though without acting upon it. We see too that a new idea of life dawns on Wilhelm when he first comes into high society at the Count's mansion. But these hints are left in the air, and we cannot discover any intention in the unfinished *Sendung* of a further development; they become all-important for the *Lehrjahre*.

The main theme of the unfinished novel is, then, Wilhelm's participation in the foundation of a national theatre, his contribution to the aesthetic education of Germany. Its charm lies in the incidents and characters Wilhelm meets in his progress. With great subtlety and humour Goethe shows how this idealistic, candid youth gets involved, by chance, with a variety of theatre-folk, and against his intention becomes a focal point for their livelihood, building up intricate personal ties in the process. The incidents have almost always an element of the accidental, the unforeseen, as in a typical eighteenth-century novel. (pp. 3-6)

In 1819 Goethe wrote:

> The beginnings of Wilhelm Meister had long lain untouched. They arose from an obscure surmise of the great truth that man would often attempt something for which nature has denied him the capacity . . . yet it is possible that all his false steps lead him to something inestimably good: a surmise that is more and more unfolded, clarified and confirmed in Wilhelm Meister, yes, and is even expressed in the clear words: 'You appear to me like Saul the son of Kish who went out to seek his father's asses, and found a kingdom'.

It is questionable whether this statement is true of the *Sendung;* but it does define the *Lehrjahre*. We now learn with surprise that Wilhelm's conception of his capacities and aim is erroneous, that he finds something quite different and much nobler than he sought. Schiller, in the admirable letters in which he commented on the novel, defines the new theme: 'Wilhelm Meister steps out of an empty and imprecise ideal into a definite active life, but without forfeiting his power of idealisation'. It could not be meant that the ideal of a national theatre was 'empty' or 'imprecise'; what we are to understand is that his ideal of himself, the idea of his personal calling, was both. Schiller's remark suggests therefore, and rightly, that all the stress is now, not on the external object of Wilhelm's life, but on his own personal self-fulfilment: that is on 'Bildung', the formation of personality. Only now does the novel become a 'Bildungsroman', *the* 'Bildungsroman'. Wilhelm is now no longer the artist who is to educate the public. The essential point is, as Grillparzer noted, that he is not an artist, not a true 'Kunsttalent', he is now a representative, not an exceptional, human being.

The *Lehrjahre* takes over much of the earlier material, altering its arrangement, making additions, and conducting the story to a new conclusion. I shall first outline the additions and the new theme, and then examine the meaning the older material acquires through the framework in which it is now placed.

A significant new note is struck through the interpolation of a long letter Wilhelm writes (Book 5, Chapter 3) to explain to Werner (and himself) why he signs the contract with Serlo. The emphasis is here on his need for personal development and purification: 'What does it help me to manufacture good iron, if my own inner self is full of flaws?' And he continues:

> 'To put it in a word, to develop myself, entirely as I am, that was obscurely my wish and intention from childhood.'

He contrasts the nobility and the bourgeoisie; in Germany only the former may achieve 'personal development', the middle class can only gain a living and at best develop the intellect.

> 'The burgher may not ask: "what are you?" but only "what have you got?"' . . . If the nobleman gives everything through the display ["Darstellung"] of his person, the burgher gives nothing through his personality and should give nothing. . . . The former must act and affect the outside world ["wirken"], the latter must perform and accomplish. . . . But it is just for that harmonious development of my nature, which my birth has denied me, that I have an irresistible bent—'

and to become 'a public person' he thinks the means for him, a burgher, is the theatre.

This letter is pivotal. Not because it gives the clue to the meaning of the book, as Korff suggests. Wilhelm's aim 'to develop himself, entirely as he is', is to be shown to be an illusion; his idea that the stage is the proper method is wrong. But the passage is pivotal since it places the objective of personal development, the fulfilment of personality, in the centre of the picture, giving quite a new importance to Wilhelm's earlier remarks about the nobility and Shakespeare, and to Jarno's reproof.

The production of *Hamlet* is a great success and Wilhelm feels himself near to his goal. But after a while the public grows weary of *Hamlet,* and more popular trivial plays are put on. The troupe grows more and more intractable. Wilhelm leaves to visit a nobleman who has played fast and loose with an actress's feelings, in order to speak plainly to him about his heartless behaviour. Before his departure he comes into possession of a manuscript, 'The confessions of a beautiful soul', which fills the whole of Book 6. It is the autobiography of a noblewoman who is carried irresistibly by her own inclinations to renounce the world and live in the contemplation of God; he reads here of a woman who discovered her own personality and lived utterly for it. The noble circle he now meets is introduced by this autobiography, and in them he discovers a group of people of distinctive character, all active in their various ways, all unhesitatingly following their own peculiar bents. Attracted first by their personalities, he learns through

them to admire practical activity. He has read what the Uncle of the 'beautiful soul' has said: 'Man's highest merit is after all to control circumstances as far as possible', and recognises with shame that he himself has both ignored and been at the mercy of circumstances hitherto. Now, conscious that he is guided by these people, the 'Society of the Tower', who unknown to him have guided him in the past, Wilhelm recognises the need for activity within a community. He learns that activity demands self-limitation, but that personal one-sidedness is compensated and rounded off in the community, in which all one-sidednesses combine into a whole. At the same time he discovers a son, the child of Mariane, and marries; the family roots him in society.

But it is necessary that we should examine more closely the goal which Wilhelm is approaching. If we leave it as 'activity', even as 'a transfigured practical life' (Korff), we are left with an unprincipled admiration of activity like Nietzsche's; if we admit 'one-sidedness' without examining what justifies, in Goethe's view, the choice of specialisation, we cannot see the difference between Werner and Wilhelm; if we say 'community' without asking 'what sort of community', we open the door to all sorts of misrepresentation.

Wilhelm enters into a society predominantly of nobles. These men and women incorporate the ideals he had defined in his letter to Werner. They follow their own inward bent, they realise their personalities, freed by their social station from sordid cares and calculations, and by their characters from convention. They are all reformers and educators. Lothario, the man they all look up to, has fought under Washington in America, and is engaged in bold schemes of agricultural improvement. He would abandon the privileges of the nobility, considering that feudal burdens should be lifted from the peasantry, noble estates should be taxed, entail abolished, and class-distinctions removed. This company of aristocrats seeks to establish a new society based on achievement, one that will make each man a full citizen and encourage the development of his potential powers. Goethe was aware that he was placing Utopian principles in the mouths of 'miserable landed gentry', and in the *Wanderjahre* we see that the whole society is to emigrate to America, where the moral and social hindrances to their schemes do not exist. Also, the *Lehrjahre* ends with four 'Missheirate', as Schiller called them, marriages between nobles and bourgeois: Lothario and Therese, Jarno and Lydie, Wilhelm and Natalie, not to forget Friedrich and Philine. Thus Wilhelm is entering a new type of society in which the best of the nobility and the bourgeoisie unite, the spirit of which is contrasted explicitly, even harshly, with the withered laborious hypochondria of Werner, with the misanthropic pietism and foolish arrogance of the Count, and with the illusoriness of the world of the theatre.

Because of the character of this society Wilhelm can see the justice of Jarno's opinions about the necessity of specialisation. Jarno tells him, and the others illustrate the theme in practice, that each individual, to be anything, must be one-sided, and that the totality he seeks can only be achieved socially, in the co-operation of one-sided individuals. But one-sidedness does not profit the individual if it is something merely imposed, by birth or necessity. Wilhelm learns from 'the beautiful soul', and from the others, that 'man is not happy until his boundless striving sets itself its own limits'; the choice he is to make is to come from within, to be determined by his personality. Thus he chooses, in the *Wanderjahre,* to become a surgeon, moved by his aesthetic delight in the body as well as by social obligations. The doctrine of one-sidedness cannot satisfy Wilhelm if it is associated with the society represented by Werner or the Count; it can do so only in relation to the new, projected society, in which one-sidedness and personality are not opposed. Activity in such a framework is also, he learns, the only way to come to self-knowledge; without it thought remains imprecise and cloudy. 'Thinking and doing, doing and thinking, that is the sum of all wisdom. . . . To test doing against thinking, thinking against doing.' These are Jarno's words in the *Wanderjahre;* more generally it is stated later on:

> How can one get to know oneself? Never by contemplation, but certainly by activity. Try to do your duty, and you will immediately know what is in you. But what is your duty? The demand of the day.

This then is the kingdom that Wilhelm finds, instead of the national theatre, or poetry: specialised activity within a worthy community, renunciation of much in the interests of what is essential, the consequent building-up of personality and true self-knowledge (in this sense the community of emigrants of the *Wanderjahre* is called the 'Renunciants'). Wilhelm emerges from his apprenticeship when he understands all this, when he prepares to enter a new life on these conditions and with these aims. This is what is meant by 'Bildungsroman', the story of the formation of a character up to the moment when he ceases to be self-centred and becomes society-centred, thus beginning to shape his true self.

In a sense, therefore, this novel is didactic. We notice, however, a great difference from the normal didactic novel. Running along with the general stress on activity, on social service, there goes an emphatic appreciation of the distinctiveness of each personality. There is no one ideal of man. What attracts and instructs Wilhelm in his new acquaintance is that each is himself, unique. 'The beautiful soul', Lothario, Jarno, Therese, Natalie, all have sharply differentiated personalities; yet each tolerates the others, realising they are complementary to one another. They do not seek to make Wilhelm like themselves, but to encourage him to find his own self. He brings, in fact, a very special element into their community. Early on, when Jarno expresses himself in his blunt way about the Harper and Mignon, Wilhelm wrongly calls him 'a heartless worldling'; but there is meaning in it when he says that his own sympathy for these unfortunates is worth more than all Jarno can offer him. Later, Wilhelm is shocked at the indifference with which Jarno and the others hear that he has discovered Felix to be his son. Therese is indifferent to imagination and art, both she and Natalie are insensitive to the beauty of nature. Lothario tramples on other people's feelings. All these nobles, even Natalie, show a certain impoverishment of the heart—Wilhelm himself had told the actors that the nobles lack that happiness which comes from inward warmth. He retains to the end his warmth of heart, his generous humaneness, which make him the confidant of people in distress. It is a true bourgeois feature in him that he will not lose.

It is one of the peculiar elements in the novel that, from the beginning of his adventures, this 'Society of the Tower' has been interested in Wilhelm's education, guiding it in certain ways. The novel here links up with the conventional mystifications of eighteenth-century literature, omniscient guardians, unexplained interventions, etc.; and it links up with the contemporary development of secret societies, the Free Masons in particular. But there is a profound and rational meaning behind this apparatus. In his letter to Werner, Wilhelm speaks of developing 'out of himself'; in actual fact he discovers that he has needed the guidance of others—'You do not remain alone, you form yourself in society' (*Urworte. Orphisch*). He, like everyone, is educated by influences from outside as well as by his own inner movement. The 'Society of the Tower' symbolises the world, and like the world its members apply different educative methods. The Abbé, the educator-in-chief, believes man is educated by his own errors; Jarno uses the corrective of caustic and blunt sarcasm; Natalie intervenes to help with a loving hand. All are right in their way, together they make up the total process of education. And again, Goethe subtly shows how precarious the results are. Wilhelm, fully in accord with his friends, makes the first really sound, clear decision of his new life. He becomes betrothed to Therese, the woman who is all practical efficiency. And immediately, through outward events and his own feeling, he discovers it was a wrong decision: 'Again and again my eyes are opened to myself, always too late and always in vain'. In the fickleness of his little son he recognises the image of himself and of man: 'You are a true man'. We are never allowed to sit back with the comfortable feeling, now all is resolved, all is plain; though much progress is made, one problem is solved, as Goethe was fond of saying, only to give rise to another. Thus the book, like so many of Goethe's works, closes (as the *Wanderjahre* closes) not with a final certainty, but with an infinite prospect, comparable with the indeterminateness of life. Goethe once called Wilhelm 'a poor dog', for as he said it was Wilhelm's indeterminateness, his infinite 'plasticity' as Schiller called it, that made it possible for Goethe to show clearly 'the interplay of life and the thousand different tasks of life'.

So far only the 'what' of Goethe's novel has been discussed; we must now turn to the 'how'. And first, the composition. How does the new intention fit on to and alter the earlier version, the *Sendung*? Here very subtle changes of pattern can be noticed, as if a kaleidoscope had been ever so gently shaken.

Instead of reading the story of Wilhelm's early passion for the theatre and drama in the form of a direct narrative, we find that it is now Wilhelm himself who tells it to Mariane. The alteration is decisive. What was a plain objective statement of a 'calling' for the theatre becomes a subjective statement made by the hero to the actress he loves. From the start we ask ourselves, therefore, is Wilhelm's devotion to the theatre a real, abiding passion, a calling, or is it a mere childish enthusiasm, even a delusion stimulated by his present situation? Mariane's attitude reinforces our doubts, for as Wilhelm tells his story she once or twice falls asleep; to her it is all an old tale, without present significance. From the beginning, therefore, there is an ambiguous element in Wilhelm's sense of mission, a gentle irony in the account, which colours all that follows.

When Wilhelm first falls in with the dispersed company of actors, he watches a troupe of acrobats performing in the little town. In the *Sendung*, as in the *Lehrjahre*, this incident serves to awaken his delight in show, it is a prelude to his real work with the theatre. But in the *Lehrjahre* it has, merely because of what precedes and follows, a further meaning, for these acrobats appear as a parody of the artist and art, their art has no soul, it is sheer skill and entertainment. This meaning is clarified by Jarno when he tells Wilhelm to read Shakespeare, instead of wasting his time on the actors: 'it is a sin that you poison your hours by dressing up these apes to make them seem more human, and teaching these dogs to dance', a blunt identification of the actors with the trained apes and dogs of the circus which takes us back to the acrobats.

On a larger scale, Wilhelm's whole life with the actors acquires a new meaning in the *Lehrjahre*. Wilhelm continually comes into conflict with them because they have no idea of the dignity of their profession but are consumed with the desire for money, applause, private favours, etc. In the *Sendung* we see these contradictions as the natural difficulties and humours of his life's work; these people are the poor clay which he has to mould into something new. But in the *Lehrjahre,* they are the actual, inescapable reality, which prove to be the rock on which he is wrecked. That the actors speak of the dignity of their profession in the *Sendung* is lightly humorous; in the *Lehrjahre* it is ironical and grating. The jealousies and follies that rend the troupe at the Count's mansion, which Wilhelm believes can still be overcome, have no longer the simple gaiety of the picaresque novel; ultimately these personal defects, and the taste of the public which is their correlative, defeat him. Wilhelm takes these difficulties to be accidental and trivial hindrances in his way, and even when he turns away from the theatre in discouragement, he fails at first to see any deeper meaning in his disappointment. But Jarno brings him up sharp. In recounting the life of the troupe, Jarno tells him, Wilhelm is merely describing the world. So, Wilhelm's delusions and failure with the actors are representative of his delusions and failure with the world, and at the same time the means of his education.

The discussions on *Hamlet* take on quite a different meaning too, although they are substantially the same as in the *Sendung*. Much attention has always been paid to Wilhelm's interpretation of the play, and it is certainly original and interesting. But the question is, what meaning have these long discussions in relation to Wilhelm's pilgrimage. Why is *Hamlet* singled out for discussion and production? Why is Wilhelm such a success in the title-role, while he fails in others? Jarno, his Mephistophelean friend, tells him outright:

> 'He who can only play himself is no actor. If you cannot transpose yourself, in disposition and figure, into many characters, you do not deserve this name. You for instance have played Hamlet and a few other parts quite well, for they suited your character, your figure, and the mood of the moment. That would be good enough for an amateur theatre and for anyone who sees no other way open to him. . . . One should guard against a talent that one cannot hope to practise in perfection'.

Jarno expressly associates Hamlet with Wilhelm himself. The point is, Hamlet engrosses Wilhelm because he is an objectivisation of Wilhelm's own inward uncertainties. Wilhelm sees him as a 'pure, noble, highly moral being destroyed by a burden he can neither carry nor shake off', a man torn by doubt; in analysing the conflicts in Hamlet's mind he unwittingly reveals the conflict within himself, of which he is not yet conscious, and the task of his life, which so far he has misunderstood. The discussions on the play, particularly those on Hamlet himself, subtly illuminate Wilhelm's own character, his own inadequacies; they circle round the issue that Goethe later called the theme of his novel—'the great truth that man would often undertake something for which nature denied him the capacity'. In the *Sendung* the deeper bearing of the Hamlet discussions is not made clear to us, and we cannot say how far the author was conscious of it. The surmise can be detected, however, in the *Lehrjahre,* if we see the discussions in the context of the whole novel. The comment on *Hamlet* in *Poetry and Truth* leaves us in no doubt about Goethe's intention. Here, discussing the influence of English melancholia and misanthropy on the young Germans of his generation, Goethe refers specifically to the meaning of Hamlet for them: 'Hamlet and his monologues remained ghosts that haunted all young minds'. It is precisely the 'ghostliness' of his artistic aims and his life on the stage that Wilhelm unconsciously reveals in his preoccupation with Hamlet. Thus the production of *Hamlet* is the climax of his theatrical career, but at the same time its conclusion; from this point he sets out to seek his 'kingdom'; the search for the 'asses' is abandoned.

The visit to the Count's mansion likewise shows the clarification of an 'obscure surmise', to such a degree that we can almost speak of a change in function. It is here that Wilhelm gets an inkling, from his first contact with high society, that the world is different from what he had thought. Here Jarno, whom he calls his friend, tells him he is wasting his time with the troupe, and in directing him to Shakespeare encourages him in his impulse to take an active part in life. But these hints do not lead, in the *Sendung,* to anything specific, nor can we guess that any new direction in Wilhelm's life was to arise out of them. The primary purpose of the visit is to show how harmful to the theatre and the actors is the dilettante, tasteless, class-proud patronage of the nobility.

In the *Lehrjahre,* however, while all these elements are present, new additions attract our attention primarily to the problem of 'Bildung'. Wilhelm is persuaded, against his better feelings, to dress up as the Count in order to play a trick on the Countess; when the Count, unexpectedly returning, sees in a mirror what he takes for his own image, he believes it to be a presage of impending death; he falls victim to an obsession, abandons all his worldly responsibilities, and joins the sect of the pietists. Wilhelm and the Countess, yielding to impulsive emotion, embrace, and in the embrace a medallion the Countess wears presses painfully on her breast. Her feeling of sin turns into an obsession that she has a cancer there, and she joins her husband in his pietism.

These two incidents flow into the main stream of the novel. Wilhelm can never overcome his remorse, for he recognises that his irresponsible and impulsive behaviour has caused irreparable harm to the two, and it is a tangible symbol of the falsity of his theatrical life and aims. And the Count and Countess, reappearing as the relatives and friends of the 'Society of the Tower', illustrate the perversities which attend a *fainéant* nobility, forming a useful foil to the rather idealised nobility that Wilhelm admires. They, like the Harper, fail to live worthily, because of 'an *idée fixe* that has no influence on active life'; the harsh mockery with which their friends speak of them startles and shocks Wilhelm, yet it tells him indirectly that he needs, equally severely, to repudiate his own earlier *idée fixe*.

Of particular interest is the later treatment of Mignon and the Harper, since Goethe's development of their characters and story has provoked the sharpest criticism. He does not leave them in the mysterious twilight in which they appear in the *Sendung*. We discover their past. The Harper is an Italian monk, and Mignon is the child of his union with his sister, whom he loved without knowing her identity. They are outcasts in every sense, morally and psychologically. The 'Society of the Tower' puts the Harper, who suffers from attacks of homicidal insanity, under the tuition of a wise clergyman, who succeeds in restoring the old man to health, though he can remain balanced only if he carries round with him a bottle of poison, the assurance that he can at any moment dispose of his life. Felix is discovered, as they think, to have drunk the poison, and the old man cuts his throat; saved in the nick of time, he tears the bandage from his throat and dies. The efforts of the Society, so successful with Wilhelm, fail with this psychosis; there are dark regions where even their wisdom is unavailing.

A more subtle process takes place in Mignon: she can be said to pass like Wilhelm through phases of development, a metamorphosis; but with her it is a purely natural, almost physical development rather than a moral one, arising from her adoring love for Wilhelm, and indicating her growth from 'a hermaphrodite' to the threshold of womanhood. After the night that Philine spends with Wilhelm, Mignon changes. Suffering a terrible shock out of childish jealousy, she sullenly submits to Wilhelm's reasonable advice to become a pupil of Natalie's, but is subject to repeated hysterical attacks. She accepts guidance, and dresses as a girl; but she is ill, and no one can restore her. She dresses in the white costume of an angel, which symbolises her withdrawal from ordinary life, her longing for death. When she sees Wilhelm in the arms of his betrothed, Therese, her heart breaks and she dies.

Schiller made rather curious observations on these two figures, Mignon and the Harper, linked both by birth and nature. He noted, with acumen, that all the other characters are ordered in a 'planetary system' at the end of the book, but these two are outside, 'linking it with something distant, something greater'; but at the same time he considered their 'monstrous fate', their psychoses, were due to the 'unnaturalness' of a superstitious religion. The statements are contradictory, and there is no evidence that Goethe intended here any criticism of Roman Catholicism. In both these persons we are made aware of obscure forces, an unmastered fate, a mysterious beauty, which do not fit into the normal world and cannot be controlled by it. There are hints in Wilhelm and Felix of forces which cannot be brought under full control by reason; here in the Harper and Mignon these forces dominate. But, while in the *Sendung* these characters represent the highest beauty, a sort of elusive, incomprehensible ideal, in the *Lehrjahre*, while they may be loved, they are not idealised, but shown as ineffectual, dangerous. It is surprising, even repellent, to find that Mignon's death passes almost without comment. Wilhelm, conscious that all his efforts to help Mignon have resulted in her destruction, dismisses the problem from his mind; a pompous funeral-ceremony is a substitute for personal feeling. Mignon is embalmed as if for ever to be removed from the natural, healthy process of life. Yet Goethe's development of the characters and the meaning of the Harper and Mignon is consistent; and we can see that it is a misreading to make Mignon the centre of the story, to call her, as did Friedrich Schlegel, in his review of *Wilhelm Meister*, 'the mainspring' of the work. Here is the core of the Romantic criticism of the book, as we find it in Novalis, who attacked the book because he observed, more accurately than Schlegel, that Goethe in a sense condemns the 'natural poesy' of Mignon's character. The idealisation of Mignon is the commonest source of a misunderstanding of Goethe's novel; few people can both appreciate the 'poetry' of her existence, and recognise that it is the beauty of immaturity, even of disease.

In reference to *Wilhelm Meister,* Grillparzer, himself much of a Romantic, made a most apt comment on the Romantic conception of beauty:

> That the Germans attribute so high a value to this unsteady dreaming, this capacity for boding without clear image or idea, is the very misfortune of this nation. . . . They think it is something peculiar to their nation, but other peoples know this state of mind too, only with them boys in the end grow into men. I do not speak as one to whom this dreamy daze is strange, for it is my state. But at least I recognise that one must work one's way up out of it if anything is to be achieved. Monks and hermits may intone 'Hymns to the Night' [Novalis], but active men need the light.

Goethe would have approved the whole of this statement as summing up the theme of his novel.

Beside all these particular problems of composition, there still remains the central question, how does the main theme of the *Sendung,* the idea of a theatrical mission, contribute to the realisation of the ultimate purpose of the *Lehrjahre.* If it is merely an 'error', it lasts an unconscionable time, and is artistically scarcely justifiable. The problem is raised directly. When Wilhelm deplores the void of his life with the troupe, the wise Abbé, his moral guardian, answers: 'Everything we encounter leaves traces behind. Everything contributes imperceptibly to our education.' He admits that it is often difficult to recognise what contribution a particular experience may make, so gives the wise advice that the safest thing is not to think over it too much, but just do the immediate task—in this spirit the 'Renunciants' in the *Wanderjahre* are pledged never to talk about the past or the distant future. The permanent

A portrait of Gottfried Keller from the 1854 edition of his Neuere Gedichte.

influences of Wilhelm's theatrical experiences are indeed difficult to perceive, and never made explicit; he drops his old acquaintances and interests completely. Only a most attentive reading will discover relationships here.

The formal link between Wilhelm's old and new life is his reading of the 'Confessions'. How is this book a spiritual bridge? We note the title, 'the beautiful soul': so, it is still a question of beauty. But the beauty is now a moral beauty, a beauty of life and temperament, not a beauty which belongs to a realm distinct from the moral and social world. It is the beauty of Iphigenie, issuing from the identity of feeling and moral purpose, from the union of duty and inclination, as Schiller defined beauty. In the case of 'the beautiful soul' herself, this beauty is still restricted, not exemplary, because the outer world, activity, is neglected, because she develops without struggle, almost without being conscious of her aim. The views of the Uncle which she reports, provide a correction of herself. He asserts that a larger harmony, a larger beauty, must be sought, that man must through activity bring his environment into harmony with himself. Hence he admires above all 'resolution and pertinacity'. The activity he pursues and recommends, like that illustrated in many characters in the *Wanderjahre*, is good because it is useful; but usefulness is the way to the true and the beautiful, for the beautiful is exactly this harmony within the character, and between the character and the outer world. Natalie is more truly a 'beautiful soul' than her aunt, because her inner self is entirely and serenely fulfilled in service to others; she is both a 'realist' and 'a purely aesthetic nature', as Schiller remarks. No man can be happy and harmonious, says the Uncle, unless he is systematically active: 'It is always a man's misfortune if he is made to strive after something with which he cannot unite himself through regular self-activity ('Selbsttätigkeit')—by 'Selbsttätigkeit' he means an activity which springs from his own character and will. For the Uncle art is a necessary condition too to moral training, for it is a means of training our 'sensuous nature', of refining it so that we do not fall a victim to an 'unregulated fancy', to false sentiment. It is not without significance that the art that most enchants this ideal group is that of choral song, where each part becomes lovely only in combination with others.

These 'Confessions' have the deepest educative influence on Wilhelm. He learns through them a new ideal of character, beauty of character based on complete inner harmony and self-certainty; and he learns of the task that faces him, of being active in such a way that a harmony is established within himself, and between himself and a community, so that practical social existence itself may be beautiful.

It is only too easy to misunderstand this theme, to ignore it, to reject it. For the Romantics it seemed the negation of beauty, which resides for them in the world of presentiment and fancy. Sentimental Philistines reject it too, for they want the beauty which is an alleviation, a leisure-time entertainment, a comforting delusion. Carlyle, on the other hand, with his puritan asceticism, could approve heartily the doctrine of activity and work, but completely failed to see the aesthetic aspect of Goethe's intention. Schiller understood it best and Korff has well brought it out in his chapter on *Wilhelm Meister*. The beauty of the harmonious, purposeful character and of his work is exemplified in a somewhat idealised form in the *Lehrjahre* through the description of the few noble characters with whom Wilhelm consorts or through that of his own appearance in contrast to the withered Werner. It emerges in the *Wanderjahre* in relation to certain characters, with their true beauty like Frau Susanna,

or their false faces like 'The Fifty-year-old Man'. It comes out also in the beauty of the well-managed estate of the Uncle, in the beauty of the operations of spinning, which Goethe describes with such loving attention. Goethe's praise of systematic and skilful work has always an element of utilitarianism in it; but he values it in the conviction that usefulness implies a harmonious relationship with society, a combination of personal and social interests, and that it alone can make a man harmonious in himself, can fuse opposing qualities in him, can give him beauty. In this sense Wilhelm's early search for beauty, his mistaken feeling of a 'mission' for the theatre, his desire to find fulfilment for his talent and to be a cultural educator, all these trends find fulfilment in his later life. His life with the troupe was not merely an error; it fostered and developed his inherent tendencies. It not only taught him the falseness of an ideal of art which is not associated with personal and moral 'Bildung', but it firmly established in him an aesthetic purpose—the purpose of making the totality of existence harmonious, beautiful. In this complex sense *Wilhelm Meisters Lehrjahre* is the fundamental document of Weimar classicism.

In a famous passage in Book 5, Chapter 7, Goethe presents the conclusions of a discussion on the relative merits of the drama and the novel which certainly represent his own views at the time he was writing *Wilhelm Meister:*

> In the novel, as in the drama, we see human nature and action. The difference between these genres does not lie simply in their outward form. . . . In the novel, opinions and occurrences are above all to be presented; in the drama, characters and actions. The novel must move slowly, and the views of the main character must, in one way or another, obstruct the unravelling of the whole. The drama must speed, and the character of the hero must drive on towards the issue, and only meet obstructions. The hero of the novel must be passive, or at least not highly effectual; we demand of the dramatic hero impact and deeds. Grandison, Clarissa, Pamela, the Vicar of Wakefield, even Tom Jones are, if not passive, yet retarding characters, and all occurrences are in a sense moulded upon their dispositions. In the drama, the hero moulds nothing upon himself, everything resists him, and he clears and shifts hindrances out of his way, or else succumbs to them.

> They agreed too that chance might properly be allowed free play in the novel, but that it must always be steered and guided by the dispositions of the characters. On the other hand, fate, that urges men without their co-operation through incoherent external circumstances to an unforeseen catastrophe, belongs only to the drama. Chance may produce pathetic situations, no doubt, but never tragic; fate on the other hand must always be terrible, and becomes in the highest sense tragic, when it brings disconnected deeds, innocent and guilty, into disastrous association.

We cannot at the moment consider how far this definition applies to the novel in general. That the distinctions drawn between novel and drama are not completely satisfactory is immediately discovered by the company, for they agree that Hamlet himself has the 'disposition' of the hero of a novel—another gentle hint at the relevance of Hamlet to Wilhelm Meister. Goethe's definitions, based largely on the English novel of the eighteenth century, lead to the conception of the 'Bildungsroman'. The hero is not a man of action or will, he does not influence the march of events, even retarding them rather than propelling them. He is interesting above all for his disposition, his moral views and sentiments, his moral personality. In the midst of apparently fortuitous occurrences, he gives the latter a unity within his disposition, he 'moulds' them though he does not cause or control them. The occurrences are of little importance in themselves, but acquire a meaning when reflected in his character. Thus Goethe lays all the stress on the disposition of the hero, on his 'Bildsamkeit' as Schiller and Friedrich Schlegel called it, his educability. There is no fatal clash between circumstances and character; the outcome is inherently there in the character from the beginning.

Hence, and here Goethe's definition leads on from the English novel to the 'Bildungsroman' proper, a moral meaning is given to the outer world, however haphazard its scenes and occurrences may appear. There is a moral logic that connects events, that leads the Harper and Mignon to their pathetic end as it leads Wilhelm to his 'happy ending'. The novel has therefore an exemplary purpose—to show 'how man, in spite of all follies and errors, led by a higher hand, yet comes to a happy ending'.

There is something 'garden-like', as G. Müller well puts it, about the composition of the *Lehrjahre*. An almost bewildering variety of characters and incidents is disposed in a plan which belongs not to nature but to a gardener, who ensures to each plant the soil and position which enable it to flourish. Wilhelm, specific as he is, demonstrates a typical process; his 'Bildung' has 'the objectivity and teleological direction of an organic process'.

Goethe's concept of 'metamorphosis' postulates two active factors: a set of influences from outside which are shaped by the formative dynamism within the organism. We see these two principles in the growth of Wilhelm. He meets a vast number of incidents, and his character gives them a meaningful shape. It is a peculiarity of Goethe's conception, and of the whole book, that events are never decisive; there are no points at which the hero is suddenly brought to change course. He develops in time, but time is not broken up into clear, distinct turning-points. Almost unconsciously he absorbs what an occurrence offers, and its result takes shape slowly or quickly, according to the tempo of his inward growth; the novel is ruled not by clock-time or historical time (its chronology is in fact rather shaky), but by organic time, the speed of which is determined by the inherent laws of the organism. Thus a confused series of accidents and incidental attachments leads Wilhelm to throw in his lot with Melina, Philine and the rest; there is no precise challenge, no moment of decision, and his decision in fact comes from an irresistible urge in him which becomes dominant at that moment of his development. Again, the experiences at the Count's mansion seem disparate and bewildering until Wilhelm, slowly maturing, gives them a meaning in the letter in which he announces to Werner that he is signing the contract with Serlo. The final decision, to enter into the circle of the 'Society of the Tower', is poorly motivated if we observe only external causes; it is explicable only if we understand an inward movement in Wilhelm which proceeds at a speed of its own. He seeks to elucidate and understand the change, in order to be assured that it is sound and permanent; but the actual process escapes analysis and is never the result of definable causes. There is the same sort of movement in Mignon. Outer events induce change, but it takes place in a way and at a speed which is determined by her own nature, primarily as the outcome of her leap from childhood to girlhood. Up to very recent times few writers have been able so subtly to represent the movement of this inward, organic time.

It is evident that with this central pre-occupation, the events of the novel have a function not met with in other novels of Goethe's time. In fact Goethe uses many of the tricks of the eighteenth-century adventure-novel, partly in order to satisfy the taste of the reading public: chance meetings in inns, abductions, robbery, fire, lost children, incest, secret societies, mysterious figures with uncanny knowledge, etc.; the reader's curiosity is tickled by wilful suspension of the narrative or arbitrary withholding of information. Straightforward narrative is often replaced by reminiscences of various characters, letters, poems, lengthy conversations and reported speech. Much of this 'dates', and the variety irritates rather than pleases. But we are the less disturbed by this paraphernalia because of the primary interest in character and in growth round which it is organised.

> Wilhelm gathers in, so to speak, the spirit, the meaning, the substance of all that goes on round him, transforms every obscure feeling into an idea and a thought, expresses each individual thing in a more general formula, brings home to us the meaning of all, and thereby fulfilling his own character, most perfectly fulfils the purpose of the whole.

Throughout the book, the author intrudes in the ways usual in the contemporary novel, through direct address to the reader, short recapitulations at the head of some chapters, references to 'our hero', comments that the hero 'did not know' certain things, etc. The presence of the storyteller is equally, though more subtly, betrayed by the composition, by the often ironical juxtaposition of events and opinions, by the prevailing clear, equable, somewhat detached style. It is noticeable for instance that Goethe gives many conversations in indirect speech, thus introducing the author's personality even here, where the characters might be expected to appear most immediately; and in any case there is extremely little differentiation in the direct speech of the characters—they are distinguished more by the content, the underlying bearing of what they say, than by the mode of expression. In this respect the novel is characteristic of Weimar classicism; the variety of life is as it were filtered through the medium of a clear, harmonious, serene personality. This personality is indeed not felt as an 'intrusive author', something separate from the story related. It is not the particular historical Goethe, but an imagined, idealised (somewhat avuncular) character, a bearer of the whole meaning of the book, and ultimately, perhaps, its most important character.

In general composition and conception the novel is a unity. Just as Wilhelm's 'Bildung' is the central interest of the novel, so he himself provides the formal centre of its composition—'the most necessary, not the most important character'. The author tells us more than Wilhelm is conscious of, but he always takes his stand-point alongside Wilhelm, so that only those events and that experience that is available to Wilhelm is presented. Thus, from a purely formal point of view, Wilhelm takes the centre of the picture and forms the focus for the reader's imagination.

Thus there is a complex and subtle unity of composition in *Wilhelm Meisters Lehrjahre;* complex and subtle because the novel does not present completed characters within a static set of values, like for instance *Tom Jones* or *Vanity Fair,* but shows a 'Bildung' in the main character, a metamorphosis of values as well as of environment. Yet no reader will feel this unity immediately, and most fail to grasp it altogether. And this is not only due to Goethe's ironical reserve, his delight in veiling himself, in testing the reader by subtle hints and connections. Nor is it due to faults in the actual composition, some of which Schiller pointed out. The main cause lies in the style; in this respect the book lacks unity.

The parts of the *Lehrjahre* which were taken over from the *Sendung* are outstanding for their fresh liveliness, the realistic descriptions, the clear delineation of a number of characters who have the startling uniqueness, almost the irresponsibility of life. Goethe writes with an amused, friendly irony of characters who refuse to obey rational principles. With this go the deeper notes of Mignon's and the Harper's songs, expressing a longing and a despair which interpret a subterranean stream within Wilhelm's own naïve and candid character and give to his apparent harmlessness a strength and substance that on the surface it lacks. Totally different is the style in the later books. In a note to guide the completion of the book, Goethe summed up in abstract terms what he intended to do with his characters. 'Wilhelm, aesthetically moral dream. Lothario, heroically active dream. . . . Mignon, madness of discordant relationships.' Useful as this note is for the interpretation of the novel, it is even more revealing from the point of view of the style. The characters are to acquire an abstract meaning, they stand for general psychological types, they become allegorical. The 'Confessions' still has the liveliness of actual experience, based as it is on documents of Goethe's friend, Fräulein von Klettenberg. But otherwise the later books are pale and abstract, the lessons and experiences are theoretical, and they do not strike home to our imagination. Natalie, for instance, is a completely ideal character, who educates and loses Mignon, who hears of Wilhelm's adventure with Philine, furthers his match with Therese, and ultimately marries him herself, with unaltered serene equanimity. Wilhelm's early life is full of the substantiality of experience; his later education is theoretical. Hence we cannot help feeling that in his adventures with the troupe he was a real person among real persons, while in the later part, and in the *Wanderjahre*, he is an unreal ghost walking among other ghosts.

And this directly reverses the theme of the book! Compared with Natalie, Philine, the whimsical light-of-love, is rooted and real; there is more harmony, confidence, wholeness in her 'If I love you, what's it to do with you?' than in any action or thought of the later characters. The haphazardness of person and incident in the first part seems solid; the subtle linking of persons and incidents in the later part seems 'romantic' and more than far-fetched. Mignon and the Harper seem sufficient in the mystery of their early appearance; when their characters are explained, they seem to lose all substance. The climax of the first version is a real event, the creation of a theatre and the production of plays; the climax of the other is a set of aphorisms (Wilhelm's articles of apprenticeship) and a marriage which is unattended by passion or even by union. This is the great weakness of the book, and it cannot be overlooked. The lack of sensuous reality in the later books is not merely a regrettable weakening of artistic quality; it almost fatally injures the whole meaning of the novel, and is the chief cause of the misunderstanding of the work.

The novel ends with the winning of an outlook, a set of values, and a set of relationships; with this Wilhelm's apprenticeship is concluded. He is now on the springboard of the social world, ready 'to mingle in the tide of fates'. How will he fare, what struggles will come? Goethe felt a conclusion was necessary. He composed the *Wanderjahre*, yet this again tells us only of preparation, moral preparation above all, for active life, represented as the New World to which all the society of 'renunciants' will emigrate. Goethe thought once of a *Meisterjahre*, but without result. In the light of the subsequent history of the German novel, we must consider this fact as being of great significance. We find again and again, in Stifter, in Keller,

in Thomas Mann (*Der Zauberberg*), that the 'Bildungsroman' leads up to the decision to take part in social life, but halts at the threshold, or deals summarily and feebly with the later fortunes of the hero. Viëtor is no doubt right in calling the 'Bildungsroman' '*the* German species of the novel'; and it is characteristic that while no other national literature can show novels comparable with the German in illuminating the moral and spiritual development of man from subjective pre-occupations to the affirmation of objective activity, German literature is extraordinarily poor in novels which present the main theme of the nineteenth-century European novel, the problems of actual social life.

It seems that the urgency of the message of *Wilhelm Meister*, so well understood by Grillparzer, remained; it provided the stimulus for Germany's greatest novelists, and limited the range of the German novel. Goethe understood something of this when comparing his work with Walter Scott's novels. The rich variety of great events in British history was lacking in German, he believed, so that he himself was forced to choose the 'most wretched material' for *Wilhelm Meister*—'itinerant theatre-rabble and miserable landed gentry'. In order to provide the Society with a worthy field of activity, he had to idealise them and send them to a Utopia. Since Goethe's time German novelists seem to have been dogged by the conviction that German circumstances were not adequate to the needs of the full personality. (pp. 7-29)

Roy Pascal, "Johann Wolfgang von Goethe—'Wilhelm Meister'," in his The German Novel: Studies, *Manchester University Press, 1956, pp. 3-29.*

DAVID H. MILES

[*Miles focuses on the evolution of the portrayal of the* Bildungsroman *hero, using Goethe's* Wilhelm Meister *and Keller's* Green Henry *as cases in point.*]

The Bildungsroman, as a novel that "educates" by *portraying* an education, automatically poses questions as to the nature and status of the hero. The standard hero of the genre, as well as the classical pattern of his progress, is perhaps best described by Hegel in his lectures on esthetics, in a remark whose condescending tone reminds us that at least the *plot* of the Bildungsroman was already very much a cliché by 1820. Following apprenticeship years of Strum-und-Drang escapades and sentimental journeying, Hegel tells us, the typical educational hero ultimately flees back into the lap of bourgeois culture, accepting its goodly philistine values of personality, profession, and marriage. . . . Wilhelm Dilthey's well-known remarks on the genre, in his 1906 essay on Hölderlin's Bildungsroman *Hyperion*, actually depart little from those of Hegel, the main emphasis once again being on the conciliatory, conservative nature of the genre—the hero's ultimate assimilation into existing society.

Yet in the *post*classical period of the nineteenth century, deep and far-reaching changes were to take place in the figure of the hero—precisely with regard to his assimilation into society—and it is these changes that I propose to investigate here. I will be concentrating in particular on the heroes of . . . Goethe's *Wilhelm Meisters Lehrjahre* (1795) [and] Gottfried Keller's *Der grüne Heinrich* (1880). . . . (p. 981)

The first great Bildungsroman in the German language, *Wilhelm Meisters Lehrjahre*, may not be a Bildungsroman at all, for one of the most curious facts about the work is that for a book purportedly describing a leisurely odyssey to self-awareness, it is strangely *un*psychological. As Heinrich Meyer has pointed out, it is a book full of "psychological impossibilities," of characters who are nothing more than mere "marionettes . . . who love one another and exchange places with one another, much as if there were no such thing as personality, as if love and passion were mere Dream- or Glassbead-Game." D. H. Lawrence, with his usual insight, has pointed to the same characteristic: "I think *Wilhelm Meister* is amazing as a book of . . . intellectualized sex, and the utter incapacity for any *development* of contact with any other human being, which is peculiarly bourgeois and Goethian" (letter to Aldous Huxley, 27 March 1928). Other critics, particularly in more recent years, have voiced similar misgivings, pointing out as well that this nonpsychological side of the novel actually locates it, in some respects, closer to such forms as the fairy tale, comic fiction, and the picaresque narrative, rather than the Bildungsroman. As D. J. Enright has observed, the first part of the novel in particular follows a definitely "picaresque path: the company moves from theatre to theatre (instead of from inn to inn), it meets with successes and failures, new people join it from time to time and we are regaled with their biographies, and the actors are even attacked by highwaymen and robbed of their clothes, like Joseph Andrews."

In sum, then, Goethe requires us to grant a good deal regarding the simplicity of Wilhelm's mental growth. Even the flashbacks in the novel, which should be most capable of psychological elaboration, appear after closer examination to be closer to Auerbach's picaresque or Homeric "foreground" reminiscences than to the "background" ones of more psychological fiction. Wilhelm's recollections of playing with puppets as a child, for instance, are motivated, not by self-questioning, but by self-satisfaction, and the rather tedious episode is excused by the narrator with a nice touch of irony: Mariane falls asleep in the middle of the story and leaves the unsuspecting Wilhelm holding forth in front of the tipsy old housekeeper in a room full of gaping puppets. Likewise, Wilhelm's days of recuperation at the village vicarage following the robber attack are filled with various potentially crucial reminiscences and vows ("more calculated steps should characterize his career from now on") and yet these vows never materialize; he reflects as little afterward as he had before. Even the final, all-important decision to abandon his lifelong dream of becoming a strolling player transpires in a dreamlike and unselfconscious manner: "he felt that he had already bid farewell and now only needed to leave."

Quite in keeping with this nonpsychological, picaresque dimension of the novel is the central tenet of Wilhelm's "education," a picaresque carpe diem. Here, as in *Faust,* activity is the key to salvation: "Everything in life contributes imperceptibly to our *Bildung,"* the Abbé assures Wilhelm toward the end of the novel, "yet it is dangerous to want to take responsibility for this . . . the safest is always to do the thing that lies directly before us." "Be active and agreeable and enjoy the present," Wilhelm himself advises Madame Melina; and, a short time later, during the ritual initiation in the tower of Lothario's castle, Wilhelm receives a very similar commandment from the hidden voice of his ghost-like father, the "King of Denmark": "You will repent none of your follies, nor wish to repeat them. No happier fate can befall a man." Most characteristic of all, however, are Wilhelm's own very last words in the novel; upon being reminded of his earlier theatrical days by his brother-in-law Friedrich, he retorts: "Don't remind me of those times now, in such a moment of great

happiness.'' Wilhelm's life in the present moment is necessarily paid for by a constant denial of the past. His aversion to reflection results even in the minor fact that he does not find time to compile a simple *Reisejournal,* which in the end must be ghostwritten for him by a friend plundering a *Baedeker.* Equally telling is the fact that the autobiography he begins to write at one point (and whose psychological import Schiller rightly discerned . . .) does not progress beyond the mere form of a sketch.

In the end, in fact, when we examine these and other instances, we see that it is actually the Tower Society, not Wilhelm, that provides the novel with its "educational" dimension and continuity. At the close of the novel, for instance, where we expect finally to discover some signs of an incipient growth in Wilhelm, we are confronted instead with the wholly outer device of the secret Tower Society. It is they who recall for him the painting of the sick prince, who write his biography (*Lehrjahre*) for him through which he becomes aware of his previous selves for the first time, who assemble an art museum for him in the sphinx-guarded Hall of the Past in Natalie's castle, who compose his pedagogic Indentures for him, and, most important, who compel him to listen to these, in spite of Wilhelm's vigorous protestations about these "pompous maxims." To arrive at the end of his "apprenticeship" and the commencement of his "journeyman" years—at the rather late age of twenty-seven—Wilhelm has had only to exhibit the patience of Hamlet (under a much happier providence) and pose the Parzival-like question of whether or not Felix ("Happiness") is his son. "Nature" then pronounces him "free"—that very same eighteenth-century Nature whose "darling" he has been since the beginning of the novel and who has served him as protectress and guide, in typically Rousseauean fashion, in place of ill-advised "bourgeois morals." After all this, we are indeed tempted to question, as Schiller did, just *how* Wilhelm can be pardoned for all of his picaresque misdeeds—particularly those involving poor Mariane (who must die, Gretchen-fashion, to make way for Helene-Natalie)—simply by a sudden display of the "paternal feelings" that have been aroused in him. The best answer to this question, perhaps, is that offered with respect to a similar lack of conscience in the life of Wilhelm's creator: Goethe, too, as one critic has observed, recognized full well the fact that since "memory and conscience are closely allied," one "secret of happy and effectual living is not to have too good a memory."

Considering all of this, we can begin to sympathize somewhat with Schiller's wish that Goethe had done a better job of bringing home to the reader the significance, for Wilhelm's inner development, of the novelistic "machinery" of the last two chapters. The Society, of course, can be interpreted in a number of ways. It can be viewed as a sort of epic deus ex machina— as what Goethe himself designates elsewhere as the modern equivalent of the ancient epic's pantheon of "gods, soothsayers, and oracles" (the Society overseeing young Wilhelm perhaps as Athene did young Telemachus?). Or, in an anachronistically modern fashion, we might even view it as the projected machinery of Wilhelm's own subconscious, much as Kafka's *Castle* could be read as merely a figment of his hero's imagination. Or, and this is undoubtedly the most appropriate interpretation, we can see it as a standard literary device of the period: Goethe most probably had lifted the device of the Tower Society from the *Trivialroman* of his time—the penny dreadfuls and Gothic novels, for the motif of the mystical *Geheimbund,* in Goethe's very Masonic century, was active in the popular genre of the *Bundesroman* (League Novel) as well as in such other works as Mozart's *Zauberflöte*, with its *Priesterbund*.

No matter how we interpret the Tower Society, however, Schiller's objection remains, and raises an extremely important question. In what respect, if at all, is the *Lehrjahre* a Bildungsroman and Wilhelm a *Bildungsheld*? To answer this, we must turn for a moment from considerations of plot, theme, and character to matters of style, form, and narrative viewpoint. As has often been observed, Goethe's novel falls, stylistically as well as thematically, into three parts. The first five books, recounting Wilhelm's picaresque adventures with the group of strolling players—a group little concerned with introspection and humanitarian ideals—are written in a lively and objective style, one approaching Auerbach's "extensive, foreground" style. The second part, comprising Book VI ("The Confessions of a Beautiful Soul"), plunges the reader into the subjective and introspective world of the Pietist confession, depicted, in Auerbach's terms, in an "intensive, background" style. In this part, the important connection between growth and the role of memory is made, for the aunt (Wilhelm's future aunt-in-law) unfolds a story of psychological *Bildung* totally foreign to the unreflective world of Wilhelm and the actors. Already at the age of eight (much like Augustine in the *Confessions*), she writes, she had suffered a severe illness that had infused her whole being with "sensitivity and memory"; the illness had laid the foundations for her entire later spiritual development. Through her, rather than Wilhelm, we come to know the truth that all genuine transitions in life tend to be "sicknesses" or "crises." . . . Following the "Confessions," Books VII and VIII bring us yet a third style: "intensive" as well as "extensive," featuring "background" as well as "foreground," at the same time meditative and descriptive, generalizing and realistic.

The triadic structure of the novel is so apparent, in fact, that several critics have spoken of actual stylistic and thematic "breaks" in the work. Yet the divisions are not, as Viëtor would have it, for instance, "fatal to its artistic effects" (*Goethe the Poet*). On the contrary, it is these very transitions in the work that provide us with signs of a genuine *Bildung*. Yet, in speaking of such structural matters, we have moved from the world of the hero to the level of the implied narrator of the work, and the fact is that *Wilhelm Meister* presents us with the *Bildung* of a narrator rather than of a protagonist.

The presence of the narrator (in technical terms, the "authorial" mode of narration) is suggested in a number of ways, the most noticeable of which is irony. From the title page on (Wilhelm, in no sense, ever becoming a "Meister") the reader is forced into viewing Wilhelm from above, through the eyes of the omniscient narrator. The narrator, for instance, often addresses us over the shoulder of his middling protagonist, to spare us embarrassing love scenes . . . or certain tediously unproductive years, or merely to impart to us general wisdoms of life. Through summary and recapitulation, he effectively filters the action of the novel, often translating the conversations of the characters into indirect speech to spare us the full extent of their harangues. At the end, with the sovereignty of a master puppeteer, he musters his characters into a trio of melodramatic marriages presided over by a patent happy end. With respect to its narrator, then, as Roy Pascal has pointed out, *Wilhelm Meister* is actually "characteristic of Weimar classicism; the variety of life is, as it were, filtered through the medium of a clear, harmonious, serene personality. This personality is indeed not felt as . . . the particular historical

Goethe, but an imagined, idealised (somewhat avuncular) character, a bearer of the whole meaning of the book and ultimately, perhaps, its most important character" [see excerpt above]. Schiller had made somewhat the same point much earlier: Wilhelm, he said, although a very important figure in the novel, was not the *most* important; ultimately, it is the *narrator* who assumes this position.

The situation is actually a common one in Goethe's works: in *Werther*, *Die Wahlverwandschaften*, and even in *Faust*, the "editor" or narrator, in the end, tends to assume the position of an omniscient guardian or alter ego of the hero himself, adopting a stance very much akin to that of Goethe's higher rhapsode, of his poet who possesses "style" in its deepest sense. In *Wilhelm Meister* the role of the narrator, for instance, is intentionally merged toward the end of the novel with the role of the Tower Society. For the "thinking Intellect," the "great Talent" that writes the story of Wilhelm's youth for him, is to be found not only in the humanists of the Tower (the fictional "authors" of the *Lehrjahre*) but also, by direct implication, in the figure of the narrator himself. (In his comments to Eckermann on 18 Jan. 1825, Goethe also speaks ambiguously of the "higher hand" that leads Wilhelm to his happy goal.) In their humanistic ideals, their abstract maxims, and their "hidden" efficacy, the Society and the narrator approach a common point of view.

In short, the only personage in Goethe's novel who truly approaches the standpoint of an "educational hero" is the narrator himself. Viewed from his standpoint (or that of the reader), the three parts of the novel form a dialectical progression in terms of both narrative content and technique: extensive-picaresque (Bks. I-V) and intensive-confessional elements (Bk. VI) combine in an ultimate synthesis of the two (Bks. VII-VIII), which both unites and transcends the elements of the two earlier parts. In terms of Goethe's own morphological esthetics, the development of the narrator has passed through a polarity to a *Steigerung*, through a diastole and systole to a rhythmic resolution of the two. The grand "synthesis of antinomies" that Novalis perceives at the end of the novel, as well as the "invisibly effective, higher Intellect" that Schiller sees in the Society, are both grounded, ultimately, in the final attitude of the narrator.

Moreover, when we recall that genuine *Bildung* involves a restructuring of recollections often analogous to the creative process itself, we can see that there is a tendency for the hero of any Bildungsroman, if he develops in a truly psychological fashion, to become a narrator—in the present case, for the narrator to become the hero. In *Wilhelm Meister* this tendency is ironically hinted at by the narrator himself, who, in an aside to us at one point, states that there are three basic stages in the development of a personality. The first and most naïve of these is that of the untutored soul, who is content "if he can merely watch something going on"; to this stage we might assign Wilhelm at the beginning of the novel. The second is that of the educated man—"der gebildete"—who not only sees, but *feels;* this might describe Wilhelm at the close of the novel. The third and highest stage is reserved for those rare individuals who are capable not only of seeing and feeling but also of thinking and *reflecting;* only this type can be called the truly educated man ("der ganz ausgebildete"), and only the narrator, in our view, may be said to qualify for this stage in the novel.

In Keller's *Der grüne Heinrich* the tendency merely implicit in *Wilhelm Meister* becomes explicit: the hero actually *becomes* the narrator. No longer do we watch the antics of a picaresque hero from the higher vantage point of an omniscient narrator, but, instead, experience such exploits directly through the eyes of the hero himself—at a remove in time rather than space. Moreover, Keller's *self*-portrait of the artist as a young man affords us, in effect, two viewpoints at once: the "I" telling the tale is also the "I" who experienced it. Together with a worldly irony of wisdom and humor, this double vision also creates the central irony of any life when seen as a whole: the dreams of the child are juxtaposed to the experiences of the man. Thanks to the narrative standpoint, Heinrich Lee's end is already present in his beginning, and the result is a far truer, far more psychological portrait of *Bildung* than that offered in *Wilhelm Meister*.

The plot of *Der grüne Heinrich* is of course similar to that of *Wilhelm Meister*: Heinrich's years as dilettante artist and bohemian student in Munich between the ages of nineteen and twenty-five parallel those of Wilhelm with the troupe of actors; and the subsequent episode, Heinrich's six-month sojourn at the castle of the German count, corresponds closely to Wilhelm's stay at the aristocratic castles of Natalie and her brother Lothario. The parallels between the two later episodes, in fact, are particularly striking. Heinrich's lover—Dorothea ("God's gift") Schönfund!—bears a marked resemblance to Natalie ("Christ-child"), for she, too, lives at the castle of her rich uncle. The paintings Heinrich discovers in the count's castle recall those Wilhelm finds in Natalie's castle; the Hall of Knights, with its ancestral portraits, resembles the Hall of the Past; and the Chaplain may also be related to the Abbé in *Wilhelm Meister*. Furthermore, just as Wilhelm first glimpses Natalie at the low point of his career (in the forest after the robber attack), so Heinrich first catches sight of Dorothea when he is selling his flute in a Munich pawnshop (Dorothea's "sunny" appearance recalling Natalie's "halo"). In fact, Keller's description to his publisher of Heinrich's stay at the castle could just as easily be a description of the closing scenes in *Wilhelm Meister*: the hero, Keller writes, "enters an aristocratic circle, regains his strength, gains . . . a firm hold, and sets out on a new career that holds the promise of a fine reward" (letter to Eduard Vieweg, 3 May 1850). Yet Keller enriches his plot by extending it temporally beyond that of *Wilhelm Meister*: at the beginning we have the story of Heinrich's youth in Switzerland, based on his Munich notebooks, and at the end we have his return home, where he assumes a job as a Swiss civil servant for the remainder of his days. The circle has a feeling of symbolic and realistic completeness to it, and lends Heinrich's life a compelling sense of psychological and social growth which is quite lacking in Wilhelm's life.

A necessary side effect of Keller's starkly psychological and social realism was a mocking and debunking of certain cultural beliefs common to the Weimar *Hofklassik*, as well as a deep sense of loss over what was replacing these. Keller's entire episode at the count's castle in particular can be read as a devastating parody of the utopian machinery of classical *Bildung* assembled by Goethe in his Tower Society. Rather than forming a "metaphysical completion" of Heinrich's education (as Georg Lukács would have it), the crucial episode would appear to represent precisely the very opposite: a sense of bitter disillusionment with life's ideals. Whereas Wilhelm's brother-in-law Lothario, for example, after fighting in the American Revolution, had retreated to his castle in Germany in order to devote himself to the humanistic schemes of the secret Tower Society, the count no longer harbors any such utopian ideals of an aristocracy voluntarily performing good deeds, and would

be happiest if he could flee to America, "to immerse himself in the rejuvenating flood of simple humanity." Fatigue—not Lukács' "mature self-confidence"—has possessed the soul of the count. He ushers Heinrich into the hallowed Hall of Knights, not with Masonic gestures, but with the casual remark that in this room "all the family junk" had been piled up. The Feuerbachian freethinkers of the castle (pace Lukács) do not initiate Heinrich into the "highest philosophy (*Denkform*) of pre-revolutionary Germany," but merely rob him of his last faith in God, immortality, and all hope of seeing his mother again. In place of Natalie's aura of priestess in a temple, before whom Wilhelm literally falls to his knees, we see in Dorothea the embodiment of a lively atheism: "With God," she tells Heinrich, "anything is possible—even that he exists!" Most unfortunate of all, perhaps, is the case of Heinrich's diary, his self-composed *Lehrjahre*: far from being treated with Masonic reverence, it is turned into a "Herbarium" by Dorothea, who fills it with leaves as bookmarks (perhaps a thrust at Goethean organicism), and, later, when Heinrich forgets it at the castle, the count informs him that there is no time to retrive it, but that he will send it on later by mail.

The deepest part of the parody, however, occurs in the events that transpire *after* Heinrich has left the castle. For a year later he receives a letter from the count berating him for not having mustered the courage to propose to Dorothea (we recall the successful *silence* of Wilhelm's connubial vows, largely foisted on him by his eager in-laws) and reporting to him the news that Dorothea—her noble heritage having come to light—had become engaged to a certain Theodore (also a "gift of God"), who would now become sole heir to the count's castle. "How long it will take," he concludes, for Dorothea "to become the subject of a novel or two is hard to say," but he has already warned her to expect at least a few "soap-operas and melodramas" on the subject. (One thinks immediately of the melodramatic and sentimental marriage tableau at the end of *Meister*.) Heinrich's idyllic interlude at the castle, in other words, culminating as it does in literary self-parody, only heightens his own realistic ending in redemptive service to the community.

In place of Wilhelm's sentimental education, then, Heinrich experiences a severely moral one. In Keller's own words, this ethical dimension of the novel lies in the fact that it indicts a particular way of life: Heinrich's demise is due primarily to an "adventurous vegetating," a "passive, awkward wandering about" (letter to Eduard Vieweg, 3 May 1850). The words could easily describe Goethe's "organic" *Bildung* and Wilhelm's lifestyle of "eternal seeking and never finding" as well. Where Wilhelm thrives on a pedagogical diet of Rousseauean permissiveness, Heinrich is destroyed by it; losing his father early in life, he is brought up by his all too permissive mother, who herself later regrets her permissiveness. Unlike Wilhelm, who receives enough money from his mercantile father (and this through his twenties!) to buy Mignon, support her and her father the harpist, and to finance Melina's theatrical ventures—and who later marries into a family of aristocratic capitalists, inherits Natalie's German castle, and is given Mignon's estates in Italy!—Heinrich incurs a lifelong sense of guilt precisely because of his unthinking use of others' money, in both the case of the painter Römer and that of his poor mother. Indeed, it is the sense of *debt*, in all senses of the word, that exercises such a moral influence on him in the book. Memory and reflection, together with their attendant phenomenon of moral guilt, are the moving forces behind his education.

In fact, we can actually point to the specific moment in Keller's novel at which this development commences—namely, in the

Munich episodes where Heinrich, plagued by financial troubles and guilt feelings about his mother, decides to isolate himself and set down his confessions. ''Suddenly I bought several notebooks and began writing,'' he tells us, ''in order to give myself a clear idea of my development and of what I was, a description of my life and experiences up to that point. . . . In the dark gloom that had surrounded me for some time I had gradually come to feel that I had actually never experienced a childhood.'' Losing all track of time, he spends days buried in the memories of his youth, recording them up to that point when he left home for Munich. When we recall Wilhelm Meister's ineptitude at writing even a short autobiography as well as his aversion to keeping even a simple *Reisejournal,* I think we perceive very clearly the psychological forces at work in Heinrich's education; moreover, we actually experience Heinrich's growth, for the confessional autobiography of his Munich days constitutes the first half of the book we have been reading. In place of a Masonic manuscript-as-initiation-prize, we have a diary-autobiography as a vital factor in an individual's growth; Heinrich grows by recollecting and writing as well as by experiencing. Even his paintings (unlike Wilhelm's favorite of the *Sick Prince*) have a direct and realistic bearing on his inner development, for they furnish, in effect, ''illustrations'' for his autobiography.

Heinrich's advance over Wilhelm as an educational hero is best summarized by looking at a chapter characteristically entitled ''Activity *and* Contemplation'' (''Arbeit und Beschaulichkeit''). ''It is the seer who finally completes the circle of things seen,'' he writes, contemplating the relationship of thought to action, ''and if he is a true seer, there will also come a moment when, like the eighth king in *Macbeth,* he will join the procession with his golden mirror.'' The statement captures perfectly Keller's departure from the form of Goethe's novel; for in allowing his protagonist to relate his own story, to *mirror* life's procession as well as to participate in it himself, he lends the portrayal of youth an added, psychological dimension. Moreover, that Heinrich develops is also evidenced by his constant awareness of time, something that removes him entirely from the timeless, fairy-tale world of the *Lehrjahre.* Whereas the conclusion of the *Lehrjahre* is open and optimistic, anticipating Wilhelm's future romantic adventures in Italy, *Der grüne Heinrich* closes on an elegiac note; having long since cast away Dorothea's ''green song of hope,'' Heinrich is left with only the ''green paths of memory.'' The novel leaves us with the image of a solitary, brooding figure, and the saddening realization that time destroys as well as creates. (pp. 981-86)

From the forward-looking, utopian close of *Wilhelm Meister* through the subdued and elegiac tones of *Der grüne Heinrich* . . ., the viewpoint of the hero in the nineteenth-century Bildungsroman shifts unerringly from the world without to the world within. The change is signaled in at least three ways: thematically, by the gradual retreat toward the days of one's childhood; structurally, by a turning toward forms dictated by the psychological time of memory—to autobiography, diary, and notebook; and, in terms of the image of the hero, by the transformation of the ''picaro'' into the ''confessor.'' From Wilhelm through Heinrich . . . the concept of the self shifts imperceptibly from its status as an assumed postulate to what Samuel Beckett has called a ''retrospective hypothesis.'' Moreover, the confessor, due to his increased attention to inner states of the self and his past, often merges with the figure of the artist; his therapeutic, cathartic act of confession actually frees him from the past by putting it into some *form.* . . .

More interesting than merely noting this change in the image of the hero, however, is to probe the question of *why* this came about. Although there are obviously many answers to this question, there are two that I feel are much more important than the rest. First of all, the change is connected with the increasing sense of alienation—most acutely sensed by artists—during the nineteenth century. It is certainly no accident that the image of the city looms ever larger in the genre, and that the crises of the hero tend to take place here: Heinrich wandering among the pawnshops of Munich. . . . Whereas Wilhelm Meister moves through a societal landscape no more problematic than that of the countryside lying ''between the forests of Thuringia and the sandy wastes of Mecklenburg,'' Heinrich makes his exit from the Goethean castle via railroad. . . . (p. 989)

The second reason, in many ways representing merely another dimension of the first factor, is the rise of what Philip Rieff has called ''psychological man,'' whose increasing burden of inwardness and self-consciousness serves to alienate him from his surroundings as much as, if not more than, sociological and economic factors. This gradual internalization or psychologization of reality during the nineteenth century can be traced in practically all areas of thought. It is signaled in philosophy, for instance, by the development from Hegel to Nietzsche; in theology, by that from Schleiermacher to Freud (the progressive demythologization of God from ''feeling'' to mere ''illusion''); in the novel, by a corresponding ''death'' of the godlike narrator (the disembodied voice of the novels of Goethe and Flaubert) and the concomitant rise of the neurotic artist, shedding his sicknesses in books; and in the visual arts, by the shift in perspective from Romanticism and Biedermeier through Impressionism to Cubism. In view of all this, it is understandable that the novelist, in order to remain mimetically true to such an increasingly inner order of reality, had to create heroes with corresponding energies of sensibility, self-consciousness, and inwardness; to borrow Stendhal's metaphor, the novelist no longer wandered down life's road with his magic mirror, but returned it to his cell, where he hung it directly above the writing desk, to catch every distortion of the world as mirrored first in his own consciousness.

The importance of recognizing these deep-lying historical changes is that it affords us, I think, a new angle of vision on the Bildungsroman as a whole. The standard view—that of Goethe, Thomas Mann, and most German critics—is that the hero of the genre is basically a modification (a ''sublimation and spiritualization,'' as Mann puts it) of the old-time adventurer figure—be this the quester hero of such medieval epics as *Parzival* or the picaresque hero of such novels as *Tom Jones.* Yet our investigations here have actually shown us that the hero, particularly in his modern guise, also represents very much a secularization of the confessional hero of religious fiction. . . . Moreover, we recall that the rise of the Bildungsroman in the late eighteenth and nineteenth centuries coincides not only with the final secularization of religious (pietistic) literature into such bourgeois, didactic forms as that of the Bildungsroman, but also with Romanticism's interest in the phenomena of consciousness and memory—in such figures as the *Doppelgänger* and the artist. Such very different works as Moritz's *Anton Reiser* (1790), Jung-Stilling's *Heinrich Stillings Jugend* (1777), and Hölderlin's *Hyperion* (1799) are all direct forerunners of the modern, confessional mode.

What of the future of the Bildungsroman, however, its forms in the twentieth century? . . . Discounting the possibilities of regression to outdated forms (as in the novels of Stifter in the nineteenth century), there are virtually only two alternatives lying open to the modern writer: either to take a final step into the world of total breakdown and psychic disorder, into that tangential sphere—Kafka's "Archimedean point"—from which *all* reality becomes problematic; or, in a less drastic move, to raise the entire narrative to the saving plane of self-parody—to write, in other words, an anti-Bildungsroman parodying both picaresque and confessional branches of the genre. It is the second solution that occurs most frequently in the Bildungs-roman of the twentieth century. Indeed, in the travesties and burlesques of traditional forms that are found in the works of Kafka, Mann, Grass, and others, there emerges a sort of literary coda, summing up, in distorted form, all that has gone before. In Kafka's *Castle,* for instance, the gulf yawning between the nameless village and the numinous castle could be read as a parable of modern man's alienation from the world of Wilhelm Meister's Tower Society (the latter now transmogrified by Kafka into a mansion housing a "company of gnostic demons"). In Thomas Mann there is, among other figures, the inimitable Felix Krull (conceived at least as early as 1911), shamelessly happy (*felix*) confessor and genially *self-conscious* picaro—an affront, as it were, to both major traditions of the Bildungsroman.

It is in Günter Grass, however, that we encounter the most radical extreme in the development of the anti-Bildungsroman, the most devastating and ruthless parody of the tradition yet to emerge from postwar German literature. For in the figure of Oskar Matzerath, Grass has sketched for us an outrageous portrait of the *Bildungsheld* as a hunchbacked dwarf. Not only is Oskar, like Felix Krull, cheerfully confessing to us from behind bars the exploits of a satanically self-conscious picaro, but his "case history" itself is a calculated affront to the entire tradition. In place of the modest account of the cultural ripening of a tender young soul, we are presented with the uninhibited tale of a dwarf whose most remarkable growth is purely phallic. Moreover, instead of dreaming of founding national theater companies or "ascending" to Tower Societies, young Oskar climbs, at a tender age, to the top of the Danzig Stock Tower (meditating all the while on the innate "absurdity of constructing towers") and shatters, with the force of his telekinetic voice, the massive lobby windows of the *Stadttheater*—the city's hallowed *Bildungstempel.*

The blow touches the very heart of the Bildungsroman tradition, and would seem to signal some sort of absolute end to the genre, even within the realm of parody. The figure of the dwarf on the cover of Grass's novel, characteristically more clown than *Bildungsheld,* seems to be mocking his entire literary parentage of the last two hundred years—the picaros, the confessors, and the various tragicomic inversions of both. The implication, very clearly, is that we must begin anew; yet neither Grass nor his grotesque hero points in a new direction. Parody, coming as it does at the end of a historical period, necessarily holds its mirror up to the art and life of yesterday, not to that of today or tomorrow. (pp. 989-90)

> *David H. Miles, "The Picaro's Journey to the Confessional: The Changing Image of the Hero in the German 'Bildungsroman',*" *in* PMLA, *Vol. 89, No. 5, October, 1974, pp. 980-92.*

MARTIN SWALES

[Swales offers a detailed analysis of the style and themes of Stifter's Indian Summer *and Keller's* Green Henry, *noting their respective places within the* Bildungsroman *genre. For additional commentary by Swales, see excerpt above.]*

[In Stifter's *Indian Summer*], Heinrich Drendorf, a young man greatly interested in botany and geology, spends his summers in the Austrian mountains, drawing and collecting details of the natural landscape which attract his interest. One summer, a storm obliges him to seek shelter at the residence of one Herr von Risach. He is immediately struck by the harmony and orderliness of this house—the Rose House—by the rightness of all its component parts, the furniture, the books, paintings, and *objets d'art*, the scientific and scholarly instruments. Everything in the house, even the very materials from which it is made, breathes a reverence for the given things of the world which appeals very powerfully to Heinrich. After three days he leaves, but he returns on frequent occasions. He meets Mathilde, a close friend of Risach's who lives on a nearby estate, and gradually he comes to know and to fall in love with her daughter Natalie. Risach and Mathilde give their blessing, as do Heinrich's parents. Risach confides the story of his past to Heinrich: he was a tutor in the house of Mathilde's parents; he and Mathilde were in love. Her parents asked them to wait before getting married. Risach agreed, out of respect for the sacred order of family life. But Mathilde would not wait, and resented Risach's acquiescence in the parental decision. So they parted. Mathilde married and had two children, Gustav and Natalie. Risach went into public life, but then withdrew to the country, buying the Rose House. Mathilde arrived later, after the death of her husband, and bought a nearby farm. Hence it comes about that Risach and Mathilde see each other frequently and live out the Indian summer of their love. Natalie and Heinrich are engaged. He goes off on a world tour which lasts two years, and then he returns to the Rose House, where the marriage is celebrated.

The plot of *Indian Summer* is not exactly alive with exciting incidents. Moreover, even the events summarized above are in large measure peripheral to the main concern of the text. The events that matter are not specific, discrete happenings; rather, they are the recurring processes and activities in which the characters engage. Narrative space and energy is expended on the house itself, on how one restores a painting, prunes a garden, measures the depth of a lake. Human behavior is significant precisely insofar as it is embedded in this gradualness and continuity of things and objects, of the natural and man-made environment. In other words, there is very little human interest, in the accepted sense of the term, in Stifter's novel. The one obvious exception is the section in which Risach recounts his past, his love for Mathilde and the breakdown of their relationship. Yet these events are securely embedded in the past; they function, in part at least, as a kind of cautionary tale, as a model of human aberration and disturbance which throws into relief the rightness of the present harmony that prevails. The foreground of the novel, existentially and stylistically, is Risach's Rose House as a temple enshrining certain values and principles. It is manifestly a limited world, insulated from the social generality outside, from any contact with urban society and the stresses and strains of historical and social change. It is a haven in which everything, every object, every detail, is held in a loving framework. And thereby the physical facts of this world are made to vibrate with abiding value: the characters of the novel and the narrator accord these objects the reverent contemplation and restorative attention commonly reserved for the work of art. The framework of Risach's world is, in a sense, the frame around a picture: the context proclaims the significance achieved by even the most humble detail.

Toward the end of the novel, Heinrich goes on a world tour:

I went first via Switzerland to Italy; to Venice, Florence, Rome, Naples, Syracuse, Palermo, Malta. From Malta I took a ship to Spain which I crossed from south to north with many detours. I was in Gibraltar, Granada, Seville, Cordoba, Toledo, Madrid and many other lesser towns. From Spain I went to France, from there to England, Ireland, and Scotland, and from there via the Netherlands and Germany back home. I had been absent for one and a half months less than two years. It was again spring when I returned.

This passage is remarkable for its deadness: the deadness is almost comically at variance with what is being reported. Here, after some five hundred pages of narration, Heinrich actually does something that would commonly be held to be interesting and exciting. Yet these experiences are reduced to a mere list reported in one paragraph, to an empty, cataloguing baldness which is never applied to the facts of the Rose House. The facts quicken with experiential affirmation only when, a few lines later, Heinrich comments on the glory of the sea—"perhaps the most splendid thing which the earth has to offer." But for this brief exception, the passage has an unmistakable inertia to it. Heinrich's description of the duration of his world tour—"I had been absent [ich war abwesend gewesen] for one and a half months less than two years"—explains the deadness of the list. He has been *absent* for nearly two years. The places visited represent an exile from the centrality of the Rose House; his tour was an interlude of inauthenticity, of "being away from being," of having left the all-encompassing ontological and moral strength of the world of the Rose House. Quite understandably, after what amounts to a package tour *avant la lettre,* Heinrich returns with relief to Risach's dwelling.

But then Heinrich always returns with relief to the Rose House. Early in the novel, after that crucial first sojourn with Risach, Heinrich comes from Vienna to the Rose House. Speaking to Risach, he explicitly contrasts the Rose House with the common world of urban life: "It is strange, but when I came from your estate into the city with its concerns, your being was as a fairy tale in my memory, and now that I am here with peace all around me, this being is real again and city life but a fairy tale. The great has become small for me and the small great." His point is that what seems to be real (the city) fades into insubstantiality before the validity of Risach's world. There are two schemes of opposition in this passage: reality and fairy tale, and great and small. Heinrich implies that both worlds have reality, that each is convincing when one is part of it, but that there is a gulf between them. They cannot both be felt to be real at the same time: as one wanes, the other waxes. Despite Risach's reply—"both probably belong—indeed everything belongs to the whole if life is to be full and happy"—the reader is left in no doubt that Risach's world exists in embattled and rightful opposition to the broader social experience beyond its confines. The Rose House, like Stifter's fiction which celebrates it, is built upon a revaluation of human modes of being and doing. Heinrich concedes the common value scale (of "great" and "small"), but goes on to revalue it completely: "The great has become small for me and the small great." These words are spoken early in the novel. The young man who speaks them might seem to be torn between two allegiances, but the conflict is not allowed to assert itself with any real urgency. . . . Stifter's novel hardly operates with psychological verisimilitude in its portrayal of Heinrich Drendorf. The young Heinrich has no scruples about abandoning the "greatness" of Vienna for the "smallness" of Risach's secluded haven. Heinrich as narrator is not really a character in any psychological individuated sense: he is simply the

voice of Stifter's article of faith. *Indian Summer* is artistically of a piece with its moral aim in that it is resistant to common norms of artistic and fictional interest. This constant intimation (as in the lifeless catalogue of the world tour) that *Indian Summer* was written against the general expectations of novel writing makes Stifter's prose the painstaking, yet incandescent, litany that it is.

Risach's morality, the heart of that litany, is one that esteems the gradual unfolding of the natural world and that attempts to house man within this sacramental gradualness. In human terms, this means the embedding of man in the continuity of the sacred, eternal sequence of family life. If man can be absorbed into that gradualness, then he may become part of the self-renewing whole that is creation itself. But this is not easy. Man is problematic, individuated, and therefore prone to aberration. Hence the stylistic intensity lavished on things: things are simply more trustworthy than people. Risach has an infinite reverence for natural objects, and for the way in which man can serve them through the work of his hands. This involves an ethos of craftsmanship, an *artistic* reverence which spills out beyond the *objet d'art* alone to become the *raison d'être* of the Rose House.

Art, as expressed in the total work that is Risach's house, is in every sense premeditated and carefully wrought. It is not a spontaneous expression of individual selfhood. Rather, it springs from an act of human submission before the *donnée* of any given material or experience. Art, therefore, is not hostile to the common universe of humble things and uses: in Hegel's terms, prose and poetry interlock. A wooden floor can be as much a work of art as a statue. Moreover, for Risach, art is part of an overall moral design: it is an expression of right living, of man's offering reverence to the given world of his surroundings and to the fundamental law of gradual continuity which makes that world possible. Art, then, grows out of a deep-seated human need: "the artist makes his work as the flower blooms: it blooms even if it is in the desert and no eye ever falls upon it." Art is part of the organic self-realization of man; it is the cipher of man's humanity. "In art," Risach comments, "if such modest things merit the name of art, a dislocation [Sprung] is as impossible as in nature." The lack of "Sprünge," of jumps, cracks, fissures, breaks, is the measure of the ontological strength of the art in question. For art, like every other aspect of man's life, must obey that general law "that in creation gradualness is always pure and wise."

Man's significance depends, ultimately, on his oneness with that gradualness. The story told by *Indian Summer* is that of Heinrich's gradual absorption into this order of being. The events are recounted in the first person by a young man who comes to the Rose House from the world outside, and who is inevitably drawn to identify that house as *the* world. The Heinrich Drendorf who first comes to the Rose House has reverence for things; he is, we learn, particularly interested in the natural sciences. He also has profound respect for the family. Risach helps him to round out these two spheres, the human and the scientific, to the point where they merge into the overarching unity of a total moral vision. Heinrich learns from Risach, but the learning process is serene, gradual, inevitable. There is no friction, no resentment, no willfulness in Heinrich. Even when Heinrich as narrator asserts the distance that separated him from Risach, we never quite believe him. The present, narrating self dominates completely, and its acknowledgment and stylistic enactment of Risach's principles is unambiguous. A characteristic moment between mentor and pupil has Risach speaking:

"Because men only want and cherish one thing, because they pursue the one-sided in order to find satisfaction, they make themselves unhappy. If we were in order within ourselves, then we would take much greater pleasure in the things of this earth. But when an excess of wishes and cravings takes possession of us, we always hear them speaking and are unable to perceive the innocence of the things around us. Unfortunately, we describe things as important when they are the objects of our passions, and as unimportant when they stand in no relation to these passions, whereas the opposite can often be the truth."

I did not then understand these words so well. I was still too young and I myself often heard only my inner self speaking—and not the things around me.

Heinrich's immaturity is anything but problematic. It is occasionally referred to, but it is never evoked with any stylistic urgency. He is the perfect pupil, and Risach the perfect teacher. Lessons are proffered and absorbed evenly and inevitably. Other people (Natalie) will be there as and when they are needed. There is, quite simply, no friction, no tension, no individuated psychological interest. The human sphere, although it is the center of the novel's purpose, remains curiously unspoken. The urgency of thoroughgoing narrative attention is directed toward things, toward the celebration of a number of modest practical activities. This is the extraordinary radicalism of Stifter's achievement: things are handled with a greater stylistic intensity than are people. People can stray from the norm, but things *are* the norm.

There is, of course, one exception to this rule, the story of Risach's love for Mathilde. It is the story of human aberration, of a love thrown away because of impetuosity on Mathilde's part, because of excessive diffidence and self-control on Risach's part. This past gives a dark relief to the harmony of the Rose House. But the darkness is exorcised by being contained in Heinrich's narration of how it is possible for youth to accept the wisdom and maturity of old age without having to go through the process of error itself. Even for Risach and Mathilde the sting of tragedy is taken out of their past experiences. They have come together late in life; the summer may have been thrown away, but there is an Indian summer. In Risach's account of the crowning of their love, there is an explicit revaluation of the modes of human affection. The Indian summer is *not* second best. Rather, it is an all-too-rare perfection:

There is a marital love which follows upon the days of that fiery, stormy love which takes man to woman: it appears as quiet, totally sincere, sweet friendship, which is beyond all praise and all blame, and which is perhaps the nearest thing to mirrorlike clarity which human relations can achieve. This love came. It is heartfelt, without self-seeking, it takes pleasure in the company of the other, it seeks to adorn and to lengthen his days, it is tender and has, as it were, no earthly source to it. Mathilde shares all my concerns. She walks with me through the rooms of my house, she is with me in the garden, looks at the flowers and vegetables, she is in the farm and watches its milk yield, she goes into the carpenter's shop and observes what we are doing, and she shares in our art and even in our scientific pursuits. I keep an eye on her house, I look at the things in the residence, in the farm, in the fields, I share her wishes and views, and I took the education and future of her children to my heart. So we live in joy and constancy our, as it were, Indian summer, without having known the preceding summer.

The key verbs here are "to share," "to be," "to look at." The love is praised in moral terms which recall the vision of Christian charity in 1 Cor. 13. Yet embedded within the passage are many practical details which suggest what activities this love entails, how it operates. There are facts, aspects of human behavior that are at one with this love. They amount to sharing interests, to walking round the house, the garden, the outbuildings, to looking at the things that are there.

For Risach and Mathilde, this wisdom was distilled out of error. For Heinrich, it represents a by-passing of youth, a shortcut to the Indian summer. Stifter seeks to persuade us of something that at first sight appears inherently self-contradictory: the Rose House in all its manifest restriction of human experience nevertheless allows for the realization of the whole man, of the totality of human aspiration. Indeed—and here is the essential paradox—the wholeness is only made possible by a drastic restriction of the self and its concerns.

Both thematically and stylistically, *Indian Summer* is manifestly a challenge to all manner of common assumptions and expectations. As W. H. Bruford so cogently points out [in his *The German Tradition of Self-Cultivation*], it is a novel written against history, yet written in an age that was obsessed with historicism. It betrays no interest in national or social problems, it allows for no questioning of the ethics of early retirement to a quasi-feudal existence in the countryside. There is no awareness of the stresses and strains of modern life, of incipient industrialization, of the increasing specialization and narrowing of man's capacities in the practicality of his social life. It is a novel that devalues all manner of human qualities that are commonly held to be significant—vitality, passion, conflict. It is a novel written against the demands of plot in that it attempts to transform man from an individuated entity into a being who exists in utopian oneness with the ontological integrity of things. Its unmistakably stylized narrative betrays no interest in the psychological resonance of first-person narration. There is no real tension between experiencing self and narrating self; there is only the systematic exorcism of common narrative and psychological expectation.

Within the context of nineteenth-century fiction, *Indian Summer* is a truly remarkable work. It is an attempt at epic totality, at oneness of facts and values, of existence and significance, that can only be achieved by the restriction of its whole concern to one overtly sacramental enclave. Within the narrow world of the Rose House we find a realm in which nature, art, and ethics are at one. Only a few years later, Gustave Flaubert was to write *Bouvard and Pécuchet*, the counterimage to *Indian Summer*. In Flaubert's novel, the protected world of humble activities and simple things congeals into grotesque bourgeois clutter. But Stifter uncompromisingly produced a novel in which limitation is transfigured into totality, in which everything man needs to know and be is realized in the modest doings of the Rose House. It is probably tempting to see *Indian Summer* as a somewhat peripheral and provincial phenomenon within the European context. But I would argue that this does not do justice to the resonance of Stifter's novel. The line in lyric poetry, from the intense outpourings of Romanticism via the attempt at motionless, static art of *l'art pour l'art,* to Rilke's concern to remove the human dynamic from poetry in order to rediscover the wholeness of things, is one of the cardinal experiences of the European nineteenth century. Stifter's novel is, it seems to me, part of this imaginative undertaking. As a *novel*, it probably fails. But then, because it was deliberately written against novel expectations, it concedes its failure while at the same time it questions the criteria for success or failure in the accepted novel mode. In a strange way, it is not harmed by its failure, for, as Risach observes, "the artist makes his work as the flower blooms: it blooms even if it is in the desert and no eye ever falls upon it." If the world is not *there* for man, it is not harmed by man's ignorance of it (just as Rilke's things are not diminished by man's ignorance of them).

Indian Summer is different from any of the other Bildungs-romane . . . in that it resolves rather than enacts that tension between restriction and totality, between the *Nacheinander* of plot and the *Nebeneinander* of the human self in all its value-heavy complexity. For Stifter there cannot be even an approximation toward human wholeness within the framework of everyday society. Accordingly, he created an alternative world, one not less, but more confined than the society he so utterly repudiated. Within that world, the limitation of human and artistic interest to a number of simple, practical activities is underwritten by an urgent, almost hectoring, sense of human and artistic wholeness. In the process, prosaic reality comes alive with the poetry of the morally and aesthetically valuable. But the overall tone is one of sacramental pedantry: the difficulty of Stifter's narrative undertaking implies a tension which the act of aesthetic exorcism cannot allay. The attempt to write an unproblematic Bildungsroman in fact serves to intimate the increasing tension to which the genre is prone, a tension which can only be resolved by converting the novel into a monolithic litany. (pp. 75-85)

· · · · ·

As a prose writer, [Gottfried] Keller is one of the great masters of nineteenth-century German literature. He can be genuinely funny, and his humor embraces a whole spectrum from the serene and conciliatory to the mordant and grotesque. Above all, Keller's prose has a sheer vitality that seems curiously at variance with his somewhat joyless life, particularly with [the] very long coda during which he followed the routine of the irreproachable bureaucrat. Out of the conflict between imaginative potential on the one hand, and the constrictions of practical social living on the other, *Green Henry*, as I hope to show, derives its principal import.

Heinrich Lee loses his father at the age of five and is brought up by his mother. In school he suffers from the poverty of his home background, and he seeks to offset his disadvantages by stealing money from a chest of silver coins which his father left him. He is a child of imaginative disposition, and he is often able to turn this to good account, finding that he can on occasion replace fact by fiction and get away with it (as in the incident when he gets older boys into trouble by accusing them of having taught him swear words). His desire for prominence in the school leads him—against his better judgment—to take part in a procession attacking an unpopular schoolteacher; as a result, he is expelled. Heinrich attempts to pursue a career as a painter, but his studies are interrupted when his mother sends him on a visit to her home village. There Heinrich meets and is attracted to two very different women: the spiritual, ethereal Anna, and the robust, sensuous Judith. On returning home, Heinrich does genuinely improve his painting by becoming the pupil of the unstable but gifted artist Römer. But a break soon comes in their relationship when Heinrich discovers that his teacher has been involved in financially dubious activities. In a fit of self-righteousness, Heinrich demands the return of a loan, thereby bankrupting Römer, who later is committed to a madhouse. Heinrich continues to visit his mother's relatives. Anna, his idealized beloved, dies, but her image

continues to exert a potent influence on him, with the result that he repudiates Judith. She leaves Switzerland and emigrates to America.

Heinrich goes to Munich to pursue his artistic career. But his attempts are dogged by failure. On learning that his mother is gravely ill, he leaves for home. He is given hospitality on the way by a Count who knows and has been collecting Heinrich's sketches (which Heinrich has been forced to sell for a song to a junk store dealer). The Count has a foster child, Dortchen Schönfund, who clearly falls in love with Heinrich and he with her. But Heinrich is unable to pluck up the courage to propose to her. He resumes his journey home, arriving in time to witness the death of his mother. Heinrich now abandons all pretensions to an artistic career. He becomes a civil servant and spends the rest of his life in the service of his community. His loneliness is alleviated somewhat by the return of Judith from America: they agree not to marry, but to remain firm and frank friends.

Such is the essential outline of the largely autobiographical plot of Keller's novel. One should note at the outset that there are two versions of the novel. The first (1854-1855), written in the third person with a lengthy first-person interpolation, is in many ways more passionate and intense than the later version (1879-1880), which is narrated in the first person. The earlier version ends with the death of the hero from grief and shame: Heinrich is obliged to recognize that both practical social reality and his artistic aspirations are insufficient to sustain his existence. The second version has (as the summary above indicates) a more conciliatory conclusion, and indeed, the conciliating mode of the recollecting hero-narrator does remove some of the friction and urgency from the incidents recounted. For this reason, many readers have felt that the first version is to be preferred. They argue that the first version, precisely because it is sustained in third person narrative, allows Keller to explore his own experience with a distance, with an imaginative radicalism, that he never allowed himself in life. There is undeniably a certain lifelessness to the closing sections of the second version, which chronicle the protagonist's espousal of the irreproachable ethic of bureaucratic hard work. Hence, one cannot dismiss out of hand the view that the later version is debilitated by being narratively too close to Keller's own evasiveness and timorousness.

Yet one must, in my view, recognize that Keller in the later version makes no attempt to claim more for the experiences depicted in its closing chapters than is appropriate. The Dortchen Schönfund episode makes abundantly clear that, in spite of his many potentialities, Heinrich is simply unable to convert his inner feelings into practical, outward expression (that is, a relationship). Deadness is the price Heinrich pays for that continuous divorcing of his imaginative life from social reality. And, as Roy Pascal and Wolfgang Preisendanz have shown in their magnificent studies of Keller's novel, this deadness is part of the central thematic concern of *Green Henry*. The novel chronicles the life of a young man whose imagination in childhood becomes so much the colorful supplanter of a drab reality that he spends the rest of his life unable to find an assent to reality that goes beyond the grudging and the pragmatic. As Pascal so well suggests, it is in this thematic sense that Heinrich's progression along this road has profound socio-psychological implications: in all his eccentricity, Heinrich becomes representative of larger social issues and problems in a way that the first version, for all its greater immediacy, cannot allow him to be. Moreover, it is the measure of the thematic resonance of the second version that we are confronted not with a simple dualism of imagination *versus* reality, but with their dialectical interaction and interpenetration. Imagination can be an escapist compensation, but it can also be the vital agent by which the contingent facts of a social environment are rounded out into the density of an embracing human reality.

Green Henry opens with one of the several crucial passages in which Keller evokes the continuity of life within the human community. Remarkably, we are told first of the graveyard, of the soil to which each inhabitant returns. This humus, we learn, is not alien to man; it is made up of the bones of his ancestors, so that even in death he inhabits the continuity of village existence:

> The little graveyard, which sourrounds the church, its whitewash still glowing despite its age, has never been extended: its earth consists literally of the dissolved bones of previous generations: it is impossible that even to a depth of ten feet there should be a grain of that earth that has not undertaken its journey through the human organism, that has not been turned over with the rest of the earth.

It is from this kind of existential shelter that Heinrich Lee will increasingly remove himself, thereby producing an isolation that will amount to devastating homelessness. The narrator can celebrate and esteem this human possibility. But as we shall see, the protagonist is unable to find such an affirmative relationship to the modest facts of social continuity. Out of this narrative tension—between the "then," experiencing self and the "now," narrating self—the novel generates its principal import.

We come next to the account of Heinrich's school days. We note the gaiety and fantasy of the child, and the authoritarian incomprehension of the elders, with their rudimentary—and largely outward—notions of right and wrong. On the first day in school Heinrich is asked with his fellows to name the letters of the alphabet. He has heard the word *Pumpernickel* at home and is fascinated by its sound. As ill-luck has it, he is asked to name the letter *P*, which he promptly identifies as "Pumpernickel." The unconventional reply lands him with a severe beating. The teacher shows no comprehension of the complex psychological processes of a child's mind: capital letters are shapes, words are sounds, mysterious entities in their own right, whose conventional value has not yet been learned or absorbed. By definition, the growing-up process involves an accommodation to the established universe of terms, of linguistic, social, and moral conventions. Yet the adult world seems unaware that in the act of accommodation individual fantasy and established rules can be reconciled. Instead, adults proceed by brute force, riding roughshod over the child's unformed self-understanding—and thereby, as the interpolated "Meretlein" incident makes clear, they can produce the self-destructive defiance of aberrant behavior. Heinrich's experience of religious instruction is particularly telling in this context. He is intelligent enough to perceive that God is defined by his elders and betters as a kind of ultimate arbiter of socially acceptable behavior. Against this God Heinrich rebels in agonized blasphemy. His blasphemy is a nervous act, born of a fear that the divinity does exist and will punish if provoked. And in a sense, the punishment would be a comfort: he would know what he was up against, he would have proved the issue one way or the other. Once again, the psychic processes within the child display a complex dialectic of acknowledgment and rejection, of association and dissociation vis-à-vis the values of the adult world.

It is, of course, the measure of Heinrich's imaginative skill and intelligence that he is able, in the swearing incident, to concoct a fantasy instantly acceptable to the adult world. Moreover, he senses that the teachers are so narrow-minded in their understanding of swearing that they will not for a moment reflect on the complexity of the phenomenon. They will punish the behavior without inquiring into its causes. Heinrich knows he is producing a fiction that is both more simple and more colorful than the reality of the situation. Thereby he can manipulate both the "real" world of adult simplification and the complex reality of his own psychic processes. As a result, his imaginative act appears powerful and dangerous. The swearing incident suggests the sheer power of the child's affective and imaginative life. This is underpinned by the whole sequence of events involving Meierlein. Heinrich's desire to have money, to be part of the schoolboy group, leads him to borrow money from Meierlein, the young moneylender. Heinrich is appalled by the bureaucratic and monetary implacability of his adversary, and the hatred he stores up for Meierlein never loses its edge. Not even the passage of time dulls it: Heinrich will rejoice when he hears of Meierlein's death many years later. Here, as elsewhere in the novel, we sense a perception—rarely expressed with such force in the Bildungsroman tradition—of the finality of experience. Heinrich's relentless hatred has indelible contours: the emotional intensity of childhood, as Keller portrays it, includes something disturbing and unsettling. It is never allowed to soften into a sentimental idyll. Moreover, Keller leaves us in no doubt that Heinrich is endangered throughout his adolescent years. He is someone who is both apart from his fellows and yet longs to be one of their number. The incident with the unpopular teacher which leads to his expulsion from school shows the uneasy spectrum of Heinrich's motivation: from being the skeptical outsider he gradually maneuvers himself (and is maneuvered) into the role of quasi ringleader. Here we sense the imbalance of his relationship to

A portrait of Adalbert Stifter.

reality: he is withdrawn and critical; yet when he is involved, it is with an excessive commitment by which he seeks to maximize his acceptance. Keller offers a remarkably subtle and differentiated understanding of the issues involved. The moral question—whether Heinrich or his rather narrow environment is to blame—is not, as Beddow would have us believe, the primary concern. Keller's unforgettable portrayal of childhood suggests precisely the problematic area of interaction between individual imagination and social norms that makes Heinrich's fate the exceptional enactment of issues inherent in the social generality around him. His psychological dislocations are symptomatic of the social uncertainties embedded in bourgeois idealism.

When Heinrich goes to visit his mother's relatives, his life acquires two centers in the contrasting figures of Anna and Judith. Anna is beautiful and frail. Heinrich's attraction to her, it has often been maintained, is an idealistic one: there is, for example, a persistent awkwardness about the physical aspects of their relationship. This culminates in the kiss after the carnival, which so troubles Anna that she faints, and which afterwards leaves them both with feelings of guilt and shame. For Heinrich, Anna more and more becomes a kind of disembodied wraith, someone to whom he can pour out all his wish-dreams, all his visions of human nobility and purity—in short, all his imaginative fantasies. The unreality of the relationship is precisely the source of its hold over Heinrich. It is a relationship that cannot grow with time, with the development of physical maturity: Anna always remains the childhood sweetheart of the first awkwardly solemn kiss by the grave of the grandmother. In this early scene the narrator beautifully suggests the theme of human continuity with which the novel opens: the gaiety of the young people, the joy in physical movement, in dancing, coexists with the death and burial of the grandparent. But from this point on, the relationship between Heinrich and Anna becomes increasingly ethereal. And it is essentially because of this appeal of the physically inadequate and insubstantial that Heinrich repudiates Judith.

For Judith he feels an immediate, natural attraction which he simply will not allow himself to trust. Yet—and this is the greatness of Keller's achievement—Judith is not just a cipher for physical vitality, womanhood, and spontaneous sensuality. On her first appearance in the novel, Judith is associated with natural growth, with apples, milk, the yield of the harvest. But she also has a mind, an intelligence of unshakable perception and tenacity, a moral sense imbued with the honesty of her physical existence. In the superlative scene at the end of Book II, Chapter 18, Heinrich is impelled to declare his love for Judith, but he does so in restrictive terms:

> For Anna I would bear every burden and obey her every sign; for her sake I would like to become a good and honorable man, transparent like a crystal. I would do nothing without thinking of her, and to all eternity I would be at one with her soul even if I were never to see her again from this day forward! All this I could not do for you. And yet I love you with all my heart, and if you were to ask me to prove it by letting you plunge a knife into my heart, I would stand quite still before you now and calmly allow my blood to flow over your lap!

This declaration of love, behind the grand rhetoric of the adolescent, amounts to an exaltation of Anna and a debasement of Judith. The feelings for Anna have to do with sublimity, integrity, eternal devotion; those for Judith are linked with passion and desperation. Judith's reply, amidst tears, is char-

acteristic in its honesty: "What am I supposed to do with your blood! Ah, never has a man wished to be good, clean, and pure before me, and yet I love truth as I do myself!" The truth Judith esteems is a moral value that is immanent in her very being, in actual living; it is not a luxuriant fantasy divorced from the real. Yet men, specifically Heinrich, will not allow themselves to see this, are ashamed of their attraction to her. The result is a dualist heresy, one which divorces the real from the valuable. The dangers inherent in Heinrich's childhood are beginning to bear fruit. And that childhood, we remember, was shaped not simply by the facts of Heinrich's personal psychology, but also by his all-important contacts with the adult social world, in particular by his school experiences. The imperfectly understood relationship between the demands of practical social living on the one hand, and the claims of the imaginative capacity in the individual on the other, emerges as an inadequacy not only in Heinrich but also in his teachers. We note, furthermore, that the dualism which vitiates Heinrich's sexual relationship with Judith is not confined to him alone. He is, apparently, one of a number of suitors whose idealism forces a debasement of the physical attraction felt for Judith. The result is a double impoverishment: ideals become vague and unfocused, actuality is dismissed as a suffocating dimension. In this sense, the troubled course of Heinrich's feelings for Judith is more than simply a personal experience. Rather, it focuses a complex of themes that has general social relevance. That complex is the inquiry into the relationship of practical living on the one hand and the individual's creative inwardness on the other. It is the center of the Bildungsroman genre, and it has its roots in the vital intellectual issues of bourgeois society.

The particular significance of Heinrich's curiously resentful dependence on Judith expresses itself in their conversations, which serve to articulate the whole spectrum of Heinrich's troubled relationship to social reality. One occasion is especially important. Heinrich goes to Judith after his betrayal of Römer. He seeks absolution from her, he hopes to shed his bad conscience. What Judith offers him is a combination of astringency and compassion that he cannot deal with:

> The reproaches of your conscience are a healthy diet for you, and on this bread you can chew for the rest of your days without my spreading the butter of forgiveness on it! And I could not even do it; because what cannot be changed is not for that reason to be forgotten, to my way of thinking, and I have experienced it often enough! By the way, I do not unfortunately feel that you have become repulsive to me because of what you have done. What are we here for if not to love people for what they are?

Judith clearly expresses the sense that Heinrich has incurred guilt through his experience. She returns to it a few lines later: "you are now grown up, and in this transaction you have already lost your moral virginity." She asserts here the growth process that is part of the traditional Bildungsroman pattern. In this sense, she could be seen as a kind of mentor figure. Yet the emphasis of her teaching is remarkable within the context of the Bildungsroman because it asserts the irrevocable nature of experience. She insists, in effect, that other people do not exist simply for the educative benefit of Heinrich; they exist in their own right. Moreover, the interaction between Heinrich and them is binding: human actions have effects, they produce results which are lasting. Judith confronts Heinrich with the fact that his life is not just an experiment which allows him to find himself in his own good time. The destruction of

Römer is a fact for which Heinrich will continue to bear moral responsibility. Römer will not, as it were, recur once Heinrich has learned his lesson: he is not a figure embedded in a beneficently providential world organized for the protagonist's benefit. And yet Judith, having issued this moral judgment, does not withdraw her affection for Heinrich. Rather, she asserts her love for him as a moral involvement which is not conditional upon good behavior. Her physicality produces more than a sensual response to the moment, an unreflected instinctuality. Rather, it is a moral truthfulness derived from physical love. But this is something Heinrich cannot acknowledge because it does not belong in his imaginative scenario. Judith's words of love—"what are we here for if not to love people for what they are"—touch the sore point. Heinrich is unable to love the world as it is, to love Judith as she is, to be loved as he is. He has lived too long in a frame of mind in which the real is insufficient when measured against inward criteria. His imagination will tell him that he must repudiate Judith in the name of an ideal. The key image associated with Anna is the star: her very unattainability makes her precious. In her he sees "such a clear and lovely star for my whole life . . . according to which all my actions can be shaped." We recall the moment when Heinrich, having kissed Judith, reflects on the difference between her kisses and Anna's: "This difference was so palpable that in the midst of violent kisses Anna's star rose."

From the time of Wieland's *Agathon* and Goethe's *Wilhelm Meister,* the German Bildungsroman has been concerned with somewhat naively idealistic young men who grope their way toward some recognition of the real in its significance. But no novel in the tradition has so powerfully documented the moral danger of unfocused idealism as does *Green Henry*. It is, moreover, part of the intensity of Keller's novel that the narrator perceives what it was not given to the experiencing self to understand and to act upon. In the context of Judith's remarks about the irreversibility of time and experience, this narrative technique acquires an ominous ring. When Heinrich turns away from Judith, we wonder whether that betrayal will ever prove redeemable.

If the relationships with Anna and Judith highlight the intrapersonal consequences of Heinrich's inability to love and trust the real, the two scenes depicting popular festivals (one in Switzerland, one in Munich) illustrate the broader social consequences of Heinrich's incapacities. The Swiss celebrations, which culminate in a performance of *Wilhelm Tell,* are portrayed by the narrator with great honesty and unsentimentality. Indeed, it is this very down-to-earthness of the Swiss carnival that offends the youthful Heinrich. He is appalled that everyday reality—haggling over money—should so overtly mingle with the high flights of patriotic and poetic drama. Yet his fastidiousness is profoundly wrong: the *Tell* performance is the expression of that imaginative allegiance to their community which makes the villagers so much more than separate individuals out for their own benefit. The coexistence of the overtly practical and the imaginative is unacceptable to Heinrich because of the disjunction of precisely those two realms within himself. This dislocation also determines the limitation of Heinrich's art: his painting and sketching is either so fussy and painstaking that the object or scene copied becomes a labyrinth of minute strokes, or it becomes vague and sentimental as the imagination renounces any concrete embodying of its vision. Precisely that middle ground, Heinrich discovers, is occupied by Goethe's art, although this insight does not serve to transform Heinrich's artistic capacities. What moves Heinrich about Goethe is the latter's ability to render the immanent poetry of the real, "something poetic or, which means the same thing, something living and sensible." Heinrich is overwhelmed by Goethe's "outgoing love for everything that has come about and lasts, a love which honors the rightness and the significance of every thing and which feels the connection and the depth of the world." The interpenetration of the concrete and the imaginative is, of course, precisely the strength and beauty of the Swiss *Wilhelm Tell* performance. That strength is highlighted by the description of the Munich carnival Heinrich attends. It is meretricious in its consciously arty quality: the pseudo-medievalism is the archly imaginative veneer covering a squalid and largely trivial actuality. All this is typified in the duel, the absurdly grandiloquent and inflated imaginative gesture overlaying small-mindedness and irritability.

Increasingly, Munich seems unable to provide the sustenance Heinrich is seeking. There are glimpses of possible fulfillment: the friendships with specific individuals, the anatomy classes which reveal to Heinrich the miracle of organic reality. But no epiphany is forthcoming; the world constantly refuses to oblige Heinrich with the desired experiences and satisfactions. News of his mother's ill health obliges him to return to Switzerland. On several occasions he has dreamed of his homeland, even glimpsing its possible beauty and significance as a constantly changing continuity, as a sacred and sustaining sequence of generations. But even the return home does not provide the fulfillment, the sense of rightness and integrity that Heinrich looks for. The clock cannot be put back; Heinrich has to pay for the falsity of his imaginative life, for the relentless encapsulation from reality that has resulted from it. One feels this also in the episode with Dortchen Schönfund. Indeed, it is almost as though novel convention becomes an overt presence here: we have the aristocratic environment, the good will toward the hero, the loving girl. We wonder whether the conclusion of Goethe's *Wilhelm Meister's Apprenticeship* is not being resurrected here. But the experiences we observe do not allow of any such resurrection: Heinrich is the "frozen Christ." The inward life, the imaginative posssibility, is there, but no outward enaction takes place. Heinrich cannot break this deadness which surrounds him, and he loses Dortchen irrevocably. Heinrich is, we remember, the man who carries around with him the skull of Albertus Zwiehahn, the emblem of a withered and wasted life.

Heinrich returns to Switzerland. Whatever his dream images of his homeland, the reality he experiences lags far behind. But then, for Heinrich, reality has always lagged far behind. The death of his mother produces guilt in him, and this in turn leads to emptiness, to the sense of watching himself dying: "it was almost as though my own self moved out of me." There is the last flickering of an attempt to make contact with living relationships: "while the lament for my mother gradually became a dark, but quietly even, background of joylessness, the image of Dorothea [Dortchen] began to assert itself with greater liveliness—but without bringing light into the darkness." He finally plucks up courage to write to Dortchen's father. His letter is oblique, diffident—and late. The reply confirms that he is *too* late: Dortchen is engaged. So Heinrich becomes "a somewhat monosyllabic and melancholy civil servant." This is the dominant note at the close of the novel.

That note is intensified by the final episode, the return of Judith from America. Her reappearance does alleviate somewhat Heinrich's isolation and anguish. Once again he confides in her, hoping for absolution. Once again Judith insists that she can only offer him her affection:

"Tell me everything, but do not think that I shall be turned against you."

"But then your judgment has no value if it is conditioned by your kindness and affection."

"But this affection is enough of a judgment and you must accept it. Now tell me."

Judith's moral toughness is the same as before. Heinrich would like to transform her into an arbiter who measures with some yardstick other than human affection and involvement. But this Judith cannot become. She insists on the integrity and truth of her feelings for Heinrich: she will not allow herself to be transformed into some *dea ex machina*, into some spiritual authority divorced from the real world.

In her affection for Heinrich, Judith retains the clearsightedness that has characterized so much of her behavior. She insists that it would be wrong for them to marry: "We will forego [entsagen] that crown and instead we will be the more certain of that happiness which delights us at this moment." The term *entsagen* sounds very hallowed and Goethean. Yet it has a specific moral rightness here, for it implies that the clock cannot be turned back. In Keller's novel there is no Indian summer without the preceding summer. Neither Heinrich nor Judith can undo what has become of their relationship. Just as Judith had insisted that she could not judge with eyes other than those of a woman who knows and feels what it is given to her to know and to feel, so now she perceives that neither of them can get outside the context and function of their own selfhood. Keller's novel has the honesty to recognize that the past life is not an experiment preparing the individual for right knowledge, for full maturity. It is binding, not only morally, but also psychologically, in the sense that what a man has been and done inalienably molds and defines his selfhood at any given time.

Judith dies some years later. Heinrich inherits from her the account he has written of his early years: "According to her wishes, I have now received it from her papers, and have added the other part in order to walk once again the old green paths of memory." The novel closes with a definition of Heinrich as narrator: in the act of recounting his life he is to celebrate the green paths of memory, the greenness suggesting life, vitality, fertility. The narrator is able to see and cherish what the experiencing self was not able to affirm and realize (in both senses of the word). It is the narrator who perceives the strength of the human community, the resonance of the *Wilhelm Tell* pageant, the glory of Judith. To so much of this the experiencing Heinrich was impervious. The interplay between the experiencing self and the narrating self gives a toughness and astringency to the whole work. The artistic (narrative) achievement is not allowed to take the sting out of the actual experiences chronicled. We are aware both of Heinrich's slow strangling of his own living substance, and of the vibrant reality around him. To modify an observation of Kafka's, one might say that there is hope everywhere—but not for Heinrich Lee.

I have on several occasions referred to ways in which Keller's novel departs from the Bildungsroman tradition as . . . [it is used] in works of Wieland, Goethe, and Stifter. Above all, Keller's moral rigor, his insistence on the ineluctability of experience in its relentless temporal flow, separates his novel from so many of the . . . [other Bildungsromane]. Yet I think it would be wrong to see *Green Henry* as a work that breaks with the Bildungsroman tradition. In the first place, we have obvious links with the tradition: the young hero as a man searching for a fuller realization of himself than that vouchsafed by the world in which he grows up; the encounter with two

different modes of erotic experience in the contrasting figures of Anna and Judith; hints of the characteristic providentiality of Bildungsroman plot in the meeting with Dortchen and her uncle and in the return of Judith at the end. Most important, we have the narrative perspective which I highlighted above. The recollecting self celebrates precisely that modest human wholeness that is the interaction of world and self, of facts and imaginative allegiance. The novel intimates, in other words, that the prose of narrow circumstances can interlock with the poetry of the individual imagination, that human reality is an existential category in which the limited world of practical affairs can come alive with inward validation. Keller is not the philistine apologist of a banal status quo. As narrator he highlights what his hero fails to recognize: the richness and poetry immanent in the real. Heinrich's quest for a fulfilling life leads him to supplant the real by the imaginative, to esteem potentiality above actuality. Keller's moral astringency illuminates the flaws for what they are, insisting that Heinrich pay the price for disregarding external reality, that is, that he condemn himself increasingly to a lifeless existence. In one sense, we can see Keller's novel as a critical debate with a novel tradition that inclines to cherish the potential rather than the actual, inwardness rather than outward self-realization, that all too frequently operates with a highly tentative relationship to facts, deeds, and the practicalities of human interaction. But in another sense, we must recognize that Keller's novel is a debate conducted from within that tradition. What the narrator affirms is not simply the joyless credo of no-nonsense hard work. Rather, it is that the world, if underwritten by the allegiance of the individual in all his inwardness, becomes the vessel for a wholeness that is the lifeblood not only of right living but also of art. Artistic and moral validation go hand in hand. Thereby, I would suggest, Keller's novel partakes of that tentative teleology inherent in the Bildungsroman tradition. The protagonist may lose his way, but the novel itself—thanks to its informing narrative presence—does not. The characteristic tension between the *Nacheinander* of plot and the *Nebeneinander* of human potential may become a complete dualism in Heinrich's actual experience, but that tension is an artistically sustained presence in *Green Henry* because of Keller's interlocking of experiencing and narrating self. (pp. 86-104)

> *Martin Swales, "Stifter: 'Indian Summer' (1857)"
> and "Keller: 'Green Henry' (1879-1880)," in his*
> The German "Bildungsroman" from Wieland to
> Hesse, *Princeton University Press, 1978, pp. 74-85,
> 86-104.*

MICHAEL BEDDOW

[*Beddow analyzes Goethe's depiction of the process of human development in* Wilhelm Meister *and comments on the philosophical underpinnings of the novel.*]

[It] is an essential part of the understanding of human nature which [*Wilhelm Meisters Lehrjahre*] sets out to portray that each individual is unique, and must work out the particular form of his own distinctive selfhood in and through experiences which are peculiarly his own. So any representation of this vision (as distinct from its gnomic formulation in maxims) will have to be a specific and concrete representation. A valid and truly representative fictional embodiment of that vision will have to be a highly specific depiction: specific in what it shows of the distinctive complexities of the individual portrayed, and specific, too, in its conveying of the particular social, historical and cultural circumstances which are the medium of that individual's self-discovery. That is why the difference between the texture of Goethe's novel and the attempted a-historical generality of *Agathon* is a concomitant of the outlook which shapes Goethe's undertaking. Nevertheless, although the process which Goethe is trying to show demands to be depicted in a representation marked by a high degree of concrete substance, it is after all *the process itself* which Goethe wishes to bring home to us, not the specific substance in which it is necessarily instantiated. The concrete specificity of the portrayal is a means to the showing-forth of the process of human development, not an end in itself. Put less abstractly: in order to show us what he holds to be the distinctive features of human nature, Goethe has to show us a specific individual, Wilhelm Meister; but the overall aim is not to make us acquainted with Wilhelm Meister in his own right, as it were, but to draw our attention to the significance of the pattern of experience which is manifested in his story. This means that if we left the novel with the impression that it was offered to us simply as the story of an interesting individual, Wilhelm Meister, or with the notion that the actual *content* of Wilhelm's represented fulfilment was being put forward as an ideal towards which everyone should aspire, we should have missed much of the point. If we bear in mind Goethe's need to safeguard his text against these misinterpretations, which concentrate on the substance of Wilhelm's nature and experiences at the expense of their form, we can see the sense of the substance of Wilhelm's final fulfilment being presented in such a markedly etiolated fashion. Such a thinning-out cannot take place until a late stage in the narrative without prejudice to the specific concreteness of the representation, which is a condition of the process of development being properly shown in the first place. But, by the closing sections of the novel, that concreteness has been sustained for long enough for the nature of the process involved to be visible to anyone who looks to find it: if we cannot grasp the lineaments of the vision of man which is shaping the narrative by the time we reach the Eighth Book, we shall never grasp them at all. So, having firmly established the necessary specificity of this instance of human development, Goethe reminds us to direct our attention to the *form* of the experiences Wilhelm goes through rather than to their content by diluting the content of those experiences as the narrative draws to a close. This dilution is noticeable in the representation of both complementary components of Wilhelm's fulfilment—his projected collaboration with Lothario and his relationship with Natalie. We are encouraged to understand in outline how both these things meet needs which have been shown to be necessary and distinctive elements of Wilhelm's selfhood; but the final satisfaction of those needs is not shown to us with anything like the fullness and immediacy which marked the portrayal of the earlier experiences in which those needs were 'only half satisfied, and led in a wrong direction'. This striking change of narrative manner invites us to re-examine the status of the specific content of Wilhelm's experiences in the rest of the text, warning us against paying excessive attention to the particularities of Wilhelm's life in its own right, rather than perceiving that life as an especially revealing instance of a more general pattern which will have as many different substantial manifestations (and hence as many different substantial conclusions) as there are individuals.

However, even a reader who is alerted to this distinction between substance and form by the deliberately etiolated rendering of Wilhelm's fulfilment might easily overlook another important aspect of Goethe's vision, were not that aspect, too, emphasised by a series of narrative devices which give rise to the remainder of the 'oddities'. . . . Goethe (who is in this

respect more tough-minded than Herder) takes all the implications of an organic model of human nature and human development extremely seriously. And one of these implications is that the full accomplishment of the developmental process, the complete realisation of the individual's immanent form, will be a relatively rare occurrence. As Goethe very well knew, in the biological domain from which the pan-organic vision of the universe is extrapolated, there is a ceaseless dynamic development and dissolution of forms, a constant passing from potentiality to actuality accompanied by the equally constant breaking down of actualised forms to release material in which new forms can then be realised. But by no means all potential attains to actuality, not all immanent forms achieve realisation as the culmination of their process of development. Indeed, relatively few organisms enjoy the full attainment of their potential: the remainder have their process of development curtailed at some stage—often an extremely early stage at that—and are destroyed through the action of precisely the dynamic influences which assist the fortunate minority of organisms to flourish. In a universe viewed as analogous to the realm of biology, we should expect to find pattern and significant order if we focus our attention either on the development of the minority of 'organisms' to whose advantage the interplay of forces happens to work, or on the functioning of the total universal system, in which nothing is ultimately wasted. If, however, we were merely to observe the 'life-histories' of a number of 'organisms' taken at random, we would see a picture dominated by what looked like quite senseless waste and destruction. But if the universe really is a system which is properly to be understood in organic terms, that picture of waste, however empirically-statistically plausible, would be a false picture, since its contents would have been conditioned by a misleading perspective which did not offer a proper sight of the true nature of the processes at work. Shunning the mechanistic understanding of nature, which allowed only for efficient causality, Goethe believed that reality was manifestly informed by teleological principles. But he conceived of that teleology, following lines of thought suggested by Herder, in biological, not theological terms: to employ the terminology which Hegel, himself strongly influenced by Herder and Goethe, adapted from Aristotle, the teleology at work in the universe was internal, not external. There was, in Goethe's understanding of how the world works, no divine power external to the universe, supervising or regulating or intervening in it from without; and *a fortiori* there was no divine Providence watching solicitously over the destiny of each and every creature, ensuring that every single human being (apart from those who chose to oppose the divine will) was in the end brought to enjoy the ultimate good for which each was created. The teleology Goethe discerned worked purely from within; each entity had an immanent form which it strove to express, and the realisation of that potential was its *telos*, its end. At the same time, the achieved self-realisation of any particular entity was a stage in the realisation of the potential form of the larger 'organisms' in which that entity participated, up to and culminating in the total 'organism' of the Cosmos. The power of emergent form to overcome the inertia of unorganised matter and adapt to obstacles produced by external factors was enormous; but this power was not always triumphant in every particular case: sometimes the forces opposing the realisation of form in an individual instance were just too strong, and the immanent end was not achieved. Nevertheless, the existence of each 'organic' entity's drive to self-realisation was, for Goethe, a fundamental truth, one which was inalienably part of the essential structure of reality; whereas the observation that, as a matter of empirical fact, the drive to self-expression was often unable fully to achieve its end reflected, in Goethe's eyes, no more than a contingent state of affairs, which had to be acknowledged as such but which was not on any account to be viewed as evidence of what reality was fundamentally like.

These considerations offer the key to understanding the peculiar providentiality of the narrative, whose course seems so solicitously shaped to foster Wilhelm's self-discovery. We appear to find in the novel a world in which 'Wilhelm's life, for all its adventurousness and wandering, is curiously sheltered and protected'. It looks, in other words, like the image of a world governed by external teleology, by the guiding hand of a benevolent deity, a fact which puts us in mind of the popular fiction of its day. Indeed, some of the agencies by which the apparently providential course of Wilhelm's life is steered seem to come straight from the pages of the contemporary 'Trivialroman'. Two salient instances are the attack by robbers, which had already figured as a hackneyed device in Wieland's novel some thirty years earlier; and the part played in the plot by a secret society watching over the hero's fortunes, a motif frequently found in novels written for a mass readership in the 1780s and 90s. Yet the novel is very far from asserting the existence of an external Providence in the real world. The ostensibly providential management of the narrative is not in itself meant as a truthful mimetic image of the 'workaday world': it is there simply to provide a suitable context in which Wilhelm's self-clarification can be shown proceeding to its immanent goal free from disturbance by contingent destructive forces. That as a matter of fact such contingent influences all too often thwart full self-realisation by individuals in the real world, Goethe does not wish to deny. But in order to show forth what he believes to be the deeper—and higher—truth of the presence of the immanent drive to form within each individual in a particularly exemplary way, he creates for his exemplary individual an especially sheltered set of external circumstances.

In the *Lehrjahre* we find, then, the representation of both external and internal teleology; but these two kinds of teleology are not of equal mimetic status. Only the representation of internal teleology through the exploration of Wilhelm's psychological processes is offered as the image of a fundamental truth about extra-literary reality: the external teleology in the 'providentiality' of the plot figures as no more than a convenient fictional means for conveying that essential truth. Just as the content of Goethe's vision derives from a biological analogy, so too this aspect of the expression of that vision can be illuminated through a comparison with biological procedures. An observer wishing to study the development of a particular living organism will often find it convenient to do so in a medium which to some degree protects that organism against destructive influences to which it is vulnerable in its natural habitat. That experimental medium will not, however, be wholly different from the conditions in which the organism normally lives, since the organism relies for its successful growth upon a set of interactions with appropriate surroundings; but it will exclude factors which would seriously impede or even halt the functioning of the organism's vital processes, and thereby vitiate the study in hand. Similarly, Goethe has placed the depiction of the working-out of Wilhelm's distinctive needs and capacities towards their proper form, the vision of internal teleology, in a narrative context in which the power of external factors gravely to hamper or to cut short that working-out has been artificially weakened; and the result is a narrative se-

quence which seems to be governed by external, as well as internal, teleology. But that external teleology, although it shields Wilhelm against radically negative forces, neither initiates, nor sustains, nor decisively shapes the internal teleology of his selfhood. That internal teleology, manifested in the restless aspiration to clarify and express potential, would still be there, we are asked to recognise, even under less favourable circumstances: it is just that under such unfavourable circumstances it might remain unactualised and therefore not visible to an observer.

The secondary, auxiliary status of the external teleology as a purely fictional device wholly in the service of a suitably clear manifestation of internal teleology is emphasised by the way Goethe brings the 'providentially' shaped narrative sequence to a close which is blatantly stylised and artificial; and it is also brought home to us by the presence within the text of a number of life-histories other than Wilhelm's in which providential tutelage is very noticeably absent.

The fairy-tale, or operetta-like character of the novel's closing tableau has often been remarked upon. The impression of a highly 'literary' conclusion produced by the simultaneous betrothals is heightened by the fact that, as Schiller was the first to point out, all three matches entered into by the siblings Natalie, Lothario and Friedrich—to Wilhelm, Therese and Philine respectively—are mésalliances between nobles and commoners, and as such would have been highly scandalous in the society in which the novel is ostensibly set. The utopian element here is not just that these marriages are proposed in the first place, but that they are envisaged without any issue being made of the socially outrageous character of the unions, even though the narrative has earlier drawn explicit attention to the 'vast gulf of birth and station' separating Wilhelm from the Countess, Natalie's sister. A world in which such matters can be so blithely ignored is plainly no longer being put forward as a realistic image of the social and political circumstances of later eighteenth-century Germany, as the earlier portions of the narrative equally plainly were. The result is, to be sure, an 'ironisation' of the ending; but it does not amount to a *radical* ironisation of Wilhelm's represented fulfilment, any more than did the deliberate 'thinness' with which the substance of that fulfilment was portrayed. What the overt stylisation of the ending tells us is that such a triumphant completion of the process of self-clarification and self-expression which has been vouchsafed to Wilhelm is far too rare an occurrence in the world outside literature to be properly conveyed in anything other than a self-consciously literary vein. But the essential claim that such a process, whether or not it as a matter of fact reaches completion, is a fundamental feature of all authentically human experience remains entirely untouched by the manifest fictionality of the plot's closure. Indeed, the pointing-up of the conventional nature of that closure is an attempt to ensure that the reader grasps that the novel does not rest its claim to truth on its external teleology, of which the ironised ending is the last manifestation, but on the unironised internal teleology, which is given greater room to disclose itself under the conditions offered by the ostensibly providential plot than it would enjoy within a more rigorously realistic external narrative sequence.

Wilhelm's represented life, the manner of the ending reminds us, is a highly exceptional case, too exceptional to lay claim to comprehensive mimetic plausibility. But it is exceptional, according to Goethe's vision, not in the actual processes which are embodied in Wilhelm's experiences, but purely in the extent to which those processes are permitted to achieve their due completion. The exceptional character of that completion is also borne in upon us when we see, alongside and around the plainly idealised outcome of Wilhelm's experiences, the very far from idealised or ideal destinies of a number of other figures in the novel. These destinies remind us that the organic model of man and the universe which the novel shows forth is significantly different from the understanding of the world as a providentially ordered system which underlay most contemporary fiction. Wilhelm's intimations of a fuller life, the driving force of his quest for self-realisation, are both given to him and brought to fruition through the workings of what is represented as an organically functioning 'Nature', whose 'darling', we are told, Wilhelm is. But unlike the Providence which is made responsible for the outcome of the events in most eighteenth-century German novels, the 'Nature' which is said to be manifest in the processes portrayed in the *Lehrjahre* has definite favourites, and is indifferent to many or hostile to some.

The harmony of the ending as far as Wilhelm is concerned should not blind us to the underlying toughmindedness of the novel. To look only slightly to one side of the main figure is to see that this is a represented world in which extremely harsh fates befall a number of characters, usually without either narrator or protagonists offering more than brief tokens of regret. This, too, is not an artistic failing, but an essential component of the novel's vision. To say that, for example, Mariane, Aurelie, Mignon and the Harper are 'disposed of' or 'written out' of the novel as soon as they no longer have anything further to contribute to Wilhelm's story is to reduce to the level of mere narrative expediency what is in fact an important part of the novel's significance. These characters are brought to grief, not primarily because they have no further part to play within the plot, but because their various ends form part of an array of destinies in which, for one reason or another, the 'natural' process of human development is impeded: and that array of destinies impresses upon us that the benevolence of 'Nature' is qualified in a way that the universal, comprehensive and omnipotent benevolence of Providence was never held to be. (pp. 132-41)

There are other, less disastrous, instances of incomplete 'natural' development as well, with a similar function in the narrative structure. Much of what we learn about Serlo's career and character has to do with the elucidation of why the professional theatre simply cannot provide a viable means for Wilhelm to realise his distinctive aspirations; but at the same time we are being asked to see in Serlo a figure who in his own way follows his sister Aurelie in wilfully perverting his own development and frustrating his own potential. Where Aurelie destroys herself by misdirected passion, Serlo prejudices his own finer qualities and his possibilities of improving the life of his fellows through giving way to calculating greed. When Serlo, in the first days of his association with Wilhelm, insists on the importance of stimulating and fostering one's own appreciation of 'the beautiful and the perfectly achieved' and of spreading that appreciation to others, the narrator assures us that such notions were 'natural' to Serlo. But Serlo's actual pursuit of these distinctive 'natural' aspirations is sporadic and fickle. Briefly inspired by Wilhelm's enthusiasm to attaining a level of achievement which is capable of setting new standards of artistic taste for the German theatre, Serlo soon proves willing to let his ideals be suppressed by the prospect of making money through productions of a deliberately debased kind, which he knows will pander to all he most disapproves of in the public's attitudes and expectations. Given the choice between arduous and devoted development of the potential of his own talents, his company and his public on the one hand, and easy accommodation to a comfortable mediocrity on the other, Serlo knowingly chooses the less artistically and humanly demanding but financially more rewarding course. The due expression of 'natural' capacities calls for a willed commitment to the effort involved in realising those capacities against the resistance of the given; and where that commitment is not forthcoming, no amount of innate talent is of any avail. Serlo's example shows us that the 'organic' model of human nature does not exclude individual human freedom. It is true that a successful realisation of potential such as Wilhelm experiences cannot be brought about by the will alone, since it proceeds from a level of the individual's being which lies deeper than the domain of conscious choice and deliberate action: but neither can it be achieved without the free and active assent of the individual to the pursuit of the ends which his distinctive nature enjoins upon him. Where that willed assent is lacking, the proper development will not be achieved and the individual's particular potential, his specific humanity, will never be expressed.

Completing this array of destinies which show incomplete development is the life-history of the Schöne Seele, whose memoirs form the Sixth Book of the novel. The incompleteness here, however, is insignificant compared to what she actually managed to achieve, and the pointing-up of her shortcomings is suitably muted. In the Schöne Seele's life we certainly find a sense of personal potential scrupulously identified and singlemindedly pursued, and it is doubtless for this reason that Wilhelm remarks that the reading of her manuscript has 'not been without influence on [his] whole life.' Natalie, too, speaks of owing a great debt to her aunt; but she identifies the character of that debt by describing her relative as an example whose spirit, rather than achievement, one tries to emulate. The Schöne Seele's story may inspire others also to seek and strive to realise their own particular potential, yet her development, Natalie feels, did not bring to full expression all her potential capacities: 'extremely frail health, perhaps too great a preoccupation with herself, and in addition a certain overscrupulousness in moral and religious matters prevented her from having the influence on the world outside which under other circumstances she might have grown to exercise.' By comparison with Natalie's combination of inner poise and outgoing activity, her aunt's somewhat isolated though highly refined spirituality is meant to appear a slightly less than perfect achievement.

It emerges, then, that the various 'oddities' which critics have taken as in one way or another ironisations or qualifications of the positive outcome of the plot can be interpreted as part of the expression of the novel's underlying vision of man, the vision which is gnomically formulated in the maxims of the Society of the Tower and bodied forth in the represented experiences of the characters, and especially, though not exclusively, in the experiences of Wilhelm. However, there remains one further feature of Wilhelm's fulfilment which many readers understandably find strange: the fact that he is allowed to enjoy that fulfilment untroubled by any lasting anguish at the cost of his formative experiences to others less fortunate than himself. In the course of his quest for self-realisation, Wilhelm plays a part in worsening the lot of Mariane, of the Count and Countess, and of Mignon. His responsibility for detrimental consequences of one kind or another to all these people is complex and defies exact assessment, but it is real enough and he recognises it as such. His discovery of Mariane's fate and of his part in it, his realisation of the effect of his behaviour on the subsequent lives of the Count and Countess, his awareness that by inadvertance and self-concern he has increased Mignon's sufferings and hastened her death, all plunge Wilhelm for a time into acute despondency. But it is a despondency from which he wholly recovers and which does not pass over into any abiding sense of guilt. The narrative offers no criticism of him on this account. Quite the reverse: his freedom from enduring feelings of guilt for the consequences of his past conduct is put forward, not as a failing, but as a sign of Wilhelm's strength, vitality and capacity for sustained creative development and activity. In this represented world, where 'natural' dynamic self-expression is the supreme principle of all existence, anything which might inhibit the individual's spirited pursuit of a fuller life is regarded as 'unnatural', inhumane, and to be shunned. Guilt for wrongs inflicted on others in the course of the quest for full selfhood, however genuine and grave the responsibility from which the sense of guilt might derive, is liable to hamper the individual's faith in the worth of his quest and lessen his readiness to embark upon further experience with unabated confidence. So the cultivation of an awareness of guilt is looked upon as inimical to the 'natural' impulse to develop oneself and the world still further: thoughts of the negative effect of one's past conduct on others would be prompted by a life-denying 'evil spirit'. This means that Wilhelm's ability to leave feelings of guilt behind him and face the future unchastened by thoughts of the damaging consequences of his past actions is one more aspect of his story which is all of a piece with the overall outlook conveyed by the novel. However objectionable one may find this, it follows quite straightforwardly from the elevation of the conception of Nature espoused in the novel to the supreme principle of existence, as Goethe makes no bones about admitting. Nature may well show a benevolent countenance towards its 'darlings'; but it is not Providence, and it is unconcerned about the numerous individuals who are crushed rather than fostered by its dynamism. Anyone who is to achieve full 'natural' development has to share Nature' dispassion, a requirement which Wilhelm amply fulfils.

The spirit to which Wilhelm's ability to cast off feelings of guilt testifies is solemnly enshrined in the Hall of the Past. Natalie's house, Wilhelm proclaims, is a temple; and this secular temple has as its holy of holies the Hall of the Past, the Uncle's finest achievement. The deity to whom this shrine is dedicated is the spirit of human creativity, shown forth in the perfection of the Hall's proportions, its exquisite decorations, and the fine sculptures and paintings it contains. Anyone who entered that place, the narrator tells us, 'seemed . . . raised above himself, as he experienced for the first time through the combined power of the works of art (durch die zusammentreffende Kunst) what man is and what he is capable of being.' Here Wilhelm is caught up in delighted contemplation of the mystery of formal perfection which 'powerfully and at the same time captivatingly' affects him 'quite apart from any meaning, quite distinct from any sympathy which [the representation of] events in human life and human destinies inspires in us.' He has finally reached that fullness of artistic appreciation which, the first Stranger hinted, he might have achieved earlier, had he not been deprived of the formative influence of his grandfather's collection. Inscribed on the Uncle's sarcophogus, which is the Hall's centrepiece, is the exhortation 'Gedenke zu leben' (be mindful to live) a deliberate reversal of the injunction 'memento mori' which is a traditional motif of Christian memorial art. The very existence of the Hall as a place of entombment is an acknowledgment of the reality of death; but, like the realities of guilt and of human aspirations senselessly frustrated, which the novel likewise acknowledges in its way, the power of death cannot be dwelt upon without prejudicing the confidence of Nature's favourites in the value of their strivings after an ever fuller realisation of human potential. Hence the place in which the dead are entombed is dominated by the imperative to put thoughts of death aside and concentrate on the pursuit of a fuller life.

The ritual of Mignon's exequies is a kind of gloss upon the Uncle's exhortation which is the Hall's keynote. The invisible choir speaks for the dead into whose company Mignon has passed; but they are concerned less to welcome her than to urge the four boys who represent the living, Mignon's grieving companions and friends, to forget their sorrow. The boys express at first the sense of irrevocable loss and a feeling that fidelity to the value of what has been lost demands abiding sorrow. Against this, the choir of the dead appeals to 'die bildende Kraft' (the creative energy) in the living, which those who are still alive must carry on into the future, leaving the dead to care for the dead. And the boys obey, symbolically leaving the sarcophogus and the Hall of the Past with the refrain 'Come, let us return to life.' Nothing the Abbé has to say in his short oration adds much to what this brief ritual expresses, and the ceremony concludes with the coffin being sealed by four youths who address to those present the choir's earlier exhortations and add a further, final injunction, in which the spirit of the Uncle is once more clearly to be felt: . . .

> Stride out, stride out into life again! Take with you your sacred gravity, for gravity, sacred gravity alone makes life into eternity.

'Nothing can be done in the world without gravity (Ernst)', the Uncle had said; and the word 'gravity' tends to misrepresent the spirit of his belief, for 'Ernst' implies a seriousness which is by no means necessarily ponderous. It denotes a kind of intensity or density of experience which comes about when the individual approaches every aspect of existence as worthy of the most exacting attention, whether what is involved is work or recreation, pleasure or suffering, life or art. This 'Ernst' is fostered by a recognition of the precariousness of the individual's life, his exposure to chance, the possible fleetingness of whatever he may achieve, the constant danger of wreaking destruction while he is trying to build. But, unlike 'Sorge'— the harrowing care, the obsessive dwelling upon the negative aspects of human endeavour, which figures as the deadliest enemy of man's self-realisation in the final Act of *Faust II*— 'Ernst' nourishes and sustains the quest for self-clarification and self-expression, the quest which Nature enjoins upon man, and which every human being must pursue if he is to actualise that specific potential which both defines his unique individuality and integrates him into the human community and the dynamic order of the natural world.

The way in which *Wilhelm Meisters Lehrjahre* engages with the philosophical issues from which it ultimately arises and to which it is chiefly addressed needs no further elaboration. As an attempt to bring imaginative literature to bear upon those issues, the novel impresses by its genuine complexity and by its honesty. Its complexity can be called genuine in that it is far more dearly bought than the apparent complexities of *Agathon*. Where Wieland contrived to make his novel *seem* complex by the ingenious manipulation of an intrinsically rather sparse set of narrative materials, Goethe lays before us a highly differentiated and variegated image of the world in general and of human action, thought and feeling in particular, which he nevertheless manages to organise into an integrated structure expressive of a coherent meaning. And the novel is honest in the sense that it contains clear indications of what the 'organic' vision of man and the world which it conveys cannot offer, indications of the harshness of that vision compared with an understanding of the world as governed by divine Providence. All these things dispose us to look favourably upon the novel's claim to offer a true account of human nature and a valid conception of human fulfilment. (pp. 146-53)

> *Michael Beddow, in his* The Fiction of Humanity: Studies in the ''Bildungsroman'' from Wieland to Thomas Mann, *Cambridge University Press, 1982, 325 p.*

THE *BILDUNGSROMAN* IN ENGLAND

SUSANNE HOWE

[*In the following excerpt from her seminal study of the* Bildungsroman *in England, Howe discusses the characteristics of the genre and cites some differences between the German and English types.*]

Man and his meeting with the world, *Mundus et Infans*, has always been good fiction material. Goethe was not the first to discover it, though no careful biographer of Goethe may be caught napping in the shadow of that admission. Even the eighteenth century did not discover it, although it sounds suspiciously like one of those good, solid, mouth-filling abstractions such as the eighteenth century loved to fasten its teeth in—Life and the Individual, *Geist und Welt, le Génie et l'Ordre Éternelle*—and the like. It seems that, long before men's minds began to work in capitals on such antitheses, the latent story material in the subject appealed to the eager author, perhaps because it implied the gaining of experience—usually the author's own—at the hands of the world, and therefore it involved action, travel. Even the younger Cyrus, that pert young Persian with an autobiographical Xenophon hard at his elbow, has to leave home to serve his apprenticeship as a soldier before he can rule a kingdom. After all—putting aside for the moment Miss Austen's *Emma* and a few other magnificent exceptions— no one can learn much of anything at home. Going somewhere is the thing. And there—in all sorts of tempting variety—is your story. You cannot come to grips with the world and be balked and disappointed and disciplined by it, and finally reach the Celestial City or become a Master in the art of living, or make your choice of life and return quietly to Abyssinia, without at least doing the grand tour and having a few adventures. It is in the certainty of the adventures that the lure of the theme lies, and later there is the passionate interest in individual human experience—if the writer's own, so much the better— which John Bunyan as well as Goethe knew he could count on. No one said to Goethe's Wilhelm Meister in the forthright style of Mr. Worldly Wiseman, ''Hear me; I am older than thou: thou art like to meet with, in the way which thou goest, wearisomeness, painfulness, hunger, perils, nakedness, sword, lions, dragons, darkness, and, in a word, death and what not. These things are certainly true, having been confirmed by many testimonies.'' No one ever spoke to Wilhelm as plainly as that. But Wilhelm too hears plenty of warning voices, and Worldly Wiseman appears to him in several guises. The apprentice formula is a good one. For we know this young man will go on just the same, and who will refuse to follow the fortunes of a pilgrim hero whose path is to be so delightfully checkered? There is the pleasing suspicion too that all this would scarcely be worth while if he were not to emerge triumphant, adjusted to life in terms of the author's own conclusions about it, but what of that? It may be a tame conclusion enough; Candide learned only that one must cultivate one's garden, but what a series of profound shocks that phlegmatic Westphalian was exposed to first! There is plenty of time along the way for discussions on all sorts of subjects—repentance, criticism, beauty versus wit, the best of all possible worlds, the relative miseries of the married and the celibate, the proper way to present *Hamlet*. Then too, if experience is the thing, it must include all sorts of people and ways of living, and so we get the *Weltbild*, the background of a whole period sketched in as Goethe and Fielding could do it—almost deliberately in each case, if we may judge by Goethe's words about *Wilhelm Meister* and Fielding's apostrophe to Experience in one of his great mock-heroic introductions. And against this eighteenth-century background certain typical figures begin to stand out, not labeled as plainly as Evangelist, Christian's watchful companion, or Good Counsel who browbeats the pleasure-loving Iuventus of the morality play into repentance, so that he may be raised by Merciful Promises. But there are mentors like Eubulus and Thwackum and Square and Mr. Allworthy and Imlac the sage and the Abbé, who try to guide the young apprentice, whether he be of the gay, irresponsible type, inclined like Euphues and Tom Jones to sing with Lusty Iuventus:

> Why should not youth fulfill his own mind,
> As the course of nature doth him bind?
> In youth is pleasure!

or of the more serious-minded seekers like Christian and Rasselas; or, like Goethe's Wilhelm, a little of both. These figures, old and young, much modified it is true, are alive in the novel today. The very titles of such novels as *Youth's Encounter* and *A Candidate for Truth* testify that Goethe's theme, not new when he came to it, has gone on through the variations of the nineteenth century and into the twentieth, partly on its own literary merits, and partly from the fresh impetus that *Wilhelm Meister* gave it.

The idea that inspired the name and the story of Goethe's hero, Wilhelm Meister—the idea that living is an art which may be learned and that the young person passes through the stages of an apprenticeship in learning it, until at last he becomes a ''Master''—is one which has had a long and complex history in the novels of two nations, Germany and England. They are preëminently the novels of youth. The adolescent hero of the typical ''apprentice'' novel sets out on his way through the world, meets with reverses usually due to his own temperament, falls in with various guides and counsellors, makes many false starts in choosing his friends, his wife, and his life work, and finally adjusts himself in some way to the demands of his time and environment by finding a sphere of action in which he may work effectively. This is the apprenticeship pattern in the barest possible outline. Needless to say, the variations of it are endless. (pp. 1-4)

The hero of such novels, whether German or English, is heir to several literary types and traditions, and may be an ingenious and bewildering compound of all his inherited and acquired characteristics. Hence his progress through the world is seldom a simple affair. His kinship with the recalcitrant hero of the moral allegory makes it necessary for him to meet certain abstract vices and virtues, often but thinly disguised as human beings, who tempt or warn or advise him. The picaresque hero, like Françion, Gil Blas, or Tom Jones, is another near relative who lends him a taste for carefree, rambling adventure of a realistic and often amorous sort—a tendency to go on long journeys and see the world, meeting in the course of his travels a motley array of characters who insist upon telling the hero their life-histories and who represent all sides of the social structure of the time. The "universal man" of the Renaissance, bent on developing all his gifts to the utmost and welding them into an artistic whole, is another part of our hero's complicated family tree, and over all this variegated group of apprentice heroes there falls, though ever so palely, the shadow of a still more remote ancestor, Parsifal, "the brave man slowly wise" through experience, learning painfully from the blows the world deals him, but a dedicated spirit destined from the beginning to reach the goal of his quest. For these heroes are, after all, the elect—a little feeble, impressionable, vacillating, perhaps, but endowed with exceptional powers of mind and spirit, though it takes them a long while to find it out. They are more sensitive and more gifted than the average young man; their perceptions are sharper, their failures more heartbreaking, their struggles for adjustment to the world more desperate than those of their fellows, but their ultimate victory is assured.

All these elements, with the addition of some others such as Pietism, peculiar to eighteenth-century Germany, went to make up what the Germans called and still call the *Bildungsroman,* the novel of all-round development or self-culture, of which *Wilhelm Meister* is the archetype, and which flourishes today in countless modern German novels. Because it came into England chiefly through the influence of *Wilhelm Meister,* we may call it, for convenience, the "apprentice"novel, but it never assumed in England the importance of a group classification or a type. The German passion for categories, as opposed to the English preference for vagueness in these matters, has enabled the *Bildungsroman* to remain in Germany something distinct from the more definite *Erziehungsroman,* the pedagogic or education novel, like *Émile,* and Pestalozzi's *Lienhard und Gertrud,* which have a definite intent, partly practical and partly philosophical. It is distinct also from the *Entwicklungsroman* which has a more general scope and does not presuppose the more or less conscious attempt on the part of the hero to integrate his powers, to cultivate himself by his experience, which is essential to the *Bildungsroman.* (pp. 5-6)

[The] so-called apprentice novel in England was derived mainly from the German *Bildungsroman* as represented by *Wilhelm Meister.* . . . Certainly the apprentice form is most clearly developed by those English writers who had either spent some time in Germany, or were familiar with German literature and thought, especially Goethe's, from their reading. . . . The line at which the direct effect of *Wilhelm Meister* ceases, and independent English variations on the theme begin, is blurred and uncertain. Two languages and literary traditions, and two national cultures during a complicated period of their history, have helped to make it so. (pp. 6-7)

In England, furthermore, the course of the apprentice theme in novel writing is modified by other factors than *Wilhelm Meister.* Its autobiographical tone is in part due to Rousseau and the "confession" literature that followed in his wake, and in part to *Werther,* which was itself affected by the *Nouvelle Héloise. Werther* undoubtedly had something to do with the world-weariness, the supersensitiveness, and the introspective tendency of many of the English apprentice heroes. At any rate, the creators of these heroes develop a skill in self-analysis and a power to expose its results in fiction that has grown steadily from the ardent effusiveness of the romantic confession to the relentless machinery of the new psychology. It is a far cry from Les Charmettes or Julie's garden at Clarens, from Werther and Charlotte at the window watching the storm clouds, to that formidable day in Dublin exposed to us by James Joyce. Between the two extends [a] long chain of British young men. . . . Their *Sturm-und-Drang* periods and learning from life by a kind of trial-and-error method, are all in some degree confessional of their authors' own experience, from the sorrows of Carlyle's Wotton Reinfred up the ascending scale of subtlety in method to Meredith's Richard Feverel and Evan Harrington. The impulse to "tell it all," in one form or another, has become more compelling, apparently, as life has grown more complex and there has been more to tell. It may be objected that these later writers are simply ringing the changes on old subject matter, that man's soul and his own interest in it have been from the beginning, that there is no more to "tell" about it now than in the days of John Bunyan or Henry Fielding. But the machine age of nineteenth-century industrial England, the growth of large cities, and the progress in transportation have surely not been without their effect on the quality of the experiences that fiction heroes undergo. The possibility of sharp contrasts, the more sensitive social conscience, the "speeding-up" of life in general, have added to their self-revelations an intensity and variety, a sharpness of outline, and an immediacy of appeal that has gradually deepened if not widened the province of the novel.

The confessional quality of these apprentice novels may also be connected with Byronism. Their heroes are often misunderstood and badly adjusted young men, unappreciated by their families, and full of loud complaints against the world. But the chief Byronic contribution to their make-up seems to be a more healthful one. A dash of Byronic pride and fine theatrical frenzy, something of his sense of the vanity and futility of all things in heaven and earth, is often just the thing that saves them. They are not, as a rule, conspicuous for their sense of proportion or their sense of humor, but an ironic defiance of circumstance sometimes takes the place of it and proves to be a safety valve. *Childe Harold* and *Manfred* have given them, also, a taste for roaming the wild waste places of the world. They take to the road with reassuring ease; even Carlyle's hero in *Sartor,* who did not hold with Byron, "quietly lifts his Pilgrim-staff . . . and begins a perambulation and circumambulation of the terraqueous Globe." Bulwer's heroes are drawn to Italy, and Disraeli's gravitate toward the mysterious East, while Butler's Ernest Pontifex gets only as far as the alien world of the London slums, but finds it far enough. "Any road," as Teufelsdröckh, using the words of Schiller's *Tell,* discovers, ". . . will lead you to the end of the world." Our heroes have a romantic, Byronic preference for stormy landscapes; even Teufelsdröckh, who was no believer in view hunting, gazes, in the course of his wanderings, "upon a hundred and a hundred savage peaks." All this does distract them—however gloomily, and however much they may still be a prey to moral reflections—from the torments of their ill-starred love affairs, so that Byron not infrequently saves them from the typical Wertherian *dénouement.*

With only the Werther-Byron strains and their inheritance of self-analysis from Rousseau, however, they might well come to grief—*zu Grunde gehen* as the more sonorous and suggestive German phrase has it—more often than they do, were it not for the admixture of *Wilhelm Meister* and the Gospel of Work which Carlyle derived from it. Without these, in fact, they would not be apprentices at all and certainly not masters of the difficult art of living in their English setting. Through Carlyle the sane and corrective power of action was the moral lesson that *Wilhelm Meister* taught its English readers and imitators, and Goethe's eighteenth-century *Bildung,* or harmonious self-development motif, became subsidiary. Our heroes became too busy finding something to *do,* to envisage life very clearly as an artistic creative process. Thus the English apprentice heroes, often derived only indirectly from Goethe through Carlyle's translation of *Meister* and his interpretations of Goethe in general, pass through their black period of Wertherism and Byronism to the Carlylean conviction that they must find something to *do* in the world, and do it whole-heartedly.

It is in the variety of things that they find to do, that the interest of this hybrid, transplanted apprenticeship theme chiefly lies. These German-English heroes, looking about them at their English world swept by industrial confusion, political reform, religious doubt, and imperial expansion, solve their common adjustment problem in strange and manifold ways. They may finally find the right woman to marry, and then settle down to a wise and beneficent rule over their ancestral estates. They may choose a career of public service as members of Parliament, or become, after many false starts and choices, successful doctors, reformers, or writers. The conclusions are as diverse as the personalities and careers of the different authors themselves. But the fascination of this whole array of novels consists in the fact that, by their very nature, they show life and philosophies of life as something moving, changing, dynamic. These authors and their heroes grow into an expanding and deepening consciousness of human experience, an increased awareness of living. Even when the hero settles down to his vocation, we get no sense of smug completeness. None of them has solved the problem; the best thing about most of them is their sense of their own inadequacy in the face of it, and of man and his destiny as an eternal mystery. Two expressions of this idea that form an interesting and perhaps somewhat significant parallel may be found at the conclusion of Carlyle's *Sartor Resartus,* and in the closing chapter of H. G. Wells's *Tono-Bungay,* both of which are, in a sense, apprentice novels. Carlyle writes:

> So has it been from the beginning, so will it be to the end. Generation after generation takes to itself the Form of a Body; and forth-issuing from Cimmerian Night, on Heaven's mission *appears.* What Force and Fire is in each he expends: one grinding in the mill of Industry; one hunter-like climbing the giddy Alpine heights of Science; one madly dashed in pieces on the rocks of Strife, in war with his fellow:—and then the Heaven-sent is recalled; his earthly vesture falls away, and soon even to Sense becomes a vanished Shadow. Thus, like some wild-flaming, wild-thundering train of heaven's Artillery, does this mysterious Mankind thunder and flame, in long-drawn, quick-succeeding grandeur, through the unknown Deep. Thus, like a God-created, fire-breathing Spirit-host, we emerge from the Inane. Earth's mountains are levelled and her seas filled up, in our passage: can the Earth, which is but dead and a vision, resist Spirits which have reality and are alive? On the hardest adamant some footprint of us is stamped-in; the last Rear of the host will read traces of the earliest Van. But whence?—O Heaven, whither? Sense knows not; faith knows not; only that it is through Mystery to Mystery, from God and to God.

And Wells, on his epic voyage down the Thames in his new destroyer, speaks in strangely echoing accents, though he speaks for the modern world:

. . . The Hills of Kent fall away on the right hand, and Essex on the left. They fall away and vanish into blue haze, and the tall slow ships behind the tugs, scarce moving ships, and wallowing, sturdy tugs, are all wrought of wet gold as one goes frothing by. They stand out, bound on strange missions of life and death, to the killing of men in unfamiliar lands. And now behind us is blue mystery and the phantom flash of unseen lights, and presently even these are gone, and I and my destroyer tear out to the unknown across a great grey space. We tear into the great spaces of the future and the turbines fall to talking in unfamiliar tongues. Out to the open we go, to windy freedom and trackless ways. Light after light goes down. England and the Kingdom, Britain and the Empire, the old prides and the old devotions, glide abeam, astern, sink down upon the horizon, pass—pass. The river passes—London passes,—England passes. . . . Through the confusion something drives, something that is at once human achievement and the most inhuman of all existing things. . . . I have figured it . . . by the symbol of my destroyer, stark and swift, irrelevant to most human interests. Sometimes I call this reality Science, sometimes I call it Truth. But it is something we draw by pain and effort out of the heart of life, that we disentangle and make clear. Other men serve it, I know, in art, in literature, in social invention, and see it in a thousand different figures under a hundred names. I see it always as austerity, as beauty. This thing we make clear is the heart of life. It is the one enduring thing. Men and nations, epochs and civilizations pass, each making its contribution. I do not know what it is, this something, except that it is supreme. It is a something, a quality, an element, one may find now in colors, now in forms, now in sounds, now in thoughts. It emerges from life with each year one lives and feels, and generation by generation and age by age, but the how and the why of it are all beyond the compass of my mind. . . .

In the great pageant of progress toward uncertainty which these novels represent, the apprentice theme quite naturally loses itself toward the end of the century in a maze of doctrines, social, political, religious, for which fiction formed a convenient vehicle. Religious uncertainty and the growing strength of scientific inquiry have given rise to a rich harvest of novels of religious controversy, or of the waning of faith before the discoveries of the new age. Edmund Gosse's *Father and Son,* Butler's *Way of All Flesh,* and Mrs. Humphry Ward's *Robert Elsmere,* with their large following, form the material of a separate study that might be based, perhaps, on the break between the two generations; the old order and the new sense of impermanence, the father who clings to the established orthodoxy and the son who struggles with doubt and finally adapts himself to some compromise—practical social Christianity, a settlement house in the slums, or other modification of the Gospel of Work. The members of the younger generation in these books may well be called apprentices too, but they are so preoccupied with religious matters that their apprenticeships have become highly specialized, and it has seemed expedient to pass them by. (pp. 7-14)

[*David Copperfield, Great Expectations,* and *Pendennis*] are autobiographical and they deal, it is true, with young men who learn from experience and who do grow up in the course of the story, but more by accident than design. David and Pip and Arthur Pendennis are, like Tom Jones, sadder and wiser young men in the last chapter than in the first, but their essential nature has not been modified. They have not developed through any inner realization of their own powers and the resolve to make their experience function. They have stumbled good-naturedly over their obstacles, righted themselves, and determined not to make that particular mistake again, but they are not imaginative or reflective enough to see the wider implications of what has happened to them. Their history leads back rather more distinctly to the eighteenth-century picaresque tradition of Fielding and Smollett than to the German form of the *Bildungsroman*. . . . (pp. 14-15)

> Susanne Howe, in an introduction to her Wilhelm Meister and His English Kinsmen: Apprentices to Life, *Columbia University Press, 1930, pp. 1-15.*

G. B. TENNYSON

[*Tennyson traces the history of the term* Bildungsroman *in German and English critical parlance, describing the various kinds of* Bildungsromane *and explaining the development of the genre in Victorian England.*]

Thirty years ago the term *Bildungsroman* was very little used in English. Germanists and students of comparative literature knew it from its increasing currency in the study of German novels of the nineteenth century, and there were readers of Susanne Howe's *Wilhelm Meister and his English Kinsmen* [see excerpt above] who had become acquainted with the term through her book. . . . [The] term appears to have found a place in the contemporary critical vocabulary. There is thus some interest in defining clearly just what it means and in examining its use and value in the study of nineteenth-century English fiction. (p. 135)

The term *Bildungsroman* is a coinage of the German critic and philosopher Wilhelm Dilthey, who first used it in 1870 in a biography of Friedrich Schleiermacher. Thus, like so many literary terms, it came into existence after the fact. When Dilthey first applied it, he wrote, "I should like to call these novels of the school of *Wilhelm Meister, Bildungsromane*"; and went on to say, "Goethe's novel depicts the development of a human being in various stages, forms, and periods of life." He elaborated a bit on the pattern of *Meister* and concluded his first discussion of the matter by citing also Jean Paul's novel *Titan* (1800-03) as another representative.

In 1906 Dilthey broadened his concept of the *Bildungsroman* in the celebrated work *Das Erlebnis und die Dichtung* in a discussion of Hölderlin's novel *Hyperion* (1797). This time he included not only Goethe's and Jean Paul's novels (in this instance he cited *Hesperus* (1795), not *Titan*), but also Tieck's *Franz Sternbalds Wanderungen* (1798), and Novalis' *Heinrich von Ofterdingen* (1802). I give the dates here to emphasize that these are all novels of the same period. In fact, these German novels of the period 1795 to 1825 have continued to serve as touchstones in all later treatments of the *Bildungsroman*, with Goethe's novel in its full form—*Meisters Lehrjahre* (1795-96) and the *Wanderjahre* (1821)—viewed as the most comprehensive and authoritative of them all. This emphasis on the primacy of *Wilhelm Meister* for the *Bildungsroman* has advantages and disadvantages. On the one hand, *Wilhelm Meister*, especially the full version, contains a God's plenty of everything, and it would be an unimaginative reader indeed who could not find just about anything he wanted in that immense and varied work. On the other hand, this very abundance mitigates against precision in the form and leads us to ask, which features in *Meister* are essential to the form and which are superfluous?

Dilthey, of course, offers more than just examples. In the Hölderlin essay he provides us with the determinative discussion of the form, even though subsequent criticism has added to his concept. Briefly stated, Dilthey's main points about the *Bildungsroman* are five: (1) the idea of *Bildung*, or formation, cultivation, education, shaping of a single main character, normally a young man; (2) individualism, especially the emphasis on the uniqueness of the protagonist and the primacy of his private life and thoughts, although these are at the same time representative of an age and a culture; (3) the biographical element, usually supplied from the author's own life in what Dilthey calls the "conscious and artistic presentation of what is typically human through the depiction of a particular individual life"; (4) the connection with psychology, especially the then-new psychology of development; and (5) the ideal of humanity, of the full realization of all human potential as the goal of life. To illustrate what Dilthey is saying, I quote his concluding remarks on the *Bildungsroman* from the essay on Hölderlin:

> [The *Bildungsroman*] examines a regular course of development in the life of the individual; each of its stages has its own value and each is at the same time the basis of a higher stage. The dissonances and conflicts of life appear as the necessary transit points of the individual on his way to maturity and harmony. And the "highest happiness of humankind" is the development of the person as the unifying, substantial form of human existence. Nowhere is this optimism about personal development . . . more cheerfully and confidently expressed than in Goethe's *Wilhelm Meister;* an imperishable glow of joy in life emanates from this novel and from those of the romanticists.

It is important to remember, then, that in Dilthey's definition the emphasis in the *Bildungsroman* is on the cultivation and harmonious development of the whole personality, the attaining of a goal that is a happy blend of the material and spiritual. Much the same idea is still with the later definitions of the *Bildungsroman* in German, and to bring us up to date I cite the following characteristics of the *Bildungsroman* (apart from story or plot elements) as set forth by Hans Heinrich Borcherdt, who has been one of the most knowledgeable German scholars on the *Bildungsroman:* first, there is a cultural goal, which is the complete unfolding of all natural qualities; then there is a clear path toward that goal, a path that Borcherdt emphasizes as itself both the means to and the realization of the goal; in sum, the movement in the *Bildungsroman* is a reasonably direct line from error to truth, from confusion to clarity, from uncertainty to certainty, from, as the Germans have it, nature to spirit.

So much for the origin and later interpretations of the terms in German. Something must be said, however, about intervening developments. If we were to consult a German literary handbook today under *Bildungsroman*, we would probably read little or nothing about Wilhelm Dilthey, but instead find that the *Bildungsroman* is dominated as a variant of the *Entwicklungsroman*, which has yet another variant, the *Erziehungsroman*. Any one of these forms, we would be told, might coexist with the *Künstlerroman*. Allowing for the fact that Germans have a heartier appetite for these things than we do, we must nevertheless be clear about what has happened to produce such an abundance of forms and terms.

Contenting ourselves with the Dilthey-Borcherdt interpretation of *Bildungsroman*, we can say that the *Entwicklungsroman* is best rendered as "novel of development," the *Erziehungsro-*

man as "novel of education," or, better, "pedagogical novel," and the *Künstlerroman* as "novel about an artist." In the flowering of critical terms there has been some expansion but also some dissipation in the idea behind Dilthey's *Bildungsroman*. Once the appropriateness of Dilthey's designation was seen, it seemed obvious to many that there were other novels about an individual's growth and development that ought to fit into the classification. English readers might think, for example, of *Tom Jones* (1749), as German readers thought of Wieland's *Agathon* (1766). But Dilthey had explicitly excluded *Tom Jones* on the grounds that, while it emphasizes the important moments in an individual life in terms of their typicality, it does not exhibit those features I cited earlier, especially the emphasis on development and culture, in short the emphasis on *Bildung*. So German critics began using the term *Entwicklungsroman*, or "novel of development," not of *Bildung*. In other words, an *Entwicklungsroman* suggests development of almost any kind, while a *Bildungsroman* implies development toward the goal of full, harmonious personality. The distinction is clear in a German definition of *Entwicklungsroman* from the nineteen-twenties. The *Entwicklungsroman* is described by Melitta Gerhard as "a narrative work that has as its subject the problem of the conflict of the individual with the world at large, his gradual maturing and growth in the world, *in whatever way the goal of his journey may be construed*" [my italics]. With such a definition it was found that the first German novel of development was nothing less than Wolfram von Eschenbach's *Parzival* from about the year 1200. Then, when the term *Entwicklungsroman* was conjoined with the already established *Erziehungsroman* (pedagogical novel) it was possible to trace the type back to the *Cyropaedia* of Xenophon from the early fourth century B. C. When the *Entwicklungsroman* was found to coexist with the story of an artist (as in Tieck's *Sternbald*), we had an *Entwicklungsroman* that was also a *Künstlerroman*. Well, the permutations are almost endless, and we would not need to trouble ourselves with them here, were it not for the fact that a good deal of the concept of the *Entwicklungsroman*, the comprehensive "novel of development" idea, seems to have come across the channel with the word *Bildungsroman* and to have strongly colored the English use of the term. Webster's Third now lists both terms. Many literary handbooks in English give *Entwicklungsroman* as a synonym for *Bildungsroman*. Thus, there has never been in English, and perhaps never can be, the same degree of precision in the use of the term *Bildungsroman* as is possible in German. *Bildungsroman* in English has come to mean by itself what the *Bildungsroman*, the *Entwicklungsroman*, and the *Erziehungsroman* mean separately in German. For this reason you will frequently encounter the term *Bildungsroman* translated as "novel of education," "novel of development," and / or "apprenticeship novel." There may be nothing to lament in this looser use of the term, provided we understand that it *is* a looser use, but I believe there will always be a tendency on the part of scholars who know the German term to apply it more readily to those works that suggest some sort of complete *Bildung* than to those which merely show development. And generally we will find that the best examples of the form in English are those that owe something to the German examples or to intermediaries based on the German examples.

One reason for examining in such detail the origin and development of the term *Bildungsroman* in German lies in the dearth of treatments of the concept in English. Although . . . the term has lately become fashionable in critical discussions of the Victorian novel, there are still very few extended examinations of the concept in English literature. Just as the precise meaning of the term is a bit shadowy in English, so there is no absolutely agreed-upon list of *Bildungsromane* in English. Nor is there a full examination of the extent to which various English authors thought they were writing in an established form or tradition. There are in fact only two full-length treatments of the English *Bildungsroman*, although there are articles and many German studies that touch upon the topic. The first of the two book-length treatments is Susanne Howe's previously cited study, *Wilhelm Meister and his English Kinsmen*, subtitled "Apprentices to Life." From her study dates the use of the term *Bildungsroman* in English; and from her study dates the expression "apprenticeship novel." The other study, by a Swiss scholar, Hans Wagner, is in German and is titled *The English Bildungsroman to the First World War*. Although Wagner's study is much more recent (1951), and in some respects more comprehensive than Howe's, it is by and large inferior to hers. Between the two, however, we can compile a reasonably authoritative list of Victorian "novels of development or education," and we can also observe the line of descent from the first English treatment.

Let us trace for a moment the main outlines of the Howe-Wagner family tree of English *Bildungsromane*. The form is Victorian rather than Romantic because it takes its rise from the work in the eighteen-twenties of that later-to-be eminent Victorian Thomas Carlyle. In 1824 Carlyle translated *Wilhelm Meisters Lehrjahre* as *Wilhelm Meister's Apprenticeship*, and in 1827 he translated the *Wanderjahre*. The two were issued together for the first time in 1839. Then in 1833-34 appeared Carlyle's own *Sartor Resartus*, containing, among so much else, a Carlylean version of the *Bildungsroman* in Book II. From Carlyle the line of descent moves through no fewer than eight novels by Edward Bulwer-Lytton, among these the chief being *Pelham* (1828) and *Ernest Maltravers* (1837); then through Benjamin Disraeli in the novels *Vivian Grey* (1826-27), *Contarini Fleming* (1832) and *Lothair* (1870). According to Wagner but not Howe, Thackery is represented by *Pendennis* (1848) and Dickens by *David Copperfield* (1849-50). A group Miss Howe styles as followers of Carlyle contributed several novels: John Sterling's *Arthur Coningsby* (1833), G. H. Lewes' *Ranthorpe* (1842) and *The Apprenticeship of Life* (1850), J. A. Froude's *The Nemesis of Faith* (1849), Geraldine Jewsbury's *Zoë* (1845) and her *The Half-Sisters* (1848), and Charles Kingsley's *Alton Locke* (1850). From these middle years of the century Wagner adds Thomas Hughes' *Tom Brown's Schooldays* (1849), and George Eliot's *The Mill on the Floss* (1860). Both Howe and Wagner agree that the next important author of *Bildungsromane* is George Meredith in *The Ordeal of Richard Feverel* (1859), *Evan Harrington* (1861), and *Beauchamp's Career* (1874-75). To finish off the century Wagner lists Samuel Butler's *Way of All Flesh* (1884), Thomas Hardy's *Jude the Obscure* (1895) and George Gissing's *Born in Exile* (1892). Miss Howe does not push her study so far in time, although she cites a few moderns. Wagner devotes some attention to post nineteenth-century authors and lists no fewer than twenty-four *Bildungsromane* in English between 1900 and 1940. But this is surely straining to find a pattern at all costs. What we have in many modern novels is a developmental motif, rather than the *Bildungsroman*.

Both Howe's and Wagner's studies are comprehensive, if capricious. Howe does not include Dickens on the wholly inexplicable grounds that *David Copperfield* is autobiographical, as though there were not warrant enough for that in the model of *Wilhelm Meister*. Neither Howe nor Wagner includes *Great Expectations*, and neither gives any reason for excluding it.

Still, the outlines are fairly clear: almost any English novel of the nineteenth century that depicts the growth and development of a central figure is likely to find itself called a *Bildungsroman,* but the ones that most repay study in terms of the form are those most concerned with portraying the way the protagonist comes to a deeper understanding of life. These are the novels that flesh out the pattern provided in *Sartor Resartus* or adapt the pattern of *Wilhelm Meister.*

It would be impossible in the present discussion to treat even the major English *Bildungsromane* individually, but let me review the pattern Carlyle offered the English public in *Sartor* with the request that you think of how well it suits the pattern in some of the novels I have cited, and also how well it suits a novel like *Great Expectations,* which I should certainly include among English *Bildungsromane.* Remember, too, that Victorians were readers not only of *Sartor* but of Carlyle's translation of *Meister,* so the pattern was doubly available to them. And of course authors like Bulwer-Lytton, Thackery, Lewes, and Meredith knew German at first hand.

So, how does *Sartor* present the pattern? It is certainly a mistake to call all of *Sartor* a *Bildungsroman,* but it seems to the point to use the term for Book II alone, the biography of Teufels-dröckh. Of the three books in *Sartor,* Book II is the one that is directly concerned with the development and education of an individual, representative man. In that book Carlyle provides us with the form of the *Bildungsroman* in outline. The day-to-day experiences, the sense of life being lived, is barely present. The chapter titles of Book II give the key: "Genesis," "Idyllic," "Pedagogy," "Getting Under Way," "Romance," "Sorrows of Teufelsdröckh," "The Everlasting No," "Centre of Indifference," and "The Everlasting Yea." In short, the protagonist is taken from birth, through childhood, to and through the educational process; he falls in love, suffers, and wanders, experiences doubt and negation, denies it, reaches a plateau of indifference, and finally affirms a belief and a mission. That Carlyle's concept of affirmation, his so-called Calvinizing of Goethe's *Entsagen,* is not the same thing as the Weimar circle's concept of *Bildung* is to be expected, and it is a measure of the way in which a somewhat aristocratic and characteristically metaphysical German notion was domesticated. For the German concept appeals at once to an aesthetic and intellectual aristocracy and to the speculative and deep-thinking mind. These dimensions are represented on the one hand by Ofterdingen's quest for the fugitive *blaue Blume* and on the other by Meister's concept of the Three Reverences. Carlyle conceives these notions in more practical and yet more religious terms, and he expresses them in the earnest quasi-Biblical language of evangelical piety ("Work thou in Well-doing," for example). The effect, however, is not a denial of *Bildung* but a transmutation into a more British frame of reference. Book II of *Sartor Resartus* thus still stands as an English *Bildungsroman* in the classic pattern. What is missing, however, is the novelistic content that we expect in the English novel, although we must acknowledge that many German works generally called *Bildungsromane* are, from an English point of view, novelistically unorthodox, such as most of the novels of Jean Paul, and certainly *Heinrich von Ofterdingen* or *Hyperion.* But in an English context, we must say that *Sartor Resartus,* Book II, *asserts* all of the things that are to be found in the *Bildungsroman,* but it does not *show* them.

Still, I believe the pattern was instructive. Dickens, in both *Copperfield* and *Great Expectations,* returns us to the realistic and abundant world of the English novel, and even lesser nov-

An engraving of Christoph Martin Wieland made in 1797.

elists than Dickens create a more conventional fictional world than Carlyle. But all seem to have drawn on Carlyle's pattern for the structure of their *Bildungsromane* or *Entwicklungsromane.* It can be discerned in the work of that group that Susanne Howe calls "Candidates for Truth," comprising Sterling, Froude, Lewes, Jewsbury, and Kingsley, and also in novels by Dickens and Meredith. Whether we are dealing with Pip's progress from the smithy to snobbery to self-understanding, or the much more carefully supervised progress of Richard Feverel at the hands of Sir Austin's "System" in a work that is both *Bildungsroman* and *Erziehungsroman,* the Goethe-Carlyle pattern can be discerned without much difficulty. As far as pattern goes, there is surely a group of novels in English legitimately called *Entwicklungsromane.*

The question that remains is whether the English *Bildungsroman* displays not only the pattern—which is after all almost inevitable when taking a protagonist from birth to manhood—but whether there is also an underlying concept of *Bildung,* English or otherwise. The question, in short, is whether we have in English the *Bildungsroman* or the *Entwicklungsroman,* the novel of harmonious cultivation of the whole personality, or merely the novel of development. This is a question that usually remains unanswered because not faced and because the business merely of tracing the pattern through the many English novels of the nineteenth century occupies so much time and attention. Moreover, to answer this question adequately one must set forth what the goal of Victorian *Bildung* is, a mighty task in itself. Yet something of the sort must be done if we are not to remain forever bogged down with minor novelists and their novels. Susanne Howe attempts to set forth such a concept in her careful analysis of *Wilhelm Meister* and *Sartor*, but the value of her groundwork is vitiated by then being applied so relentlessly to minor novels. To abide so consistently, as Howe and Wagner do, with novelists like Disraeli, Bulwer-Lytton, Sterling, Froude, Lewes, Kingsley, and Jewsbury is to admit tacitly that the *Bildungsroman* as a form did not attract the major English talents outside of Carlyle (who was not a novelist) and that the question of the *Bildungsroman* in English must ever remain one of marginal interest.

The historians of the English *Bildungsroman* do not consider any major works other than *Sartor* and *The Ordeal of Richard Feverel*. Indeed, when they have said all, Meredith emerges as the only consequential English writer of *Bildungsromane*, and most of these are among his lesser works. Yet Meredith already represents a second generation of the Victorian novel and the English *Bildungsroman*, comparable more to Keller and Mörike in German than to Goethe and Novalis. In Meredith the optimism and drive of the earlier Victorians has been supplanted by a skepticism that borders at times on the cynical, and the Romantic and early Victorian organicism has been transmuted into an impersonal, almost mechanical life-force evolutionism. *Feverel* is even a kind of anti-*Bildungsroman* that comes to no positive assertions about education or culture or experience, but instead brings the protagonist to grief and emptiness. Small wonder that Howe places Meredith with the moderns. Dilthey marked an "imperishable glow of joy in life" in the *Bildungsromane* of Goethe and his contemporaries. There may not be as much of that in the early Carlyle at the dawn of the English *Bildungsroman* as in Goethe, but surely there is more than in Meredith and Samuel Butler at the twilight.

So we return to the question of whether there is a substantially coherent Victorian *Bildung* which is exhibited in any major work of the middle years of the century. Knowing that we cannot at present answer such a question fully, we can still seek some hints toward an answer. They may be found in that handbook of the Victorian *Bildungsroman*, *Sartor Resartus*. Following his experience of life, his wanderings, his "education," Teufelsdröckh affirms the necessity for "working in Welldoing," for accepting the common humanity of man, for standing by the "sanctuary of Sorrow" in recognition that the "din of many-voiced Life" that seems a maddening discord is in reality the sound of "prayers to Heaven," for finding something in man that is "higher than Love of Happiness," and for "doing the duty which lies nearest thee."

We can recognize at once the differences between Carlyle's emphases and Goethe's: Wilhelm Meister is often spoken of as a man who sought to become an "artist at living," while we should have to say of Teufelsdröckh that he is more concerned to become an artist at believing. The world, against which so many Romantic heroes cast themselves confidently, is already seen as a sadder place by the early Victorians; but not as a hopeless one. Both Meister and Teufelsdröckh are set on a spiritual goal, and this is central to the *Bildungsroman*. When the goal becomes too secularized we wander off into such thickets as Bulwer's novels of Dandyism; and when the spiritual element becomes actualized in specifically religious forms we stray into the realm of the Victorian religious novel, such as Mrs. Humphry Ward's *Robert Elsmere* or the novels of the Oxford Movement. But there is a *via media* in the Victorian novel of development, and it is represented at its best by such characters as David Copperfield and Pip, by Dickens of the early and middle years and the early George Eliot, before the early Victorian optimism had clouded over.

Although *David Copperfield* and *Great Expectations* are frequently listed in German compilations of the English *Bildungsroman*, neither is much talked about. Yet either novel could be taken as a representative English *Bildungsroman*. (The two are in any case intimately related, as Dickens' own testimony reveals.) To my mind the most complete expression of the English *Bildungsroman* is *Great Expectations*. We must ask, in what way is *Great Expectations* a *Bildungsroman*? G. Robert Stange's treatment of *Great Expectations* as a moral fable [in his article in *College English*, October 1954] seems almost to have been written to answer these questions. Without mentioning the *Bildungsroman* or *Entwicklungsroman*, Stange nevertheless writes as though he had the form in mind, and he does cite the parallel French novels. Of *Great Expectations* he says: "*Great Expectations* is conceived as a moral fable; it is the story of a young man's development from the moment of his first self-awareness to that of his mature acceptance of the human condition." And he adds later: "*Great Expectations* belongs to that class of education or development-novels which describes a young man of talents who progresses from the country to the city, ascends in the social hierarchy, and moves from innocence to experience." He compares it to Stendhal's *Le Rogue et le noir*, and Balzac's *Le Père Goriot* and *Les Illusions perdues*. Stange also notes the process of growth as the form-giving element and the use of folklore motifs. Beyond that, he points out that "Pip's career is a parable which illustrates several religious paradoxes: he can gain only by losing all he has; only by being defiled can he be cleansed." We may add that Pip must also "die" to the world in order to be reborn; he must become a child again and be led by a child (Joe) in order to be a man.

It is worth noting that Carlyle is fond of even more overt religious paradoxes than Dickens, and the same thing can be discerned in Goethe. More important, however, is the spiritual dimension these relationships give to *Great Expectations* without at all turning it into a religious novel. Pip's story is, as a result, far from being merely a "snob's progress"; it is rather the progress of the individual yet representative man as he forms his whole being. What Pip undergoes is a self-education that is of necessity painful, but also ultimately spiritually fortifying. I think we can ignore the churlish dismissals of Pip's culture as not sufficiently "cultured" when we recognize that the true goal of *Bildung*—certainly of a Victorian *Bildung*—is not the kind of culture taught at the university (it is noteworthy that formal education plays no significant role in the *Bildungsroman*), but a culture of the spirit, which Pip acquires in even greater measure than *David Copperfield*. Perhaps the best example is the Sunday scene toward the end of *Great Expectations* as Pip recovers from his "death" to the old world to find a new and beautiful one instead:

> . . . we drove away together into the country, where the rich summer growth was already on the trees and on the grass, and sweet summer scents filled all the air. The day happened to be Sunday, and when I looked on the loveliness around me, and thought how it had grown and changed, and how the little wild flowers had been forming, and the voices of the birds had been strengthening, by day and by night, under the sun and under the stars, while poor I lay burning and tossing on my bed, the mere remembrance of having burned and tossed there, came like a check upon my peace. But, when I heard the Sunday bells, and looked around a little more upon the outspread beauty, I felt that I was not nearly thankful enough— that I was too weak yet, to be even that—and I laid my head on Joe's shoulder, as I had laid it long ago

when he had taken me to the Fair or where not, and
it was too much for my young senses.

This, I submit, is closer to a Victorian concept of *Bildung,* and
certainly more eloquently expressed, than most of what is found
in the novels usually treated under the heading of English
Bildungsromane. Further, does it not echo, though in a thoroughly Dickensian way, the message of Teufelsdröckh in the
"Everlasting Yea," or "Natural Supernaturalism"? Is it not,
finally, the conviction that the world is a harmonious organic
whole that permeates the great *Bildungsromane* of Germany
and England alike? Only with such a conviction could a novelist
like Dickens lead a character like Pip from error to truth, from
confusion to clarity, uncertainty to certainty, nature to spirit,
to use once again Borcherdt's categories for the German
Bildungsroman.

It would take a more extensive study than the present one to
illustrate the variety of ways in which some major Victorian
novels reveal not only the development pattern but also a Victorian developmental ethos. But as much as there is a uniform
concept of *Bildung* to be extracted from Goethe, Jean Paul,
Novalis, Tieck, and Hölderlin, I think there may be a Victorian
ethos that permeates the great nineteenth-century treatments of
the development of the individual representative man, from
Carlyle to Dickens, to George Eliot, to Meredith. If such a
conception can be affirmed as the true common ground of
Victorian novels of development, then we have returned to
something close to Dilthey's concept, and have found that the
English *Entwickslungsroman* is also the English *Bildungsroman.* (pp. 135-45)

> G. B. Tennyson, "The 'Bildungsroman' in Nine-
> teenth-Century English Literature," in Medieval Epic
> to the "Epic Theater" of Brecht: Essays in Com-
> parative Literature, *edited by Rosario P. Armato and
> John M. Spalek, University of Southern California
> Press, 1968, pp. 135-46.*

JEROME HAMILTON BUCKLEY

[*In the first part of the following excerpt, Buckley describes the
forms that the* Bildungsroman *took in English literature; in the
second part, he discusses Dickens's* David Copperfield *and* Great
Expectations *as significant examples of the English* Bildungsroman.]

Wilhelm Meister . . . [differs] sharply in manner and matter
from . . . the English Bildungsromane that followed—from *Great
Expectations,* for example, or *The Way of All Flesh* or *Sons
and Lovers,* each of which in turn has its own distinctive style
and substance. Yet from all these books and many others we
may abstract the broad outlines of a typical Bildungsroman plot
and so determine the principal characteristics of the genre. A
child of some sensibility grows up in the country or in a provincial town, where he finds constraints, social and intellectual,
placed upon the free imagination. His family, especially his
father, proves doggedly hostile to his creative instincts or flights
of fancy, antagonistic to his ambitions, and quite impervious
to the new ideas he has gained from unprescribed reading. His
first schooling, even if not totally inadequate, may be frustrating insofar as it may suggest options not available to him
in his present setting. He therefore, sometimes at a quite early
age, leaves the repressive atmosphere of home (and also the
relative innocence), to make his way independently in the city
(in the English novels, usually London). There his real "education" begins, not only his preparation for a career but also—
and often more importantly—his direct experience of urban

life. The latter involves at least two love affairs or sexual
encounters, one debasing, one exalting, and demands that in
this respect and others the hero reappraise his values. By the
time he has decided, after painful soul-searching, the sort of
accommodation to the modern world he can honestly make,
he has left his adolescence behind and entered upon his maturity. His initiation complete, he may then visit his old home,
to demonstrate by his presence the degree of his success or the
wisdom of his choice.

No single novel, of course, precisely follows this pattern. But
none that ignores more than two or three of its principal elements—childhood, the conflict of generations, provinciality,
the larger society, self-education, alienation, ordeal by love,
the search for a vocation and a working philosophy—answers
the requirements of the Bildungsroman as I am here seeking
to describe and define it. Thus *Lord Jim* and *Emma, The Old
Wives' Tale* and *The Ambassadors, Tom Jones* and *The Egoist,*
though each splendidly develops some of the characteristic
themes, all belong essentially to other categories of the novel.
Yet, when we have made all such necessary exclusions, we
still have left for consideration a large and impressive body of
fiction, remarkable for its freshness and variety, both of style
and content, within the recognizable genre.

In the dedication to his autobiographical *Sinister Street* (which
carries as its epigraph the passage by Keats about childhood,
manhood, and the space between), Compton Mackenzie defended the great length at which he had explored his hero's
growth. "Yet are a thousand pages," he asked, "too long for
the history of twenty-five years of a man's life, that is to say
if one holds as I hold that childhood makes the instrument,
youth tunes the strings, and early manhood plays the melody?"
After all, he insisted later, he had carefully picked and chosen
among his memories: "If I were to set down all I could remember of my childhood, the book could not by this time have
reached much beyond my fifth year." His intention, he said,
was "not to write a life, but the prologue of a life," and the
conditioning of childhood was clearly of first importance in
his hero's development. To Byron, as to Fielding, the young
child was little more than the small adult. To the authors of
the Bildungsromane, as to Wordsworth, the child was an entity
in himself responsive to experiences that might alter the entire
direction of his growing mind and eventually influence for
better or for worse his whole maturity. Not until the psychology
of the child was taken seriously as an appropriate literary concern was the writing of the English Bildungsromane a possible
enterprise.

The growing child, as he appears in these novels, more often
than not will be orphaned or at least fatherless, like David
Copperfield, Pip, Jude, Pater's Marius, George Ponerevo in
Tono-Bungay, Philip Carey in *Of Human Bondage,* and Sammy
Mountjoy in *Free Fall.* But if not deprived by death of a father,
who presumably would have been a true guide and protector,
he will almost certainly be repelled, like Richard Feverel and
Stephen Dedalus and Paul Morel, by a living father who mis-
trusts and seeks to thwart his strongest drives and fondest desires. "A man," says Ernest Pontifex (when he has learned to
talk like Samuel Butler), "first quarrels with his father about
three-quarters of a year before he is born. It is then he insists
on setting up a separate establishment. When this has been
once agreed to, the more complete the separation forever after
the better for both." The loss of the father, either by death or
alienation, usually symbolizes or parallels a loss of faith in the
values of the hero's home and family and leads inevitably to

the search for a substitute parent or creed, such as Julien Sorel expects to find in his mentors or Wilhelm Meister discovers in the masonic secret society. The defection of the father becomes accordingly the principal motive force in the assertion of the youth's independence. It links him immediately with the traditional heroes of romance and folklore, the exiled Joseph and the boy David, Romulus and Oedipus, Aladdin and Jack the Giant-Killer, each of whom, fatherless, must make his own way resolutely through the forests of experience.

The journey from home is also in some degree the flight from provinciality. But the English hero is much less aggressive than his French counterpart, "the young man from the provinces" like Julian Sorel or the ruthless, self-seeking Eugène Rastignac of Balzac's *Père Goriot*. He first enters the city, as Pip or Ernest or Jude does, with bewilderment and naiveté; and the city plays a double role in his life: it is both the agent of liberation and a source of corruption. In nineteenth-century English poetry the city is likewise an ambiguous symbol. It may stand as a citadel of light, like Tennyson's Camelot, the protest of a civilization against wilderness, barbarism, and bestiality. But more often it may be the dark hell of James Thomson's City of Dreadful Night. In *The Prelude* the young Wordsworth finds London a crowded and exciting panorama of modern society, but also a lonely and strangely insubstantial place, a Bartholomew Fair, all illusion and confusion, in fact not unlike T. S. Eliot's urban Waste Land, "Unreal City,... I had not thought death had undone so many." In the Bildungsromane the city, which seems to promise infinite variety and newness, all too often brings a disenchantment more alarming and decisive than any dissatisfaction with the narrowness of provincial life.

The novel of youth, at least in the Victorian period, is frequently the equivalent of the Renaissance conduct book, insofar as one of its recurrent themes is the making of a gentleman. But in the busy world of middle-class progress the gentlemanly ideal becomes increasingly difficult to discover or define; struggle for survival in the atomistic modern city is hardly conducive to good manners and quiet consideration of others; the urban is seldom the urbane. In the jargon of the time, to "make good" is to make money; and the gentleman, especially if his resources are limited, commands less respect than the financial "success." Money therefore assumes a new and pervasive importance in the Bildungsroman. If Richard Feverel and Harry Richmond can take a considerable wealth for granted, most of the other heroes from Pip and Jude to Stephen Dedalus and Sammy Mountjoy must resist, sometimes ineffectually, the menace of a real poverty. The "great expectations" of Dickens's title are more or less delusive "prospects of inheritance." A bankruptcy is central to the plot of *The Mill on the Floss*. Money-worries plague the Morel family in *Sons and Lovers*. And reckless speculation brings the collapse of Uncle Teddy's empire in *Tono-Bungay*. Mr. Overton, the narrator of *The Way of All Flesh*, who declares money more desirable than health or reputation and believes the loss of money the root of all evil, withholds Aunt Alethea's legacy until Ernest is mature enough to appreciate a beautifully managed portfolio. Goethe long before commented that his Wilhelm had been foolish to remain indifferent to his property and money: "He knew not that it is the manner of all persons who attach importance to their inward cultivation altogether to neglect their outward circumstances. This had been Wilhelm's case: he now for the first time seemed to notice, that, to work effectively, he stood in need of outward means." Most of the later heroes, however, are less able than Wilhelm or Ernest to reconcile the outward

and the inward, to see how the processes of money-making contribute to their true enrichment of spirit. The sensitivity that made for childhood alienation from father and home leads many to the larger repudiation of a materialistic society. (pp.17-22)

If he survives his trial by parents, by money, by the city, the hero, like the knights of the old romances, may still have to undergo further testing before his initiation is completed. "Love of any object," Sir Austin Feverel tells Richard, "is the soul's ordeal; and [women] are ours, loving them, or not." But Richard's ordeal is largely self-induced—by his wilful neglect of love and his determined dabbling in passion. And the central conflict in nearly every other Bildungsroman is likewise personal in origin; the problem lies with the hero himself. Thus David Copperfield has an errant heart, and Pip misdirects his ambitions and affections. Ernest Pontifex like Wilhelm Meister at first misconceives his vocation. George Ponderevo is willing to abandon scientific truth for the promotion of the fraudulent Tono-Bungay. And Sammy Mountjoy deliberately compromises his freedom when he lets himself be governed by a selfish lust. Yet each of these young men experiences privileged moments of insight, epiphanies, spots of time, when the reality of things breaks through the fog of delusion. And each then feels a responsibility for change of heart and conduct. For each is what we should now call "inner-directed"; each is guided by a sense of duty to the self and to others, a sense perhaps inculcated or sharpened by parents and childhood conditioning, and perhaps never freely admitted, but nonetheless remaining latent and strong through all the rebellions of adolescence.

Yet even when he sees the error of his ways and judgments, the hero is by no means guaranteed a resolution to his problems at all comparable to the joyous denouement of *Wilhelm Meister*. Like *The Red and the Black*, some of the Bildungsromane—*The Mill on the Floss, Marius the Epicurean, Jude the Obscure, Jacob's Room*—end with the death of the protagonist. Others, like *The Ordeal of Richard Feverel* or *Tono-Bungay*, leave us speculating on the defeat of all positive emotion. Perhaps most—*Great Expectations, A Portrait of the Artist, Free Fall*, for example—conclude more or less uncertainly, with an open question about the hero's final choice. Only a few—*David Copperfield, The Way of All Flesh*, and *Of Human Bondage*—reach a recognizably happy ending. (pp. 22-3)

Like *Of Human Bondage*, the typical novel of youth is strongly autobiographical and therefore subject at any time to intrusions from areas of the author's experience beyond the dramatic limits of the fiction. As a rule it is a first or second book in which the novelist is still very close to his orientation, often indeed too close to achieve an adequate perspective. Since his career is still in progress, perhaps only beginning, he can hardly be sure that the initiation of a hero in many ways so like himself has been an unqualified success. He may, therefore, choose to leave the hero's future ambiguous; he may, in a sort of self-justification, seek to reward the hero beyond his deserts; or, again, he may evade the problem altogether by bringing the hero to an untimely death. But whatever course he follows, he will not find it easy to give his novel a cogent and organic ending.

There are of course many degrees of identification between author and hero and of detachment from each other. In his comments on *Of Human Bondage*, Maugham makes a distinction we should bear in mind when approaching any Bildungsroman: "It is not an autobiography, but an autobiographical novel; fact and fiction are inextricably mingled; the emotions are my own, but not all the incidents are related as they happened and some of them are transferred to my hero not from my own life but from that of persons with whom I was intimate.'' As the ending of that book demonstrates, the involvement of the personal emotions of the novelist can impair the integrity of a novel. But it can also, if properly controlled, lend a peculiar vibrancy to character, setting, and incident. (pp. 23-4)

The autobiographer is typically the older man . . . indulging in fond retrospect, often more than a little sentimental in his view of his youth, recalling what it pleases him to remember. The autobiographical novelist is usually a younger man, nearer in time to his initiation, self-protectively more ironic, still mindful of the growing pains of adolescence, reproducing as accurately as possible the turbulence of the space between childhood and early manhood. The autobiographer must account, at least to himself, for the omissions from his life story; he must be to a considerable degree self-conscious—through modesty, through fear of unwanted self-exposure, through the desire not to be judged excessively egotistical; and he must know that he can paint only a partial self-portrait, for he can describe his experience only from his own point of view, and his life changes even as he records it. The autobiographical novelist is patently freer to conceal or reveal what he will of his past by assigning to his hero some of his own acts and feelings and inventing as many others as he chooses to complete a dramatic characterization. He thus has a distinct advantage over the direct autobiographer. But he has a special responsibility as a novelist to make his book aesthetically independent of its author. Both the strength and the weakness of the Bildungsroman, insofar as it is subjective at all (and very few examples of the genre are not), lie in its autobiographical component. It gains in immediacy and authenticity from the novelist's intimate knowledge of his materials. It suffers whenever the novelist's engagement leads to special pleading for a self-interest outside the frame of the fiction or when the motivation of the hero is determined by forces in the novelist's experience for some reason excluded from the novel. In such cases we must know something of the author's life, as the most objective of his biographers have been able to present it, if we are adequately to understand and appraise his book.

Whereas Wordsworth had declared *The Prelude* ''unprecedented'' in its subjectivity, Walter Pater, writing *Marius the Epicurean* some eighty years later, claimed that it was one of his hero's ''modernisms'' to keep a diary or journal in which he might confess to himself his private thoughts and feelings. In the interim between the poem and the novel there appeared innumerable examples in both verse and prose of what Matthew Arnold was calling ''the dialogue of the mind with itself,'' a new and unabashedly subjective literature. Perhaps the most successful of the autobiographical forms, because the most oblique and richly creative, was the Bildungsroman, which attracted most of the major Victorian novelists and a number of their twentieth-century successors. An examination of some representative Bildungsromane . . . should indicate how each writer in turn learned to accommodate a powerful personal vision to the developing conventions of the genre. And it should uncover, along the way, some fresh perceptions of the unpredictable vitality of youth. (pp. 25-7)

· · · · ·

David Copperfield . . . is to be read as David's autobiography, not Dickens's. Some of the trial titles sent to Forster suggest the literary tradition to which the first-person narrative should be related: *The Copperfield Disclosures, The Copperfield*

Confessions, The Last Will and Testament of Mr. David Copperfield. Another, however, *The Copperfield Survey of the World as It Rolled,* might seem to us more accurate, for David's personal confessions and disclosures occupy but a small part of a long book, and we are less immediately struck by them than by the gentle irony and good humor with which he introduces us to the people and places he has observed in the rolling world. From the beginning he feels compelled to account for an extraordinary, indeed quite Dickensian capacity as observer: ''If it should appear from anything I may set down in this narrative that I was a child of close observation, or that as a man I have a strong memory of my childhood, I undoubtedly lay claim to both of these characteristics.'' Though the novel is never egotistical, ''I'' and ''My'' dominate the early chapter headings, and in the first half of the novel the narrator is indeed usually at the center of the action; but in the last half, where the first person rarely enters the titles, David sometimes seems to have become simply the recessive spectator. Yet we miss the point if we forget that *David Copperfield* is designed as a Bildungsroman and fail to see that almost every character and incident may have some final relation to the development of the hero.

Like Wordsworth in *The Prelude,* David presents his autobiography as the product of a powerful memory working over his experience from childhood to early maturity. Though the suffering at Murdstone and Grinby's proves less traumatic than its parallel in Dickens's life, David describes it as something quite unforgettable: ''I now approach a period . . . which I can never lose the remembrance of, while I remember anything; and the recollection of which has often, without my invocation, come before me like a ghost, and haunted happier times.'' Later, writing of the Yarmouth storm and the death of Steerforth, he confronts an ever-present reality: ''As plainly as I behold what happened, I will try to write it down. I do not recall it, but see it done; for it happens again before me.'' The strength of the memories derives from the vividness of the original sense impressions; what has been observed intensely becomes forever a part of the observer. Thus sound, sight, and smell recreate the scene of David's mother's funeral:

> If the funeral had been yesterday, I could not recollect
> it better. The very air of the best parlour, when I
> went in at the door, the bright condition of the fire,
> the shining of the wine in the decanters, the pattern
> of the glasses and the plates, the faint sweet smell
> of cake, the odour of Miss Murdstone's dress, and
> our black clothes. Mr. Chillip is in the room, and
> comes to speak to me.

Often, as in Proust—though David's effort at recall requires no Proustian deliberation—the present impression will help recover the buried past. The scent of a geranium leaf strikes David ''with a half comical, half serious wonder as to what change has come over [him] in a moment,'' for it brings back years later a vision of Dora in a straw hat with blue ribbons, and a little black dog in her arms, against a bank of bright blossoms. And the splash of the rain on the road by the Wickfield house reminds him, on his return after long absence, of the mood in which he once used to regard vagrants limping into town on wet evenings, a mood ''fraught, as then, with the smell of damp earth, and wet leaves and briar, and the sensation of the very airs that blew upon [him] in [his] own toilsome journey.'' Such moments of recollection are virtually ''spots of time,'' suggesting to David a unity, or at least a continuity, amid all the diversity of his experience.

Occasionally the pressure of the present impression is so intense that it, too, seems to him a sort of memory of some lost larger life, carrying with it a sense of *déjà vu*, "a feeling . . . of what we are saying and doing having been said and done before, in a remote time—of our having been surrounded, dim ages ago, by the same faces, objects, and circumstances—of our knowing perfectly well what will be said next, as if we suddenly remembered it!" The feeling, twice related to the fleeting awareness that he has neglected or misunderstood Agnes Wickfield, is accompanied by a certain bewilderment, a half-conscious sense of misdirection, intimating that he has misread the signposts of his life. David has much of the poet's sensibility, a delight in sensuous concretions, a fascination with the miracle of memory, but he shows nothing of Wordsworth's concern for the development of the artist as such or the shaping of an aesthetic theory. His autobiography describes the education, through time remembered, of the affections; his growth lies in the ordering of his "undisciplined heart."

David experiences a moment of great qualitative depth, a half-understood troubling self-revelation, when he hears Annie Strong's defense of her marriage to the elderly schoolmaster. Annie might at one time, she confesses, have given herself to the indolent, self-seeking Jack Maldon, had not the love of Dr. Strong persuaded her that "there can be no disparity in marriage like unsuitability of mind and purpose" and so protected her from "the first mistaken impulse of [her] undisciplined heart." The phrase lingers with David, like the perpetual judgment on his own life and conduct, and he applies it before long to the disparity of temperament between himself and his childwife:

> "The first mistaken impulse of an undisciplined heart." Those words of Mrs. Strong's were constantly recurring to me, at this time; were almost always present to my mind. I awoke with them, often, in the night; I remember to have even read them, in dreams, inscribed upon the walls of houses. For I knew, now, that my own heart was undisciplined when it first loved Dora; and that if it had been disciplined, it never could have felt, when we were married, what it felt in its secret experience.

Later, when Dora lies dying, he remembers all his unspoken dissatisfactions, and his "undisciplined heart is chastened heavily." Finally, in bereavement, "left alone with [his] undisciplined heart," he must learn to redirect his impulses and energies.

As in Annie's use of the term, describing the possible appeal of Maldon, the undisciplined heart is clearly associated with a wayward sensuality, which is so central to a number of relationships as to constitute a major theme in the novel. David's frail mother seems "very fond" of the monstrous Mr. Murdstone and submits only too eagerly to his possessive embrace:

> He drew her to him, whispered in her ear, and kissed her. I knew as well, when I saw my mother's head lean down upon his shoulder, and her arm touch his neck—I knew as well that he could mould her pliant nature into any form he chose, as I know, now, that he did it.

Aunt Betsey, disciplined at last by kindness to Mr. Dick and true affection for David, has years ago made an impulsive marriage to a wastrel. Little Em'ly, at the cost of all that should be dear to her, is attracted to the ruthless Steerforth, the irresistible Byronic *homme fatale*. Steerforth in turn can exploit her innocence as if in "a brilliant game, played for the ex-

citement of the moment, . . . in a mere wasteful careless course of winning what was worthless to him," and yet, in a mood of dejection that David is unable to fathom, he can also deplore his lack of discipline: "I wish with all my soul I had been better guided! . . . I wish with all my soul I could guide myself better!" Rosa Dartle is consumed forever by a sexual frustration she herself has wilfully nurtured. And Uriah Heep, "umble" as he is, blatantly avows his designs upon Agnes. All of these should have taught David his lesson; instead they provide parallels to his experience, an ambiance in which undisciplined choice may prove disastrous.

David's most serious mistaken impulse is his immediate and complete commitment to Dora, at the first sight of whom he feels his fate sealed forever. On entering Mr. Spenlow's house, he hears a voice making introductions:

> It was, no doubt, Mr. Spenlow's voice, but I didn't know it, and I didn't care whose it was. All was over in a moment. I had fulfilled my destiny. I was a captive and a slave. I loved Dora Spenlow to distraction!
>
> She was more than human to me. She was a Fairy, a Sylph, I don't know what she was—anything that no one ever saw, and everything that everybody ever wanted. I was swallowed up in an abyss of love in an instant. There was no pausing on the brink; no looking down, or looking back; I was gone, headlong, before I had sense to say a word to her.

In itself this passage has the charm and vitality of extravagant youth; though we know that first love so delirious often proves illusory, we nonetheless feel it beautiful and harmless, especially if the lover is such a pleasant young man as David seems to be. In the context of the whole novel, however, the passage has darker overtones; it indicates a precipitancy that may injure others as well as David, a naiveté that threatens to leave him defenseless and amorphous. With it should be contrasted the first description of Agnes Wickfield, which appears in a much earlier chapter:

> Although her face was quite bright and happy, there was a tranquillity about it, and about her—a quiet, good, calm spirit,—that I have never forgotten, that I never shall forget. . . .
>
> I cannot call to mind where or when, in my childhood, I had seen a stained glass window in a church. Nor do I recollect its subject. But I know that when I saw her turn around in the grave light of the old staircase, and wait for us, above, I thought of that window; and I associated something of its tranquil brightness with Agnes Wickfield ever afterwards.

Though the idealization and especially the placing of the girl in an angelic stained-glass attitude make it difficult, here and sometimes elsewhere, to believe in Agnes as a flesh-and-blood creation, David gives priority to the object rather than to his own immediate response. The sight of Agnes does not intoxicate him; he will only gradually come to know his love. But Agnes will remain the model of the calm considerateness he must achieve in his own heart if he is to reach his maturity. From the beginning, as Dickens's plan notes make clear, Agnes is to be understood as "the real heroine" of the novel.

Like other Victorians, David endures a dark night of despair before he finds hope and purpose and even true identity; he moves through the "pattern of conversion" traced by Carlyle in *Sartor Resartus* and seen with variations in *In Memoriam* and later, after *David Copperfield*, in other Bildungsromane and in the autobiographies of John Stuart Mill and John Henry Newman. After the deaths of Dora and Steerforth and the emigration to Australia of the Peggottys and the Micawbers, David wanders disconsolately through Italy and Switzerland. "Absence," the chapter devoted to his three-year exile, differs in style from the rest of the narrative; it is the one section given over to sustained analysis and introspection, a subjective, almost lyrical account of a crisis which, in accordance with Dickens's working notes, must be "dreamily described."

In his Everlasting No David sees his whole life now "a ruined blank and waste, lying wide around [him], unbroken, to the dark horizon." He is once again the homeless alienated orphan, like the child in the warehouse, but now without the will to find distractions from his sorrow. His despondency hardens into despair, and he comes to think death the only possible escape. He passes the great shrines of history in a trance, "as a dreamer might," observing nothing. "Listlessness to everything, but brooding sorrow," he explains, "was the night that fell on my undisciplined heart." The first faint break in the darkness comes when suddenly, as he descends into an Alpine valley, he is stirred by "some long-unwonted sense of beauty and tranquillity," a feelng far less intense than Wordsworth's epiphany at the Simplon Pass, yet sufficient, when he enters the valley village, to make him responsive, with a quite Wordsworthian reverence, to the singing of shepherds as if he were hearing the voice of "great Nature" herself. A letter from Agnes then helps restore his perspective on the purposes of human life and society, somewhat as the more mystical letters from Hallam in In Memoriam help affirm the continuity of the living soul. As Tennyson sees the darkness dissolve, so, in reading, David feels "the night . . . passing from [his] mind." Again like Tennyson, who resolves to "take what fruit may be / Of sorrow under human skies," he now cultivates "the human interest" he has "lately shrunk from," and before long he has many friends in the Swiss valley. His Everlasting Yea, as Sartor prescribed, is the discovery of his life's work; already a writer, he becomes the dedicated novelist—presumably first of all the author of a Bildungsroman:

> I worked early and late, patiently and hard. I wrote a Story, with a purpose growing, not remotely, out of my experience,. . . and the tidings of my growing reputation began to reach me from travellers whom I encountered by chance. After some rest and change, I fell to work, in my old ardent way, on a new fancy, which took strong possession of me. As I advanced in the execution of this task, I felt it more and more, and roused my utmost energies to do it well.

Having made the saving adjustment to work and society, David has conquered self-indulgent sorrow and is prepared at last to discipline his affections. In a new self-knowledge he recognizes his lifelong love of Agnes, which was strong, he now admits, even when, in blindness, he "bestowed his passionate tenderness upon another object." Returning to England consciously "a better man" for the change he has undergone, he can eventually tell Agnes, "There is no alloy of self in what I feel for you." Agnes is indeed his necessary complement; she is both the clear-eyed understanding for which he has always groped and the unselfish fortitude necessary to give his sensibilities purpose and direction. In marriage to Agnes, David achieves the integration of personality to which the hero in the novel of youth typically aspires.

"Of all my books," said Dickens, "I like this the best. . . . Like many fond parents, I have in my heart of hearts a favourite child. And his name is David Copperfield." From other com-

ments it seems clear that his fondness extended from the book to the character, perhaps with the sense of satisfaction that through art David could be granted "the one happiness" Dickens felt he had missed in life. Yet he could hardly have considered the bland David of the last chapters an adequate surrogate for his tempestuous self, and he knew from his own experience that a young man's development might be troubled by a guilt and inner conflict which David had never suffered. When he returned to the Bildungsroman as a genre ten years later, he was ready to deal not in wish-fulfillment but in forces precluding a tranquil resolution, in errors of pride and self-interest, far more insidious than the well-intentioned but undisciplined heart.

Dickens himself was the first to compare Great Expectations with David Copperfield. In October 1860 (the serial publication began in December), he told Forster: "The book will be written in the first person throughout, and during the first three weekly numbers you will find the hero to be a boy-child, like David. Then he will be an apprentice. . . . To be quite sure I had not fallen into no unconscious repetitions, I read David Copperfield again the other day, and was affected by it to a degree you would hardly believe." Though popular from the beginning, Great Expectations was never as dear to Dickens as his "favourite child." Yet, largely because he approached it with complete dispassion and no vestige of self-pity and proportioned it with matchless logic, it strikes most modern readers as the better book, and many indeed as Dickens's finest work. Some would agree with Bernard Shaw that it altogether "wiped out" Copperfield. Others, less exuberant, might prefer Humphry House's description of Great Expectations as "the pendant to the first part of David Copperfield, the more mature revision of the progress of a young man in the world." But even the first part of David Copperfield differs sharply in tone and method from Great Expectations, and the whole of it—by no means expunged—remains remarkable for its own distinct qualities. Still, considered simply as a study of a young man's progress—that is, as a Bildungsroman—Great Expectations is undoubtedly the more impressive novel, for its narrower, sharper focus allows a much fuller characterization of the narrator, who is once again the protagonist. Like David, Pip, in telling his story, has the virtues of Dickens the novelist; but unlike David, who is relatively reticent, Pip in his acute self-analysis reveals much of the temper of Dickens the man.

As in David Copperfield, many of the settings in Great Expectations are drawn from scenes familiar to Dickens since his boyhood. Pip's village has been identified as Cooling; the nearby town is clearly Rochester; the hulks were the prison ships once anchored at Chatham; we can trace the original of Miss Havisham's weird Satis House; and we may be sure that the marshes have been evoked in all their gray miasma by one who knew the ooze of real Thames mud beneath his feet. Yet there is none of the direct autobiography that from time to time invades Coppperfield. Pip's conduct at no point coincides precisely with that of Dickens; the personal has become oblique, distant and ironic. We may find the true measure of the difference between the two novels in an incidental comment by the blacksmith Joe Gargery, who, to the great embarrassment of Pip, has just arrived in London. When Pip's friend Herbert asks him if he has seen anything yet of the city, Joe replies, "Why, yes, Sir, . . . me and Wopsle went off straight to look at the Blacking Ware'us. But we didn't find that it come up to its likeness in the red bills at the shop doors: which I meantersay, . . . as it is there drawd too architectooralooral." Here the warehouse that Dickens previously could not bring himself to mention except under the fictional guise of Murdstone and Grinby's is reduced from a menace to a joke by a fearless, almost self-mocking disengagement. In *Great Expectations,* of course, the parallel to David's misery in the warehouse, or to Dickens's, is Pip's revulsion from the forge after a brief acquaintance with the faded pomp of Satis House:

> I had believed in the forge as the glowing road to manhood and independence. Within a single year all this was changed. Now, it was all coarse and common, and I would not have had Miss Havisham and Estella see it on any account. . . . What I had dreaded was, that in some unlucky hour I, being at my grimiest and commonest, should lift up my eyes and see Estella looking in at one of the wooden windows of the forge. I was haunted by the fear that she would, sooner or later, find me out, with a black face and hands, doing the coarsest part of my work, and would exult over me and despise me.

But whereas David's feeling of degradation was intended to elicit our deepest sympathy, Pip's distaste and dread, presented with a relentless detachment, are far more ignoble than the work of which he is ashamed. The mature Pip's account of his unhappy apprenticeship is decidedly not to be confused with an apologia for the young Dickens.

Yet, for all its objectivity of manner, *Great Expectations* comes closer than *Copperfield* to being a portrait of the author. Not only does Pip, like David, have a keen Dickensian memory, apparent in the vividness of the physical details he recalls and in scattered remarks on the persistence of an emotion through time ("To the present hour, the weary western streets of London on a cold dusty spring night, with their ranges of stern shut-up mansions and their long rows of lamps, are melancholy to me from this association"). He also shares with Dickens—and not with David—several obsessive drives and passions, which as narrator he describes with cogency and great candor. He has an excessive respect for the power of money, a naive confidence that he can somehow buy real security and peace of mind. He loves against all reason a proud beauty who never can or will adequately reciprocate his affection: Estella, clearly modeled on the actress Ellen Ternan, whom the mature Dickens could neither acknowledge nor relinquish. And he nervously strives to conceal his past in the dread that public knowledge of his humble beginnings might debar him from the society of "gentlemen" toward which he too aggressively aspires. Pip's sense of guilt and his involvement, conscious and unconscious, with criminals surely reflects Dickens's remembrance of his father's humiliation before the law and his lifelong awareness of the thin line between respectability and illicit impulse. Pip's vanity and wilful self-delusion echo a fiercer pride tempered by a stronger imagination. And his restless ambition dimly mirrors a more alarming, because unremitting and ultimately self-destructive, energy.

But whatever was subjective in origin, the product of an acute self-knowledge, has been assimilated to a beautifully controlled work of art. If *Great Expectations* comments dramatically on Dickens's uncertainties and moral misgivings, it nonetheless, in the very act of doing so, abundantly illustrates his aesthetic confidence and power. It moves in three equal parts with a dialectical precision: the first presents Pip in a state of relative innocence and naiveté, driven at length from Eden by his worldly "expectations"; the second depicts his corruption in the city, where he hopes, though realized, prove delusions; the third records the utter loss of material wealth and the concomitant recovery of spiritual integrity. . . . Like a poem, the novel

exacts our willing suspension of disbelief by its texture, the coherence of its symbols, and the sense that it is exploring through metaphor a real and pertinent psychology. We can thus accept the improbable fantasy of Satis House, where Miss Havisham strikes Pip at one moment as a witch, at another as his fairy godmother; and we scarcely question the unlikely melodrama of Pip's struggle with Orlick at the lime kiln as if with a devil at the gate of Hell. *Great Expectations* boldly invokes any device, realistic or not, that will advance its central object, the depiction of its hero's development.

That Dickens was aware of the particular conventions of the Bildungsroman, though unfamiliar with that label, is, I think, apparent from his statement that, when beginning the new book, he reread *David Copperfield* to make sure he would not indulge in unconscious repetition. What he wished not to repeat was not, I assume, personal detail (for it was no longer his intention to be circumstantially autobiographical), but rather the same use of the standard motifs of the genre as it was defining itself in nineteenth-century fiction. *Great Expectations* as a Bildungsroman shares many characteristics of the form with *Copperfield* and still more with *The Red and the Black,* which Dickens perhaps never read. But it gives each element fresh interpretation and new vitality.

Pip, like many other apprentice-heroes, is an orphan, but that condition instills no conventional independence or self-assertion. Instead, it is the source of a distinct resentment and a sorry lack of initiative:

> Within myself, I had sustained, from my babyhood, a perpetual conflict with injustice. I had known, from the time when I could speak, that my sister, in her capricious and violent coercion, was unjust to me. I had cherished a profound conviction that her bringing me up by hand, gave her no right to bring me up by jerks. Through all my punishments, disgraces, fasts and vigils, and other penitential performances, I had nursed this assurance; and to my communing so much with it, in a solitary and unprotected way, I in great part refer the fact that I was morally timid and very sensitive.

Like other orphans, Pip must find a substitute father; but he has not far to look, for one is literally thrust upon him in the opening scene as he lingers over the graves of his departed parents. Magwitch's first positive act is to protect the child by assuming guilt for the theft from Mrs. Joe's pantry. Thereafter he lives and works only for his "boy," and if his money proves nearly disastrous to Pip, his love is ultimately the agent of Pip's redemption.

Pip travels the familiar highway from the provinces to the city. But he has less vivid reasons for leaving his native village than Julien Sorel's for deserting mean-souled Verrières. His early faith that the forge is "the glowing road to manhood and independence" is far nearer the truth than the illusions that shatter it, and he can eventually look back on his naive farewell to the country only with deep irony: "No more low wet grounds, no more dykes and sluices, no more of these grazing cattle—though they seemed, in their dull manner, to wear a more respectful air now, and to face round, in order that they might stare as long as possible at the possessor of such great expectations—farewell, monotonous acquaintances of my childhood, henceforth I was for London and greatness: not for smith's work in general and for you!" The city, as in other Bildungsromane, proves a sad disappointment; but its menacing drabness is now caught with an incomparable intensity. The dismal offices of Little Britain, the forlorn houses of Barnard's Inn, the crowded streets, the ominous riverside are more than setting; all relate expressionistically to the mood and theme of the novel. Pip wryly recalls his mixed feelings on arrival in London: "We Britons had at that time particularly settled, that it was treasonable to doubt our having and our being the best of everything: otherwise, while I was scared by the immensity of London, I think I might have had some faint doubts whether it was not rather ugly, crooked, narrow, and dirty. He can scarcely afford to admit what a dreary foggy dust-hole he considers the lodgings Mr. Jaggers has procured for him. The most candid opinion of the apartment, even after Pip has tried at reckless expense to make it presentable, comes from Joe on the occasion of his unwelcome visit: "For the present may be a wery good inn, according to London opinions, . . . and I believe its character do stand i; but I wouldn't keep a pig in it myself—not in the case that I wished him to fatten wholesome and to eat with a meller flavour on him. Joe fears that the close stale atmosphere of London may be injurious to the health; actually Pip's life in the city threatens his body less than his whole moral being.

The chief agent of his corruption is money, a familiar theme here given unusual prominence. Money seems to be the central objective of most of the Londoners Pip meets, from his predatory houseboy to Mr. Jaggers, with his sharp eye to business, and Wemmick, with his awesome regard for portable property. But even before coming to the city, Pip has a "first decided experience of the stupendous power of money" when he sees it utterly confound Trabb's boy. So dazzled is he himself by his great expectations that he is willing for the moment to take the mercenary, hypocritical Pumblechook at face value as "a sensible practical good-hearted prime fellow." Pip might have learned a lesson from Joe's angry retort to Mr. Jaggers that no money could possibly compensate him for the loss of his apprentice. Instead, he shares (at least until he knows he is sharing it) Magwitch's assumption that money can buy all things desirable. Magwitch desires most a well-bred son, and he comes to believe that that is precisely what his money has bought. Pip's ambition is strikingly similar: to buy for himself the status of a gentlemen.

From the moment he hears Estella call him "a common labouring boy" with "coarse hands" and "thick boots," Pip is ashamed of all things "coarse and common" in his background and in his present life at the smithy. To be worthy of the disdainful Estella, whom he identifies at first sight as "a young lady," Pip must clearly improve himself—"Biddy," he tells his honest confidante, "I want to be a gentleman." His unknown benefactor has the same ambition for him, and eventually Mr. Jaggers comes to rescue him from the laboring village: "Well, Mr. Pip, I think the sooner you leave here—as you are to be a gentleman—the better." Pip's deliberate pursuit of his objective recalls Wilhelm Meister's dedication to self-culture. But whereas Wilhelm's ideal was reasoned and coherent, Pip's is ill conceived and naively developed. It rests on a contemptible snobbery, which leads Pip to repudiate the best man he has known ("I wished Joe had been rather more genteelly brought up," or again, "I wanted to make Joe less ignorant and common that he might be worthier of my society"). Biddy recognizes his unkindness and reminds him, "Yet a gentleman should not be unjust neither." And Herbert Pocket commends to him the principle that "a true gentleman in manner" must be "a true gentleman at heart," for "no varnish can hide the grain of the wood." Herbert himself, with his nonchalance and charm and "natural incapacity to do anything secret and mean," provides an immediate gentlemanly example

Pip might well emulate. But Pip has his own more superficial notions of the role he is determined to play. His idea of a gentleman is not unlike Carlyle's concept of the Idle Dilettante, the mannered rather than mannerly spender of unearned income, content to "go gracefully idle in Mayfair," untroubled by the drudges supporting his existence. Pip may or may not be a Carlylean dandy (we are not told what sort of appearance he affects), but the livery he designs for his houseboy—a "blue coat, canary waistcoat, white cravat, creamy breeches," and high boots—suggests a taste more flamboyant than discreet. On first coming to London he is told that he is "not designed for any profession" and will "be well enough educated" if he can hold his own "with the average of young men in prosperous circumstances." He assumes without question that this golden mediocrity satisfies a gentlemanly requirement; but when his expectations evaporate and he is forced to consider a vocation, he is overcome with dismay: "I have been bred to no calling, and I am fit for nothing."

At no time does it occur to him that the gentleman, as Newman defined the ideal for the Victorians, must be tolerant, open to new ideas, devoted to the free play of the intellect, sympathetic, considerate of the feelings of others. On the contrary, in spite of his better instincts, he forces himself to accept the credentials of the brutish Bentley Drummle, a thick-skulled sadist with a pedigree and a good deal of money, whom he both envies and despises. Magwitch, however, is entirely satisfied with Pip's success, and on his return from Australia is eager to claim credit for making it possible: "Yes, Pip, dear boy, I've made a gentleman on you! It's me wot has done it! . . . I lived rough, that you should live smooth; I worked hard that you should be above work." Later, tracked down, caught and manacled, Magwitch can console himself, "I've seen my boy, and he can be a gentleman without me." Pip thinks he knows better, for he has already decided to give up the money that sustains his social pretensions. But love and devotion have now changed the young man's scale of values, and Magwitch is actually not far wrong: without him, without his money, Pip has at last a chance to become a real gentleman. Eventually he approaches that objective, when, to tell his story, he sets his experience in perspective and candidly deplores "all those wretched hankerings after money and gentility that . . . disturbed [his] boyhood.

Pip the narrator differs more sharply from Pip the adolescent than the mature David Copperfield from his younger self. Though the young David has to learn the value of the disciplined heart, he commands a large measure of sympathy from the beginning; if sometimes impercipient, he is essentially kind and good, a gentleman by nature and without deliberate effort. Pip as autobiographer has a more complex development to describe, a conquest of selfish pride and self-delusion, snobbery, hypocrisy, and timorous feelings of guilt. So eager is he to trace the effects of his shortcomings that he is reluctant to mention his virtues. His tale accordingly has the quality of a dramatic monologue; we must deduce his whole character from what he leaves unsaid as well as from his frank confession, and we must establish the necessary continuities between his past and the present in which he is writing. George Orwell complained that the child Pip speaks a perfect English rather than the broad Essex of his companions. But most of Pip's speech throughout the novel is recorded in indirect discourse properly consonant with the educated style of the narrator, and the few direct quotations, it seems to me, fit better into place in the same language than if the mature man had tried to present the child as a third person objectively distinct from himself. The concentrated purpose of *Great Expectations* is to depict the moral growth of a single character, the painful initiation, as he himself remembers it.

Magwitch in his last illness may have wondered "whether he might have been a better man under better circumstances," but "he never justified himself by a hint tending that way, or tried to bend the past out of its eternal shape." Pip in the retrospect that is his story is likewise able to examine his whole experience without evasion, excuse, or denial. But as he presents himself in the process of growing up, he is much given to apology and self-deception; he is eager at any given moment to forget or escape his past and to rationalize his present course of action; and he is slow to learn the truth that "all other swindlers upon earth are nothing to the self-swindlers." Yet he has been shaken as a child by a terror that remains for years to haunt his imagination:

> Since that time, which is far enough away now, I have often thought that few people know what secrecy there is in the young, under terror. No matter how unreasonable the terror, so that it be terror. I was in mortal terror of the young man who wanted my heart and liver; I was in mortal terror of my interlocutor with the iron leg; I was in mortal terror of myself, from whom an awful promise had been extracted; I had no hope of deliverance through my all-powerful sister, who repulsed me at every turn; I am afraid to think of what I might have done on requirement, in the secrecy of my terror.

And the terror, exacting the pledge of secrecy, leads to an abiding sense of guilt. Pip has aided a criminal, made himself involuntarily an accomplice, and so begun a career in which he will one day find himself "encompassed by all this taint of prison and crime." When his sister is assaulted with the convict's leg-iron, he persuades himself not to reveal the source of the weapon: "the secret was such an old one now, had so grown into me and become a part of myself, that I could not tear it away." But he feels partly guilty of the attack as well as the concealment, for he has often wished to see Mrs. Joe silenced and has now inadvertently supplied the means. Later Orlick, the real assailant, makes him face up to the possibility of his guilt in thought if not in word or deed. By that time, however, he is ready to abandon self-swindling and to confront the inexorable truths of his development.

Orlick has been construed as Pip's double, the agent carrying out his subconscious wishes, and so a witness to the fact that Pip has good reason to experience criminal guilt. But to pursue such an argument is to suggest that Pip's sins are offenses against society rather than moral failures, and Pip the narrator, who seems to me a trustworthy guide, makes it emphatically clear that they are the latter. Pip indicts himself for ingratitude, selfishness, and emotional dishonesty. He declares himself in his snobbery "capable of almost any meanness towards Joe or his name." He recognizes an "ungracious condition of mind" in his being ashamed of home and of Joe's occupation—"ungracious" perhaps with the overtone of meaning "cut off from heavenly grace and charity." He is vain about his few calculated gestures of magnanimity, as when, home for his sister's funeral, he asks if he may sleep in his own little room—"I felt that I had done rather a great thing in making the request." His departure the next morning shows him at his worst, not the criminal but the deficient human being; he has been annoyed at Biddy for asking if he really means to keep his promise to return, and he now bids farewell showily to her and to Joe:

> "Good-bye, dear Joe!—No, don't wipe it off—for God's sake, give me your blackened hand!—I shall be down soon and often."

> "Never too soon, sir," said Joe, "and never too often, Pip!"

> Biddy was waiting for me at the kitchen door, with a mug of new milk and a crust of bread. "Biddy," said I, when I gave her my hand at parting, "I am not angry, but I am hurt."

> "No, don't be hurt," she pleaded quite pathetically, "let only me be hurt, if I have been ungenerous."

> Once more, the mists were rising as I walked away. If they disclosed to me, as I suspect they did, that I should *not* come back, and that Biddy was quite right, all I can say is—they were quite right too.

Pip needs no instruction in moral cowardice and following the course of least resistance; as a child, "quite an untaught genius," he has discovered baseness for himself. But he is certainly abetted in meanness of spirit by Estella, who engenders in him false pride, false hopes, and a woeful contempt for his origins. Estella entices and rebukes, tortures and torments, and Pip is aware of "all the pain" she has cost him and of being "always miserable" in her presence. She speaks with the cold logic of Louisa in *Hard Times:* love is a fancy she can not comprehend, "a form of words, but nothing more." She has, she insists, no heart, "no softness, . . . no—sympathy—sentiment—nonsense." Herbert, who is normally generous in his judgments, describes her as "hard, haughty and capricious to the last degree." Pip knows only too well the validity of this indictment; but from the moment he first sees Estella, he feels bound to her beyond all rational argument or persuasion, and she remains through all his growing years a fever in the blood, an image of what he selfishly desires and cannot have. The intensity of the commitment is paralleled in the English Bildungsroman only by Philip Carey's abject surrender to Mildred in *Of Human Bondage* and Sammy Mountjoy's ruthless determination to possess Beatrice in *Free Fall.* "The unqualified truth," Pip admits, "is that when I loved Estella with the love of a man, I loved her simply because I found her irresistible. Once for all; I knew to my sorrow, often and often, if not always, that I loved her against reason, against promise, against peace, against hope, against happiness, against all discouragement that could be. Once for all; I loved her none the less because I knew it, and it had no more influence in restraining me, than if I had devoutly believed her to be human perfection." But love in such terms, appetite without sympathy, proves destructive and demeaning; Pip cannot reach his moral maturity until he can recognize the claims of a love which involves disinterested charity, and so rid himself of his old obsession.

Yet even when most deluded, he retains enough judgment to be frequently dissatisfied with his conduct. He knows in his heart that Biddy is "immeasurably better than Estella" and that life at the forge is healthier than the death-in-life of Satis House, and he suffers a serious ambivalence of emotions, what he calls a "confused division of mind," as he faces his moral choices. Whether or not he often chooses badly, the fact that he experiences conflict and remorse is itself some indication of his potential for spiritual change. Though he has a strong recurrent sense of guilt, his errors are largely sins of omission, and these coexist with undeniable positive virtues. If he neglects Joe, he is nonetheless loyal to Herbert, whose career in business he manages quietly to advance; and Herbert in turn values his friendship, with no expectation of personal advantage. He is alert, quick to associate ideas and impressions, sensitive to the patterns of memory that unify his experience. He has, as long as he is not thinking of Estella, a pleasant sense of humor; he enjoys the absurdities of Mr. Wopsle's Hamlet and joins convivially in Wemmick's wedding party. And despite his unkindness to Biddy, he readily discerns and rejects the brutal and the fraudulent, Drummle, Pumblechook, and the grasping hangers-on at Miss Havisham's. The city is clearly a force of corruption, but it also sophisticates Pip in ways not wholly bad, by widening his range of knowledge and giving him glimpses into the complexities of modern society. Whatever his moral condition, he will not be able to return for long to the simplicities of the village.

Pip's regeneration begins when his fear of Magwitch becomes a fear for Magwitch, when his selfish recoil from his protector yields to an anxious and selfless solicitude; as he hides the convict from the law, he risks his own comfort and safety in a way he himself would not have believed possible. He can now feel compassion also for Miss Havisham, who asks him to forgive her: "My life," he tells her, "has been a blind and thankless one; and I want forgiveness and direction far too much to be bitter with you." But he must be tested further. Orlick at the lime kiln forces him in extremity ("I felt," Pip says, "that I had come to the brink of my grave") to an honest and dreadful confrontation of his whole past. Finally a narrow escape from drowning, when the river police capture Magwitch, dissolves his last grain of repugnance and pride: "in the hunted, wounded, shackled creature, . . . I only saw a man who had meant to be my benefactor, and who had felt affectionately, gratefully, and generously, towards me with great constancy through a series of years. I only saw in him a much better man than I had been to Joe." At the trial he endures the horror of standing by Magwitch as the judge pronounces the death sentence and the audience rises and points down at both of them. He tends the prisoner lovingly until the end and then falls into his own little death, a serious illness that leaves him for weeks in delirium. From this he eventually recovers, as if reborn, feeling, he says, like a child again. For watching over his progress is his childhood friend and foster-father, Joe, whom he now recognizes for what he is, if not a perfect gentleman, then something finer, "this gentle Christian man." Joe at last carries him down to an open carriage and drives him into the country, where he rejoices in the fullness of life, much as the self in Tennyson's debate: "The Two Voices," emerging from the dark night of the soul, is admonished by the fields bathed in the light of a Sunday morning:

> The day happened to be Sunday, and when I looked on the loveliness around me, and thought how it had grown and changed, and how the little wild flowers had been forming, and the voices of the birds had been strengthening, by day and night, under the sun and under the stars, while poor I lay burning and tossing on my bed, the mere remembrance of having burned and tossed there, came like a check upon my peace. But, when I heard the Sunday bells, and looked around a little more upon the outspread beauty, I felt that I was not nearly thankful enough—that I was too weak yet, to be even that—and I laid my head on Joe's shoulder, as I had laid it long ago when he had taken me to the Fair or where not, and it was too much for my young senses.

By losing himself, Pip thus retrieves his identity; his rediscovery of his first affections is his passport to maturity.

Physically rehabilitated, Pip goes back to the village in the hope of offering his once "errant heart" to Biddy (the epithet recalls *David Copperfield,* though Pip's waywardness has been far more self-conscious and deliberate than David's). His story is now near its end; the result of the proposal will, he says, be all he has "left to tell." Biddy, however—the irony is most appropriate—has just married Joe, and Pip accordingly goes abroad alone as a representative of Herbert's import-export company. When he returns to England eleven years later, he finds the Gargerys the happy parents of a son named in his honor, but assures them that he himself will not marry and that he has conquered his old obsessive love for Estella: "That poor dream, as I once used to call it, has all gone by, Biddy, all gone by!" Here would be a wholly satisfying conclusion to the novel, a final testimony to Pip's mature self-knowledge.

But Dickens has given us two endings beyond this logical stopping-place, neither, I think, altogether adequate. The first, more laconic and surely stronger than the alternative, shows us Pip, on another visit, with little Pip in London, where he is greeted by Estella, now widowed and remarried, who mistakes the child for Pip's own. Pip does not linger long enough to correct her impression, but he is nonetheless, he tells us (with a slight and rather unpleasant resurgence of self-regard), pleased to have seen her: "I was very glad afterwards to have had the interview; for, in her face and in her voice, and in her touch, she gave me the assurance that suffering had been stronger than Miss Havisham's teaching, and had given her a heart to understand what my heart used to be." The second and standard ending, supplied when Bulwer Lytton thought the original too severe, brings Pip to reunion with Estella in the dank ruined garden of Satis House. The scene, though skillfully contrived to echo the imagery of Pip's first departure from the marshes, is neither probable nor convincing. Though we gather that Estella has suffered and "been bent and broken . . . into a better shape," we are given no reason to believe that she has ever learned the meaning of selfless love. Pip's attraction to her is acceptable only if we discount the significance of his "conversion." Yet the logic of the novel as a whole demands that Pip, properly to complete his initiation, sacrifice Estella along with all his other false expectations. And the technique of the narrative itself points in the same direction. Pip as narrator would certainly have had something "left to tell" in the last pages if he knew he would woo and win Estella when he found it was too late to marry Biddy. Moreover, unless he is deceiving us from the beginning, it is difficult to see how he could arraign Estella so consistently and emphatically throughout his story and all the while assume that she will provide its happy denouement. Fortunately the existence of the alternatives allows us to choose the one that does little harm to the integrity of the book, and to ignore the other as an inorganic afterthought.

With *David Copperfield* and *Great Expectations* Dickens gave the English Bildungsroman both personal intensity and objective power. From his own strenuous experience and his sharp insight into the processes of his mind and memory, he drew moods and incidents which his creative imagination worked into new forms. His mastery in both novels of first-person narration enabled him to give each an inward dimension by dramatizing the consciousness of the narrator, by letting David or Pip interweave memories and past fears with present observations or pause to consider the mysteries of time which help shape his identity. In Pip especially he created a rounded character, interesting as hero and persuasive as narrator. Though not a professional novelist like David, Pip commands an equally fine prose style, less serene and meditative, but wittier, more ironic, more precise in both description and analysis. We do not know what Pip read during his period as Idle Dilettante in London, but we can credit his claims to literacy: "through good and evil I stuck to my books," and again, "Notwithstanding my inability to settle to anything, . . . I had a taste for reading, and read regularly so many hours a day.'' Whatever he may have read, he clearly learned from some sources how to write—though very few of the books he encountered could have been nearly so well written as his own story. (pp. 34-62)

> Jerome Hamilton Buckley, "Introduction: The Space Between" and "Dickens, David and Pip," in his Season of Youth: The "Bildungsroman" from Dickens to Golding, *Cambridge, Mass.: Harvard University Press, 1974, pp. 1-27, 28-62.*

THE FEMALE *BILDUNGSROMAN*

ELAINE HOFFMAN BARUCH

[*Arguing that "the authentic feminine* bildungsroman *is still to be written," Baruch explores how women seek vicarious knowledge through marriage in Brontë's* Jane Eyre, *Flaubert's* Madame Bovary, *and Eliot's* Middlemarch.]

It has long been a critical commonplace that there is no feminine *bildungsroman*. But if the central theme of the *bildungsroman* is the education of the hero who is brought to a high level of consciousness through a series of experiences that lead to his development, then many of the great novels that deal with women treat similar themes. From *Emma* to *Jane Eyre* to *Madame Bovary* to *Middlemarch* to *Anna Karenina* to *Portrait of a Lady* to *Lady Chatterley's Lover* and beyond, the novel presents a search for self, an education of the mind and feelings. But unlike the male *bildungsroman*, the feminine *bildungs* takes place in or on the periphery of marriage. That is its most striking characteristic.

In his important book *The Rise of the Novel*, Ian Watt made the point that, starting in the eighteenth century, marriage determined woman's social, economic, and geographic future. In the Pamela tradition, which mirrors this social reality, the heroine seeks upward mobility in marriage. In the tradition that I am here treating, which is perhaps equally important, if not as widely recognized, the heroine longs for a marriage that will increase her knowledge, often in some wide experiential sense.

It is perhaps an index of how much we have changed that we can now dissociate women's education from marriage. However, throughout the nineteenth century things were quite otherwise. Hegel, who is merely one of many spokesmen for the idea, writes that women have their essential destiny in marriage and there only. In a seemingly unrelated passage, he speaks of women and learning:

> Women acquire learning—we know not how—almost as if by breathing ideas, more by living really than by actually taking hold of knowledge. Man, on the other hand, achieves his distinction only by means of advancing thought and much skilled exertion.

Hegel, who admittedly idealizes intuitive knowledge, doesn't recognize the causal connection in the two passages. What other way could women acquire knowledge than to "breathe" it? And what was more natural than for them to seek to make of their marital destiny a means of education since almost without exception every other institution of higher learning was closed to them?

Even in Mary Wollstonecraft's revolutionary *Vindication of the Rights of Woman*, a basic argument for equal education for women is that it will make them good mothers and faithful wives. Perhaps the least sexist of nineteenth-century novelists, Stendhal, advocates equal education (in his treatise *On Love*) so that women will be more desirable and lovable companions for men. Of course it is possible that these arguments were designed with subversive intent. Their authors may have deferred to the populace in order to get women into the ivory tower by way of the kitchen door, so to speak. This seems entirely probable when one considers that Wollstonecraft also speaks of opening up all professions to single women and that Stendhal laments that all geniuses born women were lost to the world, hardly conservative statements, either one of them.

One must admit, however, that these writers' enemies have turned out to be right. Women's education *has* led to the neglect of household tasks and the decline of motherhood. Still, critics today would hardly venture to return to the most popular mid-nineteenth-century position on women's education, that of Mrs. Sarah Stickney Ellis, who claimed that no husband was ever happy that his wife could read Virgil without a dictionary and who urged that women be educated for "disinterested kindness."

In the great, if not the popular, novels of the nineteenth century, it is the search for self rather than selflessness that takes place, in contrast to the prevailing educational theory and in contrast also to literary genres other than the novel, where woman is child, animal, housemaid, angel, femme fatale—almost everything on the great chain of being except the human.

Yet in some respects, it is no surprise that woman's search for self becomes important in the nineteenth century, for as the Marxist critic George Lukacs says, once the outside world is no longer seen as the ground upon which the hero tests himself, then woman's soul becomes worthy of examination.

What happened in the novel is perhaps similar to what happened in Greek tragedy. According to classicist Werner Jaeger, once Sophocles revealed an interest in men's souls, it was only a matter of time before women's souls compelled interest as well. It seems possible, however, that among moderns, emphasis on the interiorization of women came first. Such, at least, is Madame de Staël's theory. It was women, says the baronness, who created an interest in private life, for they were allowed to explore it without limit. The advantage that the moderns thus have over the ancients is that of expressing a more delicate sensibility, a more various characterization because of a knowledge of the human heart, a knowledge that men owe to women. De Staël implies that women discovered the self.

Whatever its origins or the sex of its hero, the novel of education emerges at the time that the individual is no longer conceived of as static, a time when process and the inner life become valued over prescribed social roles.

Although most of the women in Austen's *Emma* fall into the Pamela tradition because of their economic dependence, Emma herself is already beginning to hint at the romantic importance of a woman's self. Having neither economic need nor romantic inclination, she eventually does consent to have her Knightley in shining armor. The question is why. Lionel Trilling rightly sees Emma as having a moral reality of her own unlike most women in fiction, and he recognizes her fault as "the classic one of hubris, which yields to the classic result of blindness," an inability to interpret experience realistically. When she realizes this, she quickly takes a husband to save her from self-destructive capacities. Whereas a traditional sign of manhood lies in the hero's ability to give up guides, the test of womanhood has resided in the heroine's ability to find a mentor. The male hero who sees the folly of his ways is allowed to correct himself, no matter what the cost in suffering. But Emma accepts a guide to lead her, after not suffering very much. It would seem that womankind cannot bear much reality. Although Emma marries for an educative reason, we do not see what happens to her after she makes her choice. Presumably, she will live happily ever after, like Pamela. Although Knightley notably enables her to retain the childhood home of her own, Emma ends up as dependent on men emotionally as the economically-deprived women of the novel are on men financially. But we must not commit the twentieth-century fallacy of finding such pedagogical dependence charmless, as Trilling points out elsewhere.

In large measure, the Pamela and Emma traditions are fused in *Jane Eyre.* The difference between the hero and heroine's social class and the reformation of the rake theme—pedagogical dependence may exist in males as well as females—are reminiscent of *Pamela.* However, *Jane Eyre* unlike *Pamela* is less about upward mobility in marriage than it is about the search for expanded experience. Brontë's work has often been labelled a moral tract, but one can hardly call the heroine's aims disinterestedly selfless. At Thornfield Hall, where Jane seeks a new life, after her miserable existence at Lowood, she speaks movingly of women's need for activity:

> It is vain to say human beings ought to be satisfied with tranquillity; they must have action; they will make it if they cannot find it. . . . Women feel just as men feel; they need exercise for their faculties and a field for their efforts as much as their brothers do; they suffer from too rigid a restraint, too absolute a stagnation, precisely as men would suffer; and it is narrow-minded in their more privileged fellow creatures to say that they ought to confine themselves to making puddings and knitting stockings, to playing on the piano and embroidering bags. It is thoughtless to condemn them, or laugh at them, if they seek to do more or learn more than custom has pronounced necessary for their sex.

Jane is attracted to Rochester, precisely because she is "weary of an existence all passive." Unlike romantic heroes who long for calm women, no doubt to provide some solace in their storm-tossed lives, romantic heroines and their real-life imitations veer towards the less safe choice in suitors, knowing that their only routes to activity and adventure lie in marital waters of some risk. The aims of men and women in marriage have been so opposed, one might say that marriage is an entirely different institution for the two sexes. While men, a Rochester, for example, have often expected marriage to root them into the social order, women, at least that type which I am here treating, have turned to marriage to achieve the goals of romantic individualism, those of increased knowledge, enhancement of feeling and experience, and precisely those dangers and adventures that men seek through marriage to escape. It is only through a male intermediary that women could attain such pleasures. This is the reason why, for all her ostensible independence and freedom of mind, Jane's world falls apart when her first engagement to Rochester does. All paths to her future development now seem closed. The fact that they are not indicates that Brontë was already transcending the rules of the genre even before they were firmly established.

After discovering that Rochester is still married to a mad woman, Jane goes on a solitary journey which brings her, rain-drenched and starving, to Marsh End. This heroine is already light years away from the socially protected Emma. Her journey, which is not so much inside as on the periphery of society, brings her knowledge as well as suffering. Rochester, too, comes to a new awareness though he remains at Thornfield Hall. The passive hero and the active heroine seem to represent a reversal of more usual literary tradition. And here Brontë underscores a brilliant perception. Unlike the male heroes of the medieval romance, for example, who go forth to encounter the monsters of sexuality that they fear, the heroine here must confront a "monster" of spirituality, St. John, whom she conquers after much temptation. Spenser offers something of a precedent here, for St. John represents false chastity. Even more important, Spenser in the *Faerie Queene* had reinforced a Renaissance convention that becomes a major theme in the novel tradition, that of the female quest for the male. Like Spenser's Britomart, although less deliberately, Jane is searching for the right man to marry. He is not the bloodless St. John but rather a reformed Rochester.

Unlike the lady of the chivalric romance who had merely to sit still in order to find a destiny in the form of some passing knight, modern woman must seek her own hero. The development of the self through marriage involves many trials, for assuredly finding the right man to be one's tutor/lover is far more difficult and dangerous an undertaking than finding the right university.

There is something else to notice as well. Although the heroines in this tradition of education through marriage look to wedlock as the primary means of educating and developing the self, they often reveal a high degree of self-development before they marry. Their very accomplishments are designed to win them the kind of mate who will finish their education. Jane is a case in point. She develops enormously, even when unmarried, particularly in the second part of the novel, where like the other heroines of this tradition, she even comes to a measure of economic independence without which she could not marry in psychological comfort. Like the male hero of the *bildungsroman,* she grows by going out into the world on her own, but the ultimate aim of her development is not life within the larger community as it is for the male hero, but rather marriage with the partner of her choice.

Some years later in another country, another dark lady—this time a beauty (Brontë is as down on beauty as any male misogynist)—does not fare as well. Like Jane Eyre, Madame Bovary is unwilling to sacrifice herself to "disinterested kindness" and seeks a self of her own. Because of this, she is often called selfish. Sainte-Beuve asks why she could not find a meaningful course of action in being useful to others or in loving her child. But why should she? Would a man who trained to be a doctor, a man who worked assiduously towards that end for which he had a gift (I do not speak here of a Charles Bovary, who was merely a hack), would such a man give up the idea of a career with calm? Emma Bovary had been training for one thing all her life. Why should she accept not achieving it?

What does Madame Bovary want? The panorama of mountains and sea, fishing villages and gondolas is only one of her dreams— the setting for one type of lover; although less prominent and often forgotten by readers, she has another dream of a man who need not be handsome or elegant or charming provided he be brilliant. Her desire is for intensity, for a heightening of experience, either through the route of the senses or through the vicarious awareness of someone else's intellectual life. In either case, a man was necessary for the fulfillment of the dream. It isn't even that the "selfish" Madame Bovary wants to be loved. What she wants is to give love to a man who is worthy of her. All her formal education (which consisted in large part of reading romantic novels), her accomplishments—the piano playing, drawing, embroidering—all her style, elegance and taste are directed towards this one end. Her type is still with us, and every little princess can say along with Flaubert, "Madame Bovary, c'est moi." Emma Bovary's entire life is taken up by the fantasy of Monsieur Right, so that even after she has made the choice (and it is pathetic how little choice she has in the one event towards which her whole being has been directed—her father answers for her and Flaubert doesn't even let us know what she is thinking at the moment that Charles asks for her hand), she is still searching. No! The selfishness must lie elsewhere than in Madame Bovary.

How many critics find her stupid. She is educated beyond her opportunities, say some, and beyond her intelligence say others. One might counter and say that she is not educated enough, and therefore she would seem to prove that the older Mme. Bovary is not so ludicrous when she suggests as a cure for Emma's nervous disorders that she be kept away from books. As long as books arouse expectations that have no means of fulfillment, they can only increase melancholy and frustration. Unless they are read with discipline as well as passion, they will become a poison.

Madame Bovary's problem was that she was educated to be one thing only—a seductress to her husband. In fact, Mme. Bovary lives out Rousseau's prescriptions for the ideal woman, and in doing so she fulfills Wollstonecraft's prophecy that a woman educated to be a seductress to her husband would end up an adulteress with someone else.

Flaubert had thought of situating Emma in Paris, and we might well ask why he didn't do so. After all, what opportunities could she have had, being stuck in the provinces? Yet one suspects that Emma in Paris would have had the same fate as many a single girl who runs to the city today. She becomes the target of every roué, at least Emma's type does.

The French critic Thibaudet finds it a stroke of bad luck that Emma has a daughter instead of a son. Bad luck or not, Flaubert's reasons for Emma's disappointment are more acute than Freud's are in analyzing similar responses. It is not that Madame Bovary wants a penis between her legs. Rather she wanted a male child so that she could participate vicariously in what her culture did not allow her to experience directly. "A man is free, at least—free to range the passions and the world, to surmount obstacles, to taste the rarest pleasure," she exclaims. One might ask *which* men, for certainly this does not apply to Charles. Unlike her husband, Emma cannot be satisfied with a vision of domestic pleasures for little Berthe. It is not that the mother is selfish so much as that she is in despair, for the one means of gaining experience through the marriage, for achieving identity, is denied her, and although this is never stated directly, perhaps she is in despair for her child too.

It is testimony to the existential reality of Mme. Bovary that the question, "What does Mme. Bovary want?" has been answered so variously and with so much conviction by so many readers. For the reader today, the salient problem is perhaps that of identity. When Mme. Bovary doesn't find what she wants in marriage, namely a god who could initiate her into passion and instruct her in life's pleasures, she turns outside it. What she learns from her lovers must still be considered

education through marriage, however, for without that institution, respectable women could not take lovers.

As part of his plan for seduction, Rodolphe says, "Madame Bovary! Everyone calls you that, and it's not your name at all. It's somebody else's. Somebody else's." For all his deceptions and conniving, he has hit on the central problem of Emma's existence, that of autonomy. (The success of the seducer often lies in his awareness, his sensitivity in fact to the other person's needs, which he then manipulates to his own advantage.) Rodolphe speaks these lines to make her feel that she is her own person and can therefore turn to him with impunity, and probably he means also to imply that he would like her to have his name. This, of course, is a ruse, but he does strike the right notes. Emma yields to him because she needs him to give her an identity, having rejected that of the bovine Charles Bovary.

In his endearments Rodolphe calls her a madonna and angle, but he thinks of her as a carp on a kitchen table, gasping for water. This counterpoint is a brilliant example of Flaubert's undercutting of the romantic ideal, but it is not Flaubert's dichotomy alone. The madonna and carp images may be seen as illustrative of much of woman's condition in the Western world. Within Christianity, she has either been the exalted, desexualized mother on a pedestal or the vulnerable object dependent for her very breath on the male. Yet one must also grant that Mme. Bovary's concept of experience would have resulted in her destruction even had she been a male. Flaubert himself said that the Bovarian problem transcends sex. A male Bovary would have struck a Faustian bargain. Yet there is a difference. Traditionally, for women, at least since Eve, the devil has merely been the husband or the lover and not the real thing, for it is to the husband or his imago that the woman is to entrust her soul. Thus women's fall as well as their development has been vicarious.

Of all the heroines that I treat, it is Dorothea Brooke in *Middlemarch* who most consciously seeks an intellectual development through marriage. Ironically, it is a sensuous development alone that she ultimately finds. Dorothea envisages a husband as an awesome tutor/parent. "The really delightful marriage must be that where your husband was a sort of father, and could teach you even Hebrew, if you wished it." Of her impending marriage to Casaubon, who is twenty-seven years her senior, she says, "I should not wish to have a husband very near my own age. . . . I should wish to have a husband who was above me in judgment and in knowledge." Eliot adds, "The union which attracted Dorothea was one that would deliver her from her girlish subjection to her own ignorance, and give her the freedom of voluntary submission to a guide she would take along the grandest path."

For Dorothea, "after that toy-box history of the world adapted to young ladies which had made the chief part of her education, Mr. Casaubon's talk about his great book was full of new vistas." But she doesn't find the "large vistas and wide fresh air which she dreamed of finding in her husband's mind but rather winding passages that seemed to lead nowhere."

Her awareness that he has nothing to offer intellectually is coupled with an awareness that he has nothing to offer in response to her feeling. One of the fascinating aspects of the search for knowledge through marriage is the unity of intellect and feeling that women envisage. But the unity is not realized:

> Her blooming full-pulsed youth stood there in a moral
> imprisonment which made itself one with the chill,
> colorless narrowed landscape, with the shrunken fur-

niture, the never-read books, and the ghostly stag in
a pale fantastic world that seemed to be vanishing
from the daylight.

It is testimony to Eliot's sensitivity that she presents not only
Dorothea's view. For Casaubon too, the marriage is a failure:
"the young creature who had worshipped him with perfect
trust had quickly turned into the critical wife; and early instances of criticism and resentment had made an impression
which no tenderness and submission afterwards could remove."

His is a revealing statement of why marriage for education so
seldom works. It is because "intellectual approbation . . . always involves a possible reserve of latent censure. A man—
poet, prophet, or whatever he may be—readily persuades himself of his right to all the worship that is voluntarily tendered."
So Hawthorne had written in *The Blithedale Romance.* The
words apply equally here.

Dorothea's first marriage is a disappointment to both parties.
But unlike the traditional male novel's solution to the problem,
in *Middlemarch,* it is not the wife but the husband, whose
theory "was already withered in the birth like an elfin child,"
that dies. His cousin, the young sensuous Will, becomes Dorothea's second husband. He would have been her adulterous
lover in continental tradition. Presumably, he is able to instruct
her in matters of feeling if not in those of intellect. But as for
Dorothea and her aspirations, we read, "Many who knew her,
thought it a pity that so substantive and rare a creature should
have been absorbed into the life of another, and be only known
in a certain circle as a wife and mother." But, as Eliot goes
on to say, "no one stated exactly what else that was in her
power she ought to have done." "For there is no creature
whose inward being is so strong that it is not greatly determined
by what lies outside it." Eliot, who has the range of a Tolstoy,
is much more consciously aware than he is, of the restrictions
of the social order on women. As Eliot points out in more than
one reference, nineteenth-century England ironically offered
fewer opportunities to Dorothea than did sixteenth-century Spain
to Saint Teresa. Notably, none of the authors that I consider . . .
saw fit to treat a heroine who was a writer, but then one must
add that few women authors deal with writers as heroines even
in the twentieth century. It is as if women have not yet achieved
the sense of self required to treat the artist as a young woman.
The one striking early exception is Mme. de Staël's *Corinne,*
whose heroine significantly refuses to marry, as if recognizing
even in 1807 that a true development of the self cannot take
place vicariously.

But most heroines are willing to give up all for love, for love
is seen as the great developer of the self. (pp. 335-47)

To my knowledge, which is admittedly fallen, the only woman
within the Western corpus of beliefs who sought knowledge
directly without the intermediary of a man, the figure who
could be the prototype of the feminine rite of passage, is Eve.
But part of her post-lapsarian punishment is that her desire
shall be to her husband, and ever after husbands have been
intermediaries.

It is only relatively recently in literary and cultural history that
critics of the vicarious life have emerged on the scene. It is
testimony to the boldness of his thought that Kierkegaard in
his *Concept of Dread* blames Eve for seeking support beyond
herself, in man. Thus his position is essentially the same as
that of current liberationists. In Hegelian terms, the consciousness of feminine consciousness has only become perceptible
at this time.

A portrait of Charles Dickens.

In "Leda and the Swan," Yeats brilliantly poses the question
of the relationship of sexuality, knowledge and power:

> Being so caught up,
> So mastered by the brute blood of the air,
> Did she put on his knowledge with his power
> Before the indifferent beak could let her drop?

As we view the central problems of gender relationships today,
it seems to us that not only did Leda not put on Zeus's knowledge, she did not put on his power. To be raped is not to have
greatness thrust upon one and though it may be our limitation,
we no longer consider it power to point to one's twins in pride.
We feel that a true development cannot be vicarious. One has
to have it oneself.

This is why traditional criticism may in fact be right. The
authentic feminine *bildungsroman* is still to be written. In validating the search for the self, the novels I have been treating
were not supportive of the status quo as some feminists claim,
but rather, incipient revolutionary statements. However, insofar as their heroines' development remained inextricably linked
to marriage, these works were less *bildungsromans* than *bildungsromans manqués.* (pp. 356-57)

*Elaine Hoffman Baruch, "The Feminine 'Bildungs-
roman': Education through Marriage," in* The Massachusetts Review, *Vol. XXII, No. 2, Summer, 1981,
pp. 335-57.*

CHARLOTTE GOODMAN

[*Goodman posits a theoretical framework for what she terms the
"male-female* Bildungsroman" *and suggests that Brontë's* Wuth-

ering Heights *and Eliot's* The Mill on the Floss *fit the pattern she describes.*]

Although the *Bildungsroman*, or novel of development, has been a genre of long-standing interest to literary scholars, critics have begun only recently to draw distinctions between *Bildungsromane* written by men and *Bildungsromane* written by women—or, indeed, to give any sustained attention to the *Bildungsromane* by women. Certainly, in discussing the historical evolution of the *Bildungsroman*, critics frequently refer to a few selected works by women, among them, perhaps, Charlotte Brontë's *Jane Eyre* or George Eliot's *The Mill on the Floss*. However, usually beginning with a discussion of Goethe's *Wilhelm Meister*, the majority of studies of the *Bildungsroman* not only focus almost entirely on novels written by males about male protagonists, but also define the genre in terms that apply exclusively to male experience. This is true, for example, of Jerome Buckley's recent study of the English *Bildungsroman, Season of Youth* [see excerpt above]. As defined by Buckley, the typical plot of the *Bildungsroman* concerns a sensitive male child who grows up in a provincial environment where he finds constraints placed upon his imaginative life. According to Buckley, the *Bildungsroman* explores the young man's progressive alienation from his family; his schooling; his departure from home; his sexual initiation; and his ultimate assessment of life's possibilities. It is true that Buckley does devote one chapter of his study to George Eliot's *The Mill on the Floss*, but the remainder of the study deals largely with novels by male writers about male protagonists, including *David Copperfield, Great Expectations, Richard Feverel, The Way of All Flesh, Marius the Epicurean, Jude the Obscure, Tono Bungay, Sons and Lovers, Portrait of the Artist as a Young Man, Of Human Bondage*, and *Free Fall*.

The fact that Buckley bases his generalizations about the *Bildungsroman* almost entirely on novels written by male novelists about male protagonists leads one to ask whether, in fact, these observations would apply equally as well to the *Bildungsromane* written by women. In their brilliant study of a group of nineteenth-century women writers, *The Madwoman in the Attic*, Sandra M. Gilbert and Susan Gubar argue persuasively that confronted by male hegemony, nineteenth-century women writers characteristically both followed and in significant ways departed from male-defined literary genres. Coining the phrase "anxiety of authorship" (as opposed to Harold Bloom's "anxiety of influence") to describe the feelings of vulnerability experienced by women writers in a patriarchal culture, Gilbert and Gubar suggest that some women writers "may have attempted to transcend their anxiety of authorship by *revising* male genres, using them to record their own dreams and their own stories *in disguise*." The observations of Gilbert and Gubar, as well as those of Elaine Showalter in *A Literature of Their Own* and Ellen Moers in *Literary Women*, strongly suggest the existence of distinctively female literary traditions which both conform to and in significant ways depart from prevailing male literary modes. If the assumptions of these feminist literary critics are correct, then one would expect to find significant differences between the *Bildungsromane* written by men and those written by women, especially since, as Buckley and others have pointed out, the *Bildungsroman* frequently draws upon autobiographical material. In a patriarchal culture where the "education" of males and the "education" of females is so vastly different, surely the *Bildungsromane* which male and female novelists respectively write would be very different.

Several critics, in fact, have suggested recently that there are significant differences between those *Bildungsromane* written by men and those written by women. For example, in her discussion of a number of nineteenth-century *Bildungsromane*, Elaine Hoffmann Baruch has observed that while the ultimate aim of a male protagonist in such novels is life within the larger community, the aim of the female protagonist of the *Bildungsroman* is marriage with a partner of her choice [see excerpt above]. Additionally, Annis Pratt maintains, "If there is a 'myth of the hero' there must also be a 'myth of the heroine,' a female as well as a male *Bildungsroman*, parallel, perhaps, but by no means identical." According to Pratt and Barbara White, one important difference between the *Bildungsroman* as written by men and the *Bildungsroman* as written by women is that the female protagonist

> does not *choose* a life to one side of society after conscious deliberation on the subject; rather, she is ontologically or radically alienated by gender-role norms from the *very outset*. Thus, although the authors attempt to accommodate their heroes' *bildung* or development to the general pattern of the genre, the disjunctions we have noticed inevitably make of the woman's initiation less a self-determined progression *toward* maturity than a regression *from* full participation in adult life.

It is worth noting, as Bonnie Hoover Braendlin has done, that the feminist movement of the nineteen-sixties and seventies has of late given rise to a number of feminist *Bildungsromane* which more closely approximate the male model of the *Bildungsroman* in their delineation of the education, reassessment, rebellion, and departure of their respective female protagonists. However, prior to the present most women authors created female protagonists who, like Charlotte Brontë's Jane Eyre, eventually accept their role as wife and mother—or end up either mad, like Sylvia Plath's Esther Greenwood, or suicides, like Kate Chopin's Edna Pontellier. (pp. 28-30)

[Emily Brontë's *Wuthering Heights* and George Eliot's *The Mill on the Floss*] clearly differ from the prototypical male *Bildungsroman*, for instead of tracing the growth and development of a single protagonist as the usual *Bildungsroman* does, they describe the evolution of a pair of protagonists, one male, the other female. The term I shall employ to describe this kind of *Bildungsroman* is "the male-female double *Bildungsroman*." While I hardly can claim that these . . . novels by women constitute a major literary tradition, I believe they are worth considering . . . nevertheless because they differ significantly in design from the typical male *Bildungsroman* that Buckley and other critics have discussed. Though female characters sometimes play an important role in male *Bildungsromane* by helping the hero to define his own identity as they do in *Sons and Lovers* and *Portrait of the Artist as a Young Man*, for example, there is no question who the real hero is. In contrast, the women novelists whom I shall consider here place virtually equal emphasis on both a male and a female protagonist in a given novel, contrasting thereby the "education" of males and of females.

The male-female double *Bildungsroman* differs significantly from the prototypical *Bildungsroman* not only with regard to its principal characters but also with regard to structure. Normally linear in design, the typical male *Bildungsroman* begins in childhood and progresses toward the moment when the mature adult, having cast off the restraints of his/her earlier life, faces the future. However, the design of the male-female double *Bildungsroman* is circular; tripartite in structure, it describes the shared childhood experience of a male and a female protagonist who inhabit a place somewhat reminiscent of a prelapsarian mythic garden world where the male and female once existed as equals; then such novels dramatize the separation of the male and the female character in adolescence and young adulthood as the male, like the hero of the typical male *Bildungsroman,* journeys forth to seek his fortune, while the female is left behind; and finally, the novels conclude with a reunion of the male and the female protagonist. I believe the reunion of the male and the female protagonist with which each novel concludes signifies a turning away from mature adult experience and a reaffirmation of the childhood world in which the male and the female protagonist were undivided.

The double form of the *Bildungsroman,* with its focus on both a male and a female protagonist, appears to be particularly congenial to the woman novelist who wishes to emphasize the way in which a society that rigidly differentiates between male and female gender roles limits the full development of women and men alike. Recalling the primordial myth of an androgynous past recorded in the sacred traditions of primitive people, the male-female double *Bildungsroman* dramatizes the limitations imposed on both the male and the female protagonist in a patriarchal society where androgynous wholeness no longer is possible. Unusually close, the paired male and female protagonist in each of these novels appear to function as psychological "doubles," for each character is intensely involved in the psychic life of his or her counterpart. Each character may also embody a separate aspect of the author's own psychic life, the female character representing the author's identification with those women who have been forced to conform to traditional female gender roles, the male character, the author's desire for learning, power, mobility, autonomy. Together the male and the female character suggest the possibility of androgynous wholeness, a state imaginable only in a mythic prelapsarian world of nature before a patriarchal culture gained ascendancy. Offering a critique of a patriarchal society in which gender roles are rigidly defined, the male-female double *Bildungsroman,* then, traces the way in which a harmonious and balanced androgynous self is fractured by a culture which assigns radically different roles to males and females. Only in the final scene of each novel is the fragmentation of the self momentarily healed as the male and the female protagonist are reunited.

The prototype for the male-female double *Bildungsroman* was established in the nineteenth century by Emily Brontë's *Wuthering Heights.* Though *Wuthering Heights* has usually been classified generically as a female Gothic novel, the section of the novel which deals with the growth and development of Catherine and Heathcliff also has certain generic affinities with the *Bildungsroman.* Telling both Catherine's story and Heathcliff's, the novel describes their shared childhood, their separation in adolescence and young adulthood, and their final reunion.

From the moment that Heathcliff is brought to Wuthering Heights by Catherine's father, the young foundling and Catherine become inseparable companions. "They both promised fair to grow up as rude as savages," remarks the housekeeper Nelly Dean. Preferring the world of nature to the world of culture, Catherine and Heathcliff conclude that the true "heaven" resembles not the Linton's elegant drawing room at Thrushcross Grange, as they first believed, but the outdoor world of the moors where, free from the constraints of culture, the female young lady of the manor and the "gypsy brat" can exist as equals.

While the first part of *Wuthering Heights* rapturously celebrates the shared childhood of Catherine and Heathcliff, the second part dramatizes their separation. As soon as Catherine's education for her adult life as a "lady" begins at Thrushcross Grange, she and Heathcliff are divided not only by the physical distance between Wuthering Heights and Thrushcross Grange but by the gender roles Catherine and Heathcliff must assume. Bitten by the Lintons' dog and taken by them into Thrushcross Grange to recuperate from her injury, Catherine becomes transformed from the independent girl who formerly ran barefoot on the moors with Heathcliff into a delicate young lady who has her feet washed by a woman servant and then, with her feet enveloped in a pair of enormous slippers, is wheeled to the fireside to feed on the rich food of the Lintons. These images of entrapment and enfeeblement powerfully suggest the way in which the vital natural energies of Catherine will be sapped when she is assimilated into the cultured Linton world. As Gilbert and Gubar point out in their illuminating discussion of the novel, this scene conjures up some "sinister ritual of initiation, the sort of ritual that has traditionally weakened mythic heroines from Persephone to Snow White." When Catherine returns home to Wuthering Heights after a five week stay at Thrushcross Grange, she is dressed in the elegant and confining clothes of a lady, and she is reluctant to kiss the flour-besmeared Nelly or to shake hand with the grimy Heathcliff because she fears she will soil her fingers, now "wonderfully whitened with doing nothing and staying indoors." Soon after, when Catherine becomes Edgar Linton's wife, her "bildung" or education is over. Brontë depicts Catherine's married life in terms of entrapment, progressive mental deterioration, and increasing physical disability, until Catherine dies, as did so many women of Brontë's day, in childbirth.

It is Heathcliff rather than Catherine who sets forth on the typical journey of the hero of the male *Bildungsroman* from the country to the city to be educated and to make his fortune. Not really interested in describing in detail the events which transform the ragged Heathcliff into a gentleman, events that usually comprise the center of the male *Bildungsroman,* Brontë notes the evolution of Heathcliff from ragged waif to rich and educated gentleman in but a few sentences. What she chooses to focus on is the way that Heathcliff subsequently does battle with the world that cast him out and changed his beloved Catherine from a robust companion into a passive lady, then an invalid, and finally a corpse.

The tripartite structure of this male-female double *Bildungsroman* is completed in *Wuthering Heights* when Heathcliff and Catherine finally are reunited. Their reconciliation begins several hours before Catherine dies in childbirth but is not really concluded until Heathcliff dies many years later. "*Wuthering Heights,* acknowledging the necessity for growing up, is a prolonged cry of anguish at the necessity," writes Patricia Meyer Spacks. The dead Heathcliff's eyes are said to express "exultation," for only in death can he and Catherine be reunited.

In her double *Bildungsroman, The Mill on the Floss,* George Eliot also describes the shared childhood, the adolescent separation, and the final reunion of a male and a female protagonist. Jerome Buckley, who calls his chapter on Eliot's novel "A Double Life," attributes her use of a double protagonist at least in part to Eliot's own relationship to her brother Isaac, and the same might be true of Emily Brontë's relationship to her brother Branwell. However, I would like to point out that many male writers had sisters, but none that I know of wrote a male-female double *Bildungsroman.* Though *Wuthering*

Heights is essentially mythic in design while *The Mill on the Floss* is firmly grounded in the conventions of literary realism, both works appear to have sprung from a common source: the imperative need of Emily Brontë, who assumed the male pseudonym Ellis Bell, and of Mary Ann Evans, who assumed the male pseudonym George Eliot, to dramatize in their respective novels the tragic fragmentation which growing up entails, particularly for creative, energetic girls whose education perforce trains them to subdue their aggressive instincts and to conform to the narrowly defined female roles assigned to them by a patriarchal society, while their male counterparts are free to journey into the larger world.

Like Catherine and Heathcliff, Eliot's Maggie and Tom Tulliver inhabit a garden world in childhood, until they are forced to pass through what Eliot calls the "golden gates." As Gilbert and Gubar have observed, Eliot's view of their childhood is hardly as blissful as Brontë's vision of the early years of Catherine and Heathcliff, for Tom, who has already entered the world of culture at the beginning of the novel, returns home to lord it over his sister and to point out his superiority to her because he is a male. Nevertheless, when Eliot describes the young Tom and Maggie sharing a piece of cake or rubbing each other's brows and nose like "two ponies" (Book I, Ch.V), or when she refers to "the golden gates" of childhood, she suggests a prelapsarian stage in Tom and Maggie's early life when they were very close. All too soon, however, Maggie and Tom are separated by their respective educational experiences. Significantly, Tom's classical education is described in great detail, whereas Maggie's experience at Miss Firniss's boarding school for young ladies is dismissed with a single sentence. As Mary Jacobus has noted, Tom's education is not only more intellectually challenging than Maggie's but it is also explicitly antifeminist. Maggie and Tom are driven even further apart when their father is financially ruined. Eliot emphasizes how limited Maggie's vocational possibilities are compared to Tom's. Whereas Tom's rise in trade is carefully documented by Eliot, Maggie's work experience as a teacher in a "third-rate schoolroom, with all its jarring sounds and petty rounds of tasks" is, like Maggie's schooling, very briefly recounted (Book VI, Chapter II). Clearly, Maggie's work as a teacher of young girls counts for little in the bustling, mercantile world of St. Ogg's.

Much has been written about the "deux ex machina" conclusion of *The Mill on the Floss* which describes the drowning of Maggie and Tom in a flood. In contrast to the "Reader, I married him" ending that Patricia Beer says is typical of many nineteenth-century novels, Eliot has Maggie marry neither Philip Wakem, who appeals to Maggie's intellect, nor Stephen Guest, to whom she is sexually attracted. Instead, as Nancy K. Miller recently has noted, George Eliot eschews the traditional plot ending of novels by women and throws Maggie into the cold river rather than into her lover's warm embrace. While this ending fails to conform to the usual novelistic pattern, however, it does conform to the pattern of the male-female double *Bildungsroman* that Brontë initiated, for the flood is the instrument by which Maggie and Tom are reunited in this novel. Previously, when Maggie almost eloped with her cousin Lucy's fiancé, Stephen Guest, a furious and vindictive Tom had accused Maggie of disgracing the family name, and refusing to offer his sister asylum under his roof, he had declared, "I wash my hands of you forever" (Book VII, Chapter I). So great is the emotional rupture between Maggie and Tom that it is only a cataclysmic event like the flood that is capable of reuniting them. With the flood, the pattern of the male-female double

Bildungsroman is completed, as the male and the female protagonist are joined once again. It is significant that the formerly passive Maggie, who was "borne along by the tide" as she joined Stephen Guest in a boat, now becomes an active agent by rowing a boat herself to rescue her brother Tom. At the moment of Maggie and Tom's death, Eliot tells us, they are returned to the days of their childhood when "they had clasped their little hands in love and roamed the daisy fields together" (Book VII, Chapter V). Maudlin though it may be, this passage calls attention to the evanescent harmony of a prelapsarian, pre-patriarchal, pastoral world where the male and the female were undivided. (pp. 30-4)

For women authors in the nineteenth century, choosing to be a serious writer was an aggressive act, defying prescribed gender roles and norms. This is still largely true of women writers today. As Gilbert and Gubar point out, the female artist, in particular, frequently suffers from "loneliness . . . feelings of alienation from male predecessors coupled with her need of sisterly precursors and successors." She experiences an "urgent sense of her need for a female audience together with her fear of the antagonism of male readers. . . ." Looking for a seemingly conventional form in which to cast their fictions without arousing "the antagonism of male readers," Emily Brontë [and] George Eliot . . . apparently found the genre of the *Bildungsroman* adaptable to their purposes. Yet by doubling the protagonist and thus comparing male and female experience, they radically altered or subverted the genre, offering a critique of patriarchy, whose values the male *Bildungsroman* supports. As Elaine Showalter has suggested about women writers in general, the novelists . . . may have channeled their own aggressiveness and desire for autonomy into their male characters. More typical of women in a patriarchal society, however, their female characters conform to socially sanctioned female roles which severely limit their possibilities. In each of these novels both the male and the female protagonist are finally shown to be incomplete, their lives restricted and damaged by the narrowly defined gender roles they have had to play. The underlying structure of union, separation, and return which I have identified as the salient feature of the . . . male-female double *Bildungsromane* emphasizes the dichotomy between male and female experience in a patriarchal culture. In childhood, the male and the female protagonists are unusually close, appearing together in an environment evoking, however faintly, an Edenic androgynous world. In adolescence, however, when culture replaces nature and sexual differentiation occurs, the male journeys forth, as does the typical hero of the single *Bildungsroman*, while the female protagonist is forced to remain close to home or in an enclosed and limited environment. As I have suggested, the conclusion of the male-female double *Bildungsroman* differs most significantly from that of the traditional *Bildungsroman*: instead of facing the future, as do the protagonists of the more conventional *Bildungsromane*, the male protagonist returns to the world of his childhood by embracing his female counterpart, allowing the male and the female halves of the divided self to be joined once again. As "brother" and "sister" are reunited at the end of each of these novels, the reader is made aware of the radically different kind of "education" each has undergone; only in this final meeting is the fragmentation of the androgynous self healed through the alchemy of the author's art. (pp. 42-3)

[The] *Bildungsromane* I have considered here articulate the longing for the "brother lost." They also indicate envy of his male prerogatives and express a desire to join him in his adventures. But Cathy and Heathcliff are reunited only in death;

Maggie and Tom, when they are drowned. . . . In the world which Brontë [and] Eliot . . . describe in their respective double *Bildungsromane*, ''androgyny'' is not possible, and the ''dream of a common language'' between the male and the female protagonist, tragically, remains unrealized. (p. 43)

> Charlotte Goodman, ''The Lost Brother, the Twin: Women Novelists and the Male-Female Double 'Bildungsroman','' in *Novel: A Forum on Fiction, Vol. 17, No. 1, Fall, 1983, pp. 28-43.*

BEVERLY R. VOLOSHIN

[*Voloshin comments on several nineteenth-century American female* Bildungsromane, *noting their shared emphasis on the conflict between domestic duties and the need to prove oneself in a man's world.*]

During the nineteenth century in the United States there emerged a new mass market for fiction—fiction which both shaped and was shaped by the attitudes and desires of its audience. Since much of this fiction of the middle decades of the century was written and read by women and pertained especially to female experience, modern scholars have analyzed women's popular fiction of the period, often labelled domestic or sentimental fiction, principally for its direct and symbolic statements about women and social organization, generally finding this fiction either deeply conservative with respect to woman's role or subversive of or antithetical to conservative values. Both judgments are accurate: I propose here to show that in a significant group of novels there is, precisely, a conflict about woman's role and that this conflict reflects the larger ideological situation of the period.

The novels I examine are of the type which Nina Baym categorizes in her useful study, *Woman's Fiction: A Guide to Novels by and about Women in America, 1820-1870.* Her subject is what we might call the female *Bildungsroman.* Baym excludes some of the women's novels of the period, such as those of Harriet Beecher Stowe, to focus on the most common sort of story. As she writes, ''In essence, it is the story of a young girl who is deprived of the supports she rightly or wrongly depended on to sustain her throughout life and is faced with the necessity of winning her own way in the world'' until the happy marriage at the conclusion of the novel. Though the domestic ideal of the period is praised in these novels, the novels also value the opposing ideal of female independence and equality. The conflict between domestic patterns and other expectations and desires, generally less overtly expressed, is central to the meaning of this fiction and is understandable in terms of nineteenth-century culture.

In American culture, the question of woman's place was far from being a settled issue. While domestic duties were becoming peripheral to economic life, Victorian culture in America glorified the role of woman as homemaker and idealized the moral influence of wives and mothers. Women, though increasingly isolated in the home, had a compensatory influence over the behavior of family members. The man's sphere of business, seen as appetitive and amoral, could be balanced and held in check by woman's love and moral tutelage in her sphere, the home. In a period when traditional kinship groups were breaking up because of westward migration and industrialization and when the nation was anxious about social instability resulting from individualism and acquisitive business practices, the home and its new ruler came to be accepted as the stabilizing force in society.

But this split in the functions of men and women, perceived to give stability to society, was itself unstable; for the natural rights theory which sanctioned the economic and political freedoms of the common man implicitly guaranteed, as the early woman's rights supporters pointed out, the same freedoms for the common woman. Given this democratic ideological premise and given the fact that the nineteenth century witnessed the shrinking of the number of occupations open to women and their increasing restriction to the home, it is not surprising that even women not associated with the women's movement should have chafed at the confines of the domestic role. The ideology of domesticity, then, existed in a state of tension with other values of the dominant culture. The popular female *Bildungsroman* gives evidence of the tension between the values of domesticity and the opposing values of independence and equality, even for those authors and readers who ostensibly accepted the domestic ideal. (pp. 283-84)

In these novels of female development, the heroine's rebellions against the domestic role are of two kinds, her attempts to be independent and her hostility to male power. The heroines are intent on developing self-discipline and self-reliance and on finding occupations which allow them to define and support themselves. Though there is almost no explicit criticism of marriage and of the domestic role in these works, the heroine is, typically, eager to educate herself and is not eager to marry. She puts her education to financial use by working as a governess, teacher, or author, until she at last accepts the hero's marriage proposal. While the heroine's independence is necessary to her own development and sense of worth and thereby to her ability to choose a good husband, her interest in having a significant vocation and in being independent is also a temporary rejection of the domestic role, an attempt not to rely on men for financial support or for self-definition.

In addition to the heroine's endeavour to achieve financial and emotional independence, she is typically hostile to male authority, sometimes openly defying it and sometimes taming it. The heroine may defy her male benefactor, who tries to keep her in the status of dependent, and leave his household, thus diminishing his domestic power. Taming the male is a way for women to increase their power in the domestic realm. Protagonists and other women characters in these novels sometimes use their role as spiritual guardian to temper male behavior; the heroine or another woman may exercise an influence over the heroine's prospective husband which guarantees his docility and his sexual faithfulness to the heroine. Woman's influence is used strategically here, not only for the good of others, as the ideology of domesticity would suggest, but also for woman's security. Thus, though the novels finally accept marriage and the legal and economic subordination of the wife to the husband, they qualify the power of the husband. Hence, the dependence on men which the heroine has attempted to reject is purged of its liabilities by the end of the novel, and the conclusion often recontains, at least partly, the heroine's expressions of dissatisfaction with the limitations of domesticity.

Analysis of five popular novels, chosen for my purposes but nonetheless representative of this genre, shows the strain between expressed approval of domestic values and more covert interest in the opposing values of female independence and equality. These novels, spanning the period of the female *Bildungsroman,* are Catharine Sedgwick's *A New-England Tale* (1822), the first exemplar of this genre; Susan Warner's *The Wide, Wide World* (1850), the first spectacular best-seller of the mid-century; Maria Susanna Cummins' *The Lamplighter*

(1854), the popular novel which Hawthorne singled out for invective in his famous diatribe against the "scribbling women"; and Augusta Jane Evans' *Beulah* (1859) and her novel of 1867, *St. Elmo*, which marks the virtual end of the genre.

Catharine Sedgwick's *A New-England Tale*, first of her four novels of female development, initiated this narrative form in the United States. In line with her didacticism, Sedgwick in *A New-England Tale* intends to create a model of womanhood and to define the functions of home. One of the articulators of the ideal of domesticity, Sedgwick pictures a culture which is woman-centered; character, Sedgwick claims, derives primarily from nurture, and the responsibility for providing proper nurture falls to women. The main source of virtuous behavior is thus not civic and religious institutions, the public world of men, but the private world of women.

But in showing the importance of home, Sedgwick gives us the story of an orphan heroine who must live for several years apart from a good home, relying primarily on her own strength and on her early moral training. With the story of the orphan heroine, Sedgwick can underscore the centrality of the domestic ideal to her view of good character and a good society while interesting the reader in a protagonist who is much freer of the restraints of domesticity than most young women. Like the novelists who follow her, Sedgwick thus taps the best of two worlds, the security of the cult of domesticity and the excitement of the radical gesture for independence, given its institutional form a little later in the century in the woman's rights movement.

A New-England Tale is the story of Jane Elton. Jane's father, a businessman of shallow character, lives beyond his means, and when he goes bankrupt, he suffers what we would now regard as a nervous breakdown and dies of a violent fever. Jane's mother, less concerned with wealth than with goodness, has given Jane vigilant and judicious training; but Mrs. Elton has her own flaw, a certain passivity, an inability to take hold of her life in her unsatisfactory marriage and then in her widowhood. True to the logic of her character, Mrs. Elton dies soon after her husband, and Jane is left an orphan in the care of her mean and hypocritical Calvinist aunt. Her aunt and cousins abuse Jane, yet she never deviates from the path of right. The question, of course, becomes what Jane will do with herself in young adulthood. She has acquired the patronage of a wealthy Quaker widower, Mr. Lloyd, who sends her to the local school, where she distinguishes herself as a scholar; she is also admired by the most eligible young bachelor of the town. When she is offered a teaching position if she can bring $100 to the job, she refuses to ask Mr. Lloyd for the money, which she knows he would give her. Later when she is engaged to the young bachelor, she is more interested in her work as a teacher than in her prospective marriage, and when she sees that she and her fiancé are not suited to each other and that she cannot reform him she breaks off the engagement, though it affords her protection from her aunt. Jane is at this time no longer at her aunt's home, but is boarding out. Jane's strong character and independence have now qualified her for the happy ending the reader has anticipated—marriage to the wealthy but unromantic Mr. Lloyd, who is suited to her in character and outlook.

Two points should be made here. The first is that Sedgwick is demonstrating a deeply felt conviction that home *is* the source of values. The narrator attributes the bad character of Jane's cousins to their improper Calvinist upbringing at the hands of their mother. As Jane's cousin David reproaches his mother

after he has escaped from jail: "My mind was a blank, and you put your own impression on it . . ."—*tabula rasa* theory with a vengeance. Sedgwick's contention that sectarian religious belief and practice are far less important than sympathy and good works also gives the home many of the functions of regulating behavior formerly performed by the church. The second point is that though home and women form a uniquely important institution, they are also uniquely vulnerable. This is the lesson of the fate of Jane Elton's mother and the lesson of the story of the woman seduced and betrayed by Jane's cousin David. Men have an awesome power to ruin the home, to ruin women. The unhappy and withdrawn life of Jane's mother, the narrator suggests, stems from her having married a man not suited to her. Jane avoids this fate when she rejects her romantic fiancé and chooses Mr. Lloyd. The destructive power of men is further underscored by Sedgwick's use of the conventional seduction and betrayal plot, in which the young woman seduced by Jane's cousin David dies with her infant.

Given the vulnerability of women and of the home, it is not surprising that salient lessons of the heroine's education are discipline and self-reliance. It is only because the heroine is strong enough to live outside of a good home that she gets a good home in the end. Jane's unwillingness to take $100 from Mr. Lloyd frees her from being his subordinate, as her interest in teaching keeps her from an unsatisfactory marriage. Jane's independence, though temporary, is what makes Jane so interesting to author and reader; it is primarily Jane's independence—her power over her own life—rather than her exercising of female "influence" which constitutes her heroineism. The novel thus endorses both the domestic ideal and its antithesis, female autonomy. Female autonomy in its own right has greater emotional appeal than female influence in *A New-England Tale* and is also attractive as an alternative to female influence, which cannot always check male power. In several later novels in this genre there is more pronounced dissatisfaction with the limitations of the domestic role, probably related to the authors' diminished belief that home can be made the source of the culture's values, for later novels, though often obtrusively pious, lack Sedgwick's moral seriousness and didactic intent. (pp. 285-89)

The conflict between domesticity and autonomy is present even in novels which portray less bold heroines than Sedgwick's. Susan Warner's first novel, *The Wide, Wide World* (1850), became one of the most popular novels of mid-century. In this novel, Ellen Montgomery is thrust into the wide, wide world of the title when she is virtually orphaned by being sent away to grow up on the farm of her rustic aunt, Miss Fortune. But despite the title, the world Ellen lives in is rather circumscribed, and Ellen is never entirely on her own. Though Ellen is not as independent as the typical heroine in novels of this sort, *The Wide, Wide World* expresses female hostility to male power over women and female desire for independence in a covert way, and this covert content is particularly notable because the overt and often repeated message of *The Wide, Wide World*, as of many of the women's novels of mid-century, is submission in affliction.

The rebellion against male authority is suggested through some actions which Ellen's mother takes for the sake of her daughter. Mrs. Montgomery is financially dependent on her cavalier husband; when he does not give her enough money to buy supplies for Ellen, who is about to be sent away to her Aunt Fortune's farm, Mrs. Montgomery circumvents his power. She sells her jewelry to buy Ellen cloth, a sewing box, a Bible, and a writing desk and supplies. The details of the selection of the Bible and writing materials are so carefully described by the author that these objects take on special significance. By reading the Bible, Ellen learns one lesson her mother had begun to teach her, trust in God. The gift of the writing desk is actually subversive. Mrs. Montgomery wants Ellen to be able to write, and in particular to write letters to her mother, without needing to rely on anyone for materials. Recalling *Clarissa,* this suggests the importance of letter writing as a means of self-expression for women. In buying the writing desk Mrs. Montgomery covertly defies her husband; her buying it so that Ellen may correspond with her mother, who is to be sent away by the father, links the daughter to the mother in this circumvention of male dominance. Through the correspondence, Mrs. Montgomery hopes to educate her daughter to the end that Ellen will be able to live properly without parental supervision. By giving Ellen the Bible and the writing desk, Mrs. Montgomery is infusing her spirit into her daughter. Ellen's writing desk is thus a veiled symbol of female independence, economic and emotional. (pp. 289-90)

In Maria Susanna Cummins' *The Lamplighter* (1854), the heroine's hostility to male power and her rejection of the limitations of the domestic role are much more striking than in *A New-England Tale* and *The Wide, Wide World.* The conflict between independence and dependency comes into sharp focus in *The Lamplighter,* as in several other novels, in the direct confrontations between women who want to be independent and men who want to control them. In this novel the neglected orphan Gerty is looked after first by the lamplighter Trueman Flint and by his neighbor, Mrs. Sullivan, whose young son Willie takes Gerty's education in hand; then in the home of Emily Graham, a rich blind woman, Gerty begins an education which will qualify her to be a teacher. Willie leaves for India to make his fortune while Gerty at home learns from Emily that those only can be happy "who have learned submission; those who, in the severest afflictions, see the hand of a loving Father, and, obedient to his will, kiss the chastening rod." While at the Grahams', Gerty strikes out for a more independent life, directing her hostility at Mr. Graham, Emily's father, who tries to keep her in his elegant home as a dependent. Gerty takes up her occupation as teacher and boards with the ailing Mrs. Sullivan in order to help her after Mr. Graham asks Gerty to be Emily's travelling companion. Mr. Graham is the only demanding male character in the novel, and he commands power through his wealth. Gerty refuses to bend to his wishes, exhibiting a passive resistance to his power. She does not practice submission here. She claims that she cannot comply with Mr. Graham's wishes to help Emily because of her duty to her other friend, Mrs. Sullivan, but her deeper motive, that of psychological independence, is unacknowledged. The dialogue between Gerty and Mr. Graham about her responsibilities neatly contrasts the heroine's desire for financial and emotional autonomy with her male antagonist's desire to exact obedience from her. Though Mr. Graham insists, "You are under my care, child, and I have a right to say what you shall do," Gerty remains adamant about leaving the Graham home, and Mr. Graham vows to withdraw his support from her. Emily, siding with Gerty, explains to her father, "I thought the object, in giving Gertrude a good education, was to make her independent of all the world, and not simply dependent upon us." Independence is thus underscored as the central benefit of Gerty's education.

One avenue, then, for expressing dissatisfaction with the limitations of the domestic role is the heroine's utilization or flaunting of her skills. Another is the familiar Victorian theme of taming the male. If the male can be tamed, independence becomes less necessary for the heroine's well-being. In *The Lamplighter* the pattern of taming a prospective husband is doubled. First, before her death, Mrs. Sullivan has a dream in which her spiritual presence keeps Willie from succumbing to the temptations of drink, gambling, and loose women. This dream, which Mrs. Sullivan narrates for Gerty, ends with Mrs. Sullivan's flying to lay her "precious boy" at Gerty's feet. The dream reconciles Mrs. Sullivan to her death, for it shows that she will always, in a sense, have possession of her son, and Mrs. Sullivan's control reinforces Gerty's control. While Gerty could not bend to all of the wishes of Mr. Graham, over whom she had no power, she can marry a man who has been brought under woman's influence.

As Mrs. Sullivan tames her son for Gerty, her adoptive daughter, so Gerty tames her father for Emily, one of her two surrogate mothers. After Mrs. Sullivan's death, Gertrude, as she is now called, gives up her teaching to rejoin Emily. The two visit the fashionable resort of Saratoga Springs, where Gerty preaches a religion of hope and love to a skeptical and jaded man. This Byronic character reveals to Gerty that he is really her father and Emily's step-brother and long-lost lover; in his youth he had accidentally blinded Emily and then had abandoned her. Willie, having made his fortune, has returned to marry Gerty, while Gerty's father, who has become rich during his melancholy wanderings, is reunited with Emily. Gerty's christianizing of her father makes him worthy of marrying Emily, while Mrs. Sullivan's spiritual influence, from beyond the tomb, over her son Willie guarantees his faithfulness to Gerty. As in *A New-England Tale* and *The Wide, Wide World,* the contrasting lives of mother and daughter in *The Lamplighter* show the way marriage has been transmuted from a vulnerable into a secure situation. In *The Lamplighter,* through marrying the dutiful Willie, Gerty will avoid the dramatic male abandonment suffered by Emily and by her own mother. The heroine can in the end give up her independence for a highly idealized domesticity in which there are no threats.

In Augusta Jane Evans' most popular novels, *Beulah* (1859) and *St. Elmo* (1867), the conflict between domestic dependency and female autonomy which we have seen in earlier novels is especially acute and cannot be entirely recontained by the marriage ending. In *St. Elmo* this dissonance is so sharp and pervasive that it is not surprising that this novel marks the virtual end of the genre.

Evans' heroines are more ambitious than Gerty Flint: Beulah Benton in *Beulah* and Edna Earl in *St. Elmo* make pronounced and prolonged bids for independence and professional achievement. After girlhood, both orphan heroines reject the hospitality and assistance of their benefactors. To be free of her wealthy male benefactor Beulah works as a teacher, while Edna works as a governess; both spend long hours, when off duty, writing for publication, and they thereby undergo stress not only physical but also emotional. As Evans' heroines invest more of themselves in their work than Gerty Flint does, so in Evans' novels there is a more explicit conflict between ambition and happiness, Beulah and Edna being warned that because of their desire for work and for recognition through writing they will have none of the comforts of the hearth which alone can make a woman's life fulfilling. As Dr. Hartwell admonishes Beulah, "Ambition such as yours, which aims at literary fame, is the deadliest foe to happiness. Man may content himself with the applause of the world and the homage paid to his intellect; but woman's heart has holier idols.'' He predicts unhappiness and continuing illness.

Even when the heroine and narrator find the heroine's aspirations worthy, other aspects of the narration show how dangerous these aspirations are. For example, after Edna's first magazine article is rejected, she wonders "whether all women were browbeaten for aspiring to literary honors.'' Edna concludes that women may rightly have intellectual and literary ambitions, but, by juxtaposing Edna to a moth consumed by light, the scene suggests the threat to her nature that these desires pose: "To abandon her right to erudition formed no part of the programme which she was mentally arranging as she sat there watching a moth singe its filmy, spotted wings in the gas flame.'' Further, the narrator implies that most intellectual ambitions are inappropriate because unwomanly and comments that literary women generally "barter their birthright of quiet, life-long happiness in the peaceful seclusion of home for a nauseous mess of poisoned pottage.'' Here the line between noble aspiration and shockingly unwomanly ambition is fine indeed, another sign of the pervasive conflict in the novel about woman's role.

What is significant about admonitions such as Dr. Hartwell's, the description of the moth, and the authorial comment on literary women, as well as the heroines' own doubts about their vocation, is precisely the ideological issue which is more subdued in the earlier novels: what is woman's place. The heroines are perceived by other characters to be putting themselves outside of "woman's sphere'': we might add that they are entering the public and commercial world of men. They are in fact competing with men, both in their circumvention of the power of their benefactors and in their work. We see in these novels the desire to escape male power over women and the desire to compete in the world of men and to prove oneself equal by winning in the competition.

In *Beulah,* Beulah Benton leaves the home of her patron, Dr. Hartwell, to become a teacher, explaining to a friend that she prefers not to be dependent on anyone; Beulah remains adamant about her independence even when on several occasions Dr. Hartwell implores and almost commands her to return. Among these heroines, Beulah in particular preaches the doctrine of psychological and economic self-reliance. Beulah's debate with another young teacher, Clara Sanders, underscores the importance of self-reliance, independence, and mission to Beulah. Clara says of Beulah's vocation, "Can the feeling that you are independent and doing your duty, satisfy the longing for other idols? Oh! Duty is an icy shadow. It will freeze you. It cannot fill the heart's sanctuary. Woman was intended as a pet plant, to be guarded and cherished; isolated and uncared for, she droops, languishes and dies.'' (This is precisely what is happening to the unwillingly self-reliant Clara at this point in the novel.) Beulah returns, "I don't believe one word of all this languishing nonsense. . . . Duty may be a cold shadow to you, but it is a vast volcanic agency, constantly impelling me to action. What was my will given to me for, if to remain passive and suffer others to minister to its needs.'' Beulah's sense of duty allows her to fulfill her personal ambition for independence and even renown. Not only does Beulah support herself by teaching but she spends her nights writing for publication, and she gains thereby salary and distinction. Beulah is an intellectual who has devoted herself to languages and literature since childhood; using her erudition in writing is a way of demonstrating her equality with men. Further, contrary to Southern practice, Beulah will not publish her magazine pieces

unless she is paid a fee, and thus she enters the commercial world run by men.

Beulah's intellectual pursuits constitute in part her heroineism, and the strenuousness and solitariness of the intellectual adventure as well as the courage necessary to meet it are shown especially when Beulah's studies precipitate her crisis of faith. Beulah's intellectual and spiritual trial has paradoxical meaning, marking her distance from the feminine ideal of living for others and providing moral guidance, which she herself espouses, even as it defines her heroineism and makes her a match for the novel's hero.

Having over the course of several years proven herself at least the equal of the men around her and emerging from her crisis with renewed faith, Beulah does finally marry the wealthy and Byronic Dr. Hartwell, and in an about-face gives up entirely her former work. Her work now, as the narrator says, is "to save her husband from his unbelief.'' The narrator makes no comment on this sharp contrast between Beulah's remarkable accomplishments in the public world and her subsequent complete removal to the private world of the home. Perhaps the ending is meant to suggest that the home is truly woman's place, but the narrator has given hundreds of pages and much intense attention to Beulah's independence, and we must conclude that the author is pulled between antithetical desires, that Evans both repudiates and accepts the limits of domesticity.

These antithetical desires are in even sharper conflict in *St. Elmo,* a novel in which the heroine lives the life of the independent woman while espousing the virtues of domesticity. A young orphan determined to leave the country for work in the city and to support herself instead of accepting charity, the heroine, Edna Earl, is injured in a train crash en route to the city and is taken into the elegant home of Mrs. Murray and her son, the Byronic St. Elmo, between whom and Edna there is a powerful attraction. At the Murray home Edna studies Latin, Greek, Hebrew, Chaldee, and that great Victorian discipline, comparative mythology; then, bent on proving that women can be as learned as men, Edna leaves the Murray home to become a governess and author. Against the advice of editors and friends, Edna writes on, straining her health; in contrast to their predictions of failure, she becomes a popular success, and, what is more important, she becomes "a power in society'' through her writing.

Edna's actions and her erudite writing embody a complicated desire to be the intellectual and social equal of men—indeed, to be their superior—and yet not to be "unfeminine'' by assailing the male fortress of politics and business. Ambivalence about women competing with men is especially intense in *St. Elmo*. Edna both wants power and abjures it. When the editor who rejects Edna's first article advises her to find a theme better suited to her "feminine ability,'' to "burn the enclosed MS . . . and write sketches of home life,'' Edna passionately rejects this counsel, yet later in the novel she proclaims and writes that woman's place *is* the home and that a woman who ventures into the male sphere would be endangering "national purity'' and "disgracing all womanhood.'' In fact, her novel *Shining Thrones on the Hearth* illustrates the proposition that "Those who rock the cradle rule the world.'' But by writing Edna herself competes with men. Her writing is not a peaceful domestic activity; through it she gains fame, high social status, and power, and her success even convinces her that she is too good for the men who want to marry her. As Edna's success puts her on a par with men of her acquaintance, it also removes her from woman's sphere. Edna does not simply serve others through her writing; she gains a unique status through the "good" of her publications, escaping the anonymity and restrictions of the feminine ideal of service which her works promulgate. Like several architects of the cult of domesticity, Edna Earl makes a career out of showing women that they should not have careers. In Edna's case, the conflict between her practice and her preaching is acute.

When Edna Earl does in the end marry the hero, St. Elmo, Edna's career is ended even more sharply then Beulah's. St. Elmo tells his bride, "To-day I snap the fetters of your literary bondage. There shall be no more books written! No more study, no more toil, no more anxiety, no more heartaches! And that dear public you love so well, must even help itself . . . You belong solely to me now, and I shall take care of the life you have nearly destroyed in your inordinate ambition." Edna's "inordinate ambition"—that is, her desire to excel in the world of men—is paradoxically both the source of her greatness as a woman and the obstacle to her becoming a true woman. When Edna's career is ended and she returns to the haven of the home, we may assume that Evans here endorses the values of domesticity, but Evans has also emphasized throughout with her heroine's ambition.

Edna Earl gives up her power in order to marry only after the conventional romantic hero of the novel has been cut down to size; weakening the opposition in part resolves the ambivalent attitudes toward female independence and competition with men. As in *The Lamplighter,* in *St. Elmo* the Byronic hero credits his conversion to the example and the power of the heroine's love and faith. Though drawn to him, Edna Earl rejects St. Elmo as a suitor because of his sinful ways. St. Elmo follows his path to regeneration and becomes a minister because of his love for Edna and because of her example of Christian goodness. Edna thus gains a devoted, responsible, and chastened husband (but one who retains much of his former virility, as shown when he forbids Edna to write again). Once the hero gives in to the heroine, the heroine in turn can submit to his rule. (pp. 291-97)

[The] orphan heroines of the female *Bildungsroman* generally internalize, at least for a time, the values of self-reliance, of liberal individualism, which the dominant culture valued in men. Indeed the orphan is an extreme version of the American individual; she is by definition independent and separate. Male self-reliance, though valued, also led to the amorality, materialism, and aggressiveness of the public realm and required the counter-balance of "woman's sphere," of the institution of the home as the source of affectional bonds and ethical relations. But the ideology of domesticity, while emphasizing women's influence, at the same time had coercive effects, denying women political rights in a period when increasing numbers of men were coming to exercise these rights, confining women to the isolation of the home, and legitimizing restrictions on their occupations. These limitations, moreover, could not be justified on democratic principles. It is not surprising that in addition to the express grievances of supporters of the woman's rights movement in this period, we find less articulate dissatisfaction with the limits of domesticity, as in the popular novel of female development. When heroines of the female *Bildungsroman* develop into independent and self-reliant women, the novels cannot maintain a clear separation between women's and men's spheres. Though in *A New-England Tale* Catharine Sedgwick intended to define and elevate the functions of the home, Sedgwick's heroine must prove herself largely outside of the home; and it is appropriate that one of the last best-

sellers of this genre, *St. Elmo,* should embody such a sharp conflict about the place of women, which even the marriage ending does not entirely mute.

But in general, the endings of these novels at least partly recontain this conflict, and they reintegrate the orphan heroine into society. In the conclusion the heroine's social rise, her material security, and the devotion of her husband compensate her for the loss of her independence. In fact, the heroines of many of the novels after *A New-England Tale* acquire the manners and beauty which make them admired in fashionable society and accepted into it even as they profess to be independent working women. The novels seem to gratify for the nineteenth-century woman reader first the desire for independence from the domestic role and then the safer desire for a romanticized and idealized domesticity.

This idealization is itself a powerful ideological force in the genre. In idealizing domesticity the popular genre of the female *Bildungsroman* betrays a class bias which prevents it from genuinely offering a new vision of women and social organization. However burdened with contradictions about the role of women, Sedgwick's aim in *A New-England Tale* and other works was to mold new social values. The novels which follow *A New-England Tale* do not fulfill Sedgwick's purpose; instead they ratify the values of the expanding middle class. The popular conception of the home as the balance to the amorality of the public sphere left the public sphere intact, and, in that sense, the ideology of domesticity sanctioned what it seemed to oppose. But more than this, in the female *Bildungsroman,* the heroine's rise generally involves in her response to the world a conflation of piety, gentility, and a feeling for material goods, suggesting that home also functioned as the showcase and justification for the acquisitiveness of the public domain, rather than as its balance. And this is perhaps the most serious limitation of the genre, and of the cult of domesticity as well. (pp. 298-300)

Beverly R. Voloshin, "The Limits of Domesticity: The Female 'Bildungsroman' in America, 1820-1870," in Women's Studies, *Vol. 10, No. 3, 1984, pp. 283-302.*

ADDITIONAL BIBLIOGRAPHY

PRIMARY SOURCES

Austen, Jane. *Emma.* London: Oxford University Press, 1966, 432 p.

Brontë, Charlotte. *Jane Eyre.* Oxford: Clarendon Press, 1975, 637 p.

Carlyle, Thomas. *Sartor Resartus.* New York: AMS Press, 1974, 250 p.

Dickens, Charles. *David Copperfield.* New York: Macmillan, 1962, 850 p.

———. *Great Expectations.* Everyman's Library, Fiction, no. 234. 1907. Reprint. New York: Dutton, 1971, 461 p.

Eliot, George. *The Mill on the Floss.* London: Pan Books, 1973, 505 p.

———. *Middlemarch.* A Norton Critical Edition. New York: Norton, 1977, 770 p.

Goethe, Johann Wolfgang von. *Wilhelm Meister's Apprenticeship and Travels.* 2 vols. Translated by Thomas Carlyle. New York: AMS Press, 1974.

Hölderlin, Friedrich. *Hyperion; or, The Hermit of Greece.* Translated by Willard R. Trask. New York: F. Ungar Pub. Co., 1965, 173 p.

Keller, Gottfried. *Green Henry.* Translated by A. M. Holt. New York: Riverrun Press, 1986, 656 p.

Meredith, George. *The Ordeal of Richard Feverel: A History of Father and Son.* New York: Charles Scribner's Sons, 1977, 455 p.

Novalis. *Henry Von Ofterdingen.* Translated by Palmer Hilty. New York: F. Ungar Pub. Co., 1964, 169 p.

Stifter, Adalbert. *Indian Summer.* Translated by Wendell Frye. Bern: P. Lang, 1985, 460 p.

Wieland, Christoph Martin. *The History of Agathon.* 4 vols. London: T. Cadell, 1773.

SECONDARY SOURCES

Bruford, W. H. *The German Tradition of Self-Cultivation: "Bildung" from Humboldt to Thomas Mann.* London: Cambridge University Press, 1975, 290 p.
> Traces the themes of inwardness and personal development in the works of several eighteenth-, nineteenth-, and twentieth-century German novelists.

Butler, R. "The Realist Novel as 'Roman d'Éducation': Ideological Debate and Social Action in *Le Père Goriot* and *Germinal.*" *Nineteenth-Century French Studies* 12, Nos. 1, 2 (Fall-Winter 1983-84): 68-77.
> Suggests a reading of Balzac's *Le Père Goriot* and Zola's *Germinal* as *Bildungsromane.*

Emmel, Hildegard. "Historical Development: Goethe and His Contemporaries." In her *History of the German Novel,* pp. 20-108. Detroit: Wayne State University Press, 1984.
> Places the *Bildungsroman* in its literary and historical context, discussing the importance to the genre of such authors as Goethe, Hölderlin, Novalis, and Tieck.

Germer, Helmut. *The German Novel of Education, 1792-1805: A Complete Bibliography and Analysis.* German Studies in America, edited by Heinrich Meyer, no. 3. Berne: Herbert Lang, 1968, 280 p.
> A detailed list of late eighteenth- and early nineteenth-century German *Bildungsromane.* Germer includes sections on such topics as the themes and formal characteristics of the works listed.

Harrold, Charles Frederick. "Carlyle and the Problem of Life: Carlyle and *Wilhelm Meister.*" In his *Carlyle and German Thought: 1819-1834,* pp. 202-08. Yale Studies in English, vol. 82. 1934. Reprint. Hamden, Conn.: Archon Books, 1963.
> Analyzes Carlyle's attitude toward *Wilhelm Meister,* asserting that from the novel he learned that "the secret of life was the effort to fill the real with the ideal, to apply one's capabilities, once they were discovered, to the materials offered by circumstances, and to achieve the expression of mind and spirit."

Minden, M. R. "The Place of Inheritance in the *Bildungsroman.*" *Deutsche vierteljahrsschrift für literaturwissenschaft und geistesgeschichte* 57, No. 1 (March 1983): 33-63.
> An essay that, in the critic's words, "explores the relationship between the motif of inheritance, the concept of art, and the notion of *Bildung* itself" in Wieland's *Agathon,* Goethe's *Wilhelm Meister,* and Stifter's *Indian Summer.*

Pascal, Roy. "'Bildung' and the Division of Labour." In *German Studies Presented to Horace Bruford on His Retirement by His Pupils, Colleagues and Friends,* pp. 14-28. London: George G. Harrap & Co., 1962.
> Discusses the idea of *Bildung* in the writings of Humboldt, Fichte, and Schiller, noting the light their works shed on Goethe's *Wilhelm Meister.*

Pratt, Annis, and White, Barbara. "The Novel of Development." In *Archetypal Patterns in Women's Fiction,* by Annis Pratt, Barbara White, Andrea Loewenstein, and Mary Wyer, pp. 13-37. Bloomington: Indiana University Press, 1981.
> Analyzes several archetypes in nineteenth- and twentieth-century novels dealing with women's development.

Schilling, Bernard N. "Realism in 19th Century Fiction: Balzac, Dickens and the *Bildungsroman.*" In *Actes du V-e Congrès de l'Association Internationale de Littérature Comparée,* edited by Nikola Banašević, pp. 251-59. Belgrade: Université Belgrade, 1969.
> Discusses moral realism as it pertains to character development in Dickens's *Great Expectations* and Balzac's *Illusions perdues,* concluding that the hero of the former novel matures, whereas the hero of the latter work fails to grow in a positive direction.

Selbmann, Rolf. *Der deutsche Bildungsroman.* Stuttgart: J. B. Metzlersche Verlagsbuchhandlung, 1984, 164 p.
> A concise but inclusive overview of the *Bildungsroman* in Germany. The work, which is available only in German, contains a section on the theoretical foundations of the *Bildungsroman,* explores Goethe's themes, techniques, and influence, and provides surveys of the German *Bildungsroman* in the nineteenth and twentieth centuries.

Waxman, Barbara Frey. "Heart, Mind, Body, and Soul: George Eliot's Female *Bildungsroman.*" *Victorians Institute Journal* 11 (1982-83): 61-82.
> Analyzes Eliot's *The Mill on the Floss* and *Middlemarch* as female *Bildungsromane,* noting that "Maggie and Dorothea emerge from their life's struggles with a modicum of domestic contentment, perhaps an hour of heroic fulfillment, and a lot of frustration."

Witte, W. "Alien Corn. The 'Bildungsroman': Not for Export." *German Life and Letters* XXXIII, No. 1 (October 1979): 87-96.
> Posits that the *Bildungsroman* genre is dependent upon the German philosophical and literary tradition, and that it constitutes "a continuation as well as a critique of it."

The French Symbolist Movement

INTRODUCTION

French Symbolism was a complex and influential literary movement that flourished during the last two decades of the nineteenth century. The works of the Symbolist school were characterized by a desire to suggest the existence of a transcendent realm of being, a concern with moods and sensations rather than lucid statements and descriptions, a hermetic subjectivity, and an obsession with the morbid or occult aspects of life. Although the term Symbolism was first applied to this school of poets by Jean Moréas in 1885, the stylistic, thematic, and philosophic tenets of the movement were established earlier in the works of Charles Baudelaire, Paul Verlaine, Arthur Rimbaud, and Stéphane Mallarmé. Collectively the writings of these poets define the major traits of Symbolism. A study of the origins and distinguishing features of the movement must also take into account its relationship to two other literary movements of the time: Decadence and Naturalism.

The Decadent movement in French literature instituted much of what came to be identified with the slightly later and more prevalent Symbolist movement. The Decadents were a group of writers who rejected conventional religious, social, and moral values and sought refuge from their ennui in novel sensations. The Symbolists had a number of characteristics in common with the Decadents—including a world-rejecting escapism, a tendency toward exoticism, and an aggressive individualism—and many writers are associated with both movements, including Verlaine and Mallarmé. In addition to its connection with the Decadent movement, Symbolism can be understood in terms of its opposition to Naturalism. Briefly, Naturalism was linked to the rise of scientism during the late nineteenth century and held that the truest manner of presenting human life was in terms of physical and biological forces, which the Naturalists considered the determining factors in shaping individuals and groups. In their fiction, the Naturalists depicted the outward existence of persons from ordinary walks of life, representing these subjects in an uncomplicated, journalistic prose style. Conversely, the Symbolists, who were for the most part poets rather than fiction writers, were primarily concerned with the expression of inward experience, and their approach often resulted in works that were intentionally obscure and highly personal. Whereas the Naturalists became expert in portraying the lives of businessmen, laborers, and criminals, the Symbolists occupied themselves with the lives of poets, saints, and aristocrats; while the works of the Naturalists were grounded in scientific materialism, those of the Symbolists followed the teachings of German idealist writers and the mystical philosophy of Emanuel Swedenborg.

The aesthetics and ideology of Symbolism are in different ways embodied in the works of Baudelaire, Verlaine, Rimbaud, and Mallarmé. Baudelaire's poetry collection *Les fleurs du mal* (*The Flowers of Evil*) represents a catalogue of qualities that would reappear in the writings of the later Symbolists: individualism to the point of misanthropy, perverse eroticism, fascination with the exotic, extreme cynicism, occult reverence for the power of language, and nostalgia for a spiritual homeland that exists beyond the visible world. In particular, Bau-

"Be a Symbolist," a caricature of Jean Moréas.

delaire's poem "Correspondances" ("Correspondences") articulates two important principles of Symbolist poetry: first, that esoteric parallels exist between the material and the spiritual worlds; second, that human senses may correspond to one another, a phenomenon known as synesthesia, resulting, for instance, in the perception of sounds as colors or colors as fragrances. Baudelaire's importance to Symbolism also resides in his translations of the works of Edgar Allan Poe, whose critical theories influenced the Symbolists's ideas on poetry as the art of suggestion and as a reflection of an ideal realm. The contribution of Verlaine to the development of Symbolism derives from the intense lyricism of his verse, which inspired an emphasis in late nineteenth-century French poetry on the musical possibilities of language, and also prompted a poetic concern with mood rather than meaning. "Music before everything else," Verlaine wrote in his poem "Art poétique." In the poetry of Rimbaud, the visionary nature of Symbolism is conspicuously revealed as the poet assumes the role of seer and advocates the abandonment of reason for the illuminations of mysticism; such works as *Le bateau ivre* (*The Drunken Boat*) and *Les illuminations* exhibit a hallucinatory mode of perception and an inventive style of expression. Similarly noted for his stylistic innovations in the service of a transcendent vision was Mallarmé, who became the central figure in the Symbolist movement both for his role as mentor to younger poets and for his poetry, which many critics regard as the epitome of Symbolist art. It was Mallarmé who most explicitly outlined and scrupulously practiced the technique of suggesting rather than clearly stating the subject matter of a poem. "To name an object," he wrote, "is to suppress three-fourths of the delight of the poem which is derived from the pleasure of divining little by little: to *suggest* it, that is the dream." With such poems as "L'après-midi d'un faun" ("The Afternoon of a

Faun'') and ''Hérodiade,'' Mallarmé not only provided supreme examples of Symbolist themes and techniques but also engaged in literary experimentation to a degree that anticipated the direction of modernist literature.

The Symbolist movement emerged in reaction to adverse criticism that had been directed at poets associated with the earlier Decadent movement. In an article of 1885, Paul Bourde, a writer for the *Temps,* attacked the ''decadent'' style of Moréas and his contemporaries, who had drawn their inspiration primarily from the works of Baudelaire and the critical theories of Poe. Moréas responded in the journal *Le XIXeme siècle* with an essay defending the search for a new language, one that progressed beyond the previous conventions of French versification to convey a poetic reality independent of rhetoric and surface descriptions. ''Thus, in this art,'' Moréas wrote, ''the pictures provided by nature, the actions of men, all concrete phenomena, cannot manifest themselves as themselves; they are perceptible appearances intended to represent their esoteric affinities with primordial ideas.'' In his essay, Moréas coined the term ''Symbolism'' in its modern sense, believing it a more accurate and less derogatory word than Decadence to describe his work and that of his contemporaries. In a continuation of the debate over the validity of the movement, Moréas published ''Manifeste littéraire de l'école Symboliste'' a year later, in effect proclaiming Symbolism as the dominant school of French poetry. The same year Moréas joined with Gustave Kahn and Paul Adam to found *Le symboliste,* a short-lived periodical formed to further the cause of Symbolist literature. Perhaps the best-known journal of the movement was the *Mercure de France,* which was cofounded by Remy de Gourmont, one of the most prominent critics to support the Symbolist movement. Gourmont also helped to make the works of the major Symbolist writers known to a wider public through his essays in *Le livre des masques (The Book of Masks).* Defining the principles of Symbolist art, Gourmont noted that Symbolism meant ''individualism in literature, liberty in art,'' and the ''abandonment of existing forms,'' as well as ''anti-naturalism'' and a ''tendency to take only the characteristic detail out of life.''

By the end of the nineteenth century, the Symbolist movement had virtually disappeared from the French literary scene. The deaths of its leading figures, including Mallarmé in 1898, as well as the involvement of former Symbolists in other literary movements, contributed to this decline. However, the influence and prestige of Symbolism endured for several decades in countries throughout the world, particularly in Russia, Germany, Eastern Europe, and Japan. Furthermore, a number of the leading French writers of the modernist period, most prominently Paul Valéry and Paul Claudel, continued to follow many of the principles of Symbolism in their work written in the twentieth century. Succeeded by various movements such as Surrealism and Expressionism, Symbolism is often recognized as the source of the modern artistic temper as characterized by formal experimentation and alienation from society. While Symbolism was a short-lived movement in French literary history, its effect on the subsequent course of world literature has been lasting and profound.

BACKGROUND AND CHARACTERISTICS OF SYMBOLISM

PHILIPPE JULLIAN

[*Jullian discusses the artistic, philosophical, and social climate in which the Symbolist, Decadent, and other aesthetic movements flourished in late nineteenth-century Europe. In addition, Jullian provides a consideration of the influence of Symbolist style in twentieth-century visual arts.*]

PESSIMISM. 'Our century is not moving towards either good or evil: it is moving towards mediocrity.' These words, uttered by Renan when the last quarter of the nineteenth century was just beginning, were scarcely calculated to encourage young people endowed with any imagination. But who at that time said anything that might be described as encouraging? Leaders of expanding industries and generals in need of soldiers to defend a province or conquer a colony: that was nearly all. The Church was losing many of its faithful, and the intransigent attitude adopted by the Vatican Council was unlikely to bring them back to the fold; the bourgeoisie, terrified by the Commune, was finding it impossible to recapture the sense of security it had known in the middle of the century; while high society felt ashamed of having enjoyed itself too much under the Second Empire. Consequently, as the century drew towards its close, a feeling of uneasiness became apparent in every class of society. There was no fear that the end of the world was in sight: at that time the possibility seemed incompatible with science. However there *was* a fear of the end of civilization, a sort of *millennium* whose destructive forces would no longer be the angels of the Apocalypse, but either Socialism or the Machine or the Yellow Peril. In the case of particularly sensitive natures, this fear became sheer anguish; it took the form either of insolent rebellion against an unstable society, or of escape into the world of dreams. But the Intellectuals were divided: some of them, led by Zola, accepted the materialism of their age, however much this might horrify more delicate souls. The *fin de siècle* malady was much less antisocial than the Romantic *mal du siècle* had been, but it was also much less widespread than in 1830, for the mass of society wanted nothing but material satisfaction. This anguish was therefore the privilege of a young élite. The form it took varied according to the country and period in which it appeared, but it found expression everywhere in the cult of death and melancholy.

England went through this crisis when, at the time of the Industrial Revolution, the spirit of competition and excessive conformism weighed too heavily on social life. The resulting revolt was more moral and artistic than literary. The idea was a return to the purity which some pious individuals and a few artists believed to have existed in the Middle Ages. The most ardent advocates of this purity founded the Pre-Raphaelite Brotherhood in 1848, having found in Ruskin a champion for their ideas. For these painters and their prophet, the idea of Beauty was inseparable from a reformed society. They accordingly depicted the Middle Ages as a mystical, Socialist period to which they attributed all the virtues they had searched for in vain in the Victorian era. They hoped to regenerate society by ridding its surroundings of vulgar industrial manifestations, and they set off with admirable courage on a crusade. Many never came back—for if William Morris became the respected patriarch of *Art Nouveau* and Millais the richest of the academic painters, Rossetti succumbed to drugs, and his admirers Swinburne and Wilde, each in his fashion, both suffered the vengeance of society. The dramas of the Pre-Raphaelite Bohemia foreshadowed the dramas of the *fin de siècle* Bohemia, just as Chelsea's fashions would be copied a dozen years later on the other side of the Channel.

Those fashions were adopted by men who were looking, above all else, for a soul, while the English Decadence was chiefly a revolt in matters of taste, and ridicule was the chief danger that it braved. Wilde, thanks to his sense of the theatre, managed to become an ill-starred poet, a *poète maudit*, at the end of a delightful life; but that was a French fashion. There were hardly any *poètes maudits* in England, only a few poor wretches who died of hunger in complete obscurity, while their French contemporaries, ill-starred or not, were famous. Thus, James Thomson, the author of ''The City of Dreadful Night,'' and Francis Thompson remained unknown. In France, only Germain Nouveau could be compared to these successors of Thomas de Quincey.

One of the greatest influences, that of Edgar Allan Poe, came from the United States, where Decadence would not set in until over a century after the poet's death. Poe had an immense influence on Redon, for example, who made lithographs entitled *Le Pèlerin d'un monde sublunaire* (and here we can see the continuity of fantasy down to Lovecraft), *La Cosmologie du poème 'Eureka'*, and *Le Souffle qui conduit les êtres est aussi dans les sphères;* many other *fin de siècle* figures saw the world lit by the cabbalistic star of Gérard de Nerval, Poe and the Victor Hugo of *Ce que dit la bouche d'ombre:* the Black Sun.

THE AESTHETES. The most important consequence of this English movement was probably the appearance of a character who was new to Europe (he had existed for a long time in China): the aesthete, the ardent servant of beauty, often incapable of creating anything himself, but skilled in devising a décor or setting a tone. Unlike the art-lover, however, he was eager to play a part in artistic creation, and he served as a link between the various forms of artistic expression. The aesthetes had no fatherland, no ideal other than Beauty, no enemies other than ugliness and stupidity. These *fin de siécle* Knights Templar were violently attacked by those who envied their gifts, and also by those who were annoyed by their insolence. The aesthetes, following in the wake of the Pre-Raphaelites, succeeded in giving Europe a new style and fashioning a new type of beauty, leaving anguish to the artists. But the aesthete, with a perversity he calls humour, sometimes makes fun of what he most admires; thus we see the rarest flower of aestheticism, Aubrey Beardsley, casually toying with all the religions and all the vices which tempted him. For forty years, thanks to the Pre-Raphaelites, and then to Beardsley, English art was to be a source of images from which all dreamers would draw inspiration. On the other hand, the ideas of the English aesthetes were less representative of the movement, in spite of Ruskin, Pater and above all Wilde, who was the Holy Ghost, or rather the Blue Bird, of the aesthetic trinity.

France, on the contrary, was to be a great source of poetic themes, thanks to Baudelaire, who was recognized by the time he died as the first modern European poet, and then, later on and to a lesser degree, thanks to Mallarmé and Verlaine. Baudelaire dominated all Swinburne's work, and the Germans admired him more than their own poets. All the themes of *Les Fleurs du Mal* were taken over by [Symbolist artists] . . . : satanism, dandyism, exoticism and above all eroticism—in fact, everything the bourgeois regarded as decadent. . . . Thus, while England was Aesthetic, France was Decadent. There were few Decadents in England, apart from certain disciples of Wilde, and few Aesthetes in France, although she can lay claim to the most exquisite of them all, Robert de Montesquiou, who was the model for the Duc Floressas des Esseintes in Huysmans's novel *A Rebours* before becoming Proust's Baron de Charlus. *A Rebours* was published in 1884, an important date also for painting, with the first *Salon des Indépendants* in Paris and the first *Salon des XX* in Brussels.

The Decadence found more remarkable expression in France than anywhere else because in that counry the *fin de siècle* anguish was rooted in two separate preoccupations. First of all, after the disasters of the Franco-Prussian War and the Commune, people had the feeling that they were living in a period of political degeneration, a suspicion confirmed by the many scandals of the Third Republic. With a democratic government, France was afraid of becoming a second Spain. One of the strangest figures of the period, Joséphin Péladan, . . . was to give vivid expression to this horror of democracy about 1890, when he declared: 'I believe in the inevitable and imminent putrefaction of a Latin world without gods and without Symbols.' Twenty years earlier, on hearing the news of the defeat of Sedan, Flaubert had written: 'We are witnessing the end of the Latin world'; and it is said that Renan once retorted to the chauvinistic Déroulède: 'Young man, France is dying: don't disturb her death-agony.' Refusing to recognize Germany's intellectual superiority, the French drew a parallel between the Byzantine Empire and the Second Empire on the one hand, and the barbarian world and Bismarck's Germany on the other.

The other reason for pessimism was one which France shared with Germany and England, for like those powers, although to a lesser degree, she was feeling the effects of prosperity, or in other words materialism. Everybody who had retained a certain sense of honour, whether religious, aesthetic or literary, felt threatened by the machine as well as by the masses who served the machine. They were conscious of the hostility of the advocates of progress typified by Flaubert's Homais and certain characters in Dickens's novels. Since the Revolution of 1848 nobody in France could seriously believe in democracy. Baudelaire and Renan both condemned it, the former on behalf of the dandies—who, it should be noted, were the progenitors of the aesthetes: 'Day after day, the rising tide of democracy, which is spreading everywhere, is drowning the last representatives of human pride.' Renan for his part wrote: 'Democracy is the most powerful solvent of virtue of any kind that the world has ever known.'

Young people who were not attracted by the nationalist movement for *la revanche* or revenge on Germany, a movement which in any case began only in the late 1880s with the Boulanger episode, could find hardly anybody to inspire them at the beginning of the *fin de siècle*. Hugo regarded himself as God, the Parnassians were first and foremost academicians, and Renan's pronouncements, as we have seen, were anything but encouraging. If they turned towards the fine arts, they met with a similar disappointment. On the one hand there was academic art, and on the other Impressionism, whose language was still difficult to understand and which offered nothing to the imagination. Gustave Moreau was to be both a Baudelaire and a Delacroix to this frustrated generation. One has only to read Huysmans's *Salon* of 1889 to realize that the youth of a whole era found their dreams and their despair reflected in Moreau:

> Spiritual onanism . . . a soul exhausted by secret thoughts . . . Insidious appeals to sacrilege and debauchery . . . Goddesses riding hippogryphs and streaking with their lapis-lazuli wings the death-agony of the clouds . . . The crushed globes of bleeding suns and haemorrhages of stars flowing in crimson cataracts . . . Contrary to Taine's theory, environment stimulates revolt: exceptional individuals retrace their steps down the century, and, out of disgust for the promiscuities they have to suffer, hurl themselves

into the abysses of bygone ages, into the tumultuous
spaces of dreams and nightmares.

All the themes of the *fin de siècle* are gathered together in
these few lines which place Moreau among the poets rather
than among the painters; and indeed, his influence was to be
greater upon the former than upon the latter.

If England provided the images of the *fin de siècle* and France
the poetic themes, Germany supplied the doctrine—that of her
philosophers, and above all the most pessimistic of them—and
also gave the world Wagner, who was the god of the time.
The young German Empire had too much self-confidence to
give birth to Aesthetes and Decadents. Even the most unusual
of its painters had something robust about them. It was the
crumbling Austro-Hungarian Empire which would provide the
German representatives of the *fin de siècle:* Rilke and Klimt.

In Russia, another crumbling Empire, mysticism occupied a
far more important place than aestheticism. The Russian Decadents are represented by Dostoevsky's *The Possessed* and the
Nihilists, while Tolstoy became the guru of a Europe which
was already drawn towards Asia. Leontiev, a writer despised
far too long as a reactionary, was a 'Knight of Beauty' like
Stefan Trofimovich in *The Possessed*, but also a narcissistic
anti-Christian without any social preoccupations who delared
that Poetry was the sole reality: his influence was confined to
only a few artists.

From the artistic point of view, the Scandinavians made a much
greater contribution: first through a revival of traditional decorative themes, and secondly through the close connections
with the Beyond which Scandinavians from Swedenborg to
Strindberg had maintained since the late eighteenth century.
The same phenomenon, incidentally, was to be observed in
Ireland, where the Celtic Revival was inseparable from
spiritualism.

THE THINKERS. Swedenborg is scarcely known today except to
readers of Balzac, who expounded his theories in the novel
Seraphita, thus becoming a hero for the Symbolists—at once
sage and aesthete, spiritualist and dandy. The Norwegian visionary found a new public when artists discouraged by a world
dedicated to progress began to seek refuge in fantasy. Baudelaire had rediscovered the first of Swedenborg's principles
when he had written in his *Paradis Artificiels:* 'Natural things
exist to only a limited degree; reality lies only in dreams,' and
again in his tribute to Théophile Gautier: 'It is this admirable,
unchanging instinct for beauty which leads us to regard the
world and its sights as manifestations of heaven. The insatiable
hunger for all that belongs to the after-life which is revealed
to us by life on earth is the clearest proof of our immortality.'
The whole outlook of Symbolism is to be found in these lines
inspired by Swedenborg, and later the theorist of the Symbolist
movement, Albert Aurier, was to cite the visionary as his
principal authority.

A few quotations from Guy Michaud's fine work, *Le Message
Poétique du Symbolisme,* will show us what the enemies of
Realism expected from the philosophers. Thus Taine introduced Carlyle to them in the following terms: 'Ideas transformed into hallucinations lose their solidity. Human beings
take on the appearance of dreams. Mysticism seeps like a
vapour through the overheated walls of the crumbling mind . . .
The distinguishing feature of Carlyle as of any mystic is his
ability to see a double meaning in anything and everything.'
Here again we note the Baudelairean idea of correspondences,
as does this dictum which sheds light on a great many figures

in the paintings of Moreau and Burne-Jones: 'The hero is a
messenger sent from the impenetrable infinite, bearing news
for us' (Carlyle).

Any theory which undermined the rationalism inseparable from
materialism was welcome. Thus Jules Laforgue, excited by
Hartmann's *Philosophie des Unbewussten,* looked forward to
'a system of aesthetics in harmony with Hartmann's philosophy
of the unconscious, Darwin's theory of evolution, and Helm-
holtz's studies on the physics of colour.' As for pessimism,
Schopenhauer's works encouraged it in its darkest forms. He
was just as popular in society drawing-rooms as he was at the
Sorbonne, and the caricaturist Caran d'Ache frequently poked
fun at his female readers . . . Schopenhauer's influence was
countered by Nietzsche's success, but in 1893 Rémy de Gourmont could still write, in connection with a Filiger drawing
entitled *Idealism:*

> Idealism is an immoral, antisocial, inhuman doctrine
> of despair, and therefore an admirable doctrine in a
> period when what matters is not preservation but
> destruction . . . Everything I think is real . . . The
> only reality is thought. Schopenhauer's pessimistic
> ideal culminates in despotism; Hegel's optimistic ide-
> alism results in anarchy. One has only to apply the
> differential method to see that Schopenhauer is in the
> right.

Two French thinkers, whose reputation in their own day as-
tonishes us now, were greatly influenced by the philosophers
we have just quoted. They were the teachers of all the *fin de
siècle* dreamers. In 1889 Edouard Schuré published his *Grands
initiés,* which for several generations was the bedside book of
high-minded Frenchmen, much as the works of Teilhard de
Chardin are now. In it he wrote: 'Deprived of the sight of the
eternal horizons, literature and art have lost the sense of the
divine. Positivism and scepticism have produced nothing but
a desiccated generation without ideals, without inspiration and
without faith, doubting in itself and in human liberty.' Schuré
wanted to rediscover 'the profound learning, the secret doctrine
and the occult influence of the great initiates, prophets or reformers'. Ernest Hello, a Breton mystic who, in Léon Bloy's
happy phrase, was 'a man of genius with flashes of the commonplace', also tended to be pessimistic. 'Between the eighteenth century,' he wrote, 'and the century I shall call the
twentieth, even if it begins tomorrow, the clock of the earth
marks a slow and awful hour, an hour of transition: the terrible
nineteenth century. Waking slowly from its nightmare, it possesses nothing, but it yearns, my God, as the world has never
yearned before.' Hello had a certain influence on the art of his
times, for, before Huysmans, he violently attacked the Sul-
pician style and all commercial art based on the work of Hippolyte Flandrin and Ary Scheffer. (pp. 25-33)

THE DECADENTS. 'I love the word "Decadence", all gleaming
with crimson . . . It is made up of a mixture of carnal spirit
and melancholy flesh and all the violent splendours of the
Byzantine Empire . . . The collapse into the flames of races
exhausted by sensation at the invading sound of the enemy
trumpets' (Verlaine). 'Slowly and surely a belief is growing
in the bankruptcy of Nature which promises to become the
sinister faith of the twentieth century, if science or an invasion
of barbarians does not save an over-reflective humanity from
the fatigue of its own thought' (Paul Bourget, *Essais de psy-
chologie contemporaine, 1884*). These quotations are taken
from K. W. Swart's interesting thesis, *The Sense of Decadence.*
We are often surprised to find that Bourget was taken seriously,
but we should not forget that Nietzsche admired him and that

Wilde, in *Intentions,* imitated his *Dialogues esthétiques* of 1883. If Bourget, famous thinker and triumphant snob, was a pessimist, what else could be expected of a poor, unknown poet such as Jules Laforgue? Here is a note found among his papers about a novel he planned to write: 'It is an autobiography of my person and my thought transferred to a painter, to a painter's life and ambitions, but to a philosopher-painter, a macabre and pessimistic Chenavard. A failed, virgin genius, who dreams of four great frescoes: the epic of mankind, the *danse macabre* of the last period of the planet, the three stages of illusion.' The same anguish in the face of the absurdity of the world, this time taking the form of frenzy, is expressed in a letter from the young Belgian poet Verhaeren to Odilon Redon: 'I fly into a fury with myself because every other form of heroism is forbidden to me. I love things that are absurd, useless, impossible, frantic, excessive and intense, because they provoke me, because I feel them like thorns in my flesh . . .'

The society of Zola's Rougon-Macquarts certainly offered the pessimists countless reasons for despair, with the result that the atmosphere of the *fin de siècle* Bohemia was more bitter and dramatic than that of the Romantic Bohemia of the 1830s. The difference is illustrated quite well by the choice of drinks: the Decadents drank absinthe, the so-called 'green fairy'; the 1830 generation, on the other hand, preferred punch. A little later, opium had had its adepts, often in the form of laudanum, as with Nerval and Rossetti. Other drugs appeared on the scene about 1880; for a time morphine was in fashion, and then ether which could produce madness fairly quickly; but more often than not, absinthe was regarded as sufficient. Consequently much of the literary life of the Decadence was spent at the café, and every group had its own, for very few *salons* were open to young artists before 1892 or 1893. . . . In the absence of any Decadent *salons,* artists' studios also played a great part. Wilde enthused over the studios, with their more or less luxurious bric-à-brac, the company of the models, chats on the divans and discussions in front of the easels. The studio was as important as the café for another reason—painters, poets, thinkers and even musicians dreamed of a mingling of all the arts, and dabbled in everything. Studios were equally suitable for costume parties and spiritualist seances, two ways of travelling 'anywhere out of this world'. (pp. 33-5)

The extravagances of the Decadents can best be seen in their language. While the Aesthetes prided themselves on speaking a precise language, studded with expressions of ecstasy, the Decadents enriched the opulent vocabulary of the Parnassians and the Goncourt brothers' *écriture artiste* with fresh neologisms. It is not always easy to see where originality ended and pastiche began, and reviews such as *La Plume* and *Le Décadent* unhesitatingly accepted hair-raising contributions from fake Rimbauds. The best known satire on the language of the Decadents is *Les Déliquescences d'Adoré Floupette;* it is worth quoting instead a few definitions from the *Little Glossary for the Understanding of Decadent and Symbolist Poets* published by Jacques Plowert (Paul Adam & Félix Fénéon) in 1887:

> AMPHICURVED: Curved on both sides. 'Age-old nightmares in love with amphicurved orbs' (Moréas).
>
> (TRANSLATION): Succubi with their feet on the ground and fond of bottoms.
>
> VESANIC: Mad. 'Tormented by vesanic neuroses' (Fénéon).
>
> BALSAMMYRRHED: Steeped in balm. 'And the solitary plic-placs of balsamyrrhed, opaline fountains' (Laforgue).

The black humour which the Surrealists would try to achieve is to be found on every page of this glossary. People laughed in 1890 too, but a little hysterically. There were countless corpses in the works of poets and painters, who were fond of describing themselves as doomed. This macabre preciosity, cultivated in the studios of Montmartre, found an echo in Beardsley, Klimt and many foreign writers, the most famous of whom was d'Annunzio, for such extravagances, which reconciled the fashionable pessimism of the period with the exuberance of youth, were successful throughout Europe. It was thanks to the Decadents—and at that time Mallarmé and Verlaine, Moreau and Redon were classified as Decadents—that France, despised and denigrated after her defeat, recovered her prestige among the European *avant-garde.* This movement prolonged the Pre-Raphaelite movement in an increasingly bizarre direction: Wilde, for instance, came to Paris to take lessons in 'deliquescence' from Rollinat and Lorrain. Thus the so-called 'mauve Nineties' derived their sinister glow from the Celtic twilight as well as from the gaslamps of Paris. 'They delight in the rare and push worship of the unique to the point of decadence.' It was in 1884, in *Taches d'Encre,* that Barrès used this last word for the first time to describe the new spirit. And satirists were quick to seize upon the Decadents' affectations. Octave Mirbeau, the great friend of the Impressionists, who was always hostile to the Aesthetes and the Decadents, was one of the first to show his teeth. He invented a painter called Loys Jambois, modelled on Whistler and Montesquiou. The bric-à-brac surrounding this character recalls des Esseintes's drawing-room, Sarah Bernhardt's studio, Dorian Gray's boudoir, and the Duke of Brunswick's palace. Exoticism and historicism combined in it to form the culture in which *Art Nouveau* would be born and the chimeras raised.

This religion had few martyrs, but it found a great many worshippers among those new phenomena in French society: the snobs. The word *snob* became current in France about the same time. The snobs were those Aesthetes who were in the latest fashion; the beauty they admired was novelty, and that is why their enthusiasms lasted so short a time. . . . [Their] influence was immense and eventually disastrous, since it thrust a number of masters into unjustified oblivion after a brief hour of fame. The alliance of the snobs and the artists created, by the end of the nineteenth century, an aristocracy of taste served by Toorop, Khnopff, Klimt, all the exponents of *Art Nouveau,* an élite which itself had been nurtured on the works of the Pre-Raphaelites and especially of Moreau.

Jean Lorrain wrote in *Sensations et Souvenirs:*

> Oh, that man [Moreau] can boast of having broken open the door of Mystery; that man can claim the honour of having disturbed his entire century. He infected a whole generation sick today with a mystical nostalgia for the Beyond, with a dangerous passion for dead beauties, beauties of bygone ages which he resuscitated in the Mirror of Time . . . And that painful obsession with the symbols and perversions of the old theogonies, that curiosity about the divine debaucheries worshipped in the dead religions, has become the exquisite sickness of the refined souls of this *fin de siècle.*

These lines state once gain the themes of the first art to be deliberately decadent: the taste for death and occultism, the combination of mysticism and eroticism. But it would be a mistake to see in these tendencies a pose or a vice: they revealed above all else a compulsive need to escape from a materialistic society. (pp. 35-7)

• • • • •

[The] last quarter of the nineteenth century developed a style peculiar to itself, a style which can rightly be called Symbolist, so close are the links between the literary school of Symbolism and those artists who rejected both academic art and Impressionism. For the painters, the name of 'Symbolist' is more suitable than the terms '*Art Nouveau*' or '*Modern Style*', which are more applicable to the decorative arts than to intellectual painting. To appreciate the unity of this style, after studying its aspects in different countries, it may be useful to compare it with two other styles which are very close to it, one a long way away in time—Mannerism—and the other so near that at times it seems a continuation of Symbolism—Surrealism.

There are many similarities between mid-sixteenth-century Italy and post-1870 France. As the Italian States declined, the Papacy was ruined by the Reformation, and Renaissance art became academic, aesthetes began to appear in the courts of the Italian princes, who wanted to be amused with strange experiments. The Mannerists' works, which were produced at this time and seem artificial unless one knows of their links with the ballet and with allusive poetry such as Bembo's, were for a long time relegated to museum store-rooms. It was only after about 1920 that critics and art historians began to realize that this despised style had produced a few masterpieces and a great many curiosities. The latter more than the former reveal the analogies between Mannerism and Symbolism: in both styles artists elongate the human body and impose on it the artificial poses of the ballet, even in the most solemn scenes. The *figura serpentinata* which the aged Michelangelo recommended to his pupils is reminiscent of Sarah Bernhardt's 'Imaginary intertwinings'. There are resemblances too between the northern mannerist Bellange and de Feure, and, on a less frivolous level, between Duvet and Redon, both of them illustrators of the Apocalypse. There is a curious kinship between Pontormo's characters, always disquieting and melancholy in spite of the bright colours of their clothes, and Moreau's, between Rosso's indulgent angels and angelic fauns and Burne-Jones's knights. And there are many links, though more psychological this time, between Michelangelo and Moreau, whose *Chimères* were a nineteenth-century *Last Judgement*.

The Mannerists, as it happened, were as devoted to the Chimeras as were the nineteenth-century Symbolists. Rosso decorated the fireplaces of Fontainebleau with them, and they can be seen too in the Boboli Gardens and in ewers designed by Cellini—incidentally, the most representative artist of his time, as Gallé was of his, for in Decadent periods decorative art is more revealing than great art. Again, both periods show a pronounced taste for monsters: on the one hand, the statues of Bomanzo and Rosso's imaginary masquerades, and on the other, Böcklin's sirens and Beardsley's transvestites. Mention should be made of one final analogy: Mannerism adapted itself much more easily to the Nordic countries, with artists such as Spranger and Goltzius, than to France; and Cornelius Van Haarlem's *Massacre of the Innocents* bears a curious resemblance to Baron Frédéric's *Torrents*. It was also an art associated with courts—the court of the Medicis in Florence, or the court of Fontainebleau—just as Symbolism was the art of an aesthetic coterie.

The links between Symbolism and Surrealism are much less artistic than intellectual. Surrealists and Symbolists had two attitudes in common, both inspired by Baudelaire: the attitude of the *poète maudit* and the desire to shock the bourgeois. The Surrealists, in their childhood, had been fascinated by the pictures of certain poetic painters which were used as illustrations in children's books, almanacs and magazines. Rackham, Mucha, and Beardsley's imitators reached a wide public which had never heard of Moreau or Redon. In Germany Böcklin always remained a leading national painter, while the Pre-Raphaelites continued to delight a broad section of the English public for many years. (pp. 217-18)

In Italy, where Symbolism enjoyed a considerable vogue thanks to d'Annunzio, monuments were put up (until the Fascist-Classical style became predominant) decorated with groups of twisted figures, in the *Salammbô* style which also inspired the architect of Milan Station and the director of the film *Cabiria*. In Norway, on the eve of the Second World War, the sculptor Vigeland was still populating a park with statues symbolizing the different stages of life. And at the same period England was coming to admire Stanley Spencer's naïve symbolism.

However, it is the cinema rather than painting which has done most to prolong the dreams of the *fin de siècle* down to our own times. Bergman, who owes so much to Maeterlinck in his allegorical films, and to Strindberg in his social films, recreates the atmosphere of both Klinger and Munch. Another Nordic director, Murnau, produced a film some fifty years ago which is strangely evocative of the Symbolist dream: *Nosferatu*, which might have been born in Poe's imagination, revives themes one had thought to be utterly hackneyed—redeeming love, lost castles, and ghost ships with dead crews—recalling Gilkin's poems and certain faces by Khnopff. In the same vein, though with less attractive images, Dreyer's *Vampire* and nearly all the films starring Conrad Veidt continued to exploit the Decadent myths, sometimes in an Expressionist setting. While making certain concessions to vulgarity, the first great film directors therefore worked as Symbolists, long before the artists whose images they borrowed were rediscovered by the public. Sometimes the cinema can contribute something which painting was incapable of giving: thus Wagner, who had never found a painter worthy of him, found in Fritz Lang the perfect director of the *Nibelungen*. Fritz Lang again, in *Metropolis*, evokes Gustave Moreau's settings and Henry de Groux's crowds. Monsters like Frankenstein may have been born in the Gothic novel, but the films of which they are the heroes are reminiscent in certain respects of Villiers de l'Isle-Adam. There is more Symbolism, this time belated and deliberate, in Cocteau's *L'Eternel Retour*, with its Ophelian heroine, Wagnerian landscapes, and Schopenhauerian theme.

The screen also revived the Pre-Raphaelite beauty: Lillian Gish was the 'flower beneath the foot' in countless Hollywood melodramas; and Georgette Leblanc, beautifully photographed by Marcel L'Herbier, brought Mélisande's features to a succession of adventure films. The Sphinx lived again in vamps such as Pola Negri and Theda Bara; while Salome was reincarnated by Nazimova in costumes worthy of Beardsley. In Hollywood, a new Sodom dreaming of the glories of Byzantium, Erich von Stroheim perpetuated the erotic and costume eccentricities of the Vienna—Klimt's Vienna—in which he had been raised. And *Atlantis* would have been an animated Gustave Moreau, if only the producer had found actors for it as beautiful as the master's models, for the heroine of the film is the younger sister of Moreau's Helens and Herodiades.

Thus the cinema gave an increasingly mechanized world the images of which Symbolism had dreamt thirty years before. Surrealism, which, unlike the cinema, was addressed to an élite, thought it was carrying out a revolution when in fact, in many respects, it was simply continuing the poetic movement begun two generations earlier. The similarities with the circumstances which had given rise to Symbolism, or rather to the Decadence, are numerous: confusion after the First World War; rebellion against society, but this time supported by the Russian example; the influence of German philosophy; and the power of dreams, this time interpreted by Freud. The public too was the same, with anarchy rubbing shoulders with *avant-garde* snobbery. Taking over from the Baronne Deslandes and Lady Archibald Campbell, strange women like Lise Deharme and Nancy Cunard surrounded themselves with artists: they too had a fatal beauty which we can see in Alastair's drawings and Man Ray's photographs. André Breton's *Nadja* could have been painted by Rossetti and praised by Swinburne.

As is well known, there were many cases of madness and suicide among the members of both movements; there were many conversions too, though it was chiefly to Communism that the Surrealists turned, in a desperate longing for order, when they felt their dreams giving way beneath them. To both Decadents and Surrealists one could apply the magnificent observation of Arthur Symons, who after describing the failures of the visionaries, Coleridge's opium, Villiers's pretensions to the throne of Jerusalem, and Blake's madness, wrote of the last: 'For he who half lives in eternity endures a rending of the structures of the mind, a crucifixion of the intellectual body.'

If there are considerable resemblances between the two movements they differ completely in the ways in which they express themselves. Surrealism is aggressive: its Baudelairean penchant for shocking the bourgeois has turned into a feeling of positive hatred, or else, as in the case of Salvador Dali, has become a systematic exploitation of snobbery. There is more vitality too in the Surrealists; they may be precious, but they are never languid. What is more, they adore women, and that constitutes another great difference. In the matter of inspiration, Freud has turned everything topsy-turvy: the analysis of dreams gives rise to a very different aesthetic from one based on aspirations towards a world of dreams. Vagueness in the Decadents is replaced by irony in the Surrealists, but both movements adopt a symbolism which, in the long run, produces clichés, such as lilies and peacocks. Freud wrote his great work in the middle of the Symbolist period; it is based on equivalents, but not, like Swedenborg's work, on celestial equivalents.

With heroes like Sade and Lautréamont, Surrealism becomes a black Symbolism. The grey period is over, and the Mona Lisa has given place to the vulture which, according to Freud, represents the libido of the child Leonardo. These equivalents, and above all a common stock of images enable us to link a large number of Surrealist painters with the chimerical artists. This is particularly true of Belgium, where the two schools offer some remarkable examples. How can one fail to think of Khnopff when one discovers the world of statues created by Delvaux? And are not some of Magritte's landscapes suburbs of Bruges-le-Morte? But there is no lack of links in other countries too, even if they are fortuitous; between Toorop, for example, and the vague, disquieting worlds of Wilfredo Lam or Matta. DeChirico's antiquity owes a great deal to Böcklin's, and it is well known that the Island of the Dead has been used more than once by Dali. This last artist, who, Breton declared, had 'died in 1938', should not be overlooked: he brought the *Modern Style* back into fashion and amusingly publicized the discoveries of his elders. It must be admitted that Dali showed a certain audacity in writing in 1933: '*Art Nouveau* objects reveal to us in the most concrete fashion the persistence of dreams in the face of reality.' We find no Dali among the

[Symbolists] . . . , for none of them, good or bad, ever thought of establishing a precise relationship between his art and money; none of them would ever have allowed one of his works to become a publicity gimmick.

Some minor artists—called 'minor' because they have devoted themselves to the art of illustration—have been and still are great Decadents; and none is more admirable than Valentine Hugo, who forms a remarkable link between German Romanticism and Surrealism. Some of Valentine Hugo's portraits, and his well-known illustrations of Rimbaud, suggest a Burne-Jones who has read Freud. Fuchs, while imitating sixteenth-century German engravings, resembles the strangest of the Rosicrucians; indeed, under the cover of Surrealism, the fantastic tradition is still very much alive in Germany. As for the sphinxes, they have always been in fashion since the eighteenth century, painted yesterday by von Stuck and Khnopff, and today by Leonor Fini. This last artist is herself a character out of Jean Lorrain, and her sphinxes would have inspired many Decadents to commit wild eccentricities. Bellmer's dolls, those rejuvenated, dislocated versions of Rops's old whores, also belong to the world of Symbolism. In the case of Max Ernst, who dominates his period as Moreau dominated his, his collages . . . have the same inspiration as Klinger's canvases, and the trees of his great petrified forests, with fearsome birds flying out of them, have the same roots as Böcklin's. Finally, Tchelichev's work *Cache-Cache* is full of esoteric symbols: the admirable draughtsmanship of that New York Russian, in the service of a philosophical art, would have won him a surer fame in the last century than in our own day.

Naturally, the differences between Symbolism and Surrealism are just as great as the resemblances. The latter movement is still very much alive after fifty years, and has not suffered the sudden disgrace of the former. This longevity cannot be explained solely by the talents of the respective artists. Surrealism is in fact an entertaining art, which was sorely needed during the boring reign of Abstract painting. We must be grateful to the painters and writers of that school for remaining aloof from Sartre's world, just as the Symbolists shunned that of Zola. The Surrealists could indeed have echoed Schuré's words: 'The abysses of the unconscious open up within ourselves, showing us the gulf from which we have emerged and the dizzy heights to which we aspire.' Thus Breton repeatedly paid homage to the Symbolist painters, writing with the serene insolence of a Magus, of a Villiers or a Baudelaire: 'Moreau, planning shortly before he died to paint that "Argo whose mast was made from a Dordona oak", consoles me for the existence of Renoir, exulting over his last dish of fruit to the extent of believing—and declaring—that he was still making progress.' And it was Moreau once again whom the best critic of contemporary painting, Lucien Alvard, quoted approvingly a few years ago in his preface to the catalogue of the *Antagonisme* exhibition: 'Art is the strenuous attempt to express inner feelings in plastic form.' (pp. 219-20, 223-26)

Today, as in the days of the silent film, it is the cinema rather than painting which is recreating the world of yesterday's poets, or rather which is giving life to their images, although without trying to give them a significance likely to strain the understanding of a child of twelve. Thus Vadim's *Barbarella*, an essay in infantile science fiction, revives all the themes of the *fin de siècle:* Barbarella is Ophelia lost among a host of Salomes; the Black Queen is the eternal Medusa; and the Angel is Péladan's chaste hermaphrodite. Many of his ideas are worthy of Villiers de l'Isle-Adam's *L'Eve Future,* and may well have been borrowed from that work; and the *Art Nouveau* sets, particularly the harem, in which the girls wear the most fantastic costumes, would have delighted the poet. The Angel's flight above a dead planet is pure Moreau, and some of the luminous shapes are reminiscent of Redon. Again, in Fellini's admirable *Satyricon* there is a deliberate imitation of Beardsley and Klimt, and sequences which reproduce pictures by Böcklin, Rochegrosse, and Alma-Tadema. The theme of the Byzantine Empire with all the perversions and superstitions of the Decadence has been revived with telling effect in a society which is growing increasingly aware of its own decline.

When the young artists of today, attracted by these images, start drawing, they adopt the style of either Beardsley or Mucha. Beardsley's admirers use stippling and blots to express a sort of naïve perversity; gentler natures prefer Mucha's elongations and soft colours. Beardsley and Mucha: these two names already enjoy greater prestige with the young than those of Pollock or Dubuffet, Monet or Renoir. 'The evocatory witchcraft of chance gives rise to similarities,' wrote Gustave Kahn. It matters little whether these repetitions of poetic themes are conscious or not, whether they are projected on a screen or a canvas, or even whether they delight a roomful of mental defectives or a theatre sparsely dotted with aesthetes. These dreams remain a living rejection of everyday life. (p. 227)

Philippe Jullian, " 'Fin de Siècle' " and "Conclusion," in his Dreamers of Decadence: Symbolist Painters of the 1890s, *translated by Robert Baldick, Praeger Publishers, 1971, pp. 25-38, 217-28.*

REMY DE GOURMONT

[*Gourmont, a French poet, novelist, critic, and essayist, was one of the founders of the influential* Mercure de France, *a journal that championed the Symbolist movement in France during the late nineteenth century. He is considered one of the most perceptive and sensitive of the Symbolist critics, and his work is noted for its detached and objective tone. In the preface to his* Le livre des masques (The Book of Masks), *excerpted below, Gourmont discusses the qualities of Symbolist writing, particularly its experimentation with literary form, its concern with the nature of art rather than with the issues of life, and its celebration of individual expression.*]

It is difficult to characterize a literary evolution in the hour when the fruits are still uncertain and the very blossoming in the orchard unconsummated. Precocious trees, slow-developing and dubious trees which one would not care, however, to call sterile: the orchard is very diverse and rich, too rich. The thickness of the leaves brings shadow, and the shadow discolors the flowers and dulls the hues of the fruit.

We will stroll through this rich, dark orchard and sit down for a moment at the foot of the strongest, fairest, and most agreeable trees.

Literary evolutions receive a name when they merit it by importance, necessity and fitness. Quite often, this name has no precise meaning, but is useful in serving as a rallying sign to all who accept it, and as the aiming point for those who attack it. Thus the battle is fought around a purely verbal labarum. What is the meaning of *Romanticism?* It is easier to feel than to explain it. What is the meaning of *Symbolism?* Practically nothing, if we adhere to the narrow etymological sense. If we pass beyond, it may mean individualism in literature, liberty in art, abandonment of taught formulas, tendencies towards the new and strange, or even towards the bizarre. It may also

mean idealism, a contempt for the social anecdote, anti-naturalism, a propensity to seize only the characteristic details of life, to emphasize only those acts that distinguish one man from another, to strive to achieve essentials; finally, for the poets symbolism seems allied to free verse, that is, to unswathed verse whose young body may frolic at ease, liberated from embarrassments of swaddling clothes and straps.

But all this has little affinity with the syllables of the word, for we must not let it be insinuated that symbolism is only the transformation of the old allegory or of the art of personifying an idea in a human being, a landscape, or a narrative. Such an art is the whole of art, art primordial and eternal, and a literature freed from this necessity would be unmentionable. It would be null, with as much aesthetic significance as the clucking of the hocco or the braying of the wild ass.

Literature, indeed, is nothing more than the artistic development of the idea, the symbolization of the idea by means of imaginary heroes. Heroes, or men (for every man in his sphere is a hero), are only sketched by life; it is art which perfects them by giving them, in exchange for their poor sick souls, the treasure of an immortal idea, and the humblest, if chosen by a great poet, may be called to this participation. Who so humble as that Aeneas whom Virgil burdens with all the weight of being the idea of Roman force, and who so humble as that Don Quixote on whom Cervantes imposes the tremendous load of being at once Roland, the four sons Aymon, Amadis, Palmerin, Tristan and all the knights of the Round Table! The history of Symbolism would be the history of man himself, since man can only assimilate a symbolized idea. Needless to insist on this, for one might think that the young devotees of symbolism are unaware of the *Vita Nuova* and the character Beatrice, whose frail, pure shoulders nevertheless keep erect under the complex weight of symbols with which the poet overwhelms her.

Whence, then, came the illusion that symbolizing of the idea was a novelty?

In these last years, we had a very serious attempt of literature based on a scorn of the idea, a disdain of the symbol. We are acquainted with its theory, which seems culinary: take a slice of life, etc. Zola, having invented the recipe, forgot to serve it. His "slices of life" are heavy poems of a miry, tumultuous lyricism, popular romanticism, democratic symbolism, but ever full of an idea, always pregnant with allegoric meaning. The idealistic revolt, then, did not rear itself against the works (unless against the despicable works) of naturalism, but against its theory, or rather against its pretension; returning to the eternal, antecedent necessities of art, the rebels presumed to express new and even surprising truths in professing their wish to reinstate the idea in literature; they only relighted the torch; they also lighted, all around, many small candles.

There is, nevertheless, a new truth, which has recently entered literature and art, a truth quite metaphysical and quite *a priori* (in appearance), quite young, since it is only a century old, and truly new, since it has not yet served in the aesthetic order. This evangelical and marvelous truth, liberating and renovating, is the principle of the world's ideality. With reference to that thinking subject, man, the world, everything that is external, only exists according to the idea he forms of it. We only know phenomena, we only reason from appearances; all truth in itself escapes us; the essence is unassailable. It is what Schopenhauer has popularized under this so simple and clear formula: the world is my representation. I do not see that which is; that which is, is what I see. As many thinking men, so many diverse and perhaps dissimilar worlds. This doctrine, which Kant left on the way to be flung to the rescue of the castaway morality, is so fine and supple that one transposes it from theory to practice without clashing with logic, even the most exigent. It is a universal principle of emancipation for every man capable of understanding. It has only revolutionized aesthetics, but here it is a question only of aesthetics.

Definitions of the beautiful are still given in manuals; they go farther; formulas are given by which artists attain the expression of the beautiful. There are institutes for teaching these formulas, which are but the average and epitome of ideas or of preceding appreciations. Theories in aesthetics generally being obscure, the ideal paragon, the model, is joined to them. In those institutes (and the civilized world is but a vast Institute) all novelty is held blasphemous, all personal affirmation becomes an act of madness. Nordau, who has read, with bizarre patience, all contemporary literature, propagated this idea, basely destructive of all individualism, that "nonconformity" is the capital crime of a writer [see excerpt dated 1895]. We violently differ in opinion. A writer's capital crime is conformity, imitativeness, submission to rules and precepts. A writer's work should be not only the reflection, but the magnified reflection of his personality. The only excuse a man has for writing is to express himself, to reveal to others the world reflected in his individual mirror; his only excuse is to be original. He should say things not yet said, and say them in a form not yet formulated. He should create his own aesthetics, and we should admit as many aesthetics as there are original minds, judging them according to what they are not.

Let us then admit that symbolism, though excessive, unseasonable and pretentious, is the expression of individualism in art. (pp. 9-15)

> *Remy de Gourmont, in a preface to his* The Book of Masks, *translated by Jack Lewis, 1921. Reprint by Books for Libraries Press, 1967, pp. 9-17.*

ARTHUR SYMONS

[*While Symons initially gained notoriety as a member of the English Decadent movement of the 1890s, he eventually established himself as one of the most important critics of the modern era. As a member of the iconoclastic generation of fin de siècle aesthetes that included Aubrey Beardsley and Oscar Wilde, Symons wholeheartedly assumed the role of the world-weary cosmopolite and sensation hunter, composing verses in which he attempted to depict the bohemian world of the modern artist. However, it was as a critic that Symons made his most important contribution to literature. His* The Symbolist Movement in Literature, *from which the following excerpt is drawn, was responsible for exposing Symbolism to the English-speaking public. In this work, Symons provided his English contemporaries with an appropriate vocabulary with which to define their new aesthetic—one that communicated their concern with dreamlike states, imagination, and a reality that exists beyond the boundaries of the senses. Symons also discerned that the concept of the symbol as a vehicle by which a "hitherto unknown reality was suddenly revealed" could become the basis for the entire modern aesthetic. A proper use of the symbol "would flash upon you the soul of that which can be apprehended only by the soul—the finer sense of things unseen, the deeper meaning of things evident." This anticipated and influenced James Joyce's concept of an artistic "epiphany," T. S. Eliot's "moment in time," and laid the foundation for much of modern poetic theory. Here, Symons seeks to define the elusive qualities of Symbolism and articulate the aims and techniques of*

the Symbolist writers. For additional commentary by Symons, see excerpt below.]

Without symbolism there can be no literature; indeed, not even language. What are words themselves but symbols, almost as arbitrary as the letters which compose them, mere sounds of the voice to which we have agreed to give certain significations, as we have agreed to translate these sounds by those combinations of letters? Symbolism began with the first words uttered by the first man, as he named every living thing; or before them, in heaven, when God named the world into being. And we see, in these beginnings, precisely what Symbolism in literature really is: a form of expression, at the best but approximate, essentially but arbitrary, until it has obtained the force of a convention, for an unseen reality apprehended by the consciousness. It is sometimes permitted to us to hope that our convention is indeed the reflection rather than merely the sign of that unseen reality. We have done much if we have found a recognisable sign.

"A symbol," says Comte Goblet d'Alviella, in his book on *The Migration of Symbols,* "might be defined as a representation which does not aim at being a reproduction." Originally, as he points out, used by the Greeks to denote "the two halves of the tablet they divided between themselves as a pledge of hospitality," it came to be used of every sign, formula, or rite by which those initiated in any mystery made themselves secretly known to one another. Gradually the word extended its meaning, until it came to denote every conventional representation of idea by form, of the unseen by the visible. "In a Symbol," says Carlyle, "there is concealment and yet revelation: hence, therefore, by Silence and by Speech acting together, comes a double significance." And, in that fine chapter of *Sartor Resartus,* he goes further, vindicating for the word its full value: "In the Symbol proper, what we can call a Symbol, there is ever, more or less distinctly and directly, some embodiment and revelation of the Infinite; the Infinite is made to blend itself with the Finite, to stand visible, and as it were, attainable there."

It is in such a sense as this that the word Symbolism has been used to describe a movement which, during the last generation, has profoundly influenced the course of French literature. All such words, used of anything so living, variable, and irresponsible as literature, are, as symbols themselves must so often be, mere compromises, mere indications. Symbolism, as seen in the writers of our day, would have no value if it were not seen also, under one disguise or another, in every great imaginative writer. What distinguishes the Symbolism of our day from the Symbolism of the past is that it has now become conscious of itself, in a sense in which it was unconscious even in Gérard de Nerval, to whom I trace the particular origin of the literature which I call Symbolist. The forces which mould the thought of men change, or men's resistance to them slackens; with the change of men's thought comes a change of literature, alike in its inmost essence and in its outward form: after the world has starved its soul long enough in the contemplation and the re-arrangement of material things, comes the turn of the soul; and with it comes the literature of which I write in this volume, a literature in which the visible world is no longer a reality, and the unseen world no longer a dream.

The great epoch in French literature which preceded this epoch was that of the offshoot of Romanticism which produced Baudelaire, Flaubert, the Goncourts, Taine, Zola, Leconte de Lisle. Taine was the philosopher both of what had gone before him and of what came immediately after; so that he seems to explain at once Flaubert and Zola. It was the age of Science, the age of material things; and words, with that facile elasticity which there is in them, did miracles in the exact representation of everything that visibly existed, exactly as it existed. Even Baudelaire, in whom the spirit is always an uneasy guest at the orgie of life, had a certain theory of Realism which tortures many of his poems into strange, metallic shapes, and fills them with imitative odours, and disturbs them with a too deliberate rhetoric of the flesh. Flaubert, the one impeccable novelist who has ever lived, was resolute to be the novelist of a world in which art, formal art, was the only escape from the burden of reality, and in which the soul was of use mainly as the agent of fine literature. The Goncourts caught at Impressionism to render the fugitive aspects of a world which existed only as a thing of flat spaces, and angles, and coloured movement, in which sun and shadow were the artists; as moods, no less flitting, were the artists of the merely receptive consciousnesses of men and women. Zola has tried to build in brick and mortar inside the covers of a book; he is quite sure that the soul is a nervous fluid, which he is quite sure some man of science is about to catch for us, as a man of science has bottled the air, a pretty, blue liquid. Leconte de Lisle turned the world to stone, but saw, beyond the world, only a pause from misery in a Nirvana never subtilised to the Eastern ecstasy. And, with all these writers, form aimed above all things at being precise, at saying rather than suggesting, at saying what they had to say so completely that nothing remained over, which it might be the business of the reader to divine. And so they have expressed, finally, a certain aspect of the world; and some of them have carried style to a point beyond which the style that says, rather than suggests, cannot go. The whole of that movement comes to a splendid funeral in M. de Heredia's sonnets, in which the literature of form says its last word, and dies.

Meanwhile, something which is vaguely called Decadence had come into being. That name, rarely used with any precise meaning, was usually either hurled as a reproach or hurled back as a defiance. It pleased some young men in various countries to call themselves Decadents, with all the thrill of unsatisfied virtue masquerading as uncomprehended vice. As a matter of fact, the term is in its place only when applied to style; to that ingenious deformation of the language, in Mallarmé for instance, which can be compared with what we are accustomed to call the Greek and Latin of the Decadence. No doubt perversity of form and perversity of matter are often found together, and, among the lesser men especially, experiment was carried far, not only in the direction of style. But a movement which in this sense might be called Decadent could but have been a straying aside from the main road of literature. Nothing, not even conventional virtue, is so provincial as conventional vice; and the desire to "bewilder the middle-classes" is itself middle-class. The interlude, half a mock-interlude, of Decadence, diverted the attention of the critics while something more serious was in preparation. That something more serious has crystallised, for the time, under the form of Symbolism, in which art returns to the one pathway, leading through beautiful things to the eternal beauty.

In most of the writers . . . [who sum] up in themselves all that is best in Symbolism, it will be noticed that the form is very carefully elaborated, and seems to count for at least as much as in those writers [who are over-possessed by form]. . . . Here, however, all this elaboration comes from a very different motive and leads to other ends. There is such a thing as perfecting form that form may be annihilated. All the art of Verlaine is in bringing verse to a bird's song, the art of Mallarmé in

bringing verse to the song of an orchestra. In Villiers de l'Isle-Adam drama becomes an embodiment of spiritual forces, in Maeterlinck not even their embodiment, but the remote sound of their voices. It is all an attempt to spiritualise literature, to evade the old bondage of rhetoric, the old bondage of exteriority. Description is banished that beautiful things may be evoked, magically; the regular beat of verse is broken in order that words may fly, upon subtler wings. Mystery is no longer feared, as the great mystery in whose midst we are islanded was feared by those to whom that unknown sea was only a great void. We are coming closer to nature, as we seem to shrink from it with something of horror, disdaining to catalogue the trees of the forest. And as we brush aside the accidents of daily life, in which men and women imagine that they are alone touching reality, we come closer to humanity, to everything in humanity that may have begun before the world and may outlast it.

Here, then, in this revolt against exteriority, against rhetoric, against a materialistic tradition; in this endeavour to disengage the ultimate essence, the soul, of whatever exists and can be realized by the consciousness; in this dutiful waiting upon every symbol by which the soul of things can be made visible; literature, bowed down by so many burdens, may at last attain liberty, and its authentic speech. In attaining this liberty, it accepts a heavier burden; for in speaking to us so intimately, so solemnly, as only religion had hitherto spoken to us, it becomes itself a kind of religion, with all the duties and responsibilities of the sacred ritual. (pp. 1-9)

Arthur Symons, in an introduction to his The Symbolist Movement in Literature, *revised edition, E. P. Dutton & Company, 1919, pp. 1-9.*

EMILE VERHAEREN

[*Today considered the most important poet in Belgian literature, Verhaeren was especially venerated during his lifetime for his energetic spirit, lofty socialism, lyrical tributes to common folk, and open faith in scientific and industrial progress. His work, particularly in its beautiful imagery and exploitation of the vers libre form, bears strong similarities to the verse of the Symbolists. In the following excerpt, Verhaeren discusses the genesis of the Symbolist movement and the main characteristics of Symbolism.*]

[All poetic reforms, from Hugo to Verlaine,] led to modifications rather than transformations; but they cleared the way, by their slow but ceaseless advance, for a deeper and more thorough reform. This was accomplished by the later modern schools, writers of blank verse, symbolists and decadents. Never were so many different names given to artistic groups. But what matter the labels, they will all be carried away when the work of these innovators has melted into the general growth of literature. Their action was a collective one, as if poetry already shared in the new mode of human activity, which depends not upon the single effort of one man, leading others, but upon the co-operation of many such agents all working towards a common end.

I will quote a few names: Rimbaud, Laforgue, Kahn, Moréas, Maeterlinck, Regnier, Viele-Griffin, Stuart Merril, André Gide, Retté, Francis Jammes, Henry Bataille, Charles Van Lerberghe, Max Elskamp, André Fontainas, Albert Mockel, Henri Ghéon. Each different from the rest—some with an individuality the more clearly defined according as their talent expands and asserts itself, they all concur in guiding in the direction of a wider freedom of form and a more truthful synthesis of matter, that crystallisation begun at the dawn of the nineteenth century, and of which their own work is the ultimate consequence.

The present school of critics explain and justify in the name of logic, the convulsion that has shaken prosody to its very depths. Granted that they have reason on their side, they yet have not sufficient reason.

They ask: Why prohibit a hiatus at the meeting of two words and allow it in the body of a word? Why prescribe *il y a (a verb)* and tolerate *Illion (a substantive)*? Why insist upon the rhyme being full, solemn and "rich," in elevated subjects, when such rhyme almost invariably leads to a punning jingle? Why talk of caesura when our language contains words of seven or eight syllables? Why permit the *enjambement* and reject with scorn lines of thirteen and fourteen feet? And any but a purblind critic arrives at the conclusion that the poets of today are doing rational work.

Granted, but in matters of art, strict logic is not a decisive argument; poetry wells up like a boiling spring from the depths of human nature, and like love and fancy it refuses to obey the mandates of pure reason. Whether or not the labour of poets is logical is quite a secondary matter. The truth is this: from its earliest beginnings, French verse has been based upon measure; today it is sought to found it upon rhythm. It is not the want of logic of the older prosody that is impugned; it is the principle on which it rested.

Rhythm, measure! Assuredly every measure is possessed with rhythm, every rhythm with measure. The distinction between these two almost identical terms is nevertheless a notable one. The form of the older French poetry, based upon measure, appears like a mould, preordained and sharply defined, into which a whole train of thought is compressed, without ever widening, restricting or doing away with a single division. The form is pre-existent; it therefore determines the length, progress and subdivision of the lyrical movements. Rhythm may also be termed a form, but a flexible form of infinite variety, literally embodying the thought, for what is it but that thought which, in finding expression, fashions out its own mould? There is not pre-existence but co-existence between the thought and its materialisation. The modern poets reject measure, the superimposed form, and adopt rhythm, the direct form. The sentiments evolved in a poem thus appear in all their original spontaneity.

But, it may be asked, not without a pardonable diffidence, is it then possible to seize in so subtle and direct a manner every thought that springs into existence? For the real poet this presents no difficulty. Alone he possesses the secret gift, at the very instant a thought takes birth in his brain, of at once conceiving it as a living entity with its inherent static or dynamic action. Now this action is rhythm itself. The true poet cannot, therefore, but be a perfect master of rhythm. All great masters were so. In spite of the guiding-strings and shackles of conventional, sterile and useless metre, Racine, Lafontaine, Lamartine, Hugo, Baudelaire, Verlaine cannot but obey the movement of the idea. (pp. 730-32)

A poem therefore appears as the notation of movements of the mind, and no longer as a development conforming to such and such a rule of prosody. A canvas to work upon is no longer needed; the knots of the work are themselves its chain and woof. Canalisation is superseded, the river is left to hollow out its own bed. Such a theory may conceivably frighten second-rate poets. Granted. In art all is either easy or impossible.

The earliest poets were free singers; they evolved from themselves the form of their emotions. They preceded all manner of criticism or laying down of laws. It is to them, to their source of youth and light, that we should return. If we examine how it came about that in those far-off times rhythm was made subservient to measure, the domination of the latter can only appear as that of an usurper.

It was the pedagogues who brought it about. When certain ancient rhapsodists, either by habit or sterility, congealed their songs into set forms, the scribes stepped in and decreed that poets yet unborn should be subjected to this restriction, thus withering up the future in the name of the past. The art of the poet is spontaneous and intensive, that of the critic rational and restrictive; there can be no agreement between them, there must be war to the knife. The critic has domesticated the lofty plant of pristine and savage beauty; he has trimmed, pruned, stunted and dwarfed it. He has grown it in conservatories, cultivated it in nurseries. He has exhibited it neat, symmetrical and glossy. Now it was meant to live in the open, affronting wind and rain, storms, mists, and sunshine; it would have thriven in the rich virgin soil, it would have shot up and spread, dropping its seed into the vast lap of Nature, to be blown away further and further to the far end of the horizon.

The story of the primitive poets is a salutary lesson to us. From the moment the critics appear, a new literary caste is formed, grounded upon irony and contradiction. If only they were content to exercise a certain supervision, if their labour were restricted to making observations and experiments. A Taine instructs but does not dogmatise. The rest appraise, pronounce, condemn. They do not understand that a poet is nothing if not a creator, that is a giver of life. And it is with dead matter, with former life now stark and cold, that they bind and confine it in the narrow coffin of their judgments.

In the seventeenth century every bold emancipation was impossible; in the nineteenth, thanks to the liberating efforts of Lamartine, Hugo, Baudelaire, Verlaine, rebellion rears its head and deliverance is at hand. Modern prosody has thus achieved liberty; modern inspiration, untrammelled truth. At the time it set out for this conquest, realism reigned supreme. From the Parnassian group a few poets had become severed, chief of whom was François Coppée. He had wandered off to meet the novelists in the by-ways of minute and direct observation. *"Le Petit Epicier de Montrouge"* was the model of that fireside poetry which he made so popular.

The Parnassians were archaeologists, historians and scientists. Exotic subjects attracted them, they revelled in the Past. They also sought after truth, but after truth as it is to be found in books. They revived old civilisations and old legends, as taught by exegesis and science. They thus reflected one of the great conquests of their age, the science of ruins. They unconsciously displayed certain affinities with the Naturalists whom they combated. Both belonged to the *documentary* school, the one exploring ages that are dead, the other the living age, and Gustave Flaubert might be said to belong to either, according as he wrote *Hérodias* or *l'Education Sentimentale.*

It was to this love of precise, clear, and wholly experimental truth, to this truth to material fact, that the building up of synthetic truth was opposed by the new school. They admit the dogma triumphantly proclaimed in philosophy by Kant and Schopenhauer: Truth cannot be found in material objects, it exists only in the idea. Though reflected to infinity in the sensible universe, the categories of our understanding—subjective forms—may perceive, but cannot penetrate it. The world is but a conjunction of appearances or symbols.

The initiator of this new literary creed, of this new mode of composition, was Stéphane Mallarmé. His verses are like the luminous semi-transparent veils of some great Isis—the underlying thought of each poem. These veils, upon which every part of the goddess's body imprints its warmth and motion, are but the exteriorisation of her beauty, and it is through them that it must be sought. The Parnassians showed, described and related. They amplified to a moderate extent. They were Romanticists grown cold and formal.

Stéphane Mallarmé does not design, he evokes. Picking out from among the theories of Baudelaire those relating to analogy and relation, he assembles and displays them in successive gradations; he evolves from them sufficient light to at last reveal the object. Further, as this process creates round each single thought a succession of different aspects, and as each of these may have its own peculiar, if superficial, significance, it results that the meaning of the poem is doubled or trebled. There is the shell and the kernel: the husk and the fruit. The tower no longer stands out rude and sharply defined in the blinding light of noon; it looms forth slowly from out the misty atmosphere, dimly felt before it is seen. And when at last it stands revealed, it rises with the more solemn majesty.

To realise the beauty of a poem by Mallarmé is a conquest of the mind. You are rebutted, you persevere, you go astray. When you reach the goal, you can never forget. All who have listened to his wondrous teaching, have imbibed something of his doctrine. All, in varying degrees, have felt the seduction of his discourse. The influence of his new method of lyrical composition is felt in the *Chansons d'Amants,* by Gustave Kahn; in the *Aréthuse,* by Henry de Régnier; in the *Cantilènes,* by Moréas; in the *Chevauchée,* by Viele-Griffin. No doubt symbolism always existed in literature, and it was not left to any of us moderns to discover it. But Stéphane Mallarmé marked it with a new and distinctive seal. Others used symbols unconsciously; he did so methodically, with the full knowledge of what he was doing. The most laboured and perfect models are encased in his poems. (pp. 732-34)

The peculiar merit of this art, which few critics understand, is to aim at the very essence—whether thoughts or feelings—to raise them to their highest and most universal power, to banish from them all that might determine them in point of space or time. It imparts to them something of the anonymous character of solemn lapidary inscriptions. You can imagine the sonnets of Mallarmé engraved upon stelas, standing by the roadside along the great thoroughfares of human thought. They provoke the lingering wayfarer to long and searching meditation; they are built up of learned syntheses and pure conceptions; and the images they suggest are infinite. If true poetry is the language of figures, of striking and well-applied analogies, his, before all others, may serve as an example.

And yet there is none but will perceive with what pitfalls this art, in spite of its undeniable advantages, is surrounded. All depends upon the skill, I had almost said the witchcraft, of the enchanter. If the veils in which he shrouds his visions are not of perfect texture, if they are too flimsy or too opaque, if, for fear of being obvious, he remains obscure and impenetrable, the charm does not operate, and those who expected a miracle cry shame upon the false prophet.

Such, then, was the upheaval of form and matter brought about by the recent schools of French poetry. It had been . . . prepared at great length. It had become inevitable. The alexandrine, broken, shattered, and crumbled by Hugo, would no longer have been recognised as a measure by its creators of the sixteenth and seventeenth century. It was now but a vain and illusive shadow. (p. 735)

Emile Verhaeren, ''French Poetry of To-Day,'' translated by C. Heywood, in The Fortnightly Review, *Vol. 75, No. CCCCXII, April 1, 1901, pp. 723-38.*

ANNA BALAKIAN

[*Balakian is a critic of French literature who has written extensively on writers of the Symbolist, Surrealist, and Dadaist movements. Here, she observes the problematic nature of the term ''Symbolism'' and discusses its development into an international literary movement.*]

Although elusive in meaning, the term ''symbolism'' has become a convenient label for literary historians to designate the post-Romantic era. At the same time, it has provided a target for those literary critics who consider symbolism an artificial classification of heterogeneous writers, separated from each other in terms of nationality, time, and literary genre.

To the French, ''Symbolism'' still denotes technically the period between 1885 and 1895, during which it became a widely espoused literary movement and as a *cénacle* produced manifestoes, sponsored literary periodicals such as *La Revue Wagnérienne, La Vogue, Revue Indépendante,* and *La Décadence,* and attracted to Paris poets and literary personalities from all parts of the Western world. As a specific literary school, ''symbolism'' may best be written with a capital ''S.''

Critics in the Anglo-Saxon world, on the other hand, taking their cue from Arthur Symons, who was a contemporary of Verlaine and Rimbaud, tend to think of French ''symbolism'' (this time it is best written with a small ''s'') in terms of the ''big four'' of French poetry of the second half of the nineteenth century: Baudelaire, Rimbaud, Verlaine, Mallarmé. Using the word ''symbolism'' in the same broad sense as Symons, T. S. Eliot added to the list such noncoterie poets as Laforgue and Corbière. C. M. Bowra, in his introduction to *The Heritage of Symbolism* links Baudelaire, Verlaine, and Mallarmé as the avant-garde of the symbolist movement on the basis of their great innovations in terms of literary techniques. In this way, Bowra encompasses within the symbolist tradition all those poets who ''attempted to convey a supernatural experience in the language of visible things, and therefore almost every word is a symbol and is used not for its common purpose but for the association which it evokes of a reality beyond the senses.'' He calls these poets ''post-symbolists,'' as does Kenneth Cornell in his book *The Post-Symbolist Period.* The prefix ''post,'' however, implies a greater separation from the symbolist tradition than there really was. This flexible use of the term embraces writers, posterior to the Symbolist generation, who accepted the Symbolist school and who, through their total or partial adherence to its poetic principles or mystical orientation, maintained the presence of symbolism as a literary convention and signature well into the twentieth century. The fact is that the heirs of Symbolism are today more prominent in the annals of literary history than those who founded the Symbolist school. Such diversified works as those of Valéry, Rilke, Hofmannsthal, Yeats, Jimenez, Wallace Stevens, A. A. Blok, and to some extent T. S. Eliot have shared the legacy.

The literary critics and historians of symbolism have been almost as numerous and as nationally diverse as the adherents themselves. Sometimes their studies have mirrored the critic's own spiritual image; sometimes they have been documentary records of the events that marked the concerted activities of the Symbolist writers. Others have scanned the far reaches in space and time of what was one of the closest intellectual alliances in European history, marked by a cosmopolitanism totally devoid of self-consciousness or political intent. Still others have traced the sources of symbolism back to the literary traditions of the common European heritage. There is not much left to be added to all these works.

From the beginning, the hybrid movement has presented a difficult research problem—the classification of writings, profuse and seemingly disparate in form and intent, held together by a label which had from the very start multiple connotations. The earliest studies, such as André Barre's *Le Symbolisme: essai historique,* classified the symbolists in tight, genealogical categories on the basis of generations, and without any attempt to distinguish major from minor poets. In fact, some of those whom time and distance have reduced to minor status were so voluble during their lifetime that they loomed great to their contemporaries and distorted critical judgment.

In opposition to this chronological classification, there has developed a tendency to demonstrate that the relationship among many of these poets was a common negative reaction to existing literary traditions which stemmed from Romantic conventions. In his study *The Symbolist Movement,* Kenneth Cornell describes this attitude: "The resolve not to accept a pattern was stronger than the desire to create a formula." This attitude, which indicates a common climate rather than a common aesthetics, has tended to show how artificial was the original hierarchy, based more or less on the self-evaluation of the theorists among the Symbolists. The most famous book on symbolism viewed as a spiritual alliance is Edmund Wilson's *Axel's Castle.* Wilson identified the symbolist image with the recluse hero of Villiers de l'Isle-Adam's poetic drama *Axël* which, unread and unperformed, has left an indelible mark as the symbol of the inhabitant of our latter-day ivory towers of inner existence. Defining the symbolist mode of writing in terms of this withdrawal into private worlds of thought and cryptic styles of communication, Wilson was able to include in the orbit of symbolism such widely varying writers as T. S. Eliot, Proust, Gertrude Stein, and the Dadaists.

Rejection of the world and revolt against the accepted ways of writing have been the theme and variations of studies on symbolism by Paul Valéry, Guy Michaud, and Albert Thibaudet, to mention but a few. Another line of symbolist studies has concentrated on the psychological traumas of the symbolist cult. . . . Still another group of critics have studied symbolism from the point of view of the differences rather than the affinities discernible among the so-called symbolists. . . . According to such studies symbolism might be considered a superficial cloak to hide realism, classicism, or simply another phase of the Parnassian ideal. Works such as these make one wonder if the word "symbolism" was indeed a face without features, an expression tossed about for the purpose of mystification. If it had no common denominator, then its validity as a critical term would be questionable. To be negotiable in critical exchange, a literary label must have either temporal significance or qualitative content. Since works dating anywhere from 1857 (the year Baudelaire's *Les Fleurs du Mal* was published) to the 1930s can be termed "symbolist," the time element is

invalid. The problem that faces us then is whether the techniques of symbolism are equally unrealiable when taken as yardsticks of literary values. Judging from recent criticism such as that cited above, it could be assumed that the qualitative element might also be discounted. One begins to wonder then to what extent "symbolism" may entirely be disqualified as a literary label!

Before we banish the term, however, we must remember that the disagreements as to its meaning are not limited to the fate of the word "symbolism" but rather are indicative of a general tendency in criticism to debunk all labels. So much, for instance, of what used to be called "classical" is now just "baroque." In reaction against previously tight classifications, there is a tendency today to disengage what is non-classical in a classicist, non-romantic in a romanticist, and—more pertinent to our subject—what is non-symbolist in a symbolist. But in this general desire to free the individuality of authors from group commitments, it is well to remember that, however arbitrary classifications may seem, they are necessary safeguards against the vagaries of impressionistic criticism and biographical digressions. If, as some believe, there is a loss of the particular identity of the author through categorization by labels, it is equally dangerous to leave him in a vacuum and to attribute solely to his personal assets or faults those traits that are in truth the stylization of a common heritage.

Negative values would not have suffced to produce an affiliation among a galaxy of poets; the fact that symbolism proved

Charles Baudelaire.

powerful enough to cross national, linguistic, and geographical barriers provides strong evidence that there existed a single fountainhead, and a primary derivative. If the name has survived while many of those who bore it have fallen into oblivion, this was more than a marriage of convenience. Many of the seeming disparities were often nothing more than a series of partial defaults or deviations from a chosen ideal and philosophy of writing. (pp. 3-8)

The major significance of the Symbolist school in relation to the study of symbolism in its vaster context is that it created a particular climate in which those poets and critics of England, Germany, Italy, Spain, and the United States who first shared the experiences and memories of the *cénacle* convened with French writers and then took back with them their own evolved versions of the attitudes and conventions developed in Paris. Actually, much of what was to be known as symbolism abroad was based not on French Symbolism but on a translation or interpretation of French Symbolism that was in fact a mutation of the original. The degree of originality and deviation can be grasped only in relation to the full texture of the original and its intention.

Mallarmé, in whom there has since been discovered much more than symbolism, was nonetheless the uncontested poet image of Symbolism. In fact, some will insist that he is the sole poet who has survived the *cénacle*. There were those who expressed their theories in a more technical fashion, but Mallarmé acted the role of the secular priest and verbal mystifier, vividly representing thereby the two arms of the symbolist scale. Symbolism was not French; it happened in Paris. Symbolism was to be a *Parisian* movement (in distinction from *French*), Parisian in terms of its cosmopolitan character, preparing that particular international climate which has proved so propitious for subsequent avant-garde coteries: cubism, futurism, dadaism, and surrealism. With symbolism, art ceased in truth to be national and assumed the collective premises of Western culture. Its overwhelming concern was the non-temporal, non-sectarian, non-geographic, and non-national problem of the human condition: the confrontation between human mortality and the power of survival through the preservation of the human sensitivities in the art forms.

Romanticism had been international in quite another sense; it was a contagion that attacked each European country at its own literary hearth, as its authors fulfilled the *mal du siècle* in a great surge of lyricism adapted to their particular national character and local color. Surely there is no mistaking a Novalis for a Coleridge or a Musset. But in the Paris of the 1890's poets lost their national identity, at least temporarily, in the esoteric attitude of art; they rejected society and, far from becoming the official voices of their countries, they moved in closed circles communicating solely with their own breed. In the aftermath of the political defeat of 1870, it was not the French republic that gave impetus to this strange communion through which France gained artistic prestige as she lost political power; it was rather that the French language—thanks to its ability to be at the same time clear and elliptical, simple and sophisticated, pure and intricate—became the universal language of poetic interchange. The artistic vision, freed from national ideals, focused on the relationship between the subjective, purely personal world of the artist, and its objective projection.

They all came to Paris: Arthur Symons, Yeats, and George Moore from England; Stefan George, Hoffmannsthal, Rilke, and Hauptmann from the German-speaking world; Azorín and the Machado brothers from Spain; D'Annunzio from Italy; Maeterlinck and Verhaeren from Belgium; Moréas from Greece; Viélé-Griffin and Stuart Merrill from the United States. Paris served as the neutralizer of diverse cultural formations, and at the same time was the fertile ground on which a philosophy of art, mutually acceptable, yet subject to individual variations, could be sown. (pp. 9-11)

The Symbolists and their international coterie agreed on accepting a common origin in the philosophy of Swedenborg, which had already succeeded in infiltrating the art forms, through such literary illuminists as Gerard de Nerval, Novalis, Blake, and Emerson. The manner of transmission had been multiple and simultaneous, as Swedenborgism became associated wih the Romantic tradition.

But the first part of the symbolist story is primarily French, for it was Baudelaire who bridged the gap between the Romantic treatments of Swedenborgism and its eventual applications to the symbolist cult. Those who came to Paris with a common philosophical orientation were able by the end of the century to take symbolism out of the confines of French literature and bring it to its apotheosis as an international literary movement. (p. 11)

Anna Balakian, "Introduction: The Meaning of the Word," in her The Symbolist Movement: A Critical Appraisal, *Random House, Inc., 1967, pp. 3-11.*

JOHN PORTER HOUSTON AND MONA TOBIN HOUSTON

[*In the following excerpt, the critics emphasize the affinity of Symbolist and Decadent aesthetics and examine the influence of the German philosopher Arthur Schopenhauer on the pessimistic world view of Symbolist writers.*]

More than other literatures, that of France has traditionally been notable for the production of manifestoes and for the formation of movements growing out of sometimes violent literary polemics. Symbolism is just such a movement: it suddenly took shape owing to the appearance, in the early 1880s, of a large number of younger poets, soon to be in an experimental mood, and to the founding of the first of a number of small reviews dedicated, at least in part, to new literature. Equally influential was the return to prominence of an important older poet, Verlaine, who emerged from obscurity to publish not only his own verse in *Jadis et Naguère* (1884) but also a series of essays, appearing in the little review *Lutèce,* on Rimbaud, Corbière, and Mallarmé, whom he designated as "accursed poets." Not only were the poets he revealed forgotten or unknown, and fascinating in the "accursed" aspects of their careers, but they were highly adventurous in style and in no way concerned wtih avoiding hermeticism. They wrote largely for themselves, ignoring what they considered a monumentally stupid and frivolous reading public, in which, moreover, these poets included all the well-known writers of their day as well as the bourgeois audience. The *poètes maudits* thus provided younger poets a model both in strictly poetic matters and in the attitude to take toward society.

The *poètes maudits* had started out in different ways. Corbière, isolated from the literary world, was, by temperament and by the misfortune of his chronic illness, inclined toward an ironic, scoffing view of things. He assumed the mask of a much older man in his verse, unlike the youthful voice of poetic tradition. The self-consciously sacerdotal view of the poet, increasingly widespread in the nineteenth century, was not his; he lacked the conventional high seriousness of his calling. Mallarmé, on the other hand, was a hieratic figure, evermore isolated from the literary world by too extreme a priestly vision of his role. Only when it became possible to accept poetry as a sacred mystery, a replacement for religion, did his central position in the world of letters become recognized. Rimbaud, finally, was a thorough revolutionary, seeking to destroy nineteenth-century poetic conventions; he brought out the iconoclast in Verlaine during their homosexual liaison in 1872-73, and the latter's verse then reached its greatest brilliance. What emerges from the collocation of these four poets is that conventional poetry, best represented by LeConte de Lisle, had for them a solemn bookishness but was basically not serious. It lacked the ironic dimension that even Mallarmé and Rimbaud found in the poet's position, and yet it did not go far enough in transmuting life into something strange and absolute.

The lesson of Verlaine's essays on the *poètes maudits* was immediately reinforced by the publication of Huysmans's novel *A rebours* (1884). The sole figure in it is an esthete, Des Esseintes, who has withdrawn from the world and whose reflections on society, painting, sex, literature ancient and modern, religion, music, and so forth, make of the work a kind of encyclopedia of "decadent" taste. There is much that is tongue-in-cheek about Des Esseintes and his opinions, but the discussion of Baudelaire, Verlaine, Corbière, and Mallarmé is thoroughly serious, as is the characterization of contemporary society in terms of adulteration and genetic decline. The significance of Huysmans's novel in the spread of the new taste in poetry—the popularity of the book astonished everyone—is confirmed by the dedication to Des Esseintes of Mallarmé's poem "Prose," which is an *ars poetica*.

The number of remarkably original volumes of verse by younger poets published between 1884 and the early '90s in France was quite without precedent, and nothing comparable has been seen since. The little reviews—*La Revue Indépendante, La Vogue, La Pléiade,* and others—had some impressive issues, especially perhaps *La Vogue,* which printed Rimbaud's *Une Saison en enfer* and *Illuminations,* then unknown. At first the term *decadent* was applied to the new literature: the word had been increasingly used to describe modern writing in the preceding decades. While *decadent* is not an altogether inappropriate word for the styles and subjects of the younger poets, the word *symbolist* came into favor after the publication in 1886 of Jean Moréas's *Symbolist Manifesto,* and it seemed better, more neutrally, to describe what the new poetry was aiming at. The notion and term of *decadence* went on to enjoy much currency in other countries, and if we speak of symbolism as a poetic manner, it would not be out of place to speak of a decadent view of the world behind much symbolist poetry and one related extensively to literature outside of France.

In any case, the real history of the symbolist movement lies not in the date this or that little review began or ceased publication but in the formation of the idea of a literature for an elite, and in the modernist acceptance of obscurity as a perhaps necessary part of a work of art. This sense of separateness from the larger public arose at a time when poets, although uninfluenced by great events the way certain romantics had been affected by the French Revolution and Napoleon's career, found themselves nonetheless in a distinctive, new era in the history of French society and one which marked them. A recent French historian, Emmanuel Todd, has said in an interview:

> If the French of 1979 were confronted with their ancestors of 1914, they might well consider them

mad. Men and women of that day, while living in a politically liberal society, had imprisoned themselves in a moral system almost pathological in its rigidity: bourgeois virtues. They saved, they accumulated gold; they were terrorized and obsessed by sexuality. . . . In France between 1835 and 1910 the suicide rate grew by 260 percent, the number of mental patients by 310 percent, the per capita consumption of alcohol by 100 percent. . . . Toward 1900, the middle classes were the ones which produced the mentally ill, the alcoholics, the suicides.

These social facts suggest the measure of alienation, constraint, and despair obtaining in the "Belle Epoque" and the impression this period might make on a sensitive individual. The sociology of late nineteenth-century literature has scarcely been touched on, but it appears to be such that systematic pessimism on the part of poets should hardly surprise us, and we shall turn now to its philosophical aspects.

One of the most useful ways to look at decadent-symbolist themes is in terms of Arthur Schopenhauer's thought, although his direct influence is not easy to establish. Schopenhauer consciously examined and rationally analyzed all manner of ideas which are found in symbolist poetry expressed with varying degrees of philosophical generality and explicitness. The world of active life was for Schopenhauer the realm of blind will, a largely unconscious force by which we, as subject, constantly reach out to seize on the objects of phenomena, which we propose to ourselves as goals. The process of living propels one continually toward unwanted death; while the will is purposeless in general, it shows up in each individual as a determining, fatalistic force. Sexuality is its most obvious form, and the decadent imagination makes much over this "fruit of death on the tree of life," as Samain called it. The prostitute is an important figure, as in Verhaeren's "Dame en noir," and in her mythic form she is Salome, as in Samain's "Des soirs fiévreux . . ." or Milosz's "Salomé."

It is characteristic of symbolist technique to represent a theme in various conventions of realism or imaginativeness. We move up the scale from the mimetic representation of the prostitute in the city to the medievalizing, symbolic realms of Retté's "Bâille la haute salle . . ." and Régnier's "Salut à l'étrangère," in which we see the fatal woman associated with that other object of libido, glory. The Chimaera is a frequent accompanying symbol of insane illusions. We are here on the grander, tragic level, where sexuality is merely part of the unfulfillment inevitable in the world of will. Retté's allegory "Sillages," in which man is the Eternal Beggar, dispenses with the prostitute, as does Régnier's "Motifs de légende et de mélancolie," a purely symbolic poem, whose tone might be characterized with Schopenhauer's comment:

> Thus between desiring and attaining all human life flows on throughout. The wish is, in its nature, pain; the attainment soon begets satiety: the end was only apparent; possession takes away the charm; the wish, the need, presents itself under a new form; when it does not, then follows desolateness, emptiness, ennui, against which the conflict is just as painful as against want.

There are shorter poems in which the world of will is depicted by a symbol: the city in Verhaeren's work or the violent, erotic, or death-giving sunset in Giraud and Rodenbach. Mikhaël's "Le Mage" is an especially interesting ironic poem on glory: the Barbarians, whose coming is the subject of various decadent poems, turn out to be really impotent, sexually as well as figuratively. The illusion of vitality is a false one: there are no conquerors of man's infirmity in the world of will.

Jules Laforgue, who makes highly conscious references to Schopenhauer and to the latter's disciple Hartmann, transposes decadent thematic material into a mode which is variously ironic, lyrical, and realistic. In the "Complainte des pianos," young girls of the bourgeoisie are under the sway of the will; "Complainte du printemps" comments further on the erotic urge in spring. Laforgue alludes to the late nineteenth century's obsessive scientific ideas of heredity, and we see how Schopenhauer's categories of thought can be nicely adjusted to different degrees of practical or imaginative, comic or serious representation in literature. The world of blind will, of sexuality and the life cycle, in which the will to live is actually the will to die, may seem at first to comprehend the whole range of human existence, but the symbolists found a great source of inspiration in its opposite: the denial of the will.

It is often in slim, symbolic lyrics that we find a striking image of a world other than that of the will. The refining process of illness, as in Rodenbach's "Les Malades aux fenêtres," the revelation of the exquisite essence of a dying flower in Lorrain's "Effeuillement," the sublimation of real women in a perfect dream of beauty in Van Lerberghe's "La Jonchée," the angel-woman of Mallarmé's "Soupir," the presentation in Maeterlinck and Rodenbach of the soul as being in a hothouse or aquarium, Valéry's dream of "Blanc"—all these are symbolic ways of depicting the individual free of sexual impulsions, unwanted death, and unfulfilled desires. The imagery of attenuation—"formes grêles" as Samain put it—characterizes them. Such poems represent not only a release, but by their quiet nature recall the technical definition of beauty in Schopenhauer's thought: the individual ceases to be a *willing* subject grasping after the fleeting objects of phenomena and becomes the contemplator of Platonic Ideas, in a relation free from the subject-object tension of the world of will.

Purity might be said to be the positive characterization of the state of being free from will, and purity has in many symbolist works a nexus of spiritual, esthetic, and chaste-erotic connotations which make it rather elusive. In an allegorical convention, we find it embodied by Mallarmé's Hérodiade. At the opposite, realistic pole, *Le Grand Meaulnes* shows a superb use of an experience of ineffable purity in the context of narrative; the mysterious contrast of Meaulnes's experience in the lost domain with the practical, provincial world of his schoolboy life makes this work an exemplary case of the simultaneously erotic, esthetic, and spiritual whole which cuts across philosophical categories and defies naming in any rational way. Finally, Laforgue, with his usual fondness for irony, presents one of his young poet figures mocking his own obsession with purity in "Complainte à Notre-Dame des soirs."

Purity is achieved through renunciation. When man arrives at philosophical awareness, he has a choice:

> This freedom . . . can now, at the point at which in its most perfect manifestation it has attained to the completely adequate knowledge of its own nature, express itself anew in two ways. Either it wills here, at the summit of mental endowment and self-consciousness, simply what it willed before blindly and unconsciously, and if so, knowledge always remains a *moving force* for it. . . . Or conversely, this knowledge becomes for it a *quieter*, which appeases and suppresses all willing.

One of the famous renunciations in symbolist poetry is that of Mallarmé's swan, despising the "région où vivre," but a more elaborate one can be found in the same poet's triptych of sonnets ("Tout Orgueil . . . ," "Surgi de la croupe . . . ," and "Une dentelle . . ."). There, we find the important symbolist motif of the last heir to the manor, who has realized that reproduction is the madness of the world of blind will and who dreams only of entering the realm of purity, symbolized by rebirth from a musical instrument. More explicit developments of the same theme are to be found in *A rebours,* where Des Esseintes, the last of his line, surveys the wretchedness of the world of will, and in *Axël,* Villiers de l'Isle-Adam's striking play:

> C'est elle [la Terre], ne le vois-tu pas, qui est devenue l'Illusion! Reconnais-le, Sara: nous avons détruit, dans nos étranges coeurs, l'amour de la vie—et c'est bien en REALITE que nous sommes devenus nos âmes! Accepter, désormais, de vivre, ne serait plus qu'un sacrilège envers nousmêmes. Vivre? les serviteurs feront cela pour nous.
>
> Vieille terre, je ne bâtirai pas les palais de mes rêves sur ton sol ingrat: je ne porterai pas de flambeau, je ne frapperai pas d'ennemis. Puisse la race humaine, désabusée de ses vaines chimères, de ses vains désespoirs, et de tous les mensonges qui éblouissent les yeux faits pour s'éteindre—ne consentant plus au jeu de cette morne énigme,—oui, puisse-t-elle finir, en s'enfuyant indifférente, à notre exemple, sans t'adresser même un adieu.

Axël's image of becoming one's own soul is a perfect example of the vocabulary of attenuation and sloughing off the material associated with the theme of purity. Renunciation, on the practical level of sexuality, is the subject of Laforgue's "Dimanches," "O Géraniums . . . ," and "Noire bise . . . ," except that in the last poem, the conclusion, following Hartmann's correction of Schopenhauer, is that one must be reconciled to the world of will or the unconscious.

The greatest of myths of renunciation is that of Parsifal (always spelled in Wagnerian fashion by the symbolists). Schopenhauer explains saints' lives in philosophical terms:

> Thus it may be that the inner nature of holiness, self-renunciation, mortification of our own will, asceticism, is here for the first time expressed abstractly, and free from all mythical elements, as *denial of the will to live,* appearing after the complete knowledge of its own nature has become a quieter of all volition.

We see here why, from the mystical imagery of Rimbaud's "Fêtes de la patience" to the frequent liturgical references of Laforgue, Christianity plays such a large role in the work of poets who, with rare exceptions like Saint-Pol Roux, were no longer Christians. Purity is a sacred concept in connotation, even when no theology lies behind it. Merrill's "Chrysostome" is an especially relevant example of the transfer of the religious to poetic purity. The peculiar concept of sin we encounter in the symbolists is also made quite clear by Schopenhauer:

> Certainly the doctrine of original sin (assertion of the will) and of salvation (denial of the will) is the great truth which constitutes the essence of Christianity, while most of what remains is only the clothing of it, the husk or accessories.

We see the significance of "regrets primordiaux" (Kahn's "Vers le plain ciel . . .") and the enormous difference separating the symbolists from Baudelaire, who, however erring, thought in modes clearly reflecting orthodox theology. Baudelaire's poetry is highly ethical in import, whereas for the symbolists good and evil are not in themselves notions of significance; what counts is the metaphysical distinction epitomized by Schopenhauer's willing and non-willing. There is no question of an afterlife for the symbolists: imagination and renunciation replace any life beyond death. Redemption is a poetic idea. These themes constitute, in a sense, a kind of mystique, making up for what Schopenhauer admits to be the inability of philosophy to achieve more than negative knowledge, at most a hint of peace in a will-less state. Essentially, one can only choose between conditions defined largely as to what they are free of:

> We freely acknowledge that what remains after the entire abolition of will is, for all those who are still full of will, certainly nothing; but, conversely, to those in whom the will has turned and has denied itself, this our world, which is so real, with all its suns and milky-ways—is nothing.

Both the life-in-death of the world of the will and the death-in-life of purity are denials of all fecundity except, perhaps, artistic creation. The peculiar character of Schopenhauerian and symbolist pessimism comes from this opposition of two realms which, from an outside point of view, may seem to add up to very much the same thing in the end.

The rendering of such things as ineffable states of purity would seem to demand a new conception of poetry, and indeed the symbolists did a considerable amount of theorizing. Aside from Mallarmé's writings, however, most of the theory is vague and wordy, with much talk of the symbol but little clarity about the actual choice and treatment of symbols.

It is not perhaps an exaggeration to see in the desire to obscure poetry, to attenuate its sense, a manner of conveying quiet, will-less contemplation: the only way hermetic poetry can be read is with a certain initial indifference to the goal of understanding. Mallarmé spoke on more than one occasion of poetry as a kind of dark evocation or suggestion of something—but not so dark that there was not some "reminiscence of the object." He varied in his notions as to whether this was a really creative artistic mode. In any case, we see that he is defining poetry in the mimetic or representational tradition but drawing as far away as possible from the actual representation of life, without completely breaking with it. Thus the renunciation of the practical world of will corresponds to a diminished perception of objects.

Mallarmé's attempt to define poetry in regard to traditional mimetic terms is not his only major way of conceiving of poetry. He also put forth a much more modern notion of poetry as a structure in which the words "illuminate one another reciprocally," that is, function in relation to each other and not denotatively. This is the "Idea," "music in the Greek sense," "a rhythm of relations." This purely structural idea of poetry is what Mallarmé refers to when he speaks of "taking back poetry's own from music," the nonrepresentational art. Mallarmé had, knowing virtually nothing about music, intuited that what makes music an art is a complex of harmonic, rhythmic, and melodic relationships among notes and that any art, beyond accessory representational values, must be analogous to music.

Mallarmé sometimes specifically states that when he speaks of music he means an ideal, silent music, which is why he also refers to Greek music, of which we have little practical knowledge. He did, however, in his early years, before the elaboration of his ultimate theories about art, make comparisons between symphonic music and complex poetry and express his admiration for the cryptic beauty of musical notes on paper: a properly esoteric means of expression for art. Mallarmé's contemporaries also were much given to musical analogies and the background to this way of thinking deserves a word or two.

Music has, to a greater or lesser degree, an intellectual and emotional content which is difficult to paraphrase in words. We can see that this elusiveness could be felt as comparable to the effect of hermetic poetry, an even excellent translation of which always seems to leave a large gap between explanation and the original statement. Notions like ineffable purity obviously suggest that analogy with unparaphrasable music. When Mallarmé spoke of music and poetry as two forms of an essential mystery, he doubtless had in mind not all music and poetry but some specific passages in each where one has an intense feeling of perfect communication without denotational values.

At the same time, Mallarmé and his contemporaries were influenced by the peculiar development of program music and music drama in the late nineteenth century, which were much discussed in the symbolist *Revue Wagnérienne*. Wagner had attacked pure music and held out as ideal a mixed mode of musical expression in which the literary element and the musical one combine in what some found to be an uneasy relation. There was a great deal of ambiguity about such music and many variations in technique (even among, for example, Wagner's operas) for conveying the programmatic aspect of it. Mahler and Debussy, who were generally identified with this movement, found themselves destroying programs or putting titles at the ends of pieces so as not to limit music through words and literality. It is obvious that poets would find, in any case, a greater degree of analogy between this new musical mode and their own art and that, without the manifestations of a kind of music one could tax with impurity and unfaithfulness to itself, the symbolist comparison between music and poetry would probably not have been pursued to any great length.

In practical terms, poets could hear only commonplace selections from Wagner in Paris around 1885; most of the symbolists were quite ignorant of music, and their thinking on it derived from written sources, such as the *Revue Wagnérienne,* rather than from any contact with music itself. Wagner as a *literary* inspiration, however, is not without importance, as one can see from precise references in poems to the libretto and stage action of *Parsifal*. In any case, Mallarmé, always more subtle than his contemporaries, criticized Wagner's music for being too grossly material, too loud or sensuous, too little the pure manifestation of the Idea.

After Mallarmé, Verlaine in his "Art poétique" made the most famous statement of the necessity of music in poetry. His equating of music with the nine-syllable line and its soft contours suggests the Wagnerian idea of the endless melody, and his rejection of rhetoric can be compared with the abandonment of conventionalized sonata form and other hackneyed musical models—except for the fact that Verlaine wrote his "Art poétique" years before such things were discussed in Paris, and he himself had no particular musical culture. Analogies between music and poetry always run the risk of being purely fanciful rapprochements, but it remains a profoundly interesting fact that both Verlaine and Mallarmé, long before they had the faintest inkling of the new European music of their day, when Offenbach was probably more familiar to them than even Beethoven, felt the need of a nonrepresentational way of describing poetry and sensed that music would provide such a vocabulary.

While music drama may be impure music, the poetry that was compared in France to contemporary music was felt to be considerably purer in more than one sense than what had preceded it. An obvious case is description: Mallarmé, Verlaine, and Rimbaud had defined their styles in contrast to the orderly, pictorial, mimetic poetry of Leconte de Lisle and other poets usually called Parnassians. Not raw sense data, but the sensation of the sensation, or a purified form of sensory experience was their preference, and we see how poetry drawing on such material can be compared with experience conveyed through the quintessential form of music. The vaguely medieval setting of many symbolist poems results from an attempt to achieve both sensory and metaphysical immediacy without describing anything remotely real. Mallarmé's angel who gives a purer sense to the words of the tribe is attempting to dissociate words from the practical world of individual material things.

Eloquence or rhetoric was the general term Verlaine used in his "Art poétique" to describe what poetry should not be, and we must understand rhetoric in the general sense of an art of rational, measured, systematic presentation and development of subject matter or themes. Most of Baudelaire's poetry, for example, reflects, in a very high form, the sense of order and division inherent in the spirit of rhetoric. Verlaine calls *literature,* in a pejorative sense, whatever obeys such principles, and we find in his work and in that of later poets some new matter and techniques which were counter to rhetoric such as it had existed up to then in French. Irrational mental phenomena presented in all their disarray constituted a new domain: a strange state of half-dreaming in Verlaine's "Kaléidoscope," delirium in Maeterlinck's "Hôpital," madness in Verhaeren's "Chanson de fou." In Verlaine's "L'espoir luit . . ." and certain of Kahn's poems there seems to be some sort of plot concealed, which we can scarcely make out. Fragments without commentary are used by Laforgue, as in "Complainte de l'orgue de Barbarie," and often syntax is fragmented, as in "Complainte de l'automne monotone." A general lack of explicit articulation between parts gives a certain mystery to Rimbaud's "Mémoire" or Kahn's "Je suis rentré . . ." The patterns of Rimbaud's "Bateau ivre" and Mallarmé's "Ses purs ongles . . ." are not the ordinary kinds of traditional allegorical-symbolic structures to which one can easily assign a single general meaning. Finally, allusion is handled in a new, surprising way in such a poem as Laforgue's "Complainte du roi de Thulé," with its pertinent but indirect reference to Goethe's ballad. In all of these cases we must do without the fullness and univocity of sense that rhetoric traditionally assured.

The form which offers the most striking potential for elliptical or implicit meaning is probably the song. While real songs, of course, may vary a great deal in the completeness and overtness of their meaning, the symbolists had as their ideal a kind of slim, allusive, even obscure song such as might have come from centuries of erosion of sense in the singing of it. Verlaine provided the model in his "songs without words," inexplicit as the expression suggests, and Rimbaud worked along with him in the same mode. In Moréas, Kahn, Merrill, and others we find attempts to create this kind of song, which seems to have been unknown, in any folkloric form it had in France, to city-bred poets. The symbolists actually felt their model was more a German one and occasionally designated their poems as *Lieder.*

It was not only the imitation of folk song which led away from the traditional rhetoric of French poetry; song poems drawing on a more urban or proletarian inspiration brought in new subject matter and forms of expression in Elskamp and Laforgue. They imported into poetry material outside the traditional domain of high culture, and in this they had a striking predecessor in Corbière, with his bohemian, argot-colored manner. This surprising range of late nineteenth-century French poetry from the exquisite, the precious even, to the popular is one of the most remarkable things about it and reminds us of the coexistence with symbolism in France of the taste for literary realism. All these forms of the antirhetorical contribute to the formation of modernist esthetics, which, we must remember, have their origins in the symbolist period: Corbière and Laforgue's use of slang obeys basically the same rejection of academic verse styles as does Mallarmé's hermetic manner, and brings us back to that contempt for the public generally considered literate which we noted at the beginning of this account of the decadent-symbolist movement. (pp. 3-14)

John Porter Houston and Mona Tobin Houston, in an introduction to French Symbolist Poetry: An Anthology, *edited and translated by John Porter Houston and Mona Tobin Houston, Indiana University Press, 1980, pp. 3-16.*

DECLARATIONS OF SYMBOLIST PRINCIPLES

M. JEAN MORÉAS

[*An eminent literary figure in late nineteenth-century France, Moréas advanced the cause of an emerging generation of Symbolist writers through the example of his poetry and through his manifestoes of the movement. The following manifesto, which originally appeared in* Le Figaro *on 18 September 1886, is often considered to have inaugurated Symbolism as a literary movement.*]

Like all the arts, literature is subject to evolution: a cyclical evolution with strictly determined turns, complicated by divers modifications brought about by the passage of time and the change of its surroundings. It would be superfluous to point out that each new evolutionary phase of the art corresponds exactly to the senile decrepitude, the unavoidable end, of the immediately preceding school. Two examples will suffice: Ronsard triumphs over the impotence of Marot's last imitators, Romanticism unfolds its banners over the classical ruins ill defended by Casmir Delavigne and Étienne de Jouy. The fact is that every expression of art tends fatally to become impoverished and outworn; from one copy to another, from one imitation to another, that which was once full of sap and freshness becomes dry and gnarled; that which was spontaneous and fresh becomes trite and commonplace.

Thus, Romanticism, after it had tumultuously tolled the bell of rebellion, after it had had its days of battle and glory, lost its power and its grace, abandoned its heroic daring, became sedate, skeptical, and replete with common sense. It sought a fallacious revival in the honorable and petty attempts of the Parnassian poets, and then, at last, like a monarch fallen into second childhood, it allowed itself to be deposed by Naturalism—to which one cannot seriously grant more than the value of a protest, legitimate but ill advised, against the insipidities of some then-fashionable novelists.

A new form of artistic expression was therefore awaited, necessary, inevitable. Long in the making, it has now broken forth and all the anodyne jokes of would-be funny newspapermen, all the discomfort of grave critics, all the ill-humor of a public caught short in its sheeplike indifference, all these merely affirm more strongly every day the vitality of the present evolution of French literature, the evolution which hasty judges have, by some incomprehensible contradiction in terms, labeled decadent. Note however that decadent literatures have always shown themselves to be essentially tough, stringy, timorous, and servile: all the tragedies of Voltaire, for instance, are tarred with the brush of decadence. Yet what can one reproach, what does one reproach, the new school? The abuse of pomp, the strangeness of its metaphors, a new vocabulary in which harmonies combine with lines and colors: characteristics of every *renaissance*.

We have already suggested the title of *Symbolism* as one that can most reasonably describe the present tendency of the creative spirit in art. This title can be maintained.

It was said at the beginning of this article that the evolutions of art present a cyclic character extremely complicated by divergencies; thus, to follow the exact filiation of the new school it is necessary to return to certain poems of Alfred de Vigny, to Shakespeare, to the mystics, and even further. These questions would need a volume of comment; so let us simply say that Baudelaire should be considered as the true forerunner of the present movement; M. Stéphane Mallarmé endowed it with a sense of mystery, and the ineffable M. Paul Verlaine broke in its honor the cruel bonds of verses which the prestigious fingers of M. Théodore de Banville had previously softened. However, the *Supreme Enchantment* is not yet consumed: a jealous and stubborn task awaits the newcomers.

Opposed to "teaching, declamation, false sensibility, objective description," symbolic poetry seeks to clothe the Idea in a perceptible form which, nevertheless, would not be an end in itself; rather, while serving to express the idea, it would remain subject to it. The Idea, in its turn, must not let itself be deprived of the sumptuous robes of external analogies; for the essential character of symbolic art consists in never going so far as to conceive the Idea in itself. Thus, in this art, the depiction of nature, the actions of men, all the concrete phenomena, could not show themselves as such: they are concrete appearances whose purpose is to represent their esoteric affinities with primordial Ideas.

There is nothing surprising about the indictments raised against such an esthetic approach by readers who take their reading in fits and starts. But what is one to do about them? The *Pythics* of Pindarus, the *Hamlet* of Shakespeare, the *Vita Nuova* of Dante, the *Second Faust* of Goethe, Flaubert's *Temptation of Saint Anthony*, were they not also taxed with ambiguity?

For the exact translation of its synthesis, Symbolism needs an archetypal and complex style: unpolluted words, firm periods to act as buttresses and alternate with others of undulating faintness, the significant pleonasm, the mysterious ellipsis, the suspended anacoluthe, every trope daring and multiform; lastly, good French—restored and modernized—the good, brisk, luxuriant French of the days before Vaugelas and Boileau-Despréaux, the speech of François Rabelais and of Philippe de Commines, of Villon, of Rutebeuf, and of so many other writers who were free and ready to hurl the sharp terms of language like Thracian archers their sinuous arrows.

RHYTHM: The old meter revived; a wisely ordered disorder; the rhyme incandescent and hammered like a shield of brass and gold, beside the rhyme made up of abstruse fluidities; the alexandrine of multiple and mobile checks; the use of certain prime numbers—seven, nine, eleven, thirteen—resolved into the different rhythm combinations of which they are the sum.

At this point I beg permission to present to you my little *Interlude,* drawn from a precious book: the *Treatise on French Poetry* in which M. Théodore de Banville, like the God of Claros, pitilessly inflicts asses' ears upon the head of many a Midas.

Pay attention!

The characters in the play are:

A DISPARAGING CRITIC OF THE SYMBOLIC SCHOOL
M. THÉODORE DE BANVILLE
ERATO [one of the nine muses and patron of elegiac poetry]

FIRST SCENE

DISPARAGING CRITIC. Oh! these decadents! What emphasis! What nonsense! How right was our great Molière when he said:

> This figurative style that people pride themselves on
> Deviates from good form and from truth.

T. DE BANVILLE. Our great Molière committed these two bad verses which themselves deviate far from good form. What good form? What truth? Apparent disorder, explosive madness, passionate emphasis, these are the essential truth of lyric poetry. There is no great harm about falling into an excess of figures and color. This is not the way our literature will perish. In its worst days, when it has altogether given up hope, as for instance under the First Empire, not emphasis and overornamentation kill it, but platitude. Taste, naturalness, are beautiful things but certainly less useful to poetry than people imagine. Shakespeare's *Romeo and Juliet* is written from beginning to end in a style as affected as that of Mascarille's marquis; that of Ducis shines with the happiest and most natural simplicity.

DISPARAGING CRITIC. But the *caesura*, the *caesura!* They are violating the *caesura!*

T. DE BANVILLE. In his remarkable prosody, published in 1844, M. Wilhem Tenint established that the alexandrine allows twelve different combinations, beginning with the verse whose *caesura* follows the first syllable and ending with the verse whose *caesura* follows the eleventh syllable. This amounts to saying that in effect the *caesura* can be placed after no matter which syllable of the alexandrine verse. In the same way, he established that verses of six, seven, eight, nine, and ten syllables admit variable and variously placed *caesuras*. Let us go farther; let us dare proclaim complete freedom and say that in these complex matters the ear alone shall decide. Defeat comes always not for having dared too much but for having dared too little.

DISPARAGING CRITIC. Horrors! No respect for the alternation of rhymes! Do you know, Sir, that the decadents dare to allow themseles the hiatus! even the hi-a-tus!

T. DE BANVILLE. Once the hiatus or the diphthong were accepted as a syllable in the verse, all the other things which had been forbidden, and especially the freedom to use both masculine and feminine rhymes, provided the poet of genius with a thousand opportunities for delicate touches, ever varied, ever unexpected, inexhaustible. But in order to make use of this complicated, learned verse form, one needed genius and a musical ear while, with the established rules, provided they stick to them closely, the most mediocre writers can, alas, produce *passable verses!* Who ever gained anything from the regulation and reglementation of poetry? The mediocre poets. And they alone!

DISPARAGING CRITIC. And yet it seems to me that the romantic revolution . . .

T. DE BANVILLE. Romanticism was an incomplete revolution. What a pity that Victor Hugo, that victorious and bloody-fisted Hercules, was not a complete revolutionary, and that he let live some of the monsters whom it was his duty to exterminate with his flaming arrows.

DISPARAGING CRITIC. All innovation is folly! The salvation of French poetry lies in imitating Victor Hugo!

T. DE BANVILLE. When Hugo had emancipated the verse, people must have thought that, inspired by his example, the poets that succeeded him would want to be free and depend only on themselves. But such is our love of bondage that the new poets endlessly copied and imitated Hugo's most common forms, combinations and turns of phrase, instead of trying to find new ones. This is how, made for the yoke, we turn from one servitude to another. After the classical commonplace, there have been romantic commonplaces, platitudes in turns, in phrases, in rhymes; and the commonplace, that is the chronic banality, is Death in poetry as in everything else. Let us, on the contrary, dare to live! And to live means to breathe the air of the open sky, not the breath of our neighbor, even if our neighbor should be a god!

SECOND SCENE

ERATO. (*invisible*) Your *Short Treatise of French Poetry* is a delightful work, Master Banville. But the young poets are in blood up to their eyes struggling against the *monsters* fed by Nicolas Boileau; you are wanted on the battlefield, Master Banville, and you keep silent.

T. DE BANVILLE. (*dreamily*) Damnation! Could it be that I have failed in my duty, both as an elder and as a lyric poet! (pp. 205-08)

Prose—novels, stories, tales, and whimsies—evolves in a direction similar to that of poetry. Apparently heterogeneous elements help it on its way: Stendhal contributes his translucent psychology, Balzac his exorbitant vision, Flaubert the rhythms of his amply spiraled phrases, M. Edmond de Goncourt his suggestive impressionism.

The conception of the symbolic novel is polymorphous: now a single character moves through spheres deformed by his own hallucinations, by his temperament, and the only *reality* lies in these deformations. Beings with mechanical gestures, with shadowy outlines, shift and turn round the solitary character: they are mere pretexts for sensations and conjectures, while he himself is a mask of tragedy or farce, whose humanity is nevertheless perfect even though rational.—At times crowds, superficially affected by the totality of the surrounding show, move through alternating clashes and moments of stagnation toward actions which remain incomplete.—At times individual *wills* express themselves; they attract each other, conglomerate, become one, while making for an end which, whether attained or not, scatters them once more into their original elements.—Then, again, mythical phantoms, from the ancient Demogorgon to Belial, from the Kabirs to the Nigromans, appear richly attired on Caliban's rock, or pass through Titania's forest to the mixolydian strains of several kinds of lyre, whether barbiton or octocord.

Thus, scorning the puerile methods of naturalism—M. Zola himself was saved by a wonderful writer's instinct—the Symbolic-Impressionist novel will build its work of *subjective deformation*, strong in this axiom: that art can only seek in the *objective* a simple and extremely succinct starting point. (p. 209)

> M. Jean Moréas, "A Literary Manifesto," translated by Eugen Weber, in Paths to the Present: Aspects of European Thought from Romanticism to Existentialism, *edited by Eugen Weber, Dodd, Mead & Company, Inc., 1960, pp. 205-09.*

STÉPHANE MALLARMÉ

[*Mallarmé was the central figure in the French Symbolist movement. In his poetry, Mallarmé sought to "peindre non la chose, mais l'effet qu'elle produit" ("not to depict the object itself, but the effect that it produces"). Though his body of work is small and, to many, obscure, Mallarmé created musical, evocative poems in which he tried to transcend the limits of language. In the following essay, Mallarmé defines many of the essential qualities of Symbolist poetry. For additional commentary by Mallarmé, see excerpt below.*]

A fundamental and fascinating crisis in literature is now at hand.

Such is the plain and present truth in the eyes of all those for whom literature is of primary importance. What we are witnessing as the finale of our own century is not upheaval (as was the case a hundred years ago), but rather a fluttering in the temple's veil—meaningful folds and even a little tearing.

This is disconcerting for the French reading public, whose habits were interrupted by the death of Victor Hugo. Pursuing his mysterious task, Hugo reduced all prose—philosophy, oratory, history—to poetry; and since he was himself poetry personified, he nearly abolished the philosopher's, speaker's, or historian's right to self-expression. In that wasteland, with silence all around, he was a monument. Yet in a crypt of equal silence lay the divinity of this majestic, unconscious idea: namely, that the form we call verse is itself, quite simply, literature; that we have verse so long as we have diction, rhythm so long as we have style. Poetry, I think, waited patiently and respectfully until this giant (whose ever more grasping, ever firmer blacksmith's hand was coming to be the definition of verse) had disappeared; then it broke up. The entire language was fitted out for prosody, and therein it re-discovered its vital sense of pause. Now it could fly off, freely scattering its numberless and irreducible elements. Or we might well compare it to the multiple sounds issuing from a purely verbal orchestration.

That was the beginning of the change in poetry which Verlaine, with his fluid verse, had secretly and unexpectedly prepared when he returned to certain primitive resources in language.

I was witness to this adventure. And although my role in it was not so influential as has been claimed (for no single person was responsible), I did at least take great interest in it. It is time to discuss it, and it seems better to do so at a distance, or, so to speak, anonymously.

It will be agreed that because of the priority on magic power which is given to rhyme, French poetry has been intermittent ever since its evolution. It shines for a moment, dies out, and waits. There is extinction—or rather wear and tear which reveal the weft; there is repetition. After an almost century-long period of poetic orgy and excess which can be compared only to the

Renaissance, the latest poetic urge (counteracting a number of different circumstances) is being fulfilled not by a darkening or cooling off process, but, on the contrary, by a variation in continuing brilliance. The retempering of verse, ordinarily a secret affair, is now being done openly: poets are resorting to delightful approximations.

The kind of treatment that has been given to the hieratic canon of verse can, I think, be divided into three graduated parts.

Official prosody has cut and dried rules; there lies its obstinacy. It gives its official approval to such ''wise'' procedures as the observance of the hemistich, and pronounces judgment on the slightest effort to simulate versification. It is like the law which states, for example, that abstinence from theft is the essence of honesty. But this is precisely what we need least to learn; for if we have not understood it by ourselves from the first, it is useless to obey it.

Those who are still faithful to the alexandrine, i.e., to the modern hexameter, have gone inside it and loosened this rigid, childish metrical mechanism; and so, now that such artificial metronomes have been abolished, there is joy for our ears alone in perceiving all possible combinations and interrelationships of twelve tones.

Consider the most recent literary taste.

Here is a rather typical and interesting example of it.

Henri de Régnier, a poet of great tact, still considers the alexandrine to be *the* gem—a gem, however, which (like sword or flower) he discloses but rarely, and even then only with some well-considered pattern in mind. He disturbs this verse form only with the greatest circumspection; he hovers and plays around it, yields to its related harmonies, and finally shows it forth in all its pride and purity. His fingering may fail at the eleventh syllable, or often linger on to a thirteenth. He excels in such accompaniments, which are, of course, the delicate, proud invention of his own original talent; they point up the temporary uneasiness of those who play the traditional poetic instrument. We discover a quite different example of knowing disobedience in the case of Jules Laforgue, who, in the beginning, abandoned the old worn-out form and initiated us in the secret and unfailing charm of defective verse.

Up to now, therefore (as shown in the two examples just mentioned), there has been either the delicacy of a Régnier or the self-indulgence of a Laforgue in metrical treatment, as a result of the fatigue brought on by the abuse of our national rhythm. That rhythm, like the national flag, must be used sparingly. There has, however, been one interesting exception: an occasional and wilful disobedience in the form of beautifully executed dissonances for the sensitive ear. And to think that, scarcely fifteen years ago, pedants that we are, we would have been outraged by this phenomenon—as if it were an illiterate's sacrilege! Let me say, finally, that the official alexandrine, like a memory, haunts about these rhythmic variations and thus adds to their luster.

Modern free verse—unlike the seventeenth-century free verse, which we find in fables or operas, and which was simply an arrangement of various well-known meters ungoverned by strophes—derives its entire originality from what we may properly call its ''polymorphic'' character. And the breaking up of official verse should now be what the poets will, should even be endless, provided there is pleasure to be had in it. For example, there might be a certain euphony which the reader's own poetic instinct could fragmentize with a sort of native and

unerring accuracy (such has been the recent verse of Moréas). Or perhaps a rhythmical gesture of languor and revery, or of startled passion (as in the work of Vielé-Griffin). Prior to these, there was Kahn's very skillful notation of the tonal value of words. But these are only a few of the names; there are others equally typical; Charles Morice, Verhaeren, Dujardin, Mockel, etc., whose works should be consulted; they will bear out what I have said.

But the truly remarkable fact is this: for the first time in the literary history of any nation, along with the general and traditional great organ of orthodox verse which finds its ecstasy on an ever-ready keyboard, any poet with an individual technique and ear can build his own instrument, so long as his fluting, bowing, or drumming are accomplished—play that instrument and dedicate it, along with others, to Language.

Thus we have won a great new freedom; and it is my firm belief that no beauty of the past has been destroyed as a result. I am convinced that the solemn poetic tradition which was mainly established by our classical genius will continue to be observed on all important occasions. But whenever it shall seem unfitting to disturb the echoes of that venerable past for sentimental or narrative purposes, we shall be careful to avoid such disturbance. Each soul is a melody; its strands must be bound up. Each poet has his flute or viol, with which to do so.

In my opinion, we have been late in finding the true condition and possibility not only of poetic self-expression, but of free and individual modulation.

Languages are imperfect because multiple; the supreme language is missing. Inasmuch as thought consists of writing without pen and paper, without whispering even, without the sound of the immortal Word, the diversity of languages on earth means that no one can utter words which would bear the miraculous stamp of Truth Herself Incarnate. This is clearly nature's law—we stumble on it with a smile of resignation—to the effect that we have no sufficient reason for equating ourselves with God. But then, esthetically, I am disappointed when I consider how impossible it is for language to express things by means of certain keys which would reproduce their brilliance and aura—keys which do exist as a part of the instrument of the human voice, or among languages, or sometimes even in one language. When compared to the opacity of the word *ombre,* the word *ténèbres* does not seem very dark; and how frustrating the perverseness and contradiction which lend dark tones to *jour,* bright tones to *nuit!* We dream of words brilliant at once in meaning and sound, or darkening in meaning and so in sound, luminously and elementally self-succeeding. *But,* let us remember that if our dream were fulfilled, *verse would not exist*—verse which, in all its wisdom, atones for the sins of languages, comes nobly to their aid.

Strange mystery—and so, equally mysterious and meaningful, prosody sprang forth in primitive times.

The ideal would be a reasonable number of words stretched beneath our mastering glance, arranged in enduring figures, and followed by silence.

Granted that individual inventiveness, in the case of a French poet, need not outweigh the influence of his poetic heritage; still it would be highly annoying if he were not able to follow his own paths, walk through their numberless little flowers, and gather up whatever notes his voice might find. The attempt to do so has been made just recently, and poets are still conducting learned research in the direction of syllable stressing, for example. But apart from that, there is the fascinating pastime of breaking the old alexandrine into still recognizable fragments, alternately elusive or revealing. This is preferable to total and sudden novelty. It was good to relax the rules, but the ardor which got the new school too far out of tune should now be cooled. Most delightfully out of tune, yes; but to go further, as a result of that liberation, and to suppose that every poet henceforth should invent his own prosody and base it on his own special musical gift—to say nothing of his own spelling system—is simply ridiculous. That kind of thing is cannon fodder for the newspaper boys. Verses will always be similar, and the old proportions and regularity will be observed, because the poetic act consists of our sudden realization that an idea is naturally fractionized into several motifs of equal value which must be assembled. They rhyme; and their outward stamp of authenticity is that common meter which the final stress establishes.

But the crisis in poetry lies less in the very interesting interregnum or rest treatment undergone by versification, than in certain new states of our poetic mind.

We now *hear* undeniable rays of light, like arrows gilding and piercing the meanderings of song. I mean that, since Wagner appeared, Music and Verse have combined to form Poetry.

Either one of these two elements, of course, may profitably stand apart in triumph and integrity, in a quiet concert of its own if it chooses not to speak distinctly. Or else the poem can tell of their reassociation and restrengthening: the instrumentation is brightened to the point of perfect clarity beneath the orchestral veil, while verse flies down into the evening darkness of the sounds. That modern meteor—the symphony—approaches thought with the consent or ignorance of the musician. And thought itself is no longer expressed merely in common language.

Thus Mystery bursts forth ineffably throughout the heavens of Its own impersonal magnificence, wherein it was ordained that the orchestra should complement our age-old effort to make the spoken word our only form of music.

Twin symbols interrelated.

The Decadent or Mystic Schools (as they call themselves or as they were hastily labeled by the public press) find their common meeting-ground in an Idealism which (as in the case of fugues and sonatas) shuns the materials in nature, avoids any thought that might tend to arrange them too directly or precisely, and retains only the suggestiveness of things. The poet must establish a careful relationship between two images, from which a third element, clear and fusible, will be distilled and caught by our imagination. We renounce that erroneous esthetic (even though it has been responsible for certain masterpieces) which would have the poet fill the delicate pages of his book with the actual and palpable wood of trees, rather than with the forest's shuddering or the silent scattering of thunder through the foliage. A few well-chosen sounds blown heavenward on the trumpet of true majesty will suffice to conjure up the architecture of the ideal and only habitable palace—palace of no palpable stone, else the book could not be properly closed.

It is not *description* which can unveil the efficacy and beauty of monuments, seas, or the human face in all their maturity and native state, but rather evocation, *allusion, suggestion*. These somewhat arbitrary terms reveal what may well be a very decisive tendency in modern literature, a tendency which limits literature and yet sets it free. For what is the magic charm of art, if not this: that, beyond the confines of a fistful of dust or of all other reality, beyond the book itself, beyond the very text, it delivers up that volatile scattering which we call the Spirit, Who cares for nothing save universal musicality.

Speech is no more than a commercial approach to reality. In literature, allusion is sufficient: essences are distilled and then embodied in Idea.

Song, when it becomes impalpable joy, will rise to heaven.

This is the ideal I would call Transposition; Structure is something else.

If the poem is to be pure, the poet's voice must be stilled and the initiative taken by the words themselves, which will be set in motion as they meet unequally in collision. And in an exchange of gleams they will flame out like some glittering swath of fire sweeping over precious stones, and thus replace the audible breathing in lyric poetry of old—replace the poet's own personal and passionate control of verse.

The inner structures of a book of verse must be inborn; in this way, chance will be totally eliminated and the poet will be absent. From each theme, itself predestined, a given harmony will be born somewhere in the parts of the total poem and take its proper place within the volume; because, for every sound, there is an echo. Motifs of like pattern will move in balance from point to point. There will be none of the sublime incoherence found in the page-settings of the Romantics, none of the artificial unity that used to be based on the square measurements of the book. Everything will be hesitation, disposition of parts, their alternations and relationships—all this contributing to the rhythmic totality, which will be the very silence of the poem, in its blank spaces, as that silence is translated by each structural element in its own way. (Certain recent publications have heralded this sort of book; and if we may admit their ideals as complements to our own, it must then be granted that young poets have seen what an overwhelming and harmonious totality a poem must be, and have stammered out the magic concept of the Great Work.) Then again, the perfect symmetry of verses within the poem, of poems within the volume, will extend even beyond the volume itself; and this will be the creation of many poets who will inscribe, on spiritual space, the expanded signature of genius—as anonymous and perfect as a work of art.

Chimaera, yes! And yet the mere thought of it is proof (reflected from Her scales) that during the last twenty-five years poetry has been visited by some nameless and absolute flash of lightning—like the muddied, dripping gleams on my windowpane which are washed away and brightened by streaming showers of rain—revealing that, in general, all books contain the amalgamation of a certain number of age-old truths; that actually there is only one book on earth, that it is the law of the earth, the earth's true Bible. The difference between individual works is simply the difference between individual interpretations of one true and established text, which are proposed in a mighty gathering of those ages we call civilized or literary.

Certainly, whenever I sit at concerts, amid the obscurity and ecstasy of sound, I always perceive the nascent form of some one of those poems which have their origin and dwelling in human life—a poem more understandable because unheard, because the composer, in his desire to portray its majestic lines, was not even *tempted* to "explain everything." My feeling—or my doubtlessly ineradicable prejudice as a writer—is that nothing will endure if it remains unspoken; that our present task, precisely (now that the great literary rhythms I spoke of are being broken up and scattered in a series of distinct and almost orchestrated shiverings), is to find a way of transposing the symphony to the Book: in short, to regain our rightful due. For, undeniably, the true source of Music must not be the elemental sound of brasses, strings, or wood winds, but the intellectual and written word in all its glory—Music of perfect fulness and clarity, the totality of universal relationships.

One of the undeniable ideals of our time is to divide words into two different categories: first, for vulgar or immediate, second, for essential purposes.

The first is for narrative, instruction, or description (even though an adequate exchange of human thoughts might well be achieved through the silent exchange of money). The elementary use of language involves that universal *journalistic style* which characterizes all kinds of contemporary writing, with the exception of literature.

Why should we perform the miracle by which a natural object is almost made to disappear beneath the magic waving wand of the written word, if not to divorce that object from the direct and the palpable, and so conjure up its *essence* in all purity?

When I say: "a flower!" then from that forgetfulness to which my voice consigns all floral form, something different from the usual calyces arises, something all music, essence, and softness: the flower which is absent from all bouquets.

Language, in the hands of the mob, leads to the same facility and directness as does money. But, in the Poet's hands, it is turned, above all, to dream and song; and, by the constituent virtue and necessity of an art which lives on fiction, it achieves its full efficacy.

Out of a number of words, poetry fashions a single new word which is total in itself and foreign to the language—a kind of incantation. Thus the desired isolation of language is effected; and chance (which might still have governed these elements, despite their artful and alternating renewal through meaning and sound) is thereby instantly and thoroughly abolished. Then we realize, to our amazement, that we had never truly heard this or that ordinary poetic fragment; and, at the same time, our recollection of the object thus conjured up bathes in a totally new atmosphere. (pp. 34-43)

> *Stéphane Mallarmé, "Crisis in Poetry," in his* Mallarmé: Selected Prose Poems, Essays, & Letters, *translated by Bradford Cook, The Johns Hopkins Press, 1956, pp. 34-43.*

THE MOVEMENT ATTACKED AND DEFENDED

LEO N. TOLSTOY

[*Tolstoy is regarded as one of the greatest novelists in the history of world literature. His* Voina i mir (War and Peace) *and* Anna Karenina *are almost universally accepted as all-encompassing documents of human existence and supreme examples of the realistic novel. Later in Tolstoy's life, he converted to Christianity, and the artistic repercussions of this conversion are reflected in* Chto takoe iskusstvo (What Is Art?), *an essay that distinguishes*

bogus art, which he called an elitist celebration of aesthetics, from universal art, which successfully "infects" its recipient with the highest sentiment an artist can transmit—that of religious feeling. In the following excerpt from What Is Art?, *Tolstoy objects to Symbolist writing primarily because it is intended to be appreciated by an exclusive audience rather than by all classes of readers. This essay was originally published in 1896.*]

When a universal artist (such as were some of the Grecian artists or the Jewish prophets) composed his work, he naturally strove to say what he had to say in such a manner that his production should be intelligible to all men. But when an artist composed for a small circle of people placed in exceptional conditions, or even for a single individual and his courtiers—for popes, cardinals, kings, dukes, queens, or for a king's mistress—he naturally only aimed at influencing these people, who were well known to him and lived in exceptional conditions familiar to him. And this was an easier task, and the artist was involuntarily drawn to express himself by allusions comprehensible only to the initiated, and obscure to everyone else. In the first place, more could be said in this way; and secondly, there is (for the initiated) even a certain charm in the cloudiness of such a manner of expression. This method, which showed itself both in euphemism and in mythological and historical allusions, came more and more into use until it has, apparently, at last reached its utmost limits in the so-called art of the Decadents. It has come, finally, to this: that not only is haziness, mysteriousness, obscurity, and exclusiveness (shutting out the masses) elevated to the rank of a merit and a condition of poetic art, but even incorrectness, indefiniteness, and lack of eloquence are held in esteem.

Théophile Gautier, in his preface to the celebrated *Fleurs du Mal*, says that Baudelaire, as far as possible, banished from poetry eloquence, passion, and truth too strictly copied (*"l'éloquence, la passion, et la vérité calquée trop exactement"*).

And Baudelaire not only expressed this, but maintained his thesis in his verses and, yet more strikingly, in the prose of his *Petits Poémes en Prose*, the meanings of which have to be guessed like a rebus, and remain for the most part undiscovered. (pp. 76-7)

[After Baudelaire] comes Mallarmé, considered the most important of the young poets, and he plainly says that the charm of poetry lies in our having to guess its meaning—that in poetry there should always be a puzzle. . . . (p. 78)

Thus is obscurity elevated into a dogma among the new poets. (p. 79)

But it is not French writers only who think thus. The poets of all other countries think and act in the same way: German, and Scandinavian, and Italian, and Russian, and English. So also do the artists of the new period in all branches of art: in painting, in sculpture, and in music. Relying on Nietzsche and Wagner, the artists of the new age conclude that it is unnecessary for them to be intelligible to the vulgar crowd; it is enough for them to evoke poetic emotion in "the finest nurtured," to borrow a phrase from an English aesthetician.

In order that what I am saying may not seem to be mere assertion, I will quote at least a few examples from the French poets who have led this movement. The name of these poets is legion. I have taken French writers, because they, more decidedly than any others, indicate the new direction of art and are imitated by most European writers.

Besides those whose names are already considered famous, such as Baudelaire and Verlaine, here are the names of a few of them: Jean Moréas, Charles Morice, Henri de Régnier, Charles Vignier, Adrien Remacle, René Ghil, Maurice Maeterlinck, G. Albert Aurier, Rémy de Gourmont, Saint-Pol-Roux-le-Magnifique, Georges Rodenbach, le comte Robert de Montesquiou-Fezensac. These are Symbolists and Decadents. (p. 80)

[Baudelaire's *Fleurs du Mal* contains] not one poem which is plain and can be understood without a certain effort—an effort seldom rewarded, for the feelings which the poet transmits are evil and very low ones. And these feelings are always, and purposely, expressed by him with eccentricity and lack of clearness. This premeditated obscurity is especially noticeable in his prose where the author could, if he liked, speak plainly. (pp. 81-2)

The production of another celebrity, Verlaine, are not less affected and unintelligible. (p. 83)

I must pause to note the amazing celebrity of these two versifiers, Baudelaire and Verlaine, who are now accepted as being great poets. How the French, who had Chénier, Musset, Lamartine, and, above all, Hugo—and among whom quite recently flourished the so-called Parnassiens: Leconte de Lisle, Sully-Prudhomme, etc.—could attribute such importance to these two versifiers, who were far from skillful in form and most contemptible and commonplace in subject matter, is to me incomprehensible. The conception of life of one of them, Baudelaire, consisted in elevating gross egotism into a theory, and replacing morality by a cloudy conception of beauty and especially artificial beauty. Baudelaire had a preference, which he expressed, for a woman's face painted rather than showing its natural color, and for metal trees and a theatrical imitation of water rather than real trees and real water.

The life-conception of the other, Verlaine, consisted in weak profligacy, confession of his moral impotence, and, as an antidote to that impotence, in the grossest Roman Catholic idolatry. Both, moreover, were quite lacking in naïveté, sincerity, and simplicity, and both overflowed with artificiality, forced originality and self-assurance. So that in their least bad productions one sees more of M. Baudelaire or M. Verlaine than of what they were describing. But these two indifferent versifiers form a school and lead hundreds of followers after them.

There is only one explanation of this fact: it is that the art of the society in which these versifiers lived is not a serious, important matter of life, but is a mere amusement. And all amusements grow wearisome by repetition. And, in order to make wearisome amusement again tolerable, it is necessary to find some means to freshen it up. When, at cards, ombre grows stale, whist is introduced; when whist grows stale, écarté is substituted; when écarté grows stale, some other novelty is invented, and so on. The substance of the matter remains the same, only its form is changed. And so it is with this kind of art. The subject matter of the art of the upper classes growing continually more and more limited, it has come at last to this, that to the artists of these exclusive classes it seems as if everything has already been said and that to find anything new to say is impossible. And therefore, to freshen up this art they look out for fresh forms.

Baudelaire and Verlaine invent such a new form, furbish it up, moreover, with hitherto unused pornographic details, and—the critics and the public of the upper classes hail them as great writers.

This is the only explanation of the success, not of Baudelaire and Verlaine only, but of all the Decadents.

For instance, there are poems by Mallarmé and Maeterlinck which have no meaning, and yet for all that, or perhaps on that very account, are printed by tens of thousands, not only in various publications but even in collections of the best works of the younger poets. (pp. 85-7)

And among the Germans, Swedes, Norwegians, Italians, and us Russians, similar verses are printed. And such productions are printed and made up into book form, if not by the million, then by the hundred thousand (some of these works sell in tens of thousands). For typesetting, paging, printing, and binding these books, millions and millions of working days are spent—not less, I think, than went to build the great pyramid. And this is not all. The same is going on in all the other arts: millions and millions of working days are being spent on the production of equally incomprehensible works in painting, in music, and in the drama. (p. 90)

People who grew up in the first half of this century admiring Goethe, Schiller, Musset, Hugo, Dickens, Beethoven, Chopin, Raphael, da Vinci, Michael Angelo, Delaroche, being unable to make head or tail of this new art, simply attribute its productions to tasteless insanity and wish to ignore them. But such an attitude toward this art is quite unjustifiable, because, in the first place, that art is spreading more and more and has already conquered for itself a firm position in society, similar to the one occupied by the Romanticists in the third decade of this century; and secondly and chiefly, because, if it is permissible to judge in this way of the productions of the latest form of art called by us Decadent art merely because we do not understand it, then remember there are an enormous number of people—all the laborers and many of the nonlaboring folk—who, in just the same way, do not comprehend those productions of art which we consider admirable: the verses of our favorite artists—Goethe, Schiller, and Hugo; the novels of Dickens, the music of Beethoven and Chopin, the pictures of Raphael, Michael Angelo, da Vinci, etc.

If I have a right to think that great masses of people do not understand and do not like what I consider undoubtedly good because they are not sufficiently developed, then I have no right to deny that perhaps the reason why I cannot understand and cannot like the new productions of art is merely that I am still insufficiently developed to understand them. If I have a right to say that I, and the majority of people who are in sympathy with me, do not understand the productions of the new art simply because there is nothing in it to understand and because it is bad art, then, with just the same right, the still larger majority, the whole laboring mass, who do not understand what I consider admirable art, can say that what I reckon as good art is bad art, and there is nothing in it to understand.

I once saw the injustice of such condemnation of the new art with special clearness when in my presence a certain poet who writes incomprehensible verses ridiculed incomprehensible music with gay self-assurance; and shortly afterwards, a certain musician who composes incomprehensible symphonies laughed at incomprehensible poetry with equal self-confidence. I have no right, and no authority, to condemn the new art on the ground that I (a man educated in the first half of the century) do not understand it; I can only say that it is incomprehensible to me. The only advantage the art I acknowledge has over the Decadent art lies in the fact that the art I recognize is comprehensible to a somewhat larger number of people than the present-day art.

The fact that I am accustomed to a certain exclusive art and can understand it, but am unable to understand another still more exclusive art, does not give me a right to conclude that my art is the real true art, and that the other one which I do not understand is an unreal, a bad art. I can only conclude that art, becoming ever more and more exclusive, has become more and more incomphrehensible to an ever increasing number of people, and that in this its progress toward greater and greater incomprehensibility (on one level of which I am standing, with the art familiar to me), it has reached a point where it is understood by a very small number of the elect, and the number of these chosen people is ever becoming smaller and smaller.

As soon as ever the art of the upper classes separated itself from universal art, a conviction arose that art may be art and yet be incomprehensible to the masses. And as soon as this position was admitted, it had inevitably to be admitted also that art may be intelligible only to the very smallest number of the elect, and, eventually, to two, or to one, of our nearest friends, or to oneself alone, which is practically what is being said by modern artists: "I create and understand myself, and if anyone does not understand me, so much the worse for him."

The assertion that art may be good art and at the same time incomprehensible to a great number of people is extremely unjust, and its consequences are ruinous to art itself; but at the same time it is so common and has so eaten into our conceptions

La vogue, *one of the leading Symbolist journals, 4 April 1886.*

that it is impossible sufficiently to elucidate all the absurdity of it.

Nothing is more common than to hear it said of reputed works of art that they are very good but very difficult to understand. We are quite used to such assertions, and yet to say that a work of art is good but incomprehensible to the majority of men is the same as saying of some kind of food that it is very good, but that most people can't eat it. The majority of men may not like rotten cheese or putrefying grouse—dishes esteemed by people with perverted tastes; but bread and fruit are only good when they please the majority of men. And it is the same with art. Perverted art may not please the majority of men, but good art always pleases everyone. (pp. 93-5)

Leo N. Tolstoy, "Chapter Ten," in his What Is Art?, *translated by Aylmer Maude, The Bobbs-Merrill Company, Inc., 1960, pp. 76-99.*

MAX NORDAU

[*In his* Degeneration, *from which the following excerpt is taken, Nordau analyzes what he considers symptoms of degeneracy in the arts and the effect that so-called degenerate artists have on society. Arguing that the Symbolists displayed "all the signs of degeneracy and imbecility," Nordau provides an extreme example of the negative reaction by some critics to the movement.*]

[With the French symbolists, we] see a number of young men assemble for the purpose of founding a school. It assumes a special title, but in spite of all sorts of incoherent cackle and subsequent attempts at mystification it has, beyond this name, no kind of general artistic principle or clear aesthetic ideal. It only follows the tacit, but definitely recognisable, aim of making a noise in the world, and by attracting the attention of men through its extravagances, of attaining celebrity and profit, and the gratification of all the desires and conceits agitating the envious souls of these filibusters of fame.

Shortly after 1880 there was, in the Quartier Latin in Paris, a group of literary aspirants, all about the same age, who used to meet in an underground café at the Quai St. Michel, and, while drinking beer, smoking and quibbling late into the night, or early hours of the morning, abused in a scurrilous manner the well-known and successful authors of the day, while boasting of their own capacity, as yet unrevealed to the world. (p. 100)

About 1884, the society left their paternal pot-house, and pitched their tent in the Café Francois I., Boulevard St. Michel. This *café* attained a high renown. It was the cradle of Symbolism. It is still the temple of a few ambitious youths, who hope, by joining the Symbolist school, to acquire that advancement which they could not expect from their own abilities. It is, too, the Kaaba to which all foreign imbeciles make a pilgrimage, those, that is, who have heard of the new Parisian tendency, and wish to become initiated into its teachings and mysteries. (pp. 100-01)

The Symbolists are a remarkable example of that group-forming tendency which we have learnt to know as a peculiarity of 'degenerates.' They had in common all the signs of degeneracy and imbecility: overweening vanity and self-conceit, strong emotionalism, confused disconnected thoughts, garrulity (the 'logorrhoea' of mental therapeutics), and complete incapacity for serious sustained work. Several of them had had a secondary education, others even less. All of them were profoundly ignorant, and being unable, through weakness of will and inability to pay attention, to learn anything systematically, they persuaded themselves, in accordance with a well-known psychological law, that they despised all positive knowledge, and held that only dreams and divinings, only 'intuitions,' were worthy of human beings. A few of them, like Moréas and Guaita, who afterwards became a 'magian,' read in a desultory fashion all sorts of books which chanced to fall into their hands at the *bouquinistes* of the Quais, and delivered themselves of the snatched fruits of their reading in grandiloquent and mysterious phrases before their comrades. Their listeners thereupon imagined that they had indulged in an exhausting amount of study, and in this way they acquired that intellectual lumber which they peddled out in such an ostentatious display in their articles and pamphlets, and in which the mentally sane reader, to his amused astonishment, meets with the names of Schopenhauer, Darwin, Taine, Renan, Shelley and Goethe; names employed to label the shapeless, unrecognisable rubbish-heaps of a mental dustbin, filled with raw scraps of uncomprehended and insolently mutilated propositions and fragments of thought, dishonestly extracted and appropriated. (pp. 101-02)

The original guests of the Francois I. made their appearance at one o'clock in the day at their café, and remained there till dinner-time. Immediately after that meal they returned, and did not leave their headquarters till long after midnight. Of course none of the Symbolists had any known occupation. These 'degenerates' are no more capable of regularly fulfilling any duty than they are of methodical learning. If this organic deficiency appears in a man of the lower classes, he becomes a vagabond; in a woman of that class it leads to prostitution; in one belonging to the upper classes it takes the form of artistic and literary drivel. The German popular mind betrays a deep intuition of the true connection of things in inventing such a word as 'day-thief' (*Tagedieb*) for such aesthetic loafers. Professional thieving and the unconquerable propensity to busy, gossiping, officious idleness flow from the same source, to wit, inborn weakness of brain.

It is true that the boon companions of the café are not conscious of their mentally-crippled condition. They find pet names and graceful appellations for their inability to submit themselves to any sort of discipline, and to devote persistent concentration and attention to any sort of work. They call it 'the artist nature,' 'genius roaming at large,' 'a soaring above the low miasma of the commonplace.' They ridicule the dull Philistine, who, like the horse turning a winch, performs mechanically a regular amount of work; they despise the narrow-minded loons who demand that a man should either pursue a circumscribed bourgeois trade or possess an officially acknowledged status, and who profoundly distrust impecuniary professions. They glory in roving folk who wander about singing and carelessly begging, and they hold up as their ideal the 'commoner of air,' who bathes in morning dew, sleeps under flowers, and gets his clothing from the same firm as the lilies of the field in the Gospel. (p. 102)

Moreover, the pseudo-artistic loafer, in spite of his imbecility and self-esteem, cannot fail to perceive that his mode of life runs contrary to the laws on which the structure of society and civilization are based, and he feels the need of justifying himself in his own eyes. This he does by investing with a high significance the dreams and chatter over which he wastes his time, calculated to arouse in him the illusion that they rival in value the most serious productions. 'The fact is, you see,' says M. Stéphane Mallarmé, 'that a fine book is the end for which the world was made.' [In his *La Littérature de tout-à-l'heure*, Charles] Morice complains touchingly that the poetic mind

'should be bound to suffer the interruption of a twenty-eight days' army drill between the two halves of a verse.' 'The excitement of the streets,' he goes on, 'the jarring of the Governmental engine, the newspapers, the elections, the change of the Ministry, have never made so much noise; the stormy and turbulent autocracy of trade has suppressed the love of the beautiful in the thoughts of the multitude, and industry has killed as much silence as politics might still have permitted to survive.' In fact, what are all these nothings—commerce, manufactures, politics, administration—against the immense importance of a hemistich?

The drivelling of the Symbolists was not entirely lost in the atmosphere of their café, like the smoke of their pipes and cigarettes. A certain amount of it was perpetuated, and appeared in the *Revue Indépendante*, the *Revue Contemporaine*, and other fugitive periodicals, which served as organs to the round table of the François I. These little journals and the books published by the Symbolists were not at first noticed outside the café. Then it happened that *chroniqueurs* of the Boulevard papers, into whose hands these writings chanced to fall, devoted an article to them on days when 'copy' was scanty, but only to hold them up to ridicule. That was all the Symbolists wanted. Mockery or praise mattered little so long as they got noticed. Now they were in the saddle, and showed at once what unparalleled circus-riders they were. They themselves used every effort to get into the larger newspapers, and when one of them succeeded, like the Smith of Jüterbock in the familiar fairy tale, in throwing his cap into an editor's office through the crack of the door incautiously put ajar, he followed it neck and crop, took possession of the place, and in the twinkling of an eye transformed it into the citadel of the Symbolist party. In these tactics everything served their turn—the dried-up scepticism and apathy of Parisian editors, who take nothing seriously, are capable neither of enthusiasm nor of repugnance, and only know the cardinal principle of their business, viz., to make a noise, to arouse curiosity, to forestall others by bringing out something new and sensational; the uncritical gaping attitude of the public, who repeat in faith all that their newspaper gossips to them with an air of importance; the cowardice and cupboard-love of the critics who, finding themselves confronted by a closed and numerous band of reckless young men, got nervous at the sight of their clenched fists and angry threatening glances, and did not dare to quarrel with them; the low cunning of the ambitious, who hoped to make a good bargain if they speculated on the rise of shares in Symbolism. Thus the very worst and most despicable characteristics of editors, critics, aspiring authors, and newspaper readers, cooperated to make known, and, in part, even famous, the names of the original habitués of the François I., and to awaken the conviction in very many weak minds of both hemispheres that their tendency governed the literature of the day, and included all the germs of the future. This triumph of the Symbolists marks the victory of the gang over the individual. It proves the superiority of attack over defence, and the efficacy of mutual-admiration-insurance, even in the case of the most beggarly incapacity.

With all their differences, the works of the Symbolists have two features in common. They are vague often to the point of being unintelligible, and they are pious. Their vagueness is only to be expected, after . . . the peculiarities of mystic thought. Their piousness has attained to an importance which makes it necessary to consider it more in detail.

When, in the last few years, a large number of mysteries, passion plays, golden legends, and cantatas appeared, when one dozen after another of new poets and authors, in their first poems, novels, and treatises, made ardent confessions of faith, invoked the Virgin Mary, spoke with rapture of the sacrifice of the Mass, and knelt in fervent prayer, the cry arose amongst reactionists, who have a vested interest in diffusing a belief in a reversion of cultured humanity to the mental darkness of the past: 'Behold, the youth, the hope, the future of the French people is turning away from science; "emancipation" is becoming bankrupt; souls are opening again to religion, and the Holy Catholic Church steps anew into its lofty office, as the teacher, comforter, and guide of civilized mankind.' The Symbolistic tendency is designedly called 'neo-Catholic,' and certain critics pointed to its appearance and success as a proof that freethought was overthrown by faith. 'Even the most superficial glance at the state of the world,' writes Edouard Rod, 'shows us that we are on all sides in the full swing of reaction.' And, further, 'I believe in reaction in every sense of the word. How far this reaction will go is the secret of tomorrow.'

The jubilant heralds of the new reaction, in inquiring into the cause of this movement, find, with remarkable unanimity, this answer, viz.: The best and most cultivated minds return to faith, because they found out that science had deceived them, and not done for them what it had promised to do. (pp. 103-05)

If we wish to know at the outset what Symbolists understand by symbol and symbolism, we shall meet with the same difficulties we [encounter] in determining the precise meaning of the name pre-Raphaelitism, and for the same reason, viz., because the inventors of these appellations understood by them hundreds of different mutually contradictory, indefinite things, or simply nothing at all. A skilled and sagacious journalist, Jules Huret, instituted an inquiry about the new literary movement in France, and from its leading representatives acquired information, by which he has furnished us with a trustworthy knowledge of the meaning which they connect, or pretend to connect, with the expressions and phraseology of their programme. I will here adduce some of these utterances and declarations. They will not tell us what Symbolism is. But they may afford us some insight into symbolist methods of thought.

M. Stéphane Mallarmé, whose leadership of the Symbolist band is least disputed among the disciples, expresses himself as follows: 'To name an object means to suppress three-quarters of the pleasure of a poem—i.e., of the happiness which consists in gradually divining it. Our dream should be to suggest the object. The symbol is the perfected use of this mystery, viz., to conjure up an object gradually in order to show the condition of a soul; or, conversely, to choose an object, and out of it to reveal a state of the soul by a series of interpretations.' (p. 115)

M. Paul Verlaine, another high-priest of the sect, expresses himself as follows: 'It was I who, in the year 1885, laid claim to the name of Symbolist. The Parnassians, and most of the romanticists, in a certain sense lacked symbols.... Thence errors of local colouring in history, the shrinking up of the myth through false philosophical interpretations, thought without the discernment of analogies, the anecdote emptied of feeling.'

Let us listen to a few second-rate poets of the group. 'I declare art,' says M. Paul Adam, 'to be the enshrining of a dogma in a symbol. It is a means of making a system prevail, and of bringing truths to the light of day.' M. Rémy de Gourmont confesses honestly: 'I cannot unveil the hidden meaning of the word "symbolism," since I am neither a theorist nor a magician.' And M. Saint-Pol-Roux-le-Magnifique utters this pro-

found warning: 'Let us take care! Symbolism carried to excess leads to *nombrilisme,* and to a morbid mechanism.... This symbolism is to some extent a parody of mysticism.... Pure symbolism is an anomaly in this remarkable century, remarkable for militant activities. Let us view this transitional art as a clever trick played upon naturalism, and as a precursor of the poetry of tomorrow.'

We may expect from the theorists and philosophers of the group more exhaustive information concerning their methods and aims. Accordingly, M. Charles Morice instructs us how 'the symbol is the combination of the objects which have aroused our sensations, with our souls, in a fiction [*fiction*]. The means is suggestion; it is a question of giving people a remembrance of something which they have never seen.' And M. Gustav Kahn says: 'For me personally, symbolic art consists in recording in a cycle of works, as completely as possible, the modifications and variations of the mind of the poet, who is inspired by an aim which he has determined.' (p. 116)

The Symbolists, so far as they are honestly degenerate and imbecile, can think only in a mystical, i.e., in a confused way. The unknown is to them more powerful than the known; the activity of the organic nerves preponderates over that of the cerebral cortex; their emotions overrule their ideas. When persons of this kind have poetic and artistic instincts, they naturally want to give expression to their own mental state. They cannot make use of definite words of clear import, for their own consciousness holds no clearly-defined univocal ideas which could be embodied in such words. They choose, therefore, vague equivocal words, because these best conform to their ambiguous and equivocal ideas. The more indefinite, the more obscure a word is, so much the better does it suit the purpose of the imbecile and it is notorious that among the insane this habit goes so far that, to express their ideas, which have become quite formless, they invent new words, which are no longer merely obscure, but devoid of all meaning.... Clear speech serves the purpose of communication of the actual. It has, therefore, no value in the eyes of a degenerate subject. He prizes that language alone which does not force him to follow the speaker attentively, but allows him to indulge without restraint in the meanderings of his own reveries, just as his own language does not aim at the communication of definite thought, but is only intended to give a pale reflection of the twilight of his own ideas. That is what M. Mallarmé means when he says: 'To name an object means to suppress three quarters of the pleasure.... Our dream should be to suggest the object.'

Moreover, the thought of a healthy brain has a flow which is regulated by the laws of logic and the supervision of attention. It takes for its content a definite object, manipulates and exhausts it. The healthy man can tell what he thinks, and his telling has a beginning and an end. The mystic imbecile thinks merely according to the laws of association, and without the red thread of attention. He has fugitive ideation. He can never state accurately what he is thinking about; he can only denote the emotion which at the moment controls his consciousness. He can only say in general, 'I am sad,' 'I am merry,' 'I am fond,' 'I am afraid.' His mind is filled with evanescent, floating, cloudy ideas, which take their hue from the reigning emotion, as the vapour hovering above a crater flames red from the glow at the bottom of the volcanic caldron. When he poetizes, therefore, he will never develop a logical train of thought, but will seek by means of obscure words of distinctly emotional colouring to represent a feeling, a mood. What he prizes in poetical works is not a clear narrative, the exposition of a definite thought, but only the reflected image of a mood, which awakens in him a similar, but not necessarily the same, mood. The degenerate are well aware of this difference between a work which expresses strong mental labour and one in which merely emotionally coloured fugitive ideation ebbs and flows; and they eagerly ask for a distinguishing name for that kind of poetry of which alone they have any understanding. In France they have found this designation in the word 'Symbolism.' (pp. 118-19)

> Max Nordau, "Symbolism," in his Degeneration, 1895. Reprint by William Heinemann, 1913, pp. 100-44.

STÉPHANE MALLARMÉ

[*Mallarmé considers the public image of the modern poet as reflected in such works as Max Nordau's* Degeneration *(see excerpt above) and discusses his conception of the poet's place in society. For additional commentary by Mallarmé, see excerpt above.*]

I should like to observe that the role of the poet is not entirely without its comic aspects.

In the public eye, he has become a pitiful prince banishing his own ghost from the sepulcher which should have buried him long since, and consigning it to legend and melodrama. And yet he is also the one we hold responsible for having confronted Society with an explosive and original idea.

Certain newspaper articles have been gossiping about my connection (oh, a very slight connection, really) with some scandal unleashed by a book which is apparently only the first installment of a general satire aimed at almost all the foremost minds of our time. It is not entirely unamusing to note how often such words as "idiot" and "madman" are used (and how seldom they are softened to "cretin" or "lunatic") and hurled like so many stones at a group of proud, obtrusive, feudal minds which are apparently threatening all Europe. But of course I dare not make fun of the good intentions of these scandal-mongers who are so stirred up over symptoms which do not exist; after all, we can never prevent people from making something out of nothing. The trouble in this particular instance is that science has seen fit to meddle with the problem—or else has been dragged into it. *Degeneration* is the title of the book in question (*Entartung* in the German); its author is M. Nordau [see excerpt above]. (I was determined to keep my statements on a general level and to name nobody. I think that I have just done so.) This popularizer has called our attention to a "fact": Nature (he notes) does not produce spontaneous or complete genius; instead, genius is in man generally and in no one particularly; She would appear, in practice (and in some occult and gratuitous fashion), to "compensate" for one exceptional faculty bestowed on man by destroying another. Now I submit that this is the kind of pseudo-righteous panacea and old wives' tale that needs clear critical judgment and some measure of pity. But to continue: this sickly genius (says Nordau) manages to draw strength from his weakness and grows toward fulfillment of his nature; in so doing, of course, he leaves enormous wreckage in his wake, i.e., his fellow citizens, like so many hospital cases or the "outs" on a voting list. Now M. Nordau's mistake is that he treats everything as wreckage; so you can see that the subtleties and arcana of physiology and destiny must not be entrusted to clean-living foremen or honest metal fitters, whose hands are somewhat too crude to treat them properly. A man like that goes only half way, you

see; and if he had only added a little insight to his other faculties, he would have discovered this particular phase of poor Mother Nature's sacred laws and therefore not written his book at all.

A quite different brand of insult has appeared in the newspapers—in rather timid and mumbling fashion, which is strange. For, after all, why shouldn't the slightest suspicion be shouted through the streets? When the propaganda machines break down, we get a brief glimpse of parliamentary procedure and, in the process, the mob is rather pitifully confounded. I find the glimpse most interesting—but, unfortunately, it is only a glimpse, and the lesson thus taught so brief that the legislators can claim ignorance of the problem. In any case, I would challenge the addition of bullets and nails to the fray. These are only my own opinions, of course. Let me add that the idea of damning out-of-line writers who happen to be for—or against—blank verse is really quite ingenious. It little matters whether they stand in or above the battle in readiness for some special moment; in either case they are considered an insult to the newspaper columnist. Regardless of their treasure, they manage to heap disgrace (you would think they were dropping bombs) on the organization that does of course keep us posted (at great expense) on the capital's most recent apotheoses. Let's just be sure that that organization has neither first nor last say in the matter of those particular splendors which human language can find within itself. I wish we would stop insinuating and speak out loud and bold, saying that we approve the inviolability and seclusion of certain outstanding men. Whenever the masses are being herded indiscriminately toward self-interest, amusement, or convenience, it is essential that a very few disinterested persons should adopt an attitude of respectful indifference toward those common motivations and, by so doing, create a minority. And be it always understood that however broad and deep those differences may be which are created by the mad struggles of the citizenry, they must all ultimately agree that the reason for their internecine warfare is of prime importance. Now, since we can grant the need for such a minority—for this salt of the earth, this truest exception to the rule, these few chosen minds working and living here to absolute perfection—what name can best praise them? Are they laborers for love, strangers, laborers in vain? Or are they, more simply, men of letters? (pp. 52-4)

[The] disinterested poet, eschewing all virtuosity and bravado, must project his vision of the world and use the languages of the school, home, and market place which seem most fitting to that purpose. Then poetry will be lifted to some frightening, wavering, ecstatic pitch—like an orchestral wing spread wide in flight, but with its talons still rooted deep within your earth. Wherever you find it, you must deny the ineffable; for somehow it will speak.

Thus if the common man, neighbor to us all, has the gift of language on his lips and follows this very ordinary—or, rather, extraordinary!—method; and if an unheard echo joins his song, he will be able to communicate in the common vocabulary with all pomp and light. For it is fitting that to each of us Truth be revealed in Her native magnificence. And so, like a dutiful son or taxpayer, he willingly contributes what he owes to the common treasure of the fatherland. (p. 55)

Throughout the centuries, *our earthly society has been seriously handicapped* because we have failed to consider brute reality—city, government, laws—as a group of symbols. Or, to put it another way, we have turned them into cemeteries and thus destroyed the paradise they should be. We have made them a terrace, hardly higher than the earth. But, despite all appearances, it is not on earth, nor in tolls and elections, that we can find the lofty drama of the formalities which create a popular cult; for these are rather the representatives of the great Law as It is miraculously instituted with all transparent purity.

Whenever you are in danger of losing this perspective, you must destroy all material substructures. Or, better still, stream fairy lights along them all—and see! Your thoughts must ask an image of your earth.

If, in days to come, a new religion rises up in France, it will be the heavenly instinct within each one of us, expanded to the dimensions of infinite joy. A relatively harmless and elementary example of this can be found on the political level: voting (even for oneself) will not be satisfying until it becomes that expansive, trumpeting hymn of joy in which no name is chosen; nor can revolutions quite provide the broil and tempest in which we must stream and sink if we would rise and be reborn as heroes. (pp. 55-6)

> *Stéphane Mallarmé, "Music and Literature," in his* Mallarmé: Selected Prose, Poems, Essays, & Letters, *translated by Bradford Cook, The Johns Hopkins Press, 1956, pp. 43-56.*

INFLUENCES AND PREDECESSORS

HENRI PEYRE

[*Peyre is a French-born critic who has lived and taught in the United States for most of his career. One of the foremost American critics of French literature, he has written works that blend superb scholarship with a clear style accessible to the non-specialist reader. In the following excerpt, Peyre examines the meaning of Symbolism and traces various predecessors of the movement.*]

No one word generated from designations for other literary or artistic movements—except perhaps *structuralism* (which, however, includes scarcely any imaginative creations)—enjoys a prestige equal to that of *symbol*. Even the amphigoric mannerisms of the manifestoes from symbolism's feverish years or the puerile scribblings that certain versifiers took for mysterious poetic expressions do not succeed in tarnishing the brilliance with which this word shines. Young readers and others who refuse to admit after years of study or of teaching that they like what the popular imagination likes, and for the same reasons that it likes them, will always feel their intellect stimulated by the process of deciphering a more secret meaning hidden beneath the surface. The very vagueness of the word, which has frequently been used in conjunction with others hardly less vague (*myth, emblem, analogy, allegory*) has done much to invest it with majesty. It could be wished—in vain— that some international congress of critics might one day propose two or three precise meanings for the word *symbol*, according to which it would henceforth be used in the several Western languages. Of course, nothing of the kind will ever happen. In each of the European languages, the word already carries the ballast of a past it cannot jettison. The word *symbolism* is even more heavily weighted, serving as it does to designate both the eternal symbolism common to many religions and the literary symbolism of the Parisian and Belgian groups of the end of the nineteenth century, as well as similar movements (similar at first sight, at least) that took place in Germany, Italy, Russia, and Latin America.

Etymology can be a fascinating science, but the accretion of meanings or of associations that a word acquires through the centuries and in the passage from one language to another transfigures willy-nilly the unadorned, primitive value of concrete terms raised to the abstract. In the case of *symbol*, etymology provides us with little information. In Greek the term meant a portion of an object (a piece of pottery, for example) broken in two; it was a gesture of hospitality on the part of a host to offer to a guest one of two such fragments as a sign of trust and as a promise of protection in the future from the host's family or tribe, whose members would welcome the outsider at the sight of this "symbol." The substantive form is derived, of course, from the verb that also produced *parable, hyperbole,* and *ballistics* and that means "to throw together," that is, to unite in an immediate fusion the concrete or external sign and the thing it signifies.

Briefly, the word was given a generalized usage in mythology and religion where it was not always distinguished from *emblem*. In 1924 an art historian, Vladimir Déonna, wrote in the *Revue de l'historie des religions* an article entitled "Quelques réflexions sur le symbolisme, en particulier dans l'art préhistorique." He states therein: "Symbolism occurs when the idea, the object itself, is translated by means of an appearance that is not its immediate copy, but that serves to evoke that object in an oblique way, more often by analogy or by some other mental process." He shows how replete with symbolism prehistoric art is. Medieval philosophy is no less so, as Etienne Gilson has explained. The same may be said for the religious art of the Middle Ages whose system of analogies has in fact been interpreted by Emile Mâle and others. J. K. Huysmans, in his strange descriptive and mystical novel *La Cathédrale,* shows his hero, Durtal, listening, absorbed, to a priest who explains to him, in accordance with Hugues de Saint-Victor, that "the symbol is the allegorical representation of a Christian principle by way of a palpable form." The symbol, the novelist goes on to maintain, is found in all religions, and in Christianity from Genesis through the Book of the Apocalypse. He adds: "The symbol comes to us, then, from a divine source . . . this form of expression responds to one of the least questioned needs of the human mind, which takes a certain pleasure in giving proof of intelligence, in solving the enigma submitted to it and, also, in preserving the solution reduced to a visible formula and a lasting configuration." In this sense, Mallarmé is, Durtal-Huysmans notes, very near to Saint Augustine.

The word *symbol* (and occasionally "the symbolic" used in French as a feminine substantive) occurs after the Middle Ages; later it is used in a less religious sense, often applied to pagan mythology that was being rediscovered and relived at the time by a few poets or sculptors. It was applied as well to Egyptian hieroglyphics and even to various emblems. An Australian critic, Lloyd Austin, who has added much to our understanding of Baudelaire and Mallarmé, has set forth a quick sketch of various uses of these words in the works of Rabelais, Henri Estienne, and, finally, in those of Diderot and his most zealous collaborator on the *Encyclopédie*, Louis de Jaucourt. Austin has especially emphasized certain curious usages given the word along with an extraordinary interest in the symbolic in the treatise of an early seventeenth-century Jesuit, Le Père Caussin. This work, *La Sagesse symbolique des Egyptiens* (1618), is in Latin and was apparently quite widely read. To be sure, Egyptian writing was known at that time only through the writings of ancient religious authors, and Father Caussin took hieroglyphics for symbols. It is possible that Friedrich Creuzer may have borrowed something from this treatise, or rather from this collection of ancient treatises. Therein, Austin tells us, nature was proclaimed ''as a collection of symbols that manifest God.'' But it is doubtful that the German romantics and the French symbolists—not so much scholars as poets—may have borrowed anything whatever from that work. Someone probably should take up the entire question of the use of the word *symbol* before the symbolists or up to Baudelaire and the meanings in which the word's content may be understood; the efforts of a thorough and systematic research project on the subject would most likely be rewarded.

It is doubtful, however, whether such a project would shed much light on French symbolism from 1885 through the years following. Neither artists nor poets are scholarly researchers and, for them, as for the great majority of us, many abstruse books from the past are as if they were never written.

That such should be true is not at all surprising if what has been asserted by Goethe, who was nonetheless an inquisitive reader who led a tranquil existence, is true: that to know a great deal or too much is harmful to creativeness. What is more, the allusions to symbolism that one encounters before what we call the symbolist period, the sometimes penetrating insights that may strike us in Coleridge, Hölderlin, Nerval, and Hugo are imbued with all the meaning they do have and, one might say, with their originality, only because symbolism came after them and reinterpreted the past. All the questions that fascinate scholars—romanticism before the romantic movement, primitivism before Diderot or Rousseau, surrealism before 1920—are based in fact on a begging of the question. Precursors' different flashes of insight, often fortuitous and set down in passing, later seem to us inspired only because others coming after have read them and, unlike their precursors and perhaps, it is said, because the time was ripe for it, have perceived their true import and what follows therefrom. The searching out of sources for esthetic theories and for ideas, as for those of poems and works of art, too much cultivated out of the erudition of learned scholars, must be seen for what it is in fact: a sometimes fascinating pastime, but one that risks putting the accent on the nonessential.

The word *symbol* was to keep from its origins and the still unsure uses that had been made of it before the second half of the nineteenth century a few connotations that, succinctly enumerated, seem to be these: It is a sign that as such demands deciphering, an interpretation by whoever is exposed to it or is struck by it and who wishes to understand it and savor its mystery. This sign represents or evokes in a concrete manner what is innate within it, the thing signified and more or less hidden. The two meanings, one concrete and the other ulterior and perhaps profound, are fused into a single entity in the symbol. The meaning hidden beneath appearances is not necessarily a single one; the symbol is not a riddle within which human ingeniousness (that of an artist, a priest, a legislator, or a prophet) or a god's careful doing has been pleased to enclose a certain meaning that would otherwise be too clear, too pedestrian, too lacking in inspiration, had it simply been stated as a moral precept or mathematical theorem. Within the symbol there is therefore a polyvalence, a multiplicity of meanings, certain ones addressed to all, others to the initiated alone. But these signs, these formulas or images, are not merely convenient mnemotechnical or iconographic instruments like some object recalling such and such a saint or martyr, some beast designating one of the evangelists, the five Greek letters meaning ''fish,'' because these form the first letters of the phrase ''Jesus Christ, Son of God, Savior,'' or whatever detail

associated with Hercules or Vulcan. Each person, on beholding a sign or symbol, may according to his turn of mind (concrete, esthetic, oniric, metaphysical, artistic) extract from it the meaning that is most enriching for him or her. This person supplements, feels, or thinks anew what he believes he perceives in the symbol. In this process there is, then, as with the fragment of pottery or other object offered as a sign of hospitality to a visitor, something shared, a duality. For the *fin de siècle* French poets this was to turn into a necessity to avoid an art intended for all and to obtain active collaboration from the reader, the listener, the viewer of a picture or a statue. It must be the task of the public that wants to penetrate the mystery and pierce the silence to go at least halfway along the path to meet the creator. Insofar as the press, textbooks, and oral means of diffusion vulgarize art more and more, since everyone who knows how to read thinks himself capable of judging a work of art, especially insofar as criticism continues so grossly to mistake its way and to renounce (out of facility or superficialness) interpreting for the public original forms of expression, nonconventional techniques, and new sensibilities, the creator will believe he has the right to refuse every concession to the *vulgum pecus*. Often the artist, while refusing to explain his intentions and weaving his ideas around a work of music, sculpture, or poetry that does not necessarily carry any ideas of its own, will call for a new watchword: to suggest, and by so doing to touch the imagination, the sensitivity, the associations of images, even the subconscious of those in whom he hopes to re-create a state analogous to the one that enabled him to create.

The consequences of that new esthetic were to be numerous and far-reaching. ''All things that are sacred and that wish to remain so swathe themselves in mystery,'' in art as well as in religion, Mallarmé observed in *L'Art pour tous* (1862), at the age of twenty. Whatever seeks to be of value to all is of little value. Prose and genius must, in their very language and in their images, be approached with a certain ''esthetic distance'' and a kind of reverence. The particular language that renders the author's vision and that strives to communicate while evoking that vision, especially that of the poet, must be a language that, if it is not necessarily out of the ordinary, is at least purified. The essence of poetry, as Valéry was to repeat in the wake of Poe and Baudelaire, must be chemically or alchemically isolated. We find a return to a poetic diction that the romantics had claimed to banish but that will be something quite different from the tired, worn-out, colorless diction of the eighteenth century, with its descriptive, didactic, gnomic poetry, stripped of its power of evocation and its musicality.

The visible, the carnal, the sensual, will not necessarily disappear from this symbolistic art. But poets and even painters (Paul Klee was later to say it in a now famous remark) today have the ambition of rendering the invisible visible. They assume, then, and will affirm, in the footsteps of various theologians, estheticians, and mystics, that there is between the visible and the invisible an often secret correspondence. To these vertical correspondences, poets (and especially musicians), harking back to a few works of romantic virtuosi (like Théophile Gautier) and borrowing certain theoretical views from Wagner, were to join lateral or horizontal correspondences. They came to speak of the ''correspondence of the arts,'' of forms of synesthesia as E. T. A. Hoffmann had already done. The arts, addressing themselves to our various senses are parallel translations of a vast and profound secret that lies within them and that transcends them.

Such ambitions could not attempt realization except through a recasting of the means of expression, whether they be musical, pictorial, or, especially, linguistic and literary, that is, through a renovation of vocabulary, syntax, of both verse and stanza forms, and by breaking with constricting rules. In France especially, and to some extent in Germany, this revolution in what is called form is what clashed most with the reading public's ingrained habits or with its intellectual comfort. That revolution is what caused the greatest uproar, but it was not to have the most lasting effect. It is doubtless regrettable that neither Mallarmé nor Valéry should have conferred upon free verse—or verse freed of constraints—the homage of their genius and that Claudel should have preferred instead the biblical verse form, that Jules Laforgue should have died too soon, and that Gustave Kahn should have had more critical and creative intelligence than musical gifts. The boldness of the liberators of verse, all the more timorous to our contemporary eyes, gave way very quickly to a return to forms of expression closer to traditional ones. At least a considerable step forward had been made, and to the symbolist movement falls the honor of having finally rendered French verse more supple and of having permitted a multitude of new experiments.

It would be contrived and obstinate to rely on chronology alone and seek to restrict the use of the term *symbolists* to those writers who openly laid claim to it around 1885, for they were very far from rejecting everything from the past. Only on rare occasions did they rise up against the Parnassian poets, there having been more marked differences of esthetics and intentions between the symbolists and the naturalist prose writers. They treated nearly all the romantics, Alfred de Musset sometimes being an exception, with deference and knew full well that they were pursuing in their own way and in a completely different intellectual climate the romantics' revolution. They say relatively little of Baudelaire, and it was not the symbolists of 1885-90 but the literary historians of the midtwentieth century who called attention to the sonnet "Correspondences" and the critical articles collected in *L'art romantique* and in *Curiosités esthétiques*. In so doing, these historians and critics doubtless went too far in isolating Baudelaire, to the exclusion of his precursors and contemporaries, and in seeing in him the departure point for all modern poetry and an innovator who broke with all that had preceded him. Yet our perspective need not coincide with that of readers of 1857-68, none of whom saw, as we think we do, the originality of this or that remark tossed out in *Les Paradis artificiels* or in the *Salons*. We cannot deal with symbolism today without devoting a few pages to what Baudelaire might have meant in those texts, no matter how uncertain may be his use of the term. His originality, moreover, is apparent only if one recalls certain uses of the word *symbol*, certain affirmations before the appearance of *Les Fleurs du Mal*, of the correspondences between heaven and earth, between the concrete and the idea. This is in no way a question of sources, for Baudelaire had not read, and did not have available to read, what had been written in the first half of the century by little-known French thinkers or by illustrious Germans whose works were rarely translated. But it would falsify the image of this period, which corresponds to the flowering of romanticism, to ignore all that it involves of speculations around the deeper meaning of art and of foreshadowings of the future for which it was preparing the way.

Lloyd Austin in his work on Baudelaire, Pierre Moreau in an essay on "Le Symbolisme de Baudelaire," and still others like Jean Pommier, in analyzing the origins of the Baudelairian mystique, have all cited certain interesting texts from the be-

ginning of the nineteenth century. It is possible to go back even further: a hundred statements on the multiplicity of meanings inherent in fables may be found in the hermeneutics of the Stoics who devoted themselves to the analysis of myths, in those of interpreters of mythology at the beginning of the Renaissance (Boccaccio, for example), and in the subtleties of Christian theologians. We know the Greek word that designated those works evolved into the word *myth*. Jean Cocteau cites as an epigraph to his *Le Sang d'un poète* a passage from Montaigne that expresses what had already been suggested by the earliest mythographers of Italy and France:

> Most of Aesop's fables have several meanings and understandings. Those who explicate them choose from them certain aspects which sum up the fables quite well. But, usually, this is only the immediate and superficial aspect; there are others that are sharper, deeper and more to the point, which they have not succeeded in penetrating.

Madame de Staël, with more precision and doubtless echoing thinking already current among German metaphysicians, went even further; the entire universe was for her a symbolic image of the human soul. In the tenth chapter of the second part of her *De L'Allemagne* (1810 and 1813) she declared:

> In order to conceive of the true grandeur of lyric poetry, one must wander, through the imagination, in the ethereal regions, forgetting the tumult of the earth while listening to the celestial harmonies and considering the entire universe as a symbol of the soul's emotions.

She paid the Germans the honor of judging them more than any other nation capable of the contemplative self-communion and boldness of thought necessary for the composition of this superior form of lyric poetry.

It is not easy to determine exactly what borrowings from the other side of the Rhine were made by French philosophers or professors of philosophy under the Empire and the Restoration. None of them knew the German thinkers as well as did Coleridge, who incorporated in his speculative writings views and entire passages "borrowed" from Schelling, Schiller, or Hegel. Pierre-Simon Ballanche, in his *Orphée* (1829), reveals an intuitive conception of a kind of symbolic poetry, that is, one that translates the divine word on the human plane. Following Le Père Castel and Diderot, he had perceived the theory of synesthesia or of the horizontal correspondences between parallel sensations, the concrete mark of a higher harmony. Two of his most interesting texts, the second of which is drawn from *La Ville des Expiations* (1832), have been cited by Herbert J. Hunt in his erudite and penetrating work of 1941, *The Epic in Nineteenth-Century France*:

> Our poetry is a symbol, and that is what all true poetry must be, for the word of God, when it is transformed into the word of man, must render itself accessible to our senses, to our faculties, become incarnate in us, become ourselves. It is invested with an obscure coloration because it is reflected by obscure organs.

And again:

> All the senses awaken one another reciprocally. There could be, in a way, an onomatopoeia of colors so much in harmony is everything in man and in the universe.

Victor Cousin, less original and less mystical than Ballanche, but more adroit at publicizing himself and in asserting his own authority, was nonetheless an influential disseminator of ideas, an eloquent and often ingenious master. He oriented many young people of the time toward Plato and Alexandrian philosophy and others toward German thought. In his course, given in 1818, which created a sensation at the time but was not published until 1836 (by his disciple Adolphe Garnier), "Du Vrai, du Beau et du Bien" (lesson eight), Cousin made use of several grandiloquent but felicitous phrases:

> The true, the good, and the beautiful are only forms of the infinite. . . . Love of the infinite substance is hidden in the love of its forms. . . . Art is a reproduction of the infinite by the finite.

He returned to a theme similar to that expressed above in lesson twenty-three while trying to characterize the imagination, and in lesson twenty-six where he said again that art is "symbolic" and, also, "sympathetic." Théodore Jouffroy, more given to reflection than his master, Cousin, and one of the best estheticians of nineteenth-century France—which counted few great ones—in 1822 taught a *Cours d'esthétique* that was only published in 1843 by Jean-Philibert Damiron. After various considerations on the beautiful, distinguished from the useful and the new, as a marriage of variety and unity, he devoted the eighteenth lesson to the symbol. He stated without reservation:

> Every object, every idea, is to a certain point a symbol. . . . All that we perceive is symbolic since it excites in us the idea of some other thing we do not perceive. . . . The romantic prefers precise symbols. . . . He tends to spiritualize material nature. . . . Poetry is only a series of symbols present to the mind in order for it to conceive the invisible.

Concerning the French romantic poets themselves, the poet's claim to the privilege of seeing everything symbolically had been set forth in *La Muse française* by Alexandre Guiraud in terms first cited by Pierre Moreau: "All is symbolic in the eyes of the poet. . . ." and afterward by Guy Michaud: "The role of the poet is in effect to rediscover the traces of a primitive language revealed to man by God." A little later, an inquiring mind, Pierre Leroux, who had directed *Le Globe* for a short while, who had later founded *La Revue encyclopédique* that for a time attracted the attention of George Sand, and who had, while the two men were in exile, undertaken to win Hugo over to socially oriented poetry, gave an interesting and prophetic article to his own *Revue encyclopédique* in November 1831. "On the Poetry of our Time," was its ambitious title. Leroux assigned to poets the eminent role of legislators and prophets, the absolute interpreters of their times. For, he claims, poets see their epoch as it truly is beneath the surface, and they glimpse as well the approaching epoch or prepare the way for it: "Poets are men of desire and it is their thought that is seminal. True poets are always prophets." An earlier article by Leroux in *Le Globe* of April 8, 1829, and yet another on Jean-Paul Richter, on March 26 that same year, had shown how much Leroux was fascinated by the notion of the symbol. In *La Revue encyclopédique* of November 1831 he came back to the subject:

> The fact is that the entire world, including that of art, which is a part of the world in the same way as natural monuments, which art supplements, becomes symbolic. The symbol: here we touch upon the very principle of art. . . . The principle of art is the symbol.

Charles de Sainte-Beuve in 1830, addressed precisely to this same Pierre Leroux, whom the young poet and critic considered at the time with respect, one of the pieces from his *Consolations* wherein the symbolic mission of poetry is affirmed. Of poets, Sainte-Beuve in fact writes:

> They understand the waves, they listen to the stars
> Know the names of the flowers; for them the universe
> Is but one idea sown in symbols diverse.

For the first time in verse a Frenchman defined the role of the poet as decipherer of analogies and translator of the unheard of, as Rimbaud was to say, the interpretation of which is given to him alone. In prose, in *Joseph Delorme*, the same Sainte-Beuve had already proclaimed no less affirmatively: "The artist received at birth the key to symbols and the understanding of forms."

If among these scattered texts, of which Baudelaire could have known only two or three (those of Sainte-Beuve and perhaps of Leroux), there are any points in common, they seem surely to be these: the poet is not content to accept the superficial appearance of things; it is not in the reality that stands before his eyes that he may find his ideal of beauty. For him everything is mysterious, and he deciphers and translates the spiritual truth toward which the material world tends. Thereby he seizes upon the unity behind multiplicity and it is through his imagination that he forms his model of a form of beauty of which the things of this world can be only a pale approximation. The latent symbolism of the romantics, then, is a form of Platonism. It expresses the aspiration of poets to a higher world: the world of ideas and the world of beauty that overwhelms the soul. Among French poets, it was not toward Alfred de Vigny that Baudelaire looked, despite his respect for the poet of "La Maison du Berger," which he sometimes recalled. Nor did the symbolists of the late nineteenth century. The wolf dying in silence, the house on wheels, "the poor little Bottle," to use Vigny's own expression in one of his letters, serve to translate certain ethical ideas in a convenient, sometimes striking way. The critic who has most astutely commented on Vigny's symbols, Pierre Moreau, declares that in *Les Destinées* "the symbol and the idea, instead of fusing into one, get in the way of one another." Nor did Baudelaire and the symbolists look to the awkwardly "symbolistic" poems of the early Hugo, before his exile ("La Vache," for example). Only later, after having formulated his own ideas, did Baudelaire speak of his admiration for Hugo's genius as a decipherer of hieroglyphs. They were rather to look to Alphonse de Lamartine, the only French romantic with a Platonic sensibility, in search of a spiritual country beyond this ephemeral and perishable world. The Parnassians had, not without reason, been severe with regard to the flaccid and vague form of the *Méditations*, although Leconte de Lisle had highly praised the grandiose philosophical epic contained within *La Chute d'un Ange;* but the symbolists of 1885-90, answering the numerous queries about their tastes in poetry in the little reviews of the period, were far from despising this poet whose imagination was "diffluent" rather than plastic, to use the distinction of the psychologist Théodule Ribot. Henri de Régnier reports in a statement cited by Henri Mondor in his life of Mallarmé, that the poet spoke of Lamartine with his customary kindness. An account of the fortune of Lamartine's poetic production has yet to be written and would be instructive. If anything might redeem Jules Lemaître's obstinate incomprehension of the young poets of his time, it would indeed be his long article on Lamartine (1893), collected in the sixth volume of *Les Contemporains*. With very keen insights, he salutes him as a "demigod" who was, for the subjective, impressionist critic that Lemaître was, "up to now, the greatest of poets."

Vigny, Musset, Baudelaire, Verlaine, Mallarmé, Valéry himself, and, later, Claudel had a less imperfect knowledge of English letters than of German literature; they felt the strongest affinities with the romantic poetry of Great Britain. Without doubt much of what is found in the author of "Correspondences" and *Les Paradis artificiels,* afterward in Verlaine's "Art poétique," and even a certain pre-Raphaelite estheticism in Mallarmé, are prefigured in English poetry between 1770 and 1870. William Blake, however, never became known to the French, and one must be satisfied with imagining what Gérard de Nerval would have found in his work, had he ever opened it. Certain of Coleridge's views were transmitted to France by way of the borrowings Poe made from him. Sainte-Beuve sought from those poets, whom he called "the Lakists," models for personal and intimate poetry. He seems not to have been very profoundly struck by the boldness of William Wordsworth's theories in certain of his prefaces or by the quest for a nearly mystical ecstasy in the greatest of Wordsworth's poems, "Tintern Abbey" and "The Simplon Pass." He knew nothing of Wordsworth's *Prelude* (for good reason, since the poet, feeling himself misunderstood, refused to publish the poem during his lifetime and did not die until 1850), that autobiography in verse in which the poet says what it was that as a child he had sought in nature: transcendence beyond the concrete and appearances toward "the light which never shines on the sea or on the earth," the aspiration toward some communion with the divine. The brilliance of Lord Byron's elegant and tempestuous verse so dazzled the eyes of French and other continental readers that they did not see the profound symbolism they might have discovered, around 1820-30, in Keats and especially in Shelley. Yeats, at the end of the nineteenth century, his imagination set afire by the French symbolists made known to him by his friend Arthur Symons, was to write the first enthusiastic article on what he then called "Shelley's symbolism." I have tried to describe in another earlier work how and why Shelley came only slowly to be known to the French and what role he played in reaffirming the poets of 1885-95 in their symbolist quest. Shelley, at a time when Victor Hugo had not yet attained his twentieth year, had prefigured symbolist formulas and beliefs, not only in his poems such as "Hymn to Intellectual Beauty," "Mont Blanc," and "Epipsychidion," but also in a theoretical piece, his *Defense of Poetry,* which gave to the poet the role of tearing away the veils that hide the invisible from us. The term *symbol* was used rarely, and the English did not take the trouble to define it with precision. They often preferred the term *allegory,* which Keats uses in a letter to his brother on February 18, 1819; he decries superficial people who take everything at face value when, he says, the life of a man of some value, the life of Shakespeare, for example, is "a continual allegory, and there are so very few eyes that know how to see the mystery of such an existence which is 'figurative' in the way the Scriptures are." Baudelaire does not seem to have known more than a very few of Shelley's works, and these are not among the most profound. Hugo apparently resisted the instances of Pierre Leroux who, during their months of closeness in exile, tried to preach to him the example of the English poet who was no less visionary than he and perhaps purer for having served the cause of oppressed peoples.

In another English-speaking country beyond the Atlantic, there flourished, however, a form of symbolism whose formulas might have attracted and assisted the French theoreticians of symbolism in the last third of the century. But the prestige of Edgar Allan Poe, praised and translated by Baudelaire, shut off the French almost entirely from the esthetic and philosophical theories, the novels and the poetics of the American Transcendentalists. Thomas Carlyle, who had been their precursor in certain respects, was cited in several symbolist reviews. Ralph Waldo Emerson is mentioned less often and rather for his sermons on morality and for his elevated viewpoint. Emerson, however, in a very fine chapter, "Poetry and Imagination," in his posthumous book *Letters and Social Aims* (1875), comes quite close to the symbolist process by which the mind projects thought and the sensibility that gives it form beyond itself. Great men express themselves entirely naturally in a symbolic or metaphorical manner; Emerson does not distinguish between the two terms and gives as examples Pythagoras, Jesus, and Napoleon. He adds:

> A happy symbol is a sort of evidence that your thought is just. . . . There is no more welcome gift to men than a new symbol . . . the higher use of the material world is to furnish us types or pictures to express the thoughts of the mind. . . . Poetry is the perpetual endeavor to express the spirit of the thing, to pass the brute body and search the life and reason which causes it to exist. . . . The invisible and imponderable is the sole fact. . . . A symbol always stimulates the intellect; therefore is poetry ever the best reading.

Emerson, the philosopher of the New England group of Transcendentalists, had, one can see, read Emanuel Swedenborg and had read him more closely than had Nerval and Baudelaire. Moreover, he states in the same work that man's life, to the extent that it is more closely wedded to the truth, directs his thought so that it becomes parallel to natural laws and finds expression through symbols and in a poetic or "ecstatic" language. His friend Nathaniel Hawthorne, echoing these Swedenborgian accents, wrote: "Everything, you know, has spiritual meaning, which to the literal meaning is what the soul is to the body." Melville, in Ahab's monologue on the skull of the whale in *Moby Dick,* has his strange character cry out:

> O nature, O soul of man! how far beyond all utterance are your linked analogies! Not the smallest atom stirs or lives in matter, but has its cunning duplicate in mind.

The most recent interpreters of American literature during those productive years of 1850-65, "The American Renaissance"—to use the expression of D. H. Lawrence, who was the first to point out the somber strangeness of these American writings, in their own way as pessimistic and metaphysical as those of Victorian England—turn to the word *symbolism* to characterize its spirit. Following in the path of F. O. Matthiessen, Harry Levin has shown how little of realism there is in this completely transcendental and symbolic area of the American novel, shot through with allegories of biblical origin, or at least derived from John Bunyan. Charles Feidelson, maintaining that these American writers are infinitely closer to symbolism than to romanticism, states that symbolism, in this sense, is even a typically American phenomenon. It is, he says, "the coloration taken on by the American literary mind under the pressure of American literary history." He adds to the list of these symbolist theoreticians and novelists the name of Henry David Thoreau whose statement he cites: "My thought is a part of the meaning of the world, and hence I use a part of the world as a symbol to express my thought."

Unfortunately, the poetry of Emerson, that of Melville, or the more troubling work of the great recluse Emily Dickinson is often gauche, moralistic, and gnomic, and does not attain the freshness of imagination and the suggestive and musical power of the best of the English romantics. Perhaps that conscious and more stubborn reflection on the meaning of symbolism to which the Transcendentalists lent themselves marred the musical and evocative qualities of their verse. Thus the American poets who were to follow, the imagists Ezra Pound, T. S. Eliot, and Wallace Stevens, were to be more than generous in paying homage to the French symbolists. Robert Lowell and Richard Wilbur, among those who were still writing after 1960, have made emulative translations of Baudelaire's poems, and Stanley Burnshaw has pondered over Mallarmé. The English of 1800-30, without so great a fondness for theories, had designated the power of suggestion—often heightened by musical fluidity—as the essence of poetry and saw in the symbol one of the elements of that magic. An eminent French specialist in English literature, Louis Cazamian, has said as much and has reinforced his remarks through his excellent translations of the English poets who were ''symbolists'' before the fact, and in various articles and a book published during World War II.

French emigrants to the German states, a few Germans who came to reside in France for political reasons or by simple affinity—or attracted by the possibilities offered by the Paris of Louis-Philippe and Napoleon III in music, criticism, or the study of religious mysticism—transposed into French the plays and poetry from the other side of the Rhine. The German lieder particularly attracted many Frenchmen besides Nerval and, later, Edouard Schuré, who wanted to introduce into their own language a lyrical form that would be more musical, more haunting, in its visionary evocativeness. About 1885-95, this process of introduction was to become one of the ways in which symbolist poetry would take hold with the greatest originality and the least disappointing results. But France devoted much less attention to the theoretical reflections, very often cryptic and too philosophical in tone to be transposed, that various Germans had made concerning the symbol.

To be sure, there have been nearly as many definitions of the symbol or declarations concerning it from Leibniz or Herder and Friedrich Hebbel, Theodor Storm and lastly, Stefan George, as there have been theoreticians in the German language. Moreover, the same thinker, depending upon the occasion that led him to express himself on the subject, might contradict himself or emphasize different aspects of his esthetics of the symbol. Goethe, especially, often changed his mind during his long life, according to whether he was more or less open to scientific thought or whether he was impatient with poorly comprehending listeners. Even a very summary overview of the Germans' successive formulations of the symbolic (or of symbolism as related to poetry) would require a specialized competence in things Germanic that we do not have, and would probably need more than an entire volume. In any case, these ideas from across the Rhine scarcely touched French symbolism from 1885 to 1892 or, before that, Baudelaire. The peculiar aspect of symbolism that pertains to correspondences between the arts (those between color and the auditory sensation, for example) impressed Baudelaire more, but he found this not in the German philosophers but in the storyteller E. T. Amadeus Hoffman. One or two symbolists around 1890 (Jean Thorel especially in his *Entretiens politiques et littéraires* of 1891) were to become aware that the movement whose triumph they were trying to ensure in France had had its precursors among the German romantics. Some, pointed in that direction by Maurice Maeterlinck, read Novalis. They knew Friedrich Hölderlin scarcely better than they had known Blake. As for Goethe, France long remained content with knowing *Werther, Faust,* and a few short lyrical love poems or ballads. It is true that Goethe's declarations concerning the symbol are to be found scattered

in minor occasional pieces or in conversations recorded by admirers of the grand old man.

It is risky to generalize about ''German romanticism'' for it arrived in several waves spaced by what is called the ''classicism'' of Weimar, and because Schiller and Goethe, once the *Sturm und Drang* had quieted down, excluded themselves from the romantic movement or disdained it. Nevertheless, among the theoreticians, whether they be erudite thinkers or poets—Goethe included—there is discernible in them, to a certain degree, the same reaction against what is static, rigid perhaps, bound by defined contours. As opposed to French literary theory or the idea the Germans had of it (Goethe took care to except Diderot), they lay claim to the privilege of pursuing the fluid, the yet-to-be, and of plunging directly to the center of things and beings. ''The artist is he who finds his center in himself,'' declared Friedrich Schlegel around 1800. Wilhelm Wackenroder and Novalis similarly affirm such descent into the depths of oneself, even if one slips vertiginously into his own internal chaos, as a prelude to the sensitive understanding of others. In like manner, all these German romantics became apostles of intuitive knowledge. It is to such knowledge that Immanuel Kant lends the name *symbolic* in his *Critique of Judgment*. The romantics often repudiate cerebral knowledge. The young Wilhelm Meister, for instance, speaking to Jarno, evokes heatedly ''this splendid epoch when what is comprehensible seems to be vulgar foolishness.'' The French, Cartesians by long tradition, had in their dualistic fashion separated the physical world from the spiritual or moral world. This tendency had led them toward the allegory that seeks determinedly, awkwardly, to envelop an already clear meaning in a concrete wrapping. In their revolt against this kind of dualism, the romantics struck down the barriers that separated true reality—that of the limitless spirit—and the finite and more material reality of the world of appearances. They rejected allegory and praised symbolism as a means toward the immediate fusion between these two worlds. The profound truth enclosed within the concrete object or in the image that gives it life becomes one with its artistic or poetic expression.

Hegel, in the first volume of his *Esthetics*, defined the *symbol* as ''an exterior manifestation present to the powers of perception but which must be understood not immediately and for itself alone, but in a broader and more general sense.'' Expression is thus sacrificed to the most intimate meaning. For all that, such a view established a too conscious and calculated separation between the two elements of the symbol. Much earlier, in 1774, Herder had declared: ''The body is the symbol, the phenomenon [the real manifestation] of the soul in contact with the universe.'' In the same year, 1774, the young Goethe (who in 1770 had met Herder at Strasbourg) wrote *Werther*, in which artistic creation (Werther draws and paints) is the mirror of the soul and the soul is the mirror of the infinite God.

The clearest of Goethe's declarations on the subject are found in his ''Maxims on Art'' (*Sprüche über Kunst*), many years later. Allegory, he writes, changes a phenomenon into a concept and the concept into an image. But the concept remains as though independent, limited, retaining its identity. By contrast, ''symbolism'' (which can also be translated as ''the symbolic'') ''transfigures the phenomenon into an idea, the idea into an image in such a way that the idea remains always infinitely efficacious within the image and beyond reach; even expressed in every language it still remains inexpressible.'' Elsewhere, in a piece entitled ''On Art and Antiquity,'' Goethe has stated even more strongly:

True symbolism is that in which the particular represents the general, not in the way a dream or a shadow does, but as the living and instantaneous revelation of the impenetrable.

In another "supplementary" piece "On the Paintings of Philostratus," Goethe defined the *symbol* thus:

It is the thing without being the thing, and yet it is the thing: an image caught in a spiritual mirror and yet identical to the object.

Hence to his eyes every dramatic work, for example, is symbolic that bears in each moment of the action its meaning in itself and that nevertheless directs us toward something still more important that lies behind it. *Tartuffe,* which Goethe so admired, is in this respect a great example; so proclaimed the poet in one of his *Conversations.* On May 2, 1824, he admitted to Eckermann to not having regretted his activities as a socially popular theatrical director, which had consumed time he could have devoted to his work:

I have always looked upon my actions and my accomplishments as purely symbolic, and, in the end, it is all the same to me whether I made jugs or porridge bowls.

However, the most striking—because the most enigmatic—and the most concise of Goethe's declarations is practically the only one known until the end of the nineteenth century by readers not especially versed in German literature: the next to last lines of the second part of *Faust:*

> Alles vergängliche
> Ist nur ein Gleichnis

("All that comes to pass is but an image," or a "symbol" as it is often translated.)

It required a laborious effort of German critics of the beginning of the nineteenth century to distinguish the notion and especially the term *symbol* from that of *allegory,* which had so long been used for architecture, miniature painting, the poetry of the Middle Ages, and in the work of the greatest of medieval poets, Dante. Goethe himself does not hold firmly to that distinction. Friedrich Creuzer, in the long introduction that he gave in the first edition of his large work on *The Symbolic and the Mythology of Ancient Peoples* (1810-12), distinguishes in Platonic and neo-Platonic contexts between mystical or religious symbols and plastic symbols. He saw in religious symbols a link that raises the human to the divine plane. He insisted on the power of suggestion the symbol must possess to stimulate our thought. Although this introduction had been translated in the voluminous adaptation in French that J. D. Guigniaut had done of the German work, it scarcely attracted the attention of French Hellenists and mythographers who used this very learned work on the religions of antiquity. It was certainly not even slightly known to any of the French symbolists unless they may have learned something of it through Ernest Renan, Louis Ménard, or Alfred Maury. Schelling's *Lectures on Art,* given in 1802-03, were published in 1859 and had no greater resonance in France. Wilhelm Schlegel in 1822-25, reworked his *Lectures on Poetry,* which had appeared in a journal in 1800, before his conversion to Catholicism. He included in it, perhaps under Schelling's influence, certain interesting views on the symbol and the imagination and on the correspondences between the human mind and the world outside and beyond it. But, here again, there is in all likelihood no case of direct or oblique influence of such theoretical views on the French symbolists of 1885-92. It is very much more

likely, as is often the case in the history of ideas and sensibility, a matter of polygenesis, or the appearance, simultaneously or staged over several decades, of comparable aspirations or parallel answers given to questions of a like nature.

In all events, between 1790 and 1840, long before Baudelaire, various minds among German authors, without having absorbed Swedenborg, had already proclaimed that art is inevitably symbolic or even hieroglyphic (Schiller, who died in 1805, had said as much in his "Theosophy of Julius"). Carlyle had doubtless read it in the German authors. The German dramatist Hebbel had noted in his Journal (*Tagebücher*) on February 2, 1842, in terms that were to be recalled by the Abbé Bremond during the controversy over pure poetry in 1924:

Every authentic work of art is a mysterious symbol and, in one sense, unfathomable. The more a certain poetic style derives from thought alone, the less of mystery it will possess and the sooner it will be understood. But its content will also be more quickly exhausted, and it will be cast aside like the oyster shell from which the pearl has been extracted. The didactic poet goes so far as to offer the unadorned solution instead of the enigma which alone is of interest.

Edgar Allan Poe was not the only one who, in 1845-50, might have been able to demonstrate to Baudelaire the wrongdoing of "the didactic heresy" in poetry. (pp. 6-20)

> Henri Peyre, "The Word and Its Antecedents," in his What Is Symbolism?, *translated by Emmett Parker, The University of Alabama Press, 1980, pp. 6-20.*

EDMUND WILSON

[*Wilson is generally considered twentieth-century America's foremost man of letters. A prolific reviewer, creative writer, and social and literary critic endowed with formidable intellectual powers, he exercised his greatest literary influence as the author of* Axel's Castle, *a seminal study of literary symbolism from which the following excerpt is drawn, and as the author of widely read reviews and essays in which he introduced the best works of modern literature to the reading public. Here, Wilson explains the elements of Symbolism and the influences on its development.*]

[An] important prophet of Symbolism was Edgar Allan Poe. It was in general true that, by the middle of the century, the Romantic writers in the United States—Poe, Hawthorne, Melville, Whitman and even Emerson—were, for reason which it would be interesting to determine, developing in the direction of Symbolism; and one of the events of prime importance in the early history of the Symbolist Movement was the discovery of Poe by Baudelaire. When Baudelaire, a late Romantic, first read Poe in 1847, he "experienced a strange commotion." When he began to look up Poe's writings in the files of American magazines, he found among them stories and poems which he said that he himself had already "thought vaguely and confusedly" of writing, and his interest became a veritable passion. In 1852, Baudelaire published a volume of translations of Poe's tales; and from then on the influence of Poe played an important part in French literature. Poe's critical writings provided the first scriptures of the Symbolist Movement, for he had formulated what amounted to a new literary programme which corrected the romantic looseness and lopped away the Romantic extravagance, at the same time that it aimed, not at Naturalistic, but at ultra-Romantic effects. There was, of course, a good deal in common between Poe's poetry and such Romantic poetry as Coleridge's "Kubla Khan," as there was between his poems in prose and such Romantic prose as that of De Quincey. But Poe, by insisting on and specially cultivating certain aspects of Romanticism, helped to transform it into something different. "I *know*," we find Poe writing, for example, "that indefiniteness is an element of the true music [of poetry]—I mean of the true musical expression . . . a suggestive indefiniteness of vague and therefore of spiritual *effect*." And to approximate the indefiniteness of music was to become one of the principal aims of Symbolism.

This effect of indefiniteness was produced not merely by the confusion . . . between the imaginary world and the real; but also by means of a further confusion between the perceptions of the different senses.

> "Comme de longs échos qui de loin se confondent . . .
> Les parfums, les couleurs et les sons se répondent,"

wrote Baudelaire. And we find Poe, in one of his poems, *hearing* the approach of the darkness, or writing such a description as the following of the sensations which follow death: "Night arrived; and with its shadows a heavy discomfort. It oppressed my limbs with the oppression of some dull weight, and was palpable. There was also a moaning sound, not unlike the distant reverberation of surf, but more continuous, which beginning with the first twilight, had grown in strength with the darkness. Suddenly lights were brought into the room . . . and issuing from the flame of each lamp, there flowed unbrokenly into my ears a strain of melodious monotone."

This notation of super-rational sensations was a novelty in the forties of the last century—as was the dreamlike irrational musical poetry of "Annabel Lee" and "Ulalume"; and they helped to effect a revolution in France. For an English-speaking reader of to-day, Poe's influence may be hard to understand; and even when such a reader comes to examine the productions of French Symbolism, it may surprise him that they should have caused amazement. The medley of images; the deliberately mixed metaphors; the combination of passion and wit— of the grand and the prosaic manners; the bold amalgamation of material with spiritual—all these may seem to him quite proper and familiar. He has always known them in the English poetry of the sixteenth and seventeenth centuries—Shakespeare and the other Elizabethans did all these things without theorizing about them. Is this not the natural language of poetry? Is it not the norm against which, in English literature, the eighteenth century was a heresy and to which the Romantics did their best to return?

But we must remember that the development of French poetry has been quite different from that of English. Michelet says that in the sixteenth century the future of French literature had hung in the balance between Rabelais and Ronsard, and he regrets that it was Ronsard who triumphed. For Rabelais in France was a sort of equivalent to our own Elizabethans, whereas Ronsard, who represented to Michelet all that was poorest, dryest and most conventional in the French genius, was one of the fathers of that classical tradition of lucidity, sobriety and purity which culminated in Molière and Racine. In comparison with the Classicism of the French, which has dominated their whole literature since the Renaissance, the English Classicism of the eighteenth century, the age of Dr. Johnson and Pope, was a brief ineffective deviation. And from the point of view of English readers, the most daring innovations of the Romantic revolution in France, in spite of all the excitement which accompanied them, must appear of an astonishingly moderate character. But the age and rigor of the tradition were the mea-

Stéphane Mallarmé. The Bettmann Archive, Inc.

sure of the difficulty of breaking out of it. After all, Coleridge, Shelley and Keats—in spite of Pope and Dr. Johnson—had only to look back to Milton and Shakespeare, whose dense forests had all along been in view beyond the formal eighteenth-century gardens. But to an eighteenth-century Frenchman like Voltaire, Shakespeare was incomprehensible; and to the Frenchman of the classical tradition of the beginning of the nineteenth century, the rhetoric of Hugo was a scandal: the French were not used to such rich colors or to so free a vocabulary; moreover, the Romantics broke metrical rules far stricter than any we have had in English. Yet Victor Hugo was still very far from the variety and freedom of Shakespeare. It is enlightening to compare Shelley's lyric which begins, "O World! O Life! O Time!" with the poem of Alfred de Musset's which begins, "J'ai perdu ma force et ma vie." These two lyrics are in some ways curiously similar; each is the breath of a Romantic sigh over the passing of the pride of youth. Yet the French poet, even in his wistfulness, makes epigrammatic points: his language is always logical and precise; whereas the English poet is vague and gives us images unrelated by logic. And it will not be till the advent of the Symbolists that French poetry will really become capable of the fantasy and fluidity of English.

The Symbolist Movement broke those rules of French metrics which the Romantics had left intact, and it finally succeeded in throwing overboard completely the clarity and logic of the French classical tradition, which the Romantics had still to a great extent respected. It was nourished from many alien sources—German, Flemish, modern Greek—and especially, precisely, from English. Verlaine had lived in England, and knew English well; Mallarmé was a professor of English; and

Baudelaire . . . had provided the movement with its first programmes by translating the essays of Poe. Two of the Symbolist poets, Stuart Merrill and Francis Vielé-Griffin, were Americans who lived in Paris and wrote French; and an American, reading to-day the latter's "Chevauchée d'Yeldis," for example, may wonder how, when Symbolism was new, such a poem could ever have been regarded as one of the movement's acknowledged masterpieces: to us, it seems merely agreeable, not in the least revolutionary or novel, but like something which might not impossibly have been written by Thomas Bailey Aldrich if he had been influenced by Browning. We are surprised to learn that Vielé-Griffin is still considered an important poet. But the point was that he had performed a feat which astonished and impressed the French and of which it is probable that no Frenchman was capable: he had succeeded in wrecking once for all the classical Alexandrine, hitherto the basis of French poetry—or rather, as an English reader at once recognizes, he had dispensed with it altogether and begun writing English metres in French. The French called this "*vers libre,*" but it is "free" only in the sense of being irregular, like many poems of Matthew Arnold and Browning.

What made Poe particularly acceptable to the French, however, was what had distinguished him from most of the other Romantics of the English-speaking countries: his interest in æsthetic theory. The French have always reasoned about literature far more than the English have; they always want to know what they are doing and why they are doing it: their literary criticism has acted as a constant interpreter and guide to the rest of their literature. And it was in France that Poe's literary theory, to which no one seems to have paid much attention elsewhere, was first studied and elucidated. So that, though the effects and devices of Symbolism were of a kind that was familiar in English, and though the Symbolists were sometimes indebted to English literature directly—the Symbolist Movement itself, by reason of its origin in France, had a deliberate self-conscious æsthetic which made it different from anything in English. One must go back to Coleridge to find in English a figure comparable to the Symbolist leader, Stéphane Mallarmé. Paul Valéry says of Mallarmé that, as he was the greatest French poet of his time, he could also have been one of the most popular. But Mallarmé was an unpopular poet: he taught English for a living, and wrote little and published less. Yet, ridiculed and denounced by the public, who reiterated that his poetry was nonsense and yet were irritated by his seriousness and obstinacy, he exercised, from his little Paris apartment, where he held Tuesday receptions, an influence curiously far-reaching over the young writers—English and French alike—of the end of the century. There in the sitting-room which was also the dining-room on the fourth floor in the Rue de Rome, where the whistle of locomotives came in through the windows to mingle with the literary conversation, Mallarmé, with his shining pensive gaze from under his long lashes and always smoking a cigarette "to put some smoke," as he used to say, "between the world and himself," would talk about the theory of poetry in a "mild, musical and unforgettable voice." There was an atmosphere "calm and almost religious." Mallarmé had "the pride of the inner life," said one of his friends; his nature was "patient, disdainful and imperiously gentle." He always reflected before he spoke and always put what he said in the form of a question. His wife sat beside him embroidering; his daughter answered the door. Here came Huysmans, Whistler, Degas, Moréas, Laforgue, Vielé-Griffin, Paul Valéry, Henri de Régnier, Pierre Louys, Paul Claudel, Remy de Gourmont, André Gide, Oscar Wilde, Arthur Symons, George Moore and W. B. Yeats. For Mallarmé was a true saint of literature:

he had proposed to himself an almost impossible object, and he pursued it without compromise or distraction. His whole life was dedicated to the effort to do something with the language of poetry which had never been done before. "Donner un sens plus pur," he had written in a sonnet on Poe, "aux mots de la tribu." He was, as Albert Thibaudet has said, engaged in "a disinterested experiment on the confines of poetry, at a limit where other lungs would find the air unbreathable."

What, then, was this purer sense which Mallarmé believed he was following Poe in wishing to give to the words of the tribe? What, precisely, was the nature of this experiment on the confines of poetry which Mallarmé found so absorbing and which so many other writers tried to repeat? What, precisely, did the Symbolists propose? I have called attention, in speaking of Poe, to the confusion between the perceptions of the different senses, and to the attempt to make the effects of poetry approximate to those of music. And I should add, in this latter connection, that the influence on Symbolist poetry of Wagner was as important as that of any poet: at the time when Romantic music had come closest to literature, literature was attracted toward music. . . . It was the tendency of Symbolism—that second swing of the pendulum away from a mechanistic view of nature and from a social conception of man—to make poetry even more a matter of the sensations and emotions of the individual than had been the case with Romanticism: Symbolism, indeed, sometimes had the result of making poetry so much a private concern of the poet's that it turned out to be incommunicable to the reader. The peculiar subtlety and difficulty of Symbolism is indicated by the name itself. This name has often been complained of as being inadequate for the movement to which it was given and inappropriate to certain of its aspects; and it may prove misleading to English readers. For the symbols of Symbolism have to be defined a little differently from symbols in the ordinary sense—the sense in which the Cross is the symbol of Christianity or the Stars and Stripes the symbol of the United States. This symbolism differs even from such symbolism as Dante's. For the familiar kind of symbolism is conventional and fixed; the symbolism of the Divine Comedy is conventional, logical and definite. But the symbols of the Symbolist school are usually chosen arbitrarily by the poet to stand for special ideas of his own—they are a sort of disguise for these ideas. "The Parnassians, for their part," wrote Mallarmé, "take the thing just as it is and put it before us—and consequently they are deficient in mystery: they deprive the mind of the delicious joy of believing that it is creating. To name an object is to do away with the three-quarters of the enjoyment of the poem which is derived from the satisfaction of guessing little by little: to suggest it, to evoke it—that is what charms the imagination."

To intimate things rather than state them plainly was thus one of the primary aims of the Symbolists. But there was more involved in their point of view than Mallarmé here explains. The assumptions which underlay Symbolism lead us to formulate some such doctrine as the following: Every feeling or sensation we have, every moment of consciousness, is different from every other; and it is, in consequence, impossible to render our sensations as we actually experience them through the conventional and universal language of ordinary literature. Each poet has his unique personality; each of his moments has its special tone, its special combination of elements. And it is the poet's task to find, to invent, the special language which will alone be capable of expressing his personality and feelings. Such a language must make use of symbols: what is so special, so fleeting and so vague cannot be conveyed by direct statement or description, but only by a succession of words, of images, which will serve to suggest it to the reader. The Symbolists themselves, full of the idea of producing with poetry effects like those of music, tended to think of these images as possessing an abstract value like musical notes and chords. But the words of our speech are not musical notation, and what the symbols of Symbolism really were, were metaphors detached from their subjects—for one cannot, beyond a certain point, in poetry, merely enjoy color and sound for their own sake: one has to guess what the images are being applied to. And Symbolism may be defined as an attempt by carefully studied means—a complicated association of ideas represented by a medley of metaphors—to communicate unique personal feelings.

The Symbolist Movement proper was first largely confined to France and principally limited to poetry of rather an esoteric kind; but it was destined, as time went on, to spread to the whole western world and its principles to be applied on a scale which the most enthusiastic of its founders could scarcely have foreseen. (pp. 12-22)

> Edmund Wilson, "Symbolism," in his Axel's Castle:
> A Study in the Imaginative Literature of 1870-1930,
> *Charles Scribner's Sons, 1931, pp. 1-25.*

JEAN ALEXANDER

[*Alexander discusses the significance of Poe's works for the Symbolists.*]

From our present perspective, as we review the life of Edgar Allan Poe, we may pass severe judgment and condemn him for weakness, for neurosis, for egotism; or we may pity his misfortune or his incomplete genius. An American tends to form one of these emotional images. If Charles Baudelaire had not decided to recast the destiny of the American poet, French opinion might have been similar. But Baudelaire did not see Poe as a deviant, defeated individual to be pitied for his weakness. Paradoxically, he cast him in the role of outlaw and saint, and he insisted on quarreling publicly about it. He tried to make an important niche for Poe in literature, and he succeeded. In order to understand the first phase of Poe's French reputation, we must examine Baudelaire's motives and his purpose.

According to his friend Asselineau, Baudelaire became acquainted with Poe's work in 1847, through the translations of Mme. Meunier. But not until nine years later did he finally make Poe the center of a bitter literary quarrel. Before 1852 there had been scattered references to Poe, but aside from the essays of Baudelaire and Forgues they were very brief and superficial; Poe was an interesting oddity. Suddenly, in 1852, Baudelaire launched a campaign to force the literary world to accept Poe on Baudelaire's terms.

Attracted by the originality of Poe's mind, Baudelaire had been desultorily translating Poe's tales for publication in the magazines, but there is a marked difference between his intellectual interest during the late 1840s and his fervor during the 1850s. Although he stated more than once that he translated and defended Poe so persistently because Poe resembled him, imitating his own thoughts twenty years before they occurred, Baudelaire developed none of the passionate intensity of his famous Poe essays until after he had seen the 1850 edition of Poe's works and knew something of Poe's life and death. In

short, his partisanship was aroused not exclusively by the artist, but by the man and his destiny. (pp. 5-6)

In his journal, Baudelaire speaks of thwarted ambitions, and in his 1852 essay on Poe he speaks of thwarted sensibility. Neither his ambition nor the specific thwarting agent can be known with certainty, but references in his journal and elsewhere lead us to assume that, having been prevented from playing the part he saw as legitimately his (that of intellectual legislator) Baudelaire intended to make himself otherwise known as a power. He reversed his tactics and chose to campaign by radical defiance. (p. 7)

Personal disappointment and bitterness led Baudelaire to construct a perverse theory concerning the relationship between the superior individual and his society, and he sought a symbol to embody his ideas. Out of his social nihilism and his stubborn estheticism he had already created one symbolic figure to resist society before he encountered Poe. The dandy was his first idol. The dandy was English in origin; he combined aristocracy, cold beauty and elegance, intellectual control, and complete alienation from society. He was stoic, enduring whatever the world meted out to him, triumphing by his refusal to be moved. His motivation was not entirely esthetic; it was also moral. "Whether these men are called fops, beaux, lions, or dandies, all come from the same source; all share the same nature of opposition and revolt; all are representatives of what is best in human pride, the need . . . to combat and destroy triviality." If Baudelaire's description had stopped here, the dandy would have been reasonably harmless, but Baudelaire makes it clear that the dandy is also criminal. The dandy is the "final burst of heroism in an age of decadence," and Baudelaire's list of heroes concludes with Balzac's immoralists and criminals, Vautrin, Rastignac, Birotteau. "One could found glorious empires on crime," Baudelaire suggests in his journal. The dandy was Baudelaire's persona: an elegant, mysterious, self-possessed enemy of society.

Yet when Poe became known, Baudelaire turned all his will to the exaltation of the new hero. Although Poe displaced the dandy, the two were not totally dissimilar. On the most superficial level, Poe was the epitome of dandyism because he could preserve his elegance in the midst of sickness, poverty, persecution, and death. In tracing Poe's background, Baudelaire made aristocrats of his ancestors; in describing Poe's appearance, Baudelaire emphasized his good looks, his intelligence, his distinguished bearing. Most of all, Poe's superior spirit and the consequent audacity of his independence from the patterns of society provide a thematic pattern running through all of Baudelaire's narrative, description and analysis.

Both Poe and Baudelaire, however, were men of imagination and intelligence, not criminals, and Baudelaire found that Poe represented his intentions and desires more fully than the dandy could. Poe was Baudelaire's double, for Poe was a poet, he lived in misery, he fought an inexorable vice, he was persecuted and betrayed by his literary world, he was a lone spirit and he was an original and astonishing experimenter. When Baudelaire thrust Poe into every conversation or quoted "The Raven" or "The Black Cat" it was as efficacious for him as a campaign for the recognition of his own genius. His power was strengthened by another and more productive brain.

These two factors determined the intensity and fidelity of Baudelaire's discipleship, and they provide what appear to be very personal and limited motives. No other poet has made a fetish of dandyism in the sense that Baudelaire used the term, and no other poet has had such fraternal resemblance to Poe. However, Baudelaire intended to immortalize Poe, and he did so by making Poe represent the poet—that is, the artist in general—as Baudelaire understood him from his own fate and from his interpretation of the literature and the society of the nineteenth century. (pp. 8-9)

• • • • •

By 1885, Poe had assumed the legendary role he was to play in France. . . . [In] that year, a new school declared itself and based its program on Poe's poetics. However, the emergence of Poe in his new position was not so sudden as it seemed. In the interval between Baudelaire's death and the ascendancy of the Symbolists, Mallarmé had been persistently translating Poe and talking of Poe in his intimate circle, and Verlaine had also admired and studied Poe and kept alive the tradition of the "accursed poet." Although the poets and theorists who were to be grouped together as Symbolists were also drawing idealist and mystic ideas from other sources, notably Carlyle and Schopenhauer, Poe was a more impressive influence for he satisfied the Symbolist inclination both as theorist and as artist. When the philosophic heritage had been assimilated and the poetic movement had maturity and some coherence, the Symbolists launched the manifestos that aroused new controversy over Poe and the concepts he represented.

In the notes to his translation of Poe's poems, Mallarmé speaks of the "new poetic theory that suddenly arrived from a distant America" and caused a crisis in French esthetics. The crisis he is apparently referring to revealed itself in the exchange of articles among the traditionalists and the new poets in 1885 and 1886. Sutter Laumann and Anatole France had attacked the new "decadent" school of poetry; Paul Adam, Jean Moréas and Gustave Kahn had asserted their identity as "symbolists" and had drawn much of their theory and support from Baudelaire and Poe.

However, Poe's two essays on poetics, "The Poetic Principle" and "Philosophy of Composition," were not equally well known or completely adopted. When Mallarmé speaks of the new poetic theory, he is referring to the key concepts of "The Poetic Principle" and the idea *behind* "Philosophy of Composition." In the first essay, the Symbolists ignored certain elaborations and examples of the major ideas—the poetic inducement, for example, of "the bright orbs that shine in Heaven" and "the sighing of the night wind"—and they gave little attention to the question of length. They pointedly ignored one idea in "The Poetic Principle": Poe has commented on naturalness of style, saying "*the tone*, in composition, should always be that which the mass of mankind would adopt." Poe's own style does not obey his edict, and the Symbolists were far from entertaining this attitude.

In limiting their acceptance of Poe's theory to its essence, the Symbolists followed Baudelaire in appropriating the two master ideas that beauty, not truth, is the province of poetry, and that true poetic effect is an exaltation of spirit through the creation of beauty. At the outset it must be acknowledged that Poe's theories had already been interpreted by Baudelaire; in the process of interpretation, he had emphasized these major ideas in such a way that their application was made easier. For example, Poe's statement that beauty brings tears of sorrow "at our inability to grasp *now*, wholly, here on earth, at once and for ever, those divine and rapturous joys" is interpolated between two of Baudelaire's own favorite ideas. First, "This admirable, immortal instinct for the beautiful makes us look

upon the earth and its spectacles as if they were glimpses or correspondences of Heaven. The insatiable thirst for the beyond—which life reveals—is our most active proof of immortality." Second, "these tears . . . testify to an aggravated melancholy, a cry of the nerves, of a being exiled in the imperfect and wanting to grasp at once . . . a revealed paradise."

"Philosophy of Composition" underwent an even greater change. Whereas Baudelaire had merely translated large passages from "The Poetic Principle," he interpreted "Philosophy of Composition" thoroughly, explaining Poe's motives and the implications of the essay. Having drawn from it the principle that the poet works in full and deliberate consciousness, he ignored such details as the dictum that the death of a beautiful woman is the most poetic subject.

The Symbolists, therefore, had the advantage of Baudelaire's interpretation of Poe's essays, as well as the original statements. They were nurtured on those theories, whereas Baudelaire had come upon them in his maturity, so that they served largely as confirmation of his own ideas. Since the Symbolists treated Poe as the Source, it is necessary to see how closely their theories coincided with his.

There were various manifestoes, but the earliest and probably the most important in presenting the central Symbolist doctrine was that of Jean Moréas, one of the lesser poets, in 1885 [see essay above]. According to Moréas, the Symbolists accepted Baudelaire, with his poetry for poetry's sake, as their master, sought "the pure concept and the eternal Symbol" with Poe's limitation of poetry to Beauty, attempted to use suggestion as a technique replacing direct statement and worked for metrical liberation beyond that of Romanticism. The first three ideas bear unmistakably the mark of Poe.

In reality, the declaration of the independence of art was a necessary preamble to the other principles. If the artist was to claim a position above society, to claim to be the spiritual and intellectual aristocrat at least, and a transcendental seer at most, he had to cease being a public servant, celebrating the values of society and humbly effacing himself. . . . [The] artists were not fighting straw men; there was a strong public opinion attempting to hold the writer to his function as the supporter and disseminator of right attitudes toward life. In rejecting Morality and Truth as the concern of the poet, Poe was protesting this rein, rather than refusing all morality and all truth. To judge by their analyses of his statements, there was never any question about this in the minds of the French adapters of his theories. As the artist became progressively more dissatisfied with his society, and as the distance between commonly accepted ideas and avant-garde ideas noticeably widened, the poets detached themselves more determinedly from the limitations of public concepts. For this reason the Symbolists found Poe's "Poetic Principle" new and prophetic, as if created for their moment, even though Baudelaire had advanced it twenty-five years earlier as a solitary protest; Poe's theory had gained little credence through being supported by such Bohemians as Charles Baudelaire and Théophile Gautier.

Having thrown out the most venerable of literary standards—the social and moral end of literature—Poe had replaced it with the statement that the esthetic experience has no other end than itself. Although Moréas spoke of "poetry for its own sake" in his manifesto, such terms suggest a false interpretation of the theory. Poe no more worshipped art than a religious man worships images. He made it clear that the experience of true poetry is the closest possible approximation to a total religious and philosophic experience that man can have. Poetry is the creation of beauty, which in turn is the gate to the supernal. The last two propositions that Moréas makes (''the pure concept and the eternal Symbol,'') are techniques for fulfilling this poetic ideal. They are an outgrowth of the first proposition and of Baudelaire's theory of correspondences, which had been added to the transcription of Poe's theory. If the beautiful object becomes a means of a transcendent experience, it follows that one task of the poet is to find and represent the essence of that object. Since it is a transcendental experience that he must convey, and not a lesson that he must teach, no direct statement will serve.

This is the basic principle of the Symbolists, and it is Poe's. Once we leave broad general statements, however, and consider specific applications, we find a great deal of variety in the temperament and inclination of the Symbolists, and consequent modifications by them of Poe's theory. Gustave Kahn, who placed more emphasis on revolutionary metrics than Moréas, suggests another area of Poe's influence. Kahn thought the poets united by ''denial of the old, monotonous techniques of verse and by the desire to vary rhythm and to give the diagram of a sensation in the design of a stanza.'' He also declared the intention of the group—similar to that of the Pléiade—to renovate and restore the French language. The latter aim is characteristic of many Symbolists (Mallarmé, Adam, Laforgue, Ghil) and provided ample grounds for satire. Brunetière, in 1891, defined the group by aping its language:

> Above all intent on pledging the art dying of secularity, in urgent reaction, or better called revolt, against the torpid bondage of Alexic and Zolist naturalism to tasks of duplication of an unfixable reality, Symbolism is the reintegration of the indefiniteness or the fluidity of things, to be registered in the comparative or the suggestive by means of a polymorphic rhythm allied to a language undulating to the incessantly promised limits of metaphorism emancipated from trivial usage.

Brunetière's parody is, of course, highly exaggerated, but he has reflected the attitude and some of the faults of Symbolism. There is some possibility of Poe's having influenced Symbolist language in his use of the jargon of science and of rare and archaic words; indirectly, he may have influenced it through his translators, for Baudelaire was accused of neologism by Pontmartin, and Mallarmé has been accused of introducing foreign syntax into French. But the convoluted syntax and forced vocabulary cannot be ascribed to Poe's poetic theory, nor can the self-determinism of line and stanza. It is very probable that Kahn is referring to free verse. If so, the statement is relevant to Poe's poetry, for Kahn speaks of Poe's verse as if it were freed from traditional laws, as if brief evocative stories such as ''Shadow'' and ''Silence'' were experiments in a new poetic form, and as if Poe had begun to evolve a form combining metric poetry and prose narrative, as in ''Ligeia.'' It is uncertain to what extent Kahn believed that Poe was an innovator in poetic form and to what extent he was constructing a convincing precedent for his own innovations. In fact, we cannot even say with assurance that Kahn was mistaken. It is quite possible that Poe *was* attempting a new form, the prose poem. It has also been suggested that Mallarmé's translation of the poems, which is in prose, caused some confusion and led to the belief that Poe was a vers-librist.

Although Poe's relation to the revolution in metrics is questionable, it is evident that Moréas and Kahn are in agreement in their fundamental concepts, and that they believed they were pursuing the course that Poe had outlined. Both poets are, in their own way, seekers after essence; they share a desire to cast off not only society's requirement of didacticism, but also the old prosody and rhetoric that served the poetry of the past. Since psychic experience is intangible and is to be captured not by photography or description but by evocation, the poets struggled against rhetorical patterns associated with dogma and description. Verlaine's exuberant ''Art poétique'' states the position:

> Prends l'éloquence et tords-lui le cou!

Mallarmé, in his preface to Rene Ghil's *Traité du verbe*, excludes the ''brute'' word from poetry, and the brute word is the word rhetorically used. Rhetoric implies personal communication, which Mallarmé rejected. ''Pure work implies the elocutionary disappearance of the poet, who gives the initiative to words, mobilized by the shock of their inequality.'' There is nothing in Poe's essays to suggest a rejection of rhetoric; the poems cited in ''The Poetic Principle'' are, in fact, largely rhetorical. But the procedure described in ''Philosophy of Composition'' clearly indicates composition by the sound and effect of words, with emphasis upon the sublimity of the evocation of an essential emotion rather than on the truth of the concrete situation which gives rise to it.

Although they were unanimous in rejecting the old rhetoric (the oratorical and direct statement), they were divergent in the means of replacing rhetoric and in the extent to which they disintegrated the old forms. Mallarmé is at one extreme, with his cult of the word and his definition of poetry which echoes Poe and Baudelaire:

> Poetry is the expression, in human language recapturing its essential rhythm, of the mysterious meaning of the aspects of existence: thus it offers authenticity to our stay and is our only spiritual task.

Mallarmé is interested in a spiritual absolute, and he goes farther than Poe in abstraction of esthetic feeling. He adheres to Idea rather than sensation:

> I revere Poe's opinion, no trace of a philosophy, of esthetics or metaphysics appears; I must add that it is necessary, inherent and latent. . . . The intellectual armature of the poem is hidden and holds—occurs— in the space that isolates the stanzas and in the white spaces of the paper.

At the other extreme, far from the occult, is Gustave Kahn. In analyzing Poe's stories according to the principle of ''Philosophy of Composition,'' Kahn evolved the theory that Poe's work, and all true modern poetry, is ''an attempt to translate pure sensation: love without the contingencies that might limit it to such and such a person. . . .'' He then defined poetry as ''the elaboration of feeling in its essence, purified of the environment and the accidentals that are the cause of error.'' The key words in Kahn's analysis are *sensation, feeling, true nature* and *essence*. For him as for Mallarmé, but on a different plane, all precisions of prosody were attempts to capture the essence of experience rather than existence.

Others elaborated Poe's theory of the calculation of verbal and musical effects. In his defense against attacks made on *Le Thé chez Miranda*, Paul Adam stated the requirements of a Symbolist poet, beginning with the major one, that the poet be a complete master of language. With that mastery he created sensation and an inscape:

> Sensations should be at once complex and single; the individual should live within the external world and

construct it according to his particular configuration. And, since dream is indistinguishable from life, the poet should portray the state of dream and also the state of hallucination and the constant dreams of memory. Then he must give the phrase the cadence of the idea; use a certain tone for one sensation, a melody for another; ban sounds that are repeated without deliberate harmony; recall a previously expressed idea by a word of a different meaning, but similar to the first through assonance.

Both Kahn and Adam, though minor poets, speak for the Symbolists as a group more than Mallarmé does, for they indicate the fundamental interest in the specifics of sensibility—sensation, knowledge, feeling—whereas Mallarmé tends to speak only of the ultimate intentions. Paul Valéry follows the tendencies of Kahn and Adam in this respect when he states: "The duty, the labor, and the function of the poet are to reveal and enact the powers of movement and enchantment, the arousers of the affective life and intellectual sensibility."

When the poet was no longer held back by the dogma of his society and by its practical demands, and had freed himself from traditional art forms he would be able to use Poe's last great principle and achieve his destiny as creator rather than entertainer or teacher. For the Creator, there could be no question of inspiration; there had to be mind in full power. Poe's "Philosophy of Composition" had various repercussions because, like "The Poetic Principle," it was fortunately susceptible to many interpretations. The influence of technical aspects of the poems will be considered briefly, but the adoption of specific techniques is less significant than the poetic intention because of the overriding metaphysical or philosophic impulse of the Symbolists in applying Poe's doctrine of conscious control.

As the preceding chapter suggests, the French poets were stirred by the idea of a scientific approach to literary creation. Paul Valéry's statement on Romanticism and the reactions against it in his essay on Baudelaire summarizes the self-determination of a literary movement and indicates Poe's vital role. First, as Valéry describes the process, the Romantics having appropriated certain large areas of poetry and exhausted them, their successors had to explore other areas; second, the excesses and enthusiasms of Romanticism brought a revulsion; third, a "reflective action" inevitably took the place of a "spontaneous action." That is, the spontaneous, in the sense of a surge of expression that has not undergone an analytic test and in which "inspiration" plays a major role, must give way to a highly intellectual action in which the original inspiration becomes the subject of an analytic construct. Poe's contribution in this literary evolution was to give the new school a method: "Before Poe, the premises of literature had never been examined, reduced to a problem in psychology, and attacked by means of an analysis in which logic and the mechanics of effect were deliberately employed."

The immediate, ponderable effect was evident in the enthusiasm with which the poets avowed their credo of poetic *calculation*. A certain possibility of cynicism is implicit in the concept of the artist's dispassionate control of his craft, especially if he is intent on affecting the reader. In a comment on a line by Baudelaire, Verlaine makes light of this attitude and avoids the problem it poses by mocking the sentimentality of the opposition. Baudelaire's line, from "Les petites vieilles," is "Have you noticed that many shrouds for old women/Are nearly as small as those of children?"

> "Have you *noticed*, etc."—a superb phlegmatic impertinence, which would have ravished Poe.... I

can hear the passionists from here, those everlastingly disappointed ones: "Damn the insolent artist, spoiling our pleasure like that, making fun of the tears he wrings from us, and trampling on our emotions, which he has aroused!" And there they are, all frothing. . . . And the inspired ones! I don't dare imagine what they think.

Curiously enough, accusations of intellectual cynicism and complaints of inconstancy have been directed against Poe and Baudelaire, more than against Verlaine, Rimbaud or Valéry. Verlaine, who is scarcely notable for his integrity or rigor of thought, comments on Poe as if he were a fellow minstrel with some rather good tricks up his sleeve.

In contrast to Verlaine's essentially adolescent attitude toward highly conscious technique, other poets employed it more intellectually or more subtly. They were turning to the exploration of the reach of man's mind. Some were engrossed in the inner drama of thought and feeling:

> We want to substitute the struggle of sensations and of ideas for the struggle of individuals, and for the scene of action, instead of the overused stage of crossroads and streets, part of a brain or all of it. The essential aim of our art is to objectify the subjective (the exteriorization of the Idea) instead of subjectifying the objective (nature seen through a temperament). . . . It is literature's adhesion to the scientific theories constructed by induction and controlled by experiment [Gustave Kahn].

On the other hand, some were intent on descending into consciousness to infinity; they found a pioneer in Poe, but, as with most pioneers, he was revered on their own terms by the men who followed him. Kahn had an almost scientific detachment; although he was fascinated by the bizarre and morbid elements in Poe, he tended to deny the powerful moral basis of such stories as "Berenice," thus denying the coherence given Poe's exploration of consciousness by his concept of evil. In contrast, Maeterlinck and Mallarmé ignored the grotesque, the baroque and the evil, equally. In Maeterlinck consciousness became a mystic unconscious; in Mallarmé it became a means of transcending consciousness.

Poe's anatomizing of the perverse and of the inverted consciousness and his exploration of the levels of the human mind, from intuition probing the subconscious to reason suing the cosmos came at a time when the relationship of mind to matter, of idea to reality and of earth to universe seemed very uncertain. Psychological conflict provided a new and unknown area of art, as Valéry implied, for writers who felt overwhelmed by their Romantic predecessors. But it was much more than that. For some idealistic poets it was a method of approaching the absolute at a time when a traditional religious approach was impossible, and for some it led to a terrible intoxication and to an inescapable and deceptively enchanting labyrinth. Albert Samain recorded the latter attitude in his two responses to *Eureka* and its effect of transcendent consciousness. In the first encounter, he felt that the realm of rarified reason was a death, and he had difficulty in re-establishing contact with his earthly routine; in the second, he had been captivated by the "compelling and vertiginous beyond" and he was exhilarated by the feeling that "space opens out. . . . One advances forever, forever." Samain's response was the reaction of the School of Good Sense exactly reversed; both felt the unearthly compulsion, but Good Sense rejected it, perceiving that the disengaged mind would refuse the world. Among the Symbolists, Charles

Morice gave strongest and clearest expression to the mystical instinct of the seeking mind:

> [People] understand that the work and the spirit of the Poet are, for society as it has decided to be, a social threat: if genius should achieve its own perfect realization—that is, its own advent in the Absolute— the embrace of Man and God would intoxicate all other men with distaste for living outside of God, and this would be the fall of appearance into Reality.

Morice interpreted the Symbolist poetics according to his own bent, which was philosophic and discursively mystical, and he was more inclined toward German masters than toward Poe. Although he relegated Poe and Baudelaire to a subordinate position as predecessors of the New Art (the philosophic ancestry of Goethe and Chateaubriand, precursors in science and mysticism, was thought to be more important), it becomes clear, as soon as Morice states the intentions of art, that Poe was also philosophically in harmony with Morice's version of Symbolism, which is an attempt to reach the "forbidden beyond." Morice's contemporaries desired "l'art pour l'art," he stated, but only as it was "pour l'au-delà."

Many of the Symbolists are evidently motivated by the desire he indicates. The poetic platform of Rimbaud, serious even in its irony, is art's calculation of the means of leaping to the absolute through words:

> I regulated the form and the movement of every consonant, and with instinctive rhythms I prided myself on inventing a poetic language accessible some day to all the senses . . . at first it was an experiment. I wrote silences, I wrote the night. I recorded the inexpressible. I fixed frenzies in their flight.

These lines are in the natural line of extension of Poe's theories. From the start, most of the French critics had seen in Poe's tales a combination of calculation and mysticism, but in the 1880s the purpose of that combination became significant. The impalpable psyche was submitted to every test-tube analysis not solely through scientific curiosity, but through a craving for ultimate knowledge. All of Poe's work bears this double character: deliberate control of means, and empyrean aim. (pp. 51-61)

In its ultimate transcendental intent, Symbolism undoubtedly failed, for a final mystic vision of the One has no need of words but takes place in silence. At its best, however, Symbolist poetry succeeds as art that communicates a sense of an absolute in inner experience and esthetic perception. Paul Valéry, in the poetry of his mature years, abandoned this transcendental goal. When the transcendental impulse took him, he refused at last: "one must try to live." Similarly, his essay on Poe's *Eureka*, written in 1923, reveals his departure from Symbolism, for he ceased to believe in the poetic mind's power to know an absolute reality. The work of imagination finally seemed a magnificent game. But in the days of his discipleship to Mallarmé, Valéry's aim was very much patterned on Poe's:

> I dream of a short poem—a sonnet—written by a subtle dreamer, a judicious architect, a clever algebrist, and an infallible calculator of the effect to be achieved. . . . Everything that he has imagined, felt, and thought will pass through the sieve, will be weighed, purified, submitted to the Form and condensed as much as possible in order to gain in power what it sacrifices in length. That sonnet will be a totality, carefully composed for its final, decisive thunderclap. . . .

In short, the truly prodigious artist for me is the livid Edgar Poe, the great genius of intuition and masterly esthetics.

(p. 73)

Jean Alexander, "The Outlaw" and "The Poet," in Affidavits of Genius: Edgar Allan Poe and the French Critics, 1847-1924, *edited by Jean Alexander, Kennikat Press, 1971, pp. 5-26, 51-74.*

T. S. ELIOT

[*Eliot, an American-born English poet, essayist, and critic, is regarded as one of the most influential literary figures of the first half of the twentieth century. As a poet, he is closely identified with many of the qualities denoted by the term Modernism, including experimentation, formal complexity, artistic and intellectual eclecticism, and a classicist view of the artist working at an emotional distance from his or her creation. As a critic, his overall emphasis on imagery, symbolism, and meaning and his shunning of extratextual elements helped to establish the theories of New Criticism. A convert to the Anglican church in 1928, Eliot stressed the importance of tradition, religion, and morality in literature. Here, he examines the influence of Poe on the Symbolists.*]

[A] book about Mallarmé must also be a book about Poe and about Baudelaire, and must not ignore Mallarmé's most illustrious disciple, Paul Valéry. It must be a book about a movement—the most important "movement" in the world of poetry since that of Wordsworth and Coleridge—and about the aesthetics of that movement.

I must surround the term "movement" with safeguards of several kinds. To say that this is the most important poetic movement since Wordsworth and Coleridge is not to exaggerate the individual importance of the poets involved in it, or to place them higher than other poets, in France, England, and other countries, who are outside of it. Nor can the term here have any of its popular associations. We usually think of a literary movement as a group of young enthusiastic writers who issue a manifesto; who have or who pretend to have certain principles in common; whose work is likely to show a family resemblance; and who are banded together in championship of a common cause, or for sociability and mutual comfort, or at worst for purposes of collective self-advertisement. We think of a "movement" as a phenomenon of youth, and we expect that the sturdier members will in time leave the group as they develop their individual styles, and that the weaker members will disappear into oblivion. By "movement", here, I mean a continuity of admiration: Baudelaire admired Poe, Mallarmé admired Poe and Baudelaire, Valéry admired Poe and Baudelaire and Mallarmé—and a continuity of development of poetic theory. Valéry was the disciple of Mallarmé: but there was no personal association among the rest. Mallarmé, I have been told, came to Paris because Baudelaire was there: he once saw Baudelaire at a bookstall on a quay, but had not the courage to address him. And of course Baudelaire never met Poe. And . . . although each of these French poets in turn found Poe intensely stimulating, there is no evidence of imitation or even of borrowing from Poe in their work.

How far Baudelaire would have been Baudelaire, or Mallarmé Mallarmé, without the stimulus provided by Poe, is a question to which the answer can never be more than conjecture. . . . To Anglo-Saxon readers it must seem that this paradoxical "movement", in which the poets from generation to generation were not greatly influenced by each other's poetry, but deeply influenced by each other's attitude toward poetry, was largely propelled by an initial misunderstanding. It is difficult for us to see how three French poets, all men of exceptional intellectual gifts, could have taken Poe so seriously as a philosopher—for it is Poe's theories about poetry, rather than his poems, that meant most to them. How good a poet was Poe? There is no poet whose status is more disputed. And as a philosopher? It is difficult for an English or American reader to regard as anything but extravagant the praise which Valéry lavishes upon *Eureka*. We suspect, indeed, that if the French poets had known the English language better they could not have rated Poe so high as a stylist; and that if they had known English literature better they might have based their aesthetics not on that of Poe but on that of Coleridge.

No matter: if the influence of Poe upon Baudelaire, Mallarmé and Valéry was based upon misunderstanding, it was a fecund and significant misunderstanding; for the aesthetic which they erected upon this dubious foundation remains valid for their own work. The time had come for a new attitude towards poetry, on the part of poets first, to be accepted by readers afterwards. It does not matter whether Poe's account of the composition of *The Raven* was a conscious hoax, or whether Poe was hoaxing himself; what it suggested to the French poets was an aesthetic which might have come into existence in some other way, if Poe had never written or if Baudelaire had never read Poe.

Any good poet, of course, can be enjoyed without our having previously informed ourselves about his relation to other poets, and without our knowing anything about his theory of poetry—if he has one. Indeed, if this were not so, we might doubt whether what he had written was poetry at all. What we get from a study of these French poets in relation to Poe, is an understanding of their aesthetic which enlarges our understanding of their poetry. And by "aesthetic" here I do not mean merely an abstract theory of what poetry should be; I mean an attitude to poetry, by poets of great critical capacity, which has affected indirectly a good deal of poetry written since and which has also affected the attitude of readers towards their poetry. What the reader of poetry has come to expect of modern poetry, and the way in which he is prepared to enjoy it, are partly due to the attitude of these French poets to their own work. Without this aesthetic I do not think that the work of some other modern writers would be quite what it is (I am thinking of Rilke, for example, and of some of my own later work) or that, if it was the same, it would find a public prepared for it. (pp. v-vii)

> *T. S. Eliot, in a foreword to* Symbolisme from Poe to Mallarmé: The Growth of a Myth *by Joseph Chiari, Rockliff, 1956, pp. v-viii.*

SYMBOLISM AND DECADENCE

ARTHUR SYMONS

[*In the following excerpt from his essay "The Decadent Movement in Literature," Symons discusses a literary school that had close stylistic and thematic affinities with Symbolism. As Symons's discussion illustrates, a number of French writers of the late nineteenth century have been associated with both the Symbolist and the Decadent movements. For additional commentary by Symons, see excerpt above.*]

The latest movement in European literature has been called by many names, none of them quite exact or comprehensive—Decadence, Symbolism, Impressionism, for instance. It is easy to dispute over words, and we shall find that Verlaine objects to being called a Decadent, Maeterlinck to being called a Symbolist, Huysmans to being called an Impressionist. These terms, as it happens, have been adopted as the badge of little separate cliques, noisy, brainsick young people who haunt the brasseries of the Boulevard Saint-Michel, and exhaust their ingenuities in theorizing over the works they cannot write. But, taken frankly as epithets which express their own meaning, both Impressionism and Symbolism convey some notion of that new kind of literature which is perhaps more broadly characterized by the word Decadence. The most representative literature of the day—the writing which appeals to, which has done so much to form, the younger generation—is certainly not classic, nor has it any relation with that old antithesis of the Classic, the Romantic. After a fashion it is no doubt a decadence; it has all the qualities that mark the end of great periods, the qualities that we find in the Greek, the Latin, decadence: an intense self-consciousness, a restless curiosity in research, an over-subtilizing refinement upon refinement, a spiritual and moral perversity. If what we call the classic is indeed the supreme art—those qualities of perfect simplicity, perfect sanity, perfect proportion, the supreme qualities—then this representative literature of to-day, interesting, beautiful, novel as it is, is really a new and beautiful and interesting disease.

Healthy we cannot call it, and healthy it does not wish to be considered. The Goncourts, in their prefaces, in their *Journal*, are always insisting on their own pet malady, *la névrose*. It is in their work, too, that Huysmans notes with delight "le style tacheté et faisandé"—high-flavored and spotted with corruption—which he himself possesses in the highest degree. "Having desire without light, curiosity without wisdom, seeking God by strange ways, by ways traced by the hands of men; offering rash incense upon the high places to an unknown God, who is the God of darkness"—that is how Ernest Hello, in one of his apocalyptic moments, characterizes the nineteenth century. And this unreason of the soul—of which Hello himself is so curious a victim—this unstable equilibrium, which has overbalanced so many brilliant intelligences into one form or another of spiritual confusion, is but another form of the *maladie fin de siècle*. For its very disease of form, this literature is certainly typical of a civilization grown over-luxurious, over-inquiring, too languid for the relief of action, too uncertain for any emphasis in opinion or in conduct. It reflects all the moods, all the manners, of a sophisticated society; its very artificiality is a way of being true to nature: simplicity, sanity, proportion—the classic qualities—how much do we possess them in our life, our surroundings, that we should look to find them in our literature—so evidently the literature of a decadence?

Taking the word Decadence, then, as most precisely expressing the general sense of the newest movement in literature, we find that the terms Impressionism and Symbolism define correctly enough the two main branches of that movement. Now Impressionist and Symbolist have more in common than either supposes; both are really working on the same hypothesis, applied in different directions. What both seek is not general truth merely, but *la vérité vraie*, the very essence of truth—the truth of appearances to the senses, of the visible world to the eyes that see it; and the truth of spiritual things to the spiritual vision. The Impressionist, in literature as in painting, would flash upon you in a new, sudden way so exact an image of what you have just seen, just as you have seen it, that you may say, as a young American sculptor, a pupil of Rodin, said to me on seeing for the first time a picture of Whistler's, "Whistler seems to think his picture upon canvas—and there it is!" Or you may find, with Sainte-Beuve, writing of Goncourt, the "soul of the landscape"—the soul of whatever corner of the visible world has to be realized. The Symbolist, in this new, sudden way, would flash upon you the "soul" of that which can be apprehended only by the soul—the finer sense of things unseen, the deeper meaning of things evident. And naturally, necessarily, this endeavor after a perfect truth to one's impression, to one's intuition—perhaps an impossible endeavor—has brought with it, in its revolt from ready-made impressions and conclusions, a revolt from the ready-made of language, from the bondage of traditional form, of a form become rigid. In France, where this movement began and has mainly flourished, it is Goncourt who was the first to invent a style in prose really new, impressionistic, a style which was itself almost sensation. It is Verlaine who has invented such another new style in verse.

The work of the brothers De Goncourt—twelve novels, eleven or twelve studies in the history of the eighteenth century, six or seven books about art, the art mainly of the eighteenth century and of Japan, two plays, some volumes of letters and of fragments, and a *Journal* in six volumes—is perhaps, in its intention and its consequences, the most revolutionary of the century. No one has ever tried so deliberately to do something new as the Goncourts; and the final word in the summing up which the survivor has placed at the head of the *Préfaces et Manifestes* is a word which speaks of "tentatives, enfin, où les deux frères ont cherchés *à faire du neuf*, ont fait leurs efforts pour doter les diverses branches de la littérature de quelque chose que n'avaient point sougé à trouver leurs prédécesseurs." And in the preface to *Chérie*, in that pathetic passage which tells of the two brothers (one mortally stricken, and within a few months of death) taking their daily walk in the Bois de Boulogne, there is a definite demand on posterity. "The search after *reality* in literature, the resurrection of eighteenth-century art, the triumph of *Japonisme*—are not these," said Jules, "the three great literary and artistic movements of the second half of the nineteenth century? And it is we who brought them about, these three movements. Well, when one has done that, it is difficult indeed not to be *somebody* in the future." Nor, even, is this all. What the Goncourts have done is to specialize vision, so to speak, and to subtilize language to the point of rendering every detail in just the form and color of the actual impression. M. Edmond de Goncourt once said to me—varying, if I remember rightly, an expression he had put into the *Journal*—"My brother and I invented an opera-glass: the young people nowadays are taking it out of our hands."

An opera-glass—a special, unique way of seeing things—that is what the Goncourts have brought to bear upon the common things about us; and it is here that they have done the "something new," here more than anywhere. They have never sought "to see life steadily, and see it whole": their vision has always been somewhat feverish, with the diseased sharpness of over-excited nerves. "We do not hide from ourselves that we have been passionate, nervous creatures, unhealthily impressionable," confesses the *Journal*. But it is this morbid intensity in seeing and seizing things that has helped to form that marvellous style—"a style perhaps too ambitious of impossibilities," as they admit—a style which inherits some of its color from Gautier, some of its fine outline from Flaubert, but which has brought light and shadow into the color, which has softened

outline in the magic of atmosphere. With them words are not merely color and sound, they live. That search after "l'image peinte," "l'épithète rare," is not (as with Flaubert) a search after harmony of phrase for its own sake; it is a desperate endeavor to give sensation, to flash the impression of the moment, to preserve the very heat and motion of life. And so, in analysis as in description, they have found out a way of noting the fine shades; they have broken the outline of the conventional novel in chapters, with its continuous story, in order to indicate—sometimes in a chapter of half a page—this and that revealing moment, this or that significant attitude or accident or sensation. For the placid traditions of French prose they have had but little respect; their aim has been but one, that of having (as M. Edmond de Goncourt tells us in the preface to *Chérie*) "une langue rendant nos idées, nos sensations, nos figurations des hommes et des choses, d'une façon distincte de celui-ci ou de celui-là, une langue personnelle, une langue portant notre signature."

What Goncourt has done in prose—inventing absolutely a new way of saying things, to correspond with that new way of seeing things which he has found—Verlaine has done in verse. In a famous poem, "Art Poétique," he has himself defined his own ideal of the poetic art:

> Car nous voulons la Nuance encor,
> Pas la Couleur, rien que la Nuance!
> Oh! la Nuance seule fiance
> Le rêve au rêve et la flûte au cor!

Music first of all and before all, he insists; and then, not color, but *la nuance*, the last fine shade. Poetry is to be something vague, intangible, evanescent, a winged soul in flight "toward other skies and other loves." To express the inexpressible he speaks of beautiful eyes behind a veil, of the palpitating sunlight of noon, of the blue swarm of clear stars in a cool autumn sky; and the verse in which he makes this confession of faith has the exquisite troubled beauty—"sans rien en lui qui pèse ou qui pose"—which he commends as the essential quality of verse. In a later poem of poetical counsel he tells us that art should, first of all, be absolutely clear, absolutely sincere: "L'art, mes enfants, c'est d'être absolument soi-même." The two poems, with their seven years' interval—an interval which means so much in the life of a man like Verlaine—give us all that there is of theory in the work of the least theoretical, the most really instinctive, of poetical innovators. Verlaine's poetry has varied with his life; always in excess—now furiously sensual, now feverishly devout—he has been constant only to himself, to his own self-contradictions. For, with all the violence, turmoil, and disorder of a life which is almost the life of a modern Villon, Paul Verlaine has always retained that childlike simplicity, and, in his verse, which has been his confessional, that fine sincerity, of which Villon may be thought to have set the example in literature.

Beginning his career as a Parnassian with the *Poèmes Saturniens*, Verlaine becomes himself, in his exquisite first manner, in the *Fêtes Galantes*, caprices after Watteau, followed, a year later, by *La Bonne Chanson*, a happy record of too confident a lover's happiness. *Romances sans Paroles*, in which the poetry of Impressionism reaches its very highest point, is more *tourmenté*, goes deeper, becomes more poignantly personal. It is the poetry of sensation, of evocation; poetry which paints as well as sings, and which paints as Whistler paints, seeming to think the colors and outlines upon the canvas, to think them only, and they are there. The mere magic of words—words which evoke pictures, which recall sensations—can go no further; and in his next book, *Sagesse,* published after seven years' wanderings and sufferings, there is a graver manner of more deeply personal confession—that ''sincerity, and the impression of the moment followed to the letter,'' which he has defined in a prose criticism on himself as his main preference in regard to style. ''Sincerity, and the impression of the moment followed to the letter,'' mark the rest of Verlaine's work, whether the sentiment be that of passionate friendship, as in *Amour;* of love, human and divine, as in *Bonheur;* of the mere lust of the flesh, as in *Parallèlement* and *Chansons pour Elle.* In his very latest verse the quality of simplicity has become exaggerated, has become, at times, childish; the once exquisite depravity of style has lost some of its distinction; there is no longer the same delicately vivid ''impression of the moment'' to render. Yet the very closeness with which it follows a lamentable career gives a curious interest to even the worst of Verlaine's work. And how unique, how unsurpassable in its kind, is the best! ''Et tout le reste est littérature!'' was the cry, supreme and contemptuous, of that early ''Art Poétique''; and, compared with Verlaine at his best, all other contemporary work in verse seems not yet disenfranchised from mere ''literature.'' To fix the last fine shade, the quintessence of things; to fix it fleetingly; to be a disembodied voice, and yet the voice of a human soul: that is the ideal of Decadence, and it is what Paul Verlaine has achieved.

And certainly, so far as achievement goes, no other poet of the actual group in France can be named beside him or near him. But in Stéphane Mallarmé, with his supreme pose as the supreme poet, and his two or three pieces of exquisite verse and delicately artificial prose to show by way of result, we have the prophet and pontiff of the movement, the mystical and theoretical leader of the great emancipation. No one has ever dreamed such beautiful, impossible dreams as Mallarmé; no one has ever so possessed his soul in the contemplation of masterpieces to come. All his life he has been haunted by the desire to create, not so much something new in literature, as a literature which should itself be a new art. He has dreamed of a work into which all the arts should enter, and achieve themselves by a mutual interdependence—a harmonizing of all the arts into one supreme art—and he has theorized with infinite subtlety over the possibilities of doing the impossible. Every Tuesday for the last twenty years he has talked more fascinatingly, more suggestively, than any one else has ever done, in that little room in the Rue de Rome, to that little group of eager young poets. ''A seeker after something in the world, that is there in no satisfying measure, or not at all,'' he has carried his contempt for the usual, the conventional, beyond the point of literary expression, into the domain of practical affairs. Until the publication, quite recently, of a selection of *Vers et Prose,* it was only possible to get his poems in a limited and expensive edition, lithographed in fac-simile of his own clear and elegant handwriting. An aristocrat of letters, Mallarmé has always looked with intense disdain on the indiscriminate accident of universal suffrage. He has wished neither to be read nor to be understood by the bourgeois intelligence, and it is with some deliberateness of intention that he has made both issues impossible. M. Catulle Mendès defines him admirably as ''a difficult author,'' and in his latest period he has succeeded in becoming absolutely unintelligible. His early poems, ''L'Après-midi d'un Faune,'' ''Hérodiade,'' for example, and some exquisite sonnets, and one or two fragments of perfectly polished verse, are written in a language which has nothing in common with every-day language—symbol within symbol, image within image; but symbol and image achieve themselves in expression without seeming to call for the ne-

cessity of a key. The latest poems (in which punctuation is sometimes entirely suppressed, for our further bewilderment) consist merely of a sequence of symbols, in which every word must be taken in a sense with which its ordinary significance has nothing to do. Mallarmé's contortion of the French language, so far as mere style is concerned, is curiously similar to the kind of depravation which was undergone by the Latin language in its decadence. It is, indeed, in part a reversion to Latin phraseology, to the Latin construction, and it has made, of the clear and flowing French language, something irregular, unquiet, expressive, with sudden surprising felicities, with nervous starts and lapses, with new capacities for the exact noting of sensation. Alike to the ordinary and to the scholarly reader, it is painful, intolerable; a jargon, a massacre. Supremely self-confident, and backed, certainly, by an ardent following of the younger generation, Mallarmé goes on his way, experimenting more and more audaciously, having achieved by this time, at all events, a style wholly his own. Yet the ''chef-d'oeuvre inconnu'' seems no nearer completion, the impossible seems no more likely to be done. The two or three beautiful fragments remain, and we still hear the voice in the Rue de Rome.

Probably it is as a voice, an influence, that Mallarmé will be remembered. His personal magnetism has had a great deal to do with the making of the very newest French literature; few literary beginners in Paris have been able to escape the rewards and punishments of his contact, his suggestion. One of the young poets who form that delightful Tuesday evening coterie said to me the other day, ''We owe much to Mallarmé, but he has kept us all back three years.'' That is where the danger of so inspiring, so helping a personality comes in. The work even of M. Henri de Regnier, who is the best of the disciples, has not entirely got clear from the influence that has shown his fine talent the way to develop. Perhaps it is in the verse of men who are not exactly following in the counsel of the master— who might disown him, whom he might disown—that one sees most clearly the outcome of his theories, the actual consequences of his practice. In regard to the construction of verse, Mallarmé has always remained faithful to the traditional syllabic measurement; but the freak or the discovery of ''le vers libre'' is certainly the natural consequence of his experiments upon the elasticity of rhythm, upon the power of resistance of the caesura. . . . In this hazardous experiment M. Jean Moréas, whose real talent lies in quite another direction, has brought nothing into literature but an example of deliberate singularity for singularity's sake. I seem to find the measure of the man in a remark I once heard him make in a café, where we were discussing the technique of metre: ''You, Verlaine!'' he cried, leaning across the table, ''have only written lines of sixteen syllables; *I* have written lines of twenty syllables!'' And turning to me, he asked anxiously if Swinburne had ever done that— had written a line of twenty syllables.

That is indeed the measure of the man, and it points a criticism upon not a few of the busy little *littérateurs* who are founding new *revues* every other week in Paris. These people have nothing to say, but they are resolved to say something, and to say it in the newest mode. They are Impressionists because it is the fashion, Symbolists because it is the vogue, Decadents because Decadence is in the very air of the cafés. And so, in their manner, they are mile-posts on the way of this new movement, telling how far it has gone. (pp. 858-64)

Imagine a combination of Swift, of Poe, and of Coleridge, and you will have some idea of [Villiers de l'Isle-Adam], the extraordinary, impossible poet and cynic who, after a life of brilliant failure, has left a series of unfinished works in every kind of literature; among the finished achievements one volume of short stories, *Contes Cruels,* which is an absolute masterpiece. Yet, apart from this, it was the misfortune of Villiers never to attain the height of his imaginings, and even *Axël,* the work of a lifetime, is an achievement only half achieved. Only half achieved, or achieved only in the work of others; for, in its mystical intention, its remoteness from any kind of outward reality, *Axël* is undoubtedly the origin of the symbolistic drama. This drama, in Villiers, is of pure symbol, of sheer poetry. It has an exalted eloquence which we find in none of his followers. As M. Maeterlinck has developed it, it is a drama which appeals directly to the sensations—sometimes crudely, sometimes subtly—playing its variations upon the very nerves themselves. The "vague spiritual fear" which it creates out of our nervous apprehension is unlike anything that has ever been done before, even by Hoffmann, even by Poe. It is an effect of atmosphere—an atmosphere in which outlines change and become mysterious, in which a word quietly uttered makes one start, in which all one's mental activity becomes concentrated on something, one knows not what, something slow, creeping, terrifying, which comes nearer and nearer, an impending nightmare. (p. 864)

Joris Karl Huysmans demands a prominent place in any record of the Decadent movement. His work, like that of the Goncourts, is largely determined by the *maladie fin de siècle*—the diseased nerves that, in his case, have given a curious personal quality of pessimism to his outlook on the world, his view of life. Part of his work—*Marthe, Les Soeurs Vatard, En Ménage, À Vau-l'Eau*—is a minute and searching study of the minor discomforts, the commonplace miseries of life, as seen by a peevishly disordered vision, delighting, for its own self-torture, in the insistent contemplation of human stupidity, of the sordid in existence. Yet these books do but lead up to the unique masterpiece, the astonishing caprice of *À Rebours,* in which he has concentrated all that is delicately depraved, all that is beautifully, curiously poisonous, in modern art. *À Rebours* is the history of a typical Decadent—a study, indeed, after a real man, but a study which seizes the type rather than the personality. In the sensations and ideas of Des Esseintes we see the sensations and ideas of the effeminate, over-civilized, deliberately abnormal creature who is the last product of our society: partly the father, partly the offspring, of the perverse art that he adores. Des Esseintes creates for his solace, in the wilderness of a barren and profoundly uncomfortable world, an artificial paradise. His Thébaïde raffinée is furnished elaborately for candle-light, equipped with the pictures, the books, that satisfy his sense of the exquisitely abnormal. He delights in the Latin of Apuleius and Petronius, in the French of Baudelaire, Goncourt, Verlaine, Mallarmé, Villiers; in the pictures of Gustave Moreau, the French Burne-Jones, of Odilon Redon, the French Blake. He delights in the beauty of strange, unnatural flowers, in the melodic combination of scents, in the imagined harmonies of the sense of taste. And at last, exhausted by these spiritual and sensory debauches in the delights of the artificial, he is left (as we close the book) with a brief, doubtful choice before him—madness or death, or else a return to nature, to the normal life.

Since *À Rebours,* M. Huysmans has written one other remarkable book, *Là-Bas,* a study in the hysteria and mystical corruption of contemporary Black Magic. But it is on that one exceptional achievement, *À Rebours,* that his fame will rest; it is there that he has expressed not merely himself, but an epoch. And he has done so in a style which carries the modern

experiments upon language to their furthest development. Formed upon Goncourt and Flaubert, it has sought for novelty, *l'image peinte,* the exactitude of color, the forcible precision of epithet, wherever words, images, or epithets are to be found. Barbaric in its profusion, violent in its emphasis, wearying in its splendor, it is—especially in regard to things seen—extraordinarily expressive, with all the shades of a painter's palette. Elaborately and deliberately perverse, it is in its very perversity that Huysmans' work—so fascinating, so repellent, so instinctively artificial—comes to represent, as the work of no other writer can be said to do, the main tendencies, the chief results, of the Decadent movement in literature.

Such, then, is the typical literature of the Decadence.... (pp. 865-66)

Arthur Symons, "The Decadent Movement in Literature," in Harper's New Monthly Magazine, *Vol. LXXXVII, No. DXXII, November, 1893, pp. 858-67.*

JOHN R. REED

[Reed discusses stylistic traits of Decadence and contrasts them with the style of Symbolism and other aesthetic schools of the nineteenth century.]

What I am calling Decadent style seems always to be associated with an autumnal, frustrated mood and hence the frequent confusion between cultural decadence and *decadence* as an aesthetic term. The former is primarily a historical and social phenomenon; the latter is traceable in the methods of artistic composition. It is a highly self-conscious dissolution of established form for the purpose of creating a subtler, pervasive, and cerebral form. Founded on inevitable frustration, it incorporates in itself techniques of sensory stimulation or irritation that are never fully resolved except through negation. The elaborate and heady manner of Decadent art resembles a Beardsley drawing: intricately composed of grotesque figures and artificial designs abstracted from nature but, when examined carefully, often focusing upon a void of white or black—all of experience reduced to design, but a design that is, in itself, compelling. (p. 11)

Decadence combines Aestheticism and Naturalism, Parnassian precision and innovative intent. In contrast, Symbolism emphasizes suggestiveness, vagueness, and free departure in form. Aestheticism, as a broad movement, recognizes the connection between beauty and evil; Symbolism, in reaching toward transcendence, seeks to shed ugliness; Decadence cultivates a fastidious affection for the disreputable. Decadence stresses the interrelationship of virtue and vice, beauty and ugliness, whereas Symbolism separates them by converting offensive phenomenal facts into symbols for an immaterial reality. Symbolism is the direct descendent of Aestheticism and Art-for-Art's Sake; Decadence is an illegitimate by-blow sired by Naturalism upon Aestheticism.

Aestheticism, an inclusive term, signifies the supersession of art over meaning, the rejection of the ugly and vulgar in favor of harmonious subject and composition, and the gratification of highly refined sensibilities, emphasizing mood and reflection over vigorous action. Decadence shares Aestheticism's basic assumptions—the fascination with objects of art, distaste for the quotidian, curiosity about the artist's nature, and a favoring of unusual settings or decorations. But Decadence is a dissolving, not a cohering, art. It is self-consciously transitional. It employs techniques of Realism to convey extreme aesthetic conditions; thus it utilizes ugly details and even brutality to convey the sense of spiritual longing. Aestheticism seeks to achieve beauty here and now; Decadence purposely embraces the impossible quest of spiritual fulfillment.

These distinctions are serviceable, but more are necessary to set Decadence apart from other outgrowths of Aestheticism. Like other forms of Aestheticism, Decadence values aesthetic effect over meaning, yet like Pre-Raphaelitism, it requires some degree of "literariness" and intellectual challenge. Like Impressionism or Pointilism, Decadent art atomizes its material to compose it anew, but it does so in an indirect, not an obvious, technical way. Intensely concerned about technique and traditional forms, after the manner of the Parnassians, it nonetheless subverts those forms. Decadence and Symbolism both use prominent symbols, reject the inelegant contemporary world, and stress the longing for another sphere of being—aesthetic, ideal, even supernatural. But Symbolism permits greater experiment in form, renounces meaning in favor of suggestion, and aspires beyond the material world to some higher realm much in the manner of the *Frühromantiker*.

Decadence shared many qualities with other artistic movements of the time and reveals connections with certain intellectual developments as well. Subjectivism, Individualism, Pessimism all were common preoccupations of the age. Although Alfred Orage asserted that decadent art led the will downward, in fact, *assertion* of the will characterizes this art, for it rests to a great extent upon the assumption that there is nothing to support man beyond himself. Richard Le Gallienne grasped this quality when he objected to decadent art's concentration on the sensuous. "*Decadence* is founded on a natural impossibility to start with," he writes in *The Religion of a Literary Man* (1895). "It attempts the delineation of certain things and aspects *in vacuo*, isolated from all their relations to other things and their dependence on the great laws of life." Le Gallienne exaggerates, and his concept of decadent art is not the same as mine, but he recognizes in this kind of art a despair that hopelessly searches for a purposefulness it cannot believe. While yearning for a dependable order, it assumes the void. Naturalistic detail becomes ornament and the artificial supersedes the natural because nature offers only savagery and disappointment. Decadence takes from Darwinism the Schopenhauerian or Hartmannian sense of struggle and illusion rather than an optimistic notion of material or racial progress. Decadence was Nietzschean in its effort at self-creation out of the chaos of existence.

Decadent art is contained by nothing. Although it employs existing conventions, it usually negates them at the same time, denying the normal grounds of interpretation and reception. Its subject matter often concerns the violation of codes. It utilizes systems or mythologies (of legend, the occult, aestheticism) to oppose what *is*, without accepting those systems and mythologies. Decadence drives toward noncontainment and disconnectedness through the paradoxical act of self-imposed restraint. To some degree it anticipates features of Surrealism and Expressionism.

The Decadent recognizes a nothingness at the center of existence and dreads the emptiness within himself. His pursuit of sensuous experience is partly an attempt to construct a substantial self through the effort of his own will, but the effort is doomed to failure since sensation remains a skin of responses over a moral or emotional void, which is itself the result of frustrated yearning after some unattainable image, ideal, or faith. The Decadent protagonist differs from his Romantic forebear. The Romantic *isolato* is frequently forced out upon a quest, often an actual journey, to solve some mystery, not unlikely the discovery of his own origins. The Decadent *isolato* is usually an artist who finds nothing in the external world intriguing enough to draw him into action and who thus accumulates experiences and sensations within himself, hoping to fill the central void. The Romantic expends internal energy outward, the Decadent feeds an inner vacuum. The Romantic projects his fecund emotions into the natural world until it seems to return his moods. The Decadent, transforming nature through artifice, finds no faithful reflection in it. The Romantic seeks a union with nature; the Decadent tries to fashion nature into an ornamentation of the self. The Romantic is impelled by the pressure of accumulated history. The Decadent, fascinated by a remote past and disenchanted by the present, is lured into the future by hopelessly elegant dreams.

The inevitability of frustration may lead the Decadent to a melancholy obsession with remoteness in space or time, especially with childhood. Or it may lead to a craving for domination sometimes of a sadistic cast. Since will replaces belief, the Decadent dreads being dominated and correspondingly seeks to assert his own command over other persons, even to the point of fashioning them the way an artist creates objects of art. Stelio Effrena's outburst of joy in D'Annunzio's *Il fuoco* at the realization that his lover, Foscarina, has become his creation is instructive: "Ah, io t'ho creata, io t'ho creata . . ." (Ah, I have created you, I have created you . . .). Like other Decadent figures, Stelio desires not merely to dominate or control others, to govern their inner lives, but to shape their very beings, to *create* them. This is, of course, the dangerous impulse that energizes *The Picture of Dorian Gray*. Lacking the force or interest to impose this creative design upon others, the Decadent concentrated upon himself. Once again, in a version of Nietzsche's philosophy, life became style—hence the frequent association of Decadence and dandyism. Yeats recommended indecisive rather than insistent rhymes as a means by which "the mind liberated from the pressure of the will is unfolded in symbols." The Symbolists sought such an escape in agogic rhythms, formlessness, and feeling, but the Decadents used rhythm, repetition, and form to imply a world in which no such escape was possible except in delirium, oblivion, or death. Unlike the Symbolists, Decadents included in their highly sophisticated art a powerful sympathy for the barbaric or primitive. Order to them was balanced by the threat of destruction, control by impulse, pleasure by pain, reason by unreason.

The Pre-Raphaelites had created symbols of the soul—usually, as with Rossetti, in a female form. But for the Decadents, as for the Symbolists, the ideal state was as often as not pictured as immobile, even inorganic. Flaubert converted his ideal woman into the static, gemlike Salâmmbo; Pater recommended a gemlike state for the self; Yeats dreamed of golden birds upon a golden bough. Frank Kermode calls this reconciling of action and contemplation the Romantic Image wherein the poem itself becomes a symbol. But if Decadence imagined the ideal as inaccessible and remote, perhaps even virgin, it preserved the Romantic craving to achieve it through an act of will rather than the Symbolist's confidence that contemplation would evoke it. Thus Decadent art emphasizes tantalization and provocation, and because the object of desire is unattainable, it dwells upon the pain that accompanies longing until the pain itself becomes an object of desire since as long as it is sustained, the object of desire is not lost. Decadent art is an itch that itches more

"A Literary Manifesto" by Jean Moréas, published in Le Figaro, *Paris, 18 September 1886.*

the more you scratch until you scratch to intensify the itch that has become your morbid delight.

The pain, tension, and irresolution of Decadent art are not simply willful but result from its transitional, ambiguous nature. No state is permanent; all is open to rearrangement. Life is a form of art but one that can never be completed. Decadent art balances between linearity and spatiality, between explicitness and suggestion, between harmony and discord, between tradition and innovation, between story and image. Hence many of its topoi emphasize ambivalence—sphinxes with their mixed bodies and dangerous mysteries, hermaphrodites, beautiful but evil women, and so forth. But Decadent art is also a consciously crafted art that depends upon predictable audience responses to manipulate. To a great extent, it is more "modern" than other styles of its time in the degree to which it violates expectations while forcing an intellectual re-creation of form in the reader's, spectator's, or auditor's mind. (pp. 14-18)

> *John R. Reed, in an introduction to his* Decadent Style, *Ohio University Press, 1985, pp. 1-18.*

SYMBOLIST THEATER

HASKELL M. BLOCK

[*Block analyzes the dramatic theories of Mallarmé and assesses his influence on the Symbolist theater.*]

From 1885 to the end of his life, Mallarmé meditated and wrote on the theater. The essays and prose poems which the poet contributed to the literary reviews that clamored for his work, and which he subsequently collected in his *Divagations,* constitute a rich and complex statement of a highly original theory of drama. It is not Mallarmé's indebtedness to such vital forces in his development as Wagner or Banville which is of primary interest, but rather the ways in which he goes beyond them to break new ground. The *"Notes sur le théâtre"* which he contributed for several months to the *Revue Indépendante* demonstrate the poet's sensitivity and depth as a critic of the drama, and it is in his criticism far more than in his dramatic compositions, written or projected, that his most far-reaching contribution to the theater was to be made.

In retrospect, Mallarmé considered his essays in the *Revue Indépendante* as programmatic, part of *"une campagne dramatique,"* an effort to change the theater, not merely to describe it. Yet, in order to reshape the theater of his day, Mallarmé had to come to know it, and this meant attending all kinds of dramatic performances. The physical demands of the *"Notes sur le théâtre"* were exhausting, and doubly so because the Paris theatrical season of 1886-87 was not a particularly distinguished one. It provided ample illustration of the dominant obsession with *"l'universel reportage"* which the poet saw in every area of contemporary writing. Scribe, Sardou, Dumas fils, Zola, and their confreres dominated the stage, relieved only by occasional revivals of classics such as Mounet-Sully's Hamlet, or by performances of pantomime or dance. Mallarmé's essays provide a valuable record of the theatrical year, but far more important, they constitute a demand for a total reorientation of the drama.

We must make a sharp distinction between the poet's view of the theater as he found it and his vision of the theater as it might become. Mallarmé's critique moves between two poles: the *"art si grossier . . . si abject,"* as Gautier had described it, and the ideal theater which Mallarmé strove to bring about. He had little sympathy for the drama of realistic prose, to which one responds *"comme par un* Ce n'est pas moi dont il est ici question." Most of the plays he felt obliged to see are, he insists, not worth talking about. They are part of the *"banal sacrilège"* of the separation of drama from poetry. Mallarmé was well aware of the role played by public taste in the degradation of the stage. The theater of realistic prose he describes as *"temple d'un culte factice"*; but it is still a temple, even when desecrated: *"le grand art quand même!"* Mallarmé found the theater of literal representation tedious and dull, *"où chacun veut être dans le secret de quelque chose ne fût-ce que de la redite perpétuelle."* And yet, he could appreciate the interest which others might have in a realistic portrayal of individual or social experience. He had high praise for Zola's dramatic adaptation of *La Curée* and was quite ready to accept the traditional *"théâtre de moeurs,"* provided that it be taken on its own terms and not as a final expression of the possibilities of the drama. The poetic theater represented for Mallarmé the "other" theater, suggested here and there on the contemporary stage, but still awaiting the establishment of new attitudes and values for its realization. The easy and empty drama of mass entertainment, *"l'art officiel qu'on peut aussi appeler vulgaire,"* was not to be supplanted overnight; but a beginning could be made by providing a sense of direction and by pointing to attitudes and techniques that would help to initiate the change. It is as part of this effort that Mallarmé's dramatic theory must be understood.

Mallarmé's ideal theater is a symbolist drama, an expression of the same principles and values shaping and directing symbolist poetry. The separation of the drama from literal reality is absolute: "Le Théâtre est d'essence supérieure." The present low estate of the stage has nothing to do with its inherent greatness. In its origin and destiny, drama is a sacred and mysterious rite, a suggestion or evocation of the hidden spiritual meaning of existence; it is an act of common participation and mutual involvement before *"la majestueuse ouverture sur le mystère dont on est au monde pour envisager la grandeur."* This mystery is revealed indirectly, through dream and reverie, and in a language of rich musicality and allusiveness. *"Remplacez Vaudeville par Mystère,"* Mallarmé declares, in answer to Gautier's appeal for a return to spectacle. The mystery of drama resides not only in its language and gesture, but also in its embodiment of the ideal, its reflection of ultimate spiritual truth.

Thus, for Mallarmé the drama is not the expression of the experiences of any particular man, but rather *"de la Passion de l'Homme"*: man in his spiritual and divine character, and not in his material and accidental state of being. In this abstract and typical representation, the poet sees the union of the drama of personal heroism on the one hand and of impersonal mystery on the other: the fusion of theater and hymn. In his highly personal reformulation of the drama, Mallarmé is not concerned with the details of the *"explication de l'homme,"* but rather with the spiritual attitudes and values that the new theater will express: the primacy of mystery, dream, and imaginative vision, projected beyond any particular time or circumstance. The magic and mystery of the theater reside within its very substance, as an evocation of the absolute, embracing the destiny of all humanity. In this sense, Mallarmé's ritual drama is the means of the propagation of a new religion, a secularization of the liturgy and rite of ancient dramatic performances.

This vision of a ceremonial theater is in fact a configuration of elements derived from a variety of sources: Greek drama, the medieval liturgical drama, Shakespeare, Wagner, Banville and the tradition of poetic drama, and the Catholic Mass. Mallarmé saw the theater of both the past and the future as a temple, wherein actor and spectator participate in a sacred rite. . . . The spectacle of the Catholic Mass was for Mallarmé the nearest analog of this liturgical conception. The audience participates in an act of mass communion, not for the sake of literal understanding, but rather as a celebration of a sacred mystery. Mallarmé's notion of *"Mystère"* is in many ways suggestive of medieval liturgical drama. The presence of mystery transforms the audience into a community sharing a common awareness of the spirituality and wonder of the universe. (pp. 83-6)

Mallarmé's notion of *"Mystère"* is no mere abstraction. In *La Musique et les Lettres,* the poet places this concept at the very center of *"cette célébration de la poésie"*: *"appelez-là Mystère ou n'est-ce pas le contexte évolutif de l'Idée"*. Mystery is a reflection of *"l'Idée,"* the realm of pure spirituality, made particular and concrete in theatrical presentation. In the notes for his vast dramatic composition, Mallarmé clarifies this concept when he declares that Mystery and Drama, Drama and Mystery *"ne sont que même chose retournées présentant l'un en dehors ce que l'autre cache en dedans."* . . . Clearly, *"Mystère"* for Mallarmé is not a mere reproduction of the medieval religious drama. It is coexistent with the art of drama and, indeed, with all literature. Just as Baudelaire insisted that we can apprehend the spirituality of the universe only through the mysteries of *"l'analogie,"* so Mallarmé declares in *"Le Mystère dans les Lettres,"* *"Il doit y avoir quelque chose d'occulte au fond de tous."* The complex allusiveness of drama, its broad symbolic and cosmic implications as well as its necessary obscurity, is part of the conditions of all artistic experience. Yet, the incarnation of *"Mystère"* in *"Drame"* takes the form of

a synthesis of the spiritual and the histrionic properties of ritualistic celebration: an idea, but also a performance, a fusion of action and incantation, mime and dance. Concretely as well as in its ideological premises, Mallarmé's vision of what the drama can become represents a total transformation of the theater, a return to the rudimentary elements of the drama in their pristine simplicity.

The reductive and elemental character of Mallarmé's dramatic theory is most apparent in his emphasis on the detheatricalization of the stage. As a consequence of the debasement of the theater in his time, the poet came to feel, at least at times, that the true value of a play could never be expressed in performance, but only through the medium of the printed page. We have seen that *"Le Livre"* for Mallarmé also constitutes a mode of dramatic expression, wherein the action is directed not so much to the senses of the spectator as to the mind or inner eye. Mallarmé's preference for closet drama is deeply rooted. In his early attempts to compose drama, he viewed the theater in intimate association with poetry. It is useful to recall his intent in the composition of the *Faune* *"Intermède"*: *"je veux conserver toute la poésie de mes oeuvres lyriques, mon vers même, que j'adapte au drame."* The separation of poetry from the theater—the indifference of the stage to the role of language—issued in the poet's rejection of the purely theatrical elements of the drama.

In this respect, Mallarmé's attitude toward the theater is essentially the same as that of the English Romantics, most of whom considered a play read as superior to a play acted. The resemblance is not fortuitous. Mallarmé was well aware of the plight of poetic drama across the channel, where Byron, Shelley, and their successors had been forced to create a theater *"fait des majestueux fantômes"* and constituting a *"fête idéale."* It is in this context that the poet praises Swinburne's verse tragedy, *Erechtheus,* in a review of 1876. Swinburne's play, like those of his predecessors, is part of that theater *"dont on n'est le spectateur que chez soi, un tome ouvert ou les yeux fermés."* It is the same notion of theater that was to reappear in Mallarmé's critical essays ten years later, and it may be a direct reflection of his reading of the critical essays of the English Romantics, whose work he knew well.

The gradual reduction of the *"Drame"* to *"Le Livre"* is itself part of Mallarmé's transference of visible action to the realm of the invisible. The physical theater was not merely corrupt; it was, at least at times, utterly superfluous. With the passage of time, Mallarmé, like Banville before him, came to place increased emphasis on *"Le Livre"* rather than the *"Drame"* as the embodiment of the art of drama. The reduction of the audience, to a single person at its extreme point, went hand in hand with the virtual abandonment of the physical theater and the elimination of the acting group. The presence in *"Le Livre"* of only a single actor—the poet—precluded any dialog. There is perhaps a trace of plot action in Mallarmé's plans for the substance of his work, but the plans provide no more than the barest outline. Anecdote went the same way as character in the poet's vision of performance in *"séances de lecture reglées comme un cérémonial."* (pp. 87-9)

The superiority of the ideal drama lies in its revelation of the meaning of human destiny. The awareness of the sense of tragedy inherent in life is for Mallarmé a condition rather than an act, a mode of being rather than a series of events. The inner drama which Mallarmé evokes is perforce a static drama, wherein linear anecdote and physical action are reduced if not altogether eliminated.

The poet's interpretation of *Hamlet* is the most striking illustration of this interiorization of the drama. Shakespeare's play, he declares, in words echoing Victor Hugo's description of his *Théâtre en Liberté,* "*est si bien façonnée selon le seul théâtre de notre esprit,*" that it is indifferent to the physical setting and may freely dispense with it. We have seen in Mallarmé's early dramatic attempts the powerful shadow of the melancholy Dane, "*personnage unique d'une tragédie intime et occulte,*" exerting on Mallarmé "*une fascination parente de l'angoisse.*" Hamlet is in fact the only character in the play: "*Son solitaire drame!*" For while Mallarmé admits the presence of secondary characters—Horatio, Laertes, Polonius—they exist only as the background for the central figure and move "*selon une réciprocité symbolique des types entre eux ou relativement à une figure seule.*" Everything in the play pivots around Hamlet and is, indeed, only him. Just as Hamlet is the universal hero, so the conflict in Shakespeare's play constitutes the only subject of dramatic presentation: "*l'antagonisme de rêves chez l'homme avec les fatalités à son existence départies par le malheur.*" In this collision of dream and destiny we have the full expression of the tragedy of the human condition. The subject of *Hamlet* is in this sense universal, independent of accidental or particular circumstances and free from the confines of anecdotal description. This cosmic symbolization may well have its origin in a deep affinity which Mallarmé, like many nineteenth-century poets, saw between himself and Hamlet: "*le spectacle d'un homme s'isolant en lui-même.*" Historically, he declares, the play is a culminating point in the development of a vision of the ideal drama, "*le Monologue ou drame avec Soi, futur.*" In this sense, Shakespeare is the great precursor of the symbolist drama. (pp. 90-1)

Detheatricalization is an important characteristic of the symbolist drama as it came to be developed by Mallarmé's followers and by other playwrights who responded to the symbolist aesthetic. This reduction of the physical attributes of the drama and particularly of the role of artifice and visual effect does not imply a total elimination of the histrionic properties of the art. Mallarmé was fascinated by the spectacle of the empty stage and could claim that reading a play is quite the same as seeing it; nevertheless, he was keenly aware of the attraction of purely theatrical effects and their claims on the attention of the audience. This is not to deny the poet's deep disdain for the fashionable theater of the day. In the last years of his life he seldom went to the theater, out of the conviction that the drama in his day was a debased art. Yet, both in his critical essays and in conversation, Mallarmé demonstrated a keen understanding of the physical theater, of the importance not only of plot action, but also of the set, costumes, and scenic effects as part of the experience of drama. There is a paradox in the poet's preference for the dematerialized stage and the vivid appreciation of its theatrical qualities which may be seen in his spontaneous expression of delight over a performance of *La Vieillesse de Scapin* at the Théâtre Français. It may be that Mallarmé's reduction of décor, gesture, and theatrical artifice was applicable only to the drama of high philosophical purpose and not to the simpler forms of popular entertainment.

In the realm of the ideal theater this paradox is apparent but not troublesome. If we view "*Le Livre*" as an absolute reduction of the play to the book, it is difficult to see how the ceremonial character of the drama would be maintained. Clearly, Mallarmé did not mean to separate the eye and the mind, the spectator and the reader, in any complete sense. "*Le Livre*" is intended for stage performance as well as for spiritual performance. It is addressed to the masses as well as to the in-

dividual. The ideal theater, Mallarmé implies, will fuse aristocratic and popular elements; it will be at once drama for an elite and drama for the public at large. The "*Ode, dramatisée*" is both poem and play. The poet may reduce theatrical elements; he cannot eliminate them. Drama for Mallarmé rises out of an interplay of the book and the theater, that is, out of the exploitation of all of the resources of both the book and the arts of the stage. In this interaction, the purely theatrical is not abandoned; rather, it is placed in a new relationship to all of the elements of dramatic performance. (pp. 92-3)

It may well be that Mallarmé's image of the theater was mainly theoretical, set forth to be realized by others and never the conscious expression of a goal to be attained by the poet himself. Even so, his dramatic theory is no little achievement. The principles underlying the development of a symbolist drama were stated and elaborated in Mallarmé's critical essays. His concern with language was of central importance, because it was through a new awareness of the function of language in the theater that poetry could regain its rightful place on the stage. If Mallarmé conceived of drama as a "*poème dialogué,*" he was also aware of the practical problems confronting the young poet-dramatist: "*il est insupportable d'entendre toujours le même vers pendant cinq actes,*" he declared; for, while the classical drama imposed respect and attention, the modern playwright who merely imitated the idiom of Corneille or Racine would run the risk of losing his audience. In the face of the rigidity of the conventions of prose realism and the incompatibility between the poet and the age, Mallarmé had no assurance that his vision of an ideal theater would find expression. . . . Nevertheless, Mallarmé does not urge the young poets of the day to flee from the theater, but rather to devote themselves to its reconstruction. The development of the symbolist drama, in France and throughout the whole of Europe, is the direct result of the response of the young poets of the turn of the last century to Mallarmé's appeal. (p. 100)

• • • • •

From Mallarmé's programmatic efforts of the 1880's to the emergence of a symbolist drama in the 1890's, first in France and then throughout Europe, is but a short step. The poet did not live to see fulfillment of his dream of a new poetic theater, but the application of symbolist poetics to the art of the stage, essentially the result of his efforts, began several years before Mallarmé's death. The starting point of symbolist dramatic theory is Mallarmé's series of chronicles in the *Revue Indépendante* in 1886 and 1887; the impact of these essays on the young poets and aspiring playwrights who read and contributed to the review was direct and immediate. Mallarmé reprinted several of the more important articles, with accompanying titles such as "Hamlet" and "Ballets," in *Pages,* published in Brussels in 1891. Subsequent reprintings, notably in the section of *Divagations* in 1897 entitled "Crayonné au Théâtre," served to give wider currency to the poet's vision of an ideal theater. Along with the continual flow of essays during the 1890's, we must also take into account the constant discussion of the theater's ways and means that took place at many of Mallarmé's Tuesday evening gatherings. The preoccupations of the critical essays of 1886-87: Wagner, Hamlet, the dance, the language of drama, the interrelations of the arts, were all constant topics of conversation between the poet and his young admirers. It is impossible to separate the influence of the man from that of his thought. The steady increase in the popularity of the poet brought new attention to his early dramatic compositions as well as to his dramatic theories. Mallarmé's writings were the starting point for the efforts of many new poets and playwrights to transform the theater of the day.

Nevertheless, it would be incorrect to attribute the symbolist venture in the theater exclusively to the author of *Hérodiade*. The impact of Mallarmé's dramatic theory coincides with a number of parallel events: the recognition of the talent of Villiers de l'Isle-Adam; the rediscovery of the theater of Alfred de Musset and of the values of fantasy and imaginative improvisation; the ever-widening diffusion of Wagner's view of the art work of the future; the deliberate efforts of young symbolists to extend the gains of poetry to all of the literary arts; as well as the large share of accident in the emergence of talented playwrights capable of drawing upon Mallarmé's legacy. The restrictions of realistic and naturalistic dramaturgy further served to stimulate experimentation in language, scenic effects, and techniques of symbolization. In his historical setting, Mallarmé is a powerful influence, but he is only one of several forces shaping the emergence of a symbolist drama. Our isolation of the poet's role may suggest that he was uniquely responsible for the course of the new drama, and this is plainly not the case. On the other hand, without Mallarmé the ideals of symbolist drama as well as their concrete realization would not have been the same. Indeed, were it not for the theory and technique set forth in Mallarmé's writings, it is doubtful that we could speak of a symbolist drama at all, any more than of a symbolist poetry.

It would be well to summarize the salient characteristics of symbolist drama as they emerge from Mallarmé's aesthetic:

1. Drama is the expression of inner life, the revelation of an "*état d'âme.*"

2. Drama is the expression of mystery: the revelation of the hidden wonder of the universe.

3. The language of drama is poetry rather than prose, evocative rather than descriptive, and relying upon suggestion as opposed to statement.

4. The stage is detheatricalized, reduced to the barest and simplest elements of histrionic performance.

5. The theater brings into play all of the arts, interrelated within a poetic structure.

Not every one of Mallarmé's followers accepted all of these tenets and, in practice, the implementation of symbolist theories was to vary considerably from one playwright to another. It is clear, however, that the programmatic demands for a reorientation of the theater that we find in France in the late 1880's and in the following decade are essentially a restatement of the values of Mallarmé's poetics and his dramatic theory.

No single volume corresponded more closely to a symbolist manifesto than *La Littérature de tout à l'heure* of Charles Morice, published in 1889. We can see Mallarmé's influence directly at work in Morice's view of the future of the drama. The young critic takes due account of Wagner's effort at "*l'union de toutes les formes artistiques,*" but he has serious reservations concerning the dominance of music over poetry. Morice is painfully aware of the gulf separating the theater of the day from what it might become, and if he views the present-day stage as vulgar, profane, and inaccessible to the artist, his vision of the theater as "*fête suprême et synthèse de l'Art et de tous les Arts*" is fully in keeping with Mallarmé's ideal.

Subsequent theoreticians were more interested than Morice in ways in which symbolist poetics might transform the theater.

Gustave Kahn, in a programmatic essay of 1889, insisted that the theater constituted "*la grande forme d'art,*" capable of multiple and varied interpretations. His plea is for a poetic conception of the theater, in accord with "*notre tissu mélodique de phrases et la position plastique de nos pensées.*" Kahn envisions a theater of "*milieu indéfini,*" embracing pantomime and ballet, and drawing upon popular as well as literary modes of theatrical expression. Mallarmé himself would not have put it differently. Other essays of the early 1890's lent further support to the idea of a symbolist drama, a theater founded on the premise of multiple interpretations: "*que chaque mystère découvert fût l'enveloppe d'un mystère toujours plus ténébreux offert à des intuitions toujours plus pénétrantes.*" Camille Mauclair in the *Revue Indépendante* for March 1892 demanded the restoration of the poet in the theater and envisaged "*une langue magnifique où la poésie resplendira.*" Pierre Valin sought to reconcile the interrelations of the arts with the principle of *correspondances* in the theater: "*harmoniser toutes choses: décors, faits, sentiments, paroles, types, de manière à obtenir sur le public la sensation la plus correspondante à l'état d'âme de l'acteur principal.*" Particularly as a repertoire of symbolist drama began to emerge, critics, playwrights, and producers sought to give meaning and direction to the new tendencies; they did so largely by returning to the principles of dramatic expression set forth by Mallarmé. As Remy de Gourmont was to declare, "*le programme d'un drame ésotérique, tout en allusions à la vie, où les idées seraient* suggérées *et non* exprimées" represents "*la pure doctrine de Mallarmé.*"

The vigor of Mallarmé's aesthetic in the literature of the 1890's is in large measure the consequence of his role as guide and counselor to the young writers of the day. Warm, sympathetic to the point of fault, eager to help young poets learn their craft, he epitomized the idea of the poet for the writers of his time. The *Album* offered to Mallarmé by his disciples and friends in March 1897 provides in its table of contributors a list of the principal symbolist poets and playwrights in France: Claudel, Gide, Maeterlinck, Régnier, Vielé-Griffin, Rodenbach, Valéry, Verhaeren, and several others. The symbolist movement in both theory and expression was a tribute to the triumph of Mallarmé's art as the principal source of "*le goût du mystère, du vague, du délicieux imprécis*" in the new literature of the day. As early as 1887, Emile Verhaeren could state, "A cette heure, il n'est qu'un vrai maître symboliste en France: Stéphane Mallarmé." With the passage of time, Mallarmé has become even more fully identified with the symbolist movement.

If we may see the groundwork of a symbolist drama in Mallarmé's dramatic projects and especially in his theoretical writings, the existence of a symbolist drama in the theater is the result of the efforts of a younger generation of writers who were more naturally inclined toward theatrical expression than was the author of *Hérodiade*. Thibaudet has described Mallarmé's vision of the theater as enveloped in a "*nuage de possibilité.*" It required the talents of Vielé-Griffin, Van Lerberghe, Maeterlinck, Claudel, Régnier, Verhaeren, and their confreres to make the poet's ideals take on actuality. As early as 1890, Adolphe Retté could assert the existence of a symbolist drama:

> Désormais, la preuve est faite: il y a un théâtre symboliste; deux drames sont à l'actif du groupe: *Ancaeus, La Princesse Maleine*. Il s'en présentera d'autres.

And in fact, other plays were not long in coming. Paul Fort's Théâtre d'Art was established in 1890 as part of a deliberate attempt to open the way to *"une littérature dramatique symboliste."* The absorption of its impulses soon afterwards in the Théâtre de l'Oeuvre provided the new symbolist drama with a sympathetic, if restricted, public and with the practical means of working toward the transformation of the theater.

The establishment and role of Lugné-Poe's Théâtre de l'Oeuvre as the temple of symbolist drama has been ably and comprehensively described by Jacques Robichez, and repetition would be superfluous. However, it would be well for us, in passing, to keep in mind the close personal as well as theoretical relationships between Lugné-Poe and Mallarmé. The conception of the Théâtre de l'Oeuvre, its founder declared, was of a theater wherein *"l'idée reste supérieure et intacte."* Lugné-Poe's ideal of a theater *"où s'associeraient poésie et silences"* reflects his deep spiritual kinship with Mallarmé. In his concern with a décor of suggestiveness and atmospheric evocation, he shared the poet's conviction that theatrical devices should be effaced, subdued, if not entirely eliminated. The reduction of décor, absence of movement, monotonous manner of speech, and low emotional pressure, characteristic of Lugné-Poe's productions of Ibsen as well as of Maeterlinck, represent the counterpart of Mallarmé's plea for detheatricalization. In his memoirs, Lugné-Poe tells of talks with the poet, evidently in the summer of 1893, in which Mallarmé elaborated a plan for a theater of open-air performances, reminiscent of the Théâtre de Valvins. . . . The open-air theater is not merely one way in which Mallarmé sought to obliterate the restrictions of the physical stage; it points unmistakably to a return to the simple and elemental conditions of performance so as to make of the theater a lay ritual, akin to the festive ceremony of the drama of ancient Greece. It is a theater wholly in keeping with the drama of Banville or of the *Faune* "Intermède." The appeal to the imaginative powers of the director must have especially attracted Lugné-Poe. The open-air theater did not originate with the symbolists, nor was it sufficiently developed by them. Nevertheless, it provides another fine example of the bold experimental attitude of Mallarmé and his followers toward the drama.

The idea of an open-air theater was dear to Lugné-Poe. In all likelihood, it was he who directed the performance of Henri de Régnier's *La Gardienne* at Presles, at the edge of the forest of l'Isle-Adam, *"sur un théâtre naturel creusé dans la montagne."* The simplicity and purity of the outdoor theater—which Lugné-Poe studied with particular interest in the English drama of the late Middle Ages—contrast sharply with the modern stage, wherein everything conspires to destroy the *"sentiment du* mystère." Like Mallarmé, he preferred the stage empty: *"Pas de décor ou peu"*; and in this radical simplification he saw a means whereby poetry could recover its purity and centrality in dramatic performance.

Lugné-Poe hailed the reduction of theatrical artifice in the drama of Maurice Maeterlinck as a sign of *"l'éclosion d'une nouvelle forme dramatique."* In retrospect we may see the intrinsic and historical limitations of Maeterlinck's drama, and even Mallarmé did not fully share Lugné-Poe's enthusiastic appreciation. Nevertheless, on the plane of achieved dramatic composition, it is fair to assert that Maeterlinck constitutes the *"représentant quasi officiel de l'apport des Symbolistes au théâtre."* This is not the place for a detailed consideration of the scope and limits of Maeterlinck's art and its significance in the modern theater, but his relationship to Mallarmé is central to any discussion of the poet's role in the development of symbolist drama.

Maeterlinck can be described as a symbolist playwright not only because of his close personal relations with the leaders of the movement in Paris, but also because his literary aims and values are a consequence of his deep familiarity with the broad tradition of symbolist theory and expression. Not only Villiers and Mallarmé, but also Swedenborg and Novalis, Carlyle and Emerson, Poe and Baudelaire, Verlaine and Laforgue, all contributed to the formation of Maeterlinck's symbolist view of life and art. In Paris in 1886 the young Flemish lawyer came under the spell of Villiers, whose reading of the newly composed sections of *Axël* impressed him profoundly. Even at the beginning of his career, Maeterlinck declared, with mingled truth and exaggeration: "Tout ce que j'ai fait, c'est à Villiers que je le dois, à ses conversations plus qu'à ses oeuvres que j'admire beaucoup d'ailleurs." On his return to Ghent it was, no doubt, mainly due to Villiers' inspiration that Maeterlinck resolved to become a writer. Yet, in Maeterlinck's art the impact of Villiers cannot be readily distinguished from the influence of all the other contributors to the symbolist movement. With Mallarmé as with Villiers, the Belgian playwright shares a common set of attitudes and values that are themselves the fruit of a long poetic tradition. These traditional elements were translated into a dramatic technique that is in close accord with Mallarmé's vision of theatrical performance. There can be no doubt that Maeterlinck was familiar with Mallarmé's work and learned from it; nevertheless, the relationship is far more one of affinity than one of influence, and it is expressed not only in a common derivation from a pervasive symbolist heritage, but also in the immediate literary and theatrical affiliations of the young Belgian playwright.

The one-act play of Charles Van Lerberghe, *Les Flaireurs* (1889), is a landmark in the symbolist drama; its importance within the broader panorama of the modern theater has seldom been adequately appreciated. This is not the place for a detailed consideration of Van Lerberghe's powerful evocation of mystery and terror. He wrote the play, he declared, *"suivant le procédé indiqué par Poe dans la genèse d'un poème en prenant pour base l'effet de terreur d'un frappement à la porte."* The drama of suggestion and dread expectation, wherein the spiritual and material realms interact and in which the presence of death dominates the atmosphere, clearly anticipates such plays of Maeterlinck as *L'Intruse* and *Les Aveugles*. Albert Mockel hailed *Les Flaireurs* as a noteworthy innovation in the drama, a play wherein *"on écoute chanter en soi l'idéal orchestre qu'on rêve,"* fully in keeping with the dramatic ideals of Mallarmé. In his programmatic utterances Mockel pointed directly toward the plays of Maeterlinck and the rise of a symbolist drama, a drama that "would use music and poetry to create rhythmic continuity, and legendary subjects to create esthetic distance."

Maeterlinck's debt to Van Lerberghe is real, even if it was somewhat exaggerated by the author of *L'Intruse* in his early career. In a letter of 1892 attached to the program for a performance of *Les Flaireurs*, Maeterlinck leaves no doubt about Van Lerberghe's priority in technique, and he even declares that *Les Flaireurs* possesses *"une puissance de symbolisation"* that *L'Intruse* lacks. The futile attempt to appease the invisible in the face of *"l'invasion des ténèbres sans fin"* is for Maeterlinck the principal source of the theme and structure of his own plays. On the other hand, Van Lerberghe pointed out, shortly after the composition of his play, that he had made certain alterations according to suggestions of Maeterlinck. Without impugning Van Lerberghe's originality, it would seem that Maeterlinck's personal influence and the genuine rapport between the two friends make it difficult to establish any sharp separation in priority or technique in their early literary efforts.

At the time of the composition of *Les Flaireurs,* Van Lerberghe's admiration for Mallarmé was passionate and sustained. With due allowance for his later rejection of symbolist poetics, as far as the late 1880's it is accurate to hold that "Mallarmé n'eut pas de disciple plus convaincu." This fervent admiration was shared by Maeterlinck. In an entry in his *Journal* in 1889, Van Lerberghe declared that the discovery of Mallarmé constituted, for both Maeterlinck and himself, a literary revolution. . . . (pp. 101-09)

The description and elaboration of Mallarmé's ideal drama constitute a direct anticipation of the plays of Maeterlinck. Indeed, Mallarmé's reduction of narrative would make for an even more thoroughgoing static drama than we can find anywhere in Maeterlinck. The language of allusion and suggestion, dream and mystery, in drama as well as in poetry, is fundamental to Mallarmé's vision of art. This mistiness and complex atmospheric evocation are present, he insists, in popular theatrical forms as well as in more intimate and more literary dramatic compositions; Mallarmé's conception of the old popular melodrama is a striking anticipation of Maeterlinck's theater. If this theater culminates in a drama of silence or at any rate in an evocation of the interpenetration of speech and silence, this suggestiveness too is wholly in accord with symbolist poetics. In a letter to Georges Rodenbach in 1888, Mallarmé declared: "*cet art consiste, n'est-ce pas? le suprême, à ne jamais en les chantant, dépouiller des objets, subtils et regardés, du voile justement de Silence sous quoi ils nous séduisirent et transparaît maintenant le Secret de leur Significance.*" This description of the essence of poetry could also be read as an account of the language of Maeterlinck's drama and the effect of this drama on its audience. (p. 112)

All of Maeterlinck's early dramas: *La Princesse Maleine, L'Intruse, Les Aveugles,* and *Les Sept Princesses,* portray essentially passive characters subject to the overpowering pressures of hidden, mysterious forces. Space and time are narrowly confined; yet the boundaries of the plane of action are fluid rather than fixed, losing clarity and even identity in their interaction with the shadowy realm of the infinite. The narrative in Maeterlinck's first play, *La Princesse Maleine* (1889), is marked by all the violence and physically induced horror of Romantic tragedy, but the action is constantly retarded by means of repetition of words or phrases, elongation of scenes, elaboration of atmospheric effects, and other devices that serve mainly to intensify the feeling of mystery and horror. The play is built around the helplessness of pure innocence in the face of absolute evil. Maeterlinck does not wholly suspend the traditional linear plot; rather, he distends it, thereby reducing its importance. The broad symbolization of experience in the drama endeared the play to Mallarmé and his followers. Albert Mockel viewed *La Princesse Maleine* as an incarnation of "*ce théâtre où tendent nos désirs, le théâtre où parmi les magies d'éclatants ou lointains décors un acte se dresse, que l'on sait totale.*" For Mockel, as for many of Mallarmé's adherents, Maeterlinck's drama represented a conception of theater as a "*réalisation plastique d'un poème*"; a cosmic drama much as Mallarmé himself had attempted and defined: not the representation of "*une anecdote et un individu,*" but rather "*l'histoire éternelle de l'Homme.*" Maeterlinck did not wholly suppress the anecdotal and individual, but his drama moves in this direction. As we may see in other symbolist plays as well, the drama of purely individual experience is at sharp variance with the new aspiration toward infinite suggestiveness.

The interpenetration of physical and spiritual planes of existence which Maeterlinck derived from occult and symbolist tradition finds expression not only in atmospheric devices reminiscent of the Gothic, but also in strident and frenzied emotion that contrasts violently on the stage with the static dramatic action. In *Les Sept Princesses,* the intensity of feeling rises from the juxtaposition of the Queen's passion to the eery suggestiveness and silence, pointing to the presence of invisible and hostile forces. This evocation of mystery is the translation into dramatic terms of the same poetics of *correspondances* which dominates Mallarmé's vision of the theater and, indeed, all of his literary endeavors.

Mallarmé's appreciation of Maeterlinck's art was genuine and profound. In the second of two theater chronicles composed for the *National Observer* (London) in June 1893, he defined the significance of the young Belgian's drama in relation to the emerging patterns of symbolist drama in France. The new playwrights conceive of the theater as the expression of "*la scène intérieure,*" wherein "*Un ensemble versifié convie à une idéale représentation,*" a theater of dream and spirituality free from the restrictions of the actual. Maeterlinck is part of this poetic current of the modern stage. The young French poets who share Mallarmé's vision of the theater, Vielé-Griffin, Régnier, and others, have constructed their plays by providing "*par la convergence de fragments harmoniques à un centre, là même, une source de drame latente qui reflue à travers le poëme.*" Maeterlinck shares their effort to restore the theater to its larger poetic context; like the French playwrights, Maeterlinck "*inséra le théâtre au livre!*" All the same, there is an essential difference in dramatic structure: whereas the French poets have attempted a fusion of poetic and operatic values in a complex symphonic pattern, Maeterlinck has turned wholly away from the Wagnerian "*polyphonie magnifique instrumentale*" to a pattern of sequential action "*avec une expresse succession de scènes, à la Shakespeare.*" In this respect, Maeterlinck's art is far more traditional in its literary affiliations.

Nevertheless, Mallarmé does not share the easy identification of Maeterlinck and the author of *Hamlet* and *King Lear.* The young playwright's salient qualities are uniquely his own, for while Shakespeare's characters "*agissent en toute vie, tangibles, . . . corporels,*" those of Maeterlinck are vague, shadowy, phantasmagoric. The stage setting itself constitutes "*un massif arrêt de toute réalité,*" devoid of any sense of concrete or literal representation: "*on est loin, par ces fantômes, de Shakespeare.*"

This is not to say that, for Mallarmé, Maeterlinck's drama is lacking in theatrical effectiveness. The simplicity of action and the striking atmospheric evocation of mystery and dread in *Pelléas et Mélisande* constitute for Mallarmé "*une variation supérieure sur l'admirable vieux mélodrame.*" If we recall the poet's earlier dramatic projects, we may view his appraisal of the rudimentary and popular elements of Maeterlinck's art as praise, not blame. Furthermore, in speaking of "*une variation supérieure,*" Mallarmé alludes not merely to the superiority of the young playwright's dramatic technique, but to the "*essence supérieure*" of the theater itself—a spiritual evocation of the mystery of existence. Mallarmé views *Pelléas et Mélisande* as an indication of but one of many ways in which a theater "*de vision et de songes*" may find expression, and clearly it is not held forth as the sole model for other symbolist playwrights; nevertheless, there can be no doubt that for Mallarmé this play, along with Maeterlinck's earlier dramas, represents a significant achievement in the modern theater.

It is again through contrast with Wagner that this significance is made clear. In sharp opposition to the composer's subordination of poetry to music, Maeterlinck's drama dispenses with instrumentation by providing its own music: *"Silencieusement presque et abstraitement au point que dans cet art, où tout devient musique dans le sens propre, la partie d'un instrument même pensif, violon, nuirait, par inutilité."* In this sense, the atmosphere of Maeterlinck's theater of magic is suffused with music; it is a living demonstration of the power of the poet in the theater, and the *"authenticité de son intime munificence."* For Mallarmé, Maeterlinck's drama was a poetic drama in the fullest sense, *"un Drame . . . réglé par les conflits mlélodiques,"* wherein poetry constitutes its own music.

Maeterlinck's subsequent career was to justify Mallarmé's belief that suspense and dramatic tension were important elements of the art of the Belgian playwright. The increasingly overt exploitation of the resources of Romantic melodrama in Maeterlinck's later work represents a deliberate rejection of the symbolist values of his early dramatic theory and technique, but it is not in his later work that his importance resides. Mallarmé saw Maeterlinck's theater in the early 1890's as part of an attempt to restore magnificence and wonder to the stage through the evocation of inner life. In this effort, the Belgian playwright joins hands with his symbolist precursors and notably with Mallarmé, whose aesthetics of the theater he shared and embodied in his work. Within the larger framework of symbolist drama, Maeterlinck is not as lyrical as Hofmannsthal nor as intense as Yeats, but his plays served as the principal source of the diffusion of symbolist theories and techniques in the modern European theater. Maeterlinck's early work is to this day important for its exploration of new possibilities of dramatic expression. With all allowance made for the undeniable talent of the playwright, what is new in Maeterlinck is his assimilation of symbolist values within a traditional dramatic setting. His early career provides yet further proof of the rich imaginative and experimental character of the legacy of Mallarmé and his followers in the theater. (pp. 113-16)

Of all the symbolist poets and playwrights perhaps the closest to Mallarmé in dramatic conception was Henri de Régnier, whom Mallarmé singled out in the Huret *Enquête* of 1891 as the most gifted young poet of the day, *"devant qui je m'incline avec admiration."* No poet gave more lyrical expression to the values of the symbolists, the *"goût du mystérieux, du fluide, de l'incertain, la magie musicale du vocable qui donne une valeur active à la suggestion"*; it was with complete accuracy that Emile Verhaeren could describe Régnier in 1890 as *"le plus net poète symboliste qui soit en France."*

Régnier's *La Gardienne,* written in 1891 and performed at the Théâtre de l'Oeuvre in 1894, is clearly a symbolist drama. Like Maeterlinck's early plays, it is essentially the evocation of a mood rather than a depiction of a series of events, but the language is far more lyrical than the idiom of the Belgian playwright, and the removal from the actual and contemporary is even more complete. The drama consists of the return of ''Le Maître'' from the battlefield and from the life of turbulent strife to the forest and castle of his youth wherein, he declares, *"mon âme est rentrée en le lieu de ses rêves."* He turns away from the vainglory of military adventure to confront himself and his destiny, a lonely old man haunted by the pathos of a lost past, a time when he loved and was loved in return. In the shadows of the forest, as in a dream vision, the veiled figure of La Gardienne appears to admit the suppliant to the *"château de songe et de sagesse,"* wherein his soul may be-

come one with its destiny. There is no dialog, no development of character relationships, only the juxtaposition of *"l'état d'âme"* of the aged hero to the image of his beloved.

Clearly, *La Gardienne* is closer to dramatic poetry than to poetic drama. A contemporary critic claimed that the pleasure of seeing Régnier's play is closer to that derived from a concert than from a theatrical performance. If the static action and purely symbolic characterization militate against traditional notions of plot and character, the staging of Lugné-Poe's production served further to disconcert the spectators: actors concealed in the orchestra pit read the lines, while other actors silently mimed the bodily movements and gestures on the stage. According to contemporary reports, the performance was almost broken up by a riot in the theater. In retrospect, this is difficult to understand. The presentation of *La Gardienne* may have seemed strange and unusual, but the drama consists only of a brief single act and should not have taxed the patience of the audience unduly. Régnier's play illustrates some of the difficulties of applying Mallarmé's doctrines to the composition of a stage play, but the effort cannot be dismissed as futile. The rich evocation of atmosphere and suggestiveness of language were new resources in the drama of the day, and in time, they came to acquire a measure of acceptance as part of a new conception of dramatic art. It is not proper to view a symbolist lyric drama in the same way we view a full-length prose drama of realistic events. Régnier's play is an interesting example of symbolist poetic drama, in striking contrast to the anecdotal reportage of prose realism or the strident melodrama derived from Wagner and the operatic tradition. Régnier has none of the broad significance of Maeterlinck or Claudel in the modern theater; yet his plays, like many experiments of the 1890's, served to call attention to the areas of expression that had been repudiated by the great majority of nineteenth-century playwrights, but which subsequently came to be incorporated into the modern drama.

Late in life, looking back on the symbolist movement, Henri de Régnier declared, *"nous étions tous mallarmistes."* In view of Mallarmé's lifelong passion for the theater, it is surely no accident that in the 1890's virtually all of his disciples attempted to write for the stage. Mallarmé gave warm support to their efforts and to the programs of the Théâtre d'Art and Théâtre de l'Oeuvre, under whose auspices many of the young symbolists gained production for their plays. In passing, we may note Mallarmé's genuine encouragement of the dramatic efforts of Rodenbach, Francis Jammes, and Emile Verhaeren, along with many others. The failure of most of the symbolists to win popular acclaim in the theater was no failure at all in the eyes of Mallarmé, for whom drama was reserved *"au seul théâtre de nous mêmes,"* the theater of mystery and of silence, incapable of reduction to descriptive statement.

The break between Lugné-Poe and the symbolists in 1897 marked the end of a deliberate attempt to extend the premises and techniques of symbolist poetry to the theater. If the Théâtre de l'Oeuvre was largely a coterie theater, demanding an act of imaginative sympathy as well as a concern with subtleties and nuances that could only be the property of an initiated elite, it was nevertheless a means by which the new poetic dramatists could find expression. And if the state of poetic drama in recent times may be described as playwrights in search of a theater, the converse was true, at least for a time, during the early years of the Théâtre de l'Oeuvre. Lugné-Poe may have passed over some symbolist drama worthy of performance in order to champion the cause of Ibsen, whose plays he presented in symbolist style, but he also made every effort to encourage the symbolists to write for the stage. A letter of Stuart Merrill's to Gros, the manager of the Théâtre de l'Oeuvre, illustrates the plight of the new dramatic impulse: "Dites à Lugné que je trouverai prochainement le titre de mon drame; après quoi je n'aurai plus qu'à trouver le drame . . . et à l'écrire." The failure of the symbolist playwrights in France to produce a sustained body of drama undoubtedly led to the break of 1897; and with the death of Mallarmé in 1898, the group lost its center of cohesion. The subsequent dramatic efforts of the symbolists were sporadic, disconnected, and primarily individual manifestations.

We cannot say that the inadequacies of the symbolist drama in France in the 1890's resulted from a lack of playwrights. There were many playwrights who shared Mallarmé's vision of a new poetic and symbolist drama and who tried to give this vision expression in their work: Vielé-Griffin, Van Lerberghe, Maeterlinck, Claudel, Régnier, Rodenbach, Jammes, Gide, Verhaeren, Saint-Pol-Roux, and many others of very considerable talent participated in this enterprise. If orthodox critics like Sarcey roundly condemned the productions of the Théâtre de l'Oeuvre as undramatic and foreign to the stage, a more perceptive observer, Bernard Shaw, could write: "In the Théâtre de l'Oeuvre there is not merely the ordinary theatrical intention, but a vigilant artistic conscience in the diction, the stage action, and the stage picture, producing a true poetic atmosphere, and triumphing easily over shabby appointments and ridiculous incidents." In the 1890's the symbolist drama was a source of vitality and freshness amid the dreary repetitions of the theater of fashionable entertainment. The values inherent in the dramatic conceptions of Mallarmé and his followers were intrinsically important, fraught with immense consequences for the art of the stage. The failure of the symbolist drama to dominate the theater of the day should not blind us to its promise and its accomplishments. Perhaps none of the symbolist playwrights was a dramatist of genius, but many were writers of considerable talent whose work can still be viewed with interest and, at times, with animation and wonder. The existence of a symbolist drama, its achievement as well as its failure, is due in large part to the effort of the poet of *Hérodiade*. After the work of Mallarmé's followers, the symbolist example might be passionately embraced or just as violently condemned; it could not be ignored. (pp. 125-27)

Haskell M. Block, "The Vision of a New Theater" and "The Early Symbolist Drama," in his Mallarmé and the Symbolist Drama, *Wayne State University Press, 1963, pp. 83-100, 101-28.*

FRANTIŜEK DEÁK

[*Deák examines representative Symbolist dramas as staged by the Théâtre d'Art.*]

Between November 1890 and March 1892, the Théâtre d'Art staged seven productions. It was during these two years that it became associated with the symbolist poets and finally came to represent the symbolist poetic in theatre. The staging of Pierre Quillard's play *La Fille aux Mains Coupées* (*The Girl with Cut-off Hands*), the first stage production of Maurice Maeterlinck's plays *L'Intruse* (*The Intruder*) and *Les Aveugles* (*The Blind*), the recitation of poetry from the stage, and the staging of *Song of Songs*—all at the Théâtre d'Art—represent four different aspects of symbolist performance.

The Girl with Cut-off Hands, a mystery in two scenes performed on March 19th and 20th, 1891, was the first distinctly symbolist production in regard to its *mise-en-scene* and design. To a great extent it influenced the staging practices of Théâtre d'Art. The play was performed on a stage separated from the audience by a gauze scrim immediately behind the footlights. The backdrop was a canvas of shining gold, framed with red draperies. On the gold canvas, Paul Sérusier painted, in an iconic style, multicolored angels in positions of prayer. This decor was greeted with bravos by the spectators.

Quillard's text consisted of both verse and prose. The verse was declaimed by actors on stage, and the prose—which explained sentiments and gestures, and gave necessary scenic information—was spoken in monotone by the Narrator in a long blue tunic, who leaned on a lectern at one side in front of the gauze scrim.

In "The Argument of the *Mise-en-scene*" published in the program, Marcel Collière explained the double function of the text: "The dialog in verse is introduced by prose, which reveals changes of place and time, indicates characters, explains their acts, and, in so doing, leaves to the verse its essential and exclusive function: to express the soul of the characters. The steady choric prose comments on the poetic action. It relieves it of all narration, of all explanation which would hinder or weigh down its flight."

Because of the gauze scrim and soft lighting, the actors, placed against the background of the painted canvas, appeared distant and dream-like. The Daughter, the Father, the Poet-King, and the Chorus of Angels were seen almost as silhouettes. The actors moved and gestured slowly, pausing in different attitudes and stage pictures when the Narrator took over. Verse was spoken in part melodiously and part of it, notably the chorus of angels, was sung. Describing Georgette Camée, who played the Daughter, R. Le Clere wrote in *L'Art au Théâtre:* "Mlle. Camée was revealed as a perfect artist, not at all an actress. Without asserting herself too much, without looking for effects, she was satisfied to render poetic verse with numerous cadences and sonority of rhymes." The distinction between "an artist" and "an actress" indicates that Camée did not project her own personality or attempt an expressionistic style of acting. This differs from the emotionalism of romantic acting and the detailed characterization of naturalistic acting.

On May 1, 1891, Quillard published in *Révue d'Art* an article entitled "On the Absolute Uselessness of the Exact *Mise-en-scene*," which was a first attempt to define the principles of symbolist *mise-en-scene* and stage design. Quillard introduced his article with the statement: "Speech creates scenery like everything else" ("La parole crée le décor comme tout le reste"), which became a slogan for the symbolists. (Paul Fort wrote in his memoirs: "It was one of our beliefs, our gospel.") The statement "Speech creates scenery like everything else" denounces verisimilitude in staging and puts the visual and audial elements of the performance on a corresponding level. It proclaims that the contribution of speech to the creation of the spectator's inner image is equal to that of the scenic elements. Quillard elaborated on the concept: "The decor should be a very simple ornamental invention that completes the illusion of the play through analogies of colors and lines. A backdrop with a moving drapery most often will suffice in order to emphasize the infinite multiplicity of time and place. The spectator will no longer be distracted from the action by the noise of the abortive scenery and jarring props. He will give himself completely to the will of the poet and will see, according to his imagination, horrible and charming appearances and dreamlands where no one but himself penetrates. Thus, the theatre will be what it should be: *a pretext for a dream.*"

Symbolist stage design became known as "synthetic" decor. The use of the term "synthetic" in painting is associated wth Gauguin and the Nabis group of painters. Paul Sérusier spent the summer of 1888 at Pont Avon, where he discussed with Gauguin synthetic and symbolist theories. Strongly influenced by Gauguin, he began to disseminate these theories among his friends in Paris and, through his work in the theatre, brought them into stage design. R. H. Wilenski in *Modern French Painters* explained: "When he first exhibited his pictures of 1881-1887 in the Café Volpini exhibition, Gauguin described his work as 'synthetist-symbolic.' This cacaphonous label was intended to describe two aspects of his attitude which characterized his painting from 1887 for some years. By 'synthesis' Gauguin meant simply the recording of form in symbolic line and color as distinguished from the imitative procedures prescribed in realist and impressionistic doctrines.... Gauguin meant symbolist in the sense that the word was used at that time and for some time later by the French Symbolist writers and poets. He used the term, that is, to indicate that certain characters in his pictures were intended to record mental images and ideas as distinguished from visual experience."

On January 30, 1891, a note appeared in *L'Echo de Paris* about the future plans of the Théâtre d'Art: "Beginning with the month of March, the performance of Théâtre d'Art will end with a *mise-en-scene* of a painting unknown to the public or with a project of a painter of the new school. The curtain will remain up on the tableau for three minutes... scenic music and combined scents suited to the subject of the represented picture will prepare for it and then will perfect the impression. 'Scent, colors, and sound respond to each other,' said Baudelaire." Even if this project was not realized, it clearly indicates Paul Fort's interest in the new school of symbolist painting as represented by Gauguin, Bernard, Maurice Denis, Vuillard, Bonnard, and Sérusier.

The announcement of the staging of pictures also includes the first mention of the theory of correspondences in the context of the Théâtre d'Art. What the note envisages is a plotless, multi-sensory (total) performance; a concept that was realized later in the staging of *Song of Songs*.

After the publication of *La Princesse Maleine, L'Intruse (The Intruder),* and *Les Aveugles (The Blind),* Maeterlinck began to be noticed by the French press in the context of the rising interest in the Symbolist movement. Paul Fort began rehearsals of *The Intruder* in April 1891 in his apartment. Later Lugné-Poe helped with the direction. From Lugné-Poe's memoirs, it is clear that the staging of *The Intruder* was not given primary importance in the fourth program of the Théâtre d'Art and the significance of the first stage production of Maeterlinck became apparent only after the fact: "During the rehearsals Maeterlinck and his actors were treated like the poor family of the theatre. We would perform or we would not perform. They put us at the end of the evening so that in case the program was too long they could cut us off. I do not have to tell you that I did not feel at all like being cut off. Our poor *The Intruder* did not even have the honor of one rehearsal on stage. Catulle Mendès took over the stage and was busy with other plays and with his own play. We were restricted to rehearsing on the zinc roof of the Vaudeville theatre. *The Intruder* began before an indifferent audience. It woke up the drowsy theatre, was a

triumph, and the next day all Paris was talking about the astonishing and tragic Flemish author.''

Maeterlinck's second play, *The Blind,* was staged on December 11, 1891, as a part of the fifth Théâtre d'Art program. It was directed by Adolphe Retté assisted by Lugné-Poe, who also played the part of the First Blind Man. The stage was in a bluish semi-darkness, an effect which Retté achieved by putting colored glass in front of lights. Some critics complained that they could not see or hear anything as the actors spoke softly and unexpressively in this light. As Paul Fort and Retté remembered in their memoirs, the performance created a powerful impression: "At the moment when Lugné-Poe put his hand on the dead body and cried out with the strangled voice 'There is a cadaver among us,' a great shiver, followed by a thunder of applause, shook the theatre.''

The recitation of poetry as a part of the evening performance began with the third program of Théâtre d'Art when G. Camér recited Mallarmé's *Le Guignon.* From that time on, the recitation of poetry was an integral part of each program except the last one. In the fourth program, four poems were recited: Edgar Allan Poe's "The Raven" (Mallarmé's translation), Lamartine's *Le Cri de L'Ame (The Cry of the Soul),* Victor Hugo's *Le Doigt de La Femme (The Woman's Finger)* and Charles Baudelaire's *La Charogne.* In the fifth program, ancient French poetry was included: fragments of the poems *La Geste du Roi (Exploits of the King), Berthe au Grand Pied (Big-footed Bertha),* and *Rolland.* Arthur Rimbaud's *Bateau Ivre (The Drunken Boat)* was recited in the sixth program.

The recitation of poetry went beyond a simple reading. It aspired to be a poetry of theatre. The *mise-en-scene* of poems consisted of two aspects: first, each poem was recited against the background of a symbolic painting whose color and pictorial qualities were supposed to be analogous to the images and sound qualities of the poem; secondly, there was an attempt to arrive at a proper vocal-musical interpretation. In *Le Gaulois* (December 14, 1891), there is an indication of what the paintings were like for three of the fragments, *Le Geste du Roi, Berthe au Grand Pied,* and *Rolland:* "The spectators had before their eyes symbolist paintings. The first was of an orange tonality, the second violet with violet stones and gold rain, the third green with gold warriors executed in that adorably awkward style that has the character and charm of the Primitives." For the staging of Rimbaud's *Le Bateau Ivre,* the decor consisted of a four-part folding screen on which Ranson painted an underwater garden in Japanese style.

The vocal interpretation of the poem can not be ascertained. The following description of the interpretation of *Le Bateau Ivre* by Retté, who directed its staging, indicates in general terms only the tone of voice used: "It is necessary in *Bateau Ivre* to use three different tones. The first part should be recited with an authoritative tone (volume) of voice without quickening the tempo or raising the voice in excess. This should continue up to the admirable lines: 'I know how lightning splits the skies, the current raves; / I know the surf and waterspouts and evening's fall; / I've seen the dawn rise like a flock of doves; / Sometimes I've seen what men believe they can recall.' After that, the diction precipitates, the metaphors grow shorter, the images, which like rockets fall in a rain of stars, should be shouted in the full voice of a tenor almost beyond the normal range. All that up to those harrowing and sublime cries: 'It is these depthless nights that your lone sleep beguiles / A million golden birds, O Vigour not yet know?' Finally, toward the end of the poem, the cadence slows down, the voice becomes somber and takes on grave intonation. And it is almost in a completely low voice that the twilight quatrain should be recited: 'If there's a water in all Europe that I crave, / It is the cold, black pond where 'neath the scented sky / Of eve a crouching infant, sorrowfully grave, / Launches a boat as frail as a May butterfly.''

Paul Napoleon Roinard based his scenario of *Song of Songs* on eight chapters of Solomon's *Song of Songs*. The biblical text was left unchanged and Roinard, in this respect, considered himself only a translator.

Song of Songs can be looked upon as an anthology of a love lyric, a fragment of a wedding ceremony, or part of a dramatic composition. Every translation is by necessity an interpretation. Roinard in the Exegesis to the scenario wrote about his interpretation: ''. . . in the *Song of Songs* where the exquisite vicissitudes of love between the human spirit with its failures and the divine spirit with its domination are developed and resolved—in a double sense real and mystical—an awe-inspiring epithalamium lives. . . . From the formal point of view, Roinard interpreted the *Song of Songs* as a dramatic poem in which the poetic conflict of the human spirit with its failures (represented by the Wife [Queen]) and the divine spirit with its domination (represented by the Husband [King]) goes through eight stages of development: The Presentation (engagement of the King and Queen), the Dream (the King appears to the Queen in her dream), the First Trial (the King tests the Queen's fidelity), Joy (the King rewards the Queen for her fidelity), the Second Trial (the Queen hesitates and having barely failed is punished), Solitude (the King pretends to refuse the Queen and remains invisible to her), the Return (the King returns to the Queen and reveals his passion), and the Departures (the King confirms his complete confidence in the Queen and entrusts her with the government of his people).

Besides the real meaning—the development of the story of the King and Queen—Roinard describes for each stage of development the analogous mystical (suggestion of a corresponding spiritual sense) and musical meaning (transposition of the sense into the interplay of musical instruments).

Roinard's scenario is divided into eight devices and three paraphrases. Each device is composed as an exact orchestration of speech, music, color and scent. The orchestration for the first device is as follows:

> Speech: in *i* illuminated with *o* (white)
> Music: in C
> Color: pale purple
> Scent: frankincense

''Speech: in *i* illuminated with *o*'' means that the vowels *i* and *o* were stressed in the declamation of verses in the first device. The music was in the key of C. The color of the stage lighting was pale purple. And the scent, vaporized among the spectators, was that of frankincense. This orchestration also implied that the vowels *i* and *o* are, in the domain of speech, analogous to the key of C in music; in the domain of color to pale purple; and in the domain of scent of frankincense.

The second device was orchestrated as follows: ''speech in *i-e* illuminated with *o*, music in D; color: pale orange; scent: white violets.'' From this point of view, the scenario does not only evolve through eight stages of development but is also a succession of eight different sensory experiences.

Roinard's orchestration of sensory data is based on one of the most important concepts of the symbolist movement: that of the correspondences. Charles Baudelaire's sonnet *Correspondences* was a source of inspiration for symbolist poets in general and for Roinard's concept of the *Song of Songs* in particular:

> Nature is a temple whose living pillars
> Sometimes give forth indistinct words;
> In it man passes through forests of symbols
> Which watch him with familiar glances.
>
> Like long echoes which from a distance fuse
> In a dark and profound unity
> Vast as the night and as the radiance of day,
> Perfumes, colors, and sounds respond to one another.
>
> There are perfumes fresh as a child's skin,
> Sweet as oboes, green as meadows,
> And others, corrupt, rich, triumphant.
>
> Having the expansion of infinite things,
> Like amber, musk, balsam, and frankincense,
> Which sing the raptures of the spirit and the senses.

Baudelaire's poem implies, first, correspondence between the material and the spiritual world by means of symbols. This correspondence is represented in Roinard's scenario by the notation of three levels of meaning: real, mystical, and musical. The second correspondence is between the different data of sensation. This refers to the phenomenon of synesthesia—a transference from one sense to another. Expressions like ''cool or hot sound,'' ''sweet or sharp tones'' are the expressions of synesthesia in language. Baudelaire, in his article ''Richard Wagner and Tannhäuser in Paris,'' writes: ''. . . what would be really surprising would be that sound would not suggest color, that colors would not convey a melody, and that sound and color were unsuited to translating ideas, things always having been expressed by a reciprocal analogy since the day God created the world as a complex and indivisible whole.''

Baudelaire's synesthesia includes color, sound, and scent but does not deal in particular with the relationship between speech and color. It was Rimbaud who, in his famous poem *Vowels,* made the analogy between particular vowels and colors. ''*a* black, *e* white, *i* red, *u* green, *o* blue—I'll tell one day, you vowels, how you come to be and whence. . . .''

What was for Rimbaud poetic intuition, René Ghil in his *Verbal Instrumentation* attempted to put into a scientifically reasoned system. He established analogies between colors, timbre of vowels and the timbre of instruments. His correspondences were : ''*a,* black, organ; *e,* white, harp; *i,* blue, violin; *o,* red, brass; *u,* yellow, flute.'' Inspired by Baudelaire, Rimbaud and Ghil, Roinard established the sensory correspondences as they appear in the scenario of the *Song of Songs.*

The performance of *Song of Songs* was part of the fifth Théâtre d'Art program on December 11, 1891. Roinard directed the play himself. He also designed and executed the decor which, since it was rather complicated, took more than two months to complete.

The decor consisted of three drops. The first drop, just behind the footlights, was transparent gauze of metallic color. On it was painted a dark blue triangular cloud that was visible or invisible, depending on the lighting. Behind the gauze drop was a second drop on which was painted part of a temple. On the right side was a cedar tree and on the left a cypress tree; their tops met in the middle. This second drop was an empty frame through which the backdrop was visible. On this third drop, in groups of threes and fours, were twenty-one lilies, which spread fumes of incense. Roinard wrote about the decor: ''With the idea of synthesizing the atmosphere of the dream that envelops the *Song of Songs,* the composition of the decor attempts to make vivid in a simple and more condensed manner the principal symbols in which the generative ideas of the great lyric poem are revealed.''

Each element of the decor aspired to represent a different abstraction. Lebanon, which was probably portrayed by the temple on the second drop, represented saintly domination; the cedar tree, incorruptibility; the cypress tree, imperishibility. Roinard mentions as part of the decor ''. . . a climbing vine that surrounds the oriental altar of the wife.'' None of the review mentions this altar as a part of the design, but it could have been a part of the temple outline on the second drop. The arrangement of twenty-one hieratic lilies in three groups of threes and fours ''. . . represents the candlestick with seven branches, that hebraic glorification of the sacred number.''

The costumes for the production were simple, white draped clothes. The entrances and exits of characters were from right and left. They were formalized as to which character appeared from which side; critics wrote of ''a hieratic monotony of entrances and exits.'' It is possible (only one critic mentions the fact) that besides each device having its dominant color, each character was accompanied by a certain colored light that belonged to him or was representative of his mood. If this is true, the color scheme of each device would have been a combination of the dominant color of the device (which was always a pale color), plus the colors of the particular characters.

The acting style, as in previous symbolist productions, was unexpressive but stylized. The movements were simple and slow. The stage action had a dream-like quality. The metallic see-through gauze drop created the impression of looking through a stained glass window. Particular attention was given to the tonality of voice and to emphasizing certain vowels in the text according to the orchestration. The different scents were vaporized into the audience from the proscenium and balconies by hand vaporizers.

The production of the *Song of Songs* was not successful. Roinard summarized some of the reasons why: ''the curtain went up at one o'clock in the morning with few people present. The choruses sang out of tune, the music got too loud, the colored projections came out badly, scents even worse, the declamation seemed long—nothing astonishing at that hour of sleep. Only the decor got applause, which the author could benefit from only within himself because nobody knew that he was its contriver.''

''About the rest, concerning the use of colored projections everybody knows what success they subsequently gained for others.''

The use of scents was attacked and ridiculed. Roinard defended it by referring to the text of *Song of Songs,* in which different scents and aromas are often mentioned. He also argued that the use of incense in the theatre can be compared to the use of incense in ancient rituals. But the fact remained that the execution was unsuccessful. First, the scents were not vaporized evenly, and, second, there was not enough time between devices for a particular scent to disappear so as to permit the perception of the new scent.

Discouraged by technical difficulties but not willing to abandon the concept of correspondences, Roinard developed a new plan for his play *The Mirrors.* The color of the lighting and the scents for each scene would be written in the program but would not be executed on stage. He believed that just by reading

the color and scent the desired sensation would be produced in the mind of the spectator. (pp. 117-22)

František Deák, ''Symbolist Staging at the Théâtre d'Art,'' in The Drama Review, *Vol. 20, No. 3, September, 1976, pp. 117-22.*

SYMBOLIST PROSE

ALINE GORREN

[Gorren comments upon the work of three Symbolist prose writers: Maurice Barrès, Francis Poictevin, and Paul Adam.]

In a recent French work on psychology—entirely distinct, it is needless to say, in method and treatment, from the empiric German work in that line, whose severe *Konsequenz* dismisses metaphysics, and the perilous, if fascinating, leaps of the same— the last word of the science at present is summed up in the assertion that we are all evanescent expressions of an eternal unity. It is scarcely a new summing. If French modern metaphysics and psychology deny the duality of matter and spirit, and German research on the same path more cautiously admits the probability that both may be differing attributes of one substance, and all forms and phenomena the manifestations of one eternal essence; if M. Fouillée and his compeers, fresh from divings into animal magnetism, assert, with respect to our much-cherished individual identity, that ''the illusion of a definitely limited, impenetrable, and absolutely autonomous '*I*''' must be given up; that it is only with the lips we can claim it, while the immense orchestra of things will always answer ''We'' in our face; if it be borne in upon us daily, from divers sources, that continuity and reciprocity are the great law and the great mystery, and that ''nothing is so one that it is not multiple . . . nothing so mine that it is not collective''—the spontaneity with which these conclusions seem to be invested is but another proof of how many times the thoughts that express a world period to itself need to be reiterated, and in how many different keys, before the aggregated atoms composing it become fairly conscious of the currents informing their life. From the picturesque pantheism of Giordano Bruno, and the beautiful idealism of Spinoza, our present descent is clear, to trace the pedigree no farther. The line of succession seems especially lucid just now, because thirty years of science and materialism have swung the pendulum the other way; at least, we begin to think that we feel the oscillation. But the materialism itself belonged to the same philosophic inheritance that has both moulded us, and enunciated us, since the seventeenth century. The only difference was that it remained studiously incurious of that hidden cause back of all. Why inquisitiveness as to what is unknowable? Other things were knowable, and sure, and the Naturalist presently brought out his documents, details, note-books. These things ye can *see.* But the Symbolist—for we have come to him at the other edge of the oscillation—now replies: ''Your documents, details, verified facts, are precisely the least worth considering. They are appearances; impalpable shadows of clouds. Nothing ye think to see is what it seems. Nothing outside of our representation exists. All visibilities are symbols. Our business it is to find out what these symbols are. Any book that does not directly concern itself with the hints concealed beneath the diversified masks and aspects of matter is a house built out of a boy's toy-blocks. Science, after promising more things than it could fulfil, has many hypotheses just now that float about one central idea—the existence of one essence, infinite in moods, by reference to which, alone, anything whatsoever can be understood. Those of our creed, only and solely, have a philosophic basis for their art.''

One of the propounders, in prose, of the Symbolistic theories, whom it is easiest to follow; one, too, whose literary quality is the most charming, is M. Maurice Barrès. To the novel, as we have come to understand it, the books of M. Barrès bear but scant resemblance. But the author espouses the designation in default of a better. At a first glance you might suppose that M. Barrès's work was of the same order as that of Paul Bourget. But no. Maurice Barrès writes metaphysical, not psychological, novels. In *Sous l'Oeil des Barbares, Un Homme Libre, Le Jardin de Bérénice,* three books which, by logical sequence, form but one, three stages are represented in the metaphysical evolution of the mind of a young man of analytic, contemplative temper. It is a picture of a human life, the only important facts of which take place in that world of sensations and illusions that is engendered by the physical happenings of existence. The point of view is made clear to the eye, from the start, by the typographical arrangement of the chapters. Each division, in *Sous l'Oeil des Barbares,* is preceded by a concordance, in which the worldly occurrences that befall the chief personage are telegraphically despatched, without more ado. Then follows, in a prose of remarkable fluidity, suppleness, and suggestiveness, the drama, determined by these incidents, in the sphere of psychological experience. You look on as the protagonist's Ego evolves, through various passional phases, aesthetic principles, and philosophies, up to the culminant dogma of Maurice Barrès's individual creed: that the whole office of men is, first, to recognize that they are so many efforts, individually and collectively, of Instinct to realize itself—*je suis un instant d'une chose immortelle*—and secondly, to jealously guard themselves from being untrue to the voice of this Instinct. From all eternity each creature has been formed to play a certain part, to express, to represent a certain phase, a direction. Sincerity to the *Inconscient* is to be secured, in Maurice Barrès's opinion, by rejecting all things that are uncongenial to the *Moi,* and by assimilating all others that would naturally adhere to it, were it left—uninfluenced by the world and the Barbarians, the *grands barbares blancs* of Paul Verlaine, the Philistines— to take its own path. Its brief moment of serving as a representation, a symbol, over, the I returns to the bosom of the *chose immortelle;* the water-drop, after the semblance of an individual career of its own, goes back to the ocean; the monad melts into the Life. Death does not set free a number of personal souls; the fragments of the One Soul break down a temporary barrier, by the process, and pass out of a momentarily dividing sphere, formed by the illusion of identity. In Maurice Barrès's three books, the things and the people that come within the circle of the protagonist's intelligence, deformed and colored according to the transient state of his soul, pass before the reader like a succession of evanescent apparitions. In the last of the three the charm is keenest; the literary art impregnated with the rarest, the most subtle, savor. There are glimpses of a girl, a woman—who has been seen repeatedly, in varying guises, when all three books are read: a ''little animal,'' all of instinct, and exquisite in spite of—or because of?—that; affiliations, connections, between the ''suave eyes'' of Bérénice and those of gentle, long-eared young donkeys; these Bérénice loves because they have the misunderstood poetry of oppressed and despised things, of which race she is, this Bérénice, who is as the voice of the inarticulate People. . . . There are evocations (no descriptions) of landscapes: Aigues-Mortes; the

plains about it; the purple and crimson of departed sunsets, flushing the damp gleams of the marsh. . . . Certain gowns that Bérénice wears, sombre purple, burnished copper, that answer the sunsets. . . . An unforgettable Museum in a dead town of southern France, small, perfect, provincial, deserted; where a little girl—the ''little animal,'' in childhood—pores, in long, unawakened curiosities, over strange, suggestive things; where relics of early French kings vibrate, in their slow passage dustward, to the step of the custodian, strolling, in the long afternoons, with a jingle of keys, through the little rooms. . . . All this swimming in a luminous haze: the reader shut in by crepuscular indications, hauntings, that beckon to unexplored outlets. If there be a rather stifled feeling, as of a want of an open window, the aesthetic mode harmonizes the more truly with the underlying dogma. It is we who create the universe, says M. Barrès. That universe is but the harmonious *ensemble* of our own thoughts. Thus are we imprisoned in a dream-cage. And this is the impression with which he manages to charge his books.

From Maurice Barrès, and his effort to compress all nature into humanity, one may turn to Francis Poictevin, a prose-writer who has gradually enrolled himself with the Symbolist movement, but who, to express the modern tendencies, has taken an inverse course from Barrès. The analysis of metaphysical experiences, which at one time held Poictevin captive, has ceased to do so; or does so very secondarily. Essential symbols are coming to be more and more widely represented for him by cloud and sea, and the physiognomic aspects of plains, forests, and towns. These are his main lines. As he apprehends the multiform moods, sounds, sights, scents of

Arthur Rimbaud. The Granger Collection, New York.

nature, everything that we are pleased to name voiceless and inanimate, breathes forth the force of a veiled meaning, thrills with a hidden life; the nervously conscious attitudes of flowers; the sonorous orchestral harmonies of color in wood and shore; the hushed mystery of lakes and ponds, over whose waters hang the liquid iris-tints of evening skies, that ''fugitive, at once, and expectant, in their profound prolongations, hide una-vowed desires, already almost deflowered by the very exqui-siteness of their intensity, of a charm that grows poignant as it declines. . . .''

All nature is a temple, filled with living pillars, and the pillars have tongues, and speak in confused words, and man walks as through a forest of countless symbols . . . the lines of Beau-delaire, the father, in a kind, of the Symbolists, serve as an epigraph for Francis Poictevin's *Paysages.* Poictevin's men and women are subordinate to these wider curves of wave and sky; they come and go, emerging from their setting, briefly, and fading into it again; they have no personality apart from it; and, amid the world-symbols of the heavens in marshalled movement and the thousand-reeded winds, they, in their human symbol, are allowed to seem, as they are, proportionately small. They are possessed, as are clouds, waters, trees, but no more than clouds, waters, trees, of a baffling significance, forever a riddle to itself. They have bowed attitudes; the weight of the mystery they carry on their shoulders. Poictevin's literary style is of the quality to be slowly degustated, with an attention to the spiritual after-flavor. In *Paysages,* and notably in *Nou-veaux Songes,* in which his symbolist tendencies become es-pecially defined, the souls of landscapes, the elusive heart of things, reach one in an essentialized form; they have gone through high dilution first. The homeopathic compression, the endeavor that never shall there be a word too many, may weary the ordinary reader, whose head and stomach are equal to any of the chemical processes. Poictevin's appeal is to the *raffiné.*

A third writer, with whom the symbolic direction of thought takes a distinctly individual shape, is Paul Adam. His is the mystic note; a mysticism adapted, under some of its aspects, to the requirements of Parisian boulevard loungers on the threshold of the twentieth century. With infinitely less literary restraint than Barrès or Poictevin, much less an artist than either, Paul Adam has nevertheless striven, in novels and short tales, to give a body to one of the most interesting of the Symbolist ideas, that of recurrent rhythms in the affairs of men and of the universe, which rhythms art must express (modern music was the first to do it) by clusters of leading themes, running through many modalities. In ''Etre,'' a romance of the fifteenth century—a historic moment selected because it saw the trampling down of an epoch the only light of which (Dante thought it a great light) was a spiritual one, under the first magnificent brute struggle for material well-being that resulted in modern civilization—the magician, Mahaud, is a woman tormented by the desire for some such powers as to-day might be coveted by the followers of a Madame Blavatsky. In harmony with the general rhythm, however—which is the foundering of the spiritual life beneath periodic, and imperious, reversions to an insistence on the supreme rights of the flesh and the individual—Paul Adam shows this desire to be thwarted by the Countess's sensuous nature. She is a woman of knowl-edge and insight far beyond the age in which she lives; as the mistress of a great castle she attains wide ascendancy over her surroundings; she becomes a rallying centre of light in the darkness of confused times. But the struggle of contending forces is too sharp; the equilibrium is lost; the mind goes down, in ruin, in the closing night.

''The science she acquired dies with her,'' says Gustave Kahn; ''the influence she unfolded impels those who lived within its circle to start off, by opposed routes, upon the pursuit of some unknowable which they contain, yet which forever escapes them. The monks absorb themselves in ecstasy; the soldiers throw themselves into the wars; and the rhythm perceived, or initially unrolled, by the Countess Mahaud, is extinguished in death and in the elements, having made nought but victims, since, resulting in nothing (because of her own faultiness), it was only agitation.'' In ''En Décor'' (a novel of the present day, but not such a one in tone or atmosphere as contemporary novelists have rendered us familiar with), Manuel dreams that in the girl whom he loves—a simple, receptive Margaret for a new Faust—he can ''symbolize the treasure of his meta-physical being.'' Their love is the immortal symbol of the union of generative forces. ''Manuel et Louise relurent la patrie pre-mière, et s'éblouirent aux communs reflets de soleils origi-nels.'' They had ''an immense joy in recognizing each other as fraternal, after the separation of centuries, and all the dis-guises of successive individuals in which the germs of their being had slept.'' The mystico-sensuous phraseology abounds in allusions to the Arcana of the Law; the Splendor of the Mystery; the elliptic flight of the Cherubim, etc. These things may be pardoned to M. Paul Adam, who is only thirty, and who believes firmly that the coming time is to be one in which, ''disdaining the solicitation of useless pleasures, man will walk toward the science of things, the contemplation of rhythms and causes. . . .'' His work merits attention because it outlines, more clearly than elsewhere has been done, the technical modes which, M. Jean Moréas prophesies, will rule the development of the novel of the future.

First, to use the words of another adherent of the school, we shall have the mode, the technique, which subjectives, in the soul of a single personage, the orchestration of worlds. ''. . . Nothing exists outside the sensations of the hero. . . . The ele-ments in the texture of this mode are: the struggle of ideas in the same brain; and the unfolding of the natural selection that determines the order of their succession.''

We have seen what M. Maurice Barrès does in this kind. ''The second mode of the novel will study the inception, in a phil-osophic brain, of thoughts calculated to modify a number of inferior brains in its surroundings. It will follow these thoughts in the human forms where the philosophic hero has sown them; and, in the successive avatars of the personalities moved by this rhythm, it will expose the series of its growth, or the reasons for its atrophy. In its third form the novel sets upon its feet as a hero no longer a definite human being, but the scheme of an Essential Idea, that, filtering through a group of human beings, acquires, in each form which it penetrates, such measure of intensity and of development as it can there find; sometimes losing some, or all, of its force, by reason of the superior power of an opposing rhythm; sometimes specialized in souls particularly affected by a preponderant cast of sen-sations, until it renders those souls all its own. . . .'' Here we recognize the methods of Paul Adam.

To these pretexts for poems, which must circumscribe a phil-osophic or moral dogma, goes on our exponent, divers styles must adapt themselves, harmonious with the subject, the sur-roundings, the rhythm, the emblems of the human forms cho-sen. . . . Chipped phrases will be used for expressing a per-sonage continually employed in exploring his own small impressions; wide phrases, with flat tints, will denote the aspect of waste, vegetating lives—the monotony of dead plains. ''So that, in the Novel of the third manner, each personage, or each group of personages, only enters the tale accompanied by a particular *motif,* in assorted propositions; which is, or, at least, tends to be, the successor of the musical *motif* of Wagner.'' (pp. 338-42)

As to the future of Symbolism?

''You will never go to the great public,'' said one of the Naturalist celebrities to Jean Moréas. How satisfactorily to answer that objection, that an art can never move the social strata which, with so exclusive an attitude, appeals only to a mental aristocracy—is not clear. Evasively, the reply was that the Symbolists must go to the great public, in time, but, by another road. And, calmly, a Symbolist manifesto, penned by Jean Moréas, thus concluded: ''All those who have suffered the revilings of contemporaries may console themselves by meditating upon the end of a letter addressed by Alfred de Vigny to Lord . . . at the time of the first performance of his translation of Othello. In it he compares society to a large clock having three hands. One, the largest, advances so slowly that one could believe it motionless; it is the mass of men. The other, somewhat lighter and swifter of movement, progresses rapidly enough to permit the eye, with a little attention, to perceive its progress: this is the mass of enlightened men. But, above these two hands there is another, incomparably more agile, and whose bounds one follows but with difficulty; sixty times it has seen the space before it ere the second hand has progressed, and the first dragged itself, thus far. 'Never, no, never, have I looked at this third hand, this little dart, so restless, so bold, so emotional, springing forward, quivering, as it were, with the sense of its own audacity, or with the pleasure of its conquest over time—never have I looked at it without thinking that the poet has ever had—ever should have— this rapid advance march in the centuries; this advance upon the general spirit of his nation, even upon that of its most enlightened part.''' (p. 352)

> Aline Gorren, ''The French Symbolists,'' *in* Scribner's Magazine, *Vol. XIII, No. 3, March, 1893, pp. 337-52.*

BERNARD C. SWIFT

[*Swift considers the prerequisites that various critics and authors have posited for the Symbolist novel and analyzes whether or not these qualities have been realized.*]

Was there a distinctive literary genre which may appropriately be called the 'Symbolist novel'? In a sense, any art and literature may be regarded as necessarily 'symbolist', that is, symbolic of intended or supposed meanings; but this broad perspective bears only indirectly upon the enquiry into the relationship between Symbolism and the novel in late nineteenth-century French literature. (p. 776)

The general arguments against the concept of a Symbolist novel are clear. If the Symbolist novel is to be regarded as a viable genre, one might well expect it to have been manifested, during the late nineteenth century, in an unambiguous exemplar of generally agreed importance. In the absence of such a novelist, the question of the Symbolist novel has seemed to be conjectural, and at best problematic. In addition, there has been much dispute about the nature and even the distinctive existence of Symbolism itself. In the narrowest sense, now largely superseded, Symbolism has been regarded as a poetic movement of revolt in the 1880s and 1890s, associated with Moréas's manifesto

of 1886 and with various experiments in verse-form, such as those of Ghil and Kahn. Symbolism, in this local sense, embodied a desire for freedom and originality in verse, involving an emphasis upon the musicality of language and upon statement by allusion. It was a reaction against the supposed artificiality of existing verse-forms, and it coincided also with a reaction against what was felt to be the pretentiousness of literary Naturalism. In historical perspective this moment— rather than 'movement'—of Symbolism appears ephemeral, when not itself pretentious and artificial. A negative reaction slips easily into the faults it condemns. Scholars today usually adopt a broader historical perspective, regarding some great poets of the nineteenth and early twentieth centuries as the proper representatives of a Symbolist spirit, which is at once an ethic and an aesthetic. Poets who were once considered to be 'precursors' of Symbolism are now looked on as the fundamental embodiment of Symbolism, notably Verlaine, Rimbaud, and Laforgue, with Baudelaire as a fountainhead and directing influence. Mallarmé is, in a sense, a case apart, since he was at once a precursor and a contemporary of the Symbolist period viewed narrowly. In this broad perspective Valéry and Claudel are accounted Symbolist poets. It is, however, the view of literature proposed by Mallarmé which seems to coincide most nearly with the theory of Symbolism, apparently precluding the novel from the range of possible Symbolist forms. The Symbolist principles were above all musicality in poetry, a tendency to reject rhetoric (or, at least, didactic rhetoric), allusiveness of 'meaning', and a preoccupation with a variously conceived ideal or 'absolute' which stood to some extent in contradistinction to the 'reality' associated with Naturalist literature.

There have therefore been both immediate historical and broader aesthetic and philosophical reasons for the dissociation of the novel from Symbolism. Historically, Symbolism is associated with a reaction against pretensions to some mode of scientific realism in literature, itself identified, however unjustifiably, with the Naturalist novel. Symbolism, viewed as a poetic method or ethic, was concerned with the mysterious or the supposedly un-knowable; whereas Naturalism, viewed as a literary extension of positivist sciences, was concerned to promulgate or explore the unknown but the knowable. Aesthetically, the poetic theory and practice associated with Symbolism, for all their diversity and internal disparities, were directed towards the evocation of moods and relationships, often by emphasizing sensory correspondences or analogies between art-forms: this involved a reaction against a literature of exposition and argument, in favour of a literature of suggestion, in which the *entities* suggested were sometimes states of mind ('états d'âme'), sometimes a reality which was imagined to be spatially or temporally transcendent. Literature so conceived, and identified with 'poetry' in the sense of 'creation', was accompanied by the rejection of a literature which derived its interest from the revelation or explanation of character, motivations, psychological and social analysis, precise or documentary settings in space and time, and the development of plot towards dénouement—that is, common features of the nineteenth-century rhetoric of fiction. Such aesthetic considerations had a certain philosophical backing. Philosophically, a vague idealism and an emotional pessimism, given some measure of dignity and philosophical import by their association especially with German Neoplatonic thinkers, led some Symbolists to reject, in theory at least, a literature of the adventitious, of the spatially and temporally transitory, in order to seek a literature which could embody more general truths. In this perspective, the novel was regarded as a facile, bourgeois form, and some writers elevated the art of poetry into a quasi-religious cult.

This polarization is deceptive. It presupposes a strict opposition between Symbolism and Naturalism, and a belief that poetry and the novel necessarily involve mutually exclusive literary operations. The blurring of distinctions between poetry and prose during the late nineteenth century has been studied in great detail by Suzanne Bernard. Of course, the term 'prose' need not include the novel as it was commonly understood at this period. Nevertheless, textual study shows that such distinctions cannot be rigidly upheld. One of the characteristic features of the literature of the late nineteenth century was an interpenetration of fairly traditional narrative techniques and methods of literary evocation more immediately associated with poetry. When writers were acutely conscious of the demands of genre, and felt that they could exploit its virtues, the principle of genre itself was in fact brought into question. Similarly, a period concept—which is what Symbolism or Naturalism may appear to be—is not in itself restrictive. When literature is conceived as a fine art which communicates essentially through intellectualization, the conventional delimitations of genre and period are weakened. This belief that literature is an intellectual medium, irrespective of the supposed reality or ideality of its reference, seems to have been a determining feature of the French Symbolist aesthetic. In this perspective the hypothesis of the Symbolist novel emerges as a justifiable area of study. At the same time, the application of the term 'Symbolist novel' calls for careful discrimination.

For example, in his work on Elémir Bourges, André Lebois has argued most insistently for the existence of the Symbolist novel. Elémir Bourges (1852-1925) is today an almost forgotten writer who enjoyed the respect and admiration of a small number of literary adepts, many of them associated with Symbolism. A bibliophile and man of learning, he had a high and demanding sense of literary vocation, with a taste for the legendary, the dramatic and the mysterious, and a desire to incorporate into fiction an ideal of literature as a philosophic art. His main works were two novels, *Le Crépuscule des Dieux* (1884) and *Les Oiseaux s'envolent et les fleurs tombent* (1893), and an epic, *La Nef,* published in two parts in 1904 and 1922. The two novels combine idealism and pessimism, in sometimes Wagnerian settings, tracing the downfall of aristocratic characters in a nineteenth-century historical context; the epic is an ambitious work, based upon the legend of the Argonauts, rich in poetic expressivity and vision, but written with great difficulty and heavy in intellectual allegory and a sense of the derivative. Bourges himself felt that his vision was beyond his powers of literary creation. One might speculate briefly that had *La Nef* been more successful, Bourges's earlier works might have been received, subsequently, with greater interest and sympathy. In the event, however, he has fallen into almost complete obscurity, despite the efforts of a few scholars during the past twenty years or so. In particular, André Lebois set himself the hazardous task of rehabilitating Bourges, and as part of his defence of Bourges he sought to broaden the critical application of the term 'Symbolist'. It is not clear, however, that the affinities between Bourges and the Symbolists are so fundamental *aesthetically* that Bourges may be regarded as a Symbolist novelist. Lebois's purpose was to show the *tendencies* of Symbolism, as seen in the work of Bourges. Designating these tendencies as late nineteenth-century developments of Romanticism, he singled out, for example, a heightened sensibility, a sense of idealism and pessimism, an interest in the unconscious mind, and a predilection for painting and for the

transposition of the arts, together with such specific interests as Wagnerism, Medievalism, and Hinduism. Proposing the view that Symbolism is to be interpreted as a wide movement in nineteenth-century literary and artistic culture—in itself a reasonable postulate—Lebois has argued that Symbolism was manifested in the novel and that Bourges, whom he calls 'un des chefs du Symbolisme, le Mallarmé de la prose', is to be accounted a Symbolist novelist: 'on est fondé à parler d'un roman symboliste tout autant que de poèmes symbolistes ou de théâtre symboliste'. While this general hypothesis of the Symbolist novel is certainly very inviting, its illustration through Bourges must be subject to reservations. In his two main novels, *Le Crépuscule des Dieux* and *Les Oiseaux s'envolent et les fleurs tombent,* Bourges adopts techniques of characterization, motivation and plot-development which belong essentially to the nineteenth-century novel as traditionally understood. Whatever kinship there may be between themes in these novels and preoccupations found in Symbolist poetry, their particular literary techniques do not defer to the Symbolist misgivings about prose-fiction, and their literary vision does not appear to be Symbolist. As Lebois has shown, Bourges shares with some contemporaries a mysticism and erudition which, combining idealism with a taste for the recondite and the bizarre, may conveniently be labelled 'Symbolist'; but the designation 'Symbolist' must take into account the writer's vision as manifested not only through the themes or subject-matter of his work, but through the various techniques of presentation and the suppositions behind these techniques. Since Bourges's fictional techniques are on the whole traditional, relying upon the stock artifices of adventitiousness in plot and characterization, his two main novels may be regarded essentially as post-Romantic rather than Symbolist works. They are Stendhalian in their approach to contemporary history and in their use of detail to create archetypal characters and situations. They are 'idealist' through this typology, and also, no doubt, through their themes of aspiration and disillusionment. They reveal preoccupations which are *also* tendencies of Symbolism; but they do not bring the literary historian any closer to an understanding of the Symbolist novel.

K. D. Uitti has approached this problem differently. In his monograph *The Concept of Self in the Symbolist Novel,* he assumes the existence of the Symbolist novel as a genre in the 1880s and 1890s and examines the effects—in novels by Barrès, Dujardin, Gourmont, and Lorrain—of a supposedly Schopenhauerian belief in the Self as Will. In these studies, Uitti dwells particularly upon what he calls 'a typically Symbolist triple point of view' in the novel (that is the author-protagonist-reader relationship), relating it to the interior monologue technique as pioneered in Dujardin's short novel *Les Lauriers sont coupés* (1887-8). However, Uitti is concerned mainly with the ideology of the Self, rather than with the technical procedures which may also be a mark of Symbolism. He cuts across the ambiguities inherent in the term 'Symbolist', deliberately setting aside the possible distinctions between, for example, Symbolist, Idealist, Spiritualist, Psychological, and Naturist writings. For Uitti, a determining characteristic of the Symbolist novel is a preoccupation with the Self, to the relative exclusion of factors which may be deemed to belong to some mode of 'exterior' reality, and he regards the genre loosely as the novel 'at its most original in the decade 1885-1895 (or slightly later)'. Recognizing certain weaknesses in this genre—insipidness, superficial characterization, a tendency towards solipsism, a particular deformation of reality—Uitti describes the Symbolist novel, compared with that of Proust, as 'an Elizabethan dumb show put on before the great play'. This approach, which does not seek to minimize the weaknesses of late nineteenth-century non-Naturalist fiction, has much to commend it, not least its demonstration that there is room for further study of 'the fascinating problem in literary history presented by the unjustly neglected *roman symboliste*'.

The notion of a Symbolist novel was occasionally proposed in the late nineteenth century, but the terms of reference were vague and theoretical. Recently, attention has been focused on the part played by Jean Moréas and Paul Adam in experimentation with a possibly Symbolist novel. In his study of Jean Moréas, Robert A. Jouanny discusses the general problems of the Symbolist novel, with particular reference to two works written in collaboration by Moréas and Adam, *Les Demoiselles Goubert, moeurs de Paris* and *Le Thé chez Miranda,* concluding that, on the whole, both works were failures. They are difficult to assess, partly because they were the products of collaboration; certainly they have attracted little attention amongst scholars, except as idiosyncratic documents in literary history, illustrating an attempt to evoke sensations and to elicit conjecture. Conjecture is inherent in a Symbolist aesthetic of suggestion rather than statement. 'Sensation', which is so vague as an aesthetic criterion, may involve an amalgam of literary and transpositional effects which is not uniquely Symbolist. Jouanny suggests tentatively that there is some analogy between the appeal to sensation in *Le Thé chez Miranda* and the general premiss of the literary-artistic theory of Teodor de Wyzewa, which states that sensation—rather ill-defined—is the basis of all aesthetic perception.

Wyzewa's theories are indeed an essential point of reference, particularly if the hypothesis of the Symbolist novel is to be related to the theory and practice of Symbolist writers in the narrower sense, rather than being only a *post hoc* investigation carried out in the perspective of later literary experiments. Bearing in mind the uncertainties of definition, both of Symbolism and of the novel, Wyzewa's reflections on the novel may be regarded as the closest approach to a developed theory of the Symbolist novel. His theories have been studied notably by his daughter, Isabelle de Wyzewska, and by Elga Liverman Duval, Paul Delsemme, and Nicola di Girolamo. Very briefly, Wyzewa proposed a theory of synthesis in the arts, imagining an application of supposedly Wagnerian or Mallarméan principles in a novel of the future. Wyzewa envisaged synthesis, a common preoccupation amongst Symbolist writers, as a combination of artistic appeals to sensation, notion and emotion. For Wyzewa, sensation corresponded initially to plastic arts and painting, notion corresponded to the intellectual art of literature, and emotion was elicited by music; certain works would appeal to a combination of these perceptions. Feeling that in the French novel no attempt had been made to produce this synthesis, Wyzewa proposed a theory of the novel designed to combine these appeals. He rejected the absolutism of Naturalist theory and advocated a non-partisan approach to literature, so avoiding, incidentally, the apparently limiting designation 'Symbolist novel'. His vision of the novel of the future involved a dovetailing of genres. This novel would evoke a single central character, the source of all the perceptions. There would be a restricted time-limit on the fictional duration of this evocation. The notional life of the character should be accompanied by an evocation of emotions, by means of interlarded poetic passages, poetry and music being virtually equated. Finally, Wyzewa recommended very cautiously that the writer should try to render hitherto unknown, that is personally original, perceptions by means of neologism—though he affirmed that neologism could in fact operate only if the standard language from which it would be a deviation were fixed and fully understood.

While this theory has many shortcomings, it raises issues which are central to the Symbolist aesthetic. The premises on which the theory is based (sensation/notion/emotion) are unclear, and the resulting division of aesthetic appeals seems to be too rigid. Wyzewa was of course establishing these categories of perception precisely in order to suggest that they are interdependent. His theory does not resolve the apparent conflict between a poetic evocation of states of mind, or of transcendent awareness, and the requirements of traditional fiction with its emphasis upon characterization and plot, and with the fragmentation and arbitrariness which often accompany them. It does, however, attempt to offset this supposed weakness in the novel form by restricting the duration and the point of view, and it also defers to the contemporary Symbolist aesthetic of replacing inferred visual stimulus by auditory suggestion. At the same time, it corrects the implication that literature may appeal by sound alone, by retaining a firm basis in immediately intelligible, that is notional, meaning. Above all, it recognizes that literature is essentially an intellectual communication, in which words are a medium of abstraction. This view weakens, but does not entirely contradict, the belief that it is a function of literature to communicate *a*-literary truths. While acknowledging that words refer back, so to speak, to some anterior truth or facts in 'external' reality, it supposes also—and perhaps more importantly—a subsequent effect in the reader, indissociable from the formulation itself. This attitude towards language has something in common with recent developments in linguistics, and more immediately it is fundamental to the aesthetic associated with Mallarmé and Valéry, and to subsequent reflections on the work of literature as artefact or monad. It presupposes a change of emphasis in one's conception of literature as an art of persuasion, and it has the special virtue of distinguishing Symbolism from the earlier Romanticism, isolating as it does immediate literary vision from intermediate literary themes. The emphasis is towards creating mood in the reader, together with speculation concerning meaning itself. It is sometimes held that it is a purpose of Symbolist writing to suggest archetypal or even essential truth, but an epistemological function does not appear to be a necessary distinguishing mark of the Symbolist aesthetic. When literature is viewed as an abstract medium, the anterior referent is of reduced importance, whether it is a tangible object, personal belief or generalized sentiment. It is evident that in such considerations problems of literary genre are relatively unimportant, and that Wyzewa's theory of uniting the genres in a successive form may be regarded as a feature of the Symbolist aesthetic.

It is not certain that the hypothetical Symbolist novel envisaged by Wyzewa was actually written, but the general principle of the single-character novel leads to literary and ideological problems which are of great interest. Wyzewa's apologists have suggested that Dujardin's *Les Lauriers sont coupés* (1887-8) and Barrès's *Sous l'oeil des barbares* (1888) may derive from the theory, but there is no conclusive evidence, and in each of these novels there are marked departures from the principles formulated by Wyzewa. The parallel with *Les lauriers sont coupés* has also suggested a tentative analogy with James Joyce's *Ulysses* and with the general aesthetic of the inner monologue, and indeed the fictional technique of point of view and the various associated techniques correspond to the emphasis upon subjectivism in Symbolist writings. 'Subjective' literature may court the danger of solipsism, or at least of a sometimes effete self-questioning, but one of its main strengths is that it accepts the principles that individual experience is limited and that both perceptions and knowledge are necessarily relative. The principle of relativism in literary communication seems to underly the Symbolist aesthetic. While it is found occasionally as a literary theme, associated with social disenchantment, philosophical pessimism, and the search for intellectual and emotional novelty, it is present fundamentally in the point-of-view technique and in the linguistic-literary medium itself. Even a belief in mysterious aspects of the universe or of the consciousness, and in transcendent and human *correspondances,* may be held to postulate the relativity of experience. It is far from certain that the Symbolists as a whole, and by definition, must have believed in the reality of some suprahuman truth, akin to the Platonic Idea, which might somehow be *suggested* by the poetry of allusion. It is true that the mystic vision of Paul Claudel, for example, depends upon a subjective awareness of cosmic unity, but far from reducing the importance of the finite and the transitory, it involves a recognition that individual perceptions are necessarily partial and relative, and that creation itself consists of constant renewal. Mallarmé's position I believe to be ambiguous, for his ideal of an absolute of beauty seems to have been indissociable from what one may call the temptation of nihilism. Be that as it may, the more general Symbolist search for novelty in literature, which provoked such great enthusiasm, is interesting today, less for any passing novelty which it may have produced, than precisely because it was a search, a spirit of questioning which was inherent in the desire to refuse received ideas. The vitality of this principle of dissatisfaction persists. The critical spirit and, in literary terms, the sense of irony are amongst the most enduring features of French Symbolism. The fictional point-of-view technique is a most appropriate medium for the expression of this ironic sense, and it is here that studies of the prose-fiction composed under the impact of Symbolism may help to focus attention more clearly upon the scepticism which, perhaps paradoxically, often characterizes the Symbolist ethic.

This matter could be illustrated through many writers, of greater or lesser importance, though it must be borne in mind that, as a technique, point of view was not exploited sytematically until the twentieth century. Notable contributors to the prose-fiction of Symbolism include Villiers de l'Isle-Adam, Paul Adam, Remy de Gourmont, and André Gide. Other writers should also be taken into account, including some whose mysticism may appear to be incompatible with moral scepticism. In this perspective, it is the early work of Gide which offers a particularly interesting insight into the general problem, illustrating an uneasy combination of belief and disbelief, and at the same time providing an invaluable source of documentation, complex and relatively authoritative, on this aspect of the Symbolist experience.

Until fairly recently Gide's earliest works had received relatively little attention from scholars, who on the whole regarded them as an immature and transitory phase of his literary creation. Although Gide's early works—from *Les Cahiers d'André Walter* (1891) to *Paludes* (1895)—are rather immature, they are of interest in documenting some Symbolist preoccupations, and they have intrinsic value as works of the imagination and as a basis for the more general study of Gide. In this last respect, it may be shown that far from being merely symptomatic of a 'Symbolist' period of *attente* preceding Gide's supposed new departure with *Les Nourritures terrestres* (1897), these works embody already the themes and often the techniques with which Gide was to continue experimenting in his subsequent fiction. Reacting against the pretentiousness associated with some

Symbolist writings, including his own, he retained a fundamental concern for an ideal literature of intellectual immediacy, while remaining aware of the limitations of prose-fiction as a means of communication. In particular the irony of Gide's later fiction is already discernible in his earliest works, including *Les Cahiers d'André Walter* and *Le Traité du Narcisse* (1891). This continuity in Gide's work illustrates further the complexity and elusiveness of his mind and enhances the interest of his Symbolist works themselves. He emerges as probably the single most important exponent of the tenuous genre, the Symbolist novel.

After completing *Les Cahiers d'André Walter,* Gide wrote that he hoped he might himself become *the* Symbolist novelist. Indeed, in the *Cahiers* he had outlined a theory of the novel which may appropriately be called 'Symbolist', but which Gide, with characteristic circumspection, relegated to a long footnote in the text, so distancing himself as author from the theoretical speculation. Nevertheless his theoretical propositions deserve attention: in some respects they are reminiscent of Wyzewa's theory, though there is no evidence of filiation. Briefly, Gide proposed a single-character novel, of indeterminate spatial and temporal setting. It would draw its expressivity from the evocation, by a lyrical or musical prose-form, of a single passion, itself the product of an internal conflict in the protagonist. Gide supposed that this would be a novel of the essential, demonstrating the character's mind with a mathematical precision. In its emphasis upon the evocation of a single character, Gide's theory is similar to that of Wyzewa, for both writers sensed the importance of respecting fictional consistency if the novel were to be both essentialist and *vraisemblable.* The indeterminate time-scale proposed by Gide may seem at first sight to conflict with Wyzewa's suggestion that the duration of the novel should be severely restricted, but both theorists seem in fact to have been pursuing, by different means, a similar general intention. This intention was to create an impression of completeness in the evocation of the protagonist, while recognizing that the novel is necessarily an arbitrary, limiting medium. Gide's idea that the demonstration in the novel should be conducted with mathematical rigour is apparently at odds with the Symbolist taste for multiple meanings in literature; at the same time Gide sought to offset this by lyricism of form. Further, he toyed with the idea of modifying spelling in order to catch novelty of meaning—an uncertain procedure which he quickly rejected, and which recalls Wyzewa's tentative remarks about neologism.

Les Cahiers d'André Walter reflect some of these preoccupations, though the work cannot be said exactly to illustrate the theory. In other early works Gide experimented with aspects of the theory. In *La Tentative amoureuse* (1893) for example, he showed his mistrust of simple *récit* and some sense of the importance of point-of-view techniques and of the role of the narrator. He also relied fairly extensively upon the equation *paysage = état d'âme,* especially in the rather heavy allegory of *Le Voyage d'Urien* (1893). This literary device, now associated with the idea of objective correlative, is a mark of literary Symbolism, and in Gide's early literary vision it suggests the complexity of the interrelationship between his sensory and his intellectual or emotional life. This technique was a most appropriate means of rendering Gide's personal spiritual conflict. It is also striking that his spiritual anguish of the early 1890s should have been accompanied by his uncertainty about literary means and ends, manifested in his simultaneous respect for and disaffection from Symbolism, and in the variety of fictional forms which he adopted in *Les Cahiers d'André Wal-*

ter, *Le Traité du Narcisse, La Tentative amoureuse, Le Voyage d'Urien,* and *Paludes. Paludes* is a particularly interesting experiment, satirizing certain literary affectations then associated with Symbolism, but deferring to Symbolist misgivings about prose-fiction. This group of works as a whole illustrates the enthusiasm which a Symbolist approach to fiction aroused in Gide, together with his impatience at the arbitrariness of traditional fiction. Gide viewed fiction as an intellectual manifestation of experience, and, in part, the originality of Symbolism lay precisely in its emphasis upon this intellectual quality.

In this respect the cerebral literature of the late nineteenth century may appear to be virtually indistinguishable from literary Symbolism. For example, the characters whom we associate with the literature of decadence and of *fin-de-siècle* aestheticism—characters such as Huysmans's Des Esseintes or Villiers de l'Isle Adam's Axël—appear to be symptomatic of some of the tendencies of Symbolism itself: living in relative isolation from society, cultivating in the main solitary intellectual pleasures, refining their tastes and their perceptions, they tend to live a life of private cerebration, often bordering on solipsism. However, the example of Elémir Bourges shows that cerebralism as a literary theme is not in itself a determining characteristic of Symbolism. The same holds for themes of idealism and mysticism. By the same token, the effete, scarcely corporeal heroines associated with Symbolist fiction seem to be incidental to the main impetus of Symbolism in extended fiction. There are, of course, dangers in close literary definitions, which perhaps serve best as an incentive to general reflections on literature and as provisional guides in the evaluation of individual works; however, one may affirm at least that the literary techniques adopted in the evocation of cerebralism or of *états d'âme* help to illuminate the specifically literary Symbolist vision. Prose-fiction tends to become Symbolist, rather than, for example, cerebral or simply escapist, when its aim is less an attempted transposition or evocation of a non-literary reality, than the communication of an intrinsically literary vision. This represents a change in emphasis rather than in subject-matter. However, in such works, a literary referent may replace such 'physical' referents as imitative characterization, or social and geographical setting. This tendency of Symbolist literature is most striking in the literary work *about* the same or an equivalent literary work and its conception. It is present, for example, in much of Mallarmé's poetry, and in such novels as Gourmont's *Sixtine* and Gide's *Paludes.* The literary act becomes its own subject-matter; in this sense the work is hermetic, and for this reason its intellectual and literary qualities are indistinguishable.

This perspective upon literature, in some ways inward-turned, and no doubt imperfectly assimilated by many writers of the late nineteenth century, has had a determining effect upon much twentieth-century fiction. While the hypothesis of the Symbolist novel must be based initially on the aims of Symbolist writers in the late nineteenth century—and there is ample evidence to justify further investigation of this period—it is conceivable that the apparently *post*-Symbolist experimental novel of the twentieth century may eventually come to be regarded as the mature manifestation of Symbolism in prose-fiction. The scepticism with which the concept of the Symbolist novel has hitherto been treated may be accounted for, at least in part, by the very success of twentieth-century experimental fiction, which has helped to draw interest away from these earlier experiments. In many ways, the work of Proust is the embodiment of Symbolist principles of fiction, especially for its psychological subjectivism, its combination of aspiration and pessi-

mism, its sense of varieties of temporal perception, and its final attempt to justify experience through literary creation, inviting the reader to participate immediately in the process of creation itself. Equivalent analogies may be found in the work of James Joyce, and, similarly, stream-of-consciousness writers such as Faulkner and Virginia Woolf developed an aesthetic which is reminiscent of the Symbolist insistence that literature is the immediate expression of states of mind. More recent developments in France, such as the aesthetic of *a*-literature and some experiments by novelists of the 1950s and 1960s, classed loosely and deceptively as the 'New Novel', were in some ways anticipated during the late nineteenth century. The essential common feature is an effort to evolve a new form of realism, supposedly distinct from social and scientific realism, with the emphasis taken away from description or plot in themselves, and redirected towards the creation of mood in a central consciousness, whose perceptions, however minute, are subject to doubt, and whose reality is entirely dependent upon the reader's re-creation. It may be that this effort is based upon the truism that a fictional character has no existence outside the reader's mind, but it does raise questions which have taxed some of the more stimulating writers and theorists of the past hundred years or so: it supposes that *fiction* may be genuine creation, and not simply a somehow reflected reproduction, and that this creation is an essentially literary communication. It is perhaps not surprising that authors, such as Marguerite Duras, whose gifts may not be entirely literary have tended to turn towards the cinema as an alternative medium of fictional communication, but some basic preoccupations in common with those of the Symbolists remain: notably, that *meaning* is a variable, dependent upon both creator and recipient, and therefore that the role of the narrator is all-important, that the notion of consecutive, temporal plot is an unreliable guide to reality, and that character itself may be ultimately indeterminate. Underlying these considerations is the postulation that knowledge is relative. The belief in the relativity of knowledge, commonly found in Symbolist fiction in the late nineteenth century, has become a central preoccupation of the twentieth-century artist-mind. It is a preoccupation which may well unite the original creator of fiction with the original scientific researcher, for both are concerned to question the frames of reference with which we ordinarily limit our concepts of reality. The hypothesis of the Symbolist novel, even when considered within fairly narrow historical limitations, has a place of some importance, not only in the history of literature, but in the history of ideas. This is not to suggest that the Symbolist prose-writers of the late nineteenth century exercised any direct influence on the later writers; rather it is much more likely that the ideas and prestige of the poets, and especially of Mallarmé and Valéry, played some part in encouraging twentieth-century novelists in their experiments. (pp. 776-87)

Bernard C. Swift, "The Hypothesis of the French Symbolist Novel," in The Modern Language Review, *Vol. 68, No. 4, October, 1973, pp. 776-87.*

THE DECLINE AND INFLUENCE OF FRENCH SYMBOLISM

CHARLES CHADWICK

[*Chadwick discusses the influence of Symbolism on twentieth-century authors of various nationalities.*]

Symbolism . . . is limited to a small number of outstanding French poets from about 1850 to about 1920 all of whom had a number of aims in common. But certain particular aspects of Symbolism, to the exclusion of other aspects, were taken up by lesser poets and by writers in other fields and in other countries so that Symbolism had extensive repercussions in one way or another, although the writers concerned may perhaps more properly be said to have been influenced by Symbolism rather than to have been true Symbolists. . . .

The technical innovations of Symbolism, for example, held a particular fascination for authors such as Gustave Kahn, the great advocate of the use of free verse in the closing years of the nineteenth century in France, and René Ghil, founder of the 'école instrumentiste', who pushed to extremes the Symbolists' ideas on musicality and on the importance of the sheer sound of words. Others were attracted more by the anti-reality side of Symbolism, such as Jules Laforgue who, in the half-dozen years before his death in 1887 at the early age of twenty-seven, looked sardonically at human life, barely concealing his despair at man's inability to bring about any change. Others again, influenced by the pessimistic and morbid nature of the later poems in Baudelaire's *Fleurs du Mal,* turned away from reality only to plunge into a horrifying nightmare world. This is the case with Isidore Ducasse, better known under his pseudonym of Lautréamont, who published as early as 1868 and 1869 his *Chants de Maldoror,* a long unfinished prose poem where the unreality of the content is matched by the originality of the form.

The largest and most important category of writers, however, turned away from reality with an optimistic attitude and set about creating their ideal world. The theatre, in particular, seemed to lend itself to this idealist side of Symbolism. Mallarmé, at an early stage in his career in about 1865 had attempted two unusual verse dramas, *L'Après-midi d'un Faune* and *Hérodiade,* both of which are entirely divorced from reality and create a strange atmosphere of mystery and hallucination, while at the same time Wagner was recreating in his operas the mysterious world of medieval legend. Wagner's enormous influence in France in the last quarter of the nineteenth century, particularly with the founding, in 1885, of the *Revue Wagnérienne,* allied to that of Mallarmé, did much to encourage dramatists to abandon realism in the theatre and to create in their plays a sense of mystery, using poetic language and unrealistic settings. Three of the most notable of these dramatists were Villiers de l'Isle Adam, with his plays *Elën, Morgane* and *Axël,* whose titles alone suffice to indicate their strong Wagnerian influence, Maurice Maeterlinck, with such plays as *La Princesse Maleine, Les Aveugles* and *Pelléas et Mélisande* which, as one critic has put it, 'portray essentially passive characters subject to the overpowering pressures of hidden, mysterious forces', and Paul Claudel, most of whose plays were written in the early years of the twentieth century although it was not until the 1940s that his epic dramas such as *Partage de Midi* and *Le Soulier de Satin,* concerned with the great Christian issues of sin and redemption, were finally staged.

The idealist side of Symbolism can be discerned in the novel as well as in the theatre. Villiers de l'Isle Adam, for example, in *L'Eve future,* looked forward to a new paradise, much as he had done in his play *Axël* that has been mentioned above, and the hero of J. K. Huysmans's novel *A Rebours,* published in 1884, lives in an exotic artificial world of jewels and perfumes not unlike the one of which Baudelaire had dreamed. But Huysmans was converted to Catholicism in the closing years of the century and his longing for another world took a course parallel to that taken by Claudel in works such as *La Cathédrale,* a fervent evocation of Chartres cathedral and of the joys of a life devoted to the service of Christianity.

The greatest novelist in whom the influence of Symbolism can be detected, and in its purest form (although the concept of a Symbolist novel is not one which has ever made any great headway among literary historians), is, however, Marcel Proust who, from 1913 to 1922, wrote his long and basically autobiographical novel, *A la Recherche du Temps Perdu* which, as the title suggests, aims at penetrating behind reality in search of an ideal world. . . . [True] reality for him springs from a fusion of the present and the past. Just as Jeanne Duval's hair awakens in Baudelaire memories of his trip to the tropics and just as this fusion of a past memory with present reality creates for him 'l'oasis où je rêve', so Proust tastes the little cake called a 'madeleine' he had tasted as a child and all the memories of his early days in Illiers, the small market town near Chartres which he calls Combray in his novel, come flooding back to him, purified and crystallized by the passage of time; or he steps on an uneven paving stone, similar to one he had stepped on in Venice many years before, and those forgotten and even unnoticed days suddenly come to life for him. 'Je dis: une fleur!', Mallarmé had said, 'et, hors de l'oubli où ma voix relègue aucun contour . . . se lève . . . l'absente de tous bouquets'; similarly, from behind the vast panorama of Parisian society that Proust depicts in *A la Recherche du Temps Perdu* emerges a new and fascinating world peopled by men situated, as the final words of the novel put it, not in space but in time.

The desire to escape from reality was, however, already taking another form during the years when Proust was slowly and elaborately composing *A la Recherche du Temps Perdu.* A number of writers led by André Breton had perceived within Symbolism a conflict between the impatient genius of Arthur Rimbaud, advocating that the poet should allow his thoughts to develop uncontrolled, and the patient genius of Mallarmé and his disciple Valéry, giving a vitally important rôle to the controlling power of the intellect over inspiration. Breton and his followers preferred Rimbaud's approach, which had also been that of Lautréamont, and these two Symbolists became the fountainheads of the Surrealist movement which, from about 1920, became the new rallying point for those who wished to penetrate beyond reality. But Surrealism is clearly distinguishable from Symbolism not only by the emphasis it lays on means rather than ends, on the use of irrational methods rather than on the nature of the super-reality thus attained, but also by its attachment to painting instead of music as having particularly close links with literature, since painting clearly lends itself far more readily to the practice of the kind of principles on which Surrealism was based.

While Symbolism was thus being modified and transformed within the frontiers of its country of origin, it was making its impact outside France. Among English writers, or, to be more accurate, writers in English, the idealist side of Symbolism made a particular appeal to W. B. Yeats who, from his early twenties was interested in the occult and in the world of Irish legend. Although his knowledge of French was slight, he acknowledged his debt to Villiers de l'Isle Adam's *Axël* and he must have known of the other French Symbolists through his friend Arthur Symons whose book, *The Symbolist Movement in Literature,* published in 1899 [see excerpt above], names Yeats as their principal heir. Yeats's imagery, of course, whether it belongs to his world of Celtic twilight or to the complex philosophical system he elaborated as a result of his interest in the occult, is very much of his own devising, but *Sailing to Byzantium,* for example, can nevertheless be said to belong to the same kind of poetry as Baudelaire's *Le Voyage,* Rimbaud's *Le Bateau Ivre,* and Mallarmé's *Un Coup de Dés* in that all these works, through an accumulation of powerful images, create an impression of the spiritual goal each poet is seeking even when the origin and meaning of the symbols used is not fully understood.

On the other hand the Imagist group of English and American poets, led by T. E. Hulme and Ezra Pound, who invented the term in 1912, were attracted by the tendency of Baudelaire and Laforgue in particular to dwell on the grimmer aspects of reality. The images of the Imagists are not, therefore, symbols in the sense that this term has been defined in the first chapter of the present study, but simply metaphors and similes which were made deliberately original and startling so as to shock the reader. But although the Imagists might therefore be said to be almost anti-Symbolist in that they are too concerned with the outward, concrete image to the neglect of any abstract idea or emotion lying behind it, this is not true of one of their number, T. S. Eliot, who joined the group in 1915 but who soon came to use such images as 'the yellow fog that rubs its back upon the window panes' and 'the burnt-out ends of smoky days' not simply for the sake of making his descriptions more powerful, but so as to convey and create a mood, in the manner of Baudelaire. One might in fact say of Eliot what he himself said of Baudelaire—that his importance lay 'not merely in the use of the imagery of the sordid life of a great metropolis, but in the elevation of such imagery to the first intensity—presenting it as it is and yet making it represent something much more than itself'. Like Baudelaire too, or like the later Baudelaire, he is not only a human Symbolist who evokes the emotion behind the image, he is also a transcendental Symbolist of a pessimistic bent who sees life for the most part as a waste land, a 'correspondance de l'enfer' rather than a 'correspondance du ciel'. But the positive side of transcendental Symbolism, the optimistic belief in the creation of an ideal world through the medium of poetry, seems to have made no appeal to Eliot and it may be for this reason that, as he once said to Francis Scarfe (see the latter's essay in Graham Martin's *Eliot in Perspective*), he was 'not particularly interested in Rimbaud' and never appears to have appreciated the achievement of Mallarmé. He found himself much nearer in spirit to Baudelaire, once the latter had sunk from 'l'idéal' to 'le spleen', and just as Baudelaire, in the last years of his life after the second edition of *Les Fleurs du Mal* in 1861, seemed to be moving more and more towards a religious rather than a poetic solution to his despondency at the world around him, so Eliot, after his adoption of Anglo-Catholicism in 1927, seems to have found in Christianity a counter to his pessimism.

But if Eliot followed the example of Baudelaire in dwelling on the sordid side of life as the 'objective correlative' of his pessimism, it was the example of a far less important poet, Jules Laforgue, vastly overrated by Eliot and his fellow Imagists, which led him to express this view of life in a form very different from Baudelaire's measured alexandrines and rhetorical style. For not only was Laforgue's pessimism tinged with a sardonic note, as has been mentioned above, which made a particular appeal to Eliot, but he also adopted Gustave Kahn's free verse techniques which were an eminently suitable vehicle for sudden changes of tone, and Eliot transposed these techniques into English with telling effect.

German literature, as well as English literature, was influenced by French Symbolism and it is the two outstanding poets of the early part of the twentieth century, Rainer Maria Rilke and Stefan George, in whom this influence can most clearly be seen. Rilke acknowledged the debt he owed to Paul Valéry, whose *Cimetière marin* he translated and whose influence left its mark in particular on his final and finest works, published in 1923, the *Duino Elegies* and the *Sonnets to Orpheus*. But, more generally, Rilke is cast very much in the Symbolist mould by virtue of his constant search for a greater reality behind and beyond the surface of experience and by virtue of his use, in the *Elegies*, of *vers libre*, well fitted, as C. M. Bowra puts it, 'to express the subtle and sinuous movements of a soul communing with itself'. George too was dedicated to the pursuit of a spiritual life and was deeply impressed by Mallarmé whom he met during the time he spent in Paris in the last decade of the nineteenth century. But his life ran curiously parallel to that of Verlaine rather than Mallarmé in his obsession with an almost Rimbaud-like figure, Maximin, whom he idolized and idealized as the symbol of a new heroic age, the coming of which he heralded in such quasi-mystical poetry as *The Seventh Ring* published in 1907, some three years after the premature death of its hero.

The influence of Symbolism extended beyond Germany to Russia where a number of writers in the 1890s and in the early years of the twentieth century enthusiastically adopted the ideas of the French Symbolists. Some leaned towards human Symbolism, such as Bryusov who wrote in 1894 that 'the Symbolist tries to arouse in the reader by the melody of his verse a particular mood', while others were transcendental Symbolists, such as Volynsky who wrote in 1900 that 'Symbolism is the fusion of the phenomenal and divine worlds in artistic representation' and Bely who stated in 1906 that 'a symbol is the integument of a Platonic Idea.' (pp. 52-8)

[If] poetry in France in the last half of the nineteenth century had not led the way in the use of outward symbols to convey unexplained emotions and ideas, and if it had not shaken off, more vigorously than Romanticism had done half a century earlier, all the old conventions as regards literary forms, then later poets, playwrights and novelists in other countries might have lacked the courage and the confidence to open up their new paths. It may well be in fact that the effects of Symbolism have not yet ceased to reverberate and that the strangely real yet unreal world of so many works of literature written at the present day, the way in which they try to create an emotional state rather than to put across an intellectual message, and the unconventional forms which they so often take will be seen, in future years, to be indebted in no small measure to the Symbolist poetry of late-nineteenth-century France. (pp. 58-9)

> *Charles Chadwick, "The Repercussions of Symbolism," in his* Symbolism, Methuen & Co. Ltd., 1971, *pp. 52-9.*

JEAN PIERROT

[*Pierrot examines the factors that contributed to the eclipse of Symbolism and also assesses the influence of the Symbolist movement on French writers of the twentieth century.*]

The disappearance of the symbolist movement has been commented upon and analyzed many times by critics who have studied that movement. In Guy Michaud's view, for instance, symbolism itself crumbled away in a very short space of time and gave way to a multitude of minor rival currents, while the decadent trends that had marked its origins reappeared with renewed force in the work of writers such as Gourmont, Schwob, Montesquiou, and Pierre Louys. William Kenneth Cornell also deals with this swift eclipse in the last chapter of his *The Symbolist Movement*. Similarly, in his thesis, *"La Crise des valeurs symbolistes,"* Michel Décaudin has undertaken a detailed analysis of the development of the symbolist movement in poetry, as revealed in the principal magazines and the attitudes adopted in verse collections published during the last years of the century, and shown very clearly how, in France, that movement did in fact continue, but adopted a very different position from that which had prevailed at its outset. Thus although most poets continued to proclaim themselves symbolists during these years, symbolism itself, as an active movement, was clearly dead, as critics of the time acknowledged again and again.

These conclusions are confirmed, moreover, by the evidence of creative writers working at that time, or slightly later, who despite having frequently been active participants in the movement, nevertheless accepted that it had now ceased to exist. The feeling, around the year 1900, that a literary era had come to an end was widespread among writers themselves. Décaudin quotes the statement made by the critic René Doumic, for example, in an article published by the *Revue des Deux Mondes* on 15 July 1900: "The Symbolist School thus appears as a school that has fulfilled its task and had its day." Similarly, in a contemporary article on *Le Symbolisme en France,* reprinted in his collection *L'Art en silence* of 1902, Camille Mauclair both issues the movement's death certificate and also attempts to provide a first summing up of its achievements. With reference to the ideal around which the principal avant-garde writers had grouped themselves, he wrote that "one can regard their movement as having terminated of its own accord". In the next few years other writers were to attempt similar accounts of the movement's achievements, with varying degrees of lucidity and self-congratulation, as for example Gustave Kahn, in *Symbolistes et Décadents* published in 1902, or Retté in his *Le Symbolisme: anecdotes et souvenirs* of 1903.

The observations made by these critics with regard to the history of the purely poetic movement can also be applied, in fact, to the general esthetic ideal and world vision that had characterized literary circles of that time as a whole. . . . One can go even further, and say that what was collapsing in those final years of the century was less the particular conception of poetry itself than, much more generally, the whole conception of the world and the state of mind that had until that point pervaded the literary world in general. For one does not have to look very hard to perceive that the main technical advances made by symbolist poetry were never in any way challenged during the next few years. One may even say, in fact, that it was during these ensuing years that they achieved definitive acceptance and a widespread influence on the French poetic movement as a whole. Thus poetry became definitively dissociated from those "impure" elements, in the sense Valéry gives that word, constituted by the expression of ideas, decorative description, or the narration of events, all things henceforth relegated, and justifiably so, to the realm of prose. It was this period, too, that saw the clear affirmation, so important for modern poetry, of the distinction between poetry and the use of verse. The same is also true with regard to the great importance henceforth granted, in the poetic use of language, to the musical value of words. One might even say that the symbolist poetic ideal, conceived and progressively clarified during the last two decades of the nineteenth century, but il-

lustrated during those years solely by poets who are today viewed mostly as minor writers, was to reach its true flowering only in the next century, with the work of writers such as Claudel and Valéry, to whom Guy Michaud devotes the final chapters of his book.

What did disappear from view once and for all with the end of the nineteenth century, however, was the entire decadent vision of the world. This vision, as we have seen, was characterized by specific traits: fundamental rejection of the world and a reality regarded as intolerable by man in general and the artist in particular; fundamental pessimism deriving from the conviction that the sum of suffering in human existence is always far in excess of possible happiness; negation, in consequence, of the reality of this despised world and affirmation of an idealism that took a variety of forms—philosophical idealism, subjectivism and solipsism, or mysticism and occultism; resolve on the artist's part to escape reality by all possible means, by creating his own paradise in one way or another, and by resorting to various methods of evasion—refinement of sensations, even taken as far as hallucination, dreams and drugs, exotic imagery and poetic reconstruction of vanished civilizations; rejection of nature in all its forms—natural landscapes, human nature—and a corresponding celebration of artificiality, pursued with the aid of drugs, the artificial aspects of modern life, or sexual perversions; last, a refusal by the artist to participate in the political or social life of his time, in the name of an artistic purity that practical considerations could only sully.

Now these particular traits were to be progressively contested, disparaged, and even condemned in an increasingly radical way, even before the end of the century, by a countermovement whose growing impetus during the 1890s can to some extent be gauged, and which has been largely isolated and identified already thanks to Décaudin's analyses of the developments within the poetic movement. Early signs of it had in fact already begun to appear as early as 1893-95. The phenomenon is particularly noticeable at the level of the refusal to take part in political action, which during these years received a first setback in favor of anarchist agitation, in which a number of writers did in fact become involved. Similarly, as early as 1893 we find a writer like Hugues Rebell contributing an article to *L'Ermitage* in which he attacks certain aspects of the symbolist movement: stylistic complications, horror of the natural, insincerity, abuse of mythological erudition, and legendary embellishments. The following year, 1894, Retté himself, who in his *Thulé des brumes* of 1891 had taken escape to its furthest limits, moved to the country near Lagny, and the resultant contact with nature was to lead him to a total reversal of his previous position: his poetry from that point on was to be directed toward a pantheist celebration of nature and an enthusiastic endorsement of life, as for example in his collection *La Forêt bruissante* of 1896. Simultaneously, he was also to launch a campaign against Mallarmé, whom he viewed as a symbol of the dead end into which literature had been led by the symbolist esthetic. After a first article in January 1895, there came a whole series of pieces, published throughout 1896 in *La Plume* and later in book form under the title *Aspects,* in which he continued his unremitting attack on the decadent vision of the world and his denunciation of Mallarmé's influence. There were also a number of other symptoms of a general reaction against the symbolist esthetic in poetic circles at this time, and Décaudin has shown: development of nonsymbolist poetic themes and sentiments in a series of provincial magazines, particularly in the south of France; the influence of

Belgian poetry via the works of Verhaeren and Max Elskamp. After 1896 this movement began to acquire considerable momentum, partly as a result of Retté's conversion, partly because of the new trend in poetry constituted by naturism, and partly because a new poetic generation had begun to emerge with works such as Francis Jammes's *De l'Angélus de l'aube à l'angélus du soir,* Paul Fort's collection of *Ballades,* and, of course, Gide's *Les Nourritures terrestres.*

The decline of symbolism, and of the esthetic upon which fin-de-siècle literature had been based, became precipitous during the last two years of the century. This decline is to be explained, in particular, by the deaths of a number of artists, those whose influence in the movement had in fact been greatest, or whose work had been most representative of it. Verlaine died in 1896. 1898 brought the deaths of Mallarmé and Rodenbach as well as those of Gustave Moreau, Puvis de Chavannes, and Aubrey Beardsley. Moreover, in the space of a few years, and for varying reasons, a number of the movement's most important writers left the Parisian literary scene for good. Huysmans, for example, after his conversion in 1894, chronicled in his *En route* of the following year, was to detach himself increasingly from literature; he ceased to frequent literary circles, and after *La Cathédrale,* published in 1898, withdrew into total silence. Gourmont, totally disfigured by the lupus that attacked him in 1891, was to lead an increasingly isolated existence, even though he continued to play an essential role on the *Mercure de France.* Schwob, whose health had always been delicate, underwent a series of operations in 1895 that failed to restore him to health and forced him to lead the life of a recluse from then on. Mauclair had contracted a chest ailment, and left Paris at the end of the century for a long stay in Marseilles, reflected in his *L'Ennemie des rêves,* and from that time continued to live either in the Midi or at Saint-Leu-la-Forêt outside Paris. In 1901, Lorrain, whose excesses, particularly his use of ether, had gradually undermined his health, likewise took up permanent residence in the Midi before his early death in 1906. Thus, in the space of a few years, the literary establishment was deprived in one way or another of a number of those who had been the avant-garde's most representative writers during the previous few years, those who had given decadent literature its distinctive tone. Finally, it should be noted that 1899 brought the final closure of the Théâtre de l'Oeuvre, which meant the end of symbolist theater. Moreover, as a consequence of Zola's famous article in *L'Aurore* of 13 January 1898, that year and the next were to witness a rising tide of unrest linked with the campaign for a review of the Dreyfus case. As the whole of French society split into two camps, so its writers were to be drawn increasingly to take sides in this ideological battle, and to repudiate their splendid isolation of previous decades, while one branch of literature, in the work of writers such as Barrès and Maurras, was to concern itself with the open expression of nationalist opinions. The disintegration of the movement was to continue through the first years of the new century with the gradual disappearance of most of the periodicals that had guided and sustained literary life during the previous decade. Very soon, the *Mercure de France* was the only remaining survivor of those original publications.

What is apparent, in fact, in all these developments, is a fundamental questioning of all the principles that had inspired the decadent mentality. First and foremost, the previous generation was sharply criticized for having shut itself away in an unreal dream world. That is certainly the meaning that emerges, for example, from Mauclair's two novels *Le Soleil des morts* and *L'Ennemie des rêves,* published in 1898 and 1899. In the first,

a poet named Callixte Armel, who is plainly Mallarmé, himself admits the failure of his life's ideal and the literary dead end into which his esthetic has led him. The second tells the story of Maxime Hersant, a decadent poet living in Bruges who, under the influence of a good woman's love, agrees to return to nature, to reality and joy, by going to live in Marseilles. Mauclair openly uses this plot to declare his disengagement from recent literary fashions. In particular, he denounces the excessive use of imaginary elements, which had become "a means of turning one's back on real life, of avoiding its chores, of reducing the duties it imposes." "It had become a drug," he continues, "a hashish creating the paradise of those who had lost heart." He no longer regards dreams as anything other than "an element of moral decomposition." In more general terms, he expressed a blistering contempt for the attitude of Parisian intellectuals:

> All of them claimed to put their faith in dreams, but none of them truly wrote about them. In their minds it was a sort of murky, undefined principle; their eyes, when they talked about it, became vague. . . . Glittering above reality, Dreams, the Idea, heralded glowing, artificial dawns that never broke, displayed countries to which there was no access. All the verbose fragments left over from a high-school-level metaphysical education were concentrated in those sonorous terms. . . . Dream was just the old romantic principle, melancholy, aristocratism, the pessimism of the Werthers and the Renés of this world.

It was not only the cult of the dream that was denounced, but also the predilection for artificiality, the cultivation of everything rare, the exaggerated refinements of sensation that led eventually to a chimerical universe wholly unrelated to life. In his *Essai sur le naturisme* of 1896, we find the principal theoretician of the naturist trend, Maurice Le Blond, launching an attack on the two writers who had been the principal masters of the decadent generation, Baudelaire and Gautier, who, he writes "scarcely succeeded in doing anything but send the contemporary soul on a wild goose chase in search of an ideal of appearances and exceptions." In a chapter headed "Artificial Literature," he also blames them for having directed literature toward the abnormal and the pathological:

> Baudelaire, impotent and neuropathic, and not unaware of the fact either, was an extremely baneful ancestor of our artificial litterateurs. It is an honor he can claim to share with Théophile Gautier and the Goncourts. The morbid, the odd, the abnormal, all attracted him. He was a wonderful art critic, a passionate analyst of complicated emotions, but he understood nothing about nature. . . . He was thus the first to initiate our avid minds into sterilizing pleasures.

Similarly, in the preface to *L'Ennemie des rêves,* Mauclair attacks "the unconsious vanity of professional writers and decadents of today, their flimsy and factitious vision of existence." In his account of the sudden crisis which leads Maxime Hersant to desert the decadent ideal, he writes: "He had a sudden intuition that those people who were rejecting everyday life, seeking out the rare and abnormal at any price, scorning to take any active role in their times, exhausting themselves with endless analysis and narcissism, were doomed to intellectual death." For the decadent writer was now being criticized not only for having shut himself away in a lofty ivory tower but also, by rejecting life and reality, for having reached a dead end of solipsism and narcissism. Thus Retté condemns "the frenzied solitudes in which poets indulge their sterile ecstasies''; Le Blond, attacking Barrès, accuses him of having ''devoted himself in silence to the delicious pastime of analysis''; and Mauclair attacks the cult of the self, which he now regards as a ''moral narcotic.'' Referring to recent poets, he also writes that ''they must learn first not to analyze themselves so much, and to concern themselves enormously with others.'' In 1896, in the preface to his collection of articles *La Crise morale*, the young Maurice Pujo also singles out solipsism as one of the causes of that crisis:

> In another phase of the crisis, the man disappointed by the external world and the inevitability of its facts renounces all attempts at acting upon that world, attempts to live inside himself, in the palaces constructed by his own imagination. But that is to feed off one's own heart. The source of dreams, if never replenished or fed by any real act, gradually dries up, along with the life of the man who has given himself up to them. Ludwig II of Bavaria sank into madness and death.

Going even further, and motivated by the violent anticlericalism he professed at this time, Retté denounced in *Aspects* not only the influence of Schopenhauer, whom he described as an ''insidious blackguard'', but also the various forms assumed by the religious unease of the period, and attacked ''those still being poisoned by Christianity in the bastard form of a suspect spiritualism''. Equally opposed to all forms of mysticism, he addressed his readers in these terms, for example:

> Do you not realize that Christianity, in its final reincarnation, the mystical rottenness exemplified all around us, constitutes one of the major determining factors of the morbid state of mind you are fighting against? I do not think myself mistaken when I suggest that most of the sado-Christian writers of today must have received a clerical upbringing. Brought into contact with followers of Science, bruised by an environment impervious to their incitements, angered by the hostility of healthy minds, they lose themselves in the most convoluted systems and the most senseless aberrations.

Reacting against the dangerous deviation constituted in their eyes by the decadent state of mind, writers were now beginning to pin their hopes to a new vision of the world characterized by a return to action. (pp. 238-44)

Whereas the decadents, setting dream and life against each other, had decided to turn their backs on the latter and abandon themselves wholly to a universe of dreams, the next generation, inverting this attitude, proclaimed its new love of life from the rooftops. The word life, usually given the benefit of a capital letter, recurs constantly in the poems, manifestoes, novels, or essays that appeared at this time, and may justifiably be regarded in its turn as the key word of postdecadent literature. Michel Décaudin has clearly shown the gradual progress of this rehabilitation of life in the poetry of the time. He points out, for example, the development in Belgian literature, beginning in 1894, of a ''poetry wholly imbued with freshness and a confidence in life.'' He also notes that Vielé-Griffin, in an article published in the October 1895 number of the *Mercure de France*, saw ''the glorification of life'' or ''the worship of life'' as the common ground shared by most recently published poetry. Even the titles of two collections published at this time are revealing: Vielé-Griffin's own *La Clarté de la vie* (''The clarity of life'') of 1897, and Max Elskamp's *La Louange de la vie* (''The praise of life'') of 1898. And one of Maurice Pujo's articles in his collection of essays *La Crise morale* was actually headed ''The Return to Life.'' Mauclair, in *L'Ennemie*

des rêves, wrote in similar vein of ''a definitive acceptance of life on the ruins of false heavens built from dreams'' and his central character, summarizing the author's own conversion, proclaims: ''I fled the factitious glow of the sun of the dead to seek the natural light of life''.

This ''life'' that such authors were attempting to rediscover, understand, and appreciate again meant, in the first place, daily life, a familiar everyday existence, contact with things and people, as opposed to the abstraction and intellectualism in which the decadent generation had delighted. It also meant, however, a renewal of contact with the life of the people, ordinary people, peasants, workers, or craftsmen, in reaction to the aristocratic individualism of the decadent heroes such as Huysmans's Des Esseintes or Gourmont's d'Entragues. In his *Trésor des humbles* of 1896, Maeterlinck had expressed the wisdom and the mystery concealed by even the most humble existence, the greatness and solemnity that can lie behind the most ordinary activities of everyday life. In the magazine *L'Enclos*, which was published from 1895 until 1898 and in which social and humanitarian concerns were openly and forcefully expressed, we find an assertion of the will to ''mingle with the people and with Nature, the principles of all art.'' The work of Saint-Georges de Bouhélier, Décaudin observes, ''celebrates, not without some grandiloquence, the magnificence

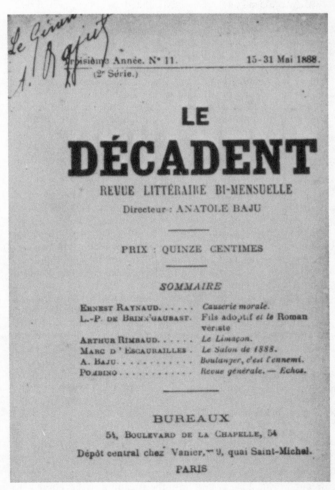

Le décadent, *a fortnightly literary review, edited by Anatole Baju, 15-31 May 1888.*

of everyday actions . . . exalts 'village folk' and 'craftsmen.' '' Maurice Le Blond, too, was to emphasize the greatness inherent, for any clear-sighted artist, in the work of craftsmen: ''Here is a craftsman, his attitude and his function, the landscape that surrounds him, the air that caresses and illuminates him, all that makes him sublime'' (*Essai sur le naturisme*). And he contrasted the abstractions and allegories that had weighed down so many symbolist works with the sight of ''that little Mouquette who presents to any passerby, so ingenuously, the double dawn of her young buttocks.'' He likewise appreciated the rehabilitation of physical health and the life of the flesh to be found in Verhaeren's *Les Flamandes:* ''Since we are so weary of those delusive settings full of wilting and anemic roses, emotional complications, and cerebral sadism, let us love *Les Flamandes* .. and feel our spirits lift among these fleshly Edens, these red idylls, these joys that may perhaps be coarse but are also wild, untamed, with a soothing and unstinting healthiness.'' In other words, the fin-de-siècle neurosis was over, and it was time to convalesce, to take the road back to both physical and moral health. (pp. 247-48)

This return to action and this celebration of energy were soon to raise the problem of the relation between writers and political life. At the outset, both symbolists and decadents had advocated and adopted an attitude of total detachment with regard to the public life of their day. Many influences had contributed to the formation of this attitude: the ancient doctrine of art for art's sake, revived by Gautier; Baudelaire's denunciation of any collusion between poetry and politics; Flaubert's contempt for electoral intrigues expressed in his play *Le Candidat* of 1875; and Renan's skepticism. Although writers had on the whole been in favor of the formation of the Third Republic, they continued to regard the new political establishment with exactly the same contempt they had expressed for officeholders under the Second Empire. Moreover, the savage repression of the Commune had made it quite clear that the price exacted from intellectuals for meddling in public affairs could be a very high one indeed.

The decadent ideology prevalent between 1880 and 1890 could only encourage this total noncommitment on the part of writers. After all, it was a generally accepted fact at the time that the defeat of 1870 had tolled the knell on French national greatness for many long years to come, perhaps forever. Since France, as a human collectivity, was by now enfeebled beyond recovery by the very refinement of its civilization, and therefore doomed to ineluctable decline, any attempt to engage in political activity would have been quite futile. It was this background of general disintegration that was viewed as precisely the precondition for the flowering of vigorous artistic individualities and daring and original works of art. The artist's contempt for the average man, generally referred to as bourgeois or philistine, not only obliged him to turn in upon himself, to cultivate his inner garden and live in a world preserved for works of art; it also made it impossible for him to engage in anything so vulgar and devoid of interest as public debate. The writer viewed himself as belonging to an intellectual aristocracy that had everything to lose by mingling with the mob. Barbey d'Aurevilly's carefully cultivated dandyism and Villiers de l'Isle-Adam's pride in his ancestry inclined them both to follow the same path. Moreover, the very fact that naturalism had advocated a much wider social spread in the novel drove its opponents, as a reaction, to depict only elite circles and exceptional people. It is hardly surprising, therefore, that the works of the period's two most representative writers, Mallarmé in the case of symbolism, and Huysmans in that of

decadence, should be almost wholly without political reference. As for Bourget, in his dialogue *Science et poésie* . . . we find him condemning the progressive equalization of wealth as ''a bad condition for the flowering of certain rare plants,'' denouncing the establishment of democracy as the triumph of mediocrity ''simply because it leads, in politics, to the imbecile sovereignty of the greatest number; in education, to a fruitless dispersal of knowlege; and in economics, to a fruitless dispersal of wealth.''

The following decade, on the contrary, was to see a perceptible change in the attitudes and behavior of writers as a whole. In its first stage, this new interest in action became apparent in the varying degrees of support that writers expressed for the anarchist movement. Between 1890 and 1894, there was a wave of anarchist agitation, beginning with demonstrations during the May Day celebrations of 1890 and 1891, then leading to a series of anarchist attacks—that by Vaillant in the Chambre des Députés in December 1893, that by Emile Henry in the Gare Saint-Lazare in February 1894, and lastly the assassination of Sadi Carnot in June 1894. These in turn led to stern repressive measures, such as the ''*lois scélérates*'' in December 1893, the arrests of January 1894, the executions of Vaillant and Casério, and the trial of the Thirty in August. And during those years an appreciable number of writers belonging to symbolist circles plainly expressed their sympathy with the anarchist movement. As early as 1890 this trend is to be found expressed in the contributions of Paul Adam, Bernard Lazare, and Pierre Quillard to the *Entretiens politiques et littéraires*, the first number of which appeared in April of that year. The following year, Fénéon, Verhaeren, Mirbeua, Mauclair, and Paul Adam all contributed to *L'En Dehors,* the paper founded by Zo d'Axa. In 1893, *La Plume* devoted its May number to a series of articles on the philosophy of anarchy, and from that point on expressed an increasing sympathy with the movement. Lastly, in 1894 Retté was arrested and imprisoned along with a number of other sympathizers or militants, and the same fate befell Fénéon, who was to be one of the accused in the trial of the Thirty, and on whose behalf many writers intervened. (pp. 251-53)

Thus, with this simultaneous return to nature, to life, to action, and to political commitment, it certainly appears that the entire world view on which the decadent esthetic had been based was crumbling away. Yet it would be illusory to believe that, once the nineteenth century had ended, the intense ferment of ideas, curiosity, and experiment in the imaginative domain that characterized the decadent period vanished without leaving any repercussions. The decadent imagination, despite a number of transformations, lived on in fact to the middle of the twentieth century, together with its interest in imagination's most anarchic forms, such as the dream, as well as its predilection for the artificial and the supernatural. It would not be impossible to demonstrate, for example, that in many ways, and despite the clear differences that distinguish them, the surrealist imagination took over and continued the imaginative heritage left by the decadents. Of course, the surrealists were vociferous in their claim to be original, and attempted to give their contemporaries the impression that the movement they were inaugurating represented a radical innovation in the history of French literature. This impression was strengthened by the connection they claimed with the Freudian theory of the unconscious, and the literary consequences they felt they had derived from it: automatic writing; the violent style of their statements; the showmanship of their demonstrations; their refusal to be merely men of letters; and their determination to establish a new conception of life in general that would lead to a simultaneous flowering of love, liberty, and revolution. Further, by nominating Lautréamont and Rimbaud as their precursors, in other words writers whose influence remained minimal during the period of decadence and symbolism, they appeared to be disposing at a stroke of all French literature between 1875 and 1914: in their eyes it was as though between those two great forebears and themselves no work of any importance had seen the light of day, apart from a few references to Apollinaire and Jarry, then later to Raymond Roussel and a few others, such as Saint-Pol-Roux. The silence they maintained with regard to the prose writers of the decadent period could give the impression that they knew nothing of them, or regarded their work as null and void. It is probable, however, that the surrealists were not as ignorant of those writers as their silence might lead one to think, even apart from the fact that the silence was sometimes broken.

We know, for example, that André Breton admitted on several occasions to an admiration for Huysmans. There is the famous passage in *Nadja* in which he confesses his sympathy for both the ideas and the personality of the author of *Là-bas*. Similarly, the preface to *Le Revolver à cheveux blancs* contains an allusion to the first dream of *En rade*. And *Les Vases communicants*, too, contains a laudatory mention of Huysmans's work. This sympathy was confirmed, moreover, by Aragon, who in an article for *Les Lettres françaises* in 1967, reminiscing about his first meeting with Breton in September 1917, tells how they discovered a shared admiration for Mallarmé, Rimbaud, and Jarry, and how Breton also talked to him about Huysmans and Francis Poictevin. It is also known that Breton felt a lifelong fascination for that other great master of the decadent imagination, Gustave Moreau, whose depiction of Dalila he describes at considerable length, for instance, in *Les Vases communicants*. Similarly, Michel Leiris has acknowledged the early influence exerted on him, particularly with regard to the genesis of *Aurora*, by Marcel Schwob's *Le Livre de Monelle*, and also, via Schwob, by the work of De Quincey. The scarcity of documentary evidence presently available, particularly of reminiscences by surrealist writers relating to the intensity of such decadent influences, means that it is probably still too early to elucidate this phenomenon completely. It remains probable, nonetheless, that such an influence was considerable in the movement's early years.

To describe and analyze in any detailed way the gradual transition, over the thirty years from 1895 to 1925, from the imaginative world of decadence to that of surrealism, to isolate the links and affinities that exist between them, would require a whole further book to itself, and certainly goes beyond the aims of this conclusion. However, I should like to sketch a number of guidelines that will indicate the general character of this development. First, it would be possible to demonstrate the continuity of imaginative preoccupations and supernatural themes in the period from the end of symbolism to the outbreak of war in 1914, by investigating the activity of a certain number of personalities, literary groups, or literary trends that form successive links in this history of imaginative life. One would have to begin by taking into account the works of Jarry and Fargue, two writers who, having belonged to the last symbolist generation, that which began to emerge in about 1895, were to remain active beyond the beginning of the twentieth century. In the case of Jarry, who died prematurely in 1907, his prose work, after *Les Jours et les nuits* of 1897 and *Les Gestes et opinions du docteur Faustroll*, written in 1898 and published posthumously, continued after 1900 with, most notably, *Mes-*

saline and *Le Surmâle,* which undoubtedly constitute important events in the history of the French novel's imaginative evolution. Moreover, the influence he exerted on surrealist writers, and the high regard in which they held his work, is known. With Fargue, who remained active for much longer, and whose work was exclusively poetic up till the 1914 war—his *Poèmes* of 1911 being a distillation of his previous work—we find at this period a predilection for both modernity and dreams that was to bear fruit later in a number of prose works. Also of major importance historically was the role played by Apollinaire and his friends, first with the *Festin d'Esope* of 1903-4, then the *Soirées de Paris* of 1912. Similar imaginative preoccupations are also apparent at this time among the group of writers that emerged from the magazine *Méditerranée,* who first came together in Marseilles in 1895 under the leadership of Edmond Jaloux, then reformed again later, after 1905, in the salon of Gilbert de Voisins. The latter had moreover published a fairy-tale novel the year before entitled *Pour l'amour du laurier.* Finally, one would need to take into account the activity and works of a number of Belgian writers, such as Jean de Bosschère and Franz Hellens. The first published a fantasy called *Béale-Gryne* in 1909 that may be regarded as representative of imaginative developments at the time. As for Hellens, in his series of novels and stories published between 1906 and 1925—*En Ville morte* of 1906, *Le Hors-le-vent* of 1909, *Les Clartés latentes* of 1912, *Nocturnal* of 1919, and *Mélusine* of 1920—he achieved a most original fusion of dream and reality.

It is possible to discern an extension of this imaginative trend in numerous narrative works published between 1920 and 1930. These include *Anicet* by Aragon (1921), *L'Autruche aux yeux clos* (1924) and *Ariane* (1925) by Georges Ribemont-Dessaignes, *Deuil pour deuil* (1924) and *La Liberté ou l'amour!* (1927) by Desnos, the large number of stories written at this same period by Benjamin Péret, in particular *Au 125 du boulevard Saint-Germain* (1923), *Il était une boulangère* (1925), *Et les seins mouraient* (1928), and lastly *Le Point cardinal* (1927) and *Aurora* (1927-28) by Michel Leiris. The majority of these works employ wildly complicated plots, derived partly from the gothic novel and partly from the contemporary novelette serial, to tell the story of the hero's quest for a woman who is at the same time a magical figure and also, quite often, unattainable. The quest moves in an atmosphere of fantasy, improbability and continual slapstick through a varied series of settings, but with a high incidence of locations in modern day Paris, locations often transfigured by dream and fantasy.

The prime characteristic of all these works is a new treatment of their imaginary content. We find that fantasy, the free play of imagination, is gradually moving closer and closer to reality. For an imaginative content cut off from life, elaborated in a world different from that of reality, a universe of legend, these writers are gradually substituting a fusion between the imaginary and the real, between dream and life, which was to lead to the surrealist type of fantasy in which the strange and wonderful can appear at the very heart of the most familiar and humdrum reality. As early as 1901, in an article in the *Mercure de France,* the critic André Beaunier was already claiming to have observed just such a development in poetry; the role of the symbolist poet, he wrote, consists in "reconstituting in the modern mind a faculty that has been lost: the sense of mystery," and in restoring to the reading public its "faculty of wonder." In other words, for Beaunier the use of symbols in poetry was essentially a means of revealing the mystery concealed in the most everyday realities:

The separation between the knowable and the unknowable is a convenient process useful in facilitating certain lines of enquiry, because human thought
proceeds analytically. But it should be clearly understood that the distinction is no more than a provisory
abstraction. For mystery is not external to the real,
it is within it. The unknowable is not in juxtaposition
to the knowable, it impregnates it. And, to use Littré's
comparison, what one should say is not that the dark
ocean batters the shores of the tranquil island, but
rather that the whole island is impregnated with the
ocean's mists. Mystery is not simply something beyond observed facts, mystery is at the very heart of
the most rigorous experimental results.

This mystery that André Beaunier, employing an abstract and
spiritualist language, was inciting his readers to perceive at the
very heart of day to day experience was, as most critics who
have studied this period acknowledge, the selfsame mystery
that an increasing number of contemporary poets and prose
writers were also attempting to reveal in their different ways.
Marcel Raymond, for instance, in his now classic work, with
reference to such poets writes of ''a reconciliation between the
real and the imaginary.'' They were encouraged, he adds, ''to
perceive strangeness, fantasy, mystery, in reality itself.'' And
it was Raymond again who observed, in the same work, with
reference to Apollinaire, that ''it is from things themselves,
from events, that the wonder should well up.'' And of André
Salmon, whose collection *Féeries* appeared in 1907, he wrote:

> André Salmon has successfully forestalled the work
> of time, the transfiguration brought about by mem-
> ory, and conjured up elements of poetry or wonder,
> like so many ultraviolet or infrared rays, in the most
> historical present. And this wonder is not that of the
> old poets. It lies at the heart of the world.

In a similar vein, referring to the work of Jean de Bosschère,
Suzanne Bernard was to write of ''a search for mystery and
wonder not in unreal legends but in life itself,'' while Décaudin
observes that ''Béâle-Gryne moves wonderstruck through a
world where the real is constantly transfigured.'' In 1911,
commenting on the recent work of Franz Hellens, Edmond
Picard speaks of ''the birth of a new talent in which the fantastic
and the real are sometimes in balance, sometimes at odds, as
in certain Flemish primitives, without either element's ever
succeeding in subjugating the other.''

These few critical comments on some of the poetry or novels
published in the first fifteen years of the twentieth century
suggest two observations. First, during those years a fundamental change had taken place in the state of mind of writers
generally. Imperceptibly but ineluctably, the barrier that previous generations believed to exist between the universe and
human consciousness, between reality and dream, was beginning to disappear. Far from trying to escape from life and
reality, these writers see them as the essential nourishment of
man's imagination. Thus the contempt for reality that characterized earlier generations was succeeded by the discovery
of new dimensions within that reality. What has become important is to know how to reveal the wonder, the unexpected,
the poetry, that lies hidden behind the superficial or banal
appearances of our familiar world. The second observation is
that the apparent isolation of the surrealist experiment from
earlier literary trends is largely a distortion and an optical
illusion. Far from being an isolated and aberrant phenomenon,
the surrealist conception of the inherent magic of the world
undoubtedly constitutes the last phase of a long and constantly

evolving trend whose roots . . . reach back as far as the height
of the romantic era. (pp. 255-60)

Thus, at the end of this long journey that has led us to contemplate the historical development of various forms adopted
by the literary imagination in France, from the romantic era to
the dawn of our present century, we find every incitement to
regard surrealism as the end result, as far as the imaginative
level is concerned, of a long and continuous development.
There is little doubt that the writers who claimed allegiance to
that movement did everything within their power to exaggerate
their originality, both in relation to previous literary trends and
to those contemporary with them. Many factors contributed to
confirm this apparent isolation: the obvious historical caesura,
in both the literary and the political fields, constituted by World
War I; the influence during surrealism's gestation period, between 1919 and 1922, of the largely foreign and certainly
international Dada movement; the vertigo caused by Freud's
discoveries relating to the unconscious, and their possible application in the realm of poetry; the surrealists' own refusal to
regard themselves as merely writers, and their widely publicized support later for extreme left-wing political groups, whether
Leninist or Trotskyite. However, it is also true that history,
including literary history, is not given to abrupt mutations.
Although the surrealist vision of the world differs radically
from that of the decadents on a number of points, for example
in its attitude to woman, it nevertheless remains true that many
key themes of the surrealist imagination—the value attributed
to dreams and the attention paid to phenomena lurking just
below the level of consciousness, celebration of the artificial,
discovery of the beauties inherent in modernity, attraction to
the bizarre and unusual—were already in gestation during the
decadent era.

It would also be desirable to establish, beyond the superficial
isolation of the surrealist movement, all the affinities that
nevertheless existed between surrealist works and those by
other writers of the time similarly fascinated by fantasy and
dreams, among whom one would have to include such men as
Jaloux, Hellens, Miomandre, and Arnoux. The result of this
would be not so much to diminish the relative originality of
surrealism as to demonstrate its exemplary and representative
character. In this way, now that time enables us to stand back
a little from it, we may be able to achieve a new perspective
on a movement that undoubtedly remains one of the richest in
modern French literature, and one that still continues to fertilize
our imagination today. (pp. 264-65)

> *Jean Pierrot, in a conclusion to his* The Decadent
> Imagination: 1880-1900, *translated by Derek Colt-
> man, The University of Chicago Press, 1981, pp.
> 238-65.*

PAUL VALERY

*[A prominent French poet and critic, Valéry was one of the leading
practitioners of nineteenth-century Symbolist aestheticism. Valéry's work reflects his desire for total control of his creation; his
absorption with the creative process also forms the method of his
criticism. In the following excerpt from an essay written in 1936
to mark the fiftieth anniversary of Symbolism, Valéry defines the
essence of Symbolism, describes its historical roots, and details
the objections that have been raised against the movement.]*

The mere name of Symbolism is already an enigma for many,
as if it had been chosen expressly to make them torment their
minds. I have known persons who attributed an imaginary depth

to the little word *symbol;* they meditated on it day after day in the hope of defining its mysterious resonance. But a word is a bottomless pit.

Those without literary training are not the only ones to be puzzled by these innocent syllables. Scholars, artists, and philosophers have sometimes revealed the same embarrassment. As for the men who were given and still bear the proud title of "Symbolists"—the men of whom one necessarily thinks in discussing Symbolism, whose lives and works would provide the clearest possible notion of Symbolism—they never adopted the name for themselves, and never used or abused it as people came to do in the time that followed their time.

It must be confessed that I too have tried to define the term (and perhaps have done so at different times in different fashions). Perhaps I shall try to define it once again, for there is no greater temptation than that of trying to resolve the nebulosity presented to the mind by the meaning of any abstract word. The word *Symbolism* makes some people dream of obscurity, strangeness, and excessive refinement in the arts; others find in it I cannot say what sort of aesthetic spiritualism or correspondence of the visible world with the unseen; while others think of liberties and licenses that they regard as a threat to the language, as well as to prosody, form, and common sense. Still others . . . but there is no limit to the suggestive power of a word. In this realm all the arbitrary tendencies of the mind can be given free rein; nobody can either disprove or confirm the different values of the word Symbolism.

After all, it is only a convention.

Conventional names of the sort often lead to misunderstandings, and these in turn to rather diverting questions, of which I find a charming example in an anecdote repeated I don't know where by the illustrious astronomer Arago.

About 1840 Arago was director of the Paris Observatory. He was approached one day by a messenger from the Tuileries—an aide-de-camp or a court chamberlain—who revealed the desire of an august personage (not otherwise identified by Arago) to visit the Observatory and there enjoy a somewhat closer view of the heavens. The visitation took place at the appointed hour. Arago greeted the royal guest, conducted him to the great telescope, and invited him to look through the eye-piece at the finest star in the sky; he announced, "That, *Monseigneur,* is Sirius." After gazing for some time, the prince raised his head and, with the air of complicity and the knowing smile of a man who cannot be imposed upon, who has seen the underside of everything, he said to the astronomer, *"Between you and me,* Monsieur le Directeur, *are you quite certain that this magnificent star is really called Sirius?"*

And so in exploring the skies of literature, in a certain region of the literary universe, which is to say in France between 1860 and 1890 (if you will), we indubitably find something there, some clearly separate system, some aggregate (I dare not say that it is luminous, lest I offend various persons) of works and authors that are distinguished from others and form a group. It would appear that the aggregate is called "Symbolism," but, like Arago's prince, I am not quite certain that this is its real name.

The men who lived in the Middle Ages did not suspect that they were medieval, and those of the 15th or 16th Century did not have engraved on their calling cards, "Messers So-and-So, of the Renaissance." The same is true of the Symbolists. That is what they are called today, not what they were.

These few remarks might help us to recognize what we are doing at this moment: we are engaged in constructing Symbolism, as others have constructed a vast number of intellectual entities, which, if they have not achieved a bodily presence, have never lacked for definitions, since everyone was at liberty to present them with a definition of his choice. We are constructing Symbolism; we are announcing its birth today at the happy age of fifty, thus permitting it to dispense with the fumbling steps of childhood, the disorders and doubts of adolescence, the problems and anxieties of early manhood. It is being born with its fortune made—perhaps, alas, after its decease. Yes, to celebrate this fiftieth birthday in 1936 is to create an entity which will always be the Symbolism of fifty years before; and the creation depends not at all on the existence in 1886 of something then called Symbolism. Nothing written, nothing remembered by survivors, existed under that name at the assigned date. It is marvelous to think that we are celebrating, as existent fifty years ago, something absent from the universe of fifty years ago. I am happy and honored to take part in the generation of a myth, in broad daylight.

Let us set to work. Let us construct Symbolism and, to be rigorous in our task, let us consult the available documents and memories. We know that between 1860 and 1900 there was certainly, in the literary universe, something. How should we undertake to isolate that something? I assume that we have formed three clear or supposedly clear ideas: one that permits us to distinguish a type of works we shall describe as classic; another that will more or less define a type we shall call romantic; a third that we shall declare to be realistic. Proceeding on this basis to explore and empty the shelves of libraries, to examine the books one by one, and then to place each of them on a pile containing others of its type—classic or romantic or realistic—we shall find that certain works cannot be included in our three categories. There is no place for them in any of the piles. Either they reveal characteristics quite different from those we had foreseen in our definitions, or else they mingle characteristics we had tried to separate. For example, how should we classify the litle volume of *Illuminations* by Arthur Rimbaud? And where should we place Mallarmé's *l'Après-midi d'un Faune*? The former resembles nothing else; the latter, in point of technique and invention, includes and surpasses everything done before its time.

We are therefore tempted to make a fourth pile for these rebellious authors—but on what principles? Quite soon we discover that the two works have nothing in common; or, to be accurate, nothing but the identical gesture that separates each of them from our first three piles. As we continue the process of classifying authors, we meet with still more puzzling questions. Verlaine, once again, brings us his specific differences; and what is there in common between Verlaine and Villiers de l'Isle Adam, or among Maeterlinck, Moréas, and Laforgue? Perhaps we might find more affinities among Verhaeren, Viélé-Griffin, Henri de Régnier, Albert Mockel. But Gustave Kahn and Saint-Pol Roux? and Dujardin?

I must go back to astronomy for the image of a nebula that, when seen through a telescope, can be distinguished from other celestial objects; it has been situated and even christened. But looking through a large telescope that brings us a little nearer to this remote system, we find it to be composed of separate stars that differ greatly in color, size, and brilliance. So it is that the closer one looks at our future symbolists, the more they seem to be marked by total differences, by incompatibilities in their styles, methods, preconceptions, and aesthetic ideals. We are forced to this double conclusion, that almost no unity of theories, convictions, or techniques is to be found among these authors, but that they are none the less related to one another, held together by something not yet visible, or at least not revealed by mere inspection of their works; on the contrary, the inspection shows that these are mutually incomparable.

What, then, is the something that holds them together, if all their possible and positive features—their doctrines, their methods, their manners of feeling and execution—seem rather to keep them separate? We could hardly be content to explain this coalescence of talents by distance alone, by a simplification resulting from the passage of time and leading to the disappearance, after fifty years, of everything that divided these individualities, while everything that combined them was emphasized. No, there is indeed something. And we know, after comparing their works and recognizing their irreconcilable differences, that the something does not reside in the perceptible qualities of their art. There is no aesthetic of Symbolism. Such is the result of our first question.

We arrive at this paradox: an event in aesthetic history that cannot be defined in aesthetic terms. The secret of their cohesion lies somewhere else. I offer one hypothesis. I suggest that in all their diversity the symbolists were united by some negation, and by one that was independent of their temperaments and their function as artists. This negation was all they had in common, but it was essentially marked in each of them. As dissimilar as they were to one another, they recognized themselves to be identically separated from the other writers and artists of their time. No matter how much they differed, opposing one another sometimes so violently that they hurled insults, excommunications, and even challenges to the field of honor, they continued to agree on one point, which . . . was foreign to aesthetics. *They agreed in a common determination to reject the appeal to a majority:* they disdained to conquer the public at large. And not only did they deliberately refuse to solicit readers in quantity or number (thereby distinguishing themselves from the realists, eager for statistical glory, who reveled in big printings and came to measure value by tonnage sold), but also they quite as sharply challenged the judgment of the groups or persons who were in a position to influence the most distinguished readers. They scorned the decrees and shrugged off the ridicule of those critics who were best established in the most imposing reviews; they inveighed against Sarcey, Fouquier, Brunetière, Lemaître, and Anatole France. With the same gesture of defiance they spurned the advantages of public esteem, disparaged public honors, and, on the contrary, exalted their own saints and heroes, who were also their martyrs and their models of virtue. Everyone they admired had suffered: Edgar Poe, found dying in the gutter; Baudelaire, hailed into court by the public prosecutor; Wagner, hissed down at the Opéra; Verlaine and Rimbaud, suspicious vagrants; Villiers, sleeping on the floor of a hovel, beside the little valise that contained his manuscripts and his title to the Kingdom of Cyprus and Jerusalem.

As for our Symbolists of 1886, without support in the press, without publishers, without access to a normal literary career and its promotions in rank, its rights of seniority, they adapted themselves to this irregular existence; they had their own reviews, their publishing houses, their intramural criticism; and step by step they created a little public of their own, which became an object of derision like the Symbolists themselves.

In this manner they effected a sort of revolution in the realm of values. For the notion of works that solicit the public, approaching it by way of its habits or inclinations, little by little they substituted the notion of works that create their public. Instead of writing to satisfy a need or a preëxistent desire, they hoped to create the desire and the need; and they did not refuse themselves any liberty that might rebuff or shock a hundred readers, if they judged it might win them a single reader of superior merit.

All this amounts to saying that they demanded a sort of active intellectual coöperation, something remarkably new and an essential feature of our Symbolism. Perhaps it would not be impossible or mistaken to deduce, from the attitude of renunciation and negation I have just described, first, the change that consisted in choosing as partner of the writer, as reader, an individual selected for the intellectual effort of which he was capable; and then a second consequence, that the laborious and refined reader could henceforward be offered texts in which there was no lack of the difficulties, the unexpected effects, and the prosodic or even graphic experiments that a bold and inventive talent might undertake to produce. A new path was open to inventors. Seen in this light, Symbolism is revealed as an era of inventions; and the simple process of reasoning I have just sketched out, starting with a consideration foreign to aesthetics, and fundamentally ethical, is one that guided Symbolism to the very principle of its technical activity, which is freedom of research, absolute adventure in the realm of artistic creation, at the risk and peril of the adventurers.

Thus, set free from the public at large, delivered from the usual type of criticism that is both guide and slave of the public, unconcerned about sales, and having no regard for the limitations and mental sluggishness of an average reader, the artist could dedicate himself without reserve to his experiments. Each artist could choose his own deities, his own ideals, and God knows if anyone denied himself the privilege. God knows the innovations of the time were numerous, varied, surprising, sometimes bizarre. Everything was requisitioned by these prospectors in search of hidden literary treasures: not only philosophy and the sciences but music, philology, occultism, and foreign literatures.

At the same time, exchanges among the different arts, which had first been practiced by the Romantics, but spasmodically, became a recognized and sometimes excessively methodical procedure. There were poets who tried to borrow from music whatever they could charm away from it by means of analogies; at times their works were arranged on the page like orchestral scores. Others, subtle critics of painting, tried to introduce into their style some imitation of the contrasts and correspondences afforded by a system of colors. Still others did not hesitate to create words or to alter French syntax, which many tried to overthrow, while a few, on the contrary, dressed it in the court robes of its ceremonious past.

Never was a literary movement more studious or preoccupied with ideas than this movement in all directions of minds whose common principle was the renunciation of any appeal to public preference. Everything I have seen produced in literature since that tormented era, in the way of audacities, ventures into an uncertain future, or brusque returns to the past, was indicated, or already attained, or prefigured, or rendered possible, if not probable, by the intense and disorganized efforts carried on at the time.

Around these authors gradually took shape a little community of disciples, analogous to the group that had formed around

Wagner after the spectacular failure of *Tannhäuser* at the Paris Opera. No doubt these disciples, "the happy few," were expected to be attentive, zealous, willing to sacrifice their habits, and disdainful of everything they had once been taught to admire—all this to a rather commendable degree; and no doubt the only reward for their fervor would be the ridicule of good society and the press, together with the handsome title of "snob" bestowed on them by scoffers with a smattering of English; but whether they appreciated or imitated, whether they explored and discovered or merely followed, they performed a genuine and useful function. Without such readers, what would have happened to many an artist of the first rank, or many a work among those of which the glory is now beyond dispute?

Let us continue our analysis. I now propose to assert that this resolution jointly adopted by men who were usually divided on all questions of art—this determination not to worship other truths than those deliberately chosen or fashioned by themselves; to turn away from the idols of their era and from those who served the idols, at the cost of all the advantages that might have been offered by their assent to public judgment—entailed the creation of *an entirely new and singular state of mind*. This could not be developed to the point of revealing its full or final potentialities, and its disappearance, which I deplore, might be assigned to the first years of the present century.

Renunciation, as we know, bears some resemblance to mortification. When we mortify ourselves, we are trying to regenerate and reconstruct ourselves by harsh and even painful methods that will raise us, we hope, to a state forejudged to be superior. The desire for such elevation, such *ascesis,* expressed itself in the domain of art, becoming a condition of the true artist's life and a prerequisite for masterpieces. Such is the quite new development and the deep-seated characteristic to be observed in all the authentic participants in this Symbolism that was still without a name.

I have explained that the unity we might agree to call Symbolism does not reside in any agreement about aesthetic principles: Symbolism was not a school. On the contrary, it included many schools of the most divergent types, and I have said: *Aesthetics divided them; Ethics united them.* It is from this point that we now advance toward another idea I should like to propose. The idea can be expressed in this fashion: At no other time did the powers of art, beauty, and form, or the virtue of poetry, come so close to providing a number of persons with the substance of an inner life that might well be called "mystical," since it proved to be sufficient in itself, and since it satisfied more than one heart *as effectively as a formal creed.* There is no doubt that some few depended on this sort of religious faith to furnish the constant nourishment of their thoughts, the guiding principle of their conduct, and the strength to resist temptation; or that, in the most difficult circumstances, it inspired them to work frenziedly on projects that had as little chance of being carried out as they had of being understood if by any chance they were ever completed.

This I say advisedly: we had the impression, in those days, that a sort of religion was nearly on the point of being born, and that its essence would have been the poetic emotion. Could anything be more understandable, to those who study the period and try to reconstitute the conditions that prevailed in the world of the intellect?

But that sort of study leads to an especially vivid type of history, because the reconstitution of an intellectual experience is a history of isolable individuals, taken one by one and not by masses; it tries to restore singularities, not human units treated collectively in statistical forms, as men are treated in histories of the usual sort. It is also especially vivid in this respect, that what it regards as events are inner events and personal reactions: an idea has the value of a battle in other histories; a man in very modest circumstances, almost unknown, assumes the stature of a hero, the power of a despot, the authority of a legislator. Hence everything takes place in the domain of the perceptible and intelligible, and is resolved into impressions, into thoughts, into those individual reactions that have just been mentioned. But the impressions are more intense, the reactions stronger and more creative, when one observes them in a new and young person at the moment when he is entering his intellectual puberty. One morning he wakens with a fresh judgment of himself, a rigorous judgment that condemns his tastes and ideas of the day before. These he suddenly finds childish; he says to himself that he has been merely accepting what he was taught, that he has been reflecting the opinions and assertions of those around him—in other words: *he now feels that he has been pretending to like what he never could like, and has been forcing himself not to like much that allures him.* He is on the point of separating himself from what had been the accepted system of his admirations, his evaluations, his borrowed ideals—and he tries to be himself, by means of himself.

But it is at the same age that he enters the world of real experiences. We know only too well what he finds there. It is seldom that he fails to suffer disappointments, to be revolted by the imperfections of the real, by all the assorted forms of ugliness that are the most frequently observable elements of reality—and these, we know, are the favorite themes of the naturalistic school.

I take this to be the essential circumstance that permits us to reconstitute, by a sort of synthesis, the spirit of the time and of the group that would bear the name of Symbolists. How could I better explain the devotion to pure art that was proclaimed and developed for a dozen years, in all countries, by a few, than by presenting to your minds the state of soul of a young man fifty years ago—whose culture, whose sensibility, and whose character I assume to be of a high enough order so that he feels at every moment the need of a second life and the desire for every form of beauty?

What does he find on completing his formal education? We must note that he feels no regret at leaving his books behind; since they served a utilitarian purpose and were prescribed by the academic authorities, they had long since revolted him. It is only natural that they should be regarded as corpses, as unhappy authors wheeled in for dissection, or else as detached fragments, dried, injected with commentaries, and reduced to the state of anatomical specimens. He has rejected these remains, these residues of century-old admiration by others. But what then does he find that will continue to serve him as spiritual nutriment?

Necessarily he samples the current fashions. In 1886 (since we have chosen that year) the bookshop windows offer him (besides a quantity of the negligible books that are always being written and displayed), on one side, a pile of novels in very active demand; the wrappers announce that a hundred, two hundred thousand copies have been printed. They are the works of the Naturalists, thick volumes usually covered with canary-yellow paper. On the other side, less patronized by customers and much less visible (for these are poets), he discovers the

Romantics, from Lamartine to Hugo. Not far away, in little white sheaves, are the fashionable rhymers: Parnassians of all dimensions. If he looks patiently, he can perhaps lay hand on a copy of the *Fleurs du Mal*.

But our young explorer of this stock of reading matter is not quite satisfied. What the realists present to him only too well, with cruel force and obstinacy, is the very world for which, having merely glimpsed it, he already feels abhorrence. Although their picture is laboriously exact and sometimes remarkably well painted, still it seems to him incomplete, since *he is not there in person,* and since he is unable or unwilling to recognize himself in this blemished humanity, burdened with hereditary evils and serving as bestial prey to these cruel observers. He does not choose to believe that men and women have more reflexes than thoughts, more instincts than depth of feeling. On the other hand, the Parnassian poets win his admiration for a little while, the time required by a nimble mind to assimilate their methods and conventions—by observing which one very soon, and with a fair degree of ease, becomes able to write verses that have the appearance of being fairly difficult. But their system, which had the merit of being opposed to negligence in form and language, the obvious fault of many Romantics, kept tempting them into a factitious rigor, into a search for effects and "fine lines," into the use of rare words, foreign names, and an ostentatious splendor that obscured the poetry under arbitrary and lifeless decorations. Rich rhymes are to be admired if they are not in contrast with the poverty of the verse; they become unbearable as soon as they are sought at the expense of all other qualities, including the general unity of the poem. That is an absolute law. The "fine line" is often the enemy of the poem: a great deal of intelligence and art is required to construct a body of work from which one is not tempted to detach, here and there, an alexandrine that makes us forget the rest of the troupe—as leading ladies often do.

Our young hero, who serves us as a touchstone, and whose sensibility helps to reveal the quality of the era in which we place him, finds little, then, in the productions of the time to gratify his needs. He is not at all dazzled by the works that everybody admires. It might be added that all intellectual activity would cease if young people were ever satisfied with *what is,* at the moment when they first look around them and, emerging from the awkward age, come forward to take their places among men.

But works derive from ideas, and the prevailing ideas appeal to him no more and offer no better nourishment to an eager spirit than do the books of the time. Neither pure criticism, which enjoys great prestige, nor the evolutionist metaphysic, which has been adopted by the naturalistic school and translated into fiction; neither dogmatic philosophy nor the orthodox creeds, which have long been under siege and against which positivism, determinism, and philosophy in general have directed so many assaults, are likely to retain his attention. He is inclined to reject indiscriminately everything that rests on a tradition or on texts—just as he is repelled by anything that depends on arguments and a more or less rigid dialectic; and just as he holds that every affirmation said to be based on scientific knowledge, whether of physics, geology, or biology, must be regarded as eternally provisional and always premature—above all, if it exploits the implications of such knowledge beyond the possibility of verification. He confronts all these doctrines; in each of them he sees only the strength of the arguments it brings forward against the others. He decides that the sum of all the doctrines is equal to zero.

What remains in his grasp? How can he escape from this intellectual stalemate and the feeling of helplessness to which it gives rise? This much remains: that he is himself, that he is young, and that he is resolved to accept nothing unless he feels its real inner necessity, its existence foreshadowed in the depths of his being; to admit nothing unless it can be expressed in words of which the meaning is an immediate experience and a value represented in the treasury of his *affections.* Idols for idols, he prefers those fashioned from his own substance to those given him to worship by others. He interrogates himself. He makes a discovery. He finds that he still has one sure possession: *the feeling imposed on him by certain aspects of nature and life, and by certain productions of men.* These he recognizes by the singular joy he derives from them, and by the strange need he finds in himself for such moments or objects, which, although perfectly useless for the preservation of physical existence, still offer him precious sensations, indefinitely varied ideas, a sometimes miraculous union of thought, sentiment, fantasy, and logic, and also delight mysteriously conjoined with energy. But might we not say that all this is "the substance of an inner life" I mentioned not long ago, as well as the nutriment that sustained a devotion to pure art? A simple description of this state compels me to use terms that are borrowed from the vocabulary of religious ecstasy.

One circumstance of the period under consideration greatly intensified the quasi-mystical type of aesthetic feeling that was inseparable from Symbolism. Among all the modes of expression and excitation, there is one particular mode that imposes itself with unmeasured power; it dominates and devalues all the others; it acts upon our nervous universe, overstimulates, penetrates, soothes and then shatters it, while lavishing upon it a wealth of surprises, caresses, illuminations, and thunderstorms; it is the master of our leisure hours, our tremulous delights, our meditations. That power is *Music;* and it so happened that the most powerful type of music was sovereign at the very moment when our fledgeling symbolist was about to enter his predestined path; he became intoxicated with the music of Richard Wagner.

As Baudelaire had already done at an earlier time, he sought every opportunity for sharing this music, which seemed to him both diabolical and sacred. It was his cult and his vice, his course of study and his poison; while it also performed the function of a liturgical office, by effecting the fusion of an entire audience, in which each member received the full force of the enchantment. Think of a thousand persons in the same hall, who, under the same compulsions, close their eyes, suffer the same transports, feel alone with themselves, and yet are identified by their personal emotions with so many of their neighbors, until these become truly their *counterparts,*—here is the essence of a religious atmosphere, that is, a unity of sentiments in a living plurality. (pp. 425-39)

One of the great disputes of the era was, as we know, the civil war about Vers Libre. The subject is such a thorny one that I scarcely have courage to grapple with it. The propriety, the opportunity, or the necessity of dispensing with the traditional rules of verse; arguments for the affirmative or the negative; proofs that one side or the other was right in theory or fact, by virtue of phonetic laws or historical experience . . . but if I tried to deal with these inexhaustible topics, I should be asking you to display more patience, attentiveness, and courage than could be rewarded by anything I might say. Moreover, we should soon find ourselves entangled in other difficulties. Even the question of who invented free verse has been hotly argued.

Battles of the sort go on forever. In this new era I should prefer not to rekindle a war that, like many others, could never be won.

But it would be impossible to discuss Symbolism, even in a summary fashion, without lingering a moment on this question of poetic technique. I shall merely indicate a few points of fact, confining myself to what is incontestable.

Regular verse is defined by a certain number of restrictions conventionally imposed on our everyday manner of speaking. These might be compared, without our intending the least disparagement, to the rules of a game. They have as their combined effect the quite remarkable virtue of separating the particular language they govern from the language in ordinary use.

At every moment they remind the man who observes them, as they also remind those who listen, that his discourse does not find its echo in the world of action, in the domain of practical life. To provide its proper meaning, explain its form, there must be another world, a universe of poetry.

It is to be noted that although this restraint imposed on language is partly an external one, it also gives us liberties. If the form I employ is one suggesting at every moment that my discourse is outside the order of real objects, then the listener or the reader can anticipate and accept all the fantasies of a mind left to its own devices. On the other hand, the form is a continual admonition; it forewarns or should forewarn us against the danger of lapsing into prose.

Another established fact: all poets from the beginning to the period now under consideration employed some conventional system of discipline. No need to speak of the ancients: Shake-

Paul Verlaine. The Granger Collection, New York.

speare's nondramatic works are sonnets and lyrics or narratives in rhymed stanzas. Dante wrote his poem in terza rima. Horace and Villon, Petrarch and Banville, all observed the rules of verse.

But a few years after 1870—that is, when the school that called itself the Contemporary Parnassus was at the height of its glory, and when, in reaction against Romanticism, it had adopted still more stringent rules than the classical poets—there began to be noted an insurrectional movement, of which the first tremors are to be found in some pages of Rimbaud and in the quite un-Parnassian air of the poems by Verlaine that followed his *Poèmes Saturniens.* Their free grace set them against the sculptural appearance and solid sonorities of Leconte de Lisle and his disciples. They introduced a simple and melodious form, sometimes inspired by folk poetry.

Still bolder innovators came forward a little later. Deliberately casting aside the conventions, they depended only on an instinct for rhythm and a delicate ear as guides to the cadence and musical substance of their verse. Some of the new experiments were the result of theoretical investigations that started with the study of phonetics or with recordings of the human voice. I cannot undertake to expound the various theories advanced at the time; but I note as a characteristic feature of Symbolism the long theoretical discussions, often developed in a scholarly manner, that accompanied or contributed to the artistic production of the period. In the years between 1883 and 1890, several rash spirits attempted to formulate a doctrine of art based on the new and fashionable science of psychophysiology. Studies of the sensibility by the methods of physical science, investigations into the (hypothetical) correspondence of colors with sounds, and the energetic analysis of rhythm were other enterprises not without their effects on painting and poetry. These attempts to substitute precise data for the vague notions hitherto utilized by criticism, and for the subjective opinions that artists are likely to hold, were doubtless premature and perhaps chimerical; but I confess that what I knew of them aroused my keen interest—less by their substance than by the tendency they represented, but also by the contrast they offered with the a-priori systems and vain affirmations of dialectical aesthetics.

The liberated poets of the time were also scholars of the past, and they found charming models in the 15th and 16th Centuries. Their borrowings from older French literature included such lyrical forms as the ode and the odelette, as well as many words that had disappeared from the language, although delightfully adapted to poetry. It so happened that these borrowings, which were suggested and carried out as a direct result of the liberties that poets were taking with the strict Parnassian forms, gradually led to a so-called romanesque or Latin revival of traditional prosody. That might serve as a rather diverting example of recurrence and of our inability to foresee.

In still another quarter, very hostile to that of the romanesque poets, a remarkable experiment was being performed: Instrumentism made its appearance. The Instrumentists preserved most of the rules for writing classical French verse, but added rules of their own, in the shape of something like a table of correspondences between the sounds of the alphabet and the tones of orchestral instruments.

All this serves to illustrate the very active life of "Symbolism" and its fertility in all sorts of inventions, but it also reveals the inner diversity of the authors whom we now classify under the same label.

Meanwhile the *Enemy* was waking; in truth he had never gone to sleep. The literary ferment . . . was not allowed to continue undisturbed. The moment its existence was suspected by those who stand guard over the interests of the public (which they manage to confuse with their own), laughter, smiles, parodies, contempt, accusations—and sometimes invectives, reproaches, regrets at seeing so much talent wasted on ridiculous fancies—began their work of depreciation and extermination. I still hear the voice of the worthy man who said, *"Sir, I am a doctor of letters and a doctor of law, and I do not understand a wretched word of your Mallarmé."*

Little by little the counts of the indictment took shape. They have not changed for fifty years; they are always the same and always three. Those who pronounce them are not too inventive. Here are the three heads of this average Cerberus speaking in turn:

> One of the mouths says to us: Obscurity.
> Another says: Preciosity.
> And the third says: Sterility.

Such is the motto inscribed on the frieze of the Symbolist temple.

What does Symbolism answer? It has two ways of exterminating the dragon. The first is to say nothing, but merely point to some figures: so many copies sold, so many new editions of Mallarmé, Verlaine, and Rimbaud. The figures have grown larger every year from the beginning, and their growth has been especially rapid since 1900.

The second way consists in saying: "You call us *obscure*? But does anyone force you to read us? If there were some decree that compelled you to do so on pain of death, one can imagine your howls of indignation.

"You call us *precious*? But the opposite of the precious is the cheap, the common. *Sterile*? But you should praise us for that. If we are sterile, there is certain to be a little less obscurity and preciosity in the world."

The confession must be made that Symbolism had other enemies than these criticisms, which disturbed only those lacking in conviction. Its own virtues were also against it, as was its ascetic ideal. Moreover, the demands of everyday life, the coming of middle age—which makes it more and more difficult, and sometimes more disheartening, to devote oneself single-mindedly to a cult that is too austere—besides the wish to broaden a reputation that had inevitably been circumscribed by the exquisite quality of works produced for the delectation of a few, and finally the coming of new generations which no longer received the same impressions or encountered the same system of circumstances, and which, by the fatal need to exist and create in their turn, were constrained to deny or ignore the aspirations and motives and values of the "symbolists"—all this would lead to a dissolution, a corruption, and at certain points a vulgarization of the spirit I have tried to explain.

In any case the great disorder of human affairs, so much accentuated since the beginning of the 20th Century, could scarcely have failed to demonstrate the utter impossibility of this attempt to create a separate culture, to preserve taste and refinement, to stand aloof from publicity, from the course of statistical values, and from the agitation that increasingly jumbles together all the elements of life. The chemistry of art no longer carries on the slow process of fractional distillation that produces pure substances, nor does it prepare the crystals that can be formed and enlarged only in perfect stillness. It now manufactures explosives and poisons.

How can we dedicate ourselves to long elaborations, how waste our time on theories and subtle distinctions, when events and manners hurry us as they do, when our days are divided between futility and anxiety, and when leisure, an assured livelihood, and the freedom to dream and meditate have become as rare as gold?

These are the circumstances that confer its present value on Symbolism, besides enhancing the value of its past—that make it, in short, a *symbol*.

The conditions for the development of talents in depth, in subtlety, in perfection, in exquisite power, have disappeared. Everything is opposed to the possibility of an independent life of art. The complaints that poets uttered sixty years ago seem to us purely rhetorical as compared with the lamentations that would be forced from poets today, if they did not feel that it would be useless to groan in the midst of the universal hubbub, the tumultuous noise of machines and arms, the cries of the crowd, and the crudely imposing harangues of those who regard the crowd as a beast to be tamed or a herd of cattle to be driven.

I shall therefore conclude by observing that "Symbolism" is henceforth the symbol that names the intellectual qualities and conditions most opposed to those which reign, and even govern, today.

The Ivory Tower never seemed so high. (pp. 442-47)

> *Paul Valery, "The Existence of Symbolism," translated by Malcolm Cowley, in* The Kenyon Review, *Vol. XIX, No. 3, Summer, 1957, pp. 425-47.*

ADDITIONAL BIBLIOGRAPHY

PRIMARY SOURCES

Engelberg, Edward, ed. *The Symbolist Poem: The Development of the English Tradition,* New York: E. P. Dutton & Co., 1967, 350 p.

Flores, Angel, ed. *An Anthology of French Poetry from Nerval to Valéry in English Translation.* Garden City, N.Y.: Doubleday, Anchor Books, 1958, 453 p.

Houston, John Porter, and Houston, Mona Tobin, eds. and trans. *French Symbolist Poetry: An Anthology.* Bloomington: Indiana University Press, 1980, 280 p.

MacIntyre, C. F., trans. *French Symbolist Poetry.* Berkeley and Los Angeles: University of California Press, 1958, 150 p.

SECONDARY SOURCES

Aubery, Pierre. "The Anarchism of the Literati of the Symbolist Period." *The French Review* XLII, No. 1 (October 1968): 39-47.
    Discusses the social awareness of the Symbolists.

Balakian, Anna, ed. *The Symbolist Movement in the Literature of European Languages.* Budapest: Akadémiai Kiadó, 1982, 732 p.
    A collection of essays on Symbolism largely devoted to the influence of the movement on twentieth-century literature, art, and music.

Bays, Gwendolyn. *The Orphic Vision: Seer Poets from Novalis to Rimbaud.* Lincoln: University of Nebraska Press, 1964, 303 p.

Assesses the poetic theories of the Symbolists, particularly Rimbaud, in light of their self-proclaimed roles as visionaries.

Bertocci, Angelo Philip. *From Symbolism to Baudelaire*. Carbondale: Southern Illinois University Press, 1964, 223 p.
Studies the work of Baudelaire and considers it the most significant antecedent of the Symbolist movement.

Block, Haskell M. "Heine and the French Symbolists." In *Creative Encounter: Festschrift for Herman Salinger*, edited by Leland R. Phelps, pp. 25-39. University of North Carolina Studies in the Germanic Languages and Literatures, edited by Siegfried Mews, no. 91. Chapel Hill: University of North Carolina Press, 1978.
Proposes that the work of the German poet Heinrich Heine influenced the writings of the Symbolists.

Bowra, C. M. *The Heritage of Symbolism*. London: Macmillan & Co., 1943, 232 p.
Analyzes the influence of Symbolism on five twentieth-century poets: Paul Valéry, Rainer Maria Rilke, Stefan George, Alexander Blok, and William Butler Yeats.

Burne, Glenn S. "Remy de Gourmont and the Aesthetics of Symbolism." *Comparative Literature Studies* IV, Nos. 1, 2 (1967): 161-75.
A detailed examination of the literary theories of Gourmont as an example of Symbolist aesthetics.

Carter, A. E. *The Idea of Decadence in French Literature: 1830-1900*. Toronto: University of Toronto Press, 1958, 154 p.
Examines themes of social, moral, and artistic decadence in nineteenth-century French literature.

Cassou, Jean. *The Concise Encyclopedia of Symbolism*. Translated by Susie Saunders. Secaucus, N.J.: Chartwell Books, 1979, 292 p.
Essays on literature, music, and the visual arts during the Symbolist period.

Chiari, Joseph. *Symbolisme from Poe to Mallarmé: The Growth of a Myth*. London: Rockliff, 1956, 198 p.
Assesses the influence of Poe on the Symbolist movement.

Cornell, Kenneth. *The Symbolist Movement*. New Haven: Yale University Press, 1951, 217 p.
An historical study of Symbolism.

Eliot, T. S. *From Poe to Valéry: A Lecture Delivered at the Library of Congress on Friday, November 19, 1948*. Washington: Library of Congress, 1949, 16 p.
Discusses the impact of Poe's poetry on Baudelaire, Mallarmé, and Valéry.

Hake, Alfred Egmont. "Symbolism and Logic." In his *Regeneration: A Reply to Max Nordau*, pp. 94-107. New York: G. P. Putnam's Sons, 1896.
Defends the Symbolist poets against the attacks of Max Nordau (see excerpt above).

Houston, John Porter. *French Symbolism and the Modernist Movement: A Study of Poetic Structures*. Baton Rouge: Louisiana State University Press, 1980, 298 p.
Examines structural, stylistic, and thematic analogies between Symbolist poetry and Modernist poetry.

Jones, P. Mansell. *The Background of Modern French Poetry: Essays and Interviews*. 1951. Reprint. Cambridge: Cambridge at the University Press, 1968, 195 p.
Discusses the literary influences that gave rise to the Symbolist movement and traces the development of free verse in France.

Kugel, James L. *The Techniques of Strangeness in Symbolist Poetry*. New Haven: Yale University Press, 1971, 123 p.
Focuses on the obscure and enigmatic qualities of Symbolist verse.

Lawler, James R. *The Language of French Symbolism*. Princeton: Princeton University Press, 1969, 270 p.

Essays on Mallarmé, Verlaine, Rimbaud, Valéry, Claudel, and Apollinaire.

Lehmann, A. G. *The Symbolist Aesthetic in France: 1885-1895*. Oxford: Basil Blackwell, 1950, 328 p.
An anatomy of the intellectual and aesthetic development of Symbolism.

LeSage, Laurent. *The Rhumb Line of Symbolism: French Poets from Sainte-Beuve to Valéry*. University Park: Pennsylvania State University Press, 1978, 267 p.
Essays on twenty poets associated with Symbolism, with untranslated selections from their works.

Nalbantian, Suzanne. "The Symbolists: The Failing Soul." In her *The Symbol of the Soul from Hölderlin to Yeats: A Study in Metonymy*, pp. 66-85. New York: Columbia University Press, 1977.
Analyzes the imagery of the soul in Symbolist verse.

Perry, T. S. "The Latest Literary Fashion in France." *The Cosmopolitan* XIII, No. 3 (July 1892): 359-65.
A contemporary reaction to Symbolism.

Peyre, Henri. "Poets against Music in the Age of Symbolism." In *Symbolism and Modern Literature: Studies in Honor of Wallace Fowlie*, edited by Marcel Tetel, pp. 179-92. Durham, N.C.: Duke University Press, 1978.
Discusses the influence of music on the Symbolists.

Poulet, Georges. "Mallarmé." In his *The Interior Distance*, translated by Elliott Coleman, pp. 235-83. Baltimore: Johns Hopkins Press, 1959.
Appraises the poetry of Mallarmé as an example of Symbolist verse.

Pound, Ezra. "A Study in French Poets." *The Little Review* IV, No. 10 (February 1918): 3-61.
A collection of Symbolist verse with commentary on the poets.

Quennell, Peter. *Baudelaire and the Symbolists*. Rev. ed. London: Weidenfeld and Nicolson, 1954, 164 p.
A study of Baudelaire and his influence on the later Symbolist poets.

Ridge, George Ross. *The Hero in French Decadent Literature*. Athens: University of Georgia Press, 1961, 195 p.
Defines the decadent hero and his role in French literature.

The Romanic Review XLVI, No. 3 (October 1955): 161-235.
An issue devoted to the poetics of French Symbolism that includes essays on Baudelaire, Mallarmé, Rimbaud, and Valéry.

Roy, G. Ross. "A Bibliography of French Symbolism in English-Language Publications to 1910." *Revue de littérature comparée* 34 (October 1960): 645-59.
A bibliography divided into two sections, the first devoted to articles on Symbolism and the second to works by and about Mallarmé, Rimbaud, and Verlaine.

Starkie, Enid. "Symbolism." In her *From Gautier to Eliot: The Influence of France on English Literature, 1851-1939*, pp. 81-100. London: Hutchinson & Co., 1960, 236 p.
Traces the development of the Symbolist movement, focusing on its major representatives and progenitors.

Temple, Ruth Zabriskie. *The Critic's Alchemy: A Study of the Introduction of French Symbolism into England*. New York: Twayne Publishers, 1953, 345 p.
Focuses on five English authors who served as transmitters of developments in late nineteenth-century French literature: Matthew Arnold, Charles Algernon Swinburne, Arthur Symons, Edmund Gosse, and George Moore.

Thibaudet, Albert. "Symbolism." In his *French Literature from 1795 to Our Era*, translated by Charles Lam Markmann, pp. 428-33. New York: Funk & Wagnalls, 1967, 510 p.
A general overview of the movement.

Uitti, Karl D. *The Concept of Self in the Symbolist Novel*. The Hague: Mouton & Co., 1961, 66 p.
> Attempts to define the aesthetic values of the novels developed in the Symbolist decade, 1885-95.

Weinberg, Bernard. *The Limits of Symbolism: Studies of Five Modern French Poets*. Chicago: University of Chicago Press, 1966, 430 p.
> Readings of works by Baudelaire, Rimbaud, Mallarmé, Valéry, and Saint-John Perse.

Wellek, René. "The Term and Concept of Symbolism in Literary History." In his *Discriminations: Further Concepts of Criticism*, pp. 90-121. New Haven: Yale University Press, 1970.
> Defines Symbolism and its role in world literature.

Opium and the Nineteenth-Century Literary Imagination

INTRODUCTION

Since the first publication of Thomas De Quincey's autobiographical *Confessions of an English Opium-Eater* in the *London Magazine* in 1821, the possible relationship between opium use and literary creativity has often been the subject of popular speculation and critical inquiry. The connection, for example, between the drug and several famous works by the English Romantic poet Samuel Taylor Coleridge has frequently been the focus of conjecture, with scholars debating the extent to which his celebrated poem ''Kubla Khan'' was the product of an opium-induced vision. De Quincey and Coleridge, however, are only the best-known members of a small but influential body of nineteenth-century English authors whose lives and works share the common influence of opium; the group also includes, among others, the poets George Crabbe and Francis Thompson. During much of the nineteenth century opium was readily available in England without prescription and widely used for medicinal purposes—not merely by writers but by a broad range of society. The drug served, according to Terry M. Parssinen, as the ''Victorian's aspirin, Lomotil, Valium, and Nyquil, which could be bought at the local chemist's for as little as a penny.'' Although scholars do not consider opium a major influence on literary history, the association between opium use, literary society, and literary creativity during the nineteenth century remains a fascinating subject for historical investigation and critical analysis, not just from a literary perspective but also from sociological, medical, and biographical points of view. The following entry provides, therefore, a range of materials for understanding the opium phenomenon in nineteenth-century literature, including selections from the most prominent works of the ''literature of opium,'' investigations of the historical background, discussions of the connection between literary society and opium use, and finally, several diverging viewpoints on the often-debated question of to what degree—if any—opium was responsible for the inspiration of those works associated in the popular imagination with the drug.

ORIGINAL SOURCES

SAMUEL TAYLOR COLERIDGE

[An English poet and critic, Coleridge was central to the English Romantic movement and is considered one of the greatest literary critics in the English language. Besides his poetry, his most important contributions include his formulation of Romantic theory, his introduction of the ideas of the German Romantics to England, and his Shakespearean criticism, which overthrew the last remnants of the neoclassical approach to William Shakespeare and focused on Shakespeare as a masterful portrayer of human character. Like his younger contemporary De Quincey (see excerpt below), Coleridge struggled with opium dependence throughout his life. Although the true nature of the relationship between his opium use and the following preface and poem is unknown and continues to inspire critical debate, Coleridge's assertion that he

The opium poppy. By courtesy of the British Museum (Natural History).

composed ''Kubla Khan'' in 1797 while dreaming under the influence of the drug has made the poem perhaps the most famous work in the literature of opium. For additional material by Coleridge, see entries below.]

The following fragment is here published at the request of a poet of great and deserved celebrity, and, as far as the author's own opinions are concerned, rather as a psychological curiosity, than on the ground of any supposed *poetic* merits.

In the summer of the year 1797, the author, then in ill health, had retired to a lonely farmhouse between Porlock and Linton, on the Exmoor confines of Somerset and Devonshire. In consequence of a slight indisposition, an anodyne had been prescribed, from the effects of which he fell asleep in his chair at the moment that he was reading the following sentence, or words of the same substance, in *Purchas's Pilgrimage:* ''Here the Khan Kubla commanded a palace to be built, and a stately garden thereunto. And thus ten miles of fertile ground were inclosed with a wall.'' The author continued for about three hours in a profound sleep, at least of the external senses, during which time he has the most vivid confidence that he could not have composed less than from two to three hundred lines; if that indeed can be called composition in which all the images rose up before him as *things,* with a parallel production of the correspondent expressions, without any sensation of consciousness of effort. On awaking he appeared to himself to have a distinct recollection of the whole, and taking his pen, ink, and paper, instantly and eagerly wrote down the lines that are here preserved. At this moment he was unfortunately called out by a person on business from Porlock, and detained by him above an hour, and on his return to his room, found, to his no small surprise and mortification, that though he still retained some vague and dim recollection of the general purport of the vision, yet, with the exception of some eight or ten scattered lines and images, all the rest had passed away like the images on the surface of a stream into which a stone has been cast, but, alas! without the after restoration of the latter!

> Then all the charm
> Is broken—all that phantom world so fair
> Vanishes, and a thousand circlets spread,
> And each misshape[s] the other. Stay awhile,
> Poor youth! who scarcely dar'st lift up thine eyes—
> The stream will soon renew its smoothness, soon
> The visions will return! And lo, he stays,
> And soon the fragments dim of lovely forms
> Come trembling back, unite, and now once more
> The pool becomes a mirror.
>   [From Coleridge's *The Picture; or, the Lover's Resolution,*
>   lines 91-100].

Yet from the still surviving recollections in his mind, the author has frequently purposed to finish for himself what had been originally, as it were, given to him. [I shall sing a sweeter song today]: but the tomorrow is yet to come.

> In Xanadu did Kubla Khan
> A stately pleasure dome decree:
> Where Alph, the sacred river, ran
> Through caverns measureless to man
>   Down to a sunless sea.
> So twice five miles of fertile ground
> With walls and towers were girdled round:
> And there were gardens bright with sinuous rills,
> Where blossomed many an incense-bearing tree;
> And here were forests ancient as the hills,
> Enfolding sunny spots of greenery.
>
> But oh! that deep romantic chasm which slanted
> Down the green hill athwart a cedarn cover!
> A savage place! as holy and enchanted
> As e'er beneath a waning moon was haunted
> By woman wailing for her demon lover!
> And from this chasm, with ceaseless turmoil seething,
> As if this earth in fast thick pants were breathing,
> A mighty fountain momently was forced:
> Amid whose swift half-intermitted burst
> Huge fragments vaulted like rebounding hail,
> Or chaffy grain beneath the thresher's flail:
> And 'mid these dancing rocks at once and ever
> It flung up momently the sacred river.
> Five miles meandering with a mazy motion
> Through wood and dale the sacred river ran,
> Then reached the caverns measureless to man,
> And sank in tumult to a lifeless ocean:
> And 'mid this tumult Kubla heard from far
> Ancestral voices prophesying war!
>   The shadow of the dome of pleasure
>   Floated midway on the waves;
>   Where was heard the mingled measure
>   From the fountain and the caves.

> It was a miracle of rare device,
> A sunny pleasure dome with caves of ice!
>
>   A damsel with a dulcimer
>   In a vision once I saw:
>   It was an Abyssinian maid,
>   And on her dulcimer she played,
>   Singing of Mount Abora.
> Could I revive within me
> Her symphony and song,
> To such a deep delight 'twould win me,
> That with music loud and long,
> I would build that dome in air,
> That sunny dome! those caves of ice!
> And all who heard should see them there,
> And all should cry, Beware! Beware!
> His flashing eyes, his floating hair!
> Weave a circle round him thrice,
> And close your eyes with holy dread,
> For he on honeydew hath fed,
> And drunk the milk of Paradise.

(pp. 307-09)

Samuel Taylor Coleridge, "Kubla Khan," in The Norton Anthology of English Literature, Vol. 2, *edited by M. H. Abrams and others, third edition, W. W. Norton & Company, Inc., 1974, pp. 307-09.*

SAMUEL TAYLOR COLERIDGE

[The following poem, written by Coleridge in 1803, is widely believed to depict the symptoms of opium withdrawal. For additional material by Coleridge, see entries above and below.]

> Ere on my bed my limbs I lay,
> It hath not been my use to pray
> With moving lips or bended knees;
> But silently, by slow degrees,
> My spirit I to Love compose,
> In humble trust mine eye-lids close,
> With reverential resignation,
> No wish conceived, no thought exprest,
> Only a sense of supplication;
> A sense o'er all my soul imprest
> That I am weak, yet not unblest,
> Since in me, round me, every where
> Eternal Strength and Wisdom are.
>
> But yester-night I prayed aloud
> In anguish and in agony,
> Up-starting from the fiendish crowd
> Of shapes and thoughts that tortured me:
> A lurid light, a trampling throng,
> Sense of intolerable wrong,
> And whom I scorned, those only strong!
>
> Thirst of revenge, the powerless will
> Still baffled, and yet burning still!
> Desire with loathing strangely mixed
> On wild or hateful objects fixed.
> Fantastic passions! maddening brawl!
> And shame and terror over all!
> Deeds to be hid which were not hid,
> Which all confused I could not know
> Whether I suffered, or I did:
> For all seemed guilt, remorse or woe,
> My own or others still the same
> Life-stifling fear, soul-stifling shame.
>
> So two nights passed: the night's dismay
> Saddened and stunned the coming day.
> Sleep, the wide blessing, seemed to me
> Distemper's worst calamity.

The third night, when my own loud scream
Had waked me from the fiendish dream,
O'ercome with sufferings strange and wild,
I wept as I had been a child;
And having thus by tears subdued
My anguish to a milder mood,
Such punishments, I said, were due
To natures deepliest stained with sin,—
For aye entempesting anew
The unfathomable hell within,
The horror of their deeds to view,
To know and loathe, yet wish and do!
Such griefs with such men well agree,
But wherefore, wherefore fall on me?
To be beloved is all I need,
And whom I love, I love indeed.

(pp. 331-32)

Samuel Taylor Coleridge, "The Pains of Sleep," in
The Norton Anthology of English Literature, Vol. 2,
edited by M. H. Abrams and others, third edition,
W. W. Norton & Company, Inc., 1974, pp. 331-32.

S. T. COLERIDGE

[*In the following excerpt, drawn from two separate letters, Cole-*
ridge describes the origins of his opium addiction as well as the
suffering and sense of shame he experienced after he had become
thoroughly dependent upon the drug. For additional material by
Coleridge, see entries above.]

The object of my present reply is to state the case just as it is.
First, that for ten years the anguish of my spirit has been
indescribable, the sense of my danger staring, but the consciousness of my GUILT worse, far worse than all. I have
prayed, with drops of agony on my brow, trembling not only
before the justice of my Maker, but even before the mercy of
my Redeemer. "I gave thee so many talents, what hast thou
done with them?" Secondly, overwhelmed as I am with a sense
of my direful infirmity, I have never attempted to disguise or
conceal the cause. On the contrary, not only to friends have I
stated the whole case with tears and the very bitterness of
shame, but in two instances I have warned young men, mere
acquaintances, who had spoken of having taken laudanum, of
the direful consequences, by an awful exposition of the tremendous effects on myself.

Thirdly, though before God I cannot lift up my eyelids, and
only do not despair of His mercy, because to despair would
be adding crime to crime, yet to my fellowmen I may say that
I was seduced into the ACCURSED habit ignorantly. I had
been almost bed-ridden for many months with swellings in my
knees. In a medical journal, I unhappily met with an account
of a cure performed in a similar case (or what appeared to me
so), by rubbing in of laudanum, at the same time taking a given
dose internally. It acted like a charm, like a miracle! I recovered
the use of my limbs, of my appetite, of my spirits, and this
continued for near a fortnight. At length the unusual stimulus
subsided, the complaint returned, the supposed remedy was
recurred to—but I cannot go through the dreary history.

Suffice it to say, that effects were produced which acted on
me by terror and cowardice, of pain and sudden death, not (so
help me God!) by any temptation of pleasure, or expectation,
or desire of exciting pleasurable sensations. On the very contrary, Mrs. Morgan and her sister will bear witness, so far as
to say, that the longer I abstained the higher my spirits were,
the keener my enjoyment—till the moment, the direful moment, arrived when my pulse began to fluctuate, my heart to

palpitate, and such a dreadful falling abroad, as it were, of my
whole frame, such intolerable restlessness, and incipient bewilderment, that in the last of my several attempts to abandon
the dire poison, I exclaimed in agony, which I now repeat in
seriousness and solemnity, "I am too poor to hazard this."
Had I but a few hundred pounds, but £200—half to send to
Mrs. Coleridge, and half to place myself in a private madhouse,
where I could procure nothing but what a physician thought
proper, and where a medical attendant could be constantly with
me for two or three months (in less than that time life or death
would be determined), then there might be hope. Now there
is none!! O God! how willingly would I place myself under
Dr. Fox, in his establishment; for my case is a species of
madness, only that it is a derangement, an utter impotence of
the volition, and not of the intellectual faculties. You bid me
rouse myself: go bid a man paralytic in both arms, to rub them
briskly together, and that will cure him. "Alas!" he would
reply, "that I cannot move my arms is my complaint and my
misery." (pp. 617-19)

• • • • •

Conceive a poor miserable wretch, who for many years has
been attempting to beat off pain, by a constant recurrence to
the vice that reproduces it. Conceive a spirit in hell, employed
in tracing out for others the road to that heaven, from which
his crimes exclude him! In short, conceive whatever is most
wretched, helpless, and hopeless, and you will form as tolerable a notion of my state, as it is possible for a good man
to have.

I used to think the text in St. James that "he who offended in
one point, offends in all," very harsh; but I now feel the awful,
the tremendous truth of it. In the one crime of OPIUM, what
crime have I not made myself guilty of!—Ingratitude to my
Maker! and to my benefactors—injustice! *and unnatural cru-*
elty to my poor children!—self-contempt for my repeated promise—breach, nay, too often, actual falsehood!

After my death, I earnestly entreat, that a full and unqualified
narration of my wretchedness, and of its guilty cause, may be
made public, that at least some little good may be effected by
the direful example. (pp. 623-24)

S. T. Coleridge, in letters to Joseph Cottle on April
26, 1814 and Josiah Wade on June 26, 1814, in his
Letters of Samuel Taylor Coleridge, Vol. II, *edited*
by Ernest Hartley Coleridge, William Heinemann,
1895, pp. 616-19, 623-24.

THOMAS DE QUINCEY

[*An English critic and essayist, De Quincey contributed reviews*
to a number of London journals and earned a reputation as an
insightful if occasionally long-winded critic. He is best known,
however, as the author of Confessions of an English Opium-Eater,
in which he chronicled his long struggle with opium addiction.
In the following excerpt, drawn from the sections of Confessions
entitled "The Pleasures of Opium" and "The Pains of Opium,"
De Quincey describes how he first became acquainted with the
drug as well as the development of his subsequent dependence
and the miseries associated with it. Although the excerpt closes
with an explanation of how he managed to give up opium, De
Quincey subsequently resumed taking the drug and remained an
addict throughout his life.]

It is so long since I first took opium that if it had been a trifling
incident in my life I might have forgotten its date; but cardinal
events are not to be forgotten; and from circumstances con-

nected with it, I remember that it must be referred to the autumn of 1804. During that season I was in London, having come thither for the first time since my entrance at college. And my introduction to opium arose in the following way: From an early age I had been accustomed to wash my head in cold water at least once a day; being suddenly seized with tooth ache, I attributed it to some relaxation caused by an accidental inter-mission of that practice, jumped out of bed, plunged my head into a basin of cold water, and with hair thus wetted, went to sleep. The next morning, as I need hardly say, I awoke with excruciating rheumatic pains of the head and face, from which I had hardly any respite for about twenty days. On the twenty-first day I think it was, and on a Sunday, that I went out into the streets, rather to run away if possible from my torments than with any distinct purpose. By accident I met a college acquaintance who recommended opium. Opium! Dread agent of unimaginable pleasure and pain! I had heard of it as I had heard of manna or of ambrosia, but no further; how unmeaning a sound was it at that time! What solemn chords does it now strike upon my heart! What heart-quaking vibrations of sad and happy remembrances! Reverting for a moment to these, I feel a mystic importance attached to the minutest circumstances connected with the place, and the time, and the man (if man he was) that first laid open to me the paradise of opium-eaters. It was a Sunday afternoon, wet and cheerless; and a duller spectacle this earth of ours has not to show than a rainy Sunday in London. My road homewards lay through Oxford Street; and near "the *stately* Pantheon" (as Mr. Wordsworth has oblig-ingly called it) I saw a druggist's shop. The druggist (uncon-scious minister of celestial pleasures!), as if in sympathy with the rainy Sunday, looked dull and stupid, just as any mortal druggist might be expected to look on a Sunday; and when I asked for the tincture of opium, he gave it to me as any other man might do, and furthermore, out of my shilling returned to me what seemed to be a real copper halfpenny, taken out of a real wooden drawer. Nevertheless, in spite of such indications of humanity, he has ever since existed in my mind as a beatific vision of an immortal druggist, sent down to earth on a special mission to myself. And it confirms me in this way of consid-ering him that when I next came up to London, I sought him near the stately Pantheon and found him not, and thus to me, who knew not his name (if, indeed, he had one), he seemed rather to have vanished from Oxford Street than to have re-moved to any bodily fashion. The reader may choose to think of him so, possibly, no more than a sublunary druggist; it may be so, but my faith is better: I believe him to have evanesced or evaporated. So unwillingly would I connect any mortal re-membrances with that hour, and place, and creature that first brought me acquainted with the celestial drug.

Arrived at my lodgings, it may be supposed that I lost not a moment in taking the quantity prescribed. I was necessarily ignorant of the whole art and mystery of opium-taking; and what I took, I took under every disadvantage. But I took it; and in an hour—oh, heavens! What a revulsion! What an upheaving, from its lowest depths, of the inner spirit! What an apocalypse of the world within me! That my pains had vanished was now a trifle in my eyes; this negative effect was swallowed up in the immensity of those positive effects which had opened before me in the abyss of divine enjoyment thus suddenly revealed. Here was a panacea, a [soothing drug], for all human woes; here was the secret of happiness about which philosophers had disputed for so many ages, at once discovered; happiness might now be bought for a penny and carried in the waistcoat pocket; portable ecstasies might be had corked up in a pint bottle; and peace of mind could be sent down in gallons

by the mail coach. But, if I talk in this way, the reader will think I am laughing; and I can assure him that nobody will laugh long who deals much with opium: its pleasures even are of a grave and solemn complexion; and in his happiest state the opium-eater cannot present himself in the character of *L'Al-legro;* even then, he speaks and thinks as become *Il Penseroso.* Nevertheless, I have a very reprehensible way of jesting, at times, in the midst of my own misery; and unless when I am checked by some more powerful feelings, I am afraid I shall be guilty of this indecent practice even in these annals of suf-fering or enjoyment. The reader must allow a little to my infirm nature in this respect; and, with a few indulgences of that sort, I shall endeavor to be as grave, if not drowsy, as fits a theme like opium, so anti-mercurial as it really is, and so drowsy as it is falsely reputed.

And, first, one word with respect to its bodily effects, for upon all that has been hitherto written on the subject of opium, whether by travelers in Turkey (who may plead their privilege of lying as an old immemorial right) or by professors of med-icine, writing *ex cathedra,* I have but one emphatic criticism to pronounce—Lies! Lies! Lies! I remember once, in passing a book stall, to have caught these words from a page of some satiric author: "By this time I became convinced that the Lon-don newspapers spoke truth at least twice a week, namely, on Tuesday and Saturday, and might safely be depended upon for—the list of bankrupts." In like manner, I do by no means deny that some truths have been delivered to the world in regard to opium; thus, it has been repeatedly affirmed by the learned that opium is a dusky brown in color—and this, take notice, I grant; secondly, that it is rather dear, which also I grant—for, in my time, East India opium has been three guineas a pound, and Turkey, eight; and, thirdly, that if you eat a good deal of it, most probably you must do what is particularly disagreeable to any man of regular habits, namely—die. These weighty propositions are, all and singular, true; I cannot gain-say them; and truth ever was, and will be, commendable. But in these three theorems I believe we have exhausted the stock of knowledge as yet accumulated by man on the subject of opium. And, therefore, worthy doctors, as there seems to be room for further discoveries, stand aside and allow me to come forward and lecture on this matter.

First, then, it is not so much affirmed as taken for granted, by all who ever mention opium, formally or incidentally, that it does or can produce intoxication. Now, reader, assure yourself, *meo periculo,* that no quantity of opium ever did, or could, intoxicate. As to the tincture of opium (commonly called lau-danum), *that* might certainly intoxicate if a man could bear to take enough of it; but why? Because it contains so much proof spirit, and not because it contains so much opium. But crude opium, I affirm peremptorily, is incapable of producing any state of body at all resembling that which is produced by al-cohol; and not in *degree* only incapable, but even in *kind;* it is not in the quantity of its effect merely, but in the quality, that it differs altogether. The pleasure given by wine is always mounting, and tending to a crisis, after which it declines; that from opium, when once generated, is stationary for eight or ten hours: the first, to borrow a technical distinction from medicine, is a case of acute, the second of chronic, pleasure; the one is a flame, the other a steady and equable glow. But the main distinction lies in this, that whereas wine disorders the mental faculties, opium, on the contrary (if taken in a proper manner), introduces amongst them the most exquisite order, legislation, and harmony. Wine robs a man of his self-pos-session; opium greatly invigorates it. Wine unsettles and clouds the judgment and gives a preternatural brightness and a vivid exaltation to the contempts and the admirations, to the loves and the hatreds, of the drinker; opium, on the contrary, communicates serenity and equipoise to all the faculties, active or passive; and, with respect to the temper and moral feelings in general, it gives simply that sort of vital warmth which would always accompany a bodily constitution of primeval or antediluvian health. Thus, for instance, opium, like wine, gives an expansion to the heart and the benevolent affections; but, then, with this remarkable difference, that in the sudden development of kind-heartedness which accompanies inebriation, there is always more or less of a maudlin character which exposes it to the contempt of the bystander. Men shake hands, swear eternal friendship, and shed tears—no mortal knows why; and the sensual creature is clearly uppermost. But the expansion of the benigner feelings incident to opium is no febrile access, but a healthy restoration to that state which the deep-seated irritation of pain that had disturbed and quarreled with the impulses of a heart originally just and good. True it is that even wine, up to a certain point, and with certain men, rather tends to exalt and to steady the intellect; I myself, who have never been a great wine-drinker, used to find that half a dozen glasses of wine advantageously affected the faculties, brightened and intensified the consciousness, and gave to the mind a feeling of being *ponderibus librata suis;* and certainly it is most absurdly said, in popular language, of any man, that he is *disguised* in liquor; for, on the contrary, most men are disguised by sobriety; and it is when they are drinking (as some old gentleman says in Athenaeus) that men display themselves in their true complexion of character, which surely is not disguising themselves. But still, wine constantly leads a man to the brink of absurdity and extravagance, and beyond a certain point, it is sure to volatize and to disperse the intellectual energies, whereas opium always seems to compose what had been agitated and to concentrate what had been distracted. In short, to sum up all in one word, a man who is inebriated, or tending to inebriation, is, and feels that he is, in a condition which calls up into supremacy the merely human, too often the brutal, part of his nature; but the opium-eater (I speak of him who is not suffering from any disease or other remote effects of opium) feels that the diviner part of his nature is paramount; that is, the moral affections are in a state of cloudless serenity, and over all is the great light of the majestic intellect.

This is the doctrine of the true church on the subject of opium, of which church I acknowledge myself to be the only member—the alpha and omega; but then it is to be recollected that I speak from the ground of a large and profound personal experience, whereas most of the unscientific authors who have at all treated of opium, and even of those who have written expressly on the *materia medica,* make it evident from the horror they express of it that their experimental knowledge of its action is none at all. I will, however, candidly acknowledge that I have met with one person who bore evidence to its intoxicating power such as staggered my own incredulity, for he was a surgeon and had himself taken opium largely. I happened to say to him that his enemies (as I had heard) charged him with talking nonsense on politics and that his friends apologized for him by suggesting that he was constantly in a state of intoxication from opium. Now, the accusation, said I, is not *prima facie,* and of necessity an absurd one; but the defense *is.* To my surprise, however, he insisted that both his enemies and his friends were in the right. "I will maintain," said he, "that I *do* talk nonsense; and secondly, I will maintain that I do not talk nonsense upon principle or with any view to profit,

but solely and simply," said he, "solely and simply—solely and simply" (repeating it three times over) "because I am drunk with opium; and that daily." I replied that as to the allegation of his enemies, as it seemed to be established upon such respectable testimony, seeing that the three parties concerned all agreed in it, it did not become me to question it; but the defense set up I must demur to. He proceeded to discuss the matter and to lay down his reasons, but it seemed to me so impolite to pursue an argument which must have presumed a man mistaken on a point belonging to his own profession that I did not press him even when his course of argument seemed open to objection, not to mention that a man who talks nonsense, even though "with no view to profit," is not altogether the most agreeable partner in a dispute, whether as opponent or respondent. I confess, however, that the authority of a surgeon, and one who was reputed a good one, may seem a weighty one to my prejudice; but still I must plead my experience, which was greater than his greatest by seven thousand drops a day; and though it was not possible to suppose a medical man unacquainted with the characteristic symptoms of vinous intoxication, yet it struck me that he might proceed on a logical error of using the word intoxication with too great latitude and extending it generically to all modes of nervous excitement, instead of restricting it as the expression of a specific sort of excitement connected with certain diagnostics. Some people have maintained, in my hearing, that they had been drunk upon green tea; and a medical student in London, for whose knowledge in his profession I have reason to feel great respect, assured me the other day that a patient, in recovering from an illness, had got drunk on a beefsteak.

Having dwelt so much on this first and leading error in respect to opium, I shall notice very briefly a second and a third, which are, that the elevation of spirits produced by opium is necessarily followed by a proportionate depression, and that the natural and even immediate consequence of opium is torpor and stagnation, animal and mental. The first of these errors I shall content myself with simply denying, assuring my reader that for ten years during which I took opium at intervals, the day succeeding to that on which I allowed myself this luxury was always a day of unusually good spirits.

With respect to the torpor supposed to follow, or rather (if we were to credit the numerous pictures of Turkish opium-eaters) to accompany, the practice of opium-eating, I deny that also. Certainly opium is classed under the head of narcotics, and some such effect it may produce in the end; but the primary effects of opium are always, and in the highest degree, to excite and stimulate the system; this first stage of its action always lasted with me, during my novitiate, for upwards of eight hours, so that it must be the fault of the opium-eater himself if he does not so time his exhibition of the dose (to speak medically) as that the whole weight of its narcotic influence may descend upon his sleep. Turkish opium-eaters, it seems, are absurd enough to sit, like so many equestrian statues, on logs of wood as stupid as themselves. But that the reader may judge of the degree in which opium is likely to stupefy the faculties of an Englishman, I shall (by way of treating the question illustratively rather than argumentatively) describe the way in which I myself often passed an opium evening in London during the period between 1804 and 1812. It will be seen that at least opium did not move me to seek solitude, and much less to seek inactivity or the torpid state of self-involution ascribed to the Turks. I give this account at the risk of being pronounced a crazy enthusiast or visionary, but I regard that little. I must desire my reader to bear in mind that I was a hard student, and at severe studies for all the rest of my time; and certainly I had a right occasionally to relaxations as well as other people; these, however, I allowed myself but seldom.

The late Duke of [Norfolk] used to say, ''Next Friday, by the blessing of Heaven, I purpose to be drunk,'' and in like manner I used to fix beforehand how often, within a given time, and when, I would commit a debauch of opium. This was seldom more than once in three weeks, for at that time I could not have ventured to call every day (as I did afterwards) for ''*a glass of laudanum negus, warm, and without sugar.*'' No; as I have said, I seldom drank laudanum at that time more than once in three weeks; this was usually on a Tuesday or a Saturday night, my reason for which was this: In those days Grassini sang at the opera, and her voice was delightful to me beyond all that I had ever heard. I know not what may be the state of the opera house now, having never been within its walls for seven or eight years, but at that time it was by much the most pleasant place to resort in London for passing an evening. Five shillings admitted one to the gallery, which was subject to far less annoyance than the pit of the theaters; the orchestra was distinguished, by its sweet and melodious grandeur, from all English orchestras, the composition of which, I confess, is not acceptable to my ear, from the predominance of the clangorous instruments and the almost absolute tyranny of the violin. The choruses were divine to hear, and when Grassini appeared in some interlude, as she often did, and poured forth her passionate soul as Andromache, at the tomb of Hector, etc., I question whether any Turk, of all that ever entered the paradise of opium-eaters, can have had half the pleasure I had. But, indeed, I honor the barbarians too much by supposing them capable of any pleasures approaching to the intellectual ones of an Englishman. For music is an intellectual or a sensual pleasure, according to the temperament of him who hears it. And, by the by, with the exception of the fine extravaganza on that subject in *Twelfth Night,* I do not recollect more than one thing said adequately on the subject of music in all literature; it is a passage in the *Religio Medici* of Sir T. Brown, and though chiefly remarkable for its sublimity, has also a philosophic value, inasmuch as it points to the true theory of musical effects. The mistake of most people is to suppose that it is by the ear they communicate with music and therefore that they are purely passive to its effects. But this is not so; it is by the reaction of the mind upon the notices of the ear (the *matter* coming by the senses, the *form* from the mind) that the pleasure is constructed; and therefore it is that people of equally good ear differ so much in this point from one another. Now, opium, by greatly increasing the activity of the mind, generally increases, of necessity, that particular mode of its activity by which we are able to construct out of the raw material of organic sound an elaborate intellectual pleasure. But, says a friend, a succession of musical sounds is to me like a collection of Arabic characters: I can attach no ideas to them. Ideas! My good sir? There is no occasion for them; all that class of ideas which can be available in such a case has a language of representative feelings. But this is a subject foreign to my present purposes; it is sufficient to say that a chorus, etc., of elaborate harmony, displayed before me, as in a piece of arraswork, the whole of my past life—not as if recalled by an act of memory, but as if present and incarnated in the music; no longer painful to dwell upon, but the detail of its incidents removed or blended in some hazy abstraction, and its passions exalted, spiritualized, and sublimed. All this was to be had for five shillings. And over and above the music of the stage and the orchestra, I had all around me, in the intervals of the performance, the music of the Italian language talked by Italian women—for the gallery was usually crowded with Italians—and I listened with a pleasure such as that with which Weld, the traveler, lay and listened, in Canada, to the sweet laughter of Indian women; for the less you understand of a language, the more sensible you are to the melody or harshness of its sounds. For such a purpose, therefore, it was an advantage to me that I was a poor Italian scholar, reading it but little, and not speaking it at all, nor understanding a tenth part of what I heard spoken.

These were my opera pleasures, but another pleasure I had, which, as it could be had only on a Saturday night, occasionally struggled with my love of the opera, for at that time Tuesday and Saturday were the regular opera nights. On this subject I am afraid I shall be rather obscure, but, I can assure the reader, not at all more so than Marinus in his life of Proclus or many other biographers and autobiographers of fair reputation. This pleasure, I have said, was to be had only on a Saturday night. What, then, was Saturday night to me more than any other night? I had no labors that I rested from, no wages to receive; what needed I to care for Saturday night more than as it was a summons to hear Grassini? True, most logical reader; what you say is unanswerable. And yet so it was, and is, that whereas different men throw their feelings into different channels, and most are apt to show their interest in the concerns of the poor chiefly by sympathy, expressed in some shape or other, with their distresses and sorrows, I at that time was disposed to express my interest by sympathizing with their pleasures. The pains of poverty I had lately seen too much of—more than I wished to remember; but the pleasures of the poor, their consolations of spirit, and their reposes from bodily toil can never become oppressive to contemplate. Now, Saturday night is the season for the chief regular and periodic return of rest to the poor; in this point the most hostile sects unite and acknowledge a common link of brotherhood; almost all Christendom rests from its labors. It is a rest introductory to another rest, and divided by a whole day and two nights from the renewal of toil. On this account I feel always, on a Saturday night, as though I also were released from some yoke of labor, had some wages to receive and luxury of repose to enjoy. For the sake, therefore, of witnessing, upon as large a scale as possible, a spectacle with which my sympathy was so entire, I used often, on Saturday nights, after I had taken opium, to wander forth, without much regarding the direction or the distance, to all the markets and other parts of London to which the poor resort on a Saturday night for laying out their wages. Many a family party, consisting of a man, his wife, and sometimes one or two of his children, have I listened to as they stood consulting on their ways and means, or the strength of their exchequer, or the price of household articles. Gradually I became familiar with their difficulties, and their opinions. Sometimes there might be heard murmurs of discontent, but far oftener expressions on the countenance, or uttered in words, of patience, hope, and tranquillity. And, taken generally, I must say that, in this point at least, the poor are far more philosophic than the rich, that they show a more ready and cheerful submission to what they consider as irremediable evils or irreparable losses. Whenever I saw occasion or could do it without appearing to be intrusive, I joined their parties and gave my opinion upon the matter in discussion, which, if not always judicious, was always received indulgently. If wages were a little higher, or expected to be so, or the quartern loaf a little lower, or it was reported that onions and butter were expected to fall, I was glad; yet, if the contrary were true, I drew from opium some means of consoling myself. For opium (like the bee, that extracts its materials indiscriminately from roses and from the soot of chimneys) can overrule all feelings into a compliance with the master key. Some of these rambles led me to great distances, for an opium-eater is too happy to observe the motion of time. And sometimes, in my attempts to steer homewards, upon nautical principles, by fixing my eye on the polestar, and seeking ambitiously for a northwest passage, instead of circumnavigating all the capes and headlands I had doubled in my outward voyage, I came suddenly upon such knotty problems of alleys, such enigmatical entries, and such sphinx's riddles of streets without thoroughfares, as must, I conceive, baffle the audacity of porters and confound the intellects of hackney coachmen. I could almost have believed, at times, that I must be the first discoverer of some of these *terrae incognitae* and doubted whether they had yet been laid down in the modern charts of London. For all this, however, I paid a heavy price in distant years, when the human face tyrannized over my dreams and the perplexities of my steps in London came back and haunted my sleep with the feeling of perplexities, moral or intellectual, that brought confusion to the reason or anguish and remorse to the conscience.

Thus I have shown that opium does not, of necessity, produce inactivity or torpor but that, on the contrary, it often led me into markets and theaters. Yet, in candor, I will admit that markets and theaters are not the appropriate haunts of the opium-eater when in the divinest state incident to his enjoyment. In that state, crowds become an oppression to him; music, even, too sensual and gross. He naturally seeks solitude and silence as indispensable conditions of those trances or profoundest reveries which are the crown and consummation of what opium can do for human nature. I, whose disease it was to meditate too much and to observe too little and who, upon my first entrance at college, was nearly falling into a deep melancholy from brooding too much on the sufferings which I had witnessed in London, was sufficiently aware of the tendencies of my own thoughts to do all I could to counteract them. I was, indeed, like a person who, according to the old legend, had entered the cave of Trophonius; and the remedies I sought were to force myself into society and to keep my understanding in continual activity upon matters of science. But for these remedies I should certainly have become hypochondriacally melancholy. In after years, however, when my cheerfulness was more fully reestablished, I yielded to my natural inclination for a solitary life. And at that time I often fell into these reveries upon taking opium; and more than once it has happened to me, on a summer night, when I have been at an open window, in a room from which I could overlook the sea at a mile below me and could command a view of the great town of [Liverpool], at about the same distance, that I have sat from sunset to sunrise, motionless, and without wishing to move.

I shall be charged with mysticism, Behmenism, quietism, etc., but that shall not alarm me. Sir H. Vane, the younger, was one of our wisest men; and let my readers see if he, in his philosophical works, be half as unmystical as I am. I say, then, that it has often struck me that the scene itself was somewhat typical of what took place in such a reverie. The town of [Liverpool] represented the earth, with its sorrows and its graves left behind, yet not out of sight nor wholly forgotten. The ocean, in everlasting but gentle agitation, and brooded over by dovelike calm, might not unfitly typify the mind and the mood which then swayed it. For it seemed to me as if then first I stood at a distance and aloof from the uproar of life, as if the tumult, the fever, and the strife were suspended, a respite granted from the secret burdens of the heart, a sabbath of repose, a resting from human labors. Here were the hopes

which blossom in the paths of life, reconciled with the peace which is in the grave; motions of the intellect as unwearied as the heavens, yet for all anxieties a halcyon calm; a tranquillity that seemed no product of inertia, but as if resulting from mighty and equal antagonisms; infinite activities, infinite repose.

O just, subtle, and mighty opium! That to the hearts of poor and rich alike, for the wounds that will never heal, and for "the pangs that tempt the spirit to rebel," bringest an assuaging balm—eloquent opium! That with thy potent rhetoric stealest away the purposes of wrath, and to the guilty man for one night givest back the hopes of his youth and hands washed pure from blood, and to the proud man a brief oblivion for

> Wrongs unredressed, and insults unavenged;

that summonest to the chancery of dreams, for the triumphs of suffering innocence, false witnesses, and confoundest perjury, and dost reverse the sentences of unrighteous judges. Thou buildest upon the bosom of darkness, out of the fantastic imagery of the braijn, cities and temples, beyond the art of Phidias and Praxiteles—beyond the splendor of Babylon and Hekatompylos; and, "from the anarchy of dreaming sleep," callest into sunny light the faces of long-buried beauties and the blessed household countenances, cleansed from the "dishonors of the grave." Thou only givest these gifts to man, and thou hast the keys of Paradise, O just, subtle, and mighty opium!

• • • • •

Courteous and, I hope, indulgent reader (for all my readers must be indulgent ones, or else, I fear, I shall shock them too much to count on their courtesy), having accomplished me thus far, now let me request you to move onwards, for about eight years, that is to say, from 1804 (when I said that my acquaintance with opium first began) to 1812.... I was never better in my life than in the spring of 1812; and I hope sincerely that the quantity of claret, port, or in particular Madeira which, in all probability, you, good reader, have taken and design to take for every term of eight years during your natural life, may as little disorder your health as mine was disordered by opium I had taken for the eight years between 1804 and 1812. Hence you may see again the danger of taking any medical advice from *Anastasius;* in divinity, for aught I know, or law, he may be a safe counselor, but not in medicine. No; it is far better to consult Dr. Buchan, as I did, for I never forgot that worthy man's excellent suggestion, and I was "particularly careful not to take above five and twenty ounces of laudanum." To this moderation and temperate use of the article I may ascribe it, I suppose, that as yet, at least (that is, in 1812), I am ignorant and unsuspicious of the avenging terrors which opium has in store for those who abuse its lenity. At the same time, I have been only a dilettante eater of opium; eight years' practice, even, with the single precaution of allowing sufficient intervals between every indulgence, has not been sufficient to make opium necessary to me as an article of daily diet. But now comes a different era. Move on, if you please, reader, to 1813. In the summer of the year we have just quitted, I had suffered much in bodily health from distress of mind connected with a very melancholy event. This event, being no ways related to the subject now before me, further than through bodily illness which it produced, I need not more particularly notice. Whether this illness of 1812 had any share in that of 1813, I know not; but so it was that in the latter year, I was attacked by a most appalling irritation of the stomach, in all respects the same as that which had caused me so much suffering in youth, and accompanied by a revival of all the old dreams. This is the point of my narrative on which, as respects my own self-justification, the whole of what follows may be said to hinge. (pp. 59-74)

[From 1813] the reader is to consider me as a regular and confirmed opium-eater, of whom to ask whether on any particular day he had or had not taken opium would be to ask whether his lungs had performed respiration or the heart fulfilled its functions. You understand now, reader, what I am; and you are by this time aware that no old gentleman ''with a snow-white beard'' will have any chance of persuading me to surrender ''the little golden receptacle of the pernicious drug.'' No: I give notice to all, whether moralists or surgeons, that whatever be their pretensions and skill in their respective lines of practice, they must not hope for any countenance from me if they think to begin by any savage proposition for a Lent or Ramadan of abstinence from opium. This, then, being all fully understood between us, we shall in future sail before the wind. Now, then, reader, from 1813 . . . rise up, if you please, and walk forward about three years more. Now draw up the curtain and you shall see me in a new character.

If any man, poor or rich, were to say that he would tell us what had been the happiest day in his life, and the why and the wherefore, I suppose that we should all cry out, ''Hear him! Hear him!'' As to the happiest day, that must be very difficult for any wise man to name, because any event that could occupy so distinguished a place in a man's retrospect of his life or be entitled to have shed a special felicity on any one day ought to be of such an enduring character as that (accidents apart) it should have continued to shed the same felicity, or one not distinguishably less, on many years together. To the happiest *lustrum,* however, or even to the happiest *year,* it may be allowed to any man to point without discountenance from wisdom. This year, in my case, reader, was the one which we have now reached; though it stood, I confess, as a parenthesis between years of a gloomier character. It was a year of brilliant water (to speak after the manner of jewelers), set, as it were, and insulated in the gloom and cloudy melancholy of opium. Strange as it may sound, I had a little before this time descended suddenly, and without any considerable effort, from three hundred and twenty grains of opium (that is, eight thousand drops of laudanum) per day to forty grains, or one eighth part. Instantaneously, and as if by magic, the cloud of profoundest melancholy which rested upon my brain, like some black vapors that I have seen roll away from the summits of mountains, drew off in one day, passed off with its murky banners as simultaneously as a ship that has been stranded and is floated off by a spring tide,

> That moveth altogether, if it move at all.

Now, then, I was again happy; I now took only one thousand drops of laudanum per day—and what was that? A latter spring had come to close up the season of youth: my brain performed its functions as healthily as ever before. I read Kant again, and again I understood him, or fancied that I did. Again my feelings of pleasure expanded themselves to all around me; and if any man from Oxford or Cambridge or from neither had been announced to me in my unpretending cottage, I should have welcomed him with as sumptuous a reception as so poor a man could offer. Whatever else was wanting to a wise man's happiness, of laudanum I would have given him as much as he wished, and in a golden cup. And, by the way, now that I speak of giving laudanum away, I remember, about this time, a little incident which I mention because, trifling as it was, the reader will soon meet it again in my dreams, which it

influenced more fearfully than could be imagined. One day a Malay knocked at my door. What business a Malay could have to transact amongst English mountains, I cannot conjecture; but possibly he was on his road to a seaport about forty miles distant.

The servant who opened the door to him was a young girl, born and bred amongst the mountains, who had never seen an Asiatic dress of any sort; his turban, therefore, confounded her not a little, and as it turned out that his attainments in English were exactly of the same extent as hers in the Malay, there seemed to be an impassable gulf fixed between all communication of ideas, if either party had happened to possess any. In this dilemma, the girl, recollecting the reputed learning of her master (and, doubtless, giving me credit for a knowledge of all the languages of the earth, besides, perhaps, a few of the lunar ones), came and gave me to understand that there was a sort of demon below whom she clearly imagined that my art could exorcise from the house. I did not immediately go down, but when I did, the group which presented itself, arranged as it was by accident, though not very elaborate, took hold of my fancy and my eye in a way that none of the statuesque attitudes exhibited in the ballets at the opera house, though so ostentatiously complex, had ever done. In a cottage kitchen, but paneled on the wall with dark wood, that from age and rubbing resembled oak, and looking more like a rustic hall of entrance than a kitchen, stood the Malay, his turban and loose trousers of dingy white relieved upon the dark paneling; he had placed himself nearer to the girl than she seemed to relish, though her native spirit of mountain intrepidity contended with the feeling of simple awe which her countenance expressed as she gazed upon the tigercat before her. And a more striking picture there could not be imagined than the beautiful English face of the girl, and its exquisite fairness, together with her erect and independent attitude, contrasted with the sallow and bilious skin of the Malay, enameled or veneered with mahogany by marine air, his small, fierce, restless eyes, thin lips, slavish gestures, and adorations. Half hidden by the ferocious-looking Malay was a little child from a neighboring cottage, who had crept in after him and was now in the act of reverting its head and gazing upwards at the turban and the fiery eyes beneath it, whilst with one hand he caught at the dress of the young woman for protection.

My knowledge of the Oriental tongues is not remarkably extensive, being, indeed, confined to two words—the Arabic word for ''barley'' and the Turkish for ''opium'' (*madjoon*), which I have learnt from *Anastasius.* And, as I had neither a Malay dictionary nor even Adelung's *Mithridates,* which might have helped me to a few words, I addressed him in some lines from the *Iliad;* considering that, of such language as I possessed, the Greek, in point of longitude, came geographically nearest to an Oriental one. He worshipped me in a devout manner and replied in what I suppose was Malay. In this way I saved my reputation with my neighbors, for the Malay had no means of betraying the secret. He lay down upon the floor for about an hour and then pursued his journey. On his departure I presented him with a piece of opium. To him, as an Orientalist, I concluded that opium must be familiar, and the expression of his face convinced me that it was. Nevertheless, I was struck with some little consternation when I saw him suddenly raise his hand to his mouth and (in the schoolboy phrase) bolt the whole, divided into three pieces, at one mouthful. The quantity was enough to kill three dragoons and their horses, and I felt some alarm for the poor creature; but what could be done? I had given him the opium in compassion for his solitary life, on recollecting that, if he had traveled on foot from London, it must be nearly three weeks since he could have exchanged a thought with any human being. I could not think of violating the laws of hospitality by having him seized and drenched with an emetic and thus frightening him into a notion that we were going to sacrifice him to some English idol. No; there was clearly no help for it. He took his leave, and for some days I felt anxious; but as I never heard of any Malay being found dead, I became convinced that he was used to opium and that I must have done him the service I designed by giving him one night of respite from the pains of wandering.

This incident I have digressed to mention because this Malay (partly from the picturesque exhibition he assisted to frame, partly from the anxiety I connected with his image for some days) fastened afterwards upon my dreams and brought other Malays with him worse than himself that ran *amok* at me and led me into a world of troubles. (pp. 76-80)

* * * * *

Reader, who have thus far accompanied me, I must request your attention to a brief explanatory note on three points:

1. For several reasons I have not been able to compose the notes of this part of my narrative into any regular and connected shape. I give the notes disjointed as I find them or have now drawn them up from memory. Some of them point to their own date; some I have dated; and some are undated. Whenever it could answer my purpose to transplant them from the natural or chronological order, I have not scrupled to do so. Sometimes I speak in the present, sometimes in the past tense. Few of the notes, perhaps, were written exactly at the period of time to which they relate; but this can little affect their accuracy, as the impressions were such that they can never fade from my mind. Much has been omitted. I could not, without effort, constrain myself to the task of either recalling or constructing into a regular narrative the whole burden of horrors which lies upon my brain. This feeling, partly, I plead in excuse, and partly that I am now in London and am a helpless sort of person who cannot even arrange his own papers without assistance; and I am separated from the hands which are wont to perform for me the offices of an amanuensis.

2. You will think, perhaps, that I am too confidential and communicative of my own private history. It may be so. But my way of writing is rather to think aloud and follow my own humors than much to consider who is listening to me; and if I stop to consider what is proper to be said to this or that person, I shall soon come to doubt whether any part at all is proper. The fact is, I place myself at a distance of fifteen or twenty years ahead of this time and suppose myself writing to those who will be interested about me hereafter; and wishing to have some record of a time, the entire history of which no one can know but myself, I do it as fully as I am able with the efforts I am now capable of making, because I know not whether I can ever find time to do it again.

3. It will occur to you often to ask: Why did I not release myself from the horrors of opium by leaving it off or diminishing it? To this I must answer briefly; it might be supposed that I yielded to the fascinations of opium too easily; it cannot be supposed that any man can be charmed by its terrors. The reader may be sure, therefore, that I made attempts innumerable to reduce the quantity. I add that those who witnessed the agonies of those attempts, and not myself, were the first to beg me to desist. But could not I have reduced it a drop a day, or, by adding water, have bisected or trisected a drop? A

thousand drops bisected would thus have taken nearly six years to reduce; and that they would certainly not have answered. But this is a common mistake of those who know nothing of opium experimentally; I appeal to those who do, whether it is not always found that down to a certain point it can be reduced with ease, that even pleasure, but that after that point, further reduction causes intense suffering. Yes, say many thoughtless persons who know not what they are talking of, you will suffer a little low spirits and dejection for a few days. I answer, no; there is nothing like low spirits; on the contrary, the mere animal spirits are uncommonly raised; the pulse is improved; the health is better. It is not there that the suffering lies. It has no resemblance to the suffering caused by renouncing wine. It is a state of unutterable irritation of stomach (which surely is not much like dejection), accompanied by intense perspirations and feelings such as I shall not attempt to describe without more space at my command. (pp. 84-5)

But for misery and suffering, I might indeed be said to have existed in a dormant state. I seldom could prevail on myself to write a letter; an answer of a few words, to any that I received, was the utmost that I could accomplish; and often *that* not until the letter had lain weeks, or even months, on my writing table. Without the aid of M., all records of bills paid, or *to be* paid, must have perished; and my whole domestic economy, whatever became of political economy, must have gone into irretrievable confusion. I shall not afterwards allude to this part of the case; it is one, however, which the opium-eater will find, in the end, as oppressive and tormenting as any other, from the sense of incapacity and feebleness, from the direct embarrassments incident to the neglect or procrastination of each day's appropriate duties, and from the remorse which must often exasperate the stings of these evils to a reflective and conscientious mind. The opium-eater loses none of his moral sensibilities or aspirations; he wishes and longs as earnestly as ever to realize what he believes possible and feels to be exacted by duty; but his intellectual apprehension of what is possible infinitely outruns his power, not of execution only, but even of power to attempt. He lies under the weight of incubus and nightmare; he lies in sight of all that he would fain perform, just as a man forcibly confined to his bed by the mortal languor of a relaxing disease, who is compelled to witness injury or outrage offered to some object of his tenderest love: he curses the spells which chain him down from motion; he would lay down his life if he might but get up and walk; but he is powerless as an infant and cannot even attempt to rise.

I now pass to what is the main subject of these latter confessions, to the history and journal of what took place in my dreams, for these were the immediate and proximate cause of my acutest suffering.

The first notice I had of any important change going on in this part of my physical economy was from the reawaking of a state of eye generally incident to childhood or exalted states of irritability. I know not whether my reader is aware that many children, perhaps most, have a power of painting, as it were, upon the darkness, all sorts of phantoms; in some that power is simply a mechanic affection of the eye; others have a voluntary or semivoluntary power to dismiss or summon them, or, as a child once said to me when I questioned him on this matter, "I can tell them to go, and they go; but sometimes they come when I don't tell them to come." Whereupon I told him that he had almost as unlimited a command over apparitions as a Roman centurion over his soldiers. In the middle of 1817 I think it was that this faculty became positively distressing to me: at night, when I lay awake in bed, vast processions passed along in mournful pomp, friezes of never-ending stories that to my feelings were as sad and solemn as if they were stories drawn from times before Oedipus or Priam, before Tyre, before Memphis. And, at the same time, a corresponding change took place in my dreams; a theater seemed suddenly opened and lighted up within my brain, which presented, nightly, spectacles of more than earthly splendor. And the four following facts may be mentioned as noticeable at this time:

1. That, as the creative state of the eye increased, a sympathy seemed to arise between the waking and the dreaming states of the brain in one point—that whatsoever I happened to call up and to trace by a voluntary act upon the darkness was very apt to transfer itself to my dreams, so that I feared to exercise this faculty, for as Midas turned all things to gold, that yet baffled his hopes and defrauded his human desires, so whatsoever things capable of being visually represented I did but think of in the darkness immediately shaped themselves into phantoms of the eye; and by a process apparently no less inevitable, when thus once traced in faint and visionary colors, like writings in sympathetic ink, they were drawn out by the fierce chemistry of my dreams into insufferable splendor that fretted my heart.

2. For this, and all other changes in my dreams, were accompanied by deep-seated anxiety and gloomy melancholy, such as are wholly incommunicable by words. I seemed every night to descend—not metaphorically, but literally to descend—into chasms and sunless abysses, depths below depths, from which it seemed hopeless that I could ever reascend. Nor did I, by waking, feel that I *had* reascended. This I do not dwell upon, because the state of gloom which attended these gorgeous spectacles, amounting at least to utter darkness, as of some suicidal despondency, cannot be approached by words.

3. The sense of space, and in the end, the sense of time, were both powerfully affected. Buildings, landscapes, etc., were exhibited in proportions so vast as the bodily eye is not fitted to receive. Space swelled and was amplified to an extent of unutterable infinity. This, however, did not disturb me so much as the vast expansion of time. I sometimes seemed to have lived for seventy or one hundred years in one night, nay, sometimes had feelings representative of a millennium passed in that time, or, however, of a duration far beyond the limits of any human experience.

4. The minutest incidents of childhood or forgotten scenes of later years were often revived. I could not be said to recollect them, for if I had been told of them when waking, I should not have been able to acknowledge them as parts of my past experience. But placed as they were before me, in dreams like intuitions, and clothed in all their evanescent circumstances and accompanying feelings, I *recognized* them instantaneously. I was once told by a near relative of mine that, having in her childhood fallen into a river and being on the very verge of death but for the critical assistance which reached her, she saw in a moment her whole life, in its minutest incidents, arrayed before her simultaneously as in a mirror; and she had a faculty developed as suddenly for comprehending the whole and every part. This, from some opium experiences of mine, I can believe; I have indeed seen the same thing asserted twice in modern books and accompanied by a remark which I am convinced is true, namely, that the dread book of account which the Scriptures speak of is, in fact, the mind itself of each

individual. Of this, at least, I feel assured, that there is no such thing as *forgetting* possible to the mind; a thousand accidents may and will interpose a veil between our present consciousness and the secret inscriptions on the mind. Accidents of the same sort will also rend away this veil; but alike, whether veiled or unveiled, the inscription remains forever, just as the stars seem to withdraw before the common light of day, whereas, in fact, we all know that it is the light which is drawn over them as a veil and that they are waiting to be revealed when the obscuring daylight shall have withdrawn.

Having noticed these four facts as memorably distinguishing my dreams from those of health, I shall now cite a case illustrative of the first fact and shall then cite any others that I remember, either in their chronological order or any other that may give them more effect as pictures to the reader.

I had been in youth, and even since, for occasional amusement, a great reader of Livy, whom I confess that I prefer, both for style and matter, to any other of the Roman historians; and I had often felt as most solemn and appalling sounds, and most emphatically representative of the majesty of the Roman people, the two words so often occurring in Livy—*Consul Romanus*, especially when the consul is introduced in his military character. I mean to say that the words "king," "sultan," "regent," etc., or any other titles of those who embody in their own persons the collective majesty of a great people had less power over my reverential feelings. I had also, though no great reader of history, made myself minutely and critically familiar with one period of English history, namely, the period of the Parliamentary War, having been attracted by the moral grandeur of some who figured in that day and by the many interesting memoirs which survive those unquiet times. Both these parts of my lighter reading, having furnished me often with matter of reflection, now furnished me with matter for my dreams. Often I used to see, after painting upon the blank darkness, a sort of rehearsal whilst waking, a crowd of ladies, and perhaps a festival and dances. And I heard it said, or I said to myself, "These are English ladies from the unhappy times of Charles I. These are the wives and daughters of those who met in peace and sat at the same tables and were allied by marriage or by blood, and yet, after a certain day in August, 1642, never smiled upon each other again nor met but in the field of battle, and at Marston Moor, at Newbury, or at Naseby cut asunder all ties of love by the cruel saber and washed away in blood the memory of ancient friendship." The ladies danced and looked as lovely as the court of George IV. Yet I knew, even in my dream, that they had been in the grave for nearly two centuries. This pageant would suddenly dissolve, and at a clapping of hands would be heard the heart-quaking sound of *Consul Romanus;* and immediately came "sweeping by," in gorgeous paludaments, Paulus or Marius, girt around by a company of centurions, with the crimson tunic hoisted on a spear, and followed by the *alalagmos* of the Roman legions.

Many years ago, when I was looking over Piranesi's *Antiquities of Rome*, Mr. Coleridge, who was standing by, described to me a set of plates by that artist, called his *Dreams*, which record the scenery of his own visions during the delirium of a fever. Some of them (I describe only from memory of Mr. Coleridge's account) represented vast Gothic halls, on the floor of which stood all sorts of engines and machinery, wheels, cables, pulleys, levers, catapults, etc., expressive of enormous power put forth and resistance overcome. Creeping along the sides of the walls, you perceived a staircase; and upon it, groping his way upwards, was Piranesi himself. Follow the stairs a little further and you perceive it to come to a sudden, abrupt termination, without any balustrade, and allowing no step onwards to him who had reached the extremity, except into the depths below. Whatever is to become of poor Piranesi, you suppose at least that his labors must in some way terminate here. But raise your eyes and behold a second flight of stairs still higher, on which again Piranesi is perceived, by this time standing on the very brink of the abyss. Again elevate your eyes, and a still more aerial flight of stairs is beheld; and again is poor Piranesi busy on his aspiring labors; and so on, until the unfinished stairs and Piranesi both are lost in the upper gloom of the hall. With the same power of endless growth and self-reproduction did my architecture proceed in dreams. In the early stage of my malady, the splendors of my dreams were indeed chiefly architectural, and I beheld such pomp of cities and palaces as was never yet beheld by the waking eye, unless in the clouds. (pp. 89-93)

To my architecture succeeded dreams of lakes and silvery expanses of water; these haunted me so much that I feared (though possibly it will appear ludicrous to a medical man) that some dropsical state or tendency of the brain might thus be making itself (to use a metaphysical word) *objective,* and the sentient organ *project* itself as its own object. For two months I suffered greatly in my head—a part of my bodily structure which had hitherto been so clear from all touch or taint of weakness (physically, I mean) that I used to say of it, as the last Lord Orford said of his stomach, that it seemed likely to survive the rest of my person. Till now I had never felt a headache even, or any the slightest pain, except rheumatic pains caused by my own folly. However, I got over this attack, though it must have been verging on something very dangerous.

The waters now changed their character—from translucent lakes, shining like mirrors, they now became seas and oceans. And now came a tremendous change, which, unfolding itself slowly like a scroll, through many months, promised an abiding torment; and, in fact, it never left me until the winding up of my case. Hitherto the human face had often mixed in my dreams, but not despotically nor with any special power of tormenting. But now that which I have called the tyranny of the human face began to unfold itself. Perhaps some part of my London life might be answerable for this. Be that as it may, now it was that upon the rocking waters of the ocean the human face began to appear; the sea appeared paved with innumerable faces, unturned to the heavens—faces imploring, wrathful, despairing, surged upwards by thousands, by myriads, by generations, by centuries: my agitation was infinite, my mind tossed and surged with the ocean.

May, 1818. The Malay has been a fearful enemy for months. I have been every night, through his means, transported into Asiatic scenes. I know not whether others share in my feelings on this point, but I have often thought that if I were compelled to forgo England and to live in China and among Chinese manners and modes of life and scenery, I should go mad. The causes of my horror lie deep, and some of them must be common to others. Southern Asia, in general, is the seat of awful images and associations. As the cradle of the human race, it would alone have a dim and reverential feeling connected with it. But there are other reasons. No man can pretend that the wild, barbarous, and capricious superstitions of Africa or of savage tribes elsewhere affect him in the way that he is affected by the ancient, monumental, cruel, and elaborate religions of Indostan, etc. The mere antiquity of Asiatic things, of their institutions, histories, modes of faith, etc., is so impressive

that to me the vast age of the race and name overpowers the sense of youth in the individual. A young Chinese seems to me an antediluvian man renewed. Even Englishmen, though not bred in any knowledge of such institutions, cannot but shudder at the mystic sublimity of *castes* that have flowed apart and refused to mix through such immemorial tracts of time; nor can any man fail to be awed by the names of the Ganges or the Euphrates. It contributes much to these feelings that Southern Asia is, and has been for thousands of years, the part of the earth most swarming with human life, the great *officina gentium.* Man is a weed in those regions. The vase empires, also, into which the enormous population of Asia has always been cast, give a further sublimity to the feelings associated with all Oriental names or images. In China, over and above what it has in common with the rest of Southern Asia, I am terrified by the modes of life, by the manners, and the barrier of utter abhorrence, and want of sympathy placed between us by feelings deeper than I can analyze. I could sooner live with lunatics or brute animals. All this, and much more than I can say or have time to say, the reader must enter into before he can comprehend the unimaginable horror which these dreams of Oriental imagery and mythological tortures impressed upon me. Under the connecting feeling of tropical heat and vertical sunlights I brought together all creatures, birds, beasts, reptiles, all trees and plants, usages and appearances that are found in all tropical regions, and assembled them together in China or Indostan. From kindred feelings I soon brought Egypt and all her gods under the same law. I was stared at, hooted at, grinned at, chattered at by monkeys, by parrakeets, by cockatoos. I ran into pagodas and was fixed for centuries at the summit or in secret rooms; I was the idol; I was the priest; I was worshiped; I was sacrificed. I fled from the wrath of Brahma through all the forests of Asia; Vishnu hated me; Siva laid wait for me. I came suddenly upon Isis and Osiris; I had done a deed, they said, which the ibis and the crocodile trembled at. I was buried, for a thousand years, in stone coffins, with mummies and sphinxes, in narrow chambers at the heart of eternal pyramids. I was kissed, with cancerous kisses, by crocodiles and laid, confounded with all unutterable slimy things, amongst reeds and Nilotic mud.

I thus give the reader some slight abstraction of my Oriental dreams, which always filled me with such amazement at the monstrous scenery that horror seemed absorbed, for a while, in sheer astonishment. Sooner or later came a reflux of feeling that swallowed up the astonishment and left me not so much in terror as in hatred and abomination of what I saw. Over every form, and threat, and punishment, and dim, sightless incarceration brooded a sense of eternity and infinity that drove me into an oppression as of madness. Into these dreams only, it was, with one or two slight exceptions, that any circumstances of physical horror entered. All before had been moral and spiritual terrors. But here the main agents were ugly birds, or snakes, or crocodiles, especially the last. The cursed crocodile became to me the object of more horror than almost all the rest. I was compelled to live with him, and (as was always the case, almost, in my dreams) for centuries. I escaped sometimes and found myself in Chinese houses with cane tables, etc. All the feet of the tables, sofas, etc., soon became instinct with life; the abominable head of the crocodile and his leering eyes looked out at me, multiplied into a thousand repetitions; and I stood loathing and fascinated. And so often did this hideous reptile haunt my dreams that many times the very same dream was broken up in the very same way: I heard gentle voices speaking to me (I hear everything when I am sleeping), and instantly I awoke: it was broad noon, and my children were standing, hand in hand, at my bedside, come to show me their colored shoes, or new frocks, or to let me see them dressed for going out. I protest that so awful was the transition from the damned crocodile and the other unutterable monsters and abortions of my dreams to the sight of innocent *human* natures and of infancy that, in the mighty and sudden revulsion of mind, I wept, an could not forbear it, as I kissed their faces.

June, 1819. I have had occasion to remark, at various periods of my life, that the deaths of those whom we love, and indeed the contemplation of death generally, is (*caeteris paribus*) more affecting in summer than in any other season of the year. And the reasons are these three, I think: first, that the visible heavens in summer appear far higher, more distant, and (if such a solecism may be excused) more infinite; the clouds by which chiefly the eye expounds the distance of the blue pavilion stretched over our heads are in summer more voluminous, massed, and accumulated in far grander and more towering piles: secondly, the light and the appearances of the declining and the setting sun are much more fitted to be types and characters of the infinite: and thirdly (which is the main reason), the exuberant and riotous prodigality of life naturally forces the mind more powerfully upon the antagonist thought of death and the wintry sterility of the grave. For it may be observed, generally, that wherever two thoughts stand related to each other by a law of antagonism and exist, as it were, by mutual repulsion, they are apt to suggest each other. On these accounts it is that I find it impossible to banish the thought of death when I am walking alone in the endless days of summer; and any particular death, if not more affecting, at least haunts my mind more obstinately and besiegingly in that season. Perhaps this cause, and a slight incident which I omit, might have been the immediate occasions of the following dream, to which, however, a predisposition must always have existed in my mind; but having been once roused, it never left me, and split into a thousand fantastic varieties, which often suddenly reunited and composed again the original dream.

I thought that it was a Sunday morning in May, that it was Easter Sunday, and as yet very early in the morning. I was standing, as it seemed to me, at the door of my own cottage. Right before me lay the very scene which could really be commanded from that situation, but exalted, as was usual, and solemnized by the power of dreams. There were the same mountains and the same lovely valley at their feet, but the mountains were raised to more than Alpine height, and there was interspace far larger between them of meadows and forest lawns; the hedges were rich with white roses; and no living creature was to be seen, excepting that in the green churchyard there were cattle tranquilly reposing upon the verdant graves, and particularly round about the grave of a child whom I had tenderly loved, just as I had really beheld them, a little before sunrise, in the same summer, when that child died. I gazed upon the well-known scene, and I said aloud (as I thought) to myself, "It yet wants much of sunrise, and it is Easter Sunday; and that is the day on which they celebrate the first fruits of resurrection. I will walk abroad; old griefs shall be forgotten today, for the air is cool and still, and the hills are high and stretch away to heaven; and the forest glades are as quiet as the churchyard; and with the dew I can wash the fever from my forehead, and then I shall be unhappy no longer." And I turned, as if to open my garden gate; and immediately I saw upon the left a scene far different, but which yet the power of dreams had reconciled into harmony with the other. The scene was an Oriental one, and there also it was Easter Sunday, and very early in the morning. And at a vast distance were visible,

as a stain upon the horizon, the domes and cupolas of a great city—an image or faint abstraction caught, perhaps, in childhood from some picture of Jerusalem. And not a bow shot from me, upon a stone, and shaded by Judean palms, there sat a woman; and I looked, and it was—Ann! She fixed her eyes upon me earnestly, and I said to her at length, "So, then, I have found you at last." I waited, but she answered me not a word. Her face was the same as when I saw it last, and yet, again, how different! Seventeen years ago, when the lamplight fell upon her face, as for the last time I kissed her lips (lips, Ann, that to me were not polluted!), her eyes were streaming with tears; but tears were now wiped away; she seemed more beautiful than she was at that time, but in all other points the same, and not older. Her looks were tranquil, but with unusual solemnity of expression, and I now gazed upon her with some awe; but suddenly her countenance grew dim, and turning to the mountains, I perceived vapors rolling between us; in a moment all had vanished; thick darkness came on; and in the twinkling of an eye I was far away from mountains, and by lamplight in Oxford Street, walking again with Ann—just as we walked seventeen years before, when we were both children.

As a final specimen, I cite one of a different character, from 1820.

The dream commenced with a music which now I often heard in dreams—a music of preparation and of awakening suspense, a music like the opening of the Coronation Anthem and which, like *that*, gave the feeling of a vast march, of infinite cavalcades filing off, and the tread of innumerable armies. The morning was come of a mighty day—a day of crisis and of final hope for human nature, then suffering some mysterious eclipse and laboring in some dread extremity. Somewhere, I knew not where—somehow, I knew not how—by some beings, I knew not whom—a battle, a strife, an agony, was conducting, was evolving like a great drama or piece of music, with which my sympathy was the more insupportable from my confusion as to its place, its cause, its nature, and its possible issue. I, as is usual in dreams (where, of necessity, we make ourselves central to every movement), had the power, and yet had not the power, to decide it. I had the power, if I could raise myself, to will it; and yet again had not the power, for the weight of twenty Atlantics was upon me, or the oppression of inexpiable guilt. "Deeper than ever plummet sounded," I lay inactive. Then, like a chorus, the passion deepened. Some greater interest was at stake; some mightier cause than ever yet the sword had pleaded or trumpet had proclaimed. Then came sudden alarms, hurryings to and fro, trepidations of innumerable fugitives. I knew not whether from the good cause or the bad; darkness and lights; tempest and human faces; and at last, with the sense that all was lost, female forms, and the features that were worth all the world to me, and but a moment allowed—and clasped hands, and heartbreaking partings, and then everlasting farewells! And, with a sigh, such as the caves of hell sighed when the incestuous mother uttered the abhorred name of death, the sound was reverberated—everlasting farewells! And again, and yet again reverberated—everlasting farewells!

And I awoke in struggles, and cried aloud, "I will sleep no more!"

But I am now called upon to wind up a narrative which has already extended to an unreasonable length. Within more spacious limits the materials which I have used might have been better unfolded; and much which I have not used might have been added with effect. Perhaps, however, enough has been given. It now remains that I should say something of the way in which this conflict of horrors was finally brought to its crisis. The reader [may be aware] ... that the opium-eater has, in some way or other, "unwound, almost to its final links, the accursed chain which bound him." By what means? To have narrated this, according to the original intention, would have far exceeded the space which can now be allowed. It is fortunate, as such a cogent reason exists for abridging it, that I should, on a maturer view of the case, have been exceedingly unwilling to injure, by any such unaffecting details, the impression of the history itself, as an appeal to the prudence and the conscience of the yet unconfirmed opium-eater, or even (though a very inferior consideration) to injure its effect as a composition. The interest of the judicious reader will not attach itself chiefly to the subject of the fascinating spells, but to the fascinating power. Not the opium-eater, but the opium, is the true hero of the tale, and the legitimate center on which the interest revolves. The object was to display the marvelous agency of opium, whether for pleasure or for pain; if that is done, the action of the piece has closed.

However, as some people, in spite of all laws to the contrary, will persist in asking what became of the opium-eater and in what state he now is, I answer for him thus: The reader is aware that opium had long ceased to found its empire on spells of pleasure; it was solely by the tortures connected with the attempt to abjure it that it kept its hold. Yet, as other tortures, no less, it may be thought, attended the nonabjuration of such a tyrant, a choice only of evils was left; and *that* might as well have been adopted, which, however terrific in itself, held out a prospect of final restoration to happiness. This appears true, but good logic gave the author no strength to act upon it. However, a crisis arrived for the author's life, and a crisis for other objects still dearer to him, and which will always be far dearer to him than his life, even now that it is again a happy one. I saw that I must die if I continued the opium; I determined, therefore, if that should be required, to die in throwing it off. How much I was at that time taking, I cannot say, for the opium which I used had been purchased for me by a friend, who afterwards refused to let me pay him, so that I could not ascertain even what quantity I had used within a year. I apprehend, however, that I took it very irregularly and that I varied from about fifty or sixty grains to one hundred and fifty a day. My first task was to reduce it to forty, to thirty, and, as fast as I could, to twelve grains.

I triumphed; but think not, reader, that therefore my sufferings were ended; nor think of me as of one sitting in a *dejected* state. Think of me as of one, even when four months had passed, still agitated, writhing, throbbing, palpitating, shattered; and much, perhaps, in the situation of him who has been racked, as I collect the torments of that state from the affecting account of them left by the most innocent sufferer (of the time of James I.). Meantime, I derived no benefit from any medicine except one prescribed to me by an Edinburgh surgeon of great eminence, namely, ammoniated tincture of valerian. Medical account, therefore, of my emancipation, I have not much to give; and even that little, as managed by a man so ignorant of medicine as myself, would probably tend only to mislead. At all events, it would be misplaced in this situation. The moral of the narrative is addressed to the opium-eater, and therefore, of necessity, limited in its application. If he is taught to fear and tremble, enough has been effected. But he may say that the issue of my case is at least a proof that opium, after a seventeen years' use and an eight years' abuse of its powers, may still be renounced, and that he may chance to bring to the task greater energy than I did or that, with a stronger consti-

tution than mine, he may obtain the same results with less. This may be true; I would not presume to measure the efforts of other men by my own. I heartily wish him more energy; I wish him the same success. Nevertheless, I had motives external to myself which he may unfortunately want; and these supplied me with conscientious supports, which mere personal interests might fail to supply to a mind debilitated by opium.

Jeremy Taylor conjectures that it may be as painful to be born as to die. I think it probable, and during the whole period of diminishing the opium I had the torments of a man passing out of one mode of existence into another. The issue was not death, but a sort of physical regeneration, and, I may add, that ever since, at intervals, I have had a restoration of more than youthful spirits, though under the pressure of difficulties, which, in a less happy state of mind, I should have called misfortunes.

One memorial of my former condition still remains; my dreams are not yet perfectly calm; the dread swell and agitation of the storm have not wholly subsided; the legions that encamped in them are drawing off, but not all departed; my sleep is tumultuous, and like the gates of Paradise to our first parents when looking back from afar, it is still (in the tremendous line of Milton):

> With dreadful faces thronged and fiery arms.

(pp. 94-102)

Thomas De Quincey, in his Confessions of an English Opium-Eater and Other Writings, *edited by Aileen Ward, New American Library, 1966, 334 p.*

ARTHUR SYMONS

[*Symons was a critic, poet, dramatist, short story writer, and editor who first gained notoriety in the 1890s as an English Decadent. In the following poem, originally published in 1889, Symons contrasts the delights of opium smoking with its miseries and degradations.*]

> I am engulfed, and drown deliciously.
> Soft music like a perfume, and sweet light
> Golden with audible odours exquisite,
> Swathe me with cerements for eternity.
> Time is no more. I pause and yet I flee.
> A million ages wrap me around with night.
> I drain a million ages of delight.
> I hold the future in my memory.
>
> Also I have this garret which I rent,
> This bed of straw, and this that was a chair,
> This worn-out body like a tattered tent,
> This crust, of which the rats have eaten part,
> This pipe of opium; rage, remorse, despair;
> This soul at pawn and this delirious heart.

Arthur Symons, "The Opium-Smoker," in his Poems, Vol. I, *William Heinemann, 1901, p. 3.*

HISTORICAL BACKGROUND

VIRGINIA BERRIDGE

[*Berridge provides an extended survey of opium consumption in nineteenth-century England, describing the sale and use of the drug in Victorian society.*]

In the first half of the nineteenth century, opium preparations were freely on sale to anyone who wanted to buy them, in any sort of shop; they were carried about the countryside by hawkers, sold in grocers' and general stores and on market stalls. Despite Britain's long-standing involvement in the Indian opium trade with China, the bulk of the drug imported into the country came not from India but from Turkey. It was freely imported (with a decreasing amount of duty); actual quantities varied in the first half of the century from 12,000 lbs. of Turkish opium in 1834 to 177,000 lbs. in 1939, out of overall import totals of 48,000 lbs. and 196,000 lbs. respectively. Turkish opium, noted for its strength and high quality, usually provided between 80 and 90% of Britain's total import of the drug, only losing some of its preeminence in the late seventies and eighties when the Persian variety was more widely imported. Opium was bought and sold on the London drug market like any other commodity. Drug brokers working with the Turkey Company, which was initially the importing organisation, controlled the sale negotiations. In 1865, for instance, Price, Gifford, and Company were offering a diverse selection, including seven cases of opium, at Garraway's Coffee House by the Royal Exchange. August bodies like the Apothecaries' Company were approached by the brokers themselves. Mr. Warrington, a director of the company, told a parliamentary committee in the mid-1850s how this was done:

> We buy the most genuine article which comes to the London Market, irrespective of price, and we test it before buying. The system of buying is this: every Saturday a public list is suspended in the outer part of the counting house, for the whole drug trade, brokers and merchants or importers, of the things which we wish to buy the following week. Before one o'clock on the following Tuesday, any one who wishes may send samples. There is a committee of medical gentlemen, which is called the Buying Committee, attended by the principal chemical officer and myself. Those samples are all laid out; they are tested, and the best of them selected.

After these frock-coated medical gentlemen made their decisions, solemnly examining and testing opium like so much tea, the drug passed through a complicated round of grinding and preparation, of sale and resale, from wholesaler to provincial wholesalers, until finally it ended up as part of the stock in trade of a local shop.

Retail sales were not limited to pharmacists, nor did sales have to be made through pharmacist's or chemist's shops. Until 1868 any person, whether qualified or not, could buy and sell opium. Pharmacists and apothecaries, grocers and general dealers all sent in their orders to the provincial wholesalers, and the carrier's carts in country districts brought out fifty-six pound lots of raw opium and gallons of laudanum for delivery. Some dealers did surround the sale of the drug with their own informal restrictions, but many of the people engaged in selling drugs and chemicals in the mid-1850s sold opium freely: "You have a great medley and variety of classes, some who will not sell at all, others who will sell under caution, and others who will sell anything on application." Many small corner shops sold opiates amid a rich profusion of other items. One such in a Manchester factory area in the 1850s was "a shop in the 'general line', in the window of which, amongst eggs, candles, sugar, bread, soap, butter, starch, herrings, and cheese, I observed a placard marked 'Childrens' Draughts, a penny each.'" The Hull coroner noted after an inquest in 1854 on an infant who had been poisoned with laudanum sold in mistake for syrup of rhubarb that the liquid opiate "was kept with several

other bottles of similar shape and appearance on a shelf in the shop window of a Grocer in a district thickly inhabited by factory operatives, and was given to a messenger between six and seven years old." Many such small corner shops were kept by people little removed in status from the population of the surrounding area they served. They, and some of the chemists in the poor areas, were often ignorant and ill-taught. For example, the prescription book of one business in Scarborough, compiled just after 1868, details not only "red oils for cattle" and methods of dressing rabbit skins, but an infants preservative remedy and one for "coff drops," based on "Loddanum, parreygorick," and other drugs.

The range of opiate preparations available in these and other shops was enormous. Medical texts of the time list opiate electuary, powder of chalk with opium, opiate confection, powder of ipecacuanha and opium (Dover's Powder), tincture of soap and opium, liquorice troches with opium, wine of opium (Sydenham's Laudanum), vinegar of opium, extract of opium, opiate clyster, suppositories, opium liniment, plaster of opium, and two of the most noted compounds—tincture of opium, or laudanum, a mixture of opium and alcohol, and the camphorated tincture, known as paregoric elixir. Many chemists had their own local recipes or compiled preparations from formulas suggested by their customers. A wide range of commercial opiate-based preparations was also available. George Meggeson, a lozenge manufacturer in Cannon Street, London, listed nine opiate-based lozenges in his wholesale list. Dr. Collis Browne's chlorodyne was introduced in 1857. There were children's opiates like Godfrey's Cordial and Dalby's Carminative. Perhaps the most popular were laudanum and raw opium itself, the latter sold often in "pills or penny sticks," the former sold also in pennyworths—twenty or twenty-five drops could be had for a penny. In a absence of other effective drugs, opiates were widely used despite a general lack of knowledge of how the drug really worked. Echoes of the eighteenth-century debate on whether its action was a stimulant or sedative one remained, and some doctors came to rather strange conclusions about its likely effects. F. Robinson, a Hammersmith surgeon, writing to the Lancet in 1846, for instance, thought that opium "would be capable of producing quicker and more deadly effects on a person of thin spare habit . . . than on a large robust individual." In general it was used, or recommended, at one time or another to treat almost every disease and condition imaginable. Up to 20% of all prescriptions dispensed by pharmacists in Islington and Holloway in the period between the 1840s and 1860s contained opiates. At the end of the 1830s, Jonathan Pereira noted in his well-known textbook that it was used "to mitigate pain, to allay spasm, to promote sleep, to reduce nervous restlessness, to produce perspiration, and to check profuse mucous discharge from the bronchial tubes and gastrointestinal canal." Opium was recommended for everything from influenza and earache, to hydrophobia, haemorrhage, and heart disease.

The way in which opiates were sold and used in the first half of the century makes it sufficiently clear that society in general had no particular fears about their use. Experiments by farmers and businessmen in growing British opium in the early decades of the century emphasised the positive attitude which many took. The most successful experimenters were, perhaps, Dr. John Cowley and Mr. Staines of Winslow who in 1823 received thirty guineas from the Royal Society of Arts for "143 pounds of opium, of excellent quality, collected by them from about eleven acres of land, planted with Papaver Somniferum." Thomas Jones, using a plot of ground near Enfield and exploiting the possibilities of child labour, established a clear pay structure for his workers based on age, while Mr. Jeston, a surgeon from Henley-on-Thames, favoured a system based on productivity with a rate of 8d. a day and 1d. for every extra bottle of opium collected. Poppy cultivation was never a wholesale commercial proposition, but such efforts were indicative of contemporary acceptance of the drug's use. Accounts of opium eating were few in number and mostly confined to descriptions provided by those like Baron de Tott who had travelled in the East at the end of the eighteenth century. Even the publication in 1821 of Thomas de Quincey's *Confessions of an English Opium Eater* in serial form in the *London Magazine* [see excerpt above], although a major literary event and a matter of much public discussion, attracted a less concerned or anxious reaction than might have been supposed.

In one area of the country, the low-lying, marshy, ague-ridden Fens, it was accepted that the sale of the drug in large quantities was commonplace. People throughout the area were to some degree dependent on opium, as Dr. Julian Hunter noted, when reporting to the Privy Council in 1864:

> A man in South Lincolnshire complained that his wife had spent £100 on opium since he married. A man may be seen occasionally asleep in a field leaning on his hoe. He starts when approached, and works vigorously for a while. A man who is setting about a hard job takes his pill as preliminary, and many never take their beer without dropping a piece of opium into it.

A growing official uneasiness about opiate use did develop, however, and eventually found expression in the restrictions of the 1868 Pharmacy Act and in changed attitudes toward the drug. Certainly there was a public health case for concern about the way in which opiates were used. This element should not be underestimated as part of the increased concern. From the late 1830s and early 1840s, opiate use became a significant, if minor, part of the general public health cause. The welter of statistics and information produced by government investigations and enquiries and by newly established government agencies, the Registrar General's Office in particular, revealed a situation which appeared worrying in its implications. Import statistics, and in particular the amount of opium entered for home consumption, were rising. In 1829, 23,000 lbs. were retained in the United Kingdom; in 1839, 41,000 lbs. But home consumption per thousand living indicated a less steep progression than a simple comparison of import totals: consumption had risen from two pounds to three pounds per thousand persons living between the 1830s and the late 1850s.

Statistics on opiate deaths caused concern too—the publication of coroner's returns of deaths by poisoning in England and Wales in 1839 revealed that 186 out of a total of 543 such deaths were the result of opium poisoning. The Registrar General's Office collected scattered figures for opiate deaths which were published in the late thirties: in the two years 1838 and 1839, there were 27 opiate deaths in London out of a total of 125 poisonings. The 1840 report revealed that 5 deaths per million living were the result of opium poisoning. The first series of figures on opium beginning in the early 1860s showed the full extent of the situation: 126 deaths from opiates in 1863, for instance, out of a total of 403 poisoning fatalities, with 80 deaths in that year and 95 in 1864 from laudanum and syrup of poppies alone. Around a third of all poisoning deaths in the decade were the result of the administration of opiates, and the relatively high accidental, rather than suicidal, death rate from opiates bore witness to the drug's easy availability. Prior to 1868, at least two-thirds of these deaths, and often a higher proportion of the general narcotic death rate, comprised accidental deaths: 5.1/million in 1863 from a total of 6.1/million for all violent opium deaths, 4.3/million in 1866 out of a total of 5.3/million living.

In some respects the poisoning statistics were less worrying than they at first appeared. The opiate death rate was in reality quite stable—it had only risen from the five deaths per million living of 1840 to six per million in the early 1860s (and the 1840 figure was probably an underestimate). But as the absolute poisoning data became common knowledge in medical and official circles, a sustained campaign began to limit the open availability and use of opiates. Expressed most clearly through enquires into the sale of poisons in the 1850s and through the reports of Sir John Simons, the medical officer to the Privy Council, in the 1860s, the protagonists' case emphasised the unguarded way in which opiates were often supplied. Alfred Taylor, professor of medical jurisprudence at Guy's Hospital, was particularly active in attacking the drug's open availability. In his book *On Poisons,* first published in 1848, in his evidence before the 1857 Select Committee on the Sale of Poisons, and in the report he compiled in 1863 for the Privy Council on *Dangers in the Sale of Drugs and Poisons,* he reemphasised the dangers involved. He agreed that "in many large manufacturing towns they put down their penny and get opium . . . in the factory districts there is a very large sale of opium. If you allow the purchase of a pennyworth, you must allow the purchase of an ounce, and the drug certainly causes a large number of deaths annually, 37 per cent." He had the full weight of medical opinion behind him, and case histories in the medical journals in the forties and fifties gave additional support to the argument that the number of accidental poisonings was too high. The haphazard way in which the drug was sold could lead to real tragedy. In 1858, for instance, a Mr. Story took a shop at Guisborough with a stock of groceries, draperies, and drugs—"Drugs he was not thoroughly acquaitned with, and objected to take the whole of them, but the person leaving pressed him to do so." A fortnight later when a servant maid, Fanny Wilkinson, sent out for an ounce of powdered rhubarb, Story, under the impression that the label "Pulv. opii. Turc. opt." on the opium bottle meant that it contained Turkish rhubarb, supplied her with half an ounce of powdered opium. She swallowed thirty grains as a teaspoonful and died the same evening. Story had to face a trial for manslaughter.

The deaths of well-known figures—that of Augustus Stafford, MP in 1857, was said to have been accelerated, despite the existence of gallstones and a weak heart, by the incautious use of laudanum—added further emphasis to the possibilities of accidental overdosing. Opiate suicides were part, too, of the public health case. The drug was said by R. Christison in his *Treatise on Poisons* to be favoured by the timid would-be suicide because of the gentleness of its operation. Other methods were more popular—1,234 people cut their own throats and 2,570 hanged themselves compared to a mere 115 opiate suicides between 1863 and 1867—but opiates were among the most popular poisons for self-destruction throughout the century. The subject could even have its lighter side. In his suicide note in 1861, Samuel Hillier, paymaster general in the Ninth Lancers, revealed the trouble that committing suicide with opium had caused him. "About ten days ago I took 1/2 an ounce of laudanum, enough to poison a horse. It had no effect on me. After that I took eight grains of opium; again, no effect, except a slight drowsiness. Then 4 grains of morphia; no effect.

I then took 5 grains of liquor opii sedativus, with the same result.'' Hillier, convinced that he was poison-proof, finally shot himself.

There were possibilities too of the criminal use of opiates. Although the published figures were minute, it was said that prostitutes in the East End of London used to add laudanum to sailors' beer and rob them of both clothes and money while the sailors were in a ''state of total stupefaction.'' Such tales could simply have been attempts at self-justification by sailors who had made fools of themselves (similar rumours circulating at the time of the cocaine ''scare'' of 1915-16 were found, on investigation, to be groundless), but opium was used in this way in other circumstances. Henry Tipper, a cab driver about to be tried at Worcester Assizes in 1856 for robbing old pensioners, tried to poison witnesses by treating them to beer laced with forty-five grains of opium. Contemporary acceptance of the prevalence of such criminal usage was reflected in the section of the 1861 Offences against the Person Act which made the giving of laudanum with such intent a criminal offence. (pp. 438-45)

Anxiety about opiate use had deeper roots than simple humanitarianism. Uneasiness was connected too with fundamental shifts in nineteenth-century society. Rapid industrialisation and urbanisation, the creation of rough and raw manufacturing towns, and the strikes, violence, crime, and political unrest which appeared endemic in such areas evoked a feeling of fear and unease. This found expression in the establishment of myths about working-class habits such as the widespread belief in official, public health, and ''respectable'' circles in general, that working people were accustomed to use opiates for ''stimulant'' or ''recreational'' purposes, as an alternative when drink was too expensive—a fundamental distortion of popular patterns of opiate use. De Quincey's statement about this practice in his *Confessions* caused as much interest and concern as the revelations about his own opium eating. His description of the use of opium by Manchester working people in the early years of the century was the starting point of the whole debate:

> Some years ago, on passing through Manchester, I was informed by several cotton-manufacturers, that their work-people were rapidly getting into the practice of opium-eating, so much so, that on a Saturday afternoon the counter of the druggists were strewed with pills of one, two, or three grains, in preparation for the known demand of the evening. The immediate occasion of this practice was the lowness of wages, which, at that time, would not allow them to indulge in ale or spirits.

This ''stimulant'' idea of working-class opium consumption was easily accepted at a time of class tension and hostility, just as later in the century, fear of the cocaine-crazed black in the American South coincided with a dread of black violence and provided useful justification for repression.

Certainly, working-class households, and middle-class ones as well, did use large quantities of opium. Edward Hodgson, a Stockton-on-Tees chemist, recorded 292 purchases of opium and laudanum during a month in 1857, with an average sale of 2½ drachms of opium and over 4 drachms of laudanum a day. A fair proportion of working people were physically dependent on opiates, with their dependence largely unnoticed unless for some reason supplies of the drug were curtailed. Those in Stockport who found themselves unable to afford their customary opiates during the cotton famine were only one example. Such use was rarely ''recreational,'' arising as it did

partly from necessity—the lack of proper medical care and the impossibility of paying for or receiving free treatment for small ailments—and also from a continuing cultural tradition of self-medication and use of opiates in various forms. In urban working-class society, commercially available opium and laudanum replaced the poppy-head tea and home-made opiate remedies of the agricultural areas.

In the absence of a valid distinction between medical and non-medical use, it is not surprising that much of the discussion on this point was confused and uncertain. There is little doubt, however, that the ''stimulant'' idea of working-class opiate use was widely accepted at the time, as in, for example, Mrs. Gaskell's *Mary Barton*, Dr. Southwood Smith's evidence to the Health of Towns Commission in the 1840s, and generally in medical circles; it has tended to be uncritically accepted ever since. Some commentators were sympathetic, but others saw it as undermining the individual effort and hard work seen as necessary for the industrial work force. The *Lancet* put this view forcefully in 1830: ''Would you add to the pangs of an aching heart, and the torture of half-cramped limbs, the frightful phantoms of a bewildering drug? . . . opium—the subtle, crafty, sleeping draught of tyrants, the courted charm of worthless sensual slaves: To make the people exert themselves to improve their conditions, pain, destitution and wretchedness, must be their stimulants!'' There existed an explicit fear of ''contamination'' by working-class opium eating and a belief that it could have a disruptive impact on middle-class society. A writer in *Chambers' Journal* commented in 1845: ''The evil is not only serious in its actual effects, but in prospect; all the inquiries made on the subject elicited proof of its alarming increase, with a tendency upwards to the middle classes. Working-class opiate use became a useful polemical weapon—whether in the debate over opium eating and longevity which started up in the 1830s, the agitation of the pharmacists to secure control of the dispensing of poisons, or in the debate over temperance in Victorian society. The ''opium eating teeto-taller'' became a standard stereotype. Opponents of licensing regulation and temperance in general argued forcibly that drink restriction would only lead to ever higher working-class opium consumption. In statistical terms alone the argument was a fallacy, but the myth remained obstinately persistent, particularly prone to break out at times when there was concern about the militancy of the temperance movement. It was indicative of the basic lack of comprehension of self-medication, for laudanum had long been known as an antidote to alcohol not only in orthodox medical practice, but also as an informal popular means of sobering up.

The dosing of children with opiates formed part of the more general working-class opium eating question. The practice undoubtedly existed: between 1863 and 1867, for instance, 292 children under five died from narcotic poisoning, against 254 adults of thirty-five or more. Even this number was probably an underestimate because, as Dr. Hunter pointed out in his report in 1864 on infant mortality in rural areas, many infant narcotic deaths were mistakenly registered as being due to ''overlying'' or ''premature birth.'' Many of the deaths attributed to opium, however, were more generally the result of unhealthy constitution and want of food. What a character in Tom Hood's 1844 novel *Out Family* called ''syruping the infants'' became part of the general anxiety about unrestricted opiate use. In novels, parliamentary investigations, and reports presented before social reforming agencies, a clearly defined stereotype of the practice emerged. In such presentations, it was not only the mothers themselves who were directly blamed;

the unqualified midwives, the old nurses who took babies to nurse while their mothers were at work, bore the brunt of criticism. They were seen as leading mothers astray, as in the *Morning Chronicle's* report on Manchester in the 1840s: "The nurses, and sometimes the mothers take to making the stuff themselves. They buy pennyworths of anniseed [*sic*], and treacle and sugar add the laudanum to it, and make the dose as strong as they like. The midwives teach them how to brew it, and if the quantity of laudanum comes expensive, they use crude opium instead. Of course numberless children are carried off in this way." Alternately, doping with opiates could be more directly the nurses' responsibility. This was Devilsdust's experience in Benjamin Disraeli's *Sybil:*

> About a fortnight after his mother had introduced him into the world, she returned to her factory and put her infant out to nurse—that is to say, she paid threepence a week to an old woman, who takes charge of these new-born babies for the day, and gives them back at night to their mothers. The expense is not great, laudanum and treacle . . . affords these innocents a brief taste of the sweets of existence . . . infanticide is practised as extensively and as legally in England, as it is on the banks of the Ganges.

Implicit in many such descriptions was a belief in the prime importance of maternal care and a condemnation both of women's factory labour and of unqualified nurses, feelings which research on family structure in industrial areas has shown to be compounded largely of prejudice and a misunderstanding of working-class child rearing customs. In industrial Lancashire, working mothers were relatively unimportant as a source of neglect, and the aged and dirty nurse was more likely to be the child's grandmother than a professional child minder. Since no patent baby foods appeared on the market until 1867, and even then they were usually priced beyond working-class pockets, something such as opium, which could effectively quiet a baby, likely to be puny and weak and made fretful and restless by unsuitable food, must have have been a godsend. The belief in the positive benefits of the drug should also not be forgotten. Opium was indeed an effective palliative for the gastro-intestinal disorders which in fact killed most infants, and working-class practice had more sense in it than the reformers realised.

· · · · ·

Doctors and pharmacists had been involved in all aspects of the debates on opiate use in the nineteenth century: in the public health issues and in the questions of popular opium consumption and child doping. Their own organisation as separate professions in mid-century also had a notable impact not only on attitudes toward opium, but also on the progress and form of legislative control of opiates. The emergence of a "professional ethic" in mid-nineteenth-century England, underpinned as it was by the expansion of the middle class in industrial society and the massive growth in incomes which increased the market for specialist services, had a particular impact in the medical and pharmaceutical worlds. As early as 1841 the Pharmaceutical Society began to form a professional body out of an amalgam of chemists and druggists and the dispensing functions of the Society of Apothecaries. The newly organised pharmaceutical chemists, granted a charter of incorporation in 1843, were at first a minority body—membership was only 2,500 in the 1850s out of a fluctuating total of between 15,000 and 26,000 chemists and druggists—but their long-term aim was to establish a tightly knit organisation, with control over entry through educational qualifications. Professional organisation among the doctors followed a similar path with the

formation of the British Medical Association in the early 1850s and the establishment, through the 1858 Medical Act, of the single medical register and the General Medical Council to oversee the conduct of the profession.

Both developments influenced the sale of drugs and, in particular, the position of such a popular and useful remedy as opium. The pharmacists wished to emphasise their metamorphosis from tradesmen and shopkeepers to professionals by demanding, and getting, control over the right to sell certain poisons, opium among them. Doctors too had designs on the sale of poisons, and the General Medical Council did at one time aim to control pharmacy as well as medicine. Doctors in general wanted to end self-medication, especially among the working class, since only by obtaining the sole right to prescribe certain drugs could their professional and qualified status be adequately established. Both professional groups argued in favour of the legislative control of such drugs, and these arguments necessarily constituted a powerful attack not only on the selling of poisons by general shopkeepers, but also on the dangerous properties of the drugs themselves. Opium naturally figured largely. (pp. 446-51)

The pharmacists finally obtained the professional control they had been seeking in the 1868 Pharmacy Act, but the position of opium in the act emphasised how professional motives rather than humanitarian feeling, or the public health issue, shaped the final form of legislation. Opium was one of the fifteen poisons selected for control, but it was finally placed in the second, not the first, schedule of the act. In the second schedule, only labelling restrictions were applicable while poisons in the first were far more closely restricted. Also, Section Sixteen of the act specifically excluded patent medicines, many opiate-based, from its operation. Doctors and pharmacists had parted company over the regulation of opium. The latter, though anxious to remove the sale of the drug from unqualified men, did not wish to restrict its sale to the extent that their own trade would be affected. The medical profession, and especially those doctors active in the public health movement, were anxious for more stringent restriction. Elias Bremridge, secretary of the Pharmaceutical Society, later told the General Medical Council's Pharmacy Bill Committee that opium had been dropped from the more restrictive first part of the poisons schedule because of protests from within the profession: "The promoters of the Bill received such strong representations from chemists residing principally in Cambridgeshire, Lincolnshire, and Norfolk, against interfering with their business—opium, as they stated, being one of their chief articles of trade—that the promoters felt compelled to strike opium out of Schedule A." The committee, after hearing this information, voiced exactly the opposite point of view: "The Committee were of opinion that the statement that regulations as to the sale of opium would interfere with the trade profits of druggists in certain parts of England, constituted the strongest ground for inserting opium in the list of poisons." The pharmacists and their trading needs won the day, and controls on opium sales remained relatively lax until the early twentieth century. The practical impact of the act was limited. Although the fall in the death rate was marked, unqualified sales continued simply because the Pharmaceutical Society had no adequate powers of enforcement and because patent medicines, many opiate-based, were left completely uncontrolled. But the act was important in the formation of attitudes toward opium. For the first time the principle that it must be controlled had received official, legislative sanction, and a decisive move had been made, in principle if not always in practice, away from the tolerant attitudes of the first half of the century.

The doctors were left dissatisfied by this outcome, and their professional moves against self-medication with opiates provided fresh impetus for changing attitudes to opiate use. Cases where opium and laudanum had been supplied without proper labels, with dire results, were continually publicised in the medical journals. Dr. E. Hartley, writing in the *Lancet* in 1873, severely criticised the position of opium under the act: ''It is no slight matter that an individual can go from chemist to chemist, procuring a deadly drug, such as laudanum, without it being compulsory for the retailer in every instance to make an entry of the transaction. We fail to see why the law should not place the same restrictions upon the sale of opium as upon strychnia, aconite, etc. when not prescribed by a registered medical practitioner.'' Both doctors and pharmacists combined in attempts to remove the glaring loophole in the act—the leeway it allowed to general dealers to continue to sell opium-based patent medicines. Publications like *Health News's Exposures of Quackery,* published in the mid-1890s, spread alarm: ''The ease with which these can be produced—we refer now more particularly to the opiate and other narcotic preparations—has led to a wide-spread system of home drugging.'' These comments coincided with a series of lawsuits against the sellers of patent medicine, culminating in the 1892 Treasury case against the manufacturers of Collis Browne's chlordyne which established that opiate-based medicines had to be sold with a poison label.

Doctors were active elsewhere, too, in formulating new attitudes toward opiate use. Medical practice itself was changing; drugs like quinine and chloral were replacing opiates as a time-honoured standby for fever and sleeplessness. Its use in other areas, such as the treatment of insanity or delirium tremens, was under attack; and there was a growing belief, particularly among younger medical men, that opiates should, as far as possible, be avoided. (pp. 451-53)

Morality had its part to play, too; the domestic implications of attitudes promoted by the anti-opium movement served further to emphasise the deviant and possibly dangerous nature of opiate use. The Society for the Suppression of the Opium Trade, founded in 1874 as the Anglo-Oriental Society for the Suppression of the Opium Trade and the successor to earlier short-lived bodies, campaigned vigorously, and eventually most successfully, for an end to what it saw as Britain's demoralising and degrading involvement in the Indian opium trade with China. The indignation which its members aroused was not entirely of a moral nature. The broad spectrum of religious interests under a Quaker leadership which the society represented found additional support in the fact that opium revenue was of declining importance in the Indian budget and that increased opportunities for British manufactured goods would present themselves in China with the ending of the opium trade. The society had its campaigning successes. Its apparent victory in the appointment of the Royal Commission on Opium in 1893 was turned into a decisive defeat by that body's decidedly pro-opium conclusions, but the Liberal election success of 1906 resulted in a firm government commitment to bring the opium trade to an end.

The society was also important in disseminating distinctive attitudes hostile to regular opiate use, which had a considerable impact in medical circles and, through them, on educated public opinion. It is not entirely accurate to say that the supporters of the anti-opium movement promoted a ''vice'' theory of opiate use in opposition to the medical disease model. There was considerable cross fertilisation between medical and moral views in the formulation of the disease model and within the medical contingent—men like Norman Kerr, Benjamin Ward Richardson, and Professor Arthur Gamgee of Manchester—which took an active part in the society. Nor was that body's propaganda concentrated solely on the question of opium smoking. The effects of both smoking and eating the drug were discussed, and the society buttressed its arguments about the Indo-Chinese trade by reference to a supposed increase in English consumption. Dr. J. Dudgeon, writing in the *Friend of China* in 1876, summed up the classical anti-opium position, stressing beliefs about inevitable addiction and ever-increasing dosage: moderate opium use was impossible and moral and physical degradation the inevitable result of the habit. ''We cannot,'' he wrote, ''get over the enthralling power of the drug, the supreme difficulty of renouncing it; the necessity for increasing the dose, the almost inevitable death that follows its sudden deprivation, and, in every case, sooner or later, the steady descent, moral and physical, of the smoker, and ultimately his self-destruction.''

Attitudes such as these, if not uncritically accepted in medical circles, helped inform public opinion on the subject of opium use. The Society for the Suppression of the Opium Trade was instrumental, too, in the association of domestic opium use with an alien minority—the Chinese seamen who lived and lodged in dockland areas, most visibly in the East End of London. Hostility toward this small group of socially and culturally dissident foreigners helped emphasise the deviant nature of opium use and hastened acceptance of the need for more formal official control of the drug. The anti-opiumists themselves often pointed out the moral that encouragement of opium smoking in China could lead to an opium smoking problem in Britain itself. Rev. George Piercy, writing to the *Methodist Recorder* in 1883, stressed that his own work in the East End had brought home to him the urgency of the matter: ''Alarms have been sounded by our cousins across the Atlantic which ought to have rung through the land. . . . Does not it demand equally careful study at the hands of Englishmen when in our metropolis for years past there have been six or eight schools for opium smoking, the presiding spirits in each being hardened opium-sodden Chinamen, confirmed smokers themselves, and earning their livelihood by teaching others also?'' This opium den stereotype had little foundation in reality, but it was taken up in the popular press and in novels. Charles Dickens's *Edwin Drood* and Oscar Wilde's *The Picture of Dorian Gray* are only the most obvious examples of the fictional presentation of the theme. The myth these accounts helped propagate was powerful in forming reactions and policies which were hostile to opiate use.

Such feelings of concern had by no means swept the board even by the end of the century. At many levels of society there was still a calm reaction to regular opiate use, whether classed as medical or nonmedical (the use of these terms was still fairly elastic). Certainly, there is some evidence that at the grass roots of the medical profession, many doctors continued to prescribe opiates as freely as they had always done. Nor was the problem of addiction a matter of much general discussion in society. Some who defended the drug's use in an Eastern context were associated with the Indian government, but many others shared the feelings that the growing prejudice against controlled opium use was misjudged. Dr. C. R. Francis spoke in 1882 for many of them. Describing a friend's lifelong consumption of opium which enabled him to do a good day's work

Samuel Taylor Coleridge in his mid-fifties.

and did him no observable harm, he commented: ''Yielding to the popular prejudice against opium eating, Mr. A. has repeatedly endeavoured to break it off. . . . Doubtless he would succeed in time, as others had, but cui bono?'' Opium, even to a pharmacist practising in the early 1900s was ''something quite normal. Nobody noticed addiction and everyone had laudanum at home.''

Addiction was not a matter of government policy, despite the advent of international narcotic control, until the First World War. An apparent wartime emergency, the danger of a cocaine ''epidemic'' at home among soldiers mixing with prostitutes in the West End of London, and the external leakage of morphine smuggled on British ships to the Far East brought strict regulation in 1916 under Defence of the Realm Act regulation 40B. This was extended and made permanent in the 1920 Dangerous Drugs Act. Addiction perceived as a pressing social problem was a phenomenon of the early twentieth century, but many of the attitudes which underlay control in England were already formed. Developments in the 1900s brought into play the complex motivations which had marked responses to opiate use in the nineteenth century. The ethic of control replaced controlled opiate use. (pp. 458-61)

Virginia Berridge, ''Victorian Opium Eating: Responses to Opiate Use in Nineteenth-Century England,'' in Victorian Studies, Vol. 21, No. 4, Summer, 1978, pp. 437-61.

TERRY M. PARSSINEN

[*In this excerpt from his study of narcotics in nineteenth- and early twentieth-century England, Parssinen explores the back-ground and development of the use of opiates as medicinal agents in Victorian society.*]

Opium's healing powers were seemingly magical. The drug could kill pain, bring sleep, ease rumbling stomachs, and stop runny bowels. This assured its growing use by healers, both inside and outside the medical profession. Opium had been known to the English medical profession since the seventeenth century. Indeed, it had been so highly praised by Dr. Thomas Sydenham that it had earned him the sobriquet ''Opiophilos.'' His widely publicized formula for tincture of opium continued to be known as ''Sydenham's Laudanum'' well into the nineteenth century. Opium had been the subject of papers by both toxicologists and clinicians throughout the eighteenth and early nineteenth centuries. Furthermore, opium was an integral part of the great medical systems of the eighteenth-century thinkers like John Brown and Benjamin Rush. Yet it was not until the 1830s and 1840s that opium assumed a crucial therapeutic role in English medicine. Medical journals wee flooded with articles touting its expanded use. Jonathan Pereira, in his influential textbook on medicine and therapeutics, echoed the dominant professional opinion when he claimed that

> opium is undoubtedly the most important and valuable remedy of the whole Materia Medica. We have, for other medicines, one or more substitutes; but for opium we have none. . . . Its good effects are not, as is the case with some valuable medicines, remote and contingent, but they are immediate, direct, and obvious; and its operation is not attended with pain or discomfort.

Opium had a wide variety of therapeutic uses, most notably as an analgesic, a febrifuge, a sedative, and as a specific for gastrointestinal difficulty, especially diarrhea. Since most medical men still prepared their own medicines, opium was available in the doctor's surgery as well as in the local pharmacy. It was compounded in prescriptions with other elements, and it was prepared on its own, in powder, in pills, or in liquid, most commonly as laudanum—tincture of opium. By the 1840s, opium had become one of the most important staples of English therapeutics.

What accounts for the increased popularity of opium in English medicine at mid-century? One factor which played a role was the influence of former East India Company medical men. Opium had long been a staple of Indian therapeutics, and was used in the treatment of cholera, which was endemic to India. When the cholera broke out in Britain (1831-2, 1848-9, and 1853-4),they promoted its use. Opium mixed with calomel was one of the most frequently used and successful cholera remedies in nineteenth-century Britain.

A second factor was the challenge to orthodox therapeutics. The early nineteenth century was a period of prolonged crisis in English medicine. Orthodox medical men were threatened by the sudden emergence of irregular practitioners in the 1830s and 1840s: homeopaths, hydropaths, ''galvanic'' healers, and mesmerists. Unlike such older rivals as herbalists, white witches, and bonesetters, these new ''quacks'' had many of the trappings of orthodoxy, from well-appointed consulting rooms and medical degrees to entire philosophies derived from medical thinkers like Hahnemann or Mesmer. They often succeeded in attracting the wealthy urban patients who were in too short supply in early Victorian Britain. The success of these irregular practitioners is easily explained. Despite the demise of the humoral etiology in the late eighteenth century, the heroic therapies which were based on it continued to be practiced by orthodox medical men well into the nineteenth century. These included such painful and unpleasant measures as bleeding, blistering, and dosing with large amounts of harsh drugs like calomel. Understandably, some patients felt that they might be better off without the attendance of orthodox medical men. Irregular practitioners benefited from this reaction since they offered therapies which were relatively painless and harmless. At first, orthodox medical men reacted angrily, claiming that mesmerists, homeopaths, and hydropaths were merely providing placebos. Eventually, however, some medical men admitted that the success of irregular practitioners was, in effect, a public rejection of the heroic therapies they had been so dependent on early in the century. This line of argument dealt the death-blow to heroic therapies by mid-century.

If medical men were no longer to bleed and blister their patients, how would they treat them? Until the revolution in therapeutics in the early twentieth century, physicians did not so much cure diseases as manage their symptoms. Given this fundamental limitation in nineteenth-century medical practice, opium was invaluable. Along with alcohol, opium became an important part of the treatment plan of noninterventionist medical practice, which urged doctors to let disease run its natural course while monitoring and managing its symptoms. Opium offered the orthodox medical man a gentle and effective means of alleviating some of his patients' most common forms of distress: pain, fever, and diarrhea. But as important as opium was in orthodox medical practice, it was even more important in the tradition of self-medication.

Until the nineteenth century, self-medication in Britain meant reliance upon the pharmacy of the woods and fields. The folk tradition of gathering, preparing, and using herbs commonly available in the English countryside dates back to at least Anglo-Saxon times, and probably much earlier. In the seventeenth century, a number of classic "herbals" were published, most notably Nicholas Culpepper's *Physicall Directory,* which continued to be sold and used well into the nineteenth century. One also finds evidence of the herbalist tradition in the manuscript "receipt" books that have survived from the seventeenth and eighteenth centuries. Typically, these are compilations of cookery, medical, and household recipes, gathered from eclectic sources, and aded to over the years. Often the distinction between a cookery and a medical recipe is unclear, indicating how often foods were used as medicaments.

Implicit in such receipt books, and explicit in published works, such as John Hill's many popular herbals and John Wesley's *Primitive Physic* is a distinct antipathy to orthodox pharmacy and medicine. "There is," according to John Hill, "no form of medicine sent from the apothecary which may not be prepared from the herbs of our own growth in the same manner as from foreign drugs." Wesley distrusted physicians and apothecaries, believing, with many of his contemporaries, that their fees were exorbitant and their knowledge was deficient. Every man, with the resources of the countryside and the aid of a readable guide, could be his own doctor. Even the Scottish physician William Buchan drew his colleagues' scorn and anger for "laying Medicine more open to Mankind," the announced purpose of his *Domestic Medicine.*

Opium, as an imported and relatively expensive drug, did not figure prominently in the herbalist literature. While opium was mentioned in many of the eighteenth-century treatises on domestic medicine, and it occasionally appears in receipt books, it clearly did not occupy as central a position in self-medication practices in the eighteenth century as it did in the nineteenth.

The herbalist tradition, both oral and written, had an important, though declining influence well into the nineteenth century. On one level, it continued as a part of the mix of good sense, empiricism, and superstition that made up village folk medicine. (pp. 22-5)

But herbalism, whether of the village or scientific variety, was clearly a marginal phenomenon in late nineteenth-century Britain. The real legacy of herbalism lay in the sense of medical self-reliance which it fostered, and which continued to thrive long after the doctrines of herbalism had disappeared.

Herbalism was the predominant form of self-medication so long as most Britons lived in villages and small towns, close to the countryside and attuned to rural folk traditions. Rapid urbanization changed that. By mid-century, the majority of the population lived in cities, cut off both from physical proximity to wild herbs, and from the culture which encouraged their use. At the same time, the population density of urban areas brought many more people into contact with chemists' shops than previously. While self-medication continued to thrive in Victorian Britain, the forms that it assumed changed significantly.

Victorians were no less reluctant than their grandparents had been to consult medical men. Although physicians' fees fell in the course of the century, they still stood at 5s. (or 2s. 6d. for a poor person) for a consultation with a general practitioner at the end of the nineteenth century. With the weekly wages of an unskilled laborer at 18s. to 25s., he would think twice before knocking on the doctor's surgery, especially for treatment of a minor problem. Where did the urbanized Victorian go to obtain relief from the ordinary aches and pains of life? There were, by the late nineteenth century, a number of clinics that treated poor patients at greatly reduced cost, or gratis. In addition, some medical men set aside one morning a week to see charity cases. But Victorian working people were often reluctant to use these services, both because they found it degrading to be patronized as a pauper, and because the inevitable wait to see a doctor could deprive a man of a half day's pay. One of the most popular sources of cheap advice and medication was the local chemist. The customer would describe his symptoms and the chemist, on the basis of his practical knowledge of therapeutics acquired over years of trade, would suggest a remedy, sometimes a patent medicine, but more often a compound of his own devising. Often the customer, on the basis of previous experience, already knew what drug or mixture he wanted. But whether or not he asked for the chemist's advice, the customer paid only for the medicine, which could usually be purchased in quantities as small as a pennyworth.

Medical men denounced these "prescribing chemists" as dangerous, untrained practitioners, and tried several times in the course of the century to force them to desist. But the chemists replied that they provided an essential service to persons whose simple complaints did not warrant a medical man's attention. At the times when prosecutions mounted by the Society of Apothecaries (the general practitioners' body) brought the issue to public prominence, the newspapers almost always sided with the chemists. In a typical comment, the *Birmingham Daily Post* published an editorial on the subject in 1878 which concluded that "it would be a great hardship, not only upon chemists, but upon poor persons, if it were made compulsory in every case where a man has a toothache, a gumboil, or a cold in the head, to pay a doctor's fee in order to obtain the necessary medicine."

The significance of chemists' counter-practice in poor neighborhoods was graphically described by an East End chemist in 1868:

> On Saturday I made an account of the customers served from eight o'clock, a.m. until twelve p.m. The amount was 400 persons:—
>
> 209 Penny Customers
> 12 at ls.
> Patent Medicines 3s. 4½d.
>
> . . . The chief part of a druggist's business in this neighborhood is prescribing for the poor.
>
> (pp. 26-8)

Since there was no significant restriction on the drugs that could be sold over the druggist's counter until 1916, narcotics of all types were dispensed through counter-practice. Opium, because of its effectiveness, was certainly the most important single drug sold by chemists. In addition to the standard version of laudanum, opium was also sold in countless local mixtures, some of which, like "Battley's Syrup" or "Black Drop," achieved such a wide popularity that they were eventually incorporated into the official British pharmacopoeia.

In 1857, a Select Committee of the House of Lords held hearings on a Sale of Poisons Bill, which produced a great deal of information about the sale and consumption of poisonous drugs, including opiates. Jacob Bell, the founder of the Pharmaceutical Society of Great Britain, testified that restrictions on the sale of opiates "would be almost impossible to carry . . . into effect in many country districts, where pennyworths of laudanum and opium are very often sold, and habitually taken by the public at large." He was supported by subsequent witnesses. W. T. Brade, Professor of Chemistry at the Royal Institution, testified that "there are a number of persons who are in the habit of keeping laudanum by them; they take 10 or 20 drops of laudanum when their bowels get out of order, or when they are apprehensive of cholera, or disorders of that kind. Mr. W. Herapath, a senior magistrate from Bristol, pointed out that chemists sell opium so frequently that it is unrealistic to ask them to keep the bottle under lock and key in a special cabinet. When questioned further, Herapath estimated that in large towns, chemists might make 100 sales of opium per day. Even John Hammill, a police magistrate distressed by the frequent use of opiates in suicides and homicides, conceded that its widespread use as a popular medicine militated against its effective regulation. (pp. 28-9)

Opium was not only effective, it was also cheap. Syrup of White Poppies, a mild opiate used as an anodyne and sedative for infants and children, sold for only 3d. per ounce. . . . Put another way, a penny would buy one-third of an ounce, enough for twenty-five to thirty doses. For working-class mothers, the cost of this medicine, as against a minimum fee of 2s. 6d. for a consultation and 1s. 6d. for a prescription from a general practitioner, must have inclined them to use it in all but the most serious cases of childhood illness. Laudanum, the most common form in which opium was consumed by adults, could be had for 8d. an ounce through the 1870s; 6d. an ounce through the mid-1880s; and 3½ or 4d. an ounce after that.

For a person who used it in doses of twenty to forty drops, for the occasional headache or stomach ailment, laudanum was a very good value. But a person addicted to, say, two ounces per day would spend 8d. to a shilling on it, a very high cost for a working-class person. In 1881, one George Dilley, a railway carpenter from Bedfordshire earning 28s. per week,

tried to have his wife committed to the workhouse. To support her habit, she had sold everything in the house, even the bedclothes. He could not provide for his children, he said, while his wife had her freedom.

The cheapness of opium was a factor which contributed to its widespread use by all segments of the population. When used therapeutically, and in moderation, opium was well within the means of most Victorian families. Indeed, opium represented a real health bargain. However, when an occasional user became a regular user, even of modest proportions, the economics turned around: addiction was riunously expensive, especially for working-class families.

A second form of Victorian self-medication was the patent or proprietary medicine, the actual ingredients of which were secret. The first patent for a medicine was issued in 1698, but proprietary medicines, or secret nostrums, had existed for centuries. In 1748, the author of an article that appeared in *Gentleman's Magazine* was able to list over two hundred readily available patent medicines. In 1783, the Government instituted a stamp duty on all patent medicines, equal to about 12 percent of an item's sale price. From revenue figures, one can appreciate how rapidly sales accelerated in the late nineteenth century. . . . From 1855 to 1905, the period of greatest growth, sales of patent medicines increased nearly tenfold, while the population just about doubled. (pp. 30-1)

The medicines offered for sale to the Victorian public ranged from headache powders and digestive aids to cures for cancer and thinly disguised abortifacients. Some were perfectly harmless, containing little more than glucose, coloring, and flavoring. Others actually contained a moderate amount of active ingredients which did in fact produce their advertised effects upon the purchaser. Still others contained powerful drugs, including narcotics, in dangerous concentrations. British Medical Association analysis of thirteen patent medicines showed that they contained varying amounts of morphine, prussic acid, strychnine, and aconite. Only four were labeled "poison" as the law required, and none, of course, actually listed the ingredients on the bottle. Even more dangerous for consumers was the fact that there was no consistency in the proportions among similar medicines. Of the seven samples that contained morphia, for example, the proportion varied from 0.2 to 3.11 grains per fluid ounce. Thus a patent medicine user, accustomed to a relatively mild opiate in one ounce of "Brand X" sleeping draught, could unexpectedly receive an intoxicating, or even lethal, dose in one ounce of the more concentrated "Brand Y" sleeping draught. The dangers of an accidental toxic dose were even greater when the manufacturer changed the morphia content of his medicine. From analyses carried out over a period of years on "Mrs. Winslow's Soothing Syrup," an infants' sedative popular in both Britain and America, it is clear that the morphia content varied from nil to one grain per fluid ounce.

Opium was not unknown in eighteenth-century patent medicines. Indeed, "Dover's Powders," one of the most famous, was a compound of ipecacuanha and opium. But opium and its derivatives came to be the most important single ingredient in Victorian patents. One of the earliest was "Godfrey's Cordial," the forerunner of all the "soothing syrups," which was recommended for infants' "colicky pains, flatus, and restlessness." Godfrey's was basically tincture of opium in a thick, sweet syrup to make it palatable to children. It became so popular that the name lost its specific designation and came to stand for any such preparation. At an inquest in 1873, a chemist in rural Yorkshire testified that he "sold about half a gallon of Godfrey's Cordial per week, and the greater portion went out in cups, which he did not label. . . . Every druggist had a formula of his own for what he called Godfrey's Cordial. This particular chemist proudly boasted that *his* Godfrey's contained no opiates whatsoever, which was fine, of course, until his customers, accustomed to swilling pints of his mixture with no ill effects, ordered Godfrey's from a chemist who used a more conventional formula. Besides Godfrey's, virtually all soothing syrups, such as "Mother's Friend" or the ominously named "Quietness," contained opiates. Opiates were also the main ingredient in many sedatives, cough syrups, and diarrhea remedies. (pp. 33-4)

It is difficult to exaggerate the importance of opium in Victorian healing. For most Britons it was invaluable. In an age in which diarrhea was one of the leading killers of children and infants; in which dehydrating diseases such as cholera were epidemic; in which overcrowding, primitive sanitation, and adulterated food produced chronic gastrointestinal problems for a large part of the population, opium was a source of cheap and effective relief. Opium was the Victorian's aspirin, Lomotil, Valium, and Nyquil, which could be bought at the local chemist's for as little as a penny. (pp. 35-6)

> Terry M. Parssinen, "The Magical Healer: Opium as Therapeutic Agent," in his Secret Passions, Secret Remedies: Narcotic Drugs in British Society, 1820-1930, *Institute for the Study of Human Issues, 1983, pp. 22-41.*

OPIUM AND LITERARY SOCIETY

ALETHEA HAYTER

[*Hayter discusses the use of opium by various nineteenth-century English authors not normally associated with the drug, including Percy Bysshe Shelley. For additional commentary by Hayter, see excerpt below.*]

Harriet Martineau recorded in her autobiography that a clergyman, who "knew the literary world of his time so thoroughly that there was probably no author of any mark then living in England, with whom he was not more or less acquainted," told her that he had reason to believe that "there was no author or authoress who was free from the habit of taking some pernicious stimulant; either strong green tea, or strong coffee at night, or wine or spirits or laudanum. The amount of opium taken, to relieve the wear and tear of authorship was, he said, greater than most people had any conception of: and *all* literary workers took something."

The second half of this pronouncement is more significant than the first half. If tea, coffee, wine, and spirits are to be classed equally with opium as "pernicious stimulants," it would be difficult to find authors in any period who never resorted to stimulus of this kind. But the statement that authors used opium with the conscious intention of "relieving the wear and tear of authorship" merits further investigation.

There is plenty of evidence that a good many English nineteenth century literary figures took opium occasionally, and a fair-number took it habitually, though their reasons for doing so, and whether these were directly connected with their approach to their work, are more debatable. The opium dependence of

Coleridge and De Quincey is notorious, and a few other writers such as George Crabbe, Francis Thompson and Wilkie Collins are fairly well known to have been lifelong addicts. But they were only the tip of an iceberg which spread its clammy shelves and shivering crevasses far and wide below the surface of the literary world. Everybody kept laudanum in the house and used it on occasion for minor ailments and aches. Many, perhaps most, writers took it a few times in their lives, generally on medical prescription and without misgiving.

Some of them (particularly the women writers) were interested in the psychological effects of this common household remedy, and recorded these in letters and journals, as they did for no other medicine. It would be hard to find two more eminently sane and well-balanced women than the novelists Mrs. Gaskell and Mrs. Oliphant, yet both of them noted and remembered the effect which a dose of laudanum had had on them. Mrs. Gaskell remembered it as "vivid and exaggerated presence of objects, of which the outlines were indistinct, or lost in golden mist." Mrs. Oliphant, who was prescribed laudanum in Rome when her husband was dying and she herself was seven months pregnant, recollected vividly many years later "the sudden floating into ease of body and the dazed condition of mind,— a kind of exaltation, as if I were walking upon air, for I could not sleep in the circumstances nor try to sleep. I thought then that this was the saving of me."

To have a confirmed opium addict among your acquaintances was an experience common to, and recorded by, many nineteenth century writers. The poet Robert Hawker had a respected country neighbour, Oliver Rouse, whose favourite tipple was gin and paregoric. Charles Kingsley knew "poor dear old opium-eating Dr. Turton." Virginia Woolf and her family, as late as the early 1900's, were used to "Professor Wolstenholme" [who] "would relapse into a drowsy ursine torpor, the result of eating opium to which he had been driven by the unkindness of his wife and the untimely death of his son Oliver who was eaten, somewhere off the coast of Coromandel, by a shark." Opium was the succour first thought of in times of domestic affliction or anxiety; we find, for instance, that that formidably strong-willed Beatrice Webb said of herself in the 1880's, when she was suffering emotional stress, that "the laudanum bottle loomed large as the dominant figure."

The general trend of opium dependence among nineteenth century English literary figures may be illustrated by short case-histories of three men and two women, some of them addicted for years, others not fully habituated but having recourse fairly often to the drug.

The first case is that of Shelley, whose fairly frequent use of laudanum has been so much overshadowed by the more famous addictions of other great Romantics that it has been comparatively little studied. If we are to believe Edward Trelawny, Shelley started taking laudanum even in his schooldays, took it at intervals all through his life, but tried to keep his habit a secret. At Eton, Trelawny suggests, Shelley experimented with various drugs.

> The power of laudanum to soothe pain and give rest especially delighted him; he was cautioned, and knew it was wrong; the seductive power of that drug retained a hold on him during the rest of his life, used with extreme caution at first and at long intervals. People who take to opiates are enslaved and never abandon them; these may be traced in some of Shelley's flights of imagination, and fancies of supernatural appearances. On one occasion in London, and

again in Italy, he so over-dosed himself that his life was only saved by those measures that are used to counteract the drug; but it must not be thought that, like De Quincey and many others, he habitually used it: he only took it on rare occasions, when in deep dejection. He was impatient of remonstrances, and so made a mystery of it. The effect of opiates is to deaden pain, but they benumb the vital powers and derange our vital organs; with Shelley they caused spasms. The professor of anatomy at the University of Pisa, Vaccà, was renowned for his skill in surgery and medicine, and he came to the conclusion that Shelley was drugging himself, and earnestly interdicted medicine in all its forms. . . . Seeking to allay the perturbation of his seething brain [Shelley] had from early life tampered with opiates. He used them in the shape of laudanum. He had always a bottle of that, which he endeavoured to conceal from everyone, disliking to be remonstrated with. He used it with caution at first, but, in time of extreme dejection or in paroxysms of passion, was heedless, and on more than one occasion his life was only preserved by remedies to counteract the poison. Whether he intended to destroy himself or no, is not clear . . . This habit of taking laudanum accounts for all his visions and occasional delusions, but startled his wife and friends, and was one cause of the pains he had in his side: for it is the effect of opiates, if not counteracted by other means, to paralyse the stomach and other vital organs.

Trelawny wrote this thirty-six years after the death of Shelley, whom he met for the first time only six months before Shelley was drowned, and everything he says about him is notoriously untrustworthy. The evidence of Shelley's more reliable and longer-standing friends is that he had only short periods of anything like addiction to opium, and that, far from making a secret of it, he positively brandished his laudanum bottle before his frightened family and friends.

The only direct references in his own letters to his taking laudanum are in January 1812, when the "nervous attack" which he suffered after his row with his friend Hogg, over Hogg's attempted seduction of Shelley's first wife Harriet, caused him to take "a quantity of laudanum"; but a fortnight later he wrote that he hoped to have no further need to resort to laudanum as "my health is re-established and I am now strong in hope and nerve."

No more is heard of laudanum-taking till the summer of 1814, when he met and fell in love with Mary Godwin, and told Harriet he must separate from her. The passion and anxiety of his situation made him take laudanum as an anodyne, and also propose its use as a suicide weapon. All his life he was inclined to keep poison by him, for possible use to kill himself, and in this crisis he made sure that everyone knew it. Mary Godwin's stepmother described his wild descent on the Godwin household in Skinner Street, where he rushed up to Mary saying " 'They wish to separate us, my beloved; but Death shall unite us' and offered her a bottle of laudanum. 'By this you can escape from tyranny; and this,' taking a small pistol from his pocket, 'shall reunite me to you.' '' Mary was terrified and implored him with tears to be calm; she refused to take the laudanum, but promised eternal fidelity. Calmed by this, Shelley left, forgetting his laudanum bottle which remained on the Godwins' table.

Mrs. Godwin was a hostile witness, but Thomas Love Peacock was a friend of Shelley's, and he too described a meeting with Shelley at this time. "His eyes were bloodshot, his hair and dress disordered. He caught up a bottle of laudanum, and said 'I never part from this.' '' Peacock adds, however, "I believe that up to this time he never travelled . . . without laudanum as a refuge from intolerable pain." This suggestion that Shelley's primary use of opium was as an anodyne against physical pain is supported by Thomas Hookham, who told Browning that at the time of Shelley's separation from Harriet, he was suffering from such intense pain that he would roll writhing on the ground, and to alleviate this "he would actually go about with a laudanum bottle in his hand, supping thence as need might be."

Shelley's next period of recourse to opium (less well documented than the 1814 one) was in 1816 to 1817 when he was suffering much mental stress over Harriet's suicide, the Chancery lawsuit which cut him off from his two eldest children, and financial worries, and was also physically ill with "a decisive pulmonary attack" which his doctors told him indicated a dangerous tuberculosis which could only be cured by removal from the damp gloom of his Marlow house to a warmer climate. Laudanum was then very often prescribed for tubercular patients, and Shelley's description of his symptoms at this time strongly suggests that he was taking it regularly.

After his move to Italy in 1818, his health greatly improved, and we hear no more of laudanum; there is nothing definite to confirm Trelawny's statement that he was still taking it in Pisa or that he nearly killed himself twice by overdoses of laudanum. Trelawny's sweeping pronouncement that "This habit of taking laudanum accounts for all his visions and occasional delusions" is clearly baseless. Shelley already walked in his sleep, had violent nightmares, and experienced some form of trance, when he was a boy of eleven or twelve at his first school, long before he could have had any opium habit. Perhaps it was Shelley's natural tendency to trance-like reveries and waking dreams in later life that made Trelawny and others suspect that he was on drugs. In fact he seems to have taken laudanum primarily as a pain-killer, occasionally as a tranquillizer. There is no evidence that he thought it affected his perceptions in any way that might be valuable to him as a poet, and certainly no man ever had less need of a stimulus to the imagination. He was forever whirled along in an incandescent chariot of visionary ideas. His occasional periods of opium-taking may possibly, as Trelawny suggested, have helped to induce the visual hallucinations, "fancies of supernatural appearances," which haunted him at intervals throughout his life. Opium may also have reinforced his fantasies of persecution, his fears that his father meant to have him shut up in a madhouse, his belief in the mysterious assailants who broke into his house in Wales and fired shots at him, or struck him in an Italian post office, his stories of diamond necklaces sent to him by post as proof of conspiracies against him. But many excitable men who have never taken opium have similar delusions of persecution, often with less justification from real events than Shelley had.

A much clearer sign of a well-known effect of opium is the hyperaesthesia which he described in a letter to Godwin written in 1817 when he was under medical treatment for incipient tuberculosis. "My feelings at intervals are of a deadly and torpid kind, or awakened to a state of such unnatural and keen excitement that only to instance the organ of sight, I find the very blades of grass and the boughs of distant trees present themselves to me with microscopical distinctness. Towards evening I sink into a state of lethargy and inanition, and often remain for hours on the sofa between sleep and waking a prey to the most painful irritability of thought."

There seems to be no correlation between Shelley's poetic impulse, or the content of the resultant poems, and his periods of laudanum indulgence. *Alastor* was written in September 1815 in an interval of tranquility and good health after a beneficial boat excursion up the Thames, when Shelley is unlikely to have taken laudanum for nearly a year; his next main work, *The Revolt of Islam,* was written in the summer of 1817 when he fairly certainly was taking laudanum for his chest complaint. Yet of the two poems, the dreamy introspective *Alastor,* rather than the sustained polemic of *The Revolt of Islam,* would be selected as the more typical of opium effects if there were no external evidence about this. Whether Shelley's imagery may have been affected by hyperaesthesia and other alterations of spatial and temporal perception produced by opium-taking is a question that would repay further study; but it seems fairly certain that he himself was not in general observant of, or interested in, any such effects, and that his motive in taking opium was not any form of experiment in modifying his poetic consciousness.

Byron's daughter, Ada Countess of Lovelace, who was a talented mathematician, was addicted to laudanum for the last nine years of her life. In 1843 she began to suffer from some kind of gastric disorder; she is also said to have suffered from asthma, but this is more likely to have been a symptom of opium dependence than a pre-existing condition. She was prescribed laudanum for her gastric complaint; she also took brandy as a stimulant to counteract the drowsiness induced by the laudanum. But in January 1844, when her doctor prescribed morphine or laudanum regularly once or twice a week, she revealed in a letter to her mother that she had in fact been taking it for some years past. "I must tell you that latterly—the last 2 or 3 years—Opium had seemed strongly to *disagree* with me. But I now understand why this has been, and why it deceived me. I was all the time taking wine or other stimulant; and the two things made a terrible jumble." She continued, however, to take laudanum (tincture of opium in alcohol), regardless of the "terrible jumble" that the mixture of opium and alcohol had produced in the past. By 1852 she was in severe pain from cancer, and was prescribed ten drops of laudanum every two hours, and in the increasing agony of her last weeks of life she took opium continally.

She often described the physical and mental effects which laudanum had on her. "The Opium has a remarkable effect on my eyes, seeming to *free* them, and make them *open* and *cool*"; "a sensation of delicious *coolness*—like a release from Hell-fire"—but the concomitant of this was that during withdrawal periods she suffered severely from the cold, and craved for warmth, a well-known withdrawal symptom. She was convinced that laudanum tranquillized and regulated her mind. "I am indebted to Laudanum for such sense and tranquillity as is really creeping over me this evening"; "it makes me so philosophical, and so takes off all *fretting* eagerness and anxieties. It appears to harmonize the whole constitution, to make each function act in a *just proportion;* (with *judgment, discretion, moderation*)."

"It makes me so philosophical"; Lady Lovelace became more and more convinced, as her opium addiction increased, that she was a prophetess born to inspire and enlighten the world, "the Deborah, the Elijah of Science". She was indeed a mathematician of remarkable ability, but in her own opinion she stood higher than that. She was convinced that her brain power was unique, phenomenal, that she was destined to make vast discoveries in mathematics and computer science, to penetrate to the uttermost secrets of the universe—a conviction she shared with other notable opium addicts such as Coleridge, De Quincey and (if he really was an opium-eater) Edgar Allan Poe. She was prescribed laudanum for physical pain, but she came to value it for cooling and calming the heated fret of anxiety, for freeing her mind to embark on vast airy voyages into the luminous clouds of inanity which seemed to her to be arcane and immortal wisdom.

Opium can be seen leaving fainter traces in the case of a very different personality, that of the Reverend Charles Tennyson Turner, brother of the poet Tennyson and himself a minor but delightful sonneteer and lyricist. He shared the isolated home life of the twelve wildly eccentric children of a half-mad father, and was as weird and untidy in his habits as the rest of his family, but he had a sounder core. He had an engaging unselfish personality, and he was the only member of the family to follow a regular calling. He was ordained and appointed curate of a Lincolnshire parish in 1833, but at this time he was prescribed laudanum for severe neuralgic pains. Opium addiction was more widespread in Lincolnshire than in any other English county, and Charles Tennyson Turner soon joined the ranks of addicts. Before long he was "making no use of body or soul" as his brother Frederick said, and his relations were convinced that he would soon kill himself with laudanum. But by 1835 he had freed himself from his opium habit, and a year later he married. Soon after his marriage he relapsed into addiction again. His wife's attempts to free him from his habit drove her into a nervous breakdown in 1839, and she had to be under medical care for years. Charles Tennyson Turner blamed himself for causing his wife's breakdown, and this gave him the courage to free himself permanently from opium. His wife eventually recovered and returned to him in 1849, and they settled down to thirty years of peaceful happiness in their remote vicarage till both of them died, within a month of each other, in 1879.

There is little in Charles Tennyson Turner's poems to indicate that opium altered his perceptions. His poetry has a fresh unforced pathos, its feeling is gently compassionate and affectionate, its style graceful. Perhaps there is a shadow of albatross-guilt about his lifelong remorse for shooting a swallow when he was a boy, a touch of De Quincey's special sympathy for outcasts and oddities in his sonnets *The Prisoner, The Drunkard's Last Market, The Little Heir of Shame* and his haunting picture of the scarecrow which is "not wholly make-believe" and might still push a human hand out from its ragged sleeve. But on the whole his addiction seems to have been a pure accident, due to an unwise prescription, which met no special need and made no special dint in his agreeable personality.

The case of Jane Welsh Carlyle is very different. She certainly needed, or was convinced that she needed, opium for a variety of physical and mental ills during ten years of her later life. As a young woman she had shunned it; she told Carlyle in 1838, when she was already suffering from insomnia, that she had asked her doctor for "any sort of sleeping-draught, which had no opium in it." But in the late 1840's, when she was tortured by insomnia, by coughs and digestive troubles, and by jealousy of her husband's friendship with Lady Harriet Baring, she took to regular doses of morphine. "Confined to my bedroom with a dreadful cough and the usual accompaniment—never getting a wink of sleep except by means of Morphia" she wrote in February 1848. In 1851 she took an overdose—probably a geniunely involuntary one, from her description.

> I merely wished to get myself some sleep after having gone without it for three nights, and took about four

> of the third morning a dose of Morphine which might or might *not* have been the right quantity—for the little black pills had melted and run all together and I had to divide them with a pen-knife. All next day I felt quite *dead*—as if I were only kept going by galvanism . . . and at night I took to fainting and having horrid spasms . . . I still feel sick and sore and miserably all-overish.

This experience perhaps frightened her; moreover in the early 1850's two doctors warned her against the injurious effects of morphia; and though she still took an occasional dose if she had not slept at all for several nights, by 1857 she had given it up altogether. She lived for another nine years, in health always bad but not apparently much affected for better or worse by her ten years' dependence and subsequent abstinence.

She left some vivid descriptions of the mental effects of opium. It seems to have bestowed on her, or stimulated in her, the power of hypnagogic visions, sharply distinct ocular spectra; ''every sad image that presents itself is thrown out in such gigantic relief on the darkness, and made so haggard by bodily weariness'' she said in a letter of condolence; she was speaking metaphorically, but it sounds as if she was using an image from her own experience. She knew the timeless Buddha-on-the-lotus sensation which Coleridge and many other addicts experienced and described; ''one night . . . I passed in as near an approach to the blessed state of Nirwana'' (sic) ''as anyone not a worshipper of Buddha need aspire to; *that* was from a dose of morphia.'' She knew the sensation of petrifaction which De Quincey, Coleridge, Baudelaire and Francis Thompson recorded; Caroline Fox noted in her journal a significant conversation with Mrs. Carlyle about this on a visit in May 1847. ''We soon settled into an interesting talk with Mrs. Carlyle. She has been very ill, and the doctors gave her opium and tartar for her cough, which induced, not beautiful dreams and visions, but a miserable feeling of turning to marble herself and lying on marble, her hair, her arms, and her whole person petrifying and adhering to the marble slab on which she lay. One night it was a tombstone—one in Scotland which she well knew. She lay along it with a graver in her hand, carving her own epitaph under another, which she read and knew by heart. It was her mother's. She felt utterly distinct from this prostrate figure, and thought of her with pity and love, looked at different passages in her life, and moralized as a familiar friend. It was more like madness than anything she has ever experienced.''

Mrs. Carlyle was a famous *raconteuse* and no doubt she heightened her story a bit to make Caroline Fox's flesh creep. But all the same it is a striking vision, obviously linked with the fully awake sensation of corpse-like lethargy, from which nothing but galvanism could resurrect her, which she experienced after her overdose of opium four years later. There seems to be no evidence, however, that she took opium in search of such visionary experiences; she valued it, and was for ten years partly addicted to it, because of the much-needed sleep which it could bring to her endless nights of insomnia.

My last case history is of a wildly eccentric personality, the violent and extraordinary poet Robert Hawker. He spent his life as vicar of an isolated Cornish parish, where one of his most frequent duties was conducting funerals of men drowned in shipwrecks. Hawker was fantastically idiosyncratic in his habits and dress (he was wont to wear a claret-coloured cassock, a fisherman's jersey and thigh boots, a yellow blanket with a hole cut for his head, a pink beaver hat and crimson gloves). He must always have been neurotic and melancholy, long before he took to opium. When he began the habit is

uncertain. He himself kept his addiction a secret. His brother suggested after his death that he began taking opium in 1863 at the time of his first wife's death, but it is likely that he began using it in the 1850's for insomnia and as an anodyne for acute neuralgia. After some years of addiction he gave it up suddenly when he got engaged to his second wife, whom he married at the end of 1864. At the end of his life, when he suffered from heart trouble, eczema, sciatica and insomnia, and was deeply worried about financial provision for his second wife and her children, he again started regularly drinking laudanum, on medical advice. He died in 1875.

Since he never owned to his addiction, there are no descriptions by him of its effects on him, but his brother reported that it

> had a most injurious effect on his nerves: it violently excited him for a while, and then cast him into fits of the most profound despression. When under this influence he wrote and spoke in the wildest and most unreasonable manner, and said things which in moments of calmer judgment, I am sure, he bitterly deplored. He would at times work himself into the greatest excitement about the most trivial matters, over which he would laugh in his more serene moments.

Hawker's son-in-law believed that his opium habit affected the way he wrote, in fact that it stimulated him to write some of his finest poetry; and it is true that *The Quest of the Sangraal,* his most substantial work, was written in the year of his first wife's death, the year in which, according to his brother, he started taking opium. But other evidence, as has been said, suggests that his first experience with opium were some years earlier, and in any case he had certainly been meditating on the subject of the *Sangraal* for many years before he actually got it down on paper, so there is no solid link between his addiction and his literary achievement. *The Quest of the Sangrall* does have more sinew, more strangeness, an incoherence shot with more imaginative significance, than his banal earlier poems, which have only an occasional powerful line among much tired conventional phraseology (it is as though all Hawker's poetic idiosyncrasy went into his way of life, none into his poetry). If *The Quest of the Sangraal* does seem richer and stranger than Hawker's other poetry, it contains none of the imagery which has elsewhere been found in common between opium-addicted poets.

A much more obvious effect of his opium addiction was his picture of himself as an inspired mystic mastering ''vast Themes'' which would enlighten all mankind. The ''Thought Books'' in which he recorded these cosmic secrets are in fact a jumble of scraps of ideas and information, not unlike Coleridge's notebooks without the genius.

Shelley, Lady Lovelace, Charles Tennyson Turner, Mrs. Carlyle and Robert Hawker had little in common with each other except that they all probably started taking opium on medical prescription as an anodyne for physical pain, a soporific for insomnia, or a tranquillizer for mental stress. Relieving the ''wear and tear'' specifically of authorship does not seem to have been among their motives for taking opium; indeed, the notion that they needed relief from what was their chief *raison d'être*, pleasure and refreshment is a diagnosis of a man who did not understand authors very well, however many of them he may have known. The fragmentary records which these five literary figures left about the effects of opium-taking on their imaginations suggest that some of them may have had glimpses into the world made familiar by Coleridge and De Quincey and others—the world of inexplicable guilts and sacred out-casts, of hierophants of cosmic mysteries, of vivid ocular spectra seen against darkness, of sensations of icy cold and petri-faction and of floating in timeless Buddha-like repose. But there is nothing to indicate that the poets among them thought of the drug, as Baudelaire did, as a tool to stimulate their imagination and promote poetic inspiration, a "machine à penser." Lady Lovelace seems to have believed that opium aided her creative thinking, but there is no sign that Shelley, Charles Tennyson Turner or Robert Hawker thought of it in this way. It was the medical observers, rather than the poets themselves, who suspected a close and sinister connection between opium and the desire for imaginative adventure. Many nineteenth century doctors bitterly complained that their patients had been seduced into experimenting with opium by reading De Quincey's *Confessions of an English Opium Eater*; the charge was so often made that De Quincey felt he had to make a public defence against it. But though no doubt most nineteenth century writers had read his work, Francis Thompson and perhaps Branwell Brontë seem to be the only instances of literary men in England deliberately experimenting with opium, inspired by De Quincey's example, in order to induce new types of sensation and imaginative experience. Nearly all the English literary figures of the age who regularly took opium did so to deaden, not quicken, their feelings and imaginations. They were seeking Nirvana, not Xanadu. (pp. 37-50)

> Alethea Hayter, "'The Laudanum Bottle Loomed Large': Opium in the English Literary World in the Nineteenth Century," in Ariel (The University of Calgary), Vol. 11, No. 4, October, 1980, pp. 37-51.

VIRGINIA BERRIDGE AND GRIFFITH EDWARDS

[In this excerpt from their full-length study of opium in nineteenth-century England, Berridge and Edwards describe the consumption of the drug both by prominent members of literary society and by middle-class society at large.]

[Popular use of opiates always attracted the most attention in nineteenth-century English society]. But at all levels of society, opium and laudanum were commonly and unselfconsciously bought and used. Few who took the drug regularly would have bothered to analyse the reasons behind their consumption. . . . [The] drug could originally have been taken for what can be called a 'medical' need—sleeplessness, headache, depression—but as it was often and quite normally self-prescribed, the use continued perhaps after the strict 'medical' condition had gone. In reality the medical uses of opium shaded imperceptibly into 'non-medical' or what can be termed 'social' ones. The type of terminology now taken for granted in discussing opiate use and abuse was not at all applicable to the situation when opium was openly available.

What would now be called 'recreational' use of opium (and what in the nineteenth century was termed the 'luxurious' or 'stimulant' use of the drug) was, however, rarely spoken of. Although . . . even working-class use could have its 'stimulant' and recreational effects, at first opium was not usually taken with such effects in mind, even if it did in practice produce them. Self-medication was the most common reason for opiate use. It is therefore surprising that historically the most attention has always concentrated on examples of recreational use. The use of opium in the early part of the nineteenth century by the circle of Romantic writers and poets, and by their friends and associates, has attracted the bulk of interest, even though . . .

popular usage was far more extensive at that time. In the Romantic circle, the opium addiction of Thomas De Quincey and Samuel Taylor Coleridge has been particularly emphasized. Some discussions have drawn very direct and unsubtle parallels between the life of these opium eaters in nineteenth-century England and the current drug 'scene'. De Quincey has been equated with a 'high-school drop-out', and his pattern of opiate use has even been related to the current American programme of methadone maintenance. A paraphrase of De Quincey's life was quite a regular component of medical journals at the height of the drug 'epidemic' of the 1960s. Calculation of his dosage of opium in current terms and analysis of his psychology, or of his experiences under the influence of opium, somehow did duty as historical input to the debate on drug use. Analysis of his untypical individual case was easier than an examination of the place of opium in nineteenth-century society as a whole.

Much more valuable work has been done from a literary point of view; and the Romantics' use of opium has been widely studied in so far as it contributed to their literary output. De Quincey and Coleridge have attracted most attention in this respect, too. Abrams, in a short study, *The Milk of Paradise* [see excerpt below], long ago stated the view that opium had affected patterns of imagery in the addicted writers, leading to 'abnormal light perception' and 'extraordinary mutations of space'. Elizabeth Schneider, however, in *Coleridge, Opium and "Kubla Khan"* [see excerpt below], discussed in some depth the poet's composition of the poem long considered the epitome of an opium reverie. Casting doubt on whether Coleridge really wrote the poem when he said he did, in the summer of 1797, she traced its origins from a 'complex literary tradition' involving pseudo-oriental writing, the Gothic fashion and even Milton. 'There is reason to believe,' she concluded, 'that its special character was not determined or materially influenced by opium.' Alethea Hayter's recent work, however, allows opium a more active role in literary creation [see excerpt below]. Her view, and Schneider's, that the 'stimulant' effects of opium were new, and largely confined to the Romantic circle, is open to criticism. A study of opiate use in eighteenth-century society indicates that such effects were widely known, but unrevealed because of 'cultural prejudices' and literary convention. The Romantic recognition of the value of the imagination brought to the fore not new, but unspoken effects. But her main assessment, that opium did indeed have an effect on literary creation, stands as the most acceptable current analysis. In her view the opium dreams of De Quincey, Crabbe or Wilkie Collins 'crystallized the particles of past experience—sensory impressions, emotions, things read—into a symbolic pattern, an "involute", which became part of the life of the imagination and could be worked into literature.' The difficulty, however, remains, in proving that it was indeed opium that aided the literary result. As De Quincey himself noted, 'If a man whose talk is of oxen should become an opium eater, the probability is that . . . he will dream about oxen.'

The poets' use of opium was also not without its wider social significance. The life histories of opium eaters like Coleridge and De Quincey are in no sense a substitute for an analysis of opium's place in nineteenth-century society; but they do indicate what were contemporary attitudes and practice. De Quincey's flight from school, his wanderings through Wales, his journey to London to raise money, his months of near starvation there in the winter of 1802-3 and his friendship with the fifteen-year-old prostitute, the famous 'Ann of Oxford Street', are well-known, and particular to his own experience. But the ease with which he could buy the drug and the self-medication thereby involved were typical of any opium user in the first half of the century. De Quincey's first purchase was in 1804, from a druggist near the Pantheon in Oxford Street: 'when I asked for the tincture of opium, he gave it to me as any other man might do; and furthermore, out of my shilling, returned to me what seemed to be a real copper halfpence. . .' [see excerpt above]. De Quincey's dose may at times have been enormous—320 grains a day in 1816, 480 grains in 1817-18 and in 1843. But the self-treatment of minor complaints involved in his story was entirely commonplace. De Quincey first took it, on the recommendation of an undergraduate friend, as a remedy for gastric pain and also to ward off the incipient tuberculosis to which he was thought to be succumbing. Indeed, at the height of the debate on Britain's involvement in the Indo-Chinese opium trade at the end of the century, Surgeon-Major Eatwell even made an analysis of De Quincey's medical history from which he concluded that he had been suffering from 'gastrodynia' and a chronic gastric ulcer—'whatever might have been the degree of abuse of opium, this drug had in reality been the means of preserving and prolonging life'.

The origin of each other's opium habit was always subject to intensive debate between De Quincey and Coleridge. Each was anxious to accuse the other of taking opium for the pleasurable sensations which resulted. After Coleridge's death in 1834, Gillman, in a life of the poet, published a letter in which De Quincey was said to have taken opium solely to obtain pleasurable effects. Coleridge, on the other hand, maintained that he himself had taken it only as an anodyne—'nor had I at any time taken the flattering poison as a stimulus, or for any craving after pleasurable sensations . . .'. De Quincey, who had become friendly with Coleridge while on a visit to Somerset in 1807, was deeply wounded. In response, his *Reminiscences of the Lake Poets* were not charitable in their treatment of Coleridge. In *Coleridge and Opium Eating*, De Quincey reiterated his view that Coleridge had begun opiate use solely as a source of luxurious sensations. 'He speaks of opium excess . . . the excess of twenty-five years—as a thing to be laid aside easily and for ever within seven days; and yet, on the other hand, he describes it pathetically, sometimes with a frantic pathos, as the scourge, the curse, the one almighty blight which has desolated his life.'

In reality, the origin of both writers' opium habits was a particular illustration of the intertwining of 'social' and 'medical' usage so much a feature of opiate use at the time. De Quincey may have begun taking the drug in self-medication—but he also took it for pleasurable sensations and as a relief from anxiety. At times of particular stress—for instance after the death of little Kate Wordsworth in 1812, of whom he was particularly fond—his opium consumption was enormous. Coleridge, too, was less than honest about his habit. His contention that he was 'seduced' into the use of narcotics during a period of painful illness at Keswick in 1801 has been widely accepted. In a letter to Poole in May of that year, he described 'the disgust, the loathing, that followed these fits, and no doubt in part, too, the use of the brandy and laudanum which they rendered necessary'. But Coleridge had been known to take laudanum before this date. It had been given to him in Christ's Hospital sick ward; and in 1796 he had taken large quantities of laudanum for toothache while at the cottage near Stowey. "Kubla Khan" was written in the following year while Coleridge was taking opium ostensibly for dysentery, but possibly, too, to combat the anxiety caused by financial problems.

Such controversies are clearly important in any evaluation of the poets' lives and writings. But they ignore the point that self-medication could easily shade into recreational use. Similarly, Coleridge's accusation, made in 1830 and repeated by Gillman, that De Quincey's *Confessions* had 'seduced' others into 'this withering vice through wantonness' ignored the established place of the drug in society. The accusation that more of the pleasures than the pains of opium eating appeared in the *Confessions* was to some extent remedied by De Quincey himself in his 1856 revised version. Examples of opium eaters who attributed their experimentation to reading the book are undoubtedly to be found. The writer James Thomson and the poet Francis Thompson both acknowledged such a debt. Certainly the author of the anonymous book *Advice to Opium Eaters* maintained that it had been hastily brought out to warn others from copying De Quincey. De Quincey's own defence against this charge stressed the links between 'stimulant' and 'narcotic' use, medical and non-medical. 'A man has read a description of the powers lodged in opium,' he wrote in 1845, 'or . . . he has found those powers heraldically emblazoned in some magnificent dream due to that agency . . . but if he never *had* seen the gorgeous description of the gorgeous dress, he would (fifty to one) have tried opium on the recommendation of a friend for toothache, which is as general as the air, or for ear-ache, or (as Coleridge) for rheumatism. . . .' The 'medical' use of the drug could, he recognized, easily develop into something more, even without specific advocacy.

The acceptability of non-medical opiate use comes out most clearly in the public response at the time. When the *Confessions* were first published in the *London Magazine* in 1821 (and republished in book form in the following year), the literary reaction was one of excitement. The opium eating of the anonymous author and his stimulant use of the drug was a matter for moral condemnation from some quarters. But in general the reaction was interested and calm rather than hysterical. The *Confessions* were the first detailed description of English opium eating, although there were earlier, less widely circulated, medical analyses. The majority of descriptions available up to that time had presented the habit, along with opium smoking, as a peculiarly Eastern custom. De Quincey's eulogy of the drug proved the reality could be different, and that English opium eating was possible. Reaction was indeed a 'mixture of intelligent appreciation and sanctimonious condemnation'. The *Confessions* undoubtedly caused a furore, but the overriding impression is of calm interest even where the reaction was condemnatory. *John Bull* mounted a libellous attack on the author in 1824; Sir James Mackintosh praised the piece. The poet James Montgomery, writing in the *Sheffield Iris,* and the *North American Review* both cast doubt on its genuineness.

Opium eating was a prime concern, but the literary value of the work and the identity of the anonymous author were as important. The *British Review* was not 'disposed to acquiesce in the justiness of this panegyric on opium'. The *Medical Intelligencer,* however, was full of admiration for the 'beautiful narrative' and concluded that opium itself should be more widely used. The *Confessions* aroused interest, not fear or a desire for control. They even became a subject for humour. De Quincey appeared as the 'English opium eater' in his friend John Wilson's "Noctes Ambrosianae", semi-humourous literary dialogues published in *Blackwood's Magazine*. General Hamley, a regular contributor to *Blackwood's,* wrote "A recent confession of an opium eater," a humorous 'take-off' of De Quincey's work, when it was republished in a collected edition in 1856. Opiumm eating as a subject for humour, however heavy-handed, indicated a relaxed reaction.

On the other hand, Coleridge's attempts to reduce or break off his habit also indicated increased medical intervention in the condition and the beginnings of changed reactions. Between 1808 and 1814 he consulted many physicians and tried to restrict his quantity without success. After a period under the care of Dr Brabant, he removed finally to Highgate in 1816 to be permanently under the medical supervision of Dr Gillman. Here too, however, he continued to obtain lesser amounts of opium secretly. Dunn, the Highgate chemist, supplied him with three quarters of a pint of laudanum at a time, enough for five days' supply. Coleridge's habit was never as notorious as De Quincey's in his own life-time, and was not well-known even to his close friends. Campbell states that his indulgence in opium may have been suspected by the Wordsworths in 1802. But it was only on his return from his stay in Malta in 1806 that his friends were acquainted with the secret. Joseph Cottle, while on a visit to Coleridge in Bristol in 1813, noted the strangeness of his look. When both men called on Hannah More, Coleridge's hand shook so much that he spilled wine from the glass he was raising to his lips. Cottle ws told by a friend that this 'arises from the immoderate quantity of opium he takes'.

The social contest of opiate use is thus implicit in the life-histories of the two men—the use of the drug in self-medication, its availability and the lack of concern evoked. But their own impact on the place of opium in society was also important. Their opium eating affected, as well as illustrated, the response to opium.

Cottle's own revelation of his friend's opium eating in his *Reminiscences of Samuel Taylor Coleridge and Robert Southey* was one indication of how later reactions to such usage were no longer as tolerant as they had once been. Cottle waited until after Coleridge's death before publishing. By the late 1830s there was more concern about the practice than there had been in the early 1820s. Taking as justification a letter of the poet's to Mr Wade in which he had expressly ordered that a 'full and unqualified narrative of my wretchedness' be given after his death, Cottle heightened, as well as expressed, the changed response. 'When it is considered also, how many men of high mental endowments have shrouded their lustre, by a passion for this stimulus, and thereby, prematurely, become fallen spirits,' he declaimed, 'would it not be a criminal concession to unauthorised feelings, to allow so impressive an exhibition of this subtle species of intemperance to escape from public notice? . . . In the exhibition here made, the inexperienced, in future, may learn a memorable lesson, and be taught to shrink from opium, as they would from a scorpion. . . .'

The 'lesson' of opium eating came increasingly to be read into the experience of the two men. Indeed in some respects the social significance of Coleridge and De Quincey was in the last, rather than the first, decades of the century. Although the *Confessions* and evidence of Coleridge's opium use were never absent from discussions on opiate use in the first half of the century, it was during the period of anti-opium debate that their experiences were most directly related to changed reactions to opiate use. De Quincey and Coleridge were an established part of the domestic evidence with which the protagonists in the debate could buttress their arguments for and against the drug's consumption. Reissues of De Quincey abounded. There were at least thirteen editions and reissues of the *Confessions* between 1880 and 1910, more than in the first half of the century. The poets' consumption of opium, their dosage, their periods of moderate addiction and their longevity were all cited as

evidence. Coleridge, De Quincey and Wilkie Collins were 'melancholy and well-known instances' of opium eating to the Society for the Suppression of the Opium Trade (even if in this case the object was to stress the harmfulness of smoking rather than eating the drug). In evidence to the Royal Commission on Opium in the 1890s, by contrast, their longevity and the consequent possibilities of long-continuing consumption were the point at issue.

De Quincey and Coleridge were, after all, only exceptional and well-publicized instances of the commonplace use of opium in respectable circles in the first half of the century. Excessive concentration on their spectacular histories of addiction, and, at times, enormous dosages, has tended to disguise the overlapping of addiction, social and medical usage throughout middle-class society at the time. Among the writers, medical men and friends of the two men, use and addiction intermingled. In the circle which gathered round Dr Thomas Beddoes of Bristol, a disciple of Dr John Brown, were Coleridge and De Quincey, Charles Lloyd and Tom Wedgwood, the photographer, whose reliance on opium was notable in the last years of his life. It was through a recommendation of opium in Beddoes' edition of Brown's *Elements of Medicine* that Coleridge was supposed to have first taken the drug. Two of Tom Wedgwood's brothers married two sisters, whose third sister was married to James Mackintosh. Mackintosh, the philosophical writer and lawyer, was, like Beddoes, also a student and admirer of Brown. He was generally reported to be an opium addict, and while out in India, as Recorder of Bombay, he was in the habit of often taking laudanum. Mackintosh was a friend of Robert Hall, the Baptist preacher. Hall, too, was an opium addict and took as much as 120 grains a day. The stirring quality of his sermons was said to result from his use of the drug.

Such a chain of inter-linking addiction is remarkable only in that it was documented; patterns of literary consumption were always the most accessible. Byron, for instance, took laudanum occasionally. When his wife, thinking him insane, had his belongings searched, she found not only a copy of *Justine,* but a phial of Black Drop. In 1821, six years later, he recorded that he was using alcohol, not opium, to raise his spirits—'I don't like laudanum now as I used to do.' Shelley was also heavily reliant on laudanum at times of excessive physical and mental stress. He recorded, after a violent disagreement with Southey in 1812, that 'I have been obliged by an accession of nervous attack to take a quantity of laudanum which I did very unwillingly and reluctantly. . . .' On his parting from his wife, Harriet, at a time when he was suffering much bodily pain in addiction, 'he would actually go about with a laudanum bottle in his hand, supping thence as need might be'.

Keats was taking laudanum in 1819 and 1820 and at one stage intended to commit suicide with the drug before his death in Italy. Sir Walter Scott wrote *The Bride of Lammermoor* in 1819 in the course of a painful illness for which he was being given up to two hundred drops of laudanum and six grains of opium a day. Branwell Brontë was overtly dependent on the drug (his consumption of it originally began in imitation of De Quincey). For sixpence he could buy a measure of laudanum at Bessy Hardacre's drug store opposite The Bull in Haworth; and he sometimes wheedled opium pills out of her when he had no money. Dickens took opium occasionally at the end of his life, in particular to mitigate the stresses and physical ailments induced by his reading tour in America in 1867-8. The drug's effects provided a notable theme in his unfinished novel,

The Mystery of Edwin Drood. James Thompson's poem ''The City of Dreadful Night'', inspired by his use of opium; the secret addiction of Francis Thompson who, taking six ounces of opium a day, had descended into destitution before Wilfrid and Alice Meynell rescued him to write for *Merry England*; James Mangan's compensation for poverty and ill-health by laudanum and alcohol—all were part of the interlocking patterns of use and addiction.

Many other writers were undoubtedly dependent on the drug. Wilkie Collins took laudanum originally to deaden the pain of a rheumatic complaint and went on taking it for the rest of his life. Towards the end of his life Collins was in almost constant pain, carrying his supply of laudanum in a silver flask with him wherever he went. He had written in 1865:

> Who was the man who invented laudanum? I thank him from the bottom of my heart . . . I have had six delicious hours of oblivion; I have woken up with my mind composed; I have written a perfect little letter . . .—and all through the modest little bottle of drops which I see on my bedroom chimneypiece at this moment. Drops, you are darling! If I love nothing else, I love you!

It was in Collins's writing that the influence of opium was most clearly expressed. *The Moonstone* itself was written under the influence of opium as Collins, aware of his mother's impending death, struggled to meet a deadline while plagued with acute pain in his eyes. Like his part-autobiographical character, Ezra Jennings, the opium addict of the novel, he found that the 'progress of the disease has gradually forced me from the use of opium to the abuse of it'.

Elizabeth Barrett Browning, whom Pickering has called 'a well-balanced addict', took opium and morphia regularly. Robert Browning was shocked to find that 'sleep only came to her in a red hood of poppies'. As she wrote to Miss Mitford, in 1840, 'I took two draughts of opium last night—but even the second failing to bring sleep. It *is* a blessed thing!—that sleep!—one of my worse sufferings being the want of it. Opium—opium—night after night—! and some nights, during east winds, even opium won't do. . . .' Muriate of morphia she called her 'elixir', but she was quite able to give up the drug altogether when she was pregnant and worried about its effect on the unborn child. Her use of the drugs was simply a fact of her life and not an important one for her literary output; Julia Ward Howe's jealous contention that Mrs Browning relied on 'pinions other than her own' for the imagery and depth of her writing remains in doubt. Jane Carlyle, too, although probably not addicted, was taking much morphia in the 1840s. She was using the drug quite regularly from 1846 to 1853 to help her depression and sleeplessness. A dose given for her cough in 1846 induced, according to Caroline Fox, 'not beautiful dreams and visions, but a miserable feeling of turning to marble herself and lying on the marble, her hair, her arms, and her whole person petrifying and adhering to the marble slab on which she lay'.

Regular middle-class use and addiction was not simply a literary matter, although evidence for it in those circles is most plentifully documented. Throughout 'respectable' society addicts were to be found, with most note being taken of the habits of the famous. Clive of India died in a fit after taking a double dose of the opium to which he was accustomed. William Wilberforce was first prescribed opium for ulcerative colitis in 1788; Lord Carrington commented of him half a century later that 'it is extraordinary that his health was restored by that which to all appearances would be ruined by it, namely the

constant use of opium in large quantities'. In 1818, thirty years after his first prescription, he was still taking the same dose, a four-grain pill three times a day. Gladstone's sister Helen, a convert to Rome, was an invalid and a laudanum addict whom Gladstone himself found in Baden Baden in 1845 'Very ill from laudanum', having taken a dose of three hundred drops. John Thomson, whose *Street Life in London* was one of the earliest documentary photographic series, was also an opium addict. He, unlike most other users, had developed the habit after a lengthy visit to the Far East. George Harley, Professor of Practical Physiology at University College Hospital and later a writer on the uses and abuses of opium, also became dependent on morphia (which he took orally) after suffering intense eye pain. 'I . . . crawled back into bed, put out my hands, laid hold of the bottle containing the draught of morphia, and drained it to the bottom.' Harley later cured himself of his addiction by an agonizing period of abrupt withdrawal. After eight sleepless nights, ten hours of oblivion left him cured.

Others, although not strictly dependent on the drug, took it for 'stimulant' purposes. Horace Walpole remembered Lady Stafford saying to her sister, 'Well, child, I have come without my wit today' when she had not taken her opium 'which she was forced to do if she had any appointment, to be in particular spirits'. Jane, Duchess of Gordon, likewise took opium regularly and was lively and gay.

Florence Nightingale took opium on her return from the Crimea, partly to counteract the effect of the ending of her work there, partly, too, for a medical reason. In July 1866, when suffering severe back pain, she wrote that 'Nothing did me any good, but a curious little new fangled operation of putting opium under the skin which relieves one for twenty-four hours—but does not improve the vivacity or serenity of one's intellect.' Southey's mother took opium in large quantities during her last illness. Southey himself took the drug for sleeplessness, as did many others. In a letter to Sir Humphry Davy, another of the circle round Beddoes at Bristol, he complained of 'nervous feelings of pain and agitation. Tonight I try if opiates will send me to sleep, and when I sleep, preserve me from broken yet connected dreams . . .'.

George IV was given opiates, too, for their narcotic effect. The Duke of Wellington commented in 1826 on the King's excessive use of spirits: 'he drinks spirits morning, noon and night; and he is obliged to take laudanum to calm the irritation which the use of spirits occasions . . .'. Jane Austen's mother had opium similarly to help her sleep. Lady Sarah Robinson, whose only daughter had recently died, was in 1826 calmed from 'an overwhelming rage' by the administration of 'a quantity of laudanum'.

Dante Gabriel Rossetti's wife, who suffered from tuberculosis and a spinal deformity, was addicted to laudanum and died of an overdose. Yet Rossetti nevertheless strongly urged Janey Morris, in the course of a romance obsessively over-concerned with ill-health, to take chlorodyne for neuralgia. Oliver, the son of Ford Madox Brown, Rossetti's associate, advised Frederic Shields, the artist and, like Rossetti, addicted to chloral, to take 'A dose of *chloral* Monday, *sour milk* Tuesday, *Laudanum* Wednesday, on Thursday a little *spirits,* while on Friday you might modestly content yourself with fifteen to twenty-five drops of *chlorodyne*. In this way you would not grow hardened to any one of them, and each would retain its full power and proper efficiency.'

There were other less famous but nonetheless 'respectable' opium eaters. In Morwenstow in Cornwall, the opium taking of the Rev. Robert Hawker was exaggerated by the stress of his wife's death in 1862. Hawker had a neighbour, Oliver Rouse, whose favourite tipple was gin and paregoric. Mostly the opium use of these less known circles went unremarked. In general, a gallery of such individual opium users and eaters is certainly no reliable guide to the incidence of usage at that time. It is, however, a valuable indication of how the situation of open availability operated before the 1868 Pharmacy Act and to a great extent beyond it. It is perhaps surprising to find that famous personalities of the period were dependent on, or regular users of, a drug the use of which is now shunned or regarded most usually as symptomatic of a diseased or disturbed personality. Many managed their dependence without the physical and mental deterioration, the social incapacity, or the early death which is the stereotype of contemporary narcotic addiction. Addiction, in fact, was not the point at issue for those users of the drug and their contemporaries. The experiences, and their publication, of Coleridge and De Quincey may with hindsight be seen as landmarks in the process of changing perspectives on opiate use, as helping gradually to engender a harsher, more restrictive response. But for their contemporaries, opium was a simple part of life, neither exclusively medical nor entirely social. (pp. 49-61)

> *Virginia Berridge and Griffith Edwards, "Opiate Use in Literary and Middle-Class Society," in their* Opium and the People: Opiate Use in Nineteenth-Century England, *Allen Lane, 1981, pp. 49-61.*

OPIUM AND LITERARY CREATIVITY

MEYER HOWARD ABRAMS

[*Abrams is an American critic best known for his writings on English Romanticism. In the following excerpt, he explores the influence of opium use on the works of De Quincey, Crabbe, Thompson, and Coleridge.*]

Four eminent English authors were addicted to opium. Each author spent a considerable part of his life in a dream world which differs amazingly from that in which we live. Each author utilized the imagery from these dreams in his literary creations, and sometimes, under the direct inspiration of opium, achieved his best writing. Thus, a knowledge of the opium world these authors inhabited is essential to a complete understanding of their work. (p. ix)

Limitations of the length allowed for this thesis have imposed limitations in subject. I have dealt with no drug but opium. . . . Foreign authors I have had to omit; and of English authors I have been able to treat at length only those four whose long addiction to the drug is certain: DeQuincey, Crabbe, Francis Thompson, and Coleridge. (p. x)

• • • • •

When Homer sang of "the drug to heal all pain and anger, and bring forgetfulness of every sorrow," he heralded a long succession of poets who paid tribute to the enchantment of opium. Vergil knew the "poppies soaked with the sleep of Lethe"; and in his *Aeneid*, the dragon which protects the distant Hesperides succumbs to this chastening gift of Somnus, god of sleep. The great English poets, too, felt the poppy's spell. Chaucer twice mentions opium; Shakespeare knows the effect

of "the drowsy syrups of the world"; Milton recalls Homer with

> The Nepenthes which the wife of Thone
> In Egypt gave to Jove-born Helena.

These poets were allured by the mystery inherent in the golden drug of Asia; but when English authors, early in the nineteenth century, actually took opium themselves, they were inspired to ecstasies. "A spot of enchantment, a green spot of fountain and flowers and trees in the very heart of a waste of sands!" So Coleridge hailed it, and found therein a refuge from the turmoil of aspiration and disillusion at the turn of the century. DeQuincey apostrophized the drug more grandly: "Just, subtle, and all-conquering opium!". . . "*Eloquent* opium!" [see excerpt above]. For he saw not only a sanctuary, but a new sphere opened to his imagination in the glowing splendors it built "upon the bosom of darkness, out of the fantastic imagery of the brain."

The great gift of opium to these men was access to a new world as different from this as Mars may be; and one which ordinary mortals, hindered by terrestrial conceptions, can never, from mere description, quite comprehend. It is a world of twisted, exquisite experience, sensuous and intellectual; of "music like a perfume," and "sweet light golden with audible odors exquisite" [see poem above by Arthur Symons], where color is a symphony, and one can hear the walk of an insect on the ground, the bruising of a flower. Above all, in this enchanted land man is freed at last from those petty bonds upon which Kant insists: space and time. Space is amplified to such proportions that, to writer after writer, "infinity" is the only word adequate to compass it. More striking still, man escapes at last from the life of a transiency lamented by poets since time immemorial, and approaches immortality as closely as he ever can in this world; for he experiences, almost literally, eternity. This is not the abstract "eternity" of the mystic, not Vaughan's vision of "a great ring of pure and endless light," but the duration of an actual, continuous experience so long that DeQuincey throws up his hands in an attempt to measure it by mundane standards:

> In valuing the *virtual* time lived during some dreams, the measurement by generations is ridiculous—by millenia is ridiculous; by aeons, I should say, if aeons were more determinate, would also be ridiculous.

This fantastic land is not the fleeting shadow of an ordinary dream, but is a reality nearly as vivid as actual experience. The important and almost neglected fact is that in "the well of memory" the fragments of this land assume as legitimate a place as any recollections from life. When the poet's selective spirit hovers over the well, these images rise to the surface as readily as any others, to be incorporated in his creation side by side with the scenes from everyday life. To reconstruct the world of dreams vividly enough to distinguish its fragments in the works of men who have roamed its exotic paths is the hazardous task I have undertaken.

In all the writings of the four men with whom I am concerned, DeQuincey's *Confessions of an English Opium-Eater* is the only acknowledged description of opium vision. Coleridge so denoted only the passing reference, in his letters, to the "green spot of fountain and trees"; we know of Thompson's recourse to opium only through the indirect testimony of Everard Meynell; and if it were not for an incidental acknowledgment by Crabbe's son, and a friend's hasty jotting on a copy of his poems, Crabbe's addiction might have escaped notice altogether.

Whether or not the impulse which caused DeQuincey to break this bond of silence was his avowed intention to be "useful and instructive," his *Confessions* may serve as a key to the mysteries of the opium world. That his descriptions of the effects of opium are authentic is verified, not only by his own reiterated insistence, but by the fact that psychological investigators still draw on the *Confessions* for data.

DeQuincey, an Oxford student of nineteen, took opium for the first time in 1804, under coercion of excruciating rheumatic pains of head and face. In accordance with accepted medical opinion, an acquaintance recommended opium, and DeQuincey tried it without question. So enticing was the "abyss of divine enjoyment" revealed to him that for ten years he tasted the delights of the drug with indulgences at three-week intervals, until in 1813 an "appalling irritation of the stomach" led to a daily resort to opium, and the addiction which lasted until his death. As with other authors, dreams of horror after long consumption of opium, rather than the pleasures experienced at the inception of the habit, stimulated most his desire for literary expression. The visions described in the *Confessions* are the "Iliad of woes" attendant upon a futile struggle against the drug; the "pleasures of opium" are lauded, but with no specific detail.

The first symptom upon which DeQuincey comments, he calls "the re-awakening of a state of eye oftentimes incident to childhood": an endless succession of scenes passing through his mind; the subject, perhaps, voluntarily chosen, but its evolution out of control. Havelock Ellis, in *The World of Dreams*, also remarks upon this "constant succession of self-evolving visual imagery," and felicitously likens it "to the images produced by the kaleidoscope." [Roger] Dupouy, describing the same effect in greater detail, notes, too, that "les pensées et les tableaux se succèdent sans arrêt, faisant défiler les vies, les générations, et les siècles."

DeQuincey then analyzes the distorted perceptions which seem to characterize all opium visions, whether of pleasure or of pain, the enormous extension of space and time.

> Space swelled, and was amplified to an extent of unutterable and self-repeating infinity. This disturbed me very much less than the vast expansion of time. Sometimes I seemed to have lived for seventy or a hundred years in one night; nay, sometimes had feelings representative of a duration far beyond the limits of any human experience.

(pp. 3-8)

In the early stages, [the] exalted splendors of DeQuincey's dreams were chiefly architectural, "such pomp of cities and palaces as never yet was beheld by the waking eye, unless in the clouds." To these succeeded "dreams of lakes and silvery expanses of water," which, by the alchemy of opium, were soon amplified: "From translucent lakes, shining like mirrors, they became seas and oceans."

Now began the affliction so horrible that it has impressed itself more deeply than any other dream experience on the work of every opium author. DeQuincey calls it "the tyranny of the human face"; but this manifestation is only one aspect of a many-sided evil, the delusion of pursuit and persecution:

> Upon the rocking waters of the ocean the human face began to reveal itself; the sea appeared paved with innumerable faces, upturned to the heavens; faces, imploring, wrathful, despairing; faces that surged upwards by thousands, by myriads, by generations.

But the many faces soon gave place to one, that of a Malay who, like a genie conjured by Aladdin's lamp, had appeared one day at DeQuincey's peaceful country cottage. Fearfully metamorphosed from that harmless vagrant, the dream fiend transports his helpless victim, night after endless night, through fantastic scenes which are the accumulations of all DeQuincey's Asiatic memories, fused under the unifying principle of guilt and horror:

> I was stared at, hooted at, grinned at, chattered at, by monkeys, by paraquets, by cockatoos. I ran into pagodas, and was fixed for centuries at the summit, or in secret rooms. . . . I fled from the wrath of Brama through all the forests of Asia; Vishnu hated me; Seeva lay in wait for me. . . . I had done a deed, they said, which the ibis and the crocodile trembled at. Thousands of years I lived and was buried in stone coffins, with mummies and sphinxes, in narrow chambers at the heart of eternal pyramids. I was kissed with cancerous kisses, by crocodiles, and was laid, confounded with all unutterable abortions, amongst reeds and Nilotic mud.

Note here the kaleidoscopic rush of scenes, and that omnipresent sensation of distorted time—"fixed for *centuries*," "*thousands* of years," "*eternal* pyramids." And later in the same vision, "Over every form, and threat, and punishment, and dim sightless incarceration, brooded a killing sense of *eternity* and *infinity*."

Into these dreams, although all before had been "moral and spiritual terrors," now entered circumstances of "physical horror":

> Here the main agents were ugly birds, or snakes, or crocodiles. . . . All the feet of the tables, sofas, &c., soon became instinct with life: the abominable head of the crocodile, and his leering eyes, looked out at me, multiplied into ten thousand repetitions; and I stood loathing and fascinated.

In the original manuscript of the *Confessions* appeared another passage which, although immediately cancelled by the writer, has since been published. . . . The dreams become so terrifying, that, DeQuincey says:

> At length I grew afraid to sleep, and I shrank from it as from the most savage torture. Often I fought with my drowsiness, and kept it aloof by sitting up the whole night and the following day.

Yet he had to sleep at times; and turning back to the published *Confessions,* we find a new series of visions, beginning with the lovely one of the "Sunday morning in May." DeQuincey is standing at what seems the door of his actual cottage; but, with the usual exaltation of space, "the mountains were raised to more than Alpine height, and there was interspace far larger between them of savannahs and forest lawns." Then suddenly "the scene is an Oriental one . . . and at a vast distance are visible, as a stain upon the horizon, the domes and cupolas of a great city."

There follows the breathless description of the finding, under Judean palms, of Ann, the forlorn little prostitute who had befriended him in London seventeen years before. Another turn of the kaleidoscope, vapors roll in, and DeQuincey, is back in London. And again a flux of scene, heralded by the welling of sounds on a drugged mentality, as he hears

> music of preparation and of awakening suspense. The undulations of fast-gathering tumults . . . gave the

feeling of a multitudinous movement, of infinite cavalcades filing off, and the tread of innumerable armies.

As the view unrolls, the scene again contorts into one of horror, with "darkness and lights; tempests and human faces." Ann reappears, but only for a moment, then—"everlasting farewells!" And as the sound is reverberated—again and again, "everlasting farewells!"—he 'awakes in struggles, and cries aloud, "I will sleep no more!"'

To those who know George Crabbe as a sedate and dignified ecclesiastic, his classification with the comparatively disreputable DeQuincey, Thompson, and Coleridge may seem a bit incongruous, even irreverent; but a touch of the poppy makes the world of poets kin. In the biography written by Crabbe's son occurs a paragraph to the significance of which most critics have been as blind as was the author. After Crabbe had experienced a fainting spell in 1790, a certain Dr. Club was called who "saw through the case with great judgment," and declared, to quote the son:

> "Let the digestive organs bear the whole blame; you must take opiates." From that time his health began to amend rapidly, . . . a rare effect of opium; . . . and to a constant but slightly increasing dose of it may be attributed his long and generally healthy life.

From Crabbe himself we learn that this "constant but slightly increasing dose" finally resulted in the usual dreams of horror. What is apparently only one of many similar experiences is narrated in his journal of 1817:

> For the first time these many nights, I was incommoded by dreams, such as would cure vanity for a time in any mind where they could gain admission. . . . Asleep, all was misery and degradation, not my own only, but of those who had been.—That horrible image of servility and baseness—that mercenary and commercial manner!

The poet Fitzgerald, who in a twenty-two year friendship with Crabbe's son had learned much about the father's habits, adds to the list of evidence. In Fitzgerald's copy of Crabbe's poems, Ainger informs us,

> there is a MS note, not signed "G.C.," and therefore Fitzgerald's own. It runs thus: "It (the opium) probably influenced his dreams, for better or worse." To this Fitzgerald significantly adds, "see also the "World of Dreams," and his "Eustace Grey."

The opening stanza of the "World of Dreams" confirms Fitzgerald's hypothesis that the visions described in the poem are of opium origin. The division of dreams into extremes of pleasure and pain at once echoes the keynote of DeQuincey's *Confessions:*

> And is thy soul so wrapt in sleep?
> Thy senses, they affections, fled?
> No play of fancy thine, to keep
> Oblivion from that grave, thy bed?
> Then art thou but the breathing dead:
> I envy, but I pity too:
> The bravest may *my* terrors dread,
> The happiest fain *my* joys pursue. . . .
>
> I feel such bliss, I fear such pain;
> But all is gloom, or all is gay,
> Soon as th' ideal World I gain.

This "ideal World" of Crabbe's diluted phraseology, it soon becomes evident, is the same twisted world of opium into which DeQuincey had entered. With characteristic phantasmagoric

succession, the restless scene shifts from "the wicked city's vilest street" to "a noble mansion," to "far-off rivers"; then, after a flash of the sea, to the land again; on and on, fading, receding, expanding, brightening.

In spite of DeQuincey's failure to give a detailed picture of his visions of pleasure, the following scene is enough like Coleridge's "green spot of fountain and flowers and trees" to indicate its type. The force of this description is lost upon those unacquainted with the usual cold restraint of Crabbe's style:

> A garden this? Oh! lovely breeze!
> Oh! flowers that with such freshness bloom!
> Flowers shall I call such forms as these;
> Or this delicious air perfume?
> Oh! this from better worlds must come;
> On earth such beauty who can meet?

Then occurs the illusion of flight, which, though new to this investigation, is an authenticated characteristic of narcotic experience:

> 'Tis easier now to soar than run;
> Up! Up!—we neither tire nor fall.
> Children of dust, be yours to crawl
> On the vile earth!

Unfortunately, these delights are soon metamorphosed into the familiar hallucinations of persecution and horror, crowded with "black Enemies," in which "the dark-brow'd throng" jostle a "female fiend" with "tainted bosom bare" and "eye of stone." Time is extended in "that sad, last, long endless day!" And again we hear the welling of noise, like DeQuincey's "undulations of fast-gathering tumults":

> Heavens! how mighty is the throng,
> Voices humming like a hive!

Although the Orient held the greatest terror for DeQuincey, Crabbe, like a true eighteenth-century man of letters, seems too have feared most the horrors of the Gothic. He is brought into a "Gothic hall," and seated with

> Kings, Caliphs, Kaisers,—silent all;
> Pale as the dead; enrobed and tall,
> Majestic, frozen, solemn, still;
> They wake my fears, my wits appal,
> And with both scorn and terror fill.

Strikingly close to similar experiences upon which DeQuincey had commented is the reappearance in Crabbe's dreams of the friends of his childhood, "all whom he loved and thought them dead." And as DeQuincey had met Ann in his dreams, so Crabbe sees

> One, the fairest, best,
> Among them—ever-welcome guest!. . .
>
> Speak to me! speak! that I may know
> I am thus happy!—dearest, speak!

But, as in DeQuincey's dream, the dear forms disappear in the tumult, the terrors become ever more unbearable, until Crabbe, by a last desperate struggle, frees himself; and so perfect is the illusion, we can almost hear him crying, as DeQuincey had done, "I will sleep no more!"

"Sir Eustace Grey," composed by Crabbe fifteen years after he had begun to take opium, again confirms Fitzgerald's judgment. This time the opium phenomena are not merely described, but are placed in a framework of plot designed to account for their peculiarities: a madman's recital of the fiendish persecution attending him since the murder of his young wife's paramour. We may detect the line, I feel certain, where the transcriptions from Crabbe's dreams begin:

> Soon came a voice! I felt it come;
> "Full be his cup, with evil fraught,
> Demons his guides, and death his doom!"

Immediately follows the usual eternal and kaleidoscopically varied persecution. Even the Malay who had been the supervisor of DeQuincey's tortures finds his counterpart in Crabbe's "two fiends":

> Then was I cast from out my state,
> Two fiends of darkness led my way;
> They waked me early, watch'd me late,
> My dread by night, my plague by day!

Space is again amplified in the "boundless plain," "vast ruins," and "pillars and pediments sublime"; and, as usual, the bonds of time are burst:

> There was I fix'd, I know not how,
> Condemn'd for untold years to stay:
> Yet years were not;—one dreadful *Now*
> Endured no change of night or day.

As DeQuincey had been fixed for centuries at the summit of pagodas, so:

> They hung me on a bough so small,
> The rook could build her nest no higher;
> They fix'd me on the trembling ball
> That crowns the steeple's quiv'ring spire.

Interminably, the tormenting fiends continue their savage game. Sir Eustace is pursued through a "bleak and frozen land," riveted to a tombstone, placed upon a shaking fen" where "danced the moon's deceitful light," hung upon "the ridgy steep of cliffs," plunged "below the billowy deep"; then abruptly, again like a sudden *awakening* from a nightmare, comes the call of grace to release him from his tortures. But before I leave the poem, one bit of imagery I wish to emphasize because of its appearance in later writers:

> They placed me where those streamers play,
> Those nimble beams of brilliant light;
> It would the stoutest heart dismay,
> To see, to feel that dreadful sight:
> So swift, so pure, so cold, so bright,
> They pierced my frame with icy wound;
> And all that half-year's polar night,
> Those dancing streamers wrapp'd me round.

That DeQuincey made no special comment on abnormal light perception in a drugged state does not prove he noticed none. It may rather be the result of an innate lack of sensitivity to light. Although ordinary dreams are prevailingly gray in color, in opium visions, as Beaudelaire affirms, occur "des échappées magnifiques, gorgés de lumière et de couleur." Dupouy, moreover, describes a sensitivity of the eye so great that it translates vivid ocular impressions in terms of actual physical pain. Thus Crabbe could speak of *feeling* light as an "icy wound."

It seems strange that Saintsbury could describe as an exponent of "the style of drab stucco" the author of the stanza above, yet this statement is not unfair when applied to almost any of Crabbe's work except the two poems most critics neglect: "The World of Dreams" and "Sir Eustace Grey." Significantly, these same two poems and no others that I could discover describe the world of Crabbe's opium dreams. These poems offer, therefore, an unexampled opportunity to observe the effect of opium on that mysterious phenomenon, poetic inspiration. On two occasions something happened to Crabbe which

"set the winds of inspiration blowing," tore him loose from the clutch of the heroic couplet, and caused the employment, in these two poems only, of an eight-line stanza with interlacing rhymes, almost as intricate as the Spenserian. This same force, in at least a score of stanzas of "Sir Eustace Grey," freed Crabbe's language from the restraint of eighteenth-century poetic diction, and gave it a simplicity and inevitability which suggest Coleridge's "Ancient Mariner." With the evidence presented, is there much doubt that this stimulus, which incited Crabbe to dash off "Sir Eustace Grey" in a single night, is the vivid recollection of an opium dream?

However admonitory were DeQuincey's intentions, the list of addicts introduced to opium by his *Confessions* is a long one, and extends even to the present day. The last gift that Francis Thompson received from his mother was a copy of the *Confessions*. He was then, in 1879, a misfit medical student wandering ill and friendless in dingy Manchester. In this condition, and under the stimulation of DeQuincey's rhapsodies, a resort to opium was almost inevitable. "Giver of life, death, peace, distress" Thompson later termed his mother, and thereby summed up the conflicting doles of the drug to which she had unsuspectingly introduced him.

Thompson rarely alluded to this surrender, but we find the records of his opium addiction in the biography written by his friend, Everard Meynell. In 1882 he was already spending money on the drug, and three years later he sold books and medical instruments to satisfy the cravings which had already become insatiable. Because of the habit, in 1887 he lost a job given him by a kindly shoemaker. Twelve years later the elder Meynell induced him to go to a private hospital for cure. Although the impression left by the biography is that this treatment succeeded, a later record indicates that its success must have been temporary at best; for in November, 1907, Thompson confessed to Wilfrid Meynell, "I am dying from laudanum poisoning."

That Thompson experienced, too, the usual opium dreams, is certain. Thus, Meynell comments, "his letters contain complaints of dreams akin to Coleridge's," and then quotes Thompson's description of "a most miserable fortnight of torpid, despondent days, and affrightful nights, dreams having been in part the worst realities of my life."

I have not space to deal in detail with Thompson's poetry, although much of it is swiftly phantasmagoric, often approaching the imagery we have come to recognize as a consequence of addiction to opium. The danger is that one may go too far and attribute, glibly, all its strangeness to a "ghostly aura from quick-burning nerves." Thompson himself has tempted such over-emphasis by the following testament in a poem suggestively entitled "The Poppy":

> The sleep-flower sways in the wheat its head,
> Heavy with dreams, as that with bread. . . .
>
> I hang 'mid men my needless head,
> And my fruit is dreams, as theirs is bread. . . .
>
> Love! *I* fall into the claws of Time:
> But lasts within a leavèd rhyme
> All that the world of me esteems—
> My withered dreams, my withered dreams.

Thompson's work also includes a prose fantasy, "Finis Coronat Opus," closely comparable to DeQuincey's visions of pain. Again, as in "Sir Eustace," the opium vagaries are moulded to fit a narrative frame designed to account for them, and again the pretext for the persecution is a murder; for the poet Florentian buys genius from an evil spirit at the price of killing his own sweetheart. Perhaps because of Thompson's inherent sensitivity, light phenomena are stressed early in the story. He describes a multitude of parti-colored lamps:

> Above them were coiled thinnest serpentinings of suspended crystal, hued like the tongues in a wintry hearth, flame-colour, violet, and green; so that, as in the heated current from the lamps the snakes twirled and flickered and their bright shadows twirled upon the wall, they seemed at length to undulate their twines, and the whole altar became surmounted with a fiery fantasy of sinuous stains.

These sinuous undulations of light rays on a narcotized retina are very like the experiences of Sir Eustace.

Dupouy treats at some length the effect of opium on auditory perceptions, of which some signs have already appeared in DeQuincey and Crabbe. . . . (pp. 9-25)

The contrasted blasting and exquisiteness of sound effects, so difficult to describe in terms of normal audition, occur within a single paragraph of "Finis Coronat Opus"; for with hearing as with sight, there is no quiescence in the opium world; everything is in a constant flux of intensification or recession. (p. 25)

Later is repeated the effect of attenuated sound on ear drums almost painfully keen. With it appears the familiar persecution theme, again through time without end, but in a new form: the hypnotic effect of accusing eyes holds the dreamer as a snake's stare holds a bird. (p. 26)

A monstrosity appears, like the crocodile which had kissed DeQuincey "with cancerous kisses": "When I recovered consciousness, it was risen from the ground, and kissed me with the kisses of its mouth." And the persecution goes on and on, sustained by an agency as persistent as the "fiends" we already know. "For two years . . . it had spoken to me with her lips, used her gestures, smiled her smile." And long afterward:

> I can fly no farther, I fall exhausted, the fanged hour fastens on my throat . . . hurrying retributions whose multitudinous tramplings converge upon me in a hundred presages, in a hundred shrivelling menaces, down all the echoing avenues of doom.

Although Coleridge, who had taken opium several times before 1791, was the first author of the four to experience the effects of the drug, I have hitherto reserved treatment of his work, in order to gain all possible momentum of evidence before approaching the contested question: did opium influence the composition of "The Ancient Mariner"? The problem hinges upon the issue whether before the conception of the poem in November, 1797, Coleridge had experienced the type of opium dreams which might have exerted such influence. (pp. 27-8)

The indubitable facts are: one, that as early as 1791 Coleridge had tried opium; and two, that the suffering which led him to do so continued until 1796, when definite proofs of addiction occur in March, and again in November and December. An investigation of the works which he composed in 1796 reveals, too, startling indications that he had experienced, even in that year, not only the pleasures, but the pains attendant either upon long addiction or upon overdoses.

In Coleridge's Note Book of random jottings, upon which Professor Lowes has based his study of Coleridge's reading, occurs a series of passages about which, Mr. Lowes confesses, except for some possible resemblances to a lightning storm in Bartram's *Travels,* he has "not the remotest notion what they are." The following quotation is a part of "one of the most wildly incoherent pages of the Note Book," spaced just as Coleridge jotted it:

> a dusky light—a purple *flash*
> crystalline splendor—light blue—
> *Green* lightnings—
> in that eternal and delirious (misery)
> wrath fires—
> inward desolations
> an horror of great darkness
> great things—on the ocean
> counterfeit infinity—

The time of the three pages of these confused entries has been definitely placed in the month or two before the composition of the "Ode to the Departing Year," written December 24-26, 1796. Upon this point, based on the inclusion of germinating fragments of the "Ode" amid the entries, Campbell, Lowes, and Brandl unhesitatingly agree. The significant thing is that in Coleridge's letters of those months, we discover more frequent references to his recourse to opium than he ever made again within the same length of time.

It is fairly clear that the disorder of these pages is due to extravagances induced by a combination of drugs and physical pain, and that at least the passage I have quoted is an excerpt from an opium vision itself. The hitherto inexplicable confusion of entries is shot through, moreover, with indications that Coleridge was preoccupied at that period with the subjects of opium and dreams. In the Note Book, immediately preceding the first fragment of the "Ode to the Departing Year," is the statement: "Dreams sometimes useful by giving to the well-grounded fears and hopes of the understanding the feelings of vivid sense." Immediately following the same fragment occurs what is evidently Coleridge's description of a dream of pain: "In a distempered dream things and forms in themselves common and harmless inflict a terror of anguish"; and this statement is in turn followed by another bit from the "Ode." Farther on, in the first draft of a scene later used in *Osorio,* occurs a mysterious reference to opium:

> It had been a damning sin to have remained
> An opium chewer with such excellent grapes
> Over his cottage.

And finally, on the same incoherent page with the "green lightnings" passage, come significant jottings of "deep sighings," and "unbind the poppy garland," which again may possibly be allusions to opium.

Even without these vanes to point the wind, internal evidence indicates the opium origin of the excerpt I quoted above. The lights and colors are certainly as close to Crabbe's "dancing streamers" and Thomson's color experiences of red, violet, and green crystal as they are to Bartram's lightnings. The rest of the passage, which an appeal to Bartram leaves entirely unexplained, is paralleled in every detail by known opium phenomena. The "eternal and delirious misery," the "wrath fires," "desolations," and "horror" represent again that omnipresent theme of persecution through eternity; and in the "great things" and "counterfeit infinity" of the ocean, space once more undergoes its limitless expansion.

In the "Ode to the Departing Year" itself—a poem in which, as Brandl puts it, Coleridge's "Gemütserregung steigert sich bis ins Fieberhafte"—are evidences of opium delirium even more definite than the confusion of the structure. In one passage

Coleridge describes a horrible vision which has appeared to him:

> And ever, when the dream of night
> Renews the phantom to my sight,
> Cold sweat-drops gather on my limbs;
> My ears throb hot; my eye-balls start,
> My brain with horrid tumult swims;
> Wild is the tempest of my heart;
> And my thick and struggling breath
> Imitates the toil of death!

If there is doubt that these lines refer to the effects of a dream of terror caused by opium, a striking parallel occurs in "The Pains of Sleep," which Coleridge himself classifies with the opium dream, "Kubla Khan" [see poems above]. Its similarities both to DeQuincey's experiences and to the excerpt above are apparent even from a few lines of quotation:

> But yester-night I prayed aloud
> In anguish and in agony,
> Up-starting from the fiendish crowd
> Of shapes and thoughts that tortured me:
> A lurid light, a trampling throng,
> Sense of intolerable wrong,
> And whom I scorned, those only strong! . . .
>
> Desire with loathing strangely mixed
> On wild or hateful objects fixed. . . .
>
> For all seemed guilt, remorse or woe.

And farther on in the same poem, he describes

> The third night, when my own loud scream
> Had waked me from the fiendish dream.

Such dreams in 1803, when Coleridge was undeniably deep in the toils of opium, are understandable; but, in view of the traditional opinion, it may still be hard to believe that the dreams also occurred as early as the "Ode" of December, 1796. A letter of Coleridge's dated September 22, 1803, clinches the case. After relating the same dreams described in the "Pains of Sleep," from which, awakening, he "blest the scream which delivered him from reluctant sleep," he makes this neglected statement: "Nine years ago I had three months' visitation of this kind." "Nine years ago" would have been in 1794. Certainly there is no reason here for conscious misstatement, and even Coleridge's fickle memory could not have recalled as "nine years" anything less than seven years. It seems probable that Coleridge is remembering, although hazily in regard to date, the very dreams of 1796 with which we are concerned.

In the afternoon of November 13, 1797, Coleridge conceived the plan of "The Ancient Mariner," and brought the poem, completed, to read to the Wordsworths on the evening of March 23, 1798. Now that we know Coleridge had already experienced opium dreams of horror in 1796 of sufficient intensity to have left their impress on his poems of that year, the question of the influence of opium on "The Ancient Mariner" must be viewed in a new light. The problem resolves itself into two distinct questions: whether opium had a part in inspiring the conception and scheme of the work; and aside from that, whether the scenery and sensations of Coleridge's dreams were utilized in the details of the poem.

Mr. John Mackinnon Robertson, in the answer to the first question which has had so much influence on the popular conception of Coleridge, represents the type of criticism I am trying to avoid. At one fell swoop he stigmatizes "The Ancient Mariner," the first part of "Christabel," and "Kubla Khan" as "an abnormal product of an abnormal nature under abnormal conditions," all having been "conceived and composed under the influence of opium."

In view of the phantasmagoric quality of all drug visions, I concur with Mr. Lowes in his denial of the specious theory that so highly wrought a piece of conscious artistry as "The Ancient Mariner" could have been "*composed* under the influence of opium," but I cannot agree with him that opium played no part in the inspiration of the poem.

There can be no question of the great gulf, both in subject and style, between "The Ancient Mariner" and Coleridge's earlier work, which had tended to didacticism and rhetoric, and had employed, in Coleridge's own scornful words, "such shadowy nobodies as cherub-winged *Death*, Trees of *Hope*, bare-bosomed *Affection* and simpering *Peace*." Reduced to baldest terms, the factors to which Mr. Lowes attributes this change are the influence of William and Dorothy Wordsworth, and "that equipoise of the intellectual and emotional faculties, which [Coleridge] christened 'joy!'"

These causes explain a gradual ripening rather than a sudden metamorphosis of technique, and leave unexplained Cole-

Scenes from an English opium factory, circa 1830.

ridge's use of the supernatural theme so foreign to Wordsworth's temperament. I put most of my faith in Mr. Lowes's final hypothesis:

> Above all, for the first time in his life Coleridge had hit upon a theme which fired his imagination, and set him voyaging again through all the wonder-haunted regions of all his best-loved books.

The point where I differ from Mr. Lowes is in my belief that this theme was not a happy accident of the imagination, but had its source and development in Coleridge's opium hallucinations. We have seen that such dreams had already influenced Coleridge's poetry, and might be very likely [to] do so again. Against this theory, too, the objection that the "superb, unwavering imaginative control" of the poem "is not the gift of opium" would not be valid. "The Ancient Mariner," I venture to say, underwent the same process to which both "Sir Eustace Grey" and "Finis Coronat Opus" were subjected: a framework of plot was constructed expressly to contain the pre-existent fabric of dream phenomena.

A careful interpretation of Wordsworth's account of the poem's origin bears out this theory. In the course of a walk, he says,

> was planned the poem of the "Ancient Mariner," founded on a dream, as Mr. Coleridge said, of his friend Mr. Cruikshank. Much the greatest part of the story was Mr. Coleridge's invention; but certain parts I suggested; for example, some crime was to be committed which should bring upon the Old Navigator . . . the spectral persecution.

Wordsworth also related to the Reverend Alexander Dyce substantially the same story of the famous walk, with the additional detail that the original dream was of "a skeleton ship; with figures in it." Wordsworth's accounts agree that his own share in the poem was limited to the suggestion of two incidents: the shooting of the albatross, and the navigation of the ship by the dead men.

The significant information here is to be read between the lines. Coleridge seized upon the detail of "a skeleton ship," but the spectral persecution is his own ideas. Wordsworth evidently added, after its conception, the detail of a crime to motivate this persecution. And by the time Wordsworth later suggested the supernatural navigation, it is apparent that the plot had been completed, up to this point, by Coleridge himself.

DeQuincey, moreover, gives evidence that such a plan had been forming in Coleridge's mind, independently of Cruikshank's dream:

> It is very possible, from something which Coleridge said on another occasion, that, before meeting a fable in which to embody his ideas, he had meditated a poem on delirium, confounding its own dream-scenery with external things, and connected with the imagery of high latitudes.

And this account, Mr. Lowes affirms, "carries its own conviction."

"A poem on delirium" "dream scenery," "spectral persecution"! These compose the structure which rose at once in Coleridge's mind at the mere suggestion of a skeleton ship. Finally, notice DeQuincey's statement that this material *preceded* the conception of "a fable in which to embody his ideas." What better confirmation could there be not only of the hypothesis that the inspiration of "The Ancient Mariner" was an opium dream of persecution, but also the plot was a consciously designed framework of later addition?

The effect of opium on the poetry of George Crabbe has already been discussed. His imagination, too, was unleashed from his desire to portray humble life "as Truth will paint it," and went soaring into the "high latitudes" with their fiends, and horrors, and spectral persecutions. But he returned at once to rustic subjects and a lukewarm style. For Coleridge, the dreams sent his creative imagination voyaging in the strange literature of Elizabethan travellers and alchemistic handbooks, which harmonized so well with his dream experiences; and all these elements, fused in the heat of his imagination, were later consciously shaped into the artistic whole which is "The Ancient Mariner."

The possibility of opium influences on the details of the poem is not eliminated by the fact that Mr. Lowes has already traced much of the imagery of "The Ancient Mariner" to parallels in Coleridge's reading. Opium dreams, as DeQuincey indicates, feed upon the fragmentary memories of earlier experience. From the Note Book it is evident that Coleridge had opium hallucinations while in the very process of reading about the material he later utilized in the poem. It is almost unbelievable that scenes which impressed him so vividly should not sink into his memory, to be later metamorphosed in the crucible of dreams; and indeed, as Mr. Lowes points out, this is the actual process recorded in "Kubla Khan"! Possibly, too, Coleridge more or less consciously clothed the bits from his reading in the new and glowing material of his dream memories. Whatever the explanation, this is a matter incapable of absolute proof. It is for me but to present parallels; the decision must be left to the reader.

Sir Eustace had murdered a friend; Florentian had slain his sweetheart; the Ancient Mariner had killed an albatross. It is the killing of the albatross which sets off the long train of "spectral persecution." As Sir Eustace had attributed his sufferings to the "two fiends of darkness," Florentian to an indescribable monster, DeQuincey to a Malay, so the Mariner places all the blame on a spirit. And significantly, some of the sailors "*in dreams* assured were" of the fiend who had engineered all the persecution. Throughout the endless duration of these tortures (no track is kept of time, but the general impression is of interminable extension) appear other characteristic phenomena.

The equivalent of DeQuincey's "unutterable abortions" occur in

> The very deep did rot: O Christ!. . .
>
> Yea, slimy things did crawl with legs
> Upon the slimy sea. . . .
>
> And a thousand thousand slimy things
> Lived on; and so did I.

And again in

> I looked upon the rotting sea.

There are, too, frequent reminiscences of the terrors of sleep:

> Fear at my heart, as at a cup,
> My life-blood seemed to sip.

And once occurs almost the very wording of the dream in the "Ode to the Departing Year," with its "my ears throb hot, my eye balls start," and the "cold sweat drops" that "gather on my limbs":

> I closed my lids, and kept them close,
> And the balls like pulses beat;
> For the sky and the sea, and the sea and the sky
> Lay like a load on my weary eye.

And later:

> The cold sweat melted from their limbs.

Perhaps the most striking descriptions are those of light and color. Remembering the serpentining mass of "flame-colour, violet, and green" in "Finis Coronat Opus," can we attribute Coleridge's perceptions to a different source?

> About, about, in reel and rout
> The death fires danced at night;
> The water like a witch's oils
> Burnt green, and blue, and white.

The same picture of writhing snakes which Thompson used to express this sinuous motion is repeated by Coleridge:

> They moved in tracks of shining white,
> And when they reared, the elfish light
> Fell off in hoary flakes. . . .
>
> Blue, glassy green, and velvet black,
> They coiled and swam; and every track
> Was a flash of golden fire.

The "dancing streamers" of Sir Eustace's visions play again in the Mariner's sky, in a passage of sound, movement, even wording amazingly close to that of Crabbe:

> The upper air burst into life!
> And a hundred fire-flags sheen.
> To and fro they were hurried about!
> And to and fro, and in and out,
> The wan stars danced between.

Later the effect is repeated:

> Like waters shot from some high crag,
> The lightning fell with never a jag,
> A river steep and wide.

Sound perception again ranges between the two extremes upon which Dupouy has commented. There is the crash of noise on abnormally sensitive ear drums:

> It cracked and growled, and roared and howled,
> Like noises in a swound! . . .
>
> The ice did split with a thunder-fit.

And at the end of the poem, sound becomes loud enough to sink the ship! But there is also the "délicatesse exquise" of hearing:

> With far-heard whisper, o'er the sea,
> Off shot the spectre-bark. . . .
>
> And every soul, it passed me by,
> Like the whiz of my cross-bow.

Yet another similarity in a detail of persecution is "the curse of the eye" which played so prominent a part in "Finis Coronat Opus." I can only summarize the Mariner's frequent references to this appearance. The first is:

> Each turned his face with a ghastly pang,
> And cursed me with his eye.

This look, we discover, "had never passed away," and was seen "seven days and seven nights"; later their "stony eyes" again gleamed in the moon; still, he "could not draw his eyes from theirs"; and finally,

> Their stony eye-balls glitter'd on
> In the red and smoky light.

Even from the quotations given, although they contain the more obvious similarities only, can be seen how significantly close is the imagery of "The Ancient Mariner" to the opium effects we already know. Such parallels can be extended, less certainly, to most of the details of the poem: for example, thirsty "Death" and "Life in Death" and the sensation of floating. (pp. 28-44)

With "Kubla Khan" we reach the end of this little pilgrimage through "straunge strondes." This poem does not merely reconstruct the world of dreams; it was itself composed within that very land. Coleridge's account of its composition is too familiar to need repetition in full. Enough that in the summer of 1798, under influence of an "anodyne" now definitely known to have been opium, he fell asleep while reading in *Purchas his Pilgrimage,* and in that state composed a poem "in which all the images rose up before him as *things,* with a parallel production of the correspondent expressions without any sensation or consciousness of effort." The recording of this dream composition upon awakening was interrupted at the fifty-fourth line, and was never completed.

Thus Coleridge's verse caught up the evanescent images of an opium dream, and struck them into immobility for all time. The dream quality of "Kubla Khan" cannot be analyzed; like the rainbow tints of a butterfly's wing, it turns to dust on the fingers. But the swift shuttling of vistas is there to perfection. From "Alph, the sacred river" the scene shifts to brilliant gardens; then, after a flash of "that deep romantic chasm," turns to the dome of pleasure; and suddenly, in that vision within a vision, emerge the glowing forms of the "Abyssinian maid" with a dulcimer, and the wild-haired youth who, like Coleridge, has "drunk the milk of Paradise."

No pain phenomena occur in the poem, for this is that rarity, a dream of pleasure purely, with all the intoxication and none of the tortures of opium. But Mr. Lowes's quick eye has caught, as most characteristic of "Kubla Khan," an effect which we know is the mark of opium: the extraordinary mutations of space. The little river at the opening of the poem expands into a mighty fountain which flings rocks like chaff; contracts into a peacefully meandering creek; then, by another dilation, becomes a huge primordial river sinking through measureless caverns—and all at once is the pellucid stream of the sunny dome of pleasure. And through all is maintained a restless ebb and flow of style, to match the eternal unrest of the dream scenery itself.

The Mrs. Barbaulds are always with us, although the criticism of the early nineteenth-century that "The Ancient Mariner" "had no moral" now gives place to the more sophisticated demand [of Jeannette Marks (see Additional Bibliography)] that the entire poem be discarded as the product of a pathological mentality. But surely the Mrs. Barbaulds are wrong. The important fact is that these four authors did an incredible thing: they opened to poetry an entirely new world. And with Coleridge and the apotheosis of this poetry in "Kubla Khan" came that rarest phenomenon, the true originality which is not just the "repristination of something old," but is something no one had conceived since poetry began. With it was struck that "new note" of lyricism of which the reverberations have not yet died away.

Alas! the vision and the flight are pitifully brief before outraged nature exacts its vengeance. For "opium gives and takes away," as DeQuincey said, and while aspirations and projects are exalted, the will to execute is soon blasted. Pathetic footnotes in the annals of literature are the tremendous metaphysical tractates both Coleridge and DeQuincey planned, but neither ever began. In Shelley's figure, ''the mind in creation is as a fading coal,'' and although the wind of opium may fan it into an instant's supernal brightness, the flame soon exhausts its fuel, wavers, and dies.

For fleeting moments of relief and revelation, Coleridge paid with a loss of creative power, even of moral sense, and with a lifetime of physical and mental torture. But to those moments we owe part of ''The Ancient Mariner,'' all of ''Kubla Khan,'' and both are like oases in our dusty lives. There is nothing frightening in their rich strangeness. Rather, they are to be the more dearly cherished because of the fearful toll exacted for beauty stolen from another world. (pp. 45-9)

> *Meyer Howard Abrams, in his* The Milk of Paradise: The Effect of Opium Visions on the Works of DeQuincey, Crabbe, Francis Thompson, and Coleridge, *Cambridge, Mass.: Harvard University Press, 1934, 86 p.*

ELISABETH SCHNEIDER

[*In the following excerpt from her full-length study of the relationship between Coleridge's drug habit and his literary works, Schneider analyzes the notion that opium use ordinarily produces dreams and visions, disputing the commonly held belief that the drug was responsible for the content, character, and creative invention of various works by Coleridge and De Quincey.*]

Accounts of nineteenth- and twentieth-century literature have been sprinkled here and there with a good many highly colored and often delusory statements about the influence of opium upon creative imagination and the life of genius. The influences are seen as twofold, the ''benign,'' as Mr. Kenneth Burke calls them, and the ''malign.'' Opium it has been thought, can inspire through dreams or trancelike reveries a special kind of poetry or poetic prose that could not be otherwise composed. Opium, on the other hand, is also held responsible for the gradual degration and final ruin of the lives and hopes of those who take it. The drug lights a bright, beautiful, and eerie light at first; then, as years go on, it dims and extinguishes the light and punishes its victim cruelly. This is quite a Gothic conception, and some of the writing about opium has been almost as imaginative as the effects attributed to it.

Literary critics, however, have usually been imperfectly familiar with modern medical accounts of the effects of opium, and earlier medical writing on the subject is exceedingly unreliable. Even the ''scientific'' writers of the past seem to have sought their information in something of that spirit of independence of mere fact that sent Rousseau to seek out the habits of primitive man by sitting in suburban woods and thinking. The lag is not solely a lag among literary critics, for the older views are still current even among physicians who have not made a particular study of opiates.

De Quincey has a great deal to answer for to the medical profession. It would have delighted his vanity to know that almost alone he dominated the scientific as well as the literary explanations of the effects of opium for nearly a hundred years. And he is still, whether they know it or not, the chief authority behind the knowledge even of many physicians. Until as late as the 1920's, many of the most competent medical accounts of addiction to opium were drawn directly from the writings of De Quincey and Coleridge or from other writers who in turn had drawn from them. Having derived their principles from these sources, moralizing physicians of the Victorian era rounded the circle of their argument by applying them back again.

Coleridge and De Quincey were held up in solemn warning as examples of how the drug leads to wretchedness and destruction. This extensive body of highly unscientific writing on the subject has not ceased to flourish. (pp. 27-8)

The old standard view, medical as well as literary, of the effects of opium runs something like this: (1) The drug injures and usually ruins the physical health and generally shortens the life of the person addicted to its use. Coleridge and De Quincey have to be taken as exceptions in the matter of longevity, since they lived to be roughly sixty-two and seventy-four, a record of survival not bad for their day. The generalization has been perpetuated, nevertheless. (2) Opium causes a gradual deterioration of intellect, psychological deterioration of the personality, and moral depravity. It is supposed thus to bring about changes in the actual character of the addict, making him a kind of person he was not and would not have become otherwise than through addiction and dooming him to unspeakable wretchedness in the end. He is supposed, further, to be easily identifiable by his pasty face, his queer look and manner, his shifty eye, and his emaciated form. (3) In the early stages the drug produces exquisite pleasure, but later the experience becomes one of horror, somewhat resembling the delirium tremens of alcoholism. (4) The drug is capable of producing dreams and visions of a most exquisite kind, utterly different in character from normal dreams. At first, they are beautiful, enchanting, their intensified sense impressions pleasurable in the highest degree. Afterwards the heightened acuteness of the senses merely accentuates their effect of horror, evil, loathing, and guilt.

Though modern medical and psychological knowledge of the effects of opium on human beings is still very incomplete, a few facts that bear upon Coleridge and De Quincey are well enough established to be summarized. As far as they go, their cumulative effect is to destroy or (on one or two points) to cast the gravest doubts upon the soundness of every one of these current beliefs. (p. 29)

• • • • •

Opium more than any other cause has been held responsible for the failure of Coleridge both to fulfil all the promise of his genius and to win his everyday living by steady labors. During much of his life he depended upon gifts and loans from friends; his path was strewn with abortive plans and fragments. He himself attributed his ''sloth'' to opium, and that cause has not been much questioned.

A ruined life, however, we now know is not an inevitable consequence of addiction to opiates. Medical writers have shown that many addicted persons live entirely normal lives for a normal life-span. No one knows how many such persons there are, but they are not rare. These people do not deteriorate psychologically, intellectually, or physically; they continue their work in the world like others, provided only a regular supply of the drug is available for their needs; and they experience no marked effects from its use. Evidence for the truth of this is plentiful, despite the necessary secrecy of modern addicts. There is no indication, either, that life is shortened by use of the drug except on occasions of a grossly careless overdose. Many addicts remain unrecognized as such, though addicted for many years. One medical writer, discussing work in the New York City Narcotic Clinic, cited as illustration the case of a signalman, obviously holding a responsible position, who had been addicted for twenty-five years without missing a day from work. He had never been reported for any sort of neglect and had never been recognized as an addict by his superior.

Cases like this have been familiar for a century and more. The poet Crabbe, for example, used opium. His son, in a memoir published in 1834, described his father's middle years: "My father, now about his forty-sixth year, was much more stout and healthy than when I first remember him." In early manhood he had had certain frightening attacks which were finally diagnosed as digestive. "You must take opiates," said his physician. The biographer continued:

> From that time his health began to amend rapidly, and his constitution was renovated; a rare effect of opium, for that drug almost always inflicts some partial injury, even when it is necessary: but to him it was only salutary—and to a constant but slightly increasing dose of it may be attributed his long and generally healthy life. His personal appearance also was improved with his health and his years. This is by no means an uncommon case: many an ordinary youth has widened and rounded into a well-looking, dignified, middle-aged man . . . health of itself gives a new charm to any features; and his figure, which in his early years had been rather thin and weakly, was now muscular and almost athletic.

In the 1830's the pasty face and emaciated frame had not yet taken possession of opium eaters. Coleridge's contemporary Wilberforce provides another instance, not quite so perfect. His sons in their biography inform us that he took opium for an illness in 1788, found it helpful, and, having become addicted, continued to use it for the remaining forty-five years of his life. He was always "sparing," they said, in his use of the drug and never felt any effect from it of any kind, good or bad, though he believed that it kept him in better health ever after. For the last twenty years, until his death at the age of seventy-four, he kept his allowance of the drug stable, though he had increased it from time to time in earlier years. Though the sons wrote more complacently than the facts warranted (Wilberforce was not always sparing in his opium-taking), the truth remains that he lived, on the whole and within the limitations of his temperament, a normal and successful life. At the time the biography of him was written (1838) little or no disgrace attended the habitual use of the drug. Though De Quincey's *Confessions* had been published and Coleridge's troubles were well known and though medical authorities were growing slightly more aware than before of the dangers of opium, it was not until toward the mid-century that the name of "opium eater" came to be thought of as a stigma.

De Quincey mentioned as opium eaters, besides himself and Wilberforce, Lord Erskine, the former Prime Minister Addington, and Isaac Milner, Dean of Carlisle; Sir James Mackintosh was said always to have taken opium to calm his nervousness when he was to speak in parliament. These are but a few stray instances of men whose health and careers seem to have been either wholly or relatively unimpaired by the use of opium. Such unspectacular figures, however, came to be quite overshadowed, not only in the view of the lay public but even among medical writers, by the histories of Coleridge and De Quincey.

Some modern studies have been undertaken to test the effect of addiction on health, physical fitness, and general efficiency. In general, the conclusions bear out the belief of Wilberforce and Crabbe that addiction *of itself* has little or no deteriorating effect. Addicts do usually deteriorate, but the cause is thought to lie in other factors than the drug itself. A few minor physiological effects are known to be brought about, but they are not permanent; they last only as long as the individual is actually under the opiate. Even under prolonged addiction, opium does not destroy the protoplasm of the tissues, as alcohol is said to do.

Probably the most carefully controlled experiment having to do with physical fitness is one conducted some years ago at a Philadelphia hospital, in which observations were made of more than five hundred addicted persons who entered voluntarily for treatment. Besides the usual medical checking for general health, the patients' ability to withstand physical exercise was tested against that of two control groups of nonaddicted persons, one made up of ordinary hospital employees accustomed to a more or less sedentary life and a second of college athletes. As tested by heart action, pulse, respiration, and so on, recorded before and after exercise, the addicts were found to equal the control group of hospital workers and withstood strenuous exercise only slightly less well than did the college athletes. From these observations (which I have oversimplified in the telling), as well as from numerous others, the authors reported that they had detected no marked physical deterioration or lack of physical fitness in addicts who were receiving their required amounts of morphine.

Approaching the problem not of health alone but of general efficiency and working by a different method, Dr. Lawrence Kolb, one of the most widely experienced investigators, studied the histories of a large group of persons who had become addicted accidentally through medical use of the drug. Some had evidently been abnormal psychologically before their addiction, and of these we shall speak later. Of the whole group, however, abnormal as well as normal, Dr. Kolb reported that three-fourths had had good employment records and that none who seemed to have been originally normal persons had had their efficiency reduced by opium. He described one alert old woman of eighty-one who had taken three grains of morphine daily for sixty-five years, yet had very successfully managed a household and reared her six children in the meantime. Addiction to opiates, it is clear, does not of itself produce an abnormal life. (pp. 31-4)

It is now well known, though it appears not to have been fully known in Coleridge's day, that all persons are subject to addiction. Everyone who takes opiates regularly for a time becomes addicted and suffers materially when the drug is withdrawn. The length of time required for habituation varies with the amount and frequency of the dose and with the individual, but it is said that three weeks of regular use will generally fix the habit. On the other hand, it is widely agreed now that persons of unstable psychological makeup are much more likely to become addicted to opiates than are normal ones; that they are much less likely to control or stabilize their lives if they remain addicted; and, finally, that they are much less likely to be cured or to remain cured. Though this view is not shared by every modern writer quite without exception and cannot be regarded as proved in the sense in which a simple chemical reaction may be proved, it is the conclusion reached by those experts who appear to have had the greatest opportunities for investigating large numbers of cases in detail and over a considerable period of time. (p. 35)

In the course of addiction, a tolerance to the drug is established, the precise physiological or chemical causes of which are not yet fully understood though the phenomenon itself is one of the earliest and most widely known facts connected with opium. The tolerance may be increased enormously, as we know from the lethal amounts taken with impunity by many habitués, but there is always a considerable gap between the limit of tolerance and the "maintenance need." The amount of opium required, that is, to keep the addict comfortably free from the miseries and cravings of abstinence is materially smaller than the amount he can take without damage. His handling of this gap is crucial for the stabilizing of his life, but it depends upon other factors than the drug. In this phenomenon is anchored one of the main bridges between the physiological and the psychological effects of opium. The deterioration of character that is so commonly associated with opium users, particularly that which shows them growing more and more irresponsible, spending hours, days, or weeks in bed, abandoning for long periods the effort expected of normal persons to work or earn a living—this is believed now to have its roots not in the drug but in the original personality of the user, where the addiction itself has most often originated. . . . The most careful and full studies of the subject tend to show that in lives which we might have supposed were ruined by opium the actual primary cause of ruin has been the original psychological makeup of the individual. The fundamentals of personality have not changed, however much aid the drug may have lent to the destructive element already at work.

The difference between psychological and medical (or accidental) addiction affects the history of individual cases broadly in two ways. The man whose need of the drug is primarily physical, having established the habit, continues to take it merely in order to avoid the discomfort or illness produced by its withdrawal. He may decide or be forced to go through the discomfort of a cure. If he does, he may remain cured permanently. But if he does not, he can continue indefinitely to take only his maintenance dose. Since tolerance increases with custom, this maintenance requirement may creep up gradually, though apparently it does not always do so. There are no reasons, however, inherent in the drug itself for the taking of extra or enormous doses such as will send the addict into a half-stupor or narcotic sleep; what might be called the "normal" craving created by opium is satisfied by the maintenance dose and does not require more. When addiction is maintained thus, it need not interfere with a perfectly normal life as long as the individual has means to purchase what he requires without becoming embroiled in crime or debt. I am not even sure that it requires an exceptionally strong will to remain addicted at this level, in control of one's addiction. This kind of addiction, at any rate, is what we have in the Crabbes and their like.

The picture of Coleridge and De Quincey and of the vast majority of other addicts is very different. With a psychological basis for addiction, the temptation is always present to increase the drug beyond the maintenance level and up to the very limit of tolerance. The studies made at the Philadelphia hospital, for example, showed that when any disturbance occurred in the narcotic ward the patients always expressed a need for a larger amount of opium than usual. During the initial period of their experiment, while the patients were supplied freely with the drug, "the slightest degree of fear on their part always resulted in a temporary increase in dosage."

These accounts bear a striking resemblance to some passages written a hundred and fifty years ago in Charles Lloyd's novel *Edmund Oliver*. Some traits of the hero were patterned after Coleridge, and, though Lloyd was writing in anger or malice and is a far from trustworthy witness, his description of his hero's use of laudanum is of interest. Its details suggest that it was founded upon firsthand information, since obviously the

modern knowledge I have been summarizing was not available to him. Lloyd's hero records in his diary: "I have some laudanum in my pocket. I will quell these mortal upbraidings," and "My brain phrensied with its own workings—I will again have recourse to my laudanum and lie down." Still later the young man of the novel, depressed, without money to pay his landlady, records of himself: "I have at all times a strange dreaminess about me which makes me indifferent to the future, if I can by any means fill the present with sensations—with that dreaminess I have gone on here from day to day; if at any time thought troubled, I have swallowed some spirits, or had recourse to my laudanum. . . ." Almost all victims of opium at some time undergo a "cure." But the unstable, even though all physical discomfort and craving for the drug have disappeared, return again to their morphine weeks or months, occasionally even a year or more, later. The words of Charles Lloyd, presumably about Coleridge, tell us why quite as accurately as the reports filtered through modern medical language, and somewhat more vividly. This evidence of the unstable or neurotic character of most persons who become addicted to opium I have set forth, however, not so much for the sake of painting a portrait of Coleridge as for its bearing upon the opium tradition. The original abnormalities of habitués came to be thought of as consequences of the drug.

The gift of extreme and mysterious pleasure is one of those powers conferred by tradition upon opiates; yet it too may be dependent partly or wholly upon the temperament of the user. Opium is known to have a pleasurable effect upon some people but not upon all; the actual proportion of each is not known. One experiment showed that from a single dose of morphine given to persons who did not know what it was, only one out of nine was pleasurably affected. On the other hand, it is generally said that this euphoria is more likely to occur after addiction begins than upon an initial dose. No studies of opiate euphoria, so far as I know, deal with a sufficient number of cases to be significant, except those of Kolb. His observation has been that, apart from natural pleasure brought about by a swift relief from acute pain, persons who are psychologically stable do not experience "mental pleasure" from opiates. In most unstable persons, on the other hand, he found that the drug does produce pleasure during the early stages of addiction. The intensity of the pleasure appeared to be in direct proportion to the degree of instability. He cites typical accounts by patients describing their euphoria:

> It makes my troubles roll off my mind.
> It is exhilarating and soothing.
> You do not care for anything and you feel happy.
> It makes you drowsy and feel normal.
> It causes exhilaration and a feelng of comfort.
> A deadening, pleasurable effect.
> . . . forgot everything and did not worry and had a pleasurable, dreamy sensation as of floating away.

One patient, typical of some others, said "it caused a buoyancy of spirits, increased imagination, temporarily enlarged the brain power, and made him think of things he otherwise would not have thought of."

The last of these is the nearest we come to finding evidence of creative powers in opium. The explanation lies, however, in the euphoria that it produces, what to De Quincey was "its deep tranquillizing powers to the mitigation of evils" and to Coleridge a green and fountainous oasis in a waste of desert. The relaxation of tension and conflict, accompanied by a sense of pleasant ease, occasionally helps to release for a time the neurotic person's natural powers of thought or imagination or (rarely) of action, though it does not give him powers that he did not have or change the character of his normal powers. Coleridge recognized this effect upon himself when he said, in a passage to be discussed later, that opium by its narcotic effect made his body a fitter instrument for his soul. With some unstable temperaments the euphoria may be intense. Its effect is usually to increase the person's satisfaction with his inner state of well-being, to turn his attention inward upon himself while diminishing his attention to external stimuli. Thus it sometimes encourages the mood in which daydreaming occurs.

The narcosis of opium has been popularly described as having the effect of heightening and intensifying the acuteness of the senses. This it quite definitely does not do. If anything, the effect is the reverse. Professor Meyer Abrams, citing De Quincey and Arthur Symons, once wrote of the "gift of opium" to these men as "access to a new world" such as ordinary mortals can never conceive, "a world of twisted, exquisite experience, sensuous and intellectual," in which "one can hear the walk of an insect on the ground, the bruising of a flower" [see excerpt above]. He notes that De Quincey mentioned no intensification of the perception of light, but thinks that this was either an accidental omission or else the result of "an innate lack of sensitivity to light."

A few experiments have been conducted for the purpose of testing precisely these things. They are not numerous enough, in my opinion, to constitute absolute proof if considered alone, but when they are weighed along with other evidence, I think we must accept them and must therefore relinquish the notion of those possible delights. Not even opium will bring us echoes of the centipede's rhythmic parade; he who would hear this must take cobra venom. The senses, it appears, are actually either unaffected or dulled—more often the latter—by opiates.

One experiment tested the acuteness of hearing in a considerable number of persons before and after the use of morphine. The injection was followed, the investigators reported, by "a marked dulling" of hearing, a decrease in acuity ranging from five to twenty decibels for various tones, the losses being greater in the upper tone registers. There vanish the shriek of the bat and the insect's footfall. In a parallel study of vision, it was observed that acuity was usually unaffected but that the field of vision was "greatly" decreased for all colors but most markedly for red and green. Opium has long been known to contract the pupils temporarily, a circumstance that would naturally account for reduction of visual range. Some earlier observers had reported that there is sometimes a reduction in acuity also. Studies in the sense of smell are few and slight; as far as they go, they suggest that keenness in the perception of odors is diminished by opiates. For the sense of touch more studies are available. All seven of the recent experiments summarized in Krueger's *Pharmacology of the Opium Alkaloids* report a very material decrease in tactile sensitiveness under opiates.

Though experimental work on some of these points has not been extensive enough to stamp the results as altogether final, they can hardly in practice be doubted because the observations are so fully consistent with each other and with other well-established facts. It is commonly known (and medically beyond doubt), for example, that addiction to opium always reduces and sometimes destroys sexual desire. Most obviously of all, the prime property of the drug is its narcosis of the sense of pain. Since the experimental work, as far as it goes, follows the same pattern as these known facts—narcosis, that is, of sensation of various kinds—and since no experiments are found to reverse this (no scientifically reputable study that I know of

reports an increase in acuity of any sense), I think we are bound to give up any notion that the drug reverses itself, acting as a sort of antinarcotic on one or two senses while it narcotizes the others.

What a man actually sees or hears, however, is no necessary measure of what he imagines. The poets know what the feeling of solitude may do with a small noise:

> when a mouse inside the papered walls,
> Comes like a tiger crunching through the stones.

And everyone must have found a bright day look the brighter because of a mood. The euphoria of opium may affect a man in such ways as this, but we have no warrant at all to believe that the outside world enters his consciousness along nerve passages more exquisitely sensitized than our own. In that respect at least, his world is ours, except that it is probably a little dimmer.

The question of sense-perception leads to the final group of phenomenon that tradition has associated with opium: kaleidoscopic imagery, the vision, and the dream. Of these it may be said in general and at once that no evidence warrants the belief that opium of itself produces any of them or that when the addict experiences them they are marked by the drug with a special character that they could not have had without it. It is surprising that even kaleidoscopic imagery should have edged its way into the opium tradition; this at least one might have supposed common enough to have escaped. Whether or not in a state between waking and sleeping everyone has seen imagery pass before his closed eyes I do not know; but certainly a great many quite normal persons do, and more would be aware of doing so if they began paying attention to it. In that half-waking state, the rational mind automatically suppresses awareness of fleeting imagery unless one deliberately notices it or unless it is for some reason especially insistent, as it is apt to be, for example, after fatiguing hours of unaccustomed motion. After walking or driving a car all day through unfamiliar scenes or working long at an unaccustomed physical task, a quite normal person may notice that his sleep is preceded by kaleidoscopic images of the day—leaf patterns or rocks, the pitching of hay, or whatever may have been going on. Such images are often vivid enough to be called "visions," however unpoetic their contents may be. One poet (who chooses to remain anonymous), whose waking life is more than usually preoccupied with visual experience, reports frequent, extremely vivid, and highly imaginative imagery of this sort. A familiar poem of Robert Frost describes a commonplace experience of the kind; his *After Apple Picking* tells over the moments before sleep in which sensations of the day are relived, the pressure of feet on a ladder, apple after apple in numberless succession. If the day's experiences have not been unusual or exhausting, the imagery is apt to be more imaginative and less exclusively tyrannized over by immediate memory.

Very likely opium addicts who indulge in heavy doses and are reduced for hours at a time to a state just this side of sleep have quantitatively more of this experience than most people; they choose (a perhaps unconscious choice) to live more of their lives in this passive state than others do. No doubt the imagery is made pleasant if the drug has produced euphoria and the stupefaction is slight. But—once more—there is no reason to suppose that their mental cinema is different in kind from that of other people as a consequence of the drug. Nor does the drug itself actively produce the cinema. Imagery of this sort is essentially the same kind of experience that we refer to as daydream or reverie, though the degree of conscious thought and control will vary greatly from time to time and much ordinary reverie is occupied with the future rather than the past, or with "wish-fulfilment." As far as opium is concerned, the truth is the same in all these forms of waking dream. Doses above the maintenance level no doubt conduce to these passive states and prolong them; but as far as is known they do no more. (pp. 36-44)

With sleeping as with waking dreams, modern medical and psychological studies do not warrant the supposition that opium of itself either causes nondreamers to dream or transforms ordinary dreams into extraordinary ones. For this latter, the chief testimony has always been that of De Quincey, whose own statements are somewhat inconsistent. He sometimes described opium as producing dreams; yet he opened his *Confessions* with the remark that "if a man 'whose talk is of oxen,' should become an opium-eater, the probability is, that (if he is not too dull to dream at all)—he will dream about oxen." The medical literature of the 1880's and 1890's does indeed record some horrible "opium" dreams by other opium eaters than De Quincey.... They can be accounted for otherwise, however. (p. 46)

An occasional reputable modern authority, particularly of the older generation, still may be found to support the notion that opium produces dreams or hallucinations. Dr. Alexander Lambert at least as late as 1914 was of the opinion that acute addiction produces "nocturnal hallucinations which render [addicts'] nights times of terror." This view, however, is not generally accepted by persons in touch with more recent studies. There are other more likely explanations of such hallucinations as may occur. (p. 47)

Pain and illness of themselves tend to make us dream, and the comfort or sleep conferred by opiates during illness may well be haunted by passing imagery—pleasant or horrible according as the relief is complete or partial, or as euphoria is felt or not. Two persons have reported to me their own experience with what they believed to be opium visions. But those of one, it turned out in response to questions, had occurred in the midst of an almost fatal illness, during which the patient had been constantly delirious. The other person was also ill, had been suffering extreme pain, and at the time of the visions still had a very high fever accompanied by intense headache. The first person reported his visions as actual hallucinations; the second reported merely vivid kaleidoscopic images. Conceivably, these phenomena might have been caused by the narcotic; but the physical condition of the patients is more than enough to account for them on the basis of well-known medical fact as well as of common experience. The dreamers' readiness to assume opium as the cause, even under these conditions, illustrates the strength in the popular mind of the De Quincey tradition, which has in fact been so embellished with romantic and oriental curlicues that my first informant, though a person well informed in many respects, explained that he was able to sort out the opium vision from the delirium by the fact, as he remembered it after recovery, that it had contained an oriental figure. De Quincey himself might have elaborated that fantasy of the poppy soaking up from oriental soil images of Eastern faces to be scattered among the dreamers of the West. It should set geneticists back on their heels. But man is a highly suggestible animal, and, the De Quincey tradition being what it is, many of us will doubtless dream an oriental dream if we but look at a grain of opium.

No tradition such as this exists in the Orient itself, I am told. The word *opium* is not, as with us, axiomatically coupled with *dream;* some Chinese visitors to this country have said, in response to a question, that though they knew opium users, they recalled no association of the drug with dreams or visions. In the West, however, since the last century, we have all been exposed to the self-hypnosis of expectation. The person who expects dreams often has them; and the mere paying attention to them either helps to produce or causes us to remember them—as with a dreamless young man of my acquaintance, who, finding himself an anomaly among friends recounting their dreams, went home and had one.

It is well known that persons under emotional stress, whether temporary or constitutional, are, roughly speaking, inclined to dream more often and more vividly than most others. Very likely, therefore, opium users as a whole may be frequent dreamers because of their original instability. Particularly the less normal ones, those least able to control their addiction, who, taking large doses for their flights into forgetfulness, neglect more and more their normal responsibilities—these people enter a vicious circle. They suffer increasingly from guilt and other emotional conflicts and in consequence may be likely to dream more and more. But the dreams would be neurotic dreams, not opium ones, the opium being causative, if at all, only in quite another sense than the traditional one. (pp. 48-50)

· · · · ·

A prime source of confusion about opium was the long delay in accurate recognition of what are called "withdrawal symptoms." Ignorance of these contributed to many false notions about the effects of the drug, including the notions about dreams. The cause of these symptoms is not fully understood even today, but at least they have been clearly described. (pp. 58-9)

Probably the fullest, certainly the most widely quoted, early account of withdrawal symptoms was that of Levinstein, which was not published until 1877. For its day it was relatively accurate, and it remained for many years the classical treatment of the subject. A mistake by Levinstein upon one important point, however, created confusion that prevailed until 1918, when W. M. Kraus published a more accurate description. The later account did not fully counteract even in medical circles the influence of Levinstein, whose misconceptions still have some currency. What he failed to understand was that withdrawal symptoms may and in fact often do occur in the midst of addiction. He therefore classified under the effects of opium itself some symptoms that are actually the effects of deprivation of opium. Levinstein's mistake was not his own but merely perpetuated for forty years more a misunderstanding already imbedded in the literature of opium. It was not realized that many, perhaps most, cases of addiction consisted not of a constant state of narcosis but rather of alternations between narcosis and incipient withdrawal illness.

Aside from relief of pain, the primary physiological effect of opiates on the human body is the functional inhibiting of some cellular and glandular activity. As tolerance develops, cells and glands become accommodated to the opium, and their functioning returns to what is approximately normal activity. After tolerance has been established for some time, if the opiate is quickly withdrawn, tissues and organs released from the influence become overactive until readjustment takes place. This is believed to be the primary, if not the whole, physiological origin of withdrawal symptoms; but there are psychological factors as well, which according to some authorities may be more important than physical sources of discomfort. As symptoms of withdrawal begin to appear about eight hours after a dose has been taken, addicts must use the drug at regular intervals three times within twenty-four hours—which they do not always do—in order to avoid daily intervals of discomfort. They suffer from deprivation too if they materially reduce the amount of their accustomed dose. If the opiate is broken off suddenly and not resumed, withdrawal symptoms run a course that rises to a peak of acuteness within two or three days and gradually subsides, the acute symptoms usually disappearing in a matter of two weeks or thereabouts.

According to the evidence of some modern studies, the acuteness of withdrawal illness may vary according to the instability of temperament among patients. In symptoms as well as in cause, physical and emotional elements are inextricably mingled. Among the milder effects of abstinence are yawning, sneezing, chills, tearfulness, semblances of a cold, copious perspiration, tremulousness, intolerable restlessness, irritability, insomnia. Other more severe effects may follow promptly: asthma-like attacks, nausea, vomiting, acute diarrhea, abdominal pains, violent pains and cramp in the limbs, sometimes a collapse of heart action. There may be other emotional effects. Besides nightmarish dreams (as one would expect), there may be hysteria, hallucination, or even delirium. These may be tied up with other psychological problems that antedate the addiction. Dr. Kolb, for example, describes the case of one man who before he became addicted to morphine had had auditory hallucinations and who during his cure again heard "voices" several times.

Many of these effects of abstinence used to be regarded as effects of the drug itself. Both constipation and diarrhea, for example—these may be particularly cited because Coleridge's frequent references to them have inspired a certain amount of amateur medical speculation—were formerly thought to be brought on by opium. Now it is known that only the first is produced by the drug; the contrary effect, however, often follows so promptly upon abstention that addicts may regulate their habits sufficiently to maintain health merely by postponing for a few hours their morning dose of morphine. A similar confusion prevailed with respect to psychological symptoms. The queer look, the pasty face, the shifty eye, and the nervous habits by which the addict has been thought to be marked out from normal human beings—these may actually appear at times when he is in need of a dose and is suffering withdrawal symptoms. So too with dreams and visions, at least of the horrible kinds. Jean Cocteau, undergoing a cure, described his own experience in psychological terms: the "tortures" of withdrawal, he said, "are caused by a return to life against the grain." Dreams inspired by this "torture" have undoubtedly sometimes been translated into "opium dreams." (pp. 59-61)

We do not know when Coleridge first took opium, when he first fell into addiction, when he first knew that he was addicted, or when he first attempted to abstain from the drug. This is rather a large order of ignorance, but we can do no better. We do not even know but that he may have gone through one or more periods of addictions and withdrawal illness without recognizing either. The habit, at any rate, was permanently fixed by 1801, and perhaps much earlier. He had used the drug more than once as early as 1791; by 1803 (probably by the preceding year) he knew only too well that it was an evil, at least for himself.

Coleridge's letters furnished a very complete account of the symptoms of opium withdrawal many years before any of the well-known medical descriptions appeared. Neither he nor his physicians could have known the full meaning of what he endured; nor has that period of his life, I think, been properly understood since then. His poem "The Pains of Sleep" [see poem above], published along with "Christabel" and "Kubla Khan" in 1816, had been composed in 1803, probably early in September. Its subject is the horrors of the poet's dreams. Almost ever since its publication it has been associated with "The Pains of Opium" in De Quincey's *Confessions,* and both together have become a textbook example of the horrifying dreams that opium produces after the pleasant dreams of early addiction have worn off. A different cause, however, was at work with Coleridge.

From about the middle of August, 1803, to the middle of October or somewhat later, Coleridge was attempting to do without opium at the same time that he was fighting an attack that he described as "atonic gout" (or gout of the stomach), complicated, it was suspected presently, by "mesenteric Scrofula." Nearly all his letters during these months describe his miseries at length and repetitively; and nearly all these miseries are classical symptoms of opium withdrawal as they are known today.

> But yester-night I pray'd aloud
> In anguish and in agony,
> Awaking from the fiendish crowd
> Of shapes and thoughts that tortur'd me!
> Desire with loathing strangely mixt,
> On wild or hateful objcts fixt.

The dream mentioned in these last two lines, though not referred to in his published letters, was probably not a poetic invention. The sexual desire that addiction inhibits is reawakened under withdrawal with increased intensity, often during sleep. The poem proceeds to other miseries:

> Sense of revenge, the powerless will,
> Still baffled and consuming still;
> Sense of intolerable wrong,
> And men whom I despis'd made strong!
>
> . . . . .
>
> Rage, sensual passion, mad'ning Brawl,
> And shame and terror over all!
> Deeds to be hid that were not hid,
> Which all confus'd I might not know,
> Whether I suffer'd or I did:
> For all was Horror, Guilt, and Woe,
> My own or others still the same,
> Life-stifling Fear, soul-stifling Shame!

These are typical neurotic dreams of fear, guilt, shame, powerlessness, and persecution, all heightened as they would naturally be by the emotional disturbances attending Coleridge's attempted cure. As his letters show, the lines were, if anything, an understatement of the actual experience. (pp. 62-4)

It is clear . . . that in 1803 Coleridge was undergoing a self-supervised "cure" but, not knowing its effects, thought he was suffering from "atonic gout." From others' accounts of Coleridge's behavior at this time and from the lengthened period of his ailments, we may doubt that his abstinence was complete or systematic. There can be no doubt, however, that he had reduced his consumption greatly or was doing without the drug altogether for much of the time. The testimony of the letters is borne out by entries in unpublished notebooks. The struggle was given up, however. On November 23 he took a large quantity of laudanum; on the twenty-sixth he was ordering a new supply through his friend John Thelwall. During part of December he was again trying to abstain, but not for long.

An entry in Coleridge's notebook for early December has been cited as an example of opium visions experienced while the dreamer is in a state of waking reverie. Evidently at this time Coleridge recaptured the euphoria from opium that most often occurs, with those who experience it at all, during the early stages of addiction or upon return to the drug after abstinence. He had apparently taken to sleeping alone in his study, an undoubted comfort in the unhappy state of his relations with Mrs. Coleridge. As his return to the drug had ended the siege of frightful dreams at least for the time being, sleep had become a delight instead of a terror. In this pleasant mood he experienced what were perhaps not so much opium visions as merely the natural imagery or recollections preceding sleep, such as anyone may have as he drifts off in a state of relief and temporary happiness after weeks of misery, but with that perfectly normal euphoria, in Coleridge's case, heightened by the return to opium.

> When in a state of pleasurable & balmy Quietness I feel my Cheek and Temple on the nicely made up Pillow in Coelibe Toro meo, the fire-gleam on my dear Books, that fill up one whole side from ceiling to floor of my Tall Study—& winds perhaps are driving the rain or whistling in frost, at my blessed Window, whence I see Borrodale, the Lake, New-lands—wood, water, mountains, omniform Beauty—O then as I first sink on the pillow, as if Sleep had indeed a material *realm*, as if when I sank my pillow, I was entering that region & realized Faery Land of Sleep—O then what visions have I had, what dreams—the Bark, the Sea, till the shapes & sounds & adventures made up of the Stuff of Sleep & Dreams, & yet my Reason at the Rudder / O what visions, . . . & I sink down the waters, thro' Seas & Seas—yet warm, yet a Spirit / . . . .

I do not find in this passage anything abnormal. Other things beside opium may put one into this half-somnolent state of physical and emotional contentment: the mere sudden cessation of an attack of acute pain will sometimes do it. Images of the sea—though dreams of bodies of water are sometimes taken to be indicative of particular neuroses—are not abnormal for anyone, still less for a man who overlooks a lake and has been a great reader of old accounts of voyages. The visions are not hallucinations, obviously, but imaginings encouraged by the will, with, as Coleridge himself says, Reason at the Rudder. (pp. 67-9)

The nearest approach Coleridge himself made to an assertion that opium had a creative or formative effect upon his imaginings, if we except the inferences generally drawn from the preface to "Kubla Khan," occurs in a later entry in an notebook of 1808:

> Need we wonder at Plato's opinions concerning the Body, at least, need that man wonder whom a *pernicious Drug* shall make capable of conceiving & bringing forth Thoughts, hidden in him before, which shall call forth the deepest feelngs of his best, greatest, & sanest Contemporaries? and this proved to him by actual experience?—But can subtle strings set in greater tension do this?—or is it not, that the dire poison for a delusive time has made the body, i.e., the *organization,* not the articulation (or instruments of motion) the unknown somewhat, a fitter Instrument for the all-powerful Soul.

Here Coleridge did express the belief that opium had formerly made him capable of thoughts he would not have had otherwise, but even in this he is far from granting De Quincey's magic

powers to the drug. He explicitly recorded his guess that it had not actually produced his fine thoughts but had merely put his body into a condition that made those thoughts possible. Even this notion he may have held only in retrospect: by 1808 he sadly needed excuses for his opium habit. He expressed the idea more succinctly in another note recently published: "Who can long remain body-crazed, and not at times use unworthy means of making his Body the fit instrument of his mind?" With all his need for self-justification, Coleridge claimed no more than this for the drug. He seems never to have suggested that opium stamped a peculiar or unique character of its own upon his creative imagination; his own statements, if read without the exaggeration encouraged by the subsequent tradition, are not as far as has been supposed from conformity to scientific modern knowledge. Once at least he expressed considerable skepticism. A certain John Webster in the seventeenth century had published an account of a witch who, by means of an ointment, put herself into "a deep sleep in which she apparently dreamed of journeys and adventures which she reported, when she woke up, as having really taken place." This, Coleridge wrote in a marginal comment, "is not the only well-attested instance of the use, and of the Cataleptic properties of, narcotic Ointments and Potions in the Pharmacy of the poor Self-be-witched." Like other "superstitions," he thought this no more than the decaying corpse of "a defunct Natural Philosophy." (pp. 71-2)

• • • • •

The fearful nightmares accompanying Coleridge's attempts at abstinence in 1803 bear some resemblance to what De Quincey, perhaps remembering "The Pains of Sleep," christened "The Pains of Opium." De Quincey may have been drawing upon a similar experience of deprivation of opium or of partial abstinence. In his literary version of his miseries, dreams or hallucinations predominate over everything else; but then he had always dreamed. His life is particularly useful to our study because it provides a well-documented before-and-after-opium record such as we do not have of Coleridge. On the whole, the evidence suggests that opium eating did no more than lead De Quincey further upon the road he had long been following. Neither his character nor the direction of his life can have been greatly altered by drugs. No doubt the elaborate accounts of his early life that he himself wrote in later years need to be read with allowance for a fictionizing memory. Many family letters survive, however, early ones of his own and of his mother especially, that give us a clear picture of him before he began taking opium.

As a boy, De Quincey was obviously unstable, though gifted. On more than one occasion in childhood, he tells us, he had fallen into a trance of some sort and had had visual and auditory hallucinations. Short of a survey of his whole early life, which is out of the question here, the most revealing document is a diary that survives from the year 1803, when, not yet eighteen years old, having run away from school and quarreled with his mother and guardians, he was permitted to live alone in lodgings on a small allowance. He spent the time brooding over fears of not making a good impression upon others, calling upon a few older people, hoping to become an author, and devouring all the Radcliffean novels he could find in the circulating libraries. He was not taking opium and, as far as is known, had never taken it. Yet the literary projects he toyed with have a familiar ring to the reader of the Opium Eater's later confessions. One entry reads: "My Arabian Drama will be an example of *Pathos* and *Poetry* united;—pathos 'not loud but deep'—like God's own head.'' Coleridge's ''The Ancient Mariner'' was evidently running in his head; and pathos, particularly of outcasts, always haunted him, for reasons not difficult for the student of his early life to guess. During the next two days he was taking home, reading, or returning to circulating libraries, besides Arabian travels, several romances whose mere titles tell us enough—*The Accusing Spirit, Castles of Athlin and Dunbayne, Sir R. de Clarendon.*

The day after this Gothic debauch, De Quincey recorded what seems to have been half a reverie and half a plan for a bit of Gothic writing on his own account. He wrote:

> Last night I imaged to myself the heroine of the novel dying on an island of a lake, her chamber-windows (opening on a lawn) set wide open—and the sweet blooming roses breathing [their] odours on her dying senses. [One of his associations for this scene, he said, was derived from ''The Farm,'' his home in earliest childhood. The entry continues:] Last night too I image [*sic*] myself looking through a glass. ''What do you see?'' I see a man in the dim and shadowy perspective and (as it were) in a dream. He passes along in silence, and the hues of sorrow appear on his countenance. Who is he?'' A man darkly wonderful—above the beings of this world; but whether that shadow of him, which you saw, be [the] shadow of a man long since passed away or of one yet hid in futurity, I may not tell you.''

There was something ''gloomily great'' about the man, De Quincey continued.

> He wraps himself up in the dark recesses of his own soul; he looks over all mankind of all tongues—languages—and nations ''with an angel's ken''; but his fate is misery such as [the] world knoweth not; and upon his latter days (and truly on his whole life) sit deep clouds of mystery and darkness and silence. . . .

(pp. 72-4)

The remainder of the diary, though it contains no other succession of ''imaged'' scenes like this, bears out the spirit in which this was written. De Quincey was living in a world half-neurotic and half-literary, a world undoubtedly of experience twisted and distorted, quite without benefit, however, of opium. He was already expanding and contracting time and space like rubber bands; his thoughts were haunted by death and persecution; he was attracted by pathetic scenes of loneliness and isolation on island or sea; he was admiring Southey's ''Ode to Horror.'' (pp. 74-5)

The eighteen years' interlude between this diary of 1803 and the *Confessions of an English Opium Eater* aged De Quincey, increased the range of his reading, and matured his tastes somewhat, though it did not perceptibly mature him as a human being. The difference between the *Diary* and the *Confessions* is obviously not the difference made by opium, for all the ''opium'' elements are already present in rudimentary form or in declared intention in the early notes. Little was needed, and that little no magic drug, to transform these youthful jottings into the highly colored *Confessions*. There was of course increased skill and experience. His great discovery in the *Confessions*, however, was the happy thought of making from his own life the thread upon which to string his preoccupations with death, loneliness, neurotic pathos, and grandeur. Evidently De Quincey had always longed to write about himself, perhaps without knowing it. The lost desolate children and little girls dying; the man dying on a rock at sea within sight of his ''paternal hills'' and home; the outcasts; the kaleidoscopic outpourings of his Gothic reading, with their mysterious, infinitely wretched and infinitely injured souls—all, clearly enough, were anagrams of himself. The chief source of his distinction as a writer may, in the long run, I suspect, prove to have been this discovery of his proper subject; without it he might have become little more than an ingenious hack writer and purveyor of only better-than-average tales of pathos and horror under the aegis of Mrs. Radcliffe and Ossian.

We cannot say to what extent De Quincey's famous dreams were fact and to what extent literary fiction. Whether the Malay who, according to the *Confessions,* came to his door and later haunted his dreams was much more than a vestige of his early plan for ''a pathetic tale, of which a black man is the hero,'' we do not know. And how much ''Ann of Oxford Street'' may have been a fictionizing of his dreams and reveries of the dead sister, who, though a little girl when she died, was nevertheless more fully his mother than that strong-minded but unsympathetic parent Mrs. De Quincey, we do not know either. We must doubt, however, that the opium legend would ever have reached its present magnitude without the influence of the Gothic novel and German Romanticism, along with books of oriental travel, to people the dreams—and without the filter of De Quincey's temperament, through which so much of it has reached us.

The native tendency of both De Quincey and Coleridge toward neurotic dreaming undoubtedly converged with a literary vogue. Dreams, both the rational or psychological analysis of them and their special character as dreams—kaleidoscopic movement, preternatural brilliance, an air of being freighted with unknown meaning, the haunting through them of a mood melancholy, fearful, persecutory, or occasionally blissful—these things were already becoming a notable feature of romantic literature in England and Germany. The conclusion seems inescapable that the ''dream'' writing of Coleridge and De Quincey derives far more from the coalescing of individual temperament with literary tradition than from consumption of opiates. (pp. 76-8)

> *Elisabeth Schneider, ''Opium and the Dream,'' in her* Coleridge, Opium and ''Kubla Khan,'' *The University of Chicago Press, 1953, pp. 21-109.*

ALETHEA HAYTER

> [*Hayter's 1968 book* Opium and the Romantic Imagination *is the most comprehensive study of the use of opium by nineteenth-century authors and its probable effect on their writings. In the following two-part excerpt from that work, drawn from both an introductory chapter and the conclusion, Hayter first investigates the effect of opium on addicts who are not writers and then examines the possible relationship between opium consumption and literary creativity, speculating about the common experiences of eight major nineteenth-century authors who used opium. For additional commentary by Hayter, see excerpt above.*]

Ever since the publication of *The Confessions of an English Opium Eater* in 1822, most statements on the effects of opium addiction on the imagination and mental processes of addicts have been either derived from the untypical case of De Quincey, or made in reaction against it. De Quincey himself gave a warning about this; he was a philosopher, he said, and therefore his opium visions were philosophical; but the plain practical man who took opium would have either no visions at all, or visions of his plain practical affairs. But the warning was disregarded. Generalizations as to how opium affects the mental operations of all addicts began and continued to be made from the individual cases of De Quincey and Coleridge. Before I discussed them and the other well-known literary addicts . . . , it therefore seemed essential to make a short survey of how opium affects the non-literary addict, for comparison. The statements in this chapter are based on reports and case-histories by doctors on the addicts under the care in hospitals, prisons and asylums and under treatment at home, and in a few cases on accounts by the addicts themselves. These drug-takers were men and women of all kinds—lawyers, clergymen, actors, soldiers, housewives, prostitutes, clerks, waiters, workers in textile factories. Some were respected figures in regular professional employment, some were convicted criminals, some were insane. None were well-known writers.

The Americans and the French have produced much of the published work on opium addiction, in both the nineteenth and twentieth centuries, though medical and general studies are now beginning to appear in Britain, as our own experience of addicts grows with the recent growth of the habit here. The recent American surveys, based on carefully controlled experiments made on statistically adequate samples, are far more valuable for the general study of the subject than the nineteenth-century reports, which were often distorted by preconception, superstition and emotion, though the writers were sometimes excellent clinical observers. But in its bearing on the nineteenth-century literary addicts, recent scientific research on opium can be misleading in another way. Most modern American research is based on addicts who take the opium derivatives heroin or morphine by injection; recent French research sometimes also includes the smoking of opium. But the early nineteenth-century literary addicts all took their opium in the form of laudanum, alcoholic tincture of opium; this has a weaker opium content than morphine or heroin, and its action is affected by the addition of the alcohol. Moreover both the pipe of the opium smoker and the hypodermic syringe of the heroin addict have come to have a mystique of their own, a complex of feeling and ritual which affects the addict's reaction to his drug in a way not known to the laudanum drinker. What the modern addict takes is different in itself, and differently administered; and he takes it in a different climate of opinion. All the American addicts on whom recent medical surveys have been based were guilty of what is now in itself a crime; they knew themselves to be legally and socially reprobated; they endured danger and ruinous expense in getting supplies of their drug. In Britain the fact of being a heroin addict is not at present in itself a crime, but even for those who get heroin legally on prescription it is an act of defiance and protest, of separation from normal society, generally dominating the addict's time and thoughts and creating a special way of life. And there are increasing numbers who depend on illicit supplies, and who therefore have the same dangers and high costs as the American addicts.

These are the states of mind and feeling on which opium now operates in those who take it, and since—as all authorities, early and recent, agree—it can only work on what is already in a man's mind, it produces different effects in the minds of the self-conscious and ever-anxious addict of today from its effects in the minds of the early nineteenth-century addicts. They indeed felt guilt and anxiety, but guilt towards God and their families and their own wasted talents, not towards society and the law; anxiety about earning their living, but not about finding the money for the drug, or how they could get supplies. Different guilts and anxieties produce different patterns in the

imagination, and not all the mental processes and limitations of a man in a prison infirmary in Kentucky in the 1950s, or a boy in a beat club in Chelsea in the 1960s, can be adduced to explain those of Coleridge, a century and a half earlier, living with his family among admiring friends beside a mountain lake. The argument works in both directions: because learned and brilliantly imaginative writers like Coleridge and De Quincey saw fantastic visions under the influence of opium, it does not follow that ordinary addicts will do so; but equally because uneducated unimaginative delinquents today see no visions under opium, it does not follow that Coleridge or De Quincey were either lying when they said they had such visions, or psychopaths because they had them. (pp. 36-8)

What do the opium eaters really get out of their drug? The most important point here is to distinguish between the earlier and later stages of addiction, and between the moments when the drug is working and when its effects are wearing off, either because the time for the next dose is near or because the addict is trying, or being made, to give up the drug. Nearly all the positive advantages, if they can be called so much as that, of taking opium belong to the first, and generally short, stage of experiment with the drug. After that, it can confer little but freedom from the torture of not taking it. I have nothing to say here about the moral implications, or about the physical symptoms, often disgusting, which follow on taking opium and on withdrawing from it. My concern is only with its mental effects, so far as these might influence the work of literary creation.

First, then, the honeymoon period, as some writers have grimly called the first embraces of this swarthy bridegroom. The first sensation from taking opium, in nearly all cases, is a relaxation of tension and anxiety, the onset of a special kind of calm enjoyment usually summarized, as far back as Dr John Jones in 1700, under the word euphoria, in its original meaning of well-bearing, the condition of being borne along by a favourable breeze. There have been cases of experimenters with opium who feel nothing at all, or nothing but nausea; but these are probably calm lethargic unimaginative characters. The more usual effect is that cares, doubts, fears, tedium, inhibitions, sink away and are replaced by a serene self-assurance, for which there is no objective justification; the opium-taker's real situation has not changed in the least, only—and transiently—his feelings about his situation. He is now in a state of listless complacent tranquillity. Nothing worries him, nothing moves him; he is at peace with his fellowmen because he does not care about them; their sorrows do not move him, their injuries and slights of which he was so conscious now rebound harmlessly off his invulnerable self-esteem. An American doctor recently summarized what his patients said when he asked what drugs did for them: 'It puts an end to my despair: it makes me feel happy; it restores my self-confidence; and it does all that in a moment, without any effort on my part. The drug is a miracle. I cannot live without it.' A French addict told his doctor that a quarter of an hour after taking opium he felt as though he were plunged in a bath of tepid milk, or in cotton-wool. Addicts have likened their feelings under opium to flying or floating, to an 'exquisite don't-care atttitude', a Buddha-like calm, an admission to paradise. Often at first there is a transient stimulus, a feeling of excitement and vivacity, of fire in the veins, but this soon gives place to the calm rêverie in which all thoughts dangerous to the cherished image of self have been annihilated, and the mind floats in its sea of warm milk.

Many drug-takers have claimed that in this early stage of addiction their mental powers and activity have been enhanced.

Their intellectual faculties are ready, vivacious, lucid, and their ideas copious and original; opium, said an addict, made him think of things he would not otherwise have thought of. The power of associating ideas is immensely stimulated, in long unfolding links and networks of thought which can be creatively revealing. Projects are formed for huge philosophical works which will be a synthesis of all knowledge and will explain the pattern of existence. The most difficult works, the most elaborate conceptions, can be read and understood with ease. Abstract ideas become images, brilliantly distinct but melting and evolving in swift metamorphoses, or the mind leaps with intrepid audacity and self-reliance across the gaps between idea and idea. Anything could be achieved—if it were worth achieving; but there is no need to make an effort, for the thing is, in effect, done already; intention and performance are no longer distinguished. Every emotional impulse—pious feeling, kindness to others, sexual love—is consummated in thought but may remain unexpressed in action. In fact, much of the supposed intellectual impetus from opium is a subjective delusion in the addict—he *feels* that he is having brilliant thoughts and doing difficult intellectual feats with extraordinary ease, but the results are not often shown by achievements objectively measurable. The unusual associations of ideas, the distinct and self-evolving images, the easy flow of words and the brilliant conversation may be powers genuinely conferred or stimulated by the drug; but the vast philosophical works which will explain everything do not get written—or if they do, explain nothing.

One of the most hotly contended facts about opium . . . is whether it stimulates artistic creation. Most nineteenth-century writers on opium were convinced that it did. (pp. 41-3)

Later authorities have almost totally rejected this theory. Nothing, they maintain, is imagined under the influence of opium which could not be imagined equally well by the same mind in a voluntary and conscious rêverie; the addict has not gained in imaginative force, he has simply deteriorated in the critical faculty which would enable him to judge the value of what he has imagined when under the influence of opium. It is, however, certain that . . . some addicts have been at any rate completely surprised when reading what they themselves have written under the influence of opium; it was unrecognizably alien even if it was not unrecognizably good.

But this leads to another mental effect of opium, the tricks it plays with the memory. There is much disagreement about these among the experts. The memory is generally asleep during an opium rêverie, so an American physician is quoted in 1862 as saying; memory is the first faculty to be affected, declared a French doctor in 1889. But addicts have maintained that under opium they could recall every note of whole symphonies, every detail of childhood experiences; and medical authorities mainly agree that though the opium addict's memory may be treacherous as to recent events and their sequence, it is phenomenally retentive of long-past ones. The opium-orientated memory selects, adapts, rearranges past experiences to a formula of its own, a magic pattern to exclude anxiety, like the pentagram on a sorcerer's floor within which the demons cannot penetrate.

There is flat contradiction between the experts as to whether opium produces hyperaesthesia or intensification of the sense perceptions. In 1871 a doctor declared that, under opium, the susceptibility of the senses may become so acute that 'not so much as an articulated sound, not the jar from a footstep, shall be endurable'; ten years later another doctor, a specialist in the treatment of drug addiction who had made experiments on

himself, reported that his tactile sensibility was much increased; and Roger Dupouy, writing in 1912, agreed that most addicts find even slight noises or bright lights painful. But an American medical report of 1941 declared that after morphine injections the hearing was dulled, the tactile sensitivity sometimes diminished, the sense of smell was not affected, nor was visual acuity, though the field of vision was sometimes decreased.

There is not much positive evidence on whether synaesthesia—that exchange of sense perceptions, by which colours are heard and smelt and sounds are seen and tasted, which was so dear to German and French nineteenth-century writers—can be induced by opium. But a good deal has been written on the question whether, at least in the early stages of addiction which I am now describing, the objects perceived by the senses are totally misreported by the brain, so as to cause hallucinations, or whether the mind under opium is a distorting mirror but one still reflecting reality. The contact with the external world is certainly attenuated during opium rêveries; sudden stimuli may still violently shock the addict, objects close at hand may be seen with painful distinctness, but general awareness of the outside world is lessened. (pp. 44-5)

Most vital to the consideration of opium and the literary imagination is the question of opium dreams and rêveries. Nearly all authorities, from De Quincey himself onwards, agree that these experiences under opium are conditioned by the addict's heredity, original education, temperament, habits of thought and of mental association, degree of talent and imagination, and innate capacity for dreaming vividly and remembering dreams. The 'silken garment of the imagination' is woven from the strands already there. Only one book on opium known to me, written by a life-long habituate, firmly rejects the theory that De Quincey had opium dreams because he had an aptitude for dreaming anyway, and issues a challenge: 'Let any one, bold enough to undertake so costly an experiment, try the virtues of opium in the capacity of producing dreams, and, my word for it, he will either claim a special aptitude for dreaming himself or, with me, give all the credit to the subtle and mighty power of opium'. But it is incontestable that many addicts have no memory of having dreamed at all, or they dream only vague subfusc scenes or sequences of monotonous slightly-varying images linked to some obsessive triviality. In any case the so-called 'dreams' of opium takers in the early stages of addiction are often not real dreams of sleep, but waking rêveries. The sleep which may overcome the addict from half an hour to some hours after taking his dose is often dreamless, but it is preceded by the rêverie state in which many of the so-called 'dreams' are enjoyed.

Opium, then, cannot give the power of vivid dreaming to those who have not got it already, and to those who have, the dreams and reveries that it brings will be mixed from the paints already on the palettes of their minds—there will be no colours entirely new, beyond the spectrum. But opium can cause the dreamer to select certain elements among the powers and experiences given to him, and to blend, deepen, heighten some and ignore or distort others. The effects of opium make these visions, even when they are experienced in waking rêverie and not in dreams of sleep, not such a fully voluntary activity as the daydreams of ordinary imagination. The addict can control them to some extent; he may start from, and even pursue, a chosen theme; one of [Roger] Dupouy's patients, an opium-smoker, said that he could evoke and control at will the mental presentations which passed before him, and some have claimed that they could choose and steer even their dreams in sleep. But something not entirely within their control is at work in the theatre of their minds, presenting to them masques and dramas which they can watch with detached fascination. (pp. 46-7)

These rêveries, since they are experienced in a partly conscious state and may be controlled, or at least steered, at will, are naturally pleasant in content for the most part, though the pleasures are limited in range. Erotic rêveries seem rare (though in the nineteenth-century case-histories this may be due to prudery in recording them); there are no dreams of eating or drinking; nothing active or aggressive, and nothing warm or companionable. All is solitary and remote. And even at this early stage, less pleasant elements sometimes intrude into dreams and rêveries—sensations of falling down precipices, of cold, of coiling snakes and grimacing countenances.

But at this stage, when a man is taking opium only occasionally, or has only been taking it for a short time, he can still stop without too much difficulty, and many who have experimented with it have in fact stopped at this stage. But with many others, this early phase of addiction, with its baseless euphoria and self-confidence, begins to fade away into the darkness that is to follow. After a period that may be only a few weeks, or may even extend to years in the case of those who space their doses very widely, the opium-taker begins to find that the drug no longer produces the euphoria for which he started taking it; but now it is too late to stop. The drug can no longer raise him above his normal level of happiness; but unless he goes on taking it, he falls excruciatingly far below his normal level, into a crater of restless misery. (p. 49)

If the authorities differ on whether opium addiction in its first stage stimulates poetic creation, there seems to be general agreement that in its later stage it makes any sustained imaginative creation impossible. It does not prevent a man from writing, or painting, or composing; many addicts have gone on earning their living to the end of their days by practising one of the arts. But the paralysis of the critical faculty makes them no longer able to distinguish their best work from their worst, and the haunting idea of the great universal masterpiece which they are one day to produce causes the work which they actually do produce to be provisional, makeshift. A very interesting analysis of the creative writer's state of mind at this stage of addiction was given by an anonymous American addict, a great admirer of Coleridge, in 1876. In the later stages of addiction, he says, a man's sensibilities are so impervious to all deep feelng that he is in a 'buried-alive condition'. 'No warmth or glow of passion or genial feeling can be aroused. Hence the poetical faculty was annihilated in Coleridge. There is a sort of vitrifying process that chills all sensibility. . . . Whatever is done, is done in pale cold strength of intellect. . . . That exquisite feeling that teaches a writer to know when the best word tips the edges of sensibility, lies buried under the debris of dead tissue'. (pp. 52-3)

An analysis of the visions of the confirmed opium addict is hampered not only by the unreliable reporting of the addicts themselves, but also by the confused terminology used by the medical writers on addiction, many of whom do not really distinguish between ordinary dreams of sleep; the special kind of dream which is known as a nightmare or 'crise nocturne' and which generally wakens the sleeper; day-time rêveries and waking visions; and hallucinations. It is probably safe to say that most advanced addicts no longer experience the partly directed waking rêverie which is the chosen activity of the early stage of addiction; rêverie is now automatic and continuous. Those who were originally non-dreamers still do not

have, or do not recall, dreams in sleep, but for those given to dreaming, nightmares may now become a misery and incubus. Opium addicts do not seem often to have actual hallucinations, in the sense that they believe in the objective reality of the visions which they see. Some morphine addicts reach that stage, but these were probably neurotic and unstable personalities originally. Most of the waking visions of opium addicts seem to be recognized as illusions, but they are inescapable tortures all the same. Some of them may be symptoms of withdrawal from the drug rather than of its presence, since most case-histories do not say whether the visions were experienced soon after taking a dose, or during abstinence. In the case of laudanum-drinkers, also, some of the visions may be due to the alcohol in the laudanum rather than to the opium.

After all these provisos, some account can be given of the more usual waking visions and nightmares of advanced addicts. They are often tortured by reptiles and insects—embraced by coiling snakes, trampled on by monsters, crawled on by worms, by ants, by microbes, thrust over precipices by tortoises or fiery dragons. Decaying things, still faintly touched with the likeness of beings once loved, stir beside them in rotting debris; their children, as they kiss them, turn to skeletons. Wandering through huge caves, they are forced to step on rotting corpses, and thousands of faces made of blood-red flame flash up and die out in the darkness. There are watching faces everywhere, grinning up through seawaves, stretching and lengthening and disintegrating, and eyes peer through holes in the wall. There are voices, threatening, insinuating, whispering, imitating each other, telling the addict his own thoughts. He is being spied on, plotted against, shot at, beaten, sawn asunder, drowned. His very identity is in danger—he is falling to pieces, his head is hollow, he is being merged with a character in a book or with the furniture in the room; he has become the opium itself and is being smoked in a pipe by the king of the island of addicts. While he is losing his living individuality, the inanimate creation is coming alive, is vibrating with secret force; the very stitches in his sheets are charged with electricity and give him shocks, and the chairs and the clothes hanging on the door are changing into fantastic animals. All that is safe, loving, stable, is decaying and suffering hideous change, but secret life and revolt are stirring in what were once humble unregarded tools and objects.

These are the miseries at which some addicts may stare daylong, or from which they may wake screaming at midnight. They do not inevitably accompany advanced addiction, there are many well-documented case-histories of addicts who even after many years of drug-taking have never had a vision or a nightmare. (pp. 55-6)

But there is no doubt or difference of opinion as to the misery of the process of withdrawal. In its early stages, it is a museum of tortures. The addict is nauseated, suffocated, ice-cold yet sweating; he yawns, sneezes, coughs, weeps, his teeth chatter; he is excruciated by restlessness, by cramps and twitches and burning pains, as though he were being pierced by needles or crawled over by ants. A woman addict subjected to forced abstinence wailed that an insect was rushing about between her skull and her brain. In the first stages of withdrawal the addict cannot sleep, he cannot stay still, he cannot concentrate or think of anything but his misery. Time seems endlessly extended, an hour lasts three months, and the ticking of a clock is unendurable—but when it is stopped, the succeeding silence is still more terrible. 'All created nature seemed annihilated, except my single, suffering self, lying in the midst of a boundless void' wrote one addict who after fifteen years of laudanum-taking finally succeeded in giving it up gradually, while another who was subjected to abrupt withdrawal treatment said that he was being 'torn by an immense void'.

But here we meet the most complete conflict of evidence between nineteenth-century and twentieth-century research. An American writing in the 1860s, an emotional but humane man with considerable knowledge of addicts, gave it as his opinion that the tortures of withdrawal were probably greater than being burnt alive. Another American writing in the 1950s, also from a wide experience in the treatment of addicts, said that though withdrawal symptoms 'are undoubtedly uncomfortable, they are seldom more severe than a bad case of gastro-intestinal influenza', and later compared them to 'a moderately severe ten-day illness', while a recent English writer has said that 'there is no need for the addict to feel more than the discomfort of a sharp dose of flu during a modern medically supervised withdrawal'. Much of course depends on the degree of addiction reached before withdrawal is attempted. Addicts vastly exaggerate their sufferings during withdrawal, according to many modern authorities, in order to be allowed some of the drug again as a palliative. Some doctors have gone so far as to say that all withdrawal symptoms are hysterical, not organic, though most experts now agree that opium produces a chemical change in the body which then depends on supplies of the drug and is disorganized by its withdrawal.

No doubt addicts lie about the tortures of withdrawal, as about every other subject; but some of the nineteenth-century accounts of withdrawal were written by cured, or temporarily cured, addicts who had voluntarily given up the drug and were writing with the express purpose of encouraging others to do the same. Such men had no reason to exaggerate the sufferings they had gone through; on the contrary, the purpose of their books required that such sufferings should be minimized. Probably the fear of discouraging addicts from making the attempt has caused some recent medical writers laudably to play down the sufferings of withdrawal. They are, of course, describing gradual withdrawal under medical supervision, helped by tranquillizing drugs, whereas the nineteenth-century accounts mostly, though not all, describe what in the addicts' jargon is called 'cold turkey'—abrupt withdrawal of the drug without palliatives. The choice is grim in any case, a choice between a sharp but probably short agony on the rack, and then freedom, or life imprisonment in a shrinking cell, since the addict who clings to his addiction gets diminishing returns from increasing doses.

I shall not try to describe the gloom, squalor and impotent suspicion of the last stages of opium addiction, since it does not apply to the opium-eating writers to whom this book is devoted, and for comparison with whom this chapter of description has been included. But since it has been suggested by some critics that the withdrawal period is the one most likely to foster literary inspiration and activity, it is worth taking a look at some of the mental symptoms of withdrawal in non-literary addicts.

The immediate effect, as has been said, is to produce a restlessness and irritability so great that concentration, even attention, are impossible. Reading or writing are out of the question; the addict is far too preoccupied with his own sufferings to use his imagination for any other purpose than dwelling on what he is enduring. He is unable to sleep, and sometimes seems to be waiting for someone who never comes. The world and everything in it seems colourless and joyless, and trifling

incidents are taken tragically, while no good fortune can win a smile from him. There may be sudden onsets of anxiety and terror, and even violence and hallucinations. These symptoms are at their height between forty-eight and seventy-two hours after the last dose of the drug, and it is unlikely that during this period any work of literature was ever consciously created.

When the first wretchedness is over, a state of mind begins to set in which may well be favourable to literary creation. The mind, so long held in lethargy, starts to work more rapidly, though the ideas flow incessantly through the brain and cannot easily be seized and worked out. One addict, describing the sleepless nights of a withdrawal period during which he lay and heard the clock tick and felt that time had been endlessly extended, says that he composed verses and hymns 'with incredible ease and rapidity', though he had never previously written a line of verse; but they were of no merit, he confessed, and he never wrote them down. Another man, describing his experiences in the later stages of withdrawal, depicts a renewed spring of energy and joy in life, when his power of thought became 'keen, bright and fertile beyond example', his imagination swarmed with ideas of beauty, his sensibility was exquisitely fine, and though he was still too restless, too much unnerved to write down his thoughts, he shone in conversation.

The shadow over this brightening state of mind is that men now again become conscious of what their addiction had concealed from them, and had been welcomed for concealing from them—their own inadequacy. Excessive self-reproach, dwelling on every sin and failure of the past life, and a consciousness of inferiority, dismay the addict who is no longer protected by the drug from these feelings, whose dismal power he had forgotten. One man describes it as 'a sickening death-like sensation about the heart; a self-accusing sense of having committed some wrong—of being guilty before God; a load of fear and trembling'.

The hyperaesthesia experienced when under opium does not disappear during withdrawal. The ticking of a clock or the jar of a heavy footstep can seem unendurably loud. The body feels sensitive all over; the lightest touch, if it is abrupt, gives pain. One man, when a barber began to cut his hair, felt as though each single hair were endowed with intense vitality, and screamed and groaned till the barber stopped. 'The least noise, the feeblest light, the faintest smell, are amplified and become obsessions'. The physical feelings of cold, the shiverings and icy sweats, transform themselves into images of icebergs and stony hands.

The evidence about dreams and visions during withdrawal from opium is most confused. Some authorities report stupendous and fearful dreams during the half-hour spells of sleep snatched during the first forty-eight hours. After that there is little opportunity for dreams in sleep, since insomnia—sometimes lasting for many months—is one of the chief miseries of the withdrawal period. But the waking visions can be terrible, and there are more cases of such visions during withdrawal periods than during addiction. There is no great difference between the visions of addiction and of withdrawal—perhaps because those reporting them have not always made it clear in which state the vision was experienced. (pp. 57-60)

• • • • •

No clear pattern of opium's influence on creative writing—always discernible, recognizable and complete in the work of all writers who took opium—has emerged from this survey. It would not be credible if it had. Opium works on what is already there in a man's mind and memory, and what was already there in the eight writers [Thomas De Quincey, Edgar Allan Poe, Charles Baudelaire, George Crabbe, Samuel Taylor Coleridge, Wilkie Collins, Francis Thompson, and John Keats] whose works have ben surveyed in this book was extremely varied. They had nothing in common except that they lived in the same century, were imaginative writers, and took opium. In every other way—literary aims and techniques, degree of genius or talent, beliefs, tastes, temperaments—they were as different as possible. Taking only a few straightforward biographical facts which can be easily compared, one can see that there was no common factor in these to account for any similarities in their work.

Their social origins varied widely. Crabbe's father was a warehouseman and fisherman, Keats's father was a groom who rose to keeping a livery stable; Poe's father was an unsuccessful actor, Wilkie Collins's was a painter, De Quincey's a prosperous merchant, Francis Thompson's a doctor, Coleridge's a clergyman, Baudelaire's a tutor in a noble family and later an official.

Coleridge, De Quincey, Baudelaire and Poe had university educations. Crabbe, Keats and Thompson had medical training, and the two former actually practised medicine for short periods. Poe and (very briefly) Coleridge were in the army. Crabbe became a clergyman. Francis Thompson worked briefly for a shoemaker; Wilkie Collins had a spell in a City office. De Quincey and Baudelaire never followed any profession or trade but that of literature, including editing and journalism.

Crabbe, Baudelaire and Thompson for short periods of their lives, and De Quincey and Poe for many years, endured extremes of poverty, including actual hunger. All of them except Collins had to borrow money at some stage; only Crabbe had an assured income for much of his life; but Coleridge and Keats were never hard up and friendless to the point of going hungry, and Collins, though he lived on his literary earnings, was never hard up at all.

Their religious beliefs were as diverse as their social origins or their education. Crabbe was a latitudinarian Anglican parson, Coleridge was at one time a Unitarian and then an undenominational Trinitarian, De Quincey was an Anglican. Baudelaire was a lapsed but, to use his own word, 'incorrigible' Catholic, Francis Thompson an ardently devout Catholic. Poe was a very problematical Deist, Keats and Collins were agnostics.

If we turn to the physical side of their lives, these prove to be equally varied. It is often said that opium produces sexual impotence, but the lives of some of these writers do not support this theory. Crabbe, Coleridge and De Quincey were married and had children; all of De Quincey's children were born after he had been addicted to opium for many years. Poe was married, but his marriage was never consummated and he may have been impotent. Keats, Collins, Baudelaire and Thompson were bachelors, but of very different kinds. We do not know what sexual experience, if any, Keats had, but Wilkie Collins kept two mistresses and had several children by one of them. Baudelaire is generally believed to have had varied sexual experience, and his poetry certainly gives that impression, though some of his contemporaries thought he was impotent. Francis Thompson was probably virgin.

Their state of health was equally unrevealing. Crabbe suffered from dyspepsia, and later from *tic douloureux*, but lived to be seventy-eight. Keats died of tuberculosis at the age of twenty-five, Poe of cardiac disease and intemperance at forty, Bau-

delaire of a paralytic stroke at forty-six, Francis Thompson of tuberculosis at forty-seven. Wilkie Collins, though suffering much from gout, lived to be sixty-five. Coleridge and De Quincey, the two most advanced addicts, lived to sixty and seventy-four, though Coleridge was prone to some form of rheumatism or gout and De Quincey to neuralgia and gastric troubles.

No common trait emerges from this confused set of biographical facts except that none of these eight writers who took opium was perfectly healthy. Otherwise, all is contrast and contradiction. Early deaths, long lives; prosperity, destitution; happy marriage and devoted fatherhood, or voluntary or involuntary chastity; a stable home, a good education, a great stock of learning, or orphanhood, unhappy adoption, early and enforced application to uncongenial work; secure literary fame or a continual struggle; calm content or anguished misery; devout faith or total unbelief; all these, not in two tidy halves but in every combination, are found among these eight writers.

These were the diverse experiences and temperaments (but with a common factor of creative imagination which is absent from all but a tiny proportion of those who take opium) on which the drug worked. Did it, as Mr M. H. Abrams believed [see excerpt above], introduce them all to a world of its own, recognizable but as utterly different from the everyday world as the life of another planet? Or did it, as Professor Schneider maintained [see excerpt above], produce no effect at all on the way they wrote?

The strongest evidence for the first hypothesis would seem to be that some who have written under the influence of opium have afterwards not recognized such writing as their own deliberate creation. It was something given, apparently from outside. But although the influence of opium seemed to have shown them something they could not recognize, which they were sure they had never seen before, it was because the action of opium had reorganized their memory, banishing some experiences and recalling others from a great distance. It did not act like a liberating government—it was a reactionary coup d'état; it was Aristides who was banished, Alcibiades or even Hippias who was recalled. These writers had not been taken to a new planet, but were being admitted to caves and prisons and secret hiding-places of their own native Earth, places whose existence they had forgotten or ignored or never observed.

It is the chance of observing these hiding-places more at leisure, and under a stronger light, that seems to be the chief contribution which opium addiction may make to a writer's imaginative equipment. The experiences of the writers described in this book show that the action of opium may unbare some of the semi-conscious processes by which literature begins to be written. These processes are analogous to, and may even be identical with, the mental processes of rêverie, of dreams in full sleep, and of the hypnagogic visions which come on the borders of sleep, and there seems sufficient evidence that opium both intensifies these processes and extends their duration, so that they can be observed while they are happening. The writer can actually witness the process by which words and visual images arise simultaneously and in parallel in his own mind. He can watch, control, and subsequently use the product of the creative imagination at an earlier stage of its production than is normally accessible to the conscious mind.

But he can only do this if he already has a creative imagination and a tendency to rêverie, dreams and hypnagogic visions; and though opium may then present him with unique material for his poetry, it will probably take away from him the will and the power to make use of it. The sophisticated inquiries of Poe and Baudelaire aimed to discover whether opium can provide a *méthode de travail* for the poet, a technique both for collecting material and for presenting it. Poe thought, for instance, that the hyperaesthesia and synaesthesia induced by opium, the intensification and alteration of sense perception, constituted a model and parallel for the intensity of concentrated interest which the writer wishes to evoke from his reader. Opium might provide a short cut, an infallible recipe for producing that immediacy, that heightening of experience, which every poet wants to feel and then to impart. The free flow of association which opium released might wash away the prosaic categories and definitions which canalize the mind, and allow symbols to melt freely into one another. For De Quincey, the way in which feelings and images are presented to the mind during opium dreams and rêveries acted as a model, a lesson in technique, for the writing of prose-poems. Dreams, for De Quincey, for Crabbe, even for Wilkie Collins, gave insight. They crystallized the particles of past experience—sensory impressions, emotions, things read—into a symbolic pattern, an 'involute', which became part of the life of the imagination and could be worked into literature, and this crystallization, in De Quincey's passionately-held opinion, was precipitated by the action of opium.

There is no way of proving whether this is true or not. We know that De Quincey took opium. We know what he afterwards wrote. We do not know what he would have written if he had never taken it. It can be no more than a hypothesis that the action of opium, though it can never be a substitute for innate imagination, can uncover that imagination while it is at work in a way which might enable an exceptionally gifted and self-aware writer to observe and learn from his own mental processes.

But it could only do so at a price which no writer of integrity would ultimately be prepared to pay. I am not referring to moral integrity, but to the poet's responsibility to his own art. One of the most obvious effects of opium addiction on a writer's powers is that it induces indolence, absence of feeling, a state in which the power to observe is detached from the power to sympathize with what is observed. At its very outset, this state of mind can be useful to a poet; there are times when he needs detachment. But in the long run it is deadly. The dislocation of objects and events from the feelings which they normally arouse is in the end destructive of poetic truth. In *Dejection* Coleridge gave, once for all, the classic description of this creeping death of the imaginative impulse, but Crabbe and Keats can also be seen fighting against it, and Poe and Collins yielding to it, and to what comes in its train—the tendency that Coleridge called 'histrionism', the resort to violent attitudes because you no longer have normal feelings. Nearly all the opium-addicted writers indulged in descriptions of violence, gruesomeness, insanity, extremes of fear. The action of opium, by its exaggeration and distortion of normal feelings, may give to one who takes it unusual insights into the mental experience of the wicked, the insane, the terrified, the tortured, the dying, which may be useful and enlightening to a writer; but it only enables him to observe, not to sympathize with, these mental experiences. He feels himself to be a pariah; he recognizes the other pariahs; but he cannot hold out a hand even to them. He is insulated from his fellow-men, and has renounced the obligation of commitment.

Nor is he any longer committed to the physical world in which he lives. Landscapes, which once to him were beautiful in themselves and part of a significant whole, are now only an expression of his mood. No identities are stable and separate, they combine and engraft on each other. There are masks and disguises everywhere, and under the mask there may be only another mask, or nothing at all. Many of these writers felt that they had been endowed with an exceptional insight into the secret of the universe, and could reveal its philosophical framework for the enlightenment of mankind; but the great work could never be finished, because the power to hold things together had gone, everything disintegrated, fell away into fragments. It did not always seem so to them themselves. Among the powers that opium damaged was the power to detect damage; judgment and self-criticism do not make their absence felt by him who has lost them.

It is the great plans that are destroyed. Writers can still write, and in fragments write well, when they have been addicted to opium for many years; and this is not necessarily only during withdrawal periods, though these do in some cases provide the energy to commit to paper the imaginative creations which may otherwise stay uselessly imprisoned in the mind. But the holding-together has gone, the great luminous images which shed light and pattern across all the wide tracts of a writer's imagination do not radiate any more. The images are still there, but some are darkened, some are luridly spot-lit, all are enclosed. The effect of what Baudelaire called the 'paysage opiacé' is produced by blotting out some of the features of a normal landscape of imagery—the groups of people, the flowing streams, the roads, the cottages, the woods, the sun—and high-lighting the solitary figure, the stagnant pools, the cliffs, the castles, the stone faces and slimy claws that show for a moment at the mouths of caves. It is not another planet, it is our own, but in a light of eclipse. . . . [Certain] images—pariahs, harlot-ogresses, quicksands, petrified landscapes, freezing cold, drowned or buried temples, watching eyes—do recur in the works of the opium-addicted writers. Some of these images—the fairly obvious poppy, the honey-dew, the temptress, the buried temple—may be conscious or unconscious equivalents for opium itself. Some—the ice-cold, the quicksands, the petrifaction, the floating lovers—may be connected with physical symptoms produced by opium dosage or withdrawal. Some—the idea of the outcast, the images of watching eyes and hybrid shape-changing creatures—may express the addict's isolation and suspicion. None of the images is peculiar to the writing of addicts, and none of the addict-writers use only these images and no others; but they form a recognizable pattern. These eight writers were differently gifted and differently experienced, and opium acted on their diverse natures and powers to produce different modifications of the way they wrote. One can only, as doctors do, deduce that a certain combination of imaginative symptoms, though they may come from separate causes, may add up to a single disease. (pp. 331-37)

Alethea Hayter, in her Opium and the Romantic Imagination, *University of California Press, 1968, 388 p.*

ADDITIONAL BIBLIOGRAPHY

Baudelaire, Charles. "An Opium-Eater." In his *Artificial Paradise: On Hashish and Wine as Means of Expanding Individuality*, translated by Ellen Fox, pp. 83-170. New York: Herder and Herder, 1971.

An English-language version of Baudelaire's translation of De Quincey's *Confessions*. Baudelaire's translation includes scattered commentary on the work.

Berridge, Virginia. "East End Opium Dens and Narcotic Use in Britain." *London Journal* 4, No. 1 (May 1978): 3-28.
    An account of the popular impression and historical reality of opium dens in the east end of London during the late nineteenth and early twentieth century.

Cooke, Michael G. "De Quincey, Coleridge, and the Formal Uses of Intoxication." *Yale French Studies*, No. 50 (1974): 26-40.
    An extended analysis of De Quincey's and Coleridge's need for and literary use of opium intoxication.

De Quincey, Thomas. "Coleridge and Opium-Eating." In his *The Collected Writings of Thomas De Quincey*, edited by David Masson, pp. 179-214. London: A. & C. Black, 1897.
    A review—first published in *Blackwood's Edinburgh Magazine* in 1845—of James Gilman's *The Life of Samuel Taylor Coleridge* in which De Quincey comments on both Coleridge's opium use and his own.

Hubble, Douglas. "Opium Addiction and English Literature." *Medical History* 1 (1957): 323-35.
    A primarily biographical account of the opium habits and supposedly opium-inspired works of Crabbe, Coleridge, De Quincey, and Thompson.

Kusinitz, Marc. "Romanticism and Decadence." In his *Drugs and the Arts*, pp. 31-45. The Encyclopedia of Psychoactive Drugs, edited by Solomon H. Synder, series 2. New York: Chelsea House Publishers, 1987.
    Discusses the use of opium, hashish, and other drugs by nineteenth-century Romantic and Decadent authors.

Lindesmith, Alfred R. *Opiate Addiction*. Bloomington, Ind.: Principia Press, 1947, 238 p.
    An influential study of opiate dependence and its social consequences.

Lomax, Elizabeth. "The Uses and Abuses of Opiates in Nineteenth-Century England." *Bulletin of the History of Medicine* 47, No. 2 (1973): 167-76.
    A survey of opium consumption in nineteenth-century English society.

Marks, Jeannette. *Genius and Disaster: Studies in Drugs and Genius*. New York: Adelphi Co., 1926, 193 p.
    Examines the use of opium and other drugs by various prominent nineteenth-century literary figures, including Edgar Allan Poe, James Thomson, Dante Gabriel Rossetti, and De Quincey.

Scott, J. M. "Opium and the Creative Mind." In his *The White Poppy: A History of Opium*, pp. 46-82. New York: Funk & Wagnalls, 1969.
    Investigates the possible connection between opium use and literary inspiration in the works of De Quincey, Coleridge, Crabbe, and Thompson.

Terry, Charles M., and Pellens, Mildred. *The Opium Problem*. New York: The Committee on Drug Addictions in Collaboration with the Bureau of Social Hygiene, 1928, 1042 p.
    An early but extensive and often discussed study of opium use as a medical and social problem.

The Pre-Raphaelite Movement

INTRODUCTION

Pre-Raphaelitism was an aesthetic movement that shaped much of the literature and art in England during the second half of the nineteenth century. The term "Pre-Raphaelite" was coined in 1848 as a derisive description of the works and aims of William Holman Hunt, John Everett Millais, and Dante Gabriel Rossetti, who were then students at the Royal Academy of Art in London. At that time, the Academy demanded a conventional, stylized method of painting that was derived from the works of Raphael and subsequent artists, most notably the eighteenth-century painter and man of letters Sir Joshua Reynolds, who, as the Academy's first president, was instrumental in establishing its traditionalist approach. Rebelling against this approach, the first Pre-Raphaelites sought inspiration in the religious works of fifteenth-century Italian painters. They also shared a love of literary themes and a determination to return to nature as the source of their art. United by similar artistic ideals, Hunt, Millais, and Rossetti formed the Pre-Raphaelite Brotherhood, or P. R. B., in 1848, a group that counted among its members the painters James Collinson and Frederick George Stephens, the sculptor Thomas Woolner, and Rossetti's younger brother, William Michael. The Brotherhood's activities included artistic collaborations and joint exhibitions as well as the publication of the *Germ*, a periodical intended to further their artistic doctrines. This short-lived journal, edited by William Michael Rossetti, contained essays, poetry, and short stories contributed by members of the Brotherhood and by such affiliates as the artist Ford Madox Brown and the poets Christina Rossetti and Coventry Patmore. While the Brotherhood was artistically stimulating for its members, their paintings elicited harsh censure: critical reaction to Pre-Raphaelite works in the early 1850s is typified by Charles Dickens's attack on Millais's realistic and detailed rendering of a religious subject in *Christ in the House of His Parents*. Although the acclaimed art critic John Ruskin took the part of the Pre-Raphaelites, repeatedly defending their artistic tenets, they had difficulty selling their works, and the P. R. B. disbanded within a few years. However, in the mid-1850s and the 1860s, a group of Oxford students who were deeply influenced by the art and poetry of the Pre-Raphaelites, and the works of Dante Gabriel Rossetti in particular, participated in a second brotherhood. Led by William Morris and Edward Burne-Jones, this coterie also included Algernon Charles Swinburne, Richard Watts Dixon, and Walter Pater. Their primary accomplishments were the publication of the *Oxford and Cambridge Magazine*, modeled after the *Germ*, and the creation of the frescoes at the Oxford Union Debating Hall, painted under the direction of Dante Gabriel Rossetti.

During the last three decades of the nineteenth century, Pre-Raphaelitism became an influential albeit controversial artistic force in England and abroad. The sensual qualities of some Pre-Raphaelite works prompted the Scottish critic Robert Buchanan to attack what he termed the "Fleshly school of poetry." Buchanan's attack, which was directed at Morris, Swinburne, and, especially, Dante Gabriel Rossetti, gave rise to an extended and well-known literary dispute featuring a series of vituperative essays by Buchanan, Swinburne, and Rossetti. Ultimately, the charge by Buchanan and others that the poetry of the Pre-Raphaelites was immoral did little to harm their reputation, and the movement continued to exert a significant influence on many aspects of Victorian aesthetics. In painting, Millais, Hunt, and Burne-Jones exhibited regularly with critical and commercial success. Morris and Dante Gabriel Rossetti produced important collections of poetry, while William Michael Rossetti published an influential translation of Dante as well as editions of the works of Percy Bysshe Shelley, William Blake, and Walt Whitman. The firm of Morris, Marshall, Faulkner and Co., which produced home furnishings, stained glass, and textiles, and Morris's Kelmscott Press, noted for its illustrated editions of Geoffrey Chaucer and other English authors, were likewise important in promoting decorative tastes and craftsmanship. Pre-Raphaelitism also had an impact in France, where parallel developments in poetry and painting were underway, and in America, where Ruskin's aesthetic doctrines together with Morris's emphasis on craftsmanship helped shape artistic thought and practice.

The works of the Pre-Raphaelites are frequently described as "literary paintings" and "painterly poems." In the visual arts, the original Pre-Raphaelites represented nature with exact fidelity, and their paintings are marked by minute detail and brilliant color. In addition, they sought to imbue their subjects with symbolic and spiritual significance, often choosing to illustrate scenes from literary sources or situations with innate narrative interest. However, Pre-Raphaelitism in art is now closely identified with the ideal of beauty represented in Dante Gabriel Rossetti's paintings of women and with the medieval and decorative elements of Morris's and Burne-Jones's works. Pre-Raphaelite poetry, like its visual counterpart, often deals with medieval and supernatural subjects and is characterized by simplicity of style, archaic diction, and attention to detail.

The following entry provides an overview of Pre-Raphaelitism; accounts of the genesis of the movement from primary sources; descriptions of the *Germ* and the *Oxford and Cambridge Magazine;* a discussion of the "Fleshly school of poetry" controversy; a selection of satires and parodies on Pre-Raphaelites and their works; surveys of the history and aesthetics of the movement; and essays on the influence of Pre-Raphaelitism.

(See also *Dictionary of Literary Biography*, Vol. 35: *Victorian Poets after 1850*.)

AN OVERVIEW

WILLIAM E. FREDEMAN

[*In this excerpt from the introduction to his full-length bibliography of materials on Pre-Raphaelitism, Fredeman provides a broad overview of the movement's adherents, major concerns, aesthetic characteristics, and influence.*]

Critics and literary historians of the Victorian period have too often been inclined to simplify the term Pre-Raphaelite to denote only those aspects of Victorian romanticism centering on the Pre-Raphaelite Brotherhood. More accurately, the term includes three stages of a congeries of literary and artistic impulse which have been used loosely and interchangeably as synonyms: the Pre-Raphaelite Brotherhood, the Pre-Raphaelite Movement, and Pre-Raphaelitism. Actually, they are not mutually exclusive but sequential terms descriptive of a continuous, if not a unified, aesthetic force.

The Pre-Raphaelite Brotherhood specifically refers to the pleiad who undertook in 1848 to bring about a revolution in English painting and poetry: James Collinson (1825?-1881), William Holman Hunt (1827-1910), John Everett Millais (1829-1896), Dante Gabriel Rosetti (1828-1882), William Michael Rossetti (1829-1919), Frederic George Stephens (1828-1907), and Thomas Woolner (1825-1892). Broader in its implications, the Pre-Raphaelite Movement incorporates not only the Brotherhood but all later aesthetic influences emanating from the doctrines of the Brotherhood and culminating in what may be called, historically and critically, a school. Pre-Raphaelitism, broader still in its applications, is essentially a generic usage, including the more common characteristics of the art and literature of such disparate figures as Rossetti, Hunt, and Millais, Edward Burne-Jones, Ford Madox Brown, and Christina Rossetti, Arthur Hughes, Simeon Solomon, and the early Algernon Swinburne—in short, the whole panoply of artists and writers for whom, roughly between 1848 and 1882, Pre-Raphaelistism was the special kind of romantic common denominator.

Definitions of Pre-Raphaelitism are almost as numerous as the persons attempting to define it. To their contemporaries the Pre-Raphaelites were either the *avant garde* of a long-anticipated artistic renaissance, foreshadowed by such artists as Maclise, Mulready, and Turner, or reactionaries seeking to undermine existing morality and to destroy the noble traditions of English art. Modern critics have distorted the significance of Pre-Raphaelitism in various ways: by attempting to popularize the movement, by depreciating it as another silly manifestation of the twentieth century's most popular scapegoat, Victorianism, or by neglecting it altogether. As an "aesthetic adventure" Pre-Raphaelitism has been dramatized beyond all proportion: it has been staged as both a "comedy" and a "tragedy"; and the Pre-Raphaelites have been etherealized, like Shelley, although admittedly on "poor" but "splendid wings." The resulting incoherence has reduced Pre-Raphaelitism to the oversimplified generalizations of anthology definitions. The failure of critics to distinguish the three phases of Pre-Raphaelitism has almost stripped the term of critical significance.

The Pre-Raphaelities, because of their critical reticence, are partially responsible for the exaggerated views of their aesthetic. Besides their "manifesto," *The Germ,* itself a vague declaration of intent, and a few scattered documents, they left no canon of critical comment by which they can be clearly identified. The numerous reminiscences, memoirs, and autobiographies, written half a century after the demise of the Brotherhood, tend, however interesting and informative they are, to be misleading; for in them old prejudices, clouding memories, and filial concern too often obscure crucial issues. Had the Pre-Raphaelites succeeded in crystallizing their aesthetic assumptions, confusion about the movement would doubtless have been appreciably lessened. Unfortunately, most of them were content to let others speak for them, or negligently to allow misconceptions and misstatements about themselves to be published without refutation.

Also responsible for the aura of confusion surrounding Pre-Raphaelite scholarship is the failure of critics to examine and explain the basic complexity of a movement which, beginning as a reform in painting, had its greatest influence in the field of English letters. In reality, Pre-Raphaelitism, a mid-nineteenth-century flowering of the Romantic Movement, is an important transitional stage between "high Victorianism" and Aestheticism. It had its roots in the reaction against the materialism of the Industrial Revolution, and it affirmed and reasserted the values of individuality in an age dominated by materialistic demands for social and artistic conformity. In art and literature, it was a revolt against the rules of the academicians and a reassertion of faith in the truth of the creative expression of the individual artist as opposed to the stereotyped and conventionalized expression of pseudo-"classical" art. Pre-Raphaelitism emphasized the artist as creator rather than as copyist, and to this end the Pre-Raphaelites insisted that the artist should follow nature, reproducing what he saw rather than what artists before him said he ought to see. Philosophically, the Pre-Raphaelities, like most romantics, were idealists, and their "medievalism," if the conscious employment of medievalisms can ever be so classified, was part of their revolt, a substitution by analogy for the materialism of the civilization around them. But the reforms they advocated were largely aesthetic, and were social only by association; for with the notable exceptions of Ruskin and Morris, whose social theories also rest ultimately on moral-aesthetic foundations, the Pre-Raphaelites were unconcerned with social reform. In stressing the individuality of the artist, they had not abandoned the possibility of reforming public taste, and they were emphatic in their belief that the artist and the poet had positive roles to fulfill, even in a materialistic age. But the projection of these basic attitudes into social reforms was a later extension which did not characterize the movement in its earlier stages.

The major difficulties in arriving at a clear definition of Pre-Raphaelitism stem from seeming and actual inconsistencies in their working aesthetic: the immediate complications of the *ut pictura poesis* concept apparent in Pre-Raphaelite art; the sometimes unclear distinction between "literary" art and genre painting; the contrast between a romantic choice of subject and the realism of technique in their scrupulous depiction of external detail; and, crucially, the unreconciled contradiction between the mimetic—"follow nature"—and the expressive—"fidelity to inner experience"—theories of art. In addition to these more obvious problems in dealing critically with the movement, there is the problem of resolving a wide and divergent range of artistic motivations within the context of the movement's aesthetic continuity: the near-aestheticism of Rossetti, the religiosity of Holman Hunt, the literal realism of Millais (a technique that continued long after his subjects had deteriorated into the sentimentalized tableaux of his Academy work), the moral-ethical sermon-paintings of Ford Madox Brown, and ultimately the medieval-socialism of Morris via Ruskin.

Much of this confusion can be resolved by confining discussion to Pre-Raphaelitism as an historical phenomenon, that is to the Brotherhood phase, or, at most, to the so-called second "Brotherhood" which flourished at Oxford between 1856 and 1859. While convenient for reducing the movement to manageable proportions, this theory in reality begs the question, for it is Pre-Raphaelitism in its generic sense with which the aesthetician or art historian must finally concern himself if he is to account for the dynamic role played by the movement in the history of nineteenth-century English art and literature.

The importance of Pre-Raphaelitism as the dominant animating force in English aesthetics through four decades of the nineteenth century is indisputable. The Pre-Raphaelites were not only the arbiters, they were often the instigators of taste—in literature, in art, in clothes, in houses, in book design, in furniture, in wallpapers—the contagion of their enthusiasm creating an atmosphere that fired the imaginations of workers in almost every field of the beautiful. A catalogue of the Movement's devotees and associates includes figures as remote as Charles Reade and William Butler Yeats. Maurice Browning Cramer has traced the influence of the group in furthering Browning's reputation between 1847 and 1856, and in kindling a devotion for Browning at Oxford during the period of the second "Brotherhood." Similarly, G. H. Ford has shown that Rossetti and the Pre-Raphaelites were largely instrumental in keeping alive the reputation and influence of Keats. Whatever else may be said of them, it is characteristic that they championed Whitman in England long before others became aware of his poetry. Dante Gabriel and William Rossetti, Swinburne, and William Bell Scott were all pioneers in the Blake revival; and Rossetti proselytized avidly for the insignificant little volume of verse that FitzGerald's publisher had disposed of, thereby retrieving the *Rubáiyát* from possible oblivion.

Not only did the Pre-Raphaelites influence Yeats who, of himself between 1887 and 1891, says, "I was in all things Pre-Raphaelite," as well they left their mark on Shaw, who in the Preface to *Candida* (1897) specifically states that he is writing a "pre-raphaelite" play. Beyond these—and the obvious attempt of Wilde and others of the *fin de siècle*, rightly or wrongly, to trace the origins of their aesthetic beliefs to the Pre-Raphaelites—the influence of the movement spread further: to Richard Aldington, to Pound, to the early Lawrence, and to the Imagists. In the final analysis, the Pre-Raphaelites must be considered as individual artists and writers, but "in the days of a deep, smug, thick, rich, drab, industrial complacency," Pre-Raphaelitism itself shone, as Max Beerbohm says of Rossetti [see Additional Bibliography], "with the ambiguous light of a red torch somewhere in a dense fog" for most of those whose lives it touched, however briefly.

Pre-Raphaelitism, then, represents a middle ground between the extremes of Victorian art morality (with its concomitants of social reform) and the Art for Art's Sake of the *fin de siècle*. More an aesthetic than an ethical movement in art and literature, it maintained, to some degree, the values of both, preserving the principles of beauty and truth so vital to the development and continuation of art in an age that had itself reacted against Romanticism. (pp. 1-5)

William E. Fredeman, in his Pre-Raphaelitism: A Bibliocritical Study, *Cambridge, Mass.: Harvard University Press, 1965, 327 p.*

GENESIS OF THE MOVEMENT FROM PRIMARY ACCOUNTS

JOHN RUSKIN

[*One of the Victorian era's most prominent art critics, Ruskin was the author of* Modern Painters *and an important influence on the Pre-Raphaelites. The following excerpt is drawn from a letter Ruskin wrote to the editor of the London* Times. *Responding to a negative critique of the paintings of the Pre-Raphaelites, Ruskin defends both their artistic goals and their works. For additional criticism by Ruskin, see excerpt below.*]

[I] regret that the tone of the critique which appeared in *The Times* of Wednesday last [7 May 1851] on the works of Mr. Millais and Mr. Hunt, now in the Royal Academy, should have been scornful as well as severe. [Ruskin's editor adds in a footnote:

"That the critique was sufficiently bitter, may be gathered from the following portions of it: 'These young artists, have unfortunately become notorious by addicting themselves to an antiquated style and an affected simplicity in painting. . . . We can extend no toleration to a mere senile imitation of the cramped style, false perspective, and crude colour of remote antiquity. We want not to see what Fuseli termed drapery 'snapped instead of folded'; faces bloated into apoplexy, or extenuated to skeletons; colour borrowed from the jars in a druggist's shop, and expression forced into caricature. . . . That morbid infatuation which sacrifices truth, beauty, and genuine feeling to mere eccentricity, deserves no quarter at the hands of the public.'"]

I regret it, first, because the mere labour bestowed on those works, and their fidelity to a certain order of truth, (labour and fidelity which are altogether indisputable,) ought at once to have placed them above the level of mere contempt; and, secondly, because I believe these young artists to be at a most critical period of their career—at a turning-point, from which they may either sink into nothingness or rise to very real greatness; and I believe also, that whether they choose the upward or the downward path, may in no small degree depend upon the character of the criticism which their works have to sustain. I do not wish in any way to dispute or invalidate the general truth of your critique on the Royal Academy; nor am I surprised at the estimate which the writer formed of the pictures in question when rapidly compared with works of totally different style and aim; nay, when I first saw the chief picture by Millais in the Exhibition of last year, I had nearly come to the same conclusion myself. But I ask your permission, in justice to artists who have at least given much time and toil to their pictures, to institute some more serious inquiry into their merits and faults than your general notice of the Academy could possibly have admitted.

Let me state, in the first place, that I have no acquaintance with any of these artists, and very imperfect sympathy with them. No one who has met with any of my writings will suspect me of desiring to encourage them in their Romanist and Tractarian tendencies. I am glad to see that Mr. Millais' lady in blue [in *Mariana*] is heartily tired of her painted window and idolatrous toilet table; and I have no particular respect for Mr. Collins' lady in white [in *Convent Thoughts*], because her sympathies are limited by a dead wall, or divided between some gold fish and a tadpole. . . . But I happen to have a special acquaintance with the water plant, *Alisma Plantago*, among which the said gold fish are swimming; and as I never saw it so thoroughly or so well drawn, I must take leave to remonstrate with you, when you say sweepingly that these men 'sacrifice *truth* as well as feeling to eccentricity.' For as a mere botanical study of the water lily and *Alisma*, as well as of the common lily and several other garden flowers, this picture would be invaluable to me, and I heartily wish it were mine.

But, before entering into such particulars, let me correct an impression which your article is likely to induce in most minds, and which is altogether false. These pre-Raphaelites (I cannot compliment them on common sense in choice of a *nom de guerre*) do *not* desire nor pretend in any way to imitate antique painting as such. They know very little of ancient paintings who suppose the works of these young artists to resemble them. As far as I can judge of their aim—for, as I said, I do not know the men themselves—the Pre-Raphaelites intend to surrender no advantage which the knowledge or inventions of the present time can afford to their art. They intend to return to early days in this one point only—that, as far as in them lies, they will draw either what they see, or what they suppose might have been the actual facts of the scene they desire to represent, irrespective of any conventional rules of picture-making; and they have chosen their unfortunate though not inaccurate name because all artists did this before Raphael's time, and after Raphael's time did *not* this, but sought to paint fair pictures, rather than represent stern facts; of which the consequence has been that, from Raphael's time to this day, historical art has been in acknowledged decadence. (pp. 85-9)

Now, sir, presupposing that the intention of these men was to return to archaic *art* instead of to archaic *honesty,* your critic borrows Fuseli's expression respecting ancient draperies 'snapped instead of folded,' and asserts that in these pictures there is a '*servile* imitation of *false* perspective.' To which I have just this to answer:—

That there is not one single error in perspective in four out of the five pictures in question [*Mariana, The Return of the Dove to the Ark,* and *The Woodman's Daughter* by Mr. Millais, *Valentine Receiving Sylvia from Proteus* by Mr. Hunt, and *Convent Thoughts* by Mr. Collins]; and that in Millais' *Mariana* there is but this one—that the top of the green curtain in the distant window has too low a vanishing-point; and that I will undertake, if need be, to point out and prove a dozen worse errors in perspective in any twelve pictures, containing architecture, taken at random from among the works of the popular painters of the day.

Secondly: that, putting aside the small Mulready, and the works of Thorburn and Sir W. Ross, and perhaps some others of those in the miniature room which I have not examined, there is not a single study of drapery in the whole Academy, be it in large works or small, which for perfect truth, power, and finish could be compared for an instant with the black sleeve of the Julia, or with the velvet on the breast and the chain mail of the Valentine, of Mr. Hunt's picture; or with the white draperies on the table of Mr. Millais' *Mariana,* and of the right-hand figure in the same painter's *Dove returning to the Ark.*

And further: that as studies both of drapery and of every minor detail, there has been nothing in art so earnest or so complete as these pictures since the days of Albert Durer. This I assert generally and fearlessly. (pp. 90-1)

> *John Ruskin, in a letter to the editor of "The Times" on May 9, 1851, in his* Arrows of the Chace: Being a Collection of Scattered Letters, *1880. Reprint by AMS Press, 1973, pp. 85-91.*

JOHN RUSKIN

[*In the following excerpt from an essay first published in 1851, Ruskin discusses the flaws prevalent in contemporary English art, praising the Pre-Raphaelites's dedication to accurate, detailed*

renderings of nature. For further commentary by Ruskin see excerpt above.]

The infinite absurdity and failure of our present training [in art] consists mainly in this, that we do not rank imagination and invention high enough, and suppose that they *can* be taught. Throughout every sentence that I ever have written, the reader will find the same rank attributed to these powers,—the rank of a purely divine gift, not to be attained, increased, or in anywise modified by teaching, only in various ways capable of being concealed or quenched. Understand this thoroughly; know once for all, that a poet on canvas is exactly the same species of creature as a poet in song, and nearly every error in our methods of teaching will be done away with. For who among us now thinks of bringing men up to be poets?—of producing poets by any kind of general recipe or method of cultivation? Suppose even that we see in a youth that which we hope may, in its development, become a power of this kind, should we instantly, supposing that we wanted to make a poet of him, and nothing else, forbid him all quiet, steady, rational labour? Should we force him to perpetual spinning of new crudities out of his boyish brain, and set before him, as the only objects of his study, the laws of versification which criticism has supposed itself to discover in the works of previous writers? Whatever gifts the boy had, would much be likely to come of them so treated? unless, indeed, they were so great as to break through all such snares of falsehood and vanity, and build their own foundation in spite of us; whereas if, as in cases numbering millions against units, the natural gifts were too weak to do this, could anything come of such training but utter inanity and spuriousness of the whole man? But if we had sense, should we not rather restrain and bridle the first flame of invention in early youth, heaping material on it as one would on the first sparks and tongues of a fire which we desired to feed into greatness? Should we not educate the whole intellect into general strength, and all the affections into warmth and honesty, and look to heaven for the rest? This, I say, we should have sense enough to do, in order to produce a poet in words: but, it being required to produce a poet on canvas, what is our way of setting to work? We begin, in all probability, by telling the youth of fifteen or sixteen, that Nature is full of faults, and that he is to improve her; but that Raphael is perfection, and that the more he copies Raphael the better; that after much copying of Raphael, he is to try what he can do himself in a Raphaelesque, but yet original, manner: that is to say, he is to try to do something very clever, all out of his own head, but yet this clever something is to be properly subjected to Raphaelesque rules, is to have a principal light occupying one-seventh of its space, and a principal shadow occupying one-third of the same; that no two people's heads in the picture are to be turned the same way, and that all the personages represented are to possess ideal beauty of the highest order, which ideal beauty consists partly in a Greek outline of nose, partly in proportions expressible in decimal fractions between the lips and chin; but partly also in that degree of improvement which the youth of sixteen is to bestow upon God's work in general. This I say is the kind of teaching which through various channels, Royal Academy lecturings, press criticisms, public enthusiasm, and not least by solid weight of gold, we give to our young men. And we wonder we have no painters!

But we do worse than this. Within the last few years some sense of the real tendency of such teaching has appeared in some of our younger painters. It only *could* appear in the younger ones, our older men having become familiarised with the false system, or else having passed through it and forgotten it, not well knowing the degree of harm they had sustained. This sense appeared, among our youths,—increased,—matured into rsesolute action. Necessarily, to exist at all, it needed the support both of strong instincts and of considerable self-confidence, otherwise it must at once have been borne down by the weight of general authority and received canon law. Strong instincts are apt to make men strange, and rude; self-confidence, however well founded, to give much of what they do or say the appearance of impertinence. Look at the self-confidence of Wordsworth, stiffening every other sentence of his prefaces into defiance; there is no more of it than was needed to enable him to do his work, yet it is not a little ungraceful here and there. Suppose this stubbornness and self-trust in a youth, labouring in an art of which the executive part is confessedly to be best learnt from masters, and we shall hardly wonder that much of his work has a certain awkwardness and stiffness in it, or that he should be regarded with disfavour by many, even the most temperate, of the judges trained in the system he was breaking through, and with utter contempt and reprobation by the envious and the dull. Consider, farther, that the particular system to be overthrown was, in the present case, one of which the main characteristic was the pursuit of beauty at the expense of manliness and truth; and it will seem likley, *à priori*, that the men intended successfully to resist the influence of such a system should be endowed with little natural sense of beauty, and thus rendered dead to the temptation it presented. Summing up these conditions, there is surely little cause for surprise that pictures painted, in a temper of resistance, by exceedingly young men, of stubborn instincts and positive self-trust, and with little natural perception of beauty, should not be calculated, at the first glance, to win us from works enriched by plagiarism, polished by convention, invested with all the attractiveness of artificial grace, and recommended to our respect by established authority.

We should however, on the other hand, have anticipated, that in proportion to the strength of character required for the effort, and to the absence of distracting sentiments, whether respect for precedent, or affection for ideal beauty, would be the energy exhibited in the pursuit of the special objects which the youths proposed to themselves, and their success in attaining them.

All this has actually been the case, but in a degree which it would have been impossible to anticipate. That two youths, of the respective ages of eighteen and twenty, should have conceived for themselves a totally independent and sincere method of study, and enthusiastically persevered in it against every kind of dissuasion and opposition, is strange enough; that in the third or fourth year of their efforts they should have produced works in many parts not inferior to the best of Albert Durer, this is perhaps not less strange. But the loudness and universality of the howl which the common critics of the press have raised against them, the utter absence of all generous help or encouragement from those who can both measure their toil and appreciate their success, and the shrill, shallow laughter of those who can do neither the one nor the other,—these are strangest of all—unimaginable unless they had been experienced.

And as if these were not enough, private malice is at work against them, in its own small, slimy way. The very day after I had written my second letter to the *Times* in the defence of the Pre-Raphaelites, I received an anonymous letter respecting one of them, from some person apparently hardly capable of spelling, and about as vile a specimen of petty malignity as ever blotted paper. I think it well that the public should know

this, and so get some insight into the sources of the spirit which is at work against these men—how first roused it is difficult to say, for one would hardly have thought that mere eccentricity in young artists could have excited an hostility so determined and so cruel;—hostility which hesitated at no assertion, however impudent. That of the "absence of perspective" was one of the most curious pieces of the hue and cry which began with the *Times,* and died away in feeble maundering in the Art Union; I contradicted it in the *Times*—I here contradict it directly for the second time. There was not a single error in perspective in three out of the four pictures in question. But if otherwise, would it have been anything remarkable in them? I doubt, if, with the exception of the pictures of David Roberts, there were one architectural drawing in perspective on the walls of the Academy; I never met but with two men in my life who knew enough of perspective to draw a Gothic arch in a retiring plane, so that its lateral dimensions and curvatures might be calculated to scale from the drawing. Our architects certainly do not, and it was but the other day that, talking to one of the most distinguished among them, the author of several most valuable works, I found he actually did not know how to draw a circle in perspective. And in this state of general science our writers for the press take it upon them to tell us, that the forest-trees in Mr. Hunt's *Sylvia,* and the bunches of lilies in Mr. Collins's *Convent Thoughts,* are out of perspective.

It might not, I think, in such circumstances, have been ungraceful or unwise in the Academicians themselves to have defended their young pupils, at least by the contradiction of statements directly false respecting them, and the direction of the mind and sight of the public to such real merit as they possess. If Sir Charles Eastlake, Mulready, Edwin and Charles Landseer, Cope, and Dyce would each of them simply state their own private opinion respecting their paintings, sign it, and publish it, I believe the act would be of more service to English art than anything the Academy has done since it was founded. But as I cannot hope for this, I can only ask the public to give their pictures careful examination, and to look at them at once with the indulgence and the respect which I have endeavoured to show they deserve.

Yet let me not be misunderstood. I have adduced them only as examples of the kind of study which I would desire to see substituted for that of our modern schools, and of singular success in certain characters, finish of detail, and brilliancy of colour. What faculties, higher than imitative, may be in these men, I do not yet venture to say; but I do say, that if they exist, such faculties will manifest themselves in due time all the more forcibly because they have received training so severe. (pp. 16-21)

John Ruskin, "Pre-Raphaelitism," in his Pre-Raphaelitism: Lectures on Architecture & Painting, &c., *J. M. Dent & Co., 1906, pp. 1-48.*

CHRISTINA ROSSETTI

[*In the following poems, Rossetti describes the members of the Pre-Raphaelite Brotherhood shortly before its dissolution.*]

THE P.R.B.

The two Rossettis (brothers they)
And Holman Hunt and John Millais,
With Stephens chivalrous and bland,
And Woolner in a distant land—
In these six men I awestruck see
Embodied the great P.R.B.

D. G. Rossetti offered two
Good pictures to the public view;
Unnumbered ones great John Millais,
And Holman more than I can say.

William Rossetti, calm and solemn,
Cuts up his brethren by the column.
    19 September 1853.

(p. 14)

• • • • •

The P.R.B. is in its decadence:
For Woolner in Australia cooks his chops,
And Hunt is yearning for the land of
Cheops;
    D. G. Rossetti shuns the vulgar optic;
While William M. Rossetti merely lops
    His B's in English disesteemed as Coptic:
Calm Stephens in the twilight smokes his
pipe,
    But long the dawning of his public day;
    And he at last the champion great Millais,
Attaining academic opulence,
    Winds up his signature with A.R.A.
So rivers merge in the perpetual sea;
So luscious fruit must fall when over-ripe;
And so the consummated P.R.B.
    10 November 1853.

(p. 27)

Christina Rossetti, "The P. R. B.: 1" and "The
P. R. B.: 2," in Pre-Raphaelite Writing: An Anthology, *edited by Derek Stanford, Dent, 1973, p.
14, 27.*

WILLIAM HOLMAN HUNT

[*Hunt, one of the founders of the Pre-Raphaelite Brotherhood,
recalls the group's early aspirations and describes the events and
individuals that shaped its history.*]

I commenced *The Eve of St. Agnes* picture on the 6th of February. A double portrait taxed my daylight very much, so that
I had to paint much of this Keats picture by candle-light. . . .
The picture was finished in Millais' studio; we worked together
late through the night for company. His picture was *Cymon
and Iphigenia,* and once, in return for some drapery I did in
his picture, he painted a hand of one of the revellers in mine,
which I can now distinguish by its precise touching, noticed
by me at the time. It is the left hand of the man throwing his
head back towards the spectator.

On the first day of the exhibition . . . , Rossetti came up bois-
terously, and in loud tongue made me feel very confused by
declaring that mine was the best picture of the year. The fact
that it was from Keats made him extra-enthusiastic, for I think
no painter had ever before painted from this wonderful poet,
who then, it may scarcely be credited, was little known. I had
never seen any but the original edition of his work (alas! since
lost by lending). Rossetti frankly asked me to let him call upon
me; before, I had only been on nodding terms with him in the
school. He had always a following of noisy students there, and
these had kept me from approaching him with more than a
nod, except when once I found him perched on some steps
drawing Ghiberte, whom I also studied; that nobody else did
so had given us subject for ten minutes' talk. It was thus *The
Eve of St. Agnes* which first brought the three future Pre-
Raphaelite Brethren into intimate relations.

In a few days more he was in my studio, talking about his
position, his work, and his prospects. He was then greatly
disheartened about his studies from still life, which his master,
Madox Brown, had insisted upon his doing. I had been content
to see F. Madox Brown's works at Westminster Hall with great
silent recognition of the genius in the picture of *The Body of
Harold brought before William the Conqueror,* but Rossetti,
with more leisure, had taken the pains to find him out and
induce the painter to take him as pupil, which he had done on
the terms of a friend. In this way Rossetti had been set, according to all sound rule, to paint still life and to copy a picture.
The repetition he had achieved, but the "*bottles*," which he
dwelt upon to me, tormented his soul beyond power of endurance; and he had turned to Leigh Hunt by letter, asking him
to be good enough to read some of his poems, and tell him
whether he would do well or not to rely upon poetry for his
bread. My namesake had replied in the most polite and complimentary manner about the verses, but he had implored him
for his own sake, if he had any prospect whatever as a painter,
on no account to give it up, for the life of a poet was too
pitiable to be chosen in cool blood, and thus he had been sent
back again to consider painting as his main means of support.
Was it necessary, he asked, to go again to the "bottles"? I
assured him of my great deference to the high judgment of his
master, but ventured to say that, although in all but extraordinary cases I should prescribe the same course to any pupil,
for him I should decide that the object might be gained by
choosing one of his recent designs (seen and admired by Millais
and myself, as they had come round a folio belonging to a
designing club of which we were members)—that this composition should be put upon canvas—that the work should be
taken up first with the still life—that, thus invested with vital
interest as a link in an idea to be developed, it would furnish
him with the exercise needful to prepare his spirit for the essential core of the poem he had to paint. This opinion he
accepted as a suggestion to be at once adopted, and, that I
might explain it in detail, he applied to me for half of the studio
which I was just taking. I agreed to this, and, after a visit
together to Rochester and Blackheath (reading Monckton Milnes'
Life and Letters of Keats on the way), we took possession of
our roughly prepared painting-room (1848). (pp. 478-80)

I gained many advantages by our partnership. Rossetti had then,
perhaps, a greater acquaintance with the poetical literature of
Europe than any living man. His storehouse of treasures seemed
inexhaustible. If he read twice or thrice a long poem, it was
literally at his tongue's end; and he had a voice rarely equalled
for simple recitations. Another gain was in the occasional visits
of F. M. Brown, the painter of the historical frescoes in the
Manchester Town Hall, who kindly gave me advice when he
had ended his counsel to Rossetti, and always explained his
judgment by careful reasoning and anecdote.

The companionship of Rossetti and myself soon brought about
a meeting with Millais, at whose house one night we found a
book of engravings of the frescoes in the Campo Santo at Pisa.
It was probably the finding of this book at this special time
which caused the establishment of the Pre-Raphaelite Brotherhood. Millais, Rossetti, and myself were all seeking for some
sure ground, some starting-point for our art which would be
secure, if it were ever so humble. As we searched through this
book of engravings, we found in them, or thought we found,
that freedom from corruption, pride, and disease for which we
sought. Here there was at least no trace of decline, no con-
ventionality, no arrogance. Whatever the imperfection, the whole
spirit of the art was simple and sincere—was, as Ruskin af-

terwards said, "eternally and unalterably true." Think what a revelation it was to find such work at such a moment, and to recognize it with the triple enthusiasm of our three spirits. If Newton could say of his theory of gravitation, that his conviction of its truth increased tenfold from the moment in which he got one other person to believe in it, was it wonderful that, when we three saw, as it were, in a flash of lightning, this truth of art, it appealed to us almost with the force of a revolution? Neither then nor afterwards did we affirm that there was not much healthy and good art after the time of Raphael; but it appeared to us that afterwards art was so frequently tainted with this canker of corruption that it was only in the earlier work we could find with certainty absolute health. Up to a definite point the tree was healthy; above it, disease began: side by side with life there appeared death. Think how different were the three temperaments which saw this clearly. I may say plainly of myself, that I was a steady and even enthusiastic worker, trained by the long course of early difficulties and opposition . . . , and determined to find the right path for my art. Rossetti, with his spirit alike subtle and fiery, was essentially a proselytizer, sometimes to an almost absurd degree, but possessed alike in his poetry and painting, with an appreciation of beauty of the most intense quality. Millais, again, stood in some respects midway between us, showing a rare combination of extraordinary artistic faculty with an amount of sterling English common-sense. And, moreover, he was in these early days, beyond almost any one with whom I have been acquainted, full of a generous, quick enthusiasm; a spirit on fire with eagerness to seize whatever he saw to be good, which shone out in every line of his face, and made it, as Rossetti once said, look sometimes like the face of an angel. All of us had our qualities, though it does not come within the scope of this paper to analyze them fully. They were such as rather helped than embarrassed us in working together.

"Pre-Raphaelite" was adopted, after some discussion, as a distinctive prefix, though the word had first been used as a term of contempt by our enemies. And as we bound ourselves together, the word "Brotherhood" was suggested by Rossetti as preferable to clique or association. It was in a little spirit of fun that we thus agreed tht Raphael, the Prince of Painters, was the inspiring influence of the art of the day; for we saw that the practice of contemporary painters was as different from that of the master whose example they quoted, as established interest or indifference had ever made the conduct of disciples. It was instinctive prudence, however, which suggested to us that we should use the letters P.R.B., unexplained, on our pictures (after the signature) as the one mark of our union.

The first work that we agreed to do after this was a series of designs for Keats' "Isabella." These were to be executed entirely on our new principles, and subsequently etched for publication. Millais chose as his subject the household of Lorenzo's brothers at meals. Rossetti at first made excuses for procrastination. I did one of Lorenzo at his desk in the warehouse, in order that thus (with Millais' design) the lover's position in the house should be made clear to the spectator from the outset. Though Millais had much oil work on hand which had to be finished in the old style, he was impatient to begin in the new manner, and he announced his determination to paint his design. But his old work still hung about, until we were almost doubtful of the time before sending-in day being sufficient for the task, when suddenly, about November, the whole atmosphere of his studio was changed, and the new white canvas was installed on the easel. Day by day advanced, at a pace beyond all calculation, the picture now known to the whole of

England [*Lorenzo and Isabella*], which I venture to say is the most wonderful painting that any youth still under twenty years of age ever did in the world.

In my studio Rossetti's plan of work promised to do all that was desired. The picture was *The Education of Mary Virgin,* and he had advanced it considerably, but, from his unchecked impatience at difficulties, the interruptions to our work, to mine, as much as to his, were so serious that once I had to go out walking with him to argue that, without more self-restraint on his part, we should certainly lose our chances of appearing, in the same season, in a band with Millais. He took this remonstrance in the best part, and applied himself with new patience to his work, which ultimately possessed in the important parts the most exquisite beauty and grace; he exhibited it subsequently in a gallery in Portland Place. Millais' picture was seen with wonder when finished, and he sold it before his "show" day. My "private view" was without any visitors, but the picture was delivered by myself in the evening, still wet, at the Academy. Before we were admitted to varnish our pictures we learned that they had been hung as pendants to one another in fair places just above the line, and in the *Times* I remember the notice of the exhibition began with two columns of comment upon our pictures as the remarkable feature of the collection. The fact itself was an unexpectedly gratifying testimony to the impression the works had made. On going to the Academy at seven in the morning (to get the longest opportunity, if necessary, for work before the public were admitted at twelve), we were received by many of the members with cordial compliments—some introducing themselves to me for this purpose—but there was an opposing spirit of indignation expressing itself loudly by some artists. (pp. 480-82)

[For the Exhibition the following year] Millais had painted his *Christ in the Home of His Parents,* and my picture was again hung as a pendant to his. While we had been quietly working the hostile feeling against us had shown itself to be wider and more extended. A newspaper had in its gossiping column revealed the meaning of P.R.B., which had been disclosed, through the weakness of Rossetti, to a rank gossiper, and far and near it seemed as if the honour of Raphael was the feeling dearest of all to the bosom of England, and that this we had impiously assailed. The leading journals denounced our works as iniquitous and infamous, and, to make our enormity more shameful in extra-artistic circles, the great Charles Dickens wrote a leading article against Millais' picture in the *Household Words* [see Additional Bibliography]. This was an attack upon the whole of us, and though my picture was not mentioned, for the prejudice excited was more practically damaging to me, since Millais had sold his work, while mine had still the duty to perform of tempting 150 guineas out of the pockets of some admirer or approver, before I could go on with a new work. Sometimes I went to the Exhibition stealthily, hoping to hear some opinion expressed, but as soon as the public arrived at my picture they invariably said, "Oh, this is one of those preposterous Pre-Raphaelite works," and went on to the next without looking again upon the canvas. (p. 484)

The treatment by the Press [grew more fierce]. . . . Our strongest enemy advised that the Academy, having shown our works so far, to prove how atrocious they were, could now, with the approval of the public, depart from their usual rule of leaving each picture on the walls until the end of the season, and take ours down and return them to us. In the schools (as we were told) a professor referred to our works in such terms that the wavering students resorted to the very extreme course of hissing us. The critic before mentioned, finding the pictures still left on the walls, then wrote that, although the *Academy* was dead to the feeling of self-respect which should prompt the Council to act on his advice, there was cause for congratulation in the thought that no gentleman of taste who valued his reputation would purchase such pictures; and, as far as I was concerned, so it seemed, since the post never brought me letters without their containing anonymous insults. There was, indeed, only one paper in London which did not join in the general cry; this was the *Spectator,* the editor of which from the first permitted William Rossetti (the brother of the painter) to defend our cause in his journal. With this exception, the public condemnation of our principle of work was universal, and at this time our cause seemed hopeless. (p. 488)

· · · · ·

Before proceeding further with my story, I should like to give some further idea of the principles of Pre-Raphaelitism, and of the hopes we had of it. In doing so, I would not trench upon the claims of others to explain from their own points of view; but I write, not as a stranger might do, gathering his conclusions from the results, but as one of the accessories before the fact, making his confessions after all his guilty companions as well as himself have had the fullest meed of punishment for their offence. I must return therefore to the studio in Cleveland Street, and give further reminiscences of Rossetti, who came rather gradually to take a retired course, out of my ken, and who can now only be known by his work and words, which give value in the eyes of the world to the records of his friends. (p. 737)

To one who lived with him he showed an inexhaustible store of accomplishments, yet from his uncontrollable temper under the trials of studio work, it was clear that he had been a spoilt child. When, however, his work did not oppress his spirits, when his soul was not tormented by some unhappy angel-model—frightened out of its wits in turn by his fiery impatience—he could not restrain his then happy memory of divine poesy. He had been a student of poetry almost to the exclusion of other pursuits, and he had feasted specially upon the verses of the tre-centists. For Homer he never betrayed great enthusiasm; of the ancients, Catullus was his favourite. He chanted with a voice rich and full of passion, now in the "lingua Toscana," and again in that of the "well of English undefiled." He delighted most in those poems for which the world then had shown but little appreciation. *Sordello* and *Paracelsus* he would give by forty and fifty pages at a time, and, what were more fascinating, the shorter poems of Browning. Then would follow the grand rhetoric from Taylor's *Philip Van Artevelde,* in the scene between the herald and the Court at Ghent with Philip in reply—a scene very much to my taste, with my picture standing on the easel designed to show the spirit of justice, inevitable in the fulness of time, on all such as being strong scourged the weak, and being rich robbed the poor, and "changed the sweat of Nature's brow to blood." Then would come the pathetic strains of W. B. Scott's "Rosabell" (which later furnished Rossetti with the subject called *Found*). These, and there were countless other examples, all showed a wide field of interest as to poetic schools.

But the studying of them had never led him to profess any respect for natural science, or to evince any regard for the remote stages of creative development or the lower steps of human progress. He regarded such studies as altogether foreign to poetry. The language used in early times to describe the appearances of nature he accepted as the exclusive and ever-

sufficient formulæ. The modern discoveries of science therefore had no charms for him; neither had the changed conditions of the people who were to be touched by art any claim for special consideration. They had no right to be different from the people of Dante's time, if I may use my own words to epitomize his meaning. (pp. 738-39)

We frequently talked over scientific and historical matters, for my previous reading and experience had led me to love them and to regard them as of the greatest poetic and pictorial importance for modern art; for then, as now, I concluded that the appeal we made could be strengthened by using the instruments of the age which human intellect had discovered. . . . [Geological and astronomical] studies seemed to me full of poetic suggestions. But Rossetti despised such inquiries. "What could it matter," he said, "whether the earth moved round the sun, or the sun travelled about the earth?" And in the question about the antiquity of man and his origin he refused to be interested. It would be beside the mark to repeat this in a narrative, which is simply professional and not personal, if it did not lead up to the view which he at that time expressed—that attention to chronological costume, to the types of the different races of men, to climatic features or influences, were of no value in a painter's work; and that therefore Oriental proprieties in the treatment of Scriptural subjects were calculated to destroy the poetic nature of a design. He would instance Horace Vernet's

An 1852 sketch of John Everett Millais by Dante Gabriel Rossetti. Birmingham Museum and Art Gallery.

pictures, painted in the East, *Rebecca giving Eleazer to Drink,* and some others, as proofs of the correctness of his opinion. But I used to meet this by insisting that Vernet, though a remarkably skilful composer and executant, was not, and could not, under any conditions or system, be anything but dull, except to the dull, and was altogether destitute of every spark of poetic fire. This Rossetti admitted, although he still held by his principle, to be fought over with fresh weapons another time. It was the question of the value of my idea, carried out five years after, to go to Jerusalem to paint sacred subjects, which brought the discussion to a head. It was profitable to try to solve such problems, although we both agreed, when it came to the last, that a man's work would be the reflex of the living image in his own mind of the idea treated, and not the icy double of the facts themselves.

While we differed so far, it may be seen that we were never, what often we have been called, *realists.* I think the art would have ceased to have the slightest interest for any one of the three painters concerned, had the object been only to make a representation, elaborate or unelaborate, of a fact in Nature. Independent of the consideration that the task would put out of operation the faculty making man "how like a god," it seemed then, as it does now, that a mere imitator gradually comes to see Nature so claylike and meaningless—so like only to what one sees when illness brings a heavy cloud before the eyes—that his pictures or statues make a spectator feel, not how much more beautiful the world is than she seemed before, but only that she is a tedious infliction, or even an oppressive nightmare.... On one other point there has been misapprehension, which it is now time to correct. In agreeing to use the utmost elaboration in painting our first pictures, we never meant more than that the practice was essential for training the eye and the hand of the young artist: we should never have admitted that the relinquishment of this habit of work by a matured painter would make him less of a Pre-Raphaelite. I can say this the better now because, although it is not true, as is often said, that my detail is microscopic, I have retained later than either of my companions the penciling of a student. When I take to large brushes, and enrich my canvases with impasto, it will imply that the remnant of my life would not suffice to enable me to express my thoughts in other fashion, and that I have in my own opinion obtained enough from severe discipline to trust myself again to the self-confident handling of my youth, to which I have already referred. If I leave uncontradicted the declaration that I have abandoned Pre-Raphaelitism, it will be because, after prolonged admiration of the power of the enemy to incite prejudice against truth by a catchword, I have at last become worldly wise enough to keep my own counsel.

Perhaps, in order to throw light upon the understanding of Pre-Raphaelitism among ourselves at the beginning, I may be excused wandering a little from the idiosyncrasies of one to the other, and to the different facts which illustrate them. Trusting to this indulgence, I still linger in the joint studio to explain the nature of the talk we had there on the subject of our future operations and influence. We spoke of the improvement of design in household objects, furniture, curtains, and interior decorations, and dress; of how we would exercise our skill, as the early painters had done, not in one branch of art only, but in all. For sculpture, Rossetti in private expressed little regard; he professed admiration for the minds of many men engaged in it, but he could scarcely understand their devotion to work which seemed in modern hands so cold and meaningless, and which was so limited in its power of illustration. He confessed,

however, that so far he had not thought of it enough, and admitted that it ought to be undertaken by painters, if only because the power of drawing on the flat seemed much wanting among the men who worked so tamely in clay and marble. Architecture also he recognized as the proper work of the painter, who, learning the principles of construction from Nature herself, could apply them to the forming and decoration of the stone, iron and wood he had to deal with. Music he regarded as positively offensive. When we obtained recognition, each of us was to have a suite of studios attached to his house; some for working in ourselves in divers branches of art; some for showing our productions to admirers when we were too busily engaged to be disturbed. Worthy pupils we were also to introduce by such means, and we should be able thus to extend our usefulness and to make art take its proper place. All this I concurred in, only I once expressed some curiosity to know how the due appreciation should be counted on from a people so committed to the idea of subdivision of labour, and so far from exhibiting Locke's spirit, never being ashamed to confess his ignorance. This Rossetti dismissed to the winds as an idle fear, asking me if I could not understand that there were hundreds of young aristocrats and millionaires growing up who would be only too glad to get due direction how to make the country glorious as Greece and Italy had been! I was fain to hope that his view was the correct one, especially as with his father's experience as a professor among the *élite* of the land, I was bound to admit he was better able than I was to judge of the possibilities, and I was glad to encourage the belief that people would in time know how to spend their money worthily. (pp. 739-42)

[To] complete the picture of Rossetti, I should say that frequently he would leave his day's appointed task to engage himself with some design or poem that occupied his thoughts. When he had once sat down and was immersed in the effort to express his purpose, and the difficulties had to be wrestled with, his tongue was hushed, he remained fixed and inattentive to all that went on about him; he rocked himself to and fro, and at times he moaned lowly, or hummed for a brief minute, as though telling off some idea. All this while he peered intently before him, looking hungry and eager, and passing by in his regard any one who came before him, as if not seen at all. Then he would often get up and walk out of the room without saying a word. Years afterwards, when he became stout, and men, with a good deal of reason, found a resemblance in him to the bust of Shakespeare at Stratford-upon-Avon, and still later, when he had outgrown this resemblance, it seemed to me that it was in his early days only that the soul within had been truly seen in his face. In these early days, with all his headstrongness, and a certain want of consideration, his life within was untainted to an exemplary degree, and he worthily rejoiced in the poetic atmosphere of the sacred and spiritual dreams that then encircled him, however some of his noisy demonstrations at the time might hinder this from being recognized by a hasty judgment.

Another aspect of our Brotherhood must not be passed over, though it lasted but a short time, and becoming meaningless was abandoned with good reason. It is the social one. Rossetti, as I have said before, was a proselytizer. He was ready to believe, and to insist upon the belief, that others should adopt our course, and those within our daily range, whom for one reason or another he cared for, he at once enrolled as Pre-Raphaelite Brothers. James Collinson had been a meek fellow-student; painstaking he was in all his drawings, and accurate in a sense, but tame and sleepy, and so were all the figures he drew. The Apollo Belvidere, the Laocoon Group, the Wrestlers, the Dancing Faun, and the Drunken Gentleman of that race, all seemed to belong to one somnolent family. No one a year later could have trusted his memory to say when he had been and when he had not been in the school, so successfully had he aimed at avoiding to disturb any one in any way. It was a surprise to all when in the year 1848 he appeared in the Exhibition with a picture called *The Charity Boy's Début*. It was a good idea to represent the shyness of a poor boy on his appearing before his family in the uniform of his parish, and although the invention did not go far beyond the initial conception, the pencilling was phenomenal throughout. It transpired that he had roused himself up of late to enter the Roman Church, and that thus inspirited he had made the further effort to paint this picture. It was natural for all the students to blame themselves for having ignored Collinson, but Rossetti went further, and declared that "Collinson was a born stunner," and at once struck up an intimate friendship with him. When the Pre-Raphaelite Brotherhood was inaugurated he at once enrolled Collinson as one who wanted only the enthusiasm which we had, to make him a great force in the battle, and accordingly he was told that he had to put the secret initials on his works, to attend our monthly meetings, and to receive us in his turn. Whether we were at his place in the Polygon, with a dragoness of a landlady six feet in height to provide quite a conventional entertainment—for he still had a liberal allowance from home—or at our Bohemian repasts in Cleveland Street, or elsewhere, he invariably fell asleep at the beginning, and had to be waked up at the conclusion of the noisy evening to receive our salutations. In figure he was far from being like the fat boy in *Pickwick,* for he was of very light weight and small measurement. He never could see the fun of anything, and I fear we did not make his life more joyful. (pp. 742-43)

The experience of trying to make men Pre-Raphaelite Brothers against their nature and will, was not an encouraging one. W. M. Rossetti had at first thought of taking to graphic art, but he had given up the study. Outside of the enrolled body, comprising with the five already mentioned, F. G. Stephens and T. Woolner (the latter had gone to Australia), were several artists of real calibre and enthusiasm, who were working diligently with our views guiding them. W. H. Deverell, Charles Collins, and Arthur Hughes may be named. It was a question whether any of these should be elected. It was already evident that to have authority to put the mystic monogram upon their paintings could confer no benefit on men striving to make a position. We ourselves even determined for a time to discontinue the flouting of this red rag before the eyes of infuriate John Bull, and we decided it was better to let our converts be known only by their works, and so nominally Pre-Raphaelitism ceased to be. We agreed to resume the open profession of it later, but the time has not yet come. I often read in print that I am now the only Pre-Raphaelite. Yet I can't use the distinguishing letters, for I have no "B." (pp. 744-45)

William Holman Hunt, "The Pre-Raphaelite Brotherhood: A Fight for Art I" and "The Pre-Raphaelite Brotherhood: A Fight for Art II," in The Contemporary Review, *Vol. XLIX, Nos. CCXCII and CCXCIII, April and May, 1886, pp. 471-88; 737-50.*

WILLIAM MICHAEL ROSSETTI

[*Rossetti was an original member of the Pre-Raphaelite Brotherhood. In this excerpt from a memoir of his brother, Dante Gabriel Rossetti, he describes the activities and aims of the group. For additional material by William Michael Rossetti, see excerpts below.*]

Some writers have said that Rossetti was the originator of Præraphaelitism. This ignores the just claims of Hunt and Millais, which I regard as co-equal with his. Rossetti had an abundance of ideas, pictorial and also literary, and was fuller of "notions" than the other two, and had more turn for proselytizing and "pronunciamentos"; but he was not at all more resolute in wanting to do something good which should also be something new. He was perhaps the most defiant of the three; and undoubtedly a kind of adolescent defiance, along with art-sympathies highly developed in one direction, and unduly or even ignorantly restricted in others, played a part, and no small part, in Præraphaelitism. But Hunt, if less strictly defiant, was still more tough, and Millais was all eagerness for the fray—"longing to be at 'em," and to show his own mettle. The fact is that not one of the three could have done much as an innovator without the other two. A bond of mutual support was essential, and an isolated attempt might have fizzed off as a mere personal eccentricity. As it was, Præraphaelitism proved to be very up-hill work. It was more abused, as being the principle of a few men in unison, than it would have been if exemplified by one of them only; but the very abuse was the beginning of its triumph. Any one of them, if acting by himself, might have been recognized as a man of genius; he would hardly have become a power in art. If the invention of "the Præraphaelite Brotherhood" was a craze, it was a craze spiced with a deal of long-headedness. Some method in that sort of madness. (p. 128)

As soon as the Præraphaelite Brotherhood was formed it became a focus of boundless companionship, pleasant and touching to recall. We were really like brothers, continually together, and confiding to one another all experiences bearing upon questions of art and literature, and many affecting us as individuals. We dropped using the term "Esquire" on letters, and substituted "P.R.B." I do not exaggerate in saying that every member of the fraternity was just as much intent upon furthering the advance and promoting the interests of his "Brothers" as his own. There were monthly meetings, at the houses or studios of the various members in succession; occasionally a moonlight walk or a night on the Thames. Beyond this, but very few days can have passed in a year when two or more P.R.B.'s did not foregather for one purpose or another. The only one of us who could be regarded as moderately well off, living *en famille* on a scale of average comfort, was Millais; others were struggling or really poor. All that was of no account. We had our thoughts, our unrestrained converse, our studies, aspirations, efforts, and actual doings; and for every P.R.B. to drink a cup or two of tea or coffee, or a glass or two of beer, in the company of other P.R.B.'s, with or without the accompaniment of tobacco (without it for Dante Rossetti, who never smoked at all), was a heart-relished luxury, the equal of which the flow of long years has not often presented, I take it, to any one of us. Those were the days of youth; and each man in the company, even if he did not project great things of his own, revelled in poetry or sunned himself in art. Hunt, to my thinking, was the most sagacious talker; Woolner the most forceful and entertaining; Dante Rossetti the most intellectual. Such men could not be mere plodders in conversation: but all—to their credit be it spoken—were perfectly free-and-easy, and wholly alien from anything approaching to affectation, settled self-display, or stilted "tall talk." And this holds good of every member of the Brotherhood. (pp. 133-34)

Had the Præraphaelite Brotherhood any ulterior aim beyond that of producing good works of art? Yes, and No. Assuredly it had the aim of developing such *ideas* as are suited to the medium of fine art, and of bringing the arts of form into general unison with what is highest in other arts, especially poetry. Likewise the aim of showing by contrast how threadbare were the pretensions of most painters of the day, and how incapable they were of constituting or developing any sort of School of Art worthy of the name. In the person of two at least of its members, Hunt and Collinson, it had also a definite relation to a Christian, and not a pagan or latitudinarian, line of thought. On the other hand, the notion that the Brotherhood, as such, had anything whatever to do with particular movements in the religious world—whether Roman Catholicism, Anglican Tractarianism, or what not—is totally, and, to one who formed a link in its composition, even ludicrously, erroneous. To say [as Esther Wood does in her *Dante Rossetti and the Pre Raphaelite Movement*] that Præraphaelitism was part of "the ever-rising protest and rebellion of our century against artificial authority," as in the cases of "the French Revolution" and Wordsworth and Darwin, etc., is not indeed untrue, but is far too vague to account for anything. Again, the so-called German Præraphaelites—such as Schnorr, Overbeck, and Cornelius—were in no repute with the young British artists. They did, however, admire very much certain designs by Fuhrich from the Legend of St. Genevieve. Neither was Ruskin their inciter, though it is true that Hung had read and laid to heart in 1847 the first volume of *Modern Painters*, the only thing then current as Ruskin's work. I do not think any other P.R.B. (with the possible exception of Collinson) had, up to 1848 or later, read him at all. That the Præraphaelites valued moral and spiritual ideas as an important section of the ideas germane to fine art is most true, and not one of them was in the least inclined to do any work of a gross, lascivious, or sensual description; but neither did they limit the province of art to the spiritual or the moral. I will therefore take it upon me to say that the bond of union among the Members of the Brotherhood was really and simply this—1, To have genuine ideas to express; 2, to study Nature attentively, so as to know how to express them; 3, to sympathize with what is direct and serious and heartfelt in previous art, to the exclusion of what is conventional and self-parading and learned by rote; and 4, and most indispensable of all, to produce thoroughly good pictures and statues. (pp. 134-35)

> *William Michael Rossetti, "The Præraphaelite Brotherhood," in* Dante Gabriel Rossetti: His Family-Letters, Vol. I, *edited by William Michael Rossetti, Roberts Brothers, 1895, pp. 125-44.*

THE *GERM* AND THE *OXFORD AND CAMBRIDGE MAGAZINE*

WILLIAM MICHAEL ROSSETTI

[*Rossetti, editor of the* Germ, *wrote the following sonnet as a declaration of the Pre-Raphaelite Brotherhood's desire to explore personal experience and express truth. The sonnet was written in 1850 for publication on the cover of the* Germ. *For additional material by Rossetti, see excerpts above and below.*]

> When whoso merely hath a little thought
> Will plainly think the thought which is in him,—
>   Not imaging another's bright or dim,
> Not mangling with new words what others taught;

When whoso speaks, from having either sought
 Or only found,—will speak, nor just to skim
 A shallow surface with words made and trim,
But in that very speech the matter brought:
Be not too keen to cry—'So this is all!—
 A thing I might myself have thought as well,
 But would not say it, for it was not worth!'
 Ask: 'Is this truth?' For is it still to tell
 That, be the theme a point or the whole earth,
Truth is a circle, perfect, great or small?

> *William Michael Rossetti, in a poem in* Pre-Raphaelite Writing: An Anthology, *edited by Derek Stanford, Dent, 1973, p. 60.*

JOHN TUPPER

[*An associate of the Pre-Raphaelite Brotherhood and a contributor to the* Germ, *Tupper wrote this statement of the periodical's purpose for publication in its third issue. For further material by Tupper, see poem below.*]

Of the little worthy the name of writing that has ever been written upon the principles of Art, (of course excepting that on the mere mechanism), a very small portion is by Artists themselves; and that is so scattered, that one scarcely knows where to find the ideas of an Artist except in his pictures.

With a view to obtain the thoughts of Artists, upon Nature as evolved in Art, in another language besides their *own proper* one, this Periodical has been established. Thus, then, it is not open to the conflicting opinions of all who handle the brush and palette, nor is it restricted to actual practitioners; but is intended to enunciate the principles of those who, in the true spirit of Art, enforce a rigid adherence to the simplicity of Nature either in Art or Poetry, and consequently regardless whether emanating from practical Artists, or from those who have studied nature in the Artist's School.

Hence this work will contain such original Tales (in prose or verse), Poems, Essays, and the like, as may seem conceived in the spirit, or with the intent, of exhibiting a pure and unaffected style, to which purpose analytical Reviews of current Literature—especially Poetry—will be introduced; as also illustrative Etchings, one of which latter, executed with the utmost care and completeness, will appear, in each number. (p. 246)

> *John Tupper, in an extract in* The Germ: A Pre-Raphaelite Little Magazine, *edited by Robert Stahr Hosmon, University of Miami Press, 1970, p. 246.*

JOHN TUPPER

[*This humorous elegy on the demise of the* Germ *was written in 1851 and is here reprinted from William Michael Rossetti's edition of his brother's letters. In a footnote, Rossetti explains that "Sloshua" in the last stanza refers to Sir Joshua Reynolds, whose style the Pre-Raphaelite Brotherhood considered "hasty, washy, indeterminate," or "sloshy." For additional material by Tupper, see excerpt above.*]

> Dedicated to the P.R.B. on the Death of
> The Germ,
> otherwise known as Art and Poetry.
>
> Bring leaves of yew to intertwine
> With 'leaves' that evermore are dead,
> Those leaves as pallid-hued as you
>   Who wrote them never to be read:

And let them hang across a thread
Of funeral-hemp, that, hanging so,
Made vocal if a wind should blow,
    Their requiem shall be anthemèd.

Ah rest, dead leaves!—Ye *cannot* rest
Now ye are in your second state;
    Your first was rest so perfect, fate
Denies you what ye then possessed.
For you, was not a world of strife,
    And seldom were ye seen of men:
If death be the reverse of life,
    You never will have peace again.

Come, Early Christians, bring a knife,
    And cut these woful pages down:
    Ye would not have them haunt the
town
Where butter or where cheese is rife!
    No, make them in a foolscap-crown
For all whose inexperience utter
    Believes High Art can once go down
Without considerable butter.

Or cut them into little squares
    To curl the long locks of those Brothers
Præraphaelite who have long hairs—
    Tremendous long, compared with
others.
As dust should still return to dust,
    The P.R.B. shall say its prayers
That come it will or come it must—

A time *Sordello* shall be read,
    And arguments be clean abolished,
And sculpture punched upon the head,
    And mathematics quite demolished;
And *Art and Poetry* instead
    Come out without a word of prose in,
And all who paint as Sloshua did
    Have all their sloshy fingers frozen.

(pp. 156-57)

John Tupper, in a poem in Dante Gabriel Rossetti:
His Family-Letters, Vol. I, *edited by William Michael Rossetti, Roberts Brothers, 1895, pp. 156-57.*

JAMES ASHCROFT NOBLE

[*In this excerpt from his introduction to an 1898 American reprint
of the* Germ, *Noble discusses significant works first published in
the magazine.*]

Most cultivated people of this generation have heard of, but
comparatively few have seen, the solitary volume of a little
magazine called *The Germ*, which was, during its short life,
the organ of a band of young art workers, who were destined
not only to become the founders of a new pictorial school, but
to exert a diffused yet very recognisable influence over the
entire region in which the artistic spirit can make itself at home.
These youthful revolutionaries—one of the most active of whom
was still in his teens, while others had only just left them
behind—had become convinced that modern traditions had led
painters away from the only true principle and the only worthy
practice of their art: that accepted conventions had taken the
place of truths of nature; that painting had therefore become
more of a handicraft and less of an inspiration; and that to find
examples of veracious and noble workmanship it was necessary
to go back to the men who were immediate predecessors of
Raphael, and whose work remained as the precious memorial
of a time when art had not ceased to be simple, sincere, and

religious. This return to mediæval antiquity suggested a name
for the reforming band, which soon became known to the world
at large as the Pre-Raphaelite Brotherhood, and to the initiated
as the P. R. B. The original Brotherhood was a company of
seven, consisting of five painters—William Holman Hunt, Dante
Gabriel Rossetti, John Everett Millais, James Collinson, and
Frederic George Stephens; one sculptor, Thomas Woolner; and
one youth who had not then entered upon any definite career,
William Michael Rossetti. Reformers are necessarily propagandists, and it would have been strange if the almost religious
ardour of the Brotherhood had not sought for some medium
of appeal to the outside unregenerate world. In a day of newspapers and reviews a periodical publication of some kind seemed
the most natural vehicle of utterance; and at the suggestion of
one or more of the Brothers—Dante Rossetti being the prime
mover—it was resolved to set on foot a small magazine, in
which the seven, and those who were in harmony with them,
should speak their message and give some indication of the
practical outcome of it. The magazine was to be the organ and,
in the main, the production of the Brethren alone, among whom
were to be divided the hypothetical profits which, it is needless
to say, never became actual; and while others were to be freely
welcomed as contributors, they were only to be regarded as
outsiders—artistic proselytes of the gate.... The approved
title, *The Germ,* testified at once to the modesty and to the
assured confidence of the Brotherhood. It was a little thing, a
seed cast into the ground, but cast there in full belief that it
would germinate, becoming, perchance, in after-days a great
tree, in whose fruit men might delight and in whose shade they
might rest. This significance was, however, hidden from the
crowd; and there is a legend to the effect that some careless
Gallio, reading the title on the wrapper as he lounged in a
bookseller's shop, did not even recognise the word, but pronounced it in a questioning sort of way as *gurm,* with a hard
g, which pronunciation was humorously adopted by two or
three of the most immediately concerned—a fact which must
have supplied a foundation for the report that it was originally
an affectation of the Brotherhood instead of the accidental error
of an alien.... When it is said that each number contained
forty-eight closely-printed large octavo pages of letterpress and
was illustrated with an etching, it will be very clear to those
having practical experience of such matters that the inevitably
small sale made the continued existence of the magazine, save
as a costly hobby, altogether impossible: and the four issues,
which when bound make a somewhat slender volume, were
all that appeared. It had, however, found its public—its "audience fit, though few,"—had done its work, and—it may be
added without exaggeration—had in a way made its mark. As
the first, and indeed the only, official manifesto or *apologia*
of Pre-Raphaelitism, it has a place in the history both of English
literature and English art; but apart from its propagandist aim,
which indeed, eludes rather than importunes recognition, it has
a permanent interest and value as a storehouse of the early
tentative experiments in critical thought and creative work of
young minds who have, since its day, in many ways impressed
the world.

The main supports of the undertaking were undoubtedly three
members of a richly-endowed family—Dante Gabriel, William
Michael, and Christine Rossetti. To the first, as has already
been said, the original idea of *The Germ* was almost certainly
due; the second acted as its editor throughout; and the third
added much to its value by contributing, under the pen-name
of Ellen Alleyn, a number of tenderly beautiful poems, in which
old chords of emotion were struck in such a way as to make
them seem new. In the four numbers there are fifty-one con-

tributions, and of these twenty-six are from the pens of the two brothers and the sister; seven being by D. G. Rossetti, twelve by Mr. W. M. Rossetti, and seven by Miss Rossetti, a series of six "Sonnets for Pictures" by the first-named being counted not as six but as one.

By far the greater number of the twenty-six Rossetti contributions are poems, a fact which betokens a keener instinct for creative than for controversial activity. Indeed, the magazine differs totally and very pleasantly from the typical sectarian organ—which is, as a rule, too polemical for endurance by non-polemical people—in addressing itself mainly to those who were already more or less sympathetic, and addressing even them, not in logical hortative fashion, but allusively through images of the imagination rather than mere conceptions of the intellect. To sweep away the malaria of false tradition by storms of sad or angry rhetoric, was not a course which seemed to commend itself to the writers in *The Germ.* They chose instead to endeavour after the purification of the atmosphere by charging it with a new emotional element, which would come not with observation, so that a man might say, "Lo, here," or "Lo, there," but should slowly transform the air of the world of art and make it once more healthful. One poem of those just mentioned, the sonnet by Mr. William Rossetti printed on the cover of each number [see excerpt above], is undoubtedly a setting forth of the unavoidably militant intellectual attitude of the Brotherhood; but there is a largeness and universality in it which forbids us to regard it as a party utterance. . . .

The writer of this sonnet was not only the editor of *The Germ;* he was also by far its most industrious contributor. His poems have subtlety and freshness of emotion and graceful firmness of handling; but they lack impressive individuality, and we recognise in them family features rather than personal expression. Already, however, Mr. W. M. Rossetti was showing his bent towards criticism; and four reviews by him—one published in each number of the magazine—if not in themselves remarkable, must be pronounced extraordinary work for a youth of eighteen, writing in the year of 1850, when in the critical region the Philistines were supreme. The books noticed were *The Bothie* of Arthur Hugh Clough; the earliest volume of Mr. Matthew Arnold's verse; Mr. Cayley's now forgotten poem, *Sir Reginald Mohun;* and the *Christmas Eve and Easter Day* of Mr. Browning. In all these criticisms one notices a studious thoroughness, an obvious attempt to catch the informing vital quality of the work under examination, which must have brought a feeling of relief and enlargement of those who were getting somewhat weary of the rough-and-ready generalising and classifying style of the literary tasters of the quarterly reviews. Perhaps the most interesting of the four was the last, which, though nominally a review of Mr. Browning's companion studies of the spiritual life, was devoted to a defence of the poet's general manner, and to an exposition of the doctrine—then little understood in England—that in all true art there is such absolute union and interdependence of matter and form as to render it impossible rightly to estimate the latter apart from the former. It was then given to but few to see clearly that to judge any style *per se,* and declare it good or bad, is always more or less absurd, just as it is absurd to judge of a garment without consideration of the person for whom or the use for which it is intended; indeed, in the case of style the absurdity is greater, for it is more than the garment of thought—it is, or ought to be, its very body, its visible incarnation. Therefore, argued the young critic, "appropriateness of treatment to subject . . . lies at the root of all controversy on style; this is the last and the whole test. . . . The question of style (manner) being neces-

sarily subordinate to that of subject (matter), it is not for the reader to dispute with the author on his mode of rendering, provided that should be accepted as embodying (within the bounds of grammatical logic), the intention preconceived." It will at once be seen how directly this doctrine, here applied only to literature, bears upon the pictorial methods of the Brotherhood; so directly that it might have been meant to meet some of the most popular objections to their work. Of course it does not cover the whole ground of the Pre-Raphaelite controversy, for satisfying completeness in the presentation of an artistic motive is never absolute but always relative, one truth having to yield to another which has a more insistent claim; but it meets the conventional sneer against the ugliness, the awkwardness, the crudity, the hundred sins of which the Pre-Raphaelites were supposed to be guilty, by the demand, which it is impossible to set aside as irrelevant, that their achievement should be judged by the measure of adequacy with which it realised its intention. That the intention might itself be unworthy was indeed possible; but to decide this an appeal must be made to a higher and finer criticism than was at that day current.

The subordination of manner to matter, of form to substance, which is implicity hinted at in this review was explicitly and much more unguardedly insisted on in two papers entitled "The Subject in Art," which were contributed to the first and third numbers of *The Germ* by Mr. John Lucas Tupper, a relative of Mr. Tupper the printer, . . . but unconnected with the popular writer and so-called poet of that name. He died in middle-age in the year 1879, and in a record of his work, written shortly after his decease, I find it stated that "his mind, in matters of art, was peculiarly scientific" a criticism amply borne out by evidence which these papers provide. The literary style of them is bald, inflexible, and even involved, resembling in many ways the style of Bishop Butler; but when the thought is once apprehended, it is seen to have the systematic logical coherence which belongs to the scientific treatment of a theme. One point is immediately made plain, that to the writer the subject is in Art almost everything; that at any rate it is the one thing which supplies us with a standard by which to award artistic precedence. "Works of Fine Art," we are told,

> delight us by the interest the objects they depict excite in the beholder, just as those objects in nature would excite his interest; if by any association of ideas in the one case, by the same in the other, without reference to the representations being other than the objects they represent. . . . At the same time, it is not disallowed that a subsequent pleasure may and does result upon reflecting that the objects contemplated were the result of human ingenuity.

As these sentences are taken from an article to which, among the prose contributions to *The Germ,* the place of honour is given, it must be taken as a sort of official utterance: and we are compelled by it to regard the Pre-Raphaelite movement as primarily intellectual and moral rather than purely artistic. Art, we are told, consists of the ingenious representation of natural objects, and the main aim of the representation is to excite the same interest and arouse the same emotions which would be excited and aroused by the objects themselves, a quite subsidiary interest being allowed to inhere in the "ingenuity" of the representation. Such a theory sounds appallingly prosaic and mechanical. It is certainly a natural outcome, not of the art temperament which thinks of creation and craftsmanship alone, and cares for nothing beyond the perfect embodiment of its conceptions; but of the grave ethical mood which regards pencil and pigment as moral agencies to be used just in the same way that the preacher uses written or spoken words. Merely "decorative works," howsoever satisfying they may be to the hunger after beauty, have no word to speak either to the conscience or to the reflective intellect; and the writer is therefore consistent in declaring of them that they "are not Fine Art at all." He ignores and really seems unable to understand the possibility of finding elevated enjoyment in the contemplation of colour as colour, or form as form, and even goes so far as to assert that the first idea suggested by a painting of dead game or of cut fruit is that it is a representation of "something to eat"; a view of the matter which would seem strange to most of us wheresoever encountered, but strangest of all, surely, in an essay written by a painter bent on unfolding the scope and purpose of his art.

I draw attention to the extravagances not for the sterile purpose of holding up to ridicule the crudities of some of the earlier disciples of Pre-Raphaelitism, but because there could be no stronger testimony to the faith of the Brotherhood in the central truth of their doctrine than the calm simplicity with which they allowed it to be pushed to extremes of application that could not fail to be stumbling-blocks in the way of those who were asked to receive it. Such deliverances are also worth quoting for another reason. Pre-Raphaelitism is vaguely identified in many minds with the dogma embodied in the familiar formula "Art for Art's sake"; and this essay of Mr. Tupper exhibits more strongly, though not more distinctly, than certain other papers in *The Germ,* the fundamental antagonism between them. Art, to the Brotherhood, existed not for its own sake, but rather "for doctrine, for reproof, for correction, for instruction in righteousness"; and this was not an accidental and separable element of their teaching, but the very heart and life of it. The ethical message of Pre-Raphaelitism is embodied, with greater beauty of form and cunning of dialectic than seem to have been at Mr. Tupper's command, in a long "Dialogue on Art," published in the last number of the magazine, and intended, had its author lived, to be the first of a series; but he was removed by death shortly before this latest fragment of his work was given to the world. His name was John Orchard, and he was a young artist whose work in painting, though unknown to me and to all but a few, was, I am assured by one in every way competent to judge it, full not only of promise, but of performance; rememberable, however, in virtue of quality not of mass. . . . (pp. 259-64)

Enough has been quoted to show the high spiritual aim of the Brotherhood, an aim to which even their passion for veracity of presentation was subordinated. Truthfulness in Art was pursued not as an end but as a means to the achievement of a great ethical purpose; and the witness of Art to holiness was declared to be as distinct as the witness of that Puritanism which, in the interests of holiness, had declared Art an unclean thing. It has, however, already been noted that dogmatic or even expository utterances form a very small portion of the contents of *The Germ,* and the portion, too, which is, as a whole, least attractive, save to those who are interested in tracing the history and development of are ideas. What is done is of more import and interest than theories of the manner in which it should be done; and one turns without regret from Mr. Tupper's scholastic definitions, and even from Mr. Orchard's eloquent dialectic, to the poems and etchings which were among the earliest blades that sprouted from the new seed—things pleasant in themselves, and pleasanter for their promise of harvest.

Midway between the purely critical and the purely creative work stands a little biographical study entitled, "Hand and Soul," a story of the days and works of a painter, one Chiaro dell' Erma, written by Mr. Dante Rossetti, and apparently meant by him to be a setting forth of his ideal of the artistic life. *The Germ* contains nothing with a more insistent charm than this piece of portraiture, which is instinct with a beautiful *naiveté,* almost unique in modern writing; with singular simplicity, austere but never bald, having that nameless grace and glamour after which elaboration often labours in vain; and with an impressive unction like that of which we are conscious as we turn over the illuminated pages of some book of devotions which has given words to the wordless sighs of generations of penitents. The little story was a prophecy in words that was to be fulfilled in lines and colours: it possessed just the pictorial qualities which years afterwards made the pictured shapes of the Palm-bearing Sybil and the Blessed Damozel for ever memorable to all who stood before them. It is the record of the outer and inner life of a painter; of how he yearned for fame, but when he found that fame was lightly won, cared no more to strive, but only to live his own life and take his own pleasure; how he was arrested in his course by hearing speech of a youth who had been faithful when he had been faithless; how he took to work diligently, so that no day more might be lost, but gaining fame, found that a weight was still at his heart; how, when he questioned himself, he feared that, being glad in his work, he had mistaken for faith the worship of beauty, and accordingly set himself to the presentment of moral greatness, not dealing, as heretofore, with the action and passion of human life, but with cold symbolism and abstract impersonation, so that men no more cared to look upon his work; and how, finally, there appeared to him an image of his own soul in the fashion of a beautiful woman in sad-coloured garments, who told him that he had erred in saying coldly to the mind what God had said to the heart warmly, that God needed not his help in strengthening Him among men, bidding him "work from thine own heart simply, for His heart is as thine is wise and humble, and He shall have understanding of thee," leaving with him this final message, "Know that there is but this means whereby thou mayst serve God with man—set thine hand and thy soul to serve man with God."

This narrative study makes manifest the essential spirit of Pre-Raphaelitism, and along with some of the poems by the same writer and by his sister, Miss Rossetti, may be accepted as a satisfying concrete embodiment of them. . . . The poems familiar to Mr. Rossetti's present-day readers which first saw the light in *The Germ* were "My Sister's Sleep," "The Blessed Damozel," four of the "Sonnets for Pictures," and a poem there called "On the Cliffs." . . . (pp. 264-66)

The remaining poetical contents of the thin volume call for no special comment; but it is pleasant to find the chief place in the first number given to two poems by the then little-known sculptor of the Brotherhood—poems which were the first instalment of the tender and gracious monody known to the world as "My Beautiful Lady." These are followed by a sonnet on "The Love of Beauty," from the pen of a now distinguished painter, not otherwise known as a poet, Mr. Ford Madox Brown. The peculiar mediæval spirituality of the new movement found a delicate metrical embodiment in a poem by another of the seven brethren, Mr. James Collinson, "The Child Jesus; a Record typical of the Five Sorrowful Mysteries," the beauty of which is at once severe, pensive, and solemn. The first and last of these poems are illustrated by etchings; Mr. Holman Hunt accompanying Mr. Woolner's work with two designs,

John Everett Millais's controversial painting Christ in the House of His Parents. *Tate Gallery, London.*

the second of which is characterized by strong, passionate realisation; and Mr. Collinson mating his own poem with a beautiful invention—archaic indeed, but not therefore unattractive to those who are generally repelled by archaism, because so evidently sincere and spontaneous. The etchings in the other two numbers have both Shakespearian motives. Mr. Madox Brown's farewell of Cordelia to her sisters is the more ambitious, and has good qualities of composition, but cannot be spoken of as pleasing or even interpretative, Cordelia having the simper of a rather silly and conceited girl delivering herself of some moral platitude, while her sisters are simply two ill-tempered women resenting the gratuitous homily. The head of Regan has character, however, but is too suggestive of Blake, and is probably a reminiscence. It is, however, only just to add that the work was executed very hurriedly to supply the place of an etching which had been prepared by Mr. D. G. Rossetti, but at the last moment rejected by him as inadequate. Mr. W. H. Deverell's "Viola and Olivia" is in no way noteworthy, and, considered as etchings, the four illustrations must be pronounced amateurish and unimpressive, being so largely deficient in that impulsive freedom of treatment which it is the glory of the etching needle to secure. What worth they have inheres in their quality as designs.

Of two suggestive articles no mention has been made. The first of these, an essay on "The Purpose and Tendency of Early Italian Art," by Mr. John Seward, another young painter, covers much of the same ground that is traversed by Mr. Tupper and Mr. Orchard; but is specially interesting as showing the true nature of the impulse which drew the Brotherhood and its associates to the work of the Pre-Raphael painters. The other article is of a very different character. It is a critical analysis

by Mr. Coventry Patmore of the character of Macbeth, intended to prove that a "design of illegitimately obtaining the crown of Scotland had been conceived by Macbeth, and that it had been communicated by him to his wife prior to his first meeting with the witches," of whose evil suggestions the action and catastrophe of the play are commonly supposed to be the results. This view of the tragedy, then novel, has of late been popularised by the subtly-conceived impersonation of Mr. Henry Irving; but Mr. Patmore was the first to break new ground, and his study really left little in the way of additional proof to be gathered together by those coming after him. In soundness, sanity, and sympathetic insight into the essential spirit of Shakespeare's portraiture, it offers a pleasing contrast to some of the eccentric *banalités* which have of late years presented themselves as contributions towards the comprehension of the great master's work.

Such are the principal contents of a magazine which will always retain its interest for lovers both of pictorial and literary art. (pp. 267-68)

James Ashcroft Noble, "Appendix 2: A Pre-Raphaelite Magazine," in The Germ: A Pre-Raphaelite Little Magazine, *edited by Robert Stahr Hosmon, University of Miami Press, 1970, pp. 259-69.*

WILLIAM MICHAEL ROSSETTI

[*Rossetti here summarizes the history of the* Germ. *For additional material by Rossetti, see excerpts above.*]

The Præraphaelite Brotherhood having been founded in September 1848, the members exhibited in 1849 works conceived in the new spirit. These were received by critics and by the public with more than moderate though certainly not unmixed favour: it had not as yet transpired that there was a league of unquiet and ambitious young spirits, bent upon making a fresh start of their own, and a clean sweep of some effete respectabilities. It was not until after the exhibitions were near closing in 1849 that any idea of bringing out a magazine came to be discussed. The author of the project was Dante Gabriel Rossetti. He alone among the P.R.B.'s had already cultivated the art of writing in verse and in prose to some noticeable extent. ("The Blessed Damozel" had been produced before May 1847), and he was better acquainted than any other member with British and foreign literature. There need be no self-conceit in saying that in these respects I came next to him. Holman-Hunt, Woolner, and Stephens, were all reading men (in British literature only) within straiter bounds than Rossetti: not any one of them, I think, had as yet done in writing anything worth mentioning. Millais and Collinson, more especially the former, were men of the brush, not the pen, yet both of them capable of writing with point, and even in verse. By July 13 and 14, 1849, some steps were taken towards discussing the project of a magazine. The price, as at first proposed, was to be sixpence; the title, "Monthly Thoughts in Literature, Poetry and Art"; each number was to have an etching. Soon afterwards a price of one shilling was decided upon, and two etchings per number: but this latter intention was not carried out. All the P.R.B.'s were to be proprietors of the magazine. . . .

The then title, invented by my brother, was "Thoughts towards Nature", a phrase which, though somewhat extra-peculiar, indicated accurately enough the predominant conception of the Præraphaelite Brotherhood, that an artist, whether painter or writer, ought to be bent upon defining and expressing his own personal thoughts, and that these ought to be based upon a direct study of Nature, and harmonized with her manifestations. It was not until December 19, when the issue of our No. 1 was closely impending, that a different title, "The Germ", was proposed. On that evening there was a rather large gathering at Dante Rossetti's studio, 72 Newman Street; the seven P.R.B.'s, Madox Brown, Cave Thomas, Deverell, Hancock, and John and George Tupper. Mr Thomas had drawn up a list of no less than sixty-five possible titles. . . . Only a few of them met with favour; and one of them, "The Germ", going to the vote along with "The Seed" and "The Scroll", was approved by a vote of six to four. The next best were, I think, "The Harbinger", "First Thoughts", "The Sower", "The Truth-Seeker", and "The Acorn". Appended to the new title we retained, as a sub-title, something of what had been previously proposed; and the serial appeared as *The Germ. Thoughts towards Nature in Poetry, Literature, and Art.* At this same meeting Mr Woolner suggested that authors' names should not be published in the magazine. I alone opposed him, and his motion was carried. I cannot at this distance of time remember with any precision what his reasons were; but I think that he, and all the other artists concerned, entertained a general feeling that to appear publicly as writers, and especially as writers opposing the ordinary current of opinions on fine art, would damage their professional position, which already involved uphill work more than enough.

The Germ, No. 1, came out on or about January 1, 1850. The number of copies printed was 700. Something like 200 were sold, in about equal proportions by the publishers, and by ourselves among acquaintances and well-wishers. This was not encouraging, so we reduced the issue of No. 2 to 500 copies. It sold less well than No. 1. With this number was introduced

the change of printing on the wrapper the names of most of the contributors: not of all, for some still preferred to remain unnamed, or to figure under a fancy designation. Had we been left to our own resources, we must now have dropped the magazine. But the printing-firm—or Mr George I. F. Tupper as representing it—came forward, and undertook to try the chance of two numbers more. The title was altered (at Mr Alexander Tupper's suggestion) to *Art and Poetry, being Thoughts towards Nature, conducted principally by Artists;* and Messrs Dickinson and Co., of New Bond Street, the printsellers, consented to join their name as publishers to that of Messrs Aylott and Jones. Mr Robert Dickinson, the head of this firm, and more especially his brother, the able portraitpainter Mr Lowes Dickinson, were well known to Madox Brown, and through him to members of the P.R.B. I continued to be editor; but, as the money stake of myself and my colleagues in the publication had now ceased, I naturally accommodated myself more than before to any wish evinced by the Tupper family. No. 3, which ought to have appeared on March 1, was delayed by these uncertainties and changes till March 31. No. 4 came out on April 30. Some small amount of advertising was done, more particularly by posters carried about in front of the Royal Academy (then in Trafalgar Square), which opened at the beginning of May. All efforts proved useless. People would not buy *The Germ*, and would scarcely consent to know of its existence. So the magazine breathed its last, and its obsequies were conducted in the strictest privacy. Its debts exceeded its assets, and a sum of £33 odd, due on Nos. 1 and 2, had to be cleared off by the seven (or eight) proprietors, conscientious against the grain. What may have been the loss of Messrs Tupper on Nos. 3 and 4 I am unable to say. It is hardly worth specifying that neither the editor, not any of the contributors whether literary or artistic, received any sort of payment. (pp. 57-9)

William Michael Rossetti, "An Account of 'The Germ' by Its Editor," in Pre-Raphaelite Writing: An Anthology, *edited by Derek Stanford, Dent, 1973, pp. 57-9.*

EDWARD BURNE-JONES

[In the following excerpt from a letter to his cousin dated 1855, Burne-Jones outlines the Oxford Brotherhood's plans and goals for the Oxford and Cambridge Magazine.]

Shall I tell you about our Magazine, as you are so good as to take an interest in it? In the enclosed envelope I have sent you a prospectus. It appeared in nearly all the magazines of the month, and will be in the *Quarterly* reviews of January and in the *Times*. We have thoroughly set ourselves to the work now, banded ourselves into an exclusive Brotherhood of seven. Mr. Morris is proprietor. The expenses will fall very heavily upon him, I fear, for it cannot be published under £500 per annum, exclusive of engravings which we shall sometimes give: he hopes not to lose more than £300, but even that is a great deal. Not one Magazine in a hundred pays, but we are full of hope. We have such a deal to tell people, such a deal of scolding to administer, so many fights to wage and opposition to encounter that our spirits are quite rising with the emergency. We shall restrict ourselves to our present contributors, and not receive any indiscriminate contributions, for we wish to keep before us one aim and end throughout the Magazine, and I question if we should find many to join us in all the undertaking, and answer for all our opinions. . . .

Two of the most able young writers of Cambridge have joined us, and for three of our Oxford contributors I should look up and down the world before I could name their peers. . . .

Such is our little Brotherhood. We may do a world of good, for we start from new principles and those of the strongest kind, and are as full of enthusiasm as the first crusaders, and we may perish in a year as others have done before. Well, if we are wanted I suppose we shall remain, and if not, what have we to want? Nothing, I know, for I can safely affirm for all that no mean and contemptible desire for a little contemporary fame, no mere purpose of writing for writings's sake has prompted one amongst us, but a sole and only wish to teach others principles and truths which they may not know and which have made us happy. (p. 77)

Edward Burne-Jones, "Introducing 'The Oxford and Cambridge Magazine'," in Pre-Raphaelite Writing: An Anthology, edited by Derek Stanford, Dent, 1973, p. 77.

WALTER K. GORDON

[Gordon recounts the history of the Oxford and Cambridge Magazine, focusing on the influence of early Pre-Raphaelites, particularly Dante Gabriel Rossetti, on the Oxford Brotherhood.]

[The Oxford and Cambridge Magazine was] a Pre-Raphaelite periodical which appeared monthly between January and December of 1856, under the editorial guidance of William Morris and William Fulford. The high ideals, youthful exuberance, and social commitment of the magazine's founders are difficult to discern now behind the loose cover, yellowing pages, and somewhat faded illustrations, but the fact is that a little over a century ago the Oxford and Cambridge Magazine sounded a vigorous note of protest against the values of life in the Victorian age. Inspired by Morris's enthusiastic leadership, the contributors to this periodical attacked the present and revered the past, shunned the materialistic chaos of the here and now and advocated a return to the spiritual and ethical unity they thought they saw in an age gone by. In so doing, Morris's group participated in what was perhaps the major leitmotif of the Victorian period—the self-conscious critical appraisal of the present in terms of the past. The Oxford and Cambridge Magazine coupled the aesthetic revolt of William Holman Hunt, John Everett Millais, and Dante Rossetti with the social dissatisfaction of Carlyle and Ruskin to become a periodical which despite its short existence, changed the direction of Pre-Raphaelite thinking and played an influential role in shaping social ideas and attitudes in the latter half of the nineteenth century.

Early in 1855 William Morris and Edward Burne-Jones, both students at Exeter College, Oxford, became acquainted with Pre-Raphaelite art through an exhibition of Rossetti, Hunt, Millias, and Madox Brown at the Clarendon Press. This led them to investigate the beliefs of this group further, and Morris's biographer records that it was at about this time that they came across a copy of The Germ and that their reading of "The Blessed Damozel" and "Hand and Soul" increased their interest in Rossetti and his school. The Germ had been defunct since 1850 when it had ceased publication with its fourth issue, but so strong was their appreciation of this Pre-Raphaelite journal that it is reasonable to assume that the conception of the Oxford and Cambridge Magazine dates from this reading, for it was at this time that Morris and his youthful group saw the possibility of publishing a periodical very similar in tone and spirit to Rossetti's in order to gain an audience for the new ideas which were already taking shape in their minds.

Interest in Pre-Raphaelitism continued through the summer of 1855 when Morris, Burne-Jones, and Fulford, who was to edit eleven of the twelve issues of the magazine, visited the Beaux Arts department of the Paris Exposition. They were overjoyed to find there Holman Hunt's "Light of the World," three paintings by Millais, and one by Charles Allston Collins. Upon their return to England the trio resumed their discussion of the art, society, and poetry of their day, but now more and more their thoughts turned toward an outlet for their ideas. These three found four others who felt as they did, Richard Watson Dixon (1833-1900), destined to become the Canon of Carlisle, a poet in his own right, and an associate of Gerard Manley Hopkins, Coventry Patmore, and Robert Bridges; Wilfred Heeley (1833-1876), later a Civil Servant in India; Vernon Lushington (1832-1912), who entered law after graduation from Cambridge and became Deputy Judge Advocate General; and Cormell Price (1835-1902), later Headmaster in several English Public Schools. These seven young men then formed what they chose to call a "Brotherhood," just as the "first generation" Pre-Raphaelites had done before them. This Brotherhood met to prepare a prospectus of aims and purposes, and after much deliberation decided that "There shall be no showing off, no quips, no sneers, no lampooning in our magazine." They further agreed that the contents of the periodical were to be mainly "Tales, Poetry, Friendly Critiques, and Social Articles," the same four categories into which The Germ had been divided. Many years later Dixon, one of the most articulate members of the Brotherhood, outlined the objectives of the Oxford and Cambridge Magazine as he remembered them in a letter to T. Hall Caine:

Of this undertaking the central notion was, I think, to advocate moral earnestness and purpose in literature, art, and society. It was founded much on Ruskin's teaching: it sprang out of immaturity and ignorance: but perhaps it was not without value as a protest against some things. The Pre-Raphaelite movement was then in vigour, and the magazine came to be considered as the organ of those who accepted the ideas which were brought into art at that time, and as in a manner, the successor of The Germ, a small periodical which had been published previously by the first beginners of the movement.

In all there were 15 contributors to the magazine, 14 men and 1 woman, all of whom submitted their articles to the editor without pay. They were all in one way or another connected with the two universities, and after 1856 most of them went their separate ways. Except for the members of the Brotherhood who did maintain mutual contact throughout most of their lives, the contributors associated very little with one another. The bonds of friendship were strong among the founders of the magazine, but the others were only peripherally associated with the venture, and the part they played in its development was a small one.

A survey of the contents of the Oxford and Cambridge Magazine shows that of the 69 contributions to its pages, there are 16 short stories (eight by Morris); 17 poems (five by Morris); 19 essays on literature, two on art, six on society and politics, two on history, one on religion, one on philosophy, and five on miscellaneous topics. Thus, it is apparent that although there was an honest effort to cover many subjects, the prevailing interest of the Brotherhood was literary in nature. The eight prose romances and five poems comprise the largest part of

Morris's contributions to the magazine and represent his earliest efforts in these genres. His settings are for the most part of indeterminate date but are feudal in tone and Norse or Anglo-Saxon in flavor. Knightly combat, trance-like states, fair ladies, and chivalric ethics are the grist for Morris's literary mill in these early pieces, and although in general they show his youth and inexperience, some like "The Story of the Unknown Church" and "The Hollow Land" exhibit a real ability to superimpose dreams upon reality, fact on fancy, to set the tangible world of actuality against an evanescent background of somnolent beauty and drowsy landscapes—a literary characteristic that was to remain with Morris throughout his life.

The most frequently discussed authors were Shakespeare, Ruskin, Tennyson, and Browning, and in the case of two issues medallions of Tennyson (January) and Carlyle (May) made by the Pre-Raphaelite sculptor Thomas Woolner were offered for sale with the magazine. Discussions of literature frequently led the contributors into analyses of social problems, and although the magazine was politically non-partisan, definite and sometimes outspoken attitudes were expressed on a variety of social topics such as over-population, women's rights, the Crimean War, the Mammonism of the Age, and the effects of the factory system. A major shortcoming of the social criticism in the periodical is that although the young collegians saw a good deal in their environment that disgusted and repelled them, at no time were they able to offer any specific measures for reform. (pp. 42-5)

Morris began as the first editor, but never really interested in the administrative aspects of the project, transferred his duties to William Fulford before the appearance of the second issue. Morris paid Fulford £100 for performing his editorial duties during the year the magazine continued to operate. With Morris's hand on the editorial helm, the Brotherhood sought popular acceptance by appeal to a wide audience in the first issue of the *Oxford and Cambridge Magazine;* thus controversial issues and doctrinaire attitudes were avoided. The issue contained the first parts of two literary essays (on Sidney and Tennyson), three short stories, three reviews (of Longfellow's *Song of Hiawatha,* Thackeray's *The Newcomes,* and Kingsley's *Sermons for the Times*), and a poem by Morris. The quality of this initial effort is not high by modern standards; indeed it is quite low. The literary essays are little more than panegyrics couched in turgid prose upon the works of favorite authors and punctuated by frequent quotation from the master; the short stories embody most of the faults of Victorian fiction at its worst. The swooning heroine, the pangs of unrequited love, the vision in a dream, expiration from a broken heart, the icy and aloof heroine—they all appear in abundance in the fiction of the *Oxford and Cambridge Magazine.*

It remained for subsequent issues to make it clear that the magazine was going to be something other than an outlet for the immature critical and creative attempts of a group of Victorian undergraduates. The first vague hint that the *Oxford and Cambridge Magazine* would have to be taken seriously came with the February issue, in which Morris wrote "The Churches of North France," an essay concerned mainly with the cathedral at Amiens. In this essay Morris described the cathedral not so much as a structure of architectural beauty to be admired by the nineteenth century but as a product of a *zeitgeist* which no longer existed, of artisans with pride in their craft and a spiritual elevation to be revered. Speaking of the workers who built the French medieval cathedrals, he wrote,

> And thinking of their [the cathedrals'] past away
> builders, can I see through them very faintly, dimly,

some little of the medieval times, else dead and gone from me forever . . . do I not love them with just cause who certainly love me, thinking of me sometimes between the strokes of their chisels; and for this love of all men that they had, and moreover for the great love of God . . . and for this work of theirs, the upraising of the great cathedral front with its beating heart of the thoughts of men . . . I think they will not lose their reward.

It was a short step from this adulation of the medieval artisan to a comparison of him with his Victorian counterpart. In his maturity Morris decried mass production, assembly line techniques, the subjugation of man to machine, and the depersonalization of the worker, and it is clear that his mature thought was to a large extent shaped by such early attitudes as that expressed in "The Churches of North France."

Another significant aspect of the *Oxford and Cambridge Magazine* consistent with Pre-Raphaelite attitudes was its defense of Browning and Ruskin at a time when it was not fashionable to admire their ideas. Browning had been defended against the charge of obscurity by William Michael Rossetti in his review of "Christmas Eve and Easter Day" in the May, 1850, issue of *The Germ,* but even six years later in 1856, the battle had not been won. When Browning's *Men and Women* was severely attacked by the critics, Morris took up the cudgel in his defense and wrote one of the two favorable reviews to appear in contemporary journals. In his review Morris placed a large share of the blame for not understanding Browning on the Victorian reader and pointed to the indolence and apathy of the age as the cause of poor communication between poet and audience. Morris asserted that Browning's obscurity resulted in large measure from a "depth of thought and greatness of subject on the poet's part, and on his readers' part, from their shallower brain and more bounded knowledge; nay often I fear from mere ignorance and idleness."

The defense of Ruskin provides an even better example of allegiance to the Pre-Raphaelite cause because it concerns the concept of the very nature of artistic expression itself. In 1855 and 1856 John Ruskin was involved in a controversy over the function and practices of art with Lady Elizabeth [Rigby] Eastlake, wife of Charles Eastlake, R. A., whom Ruskin had criticized in his *Academy Notes* of 1855, and when Lady Eastlake attacked Ruskin in her review of *Modern Painters* for the *Quarterly Review,* Edward Burne-Jones resolved to answer it in the June issue of the *Oxford and Cambridge Magazine* by pointing out that her view of art had overlooked its moral and spiritual elements, debasing it to a level of purely material and sensuous consideration: "Yet this is dismally certain that on the whole this is what the reviewer degrades the art of painting to— something which amuses men, at best refreshes them when they are tired; think of a man spending his life in this kind." The entire concept of purely utilitarian art was totally repugnant to the Brotherhood, and of course, in Ruskin they saw an advocate of the divine in art, an attitude to which they subscribed wholeheartedly. Burne-Jones, after refusing to admit the truth of any part of the *Quarterly's* attack on *Modern Painters,* lamented the fact that a figure of such a petty nature as the reviewer would dare attack John Ruskin, "a Luther of the Arts. Thenceforward, let no one wanting to be listened to, or even respected, write twaddle upon art, for we will not have it."

Another of Ruskin's views which Burne-Jones admired and one which he felt was lacking in Lady Eastlake's review was a concept of the essential *unity* of all the arts. It is certainly no accident that the members of the Pre-Raphaelite movement, unlike most other literary figures, were as much at home in the fields of painting, sculpture, printing, and woodcarving as they were in literature; and the common denominator among the diverse individuals who comprised this movement was not the *form* in which their artistic productions were expressed, for this varied greatly, but the *function* which they sought to voice, that art was essentially the evocation of an emotional stimulus through the medium of direct narrative. Both the Pre-Raphaelites and Ruskin made this alliance of art and literature, and this was another legacy of *The Germ* to Morris's group. Although most of the contributors to the *Oxford and Cambridge Magazine* left the field of art and letters, the few who remained gave evidence of having learned their lessons well. In his entire life Morris never really wrote any poetry that was not narrative in nature, and Burne-Jones's paintings are, to a very large degree, pictorial stories. In this defense of Ruskin against Lady Eastlake's attack, Burne-Jones was motivated by an attitude which was to remain with him and his fellows for the remainder of their lives.

Pre-Raphaelite fever continued to burn in the August issue of the *Oxford and Cambridge Magazine,* which was especially noteworthy for two reasons: first, because it contained the only article in the life of the magazine to discuss *specific* Pre-Raphaelite paintings, and secondly, because it marked the appearance of the poetry of Dante Rossetti in Morris's journal. Written by Vernon Lushington, the article entitled "Two Pictures" attempted to show the world that "the Academy does not contain *all* the good pictures that have been painted this year or last," and by analyzing Rossetti's *Dante's Dream* and Madox Brown's *The Last of England,* Lushington sought to gain a wider audience for paintings which, whether they be of the past or present, "quicken our faith in God and man." He especially decried the current practice of the Royal Academy of specializing in portrait and landscape paintings and clamored for more paintings which revealed the fusion of spiritual sense with material form. Rossetti himself had noted this resurgence of the Pre-Raphaelite spirit in the *Oxford and Cambridge Magazine* and had been first attracted to the new periodical by a complimentary reference to him which he had seen in the January issue. Edward Burne-Jones, in the course of reviewing Thackeray's *The Newcomes,* referred to Rossetti's ability to tell a story in his paintings and asked the question, "Why is the author of "The Blessed Damozel" and the story of Chiaro so seldom on the lips of men? If only we could hear him oftener, live in the light of his power a little longer." Rossetti remembered this passage when Burne-Jones called on him in June of 1856, to show him some designs he had done and to ask his opinion of their merit. It was as a direct result of this meeting that Rossetti became acquainted with Morris, Lushington, and Dixon. This meeting was an especially significant one, for not only did it bring Morris's Brotherhood into contact with the leading Pre-Raphaelite of the day but it also introduced them to some of the other major literary figures of the nineteenth century as well.

Rossetti's three contributions to the *Oxford and Cambridge Magazine,* "The Burden of Nineveh" (August), "The Blessed Damozel" (November), and "The Staff and the Scrip" (December), are undoubtedly the highest poetic achievement of the periodical. None, however, was written specifically for Morris's journal, and all underwent various degrees of revision in subsequent publications. . . . But even while Rossetti's poetry was enhancing the reputation of the *Oxford and Cambridge Magazine,* Rossetti himself was leading the interests of its

founders along lines which were to bring about the discontinuance of the magazine. He was using all his powers to exhort Morris and Burne-Jones to turn their attention to the field of art, and he sought to enlist their help in painting the ceiling of the Oxford Union with murals. Burne-Jones' journal records the venture:

> Rossetti and Morris . . . were full of a scheme, and I was to put everything aside and help it. . . . There were bays above the gallery that ran around the room hungry to be filled with pictures—Gabriel equally hungry to fill them, and the pictures were to be from the Morte D'Arthur, so willed our master.

So overjoyed were the members of the Brotherhood to work with Rossetti that his personality seems to have dominated their thought and action at this time. This shift of interest coupled with the gradual dissolution of the group which had conceived of the *Oxford and Cambridge Magazine* made the Brotherhood decide to discontinue publication at the end of the year. This decision came as early as August, however, for in that month Burne-Jones wrote, "The Mag is going to smash—let it go. The world is not converted and never will be. It has had stupid things in it lately. I shall not write for it again, no more will Topsy [Morris]—we cannot do more than one thing at a time, and our hours are too valuable to spend so."

In December, 1856, the twelfth and final issue of the *Oxford and Cambridge Magazine* appeared. The deficit for the entire year was several hundred pounds, all of which Morris had to pay out of an inheritance. Lured by Rossetti's magnetic personality, Morris and Burne-Jones threw themselves wholeheartedly into painting. Writing to Allingham, Rossetti announced the demise of the last of the Pre-Raphaelite journals: "You will see no more of the *Oxford and Cambridge*. It was too like the spirit of *The Germ*. Down! Down! and has vanished into the witches' cauldron. Morris and Burne-Jones are both wonders of their kind." By the spring of 1857, the *Oxford and Cambridge Magazine* was all but forgotten by the disbanded Brotherhood, but the periodical did not disappear before it had made its mark on Victorian intellectual history in several ways. First, by championing the cause of Ruskin, Carlyle, Rossetti, and Browning, the magazine gained for them an audience they would otherwise not have had and thus materially contributed to the development of their reputations. Secondly, the *Oxford and Cambridge Magazine* provided a workshop for the early efforts of Morris and gave him an opportunity to form the ideas, values, and attitudes which were to determine the course of his mature life; and finally, and most important, the magazine added a new dimension to Pre-Raphaelite thinking by fusing social unrest with aesthetic revolt, thus laying the groundwork for such subsequent Victorian movements as Anti-Scrape, the Guild of St. George, and the Socialist League. (pp. 46-51)

Walter K. Gordon, "Pre-Raphaelitism and the 'Oxford and Cambridge Magazine'," in The Journal of the Rutgers University Library, *Vol. XXIX, No. 2, June, 1966, pp. 42-51.*

CONTROVERSY: ROBERT BUCHANAN AND THE "FLESHLY SCHOOL OF POETRY"

JOHN A. CASSIDY

[Cassidy provides a detailed account of the literary controversy that began with Robert Buchanan's attack on the "Fleshly school

of poetry." He examines the factors that provoked Buchanan to attack Pre-Raphaelite poetry in general and Dante Gabriel Rossetti's works in particular, reviews the hostile exchanges published by Buchanan and the Pre-Raphaelites, and closes with a consideration of the repercussions of the dispute on the careers and reputations of those involved.]

In the long history of literary polemics none has been more savage or more far-reaching in its consequences than the Fleshly Controversy, which raged in Victorian England during the 1870's with Robert Buchanan on one side and Swinburne, William Michael Rossetti, and the unfortunate Dante Gabriel Rossetti on the other. (p. 65)

As in the case of larger human conflicts, it is impossible to say just when the Fleshly Controversy began and what was its specific incitement, but it may have been a mutual antipathy experienced by Robert Buchanan and Swinburne. It would be strange indeed if the two had not been thrown together at some time during the 1860's, for both were living in London as ambitious young men of letters, both knew Lord Houghton and were befriended by him, and both came to prominence during the middle years of the decade. Indeed, it may have been at Lord Houghton's home, sometime between 1862 and 1866, that the groundwork for the Controversy was laid, for that nobleman was fond of bringing opposite personalities together, introducing subjects on which he knew them to disagree, and then watching the sparks fly. He would not have found it difficult to set two such gamecocks as Swinburne and Buchanan upon each other. Swinburne was known as a literary representative of the Pre-Raphaelites, a cultural and artistic coterie to whose foreign flavor Buchanan's sturdy Scottish spirit was naturally opposed. As early as 1862 he expressed some of his contempt by satirizing them in *Temple Bar* in his farcical novelette, "Lady Letitia's Lilliput Hand," in the character Edward Vansittart, whom he described as a painter "whose 'Donkey feeding on Thistles' was so much commended by Mr. Buskin for the Pre-Raphaelite vigour of its drawing" (IV, 554). If they did meet, Swinburne, with his halo of red hair, his birdlike mannerisms of hopping on and off articles of furniture when he was talking, and the flutelike tones of his voice, probably affected Buchanan unfavorably. Swinburne's outspoken pride in his French ancestry would not have moved him to admiration, while his better circumstances and aristocratic connections would have earned Buchanan's envy. Temperamentally, both were vain, opinionated young men with little tolerance of any opposition to their beliefs and theories and no disposition to heed the advice of their elders.

But whatever may or may not have taken place behind the scenes, the printed war begins properly with the publication of Swinburne's *Poems and Ballads* near the end of July 1866. Two reviews written from advance copies were published before the book was available in the bookshops, John Morley's in the *Saturday Review* (XXII, 145-147) and Buchanan's in the *Athenaeum*. Morley regarded the volume with horror, but Buchanan's personalized remarks verged close to insult [see excerpt in Algernon Charles Swinburne entry, *TCLC*, Vol. 8]:

> When . . . we find a writer like the author of these *Poems and Ballads*, who is deliberately and impertinently insincere as an artist,—who has no splendid individual emotions to reveal, and is unclean for the mere sake of uncleanness,—we may safely affirm, in the face of many pages of brilliant writing, that such a man is either no poet at all, or a poet degraded from his high estate and utterly and miserably lost to the Muses. How old is this young gentleman,

whose bosom, it appears, is a flaming fire, whose face is as the fiery foam of flowers, and whose works are as the honeyed kisses of the Shunamite? He is quite the Absalom of modern bards,—long-ringleted, flippant-lipped, down-cheeked, amorous lidded. He seems, moreover, to have prematurely attained to the fate of his old prototype; for we now find him fixed very fast indeed up a tree, and it will be a miracle if one breath of poetic life remain in him when he is cut down. Meantime he tosses to us this charming book of verses, which bears some evidence of having been inspired in Holywell Street, composed on the Parade at Brighton, and touched up in the Jardin Mabile. Very sweet things in puerility . . . fine glaring patterns after Alfred de Musset and Georges Sand,—grand bits in the manner of Hugo, with here and there a notable piece of insertion from Ovid and Boccaccio. Yet ere we go further, let us at once disappoint Mr. Swinburne, who would doubtless be charmed if we averred that his poems were capable of having an absolutely immoral influence. They are too juvenile and unreal for that. The strong pulse of true passion beats in no one of them. They are unclean, with little power; and mere uncleanness repulses. Here, in fact, we have Gito, seated in the tub of Diogenes, conscious of the filth and whining at the stars. (4 August 1866, pp. 137-138)

The description of Swinburne, caricature though it is, furthers the conjecture that Buchanan was personally acquainted with him. The note of personal animosity is strong, and unfairness of comparing him to Gito Buchanan admitted privately. The patronizing manner in which he refers to Swinburne's immaturity contains a grain of sardonic humor in that Buchanan was three years younger than the "young gentleman" he was advising to mend his poetical ways.

There can be little doubt that literary gossip must have made known to Swinburne the name of at least one of his detractors. Buchanan implied this when he said later that this review led to Swinburne's slur on David Gray. Further proof is the slight on Buchanan contained in William Rossetti's defense of Swinburne published later in 1866 and titled *Swinburne's Poems and Ballads*, a slight otherwise so gratuitous that it can be explained only on the ground that Rossetti knew Buchanan to be one of the offending reviewers. If Swinburne entertained any doubts on the personal bias of his assailant, they were dissipated when Buchanan let fly another shaft at him in his mocking poem, "The Session of the Poets," published in the *Spectator* on 15 September 1866 and an obvious imitation of Sir John Suckling's "A Session of the Poets" (XXXIX, 1028). In Buchanan's version Browning, Arnold, Lytton, Bailey, Patmore, Alford, Kingsley, and Ingelow are dealt with lightly. Of himself Buchanan says:

> There sat, looking moony, conceited, and narrow,
>   Buchanan,—who, finding, when foolish and young,
> Apollo asleep on a coster-girl's barrow,
>   Straight dragged him away to see somebody hung.

Buchanan's poem differs from Suckling's in that he deals more severely with himself than does the older bard—possibly the better to preserve his anonymity—and in that, whereas Suckling's barbs are scattered impartially among his brethren, Buchanan's most telling blows are directed at Swinburne, whose actions furnish an unmistakable climax.

> What was said? What was done? was there prosing or rhyming?
>   Was nothing noteworthy in deed or in word?—
> Why, just as the hour of the supper was chiming,
>   The only event of the evening occurred.

Up jumped, with his neck stretching out like a gander,
   Master Swinburne, and squeal'd, glaring out thro' his hair,
"All Virtue is bosh! Hallellujah for Landor!
   I disbelieve wholly in everything!—There."

With language so awful he dared then to treat 'em,—
   Miss Ingelow fainted in Tennyson's arms,
Poor Arnold rush'd out, crying "Soecl' Inficetum!"
   And great bards and small bards were full of alarms;
Till Tennyson, flaming and red as a gypsy,
   Struck his fist on the table and utter'd a shout;
"To the door with the boy! Call a cab! He is tipsy!"
   And they carried the naughty young gentleman out.

After that, all the pleasanter talking was done there,—
   Who ever had known such an insult before?
The Chairman tried hard to rekindle the fun there,
   But the Muses were shocked and the pleasure was o'er.
Then "Ah!" cried the Chairman, "this teaches me knowledge
   [sic]
   The future shall find me more wise, by the powers!
This comes of assigning to younkers from college
   Too early a place in such meetings as ours!"

                                          Caliban.

That Buchanan realized Swinburne would regard the "Session" as a deliberate insult is shown by his use of the pseudonym, when for several years all his poems had been signed. Further reasons for wishing to conceal his identity probably lay in his unwillingness to anger Lord Houghton, Swinburne's literary sponsor, and in his fear of reprisals from the powerful Pre-Raphaelites. At any rate, Swinburne soon learned that the inimical poet and the *Athenaeum* reviewer were the same.

In his defense published late in 1866 as "Notes on Poems and Reviews," Swinburne displayed, for him, remarkable forbearance, for though he styled his critics "vultures," his times an "age of hypocrites," and retorted that his poems were not meant to be read by girls, he chose to overlook personalities and treat the matter as a question of literary criticism. Not so, however, William Michael Rossetti, who chose to enter the fray by publishing at about the same time as Swinburne's "Notes" his defense of *Poems and Ballads*. In his very first sentence he went out of his way to deal Buchanan a malicious blow; in his second he praised Swinburne:

> The advent of a new great poet is sure to cause a
> commotion of one kind or another; and it would be
> hard were this otherwise in times like ours, when the
> advent of even so poor and pretentious a poetaster
> as a Robert Buchanan stirs storms in teapots. It is
> therefore no wonder that Mr. Swinburne should have
> been enthusiastically admired and keenly discussed
> as soon as he hove well in sight of the poetry-reading
> public.

Had William Michael foreseen the far-reaching consequences of his slur at Buchanan it is doubtful that he would have written it. Coming from Swinburne, Buchanan would not have relished it certainly, but he would have had to acknowledge it as not unearned. As the work of Rossetti, a man who was not directly concerned in the quarrel, Buchanan could have viewed it in no other light than as the stiletto blow of a meddlesome and treacherous bystander. In this instance the bystander was all the more a *persona non grata* because of the foreign flavor of his name. With a horizon no broader than that of most Victorians, Buchanan saw anything British as basically good and honorable, while that which smacked of the foreign was to be distrusted and attacked. This concept is borne out in his novels, where the foreigner is often the villain, thoroughly treacherous and despicable. From here on, Buchanan regarded any member of the Pre-Raphaelites as fair game and certainly the name Rossetti was singled out for special attention.

The "storms in teapots" was undoubtedly a reference to the popularity of Buchanan's *London Poems*, which had been published in 1866 and had met with considerable enthusiasm in the critical press. His rise to fame had not been easy. Almost penniless and friendless, he had arrived in London in 1860 as a boy of eighteen with no more than a fair education from the University of Glasgow and with a consuming ambition to win literary renown. By dint of hard work and a dogged determination which refused to give up he made his way slowly up the literary ladder with an occasional helping hand from Charles Dickens, George Lewes, and Hepworth Dixon, who admired his courage and thought they discerned in the young Scotsman an inherent literary ability. His *London Poems* marked the apex of his career and was hailed as the work of budding genius which would certainly achieve great things. Small wonder that he regarded Swinburne and his friends as poseurs who sought to conquer the literary world by subterfuge and the mutual assistance of a coterie rather than by merit and hard work.

His reply to Swinburne and Rossetti would probably not have been long in appearing had not his attention been diverted by other and more pressing affairs. The death of his father in the spring of 1866 together with the strain of overwork and mounting family responsibilities precipitated toward the end of the year a nervous breakdown which amounted to a light stroke. In search of health he moved his family from London to the resort town of Oban, a gateway to the Hebrides on the northern coast of Argyle. Here he lived the life of a recluse from 1866 to 1873, with only occasional short visits to London for business reasons. His recovery was discouragingly slow and was complicated by a disposition to brood on religious questions. Since his father had been an avowed atheist, his death had brought a whole host of morbid imaginings and fancies with which Buchanan wrestled in a vain endeavor to develop for himself a solid philosophy and faith. He continued to write sporadically in order to meet his mounting expenses and sought relaxation by sailing his small boat among the islands of the Hebrides. In 1869 two attempts to supplement his earnings by public readings of his poems in London brought about so severe a recurrence of his nervous disorders that he was forced to return to Oban and to refrain from work of any kind.

In the meantime the Controversy languished. Swinburne's essay on Arnold's poetry was published in the *Fortnightly* in October 1867, with a remark in connection with his disapproval of Wordsworth's doctrine that if a poet were inspired he did not need to master the technique of his craft that "such talk as this of Wordsworth's is the poison of poor souls like David Gray." There was hardly any malice intended in such a statement and it is difficult to believe that Buchanan could have had his ire aroused by it. But when Swinburne republished this essay in his *Essays and Studies* of 1875 much fuel had been added to the Controversy and Swinburne's temper was at such a heat that he appended to this reference to Gray a lengthy footnote in which he attacked the dead poet with the utmost scorn and ill-feeling. In later years when Buchanan was laboring to find some explanation for his attack upon Dante Rossetti he cited this footnote as his provocation. He is unquestionably in error, for his attack antedated the footnote by four years. That his feeling toward Swinburne in 1867 and 1868 had simmered down to little more than aversion is evidenced by a letter to his friend Roden Noel in 1868 in which he admitted that his failure to appreciate Swinburne's work was probably attributable to an artistic blind-spot in himself more than to any fault in the poetry. In 1868 Buchanan published an essay ''On My Own Tentatives'' in his *David Gray and Other Essays* in which he said regretfully that ''a gifted young contemporary, who seems fond of throwing stones in my direction, fiercely upbraids me for writing 'Idyls of the gallows and the gutter, and singing songs of costermongers and their trulls'.'' In his ''Under the Microscope'' of 1872 Swinburne admitted that he was the offending critic.

Buchanan finally got around to evening accounts with Rossetti in 1870 in another *Athenaeum* review, this time of William Michael's edition of Shelley. Again the review was unsigned, as was the custom of the *Athenaeum*, but Rossetti was not long in ferreting out the author. The article was lengthy and in a more scholarly tone than Buchanan was in the habit of using when discussing his enemies, but his opinions were almost entirely negative. He stated that Rossetti had neither sufficient material, critical insight, nor the good taste requisite for such a task. He accused him of misinterpreting the facts and objected to his attempts at revising the juvenilia. His conclusion was quite patronizing:

> Mr. Rossetti has, in our opinion, mistaken his vocation in undertaking the role of commentator. Still, there can be no doubt that he has pointed out a considerable number of errors in the existing text; his book therefore cannot fail to have a certain value in the eyes of future editors, and of readers who are fond of textual criticism'' (29 January 1870, pp. 154-156).

Here the Tragic Muse took a hand in what had hitherto been only light comedy. Another actor entered the scene in the person of William Rossetti's brother, Dante Gabriel. He, in a precarious condition of mind and body from overdoses of laudanum and alcohol, suffered himself in 1869 to be persuaded to resuscitate the verses which, in an act of self-imposed justice, he had buried in his wife's coffin in 1862. In 1870 after insuring a favorable reception for the volume by arranging that members of his circle should review it in most of the prominent critical journals—he seems to have been warned by William Michael and Swinburne that his book would probably be attacked by Buchanan—he published it. The venture fared exceedingly well. The reviews, paced by Swinburne's eulogy in the *Fortnightly*, were predominantly favorable; the looked-for attack by Buchanan did not materialize; and Rossetti found himself in short order in the first rank of contemporary poets.

The reasons for the delay in Buchanan's expected attack are not difficult to find. A reliable barometer of his physical condition during these years is his contributions to periodicals, and a survey of these shows that throughout 1869 and 1870 he did very little. For another reason, his collapse had prompted his friends, and probably chief among them Lord Houhgton, to plead his case with Gladstone for a Civil List pension, and this matter was quite evidently under consideration during 1869 and 1870. Because his breakdown took place during the early part of 1869, and because of the general slowness of governmental machinery, it was probably not until late in 1870 that he was placed on the Civil List for a pension of a hundred pounds a year for life. Even one of Buchanan's impetuous nature would reason that discretion was the better part of valor, at least until the pension was safely his; for Lord Hougton was a friend to the Swinburne faction as well as to Buchanan, and even had he not been so, literary polemics, had they come to Gladstone's attention, would hardly have recommended Buchanan as a worthy recipient of a pension. A third reason lay

in the fact that his ailment had brought an intensification of the religious doubts which had plagued him since the death of his father in 1866. In the solemn fastnesses of the Hebridean mountains he went into a morbid communion with himself and nature to try to arrive at some solution. His ruminations and soul-searchings he published in rough, inchoate verse which he hoped would mean as much to his fellowmen as the experiences leading to its composition had to him. This book, *The Book of Orm*, came out within a few weeks of Rossetti's *Poems* and with a preface which indicated that Buchanan considered he had achieved something new and great in poetry. Early in 1871 he rushed into print with his hastily conceived and even more hastily written interpretation of the Franco-Prussian War, *Napoleon Fallen*, done in the same rough, abstruse style as the *Orm*. Then he sat back to await the accolade he felt certain would be his.

How rude was his awakening, when the critical returns began to come in, to find that while his own ambitious offerings were ridiculed as formless and meaningless, those of Rossetti were eulogized! To add gall to the wormwood, often the notices were in such juxtaposition that they appeared on the same page. The *Westminster Review* dismissed the *Orm* with a curt and unfavorable paragraph, and right beneath it compared Rossetti's *Poems* favorably with those of Shakespeare and Goethe (XCIV, 107-108). The *North British Review* drew an odious comparison of the *Orm* with Swinburne's ''Atalanta'' by saying, ''In these unfortunate verses Mr. Buchanan has exceeded the irreverence, while he has none of the fiery and fitful music, of the choruses of *Atalanta in Calydon*.'' Then it immediately turned its attention to Rossetti with,

> Mr. Rossetti's *Poems* have the unwonted and personal qualities of all really original work. The sense of strangeness is soon lost in admiration of the great beauty of the verses, of their wide range of subject, their various and appropriate music, their lyric fire, their lofty tone, and their high level of common perfection (LII, 596-601).

In April 1871, the *Westminster Review* extolled Swinburne's *Poems and Ballads* as approximating the verse of Shelley and Chaucer and harshly castigated Buchanan for writing his *Orm* and *Napoleon Fallen* too rapidly (XCV, 275-276).

Buchanan was quick to discern a plot in all this. It appeared to him that his enemies had gained control of nearly all the critical journals and that they were determined to exalt Rossetti while debasing him. In an angry mood and still sick mentally and physically, he secured a copy of Rossetti's *Poems* in the summer of 1870 and read it. Seen through his jaundiced eyes and against the beautiful natural backdrop of sea, sky, and mountains of the Hebrides, these verses struck him as the work of ''an affected, immoral, and overpraised writer.'' In 1871 his health improved to the point that he resumed his writing for the periodicals; in the fore part of the year he was occupied with seeing his *Land of Lorne* through the press, but in the fall he finally got around to his belated attack on all his enemies by striking at Dante Gabriel Rossetti. Although Dante Gabriel had given Buchanan no offense he bore the name and was the brother of one who had; and although Buchanan's attack upon Dante was unwarranted, so had been William Michael's attack upon Buchanan. One unwarranted attack deserved another in Buchanan's code, and so he set about his work with a will.

''The Fleshly School of Poetry; Mr. D. G. Rossetti'' appeared under the pseudonym Thomas Maitland in the *Contemporary Review* for October 1871, and filled some seventeen pages of

William Holman Hunt in 1852, portrayed by Dante Gabriel Rossetti. Birmingham Museum and Art Gallery.

that journal [see excerpt in Dante Gabriel Rossetti entry, *NCLC*, Vol. 4]. Buchanan began by imagining the poets of the day as the cast of *Hamlet* with Tennyson and Browning alternating as the immortal Dane, himself as Cornelius, Swinburne and Morris as Rosencrantz and Guildenstern, and Rossetti as Osric. Then he accused the Pre-Raphaelites of overplaying their parts in a vain attempt to rival Tennyson and Browning. The Fleshly School he found to be a grotesque offshoot in style and matter from two of Tennyson's poorer poems, "Maud" and "Vivien." He disparaged Rossetti's paintings and added that his poetry was equally thin and uninspired. He found him inferior to Swinburne, even though extolled by his family and friends. He clearly showed his bias and his recollection of William Rossetti's slight of 1866 by remarking that Dante had dedicated his *Poems* to William Michael, "who. . .will perhaps be known to bibliographers as the editor of the worst edition of Shelley which has ever seen the light." Marvelling that Dante had not been taxed with sensuality as Swinburne was in 1866, he condemned Rossetti's as the worst offense because he was a mature man, whereas Swinburne had been a boy in 1866. Of Rossetti's "Nuptial Sleep" he said:

> Here is a full-grown man, presumably intelligent and and cultivated, putting on record for other full-grown men to read, the most secret mysteries of sexual connection, and that with so sickening a desire to

reproduce the sensual mood, so careful a choice of epithet to convey mere animal sensations, that we merely shudder at the shameless nakedness.

This attack was manifestly unfair. As Buchanan said later, he had no idea he was assailing an unwell man—a man who today would be put under the care of a psychiatrist—or that he was causing untold pain by unwittingly heaping obloquy upon Rossetti's marriage relationships. He saw in Rossetti the same kind of an affected esthete he later scorned in George Moore, an esthete surrounded by a powerful group of friends who were determined to laud his works far above their true worth. To him Rossetti's poems were of a piece with those of Swinburne's *Poems and Ballads,* and his onslaught upon Rossetti was not more severe than his berating of Swinburne in 1866.

He realized, however, that he had to do with powerful foemen who would not be slow to retaliate if they learned his identity. William Rossetti claimed he had evidence to prove Buchanan was urged to sign the article but refused. Harriett Jay said Buchanan meant to acknowledge it sooner or later, but this is doubtful. Buchanan himself implied that the signature "Thomas Maitland" was not his idea, but had been affixed by Alexander Strahan, editor of the *Contemporary,* without Buchanan's knowledge. This, too, is doubtful. There is in the literature of Scotland a dissertation titled *De Jure Regni apud Scotos Dialogus* published in 1579 by George Buchanan and dedicated to King James VI of that country. The whole thing took the form of a debate or flyting between Buchanan and his friend Thomas Maitland and advanced the then daring thesis that all law originates with the people and that a tyrannical king who refused to obey it could rightfully be killed. The underlying premise, the peril of men being corrupted by evil influences, is somewhat akin to the central thesis of the "Fleshly School" article. It is hardly likely that a businessman like Strahan would have known of this recondite work or would have used the pseudonym without Buchanan's consent if he had. It is more probable that Buchanan had come across the old flyting in his browsing around the British Museum reading room, had looked into it, noted the association of the names, and had filed away "Thomas Maitland" for future reference. This is, of course, conjecture and cannot be proved; there is, however, no other association of the names Buchanan and Thomas Maitland in literary history prior to the Fleshly School article, and this fact alone adds considerable weight to the supposition. Added to this is the point that Buchanan did not at first unreservedly deny that he had conceived of the pseudonym and suggested to Strahan that it be used. He simply said, " . . . the pseudonym 'Thomas Maitland' was affixed to my article when I was out of reach—cruising on the shores of the Western Hebrides." He could have written the name on paper, left it with Strahan or mailed it to him, and suggested its use. This would be quibbling of course, but such quibbling he could have justified to himself as a fair enough expedient in the war in which he was engaged. Actually, although the Rossetti faction made much of the pseudonym and fastened upon it as incontrovertible evidence of Buchanan's perfidy, there was no literary law, written or unwritten, which prohibited its use, even in a journal where the articles were usually signed with the author's name. English literary history affords numerous instances of similar employment of the pseudonym. True enough, to throw his enemies off the scent he assigned himself the insignificant role of Cornelius in the literary cast of *Hamlet* with which he opened his article, but this was for reasons of camouflage rather than from egoism.

His article had the effect of a bombshell among his enemies. The man he attacked was in no condition to bear such blows with equanimity and when he learned that the assailant was the hated and feared bogey, Buchanan, his rage was Homeric. Fear of legal reprisals, however, prevented all-out warfare upon Buchanan until he could be driven from ambush and forced to acknowledge his guilt. Here the resources of the far-flung Rossetti clan were employed. On 2 December 1871 the *Athenaeum* printed a short paragraph in its "Literary Gossip" column stating that Sidney Colvin was shortly to publish an answer to "'The Fleshly School of Poetry,' by Thomas Maitland, a *nom de plume* assumed by Mr. Robert Buchanan." To this, one week later, Colvin printed a disclaimer couched in language so ironic that it was obviously designed to flush the quarry from his hiding place.

> You learn . . . that the same Mr. Buchanan is himself the author of this spirited performance, only he has been too modest to acknowledge it, and has had the happy thought of delivering his thrust from behind the shield of a putative Thomas Maitland. Still, what then? Do you "prepare an answer"? Rather you stand off, acknowledging it out of your power to accost Mr. Maitland-Buchanan on equal terms. You admire his ingenious adaptation of the machinery of candour to the purposes of disguise; you inwardly congratulate a pertinacious poet and critic on having at last done something which his friends may quote concerning him; and you feel that his achievement need only be known to be appreciated. If your announcement, together with this disclaimer, may in any way contribute towards such publicity, I shall the less regret the original inadvertence in your columns. (9 December 1871, p. 755).

The ruse worked even better than its perpetrators could have hoped. Quite evidently, Buchanan and Strahan had agreed to maintain silence, and Strahan accordingly sent this letter to the *Athenaeum:* "In your last issue you associate the name of Mr. Robert Buchanan with the article 'The Fleshly School of Poetry,' by Thomas Maitland, in a recent number of the *Contemporary Review.* You might with equal propriety associate with the article the name of Mr. Robert Browning, or of Mr. Robert Lytton, or of any other Robert." Buchanan was not so circumspect. With a characteristic flash of anger he penned a heated letter to the *Athenaeum* defiantly admitting his authorship. His letter is dated 12 December, the publication date of the issue which contained Colvin's letter, an indication that Buchanan wrote in hot haste and without deliberation.

> Russell Square, W., Dec. 12, 1871.

> I cannot reply to the insolence of Mr. "Sidney Colvin," whoever he is. My business is to answer the charge implied in the paragraph you published ten days ago, accusing me of having criticized Mr. D. G. Rossetti under a nom de plume. I certainly wrote the article on 'The Fleshly School of Poetry,' but I had nothing to do with the signature. Mr. Strahan, publisher of the *Contemporary Review,* can corroborate me thus far, as he is best aware of the inadvertence which led to the suppression of my own name.

> Permit me to say further that, although I should have preferred not to resuscitate so slight a thing, I have now requested Mr. Strahan to republish the criticism, with many additions but no material alterations, and with my name in the title-page. The grave responsibility of not agreeing with Mr. Rossetti's friends

as to the merits of his poetry, will thus be transferred, with all fitting publicity, to my shoulders.

> Robert Buchanan.

The *Athenaeum* was not slow to capitalize upon this windfall. At the end of Rossetti's "Stealthy School of Criticism" in the issue for 16 December 1871 it printed first Strahan's denial, then Buchanan's admission, and finally its own acrimonious comment:

> Mr. Buchanan's letter is an edifying commentary on Messrs. Strahan's. Messrs. Strahan apparently think it is a matter of no importance whether signatures are correct or not, and that Mr. Browning had as much to do with the article as Mr. Buchanan. Mr. Buchanan seems equally indifferent, but he now claims the critique as his. It is a pity the publishers of the *Contemporary Review* should be in such uncertainty about the authorship of the articles in that magazine. It may be only a matter of taste, but we prefer, if we are reading an article written by Mr. Buchanan, that it should be signed by him, especially when he praises his own poems; and that little "inadvertencies" of this kind should not be left uncorrected till the public find them out.

With the identity of the enemy clearly established, the way was open for a shot at him. Dante composed a pamphlet in answer to Buchanan's accusations, but, fearing a charge of libel if it were printed, suppressed it. From the pamphlet he made up a letter called "The Stealthy School of Criticism," which he published in the *Athenaeum* on 16 December 1871 [see excerpt in Dante Gabriel Rossetti entry, *NCLC*, Vol. 4]. Written in a quiet tone of gentlemanly protest, it contrasted favorably with the angry vitriol of Buchanan's attack. Not contented with this, he composed a ballad ridiculing his enemy which he intended to publish in the *Fortnightly*, but on Colvin's advice changed his mind and suppressed it.

Clearly uncomfortable because the *Athenaeum* had caught him in a falsehood, Alexander Strahan printed in *Pall Mall* on 23 December 1871, one week after the *Athenaeum's* damaging arraignment, a letter of defense. His weak expostulations were about as effective as those of a small boy caught with his hand in the cookie jar. He protested that his "short and hurried note" was not meant to enter into the question of authorship, but "was simply intended as a protest against the intolerable system of gossip-mongering to which our firm has been so frequently subjected." He complained that the *Athenaeum* had done him an injustice by printing his letter with Buchanan's so that "by putting the two together, an appearance of contradiction could be established, and Strahan and Co. be thus made to look ridiculous." He based his complaint on the childish contention that since he had written his letter earlier than had Buchanan, it should have been printed earlier. This blustering retort was seconded by one from Buchanan which was equally blustering and which had enough in common with Strahan's to indicate that they had profited from their former blunder of writing independently of each other. The issue of the *Athenaeum* for 23 December 1871 contained an angry letter from Buchanan in which he denied the statement of the editorial comment upon his letter of the week before. He pointed out that he had not praised his own poetry, but had instead disparaged it. He added a vainglorious insult to the editor which could do him no good with impartial readers: "It is in vain, perhaps, to protest against the comments of such a judge as you, but for every one who reads your journal a dozen will read my reprinted criticism, and will be able to see you in your true colours."

True to his defiant promise, Buchanan published his long-heralded book, *The Fleshly School of Poetry and Other Phe-*

nomena of the Day, early in 1872, this time under his own name. Strahan was the publisher of what turned out to be the magazine article revised and blown up to three times its original size. The more inclusive title is significant of the broadening of the base of his attack which accounts for most of the additions. In his preface he reviewed the history of the original article, reiterated his contention that the pseudonym was used without his knowledge, and then added grandiloquently, " . . . *in order that the criticism might rest upon its own merits and gain nothing from the name of the real writer.*" He defended himself from the charge of vanity by saying that whereas he took the character of Cornelius, who speaks only one line in *Hamlet,* he might have taken that of Fortinbras or the First Gravedigger. He said that the charge of vanity was but a red-herring to distract the attention of the public from the real issue, and exclaimed in disgust that, because Rossetti's poems were labeled "nuptial," they seemed to "have actually become favourites with that prude of prudes, the British matron; and several gentlemen tell me that their aunts and grandmothers see no harm in them!" The conclusion of the preface served notice that he had taken the bridle off his pen and permitted it to gallop at will through invective and savage insult, for he insisted, "Animalism is animalism, nevertheless, whether licensed or not; and, indeed one might tolerate the language of lust more readily on the lips of a lover addressing a mistress than on the lips of a husband virtually (in these so-called 'Nuptial' Sonnets) wheeling his nuptial couch out into the public streets." From this he proceeded to his attack, which was so farfetched, so ridiculous and phantasmagoric that the only conclusion one can reach is that it was the product of an abnormal mind. The record of his physical and mental troubles from 1866 to 1874 shows that he was neurotic and unstable; the *Fleshly School* pamphlet is proof that he had gone far toward catastrophe. His notes to the pamphlet are interesting. They include an excerpt from an article in the *Quarterly Review* in condemnation of "Jenny" and another called "Coterie Glory" from the *Saturday Review,* which took Rossetti and his friends to task for praising each other's works under the guise of criticism. Finally, there was a lengthy note praising Whitman and explaining that although he had written a few lines of indecent verse, he was by no means a fleshly poet.

The reactions to the Controversy were many and varied. One of the earliest replies to Buchanan appeared in R. H. Horne's preface to his poem *Orion,* written in November 1871, and published in 1872. Deprecating the recurrence of prudery, Horne argued that since the body came from the Creator it and its appetites could not be denied. Henry Buxton Forman, a scholarly friend of William Rossetti, published in *Tinsley's Magazine* in February 1872 an answer to the *Contemporary* article. In it he replied patiently and painstakingly to Buchanan's charges one by one, explaining the background and context of each one of Buchanan's quotations. *Temple Bar* agreed with Buchanan's viewpoint: ". . . Mr. Rossetti and his admirers have been told a few wholesome truths. There is in all the writings of this school a *fleshliness* which is meant to be natural, but is exaggerated and unwholesome . . ." (XXXIV, 99-100). It agreed that the system of friends writing approving criticism of the work of friends was evil and should not be condoned. The consensus, however, was against Buchanan. *The Illustrated News,* noting that a current issue of *St. Paul's Magazine* contained several of Buchanan's sonnets, sneered: "Mr. Buchanan, having quarrelled with Mr. Rossetti, appears ambitious of proving that he can write sonnets too, and has produced a string of these compositions, which assuredly run no risk of being mistaken for the production of his rival" (LX, 490).

Fraser's, after a scholarly discussion of the merits of the poetry of Rossetti, Swinburne, Morris, and Tennyson, said of Rossetti: "Mr. Rossetti has come nearest to the embodiment of the heart's desire of the school; but though he is often artificial, fantastic, and wilfully obscure, he has a real power which cannot be explained away by calling him fleshly, sub-Tennysonian, or any other names" (N.S. V, 588-596). The *Athenaeum* reviewed the matter of the pseudonym, calling it an alias and implying that Buchanan had lied in his disclaimer (25 May 1872, pp. 650-651). It deplored his lack of judgment in republishing his charges and the ridiculous lengths to which he had gone in expanding them. It concluded that "malicious friends" must have advised him to publish the pamphlet, and quipped:

> Mr. Buchanan tells how the miasmic influence of Italy 'generated madness even far north as Hawthornden and Edinburgh.' What influences may have generated so much foolishness even as far north as the Hebrides we cannot tell; but only that the foolishness is there, and has ended in a worthless and discreditable treatment of what might have been made a perfectly just and interesting question of criticism.

The *Saturday Review* began by agreeing with Buchanan's accusations that Rossetti and Swinburne resented all adverse criticism, that their poetry was "fleshly" and effeminate, and their influence "mischievous." Then it lashed Buchanan for his egoism and bad taste in printing the pamphlet. Ironically, it observed of his excuse that the pseudonym was used to avoid giving the article the added power of his name:

> In the old romances we occasionally read of a knight of tremendous prowess and overpowering reputation, who found it necessary, in order not to alarm antagonists too much, to enter the lists with closed visor and borrowed shield; but Mr. Buchanan is hardly a combatant of this description. There is no reason to suppose that his name carries with it an oracular authority which would be fatal to the free exercise of private judgment; and, on the other hand, it is conceivable that the general reader would appreciate the necessity of examining his dicta more cautiously when aware of the peculiar relations of the critic to the objects of his criticism.

It satirized his morbid imagination in fancying sensuality in everything about him, and thought that most of the trouble lay in his own head. It scoffed at the inconsistency of his admiration for Whitman and concluded: "There is unhappily a spreading taint of sensualism, which may be traced in various directions at the present moment, but it may be seriously doubted whether such productions as this pamphlet are not calculated rather to minister to than to check it" (XXXIII, 700-701). The *Graphic* thought that the pamphlet contained "more objectionable stuff than in anything we have seen lately" (V, 606). It was of the opinion that Buchanan had forfeited his right to a serious hearing by the ridiculous lengths he had gone to in proclaiming some of the most beautiful poetry in English literature tainted with sensuality, and then praising Walt Whitman and Paul de Kock.

Buchanan fired one last shot at Rossetti in an article published in *St. Paul's Magazine* in March 1872. His main object was patently to repair the slight on Tennyson in his article and pamphlet, for he flattered the Laureate by eulogizing him for the nobility of his verse as exemplified in his "The Parting of Arthur and Guinevere." Then, by way of contrast, he appended a footnote with several illustrations of what he considered Rossetti's affected language and concluded: "Here is Euphues come again with a vengeance, in the shape of an amatory foreigner ill-acquainted with English, and seemingly modelling his style on the 'conversation' of Dr. Samuel Johnson.'' The epithet, ''an amatory foreigner,'' betrays Buchanan's prejudice and reveals the reason why he set upon the Rossettis with such savagery, while by comparison his style of address to his arch-foe, Swinburne, is almost courteous.

Buchanan soon learned that the *Athenaeum* had spoken with the voice of prophecy and that the publishing of the pamphlet had been a grave error. He had expected powerful forces to rally to his support, but none did. (pp. 65-81)

Matters went even worse for the man he had attacked. He attempted suicide with an overdose of laudanum in 1872, and from that date until his death in 1882 he lived a broken man whose course, though he occasionally revived sufficiently to do a little painting and writing, was steadily downward.

But although Rossetti was incapable of answering his attacker, Swinburne was not. In 1872 he wrote and published his ''Under the Microscope,'' one of the most savage lampoons in the language, inspired principally by Buchanan's taunts. He did not honor his foe by deigning to argue with him as Rossetti had done in ''The Stealthy School''; he belabored him with epithets, insults, and scurrilous insinuations; he left him not one shred of dignity as a human being; but cast him aside at the conclusion as a foul serpent too loathsome to touch. To do justice to Swinburne, it must be noted that he had had ample provocation for his reprisal and that he, too, having begun the bibulous practices which were to lead almost to his undoing, was by no means in complete possession of himself. In ''Under the Microscope'' he more than evened the score for anything Buchanan had said or done. With some justice Buchanan could say in later years that, had he not been made of sturdy fibre, he might have suffered a fate like that of Rossetti.

Although his armor was dented and his head reeling from Swinburne's doughty blows, he still had spirit to fight back. In *St. Paul's Magazine* he published his retort, ''The Monkey and the Microscope,'' in which he once again satirized Swinburne's vanity and amorous proclivities:

Once, when the wondrous work was new,
I deemed Darwinian dreams untrue,
But now I must admit with shame
The caudal stock from which we came,—
Seeing a sight to slay all hope:
A Monkey with a Microscope!

A clever Monkey—he can squeak,
Scream, bite, munch, mumble, all but speak;
Studies not merely monkey-sport
But vices of a human sort;
Is petulant to most, but sweet
To those who pat him, give him meat;
Can imitate to admiration
Man's gestures, gait, gesticulation;
Is amorous, and takes no pain
To hide his Aphrodital vein;
And altogether, trimly drest
In human breeches, coat, and vest,
Looks human, and upon the whole
Lacks nothing, save perchance a Soul.
For never did his gestures strike
As so absurdly human-like,
As now, when, having found with joy
Some poor old human Pedant's toy,
A Microscope, he squats to view it,
Turns up and down, peers in and thro' it,

Screws up his cunning eye to scan,
Just like a clever little man!
And from his skin, with radiant features,
Selecting small inferior creatures,
Makes mortal wonder in what college he
Saw real Men study entomology?

A clever monkey!—worth a smile!
How really human is his style;
How worthy of our admiration
Is such delicious imitation!—
And I believe with all my might
Religion wrong and science right,
Seeing a sight to slay all hope:
A Monkey use a Microscope!

The controversy lay dormant through 1873 and 1874 and might have expired altogether had it not been for Swinburne, who published his *Essays and Studies* in 1875 with the addition of the ill-natured footnote on Gray in his ''Matthew Arnold's New Poems.'' While outwardly interested only in identifying Gray, he called him ''a poor young Scotchman'' who received aid from Dobell and Houghton, referred to his poems as ''his poor little book,'' accused him of plagiarizing ''some of the best known lines or phrases from such obscure authors as Shakespeare and Wordsworth into the somewhat narrow and barren field of his own verse . . .'' and railed upon his ''hysterical self-esteem.'' By way of explaining why he used Gray to illustrate his point, he added unconvincingly:

I may add that the poor boy's name was here cited with no desire to confer upon it any undeserved notoriety for better or for worse, and assuredly with no unkindlier feeling than pity for his poor little memory, but simply as conveying the most apt and the most flagrant as well as the most recent instance I happened to remember of the piteous and grievous harm done by false teaching and groundless encouragement to spirits not strong enough to know their own weakness.

Buchanan could hardly have doubted that Swinburne's prime objective was himself. If knowledge of Buchanan's sentimental relationship to the deceased Gray had not come to him through his association with Lord Houghton, Buchanan's memoir of Gray published in 1864 would have apprised him of the fact. The footnote was unworthy of Swinburne and shows that on his side also the Controversy was being conducted without any pretense to literary sportsmanship. This is the note which Buchanan erroneously said led to his original *Contemporary* article of 1871. One point which cannot be doubted is Buchanan's assertion that the note enraged him to the point of desiring revenge. The blows at himself in the essay of 1872 he had taken, but this attack on his dead and innocent friend was another matter. He sought eagerly for an opportunity to strike back and subsequent events gave his enemy into his hands.

In the summer of that same year, 1875, was published an anonymous poem entitled *Jonas Fisher*. The author was actually James Carnegie, the Earl of Southesk, but it is not surprising that it was attributed by Swinburne and the Rossetti circle to Buchanan because Buchanan had announced that his *Orm* was a prelude to an epic poem which was to follow, after the manner of Wordsworth; *Jonas Fisher*, while it is not called an epic, is a poem which fills a book of 243 pages and is as prolix and verbose as the *Drama of Kings;* also, the style of the verse closely resembles Buchanan's: it is of a rough and unfinished quality and is really only prose set to rime with many stumbling lines and marks of hasty and inept composition. In content the resemblance is even closer. The entire poem is a versified criticism of the times, much after the manner of the *Spectator* of Addison and Steele and in the same vein as the *Fleshly School* pamphlet; particularly, it deplores the immorality of current literature and hints at France as the fountainhead of all such pernicious tendencies. If Swinburne required any further proof that *Jonas* was Buchanan's handiwork, he found it in its appearance at exactly the right time for the expected riposte to his thrust at Gray. He was quick to retaliate with four lines of scornful verse in the *Examiner* on 20 November 1875, which show to what depths a great poet could descend when under the joint influence of malice and alcohol:

> He whose heart and soul and tongue
> Once above-ground stunk and stung,
> Now less noisome than before,
> Stinks here still, but stings no more.
>
> A. C. SWINBURNE

A week later the same paper came out with a review of *Jonas,* devoting its first long paragraph to speculating that Buchanan was the probable author:

> This anonymous poem is said by the "London Correspondents" to be the work either of Mr. Robert Buchanan or of the Devil; and delicate as may be the question raised by this double sided supposition, the weight of probability inclines to the first of the alternatives. That the author, whichever he is, is a Scotchman, may be inferred from one or two incidental sneers at the characteristic virtues of his countrymen. If a prophet has no honour in his own country, it must be said on the other hand that a country seldom gets much honour from its own prophet; the worst things said about countries have been said by renegade natives. (27 November 1875, p. 1336).

That the review had come to Buchanan's attention is evidenced by his printing in the *Athenaeum* on 4 December 1875 a flat denial that he had even seen *Jonas Fisher*. The denial brought forth an acrid retort from the *London Quarterly* that since the real author had not signed the poem, he "thus afforded Mr. Robert Buchanan a favourable opportunity (not altogether lost) of getting up another fuss about himself" (XLV, 527-528).

Either the disclaimer did not convince Swinburne, or he chose to overlook it in his desire to use the opportunity to burlesque the whole matter of the original *Contemporary* article and the pseudonym. In the *Examiner* for 11 December 1875 he printed a letter titled "The Devil's Due" and signed "Thomas Maitland." The letter opened with a long paragraph imitating the style of Buchanan's critical essays with a bewildering number of reservations, insinuations, and definitions; after some scornful references to the poem it came to an end with the pseudonymous signature and the date-line "St. Kilda, December 28, 1875," all of which was, of course, directed at Buchanan's excuses for the use of the original pseudonym. That his readers might not overlook the implication of dishonesty, Swinburne added a postscript purporting to be Buchanan's instructions to his publisher: "P.S.—On second thoughts, it strikes me that it might be as well to modify this last paragraph and alter the name of the place affixed; adding at the end, if you please— not that I would appear to dictate—a note to the following effect:—" What follows is a malicious parody of both Buchanan's and Strahan's notes to the *Athenaeum:*

> The writer of the above being at present away from London, on a cruise among the Philippine Islands, in his steam yacht (the Skulk, Captain Shuffleton master), is, as can be proved on the oath or the solemn word of honour of the editor, publisher, and propri-

etor, responsible neither for an article which might with equal foundation be attributed to Cardinal Manning, or to Mr. Gladstone, or any other writer in the *Contemporary Review,* as to its actual author; nor for the adoption of a signature under which his friends in general, acting not only without his knowledge, but against his express wishes on the subject, have thought it best and wisest to shelter his personal responsibility from any chance of attack. This frank, manly, and consistent explanation will, I cannot possibly doubt, make everything straight and safe on all hands.

Buchanan took his time about entering suit, perhaps because he was living in Ireland and did not wish to undertake an unpleasant winter journey to London to set legal machinery in motion. However, his intentions were advertised early enough to bring about the immediate suppression of Swinburne's pamphlet of "The Devil's Due," which he had published concurrently with the newspaper article. With the advent of summer he proceeded to bring his tormentor to justice by suing Mr. P. A. Taylor, owner of the *Examiner,* for five thousand pounds for libel done him in the review of *Jonas Fisher* and in the anonymous "The Devil's Due," with most of the charge resting upon the latter. The formal charge read: ". . . that the said letter was written . . . with the malicious intention of injuring the plaintiff's position and abusing his personal character . . . ." The hearing began on Thursday, 29 June, and lasted until Saturday, 1 July 1876. It was held in the Common Pleas Division of the High Court of Justice before Justice Archibald and a Special Jury. Charles Russell and a Mr. MacClymont represented Buchanan, while Taylor retained as his attorneys the Messrs. Murphy, Nathew and Hawkins, and Williams. Despite considerable dodging about England to avoid being dragged into the trial, Swinburne was subpoenaed on 18 or 19 June, he and the Earl of Southesk being the only witnesses called. Because Swinburne freely acknowledged the letter, Taylor's counsel attempted to save their man by suggesting that the suit against the publisher be dropped in favor of one against the author, but Swinburne had a friend in the enemy's camp in MacClymont, who prevailed upon Buchanan not to change his suit. In response to the Justice's question as to why they were unwilling to do this, Counsellor Russell replied for Buchanan, irritating Swinburne by stating that he "was a man of straw who presumably could not be made to pay up, and therefore they had fallen back on the proprietor of the paper as a scapegoat . . . ." This last is Swinburne's angry interpretation of the attorney's answer rather than the actual words used in court.

With this point settled, the trial proceeded and entered upon some amusing ramifications. In order to prove the libel Buchanan's attorneys had to review the facts attendant upon the original *Contemporary* article. Their man, they said, "in the course of his public duty as a critic and writer had had occasion to examine the works of certain writers of English verse, and to point out that some of the works of those writers were obscene, indecent, and offensive to sound moral and religious taste." This gave the defense attorneys an opportunity they quickly seized. Reading excerpts from "The Session of the Poets," Hawkins tried to prove that Swinburne had had ample provocation for his letter; and when Buchanan unblushingly offered the makeshift excuse that his poem had been directed at Swinburne's writings and not his person, even the Judge was moved to comment incredulously. Finally, to prove Buchanan's insincerity in his attack on the Fleshly School, Hawkins forced him to acknowledge his praise of Whitman's poetry;

whereupon the attorney, producing an unexpurgated edition of those poems, triumphantly submitted them to the Judge and the jury for silent examination because they were considered too evil to read aloud. To this poser Buchanan replied that he still considered Whitman a "colossal mystic" and fundamentally "a spiritual person."

In his summation to the jury, Justice Archibald indicated rather clearly that he sided with Taylor. He carefully defined libel and warned that something written simply in bad taste could not be construed as libellous. Although he pointed out that Taylor was responsible for anything printed in his paper, he advised that if the jury was of the opinion that Swinburne rather than Taylor should have been sued, this point might affect the amount of damages charged against Taylor. Then he blandly stated that the matter of Buchanan's provoking the alleged libels could not affect the case of Taylor since it had not concerned the publisher but only Swinburne, *who should have been sued in his stead.* Turning his attention to the two poets, he observed that many of the works of the so-calld "Fleshly School" would have been better unwritten; but since they had been written, "they were not too be rebuked except in a grave and serious way; and if, instead of this, they were made the excuse of a sensational essay, and the same faults were reproduced by repetition and unnecessary quotation, such a mode of treatment must be taken into account by the jury in assessing damages." He followed this by reading passages from the *Contemporary* article and "The Session of the Poets," commented adversely upon Buchanan's defense of Whitman, and asked the jury if they thought the author capable of honest criticism of the Pre-Raphaelites.

The jury, however, were of a different mind and stood upon their constitutional rights to arrive at their own verdict. The *Athenaeum* summed up the trial by explaining that they were swayed by Swinburne's unsavory reputation, by Taylor's being a radical and his paper having radical and deistic principles, and by the fact that Buchanan was poor and Taylor rich. They deliberated only twenty minutes before awarding Buchanan damages of one hundred and fifty pounds.

The trial created a sensation in London literary circles and, by virtue of the humorous comments upon it, was viewed as somewhat of a comedy. Only *The Times* dignified it with a long, detailed report. The *Illustrated News* regarded it as a "dolorous lawsuit" of quarrelling poets which made nobody happy, not even Justice Archibald, becuase he wore a white hat and a quotation was read from one of Buchanan's poems ridiculing judges in white hats (LXIX, 42). *Once a Week* agreed it was a mistake for poets to attack each other and that the trial had done only harm in advertising a deal of obscene poetry (IV, 265). The *Athenaeum* regarded Buchanan's triumph as a hollow victory brought about by a biassed jury and inept counsel rather than by the merits of his case (8 July 1876, pp. 50-51). *Pall Mall* made its report in the form of a dialect poem in which an imaginary cockney named Samuel Perkins—a lineal descendant of Dickens' Sam Weller—used the incident as the basis of a lengthy sermon to his son on the evils of writing poetry and the futility of human strife. After reviewing the history of the Controversy and the incidents leading to the trial, Perkins said:

> That you see's what comes of printin' what a hangry poet writes.
> Lor! what larks to see them lawyers overaul Buchanan's lines
> Dippin' in their scoops to try 'em like my cheeses, through the rines!
> Tastin' this and smellin' t'other. "Isn't this a little strong?"

"Call that pure?" "Well, what of this now, for a hammatory song?"
Yes, by George, I never laughed so 'earty, nor I never shall,
As at 'earing Mr. 'Awkins read about that Injin gal,
And the cuddlin' in the forest! Well, per'aps it meant no harm,
Still the author owned hisself the scene was just a trifle warm.
Then, of course, Buchanan's counsel—he was not a goin' to fail;
So he dropped upon the "fleshlies" right and left and tooth and nail!
"Grossly senshal," "most indecent," "hanimal passion consecrated."
Says the judge, "A style of poitry 'ighly to be deprecated!"
Well, the upshot was Buchanan gets his verdic safe and sound,
And he comes on Mr. Taylor for a hundern-fifty pound.
But, Lord love you, my dear Dudley, what a foolish price to pay!
What a terrible exposy for the poets of the day!

(3 July 1876, p. 5)

The trial ended all activity along the fleshly front until 1881 and the appearance of Buchanan's novel, *God and the Man,* some six months before Rossetti's death. It is impossible to delineate the circumstances which led up to Buchanan's apology to Rossetti contained in the dedication of his novel, but it is probable that in the intervening years since his pamphlet of 1872 he heard rumors and gossip in literary circles of the pitiable condition of the man he had attacked. Always tenderhearted toward any unfortunate, his conscience must have plagued him with the thought that he had contributed to Rossetti's unhappiness. More accurate and detailed reports of his enemy's condition probably came to him from Westland Marston, who was a long-term friend of both Rossetti and Buchanan, and from Hall Caine, who became intimate with Rossetti in 1879. There was at least one other factor involved: in 1881 Buchanan was a very different man from the neurotic and psychotic disputant of 1871 and 1872. Not only had he regained most of his mental stability, but the impending death of his wife sharpened his sympathies with his fellowman, especially a fellowman who, like Rossetti, had more than an ordinary claim upon his commiseration. The result of all these influences is the two verses with which he dedicated his novel of hatred and forgiveness:

> To An Old Enemy.
>
> I would have snatch'd a bay leaf from thy brow,
>   Wringing the Chaplet on an honoured head;
> In peace and tenderness I bring thee now
>   A lily-flower instead.
>
> Pure as thy purpose, blameless as thy song,
>   Sweet as thy spirit, may this offering be:
> Forget the bitter blame that did thee wrong,
>   And take the gift from me.

Before his death Rossetti had heard of the verses and was moved by them as he was also by Buchanan's poem, "The Lights of Leith," which Caine read to him. After his death Buchanan added two more stanzas for a later edition, this time placing Rossetti's name above them:

> To Dante Gabriel Rossetti.
>
> Calmly, thy royal robe of Death around thee,
>   Thou sleepest, and weeping Brethren round thee stand—
> Gently they placed, ere yet God's crown'd thee,
>   My lily in thy hand!

> I never knew thee living, O my brother!
>   But on thy breast my lily of love now lies;
> And by that token, we shall know each other,
>   When God's voice saith 'Arise!'

Not satisfied even with this, he prostrated himself at his enemy's feet in a final prose paragraph:

> Since this work was first published, the 'Old Enemy' to whom it was dedicated has passed away. Although his name did not appear on the front of the book, as it would certainly have done had I possessed more moral courage, it is a melancholy pleasure to me to reflect that he understood the dedication and accepted it in the spirit in which it was offered. That I should ever have underrated his exquisite work, is simply a proof of the incompetency of all criticism, however honest, which is conceived adversely, hastily, and from an unsympathetic point of view; but that I should have ranked myself for the time being with the Philistines, and encouraged them to resist an ennobling and refining literary influence (of which they stood, and stand, so mournfully in need), must remain to me a matter of permanent regret.

In a somewhat different tone is the letter written to Caine by Buchanan after Rossetti's death and published in a footnote in Caine's *Recollections*. Here he reviewed the quarrel, confessing his error and not in any way rescinding his apology to Rossetti, but defying "the horde of slanderers who hid within his shadow" and left no epithet unturned to injure Buchanan. Quite evidently his forgiveness and apology did not extend to Messrs. Swinburne, William Rossetti, and others of the enemy forces.

His final word on Rossetti was said in his "A Note on Dante Rosetti," an essay published in 1887 in his *A Look Round Literature,* wherein he showed how far he had moved with his times under the impact of Zolaism and Ibsenism by boldly stating that all love, even the fleshly variety, was the highest human pleasure.

But Buchanan was to discover he had raised a genie he could not command. Within a few months after Rossetti's death the staid *British Quarterly* in a review of Rossetti's "House of Life" sonnets described him as coarsely sensual and everything he had been called in the "Fleshly School" (LXXVI, 54-63). This so angered Buchanan that he reiterated his apology with added emphasis in *A Look Round Literature*. Again in 1882 in a review of his novel, *The Martyrdom of Madeline*, the *Academy* mistook what was probably an attack upon George Moore and the cult of aestheticism for a ghoulish lampooning of the dead Rossetti (XXI, 428-429). This brought a speedy and bitter denial from Buchanan in a letter to the *Academy* in which he remarked that Swinburne had now forsaken fleshliness and Morris and Rossetti had never embraced it. Sarcastically he asked the readers of the *Academy* to reexamine his novel

> to compare the lineaments of my Blanco Serena, a society-hunting, worldly minded, insincere, but good-humoured, fashionable painter, with the literary image of Mr. Rossetti [,] a solitude-loving, unworldly, thoroughly sincere and earnest, if sometimes saturnine man of genius, in revolt against society. The blundering of windmill-criticism could surely go no further. (XXII, 11-12).

Strategically Buchanan's several apologies were the worst thing he could have done for his own cause. Rossetti's friends might have blamed his death upon Buchanan even so, but the unre-

served admission of error, instead of placating them by its manliness and straightforwardness, brought them down upon him in a veritable avalanche of accusation and imprecation. The incongruous fact that Rossetti's demise did not take place until a full ten years after the *Fleshly School* pamphlet, was overlooked. They were quick to clothe him in the white robes of a martyr and to cast Buchanan in the sinister garb of executioner, pointing to his recantation as conclusive proof of his guilt. The various matters of provocation given Buchanan by William and Swinburne were conveniently relegated to the background or forgotten altogether. Minimized were the long and increasing use of chloral and alcohol by Dante Gabriel, his haunting memory of his wife's death with the corroding suspicion that his neglect had caused her to commit suicide, the subsequent desecration of her grave to recover his poems—all of which were certainly factors in the poet's catastrophe. His defenders stubbornly insisted that Buchanan's attack was the major cause of his collapse, probably from a desire to cover up Rossetti's shortcomings on the one hand and to damn a common enemy on the other. The melodramatic quality of their claims undoubtedly appealed to the Victorian audience, trained as it was to love melodrama and to think in its terms. Another propaganda device was employed in that the story was told so often and with such vehemence by so many different persons that even the skeptical were convinced. As for Buchanan, his several apologies had robbed him of the power to speak out in his own behalf without appearing to give the lie to himself, so he was forced to endure in silence the slings and arrows of his outrageous fortune which pelted him from all sides from Rossetti's death in 1882 until his own passing in 1901.

Within a year after Rossetti's death Theodore Watts published an article in the *Nineteenth Century* comparing the attack upon him with those upon Keats and Poe and calling upon the poet's friends to stamp out any lingering traces of the charge of sensuality which yet might cling to his name (XIII, 404). In its review of *Foxglove Manor* the *Spectator* sneered that no member of the Fleshly School had ever done anything more morally obnoxious (LVII, i, 652-653). George Moore aimed a cut at the old wound in his passage at arms with Buchanan in 1889, when he described Buchanan as a failure rejected by Moore and all other true descendants of Rossetti and Swinburne. William Rossetti in his book, *Dante Gabriel Rossetti As Designer and Writer,* published in 1889, implied that Buchanan should have admitted his error much sooner than he did and pointed to the apology as complete justification for William's having labeled the attack unfair and uncalled for all along. In the same year William Bell Scott published in his *Autobiographical Notes* his account of the events leading up to and following the "Fleshly School." While he admitted the precarious condition of Rossetti's mind before 1871, the use of chloral and alcohol, and the controlled criticism of the *Poems,* he stated flatly and arbitrarily that Buchanan's onslaught was the deciding factor in the artist-poet's breakdown. Tenacious and unimaginative William Rossetti re-entered the fray in 1895 with a *Memorial* to his brother which is chiefly remarkable for its display of that strong family loyalty not uncommon to people of Italian blood. Denying the truth, that Dante had shepherded the criticisms of his *Poems,* he argued that Buchanan's own words in his apology proved his attack a "miserable" and "disgraceful" matter inspired only by jealousy of Dante's success. He insisted his brother had been a well man until 1872, that the attack had brought on increased use of chloral, and that it had been a direct cause of Dante's subsequent misfortunes and torments. (pp. 81-92)

The Fleshly Controversy passed into history with most literary people holding the view crystallized by William Rossetti and the *Saturday Review* [LXXX, 838-839]: that the death of Dante Rossetti had been brought about by the action of a disagreeable and envious man who had had none but the basest of motives for his attack. Buchanan's later polemics against a variety of people and institutions did much to solidify this opinion. With the advent of modern realism in all forms of art and with the progress of science, the mind of the times became more frank and liberal, so that subjects which had called forth shocked revulsion in the 1860's and 1870's were regarded with equanimity in the '80's and '90's. Buchanan's attack, therefore, assumed a more and more ridiculous aspect even to periodicals which had agreed with him in 1871 and 1872. (p. 92)

John A. Cassidy, "Robert Buchanan and the Fleshly Controversy," in PMLA, Vol. LXVII, No. 2, March, 1952, pp. 65-93.

SATIRES AND PARODIES

JOHN BURLEY WARING

[*Waring satirizes the Pre-Raphaelite Brotherhood and Ruskin, referred to as "Buskin," in this 1857 poem.*]

William Holman Hunt's 1852 painting The Awakening Conscience. *Walker Art Gallery, London.*

Oh, we live in wretched days, there are few whom we can praise,
Save the happy band of brothers, who "Pre-Raffaelleite" are called;
All the rest will come to grief, with no hope of relief,
And by our prophet, Buskin, will be regularly mauled.

Still no more will we say, of the painters of to-day,
Who, if they only join our ranks, may yet perhaps be saved;
But for Raffaelle and his crew, we will pink them through and through,
And Buskin's name in blood upon their souls shall be engraved.

That Raffaelle was a fool, like all others of his school,
Without sentiment or soul,—a sensual heathen brute;
But although he has a name, yet Buskin soon his fame
Shall scratch and tear to tatters, and trample under foot.

As for wretched Buonarotti, so contorted, coarse, and dotty,
Such a humbug diabolical has never yet been known;
As emissary from Hades, from whom gentlemen and ladies
Should turn in proper horror, and entirely disown!

There's that satyr, J. Romano; that immoral Tiziano;
Giorgione, Tintoretto, Guido,—demons one and all,
Whom we loathe, abhor, detest; and we swear to take no rest
Till we dance upon their monuments, both great and small.

Oh, Rembrandt's simply bosh; and Ruben's actual slosh;
And those who dare say otherwise are fools, and dogs, and slaves.
Vandyke, Ostade, and Snyders, with the squad of Dutch outsiders,
Were a set of heartless, pagan, drunken, muddle-headed knaves.

As for poor old Claude Lorraine, Buskin makes it very plain
That a muff more unartistic we couldn't well conceive;
Whilst dull Salvator Rosa is a "maladetta cosa,"
And they and all who follow them are doomed without reprieve.

The Poussins and Le Brun, we will show you very soon,
Were nothing more than pagans of the deepest, blackest dye,
In fact, throughout the century, to take an oath we venture, ye
Will find no Christian sentiment, or anything that's high.

And every single Spaniard is ridiculously mannered;
Velasques and Murillo, with Zurbaran as well;
Old Cano and El Greco, would a pretty party make, oh!
In a place that mayn't be mentioned, as I need not tell.

In that *place* they all have got, let us hope, a fiery lot,
For the dark artistic crimes which they committed here on earth,
Whilst we shout with might and main, till the heavens vibrate again,
That High Art in Great Britain has at last been brought to birth.

And Buskin swears that now, if your knee you do not bow,
And humbly; to the Genius of this Infant so divine,
He will give you such a slashing,—such a mashing, crashing, thrashing,
As befits a set of donkeys, or a herd of filthy swine.

So, you see, we must be right; and, having put you in a fright,
Go, burn your stupid ancient daubs, and come to us to school;
Then perhaps you may, some day, find out the proper way
To look on Art and Nature, and cease to be a fool.

(p. 122)

John Burley Waring, "Pre-Raffaelleite Chorus," in Pre-Raphaelitism: A Bibliocritical Study by William E. Fredeman, Cambridge, Mass.: Harvard University Press, 1965, p. 122.

GEORGE DU MAURIER

[*Du Maurier's parody of Morris's poetry, excerpted below, was first published in* Punch *in 1866.*]

Tall Braunighrindas left her bed
At cock-crow with an aching head.
    O miserie!
"I yearn to suffer and to do,"
She cried, "ere sunset, something new!
    O miserie!
To do and suffer, ere I die,
I care not what. I know not why.
    O miserie!
Some quest I crave to undertake,
Or burden bear, or trouble make."
    O miserie!
She shook her hair about her form
In waves of colour bright and warm.
    O miserie!
It rolled and writhed, and reached the floor:
A silver wedding-ring she wore.
    O miserie!
She left her tower, and wandered down
Into the High Street of the town.
    O miserie!
Her pale feet glimmered, in and out,
Like tombstones as she went about.
    O miserie!
From right to left, and left to right;
And blue veins streakt her insteps white;
    O miserie!
And folks did ask her in the street
"How fared it with her long pale feet?"
    O miserie!
And blinkt, as though 'twere hard to bear
The red-heat of her blazing hair!
    O miserie!
Sir Galahad and Sir Launcelot
Came hand-in-hand down Camelot;
    O miserie!
Sir Gauwaine followed close behind;
A weight hung heavy on his mind.
    O miserie!
"Who knows this damsel, burning bright,"
Quoth Launcelot, "like a northern light?"
    O miserie!
Quoth Sir Gauwaine: "*I* know her not!"
"Who quoth you *did?*" quoth Launcelot.
    O miserie!
"'Tis Braunighrindas!" quoth Sir Bors.
(Just then returning from the wars.)
    O miserie!
Then quoth the pure Sir Galahad:
"She seems, methinks, but lightly clad!
    O miserie!
The winds blow somewhat chill to-day.
Moreover, what would Arthur say!"
    O miserie!
She thrust her chin towards Galahad
Full many an inch beyond her head. . . .
    O miserie!
But when she noted Sir Gauwaine
She wept, and drew it in again!
    O miserie!
She wept: "How beautiful am I!"
He shook the poplars with a sigh.
    O miserie!
Sir Launcelot was standing near;
Him kist he thrice behind the ear.
    O miserie!

"Ah me!" sighed Launcelot where he stood,
"I cannot fathom it!" . . . (who could?)
    O miserie!
Hard by his wares a weaver wove,
And weaving with a will, he throve;
    O miserie
Him beckoned Galahad, and said,—
"Gaunt Braunighrindas wants your aid . . .
    O miserie!
Behold the wild growth from her nape!
Good weaver, weave it into shape!"
    O miserie!
The weaver straightway to his loom
Did lead her, whilst the knights made room;
    O miserie!
And wove her locks, both web and woof,
And made them wind and waterproof;
    O miserie!
Then with his shears he opened wide
An arm-hole neat on either side,
    O miserie!
And bound her with his handkerchief
Right round the middle like a sheaf.
    O miserie!
"Are you content, knight?" quoth Sir Bors
To Galahad; quoth he, "Of course!"
    O miserie!
"Ah, me! those locks," quote Sir Gauwaine,
"Will never know the comb again!"
    O miserie!
The bold Sir Launcelot quoth he nought;
So (haply) all the more he thought.
    O miserie!

(pp. 1-2)

George Du Maurier, "A Legend of Camelot," in his A Legend of Camelot: Pictures and Poems, *Harper and Brothers, Publishers, 1898, pp. 1-12.*

WILLIAM HURRELL MALLOCK

[*Offering a "recipe" for Pre-Raphaelite poetry, Mallock ridicules the archaic diction, imagery, and style that characterize many Pre-Raphaelite poems. This piece was first published in 1872.*]

Take a packet of fine selected early English, containing no words but such as are obsolete and unintelligible. Pour this into about double the quantity of entirely new English, which must have never been used before, and which you must compose yourself, fresh, as it is wanted. Mix these together thoroughly till they assume a color quite different from any tongue that was ever spoken, and the material will be ready for use.

Determine the number of stanzas of which your poem shall consist, and select a corresponding number of the most archaic or most peculiar words in your vocabulary, allotting one of these to each stanza; and pour in the other words round them, until the entire poem is filled in.

This kind of composition is usually cast in shapes. These, though not numerous—amounting, in all, to something under a dozen—it would take too long to describe minutely here; and a short visit to Mr.——'s shop, in King Street, where they are kept in stock, would explain the whole of them. A favourite one, however, is the following, which is of very easy construction. Take three damozels, dressed in straight night-gowns. Pull their hairpins out, and let their hair tumble all about their shoulders. A few stars may be sprinkled into this with advantage. Place an aureole about the head of each, and give each a lily in her hand, about half the size of herself. Bend their necks all different ways, and set them in a row before a stone wall, with an apple-tree between each, and some large flowers at their feet. Trees and flowers of the right sort are very plentiful in church windows. When you have arranged all these objects rightly, take a cast of them in the softest part of your brain, and pour in your word-composition as above described.

This kind of poem is much improved by what is called a burden. This consists of a few jingling words, generally of an archaic character, about which we have only to be careful that they have no reference to the subject of the poem they are to ornament. They are inserted without variation between the stanzas.

In conclusion, we would remark to beginners that this sort of composition must be attempted only in a perfectly vacant atmosphere; so that no grains of common-sense may injure the work whilst in progress. (pp. 471-72)

> William Hurrell Mallock, *"How to Make a Modern Pre-Raphaelite Poem,"* in The Pre-Raphaelites, *edited by Jerome H. Buckley, The Modern Library, 1968, pp. 471-72.*

WILLIAM SCHWENCK GILBERT

[Gilbert is best known for his collaboration with Sir Arthur Sullivan on a series of comic and satirical operas. In the following lyrics from the 1881 opera Patience, *Gilbert describes the aesthete Bunthorne with many Pre-Raphaelite features.]*

BUNTHORNE'S RECITATIVE

Am I alone,
    And unobserved? I am!
Then let me own
    I'm an aesthetic sham!

This air severe
    Is but a mere
      Veneer!

This cynic smile
    Is but a wile
      Of guile!

This costume chaste
    Is but good taste
      Misplaced!

Let me confess!
A languid love for lilies does *not* blight me!
Lank limbs and haggard cheeks do *not* delight me!
I do *not* care for dirty greens
    By any means.
I do *not* long for all one sees
    That's Japanese.
I am *not* fond of uttering platitudes
    In stained-glass attitudes.
In short, my mediaevalism's affectation,
Born of a morbid love of admiration!

BUNTHORNE'S SONG

If you're anxious for to shine in the high aesthetic line as a
    man of culture rare,
You must get up all the germs of the transcendental terms, and
    plant them everywhere.
You must lie upon the daisies and discourse in novel phrases
    of your complicated state of mind,
The meaning doesn't matter if it's only idle chatter of a
    transcendental kind.

And everyone will say,
  As you walk your mystic way,
"If this young man expresses himself in terms too deep for
    me,
Why, what a very singularly deep young man this deep young
    man must be!"

Be eloquent in praise of the very dull old days which have
    long since passed away,
And convince 'em, if you can, that the reign of good Queen
    Anne was Culture's palmiest day.
Of course you will pooh-pooh whatever's fresh and new, and
    declare it's crude and mean,
For Art stopped short in the cultivated court of the Empress
    Josephine.
  And everyone will say,
  As you walk your mystic way,
"If that's not good enough for him which is good enough for
    me,
Why, what a very cultivated kind of youth this kind of youth
    must be!"

Then a sentimental passion of a vegetable fashion must excite
    your languid spleen,
An attachment *à la* Plato for a bashful young potato, or a not-
    too-French French bean!
Though the Philistines may jostle, you will rank as an apostle
    in the high aesthetic band,
If you walk down Piccadilly with a poppy or a lily in your
    mediaeval hand.
  And everyone will say,
  As you walk your flowery way,
"If he's content with a vegetable love which would certainly
    not suit *me,*
Why, what a most particularly pure young man this pure
    young man must be!"

(pp. 476-78)

> William Schwenck Gilbert, *"From 'Patience',"* in The Pre-Raphaelites, *edited by Jerome H. Buckley, The Modern Library, 1968, pp. 476-78.*

HENRY DUFF TRAILL

[Traill's 1882 parody of Dante Gabriel Rossetti's "Sister Helen" and "House of Life" sonnets appears below.]

"Why do you wear your hair like a man,
           Sister Helen?
This week is the third since you began."
"I'm writing a ballad; be still if you can,
           Little brother.
    (O Mother Carey, mother!
What chickens are these between sea and heaven?)"

"But why does your figure appear so lean,
           Sister Helen?
And why do you dress in sage, sage green?"
"Children should never be heard, if seen,
           Little brother.
    (O Mother Carey, mother!
What fowls are a-wing in the stormy heaven!)"

"But why is your face so yellowy white,
           Sister Helen?
And why are your skirts so funnily tight?"
"Be quiet, you torment, or how can I write,
           Little brother?
    (O Mother Carey, mother!
How gathers thy train to the sea from the heaven!)"

"And who's Mother Carey, and what is her train,
　　　　　Sister Helen?
And why do you call her again and again?"
"You troublesome boy, why that's the refrain,
　　　　　Little brother.
　(O Mother Carey, mother!
What work is toward in the startled heaven?)"

"And what's a refrain? What a curious word,
　　　　　Sister Helen!
Is the ballad you're writing about a sea-bird?"
"Not at all; why should it be? Don't be absurd,
　　　　　Little brother.
　(O Mother Carey, mother!
Thy brood flies lower as lowers the heaven.)"

　　(A big brother speaketh:)
"The refrain you've studied a meaning had,
　　　　　Sister Helen!
It gave strange force to a weird ballàd,
But refrains have become a ridiculous 'fad,'
　　　　　Little brother.
　And Mother Carey, mother,
Has a bearing on nothing in earth or heaven.

"But the finical fashion has had is day,
　　　　　Sister Helen.
And let's try in the style of a different lay
To bid it adieu in poetical way,
　　　　　Little brother.
　So Mother Carey, mother!
Collect your chickens and go to—heaven."

(A pause. Then the big brother singeth, accompanying
　himself in a plaintive wise on the triangle:)

"Look in my face. My name is Used-to-was,
　I am also called Played-out and Done-to-Death,
　And It-will-wash-no-more. Awakeneth
Slowly, but sure awakening it has,
The common-sense of man; and I, alas!
　The ballad-burden trick, now known too well,
　Am turned to scorn, and grown contemptible—
A too transparent artifice to pass.

"What a cheap dodge I am! The cats who dart
　Tin-kettled through the streets in wild surprise
　Assail judicious ears not otherwise;
And yet no critics praise the urchin's 'art,'
Who to the wretched creature's caudal part
　Its foolish empty-jingling 'burden' ties."

　　　　　　　　　　　　　(pp. 473-75)

Henry Duff Traill, "After Dilettante Concetti," in
The Pre-Raphaelites, *edited by Jerome H. Buckley,*
The Modern Library, 1968, pp. 473-75.

L. E. JONES

[In this bogus extract from Millais's diary, Jones caricatures
Millais, Dante Gabriel Rossetti, Ruskin, and his wife, Effie.]

June 11th. Began "Ophelia". Effie and I read together the
passage beginning: "There is a willow grows aslant a brook."
We both cried a little.

June 12th. Effie brought me nettles and daisies, but no crow-
flowers or long purples. D.G.R., who was here, advised her
to consult some liberal shepherds. I threw him out. Effie refused her lunch.

June 18th. J. said:"Clothes can't hold a person up in fresh
water; that could only happen in the Dead Sea." I said, "How
could O. get from Denmark to the Dead Sea?" That shut him

up. But may he be right? Ruskin, with his confounded "truth"
would never let it pass.

June 20th. Overheard Effie telling the footman, who had re-
ferred to the painting as "Ophelia," to call it "Miss Ophelia."
Felt this going rather far, since O. is in Shakespeare. E. said,
"But your O. isn't." Not very happy about it.

June 25th. Dean Stanley brought young P. Albert Edward to
studio. Asked who the lady was, the P. said, "The Lady of
Schallott?" Stanley reproved him, rather harshly, I thought.

June 26th. Article by Ruskin praising my Academy picture,
d—— him. Effie cried.

June 27th. D.G.R. came. Said "Corpses float face-down-
wards." I said, "Not when singing." That shut him up.

L. E. Jones, "Sir John Millais: While Painting
'Ophelia'," in his À La Carte, *Secker & Warburg,*
1951, p. 23.

HISTORICAL AND CRITICAL SURVEYS

R. L. MÉGROZ

[Mégroz relates the poetry of the Pre-Raphaelites to that of the
Romantic movement.]

The almost threadbare term "Pre-Raphaelite", since it cannot
conveniently be dispensed with, affords a notable instance of
the ambiguity in literary labels. Robert Bridges, in his well-
known essay on Keats, stressed the importance of Keats as an
influence in the Pre-Raphaelite movement. Perhaps he over-
stressed that influence, for where poetry is concerned, owing
to Rossetti, both Blake and Coleridge were also potent forces
throughout the latter half of the nineteenth century. In Keats's
"Isabella" Bridges found

> a characteristic agritude of passion, which makes the
> best occasion to speak of the curiously close simi-
> larity which exists between him and the school of
> painting which had Rossetti for its head. The lovers
> who "could not in the self-same mansion dwell with-
> out *some malady*", the "sick longing" of Isabella,
> the "passion both meek and wild", the "little sweet
> among much bitterness", the consciousness of some-
> thing too horrible to speak of behind the scene, and
> all the passionate faintness of the personages of the
> romance,—in whom, as in a faded tapestry, the bril-
> liance of the raiment has outlasted the flesh-colour,—
> have a likeness to the creations of this school so
> remarkable, that Keats may be safely credited with
> a chief share of parentage.

Bridges' plausible phrasing of second-hand opinions (he obviously knew very little about nineteenth-century painting) is
none the less misleading for coming from such an authoritative
source. All that generalization about the 'school' of painting
seems very flimsy in view of the fact that Rossetti's pictures
have so little in common with the work of the other recognized
Pre-Raphaelite painters. Except for two only of Millais's early
and uncharacteristic paintings (the Ophelia and that of a Nun-
nery garden), Bridges' description of the pictured figures cannot be applied to the work of any other important painter besides
Burne-Jones. The dream-like figures in the immature work of
Lizzie Siddal, which owe so much to Rossetti's early water-
colour paintings, correspond most fully with the critic's ret-

rospective impression of the school. As for Pre-Raphaelite poetry, where is the comparison (to begin with) in morbidity or decorated languor between the figures in 'Isabella'' and the tragic passions of the persons in Rossetti's narrative and ballad poems—"Sister Helen'', "The Bride's Prelude'', "A Last Confession'', "The Staff and Scrip''? Can it be that the gorgeous texture of such poems still obscures their tremendous energy?

That view of Pre-Raphaelite poetry as a sort of wish-washy emotionalism became hardened into a critical habit after the chief work of the movement was done, and imitators were hastening its decline. The associations with languid lilies and exotic sin, when not traceable to Swinburne's *Poems and Ballads,* is derived from the completely different later cult of Wilde and Pater. Nevertheless, since the label obviously has a meaning, if only it calls to mind Rossetti and Swinburne, the significance of it has to be differentiated both from the intentions which led to its original adoption and to the ultimate degradation of the slogan.

Three young painters, Rossetti, Millais and Holman Hunt, formed themselves into a "Pre-Raphaelite Brotherhood'' as a gesture of defiance to the prevailing academic principalities and powers. Their not-well-considered choice of a name was largely due to Rossetti's transient admiration for Ford Madox Brown's imitation of the German pseudo-primitive school, represented by the sugary Overbeck. This led to his interest in the genuine Italian primitives, whom he alone could fully appreciate. It was, however, only through the friends seeing some engravings by Lasinio from the Campo Santo frescoes in Pisa that their violent but vague feeling of revolt against the contemporary academic style of painting took shape as an attack on Raphaelism. Crude as were the engravings, the young men detected a sincerity in the original artists which was lacking in the effete style of the academicians. The work of the young painters was soon to show that apart from enthusiasm they had little in common. Moreover, the genius of Rossetti soon drew him into a renaissance in poetry as intense as the renaissance in painting.

In the perspective of a century the decline in painting and poetry appears to be due simply to the persistence of powerful influences expressed as a prevailing taste for schools that had ceased to be vital. Behind such an explanation, as always, there is the real cause, a temporary hiatus in the recognition of new work of genuine originality. The lesser artists are dominated by the contemporary taste, and the crowd of unoriginal practitioners are not so much dominated as inspired by the echoes of what is already concluded. They busy themselves in giving the public what it wants or what the academic critics of the time want. (What the public wants *in the long run* is not so very different from the enduring new work which only a few recognize at the moment of its appearance.) Here and there a genius of strong originality remains for a while as a voice crying in the wilderness.

Little might have been heard of the Pre-Raphaelite movement in painting (for the Brethren soon broke apart) had not Ruskin stamped it by his championship with some sort of critical meaning, which ultimately he found very difficult to apply to the new work being done. In poetry, however, the forceful personality of Rossetti imparted a directional impulse so strong that it has been described as a second romantic revival. How much truth there is in this we shall see. Note that the impulse owed little to any other member or associate of the original P.R.B. except Christina Rossetti, whose poetry conveys with

the least mixture of other elements the refined luxury and clarity of the Pre-Raphaelite ideal. The width of this term when used for criticism is indicated by the fact that an important painter and an important poet—Ford Madox Brown and Tennyson—who both stood apart from the P.R.B.s, did work almost as clearly Pre-Raphaelite as any later painters and poets, although their inspiration in this vein quickly exhausted itself. Some of the earliest work of Coventry Patmore also betrayed the common influence, and though he went beyond the Pre-Raphaelite standards of naturalism with his *Angel in the House,* he came back later into sympathy with other Pre-Raphaelite qualities in his Odes. There is no doubt at least that Tennyson's best early poems, in the vein of "The Lady of Shalott'' and "The Lotos-Eaters'', and Brown's middle-period work, like *The Carpenter's Shop,* which caused such a hullabaloo in the Press, not only have a family likeness to poetry and painting by recognized Pre-Raphaelites but take a fairly high place among such works.

Two younger poets, Swinburne and Morris, and a young painter, Burne-Jones (he was practically forced into painting by the enthusiasm of the others), became disciples of Rossetti after the original P.R.B. and its organ *The Germ* had fallen into desuetude. It was the work of this second boisterous group which centred itself round Rossetti at Oxford during the painting of the Union Hall, plus Christina Rossetti's poetry, that constituted the chief contributions to a "Pre-Raphaelitism'', which had, except for Rossetti, lost touch with Italian archaism and found new fields in medieval legends and neo-classicism. The almost forgotten work of lesser poets shows how extensively the literary atmosphere was pervaded by similar aims. Thomas Woolner, the sculptor, was one of the contributors to *The Germ* and his verse, although it differs from that of his early associates, in owing more to Shelley than Keats, has often the family likeness. His superiors in poetry, the Irish William Allingham; and Richard Watson Dixon and John Nichol, who came under the Rossetti-Swinburne-Morris spell, also reveal their kinship. Allingham might be described almost as a lesser Christina Rossetti, Dixon a smaller Rossetti (but in part he was quite unlike Rossetti in his inclination for metaphysical thought), and Nichol, a fraction of a fraction of Swinburne. There were also Arthur O'Shaughnessy (1844-1881), Lord de Tabley (1835-1895) and Philip Bourke Marston (1850-1887), the blind poet, who, like Dixon and several other lesser men of the age, received the stimulus of Rossetti's forceful praise. Such poets might be regarded as precursors of the later and less original group of decadents in which Oscar Wilde occupied a position comparable with Rossetti's in the Pre-Raphaelite movement. (pp. 13-17)

A definitely Pre-Raphaelite anthology could be made of poems written in the quarter-century roughly between 1845 and 1870. Such a collection would illuminate the source of much of the best poetry written during the period we are surveying. . . . It might assist in the distinguishing of certain traits that we perhaps feel rather than logically isolate in Pre-Raphaelitism to name first some poems of the preceding Romantic Revival which occur to the mind as models or presages of the Pre-Raphaelite style.

> KEATS: "The Eve of St. Mark'', *Hyperion* (first draft), "La Belle Dame Sans Merci'' and "The Eve of St. Agnes'' (in spite of its merely factual errors) and several sonnets.
>
> COLERIDGE: "Christabel'' and "The Rime of the Ancient Mariner''.

WORDSWORTH: "The Leech-Gatherer", "The Reaper", "The Reverie of Poor Susan" and the sonnet "Composed on Westminster Bridge".

SHELLEY: *Alastor, The Cenci*, and a few lyrics.

This group of poems is marked by what we may describe as sharpness of sensory impressions made auxiliary to ideal (or imaginative) perception. The composition often has a dream-like effect, not only by the familiar yet far-away imagery, but also by the associational freedom of fantasy which is inseparable from the successful creation of such imagery.

Another characteristic, largely arising out of the one just noted, is the freshness of colour and naturalism of feeling. The word "naturalism" at once provokes a query about the weird or "supernatural" atmosphere which pervades poems like "Christabel" and "La Belle Dame". The fascination of weirdness in such poems is not due to any sacrifice of naturalism in the psychology or imagery; it is actually enhanced because of the naturalism; as in Shakespeare's tragedies, universal emotions of love, hate, and fear are raised to extraordinary tension by an environment of natural imagery luridly displayed in a fantastic light by the more or less obvious use of the pathetic fallacy. But for this inward truth to nature in the double sense of realism, in description and psychology, the Romantic Revival through Coleridge would have made no progress from the already abundant eighteenth-century "Gothic" literature of strangeness and horror, in which dream-like imagery is exploited vainly in crude and falsely "romantic" themes. Just as Coleridge was the chief Romantic creator of mysterious atmosphere, so Rossetti is the fount of the mid-century revival of such hauntings of the unseen. The "supernatural" element therefore cannot be subtracted from what we envisage as Pre-Raphealitism. Nevertheless the emphasis on accuracy of perception and a fresh naturalism of sentiment is clearly an equally important and a more exclusively Pre-Raphaelite characteristic. A strong sense of occult forces is a matter of temperament, but freshness of perception is possible to artists as different in temperament as Holman Hunt and Rossetti, or Coleridge and Wordsworth. There is nothing of a photographic realism in the art of either, at their best. In the *Prelude* Wordsworth stresses the idealizing process of the creative imagination, attributing to the poet's newly created world the poise of fixed laws, according to which is maintained

> an ennobling interchange
> Of action from without and from within;
> The excellence, pure function, and best power
> Both of the objects seen, and eye that sees.

No doubt an emphasis upon the "eye that sees" helped to give poetry of the early nineteenth century the character we label as Romantic. . . . (pp. 24-5)

The imaginative idealism which imparts to realistic imagery a symbolic or dream quality can be seen in the Pre-Raphaelite poetry as clearly as in the poems typical of the Romantic Revival which have been enumerated. What did alter considerably were the poetic "properties". There was much more borrowing from medieval and archaic themes, of the type of the *Morte d'Arthur*, and also, owing to Rossetti, from Christian hagiology. Rossetti's "Blessed Damozel" and translations from Dante led to Morris's invocation to his lady as "Madonna", and after Morris came a host of minor singers of Madonnas and lilies.

Patmore in his *Unknown Eros* odes (1877) opened a way in a new direction, for he was the least Romantic of the poets who contributed (as he does in the Odes) to Pre-Raphaelite poetry,

and the most original after Rossetti. In the *Unknown Eros* he took the liturgical eroticism of Rossetti's "House of Life" from a blind-alley of passion and linked it to the wisdom of religion, with of course an authentic art of his own which certainly cannot be described as Romantic without straining the term. If in the long run the Romantic character seems to predominate in Pre-Raphaelite poetry, that is solely due to the temperamental leanings of the chief Pre-Raphaelite poets, notably Rossetti and Swinburne.

Against that previous list of poems we may put a list that roughly belongs to dates a quarter of a century later:

TENNYSON: "The Lady of Shalott", "The Palace of Art", "The Gardener's Daughter", "St. Agnes' Eve", "Mariana in the South".

(It is noteworthy how Tennyson always fails to come to grips with reality if he deals like Wordsworth with homely and contemporary characters. His irrepressible moral humbuggery makes most of his narratives absurd, and undermines the vitality of the otherwise "Pre-Raphaelite" *Idylls of the King*.)

D. G. ROSSETTI: "The Blessed Damozel", "The Bride's Prelude", "Jenny", "A Last Confession", "Sister Helen", "The Burden of Nineveh", "The Staff and Scrip", "A Trip to Paris and Belgium; (i) London to Folkestone", and several sonnets.

CHRISTINA ROSSETTI: "An Apple Gathering", "The Pink Mezereon", "Sleep at Sea", "The Convent Threshold", "Goblin Market", "Dream Love", "Remember Me".

A. C. SWINBURNE: "In the Orchard (Provençal Burden)", "At a Month's End", "The Leper", "The Garden of Proserpine", "Before the Mirror", *Atalanta in Calydon*.

COVENTRY PATMORE: *To the Unknown Eros.*

WILLIAM MORRIS: *The Defence of Guinevere*, and other Romances. Tensely dramatic narratives like "The Haystack in the Floods" as well as the picturesque and dream-like "Rapunzel" and "Two Red Roses across the Moon". His prose romances, like "The Hollow Land", are also seen to have close affinities with Rossetti's small quantity of poetry in the form of prose fantasies.

DIXON: "St. Mary Magdalene", "St. John", "Cephalus and Procris".

DE TABLEY: "Ophelia", much of *Philoctetes*, the Ode to Pan.

MEREDITH: *Bellerophon*, "Love in the Valley", "The Lark Ascending".

We have now to note that as early as 1866 Rossetti was already denying the relevancy of the term "Pre-Raphaelite" applied to himself, and a decade later Swinburne says in an unpublished letter:

> Before 1860 my early work had no doubt a savour of the same influences as the earlier work of Morris and Rossetti,—but from the date of *Chastelard* and *Atalanta* onwards I cannot trace in any part of my work, classical, modern, or historic, a trace of any quality that could correctly or even plausibly be labelled "Pre-Raphaelite" either for praise or blame.

Swinburne carefully excludes *Atalanta in Calydon*, presumably because of the classical theme and the brilliant improvisation on traditional metres, but the predominantly romantic colour of the poem is recognized at once in a contrast with his later

Erectheus which he came to look upon as more Greek in spirit. And its association with Pre-Raphaelite poetry becomes inevitable when we compare it with the unmistakably Pre-Raphaelite *Philoctetes* by Lord de Tabley which was, unfortunately for the lesser poet, published less than a year before *Atalanta in Calydon.*

As M. Lafourcade reminds us, the definitely ''Pre-Raphaelite'' portion of Swinburne's work, even excluding *Atalanta,* is no inconsiderable one if it only includes most of the first series of *Poems and Ballads.* In fact, however, there is a good deal more of the ''Pre-Raphaelite'' in Swinburne than this, not only in many later lyrics and ballads but in the choice of a theme like that of *Tristram of Lyonesse.* Very different from Morris's treatment of a similar theme in *The Defence of Guinevere,* and owing little if anything to Malory, Swinburne's *Tristram,* it may be said, is medieval in theme and resplendently coloured because of the dominant influence over him of his Pre-Raphaelite friends. So a similar literary mood is felt in the more classical Arnold's poem, ''Tristram and Iseult''. Without the plaster morality of Tennyson's *Idylls of the King,* Arnold's poem shows the same reaching back to an archaic glamour and a definitely Pre-Raphaelite naturalism in sentiment and details. The glamorous atmosphere has faded almost away; it is not to be compared with the dream stillness and clarity of Morris and the early Swinburne, but the hints of it are strong enough to occupy the gap between those later Pre-Raphaelites and Francis Thompson, who is the next great poet in a succession which goes back past Rossetti and the youthful Tennyson to Keats and Coleridge and Blake, and thence to the old ballads and Malory. If the glamour of atmosphere and old and far-off things is sought in still later poetry, it can be traced in the eccentric and often powerful work of Charles Doughty, and in much of the work of Irish poets which has been grouped, thanks to W. B. Yeats, as belonging to the ''Celtic Twilight''. It is continued in such diverse modern English poets as Walter de la Mare, Gordon Bottomley and Edith Sitwell. Much of Edith Sitwell's poetry will be found undeniably descended from Pre-Raphaelitism, not in spite of her modern sources, but partially because of these, for the element shared in common between Rossetti and Keats, Wordsworth and Coleridge, is also a distinctive strain in Baudelaire and his French successors. Fromentin, who died in 1877, was a French painter and writer contemporary with the Pre-Raphaelite Brotherhood whose ideas often seem to agree with Rossetti's. He is significantly quoted by Ribot [in *The Creative Imagination*] as saying:

> My recollection of things, though very trustworthy, by no means has the exactness and general validity of an absolute record. As the exact form goes on it gradually becomes a new form, half-real, half-imaginary, which I consider more advantageous.

This declaration would not have gained the assent of the P.R.B.s, but it would nevertheless have served as a text for their best work, which they intended to be realistic in detail but which was actually the product of imaginative perception, the deliberate attention of the reason being given to observing facts. The kind of academic painting which the early P.R.B.s had revolted against was both prosaic and lacking in realism, though shallowness of sentiment and confusion of ideas were obvious enough in it.

In the contemporary poetry a good example of what the P.R.B.'s called ''slosh'' is afforded by a competent piece of inanity like ''The Poet's Heart'' by Samuel Laman Blanchard (1804-1845). It is typical of ''slosh'' in the arts to smother potentially moving or profound themes with treacle and ''The Poet's Heart''is therefore quite in character.

More instructive than such an example is the evident deterioration in the style of a great poet like Swinburne. Long before he died in 1909 he had lost contact with the deeper sources of his inspiration. Nearly all his good poetry indeed had been published by 1882, the year which saw Rossetti's death and the publication of his own *Tristram of Lyonesse.* His *Songs before Sunrise* containing the wonderful ''Hertha'' appeared in 1871. There were a few things in the third series of *Poems and Ballads* (1889) and some notable passages in *Astrophel and Other Poems* (1894).

Swinburne still in ''A Nympholept'' beautifully weaves into the music of his thrumming lyre accurate and lovely impressions with exact ideas. But the exact ideas can rarely be grasped in sequences because usually a definite image is the prelude to some evanescent and half-seen outlines of ideas that rush after it:

> The face of the warm bright world is the face of a flower,
>   The word of the wind and the leaves that the light winds fan
> As the word that quickened at first into flame, and ran,
> Creative and subtle and fierce with invasive power,
>   From darkness and cloud, from the breath of the one god,
>   Pan.

Here the first line is both definite and comprehensive, but the succeeding ones are complicated not by thought so much as by the style itself. The double use of 'that' as a relative and then adjectivally is confusing though logical in the musical sense. The repetition of the same sound in ''that'' as of other sounds—''bright'' and ''light'', and the assonances of ''face''— ''flame'', ''creative''—''invasive''—all of them as strong as the alliterations—serves to echo the developed idea. The subsidence of the idea under the half-transparent surface of linked images encourages the reader's submission to the hypnotic spell of the metre, and after a few long stanzas one's mind seems to drown in a shimmering pool, and one longs for more projecting branches of statement to break up or shade the inconclusive brightness. ''A Nympholept'' is really a hymn to Pan and it is evidently imitated from the classical invocation which was accompanied by dancing. This affords a clue to what our attitude as readers should be. Nevertheless, the increased potency of the poetry can be felt at once when the poet unfolds his argument in a series of definite ideas:

> The whole wood feels thee, the whole air fears thee: but fear
>   So deep, so dim, so sacred, is wellnigh sweet.
> For the light that hangs and broods on the woodlands here,
>   Intense, invasive, intolerant, imperious, and meet
>   To lighten the works of thine hands and the ways of thy
>   feet,
> Is hot with the fire of the breath of thy life, and dear
>   As hope that shrivels or shrinks not for frost or heat.

The last quoted line reminds us how readily Swinburne, by using words as musical notes, also attenuates the idea, for the eleven words of that line are not only a prolix paraphrase for an invulnerable hope, but they bring no fresh image with them, and except for fulfilling a metrical necessity their ensemble is decidedly cacaphonous. (Just try saying them over.) It is no wonder that ''A Nympholept'' contains two hundred and seventy-three lines to express a mood and vision which might have been more powerfully expressed in half the length. The tendency to wordiness is still more evident in the descriptive and occasional pieces, e.g. ''Loch Torridon'' and ''Grace Darling'', although even in such pieces there is actually as much rational thought as one could find in the majority of poems. Thought often more searching indeed than one would find in most of Tennyson's or Browning's poems, but the ideas jostle one another and are repeated, and the words often fail to carry additions to the ideas when such developments would increase the force of the poem. The mind is similarly jostled at the same time by another stylistic effect of Swinburne's verse. The couplets of *Tristram of Lyonesse,* in spite of the poet's skill in varying pauses and stresses, become very monotonous and every now and again make a din in the mind, so that Swinburne's allusive and adjectival manner often submerges the argument and the tale itself underneath that same half-transparent surface of weakly linked images which are found in "A Nympholept". Take this brief example from the first section, "The Sailing of the Swallow":

> And with her sweet eyes sunken, and the mirth
> Dead in their look as earth lies dead in earth
> That reigned on earth and triumphed, Iseult said,
> "Is it her shame of something done and dead
> Or fear of something to be born and done
> That so in her soul's eye puts out the sun?"

The dramatic inappropriateness of the language put into Iseult's mouth troubles the reader; but still more does the almost absurd employment of the word "dead" three times in these few lines, each time except the first without meaning other than that of a vague rhetoric. If earth that "lies dead in earth that reigned on earth and triumphed" means a corpse buried under a grave covered by grass and flowers, the imagery is a stylistic affectation that makes a clear idea vague; but the injury to the poetry is even deeper than this, because the image of the triumphant earth, although the poet means beauty alone, suggests a glad beauty, which is the opposite of that intended by the description of Iseult's mirthless look. When he is at his best as in the noble "Ave Atque Vale" to Baudelaire, rhetoric is a perfection of the style, a light blowing on the flame of poetry:

> For sparing of his sacred strength, not often
>   Among us darkling here the lord of light
>   Makes manifest his music and his might
> In hearts that open and in lips that soften
>   With the soft flame and heat of songs that shine.
>   Thy lips indeed he touched with bitter wine,
> And nourished them indeed with bitter bread;
>   Yet surely from his hand thy soul's food came,
>   The fire that scarred thy spirit at his flame
> Was lighted, and this hungering heart he fed
>   Who feeds our hearts with fame.

But it was Swinburne's rhetorical faults that minor poets were to echo for nearly two decades because the Swinburnean style in all its richness and its metrical force cannot be adapted to ecstasies less keen and intelligence less richly furnished than those of Swinburne at his highest level.

The deterioration in Swinburne's individual style has much in common with the insidious disintegration which belongs to a literary decadence, and is to be distinguished from the more consistent crudities in the style of William Morris, which prevent one ranking him with the great poets of the last century, just as in the succeeding generation the inadequate technique of John Masefield robbed us of another major poet. Morris always lacked the artistic mastery of the literary medium which might have made his poetic fame secure, but his genius as a poet of the day-dreaming imagination, like Masefield's indeed, is not to be denied, and will for a long time yet hold youthful readers in thrall. But Swinburne's always eclectic diction and metrical skill are seen beginning in *Tristram of Lyonesse* to

lack the divine necessity of expression. Many of the French experiments, from Mallarmé's musical symbolism to Verlaine's marvellous fluting with vowels, are due less to urgent needs of developing art than to the weakening of spiritual motives for great poetry.

If great poets can by example as well as influence encourage the writing of pseudo-poetry, it is not astonishing that every original impulse in poetry should be distorted or diluted by unoriginal writers, and "slosh" derived from the Rossetti-Morris-Swinburne movement is to be found at the end of the century even more easily than we can still find (in anthology selections, too) the "slosh" half a century earlier derived from the Romantic Revival. For pseudo-poetry quickly absorbs the preciosities of a literary decadence. (pp. 28-36)

R. L. Mégroz, "Pre-Raphaelite Poetry," in his Modern English Poetry: 1882-1932, *Ivor Nicholson & Watson, Ltd., 1933, pp. 13-36.*

W. W. ROBSON

[Robson discusses the stylistic qualities of Pre-Raphaelite writing in this excerpt from his survey of the major poets of the movement, Dante Gabriel Rossetti, Christina Rossetti, and Morris.]

The poets of the Victorian age were numerous, and they included some people of talent and even of genius. But the greatest imaginative writers of the period are novelists, not poets. The reasons for this decline of poetry are disputable, but the fact of the decline itself can hardly be questioned. For Victorian poetry, though it often reaches a high degree of sophistication and shows a conscious care for style and form,

Dante Gabriel Rossetti's self-portrait in 1847.

does not satisfactorily embody the life of the age; it is not at its best when it tries to put to poetic use a wide range of the emotional, intellectual, and moral interests of an intelligent adult. It is usually more successful when it either ignores these or transposes them, by more or less subtle means, into some mode of evasion. And this is true even of the poets who dutifully attempt to grapple with the world they lived in; who offer thought, or a moral burden for the times; since their success as poets, when they are truly poets, is significantly *like* the achievement of their avowedly un-didactic successors: in creating a dream world; in withdrawing to memories of childhood over which a glamour of ideality is thrown; or in making incantation, decoration, emotional overtones, and other incidental beauties of style, serve as beguiling substitutes for the centrality of themes, and completeness of command of them, characteristic of great poetry. (p. 352)

Perhaps Arnold had this contemporary situation in mind when he made his celebrated formulation: 'Poetry is at bottom a *criticism of life.*' Certainly he was the opponent, in his critical propaganda, of a trend which he discerned in the work of the great Romantic poets: a separation between 'poetry' and 'life'. It is these poets whose joint influence constitutes the Victorian poetic tradition. And the influence of none of them—not even Wordsworth's—was such as to counteract the trends which Arnold saw. One of them, indeed, was a chief inspiration and sanction to poets in the phase of Victorian Romanticism succeeding that of Tennyson and Ruskin; the original high priest of their Religion of Beauty was John Keats.

The Religion of Beauty is today somewhat *en baisse.* The work of the Pre-Raphaelites (like that of their successors in the Aesthetic Movement) is now generally judged to be not only inferior to, but in some ways deeply unlike, that of Keats. Pre-Raphaelite poetry is seen to bear a derivative and subordinate relation to that of the great Romantics, and even to the contemporary poetry of Tennyson and Browning. . . . My purpose here is not to suggest reasons for reversing this implicit verdict; nor to discuss whether other poets—notably Hopkins, but perhaps also Beddoes, Darley, or John Davidson—have better claims to be regarded as the true heirs of the great Romantics. I wish rather to consider what kind of interest Pre-Raphaelite poetry can be made to yield to the reader who shares, substantially, Arnold's view of the right relation between 'poetry' and 'life.'

By 'Pre-Raphaelite poetry' I mean the poetry of Dante Gabriel Rossetti (1828-82), of his sister Christina (1830-94), and of William Morris (1834-96)—though other poets, from Swinburne to Yeats, have Pre-Raphaelite connexions. D. G. Rossetti, the strongest personality and effective organizer of the group, deserves the chief critical attention. But he has hardly received it: his picturesque life and habit of confession have proved a biographical lure too strong for most critics. What is now known as the 'cult of personality' existed among the Pre-Raphaelites themselves and their followers; and the flood of autobiography, memoirs, and letters has not yet subsided. I am not of course saying that Rossetti's private life is irrelevant to the study of his poetry; any more, or any less, than the relation between devoutness and morbidity in Christina Rossetti, or the activity of Morris as designer, printer, or propagandist of Socialism, is irrelevant to the study of theirs. These things have their importance even for the literary critic: but they must be recalled in their due place, as ancillaries, not as substitutes, for the study of poetry, which is the study of what poets do with words.

But at this point an obvious objection must be met. Is it proper, or useful, to discuss Pre-Raphaelite poetry without discussing Pre-Raphaelite theory and practice in painting? The term 'Pre-Raphaelite' itself, as is well known, came to be used when the young Holman Hunt and the young J. E. Millais adversely criticized Raphael's *Transfiguration*, challenged the 'classical' doctrines expounded by Sir Joshua Reynolds, and extolled the superior purity and simplicity of the Italian primitives. And the movement began, at the close of the 1840s, as an attempt to introduce into visual art, not only the qualities of medieval Italian painting, but the naturalistic accuracy of detail thought appropriate to the dawning age of science. But by the 1850s what is now associated with Pre-Raphaelite painting—the merely decorative neo-medievalism, the subjectivity, the dreaminess—had become its dominant style. Painters were turning their eyes away from a contemporary industrial and urban world which was *ipso facto* hideous and hence, on Ruskinian principles, intractable to treatment in art. In any case, Rossetti himself—who is the literary critic's first concern—seems to have had no very intense interest in the philosophical basis of the early naturalism of Hunt and Millais. (The general lack of wide intellectual interests in the circle of Rossetti and Morris comes out clearly in contemporary accounts.) And that dogmatic concern with precision of detail, which excited the admiration of Ruskin and the scorn of Dickens, appears in Rossetti—the Rossetti of *Ecce Ancilla Domini*—only as a transient phase of style. He was always essentially a 'literary' painter, and the Pre-Raphaelite Brotherhood was fundamentally literary and preoccupied with literature. A literary approach, therefore, seems to be quite in order.

The adjective 'Pre-Raphaelite' in *literary* criticism suggests certain idiosyncrasies of style—sometimes they are hardly more than tricks—associated with the Rossettis and the early Morris. Yet many of them are to be seen in earlier poetry: in Tennyson's "Mariana" poems; in Coleridge's "Christabel" (which might be called the first Pre-Raphaelite poem); or in Keats's "The Eve of St. Mark". There is the deliberate simplicity (or *simplesse*) of manner, often found in conjunction with that curious trick of particularizing, e.g. numbers:

> She had three lilies in her hand,
> And the stars in her hair were seven.
>> (Rossetti, "The Blessed Damozel")

> There were five swans that ne'er did eat
> The water-weeds, for ladies came
> Each day, and young knights did the same,
> And gave them cakes and bread for meat.
>> (Morris, "Golden Wings")

There is the particularity of sensory detail, of which again the thematic relevance is not obvious; visual detail, as here:

> Without, there was a cold moon up,
> Of winter radiance sheer and thin;
> The hollow halo it was in
> Was like an icy crystal cup.
>> (Rossetti, "My Sister's Sleep")

Or auditory detail:

> Twelve struck. That sound, by dwindling years
> Heard in each hour, crept off, and then
> The ruffled silence spread again,
> Like water that a pebble stirs.
> Our mother rose from where she sat;
> Her needles, as she laid them down,
> Met lightly, and her silken gown
> Settled: no other noise than that.
>> ("My Sister's Sleep")

There is the archaizing and medievalizing, the cultivation of the ballad-mode and similar archaic forms, accompanied (especially in Morris) by a liking for archaic technical vocabulary:

> 'They hammer'd out my basnet point
>   Into a round salade,' he said.
> 'The basnet being quite out of joint
>   Natheless the salade rasps my head.'
>
> (Morris, "Old Love")

There is a characteristic Pre-Raphaelite taste in decoration, as in:

> Raise me a dais of silk and down;
>   Hang it with vair and purple dyes;
> Carve it in doves and pomegranates,
>   And peacocks with a hundred eyes;
> Work it in gold and silver grapes,
>   In leaves and silver fleur-de-lys;
>
> (Christina Rossetti, "A Birthday")

But these are superficial traits of style. More important for the critic is the recurrence of certain habits of feeling; especially a mood associated with autumn, regarded as the season of listlessness, decay, desolation, death; never, in Pre-Raphaelite poetry, the 'close bosom-friend of the maturing sun', but Tennyson's 'spirit' that 'haunts the year's last hours, Dwelling amid these yellowing bowers'; as in

> . . . the sere
> Autumnal springs, from many a dying year
> Born dead;
>
> (Rossetti, "The Stream's Secret")

> . . . the year grown old
> A-dying mid the autumn-scented haze,
> That hangeth o'er the hollow in the wold,
> Where the wind-bitten ancient elms enfold
> Grey church, long barn, orchard, and red-roofed stead,
> Wrought in dead days for men a long while dead.
>
> (Morris, "The Earthly Paradise: October")

> [Life's] very bud hangs cankered on the stalk,
>   Its very song-bird trails a broken wing,
>   Its very Spring is not indeed like Spring,
> But sighs like Autumn round an aimless walk.
>
> (Christina Rossetti, "Later Life")

Finally, there is the habit suggested by such passages as these:

> O thou who at Love's hour ecstatically
> Unto my lips dost evermore present
> The body and blood of Love in sacrament;
> Whom I have neared and felt thy breath to be
> The inmost incense of his sanctuary;
>
> (Rossetti, "Love's Redemption")

> This feast-day of the sun, his altar there
>   In the broad west has blazed for vesper-song;
>   And I have loitered in the vale too long
> And gaze now a belated worshipper.
>
> (Rossetti, "The Hill Summit")

This is religiosity: the use of religious language for evocative purposes, by a man to whom real religion means nothing. But with this example we have left the Pre-Raphaelite group as a whole and become aware of the need to make distinctions; religiosity is not a characteristic of Morris's poetry: formal religion meant little to him, and he was not tempted to exploit its language in this way; neither was Christina Rossetti—though for an opposite reason. But it is significant that the last two passages quoted from Rossetti could be endlessly paralleled in other Victorian poetry.

One feature all these examples have in common with each other, and with mid-Victorian poetry in general: their obvious literariness. In Rossetti especially, whether in his simple or his elaborate manner, one is conscious all the time of the artifice, the sophistication, of a poet using a diction and movement which he well knows to have been used before by other poets. There is little that is fresh, spontaneous, un-literary, immediate. The contrast with another poet-painter, William Blake, is illuminating. In reading Blake's successful poems ("O Rose, thou art sick", for example) we do not merely hear words, we 'see' things, and our 'seeing' is not confined to mere visualization ('In my mind's eye, Horatio'); since Blake's own 'seeing' is an activity of the intelligence, manifesting itself in an almost clairvoyant power of notation of mental and spiritual realities. In a Rossetti sonnet—to show the contrast with Blake at its most extreme—our response is predominantly a response to *words*, words heavily charged with literary association and reminiscence; there is nothing that is strong in imagery or concrete in evocation:

> So it happeneth
> When Work or Will awake too late, to gaze
> After their life sailed by, and hold their breath.
> Ah! who shall dare to search through what sad maze
> Thenceforth their incommunicable ways
> Follow the desultory feet of Death?
>
> ("Known in Vain")

We have only to ponder the metaphorical value of 'sailed' or 'maze' here, or the literal meaning of 'incommunicable', to see how small a part they play in the total effect. The words seem to be 'saying' a great deal, but to be 'doing' very little; and when we look up the passage in its context, the impressiveness of this 'saying' seems to be the *raison d'être* of the whole poem.

A care for finish of style and polish of phrasing takes the place of a scrupulous effort at definition of meaning. And when we admire the phrasing and music of

> Thenceforth their incommunicable ways
> Follow the desultory feet of Death?

and try to characterize more exactly the spirit of Rossetti's manipulation of the language, it is tempting to recall his Italian origin. But this use of English is an important part of English poetic history from Spenser and Milton to Keats and Tennyson. And the reservation we have about this use of language is not only that it leaves out, or does not employ creatively, so much that is centrally characteristic of English, the language of Shakespeare: its concrete expressiveness and mimetic vigour, its colloquial force, and the much richer music that arises from the playing-off of its speaking rhythm against the patterns of formal metre. It is not merely that the 'Italianate' use of English deprives it of the typically English energy of the verbs. The great limitation of the 'music' cultivated by Tennyson and Rossetti is that it is a medium unsuited to precise expression *of any kind*. This, no doubt, could be said to some extent of its earlier phases of development, in Spenser or in Milton. But it would be easy to find passages from those earlier poets in which there is plenty of general mental activity going on; whereas the Victorian development of this use of English, even in a 'sage-poet' like Tennyson, tends towards confusion, vagueness, and a progressive emaciation of the *content* of poetry. Thus, while Swinburne has his own music, which is not Tennyson's or Rossetti's, his well-known sacrifices of sense to sound, his rhythmic self-intoxication, his hypnotic cadences, his hallucinations of meaning dissolving inextricably into one another, may be considered as an exotic variant of the same tradition.

What is most important, for critical purposes, in this verbal music, appears not so much in frankly incantatory poetry like much in the early Morris ("The Blue Closet", for example), but in passages where the poet is making a sustained offer of thought and 'message'. It will be noted that the passage quoted above from Rossetti is sententious. And though Rossetti does not come before us, as Tennyson sometimes does, in the role of the Sage, but rather as a fellow-sufferer, his mature poetry is quite as sententious as Tennyson's, and ostensibly stakes quite as much on the reader's thoughtful acceptance of a message solemnly delivered. (Rossetti is never humorous or ironic in his successful poetry—at any rate, not in the "House of Life" sequence, where the moral-philosophical ambition is as apparent as the stylistic virtuosity.) And the admirer of Rossetti discovers 'fundamental brainwork' even in the more lush and mannered specimens of his later style ("The Stream's Secret", for example). But it seems fairest to verify the attribution of 'fundamental brainwork' by considering a poem in which Rossetti appears to be offering a deliberated and credal affirmation of his religion of beauty. This is the famous sonnet "Sibylla Palmifera", from which I quote the sestet:

> This is that Lady Beauty, in whose praise
> Thy voice and hand shake still,—long known to thee
> By flying hair and fluttering hem,—the beat
> Following her daily of thy heart and feet,
> How passionately and irretrievably,
> In what fond flight, how many ways and days!

Those who do not dislike this poem are not likely to be persuaded to do so by detailed fault-finding. But such is not my intention: I wish merely to show, by a particular inspection of the way Rossetti uses words, that the poem does not owe what impressiveness it has to 'fundamental brainwork', to the communication of anything precisely defined or clearly imagined; it is, rather, a gesture in a *general* direction, depending for its effect on the reader's anterior readiness for vague sympathy with the attitude suggested. Poetic skill is certainly there, in the means by which the despairing yet unchecked pursuit of 'Beauty' is communicated by the delayed caesura of the fourth line, the assimilation through alliterativeness of the '*flying* hair' and '*fluttering* hem' to the poet's 'Following'; and, more subtly, by the breathlessness conveyed in the associated aspirates in 'hair' and 'hem' and 'heart and feet'. But it is a skill which does little but display itself; we are merely *told* what this ardent though desperate pursuit, of which we are given a general sense, is a pursuit *of*; 'Beauty' remains something only vaguely gestured at, as in the poem's opening:

> Under the arch of life, where love and death,
> Terror and mystery, guard her shrine, I saw
> Beauty enthroned . . .

If we dislike the poem, we will be inclined to say that 'Beauty' from beginning to end remains as much a mere word as 'life', 'love', 'death', 'terror', and 'mystery' in this poem. And if we find ourselves resisting the hierophantic manner of the opening lines, we may be provoked in reaction to a closer examination of the seeming impressiveness of phrasing, the appearance of lapidary conciseness, exemplified in the sestet—'. . . in whose praise / Thy voice and hand shake still'. If we reflect for a moment—which the lines do not encourage us to do—on the meaning of 'shake' here, it will appear that whatever propriety the verb has in regard to the 'voice' of the poet trembling in praise of 'Beauty', it cannot have in regard to the 'hand' (of the painter); the word 'shake', in fact, represents the articulation of one vague meaning with another even vaguer. There is no real gnomic or graphic precision, only an appearance of it. Similarly with '. . . the beat / Following her daily of thy heart and feet': the appearance of compression, or effective zeugma, dissolves immediately [when] we bring the meaning of the word 'beat' here into focus. But bringing into focus is not, of course, what we are supposed to do. It is only the general effect that matters to the admirer of this poem; the predisposition to accept an attitude which is never more than suggested by the poet. But in compensation, the tone in which the suggestion is made combines grandiloquent expansiveness with unction. And it is on this tone of voice that objections will primarily centre; even the most sympathetic reader-aloud of the sonnet will find it hard to play down its unctuous rectitude:

> The allotted bondman of her palm and wreath.

It is significant that those who dislike this poem are usually told that they have an initial prejudice against its subject ('aestheticism'). But this retort in a way itself confirms the observations made above about the character of this sonnet; what is approved, or disapproved, by one reader or another, remains something *general,* something outside the poem which the poem itself merely gestures at; what is found impressive, or unimpressive, as the case may be, is nothing more specific than a manner and a tone of voice.

Rossetti, of course, wrote much better poems than "Sibylla Palmifera". Nor is the range of his powers best seen in things like "The Blessed Damozel", charming as that is. His most interesting work, in my opinion, is his turbid, mannered love-poetry, with its characteristic alternation of the hectic and the languid, of overripe voluptuousness and the chill of desolation.

> Stand still, fond fettered wretch! while Memory's art
> Parades the Past before thy face, and lures
> Thy spirit to her passionate portraitures:
> Till the tempestuous tide-gates flung apart
> Flood with wild will the hollows of thy heart,
> And thy heart rends thee, and thy body endures.
>
> ("Parted Love")

Over-sophisticated as this is, it has a certain power, though perhaps not of a very pleasing kind: the power of

> 'O ye, all ye that walk in Willowwood,
> That walk with hollow faces burning white;' . . .
> Alas! the bitter banks in Willowwood,
> With tear-spurge wan, with blood-wort burning red.
>
> ("Willowwood")

Willowwood is everywhere in this poetry: romantic idealization, and half-glimpsed behind it, its corollary of selfishness, and incapacity for a mutually respecting relation with another; ahead of it, the nemesis of inevitable disappointment, weariness with oneself, a sense of irretrievable waste and loss. The Rossetti of "Barren Spring", of "Lost Days", of "Retro Me, Sathana!", could have echoed Baudelaire's:

> Mais mon cœur, que jamais ne visite l'extase,
> Est un théâtre où l'on attend
> Toujours, toujours en vain, l'être aux ailes de gaze!

But the comparison with Baudelaire reminds us that the Rossetti of such poems is still the Rossetti of "Sibylla Palmifera". They reveal subtler ways in which the poetry insinuates an over-valuation of the experience it presents, but their limitation is essentially the same; the temptation, yielded to by the poet, to find in spiritual sickness the occasion for suggesting a spiritual superiority. That temptation is insidious, and I do not say that Baudelaire always overcame it; but his greatness is surely that he succeeded, in his finest poems, in diagnosing his own malady, and thereby making us see his own very special case in relation to more universal feelings, principles of health, and moral judgements. If Baudelaire's weaknesses as a poet are due to his Romanticism, his strength is that he was able at times to turn it into a creative force. Rossetti's guilt, remorse, and sensation of spiritual bankruptcy remain egocentric. The result is that doom of the emotionalist: monotony; the monotony which so soon afflicts the reader of his poetry, small in bulk though it is. Worse still is the pretentiousness which commonly accompanies the over-valuing of one's experience:

> Because our talk was of the cloud-control
> And moon-track of the journeying face of Fate,
> Her tremulous kisses faltered at love's gate
> And her eyes dreamed against a distant goal:
> But soon, remembering her how brief the whole
> Of joy, which its own hours annihilate,
> Her set gaze gathered, thirstier than of late,
> And as she kissed, her mouth became her soul.
>
>   ("Secret Parting")

The relation of the highfalutin of the opening to what follows is very obvious and very distasteful; the last line of the quotation is curiously vulgar. It is clear that the Meredith of *Modern Love* had forerunners.

But that is Rossetti at his worst. And there is at least one poem in which we glimpse a remarkable freshness and directness of perception, which suggest that Rossetti's potentialities as a poet were greater than his achievement. I am thinking of *Song IV* in the "House of Life", the poem called "Sudden Light", which begins:

> I have been here before,
>   But when or how I cannot tell:
> I know the grass beyond the door,
>   The sweet keen smell,
> The sighing sound, the lights around the shore.

From the first line onwards we have an unusually direct presentment of an individual's experience in a sensitively particularized situation. This particularity is very different from anything in "The Blessed Damozel": it contributes functionally to the recreation of that peculiar state, at once one of bewilderment and of clarity ('sudden light'). We notice how it brings in lightness, a fresh air, 'the sweet keen smell'—so un-Rossettian, un-Pre-Raphaelite, un-Tennysonian. The 'sighing' is no mere poeticality; it is precise in evocation, and the stanza as a whole, with all its rich suggestiveness, has no incantation, but rather the effect of statement.

But for critical purposes, the stanza in its context can only confirm the general judgement on Rossetti's poetry. For the poem modulates back into a familiar Pre-Raphaelite key: the static, dreamy atmosphere, which has not the transitory vividness of real dreams, but rather the insubstantiality of a waking dream or reverie:

> Shall we not lie as we have lain,
>   Thus for Love's sake,
> And sleep, and wake, yet never break the chain?

In view of Rossetti's love-poetry in general, with its ardours, hungers, opiates, and derelictions, it is interesting to note the plausibility here lent to Freud's theory that the *déjà vu* sensation is associated with the wish to return to the mother. But here we reach the frontier between criticism and psychiatry. And

we may leave Rossetti to pass the final judgement on his own work in those characteristic lines:

> Look in my face: my name is Might-have-been;
> I am also called No-more, Too-late, Farewell.
>
>   ("A Superscription")

Christina Rossetti's poetry has the Rossetti skill and the careful concern with form and design, and it has a Pre-Raphaelite vocabulary and colouring. But it has none of the over-sophistication and artificiality of her brother's poetry; it is never lush or mannered; nor does it succumb to the temptations, gross or subtle, which beset the poet who must seek, as becomes a devotional poet, to express an attitude of humility and self-forgetfulness. It is significant that one finds oneself appraising her work in these negative terms. For negation, denial, deprivation are the characteristic notes of Christina's religious poetry: and it must be admitted that an extensive reading of it is depressing. The sadness, often morbidity, which is felt even in her delightful poetry for children, even in *Goblin Market,* certainly in "The Prince's Progress"; the felt absence of any outlet for aggressive impulses, deepening into depression or resignation; the compensating yearning for death imagined as an anodyne, an eternal anaesthetic—these are familiar to every reader of her poetry. And it is difficult to find many poems in which she either transcends them or turns them into the conditions for major creation.

One of the rare occasions on which her religion appears in her poetry as a source of revival and refreshment is the (significantly titled) sonnet "A Pause":

> They made the chamber sweet with flowers and leaves,
> And the bed sweet with flowers on which I lay;
> While my soul, love-bound, loitered on its way.
> I did not hear the birds about the eaves,
> Nor hear the reapers talk among the sheaves:
>   Only my soul kept watch from day to day,
>   My thirsty soul kept watch for one away:—
> Perhaps he loves, I thought, remembers, grieves.
> At length there came the step upon the stair,
>   Upon the lock the old familiar hand:
> Then first my spirit seemed to scent the air
>   Of Paradise; then first the tardy sand
> Of time ran golden; and I felt my hair
>   Put on a glory, and my soul expand.

The simplicity and naturalness of this writing, the trace of the speaking (not intoning) voice:

>   Perhaps he loves, I thought, remembers, grieves

the exquisite good taste and spiritual good manners (if the expression be permitted) of the way in which the two worlds are related—the religious and the everyday—are characteristic distinctions of Christina's poetry. And a comparison of her better-known "Spring Quiet" ('Gone were but the Winter') with Hopkins's early "Heaven-Haven" ('I have desired to go') brings out a certain community of temperament (though even the latter, slight as it is, has Hopkins's idiosyncracy—'sharp *and sided* hail'). But it reminds us also that "Heaven Haven", unlike "Spring Quiet", by no means represents a high point of its author's achievement.

The distinctiveness and the limitation of Christina Rossetti's talent are alike illuminated by the parallel her sonnet "Remember" offers to Shakespeare's 71st sonnet ('No longer mourn . . .'). Perhaps, indeed, she was remembering Shakespeare's poem when she wrote it.

> Remember me when I am gone away,
> Gone far away into the silent land;
> When you can no more hold me by the hand,
> Nor I half turn to go yet turning stay.

> Remember me when no more day by day
> You tell me of our future that you plann'd:
> Only remember me; you understand
> It will be late to counsel then or pray.
> Yet if you should forget me for a while
> And afterwards remember, do not grieve:
> For if the darkness and corruption leave
> A vestige of the thoughts that once I had,
> Better by far you should forget and smile
> Than that you should remember and be sad.

The superficial similarity of theme does not disguise the deep difference between the two poems. Shakespeare's sonnet, though not one of his greatest, is characteristic of his best work in the Sonnets, in the effect it produces of a mind intent upon its argument, charged with the determination to deliver its meaning, and taking the emotional effect of that meaning so much for granted, that the poet can afford to deploy his statement in a highly formal, 'logical' progression. For all the element of poignancy, the total effect is therefore akin to wit; the satisfactory following-through of an exaggeration, a hyperbole, to its completion. The result is that a poem which, on the face of it, expresses as much loving self-abnegation and tender humility as Christina's, conveys at the same time a graceful compliment and a hint of rebuke. And thus the *precise* value we are to give to Shakespeare's overt humiliation of himself and his poetry has been beautifully defined, and the beauty of this defining is the beauty of the poem. Christina's poem calls for no such subtle adjustment; the shy reserve, tenderness, and wistfulness of the speaker are presented simply and truthfully, and our acceptance of her truthfulness is bound up with our recognition of her authentic speaking voice:

> Yet if you should forget me for a while,
> And afterwards remember, do not grieve . . .

But by the time we reach the closing lines, with their (hardly successful) epigrammatic turn of phrasing which sends us back to the Shakespeare sonnet, we feel a slight discomfort with the poem; its modest acceptance of very limited pretension which makes it seem, if not mawkish, a little *mièvre:*

> Better by far you should forget and smile
> Than that you should remember and be sad.

The comparison with Shakespeare's sonnet leads us to call the other sonnet, with a limiting intention, 'feminine': in the absence of the verve and chargedness there is felt to be a thinness, a lack of substance.

But what is also evident in this poem is the very welcome absence of anything like the sonorous and vatic manner, at one and the same time declamatory and embarrassingly intimate, which we associate with Mrs Browning—and, perhaps, with one or two later women poets. If we pay Christina Rossetti the archaic compliment of calling her a lady, this will be understood to have no implication of snobbery.

The deprived, depressed, monotonous quality of her poetry is to be accounted for, as we know, very largely by the circumstances of her life and her renunciation. But in one form or another this is a common feature of Victorian Romantic poetry. And if we ignore the personal accent of Christina Rossetti, and the devotional vocabulary and setting of her poems, their moods and tones are immediately recognizable as moods and tones of the period. This is certainly not because of any affectation of fashionable melancholy on Christina'a part: no poet could be more touchingly sincere and disinterested. Yet we may wonder if, had she been in contact with a tradition allowing the exercise, in serious verse, of her sharp wits and her astringency,

the substance of her work might not have been more considerable and its styles more various. Certainly, after reading her poetry, we are keenly reminded of the advantages enjoyed by some seventeenth-century religious poets.

William Morris is, in my opinion, much the least interesting of the three poets considered here. What he can do best is illustrated in the early (1858) *Defence of Guinevère* volume, especially the title poem; yet we may find even that poem plaintive and picturesque, rather than rising to the tragic possibilities of its subject; and for the other poems in the volume only a limited compliment seems appropriate, such as that implied when we say they are 'charming'. Arnold, regretting Burns's background, remarked that it is a great advantage to the poet to live in a beautiful world; and so it must have seemed to the Morris of "Golden Wings":

> Midways of a walled garden,
> In the happy poplar land,
> Did an ancient castle stand,
> With an old knight for a warden.
>
> Many scarlet bricks there were
> In its walls, and old grey stone;
> Over which red apples shone
> At the right time of the year.
>
> On the bricks the green moss grew,
> Yellow lichen on the stone,
> Over which red apples shone;
> Little war that castle knew.
>
> Deep green water fill'd the moat,
> Each side had a red-brick lip,
> Green and mossy with the drip
> Of dew and rain. . . .

This is certainly charming. But the 'beautiful world', from which everything harsh or disagreeable is excluded, turns out to be day-dream world and, in no very long run, an uninteresting one. Morris, of course, has his characteristic emotional tone, his pathos, in these shorter poems, and it might well be said that even the happier ones imply the sadness from which they withdraw. But in his poetry Morris's protest against the actual world is confined to the protest of ignoring it.

The Life and Death of Jason makes pleasant reading, but again one cannot feel that Morris has glimpsed the tragic power of the story he is telling; the sin of Jason seems to have little moral significance; the poet's activity as poet is directed, again, to charming incidentals of visual observation, of costume, colour, and landscape. In *The Earthly Paradise,* however much Morris may have felt himself the successor of Chaucer, there is none of Chaucer's vigorous interest in and command of life in so many of its forms, the sense of *nihil humanum a me alienum puto.* Morris's interest is always in the picturesque, the decorative, in the romantic 'feel' of the legends, as in the 'northernness' of *Sigurd the Volsung.* When human beings are at the ostensible centre of interest, there is a queer externality, difficult to illustrate convincingly just because it is so pervasive. Hence it would be futile to enter the controversy about *The Earthly Paradise*—is it not really poetry of escape, but a sociological sermon in the form of an allegory? Whatever Morris's deeper intention, no effective message of the kind he is credited with could be delivered in such verse.

We almost always have the sense in reading Morris's poetry—and indeed his prose romances, too—that what he is doing is quite marginal, quite apart from the main activities of his life. Outside his poetry we know Morris as an energetic, strenuous figure and strong character, the last of the great Victorian 'prophets', and more than a 'prophet' in being a man of action and a maker. But in his poetry—even after his 'Pre-Raphaelite' phase—we observe in an extreme, and a naïve form, the Pre-Raphaelite separation of 'art' from 'life'. 'Art' for Morris was essentially a relaxation, an amusement, something to do; writing poetry came easily to him, and he was not the poet to resist the temptations (or profusion and careless workmanship) inherent in being one's own publisher and printer:

> The fascination of what's difficult
> Has dried the sap out of my veins, and rent
> Spontaneous joy and natural content
> Out of my heart.

Morris the poet could not have applied to himself these words of Yeats. And it is significant that there is no parallel between *his* development and that of Yeats—who also began as a Pre-Raphaelite, born out of due time. Indeed, 'development' is not a word with any obvious application to Morris's poetry. His work as translator of epic and saga—and the greater part of his verse is translation—shows him as responding to certain 'romantic' qualities which may well be in his originals but which are not necessarily the most important there. The socialist songs have their merits, but they hardly concern the student of poetry.

It is difficult, then, to give Morris a high place purely as a writer. Even in the prose work, *News from Nowhere*, in which his dream-world is realized more interestingly than in his poetry, it is still the impulse to 'Forget six counties overhung with smoke' that predominates. His lack of human centrality, the lack of concentration and pressure in all his imaginative writing, the day-dream habit of his verse, may be mainly attributed to his having other things to do. The expression of the robuster side of his nature was to be reserved for the Anti-Scrape Society, the settlement-house, and the socialist meeting; above all, for the noble effort to fulfil (in the world of Victorian industrialism, Karl Marx, and Mr Podsnap) the prophecy of John Ruskin. But the poetic tradition which he accepted was not, anyway, calculated to encourage the expression of anything robust, and one of the most telling criticisms of it may be that it confined William Morris to minor poetry. (pp. 352-70)

W. W. Robson, "Pre-Raphaelite Poetry," in From Dickens to Hardy, *edited by Boris Ford, revised edition, Penguin Books, 1960, pp. 352-70.*

LIONEL STEVENSON

[*Stevenson was a respected Canadian critic and biographer. In his* The Pre-Raphaelite Poets, *from which the following excerpt is drawn, Stevenson considers the movement as an influential and revolutionary force in English literature. Here, he examines the lives, works, and personal relationships of some of the lesser-known Pre-Raphaelite poets and of others who were briefly affiliated with the movement. For further criticism by Stevenson, see excerpt below.*]

A center of energy as potent as the Pre-Raphaelite movement was bound to attract satellites into its magnetic field. Few poets in the second half of the nineteenth century were totally unaffected, as a cursory survey will suffice to indicate. (p. 253)

It will be convenient to begin with the Pre-Raphaelite Brotherhood itself. With the establishment of the *Germ*, Dante Gabriel Rossetti gave notice to his coterie that they were expected to wield the pen as well as the brush. Even Madox Brown contributed a sonnet. Since Rossetti's brother, William Michael (1829-1919), who showed little promise as a painter, had pre-

sumably been recruited mainly to complete the mystic seven, he felt the poetic responsibility strongly. The cover of the *Germ* bore a sonnet of his, modestly emphasizing the priority of sincerity in poetry: "Be the theme a point or the whole earth, / Truth is a circle, perfect, great or small" [see poem above]. Being the editor, he was obliged to fill up the pages with his own work when more temperamental contributors defaulted. For an illustration of *King Lear*, by Brown, he had to write a poem, "Cordelia." Eight of his brief pieces had originally been composed in the games of *bouts rimés* which were a family pastime of the young Rossettis. In the circumstances, it is astonishing that his contributions were as good as they were. A fairly extensive blank-verse poem, "To the Castle Ramparts," as well as shorter descriptive pieces shows precise observation, and his sonnets are neatly turned; but his diction lacks distinction and his lines move with none of the melody inherent in those of his brother and sister. Not published until twenty years later, his blank-verse poem, "Mrs. Holmes Gray," was his most ambitious effort to practice Pre-Raphaelite realism. Reporting a coroner's inquest, it aroused in Swinburne a mixture of fascination and disappointment. "That idea of yours," he told his friend, "beats everything but Balzac. I can't tell you—not what I think of the poem done—but what I think of the poem feasible. Do write something more in my line and I'll be the first to admit your superiority."

Swinburne might have approved more strongly of one sonnet that came out in the *Germ*, "The Evil under the Sun," a bitter protest against the suppression of the Hungarian insurrection. Long afterward, in 1881, the poet planned to publish this and other expressions of political protest in a volume to be called *Democratic Sonnets,* but his brother took fright at the idea that such subversiveness might cost William his government post, and so the book did not appear until 1907, whhen the writer was a reverend senior.

With characteristic common sense, he accepted the evidence that his literary talent was not creative. "To be a quasi-poet," he remarked in his *Reminiscences*, "a pleasing poetaster, was never my ambition; I felt that in the long run I should stay outside the arena of verse altogether. And so, after making some few experiments, I did." For fifty years he earned his living in a routine civil service post, and functioned as balance wheel for the erratic family. He published inexhaustibly as an editor of literary texts, a reviewer, and a biographer. After his marriage to a daughter of Ford Madox Brown he was the chief contact point between the artistic and literary wings of the movement, and his industrious documentation provides almost all the basic information about it. After his death at the age of ninety, his daughter, Helen Rossetti Angeli, sustained his record, both in longevity and in literary productivity as chronicler of Pre-Raphaelitism, until 1969.

Among the other members of the Pre-Raphaelite Brotherhood, the one who emulated Dante Gabriel Rossetti in being both artist and poet was Thomas Woolner (1825-92), who was also its only sculptor. An opinionated radical and a devotee of Shelley, he constantly brooded on plans for heroic statuary, but his ambition exceeded his power of execution. Two poems by Woolner, "My Beautiful Lady" and "Of My Lady in Death," were the longest specimens of verse in the first issue of the *Germ*. Able pieces of Pre-Raphaelite decoration, they established the style of archaic naïveté, with short words, lines, and stanzas, that later was picked up in Morris's "Blanche" and

Swinburne's "Queen Yseult." The awkward charm of Woolner's diction was apt to verge upon bathos:

> My lady's voice, altho' so very mild,
> Maketh me feel as strong wine would a child;
>   My lady's touch, however slight,
>   Moves all my senses with its might,
>   Like a sudden fright. . . .
>
> Whene'er she moves there are fresh beauties stirred;
> As the sunned bosom of a humming-bird
>   At each pant shows some fiery hue,
>   Burns gold, intensest green or blue:
>   The same, yet ever new. . . .

The use of unpoetical words was so frequent as to seem intentional. It pervades another of his *Germ* contributions, "Emblems":

> . . . Where lay a rotting bird, whose plumes
>   Had beat the air in soaring.
>   On these things I was poring. . . .
>
> On swamps where moped the lonely stork,
>   In the silent lapse of time
>   Stands a city in its prime. . . .

Coventry Patmore "praised Woolner's poems immensely, saying however that they were sometimes slightly over-passionate, and generally 'sculpturesque' in character" (meaning that each stanza was a separate unit).

Woolner's failure to obtain commissions or to sell the statues he exhibited led him to despise the whole bourgeois taste and commercial orientation of his time, and in 1852 he emigrated to Australia, confident of making his fortune in the gold fields. When he found no nuggets he had to support himself meagerly by modeling portrait medallions of newly prosperous citizens,

Dante Gabriel Rossetti's 1854 painting Found. *Samuel and Mary R. Bancroft Collection, Delaware Art Centre, Wilmington, DE.*

and after two years he returned ignominiously to England. Ironically, it turned out that he had discovered his métier. His medallion likenesses of literary friends became popular, and he began to receive orders for life-sized statues of celebrities. Within a few years, like his former comrade Millais, he was wealthy and was accorded the accolade of artistic respectability—election to the Royal Academy. With his rise in the social scale he abandoned the bohemian Pre-Raphaelites and attached himself to the more distinguished coterie of Tennyson. In 1863 he published a volume, My Beautiful Lady, in which his two *Germ* poems of that title, with their haunting echoes of "The Blessed Damozel," were expanded with a dozen other pieces about love and nature and encrusted in a tedious prelude and conclusion in didactic blank verse. Much later, completely under Tennyson's influence, he published several other books of poetry, mainly on mythological subjects: *Pygmalion* (1881), *Silenus* (1884), *Tiresias* (1886). They were as marmoreally lifeless as his statues.

Though never officially a member of the Pre-Raphaelite Brotherhood, the poet-painter who was closest akin to them was William Bell Scott (1811-90). In spite of his aggressive and jealous disposition, he contrived to retain the affection of Rossetti, Morris, and Swinburne until the end of his life, long after they had drifted apart from each other.

The son of a Scottish artist, he was brought up to worship Blake and formed an ambition to emulate him in both arts. Overshadowed as a painter by a successful elder brother, he took to writing reflective poetry in the model of the eighteenth-century graveyard school until the literary dictators of Edinburgh, Christopher North and Sir Walter Scott, advised him to choose a less pretentious manner. Handsome in physique and dramatic in manner, he was popular in the Edinburgh artistic and literary circle, but made little headway with a career. His first book, *Hades; or, The Transit, and the Progress of Mind,* was published in 1838, shortly before Philip James Bailey's *Festus,* which somewhat resembled it in efforts to versify metaphysical speculation. He spent five years in London, making friends with various writers, and in 1842, when he was thirty-one, he finally had a picture accepted for exhibition at the Royal Academy. The next year he was appointed headmaster of an art school in the commercial city of Newcastle-on-Tyne, which doomed him to exile from intellectual stimulus.

Four years later the young Gabriel Rossetti, reading an obscure magazine, came across two poems by Scott, "A Dream of Love" and "Rosabel," the latter inspired by a prostitute he had known in his Edinburgh days. Perhaps struck by some resemblance to his own "Jenny," Rossetti decided in his usual precipitate way that the poem was the work of an important unrecognized author; and just at that time Scott's next book provided more of his work. *The Year of the World* was another of his tedious allegorical poems, "treating the different forms of religion underlying the periods of time occupied by the civilization of the world," and strongly resembling Shelley's *Prometheus Unbound.* Rossetti, who just at that time obtained a volume of Shelley and "surged through its pages like a flame," devoured Scott's book ecstatically and wrote him an incoherent letter asking where his other writings could be found. On receiving a guarded reply, he sent Scott a manuscript of his own poetry, and on Scott's next visit to London he called at the Rossettis' home. The family, and soon the whole Pre-Raphaelite circle, were impressed by his saturnine good looks and his gloomy manner; if Lona Mosk Packer's hypothesis is to be accepted, Christina Rossetti promptly fell in love with him. He was asked to contribute to the *Germ*, and supplied a long blank-verse poem entitled "Morning Sleep" and a sonnet, "Early Aspirations." The next year he expressed his appreciation for the new friendships in a sonnet "To the Artists Called P.R.B.":

> I thank you, brethren in Sincerity—
>   One who, within the temperate climes of Art
>   From the charmed circle humbly stands apart,
> Scornfully also, with a listless eye
> Watching old marionettes' vitality;
>   For you have shown, with youth's brave confidence,
>   The honesty of true speech and the sense
> Uniting life with "nature," earth with sky. . . .

This portrayal of himself, at the age of forty, as a disgruntled outsider is confirmed in his autobiography: "Introspection was my curse. Action was hated by me; I was an absentee, a somnambule, and gave myself much to subjects no one else cared for. I had thus a private interest apart from success, and was indeed possessed of a mystery, as it were. Untiring industry I certainly had, but it was only to meet the necessities of the hour. That accomplished, I fell back upon my secret speculations in an ocean of regrets and tobacco smoke; and on my poetry, which shared in all the peculiarities of my nature." Here clearly is the pose of the artist as social exile, which emerged as one of the consequences of Pre-Raphaelitism and kindred tendencies.

About this time he was producing a series of love poems to a woman he called "Mignon," whom Mrs. Packer identifies as Christina Rossetti; the lyrics move with a charming lightness that contrasts with Scott's usual solemnity. They appeared in his 1854 volume, *Poems of a Painter*, which won some commendation. As a painter, too, he was encouraged by a commission for a series of murals depicting episodes in the history of Northumberland for the castle of Sir Walter and Lady Trevelyan, and, like Ruskin before him and Swinburne a little later, he fell under Lady Trevelyan's spell. These murals, and similar ones illustrating *The King's Quair*, which he made for his later patroness, Alice Boyd, represent his principal work in the Pre-Raphaelite medieval style.

After 1864, when he gave up his art school position, he settled in London, where he saw much of the Rossettis and their circle. He also entertained them as guests during the summer months when he was with Miss Boyd at Penkill. In 1875, when he published his next volume of *Poems*, his dedicatory sonnet expressed his gratitude to Rossetti, Morris, and Swinburne for their encouragement:

> Now many years ago in life's midday,
>   I laid the pen aside and rested still,
>   Like one bare-footed on a shingly hill:
> Three poets then came past, each young as May,
>
> Year after year, upon their upward way,
>   And each one reached his hand out as he passed,
>   And over me his friendship's mantle cast,
> And went on singing, everyone his lay.

Scott's poetry is representative of the Pre-Raphaelite rank and file. His descriptive blank-verse pieces are precise and decorative, his ballads have a touch of eerie horror, his sonnets are always shapely, and his love lyrics often convey a real sense of passion. A series of sonnets called "Parted Love," written in 1868-69, though not published until he was in his seventies in *A Poet's Harvest Home* (1882), and possibly recording his

feelings for Christina Rossetti, catches something of the Rossettian intensity:

> In vain I wish again within those arms
> To fold thee, once more feel there those shoulders soft
> And solid, but that is no more to be:
> Unless perchance—(*speak low*) beyond all harms
> I may walk with thee in God's other croft,
> When this world shall the darkling mirror be.

The hundred lyrics in the 1882 volume had almost all been written during the preceding few months, a remarkable achievement for a man of his age. He reported to Swinburne that "every one was produced with a spontaneity and energy, quite a new experience to me. They (for the major part) record, or relate to actual incidents." Mrs. Packer assumes that his impetus came from the publication of Christina Rossetti's *A Pageant and Other Poems*, and particularly from his response to her "Monna Innominata" sonnets. Certainly one of his lyrics, "Once a Rose," was an explicit reply to her "Summer Is Ended."

Quite apart from his putative romance with Christina, Scott played an ambiguous role in the Pre-Raphaelite drama. During the last decade of Rossetti's life he was a favorite whist partner, and the poet always enjoyed his holidays with Scott at Penkill, away from his depressing surroundings in Chelsea; it was on one such visit that Scott and Miss Boyd persuaded him to exhume and publish his poetry. On the other hand, even on these occasions Scott can be blamed for drinking brandy with Rossetti and for disturbing his morbid fancies with superstitious tales.

Scott's *Autobiographical Notes* are among the most candid and vivid sources of first-hand glimpses of the Pre-Raphaelite circle, but the book reveals his egoism, envy, and malice. His death in 1890 had been observed by Swinburne with affectionate "Memorial Verses":

> Poet and painter and friend, thrice dear
>   For love of the suns long set, for love
> Of song that sets not with sunset here,
>
> For love of the fervent heart, above
> Their sense who saw not the swift light move
>   That filled with sense of the loud sun's lyre
> The thoughts that passion was fain to prove
> In fervent labour of high desire. . . .

The posthumous publication of Scott's recollections, though edited by Swinburne's old friend John Nichol, changed the poet's devotion to fury, particularly because of his unflattering portrayal of Elizabeth Siddal. He branded Scott as "a man whose name would never have been heard, whose verse would never have been read, whose daubs would never have been seen, outside some aesthetic Lilliput of the North, but for his casual and parasitical association with the Trevelyans, the Rossettis, and myself."

A poet of more substance than Scott, Coventry Patmore (1823-96), was another early recruit to the Pre-Raphaelite troop. The son of a minor figure in the "Cockney" literary circle that included Keats, Hunt, Lamb, and Hazlitt, Patmore was brought up in the Romantic tradition of uninhibited self-expression, and readily accepted his family's assumption that he was a genius. He had some thoughts of becoming a painter or a scientist, but his first love affair turned him into a poet. At the age of sixteen, while in Paris to learn French, he was captivated by a coquettish society beauty two years older, and when she ridiculed the youth's adoration he vented his despair in two long ballads which, though derivative, showed remarkable promise. Both are composed in the extended six-line ballad stanza later used memorably by Rossetti in "The Blessed Damozel" and "The Card Dealer." "The River" employs atmospheric suggestion to convey the suicide of a rejected lover who drowns himself on the night of his beloved's wedding to a rich rival. "The Woodman's Daughter," in the Wordsworthian tradition of rustic tragedy, again uses implication (somewhat like "The Thorn") to indicate that a seduced girl drowns her infant.

Two years later he encountered Tennyson's poems and was moved to emulation. In the mood and heptameter of "Locksley Hall" he composed "The Yewberry," a morbid young man's account of how he discovered his sweetheart's liaison with another lover. More closely identified with his disaster in Paris was "Lillian," in which a young woman rejects her suitor because she has been corrupted by reading French literature. He inveighs bitterly against "These literary panders / Of that mighty brothel, France." At this juncture Tennyson's publisher offered to bring out a book of Patmore's poems if he could supply enough material. He hastily terminated "Lillian" and set to work on a longer narrative poem in the same heptameter triplets as "The Yewberry." Based on a story by Boccaccio, it was first called "Sir Hubert" but in later editions became "The Falcon." It is an implausible tale of a baronet whose beloved marries another when he loses his wealth and becomes a farm laborer. He retains only his best falcon, because its eyes remind him of his lost Lady Mabel. After she is widowed she visits his cottage, and to provide lunch for her he has to kill and broil the bird. Subsequently she convinces him that she now reciprocates his love, and so he acquires not only his longed-for bride but all her husband's property too. The solemn absurdity of the tale exerts a strange sort of guileless charm.

Eked out with a few competent sonnets, the poems sufficed for a slim volume, which was published before Patmore was twenty-one. His ecstatic father escorted him on a round of the literary salons and pleaded for favorable reviews. Browning reported that "a very interesting young poet has blushed into bloom this season," and Patmore was accorded the rare distinction of a visit to Elizabeth Barrett (before Browning was so privileged). The two-volume edition of her poems came out just at this time, and along with Tennyson she was the most obvious model of Patmore's poetry. Bulwer Lytton gave him both praise and advice: "I honestly . . . think the promise you hold out to us is perfectly startling, both from the luxuriance of fancy, and the subtle and reflective inclinations of your intellect. . . . As yet you seem to me to lean more towards that class of Poets who are Poets to Poets—not Poets to the Multitude." The aged Leigh Hunt published a laudatory review, as did Dickens's dramatist friend, Thomas Noon Talfourd, who termed the book "a marvellous instance of genius anticipating time." *Blackwood's Magazine,* still rampant after a quarter century of berating the Cockney school, distinguished the innocent little book with a ferocious blast: "This is the life into which the slime of the Keateses [*sic*] and Shelleys of former times has fecundated. . . . Nothing is so tenacious as the spawn of frogs. . . . His poetry (thank Heaven!) cannot corrupt into anything worse than itself."

Within a year triumph gave place to catastrophe. Patmore's father lost all his money in railway speculation and decamped to France. Untrained in any vocation, the young poet had to set about supporting himself, and during a year of hack writing he barely avoided starvation. Then Monckton Milnes, describing his poetry as "of the highest genius and with the due amount of absurdity which youth demands and excuses," managed to have him appointed as a junior assistant in the British Museum Library. On the strength of this meager income he married a penniless orphan girl who shared his literary tastes, and they were blissfully happy. Their tiny house became a meeting place for such paladins as Tennyson, Browning, Carlyle, and Ruskin. Meanwhile, Leigh Hunt's review had brought Patmore's book to the attention of the omnivorous Rossetti; he and his brother "read and re-read it . . . and delighted in it much."

When his Cyclographic Society, precursor of the Pre-Raphaelite Brotherhood, in 1848 made a "List of Immortals," Patmore's name received one star, along with Tennyson and Mrs. Browning (her husband was honored with two, equaling Homer, Dante, and Chaucer). It was natural for Rossetti to be so moved by the lush romanticism of Patmore's poetry that he ignored its immaturity and extravagance. Especially it appealed to him by its insistence on the absolute priority of love before all other concerns. In one of the sonnets Patmore had declared, "At nine years old I was Love's willing Page; / Poets love earlier than other men." In "Sir Hubert" he said of "Love's brand":

> For ever and for ever we are lighted by the light:
>
> And ere there be extinguish'd one minutest flame, love-fann'd,
> The Pyramids of Egypt shall have no place in the land,
> But as a nameless portion of its ever-shifting sand.

Patmore's naïve sexuality was fully congenial to Rossetti. The specific detail in the poems' settings was also consistent with Pre-Raphaelite realism.

At one of the discussion sessions of the Pre-Raphaelite Brotherhood, Rossetti recited "The Woodman's Daughter" so movingly that Woolner was delegated to ask the author whether a copy of his book was available. When they met, Woolner showed Patmore some of his manuscripts, and a warm friendship ensued. Within a year Woolner was busy making medallions of the Patmore couple. Finally, late in 1849, Patmore attended a meeting of the brotherhood, and was gratified by their adulation. Soon they were assembling at his house as often as in their studios, and through him they first met some of the leading writers whom they most admired, notably Tennyson. To the *Germ* Patmore contributed an essay on *Macbeth* and two short poems: a graceful lyric, "The Seasons," and a pleasant conversation piece, "Stars and Moon."

For the next year or two he seemed to be almost their literary mentor. Millais painted Mrs. Patmore's portrait and also a picture illustrating "The Woodman's Daughter," which he exhibited at the Royal Academy in 1851. When the *Times* virulently condemned Millais's canvases, it was Patmore who persuaded his friend Ruskin to come to the defense, and thus turned the critical tide in favor of the brethren. Looking back in old age, Patmore summed up those exciting days: "I was intimate with the Pre-Raphaelites when we were little more than boys together. They were all very simple, pure-minded, ignorant and confident."

In his next book, *Tamerton Church Tower and Other Poems* (1853), the title piece is a strangely desultory performance. Written in the simplest ballad meter and the plainest of colloquial diction, it is mainly a leisurely account of rides back and forth across Cornwall and Devon, with extensive descriptions of summer weather. Imbedded in the middle of it is a concise page or two of action, in which the narrator falls in love, marries, and loses his bride by drowning when they are caught in a squall while rowing in the bay. Among the other poems, the most remarkable is "A London Fête," a chillingly callous depiction of a public execution. In view of Patmore's major concern, however, the significant pieces are "Honoria: Lady's Praise" and "Felix: Love's Apology," for they were brief samples extracted from a large project that he had been working on for several years.

During his engagement he had written to his fiancée, "I have been meditating a poem for you, but I am determined not to give you anything I write unless it is the best thing I have written." After their marriage, he formulated a theory of Nuptial Love as a sublimation of erotic passion into aesthetic beauty, and he decided that no previous poet had done justice to the topic:

> I, meditating much and long
>   What I should sing, how win a name,
> Considering well what theme unsung,
>   What reason worth the cost of rhyme,
> Remains to loose the poet's tongue
>   In these last days, the dregs of time,
> Learn that to me, though born so late,
>   There does, beyond desert, befall
> (May my great fortune make me great!)
>   The first of themes, sung last of all.

In high excitement over his resolve, he hurried to tell his poet friend Aubrey de Vere about this great theme,

> the more serious importance of which had been singularly missed by most poets of all countries, frequently as they had taken its name in vain. That theme was Love: not a mere caprice of fancy, or Love as, at best, a mere imaginative Passion—but Love in the deeper and softer sense of the word. The Syren woman had been much sung. . . . But that Love in which, as he affirmed, all the Loves centre, and that Woman who is the rightful sustainer of them all, the Inspiration of Youth, and the Consolation of Age—that Love and that Woman, he asserted, had seldom been sung sincerely and effectually.

In March 1850, William Rossetti reported that Patmore "has been occupied the last month with his poem on Marriage, of which, however, he has not meanwhile written a line; but, having meditated the matter, is now about to do so. He expresses himself quite confident of being able to keep it up at the same pitch as the few astonishing lines he has yet written."

The enthusiasm of his young friends gave him the needed stimulus. Lecturing them dogmatically, "he insists strongly on the necessity of never leaving a poem till the whole of it be brought to a pitch of excellence perfectly satisfactory; in this respect of general equality, and also in regard to metre, he finds much to object to in Woolner's poem of "My Lady." . . . He himself spent about a year (from the age of sixteen to seventeen) on "The River," with which, and "The Woodman's Daughter," he is contented in point of finish. . . . Patmore holds the age of narrative poetry to be passed for ever, and thinks that probably none such will again appear. . . . He looks on the present race of poets as highly 'self-conscious' in comparison with their predecessors, but yet not sufficiently so for the only system now possible—the psychological."

Holding these doctrines, he started to write his new poem in alternately rhyming tetrameter and in subdued everyday speech, a form that proved so easy that, as he said later, "the first book . . . took only six weeks in the writing, though I had thought of little else for several years before." He confidently told Rossetti that the completed work would be bigger than *The Divine Comedy*. Under Tennyson's counsel, however, he

paused for revisions, and so the first installment, *The Betrothal*, was not ready for publication until 1854. He sent the proof-sheets to Tennyson for final approval, and was told, "You have begun an immortal poem, and, if I am no false prophet, it will not be long in winning its way into the hearts of people." Book 2, *The Espousals*, came out in 1856, and thereupon the two parts were combined under the title that became famous, *The Angel in the House*.

The poem was an outstanding example of a genre that flourished briefly in the mid-Victorian years, the novel in verse. . . . The first important examples were by Arthur Hugh Clough, *The Bothie of Tober-na-Vuolich* (1848) and *Amours de Voyage* (written in 1850, published in 1858). Tennyson's *Maud* (1855) was allied with the genre, and the two most popular specimens, along with Patmore's, were Mrs. Browning's *Aurora Leigh* (1857) and Owen Meredith's *Lucile* (1860). Clough's remain acceptable to modern taste because his ironic tone saves the commonplace details and diction from absurdity. Tennyson avoided the pitfalls by providing emotional intensity through the monodrama technique. This is true also of Meredith's *Modern Love*, a condensed variety of the genre. In the others, emotion lapses too often into sentimentality, and the use of meter and rhyme for trivial details and conversations is often ludicrous.

Insofar as the art of literature is concerned, the novel in verse is the reductio ad absurdum of Pre-Raphaelite realism. If absolute fidelity to observed experience is the primary requirement of art, then such tales of ordinary people in familiar surroundings, set forth in technically accurate meter, must be aesthetically valid. Yet somehow a more essential element of beauty is absent—what Ruskin or Arnold would have termed "the grand style." In revulsion against the platitudinous language and trivial domesticity of *The Angel*, critics are apt to overlook Patmore's profoundly earnest spiritual purpose. As Osbert Burdett says, he believed that "marriage was not the end nor anti-climax of love, but its fulfillment; and he showed . . . that within its narrow circle, and because of its limitations, it was capable of delights, and discoveries, more wonderful than the extravagant adventures of Don Juan." In the words of Frederick Page, "The Angel in the House, then, is conscious love, uniting its subject and object, Man, Woman, God."

Patmore's version of love between the sexes was, as he himself insisted, totally unlike the two conventional aspects depicted by Rossetti and Swinburne—the unattainable saintly lady (derived from the chivalric tradition of Courtly Love) and the diabolical temptress (derived from the Christian equation of sex with sin). Nevertheless he was just as much an erotic poet as they were, and *The Angel* was another contribution to the deeply probing Victorian revaluation of woman's status.

Patmore's intimacy with the group diminished after the brotherhood broke up. In 1857 he went to Oxford to see the murals in the union, and wrote a vivid report of them for the *Saturday Review*, but he did not become a friend of Morris, Jones, and Swinburne, and his own career took a different direction. His adored wife died in 1862 after a long illness, leaving him with six young children. Two years afterward he joined the Church of Rome and married a well-to-do woman, also a convert. He could now afford to give up his librarian's work and settle in the country. His new prosperity, his orthodox religion, and his Tory politics all set up a barrier between him and the irresponsible Rossetti circle.

He published a sequel to *The Angel*, again in two parts, in 1860 and 1861, *Faithful for Ever* and *The Victories of Love*.

Using the epistolary technique, he narrated the marital history of the man who had been the rejected rival in *The Angel*. Having thus exhausted the potentialities of domestic fiction, he spent several years in working on a sequence of irregular odes which expounded his amatory philosophy, no longer in realistic narrative but in mystical symbolism. Nine of them were privately printed in 1868, but Tennyson and his other friends did not appreciate them, and so he burned most of the copies. Not until 1877 did a volume of the odes, now expanded to thirty-one, appear anonymously under the title *The Unknown Eros*. When reissued the next year, with the author's name, a number of others were added.

By coincidence, the privately printed edition of the first odes was at the same time as the first publication of "The House of Life," and thus the contrast between the two major erotic poets of the Victorian age is brought into sharp focus. Both were proclaiming a religion of sexual love, but Rossetti's was persistently physical, whereas Patmore interpreted it as a transcendent spiritual experience, an analogue for mankind's communion with God. As in Rossetti's sonnets, some of the odes are profoundly melancholy—those which record the agony of the poet's grief for his first wife and reveal the complexity of his emotions toward his second marriage; but there is none of the morbidity that haunts *The House of Life*.

It was Patmore who introduced to Rossetti a young poet who proved to be one of his most loyal admirers. William Allingham (1824-89) was born in the tiny town of Ballyshannon, in the remote northwest of Ireland. His father was the local bank manager, and after elementary schooling Allingham went to work in the bank at the age of fourteen. Determined to become an author, he read widely, and when he was about twenty he began sending contributions to London periodicals. From 1846 he was an official in the customs service in Ireland, and managed to pay vacation visits to London. Leigh Hunt introduced him to Carlyle and other writers, and Patmore made him acquainted with Tennyson and Rossetti. Allingham, in turn, took Rossetti for the first time to meet Browning. The Pre-Raphaelite group were charmed with the Irish poet's ingenuous enthusiasm for poetry and with the simple, melodious melancholy of his own verse.

In 1850 he brought out a volume of poetry, dedicated to his original patron, Leigh Hunt, but he soon withdrew it from circulation in order to revise the poems extensively. A few of them reappeared in *Day and Night Songs* in 1854, and the success of this book led him the next year to combine it with a long narrative poem, "The Music Master," drastically revised from the 1850 book. This edition was provided with Pre-Raphaelite illustrations—one by Rossetti, one by Millais, and the rest by their protégé Arthur Hughes.

Allingham's songs and ballads had the unique advantage of possessing the authentic tone of folk poetry, which the Pre-Raphaelites strove to achieve by sheer will power. He explained in the preface to the 1854 volume: "Five of the songs or ballads . . . have already had an Irish circulation as 'ha'penny ballads.'" In fitting these to traditional tunes, following the example of Burns and Moore, he echoed the true lilt; but his language usually conformed to the faceless triteness of the peddlers' broadsides so closely that he only occasionally touched the inimitable hyperbole of peasant Irish rhetoric. A dim forecast of Synge may be detected in lines such as these from "Lovely Mary Donnelly":

> When she stood up for dancing, her steps were so
>   complete,

> The music nearly kill'd itself to listen to her feet;
> The fiddler moan'd his blindness, he heard her so
>   much praised,
> But bless'd himself he wasn't deaf when once her
>   voice she raised.

Allingham was handicapped by anxiety to avoid dialect; he remarked in his preface that "I found it not easy, in ballad-writing, to employ a diction that might hope to come home to the Irish peasant who speaks English (as most of them now do), using his customary phraseology, and also keeping within the laws of poetic taste and the rules of grammar."

The more literary poems are apt to contain traces of eighteenth-century formal language and moralizing, and only a handful achieve distinction. Allingham is usually represented in anthologies solely by "The Fairies," which with its tripping meter and touches of homely detail conveys the "natural magic" of Celtic legend:

> Down along the rocky shore
>   Some make their home,
> They live on crispy pancakes
>   Of yellow tide-foam;
> Some in the reeds
>   Of the black mountain-lake,
> With frogs for their watch-dogs,
>   All night awake.

The weird quality of the Irish imagination appears in "A Dream":

> I heard the dogs howl in the moonlight night,
> And I went to the window to see the sight;
> All the dead that ever I knew
> Going one by one and two by two.

> On they pass'd and on they pass'd;
> Townsfellows all from first to last;
> Born in the moonlight of the lane,
> And quench'd in the heavy shadow again.

An ornate ballad in the Morris style, "The Maids of Elfenmere," with its decorative detail and its haunting refrain, was sufficiently Pre-Raphaelite to be chosen by Rossetti as the one to illustrate. An unexpected specimen of the comic-grotesque is "The Dirty Old Man" (which incidentally may have given Dickens a hint for Miss Havisham).

The narrative poem, "The Music Master," is a discursive, pathetic pastoral. The story is uneventful: the heroine is equipped with a malicious elder sister, who turns out to play no part whatsoever in the action; the hero emigrates to America for no adequate reason and leaves his sweetheart to pine away and die. The model is Goldsmith and Crabbe rather than Wordsworth, and the poem is redeemed from tediousness and sentimentality only intermittently by the loving portrayal of humble life in an Irish village.

In 1863 Allingham was transferred in the customs department from Ireland to England, and propinquity to the literary world stimulated his activity in writing. Following the fashion of the preceding decade, he composed a novel in verse, *Laurence Bloomfield in Ireland*, which came out as a serial in *Fraser's Magazine* before being issued in book form. The use of rhyming couplets lends a touch of aesthetic distance to the otherwise commonplace account of a philanthropic landlord who is trying to improve the condition of his tenants.

Allingham continued to see Rossetti for several years. We hear of them spending an evening together talking about Chistina's poetry while they lay on the grass of Lincoln's Inn Fields. In his diary for 1866, mentioning a visit to the house in Cheyne

Walk, Allingham remarked, "My old regard for D.G.R. stirs within me, and would be as warm as ever *if he would let it.*" A year later, when Rossetti was in a neurasthenic depression because of anxiety over his eyesight, he volunteered to visit Allingham at his home in Hampshire. For more than a week, the host made superhuman efforts to entertain and stimulate him, but to no avail; Rossetti was incurably lethargic and hypochondriac. After Allingham with difficuly arranged for a visit to Tennyson in the Isle of Wight, Rossetti balked at the last minute on the pretext that the five-mile crossing of the Solent might make him seasick. Discouraged by his failure to reestablish genuine communication with his former idol, Allingham confided to his diary that "it is plain that the simple, the natural, the naïve are merely insipid in his mouth; he must have strong savours, in art, in literature, and in life. Colours, forms, sensations are required to be pungent, mordant. In poetry he desires spasmodic passion and emphatic, partly archaic, diction." Rossetti, however, dismayed by solitude after his return to London, begged Allingham to visit him. The days he spent in Cheyne Walk merely confirmed Allingham's disillusionment. The disorderly household, Fanny Cornforth's vulgarity, even Rossetti's profane language, got on the nerves of the precise and unsophisticated guest. The fact was that in his indiscriminate hero worship Allingham was more devoted to Tennyson and Browning than to Rossetti, and such eclecticism was not to Rossetti's taste. Summing up the uncomfortable visit, Allingham said that "in art, and still more in life, Rossetti and I have discords not to be resolved."

In 1870 Allingham gave up his civil service position and settled in London as editor of *Fraser's Magazine*. He continued to revise his poems and to write new ones, but added nothing significant to his previous achievement. He dined a few times with Rossetti, but saw him seldom if ever after 1871, as the poet's alienation from old associates intensified.

Though Allingham's talent was slender, it was individual, and his early admiration for Pre-Raphaelite poetry never seduced him into sheer imitation. He had memorized Woolner's "My Beautiful Lady" when it came out in the *Germ*; rereading it thirteen years later he still found it "tender and sweet," but added, "with the quaint guild-mark, so to speak, of the P.R.B. (I can't bear to be verbally quaint myself, yet often like it in another)."

Another poet who moved for a while in the Pre-Raphaelite orbit before finding his own literary métier was Richard Watson Dixon (1833-1900). Having been at school with Edward Burne Jones in Birmingham, he remained his close friend at Oxford, and thus became intimate also with Morris. It was he who proposed to them the founding of the *Oxford and Cambridge Magazine*. A letter of Jones's depicts him at this time: "Dixon is another fine fellow, a most interesting man, as ladies would say—dark-haired and pale-faced, with a beautiful brow and a deep, melancholy voice. He is a poet also. I should be sorry to dash the romance of his character, but truth compels me to say he is an inveterate smoker." Jones escorted him to Rossetti's studio in London, assuring him that "we shall see the greatest man in Europe," and Dixon was duly captivated. He took some lessons in painting, and was among the band of undergraduate novices who wielded brushes under Rossetti's direction on the murals for the union. For a while he shared the London studio of Jones and Morris in Red Lion Square, until he became convinced of his incompetence as a painter. Like them, he had been committed to a career in the church, but unlike them he did not relinquish his faith. Ordained in 1858, he went to work as a curate in a London slum. It was he who performed the marriage ceremony in 1859 for William Morris and Jane Burden.

His first book, *Christ's Company and Other Poems* (1861), was strongly Pre-Raphaelite in its pictorial precision, its formal verse patterns, and its melancholy cadences. The opening stanzas of "St. Mary Magdalene" suffice to display the Rossetti-Morris dominance:

> Kneeling before the altar step,
>   Her white face stretched above her hands;
> In one great line her body thin
> Rose robed right upwards to her chin;
> Her hair rebelled in golden bands,
>   And filled her hands;
> Which likewise held a casket rare
>   Of alabaster at that tide;
> Simeon was there and looked at her,
> Trancedly kneeling, sick and fair;
> Three parts the light her features tried,
>   The rest implied.

The poem goes on to recount her guilt-ridden hallucinations in gruesome detail.

The longest piece, "St. John," is a dramatic monologue of apocalyptic visions and mystical meditation, adorned with medieval details of emblems, heraldry, and general Pre-Raphaelite pictorialism:

> Came Gabriel, with his banner over him,
>   White lilies, brass-bright flowers, and leaves of green;
> A lily, too, he carried seemed to brim
>   With golden flames, which mounted pure and clean
> To touch his blessed mouth, and then would trim
>   Themselves within the lily leaf again:
> Gabriel's fair head sank even with dream-pain.

Another long religious poem, "St. Paul, Part of an Epistle from Gallio," is a slavish imitation of Browning. An older model, Chaucer, was chosen for what was to have been a sequence of nine symbolic narratives of "The Crosses of Love," but only the prologue, "Love's Consolation," was written in time for inclusion in the book. The narrator is a garrulous old monk, and his word-pictures of lovely ladies and gallant knights, in the vein of "A Legend of Good Women," foreshadow the subsequent style of Morris in *The Earthly Paradise*.

Some of the shorter poems are notable for weird, elusive evocations of nightmare landscapes and moods of spiritual blackness:

> I mark a woman on the farther shore
>   Walk ghost-like; her I shriek to with my might;
> Ghostlike she walketh ever more and more;
>   Her face how white!
> How small between us seems the Infinite!

In spite of the obvious resemblances to Morris's work, the mixture of religious devotion and emotional gloom links Dixon with Christina Rossetti rather than with the more secular-minded Pre-Raphaelites.

Dixon's promising start as a poet was not fulfilled. In 1861 he married a widow twelve years his senior, with three children, and gave up his curacy to become a schoolmaster, at which he persisted for six years, though he proved to be far too gentle and absent-minded to maintain discipline over unruly boys. His employment is chiefly memorable for setting up a fortuitous connection with the poetry of the next era. One of his first pupils was a seventeen-year-old youth named Gerard Manley Hopkins, who was greatly impressed by his teacher's recent book of poems. Seventeen years later, Hopkins sent Dixon a request for advice in his writing of poetry, and the outcome was a close friendship and a body of important correspondence. It was probably mainly through this intermediary that Hopkins acquired his contact with Pre-Raphaelite poetry.

Dixon's next book, *Hisorical Odes and Other Poems* (1864), added little to his achievement, though it showed clearer evidences of his religious mysticism. The four historical poems are pretentious, and two stories for the abortive "Crosses of Love" series are notable chiefly for their antagonism to carnality. The Pre-Raphaelite influence was diminishing in favor of Keats. Four philosophical odes are dignified and ornate, but a few of the short lyrics show something of Blake's engaging simplicity.

Thereafter Dixon vanished from the literary arena for twenty years. By 1866 he had material for another volume of short pieces and had almost finished a "Northern Epic" which he later destroyed because it was forestalled by Morris's saga poems. He asserted that "I stick to poetry and ever shall," but nothing got into print. In 1868 he resumed clerical duties as a minor canon of Carlisle Cathedral and began research on Anglican church history. In 1874 he published a biography of his father, who had been an eminent Methodist minister. Though he had faded into the obscurity of theological scholarship, he maintained some contacts with his old Pre-Raphaelite friends. Rossetti belatedly read his two books of verse in 1875 and wrote him a long and enthusiastic letter: "You are one of the most subtle as well as varied of our poets, and . . . the neglect of such work as yours on all hands is an incomprehensible accident. . . . Surely there must be more in store by this time." Dixon replied ruefully: "My work has met with nearly absolute neglect, but along with this there has been some censure of a very ignorant sort. . . . I have several volumes of poems in MS, but no immediate prospect of publishing. I can hardly yet believe that I have received so much commendation from the author . . . whom I have always regarded as the greatest master of thought and art in the world."

By this time he was settling down in a quiet country parish and working on his massive *History of the Church of England*, the six volumes of which came out at intervals over a quarter of a century. The unexpected tribute from Hopkins in 1878, leading to an introduction to Hopkins's friend Robert Bridges, restored a vital connection with poetry, and he felt encouraged to disinter and publish in 1883 an ambitious historical novel in verse, *Mano: A Poetical History*, which he had written several years before. Composed in terza rima, it deals with the exploits of a Norman knight at the close of the tenth century, when he is involved in the defense of Italy against the Saracens. The historical background is the apocalyptic expectation of the imminent millennium, and the narrator, an aged monk, shares the fatalistic and superstitious assumptions of the time. Hence a remarkable sense of immediacy emerges in spite of fantastic supernatural episodes and the whole Gothic issue of imprisoned maidens, valiant knights, defiant outlaws, and mysterious parentage. Elements of Dante, the monastic chronicles, and the metrical romances contribute to the convincing medieval impression. Like Morris, Dixon was fully capable of identifying himself imaginatively with the Middle Ages.

Mano marked the end of Pre-Raphaelite influence in Dixon's work. The world-weary mood, the inevitable frustration and misery of earthly love, the word-pictures of the melancholy heroine nursing her secret passion, and the many other pictorial passages, all are in the Rossetti-Morris tradition. Thereafter,

under the influence of Bridges, Dixon wrote in a simpler, more fastidious style. (pp. 253-75)

Lionel Stevenson, in his The Pre-Raphaelite Poets, *The University of North Carolina Press, 1972, 330 p.*

AESTHETIC TENETS

HUMPHRY HOUSE

[*In these comments from a 1948 broadcast commemorating the centennial of the Pre-Raphaelite Brotherhood, House focuses on the medieval qualities of the movement. He suggests that archaism appealed to the Pre-Raphaelites as a means of recapturing symbolic spiritual values and restoring a harmony lost to the modern world.*]

When *The Germ* appeared in January 1850, there was printed on its cover a sonnet by William Michael Rossetti intended to declare the purpose of the paper [see excerpt above]; he later said the sonnet meant that

> A writer ought to think out his subject honestly and personally, not imitatively, and ought to express it with directness and precision; if he does this, we should respect his performance as truthful, even though it may not be important.

And he added that this was meant to indicate for writers much the same principle which the PRB professed for painters. But it *is* startling to see that the whole of this sonnet professing the need for personal honesty, directness, precision, etc., together with the title of the paper and the sub-title including the words "Thoughts toward Nature", should all be printed in heavy black Gothic type, so that the cover looks like that of a Puseyite parish magazine.

This sense of duality, even of incongruity, in artistic idiom is perpetuated in much of the contents of all the four numbers of *The Germ*. For instance, there is a poem in the first number by John Tupper, called "A Sketch from Nature": its main theme is a description, in what was later called "word-painting", of sunset over the landscape seen from Sydenham Wood in 1849; it opens with a piece of blatant ballad-mongering:

> The air blows pure, for twenty miles,
>   Over this vast countrie:
> Over hill and wood and vale, it goeth,
>   Over steeple, and stack, and tree.

It then appears that the Surrey birds of 1849 included species called corbies and merles. This sort of archaism was a product of literary medievalising which already had a long history in several different modes.

In the past fifty years English poetry had developed more strongly and variously and had changed more radically than English painting. The academic painting against which the Pre-Raphaelites revolted was a long-delayed hang-over from the eighteenth century, a tradition which had failed to assimilate Blake, Constable, Turner, Palmer, and others. To have attempted an exactly parallel revolt in literature would have meant attacking very little more than University Prize poems. . . . [The] Pre-Raphaelites' painting was very literary painting; in fact they deliberately went to literature for their themes, and their treatment and style of vision were deeply influenced by the poets—especially by Keats and Tennyson. It is thus not surprising that much minor poetry written by Pre-Rapahelites or fellow-travellers shows an exaggeration of Tennyson's mannerisms. Woolner's *"My Beautiful Lady"*, for instance, is full of such echoes:

> I see a lurid sunlight throw its last
> Wild gleam athwart the land whose shadows lengthen fast.

One could well illustrate from Tennyson all the Pre-Raphaelite principles as they were explicitly put forward; and this has led people to say over and over again this year that Tennyson was a Pre-Raphaelite poet. If one has to use these labels it makes more sense to call the Pre-Raphaelites Tennysonian painters; but I want to suggest that the most important Pre-Raphaelite poetry was not Tennysonian, and that it attempted something which was never quite explicitly put forward as a Pre-Raphaelite purpose.

In its simplest form Pre-Raphaelite medievalism was merely one aspect of Pre-Raphaelite naturalism. This is made very plain in the second number of *The Germ* in an article by F. G. Stephens, under the pseudonym "John Seward": its title is "The Purpose and Tendency of Early Italian Art". Its whole argument is that the early Italian painters *were* naturalistic, that they showed "the simple chastity of nature" before "the introduction of false and meretricious ornament". Stephens understood them to be motivated by a desire for "truth in every particular", and he argued that nineteenth-century science had given a new stimulus to just this same motive. This is the purest and simplest pre-Raphaelite doctrine.

But it at once raises two questions:

(1) Was medieval freshness and naturalism really governed by similar motives and backed by similar mental processes to those of nineteenth-century science?

(2) Was the cultivation of nineteenth-century scientific naturalism an adequate or interesting formula for the production of works of art?

The most important Pre-Raphaelite poetry implied an emphatic answer "No" to both these questions. It was searching through the mixture of modernism and medievalism after deeper purposes.

When a medieval artist painted a religious or scriptural theme he dressed the figures in the normal clothes of his own time. James Smetham, a painter on the edge of the Pre-Raphaelite circle, recorded a conversation with Ruskin about this in 1855. Ruskin admitted that on his principles in nineteenth-century religious pictures the people should be in modern dress, adding that "if it would not look well, the times are wrong and their modes must be altered".

> J. S. "It would be a very great deal easier (it is a backward, lame action of the mind to fish up costume and forms we never saw), but I could not do it for laughing."
>
> J. R. "Ha! but we *must* do it nevertheless."

"I could not do it for laughing." There is a main clue to what I am trying to discuss.

One of the big problems for the Pre-Raphaelites and for all their generation was to try to see the daily life of Victorian England—complete with all its keepings of dress and furniture and social habits—as having an equivalent spiritual and human significance to that which medieval life had in all its details for medieval poets and painters. One method was to use modern themes to bring out the moral and social tensions which underlay the surface of slick prosperity; but there were also personal, psychological, sexual and religious tensions which became more apparent in the life and literature of the later fifties and the sixties.

The series of poems which best illustrates this dilemma in the poetry of the mid-century is Coventry Patmore's long work *The Angel in the House*; and it is significant that Patmore at once found sympathy for the Pre-Raphaelites and contributed to *The Germ*. Now, *The Angel in the House* is an attempt to invest an ordinary Victorian courtship and marriage in the prosperous educated classes with as deep a spiritual and psychological significance as was felt to attach to the great poetic loves of the past; the main narrative stresses all the details of modern dress, archery parties, passing the port after dinner, etc. etc., while the running comment in the Preludes and lyrical parts attaches to these details a highly wrought passion more delicate and sustained than the gusty discontent in *Maud*. The trouble was that people laughed; they felt as Smetham did about Lord John Russell portrayed paying homage to the Infant Saviour with his top hat standing by on a pedestal. There seemed to be an irreparable cleavage between the facts of modern society and the depths it was recognised poetry ought to touch. This cleavage is not yet healed; all our living poets have been conscious of it; so were the Pre-Raphaelites.

The medieval world attracted them not from a mere love of archaic patterns and forms or by a nostalgia for more colourful ways of life (though these things entered into it) but because medieval art did not betray any such cleavage between daily visible fact and accepted truth and values. They saw that medieval modes of apprehending reality were productive of great and satisfying works of art, as the modern modes of mixed science and sentimentality were not. They attempted, by exploring the possibilities of allegory and symbolism, to restore a harmony they thought modern life had lost.

A proper discussion of this attempt would involve many complex problems of metaphysics and theology that I am not competent to tackle: I can only just suggest certain untechnical lines of thought. We have to consider the status of symbols, allegories and emblems; by status, I mean the kind of significance they were supposed to have, and the means by which they were supposed to have any significance at all. This discussion is closely linked to the revival of sacramental doctrine in the Oxford Movement.

The Sacrament of the Eucharist provides the clearest example of what I mean, and best illustrates what I mean by status: there was (and is) a "High" and a "Low" view of this sacrament. The High view maintains that after consecration there is some kind of identity between the elements and the body and blood of Christ, and because of this, extreme reverence and care are shown for the physical elements; this is almost exaggeratedly stressed, with medieval quotations, in the Anglo-Catholic books of ceremonial and devotion of the 1850's. The elements are much more than mere symbols, mere reminders of Christ's sacrifice; they do in some way embody it.

In medieval life this sacramental view of things was not confined to the theological sacraments; the mere making of the sign of the Cross could be potent in exorcism; holy water had special powers; miraculous power inhered in physical relics and holy places; every detail of Nature was in some sense a sacramental embodiment of spiritual reality. Language itself, in the words of consecration, forgiving, blessing, and cursing had theological power, and magical power in spells. The words

John Everett Millais's Ophelia, *an illustration for William Shakespeare's* Hamlet. *From the Art Collection of the Folger Shakespeare Library.*

of Scripture were interpreted in various ways, ranging from the literal-historical to the mystical. Thus both painting and literature were charged with significance at many different levels. Most of this wealth of implication was slowly destroyed in the sixteenth and seventeenth centuries. The Anglo-Catholic and Roman Catholic revivals of the nineteenth involved in various ways the recovery of some part of it. But science and history had utterly transformed the ways in which men could be said to ''believe in'' sacraments, in the sacramental view of Nature, symbols, and myths. The Catholic countries failed no less than the Protestant to produce any great religious art.

For the members of the Rossetti family this whole question of symbolism was conditioned by the intensive study of Dante in which they were brought up by their father. In Dante was to be found the fullest development of medieval symbolism, of every kind of status, from the theologically sacramental, through the cosmological to the conventions of courtly love and their private development in the Beatrice theme. All the children knew Dante better than they knew any English poet. William Bell Scott wrote of Dante Gabriel Rossetti:

> He had never thought of pietistic matters except as a sentiment, theology being altogether ignored by him. . . . He had no idea of the changed position of historical forms or cosmogony of religion by geological and other discoveries; and, indeed, was himself not sure that the earth really moved round the sun! ''Our senses did not tell us so at any rate, and

what then did it matter whether it did move or not?'' What Dante knew was enough for him. He then remembered Galileo, another Italian, and gave in! It might matter in a scientific way, oh yes!

This is an interesting story, but not for Scott's reasons. Rossetti was not apparently in any accepted nineteenth-century sense a believing or practising Christian; but to say he thought of ''pietistic matters'' as a ''sentiment'' gives just the wrong turn to his unscientific views of the universe; this may be partly a matter of the changed force of words—even Pater said that with Rossetti common things are full of ''sentiment''; but Pater also acknowledged the force of the likeness to Dante; and ''sentiment'' is one of the last words to apply to Dante. It is more important to say of Rossetti that he had some power of making spiritual things and the details of religious myth concrete, than that he had an etherealised apprehension of the physical. It is this latter method that leads to an aestheticism for which poppies and lilies are nothing but gestures. But Rossetti lived in a society in which little of the Dante symbolism was generally accepted; in which his own sense of identity between symbol and thing symbolised was little understood. This sense was not continuous or absolute even in himself: he darted from one level to another, sometimes appealing to a knowledge in his readers which might not be there, sometimes using with tremendous effectiveness a symbolic image which carried its own interpretation in itself. Thus in ''The Blessed Damozel'' it is rather ineffectual and merely decorative to say that she had seven stars in her hair; but it is quite another matter to say she looked down from "the fixed place of Heaven", or to describe the souls rising up as being like "thin flames". These phrases both stand by themselves and become richer by association and knowledge. In "Jenny" the roses and lilies are brought in with awkward explanations of their purpose; but here is Victorian London at night-time, charged with meaning by a single symbol:

> you stare
> Along the streets alone, and there,
> Round the long park, across the bridge,
> The cold lamps at the pavement's edge
> Wind on together and apart,
> A fiery serpent for your heart.

Dante Gabriel became a father of aestheticism through others' misunderstanding of the poetic problem with which he was trying to deal.

His sister Christina solved the problem within her own compass almost to perfection. She had no strong predilection for Dante references or for historical themes; but she seems to have assimilated in her youth something of the essential quality of the medieval method and to have adapted it without strain or affectation to contemporary feelings; in her religious poems she avoids the problem of modern or medieval dress and keepings by emphasising neither; but still her persons and situations and scenes have a clarity and sharpness which belong with the Pre-Raphaelite aims. Two of her longest poems—"Goblin Market" and "The Prince's Progress"—are allegories which have the greatest virtues of all allegory, that they can be apprehended at a number of different levels and demand no gloss. Because Christina was a devout Anglo-Catholic of utterly unquestioning faith she was able to use Catholic symbolism with complete internal conviction; there is no uncertainty about her levels. It is no accident that Gerard Manley Hopkins was devoted to her poems in his youth; for it was he, not the aesthetes, who truly developed Pre-Raphaelite aims. (pp. 151-58)

> Humphry House, "Pre-Raphaelite Poetry," in his
> All in Due Time: The Collected Essays and Broadcast
> Talks of Humphry House, *Rupert Hart-Davis, 1955,
> pp. 151-58.*

JOHN HEATH-STUBBS

[*In this excerpt from his study of the Romantic tradition in late nineteenth-century English literature, Heath-Stubbs discovers a withdrawal to a world of dream and aesthetic contemplation in the poetry of Dante Gabriel Rossetti, Christina Rossetti, Dixon, Morris, and Swinburne.*]

In the second half of the [nineteenth] century the general tendency of English poetry was to abandon the attempt either to deal with the external world, or to express any "philosophy". The poets withdrew into the contemplation of purely decorative beauty. This movement, in England, had two phases. The first and most important was the pre-Raphaelite movement which took shape in the 'fifties, and which had spent its force by the middle of the 'eighties. It was a movement which primarily affected painting and the arts of decoration, but also found its expression in the sphere of poetry. If its products look dated to-day, it is well to remember the massed forces of Victorian middle-class Philistinism with which the pre-Raphaelites had to contend. A real insistence on purely aesthetic values was necessary, and it is to the pre-Raphaelites's credit that this reform was to a large extent effected. The name of the "Aes-

thetic Movement" is generally restricted to the literature and art of the 'nineties. But in the field of poetry this was essentially a resumption of pre-Raphaelitism. The movement had now acquired a sort of metaphysic, though its sources were diverse, its development complex, and its genealogy hard to trace. Matthew Arnold, with his gospel of "Culture", and Ruskin may to some extent be regarded as its prophets and forerunners. But both of these men were essentially Puritans, by upbringing and by temperament. Ruskin had tended to identify moral and aesthetic values, but the latter, for him, arose out of a consideration of the former. But the real philosopher of the later Aesthetic Movement was Pater, whose thought combined elements of German aesthetic Hellenism with a religiosity whose source must be looked for in the "ritualist" tendency which had followed up the Oxford Movement, and which had affinities, also, with the aesthetic Catholicism of Chateaubriand. But above all, for Pater, moral considerations disappear; the moment of aesthetic experience becomes the sole significant reality. (pp. 148-49)

To both these movements, the pre-Raphaelites, and that of the 'nineties, the general term "Aesthetic" may conveniently be applied—though properly it belongs only to the latter. These trends offer certain analogies with the Symbolist Movement, more or less contemporary with them, which originated in France with Baudelaire, though the formula "art for art's sake" was coined by Gautier, and accepted by the Parnassian poets in France, as well as by the Symbolists. It is instructive to compare the poetry of the Symbolists and that of the pre-Raphelites and their successors. One cannot consider the work of the latter without reference to the painting of Rossetti, Morris, and Burne-Jones, while a major inspiration of the Symbolists was the music of Wagner. Now painting—as understood in the nineteenth century—is the more decorative, music the more abstract, art. The more intellectual character of the French genius is seen even in this poetry of withdrawal, and Symbolist work tended to be increasingly metaphysical in its preoccupations.

It is fashionable to dismiss these two parallel movements in English and French poetry as decadent and escapist, with the implication that the poets should have resisted the temptation to withdraw from reality, and have evolved a style of verse capable of dealing adequately with the social problems of the day. But this, for most of them, would have been impossible. The changes going on in the social structure were too rapid, and the answers which the science offered to the questioning mind too uncertain and conflicting to provide an adequate metaphysical structure upon which the poets could have based their criticism of life. Yet, for most of them, the foundations of traditional faith, which had sanctioned a more imaginative vision of the world, seemed irreparably shaken. In these circumstances the only course for the artist who sought to retain his integrity was a withdrawal from the confused and unintelligible reality which lay without. The subjectively apprehended reality of aesthetic experience could at least not be explained away by science. By concentrating upon this, a coherent vision might yet be attained.

But this course was followed with greater consistency by the more intellectual poets of France. They lived in a country more acutely (or at least more openly) disturbed by social change than that of their English contemporaries, in their relatively sheltered and prosperous middle-class security. When the Symbolists entered their Otherworld of pure Art, they did not abandon all attempt to fuse intellectual thought with their imaginative vision. Baudelaire's *Fleurs du Mal*, though his satanism is partly a pose, does represent an attempt, only half-consciously carried out, to explore the metaphysical nature of evil, through the medium of the senses. Rimbaud went further and attempted to pass beyond Good and Evil. Mallarmé is of all the group the most withdrawn from common experience, but he is also the most intensely intellectual. His poetry deals with a very restricted and remote part of reality, yet the tract of feeling dealt with in his poems forms an integral portion of the great whole of possible human experience, and the poet is making a genuine philosophical attempt to explore it. The acrid satirical poetry of Corbière and Laforgue, though apparently only exposing a state of futility, is, fundamentally, an attempt to measure the confusion of external reality against the aesthetic standards that Symbolist poetry had begun to rediscover. It foreshadows the time when poetry can once more be integrated with the exterior world. The outcome of this metaphysical courage of the French poets is a far greater originality, precision, and freedom of style than is to be found in their English contemporaries. Despite the suspicious attitude of the critics, the best of the poetry of the French Symbolists retains vital qualities which recommend it to modern readers. Such qualities are hardly to be found in any of the English pre-Raphaelite and Aesthetic poets before the time of Yeats.

In painting, and also in poetry, the overt aim of the pre-Raphaelites was—as with the first Romantics—a "return to nature", in all her simplicity. They aimed at precision of detail, and indeed, many of the longer narrative poems of Rossetti are difficult to read because the succession of minutely observed natural details distracts from the apprehension of the subject-matter as a whole. Another characteristic of the pre-Raphaelites—that which the name of the group denotes—is their preference for mediæval subject-matter, and their revival of mediæval metrical and literary forms. A sympathy with the older literature, involving its more or less close imitation, had formed an integral part of Romanticism from Chatterton and the "Gothic" writers of the eighteenth century downwards. Such poems as those of Chatterton, Coleridge's "Christabel", and Keats's "Eve of St. Mark's" in particular, furnished models for the pre-Raphaelites, in its decorative treatment of mediæval scenes. Historical scholarship and the criticism of Ruskin had now revealed a much clearer picture of mediæval civilization, and the excellence of its art; the traditional view of the Renaissance Humanists and the men of the Age of Reason that the Middle Ages had been wholly a period of Gothic barbarism and monkish superstition was no longer tenable. Nor could the sentimentalized picture of feudalism and chivalry furnished by Scott's novels or even Tennyson's *Idylls of the King* wholly satisfy readers any longer.

But the pre-Raphaelites did not altogether succeed in piercing through to the life of earlier ages. While they employed the religious and other symbols of the old poetry, they rejected the faith which had given these symbols relevance. Hence their work is often at the same time both sentimental and vulgar, lifeless and unreal.

That this is so will become apparent if we analyse intellectually that most typically pre-Raphaelite poem, Rossetti's "The Blessed Damozel". The heroine—the poet's dead mistress—is represented as in Heaven. But instead of enjoying her felicity, she continually awaits the time when her lover will be reunited to her. Seeing a flight of angels approaching, she expects the event,

> . . . but soon their path
> Was vague in distant spheres:
> And then she cast her arms along

> The golden barriers,
> And laid her face between her hands,
> And wept. (I heard her tears).

But if we take it at its face value, the whole conception is cheaply sentimental and muddled to the point of absurdity. For by any definition of bliss it is impossible to suppose a soul in heaven capable of the emotions in which the Blessed Damozel is represented as indulging. And by the standards of meadiæval theology—which the whole framework of the poem implies—her longing for her earthly lover, to the exclusion of her joy in the contemplation of God, is as much a sin—a thing impossible in a redeemed soul—as the excessive grief for the dead of which the poet is himself guilty. The poem was written by Rossetti in his very early years, but it seems almost prophetic of the state of mind which was to be actually his, many years later, after the death of Elizabeth Siddal. The story of how he buried the manuscripts of his poems with her in her coffin, and was then persuaded to make nonsense of this romantic gesture by allowing them to be exhumed, is pathetic, appalling, and not a little nauseating. It bears the same sort of witness as does "The Blessed Damozel" itself to the atmosphere of unreasoned, muddled, romantic sentiment in which Rossetti's passion exercised itself.

In mediæval poetry, the dead always exhort the living to lay aside grief, remembering that those they have loved are in the hands of God. So speaks the voice from the Unquiet Grave in the old ballad, the dead child in the fourteenth-century allegory of *The Pearl*, the Laura of Petrarch's devotion:

> Di me non pianger tu; ch'e' miei di fersi,
> morendo, eterni; e nell' eterno lume,
> quando mostrai di chiudar, gli occhi apersi.

Perhaps this quiet voice cannot satisfy the restless and passionate mind of man. We are troubled when we try to imagine what place the individual human affections ultimately take beneath the light of eternity. The problem exists for all who think and feel intensely, whether they accept the myth of survival after death as objectively true or not. Patmore also, with his intense intellectual faith, in "Tristitia" explores the possibility that the Blessed may grieve for those they have loved on earth—not indeed from a temporary sense of separation, but if the latter should be eternally exiled from Heaven. For Patmore this bare possibility is an awful mystery, hardly to be thought of or expressed in words; a contradiction of the order of things, which will react terribly upon the damned soul who has been its cause. The distance between Patmore's sensitive Ode, and Rossetti's decorative and overloaded poem, measures the distance between the metaphysical and the merely sentimental treatment of love.

Judged by the standards I have suggested above, "The Blessed Damozel" must simply be dismissed as a sentimental and silly poem. There is, however, another line of approach, which may help us to a more sympathetic understanding of this and of the rest of Rossetti's work. The world of this poetry is a kind of limbo, a half-sensuous, pagan dream-world, such as was explored by Edgar Allan Poe, and sometimes, by Shelley. The Christian imagery, derived from Dante and the other early Italian poets, is used merely decoratively and is not really of a piece with this world. Rossetti is an explorer of the subconscious, of subtle states of mind between waking and sleeping:

> There the dreams are multitudes:
> Some that will not wait for sleep.
> Deep within the August woods;

> Some that hum while rest may steep
>   Weary labour laid a-heap;
>   Interludes,
> Some, grievous moods that weep.
>
> Poets' fancies all are there:
>   There the elf-girls flood with wings
> Vallies full of plaintive air;
>   There breath perfumes; there in rings
> Whirl the foam-bewildered springs;
>   Siren there
> Winds her dizzy hair and sings.

In his last years Rossetti was a scarcely sane man. And to this period belongs his fragmentary prose tale, "The Orchard Pit", telling of a strange Siren dwelling in an apple-tree, who lured men to their doom. This is perhaps Rossetti's most intensely imagined work, and the unfinished lyric which forms part of it, well presents the state of Death-in-Life to which his exploration of the dream-world finally lead him:

> Piled deep below the screening apple-branch
>   They lie with bitter apples in their hands:
> And some are only ancient bones that blanch,
> And some had ships that last year's wind did launch,
>   And some were yesterday the lords of lands.
>
> In the soft dell, among the apple-trees,
>   High up above the hidden pit she stands,
> And there for ever sings, who gave to these,
> That lie below, her magic hour of ease,
>   And those her apples holden in their hands.
>
> This in my dreams is shown me; and her hair
>   Crosses my lips and draws my burning breath;
> Her song spreads golden wings upon the air,
> Life's eyes are gleaming from her forehead fair,
>   And from her breasts the ravishing eyes of Death.
>
> Men say to me that sleep hath many dreams,
>   Yet I knew never but this dream alone:
> There, from a dried-up channel, once the stream's,
> The glen slopes up; even such in sleep it seems
>   As in my waking sight the place well-known.
>
> . . . . .
>
> My love I call her, and she loves me well:
>   But I love her as in the maelstrom's cup
> The whirled stone loves the leaf inseparable
> That clings to it round all the circling swell,
>   And that the same last eddy swallows up.

It is this kind of dream-poetry, rather than the formal peculiarities of their style, or their mediævalism, which is, I think, really characteristic of the pre-Raphaelites. In a sense their movement may be regarded as a resumption of the romantic impulse from the point it had reached in the dream-poetry of Hood, and Darley. . . . But in the poetry of the pre-Raphaelites it has more the quality of reverie. Their very insistence upon visual exactness in their imagery gives to their work a kind of detachment and remoteness. We seem to be gazing at something a long way off, as through the wrong end of a telescope—something, too, which is at a great distance in time, as well as in space. The sense of urgency, of relevancy to the waking world is gone. The symbols (the poem quoted above is perhaps an exception) seem to be robbed of their significance.

In some respects "The House of Life" contains the most satisfactory of Rossetti's work. His familiarity with the early Italian poets gave him an insight into the true nature of the sonnet form. Milton, in whose hands "the thing became a trumpet", and Wordsworth, following his example, by obscuring the outlines of its internal structure and its original lyrical character, had tended to make the sonnet too much a vehicle for rhetorical declamation, and furnished dangerous models for later English poets. The essential balanced structure and formal development of the sonnet are restored by Rossetti, and it again becomes a species of poem in which form and thought develop logically together. Nevertheless, an undisciplined, rootless man like Rossetti was incapable of attaining the crystalline clarity and perfect balance of his models. His archaic and affected diction, the movement of his lines, clogged with lifeless monosyllables, the vagueness of his sensuous images—all these tend to blur his picture, and make his passion seem strained and unreal. His true merit lies less in direct expressive power, than in his gift for evoking transient and half-defined states of feeling. This is seen sometimes in the sonnets of "The House of Life", more frequently in the songs that are contained in the same work—notably in the well-known "Wood-spurge", and "Sudden Light":

> I have been here before,
>   But when or how I cannot tell:
> I know the grass beyond the door,
>   The sweet keen smell,
> The sighing sound, the lights around the shore.

In poems such as these Rossetti captures a delicate sublety of emotion, rather in the manner later brought to perfection by Walter De la Mare. (The latter, a minor poet of our own time, might almost be called the last representative of the pre-Raphaelite "Renaissance of Wonder".) This visionary quality of Rossetti, both as poet and painter, gives him an affinity with Blake, whose merits he was one of the first to discover. Yet he lacks Blake's essential religious vision, and with it the lyrical intensity, clarity, and freshness which Blake, at any rate in his purely poetical, as distinct from his "prophetic" work, achieves. Rossetti's vision is blurred, lacking any unifying principle. He moves unhappily in a world of dream-symbols, and the weary, clogged rhythms of his verse indicate how imperfectly they are imaginatively apprehended.

It is a relief to turn from Rossetti's poems to those of his sister Christina. She has all the qualities which he lacks—restraint, poise, lightness of touch, a feeling for clean, bright colour. These features arise, no doubt, from her own temperament—a personality more finely constituted than her brother's, for which suffering provided a discipline, and religion an intelligible pattern by which life might be ruled. It is true that her religion—a High Anglican piety—when it impinges directly upon her poetry, produces a certain chill, as it seems to have narrowed and frustrated her emotional life. She rejected two suitors, apparently because she doubted the stability of their religious views. Quite possibly some deeper-seated psychological twist in her emotional nature prompted her to make this rejection. It is obvious from her poetry that it caused her profound suffering. In poem after poem we find this rejection symbolized—the heroine is cheated of her lover by a jealous sister (in whom we may see perhaps Christina's own "superego" personified?) or she is snatched from his arms by a mysterious demon, the "Love from the North". Again, in "The Prince's Progress", the princess dies unwedded, because the prince has delayed too long in crossing the desert to find her. Nevertheless, some of her religious verse is, in its kind, often admirable—note particularly the fine economy and dramatic movement of "The Three Enemies", in which the resolved soul resists the temptations, progressively more insidious, of the Flesh, the World, and the Devil:

The Flesh

"Sweet, thou art pale."
                    "More pale to see,
Christ hung upon the cruel tree
    And bore his father's wrath for me."

"Sweet thou art sad."
                    "Beneath a rod
More heavy, Christ for my sake trod
The winepress of the wrath of God."

"Sweet thou art weary."
                    "Not so Christ:
Whose mighty love for me sufficed
For strength, salvation, Eucharist."

"Sweet, thou art footsore."
                    "If I bleed,
His feet have bled: yea, in my need
His heart once bled for mine indeed."

The World

"Sweet, thou art young."
                    "So He was young
Who for my sake in silence hung
Upon the Cross with Passion wrung."

"Look, thou art fair."
                    "He was more fair
Than men, who deigned for me to wear
A visage marred beyond compare."

"And thou hast riches."
                    "Daily bread:
All else is His; Who living, dead,
For me lacked where to lay His head."

"And life is sweet."
                    "It was not so
To Him, Whose Cup did overflow
With mine inutterable woe."

The Devil

"Thou drinkest deep."
                    "When Christ would sup
He drained the dregs from out my cup:
So how should I be lifted up?"

"Thou shalt win glory."
                    "In the skies,
Lord Jesus, cover up mine eyes
Lest they should look on vanities."

"Thou shalt have Knowledge."
                    "Helpless dust!
In Thee, O Lord, I put my trust:
Answer Thou for me, Wise and Just."

"And Might."—
                    "Get thee behind me. Lord,
Who has redeemed and not abhorred
My soul, oh keep it by Thy Word."

But when she allows her imagination free play in spheres of feeling not directly affected by her piety, the basic religious instinct lying behind the work gives to it a clarity and an inner logic of design not to be found in that of her agnostic brother. Let us take, for example, her best-known narrative poem, "Goblin Market". This is not directly a religious poem. Laura, the younger of two sisters, is tempted by the powers of evil, the Goblins, and tastes their forbidden fruit. As a result, she pines away, almost to the point of death. Having once savoured its sweetness, she is filled with an overpowering longing to do so again, but no person may a second time meet with the goblin merchants—this is a most accurate psychological description of the nature of sensual sin. The elder sister, Lizzie, saves Laura by her self-sacrifice, herself braving the dangers of the goblins' glen. She demands to buy the goblins wares, but will not herself taste of them. They try to force her, pressing the fruit upon her mouth and face, and because of this, she is able to carry some of the juices of the fruit back to Laura, who recovers when she has tasted them. The whole story might be read as an allegory of the Fall and Redemption of Man, represented by Laura, the action of the elder sister being analogous to the guiltless self-sacrifice of Christ. There is even, perhaps, a suggestion of the Eucharist in Lizzie's words to Laura on her return:

> She cried "Laura," up the garden,
> "Did you miss me?
> Come and kiss me.
> Never mind my bruises,
> Hug me, kiss me, suck my juices
> Squeezed from goblin fruits for you,
> Goblin pulp and goblin dew.
> Eat me, drink me, love me;
> Laura, make much of me:
> For your sake I have braved the glen
> And had to do with goblin merchant men."

But there is no need to suppose that Christina Rossetti consciously, or even unconsciously, intended this. Lizzie, giving herself for the one she loves, may be taken as a type of the Christian as well as of Christ. The point to note is that the central Christian doctrines of guilt, self-sacrifice, and substitution inform the whole poem, giving significance to what seems at first sight no more than a dream-fantasy or a pastiche of folk-tale.

As a pre-Raphaelite, Christina Rossetti, like Dante Gabriel Rossetti and Morris, creates for herself an aritifical dream-world by re-evoking the poetic forms of older romance. But, within its smaller compass, her world has more of the genuine life of the world of romance and folk-tale than theirs. Dante Gabriel Rossetti's ballads—"The White Ship", "Eden Bower" and the rest—especially "Sister Helen"— are exciting enough, but they will not bear comparison with the genuine old ballads. There is much of melodrama about them; their effects are too obviously laboured, the refrains over-artfully introduced. Christina Rossetti's "Sister Maude"—short as it is—comes much nearer to the genuine spirit of the traditional ballads, and to this is added a peculiar personal poignancy of emotion. Simple though it appears, this is one of the poems which, as I have already suggested, may be interpreted in the light of modern psychology. It is the retort of the imaginative, emotional side of Christina Rossetti's nature upon the narrowly pious super-ego which thwarted her:

> Who told my mother of my shame,
>   Who told my father of my dear?
> Oh who but Maude, my sister Maude,
>   Who lurked to spy and peer.
>
> Cold he lies, as cold as stone,
>   With his clotted curls about his face:
> The comeliest corpse in all the world,
>   And worthy of a queen's embrace.
>
> You might have spared his soul, sister,
>   Have spared my soul, your own soul too;
> Though I had not been born at all,
>   He'd never have looked at you.
>
> My father may sleep in Paradise,
>   My mother at Heaven-gate;
> But sister Maude shall get no sleep
>   Either early or late.

My father may wear a golden gown,
   My mother a crown may win;
If my dear and I knocked at Heaven-gate
   Perhaps they'd let us in:
Not sister Maude, oh sister Maude,
   Bide *you* with death and sin.

The autumnal languor of pre-Raphaelite poetry—the slow lines with their weary monosyllables, the faint colours, the indirectness of emotional expression—symptomatic of a late phase of Romanticism, and contrasting so strangely with that of the mediæval writers which are the poets' models—is not to be found in Christina Rossetti. Her best work has a lilting, lyrical movement and an April freshness of imagery:

Long ago and long ago,
   And long ago still,
There dwelt three merry maidens
   Upon a distant hill,
One was tall Meggan,
   And one was dainty May,
But one was fair Margaret,
   More fair than I can say,
Long ago and long ago.

It is artificial, of course, but it really does recapture a note from the very beginning of modern European literature—the songs which, seven hundred years before, the women of France had sung as they worked at their embroidery. The poem of which the lines quoted above are the opening, "Maiden Song", seem to belong to a golden age of freshness and innocence.

The wide range and consistently high standard attained by Christina Rossetti are more considerable than anyone who has read only those of her poems which have been made over-familiar by the anthologists may imagine. Besides writing romantic and devotional poems, she occasionally displays a certain delicate power of wit, peculiarly feminine, which, nevertheless, women poets have too seldom exercised. Here is her poem "The Queen of Hearts":

How comes it, Flora, that whenever we
Play cards together, you invariably,
   However the pack parts,
   Still hold the Queen of Hearts?

I've scanned you with a scrutinizing gaze,
Resolved to fathom these your secret ways;
   But, sift them as I will,
   Your ways are secret still.

I cut and shuffle; shuffle, cut again;
But all my cutting, shuffling, proves in vain;
   Vain hope, vain forethought too;
   That Queen still falls to you.

I dropped her once, prepense; but, ere the deal
Was dealt, your instinct seemed her loss to feel;
   "There should be one card more"
   You said, and searched the floor.

I cheated once; I made a private notch
In Heart-Queen's back, and kept a lynx-eyed watch;
   Yet such another back
   Deceived me in the pack:

The Queen of Clubs assumed by arts unknown,
An imitative dint that seemed my own;
   This notch, not of my doing,
   Misled me to my ruin.

It baffles me to puzzle out the clue,
Which must be skill or craft or luck in you;
   Unless indeed, it be
   Natural affinity.

These lines have a perfection that reminds us of the most delicate art of the eighteenth century.

A brief note may be appended on Richard Watson Dixon, another Anglican poet who was associated with the pre-Raphaelite movement. Dixon was a member of the original "brotherhood"—which included, besides Dixon himself, Morris and Burne-Jones. These three shared in common a vague aspiration to regenerate the world by the cultivation of beauty. . . . (pp. 151-65)

[Dixon] has been neglected by readers of poetry, and ill-served by anthologists. His principal work, *Mano,* a long narrative poem in *terza rima* on a mediæval subject, is, it must be admitted, not very readable. Much of his other work is unadventurously descriptive, or too closely imitative of the manner of Keats, but the best of his religious verse has quite remarkable qualities, which remind us of Coleridge or Blake. His poem, "The Wizard's Funeral", will serve to illustrate how he endues a romantic theme with a more than usual consciousness of the presence of Good and Evil:

For me, for me, two horses wait,
Two horses stand before my gate:
Their vast black plumes on high are cast,
Their black manes swing in the midnight blast,
Red sparkles from their eyes fly fast.
But can they drag the hearse behind,
Whose black plumes mystify the wind?
What a thing for this heap of bones and hair!
Despair, despair!
Yet think of half the world's winged shapes
Which have come to thee wondering:
At thee the terrible idiot gapes,
At thee the running devil japes,
And angels stoopt to thee and sing
From the soft mignight that enwraps
Their limbs so gently, sadly fair;—
Thou seest the stars shine through their hair.
The blast again, ho, ho, the blast!
I go to a mansion that shall outlast;
And the stoled priest who stops before
Shall turn and welcome me at the door.

Dixon's style is not greatly influenced by that of the pre-Raphaelites—though his poem on Saint Mary Magdalen has something of the same detailed, pictorial quality as has theirs:

Kneeling before the altar step,
—Her white face stretched above her hands;
In one great line her body thin
Rose robed right upwards to her chin;
Her hair rebelled in golden bands,
   And filled her hands.

He is rather a scholarly, visionary mediævalist. . . . His work serves to remind us of the close connection between the pre-Raphaelite aestheticism and visionary and mystical tendencies within the Church which were contemporary with it.

The character of William Morris, the vigorous advocate of Socialism and the practical craftsman, presents a striking contrast to that of Rossetti. His personality was fuller, saner, more "rounded", than that of almost any other of his contemporaries. But his poetry represents only a fragment of that personality, and in some ways the least vital part of it. The withdrawal from the external world is more complete in William Morris, the poet, than in any other of the pre-Raphaelites, and his treatment of mediæval subject-matter is more consistent. It is often said that he had a "mediæval mind"; but he lacked the spiritual sense of the mediæval man, and with it, that very earthy realism which is its complement. It is significant that there is no humour in Morris—least of all the gross, animal comedy of the *Fabliaux;* no Wife of Bath, no Miller of Trumpington, no *buttocks;* not even the comic Skelton, that postures and capers through the poetry of the fifteenth century, as the curtain falls upon the mediæval scene. Morris's world is illuminated by an unreal light. He does not, indeed, sentimentalize the Middle Ages—he knew his mediæval literature too well for that; there is the real passion and brutality of primitive times in the "Haystack in the Floods". The delineation of the knights and squires of his stories is masculine—perhaps too masculine. Was there not, for all the bloody times in which they lived, a streak of adolescent femininity in the members of a class who delighted to hear stories and songs of Courtly Love, even if this strange code was always more a matter of theory than of practice? It is not his which gives to Troilus or to Arcite—they were little more than boys, after all—their pathos? And we remember too Richard II—and Edward II.

Morris's love for Chaucer was genuine, and he often set out deliberately to imitate his style. But in truth he was less at home in Chaucer's complex and sophisticated world, than in that of the Icelandic Sagas and the oldest poetry of the North— a world untouched by the new flowering of intellectualism which arose in twelfth-century Paris, or by the strange imaginative movement that spread from Provence at about the same time. The Iceland of the Sagas preserved an older and simpler social structure than the rest of Europe; it received its Christianity late, and much of the tradition, at least, of pre-Christian times lingered on.

The response of these men to life was, like that of Morris himself, simple, direct, temperate. Getting a living on the island was too strenuous a business to allow time for speculation, metaphysical or emotional; the Icelanders were not tormented by the problems which beset the men of the later Middle Ages throughout the rest of Europe. Even so apparently cheerful and unintrospective a mind as Chaucer's is obsessed by the philosophical problem of Free Will, and how it may be reconciled with God's foreknowledge. For the men of the Sagas, Fate is important; but it is something that can only be met with steadfast courage—like that half-pagan concept of *Wyrd* of the Anglo-Saxons.

Morris's translations and adaptations from the Sagas are much more vigorous than his earlier work; the languid style of the *Early Romances* gives place to the galloping metre of *Sigurd the Volsung*. But we miss the matter-of-factness, the plainness, the gruff and sometimes grim humour of the Saga-men. Above all, Morris's deliberate quaintness in his choice of language blurs the outlines of his originals.

In his treatment of stories from antique sources, Morris hardly either gives them a new significance for his own age, or penetrates to their living core. Let us remember that the legends of the mediæval story-tellers, like the myths of the Ancients, however remote from reality they may seem to us, had, as their background, the manners and social life of the times that produced them. In the Romances of chivalry the heroes often seem to us to be placed in fantastic situations, but these situations, and the problems of conduct arising out of them, reflected those which might occur in real life. To take a rather trite example: a princess in real life might not require rescuing from a dragon or giant, but an heiress or a widow might, under circumstances in all respects parallel, have need of a champion against a powerful neighbour who ravaged her lands, or who sought to coerce her into marriage in order to force her to join

her fiefs to his. Similarly, when a mediæval poet speaks of fighting, or armour, or fortification, he does not allow his eye to stray from what he is describing. He has too much professional interest in these matters. A modern poet treating an archaic subject, has either to give such things and the whole scene of his story a fresh significance for his readers, or by an effort of the imagination, pierce through to what was vital for the men of former times. Neither of these was Morris's mind strenuous enough to affect. His treatment of the old stories is fundamentally decorative; he tells them as he wove tapestry, or designed wallpaper. They are spun out at too great a length, and their beauty is merely a surface beauty of imagery with nothing lying beneath to satisfy the intellect and emotions. Archaicisms and affectations of language apart, he has probably one of the purest poetical styles, in its natural easy flow, of the century—in striking contrast to the vulgarity and heaviness of Rossetti; but it is too diffuse to leave any definite impression on the mind. It is the same with his characters; only the queen in the early *Defence of Guenevere* seems to have a vitality of her own. At moments in this poem does Morris achieve that concentrated passion, an image which continually haunts the memory.

It is significant that nearly all the members of the original Oxford "Brotherhood", among which the germ from which the whole pre-Raphaelite movement sprung was nursed, were young men intending to enter Holy Orders, and of the High Church party. Morris was no exception to this, but he seems to have changed his intention and wandered into the by-paths of agnosticism without any of the spiritual torments which usually accompanied loss of religious convictions among the Victorians. It would be true to say, perhaps, that his Christianity slipped from him, and was never missed. Whereas Rossetti is a visionary, without any clear basis of faith that might give reality to his visions, Morris has been described as a natural pagan. His was a primitive mind, not troubled by the complexities suggested by the existence of suffering and evil. He saw these things, indeed, embodied in the industrialism that lay about him, but he did not apprehend them imaginatively, as Blake apprehended the "dark, satanic mills", or even as Tennyson had expressed them in *Maud*. Following Ruskin, he simply envisaged the machine as banished from the ideal society of the future. His natural belief was on the capacity of men spontaneously to develop and to attain happiness, if only those things which check that development can be removed. Hence he advocated a form of Socialism, in its essential ideals nearer to Anarchism. The world he represents in his poetry is really less mediæval than pagan, and embodies his vision of a simple, spontaneous life.

The story-telling pilgrims of Chaucer are journeying to find the shrine of saint and martyr. The shrine is situated in a definite place in England, and the martyr suffered at a definite time. The narrators of Morris's longest poem sail away from a vague mediæval world, to seek an Earthly Paradise. They do not find it, but discover instead a fragment of pagan antiquity, timelessly surviving in the western ocean. The ideal society which Morris envisaged in *News from Nowhere* is also an earthly paradise—a mediæval dream-world, very unlike the actual Middle Ages. The only deeper emotion which disturbs the vision of Morris's poetry is the fear of death, a subdued undertone which sounds through much of his verse like the sound of the sea which echoes beyond the garden of bare apple-trees in the nymph's song to Hylas.

Swinburne is, rightly, classed with the pre-Raphaelite poets. He was a close friend of Morris and Rossetti, with whom he first came into contact in his Oxford days. His early poetry especially—notably "A Ballad of Life" and "The Mask of Queen Bathsabe"—has much the same languorous, decorative quality as theirs, the same attitude to mediæval subject-matter, and many of the same tricks of diction. But unlike them, he was never a visual poet. He was incapable of their minute concentration or particular natural images, and uses words in an almost purely aural manner. Moreover his poetry seems to stand in a wider context than theirs. At first sight it looks like a continuation of the Romantic tradition of Shelley and Byron, which brought a lyrical rhetoric and devotion to liberty, as well as purely private experience, within its scope. Swinburne's verse exhibits the appearance of a development from a preoccupation with merely erotic themes, in *Poems and Ballads*, to the public poetry of *Songs before Sunrise*. But this is largely an illusion. Throughout his writings, Swinburne remains virtually cut off from any save literary and verbal experience. His political poems, read to-day, betray, by their vague rhetoric, their unreality. He is an almost purely aesthetic poet.

None of the more important Victorian poets is more difficult to read, with any pleasure, to-day, than Swinburne. His contemporaries, and the generation which followed, even though they objected to the content of his poetry, or to its lack of definite meaning, were unanimous in according the very highest praise to the music of his verse. But the modern ear is attuned to more subtle rhythms. We have been taught by Hopkins and by the poets of our own day to expect in the music of poetry, however intricate, an underlying basis of natural speech-rhythms. We have also rediscovered the exquisite variety produced by the skilful arrangement of pause and syllable within the narrow framework of Pope's couplet—which the nineteenth century voted monotonous—and in Donne, not the harshness which had come to be traditionally associated with his name by critics, but a fine, natural music. For us it is precisely in the matter of musical delight that Swinburne fails to satisfy. His rhythms are mechanical, his heavily stressed anapæstic and dactylic metres vulgar, his use of pause often lacking in subtlety; though a certain facility in the melodic arrangement of vowel sounds must be granted him—it comes out best in his slower-moving pieces, such as "A Leave-Taking":

> Let us go hence, go hence; she will not see.
> Sing all once more together; surely she,
> She too, remembering days and words that were,
> Will turn a little towards us, sighing; but we,
> We are hence, we are gone, as though we had not been there,
> Nay, and though all men seeing had pity on me,
>   She would not see.

In order to appreciate Swinburne's style, it is best to read his poems in chronological order, as they came before the Victorian public, and with the poetic standards against which his verse instituted a reaction in mind the while. Here is Tennyson's "classical" style at its best—the much and deservedly praised "Ulysses":

> I cannot rest from travel; I will drink
> Life to the lees; all times I have enjoyed
> Greatly, have suffer'd greatly, both with those
> That lov'd me and alone; on shore, and when
> Thro' scudding drifts the rainy Hyades
> Vext the dim sea; I am become a name;
> For always roaming with a hungry heart . . .

But here are the opening lines of *Atlanta in Calydon:*

> Maiden and mistress of the months and stars
> Now folded in the flowerless fields of heaven,
> Goddess whom all gods love with threefold heart,

> Being treble in thy divided Deity,
> A light for dead men and dark hours, a foot
> Swift on the hills as morning, and a hand
> To all things fierce and fleet that roar and rage
> Mortal, with gentler shafts than snow or sleep;
> Hear now and help . . .

There is a swiftness and grace of movement, a clear melodic quality, about these lines, that must have seemed a fresh wind after the dusty academicism of much of Arnold and Tennyson's Hellenizing, the fusty antiquarianism of Browning—and, above all, the monstrous unpruned growths of Mrs. Browning and the now forgotten "Spasmodic" school. We read on, with this in mind, till we reach the famous choruses; and they—even the hackneyed "When the hounds of Spring . . ."—seem to leap from the page with a new lyrical vitality. We begin to wonder whether we had not too harshly condemned Swinburne. This hesitation, alas, does not survive a methodical critical scrutiny of the poetry. We soon detect the unnecessary diffuseness, the meaninglessness of phrase after phrase, the vagueness of the sensuous imagery, the cheap tricks of pointless antithesis, the tasteless affectation of pseudo-biblical diction. These choric rhythms too—they are not really *alive:* they repeat themselves indefinitely—there is no sense of climax, musically led up to and achieved. The long breathless sentences sprout subsidiary clauses and phrases, without providing logical cadence for the mind, or—read them aloud—pause for the voice. Moreover, in the course of the rapid flowering and long running to seed of Swinburne's genius, these initial faults become more marked. There are traces of genuinely imaginative, though immature passion in *Atalanta;* but it gives place first to the crude sensationalism of *Poems and Ballads* and then to the vague rhetoric of *Songs before Sunrise*. But his later work—for he continued to write industriously right up to the time of his death—consists largely of mere agglomerations of words, moving with a kind of spurious life of their own—it can hardly be called poetry at all.

Swinburne's psychological abnormality is quite clearly seen throughout his work, but especially in the first series of *Poems and Ballads*. He was an epileptic and a sado-masochist. It is also probable that he was sexually impotent. Such a sensibility will only respond to the crudest physical stimuli; the astonishing effect of his poetry upon an emotionally inhibited age is significant. He is continually striving in vain to render sensuous experience in imaginative terms; but the objects of sense are always slipping from him, and his imagery becomes vague and generalized. Hence Swinburne, setting forth a creed of pagan enjoyment and freedom from restraint, is himself a poet of frustration and impotence.

It is impossible to gloss over the fact that sadism, often of a crude type, forms the dominant inspiration of most of Swinburne's poetry, at any rate in his best period, and expresses itself, in a sublimated form, as Mario Praz has pointed out in his *The Romantic Agony,* in the political idealism of *Songs before Sunrise*. This aspect of his genius is pathological, but nevertheless one cannot separate his poetry from the diseased nature of his sensibility, if we are to consider the former seriously. The exploitation of "sin" and perversion which marks the first series of *Poems and Ballads* is too systematic to be dismissed, as most English critics have been content to do, as the result of a mere youthful desire to shock. Swinburne had become acquainted with the works of the Marquis de Sade in the library of his friend Lord Houghton, and their influence on him was profound, and moreover lasting. From this source he took over this conception of God as a hostile, deliberately cruel power, which permeates *Atalanta*; among the *Poems and Ballads*, ''Anactoria'' is full of echoes of de Sade's doctrine:

>   . . .but were I made as he
> Who hath made all things to break them one by one,
> If my feet trod upon the stars and sun
> And souls of men as his have always trod,
> God knows I might be crueller than God.
> For who shall change with prayers of thanksgivings
> The mystery of the cruelty of things?
> Or say what God above all gods and years,
> With offering and blood-sacrifice of tears,
> With lamentations from strange lands, from graves
> Where the snake pastures, from starved mouths of slaves,
> From prison, and from plunging prows of ships
> Through flamelike foam of the sea's closing lips—
> With thwartings of strange signs, and wind-blown hair
> Of comets, desolating the dim air,
> When darkness is made fast with seals and bars,
> And fierce reluctance of disastrous stars,
> Eclipse, and sound of shaken hills, and wings
> Darkening, and blind inexpiable things—
> With sorrow of labouring moons, and altering light
> And travail of the planets of the night,
> And weeping of the weary Pleiads seven,
> Feeds the mute melancholy lust of heaven?

The idea of the essentially sadistic nature of love dominates not only such poems as ''Dolores'', ''Faustine'', etc., but also the whole of the drama of *Chastelard*. In the first *Poems and Ballads* indeed, Swinburne introduces us into a world of sterile perversity, which, nevertheless, has a kind of lifeless reality of its own. Perhaps the best of the series is ''Hermaphroditus'', which consists in reality of a group of sonnets, to which form Swinburne has given back the essential lyrical quality which had been lost for it. Something more than mere verbalism is realized in this poem. The hermaphrodite, ambiguous and virginal, because unable to respond to the desire of either sex, yet apt to satisfy both, really does represent a *moment* in the history of European Romanticism, and links Swinburne to such Continental decadents as Lautréamont.

> Love stands upon thy left hand and thy right,
>   Yet by no sunset and by no moonrise
>   Shall make thee man and ease a woman's sighs,
> Or make thee woman for a man's delight.
> To what strange end hath some strange god made fair
>   The double blossom of two different flowers?
> Hid love in all the folds of all thy hair,
>   Fed thee on summers, watered thee with showers
> Given all the gold that all the seasons wear
>   To thee that art a thing of barren hours?

If the ''Hermaphroditus'' sonnets reveal the core of Swinburne's poetry—the prenatal, undifferentiated, embryonic form to which his maladjustment leads him to desire a return—''The Triumph of Time'', from another point of view, provides the key to his peculiar experience. It has often been singled out as showing more genuine personal feeling than his other poems. It celebrates, as is well known, his feelings when rejected by Jane Simon, to whom he had proposed marriage. It is too long, and there is a good deal too much self-pity in it. But here, at least, the Swinburnian deadness and monotony of rhythm— that wave-like, rocking rhythm—is appropriate. This unhappy love affair represented for Swinburne his defeat. Henceforward for him there was no possibility of a normal adjustment to life, and he turns from the girl who has failed him and left him unprotected against the sadistic passions within him, to the sea, which is at once a mother and womb symbol, and the image

of the cold, grey, harsh, and salty sterility which was to be henceforward his.

> I will go back to the great sweet mother,
>   Mother and lover of men, the sea,
> I will go down to her, I and none other,
>   Close with her, kiss her, and mix her with me;
> Cling to her, strive with her, hold her fast:
> O fair white mother, in days long past
> Born without sister, born without brother,
>   Set free my soul as thy soul is free.

To appreciate Swinburne to-day we must not only bear his abnormal nature in mind, but also read him less in relation to his English forerunners, Shelley and the pre-Raphaelites, and as an outlier of the Continental Romantic-Decadent Movement. We remember his mother, Lady Swinburne, and her enthusiasm for French and Italian poetry, and Swinburne's own interest in European politics. (He is really our first poet since Byron who showed himself genuinely aware of Europe.) Above all we must bear in mind the influence on him not only of Gautier and Baudelaire but also of Hugo (for whom Yeats also, in spite of his symbolist doctrines, retained a lifelong admiration, and whose vatic conception of the poet's function the Irish poet largely adopted for himself).

William Holman Hunt's The Light of the World, *which employed him from 1853 to 1856. City Art Gallery, Manchester.*

It is, however, especially when we compare him with Baudelaire that the inadequacy of Swinburne as a poet becomes apparent. Swinburne celebrated Baudelaire in "Ave atque Vale" as a "brother", but the difference between them is in reality profound. The psychology of both gives ample evidence of a sado-masochistic tendency, and both show direct acquaintance with the ideas of the Marquis de Sade. The deep-rooted connection between love and the infliction, or receiving of pain which formed the basis of de Sade's crude speculations, is a fact of which the Christian religion had preserved the intuition. The psychology of Baudelaire and Swinburne was abnormal, but their abnormality only brought into prominence what is a normal condition of human nature. But whereas Baudelaire's genius leads him to a profound poetical investigation of the nature of evil, Swinburne's abnormality merely drives him into a sterile verbalism and sensationalism. (pp. 166-78)

> *John Heath-Stubbs, "Pre-Raphaelitism and the Aesthetic Withdrawal," in his* The Darkling Plain: A Study of the Later Fortunes of Romanticism in English Poetry from George Darley to W. B. Yeats, *Eyre & Spottiswoode, 1950, pp. 148-78.*

CAROL T. CHRIST

[Christ's The Finer Optic, *excerpted below, focuses on the significance of detail and particularity in Victorian poetry. Christ here compares the works of Alfred, Lord Tennyson with those of the Pre-Raphaelites, examining their common use of acute sensory detail.*]

Much of the change in sensibility that distinguishes the middle from the early Victorian period can be seen in the relationship of the Pre-Raphaelites to Tennyson. They were fascinated by Tennyson's early poetry. Its sensuousness, its medievalism, its morbidity powerfully stimulated their imaginations: Rossetti and Millais both painted Marianas, the Pre-Raphaelites all contributed to Moxon's illustrated Tennyson, and Holman Hunt did a large oil of the Lady of Shalott. But in all their Tennysonian works, they made subtle changes in the values attached to Tennyson's symbols. They upset the delicate balance of fascination and withdrawal that is Tennyson's response to absorption in personal or aesthetic emotion and sought out this absorption wholeheartedly. Tennyson went to the land of the Lotos but returned; the Pre-Raphaelites forgot all thoughts of home and stayed.

Perhaps with the different value the Pre-Raphaelites attached to absorption in intense emotion, my terms should change. What Tennyson saw as morbidity, the Pre-Raphaelites were to seek out as a kind of sensationalism. But I retain the term morbidity to suggest the connection between them and Tennyson. Even if they did not see their art as morbid, their Victorian critics certainly did, and Tennyson's preoccupation with morbidity shows the new kind of interest in perception the Pre-Raphaelites were to further develop.

Just as in their painting the Pre-Raphaelites were drawn to Tennysonian subjects, so in his poetry Rossetti often treats situations similar to Tennyson's. Like Tennyson, he was fascinated with states of intense emotion, and like him again, he often uses an abnormal sensitivity to detail as a means of portraying such states. "The Bride's Prelude," for example, one of Rossetti's earliest poems, centers upon a very Tennysonian situation. Aloÿse, a deserted maiden obsessed with her betrayal and guilt, could well become an archetypal Tennysonian woman who lives imprisoned in some emotional ob-

session, like Mariana or Oenone. Yet Rossetti handles the situation very differently. He presents not only Aloÿse's point of view but also that of her younger sister Amelotte, so that the poem shows us not a timeless, changeless, totally exclusive emotional imprisonment, but a crisis point where we see both Aloÿse's reluctant recital of her past and Amelotte's sense of dread in hearing her sister's story.

Rossetti uses an intense sensitivity to detail to convey Amelotte's state of mind in listening to her sister.

> Although the lattice had dropped loose,
>   There was no wind; the heat
> Being so at rest that Amelotte
> Heard far beneath the plunge and float
> Of a hound swimming in the moat.
>
> Some minutes since, two rooks had toiled
>   Home to the nests that crowned
> Ancestral ash-trees. Through the glare
> Beating again, they seemed to tear
> With that thick caw the woof o' the air.
>
> But else, 'twas at the dead of noon
>   Absolute silence; all,
> From the raised bridge and guarded sconce
> To green-clad places of pleasaùnce
> Where the long lake was white with swans.
>
> Amelotte spoke not any word
>   Nor moved she once; but felt
> Between her hands in narrow space
> Hew own hot breath upon her face,
> And kept in silence the same place.

Insignificant details that usually pass unnoticed—the splash of the hound plunging into the moat, the cry of the rooks flying through the air, her own breath against her face—strike Amelotte's sense with a new violence. Her emotional state resembles the one Aloÿse describes when she first becomes sick.

> Motion, like feeling, grew intense;
> Sight was a haunting evidence
> And sound a pang that snatched the sense.

The intensity with which sense impressions strike Amelotte reflects the tension of her mind in trying to assimilate the experience she is having. Her effort to understand what her sister is saying, her dread of it, the disintegration of her former consciousness of things all make her senses extraordinarily receptive to any stimulus. The sharpness of the impressions of slight details conveys the terrible tension of her mind to the reader.

Rossetti, like Tennyson, thus turns sensitivity to natural detail to expressionistic uses. He portrays the way emotion can change our sense of the landscape, can make us perceive it in its particularity or its vagueness, or can cast strange meanings over the details of everyday life. Michael Rossetti once said his brother cared little for descriptive poetry because it exhibits and extols objects instead of turning them into "the medium of exchange between the material world and the soul." In other words, Rossetti is interested not in nature but in the way our vision of the landscape reflects our subjectivity.

Despite his concentration on the way psychology shapes our sense of the external world, the details in Rossetti's poetry remain remarkably superfluous. What strikes us about the details of which Amelotte is so acutely conscious in the passage quoted above is their lack of resonance or symbolic depth. Although there is a sense of violation in the cry of the rook Amelotte hears, much like the violation of her sense of innocence, the cry never really attains the depth of a symbol. The details of the passage have an irrelevance, almost a randomness, about them which keeps them from being absorbed into Amelotte's consciousness. This differs considerably from Tennyson's use of detail. In "Mariana," for example, emotion so fills the details of the landscape that we lose a firm sense of their phenomenal existence. The details in Rossetti's poems, on the other hand, have a much firmer location in time and space. The following stanzas, for example, describe the room in which the two sisters are sitting immediately before Aloÿse begins her story.

> She paused then, weary, with dry lips
>   Apart. From the outside
> By fits there boomed a dull report
> From where i' the hanging tennis-court
> The bridegroom's retinue made sport.
>
> The room lay still in dusty glare,
>   Having no sound through it
> Except the chirp of a caged bird
> That came and ceased: and if she stirred,
> Amelotte's raiment could be heard.

The unnatural clarity of slight sounds—the tennis game, the chirp of the bird, the rustling of Amelotte's dress—conveys the silence and tension in the room. The separate mention of each item extends our sense of the duration of the moment before Aloÿse speaks just as the tension of the moment extends it for the two girls. Occasionally an image seems to tremble on the brink of symbolic signification. The caged bird, for example, could suggest Aloÿse's situation. But if images portend meaning, that meaning is rarely developed. This failure to develop images into a symbolic pattern gives the poem a shallowness of surface in which objects have a purely phenomenal existence. Images function not to explore the meaning of the sisters' experience but to extend the sense of time and psychological tension before Aloÿse begins her story.

In his essay on Rossetti, Pater praises Rossetti for trying to create in his poetry "an exact equivalent to those data within." His praise defines Rossetti's artistic ideal. In much of his early poetry, Rossetti strives to attain a minute realism of perception and sensation. He tries to capture the way stimuli first hit the mind, before going through any process of assimilation toward meaning. The shallowness of surface I have described in "The Bride's Prelude" keeps the focus of the poem on what Pater calls "pure perception." The purely phenomenal existence of objects ensures a constant awareness of each moment's location in time and space. The mention of sounds creates an almost physical feeling of time passing from moment to moment. Rossetti uses the sounds to convey not only the progression of time, however, but the sisters' experience of it. The slightness of sense impressions and the large amount of space between them slow the movement of the poem in a way that portrays the sisters' intense consciousness of the present and their dread of the future. Thus, through his use of detail Rossetti creates a tension between the elongation of time the sisters feel and its constant movement forward toward Aloÿse's revelation, which conveys the moment-to-moment process and sensation of psychological change with a radical realism.

"My Sister's Sleep," a poem written at about the same time, also uses acute sensitivity to detail to portray a state of intense emotion. A young man and his mother have been sitting up a number of nights to watch over a sick sister. Rossetti describes the room as it looks to the boy.

> Through the small room, with subtle sound
> Of flame, by vents the fireshine drove
> And reddened. In its dim alcove
> The mirror shed a clearness round.

> I had been sitting up some nights,
>   And my tired mind felt weak and blank;
>   Like a sharp strengthening wine it drank
> The stillness and the broken lights.
>
> Twelve struck. That sound, by dwindling years
>   Heard in each hour, crept off; and then
>   The ruffled silence spread again,
> Like water that a pebble stirs.
>
> Our mother rose from where she sat:
>   Her needles, as she laid them down,
>   Met lightly, and her silken gown
> Settled: no other noise than that.
>
> 'Glory unto the Newly Born!'
>   So, as said angels, she did say;
>   Because we were in Christmas Day,
> Though it would still be long till morn.
>
> Just then in the room over us
>   There was a pushing back of chairs,
>   As some who had sat unawares
> So, late, now heard the hour, and rose.

Here the details have a clearness and a bareness that deny any meaning but their sensation. They totally resist symbolic interpretation. Yet Rossetti places these details in the religious context of the coming of Christmas morning and the sister's death. The pushing back of chairs in the room overhead, for example, is merely an incidental sound from another room that might have disturbed the sister's sleep, but it coincides exactly with the coming of Christmas morning and the discovery of her death. Most readers of the poem have seen this combination as an example of the flabbiness of Rossetti's poetic technique, but one critic, Jerome McGann, argues that by making the sensory details resist explication in terms of the religious experience, yet occupy at least as emphatic a place, Rossetti creates a deliberate tension between the religious and sensory experiences of the poem that forces us to see the importance of the pure and nonsymbolic detail [*Victorian Poetry* 7 (1969):44]. The details become almost antisymbols in the aggressiveness with which they resist interpretation.

In his definition of the pathetic fallacy in *Modern Painters,* Ruskin asserts that the highest order of poet does not let human emotion color the facts of the external world, but keeps subject and object distinct, making sure, even in the midst of powerful emotion, "to keep his eyes fixed firmly on the *pure fact.*" In maintaining a separation between human emotion and the objects of the landscape, Rossetti creates a poetic technique that suggests Ruskin's ideal. The change in poetry and in philosophy that Rossett's technique and Ruskin's criticism imply is a significant one. To see the attribution of emotion to the environment as a fallacy, one must have discarded the Romantic sense of the correspondence between the realm of human experience and the realm of nature. Because the Victorians no longer feel a correspondent breeze within, they see correspondence between man and nature as false. In her book *The Pathetic Fallacy in the Nineteenth Century* Josephine Miles analyzes poetic vocabularies through the century to demonstrate a change in poetry from a focus on objects as associates of human emotions to a focus on the perceived qualities of objects. This change in focus obviously reflects a change in belief, a gradual separation between the order of man and the order of nature. The focus upon sensed qualities reaches its height in Pater's impressionism. . . . [The] gradual separation of subject and object and the growth toward impressionism is one of the ways in which Victorian poetry anticipates modern literature. Imagist poetry, for example, and its ideal of precisely visualizing concrete impressions, or, to choose a more recent example, the nouveau roman, whose aim Robbe-Grillet describes as making objects refuse signification and establish themselves only by their phenomenal presence, both imply a belief, which Rossetti's poetry anticipates, that the only meaning objects offer is the mere fact of their sensation.

I do not mean to imply that Rossetti sees the sole end of poetry as the representation of mere sensation. Despite its use of detail, ''My Sister's Sleep'' does not deny the meaning of the religious experience it portrays but forces upon us a new perspective toward it. We see it as it is experienced together with all the concrete sensuous impressions, irrelevant in a traditional sense, that accompany it. In his essay on the metaphysical poets, T. S. Eliot asserts that the mark of a poet's mind is the ability to amalgamate disparate experiences which for the ordinary man have nothing to do with each other. The poet reads Spinoza, falls in love, hears the noise of a typewriter, and smells the cooking in the next room, and unites these experiences to form new wholes. Eliot feels that poets since the seventeenth century have lost this ability, but as Rosamond Tuve argues [in her *Elizabethan and Metaphysical Imagery*], the ideal he describes, psychological realism as a sufficient end of poetry, is essentially a modern, not a Renaissance ideal. In creating a poetry whose unity is based on perception rather than idea, Rossetti anticipates this development in modern poetry. He attempts to show experience as it presents itself to consciousness, in all its apparent disunity, and to form a new kind of poetic unity based on perception.

We can thus see from Rossetti's poetry that although he at first seems to have preoccupations similar to Tennyson's he builds from them in very different ways. Both poets were fascinated with morbid and obsessive states of emotion, one of whose symptoms was an extreme and distorted sensitivity to detail. Tennyson sees such states as having a timeless, changeless, totally self-enclosing quality, which shows the threat of self-imprisonment they posed for him. Rossetti explores the relation between perception and morbid emotion in a much more neutral way. He emphasizes the medium of time in which the processes of perception and feeling take place. The crucial role time plays in his poetry shows how much greater the possibilities of movement and change are in his poetic world, possibilities that remove the threatening element Tennyson attaches to states of morbid emotion. The protagonists of both poets reflect the change between the two. Tennyson's morbid characters—Mariana, the hero of *Maud,* Oenone—are permanently alienated; they live ''without hope of change.'' Rossetti's characters— Amelotte, the speaker of ''My Sister's Sleep''—are more often possessed by a temporary state of strong emotion. His poems, much like ''Mariana,'' contain a strong sense of the prolongation of time; nevertheless, his characters are experiencing some crisis point of change. While morbid emotion and the consciousness of particularity it entails shows a singularity of perception, they involve not the threat of permanent imprisonment but a new awareness that can be freely explored.

Rossetti's unqualified acceptance of absorption in strong emotion signifies a great change in the role of the artist in society. Rossetti himself provides an allegory for this change in his prose tale, ''Hand and Soul.'' The tale describes the career of Chiaro, a medieval Italian artist. One day while looking out his window, Chiaro sees a bloody battle taking place in front of his great fresco *Peace.* Seeing the painting streaked with blood at the end of the battle, Chiaro despairs of his attempt to teach his generation by painting myths of faith. He then has

a vision of a beautiful woman, who tells him to paint only his soul. Tennyson resembles the earlier Chiaro; he feels a vocation to be a social poet. One of the prevailing themes of Tennyson's poetry is the danger of isolation in private emotion and the virtue of social commitment. Rossetti, on the other hand, sees only Chiaro's vision of the woman telling him to paint his own soul. He is an intensely private poet, oblivious of any social role. In fact his strongest values, intense emotion and pure perception, are those later to become the foundation of the aesthetic movement. Tennyson's characters are socially alienated; Rossetti himself is. His alienation results in a more radically subjective poetic voice, in which he explores the processes of emotion and perception for their own sakes.

Nowhere does Rossetti assert the value of pure perception more clearly than in ''The Woodspurge.'' In this lyric, the poet, distressed by some unnamed grief, walks out at random, following the wind. When the wind falls still, he sits down, drops his head between his knees, and looks at the ground.

> My eyes, wide open, had the run
> Of some ten weeds to fix upon;
> Among those few, out of the sun,
> The woodspurge flowered, three cups in one.
>
> From perfect grief there need not be
> Wisdom or even memory:
> One thing then learnt remains to me,—
> The woodspurge has a cup of three.

The only thing the poet has and gives the reader is the simple sight of the woodspurge. Rossetti does not assert any symbolic or intellectual content to his vision. If the fact that the woodspurge has ''three cups in one'' seems to suggest the trinity, the poem is conspicuous in its failure to develop that implication—almost as if Rossetti is suggesting the religious allusion only to deny it, to transform it into a mere visible fact. Yet the memory of that fact is indelible, and simply in itself offers the poet a possibility of renewal. The way the poem is written reflects the value placed on perception. It offers no prior history or setting, no explanation of the poet's grief, but merely records his actions and sensations in the simplest possible terms.

''The Woodspurge'' reflects the distance Rossetti has traveled from the Romantics. Blake wanted to find ''Heaven in a Wild Flower,'' and Wordsworth found proof of Peter Bell's moral insensitivity in the fact that ''A primrose by a river's brim / A yellow primrose was to him / And it was nothing more.'' Although the Romantics started with the particular, they wanted to transcend it by discovering in it the symbol of a general truth. Even Tennyson has this desire, although he has more difficulty in understanding the meanings his symbols carry. He is sure his flower in the crannied wall would provide the clue to ''what God and man is'' if he could only discover it. Rossetti, however, insists on the fact that a woodspurge is a three-cupped woodspurge, and it is nothing more. Rossetti again recalls Ruskin's poetic ideal. Using the passage from *Peter Bell* I quoted, Ruskin distinguishes three ranks of men:

> the man who perceives rightly because he does not feel, and to whom the primrose is very accurately the primrose, because he does not love it. Then, secondly, the man who perceives wrongly, because he feels, and to whom the primrose is anything else than a primrose: a star, or a sun, or a fairy's shield, or a forsaken maiden. And then, lastly, there is the man who perceives rightly in spite of his feelings, and to whom the primrose is for ever nothing else than itself—a little flower apprehended in the very plain and leafy fact of it, whatever and how many

soever the associations and passions may be that crowd around it.

Ruskin feels that the best poets belong to this third class of men, and certainly ''The Woodspurge'' demonstrates just such a separation between the very plain and leafy fact of a plant and the human emotion associated with it.

But despite the fact that Rossetti's poetry and Ruskin's criticism reflect a similar sense of the separation between human emotion and natural objects, Rossetti and Ruskin pursue this separation for different ends. Ruskin urges poets to avoid the pathetic fallacy, so as to attain both truth to nature and an emotional containment that he feels necessary for moral strength. The separation between natural facts and human emotions in Rossetti's poetry, on the other hand, results from his attempt to portray the act of perception in its most immediate and elementary form. In her essay ''Against Interpretation,'' Susan Sontag asserts that criticism should not interpret the work of art to show what it means but describe it in all its sensuous immediacy to show how it is. Rossetti is against interpretation of natural objects for a similar reason. He does not attempt to convert them into emblems of general truths. Rather, he tries to portray the sensuous immediacy of a particular moment of perception.

Rossetti's effort to attain a sensuous immediacy in art often brought him into a position subversive to Victorian art and morality. Nowhere is this more evident than in ''The Blessed Damozel.'' The subject of the poem is a conventional one: the mutual longing for reunion of an earthly lover and a dead and emparadised lady. The extraordinary element of the poem that stirred controversy both then and now is the image of the blessed damozel. Pater remarked of the poem that one of its peculiarities ''was a definiteness of sensible imagery, which seemed grotesque to some, and was strange, above all, in a theme so profoundly visionary.'' Indeed, the poem presents the blessed damozel with a startling combination of religious iconography and distinct sensuous detail.

> The blessed damozel leaned out
>   From the gold bar of Heaven;
> Her eyes were deeper than the depth
>   Of waters stilled at even;
> She had three lilies in her hand,
>   And the stars in her hair were seven.
>
> Her robe, ungirt from clasp to hem,
>   No wrought flowers did adorn,
> But a white rose of Mary's gift
>   For service meetly worn;
> Her hair that lay along her back
>   Was yellow like ripe corn.
>
>   . . . . .
>
> And still she bowed herself and stooped
>   Out of the circling charm;
> Until her bosom must have made
>   The bar she leaned on warm,
> And the lilies lay as if asleep
>   Along her bended arm.

The sensuous details of these stanzas have a realistic particularity that makes them jump out of the religious iconographical context. By using sensuous imagery in such a visionary theme, Rossetti cannot help but affect how we see the traditional religious symbols. The blessed damozel's breast making the gold bar of heaven warm turns the gold bar of heaven, a clichéd symbol like ''pearly gates'' or ''golden streets,'' into a concrete physical object. The image of her hair lying along her back

like ripe corn gives a physical presence to her beauty that causes us to sense the religious symbols that adorn her—the three lilies, the seven stars, the white rose—as physical objects. She seems to be a Pre-Raphaelite ''stunner'' artfully posed in an angel's costume. Rossetti empties the symbols of their traditional religious meaning by making them so startlingly physical.

By making religious emblems an adornment and aspect of the damozel's physicality, Rossetti creates in the image itself a fusion of the holy and the sensuous. The traditional religious connotations of the symbols give the blessed damozel a sacred value, but this value is redefined in sensuous terms. She thus becomes an image of the sacredness of the human union of spiritual and physical love. Her image anticipates the lyric she sings later in the poem in which she imagines how heaven, when her lover arrives, will become merely the setting in which the two will realize their earthly love. Heaven centers upon them, not they upon God, and all its possibilities are turned to use in the fuller realization of their love. The poem redefines the holy, and it is through his manipulation of detail that Rossetti creates a symbol for his redefinition in the blessed damozel.

By interpreting the poem in this way, however, I am in a sense undermining its use of detail. The poem aggressively insists that an image is a particular sensuous presence not reducible to its signification. By using details like the damozel's yellow hair with an intensity and clarity far greater than that of anything else in the picture, Rossetti makes them stand out with a hypnotic sensuous presence not integrated with the whole. Susan Sontag declares in her essay that ''in place of a hermeneutics we need an erotics of art.'' ''The Blessed Damozel'' says much the same thing. It implies that the only way to imagine an object is as a particular physical presence. The relation between the soul and the material world is sensation, and because sensation must be of particulars, this view of the relation necessarily implies a nominalistic view of the world. It thus rejects generality for particularity as our mode of knowledge.

Rossetti's nominalism undermined many Victorian aesthetic assumptions. The principal Victorian critics—Carlyle, Arnold, Ruskin—prized art's ability to show us truth and to present great ideas. The emphasis of their poetic theories was almost entirely on art as statement. They were preoccupied with the content, the meaning, the practical ends of poetry. As a result of their moral aesthetic, directed so strongly toward content, they intensely distrusted the sensuous medium of art. Any affirmation of its independent value implied a trust in sense, which they saw as undermining both morality and reason. Rossetti's insistence upon its value thus seemed to endanger both moral principle and intellectual knowledge. Although Robert Buchanan's infamous essay, ''The Fleshly School of Poetry,'' certainly contains a warped view of Rossetti's poetry, it shows very clearly the ways Rossetti's aesthetic threatened these Victorian values. ''To aver that poetic expression is greater than poetic thought'' means ''by inference that the body is greater than the soul, and sound superior to sense.'' The Victorians wanted to look at the palace of art only from the outside. When Rossetti tried to live in it, they condemned him for his fleshliness. Because of its assertion of the sensuous value of the image, ''The Blessed Damozel'' was both morally and aesthetically subversive, and it was through the particular that Rossetti accomplished his subversion.

In ''The Card Dealer,'' Rossetti makes the subversiveness of his use of the image implicit by associating it with a seductive and sinister woman. The poem describes a painting by Theodore von Holst of a beautiful woman, richly dressed, who is sitting at a lamp-lit table dealing cards, with a peculiar fixedness of expression. The symbolic significance of the poem is difficult to determine. Rossetti once said the woman represented intellectual enjoyment, but the poem does not support this interpretation. The speaker comes to see her as something closer to fate or life, yet even this interpretation is strangely detached from the sheer fascination the image holds for him. The details of his description of the painting are much more convincing than any of his speculations upon its meaning. Here, for example, is an image of the lights reflected onto the cards from the woman's rings:

> Her fingers let them softly through,
>   Smooth polished silent things;
> And each one as it falls reflects
>   In swift light-shadowings,
> Blood-red and purple, green and blue,
>   The great eyes of her rings.

The unnatural clarity of this slight detail conveys an almost hypnotic fascination with the image itself that transcends any of his later attempts to affix a meaning to it. The way the woman draws the viewer into her game gives the image a seductively sinister quality, which springs not from whatever meaning she has but from the sensuous power of the image. Many of Rossetti's poems associate a beautiful and evil woman with an art object holding magic powers. Rose Mary and her beryl stone, Sister Helen and her wax doll, Helen of Troy and the cup in the shape of her breast—all suggest Rossetti's vision of art as a necessarily erotic experience. Just as in Rossetti's view of love souls can know souls only through bodies, so in art the sensation of the image is an essential and self-sufficient part of our understanding of it.

Rossetti's insistence upon the value of sensation and his attempt to make art mirror its processes had little to do with any interest in the external world. Nature frankly bored him. "D. G. Rossetti," wrote his sister Christina, "shuns the vulgar optic." What did interest him were just those introspective morbidities Tennyson warned upstanding young men to cast aside. Rossetti was not an upstanding young man in Victorian eyes, and he was certainly the lesser poet, but the shift of value is nonetheless significant. Rossetti glorifies intensity of sensation; he wants to "smart and agonize at ev'ry pore," to "die of a rose in aromatic pain." His preoccupation with extreme emotion and minute movements of perception may still strike us as morbid, but he luxuriates in his own morbidity.

In addition to using the particular in poetry, Rossetti helped begin a movement toward particularity in painting. Hunt, Millais, and Rossetti first banded together to form the Pre-Raphaelite Brotherhood in revolt against the academic art of their day, which was largely based on the teachings of Sir Joshua Reynolds. One of the basic principles of "Sir Sloshua," as they called him, was that art should avoid particularities and details of every kind in order to create ideal forms more perfect than any actuality. The Pre-Raphaelites vigorously rejected his idea that art should represent generalizations and insisted that the artist should go directly to nature, "rejecting nothing, selecting nothing, and scorning nothing." The Pre-Raphaelites found support for their doctrine of truth to nature in Ruskin, who was just as vehement as they were in his rejection of Reynolds' artistic neo-Platonism. The highest art, according to Ruskin, is that which contains the most truth to nature, and truth to nature demands not getting above particular forms, but showing the specific character of every kind of rock, every

class of earth, every form of cloud, every species of herb and flower.

The Pre-Raphaelites pursued their doctrine of truth to nature by a fanatic insistence upon absolute accuracy in the slightest detail. Millais looked all over London for a carpenter to serve as the model for the figure of Joseph in *Christ in the House of His Parents,* in order to get the development of the muscles just right. Holman Hunt spent weeks on the shore of the Dead Sea, a rifle over his knees as protection against bandits and wild animals, to paint the landscape for *The Scapegoat* with absolute accuracy. To paint *The Eve of St. Agnes* Millais posed his wife in the bedroom of James I at Knole on a freezing winter night, and when he found out the moonlight was not strong enough to shine through the stained glass and throw warm gules on Madeleine's fair breast, he rushed back to London to get a bullseye lantern, indignantly insisting Keats was wrong. The Pre-Raphaelites worshipped the vulgar optic to the point of self-parody.

Through a combination of laziness, lack of skill, and the discovery of his personal artistic bent, Rossetti gradually drifted away from the original principles and members of the brotherhood. In later life, he took pains to dissociate his aesthetic from theirs, insisting that his works did not bear any resemblance to Hunt's and that the brotherhood was merely the result of "the visionary vanities of half-a-dozen boys." The extreme stylization, the absorption of detail into decorative motif, and the concentration on medieval and mythical subjects of Rossetti's later work separate it from that of the naturalistic Pre-Raphaelites—Hunt, the early Millais, Ford Madox Brown, Arthur Hughes, and their imitators. Even in Rossetti's earliest paintings, such as *The Annunciation* or *The Girlhood of Mary Virgin,* the pale color, the idealized figures, and the lack of detail show how little he was interested in courting Hunt's and Millais's nature. Typically, he painted the lily in *The Annunciation* from an artificial flower. He never completed the one picture, *Found,* in which by painting a wall brick by brick he made a desultory attempt to justify his Pre-Raphaelite credentials. Because Rossetti's paintings do not show the sensitivity to detail that those of the other artists do, I will deal only with their paintings here.

Hunt bitterly resented what he saw as Rossetti's apostasy. Not only, according to Hunt, did Rossetti betray the original principles of the moment, but by his greater notoriety, he clouded the public's conception of true Pre-Raphaelitism. The contradictions in their articulated theories, however, make the impulses behind the art of Rossetti and the naturalistic Pre-Raphaelites seem much more distant than they actually are. Despite the fanatic adherence of the Pre-Raphaelites to the doctrine of truth to nature, their pictures most often strike us with their lack of realism. Pound once described a Pre-Raphaelite painter who in preparation for painting a twilight scene rowed across the river in daytime to see the shape of the leaves on the further bank, which he then drew in full detail. Pound's satire points to the unnaturalness of painting each object, no matter how near or far, how central or insignificant, with the same microscopic clarity. Not only is this uniform clarity of detail across the total field of vision untrue to the way we see, but it constantly distracts our attention from the main subjects of the pictures. When we look at a painting such as Hunt's *The Awakened Conscience,* whose subject is the sudden moral awakening of a kept woman to the reality of her position, our interest is continually diverted from the picture of the woman and her lover to the intricate portrayal of the furniture of the room (which a friend of Hunt's assures us was painted from an appropriate model). We see the rosewood of the piano, the hem of her dress, the glove on the floor, even the wallpaper in the farthest corner of the picture with equal distinctness. Or when we see Millais's *Ophelia,* we see each twig, leaf, and flower on the bank with a clarity so distinct that the brilliance of the picture's botanical scrupulousness threatens to over-whelm Ophelia herself. The effect of his unnatural clarity is to create the impression of a morbid intensity of vision. Robin Ironside [in his *Pre-Raphaelite Painters*] describes this effect.

> It was, at first, as if the Brotherhood looked at the world without eyelids; for them, a livelier emerald twinkled in the grass, a purer sapphire melted into the sea. On the illuminated page that nature seemed to thrust before their dilated pupils, every floating, prismatic ray, each drifting filament of vegetation, was rendered, in all its complexity, with heraldic brilliance and distinctness; the floor of the forest was carpeted not merely with the general variegation of light and shadow, but was seen to be plumed with ferns receiving each in a particular fashion the shafts of light that fell upon them; there were not simply birds in the branches above, but the mellow ouzel was perceived fluting in the elm. . . . The Pre-Raphaelites transcribed nature analytically, "selecting nothing and rejecting nothing," and the labour that went into the copying of each particle was sharpened by a kind of frenzy which goaded them into a bur-nishing and polishing of their handiwork to a point beyond representation, at which it shone with a fe-verish clarity.

The unnaturalness of vision created by the clarity of detail in their paintings is increased by their choice of subjects. Al-though they take truth to nature as their battle cry, they most often choose for their subjects not natural objects but aesthetic images. Ophelia, the scapegoat, Claudio and Isabella, the Lady of Shalott, Christ in the house of his parents, Lorenzo and Isabella, the hireling shepherd, Ferdinand and Ariel—all are literary images or religious symbols. The viewer feels a tension between the symbolic nature of the subject, which produces certain expectations of representation, and the naturalism of its portrayal. Even when the Pre-Raphaelites choose scenes from modern life for their paintings, they pose characters in such stylized attitudes of extreme emotion, like the woman in *The Awakened Conscience,* that the ultimate effect is quite unrealistic.

Struck by such obvious contradictions in their work, most crit-ics have stressed the inconsistency of the Pre-Raphaelite aes-thetic. Realistic techniques, carried to such an extreme that they cease to create a realistic effect, combined with unrealistic subjects have made most critics conclude that the poor men were dreadfully confused, perhaps even stupid, and that their art suffers from a fatal lack of focus. Part of the problem is the inability of critics to understand Pre-Raphaelitism in the Pre-Raphaelites' own terms. Despite all their talk about aes-thetics, the Pre-Raphaelites were not very good theorists. Most of the time what they were doing was different from what they said they were doing. The important task for critics is not to show the inconsistency of their aesthetic but to concentrate on why the Pre-Raphaelites never seemed to feel any inconsistency in their works, and to discover what kind of art this strange combination of seemingly contradictory impulses pro-duces. . . . [As Herbert Sussman, writing in *Victorian Studies* 12 (1968)] said, "The important question is, by what means did the Pre-Raphaelites, not only with equanimity but with a sense of mission, combine attention to detail with religious

William Morris's 1858 painting Queen Guinevere, *modeled by his wife, Jane Burden Morris. Tate Gallery, London.*

symbolism, fidelity to inner experience with social realism, an historical approach to the Bible with Evangelical Faith."

Of course part of the answer lies in certain scientific assump-tions about reality some artists acquired during the nineteenth century. In his book on Victorian poetic theory, Alba Warren demonstrates that most Victorians held the conviction that truth was the end of art and that the amount of truth in a work of art measured its quality. Ruskin, of course, is the critic most zealous in his belief that great art is that art which contains the largest amount of truth. As part of his demand for truth he insisted on scientific accuracy in the representation of detail. His long chapters in *Modern Painters* on the truth of skies, of earth, of water, of mountains, and of plants are designed to aid painters in their pursuit of accurate natural detail. Ruskin was far too sensitive an artist and critic, however, to let his definition of truth get in the way of what he felt was good art. He always qualifies his demand for truth by asking for only as great an amount as would be consistent with beauty or harmony. The mental gymnastics he performs in proving that Turner was the first of the Pre-Raphaelites show how flexible Ruskin could make his definition of truth to nature. Other artists failed to adjust their beliefs to their judgment with his agility. Certainly part of the Pre-Raphaelite demand for absolute ac-curacy in the representation of minute detail resulted from a pseudoscientific insistence upon the quantity of truth in art. In reaction to the discredit science had cast on other forms of truth, they tried to represent religious symbols through the medium of "scientific truth," which they defined as accuracy in the representation of natural detail. Holman Hunt, for example, the primary Pre-Raphaelite theorist, felt each age was given its quota of knowledge and wisdom to contribute toward the final truth. The nineteenth-century quota was truth of the accurate representation of natural fact. If artists made use of that truth in their paintings, they would increase the total sum of truth the paintings communicated. Hunt's sense of mission about representing religious symbols with minute scientific realism springs from his conviction that the kind of truth most meaningful to the nineteenth century is scientific truth, and that religious symbols portrayed with scientific accuracy will thus acquire a new cogency.

If the Pre-Raphaelites confusedly applied scientific criteria of truth to other areas of experience, they also turned detail to uses completely independent of science. Their use of nature in many ways resembles Tennyson's. The sensibility of the age led both Tennyson and the Pre-Raphaelites to an extraordinary interest in the minutiae of nature. Tennyson's charts of isobars spring from the same impulse as Hunt's sitting long hours after midnight, his feet wrapped in rags for extra warmth, to copy weeds in moonlight for *The Light of the World,* but the overly acute consciousness of detail in Tennyson's poetry and in Pre-Raphaelite painting was more than a blunder of their enthusiastic fervor for scientific accuracy. Like Tennyson, the Pre-Raphaelites managed to turn natural detail to purely expressionistic uses essentially independent of nature.

In their paintings with religious or literary symbols as subjects, the Pre-Raphaelites create a startling effect by the minute realism of their portrayal. The vulgarization of representational skills in the twentieth century makes it hard for us to realize how revolutionary the impact of these paintings was. The prosaicness of Millais's *Christ in the House of His Parents* shocked the major art critics and even Charles Dickens into passionate indignation [see Additional Bibliography]. *Blackwood's* review announced that "such a collection of splay feet, puffed joints, and misshapen limbs was assuredly never before made within so small a compass." Within a week after the picture was displayed, *Punch* printed a note, apparently by a doctor, who diagnosed the sacred figures of the painting as displaying every symptom of "scrufulous or strumous diathesis," and Dickens called the carpenters men such as "might be undressed in any hospital where dirty drunkards, in a high state of varicose veins, are received." By their insistent realism, the Pre-Raphaelites overturned the conventional iconography of the day. They created a tension in their pictures between the symbolic nature of the subject and the realism of its portrayal. Marianne Moore has said that poets should present "imaginary gardens with real toads in them," and the Pre-Raphaelites do precisely this. Furthermore, they make the warts on the toads so clear the garden no longer seems imaginary. Religious symbols are portrayed so realistically they become almost irreligious because, like Rossetti's blessed damozel, they insist so strongly on the fact of their physicality. By this exaggeratedly realistic portrayal of symbols, the paintings startle the viewer into rethinking those symbols' concrete meaning. Ruskin seems to understand this aspect of Pre-Raphaelitism when he asserts the value of representing symbolic events in their material veracity. The artist will either compel the spectator to believe the event really happened or make him detect his own incredulity and recognize that he had never asked himself if the event indeed was so.

By their realistic portrayal of symbols, the Pre-Raphaelites were trying to create a viable symbolic art for the nineteenth

century. Nineteenth-century artists had difficulty seeing the details of daily life as carrying a spiritual and human significance comparable to the significance they had carried in older cultures such as that of the Middle Ages. When artists attempted to make these details carry a sacramental value a sentimentalism resulted, in which events were laden with an emotional and spiritual significance far too heavy for them, as in Coventry Patmore's domestic epic, for example, *The Angel in the House.* In *Art and Visual Perception,* Rudolf Arnheim argues that a union between basic beliefs and the daily activities of living is necessary for a rich art and culture.

> the main virtue of any genuine culture would seem to be the capacity to experience the practical activities of living as tangible manifestations of basic principles. As long as getting a drink of water is felt— consciously or unconsciously—as obtaining sustenance from nature or God, as long as man's privilege and fate are symbolized for him in his labor, culture is safe. But when existence is limited to its specific material values, it ceases to be a symbol and thus loses the transparency on which all art depends. The very essence of art is the unity of idea and material realization.

The deadness of conventional symbols and the inability to see the details of modern life as having symbolic resonance led to both Pre-Raphaelite medievalism and the Pre-Raphaelite attempt to portray these conventional symbols with scientific naturalism. "The Blessed Damozel" and *The Scapegoat* are different paths to the same goal. Both try to restore a harmony between idea and visible fact that their artists were convinced modern life had lost, and by their use of detail both try to restore emotive power and physical presence to the symbol.

In an article on *The Scapegoat,* Herbert Sussman asserts that the central principle of Hunt's art, as well as that of the other naturalistic Pre-Raphaelites, was the fusion of representational accuracy and religious meaning in what may be called the naturalistic symbol. Sussman argues that this principle rests upon the transcendental assumption that material facts carry spiritual meanings. The Pre-Raphaelites pursue accurate representation so zealously because they believe as a result of this assumption that the more physically accurate a painting, the more spiritually meaningful it will be. According to Ruskin, the better the hoof and hair painting in a portrait of a goat, the more powerful it will be as a symbol.

Ruskin, no doubt, did believe in the concept of the naturalistic symbol, and interpreted Pre-Raphaelite art accordingly. His assertion that painting should be particular, however, springs from very different impulses than does the Pre-Raphaelites' insistence upon particularity. Ruskin never argued that artists should pursue the accurate representation of detail to the neglect of other considerations; he said only that accurate representation of particulars created more truthful and consequently greater art. He saw preoccupation with detail as morbid: the German and Flemish painters, for example, had "a morbid habit of mind" that caused them "to lose sight of the balance and relations of things, so as to become intense in trifles, gloomily minute." His view of extreme consciousness of detail suggests Tennyson's understanding of it rather than the Pre-Raphaelites'; he saw the Pre-Raphaelite passion for representing minute detail as a rather laudable excess in their scientific passion for truth. He felt they were occasionally negligent and fell into a "morbid indulgence of their own impressions," but he never saw this morbid intensity of vision as essential to their art.

Ruskin and Sussman completely misunderstand the Pre-Raphaelite use of detail. No doubt Hunt and the other Pre-Raphaelites were looking for naturalistic symbols. Hunt goes to great pains to assert that the details in *The Light of the World* were not derived from ecclesiastical or archaic symbolism but from "obvious reflectiveness." Yet what is interesting about Pre-Raphaelite paintings is the way the minute realism of representation interacts with the "naturalistic symbols." The superabundance and unnatural clarity of detail together with the frequent artificiality of the attitude of the subject, far from pushing the painting further toward natural representation, push it back toward the realm of art. Both the amount of detail and the posing of the subjects have a stilling effect that makes the painting seem more like an emblem than a natural object. The full presentation of each element of the scene, like the simultaneous presentation of all elements of a scene in the landscapes of medieval art, emphasizes the symbolic aspect of the objects. We do not see a Pre-Raphaelite painting as a single impression of a scene as it looks from one point of view at one moment. Rather, the fullness of the presentation of each detail makes it fall apart into pieces that can be individually explicated. Most critics see this as a fault and conclude that the Pre-Raphaelites had a very naive notion of realism, but it is an essential element of the kind of art that they were trying to create. The detailed representation of even the smallest objects in each painting makes each one a possible focus of contemplation. The paintings thus imply a symbolic view of the world, in which each object can become instinct with meaning. By thus singling out each object, the Pre-Raphaelites build into their painting stylistically the impetus to a sacramental view of reality. At the same time the naturalism of the portrayal pushes what had been a symbol toward status as a natural object, the sheer quantity of detail pulls it back toward status as a symbol. Images are thus poised precariously and deliberately on the brink between being aesthetic objects and being natural objects. Such portrayal reflects an assumption about the way man perceives. Faced with a world of natural objects instinct with symbolic meaning, man can understand that meaning, by intensity of contemplation. The conscious elaboration of detail in Pre-Raphaelite art reveals just such a consciously symbol-making effort. Far from producing a fatal lack of integrity of focus, the combination of allegorical and highly realistic details suggests the process of symbolic perception.

The superabundance of detail also has an emotional effect. Its excessive clarity and brilliance echoes the intensity in the emotional attitude of most of the subjects and thus intensifies the emotional response of the viewer. In *The Scapegoat*, the sharply detailed representation of the salt, the goat's footprints, the broken twigs, and the bones of old goats suggests a morbid clarity of vision which increases the pathos of the image of the scapegoat. In *Ophelia*, the brilliance of the landscape almost absorbs Ophelia. She seems to be literally dying into the life of nature, and its vitality increases the poignancy of her human death.

This emotive use of detail is even more pronounced in Pre-Raphaelite pictures based on scenes taken from modern life. *The Awakened Conscience; The Long Engagement,* Arthur Hughes's painting of two lovers looking up at the sky with an expression of maudlin but genteel mournfulness; William Henry Windus's *Too Late,* a picture of a young swain returning to his village sweetheart to find her dying of consumption; Ford Madox Brown's *The Last of England,* a picture of two departing Australian emigrants—these pictures strike us as quintessentially Victorian. And what is so peculiarly Victorian about them

is the combination of an intense emotion compressed into a small but melodramatic gesture, such as raising the eyes or clasping the hands, with a crowded, busy surface. They bring together the sentimentality of the era with the undigested detail of its decor and its architecture.

In these pictures, the Pre-Raphaelites were trying to represent inner states of strong feeling, to portray invisible areas of human emotion, and they found the resources of human gesture and expression very inadequate. This inadequacy explains the frequency of grotesque expressions and rigidly stylized attitudes in these pictures. The ghastly joy that possesses the face of the woman in *The Awakened Conscience* was the best Hunt could do to show what a moral transformation felt like. Because of the inadequacy of bodily posture and facial expression to convey states of extreme emotion, the Pre-Raphaelites turned to the use of landscape to convey the emotional intensity of their subjects. Ford Madox Brown describes exactly this strategy in talking about *The Last of England;* "The minuteness of detail which would be visible under such conditions of broad daylight I have thought necessary to imitate as bringing the pathos of the subject home to the beholder." In other words, Brown depicts objects in the painting with unnatural distinctness in order to suggest the poignant clarity they have to a mind at a crisis such as leaving home forever. The clarity of detail thus helps express the peculiar emotional stress of the emigrants' situation to the beholder. Ruskin makes a similar analysis of the use of detail in Holman Hunt's *The Awakened Conscience:*

> . . . the careful rendering of the inferior details in this picture . . . is based on a truer principle of the pathetic than any of the common artistical expedients of the schools. Nothing is more notable than the way in which even the most trivial objects force themselves upon the attention of a mind which has been fevered by violent or distressful excitement. They thrust themselves forward with a ghastly and unendurable distinctness, as if they would compel the sufferer to count, or measure, or learn them by heart.

Though we may be amused that, as one critic put it, "the inner movement of soul is so richly and factually a social vision of upholstery and interior decor," nevertheless, the particularity with which Hunt portrays the interior of the room conveys the emotional intensity of the moment as it heightens the woman's sensitivity to the objects that surround her. The distinctness of such banal tokens of her life as the rosewood furniture, the discarded glove, the freshly bound books suggests the terrible clarity of her awareness of what her life really is.

The use of detail in these pictures resembles the poetic use of detail to portray a morbid state of emotion in *Maud* or "The Bride's Prelude" or "My Sister's Sleep." Significantly, James Smetham, a minor Pre-Raphaelite painter, wrote that the stanzas about the shell in *Maud* "[answer] well to an unvarying condition of mind in anguish, viz., to be riveted and fascinated by very little things." The Pre-Raphaelite use of detail springs from a similar psychological insight. This use of detail in painting, however, depends upon the main figure of the painting functioning as a narrator would in a poem. We must see the landscape through his eyes, as a reflection of his emotion, much as we seem to see the house in Mariana through her eyes. But because this kind of projection is very difficult to attain in painting, the Pre-Raphaelite painters fail to manipulate detail to this effect as successfully as do the poets.

Humphrey House once defined the peculiar quality of the Victorian sensibility as a combination of hysteria and extreme literalness, a combination that perfectly defines Pre-Raphaelite art. The Pre-Raphaelites were seeking expressionistic art to portray strong states of emotion, and by an accident of history they wound up seeking it through naturalism. As a result, they created a realism so exaggerated it became expressionistic. They use detail, much like Rossetti, to attain a subjective intensity in art and to give symbols a concrete sensuous immediacy, but Rossetti's poetry is ultimately more successful than Pre-Raphaelite painting in the ways it uses detail and more radical in the significance it attaches to it. Despite their emphasis on the physical reality of religious symbols, the Pre-Raphaelites want to maintain and even strengthen the symbolic dimension. They do not share Rossetti's insistence on the independent value of the sensuous immediacy of the image, but rather use that immediacy to make the symbol convincing and thus meaningful to the viewer. Furthermore, Rossetti's subjective selectivity in his use of detail is psychologically more profound and aesthetically more capable of development. The Pre-Raphaelites went to nature, as did Tennyson, to communicate states of hysterical and morbid emotion essentially independent of it, but in doing so tried to make nature communicate things difficult for it to convey. Despite this aesthetic failure, their connection of aggressive particularity with extreme, often morbid emotion bears a fascinating similarity to this connection in the poetry of Tennyson and Rossetti. But to the Pre-Raphaelites this intense consciousness of particulars did not suggest, as it did to Tennyson, loss of balance and relation in a world whose center could not hold. Rather, in their painting, as well as in the poetry of Rossetti, it gradually came to reflect the discovery of a new center in the subjective perception of each individual. (pp. 37-64)

> Carol T. Christ, "The Microscopic Eye: Particularity and Morbidity," in her The Finer Optic: The Aesthetic of Particularity in Victorian Poetry, *Yale University Press, 1975, pp. 17-64.*

HERBERT L. SUSSMAN

[In this excerpt from his book-length study of typology in Victorian aesthetics, Sussman traces the influence of Ruskin's thought on the Pre-Raphaelites. Sussman considers the Pre-Raphaelite concern with scientific historicism and accuracy of representation as a quest for spiritual and artistic revitalization.]

[Much] in the history of the Pre-Raphaelite Brotherhood is rather droll. The thought of Elizabeth Siddal freezing in a tub of cold water while posing as the drowning Ophelia, or of Holman Hunt, his feet wrapped in straw against the cold, waiting in the freezing night to paint the proper shade of moonlight on a wall, is so curious to the modern mind that commentators have often found it difficult to move beyond anecdotal accounts of the Brotherhood to serious consideration of its principles. That the Brothers were earnest no one can doubt; indeed, their earnestness is the very source of their drollness. But that their curious behavior manifests an aesthetic and a style consistent within their own terms if not within ours, and that the Brotherhood's communal enterprise engaged serious issues within the artistic and literary culture of Victorian England, is a proposition that is less often accepted.

One reason for the air of drollness, the attitude of condescension, that still inform modern accounts of the Brotherhood is the assumption by many modern critics of an art-historical model that, with a Hegelian determinism, evaluates nineteenth-century art according to how closely it anticipates the "modern." Within this historical scheme, Brotherhood work comes to be seen merely as a "dead-end" in the evolution of nineteenth-century art toward impressionism and abstraction. But in the history of the arts there is not cumulative progress but rather the destruction of one paradigm and its replacement by another. The historian of artistic and literary movements can, like the historian of science, seek not to demonstrate how the past failed to anticipate the present but, instead, to reconstruct the coherence of styles and theories that have long since disappeared.

It is precisely because the aesthetic that the members of the Brotherhood shared has disappeared so completely, has become to the modern mind even more remote than the vision of the early-Renaissance artists the Brothers believed they were emulating, that the work of the Brotherhood appears to offer such a striking series of paradoxes. Although adopting an avant-garde role in opposing the teachings of the Royal Academy, the Brothers conceived of their own mission as the restoration of the authentic Western artistic tradition. Attacked intensely by the general periodicals on the exhibition of their early paintings, the Brothers nevertheless saw themselves as public artists, Victorian sages delivering highly orthodox sermons to a wide audience. Furthermore, their effort to emulate Italian artists of the fifteenth century generated a style that in its detailed naturalism and historical accuracy is distinctly of the nineteenth. To the modern sensibility, the virtually obsessive detailing of the physical world works against the transcendental significance and the personal impulses underlying the art against its public meaning. Finally, there is the historical irony that this group so self-consciously devoted to the revitalization of a didactic, orthodox sacramental art should become the germ of the modern movements that developed in later nineteenth-century England. And yet, the communal quality of their activity, the publication of *The Germ* as a manifesto, the stylistic similarities in the work produced by the circle between 1848 and 1853, all indicate that the Brothers themselves did not feel the contradictions so apparent to the modern mind, but rather held to artistic beliefs and to stylistic practices that were so deeply shared as not to require explicit articulation. (pp. xv-xvi)

Once the Brothers are no longer forced into the role of precursors, but set within their immediate cultural context, their work emerges not as misguided groping toward modernism but as participation in a widespread effort in the 1830s and 1840s to revive sacramental forms of art and literature through the adaptation of figural methods. Like Carlyle and Ruskin, the Brothers sought to reconcile through their art the fading belief in the sacramental quality of the natural world and in the providential nature of history with the powerful new attitudes generated by a wholly materialistic science and an avowedly scientific history. Rather than seeing the visible world as less significant than the transcendent reality that it symbolizes, these Victorians saw both natural fact and historical event as figure, as simultaneously tangible reality and symbol of the transcendent. Within these assumptions, the end of art is neither allegory in the religious sense of leaving the "given to find that which is more real" nor realism in the secular sense of representing tangible phenomena in a world from which God has disappeared. Instead, the Brotherhood, deeply influenced by Carlyle and Ruskin, employed a symbolic realism that sees fact as spiritually radiant and assumes that only through detailed representation of this natural and historical fact can the phenomenal be seen as figuring the transcendent. The highest power of the imagination, then, lies neither in the accurate perception of the phenomenal nor in the unmediated vision of the transcendent, but in the integrated sensibility that can see with the greatest acuity the phenomenal fact while simultaneously reading the fact as sign of a higher reality. At its most successful, figural art depicts the hard, tangible reality of individual lives in historical time while pointing to the providential design that lies beyond history.

Interest in a contemporary version of figural theory developed in the early 1830s with Carlyle's fusion, in such works as "History" (1830), "Biography" (1832), and *Sartor Resartus* (1833-34), of the new historicism with typological reading of Scripture, the most available form of figuralism in Protestant England. By 1843, Carlyle developed in *Past and Present* a literary-historical form adequate to express his vision of the facts of secular history and even of contemporary urban life as manifesting operations of the Divine. In the same year, *Modern Painters I* appeared offering a sacramentalist defense of Turner's landscapes and in 1846 *Modern Painters II*, a work that in its explication of Renaissance religious painting through Protestant typological exegesis exerted the single most important theoretical influence upon the Brotherhood. Indeed, Hunt dates the origin of the Brotherhood to his 1846 conversation with Millais about the possibilities of a truly contemporary, yet distinctly Protestant, religious art based upon the figural principles expressed by Ruskin in *Modern Painters II.* (pp. xvi-xvii)

Looking back at the end of the century, Hunt . . . shared his own intense excitement on reading the second volume of *Modern Painters:* "Lately I had great delight in skimming over a certain book, *Modern Painters,* by a writer calling himself an Oxford Graduate; it was lent to me only for a few hours, but, by Jove! passages in it made my heart thrill." Hunt's sensibility focused on Ruskin's discussion of "Imagination Penetrative," and particularly on Ruskin's typological reading of Tintoretto's *Annunciation:* "The Annunciation takes place in a ruined house, with walls tumbled down; the place in that condition stands as a symbol of the Jewish Church—so the author reads—and it suggests an appropriateness in Joseph's occupation of a carpenter, that at first one did not recognise; he is the new builder!" During his Brotherhood phase, Rossetti shared this enthusiasm for Ruskin's historicist theory of scriptural painting. As late as 1856, he writes to Browning praising the anti-Raphaelite arguments in the latest volume of *Modern Painters:* "I'm about half-way through Ruskin's third volume which you describe very truly. Glorious it is in many parts—how fine that passage in the 'Religious false ideal,' where he describes Raphael's *Charge to Peter,* and the probable truth of the event in its outward aspect. A glorious picture might be done from Ruskin's description."

For Hunt, Rossetti, and Millais, then, the primary issues in the formation of the Brotherhood were not only the achievement of a more accurate representationalism in opposition to Academic conventions but the revitalization of religious art through methods appropriate to their own age. Hunt recalls confessing to Millais in this 1846 conversation: "You feel that the men [the Venetian painters] who did them had been appointed by God, like old prophets, to bear a sacred message, and that they delivered themselves like Elijah of old." In their theory, if not always in their practice, the Brothers too sought to "bear a sacred message." From the essays in their single public manifesto, *The Germ,* and scattered statements of the circle during the Brotherhood period there emerges a coherent, self-conscious position that calls for the continuation of the pure tradition of sacramental Christian art through the distinctly contemporary mode of figuralism articulated by Carlyle and

Ruskin. Within this context, the paradoxes that puzzle the modern mind—the joining of minute realism with sacramental intention, of archaeological accuracy with faith in Scripture as revelation, of revivalist purpose with nineteenth-century style— are reconciled through the intellectual models used by Carlyle and Ruskin: the analogy of the artist to the religious scientist and a figural approach to history. And yet, ironically, this effort to restore at the midpoint of the nineteenth century what they saw as the single authentic tradition of sacred art brought the Brothers, for a time, into a stance of opposition toward their audience and a distinctly modern relationship to artistic tradition.

To the formation of their aesthetic, the Brothers brought sensibilities shaped by varying modes of figuralism. Hunt, the most authentically religious of the group, came from a firmly Protestant, deeply puritanical background. Like Carlyle and Ruskin, Hunt grew up in a family in which Bible-reading was a major family occupation. In the most recent biography, his granddaughter says, "At the age of five, his favorite day of the week was Sunday. . . . Like all their neighbours, the Hunts put on their best clothes and went to church. After the evening meal and family prayers, his father read aloud from the New Testament." Hunt himself remained self-consciously proud of his Calvinist heritage, noting in his autobiography that "our earliest recorded ancestor had taken part against King Charles and at the Restoration had sought service in the Protestant cause on the Continent." Having rebelled against his father in following an artistic rather than commercial career, Hunt justified his work as a form of ministry engaged in painting visual sermons based upon Scripture, contemporary life, or imaginative literature. Always, he thought of himself as working in the tradition of English Protestant art. He notes with pride and a hint of prefiguration, "I was christened at the church of St. Giles, Cripplegate, in which Cromwell was married, and where the toil-worn body of Milton lies."

Dante Gabriel Rossetti was neither English nor Protestant, yet the mental habits he brought from his own background drew him, for a time, toward figural methods. As a young man, Rossetti attended with his family churches known for their Tractarian leanings; and in the late 1840s and into the early 1850s, he seems to have been caught up in the resurgence of religious feeling brought about by the Oxford Movement. But for Rossetti, the figural tradition was mediated primarily through Dante, particularly through the *Vita Nuova.* Auerbach's comments on the *Vita* in his essay "Figura" exactly describe the young Rosetti's sense of this work:

> For Dante the liberal meaning or historical reality of a figure stands in no contradiction to its profounder meanings, but precisely figures it; the historical reality is not annulled, but confirmed and fulfilled by the deeper meaning. The Beatrice of the *Vita Nuova* is an earthly person; she really appeared to Dante, she really saluted him, really withheld her salutation later on. It should also be borne in mind that from the first day of her appearance the earthly Beatrice was for Dante a miracle sent from Heaven, an incarnation of Divine truth.

It is this same sense of the interpenetration of sacred and historical reality that not only informs Rossetti's Brotherhood illustrations of the *Vita* but also shapes his biblical paintings and treatments of contemporary events. And yet, the close connection of figural methods with erotic feelings in Dante's *Vita* was also absorbed by Rossetti, leading him, even within his Brotherhood work, toward the use of Dantean material as a vehicle for private emotions.

Millais brought to the Brotherhood little feeling for the sacred. His father was a person of inherited wealth and no occupation; the description of him as "a man of no ambition save where his children were concerned, and who desired nothing more than the life he led as a quiet country gentleman" prefigures elements in his son's career. With no firm religious or intellectual background to draw upon, Millais did not shape the Brotherhood aesthetic, but rather joined the group out of youthful enthusiasm and carried out its aims with his almost preternatural technical skill. But painting was always to Millais less a calling than the career track leading to the prosperous life of a country gentleman, and he left the Brotherhood as easily as he originally joined.

For all their varied backgrounds, during the Brotherhood years the members of the group thought of themselves as, and acted as, artist-scientists. In the major theoretical essay in *The Germ*, "The Purpose and Tendency of Early Italian Art," F. G. Stephens, one of the original Brothers, quite explicitly identifies the mission of the Brotherhood with that of contemporary science:

> The sciences have become almost exact within the present century. Geology and chemistry are almost re-instituted. The first has been nearly created; the second expanded so widely that it now searches and measures the creation. And how has this been done but by bringing greater knowledge to bear upon a wider range of experiment; by being precise in the search after truth? If this adherence to fact, to experiment and not theory . . . has added so much to the knowledge of man in science; why may it not greatly assist the moral purposes of the Arts?

In working to reproduce the particular object set before him, whether a beech post in the studio, a hedge in Knole Park, or the masculature of a carpenter's arms, the Brotherhood artist is emulating the scientist's "adherence to fact," to the visible truth of the particular specimen before him. In moving from the studio to work *en plein air,* in the obsessive search for the perfect wall or riverbank, he is following the scientist's "adherence . . . to experiment," to the observation of natural phenomena *in situ*. And in reporting on canvas the results of his direct observation, the Brotherhood artist is demonstrating a scientist's "adherence . . . to experiment and not theory"; he is testing the authority of Academic conventions against observed fact much as the scientist tests received theory against experimental observation.

It even appears that the Brotherhood in their practice consciously drew upon the scientific theory of their time. In his *Memoir* of Hunt, Stephens describes Hunt's purposes in representing light and shadow in *The Hireling Shepherd* as the "scientific elucidation of that particular effect which, having been hinted at by Leonardo da Vinci . . . was partly explained by Newton, and fully developed by Davy and Brewster. He was absolutely the first figure-painter who gave the true colour to sun-shadows, made them partake of the tone of the object on which they were cast, and deepened such shadows to pure blue where he found them to be so." Although Stephen's comment does provide a "rather muddled assessment" of the origins of Hunt's style, the remark does indicate how much the Brothers saw their own technical innovations, in this case the use of colored shadows, as participating in the scientific progress of their own age.

This effort to see the world directly by shedding the visual preconceptions of the past also led the Brothers to emulate the style of the scientist as artist, in particular that of the scientist, like Philip Gosse, who illustrated hiw own texts. As the testimony of Edmund Gosse suggests, the Brotherhood style closely approaches that of scientific illustration. The hard-edge manner and full modeling emphasizes the separateness of the physical object, its importance as a specimen. The minute particularity and the pushing of the object to the front of the picture plane as well as the rejection of chiaroscuro for a bright overall illumination indicates the necessity of observing and recording each detail of each specimen. Again, we may note the shock of recognition of Philip Gosse and his son in finding "the exact, minute and hard execution of Mr. Hunt to be in sympathy with the method we ourselves were in the habit of using when we painted butterflies and seaweeds."

This identification with the scientist also provided a moral justification for their minute realism. The Brothers shared Stephens's assumption that if "adherence to fact, to experiment and not theory . . . has added so much to the knowledge of man in science," the same scientific modes would inevitably "greatly assist the *moral* purposes of the Arts" (italics added). Using a Ruskinian vocabulary that fuses mimetic and moral criteria, Stephens speaks of the new school of English artists as "producing pure transcripts and faithful studies from nature." He urges artists to "believe that there is that in the fact of truth, though it be only in the character of a single leaf earnestly studied, which may do its share in the great labor of the world." His language assumes an inherent significance that will emerge from the accurate transcript of the natural world and of human events as surely as from the fact itself. He praises "the power of representing an object, that its entire intention may be visible, its lesson felt." And he exhorts the reader, "Never forget that there is in the wide river of nature something which everybody who has a rod and line may catch, precious things which everyone may dive for."

In his two *Germ* essays on "The Subject in Art," John Tupper also assumes the moral value of the scientific method in arguing for the Brotherhood belief in an art of high moral dignity derived from close observation of modern life. For Tupper, the science that the artist must follow is that of natural theology: "Science here does not make; it unmakes, wonderingly to find the making of what God has made. . . . But though science is not to make the artist, there is no reason in nature that the artist reject it." The artist, then, like the religious scientist, must find God through accurate representation of the world about him, rather than in rehearsing artistic traditions passed down by the Academy: "Thus then we see, that the antique, however successfully it may have wrought, is not our model; for, according to that faith demanded at setting out, fine art delights us from its being the semblance of what in nature delights." Faithfully imitated on canvas, the visible world will create the same response as the divinely created natural fact itself: "Works of Fine Art affect the beholder in the same ratio as the *natural prototypes* of those works would affect him."

In their scattered statements about their own work, the major Brotherhood artists also connect the close observation of natural fact with religious purpose. In his sonnet "St. Luke the Painter," written in 1849, Rossetti writes of early-Renaissance art as knowing

> How sky-breadth and field-silence and this day
> Are symbols also in some deeper way,
> She looked through these to God and was God's priest.

Characteristically, Hunt uses a Ruskinian vocabulary: "Our object was to be enslaved by none, but in the field of Nature and under the sky of Heaven frankly to picture her healthful beauty and strength." Both "field" and "sky" are modified by a capitalized possessive to show the visible fact as the creation of, and sign of, a transcendent power. And "beauty" is modified by "healthful" to emphasize the Ruskinian principle that the accurate representation of the visible landscape is not merely an aesthetic occupation but a means of restoring moral vigor.

The belief that each detail of nature figures the transcendent appears to be the message of *Convent Thoughts,* by Charles Collins, a young artist who, while executing this work, was part of the Brotherhood circle. Here, the nun lays aside the Book of God, an illustrated missal, to read from the Book of Nature, to examine closely a daisy plucked from the convent garden. In her chaste holiness, figured by the lily, able to find God not only through His revealed word but also through Wordsworthian observation of a common flower, the nun represents the integrated sensibility toward which the Pre-Raphaelite artist aspired. The very style of the painting, its detailed realism, becomes significant, then, in illustrating the mode of perception symbolized by the nun. To Ruskin, this naturalistic accuracy was the chief virtue of the work. In one of the letters to the *Times* of 1851, he praises the painting as a scientific illustration: "As a mere botanical study of the water lily and *Alisma,* as well as of the common lily and several other garden flowers, this picture would be invaluable to me." [see first excerpt by Ruskin above]. But, using the religiously resonant vocabulary of *Modern Painters,* he also notes that the scientific style in which the specimens are "so well drawn" shows that these artists do not "sacrifice *truth* as well as feeling to eccentricity."

This equation of detailed realism and sacred purpose is also implicit in the group's choice of a name. Drawing upon new models of art history popularized in the 1840s by such writers as Mrs. Jameson, Lord Lindsay, and, of course, Ruskin, the Brotherhood sees the pre-Raphaelite artists, those representational painters that have moved beyond medieval style and yet precede Raphael—"Gozzoli . . . Ghiberti . . . Fra Angilico . . . Masaccio . . . Ghirlandajo . . . Orcagna . . . Giotto"—as the last to have confronted the visible world directly, to have perceived it clearly, to have represented it exactly. For, just as the true scientist confronts the natural world openly, freed from the

distorting effect of false theories passed down on the authority of tradition, so, according to the Brotherhood, the early Italian artist perceived nature with a similar directness by not having imposed between the eye and the visible fact the distorting artistic conventions created by Raphael, imposed by his followers, and fossilized into the theory and educational practice of the Royal Academy. Stephens, in "The Purpose and Tendency of Early Italian Art," lauds these early-Renaissance artists for their "success, by following natural principles, until the introduction of false and meretricious ornament led the Arts from the simple chastity of nature, which it is as useless to attempt to elevate as to endeavour to match the works of God by those of man."

To the Brotherhood, as to Ruskin, the clarity of mimesis in the artists immediately preceding Raphael is a sign of religious strength. The work of these artists represents to the Brotherhood what the facade of Saint Mark's does to Ruskin, the manifestation of the integrated faculty in which visual acuteness and religious awareness are fused. Within this model of art history, then, the work of Raphael, praised by the Academy as the highest achievement of Western art becomes, instead, the point of decline. For the Brotherhood, as for Ruskin in *Modern Painters II* and *The Stones of Venice,* the failure of mimetic accuracy in the Grand Style, particularly its non-historicist idealization, demonstrates the secularization of the artistic consciousness. Stephens praises Masaccio as differing from a High Renaissance artist in manifesting the visual awareness that comes from a sense of the natural world as the creation of God: "For as the knowledge is stronger and more pure in Masaccio than in the Caracci, and the faith higher and greater,—so the first represents nature with more true feeling and love, and with a deeper insight into her tenderness; he follows her more humbly, and has produced to us more of her simplicity; we feel his appeal to be more earnest." For Stephens, "the introduction of false and meretricious ornament" by Raphael "led the arts from the simple chastity of nature." In John Orchard's "Dialogue" in *The Germ,* Christian says, "Nature itself is comparatively pure; all that we desire is the removal of the fictitious matter that the vice of fashion, evil hearts, and infamous desires graft upon it."

It is this historical scheme that Rossetti allegorizes in "St. Luke the Painter." In this poem, the early Italian painters alone are able to be simultaneously representational and devotional by painting "sky-breadth and field-silence" as "symbols." The early Renaissance, then, becomes the apogee of Western art. In the High Renaissance, "past noon," when the artist rejects the service of a religious art, when "her toil began to irk," he inevitably turns from the direct observation of the natural world to the mere reiteration of humanly created artistic formulas. In Rossetti's terms, the Raphaelite artist "sought talismans, and turned in vain / To soulless self-reflections of man's skill."

If the Brotherhood saw sacred meaning as emerging from the accurate representation of natural fact, the artists looked for the same divine significance to emerge from the equally scientific recording of historical fact. In their extensive treatment of both biblical and postbiblical history, the Brothers sought not to revive the style of the painters preceding Raphael but to achieve a sacred art through the historical methods they saw as characterizing the spirit of their own age. In his essay "On the Mechanism of a Historical Picture" in *The Germ,* Ford Madox Brown outlines the methods of achieving archeological accuracy carried out by the group:

A Max Beerbohm caricature of William Morris and Edward Burne-Jones titled "Topsy and Ned Jones settled on the settle in Red Lion Square." Reproduced by permission of Eva Reichmann.

The first care of the painter, after having selected his subject, should be to make himself thoroughly acquainted with the character of the times, and habits of the people, which he is about to represent; and next, to consult the proper authorities for his costume, and such objects as may fill his canvas; as the architecture, furniture, vegetation or landscape, or accessories, necessary to the elucidation of the subject.

The puzzling association of this distinctly nineteenth-century historicism with the early-Italian painters derives from the Ruskinian model of art history. To the Brothers, the chief failure of the Raphaelite manner is that the idealizing style, exemplified in Raphael's cartoons for the Vatican tapestries, appears to repudiate the historicity of scriptural events. To the Brotherhood, it seemed that only the artists immediately preceding Raphael, those painting in a realistic manner, but as yet uncorrupted by the heroicizing conventions of the Grand Style, could still feel the quotidian reality of biblical events while still realizing their sacred meaning. In his essay on early-Italian art, Stephens illustrates how these "earlier painters came nearer to fact," how they "were less of the art, artificial," through the example of a Florentine Pietà. His main point is that the work achieves its religious power through historical accuracy. In this Pietà, the Virgin "is old, (a most touching point); lamenting aloud, clutches passionately the heavy-weighted body on her knee; her mouth is open." Stephens notes that this realism, "this identification with humanity," is far superior to any Raphaelite idealization, to any "refined or emasculate treatment of the same subject by later artists, in which we have the fact forgotten for the sake of the type of religion, which the Virgin was always taken to represent, whence she is shown as still young."

Although it is difficult to share the Brotherhood's excitement over Carlo Lasinio's engravings from the Campo Santo, the group appreciated these fourteenth- and fifteenth-century works as representing the power of a historical, as opposed to Raphaelite, treatment of scriptural subjects. The subjects themselves are clearly typological. *The Departure of Hagar from the House of Abraham* is mentioned by Saint Paul as prefiguring the replacement of the Old Covenant by the New (Gal. 4:22-31); *The Sacrifice of Isaac* is a type of the Sacrifice of Christ. Although these works do not show the nineteenth-century archeological accuracy that the Brotherhood sought, they do give the sense of random daily reality by showing the central action as occurring within domestic, rather than generalized, heroic settings. In *The Sacrifice of Isaac,* as Abraham prepares for his journey, two young boys playfully fight and the servant readies the mule. After the intervention by the angel, Abraham and Isaac eat together attended by their servants, while the mule grazes peacefully nearby. Nor were the Brothers the only Victorians to be impressed by the figural quality of these works. In a letter to his father from Pisa in 1845, Ruskin writes with enormous enthusiasm of the power of these frescoes, particularly of *The Departure of Hagar,* in impressing upon the viewer the historical reality of scriptural events:

The Campo Santo is the thing. I never believed the patriarchal history before, but I do now, for I have seen it. . . . In spite of every violation of the common, confounded, rules of art, of anachronisms & fancies . . . it is Abraham himself still. Abraham & Adam, & Cain, Rachel & Rebeka, all are there, the very people, real, visible, created, substantial, such as they *were,* as they must have been—one cannot look at them without being certain that they have lived. . . . Abraham sits *close* to you entertaining the angels—you may touch him & them—and there is a woman behind bringing the angels some real, *positive* pears.

Hoping, like Carlyle and Ruskin, to find spiritual as well as artistic regeneration through historicism, the Brotherhood sought to re-create in the present the moralized imagination represented by the early-Italian artists. The very drive to create a close, fraternal group with the religiously resonant name of "Brotherhood," the paraphernalia of rules, the regular meetings, and the secrecy transcend their evident juvenility as attempts to re-create a communal consciousness in their own lives that would inevitably be expressed in their art. Although the Brothers knew, primarily through Ford Madox Brown, of the methods and the living habits of the Nazarenes, they were too Protestant, too imbued with the Victorian idea of historical development, perhaps simply too young and sexually vigorous, to don the monk's robe of the pre-Renaissance artist. In his essay on early-Italian art, Stephen takes direct issue with the Nazarene attempt to duplicate the life of the medieval artist: "The modern artist does not retire to monasteries, or practise a discipline; but he may show his participation in the same high feeling by a firm attachment to truth in every point of representation."

Stephens thus articulates the paradox at the center of the Brotherhood enterprise—that the artist can express the "high feeling" or religious imagination of the past through the use of artistic modes characteristic of the present, in particular through a "firm" scientific and historicist "attachment to truth . . . of representation." The aim of the Brotherhood, then, was not to mimic the style of fifteenth-century art but to employ the perceptual and artistic modes of the present to restore the integrated sensibility that, looking through Ruskin's eyes, they saw exemplified in the past.

Ironically, the Brotherhood effort to restore a public religious art set them, for a time, in a role defined by opposition. The choice of a name, the formation of a society as an alternative to the Royal Academy, the issuing of *The Germ* as a manifesto, the un-Academic use of brilliant color, hard-edge outline, and random composition clearly indicate the Brothers' rejection of the one institution through which one could, in mid-Victorian England, hope to become a successful artist. And yet, in opposing the Academy, the Brothers did not see themselves in the avant-garde model of breaking entirely with artistic tradition in order to create an art that is entirely new. Instead, they speak only of rejecting the false tradition codified by the Academy in order to restore the authentic tradition cut off by the High Renaissance. This justification of innovation as the continuation of the true tradition found far back in history links the Brotherhood with movements of the later-nineteenth and early-twentieth century. William Morris, while creating highly Victorian designs, saw himself as restoring the pure tradition of English folk art destroyed by the introduction of foreign styles and the division of labor in the High Renaissance. Early in his career, Yeats looked beyond late-nineteenth-century aestheticism to the disappearing traditions of Celtic Ireland. And T. S. Eliot, the most influential modern writer on the uses of tradition, postulates the theory of a dissociation of sensibility in the seventeenth century remarkably similar to the idea of a dissociation of visual and moral awareness in the Renaissance that informs the historical model of Ruskin and the Brotherhood. For the Brotherhood, as for these later writers, the appeal to the single authentic tradition expresses their sense of a complex relation to history. It is true, but only partly true, that the Brotherhood invocation of the early-Italian painters is a means of finding what Renato Poggioli calls "patents of nobility" for innovations in the present. It is equally true that their name indicates their own perception that for all their originality of style and participation in the scientific and historicist impulses of their own age, there is a genuine continuity between their work and an earlier sacramental art. (pp. 33-45)

> *Herbert L. Sussman, in an introduction and "The Brotherhood Aesthetic," in his* Fact into Figure: Typology in Carlyle, Ruskin, and the Pre-Raphaelite Brotherhood, *Ohio State University Press, 1979, pp. xv-xix, 33-46.*

THE SISTER ARTS OF PRE-RAPHAELITE POETRY AND PAINTING

LAURENCE HOUSMAN

[*In this excerpt from his acclaimed address to the Royal Society of Literature in 1929, Housman treats Pre-Raphaelitism as an outgrowth of the Romantic movement, arguing that Pre-Raphaelite literature and visual art exhibit the Romantics' characteristic emphasis on nature, individualism, detail, and emotion.*]

Pre-Raphaelitism is no longer so importantly regarded as it was twenty or thirty years ago. As a form of Art it is reckoned out of date; we find other forms more interesting—more significant of what we are now after. But as a fact—a portent—coming where it did, it is as important as ever.

One might compare the past and present value of Luther and Lutheranism. Lutheranism has not any crucial importance to-day—nor has Luther. As a theologian he has become negligible; but as an historic figure—a revolutionary—he remains tremendously important.

And so, in a narrower, more insular degree, as affecting our own history in art and literature, so it is with pre-Raphaelitism. It is very English; and it makes a very definite stage in the development of English Art.

The Pre-Raphaelite Brotherhood has a fixed date from which it started; but the Pre-Raphaelite movement belonged to something older than itself by more than half a century; and when it found its name in the year 1848, it was merely the pictorial expression of influences which had already made their mark in literature, and would perhaps have made their mark in painting much earlier had not all the tradition and training of the Royal Academy been against them.

Pre-Raphaelitism was ostensibly a revolt against the approved canons of Early Victorian art; and its name arose from the desire of a group of young painters of genius (Rossetti, Millais, Holman Hunt, and others) to adopt some watchword or battle-cry expressive of the combative energy of their conviction that things in the art world of their day were all wrong. So they chose, quite naturally, a word which had to do with that branch of art which more particularly concerned them—the art of painting.

But though it thus acquired a name for purposes of publicity, the thing itself had been in full cry for over forty years. A similar spirit had, at that earlier date, stirred literature to much the same effect, and had found expression in the poems of Coleridge, Wordsworth, Shelley, and, above all, Keats—in the whole of that part of the Romantic movement, in fact (or

of what has been well-called "The Renaissance of Wonder")—which tended to reach back to natural origins, to individual impulse and feeling, from the conventions and formulæ of the schoolmen of an established classicism.

And that being so, what I have to speak of to-day will come under the two separate headings of literature and painting; though generally speaking we shall find that the whole movement tends to draw these two together under a common bond.

But since it is the word "Pre-Raphaelitism" which gives us our text, let us (although that aspect of the revolt came later) take first the pictorial side, and see if, in any way, that name (impulsively chosen by a few young men in their late 'teens and early twenties) serves to tell us what the revolt really meant.

"Pre-Raphaelitism" seems to imply the rejection of Raphael as a great master; to suggest that those who came before him were his superiors in art; and I daresay good headstrong phrases from the early pronouncements of the P.R.B. could be found to support that idea. But, as I shall show you presently, headstrong, but quite untenable pronouncements were one of the delightful characteristics of the movement; and nobody who values the spirit of youth, with all its stimulating illogicality and contradictions, will wish those headstrong utterances expunged. They form a part of the meaning of the revolt.

But why Raphael's name crops up for apparent rejection is because he was the 300-year-old godfather of a dead school of painting—so dead that it had begun to stink. Raphael, that great creator of form, had been reduced to a recipe, and had become accountable for painters like Benjamin West, and Eastlake, and Ary Schafer; and what they made him stand for had become an embedded code. "Style" and "the grand manner" were things fixed in mediocrity, and a mannerism too grandmotherly for words. And therefore, "Pre-Raphaelitism"; so, at least, we get away from that.

The Pre-Raphaelites in their young enthusiasm of revolt against a form of art which had come to mean the elimination of all truth, valiantly declared their intention to "select nothing and to reject nothing"; good enough as a cry of protest, but in practice utterly impossible. Art cannot move an inch toward self-expression without selection. It must select and reject—something. If it selects nature, it rejects convention; if it selects impulse, it rejects rule; if it selects green as the pictorial colour for grass and trees, it rejects brown.

But, in the main, what the pre-Raphaelites meant when they said that was, "For God's sake let us use our own eyes, and trust to our own feelings. Don't let us shut our eyes, or bandage them with grandmotherly traditions". And the will and the power to use their own eyes, away from all tradition, was their means of self-discovery; and its courageous application gives the whole complexion of their revolt.

I said just now that all art must necessarily be selection. And as any great school of art rises and develops, selection and selection is always going on, always moving resolutely toward some conscious end; and toward that end (whatever it may be)—whether it be the glorification of the significance of form, or colour, or movement, or light, or character—it makes always for economy of means, by the removal of accidentals, the elimination of superfluities or excrescences, for the more definite discovery and expression of the type toward which it is seeking. And so long as the school of any period is really a living and authentic growth—arising from within—its development is safe, its changes are organic, and it remains living and significant.

And in that process of searching for its ultimate form it continues to evolve a type by the elimination of whatever is non-essential; it focusses upon its aim.

But directly you have substituted copy, imitation, repetition, instead of living growth—there you are beginning to substitute death for life, stagnation for movement, decadence for progress.

If I were able to show you here a Greek marble of the time of Pericles or after, and side by side with it a copy of the late Roman period, in which (quite wilfully) type has become convention and selection reduced to rule, you would see at work a process making steadily for death—the negation of real expression.

And it is just the same with what followed after Raphael. Raphael is the final expression of a process (quite fine and noble) toward the elimination of all accidentals and superfluities in a given direction for a given end—the expression of an ideal type of humanity—a sort of deification of the human race charged with a great deal of symbolic significance, and formulated with a gracious dignity and serenity of style which have never been surpassed. And for that end Raphael eliminated or subordinated a great many accessories, and qualities and details which did not help to bring him nearer to the thing he was out to express; and just as he broadened selectively the folds of his drapery, so that it lay broadly and composedly and without too much flutter of detail over the clothed limbs of his demi-gods and saints, so he broadened out the face of nature, making it unobtrusive and subordinate, enhancing thereby the scale and grandeur of the human form he wished to celebrate. And he did all this so wonderfully that, for 300 years, painters with no new ideas of their own went on copying him.

Thus you got a stereotyped removal from nature, a recipe for what was called "the grand manner"; and a part of the recipe was that draperies should have no texture, and backgrounds no detail, and that sacred art must have no date and no local colour, except a washed-out reminiscence of the date and local colour given to it by Raphael.

A similar thing happened in England with Peers' robes and Judges' wigs. From a certain date in the eighteenth century, when the House of Lords had become most powerful, and the science of jurisprudence had reached a very notable development—from that date on these external emblems of dignity became stereotyped, and remain with us to this day; and in consequence a sort of Georgian atmosphere clings about both institutions, giving them an obsolescent character, which nothing but a social revolution will ever get rid of. You can't stereotype anything, however beautiful, without turning it into something of a mummy. When you begin embalming you are dealing with a dead body, and what you are trying to perpetuate is not life, but death.

Now that was the position to which Raphael had been reduced in the world of art in the early nineteenth century; Art was a coffin in which Raphael lay embalmed. Therefore, in order not to remain mutes at a funeral, the men of the new movement had to become Pre-Raphaelites: get rid, not of the living Raphael, but of his corpse. First and foremost they had to find themselves; and so, in some sort, once more become primitives.

Now you have only to bear in mind what were the things which the Raphaelesque tradition had dismissed from its categories as incompatible with "style" or the "grand manner", and you will see on what lines intelligent revolt was likely to take shape. And that is just what happened. The fingers of these young men itched with power; they had abilities for which the nerveless generalities of contemporary art offered no scope. That mummy chamber into which, at the Royal Academy School, they had been so carefully inducted had no further exit. The grave has only a way in; there is no way of quitting it except by backing out. And the Pre-Raphaelite movement was the backing out process—very swiftly and resolutely effected.

In 1846 Millais and Holman Hunt were painting according to the mummy-chamber tradition in which they had been trained, while Rossetti was imitating the pseudo-Gothic German illustrators of Faust. In 1848 the P.R.B. was in full career with all the critics howling at its heels. And Ford Madox Brown, their senior by some years—quitting the gothic shades in which he had so long been hiding himself—had become a companion of the group.

They began painting blades of grass, trees leaf by leaf, dewdrops, insects, the texture of wearing apparel, the individual hairs of a man's head and beard—kind of weather, time of day, all the accidents and incidents of background as well as foreground, which the grand manner had ruled out. And they painted all these things with the intensity of feeling and freshness of discovery which we can imagine to have been the state of mind—of Noah's family, let us say, when they emerged from the Ark and found their feet once more upon natural ground and their eyes on the open heaven.

But all those brilliant minutiæ of detail and incident were but the accessories and accompaniments of their self-discovery. It would be a mistake to imagine that they were merely naturalists suddenly let loose; they were also romantics, bent upon giving romance a new pictorial outfit. Many of their subjects were subjects belonging by tradition to the "grand manner", to which, therefore, a conventional deference was due. But lo and behold, instead of so deferring, they treated their romantic and sacred figures as though they were real people, with real clothes and real characters. Blasphemy could no further go; and the outcry was great.

Now this individualistic treatment of romantic and ideal subjects we have to bear well in mind, because it is a marked characteristic of the school—a characteristic shared by its literary predecessors of the romantic revival in poetry half a century earlier, and more markedly still by the literature which accompanied the movement in its development. In both branches alike (the poetic and the pictorial) there was the same sudden discovery and the same close linking together of nature and romance—the same determination to treat romance in terms of natural feeling; to assume, in choosing a romantic subject, that its characters were real people, and that if they were without reality—did not act, move, and appear humanly—they were without significance. All of which was in flat contradiction to the "grand manner" as hitherto understood. (pp. 1-8)

Romantic individualism is, I think, the key to Pre-Raphaelite painting, and to its choice and treatment of subject; and, as I shall hope to show presently, that is also the key to Pre-Raphaelite poetry.

Putting romance first, then, in point of importance, I would describe Pre-Raphaelitism as an endeavour to express romance in terms of nature, with great intensity of individual feeling, and with a strong sense of character. On the one hand it imported romance into subjects of modern life, and on the other natural feeling into subjects drawn from the Middle Ages. And in doing this it discovered in its drama of life a new point of accentuation. Rejecting rhetorical movement and conventional gesture for the pictorial rendering of passion, it gave emphasis to the eloquence of quiet attitudes and the interchange of the human glance. In Pre-Raphaelite pictures, closely grouped faces and hands have a new and curious significance; and the figures are generally arrested figures, brought to a standstill by some appeal to the emotions, often as though they were trying deeply to read each other's thoughts. The forces born of an emotional conflict (holding the body in arrest) have passed into the face; and though some slight exceptions occur, it will be found that the central interest of picture after picture, produced while Pre-Raphaelitism was at its red heat, consists in the exchanged regards of friends and lovers, or in strong restrained pose from which all gesticulation is banished, or even in the deeply-divined expression of a single face.

Define it how you will, here is the heart of Pre-Raphaelitism; let it be regarded as dramatic portraiture, or as a deep intuition into how things really might have happened to creatures of emotion, of flesh and blood. What it comes to in result is romantic drama, and drama of a new school and quality, sincere, human, and intense.

Startling in its suddenness, this new form of expression follows immediately upon work in which they had accepted the old formula of broad rhetorical gesture. What Sir Walter Scott in self-caricature described as ''the big bow-wow style'' was at that time the only mode of pictorial drama; for every given emotion a conventional and perfectly false attitude could be evolved by rule.

Pre-Raphaelitism changed all that entirely; and it adopted the change in the course of a single year. The prevailing influence I believe to have been Rossetti's; and it is in Rossetti's work more than in that of others that this sense of intense but quiet drama persists through after years.

But bearing in mind that here you expect to be talked to rather about poetry than about painting, I will now come to that parallel side of Pre-Raphaelitism as expressed in literature, which had so much older a beginning.

The romantic individualism, which I have indicated as the key to Pre-Raphaelitism, was the distinguishing mark as well of that great poetic revival, which we associate with the names of Coleridge, Wordsworth, and Keats. For though in Wordsworth the romantic note was less strong than in the others, his method, as opposed to the poetry of the preceding generation, was all part of the effort to make a new discovery of first principles on individualist lines.

But though I might quote Wordsworth also in proof, I can name no poem in which that individuality of touch is so insistent as in Coleridge's ''Ancient Mariner'', with its curiously intent focus upon quiet small objects, and its sharp arrest of attention to accessories or to natural phenomena, giving them a strange significance in their poetic setting such as they never had before.

Take, for instance, such passages as these:

> Day after day, day after day
>   We stuck, nor breath nor motion,
> As idle as a painted ship
>   Upon a painted ocean.

> The very deep did rot: O Christ
>   That such a thing should be!
> Yea, slimy things did crawl with legs
>   Upon a slimy sea.

. . .

> Nor dim nor red, like God's own head,
>   The glorious sun uprist:
> And all averred I had killed the bird
>   That brought the fog and mist.

. . .

> The sun's rim dips, the stars rush out:
>   At one stride comes the dark;
> With far-heard whisper, o'er the sea,
>   Off shot the spectre-bark.

. . .

> The moving Moon went up the sky
>   And nowhere did abide:
> Softly she was going up,
>   And a star or two beside.

. . .

> Beyond the shadow of the ship
>   I watched the water-snakes:
> They moved in tracks of shining white;
> And when they reared, the elfish light
>   Fell off in hoary flakes.

> Within the shadow of the ship
>   I watched their rich attire:
> Blue, glossy green, and velvet black,
> They coiled and swam; and every track
>   Was a flash of golden fire.

> O happy living things! no tongue
>   Their beauty might declare:
> A spring of love gushed from my heart,
>   And I blessed them unaware.

. . .

> The silly buckets on the deck,
>   That had so long remained,
> I dreamt that they were filled with dew;
>   And when I awoke, it rained.

. . .

> The coming wind did roar more loud
>   And the sails did sigh like sedge;
> And the rain poured down from one black cloud,
>   The Moon was at its edge.

. . .

> Like one that on a lonesome road
>   Doth walk in fear and dread,
> And having once turned round walks on,
>   And turns no more his head;
> Because he knows a frightful fiend
>   Doth close behind him tread.

Now all those passages I have read to you are of Pre-Raphaelite quality; original in simile, pictorial in phrasing, they achieve an almost unexampled visibility to the mind's eye; and by a combination of strongly individualized expression with intense feeling they bring the things of nature within the charmed circle of romance in a way that was then wholly new in literature.

With those stark, vivid phrases and similes fresh in your mind, compare—it is the comparison of moonlight to sunlight, but the source is the same—compare these phrases and similes from Rossetti's "Blessed Damozel":

> Her eyes were deeper than the depth
>   Of waters stilled at even.
>
>   .   .   .
>
> Her hair that lay along her back
>   Was yellow like ripe corn.
>
>   .   .   .
>
> Beneath, the tides of day and night
>   With flame and darkness ridge
> The void, as low as where the earth
>   Spins like a fretful midge.
>
>   .   .   .
>
> Around her, lovers newly met
>   Mid deathless love's acclaims:
> And the souls mounting up to God
>   Went by her like thin flames.
>
> The sun was gone; the curléd moon
>   Was like a little feather,
> Fluttering far down the gulf....

All those similes, so vivid, pictorial and unexpected—"the earth a fretful midge", "souls mounting like thin flames", "the moon like a little feather"—fall into sequence with the romantic inventiveness of Coleridge's great Rime. It is a new mode, and he, in a single poem, was the father of it.

I do not think one can be wrong in saying that "The Ancient Mariner" and all it stood for was one of the moving forces behind Pre-Raphaelitism.

And another of its directing influences was Keats, who, until the Pre-Raphaelites established him as their poetic leader, had hardly come by his own, or secured the standing in English literature which he holds now.

Keats (not only in his poetry but in private letters to friends) had expressed the Pre-Raphaelite standpoint with singular exactness. "The excellence of every art," he wrote to his friend Reynolds, "is its intensity, capable of making all disagreeables evaporate, from their being in close relationship with beauty and truth."

And here are further passages with reference to his chosen method of production:

> I have given up *Hyperion:* Miltonic verse cannot be written except in an artful (or rather an artist's) humour. I wish to give myself up to other sensations.... If poetry comes not as naturally as the leaves of a tree it had better not come at all.

And again:

> I have had lately to stand on my guard against Milton. Life to him would be death to me. Miltonic verse cannot now be written, but it becomes the verse of art. I wish to devote myself to another verse alone. The genius of poetry must work out its own salvation in a man; it cannot be matured by law and precept, but by sensation and watchfulness.

For "Milton" read "Raphael", and you have here the attitude of the P.R.B. toward tradition and precept accurately expressed.

Without quoting to you at length from the poetry of Keats, I will only ask you to remember how consistently it went on the lines of substituting impulse for rule, safeguarded always by that "intensity of feeling" which he predicates; how extraor-dinarily vivid and pictorial is the outcome of its individualistic phrasing and concrete imagery; and how extravagantly he was abused for his desertion of the accepted canons of art not only by the professional critics, but by some of the poets his contemporaries. (pp. 12-18)

Those principles enunciated by Keats which I have just read to you were probably unknown to the P.R.B.; for they all come from letters which were only published much later. But they account for the strong attraction his verse had for them; Keats's method of getting at things was their method—sensation, openness to impressions, watchfulness, intensity of feeling, were the lines upon which they found themselves.

How right Keats was, in his own case, to trust to impulse rather then to calculation or rule, is well proved to us by the deep inferiority of his second version of "La belle dame sans merci", a poem which was declared by William Morris, one of the later disciples of Pre-Raphaelitism, to have been the germ from which all the poetry of the group sprang.

That is, I think, an excessive statement, but it contains a good deal of truth.

In Keats's second version the "Knight-at-Arms" becomes a "weary wight", which is not much better than a "weary Willie". "And there she lullèd me asleep" is changed into "And there we slumbered on the moss"; while the preceding verse which, as you probably know it, runs thus:

> She took me to her elfin grot,
>   And there she wept and sighèd full sore;
> And there I shut her wild, wild eyes
>   With kisses four.

That is polished down into the following:

> She took me to her elfin grot,
>   And there she gazed and sighèd deep,
> And there I shut her wild sad eyes
>   So kissed to sleep.

No wonder Morris raged when he caught some anthologist reprinting such second thoughts as these. Keats was right to rely upon impulse for his poetic guidance.

And now that I have mentioned Morris, I am really brought to my main point. For in no book of verse is the poetry of Pre-Raphaelitism so completely illustrated as in William Morris's first early book of poems, *The Defence of Guenevere,* written before he also indulged in second thoughts, which turned him into a different sort of poet altogether.

Morris comes upon the scene at Oxford, where, under Rossetti's leadership (a few years after the founding of the Brotherhood), certain members have undertaken to decorate the walls of the Oxford Union. Morris's value as an exponent of the Pre-Raphaelite spirit consisted largely in the fact that he was virgin soil. He had a great simple nature, hugely receptive and abounding in vitality; he was at once extraordinarily alive and extraordinarily susceptible to the influence of a bigger and subtler intellect; and when the spirit of the thing was instilled into him by Rossetti, he tumbled to it like a ripe plum, and found it, as he naïvely confessed, astonishingly easy. The story goes that he went away from one of their evening gatherings and returned a few days later with a sheaf of poems. These were passed round among the members: "'Topsy' is a great poet" they excitedly exclaimed; to which "Topsy" (quite as much surprised as anyone) replied ingenuously, "Well, if that's poetry, all I can say is, it's damned easy."

And its quite true; it was. All he had found it necessary to do was to put himself back into the Middle Ages, and realize with that intensely concrete vision which he possessed, that knight-errants and damozels were real people, capable of being really treated, saying and doing quite individual things, even though they wore the livery of a vanished age. And, putting it all rather archaically (as far as material form and language were concerned), he gave us as a result these strange figures stepping as it were out of an illuminated missal, all startlingly alive, all doing things, as if each one had a separate character, with head and heart fixed, and all their senses about them, aware of life.

> "Swerve to the left, son Roger," he said,
> "When you catch his eye through the helmet-slit:
> Swerve to the left, then out at his head,
> And the Lord God give you joy of it!"

That is how one of the poems begins; the story of a rather bad young man fighting in a thoroughly bad quarrel. It is called "The Judgment of God"—and before you have done reading it you want the bad young man to win. A thoroughly immoral poem: but it's alive. (pp. 18-21)

I have said that Morris used archaic forms, and old metrical devices. He did this, I suppose, in order to secure a formal setting for poems mediæval in character. But having made his verse resume the old rich attire, he then plays upon it in such a way as to bring it to new life. (p. 22)

It was Morris's method never to allow the occasional weakness of his technique to bother him. He just took it as it came, and went on, content so long as he got life into the thing. Sometimes he is momentarily quite annoying; often his verse goes lame, sometimes into bad lines, sometimes into bad rhymes. But in that little volume, with all its imperfections and inequalities, the Middle Ages have sprung to life as in no other book that I know; and only in the Pre-Raphaelite spirit and method could it have been done.

It is a method of pictorialism and realistic individualism curiously blended in a decorative setting; to see and to feel are his two main aims. So long as he makes you see, so long as he makes you feel as he wishes you to see and feel, he claims for his poetry that it has done its work. And his contention is, I suppose, very much the contention of those who write "free verse" to-day; so long as you get your result, what matter the means or the technique?

Of his keen visualizing tendency I want to give you one curiously extreme example. It is touch-and-go whether you regard it as success or failure. I myself have been of two minds about it, and I don't know that I thoroughly like it; yet when I last read it to myself, while deciding whether to quote it in this connection, it seemed to me wholly admirable.

It is that passage from "Sir Peter Harpdon's End" where Clisson's Squire has brought word to the Lady Alice that her good Knight has been hanged by the besiegers of his castle, and now lies buried.

> "Wherefore I bring this message: that he waits,
> Still loving you, within the little church
> Whose windows, with the one eye of the light
> Over the altar, every night behold
> The great dim broken walls he strove to keep.
> There my Lord Clisson did his burial well.
> Now, lady, I will go. God give you rest!"

Alice:
> "Thank Clisson from me, Squire; and farewell!
> And now to keep myself from going mad.
> Christ! I have been a many times to church,
> And, ever since my mother taught me prayers,
> Have used them daily; but to-day I wish
> To pray another way. Come face to face,
> O Christ, that I may clasp your knees and pray—
> I know not what: at any rate come now
> From one of many places where you are;
> Either in Heaven amid thick angel wings,
> Or sitting on the altar strange with gems,
> Or high up in the dustiness of the apse:—
> Let us go—you and I, a long way off,
> To the little, damp, dark, Poïtēvin church;
> While you sit on the coffin in the dark,
> I will lie down, my face on the bare stone
> Between your feet, and chatter anything
> I have heard long ago—what matters it,
> So I may keep you there, your solemn face
> And long hair even-flowing on each side,
> Until you love me well enough to speak
> And give me comfort; yea, till o'er your chin
> And cloven red beard the great tears fall down
> In pity for my misery, and I die
> Kissed over by you."

There is your Pre-Raphaelite picture, with its strange blend of detailed externality and intense inwardness of feeling. The method is full of candour, and *naïveté*, touched now and again with crudity; but that result could not be obtained by the mere following of a recipe, in which candour and *naïveté* were the prescribed ingredients—it requires also a great pressure of feeling, of sincerity and conviction, before anything so consistently good as these poems can come out of it.

Amongst other qualities they show a deep reverence for life, and especially for life that proves itself noble under adverse circumstances. Knights in prison, knights who die a felon's death, knights who fight well in a wrong cause; knights in feeble old age remembering lost strength and vanished beauty; and a constantly recurring sense of the civilizing touch which love and chivalry toward women had laid upon that rough age whose essentials these poems sought to reconstruct. (pp. 24-7)

I have taken this single book of the early poems of William Morris as my main illustration, partly because I think its beauty is insufficiently recognized, partly because in no other does the spirit of the Pre-Raphaelite movement so clearly declare itself.

In his later life Morris became a designer of patterns and a weaver of textiles and tapestries, and the craft of the loom found its way into his verse; thenceforth his poems, graceful and visual though they remained, became too spun out, too much the outcome of a recipe to retain the full Pre-Raphaelite flavour, with its headstrong qualities of enthusiasm and youth.

English Pre-Raphaelitism was but a phase, a passing revival, full of weakness and mannerisms in its mode of setting forth. But what it stands for is, I believe, something which, in one form or another, will forever recur in the evolution both of poetry and of painting. You can't shut out romance from the human heart; you can't shut out wonder. And the romance and the wonder of life will always find in Art an instrument ready to hand. It may all be illusion, but if it is, so is life. (p. 29)

Laurence Housman, "Pre-Raphaelitism in Art and Poetry," in Essays by Divers Hands, n.s. Vol. XII, 1933, pp. 1-29.

Dante Gabriel Rossetti's painting The Blessed Damozel, *which illustrates his poem of the same title. Lady Lever Art Gallery, Port Sunlight.*

STEPHEN SPENDER

[*Spender, an English poet and critic, discusses the integral connections between Pre-Raphaelite literature and art, focusing on the works of Millais, Hunt, and Dante Gabriel Rossetti.*]

Questions which have puzzled many people about the Pre-Raphaelites all have [the] . . . aim of isolating from the propaganda of the movement and its supporters and opponents, from the behaviour and history of personalities, the right real thing, the essential Pre-Raphaelite achievement, and attempting to estimate its significance. What was the true aim of Pre-Raphaelitism? Is the supposed Pre-Raphaelite quality in the works of the Pre-Raphaelite artists an aesthetically distinguishing feature, or is it superficial and almost irrelevant? If there are such things as specifically Pre-Raphaelite works of art, how do they compare with works produced by other artists belonging to other movements? Do we accept the definition of Pre-Raphaelitism invented by the Pre-Raphaelites, or shall we discover that really the movement was united by some common factor or factors quite other than their declared aims? (p. 125)

[The] inspiration of Pre-Raphaelitism was verbal, literary, poetic, rather than of painting. The influence which the Pre-Raphaelites shared far more than their pedantic formulæ for the technique of painting were Keats's "Isabella" and "La

Belle Dame Sans Merci." Keats, Shakespeare, the Bible, Dante, suggested to them the subjects and scenery of their pictures. The truest experience which they shared was literary, and Millais betrayed the Pre-Raphaelites not when he abandoned their rules for imitating nature, but when he lost touch with the Pre-Raphaelite communication with the spirit of Romantic poetry and produced paintings which were as badly poetic as *The North-West Passage* and *Bubbles*.

It is understandable, therefore, that Pre-Raphaelitism went out of fashion at a time when painters and critics demanded an unmitigated painter's vision in painting; and that it has become rather fashionable again now that literature has crept back into painting by the back door of Surrealism.

If one were to ask what is the supreme example of Pre-Raphaelite achievement, the answer would surely be some such poem as Tennyson's "Mariana," with pictures such as this:

> About a stone-cast from the wall
>   A sluice with blackened waters slept,
> And o'er it many, round and small,
>   The clustered marish-mosses crept.
> Hard by a poplar shook alway,
>   All silver-green with gnarled bark
>   For leagues no other tree did mark
> The level waste, the rounding gray. . .

Nothing could be more perfect here than the creation of detail which stimulates the inward eye of the reader as with a muscular movement. Again, in the "Lady of Shalott":

> Willows whiten, aspens quiver,
> Little breezes dusk and shiver . . .

The reader creates a picture of this out of his own store of memories of things half seen which he is now stimulated to see as though for the first time. Yet it is literary observation, too sharply emphasized on one detail of expression for painting, for the painter's skill unlike the poet's lies in suggesting detail by giving the whole landscape, instead of suggesting a landscape by evoking one detail. There is a difference of emphasis between the poetic effect and the effect in painting. Poetry must be sharp and particular exactly in the situation where painting must be vague. What could be more perfect in poetry than Shakespeare's famous 'the swallow dares.' The force of this is that it gives us a thrilling sensation of the word 'dares.' True, the swallow does 'dare' to come at the approach of summer, but how passionate, tender, warm, are the feelings which crystallize around this word 'dare,' which seems keen and sensitive as though balanced on a razor edge of meaning when used in conjunction with the swallow, soaring in a heaven of our minds, as it seems.

Yet imagine painting the audacious swallow, and one envisages at once the difference between the poet's and the painter's visual imagination. Detail in poetry is an illusion of particularity, it is a generalized conception imprisoned within narrow limits of sensation. The aspens that quiver and the little breezes that dusk and shiver are aspens and breezes that the reader thinks for himself, though sharpened and shaded by Tennyson to the pitch of poignancy. Paint them and they become what the artist sets before the onlooker's eyes. The limitation of poetry is that the poet can, in fact, never make the reader see exactly what he sees in his own mind; he can only stimulate him to focus the same sensations around an object which is really an invisible *x* in a kind of equation of qualifying experience. It is the sensation of *quivering* and *dusking* and *shiv-*

ering that sets up a shudder of comprehension in the reader's whole being as it focuses upon an object which it projects.

Thus, the attempt to paint poetry according to the Pre-Raphaelite formula of truth makes the mistake of *copying* poetry in painting. To-day the Victorian criticisms of the Pre-Raphaelites amaze us. They are nearly all devoted to attacking the distorted faces and bodies of the figures in Pre-Raphaelite paintings. The most famous of all these attacks is Dickens's in *Household Words* on Millais's *Carpenter's Shop*. He describes the figure of the Virgin Mother as

> a kneeling woman so horrible in her ugliness that (supposing it were possible for any human creature to exist for a moment with that dislocated throat) she would stand out from the rest of the company as a monster in the vilest cabaret in France or the lowest gin-shop in England.

The extravagance of this and other attacks should not blind us to the fact that there is a certain truth in them which we ignore, because we have long grown accustomed to discount the expressions of the Pre-Raphaelite figures which are usually irrelevant or disconcerting, so that we look to Pre-Raphaelite pictures for other qualities. Yet the Victorian attacks point to a very fundamental criticism of Pre-Raphaelite painting. This is, that the Pre-Raphaelite 'truth to nature,' that is to say, photographic exactitude, fails when it attempts to illustrate poetic truth and produces effects of ugliness, absurdity and inane irrelevance in the paintings which followed strictly the Pre-Raphaelite formulæ. There is a youthfulness and sincerity about Millais's early work (Millais was obviously a very nice person) which puts his later painting in the shade: yet *The Carpenter's Shop* is on the wrong tack because it fails to create visual symbols: instead it introduces truth on two contradictory levels, poetic atmosphere and an attempt to create photographic likenesses of the Virgin Mother, Joseph and Our Lord. Poetic truth and photography are at war in it as in so many Pre-Raphaelite paintings. The Pre-Raphaelite formula for painting *The Carpenter's Shop* was to get every detail of a carpenter's shop right, buy a sheep's head from the local butcher's and paint several dozen of it, crowding each other out in such a way that one did not have to paint any of the sheep's body (which the butcher could not provide) then find a suitable carpenter and a suitable Mary and a suitable Christ, get them to have the right dramatic expression on their faces, and paint it exactly. Often one notices in Pre-Raphaelite painting that just when the painter should be endowed with transcendant imagination, the model is expected to supply it by assuming an expression which the painter then imitates, with perfect truth to nature. Much of Pre-Raphaelite painting is just painted charades or dumb crambo by friends of the Pre-Raphaelites dressed up to fill the rôles.

Rossetti, however, who never followed the Pre-Raphaelite precepts so rigidly observed by Holman Hunt, was a poet who invented poetic symbols in painting. If one grants that *The Light of the World* and the *Scapegoat,* with their vacuous expressions, are faithful to the letter of Pre-Raphaelitism, it is Rossetti who really understood something of the spirit of fourteenth-century poetry in his painting. He was by nature a poetic symbolist painter. The crowded repetitious objects in his paintings are put there not because they are considered necessary according to the Pre-Raphaelite precepts, but because he collected objects which he loved, and their images in his pictures are crystallizations of aspects of his own personality, having the same symbolic significance of a projected egotism as the tower, the sword, the winding stair, etc., in the poetry of Yeats.

Rossetti, who was truly a literary painter—with all the limitations and defects of one—hated painting out of doors, regarded Holman Hunt's painstaking pilgrimages to Palestine and elsewhere as ludicrous, cared little for the countryside, collected bric-à-brac, was as far removed from the 'nature artist' as it is possible to imagine anyone being; he was a lovable and rather monstrous personality.

Romantic poetry then was and is the 'irreducible mystery' of Pre-Raphaelitism, a poetry that lends a strange beauty to the work of some of the minor Pre-Raphaelites, such as the exquisite *Death of Chatterton* in the Tate Gallery. A thin vein of poetry shines through the early painting of Millais, though I find it difficult to regard Millais as a 'traitor' to Pre-Raphaelitism, for he was too much a painter to be a poetic illustrator like Rossetti, and, of course, too much a painter also to be a fanatic of obsessive rules like Holman Hunt. Pre-Raphaelitism introduced him to Keats, but to little else. In his later life, whenever he wished to show that he had not forsaken his Pre-Raphaelite origins, he attempted an illustration of poetry, but the little trickle of poetry of his own had long ago dried up, and, in any case, was not relevant to his great gifts which lay in the direction of painting for its own sake. Advertising is a debased form of poetry, having about the same relation to the real thing as jazz music has to music, and it is natural that the weak poetic painter of *The Carpenter's Shop* and the *Boyhood of Raleigh* should end by painting the most staggeringly successful pictorial advertisement for soap that appeared in the nineteenth century in England. (pp. 126-29)

Rossetti was a poetic illustrator with a highly individualized style of his own. His skill, and that of the lesser Pre-Raphaelites, cannot be compared with the great continental achievements of the time. In painting, most of the Pre-Raphaelites should perhaps be regarded as poetic amateurs corresponding to the charming Sunday painters of France. The æsthetic aims of the movement were too unpainterly to produce anything but amateurs. A larger talent must either break away, like Millais, or unconsciously reveal the absurdity of the movement, like Holman Hunt. The lesser Pre-Raphaelites, Ford Madox Brown, Arthur Hughes and Charles Collins, produced pictures having a charming home-made quality, such as Brown's *The Last of England,* which must be judged as something entirely by itself, not related to any main tradition.

Yet, as Mr. Gaunt points out [see Additional Bibliography], Pre-Raphaelitism, even if not in the main line of achievement, canalized a considerable impulse in English life. This was the resistance of poetic ideas to the nineteenth century and to the Industrial Revolution. There is a clear and pure stream here which flows from Goldsmith's ''Deserted Village'' through the paintings and poetry and letters of Blake and his circle, through the Pre-Raphaelites and Ruskin, William Morris and the early socialist movement to the Aesthetic Movement of the nineties, where it becomes somewhat muddied, but not, in the last analysis, corrupt. Indeed, the strength and the weakness of this tendency in English life is its insistence on the value of a childlike, sometimes childish, innocence. If one compares it with the corresponding stream of imaginative life in France, one sees that the French and the English movements flow in opposite directions.

The difference is that between puritan protestantism and Latin catholicism. The Latin catholic tendency is to accept evil as a reality of existence, damnation as part of the whole human condition and hell as part of the divine hierarchy; the protestant puritan tendency is to refuse to touch evil or to be conscious of having touched it. The Pre-Raphaelites represented the cult of a misconceived mediævalism, an attempted refusal to be contaminated by the modern world which was, in fact, a refusal to recognize that the basic condition of the life of every contemporary is that he is involved in the guilt of the whole society in which he lives. Thus the Pre-Raphaelite poetry maintained the balance of a precarious innocence which was a refusal to recognize facts, an innocence which only Holman Hunt, who never grew up, entirely accepted, which, with Rossetti, toppled over into morbidity, with Ruskin into madness, and which collapsed into the success story of Millais.

Yet somehow the Pre-Raphaelites and even the æsthetes after them, retained a certain innocuousness, an unworldliness, surrounded as their poise, which later became a pose, was with abysses. The sins of Rossetti and Wilde were the sins of children, and so were their punishments. Under his veneer of worldly wisdom and cynicism, Oscar Wilde also retained the belief in youth and innocent purity and, when he had failed to preserve his ideal, he sought out punishment. Never did a man so openly court retribution for a crime which, after all, society need never have noticed.

One of the worst penalties of Pre-Raphaelitism was that it cut English painting almost completely off from the continent. In his volume *The Aesthetic Adventure* Mr. Gaunt amusingly shows how little the English artists who went to Paris at the end of the century knew of the great movement in French art.

The French view of life was exactly the opposite of that of the English. It was, in brief, the idea of redemption through corruption with the world instead of self-preservation from corruption. Criticisms of both attitudes can, with justice, be made. But it may be said in favour of the movements in French art and literature during the nineteenth century that the poets and artists did not lay themselves and their work open to the charge that they were too inexperienced, innocent, unworldly for this era of industry and commerce and great scientific purposes. The French artists wrung their triumphs of transcendant beauty from a hard realization of the standards of the age in which they lived. Thus, more than any other people in the world, they saved poetry and painting from the most dangerous of all charges that have been laid against the arts in England; that they belonged to a childishly imaginative and undeveloped level of consciousness which man had outgrown in the scientific and industrial era of Victoria, and of Bismarck, and of Napoleon III. (pp. 129-31)

> *Stephen Spender, "The Pre-Raphaelite Literary Painters," in* New Writing and Daylight, *No. 6, September, 1945, pp. 123-31.*

D. S. R. WELLAND

[*Welland discusses the importance of social and moral concerns, detail, and medievalism to the painting and writing of Dante Gabriel Rossetti, Ford Madox Brown, Hunt, Millais, Morris, and Burne-Jones.*]

Robert Buchanan, the bitterest opponent of Pre-Raphaelite ideals, committed himself to the generalization, "The truth is that literature, and more particularly poetry, is in a very bad way when one art gets hold of another, and imposes upon it its conditions and limitations." He is writing as a literary critic, and his prejudice is disclosed by the assertion that "Poetry is something more than painting." This falacious value-comparison of the two arts, current in the Victorian period, is echoed

by Oscar Wilde's opinion that the prose appreciations of Ruskin and Pater were greater than the pictures that inspired them:

> . . . greater, I always think, even as Literature is the greater art. Who, again, cares whether Mr. Pater has put into the portrait of Monna Lisa something that Lionardo never dreamed of? . . . And so the picture becomes more wonderful to us than it really is, and reveals to us a secret of which, in truth, it knows nothing, and the music of the mystical prose is as sweet in our ears as was the flute-player's music that lent to the lips of La Gioconda those subtle and poisonous curves.

Ruskin on one occasion classifies painters in the belief that

> . . . a certain distinction must generally exist between men who, like Horace Vernet, David, or Domenico Tintoret, would employ themselves in painting, more or less graphically, the outward verities of passing events—battles, councils, etc.—of their day (who, supposing them to work worthily of their mission, would become, properly so called, historical or narrative painters); and men who sought, in scenes of perhaps less outward importance, "noble grounds for noble emotion";—who would be, in a separate sense, *political* painters, some of them taking for subjects events which had actually happened, and others themes from the poets; or, better still, becoming poets themselves in the entire sense, and inventing the story as they painted it. Painting seems to me only just to be beginning, in this sense also, to take its proper position beside literature, and the pictures of the *Awakening Conscience, Huguenot,* and such others, to be the first fruits of its new effort.

Implicit in this is a characteristically Victorian moral judgement: literature is superior to painting in proportion to its greater power of creating "noble grounds for noble emotion," or, as Arnold put it, of "forming, sustaining and delighting us." Painting is seen as less capable of the positive, didactic communication of an uplifting moral message; it is thus an inferior art which must not be allowed to "get hold of" poetry.

Less inhibited than Buchanan by these moral considerations, we may be in a better position to seize the opportunity offered by the Pre-Raphaelites—unique in English literature except for Blake—of studying the inter-relationship between the two arts when both are practised concurrently by the same artists. Without Buchanan's prejudice, we may find that the interaction of the two is more complex than the mere imposition upon poetry of the "conditions and limitations" of painting. It is a two-way process, and in many respects poetry gains more by it than does Pre-Raphaelite painting, which is often overburdened by excessive literariness. (pp. 13-14)

PRE-RAPHAELITE BOOK ILLUSTRATION

It was, of course, in painting that Pre-Raphaelitism received its first impetus, and from art that it took its name, a nickname half jestingly applied to Hunt and Millais and adopted by them in a spirit of defiance. Dissatisfaction with what seemed to them the stereotyped artificiality of subject painting since Joshua Reynolds' Presidency of the Royal Academy at the end of the previous century had led them to seek their inspiration in a tradition other than that inaugurated by Raphael. Ruskin in *Modern Painters* had voiced a plea in 1843 for the introduction of motivating ideas into art, and this occurred also to the Pre-Raphaelites as a means of re-vitalizing subject-painting. Their insistence on every picture telling a story was the first step towards the affiliation of painting and literature and was to become even more important than their avowed adherence to Reynolds' neglected counsel of following nature. However perfunctory subject-painting may have become in the first half of the nineteenth century—and its unnaturalness has often been well-meaningly exaggerated—the landscape painting of Constable and Turner had followed nature closely enough to make Pre-Raphaelite naturalism less new than their literariness.

The pictures that best tell a story are book illustrations, and the favourite source for these was Shakespeare. Hunt's *Two Gentlemen of Verona*, Millais' *Death of Ophelia*, and Madox Brown's *Cordelia's Portion* are the best known, but Rossetti attempted many scenes, mostly from the tragedies, while Millais and Hughes both treated Ferdinand and Ariel in oils. Similarities of composition, particularly in the central figure, in these two pictures demonstrate the closeness of connection between the Pre-Raphaelites, as does the magnificent richness of colour in the skirts of Millais' *Mariana* and Hughes' *April Love*. After Shakespeare Keats was a fertile inspiration for Hunt's *Isabella*, Millais' fine *Lorenzo and Isabella* (which gains added interest by its use of members of the Brotherhood as models), and for minor works by others. Among contemporary poets they illustrated Browning and Edgar Allen Poe (especially in Rossetti's earliest period), Christina Rossetti, Allingham, and, most notably, Tennyson. The famous Moxon edition of his poems published in 1857 contained work by Millais, Hunt, and Rossetti, as well as other famous Victorian painters.

Writing to Allingham in 1855 about this venture, Rossetti puts his finger on the chief danger of illustration:

> I have not begun even designing for them yet, but fancy I shall try the *Vision of Sin*, and *Palace of Art*, etc.—those where one can allegorize on one's own hook, without killing for oneself and everyone a distinct idea of the poet's.

His designs for *The Palace of Art*, executed by the Dalziel brothers, have deservedly become classics of Victorian book illustration, for they have a spontaneity and originality that would have been impossible had he chosen such a poem as "Mariana," which is pictorially complete in the Pre-Raphaelite manner as it stands:

> With blackest moss the flower-plots
> Were thickly crusted, one and all:
> The rusted nails fell from the knots
> That held the pear to the gable-wall.
> The broken sheds look'd sad and strange:
> Unlifted was the clinking latch;
> Weeded and worn the ancient thatch
> Upon the lonely moated grange.
> She only said, 'My life is dreary,
> He cometh not,' she said;
> She said, 'I am aweary, aweary,
> I would that I were dead!'

Richly pictorial poets do not lend themselves to illustration, and the Brotherhood's admiration for Tennyson and Keats shows itself more satisfactorily in their writing.

This desire to "allegorize on one's own hook" explains Rossetti's preference for Dante as a subject for illustration: time and again he turned to the theme of Dante and Beatrice, feeling a strong affinity with the poet whose name he bore and whose work he had studied and translated, and using the situations of that story as the vehicle for the communication of his own passionate intensity. Such works as his *Dantis Amor* and the celebrated *Beata Beatrix* are far more than illustrations: they

have become expressions of a personal emotion and a mystical awareness of love that are enhanced by their literary reference instead of being subservient to it. Elizabeth Siddal is more than the model for Beatrice: she takes on the identity of Beatrice in these paintings in a wholly successful and deeply moving way, and here, far from cramping the painter's original genius, the literary subject has fired it and brought it to consummate perfection. Something of the same sort is true, though less unfailingly, of Rossetti's response to Arthurian themes.

The desire to allegorize is common to all the Pre-Raphaelites in their anxiety to transcend the limitations of illustration. Depicting an episode is not wholly the same thing as telling a story or expressing a motivating idea: to do this some machinery of reference is necessary, by which the rest of the story can be brought to the reader's mind, and this need they met by their use of significant details or "inventions" as they called them. Thus Millais' *Christ in the House of His Parents* is much more than the portrayal of an incident in the boyhood of Christ: the blood on the boy's injured palm that has dripped on to his foot prefigures the Crucifixion, just as the dove perched on a ladder at the back has a Pentecostal reference and the flock of shepherdless sheep outside the door extends still further the picture's allusiveness. Sometimes the method was employed with less subtlety than here, as in Rossetti's heraldically colourful *Wedding of St George and the Princess Sabra* where the earlier part of the story is indicated by the incongruous introduction into the bridal chamber of a grotesque dragon's head in a wooden box. Sometimes it is too subtle, as in Hunt's *The Hireling Shepherd* which can so easily be enjoyed as a sensuous study of bucolic courtship that the spectator may learn with some surprise of Hunt's conception of it as "a rebuke to the sectarian vanities and vital negligencies of the day," the shepherd representing "muddle-headed pastors."

Always the affinities between painting and writing were uppermost in their minds. If their painting was not an illustration to a piece of literature they would either compose a sonnet for their picture, as Rossetti did for *Found* and his two pictures of the Virgin and as Madox Brown did for *Work*, or they would elucidate the theme of a picture in prose comment, as Madox Brown also did for *Work* and as Holman Hunt did throughout his memoir. In January 1850 they brought out the first number of *The Germ*, a regrettably short-lived monthly which, in changing its title to *Art and Poetry* in March, defined its aim thus:

> Of the little worthy the name of writing that has ever been written upon the principles of Art, (of course excepting that on the mere mechanism), a very small portion is by Artists themselves; and that is so scattered, that one scarcely knows where to find the ideas of an Artist except in his pictures.
>
> With a view to obtain the thoughts of Artists, upon Nature as evolved in Art, in another language besides their *own proper* one, this Periodical has been established. Thus, then, it is not open to the conflicting opinions of all who handle the brush and palette, nor is it restricted to actual practitioners; but is intended to enunciate the principles of those who, in the true spirit of Art, enforce a rigid adherence to the simplicity of Nature either in Art or Poetry, and consequently regardless whether emanating from practical Artists, or from those who have studied nature in the Artist's School [see first excerpt by Tupper above].

This is as near as the Pre-Raphaelites came to the publication of a manifesto except in F. G. Stephens' essay on "The Purpose and Tendency of Early Italian Art'' in the second number of *The Germ.*

''The truth is that it is too good for the time. It is not *material* enough for the age,'' was the verdict of one reviewer upon the first two numbers. W. M. Rossetti, its editor, records that in November 1849 the Brotherhood ''spoke of not admitting anything at all referring to politics or religion'' into *The Germ,* and it is tempting to see this apparent indifference to social problems as the cause of its failure and as a besetting sin of the whole movement. Millais, whose early reputation as a boy-genius and whose facility of execution had brought a greater degree of popular recognition than the others had enjoyed, was soon turning out the accomplished, commercialized subject-pictures like *The Boyhood of Raleigh* and the *Bubbles* that became a soap-advertisement, pictures devoid of any reference to the world about him, but these are not Pre-Raphaelite in spirit at all. 'Escapist' as it has often been dubbed, the original Brotherhood was not as far removed from actuality as its detractors imply. The point merits some attention.

PRE-RAPHAELITISM AND CONTEMPORARY
SOCIETY

The world into which Pre-Raphaelitism was born was far from pleasant. 1848 has been characterized as ''the year of great and general revolt.'' At the beginning of the year there was serious apprehension of a French invasion. Then in February revolution broke out in Paris and Louis Philippe was overthrown. Rioting continued sporadically in France, and civil war raged in Hungary, in Austria, in Poland, and in Italy. This conflict of ideologies and classes throughout Europe is best epitomized by one fact: 1848 saw the publication of the Communist Manifesto by Karl Marx and Friedrich Engels. England was in the grip of the 'hungry forties': it was the aftermath of the Industrial Revolution, when working-class unrest had found expression in the Chartist risings. The panic-stricken fears of mob-violence that these aroused in higher levels of society had inspired *Barnaby Rudge* in 1841; they survive as the nightmare ideas of the Reign of Terror in *A Tale of Two Cities* (1859) and were still implicit ten years after that in Arnold's *Culture and Anarchy.* But domestic uneasiness was not only due to political causes: in 1848 the dangers of over-industrialization were emphasized in the grim form of an outbreak of cholera.

It is easy to criticize Millais' attitude, but less easy to define what the creative artist should be doing in the face of such events. Should he record them dispassionately, criticize them analytically, or ignore them entirely? On this point the Pre-Raphaelites, like all their contemporaries, were divided. W. M. Rossetti mentions a burlesque poem of his brother's, *The English Revolution of 1848,* which ''ridicules the street-spoutings of Chartists and others in that year of vast continental upheavals.'' Twenty years were to elapse before the publication of William Morris's *The Earthly Paradise,* but some familiar lines from that effectively indicate the æsthetic antidote to the squalor, misery, and unrest of the time that Pre-Raphaelitism at its best represents:

> Forget six counties overhung with smoke,
> Forget the snorting steam and piston stroke,
> Forget the spreading of the hideous town;
> Think rather of the packhorse on the down,
> And dream of London, small, and white, and clean
> The clear Thames bordered by its gardens green.

We are to forget the ugliness of mid-Victorian England, but we are still to think of London—the idyllically purified London of Morris's medieval dream-world or, in *News From Nowhere,*

the London that might follow the universal acceptance of Morris's vision. The æstheticism of Rossetti and Burne-Jones is not a creed of 'Art for Art's sake,' though in some ways they anticipate the 1890's; rather is it a spirited reassertion of those principles of colour, beauty, love, and cleanness that the drab, agitated, discouraging world of the mid-nineteenth century needed so much. It is more accurately defined as a protest against existing conditions than as an escape from them, a protest none the less sincere for the preference of some of its exponents for a world of the æsthetic imagination.

Among the early Pre-Raphaelites the one whose paintings are most clearly based on contemporary events was Ford Madox Brown. *The Last of England* and its accompanying sonnet comment on the prevalent emigrations, but more important in this respect is the larger canvas *Work* which celebrates the truly Victorian theme of honest toil. Brown's sonnet for it begins with the lines:

> Work, which beads the brow and tans the flesh
> Of lusty manhood, casting out its devils,
> By whose weird art transmuting poor men's evils,
> Their bed seems down, their one dish ever fresh.

Unemployment is represented as the only evil, and the excavating labourers are held up for admiration as the pillars of English society, while for the ragged, shifty-looking flower-collector in the left foreground our sympathy is invited in Brown's commentary as ''the ragged wretch who has never been *taught* to *work.*'' Here again, for all its social comment, the genesis of the picture is incorrigibly literary. First-hand acquaintance with less-contented artisans might have disabused Brown of his conviction that employment was all that mattered to keep ''their one dish ever fresh,'' but the picture leaves no doubt as to the source of that illusion. The two men in the right foreground, ''the brainworkers'' who ''seeming to be idle, work, and are the cause of well-ordained work in others,'' are Thomas Carlyle and Frederick Denison Maurice. The ragged wretch has heedlessly passed a poster advertizing Maurice's Working Men's College, while the sandwich-men bear placards urging electoral support for Bobus. The identity of Bobus is to be traced to Chapter IV of the Proem to Carlyle's *Past and Present,* where he is a ''Sausage-maker on the great scale . . . with his cash accounts and larders dropping fatness, with his respectabilities, warm garnitures, and pony chaise,'' the Victorian bourgeois capitalist who is always ''raising such a clamour for this Aristocracy of Talent'' which Carlye demonstrates as non-existent. Small wonder that Rossetti described *Work* as full of ''all kinds of Carlylianisms,'' for this doctrine of the blessedness of work even if it means the renunciation of happiness is the Everlasting Yea of *Sartor Resartus:*

> Close thy *Byron;* open thy *Goethe.* . . . there is in man a *higher* than Love of Happiness: he can do without Happiness, and instead thereof find Blessedness! . . . Most true is it, as a wise man teaches us, that ''Doubt of any sort cannot be removed except by Action'' . . . Produce! Produce! Were it but the pitifulest infinitesimal fraction of a Product, produce it in God's name! 'Tis the utmost thou hast in thee: out with it then. Up, up! Whatsoever thy hand findeth to do, do it with thy whole might.

To the modern reader there is a certain unreality in this shrilly-enunciated doctrine, and that unreality is intensified when it is retailed to us second-hand in Brown's painting, for all its technical interest. The doctrine was, moreover, being questioned even when the picture was being painted (1852-1865), for in

1851 Ruskin had begun his pamphlet *Pre-Raphaelitism* with the words:

> It may be proved, with much certainty, that God intends no man to live in this world without working: but it seems to me no less evident that He intends every man to be happy in his work.

That this is closer to the belief of the other Pre-Raphaelites may be shown by the juxtaposition of this passage written by Morris in a pamphlet in 1887:

> Therefore the Aim of Art is to increase the happiness of men, by giving them beauty and interest of incident to amuse their leisure, and prevent them wearying even of rest, and by giving them hope and bodily pleasure in their work; or, shortly, to make man's work happy and his rest fruitful.

Morris goes on to point out that "art is, and must be, either in its abundance or its barrenness, in its sincerity or its hollowness, the expression of the society amongst which it exists." It is on that realization that all his later work is founded, for his preoccupation with the dream-world of romance had led him back inexorably to the society of the present, about which he knew far more and knew it more realistically than ever Carlyle did.

Some awareness of the limitations of Carlyle's influence is perhaps implicit in *Work,* for, speaking of the rich man on the horse, Brown writes:

> . . . could he only be got to hear what the sages in the corner have to say, I have no doubt he would be easily won over. But the road is blocked. . . .

Does Brown intend, in the composition of his picture, to hint at the inability of the Carlyles and the Maurices to establish contact with the upper, influential classes of society? The commentary does not increase our enjoyment of the picture even if it extends our understanding by revealing the unsuspected complexity of its potential 'messages.' Pleasing as the design is, it may be that Brown attempts too much in it and allows social significance to interfere with its æsthetic appeal. Even his grandson, usually staunch in his admiration, complains that it is "difficult for the eye to find a point on which to settle."

The concluding pages of Holman Hunt's *Pre-Raphaelitism and the Pre-Raphaelite Brotherhood* show his recognition of the relation between art and society, but show too that he thought of that relation in moral terms:

> All art from the beginning served for the higher development of men's minds. It has ever been valued as food to sustain strength for noble resolves, not as that devoured by epicures only to surfeit the palate.

The Awakened Conscience is Hunt's best practical expression of this belief, and like many other Pre-Raphaelite pictures its morality has a dual source of literary inspiration in the Bible and in contemporary writing:

> When *The Light of the World* was on my easel at Chelsea in 1851, it occurred to me that my spiritual subject called for a material counterpart in a picture representing in actual life the manner in which the appeal of the spirit of heavenly love calls a soul to abandon a lower life. In reading *David Copperfield* I had been deeply touched by the pathos of the search by old Peggotty after little Emily, when she had become an outcast, and I went about to different haunts of fallen girls to find a locality suitable for the scene of the old mariner's pursuing love. My object was

John Everett Millais's Mariana, *an illustration for Alfred, Lord Tennyson's poem of the same name.*

not to illustrate any special incident in the book, but to take the suggestion of the loving seeker of the fallen girl coming upon the object of his search. I spoke freely of this intended subject, but, while cogitating upon the broad intention, I reflected that the instinctive eluding of pursuit by the erring one would not coincide with the willing conversion and instanteous resolve for a higher life which it was necessary to emphasise.

As Hunt himself points out, the theme of the lover finding his former sweetheart as a prostitute was treated by Rossetti pictorially and in sonnet form under the title *Found.* The drawing for the never-completed oil painting is an excellent example of his draughtsmanship, but Hunt is right in seeing that this situation lends itself to pathos and pity rather than to the moral earnestness at which Hunt aimed: it remains a moving, human story, which is how the twentieth century will see many of these pictures, finding their didacticism embarrassingly overemphasized. The sonnet, with its Keats quotation, sentimentalizes the subject far more than the drawing does. Hunt continues:

> While recognising this, I fell upon the text in Proverbs, "As he that taketh away a garment in cold weather, so is he that singeth songs to a heavy heart." These words, expressing the unintended stirring up of the deeps of pure affection by the idle sing-song of an empty mind, led me to see how the companion of the girl's fall might himself be the unconscious utterer of a divine message. In scribbles I arranged the two figures to present the woman recalling the memory of her childish home, and breaking away from her gilded cage with a startled holy resolve,

while her shallow companion still sings on, ignorantly intensifying her repentant purpose.

In characteristic Pre-Raphaelite manner the moral of this picture is underlined by 'inventions': the cruelty of the human
situation is copied in the cat who plays beneath the table with
a maimed and dying bird, the discarded glove suggests the
eventual discarding of the mistress by the seducer, the freshness
of the mirrored garden scene contrasts with the oppressive
luxury of the interior of gilded iniquity. Ruskin exclaimed with
enthusiasm:

> There is not a single object in all that room—com-
> mon, modern, vulgar (in the vulgar sense, as it may
> be), but it becomes tragical, if rightly read . . . nay,
> the very hem of the poor girl's dress, at which the
> painter has laboured so closely, thread by thread, has
> story in it, if we think how soon its pure whiteness
> may be soiled with dust and rain, her outcast feet
> failing in the street.

This is allowing the fancy excessive liberty, but Hunt and the
Brotherhood must have approved wholeheartedly this way of
"reading" a picture for the "story in it." Yet, valuable as
these contributory factors are, the real key to the situation so
dramatically presented is a literary one, and is to be found in
the title of the song on the music-rest: it is Thomas Moore's
"Oft in the Stilly Night," the nostalgic fragrance of which is
in perfect harmony with the picture's mood and evokes the
sentimentalism that Hunt manages to stiffen with his moral
comment:

> Oft in the stilly night,
>   Ere slumber's chain has bound me,
> Fond Memory brings the light
>   Of other days around me:
>   The smiles, the tears
>   Of boyhood's years,
>   The words of love then spoken;
>   The eyes that shone,
>   Now dimm'd and gone,
>   The cheerful hearts now broken!

There is also a roll of music in the case on the floor in the left
foreground, and from what is visible of its title it would appear
to be a setting of Tennyson's "Tears, Idle Tears," a lyric that
had been published in *The Princess* only five years before Hunt
began work on *The Awakened Conscience*, but which, for the
spectator who has the familiarity with it that Hunt expected,
epitomizes the mood and heightens the poignancy of the situation very effectively:

> Tears, idle tears, I know not what they mean,
> Tears from the depth of some divine despair
> Rise in the heart and gather to the eyes,
>
> .   .   .   .   .
>
> Dear as remember'd kisses after death,
> And sweet as those by hopeless fancy feign'd
> On lips that are for others; deep as love,
> Deep as first love, and wild with all regret;
> Oh Death in Life, the days that are no more.

The whole passage has a striking relevance to the picture, yet
it is only incidentally introduced into it and might easily be
overlooked.

If *The Awakened Conscience* is a literary painting, a poem that
challenges comparison with it, Rossetti's "Jenny," is essentially the product of a painter, despite the literary suggestion
of its Shakespearian epigraph. Less Browningesque than "A
Last Confession," it has a sincerity and individuality, and a

kindly tolerance not wholly to be expected of that time. What
is admirable is the alternation between sentiment and realism,
between a warm sympathy for the individual and an involuntary
shrinking from the degradation she embodies, as well as the
suspicion of moral judgment which still does not condone
the way of life, and the tempering of romanticism with quiet
irony in such lines as

> Poor shameful Jenny, full of grace
> Thus with your head upon my knee;
> Whose person or whose purse may be
> The lodestar of your reverie?

The complexity of the attitude to the prostitute is true to life;
the method of presentation and its unforcedly easy colloquial
manner suggest the actual process of thought. Dramatic as it
is, a scene like this is unmistakably a painter's composition,
and a Pre-Raphaelite painter's:

> Why, there's the dawn!
>
> And there's an early waggon drawn
> To market, and some sheep that jog
> Bleating before a barking dog;
> And the old streets come peering through
> Another night that London knew;
> And all as ghost-like as the lamps.
>
>   Soon the wings of day decamps
> My last night's frolic. Glooms begin
> To shiver off as lights creep in
> Past the gauze curtains half drawn-to,
> And the lamp's doubled shade grows blue,
> Your lamp, my Jenny, kept alight
> Like a wise virgin's, all one night!
> And in the alcove cooly spread
> Glimmers with dawn your empty bed;
> And yonder your fair face I see
> Reflected lying on my knee,
> Where teems with faint foreshadowings
> Your pier-glass scrawled with diamond rings:
> And on your bosom all night worn
> Yesterday's rose now droops forlorn,
> But dies not yet this summer morn.
>
>   And now without, as if some word
> Had called upon them that they heard,
> The London sparrows far and nigh
> Clamour together suddenly;
> And Jenny's cage-bird grown awake.
> Here in their song his part must take,
> Because here too the day doth break.

The convenient placing of a mirror so that the reflected image
can play its part in the picture recalls the Dutch school, but it
will be found similarly used in Madox Brown's unfinished
Take your son, Sir!, in Holman Hunt's *Lady of Shalott*, and,
more significantly, in *The Awakened Conscience*. There is the
painter's eye for light and the same dramatic use of the cold
greyness of dawn that was to have set the keynote of *Found*
with its subject so similar to this—"London's smokeless resurrection light," as he described it in the sonnet—and the sheep
in this passage are fulfilling a symbolic function similar to that
of the tied calf in *Found* as well as recalling the market references elsewhere in "Jenny". Here, too, are all the other
'inventions' that would have had their place in a painting of
the scene: the lamp still alight (with an ironical glancing Biblical allusion), the drooping rose which also has its relation to
the flower-imagery throughout, and the caged bird singing because he must. If these things recall *The Awakened Conscience*,
so too does the device of using the purity of external nature
to contrast with the impurity within: there it was the reflected

garden, here it is the London sparrows and the drooping rose. One of the most felicitous instances of the complete fusion of painting and poetry, this is the key passage in the poem and it gains greatly from the pictorial associations it evokes.

This theme of the fallen woman had a peculiar attraction for the Pre-Raphaelites. Hunt devotes a good deal of time to demonstrating that *The Awakened Conscience* was complete before *Found* was begun, Ruskin's correspondence with Rossetti believes it, while William Bell Scott in his *Autobiographical Notes* asserts that *Found* was first thought of as an illustration to his own "Rosabell," a poetically uneven product of what Buchanan would have called the "sub-Tennysonian school." Which of these came first is a matter of minor importance; more worthy of attention is their common interest in the theme. That one source of this is moral has been seen already, but Millais' pen-and-ink *Retribution,* with its sharply delineated agonizing conflict of emotion, by changing the setting throws fresh light on the subject. Here the seducer is confronted in the presence of his horrified wife and curious maidservant by his mistress and their illegitimate children, and illicit sexual relations are denounced for their violation of the sanctity of the home. The Victorian apotheosis of the domestic virtues was at its height at this time. The year 1854, which saw the exhibiting of *The Awakened Conscience,* is the date of *Retribution* and also of the beginning of Coventry Patmore's *The Angel in the House.* Already art was being assessed by its suitability for family consumption; family fiction was established, and Trollope had begun the writing of those novels for which he was later to claim with pride, "I do believe that no girl has risen from the reading of my pages less modest than she was before"; while in music the forms most characteristic of the age were the piano solo and the sentimental ballad—domestic forms, simple enough for convincing amateur performance and not over-subtle in their emotional appeal. The works of the Pre-Raphaelites and of Patmore, which, as might be expected, had much in common, had the necessary probity to constitute family literature. In his novel, *The Unclassed* (1884), George Gissing allows Waymark to recommend to Maud Enderby at a particular crisis in her emotional development the poems of Rossetti:

> These gave her much help in restoring her mind to quietness. Their perfect beauty entranced her, and the rapturous purity of ideal passion, the mystic delicacies of emotion, which made every verse gleam like a star, held her for the time high above that gloomy cloudland of her being, rife with weird shapes and muffled voices. . . . Rossetti put into utterance for her so much that she had not dared to entrust even to the voice of thought.

Similarly, as late as 1903 in *Man and Superman* Jack Tanner declines in advance "the copies of Patmore's *Angel in the House* in extra morocco" which it was still fashionable to give as wedding presents.

Yet the Pre-Raphaelite treatment of the theme of the fallen woman is not to be attributed solely to a moral championing of marital fidelity. Their paintings show a marked interest in *Measure for Measure,* the play of which Pater was to write so sympathetically later, and for them as for Angelo the sin they denounce has its fascination. Pulling against Victorian morality was the Romantic delight in passion, and it was this passion to which an illogical prudery denied artistic expression even in a conjugal setting. Patmore was accepted only because he sublimated passion into something more ethereal, and when Rossetti's "House of Life" was published in 1870 the outcry against the sonnet "Nuptial Sleep" was so great as to force

its suppression. At the same time the "discreet establishment" was receiving greater publicity from social opprobrium than it had had in the past when its existence had been tacitly ignored, and as Angelo's desire for Isabella was stimulated by his moral indignation against Claudio, so the Pre-Raphaelites became even more conscious of the irrational power of sexual attraction in a society that strove to repress it. Much of their work is characterized by a pent-up passion struggling to confine itself within the romantically idealized bounds of Arthur Hughes's delicate and fragrant *April Love,* in the sentimentalized frustration of his *Long Engagement,* or in the allegorical form of *The Hireling Shepherd,* until here again the cult of medievalism came to the rescue. The convention of courtly love made it possible for William Morris to undertake the *Defence of Guenevere,* the literary associations and background allowed Rossetti to paint the story of Paolo and Francesca as well as the Guinevere theme, and, most valuable of all, gave him in the figures of Dante and Beatrice the perfect symbolic expression of his deepest emotions.

DETAIL IN PRE-RAPHAELITE DESCRIPTION

It was not only the fragile, spiritual beauty of an Elizabeth Siddal that moved Rossetti. Some of his other "stunners" (the word is his own) were of a more sensuous type, and it was his portraying of women such as the Fanny Cornforth of *Found* and the strikingly lovely Jane Morris, wife of the poet, that earned the charge of "fleshliness" from Buchanan. His treatment of these is characterized by the curving rhythmic grace he imparts to them by his accentuation of rich auburn hair, the lushness of the lips, and the stately sweep of the long neck, as well as the sultry use of colour in oils like *Proserpine* or the quite differently bold and brilliant use of it in the luxuriant *The Beloved.* The pose with the head thrown back and the neck elongated, the hair falling in profusion on the shoulders and the eyes charged with emotional intensity, was used so often as to make parody inevitable, and no one could have parodied it less maliciously or more effectively than Max Beerbohm in *Poets' Corner* [see Additional Bibliography]. Yet Rossetti achieved some remarkably powerful effects from it in words as well as in line. . . . "A Last Confession" demands comparison with the exquisite pen and ink study of Mrs Morris: the imagery, the loving detail, and the whole tone is so evocative of the picture as to make the two complementary. Everything is visualized pictorially, and the closing lines extend the portrait into a minute but perfectly drawn landscape where again the light is as important and as clearly defined as it was in "Jenny."

Throughout his poetry Rossetti instinctively describes in pictorial terms anything that his imagination seizes on. It is not a question of "one art getting hold of another" and imposing "upon it its conditions and limitations" so much as of a gifted artist transferring unconsciously to one medium the means of expression he would have used in another. This description of a sick-bed vigil from "My Sister's Sleep" is an example:

> Twelve struck. That sound, by dwindling years
>   Heard in each hour, crept off; and then
>   The ruffled silence spread again,
> Like water that a pebble stirs.
>
> Our mother rose from where she sat;
>   Her needles, as she laid them down,
>   Met lightly, and her silken gown
> Settled: no other noise than that.

Sounds here are described entirely in terms of visual imagery: the sound *crept* off, the *ruffled* silence spreads like the ripples of a pool, and in the second stanza the noises are not suggested by onomatopaeic words like 'clicked' or 'rustled,' but the actual movement is described as it would be seen, and the reader, visualizing it, supplies the sound himself. Again, the sonnet "Silent Noon" may be compared, if we make allowances for the erotic atmosphere present only in the poem, with Millais' *The Blind Girl,* which Rossetti described as "one of the most touching and perfect things I know." Both have the same sensuous quality, the same fullness of colour, the same detailed accuracy of observation. The butterfly on the blind girl's shawl is unmistakably a Red Admiral; there is the same exactness of reference in the flower descriptions of the sonnet. Her blindness is touchingly brought out by the way in which she fingers the blades of grass; there is a parallel in the tactile imagery with which the sonnet opens, while both picture and sonnet are excellently epitomized by the telling pictorial phrase "visible silence, still as the hour-glass."

This interchange of ideas and manner between artists was one of the most striking features of the early Brotherhood. Both Rossetti and Millais caught something of Hunt's moral fervour, and drawings such as *Retribution, The Ghost,* and *The Race-Meeting* suggest in Millais the potentiality of a moral artist of some power. Hunt in his turn was influenced by Rossetti's sensuousness, while contact with Millais, unquestionably the most accomplished of them technically, must have improved both Hunt's and Rossetti's craftsmanship and encouraged their treatment of detail. It is in this respect that they followed Nature, in their meticulous concentration on the accuracy of every detail. The wood shavings on the floor of *The Carpenter's Shop* still evoke admiration for their execution and observation; the flowers and foliage that surround the drowning Ophelia are botanically correct, and the background to *The Blind Girl* is recognizably Winchelsea. Bell Scott records Millais, in about 1850, commenting to him on the elaborate detail of an Italian engraving: "That's P.R.B. enough, is it not? We haven't come up to that yet. But I for one won't try: it's all nonsense; of course nature's nature, and art's art, isn't it? One could not live doing that," but Millais did live by doing something very close to that for many years and so did the others, so that Scott is over-hasty in observing, "So soon had the principal executive tenet of the bond fallen off." Their desire for authenticity led them to a quest for models that would often be laughable were it not inspired by such seriousness of purpose. Only a carpenter could serve Millais as a model for Joseph to ensure correct muscular development; Hunt, revolving the idea of a Little Emily picture, sought an appropriate background among the haunts of fallen women, and his arrangements for nocturnal work on *The Light of the World* in order to get the right blend of light and shade were equally elaborate, while the posing of Miss Siddal as Ophelia in a bath of water heated by an oil-lamp nearly had serious consequences. Whether all this is attributable, as Scott suggests, to the indirect influence of the Daguerrotype, invented a few years earlier, is debatable. They may have been anxious to demonstrate that science and the camera could do nothing that could not be done as well or better by a skilled craftsman with a brush. On the other hand it was an age given to leisureliness in art and taught by the development of scientific knowledge to demand fidelity to nature as a proof of excellence and to equate thoroughness with sincerity of purpose. The same absorption with detail is apparent in fiction and was later to find its way on to the stage in the vogue for detailed realism of setting that followed the success of T. W. Robertson's *Caste* in 1867.

In literature this concern with detail was valuable because wise selection ensured the use only of significant detail; in pictorial art this meticulousness was of more questionable value. Thus *The Death of Ophelia* has been described as an instance of 'consecutive vision,' each detail being painted in with an exactness only possible if the artist were standing opposite to each piece of foliage simultaneously: in other words, the spectator is encouraged, as with *Work,* to a piece-by-piece approach to the picture rather than to a whole, focused view of it. It is thus that one is tempted to study the *Ramsgate Sands* or *Derby Day* of Frith, but as Frith is not concerned with the communication of a moral it matters less there. Ruskin, defending *The Awakened Conscience* in *The Times,* anticipated this objection:

> But I can easily understand that to many persons the careful rendering of the inferior details in this picture cannot but be at first offensive, as calling their attention away from the principal subject. It is true that detail of this kind has long been so carelessly rendered, that the perfect finishing of it becomes a matter of curiosity, and therefore an interruption to serious thought. But without entering into the question of the general propriety of such treatment, I would only observe that, at least in this instance, it is based on a truer principle of the pathetic than any of the common artistical expedients of the schools. Nothing is more notable than the way in which even the most trivial objects force themselves upon the attention of a mind which has been fevered by violent and distressful excitement. They thrust themselves forward with a ghastly and unendurable distinctness, as if they would compel the sufferer to count, or measure, or learn them by heart. Even to the mere spectator a strange interest exalts the accessories of a scene in which he bears witness to human sorrow.

True as this is, it remains a piece of special pleading not applicable to other pictures where the fussiness of detail can be distracting, although in the landscape work of Brown and in the backgrounds of Hunt, Millais, and Hughes that detail does contribute in no small way to the hard clarity of light in which they saw the world about them and which gave their work another of its distinguishing features.

As we see it, Pre-Raphaelite painting gives the imagination far too little to do, and indeed much of it could be adduced as evidence of a mid-Victorian deficiency of imagination. The use of 'inventions' offsets this in some ways, although even with these it is the imagination of the painter that is exercised primarily, and the spectator is asked to use his intellect. All the clues are painstakingly given to us, and we are left to piece them together in our mind to arrive at an understanding of the picture's message. The technique, though less subtly and less ironically employed, is analogous to the method of literary allusion with which the poetry of T. S. Eliot has familiarized the modern reader, and if the pictures are sometimes open to the same objection as that poetry—"what right has he to expect us to have read these things or to see his inference?"—it is open also to the same answer. Poetry is not the only art that can communicate before it is understood, and there are few Pre-Raphaelite paintings that do not make some immediate appeal to the spectator as pictures by virtue of their composition or their use of colour even before the various allusions have been intellectually apprehended. Rossetti, the most literary of them all, proves that Pre-Raphaelitism need not lead, as it did with Millais, to popular facility and over-obviousness. It is for the imaginative strength of his poetry and painting that Rossetti is remarkable, for the *minutiæ* of his work are managed with too much skill to deaden the reader's response. It would have been too much to expect the original Brotherhood to maintain over many years their relationship of interaction, idealism, and co-ordination of viewpoint; when it did begin to disintegrate, although Hunt remained closest to its original tenets, it was the mercurial, colourful personality of Rossetti that found new disciples and his ideas that gained such currency as to lead people still to speak of Pre-Raphaelite qualities when it is pre-eminently to the idiosyncrasies of Rossetti that they refer.

PRE-RAPHAELITE MEDIEVALISM

In the second phase of Pre-Raphaelitism the functions of painter and writer were not combined in the same person (except of course for Rossetti), since Morris did little painting or drawing except for his decorative work, and Burne-Jones was not a man of letters. The medievalism popularly associated with Pre-Raphaelitism, a manifestation rather of this later phase than of the original Brotherhood, is the only aspect of it requiring comment. Rossetti's veneration for Dante remained personal to him but his delight in Arthurian legend was shared by the others, and it was the ill-fated, because technically inexpert, attempt in 1857 to translate that delight into murals for the Oxford Union that first brought Rossetti, Morris, and Burne-Jones into active co-operation. Again Rossetti dominated the group. Burne-Jone's interest had been aroused by Rossetti's illustration for Allingham's *The Maids of Elfin Mere,* and Morris, who had already acquired a love of Chaucer, the ballads, and the medieval world of his imagination, was ready to surrender to this exciting, exotic personality. For them medievalism began as an escape from the constricting drabness of the contemporary world. Hunt and Madox Brown would not without protest have allowed the term Pre-Raphaelite to be applied to lines such as these:

> Dreamer of dreams, born out of my due time,
> Why should I strive to set the crooked straight?
> Let it suffice me that my murmuring rhyme
> Beats with light wing against the ivory gate.

For Burne-Jones the Middle Ages was essentially "such stuff as dreams are made on," and his pictures of it are coloured by "a light that never was on sea or land," so that at times it becomes little more than an irritating affectation—"Wardour Street medieval," as one modern critic has not undeservedly called *King Cophetua and the Beggar Maid.*

Despite a technical skill far in excess of Rossetti's, some of Burne-Jones's etherealized and emasculated paintings have an insipidity that Rossetti usually avoids, but Rossetti, Burne-Jones, and Morris were all capable of a spurious medievalism that rings particularly hollow against their more genuine work. The contrast is shown felicitously by two sentences from Morris's *The Water of the Wondrous Isles.* The romance opens on a note of debased pastiche:

> Whilom, as tells the tale, was a walled cheaping-town hight Utterhay, which was builded in a bight of the land a little off the great highway which went from over the mountains to the sea.

This pales quickly before the virile directness and poetic dignity of the fine passage that closes the tale:

> Now when all this hath been said, we have no more to tell about this company of friends, the most of whom had once haunted the lands about the Water of the Wondrous Isles, save that their love never sundered, and that they lived without shame and died without fear. So here is an end.

If the first recalls some of Burne-Jones's paintings, it recalls also the pseudo-medievalism of much Victorian architecture and the affectation that Browning pilloried in his "Middle-Age-manners-adapter" of *The Flight of the Duchess.* The second passage has more in common with the admirable directness of some of Burne-Jones's drawings. This contrast between his paintings and his drawings is not wholly accounted for by the difference of medium, because many of his oils and water-colours are unquestionably fine, but in medieval subjects he seems better able to discipline his fancy in line. The drawings from the Kelmscott Chaucer and the early *Going to the Battle,* with its wealth of carefully executed decorative detail, have a freshness and individuality that become hackneyed in the larger works; his illustrations for Chaucer, vividly realized and clean in their outlines, have a happy appropriateness, whereas in his *Love among the Ruins* the painter's medievalizing habit has lost the exhilaration of Browning's poem and blunted the contrast of the poet's juxtaposition of modern and antique in a scene that is closer to the amphitheatre scene in *The Mayor of Casterbridge* than to Burne-Jones's picture. It is as the decorative artist of tapestry and stained glass, and as the illustrator of Chaucer that Burne-Jones's affinities with the original conception of the Pre-Raphaelites are seen to best advantage, for there literature furnishes motivating ideas for works of art which are nevertheless well capable of standing alone.

The link between painting and literature was maintained in their treatment of medieval subjects, as may be seen from the pictorial quality of Morris's prose and poetry as a whole, of which this extract from the romance *Golden Wings* is representative:

> Then I said to her "Now, O Love, we must part for a little; it is time for me to go and die."
>
> "Why should you go away?" she said, "they will come here quick enough, no doubt, and I shall have you longer with me if you stay; I do not turn sick at the sight of blood." . . . She threw herself down and kissed my feet, and then did not get up at once but lay there holding my feet. And while she lay there, behold a sudden tramping that she did not hear, and over the green hangings the gleam of helmets that she did not see, and then one pushed aside the hangings with his spear, and there stood the armed men. "Will not somebody weep for my darling?" She sprung up from my feet with a low bitter moan, most terrible to hear, she kissed me once on the lips, and then stood aside, with her dear head thrown back, and holding her lovely loose hair strained over her outspread arms as though she were wearied of all things that had been or that might be.

The pose is that of a Pre-Raphaelite picture, and the situation and mood of this passage are remarkably similar to Rossetti's drawing of *Launcelot in the Queen's Chamber.*

The work of Burne-Jones and Morris at its best re-established the link between art and society that Rossetti's subjective mysticism had weakened at times, and, in re-establishing it, widened it from being purely moral as with Holman Hunt into something aesthetic and yet practical. Morris's designs for furniture and furnishings put into practice his own dictum: "Have nothing in your houses that you do not know to be useful, or believe to be beautiful." Designs and dictum alike combine the æsthetic with the realistic just as the medieval imaginary world of *The Haystack in the Floods* is brought to life by its touches of realistic detail, and just as Pre-Raphaelite painting has always tried to temper escapist beauty with factual observation. Dissatisfaction with the drabness and dirt of Victorian England made Morris a Pre-Raphaelite, and Pre-Raphaelitism led him to an artistic re-statement of the principles necessary to the revitalization of that England and to an active awareness of the craftsmanship by which he could contribute to that revitalization.

To say that a more sparing use of literary apparatus would have entitled the Pre-Raphaelites' pictures to be ranked more highly as art may be true. Sir Thomas Bodkin dismisses them for having "helped to spread the pernicious contagion" of "anecdotage" and an "unhappy insistence upon extraneous illustrative matter"; he considers that "none of these efforts illumined the writer's work, and few of them had valid claims to justify their independent existence," and speaks of "the moral or didactic implications which always follow on conscious illustration." From the viewpoint of the art connoisseur the objection is understandable, but it underestimates the pressure of the spirit of the age. In Holman Hunt and Madox Brown, as well as in the others to a lesser extent, moral didacticism did not "follow on conscious illustration": it was the motivation of their work, and the literariness of their painting is the outcome of it, the best means to hand of making art serve their moral purpose. From an historical estimate, their art did what their age required of it, and although it is not without intrinsic merit it remains the product of a particular age.

In painting, the moral realism and clarity of colour that distinguished Pre-Raphaelitism were soon to give way to the Impressionism that aimed primarily at the communication of pleasure and at the avoidance of sharp definition of outline, but the art of the Brotherhood was to influence English literature for several decades. The young W. B. Yeats found a strong poetic stimulus in their æstheticism, their love of a legendary past, and their craftsmanship. Bernard Shaw, undeterred by the fact that their art was moral and didactic (he might have applied to it his comment on the reception of *Pygmalion:* "It goes to prove my contention that great art can never be anything else"), tried in *Candida* to write "a modern Pre-Raphaelite play." The Pre-Raphaelites fired the imagination of many writers of Edwardian England, and of none more than the young D. H. Lawrence. He wrote to a friend in 1910: "Somewhere I have got the ballad of *Sister Helen*—Rossetti's—beating time. I couldn't repeat it, but yet I beat through the whole poem with now and then a refrain cropping up." By 1929 their spell was less strong because of their attitude to sex, and in the "Introduction to his Paintings" he writes, "As far as I am concerned, the Pre-Raphaelites don't exist," but there is no doubt that they existed vividly for him when he wrote his early poems, and such novels as *The White Peacock* (1911) are markedly Pre-Raphaelite, especially in their descriptive passages.

The Pre-Raphaelites were symptomatic of the leisured culture that largely disappeared with the Great War, and their didactic earnestness has not always been to the taste of later generations (although the exhibitions and publications occasioned by their centenary in 1948 indicate a renewal of interest in them). An exhibition before the first war moved Isaac Rosenberg, himself a painter-poet of promise, to a critical essay on the relationship between the two arts, with a quotation from which this introduction can usefully end:

> We are apt to confuse imagination with literature, with the psychological interest of a picture, as a quality apart from its technical qualities. Literature, I think, is permissible if it enhances the interest of a picture, but it only increases the difficulties of imagination. A picture must be a perfect consistency of thought and execution, of colour and design and conception; the more dramatic or psychological a picture

is the more intense must be the imagination of colour and design to harmonise with the idea. The psychology is helpless without the other elements; the psychology itself is only part of the imagination and perhaps the smallest. Whatever the subject, nature is always our resort, a basis for creation. To feel and interpret nature, to project ourself beyond nature through nature, and yet convince of our faithfulness to the sensation, is imagination.

> The ultimate end of all the arts should be beauty. Poetry and music achieve that end through the intellect and the ear, painting and sculpture through the eye. The former possess advantages which the latter do not; and the latter *vice versa*. Painting is stationary while poetry is in motion. Through the intellect the emotion is enchained; feeling made articulate transmits its exact state to the reader. Each word adapts itself to the phase of emotion (I include sensation of the soul), and carries one along from degree to degree. Painting can only give the moment, the visual aspect, and only suggest the spiritual consciousness; not even a mood, but the phase of a mood. By imagination in paint we do not encroach on the domain of the writer; we give what the writer cannot give, with all his advantages, the visible aspect of things, which the writer can only suggest, and give that aspect a poetic interest; and by that a more intensely human interest: for here the body and the soul are one, and beauty the crown thereof.

> (pp. 16-44)

> *D. S. R. Welland, in an introduction to his* The Pre-Raphaelites in Literature and Art, *George G. Harrap & Co. Ltd., 1953, pp. 13-44.*

WENDELL STACY JOHNSON

[*In this essay, Johnson explores parallels between the Pre-Raphaelite arts of painting and poetry, focusing much of his discussion on the "Blessed Damozel" works of Dante Gabriel Rossetti.*]

In the middle of the Victorian period, the idea of the "sister arts" of painting and poetry, an idea associated during the eighteenth century with landscape "painting" in verse, was given by John Ruskin and others a new emphasis. It could now be used to justify story-telling pictures largely on the basis of their stories: Ruskin's conception of the visual arts as constituting a "noble and expressive Language" was literally carried out in the popular taste for painting that either illustrated well-known narratives or told new anecdotes. But this was only one of the senses in which literature and the fine arts were closely related. From the 1840's to the 1870's there flourished a surprising number of writers who were also painters, sculptors, draftsmen, or architects: Thackeray, Lear, Butler, Hardy, Hopkins, and the most obvious examples, William Morris and Dante Gabriel Rossetti. In such an age, it might seem, when parallels between one art and the other were often drawn, there should be ample material for making comparisons of the literary with the visual.

Yet these comparisons are difficult to make in general terms. Even generalizations about a state of culture which is expressed in the several arts have to be undertaken cautiously, as do all large assertions about the most complex and contradictory of ages. Wylie Sypher, observing that "Pre-Raphaelite painting and poetry began by being narrative or illustrative and ended by being frankly and consciously ornamental," wisely declines to become more dogmatic about that so-called school in what he recognizes as "a century without a style" [see Additional

Bibliography]. In fact, and perhaps this is saying the same thing, the nineteenth century had almost every possible style—including both the Pre-Raphaelite clarity and simplicity of the very late forties and the lush decoration of the seventies and eighties, which is now generally (if mistakenly) thought of as Pre-Raphaelite.

By looking closely at the work in both arts of painter-poets, especially that of the major figures Morris and Rossetti, we can observe some significant similarities between picture and poem in the choice of subject, the use of patterned detail, and a certain dream-like quality of tone. Morris' poetry and design both use medieval subject matter, along with the matter of the northern sagas. In his shorter poems, as in his drawings and flat patterns, he uses repeated details, formal reiteration: the words of the ballad refrain recur insistently in something like the way flower forms recur in a design for paper or fabric, or in the background of a stained-glass window. The coolness of the poet's tone in telling such tales of violence and terror as "The Haystack in the Floods" and "The Defence of Guenevere" may find its counterpart in the flatness with which even intense and heroic figures are treated by the designer's art.

Something of the same can be said about Rossetti, who also takes medieval subjects for both his ballads and pictures, also uses the refrain and the repeated design for pictorial background, also produces an almost hypnotically "flat" tone in his narratives of death and destruction, as in his pictures of the blessed damozel and brooding Lilith. But Rossetti offers a problem in parallels that is both more complicated and more interesting. Morris' is latter-day "Pre-Raphaelitism," and however much he echoes, in the late fifties and afterward, the doctrines of the 1848 brotherhood, he remains consistently a decorative artist. When he expresses moral fervor, as in his socialist writing, it is hardly as an artist at all: he is influenced not by the Ruskin of *Modern Painters I* and *II* but by Ruskin of *Unto This last*. Rossetti, on the other hand, moves from the pictures of his sister Christina as the Virgin Mary, pictures that were praised in 1850 for an unfleshly "pious feeling," to the later drawings and paintings of his mistresses, pictures quite as "fleshly" as the poems Robert Buchanan attacked in 1871. And Rossetti, in whose art both the flat and fleshly elements are always present or implicit, embodies other contradictory elements: the man who was willing to leave all his unpublished poetry in his wife's grave came later to believe himself primarily a poet, and to argue—along with a good many other Victorians—that a picture should be only "a painted poem." If he seemed to shift from one style to another, he could seem as well to vacillate between one art and another.

Still, between the two arts there are specific similarities and consistencies: a complex personality, Rossetti is as an artist a complex whole. Close scrutiny of the subjects and images in poem and picture, of the compositions, and of techniques may help to suggest something of that whole.

Rossetti's favorite subjects in both arts are women—and not ordinary women. In this as in several respects he is an artist of opposites. In one group of extraordinary women are the dying sister, the blessed damozel, and Dante's Beatrice, all pure and all directly related to Heaven. In the other group are Sister Helen, Helen of Troy, Lilith, and the less sinister Jenny, all involved in sensuality if not in morbid passions. The archetypal virgin stands at one extreme, the prostitute or siren at the other. These extremes are represented by the Virgin Mary in his first important pictures and by the pagan Venus, who came increasingly to fascinate Rossetti, and who appears in

verse and pictures as both "Venus Verticordia" and "Astarte Syriaca." The tension between these two appealing figures can be embodied within a single work, as it is in the later and rather lush versions of the heavenly maiden, especially the damozel, and in the poem "Rose Mary." Rose Mary, who must look into a magic stone to detect her lover's danger, proves not to be a maiden at all—she is, in fact, a fleshly and a fallen woman—but at the end of the verse narrative, in Heaven, she can be forgiven and can forget the faithless lover. Rossetti's two ways of seeing women may suggest the two attitudes of Tennyson, in the *Idylls* as well as in *Maud*, where feminine figures are viewed with the eyes of desire in the image of the rose, and with the eyes of awe if not of worship in the image of the pure white lily. Rose Mary, whose very name combines the idea of woman's sexuality with that of virginity, is at last the rose redeemed.

Now we are touching on an aspect of the two arts that we might expect to provide the most striking point of comparison between poems and paintings, the aspect of imagery. Rossetti does repeatedly use the same images in his painting and his verse—not only in the poems inspired by pictures but also in his other lyric pieces. These reveal again and again, as his pictures do, a fascination with flowers, with stars, and with women's hair. But these and less obviously repeated images are usually dictated by the subject. Some of the poet's memorable images are wholly literary and do not enter into the backgrounds of his pictures; an important example is the sea, which Rossetti describes and reflects upon, following Carlyle and Swinburne, as "Time's self" in "The Sea Limits," but which does not appear in his frequently static and almost timeless paintings. When important images are common to poems and pictures, they are likely to be traditional images which are both visual and literary: the lily, rose, and dove, golden apple and blossom, all are used for the sake of symbolic meanings, religious or mythical. The inspiration for Rossetti's pictures is not often his own poetry—except for "The Blessed Damozel," the poems follow the pictures they are linked with—but it is very often literary, deriving from the Bible, Dante, or classical epic and tale. And Mary Magdalene, Beatrice, Cassandra and Pandora carry their own iconographies with them.

Eva Tietz deals with composition and technique, rather than subject and imagery, in the only analytical study of Rossetti's poetry in relation to his painting, "Das Malerische in Rossettis Dichtung" [*Anglia*, LI, 1927]. Dr. Tietz considers the detailed poetic description of light effects and contrasts in color, as well as the use of vertical and horizontal forms to achieve pictorial and decorative results. She cites examples from the verse of perspective as a painter would see it, and descriptions of objects that grow weak and grey as they recede, "green grass / Whitened by distance" ("Boulogne to Amiens and Paris"). Finally, she suggests that in both Rossetti's pictures and his poems, with their feminine figures and moonlit landscapes, the figure is the visual center, graphically described and surrounded by minute decorative detail with the landscape as a distant and subordinate background.

This last point—precise realization of the human figure in the foreground and reduction of the landscape to a distant or shadowy backdrop—is an important comment not only on Rossetti's but on the other Victorian painters' frequent composing of pictures. The Pre-Raphaelites were not alone in their inclination to paint either genre or seriously illustrative works; in spite of Ruskin's love of landscape, and perhaps in part because of Ruskin's interest in art's having "thought" and telling truths,

English artists from the late forties through the seventies very often relegated landscape to a minor role in their canvases, or, at best, used it as a means of commenting symbolically on the people in the picture. Rossetti reveals the extreme form of this tendency in his compositions. The natural settings in his paintings are either (like that he did for *Found*) quite separately studied and painted so that they seem like "flats" behind the leading characters in his scenes, or they are slight and sketchy, including some details that reflect the human situation. So Rossetti and his fellow Pre-Raphaelites domesticate (or tame to moral purpose) the landscape which they show instead of expressing the overwhelming power of external natural as Turner had done. Likewise, Rossetti's poems use the natural setting only for selected detail that is relevant to his human characters; his interest as a poet is in the psychology of persons and not in the grandeur of scenery, in the ego and not in the cosmic image.

A few familiar "pairs" can best demonstrate the degree of relationship between picture and poem. Rossetti's poem on the Virgin Mary follows and comments on pictures in a style comparable to the paintings' own styles. His longer poem on "The Blessed Damozel" precedes and is illustrated by a picture which may seem richer and more sensuous, in the manner of, say, "The Kiss" or "Nuptial Sleep." But, again, diverse elements are present in the picture of Mary and in the poem of the damozel: the vision of a religious figure on earth contains bright colors and clear decorative elements, as well as a psychologically very human, rather than transcendent, quality; the verbal description of a secular-minded maiden in Heaven carries overtones of the divine Dante as well as the morbid Poe.

Dante Gabriel Rossetti's 1864 painting Beata Beatrix. *Tate Gallery, London.*

"Mary's Girlhood (For a Picture)" actually is a pair of sonnets for a pair of pictures, the 1849 *Girlhood of Mary Virgin* and the 1850 Annunciation scene. The decorative artificiality of the sonnet scheme appears to be appropriate, for both the paintings, though tense and luminous, have a curiously flat and artificial quality. The repeated forms, natural and yet somehow de-natured already suggest the entirely formal design of later Rossetti backgrounds and of Morris paper or fabric. The vine being pruned by St. Joseph in the first picture is like a Jesse tree in a stained-glass window; the two stalks of lilies, one in a vase and the other on a tapestry which the Virgin and St. Anne work at, set up a repeated pattern. The pattern is even more striking in *Ecce Ancilla Domini* (probably the best picture Rossetti ever painted), where the lily in Gabriel's hands, almost an enameled wand, becomes reversed in the lily on the now completed strip of embroidery. This detail, making the flower into a flat decoration so that life is stylized wholly into the form of art, implies the development of latter-day Pre-Raphaelitism—or what might even be called post-Pre-Raphaelitism.

Like these pictures, especially the second, Rossetti's pair of sonnets give the impression of being strained in austerity: the decoration is clear and clearly symbolic, and the slightly awkward simplicity of syntax—"Gone is a great while, and she / Dwelt young in Nazareth of Galilee"—is related to the nervous rigidity of the figures in both paintings. But in another sense the poetry is hardly pictorial at all. It is filled with abstract nouns and adjectives, compiling—like the titles on three allegorical volumes in Rossetti's first picture—all the virtues of Mary: "devout respect, / Profound simplicity of intellect, / And supreme patience." The poet's only images, taken from his two paintings, are "an angel-watered lily," "a white bed," and, to stretch a point, the dawn, the sunshine. Certainly no one of these visual suggestions is at all precisely realized, and the most striking, the lily, in effect explicates and makes metaphorical the actual flower and small angel in the picture. It is as if the poet believed his subject too pure to be expressed in the language of the senses, and had to prove that even the flower in the picture was abstractly justified. There is the same abstract diction in Rossetti's sonnet for Leonardo's "Our Lady of the Rocks"; by way of telling contrast, "Venus" and "Lillith"—both poems for later pictures—are filled with the images of eyes, fire, the apple, golden hair, the rose and the poppy.

The painter and poet of the Virgin may feel something of that deep uneasiness about the flowers and fruits of this world (to say nothing of maidens in bed), which gives such tension to the poetry of his maiden model, his sister Christina—especially in her "Goblin Market," where lush forbidden fruits are deliciously pictured in virtually sexual language, and are ascetically rejected. But the same painter-poet can combine the elements of earth and Heaven, flesh and soul, image and abstraction, in his picture and poem on "The Blessed Damozel."

The familiar version of this work which appeared in the 1870 *Poems* is somewhat altered from the two earlier printed texts; but it is not so altered that it cannot still represent the spirit which produced the Pre-Raphaelite magazine of 1850, *The Germ*, as well as that vaguely, dreamily erotic quality which caused Rossetti to be attacked in 1871 for "fleshly" preoccupations. One oil painting of the subject was apparently done in 1874, and the other begun in 1873 but finished in 1879. But, as F. G. Stephens remarked in 1894, the pictures illustrate the poem in close and faithful detail; if there are contrasts between painting and lyric, they are not contrasts of definite imagery. The fact that in this important instance the literal images follow from the literary, the pictures having been painted after the poem was written, even makes the relationship closer: *The Blessed Damozel* is actually what Rossetti declared every picture should be, a "painted poem."

This painted version, which emphasizes the rich and sensual feeling of the poem more than its rigid form (not surprisingly, as the painting is later), nevertheless contains both qualities. If the lines in the main part of the picture are all flowing curves, the figure of the lover in the lower part (of the Leyland version), has, with his crossed legs and arms bent at right angles, the stiffness we find in early Holman Hunt figures and in Rossetti's two pictures of Mary. The painting of the damozel can, in fact, be seen as a later illustration not only of the poem's explicit subject but also of its implicit themes, style, and tone: and the themes are double, the style mixed, the tone complex. For the picture and the poem are both partly successful attempts to relate, to balance, opposites: earthly man in time and blessed woman in eternity, or the temporal and the ideal.

Certain traditional dualities introduced by the very subject of a lover on earth and a beloved in heaven become merged in the styles and imageries of picture and poem. There is no dramatized distinction of body and soul, for the heavenly is concretely embodied. The lush coloring of the picture and the definiteness of its images are counterparts for the emotional language of the poem and its definiteness of imagery: Rossetti's damozel is chaste, with her white rose and her three lilies, but she is also quite physical, with her yellow hair and her warm bosom. As for the possible sexual contrast between man and woman, Rossetti's tendency, accentuated in later pictures and seen also in Morris and sometimes in Burne-Jones, is to picture heroic women who have remarkably masculine jaws and shoulders, and delicate men who have remarkable feminine lips and eyes, so that the sexes seem virtually interchangeable and in that sense virtually sexless. This clear tendency in the painting of the damozel, where it is impossible for instance to tell if the angels are male or female, may reflect an element in the verse. Most of the men in Rossetti's poetry are awed or otherwise dominated by their women, and in the poem of the damozel the role of speaker, wooer, and teacher is hers. If body and soul, and male and female, are not strikingly distinguished, the distinct ideas of time and eternity are both clearly implied in the picture and given in the poem, ideas that cannot seemingly be so easily merged. And yet even these ideas tend to coincide with each other, or to co-exist, rather than to be contrasted.

The painting reveals an element of time in its vision of heaven if only because the blooming flowers, the gracefully waving windblown garments, and the flowing hair of the maiden all show movement instead of stillness. These are not the tranquil forms that are likely to surround a madonna or saint; and certainly the lyric lines of arm and neck, the rich living glow of the damozel's skin, seem as unlike any Byzantine or Gothic "eternalizing" of form as they can be. In the bottom panel of the Leyland picture, however, the tense earthly figure appears paradoxically to be like a statue, more still than the heavenly maiden. If, on the other hand, some element of, say, limited time is in the main part of Rossetti's picture, it is communicated by the limited space, the lack of depth in the scene. The flattening of images, a virtual denial of distance in heaven, may well work because of our association of time with space to flatten and to deny the absolute relevance of historical depth and movement to a central figure, for all its own movement. Again, by way of contrast, the rigid lover's figure in the lower

part of this picture is set against a vista of leaves and a winding river, two familiar images for seasonal change and the constant flowing of time. The damozel strikes us as warm, as breathing and moving, in a flat setting with little dimension of time and space; the lover appears almost like a carved figure seen against a landscape that provides both distance and images of time and change.

Something of this paradoxical treatment of fixedness and movement, of flatness and depth, of eternal form and flowing time, has already been given by the poem. The curious sense of temporal passion in heaven and of a timeless trance on earth is reinforced by the rhetorical structure of Rossetti's verse. "The Blessed Damozel" consists largely of a narrative voice using the conventional narrative past tense. But there are two other voices: the damozel's, set off by quotation marks, and the earthly lover's, contained in parentheses. And the damozel's speech is almost entirely in the future tense, anticipating her lover's arrival in eternity, while his interpolated speech is almost entirely in the present tense, which might ordinarily seem more appropriate to the eternal present than to the world of time in which he exists. Apparently the bereft lover can have only a dim impression, a partial vision and hearing, of the lady in heaven whom we see and hear; yet his mind is fixed on that impression so intently as to take him out of time. As for the maiden, she is so intent upon his moving toward the future that she is concerned only with the movement and the promise of time, not with her own eternity:

> From the fixed place of Heaven she saw
> Time like a pulse shake fierce
> Through all the worlds. Her gaze still strove
> Within the gulf to pierce
> Its path.

This poem touches upon the idea of time repeatedly and in various ways: ten years seem like a day in eternity, it declares, and can seem like a hundred years on earth. It repeats, in the damozel's words, the last theme of "My Sister's Sleep," that to die is to be born into new life—to leave, as it were, the trance-like present and enter into an eternity conceived of not as timeless being but as intensified time. Although the very end of the poem, which represents weeping in heaven, may appear to be the most clearly unorthodox thing about it, the paradoxical and unorthodox view is evident throughout; and it is evident most of all in the use of tense and in the treatment of past, present, and future. In contrast with other visions of the blessed in eternity—such visions as Dante's and the *Pearl* poet's—this one has a narrative describing not a visionary's growing comprehension of heaven but rather the actuality of heaven. It allows the heavenly maiden to speak not of integrity and not of the present, but of longing and of the future. The man on earth, in his fleeting glimpses of the vision, is absorbed in the present, using the words "now" and "even now." So time and eternity, in the poetic tenses as well as in the pictorial images, are blurred, are redefined, are even in part reversed.

The picture and the poem, then, both bring together and tend to merge opposing elements, in several ways; in their compositions, their images, their uses of color and line, and of diction and tense, they produce parallel effects.

John Ruskin's doctrine in the early volumes of *Modern Painters*, along with the principles of the Pre-Raphaelite brotherhood which were largely inspired by Ruskin's words, are calculated to encourage visual art that is at once literally representational in its method and either elevated or otherwise edifying in its subject matter. Pictures, that is, should tell high truths in scrupulous detail; and art should truly be, in Ruskin's famous phrase, "nothing but a noble and expressive language"—the language of the botanist or of the moralist, or both. But the tendency of much of Victorian painting is away from representing landscape nature as it reveals a divine message, toward representing both art itself (the later Rossetti's and Morris' pictures are filled with elaborately patterned tapestries, clothes, and other decorated surfaces) and human nature for its own sake.

As painter and as poet, Dante Rossetti represents something of the old Pre-Raphaelite strain and more, perhaps, of the later tendency. At his most characteristic, he combines the two interests, one in religious or moral subjects realistically portrayed, and one in earthly, even voluptuous, images artfully realized. "The House of Life" includes a sonnet on "St. Luke the Painter," whose art "looked through [symbols] to God" instead of achieving, as later painters' did, only the "soulless self-reflection of man's skill"—and this sentiment is pure Ruskin. And, of course, "The House of Life" also includes such earthly, fleshly lyrics as "Silent Noon."

Finally, if Rossetti's pictures often have extremely literary purposes, either illustrating or telling stories, his poems often have extremely visual qualities which are purely pictorial; we are probably less likely to "read" his simple physical images as psychologically or morally or philosophically symbolic than we are the images of any other important Victorian poet. The parallels observed here may support Rossetti's own inclination to think of himself as a poet who painted. Certainly he is a literary artist. But the accent hovers between the two words in that ambiguous phrase when we consider his work as a whole. (pp. 9-18)

Wendell Stacy Johnson, "D. G. Rossetti as Painter and Poet," in Victorian Poetry, Vol. III, No. I, Spring, 1965, pp. 9-18.

INFLUENCE OF THE MOVEMENT

CAMILE MAUCLAIR

[*Mauclair discusses the influence of the English Pre-Raphaelites on late nineteenth-century French painting and poetry.*]

The English pre-Raphaelite movement has been considered in France, from the pictorial point of view at least, as a reasoned protest against the abuse of realism and against the exclusion of intellectuality from painting. Horror of the academic spirit, of false nobility, of cold allegory, had led the realists strictly to adhere to the copying of Nature; the pre-Raphaelites resolved to show that nobility of soul and profound comprehension of allegories, of symbols, and of legends could be combined with sincere and realistic study of Nature. For that reason they stepped back, across academic taste and the degenerated Italian tradition of the last three centuries, to the primitives of the XIVth and XVth centuries, who were at the same time minute realists and dreamers fascinated by symbolism and decorative art. It was to them quite natural to paint 'subjects,' without falsifying life, and their art was infinitely superior to a realism that may be splendid and rousing through sheer force of talent, but can only satisfy taste by science, without touching the soul by emotion and the spirit by thought. Thus the motive of the pre-Raphaelite movement was first of all a moral and intellectual protest. (p. 169)

A movement parallel to that of Rossetti's friends has been proceeding in France. From the beginning of the last century a number of artists have been . . . desirous of preserving an idealistic art, equally removed from academic tradition and from realism falsely so-called. Realism has produced far more painters; it has been illustrated by some admirable talents who have created schools, like Courbet, Manet and his followers, Degas, Renoir, Monet, Besnard. But the intellectual painters—for that is the name they really deserve—have never ceased to follow their ideal. Delacroix has, in many of his works, proved himself their founder. He was a great lyric poet whose intellect often surpassed even his talent, not in richness of colouring, but in his drawing which was frequently below the heroic energy of his intention. Delacroix was an emotional thinker, a brilliant and tragic visionary. After him Th. Chassériau, who, unfortunately, died very young, was an imaginative painter of the first rank. His work is manifold and embraces all intentions, all subjects; it has always style and is full of ideas; it always goes further than realism. Chassériau is a surprising decorator, of imposing grandeur, and his work shows a crowd of figures of violent and original expression. Chenavard, too, more grave and sober, was a man preoccupied with pure thought; he leads up to Puvis de Chavannes, as Chassériau leads up to Gustave Moreau. Puvis will always remain the French painter, who best knew how to realise perfectly an idealistic art. He owned the secret of a pale and clear harmony, admirably adapted for mural decoration, to which all the impressionists bowed, though he was quite opposed to their ideas. He is a mystic and an absolute idealist. His figures and his decorations are real, simple, and inspired by sincere love of Nature, but they are conceived in an atmosphere of dreams, and he expresses not so much individual sentiments by facial expression, as general sentiments by his grouping of the figures. This great poet kept himself at equal distance from academic artificiality and from realism, for he always sacrificed pictorial interest to the search for general expression and for the intellectual character of his work.

He has left no disciples. But I must now speak of a man who has exercised a profound influence: Gustave Moreau, an interesting painter, a deep thinker and distinguished aesthete. Of all French artists Moreau had most in common with the pre-Raphaelites whom he admired. He, too, was a very learned man, well up in ancient literature and Oriental symbolism, fond of luxurious art, of myths and legends. Moreau's thought was that of a man of superior intellect, who considers a picture as the slow and deliberate expression of an idea with all its details. . . . The teaching of Moreau revolutionised the school to which he belonged. His liberal spirit made him bring up pupils who did not confine themselves to imitating him, but have largely profited by his generous ideas. Some have taken up modern subjects like the portrait-painter Brant, the landscapist Bussy, the painter of peasant-life E. Martel, and Sabatté and Besson, both of whom excel in interiors. The others have continued their master's heroic and legendary tradition and have also felt the influence of the idealist painters across channel. Amongst them is, first of all, G. Desvallières, who commenced by painting fine and solid works and raised himself afterwards to a very interesting idealistic and decorative art. His colour is strange, generally sulphurous and bluish. He draws with great and serious knowledge. . . . Desvallières is a powerful artist of great intelligence, and certainly the most complete and remarkable of Moreau's pupils.

Next to him should be placed Henry-Georges Ronault and Réné Piot. The former is an important religious painter; among his pictures are a *Dead Christ* and a *Jesus among the Doctors,* both distinguished by fine sentiment, rich colour, and touching expression.... So far as Réné Piot is concerned, his art is at the same time subtle and vigorous. He has painted some religious pictures, for example a fine *Adoration of the Magi,* some mythological canvases, and some decorative water-colours which reveal an artist fond of archaism and enamel-like colouring. He also is a man of the future, closely related to the pre-Raphaelites, though he does not draw his inspiration direct from Nature. He is an absolute symbolist who touches the extreme limits of refined and literary art.

I must also mention Milcendeau and Maxence, both interesting pupils of Moreau. The one seems to turn towards realism, the other towards decorative art.... Another great and well-deserved success was *The Farewell,* by Louis Ridel, an exquisite and suave colourist, a painter of ladies' portraits of almost unique delicacy. His faces are of an elegance, of a poetic, sad and pure expression, closely akin to that of Burne-Jones. This group of Moreau's pupils is, perhaps, the only homogeneous group of modern French idealists. Moreau has really transmitted his soul to these young men. He has also strongly influenced the new poets, though his work was difficult to see, since it generally went straight from his easel to some private collection. The few photographs, which circulated among the public, have produced a great impression on the French symbolist writers, who were at the same time moved by Burne-Jones, Rossetti, Morris, and Maddox Brown. The influence of the English upon the French was entirely literary, and if it was transmitted to the art of painting it was mainly through the intervention of Moreau and his disciples. They are the connecting links between our symbolists and those across the channel.

I come now to some painters outside Moreau's influence, who have produced interesting idealistic works. One of them is Armand Point, whose career is strange and fruitful. He began with charming pastels of Paris, female figures in Parisian landscapes of great delicacy, then decorative figures which already showed the desire for abstract meaning. Then he visited the museums of Italy, and he returned a changed man. He started painting in fresco with wax and egg, and developed a grand sense of style, modern and archaic at the same time. On this new road he was first powerfully influenced by Botticelli, and painted a long series of pictures of women in hieratic robes, with complicated headdress and lyric expression, some of which *The Swan-woman, Eve,* the *Charmeuse de Libellules*—will always remain exquisite pictorial inventions. It must be noted that Point had also painted, when he first started, some Algerian views, which are, without doubt, together with Dinet's, the truest and most luminous modern works of this kind. His new groove of thought led him to symbolism, and he painted legendary and religious scenes, *St. George,* and the *Magi,* in Italian manner, very gay, very conventional. Finally he searched for power under the influence of Michelangelo, and he became a confirmed symbolist fresco-painter. At the same time Point produced some jewellery, pottery, enamels; he formed a group of art-workers, and founded in the country a kind of little colony called *Hauteclaire,* to which he applied Morris's principles. Point has often annoyed the critics, and has been the victim of the same gibes as the English pre-Raphaelites. But nobody can deny the sincerity of his efforts, his power of production, his feeling for gracefulness, his seductive colour, and the extreme thoughtfulness of all his work. He is a savant, a student

of symbolism and occultism, an original artist. His jewellery and goldsmith-work are of very real beauty, and have been frequently imitated. He is the representative *par excellence* of pre-Raphaelism in France. He has all the characteristics of a disciple of Rossetti and Ruskin; he has all Morris's ideas on industrial art and socialism. He is a very interesting worker, and personifies a whole reaction against the realism and narrowmindedness of the impressionists. Having started as a modern, absorbed by the simple appearance of things, he tried gradually to raise himself above this point of view in order to arrive at abstract conceptions, always within the logic of plastic art. It is this progression which makes his personality so important.

Another artist who passed through the same stages is Valère Bernard, who lives in seclusion at Marseilles. He was a pupil of Rops and Puvis de Chavannes, and began by painting luminous Provence landscapes. Some of them are fine specimens of impressionist painting. Then he put his name to some remarkable etchings. Then he arrived at decorative painting in very light tones, and occupied himself with grand simplification of design and of colour. Finally he has touched upon symbolic art. Bernard's engravings are vigorous, treated in a black manner, and include Satanic fancies, allegories in the spirit and style of Félicien Rops, who knew so well how to unite idealism and realism. And his paintings, minute in execution and brilliant in colour, have a very personal legendary and mystic character. He is another artist who has followed the pre-Raphaelite lead, and has been strongly attracted by the English movement. He is a learned designer of great intelligence, who has also gone in successfully for sculpture and pottery. One of his paintings is the *Town Hall of Maillane,* near Tarascon, the home of the great poet, Mistral. This picture may well be said to represent the whole soul and colour of this beautiful country. (pp. 170-78)

Here we have a number of artists anxious to express ideas and the intuition of the soul, far removed from a narrow realism. Instinctively they have founded French pre-Raphaelism, less cohesive than in England, but all the same sufficiently energetic to be distinguished from academic art. There have been attempts to imitate them, such as the one instigated by J. Péladan, who started the Rosicrucian Salon based on the principal English pre-Raphaelite ideas. The programme was quite logical and elevated, but it could neither be kept up, nor made acceptable to the public, because the founder's personality was too obtrusive. Péladan is certainly a very intelligent writer and an art expert. He has written some fine essays on primitive art which he knows thoroughly. But he has grave faults, a sectarian spirit, and his frenzied taste for self-advertisement makes him antipathetic to the majority of intellectual Frenchmen. He was wrong in introducing the 'Rose-Croix' religious elements, for which there is no place because of their exclusively mystic character. Many sympathisers with the idealist art movement would neither exhibit under the sign of the 'Rose-Croix,' nor mix themselves up with Péladan's esoteric intentions, nor appear to belong to a sect or adopt its somewhat ridiculous signs. The 'Rose-Croix' included some good painters, notably A. Point and Ronault, but there were far too many mediocre, more or less symbolic and fantastic, paintings, without any merit save their exaggerated extravagance, which lent themselves to ridicule. Both Puvis and Moreau were invited, but refused to exhibit for the said reasons. Then Péladan arranged performances, concerts, and even occult *séances,* which completed spoiled the character of these shows. The 'Rose-Croix' had first a success of curiosity, but collapsed for want of interesting works. The idea was right, the application disastrous. (p. 178)

The pre-Raphaelite ideas have particularly affected the poets. The new school of poets has developed quite a cult for Tennyson and Swinburne, Rossetti and Burne-Jones. Burne-Jones especially has been the subject of much comment. All the young symbolist poets have lived for years surrounded by photographs of this great idealist's works, and their poems bear witness to this. The only volume of Swinburne that has been translated into French, his *Poems and Ballads,* has been read and admired by all, and Sizeranne's work on "Ruskin and the Religion of Beauty" has been an intellectual gospel for many. One may say that the road has been opened in France for a close union with English idealist art, because the ideas on which it feeds have been kept alive for a long time, in spite of the strong realistic tendency of French painting. I have mentioned the main supports of these ideas. They are decidedly in the minority, but this minority will suffice to maintain a tradition which is, at the bottom, the greatest and loftiest of all. We live in a period of technical evolution, where the painters are hypnotized more by the *métier,* than by the ideas which the *métier* is to serve. Yet it is equally certain that even the most admirable skill cannot by itself uphold the greatness of Art, and that the study of technique has only sense or meaning as a preparatory step towards the future expression of human emotions. We shall soon find ourselves in a period when knowledge and skill will tend once more towards idealism, lest they become mere sterile playthings. That will be the moment when the minority of idealists will take their proper place and when we shall watch a general renascence of the pre-Raphaelite conception. (p. 180)

> Camile Mauclair, "The Influence of the Pre-Raphaelites in France," in The Artist, *Vol. XXXII,* October, 1901-January, 1902, pp. 169-80.

DAVID HOWARD DICKASON

[*In the introduction to his book on Pre-Raphaelitism in America, excerpted below, Dickason outlines the impact of the movement on American culture.*]

Just a century ago a group of young British artists and writers became spontaneously vocal and derogatory. They produced some paintings and poetry of varying merit in defiance of the dominant artistic conventions, made a sharp but temporary impact on their cultural milieu—"fought their way into public disfavor," as William Michael Rossetti put it—and, after a mature apology for their youthful fervor, completely disappeared. Thus, in the popular view, the Pre-Raphaelite Brotherhood.

It may indeed be true that for many individuals the English P.R.B. art and artifacts now seem outmoded. Pre-Raphaelite poems are read chiefly in required college courses; their paintings, typified by the meticulous, photographic rendition of detail and by the seraphically vacuous expression on the face of the constant heroine, have suffered from Ruskin's misinterpretation of art principles and from changes in public taste, and so have sunk into some neglect; and original Morris designs in wallpapers and tapestries and examples of his fine printing are now only collectors' items. For Pre-Raphaelite art, itself originally a revolt against convention, soon became conventionalized—"the high finish," as Madox Brown admitted, became "too obtrusive." Even W. M. Rossetti himself in 1899 looked upon the once-solemn code of rules which the young

Brotherhood had drawn up as now "almost comic"; and concerning the early exuberance of his fellow P.R.B.'s he further commented:

> It may be freely allowed that, as they were very young, and fired with certain ideas impressive to their own spirits, they unduly ignored some other ideas and theories which have none the less a deal to say for themselves. They contemned some things and some practitioners of art not at all contemptible, and, in speech still more than in thought, they at times wilfully heaped up the scorn. You cannot have a youthful rebel with a faculty who is also a model head-boy in a school.

Nevertheless, the ultimate significance of the British Pre-Raphaelite movement should not be minimized. Insular and transient though it may have been in some of its aspects, it actually marked a very definite though limited artistic revolution. For at its inception the new Pre-Raphaelite view was [in R. W. Macan's words] "an artist's protest . . . a recall to nature, to simplicity and sincerity" in art—a declaration of independence from the long-continued and dogmatic dictates of the Royal Academy in painting and from "genteel" taste in literature.

Furthermore, the Pre-Raphaelite movement was not a solely British phenomenon. Across the Atlantic a ferment was working among certain young American painters, authors, and architects who were directly inspired by the English P.R.B. attack on sterile conservatism. This progressive group in turn denounced what they considered the slavish adherence to mere tradition. They too became less polemic, but through the latter half of the nineteenth century and into our own times they and their followers did succeed in exerting an influence on the artistic expression and even on phases of the economic life of the United States that cannot be ignored.

Three noteworthy periodicals in this country stemmed directly from the tenets of Ruskin and the British Brotherhood. The first journal clearly Pre-Raphaelite in its origin and sympathies was the *Crayon,* edited by William James Stillman, a painting-companion of Ruskin and a close associate of the whole Rossetti family. This review appeared in the 1850's and conveyed to American readers the heart of the P.R.B. theories. Another little magazine, the *New Path,* was the organ of a superbly self-confident American Brotherhood known as the "Society for the Advancement of Truth in Art," which centered in New York City in the Civil War years. Charter members of this group included several young men of a liberal cast of mind, who were to gain some public recognition: Clarence King, later the good friend of Henry Adams, author of *Mountaineering in the Sierra Nevada,* and first Director of the U. S. Geological Survey; Charles Herbert Moore, subsequently a respected art historian in the Norton tradition and the first administrator of Harvard's Fogg Museum; Clarence Cook, who became editor of the old *Studio;* and two men who made names as architects and critics, Peter B. Wight, a proponent of the Gothic Revival in America, and Russell Sturgis, art editor for *Scribner's* and designer of four Gothic buildings for Yale University. A third American magazine deriving from British sources, in this case from William Morris and his Arts and Crafts movement, was the *Craftsman,* which achieved the impressive circulation of 60,000 before ceasing publication during the First World War. Its pages gave a comprehensive account of the American handicrafts revival that flourished for over two decades and was inspired chiefly by Morris's "Red House" and the London Arts and Crafts Exhibition.

In a socio-economic direction not only the Arts and Crafts movement may be largely credited to P.R.B. origins, but, in its wider ramifications, the founding in this country of an experimental Utopian community, the ill-fated "Ruskin Commonwealth," which flowered for a few years in Tennessee and Georgia.

In the more specific field of the visual arts the spirit of Rossetti and Morris is definitely recognizable in the painting and stained-glass work of John La Farge and in the varied products of Louis Tiffany, "the William Morris of his generation in America." Richard Watson Gilder of the *Century,* who acknowledged Rossetti as his literary godfather, likewise was linked directly with the liberal art movement through the activities of his artist wife and their "little salon" in their New York home, "The Studio." Several other less known painters, such as Thomas Charles Farrer, a student of Ruskin, and J. Henry Hill, were of the American Pre-Raphaelite school. The exceptional collections of manuscripts, sketches, and paintings made by the late Samuel Bancroft, Jr., of Wilmington, Delaware, and by Grenville L. Winthrop, who bequeathed his extensive holdings to the Fogg Museum of Art, are further evidence of a continuing American interest in original Pre-Raphaelite materials.

Literary contacts, too, were frequent. Personal associations, some fugitive but others of lasting significance, were established between the British P.R.B.'s and their American sympathizers. Thomas Buchanan Read, for example, was Dante Gabriel Rossetti's first friend among writers from this country. Joaquin Miller worked his eccentric way to the dinner-table of "The Master," as he labeled Rossetti. W. J. Stillman, already recognized as the editor of the *Crayon,* later displayed talent as an autobiographer and critic, and added intimate details to the Rossetti canon; and both Stillman and his beautiful Greek wife, Marie Spartali, were themselves artists of some ability and served as models for Dante Gabriel. Hawthorne, Emerson, Whitman, Longfellow, Moncure Conway, and others knew the Pre-Raphaelites individually, and were concerned with their ideas. Some later American writers also owe something to the concepts of Ruskin and the young Brotherhood. The verse of Christina Rossetti, on the periphery of the group, was among the models for Sara Teasdale's poetry. D. G. Rossetti and Morris had a considerable effect on such diverse figures as Richard Hovey, Josephine Preston Peabody, and Ezra Pound; while Vachel Lindsay in his "Gospel of Beauty" expounded much of the Ruskinian aspiration for the better life.

These Britishers and Americans were, in the main, exponents of the second of the two chief aesthetic attitudes of the latter half of the nineteenth century. Put simply, one view held that the effective creation of artistic beauty, in whatever form, was an adequate and justifiable end in itself—art for the sake of art was enough. But to many sensitive persons this interpretation seemed too precious, too other-worldly, too esoteric. Beauty is not a supreme and absolute value. Art cannot be abstracted from the conditions of art, but must take its inspiration from its time and place, and must, in full circle, bear a constructive relationship to its surroundings.

Although pioneering chronologically, Poe's dreamworld, "out of space, out of time," demonstrated little visible connection with the American environment; and through its sensuous vividness and easy intelligibility, it led a reader smoothly into the convolutions of Walter Pater and Oscar Wilde. The purity and aloofness of art might be even better illustrated by the French, with whom the "art for art's sake" movement largely began: Flaubert, Gautier, Baudelaire, and the brothers de Goncourt.

But other writers and artists, sometimes labeled as mere sociological thinkers, looked about them at the masses of humanity struggling for a better life or even for mere existence, and believed that an artist had a moral as well as an aesthetic duty. To lead the masses the artist must serve the masses. The majority of mankind laboring under inescapable pressures must still be awakened to the power of beauty. And the materialistic proprietors of the new machine-made wealth must likewise be made to see the artistic and humanitarian light. Victor Hugo and Zola in France; Carlyle, Ruskin, and Morris in England; Whitman, Emerson, and many of the later, lesser writers in America saw what they considered the logical and inevitable link between art and literature and common, everyday life.

The core of the Pre-Raphaelite attitude, however, was a more inclusive desire than merely to apply art to society to bring about visible improvements. The touchstone, if one well-worn phrase must be selected, was "truth to nature," to Nature capitalized. Empty and trite interpretations, deliberate manipulations of subject matter to gain meretricious effects—in a word, artistic insincerity, illogicality and dishonesty in all their guises and applications—these were the foes of the Pre-Raphaelites on both sides of the Atlantic. And against them they rode manfully—and loudly—to battle.

This attitude of the Americans . . . is of particular significance when viewed against the backdrop of its historical period. The low estimate of human nature and its potential which was inherent in the theological determinism of the Puritans had yielded to the optimistic faith in man and his perfectibility through reason which the Enlightenment had offered. This "rational" attitude had found magnificent political expression in "life, liberty, and the pursuit of happiness," and had found brief philosophical application in Deism, and thereafter in the more organized concepts of Unitarianism. In the Transcendental mode man achieved an even nobler level, sharing a spark of the Divine fire, himself but little lower than the angels. And on a practical level the rich new continent seemed to stretch out endlessly, with equal opportunity and success and satisfaction for all comers.

But some acid facts of American life, both national and individual, began by the middle of the century to corrode the foundations of this high faith and hope. The cynicism evidenced in the acquisition of the great Southwest from Mexico; the self-interested regional economic struggles (as well as the genuine humanitarian concerns) of the Civil War; the corruption and self-seeking of Grant's administration and the era of the carpetbaggers; the incredible "robber barons" and their shameless pride in exploiting the nation's wealth; the thin tinsel and superficiality and "conspicuous waste" of the Gilded Age; the shock of Darwinism, biological determinism, pragmatism, and literary naturalism; the disconcerting ideas of Karl Marx and his exponents; the mushroom growth of grimy industrial centers and workers' slums; the acquisitive overseas activities and imperialism in the Philippines, the Caribbean, and Panama—these and other crises and problems seemed to leave little energy or opportunity for a serious consideration of art and the role of aesthetics in nineteenth century America.

So, whatever the ultimate residue from their efforts, [the American proponents of Pre-Raphaelitism] . . . were at least a lively, corporate antidote to the materialism and artistic stagnation of "American Victorianism." As Russell Sturgis, one of the most outspoken of the New York group in the 1860's, later viewed the Pre-Raphaelite movement in both England and the United States:

Edward Burne-Jones's 1874 painting The Beguiling of Merlin. *Lady Lever Art Gallery, Port Sunlight.*

We may gravely doubt whether it occupies an exceptionally high rank among the fine arts of the nineteenth century, and yet it is necessary to admit its intensity, its narrow and simply acting force, its vigorous attempt to make painting into a vehicle for religious, literary and patriotic sentiment, and its profound interest to the student of intellectual experiments.

(pp. 3-10)

David Howard Dickason, in his The Daring Young Men: The Story of the American Pre-Raphaelites, *Indiana University Press, 1953, 304 p.*

LIONEL STEVENSON

[*Here, Stevenson discusses the influence of Pre-Raphaelitism on later developments in the arts. For further criticism by Stevenson, see excerpt above.*]

The primary significance of the Pre-Raphaelite poets is that they stood at the epicenter of an upheaval that shattered literary placidity in the middle years of the nineteenth century. First of all, they served as the shock troops in the assault on bourgeois complacency. Carlyle, the unrepentant peasant, brandishing the weapons of romantic primitivism, had introduced from German the pejorative sense of the word "philistine," and had condemned every manifestation of middle-class prosperity, commercial vulgarity, materialistic greed. His earliest recruit was Ruskin, who transformed Carlyle's moral austerity into a cult of beauty; and later came Arnold to proclaim the need for disinterested detachment. To some degree, however, both Ruskin and Arnold were of philistine origins themselves, and their aestheticism was uncomfortably yoked with moralistic doctrines.

The Pre-Raphaelites suffered from no such inhibitions. Rossetti, a dissolute foreigner; his sister Christina, a cloistered devotee in an era of rationalistic doubt; Morris, a fugitive from the middle class who dressed like a laborer and swore like a trooper; Swinburne, a renegade aristocrat proclaiming himself a republican and a pagan; Meredith, a sardonic intellectual gadfly—to all these the keenest pleasure in life was *épater les bourgeois*. When they published their first major poetry during a few years between 1858 and 1866 the literary landscape was permanently reshaped.

It is not necessary to argue that any one of the Pre-Raphaelite group should be accorded rank among the greatest English poets. The remarkable phenomenon is that jointly they achieved a literary eminence that none of them could have gained alone. In the authentic Romantic model, each was intensely individual, so that no prototype of "the Pre-Raphaelite poet" can be constructed; but it was their diversity that provided their vigor and visibility. The nearest parallel, perhaps, is the Coleridge-Southey-Wordsworth axis that gave direction to the Romantic revolt. A major breakthrough, in defiance of accepted standards, demands more assurance than even the most gifted individual can command by himself; mutual support and stimulation entail a pooling of courage and resources, an access of self-confidence, producing a total impetus that is more than the sum of its parts. In Swinburne's words from "A Song in Time of Order," "When three men stand together / The kingdoms are less by three."

Though the epithet "Pre-Raphaelite" was of course derived from visual art, it was soon adopted by the literary critics. Sometimes the reference was merely to archaisms; a review in the *Athenaeum* in 1860 scolds an author because "she adopts . . . the Pre-Raphaelite spelling of Mr. Landor more than is agreeable. By his 'nipt,' 'clipt,' 'cropt,' 'stopt,' 'dropt' way of treating the tenses, all elegance is 'snipt' from the music." More often, however, the allusion was to precision of detail. Peter Bayne's essay on "The Modern Novel" (1857) refers to Thackeray's realism as "a Pre-Raphaelite school of novel writing." Two years later a reviewer in the *Athenaeum* remarks that Browning's "Saul" is "rich in its Pre-Raphaelite accuracy as a study of oriental scenery." In a review of Swinburne's *Poems and Ballads* in 1866, finding the voluptuous descriptive language in bad taste, John Skelton objected to the "Pre-Raphaelite distinctness of delineation in some of his pictures."

The foregoing random citations indicate elements in the Pre-Raphaelite complex. Inspired by Carlyle's *Past and Present* and Ruskin's "Nature of Gothic," the group glorified medieval honesty at the expense of Victorian hypocrisy. They refused to accept the easy compromise by which the contemporary public relegated the arts to a minor role of elegant dilettantism, unrelated to the solid realities of finance and industry. At the same time, they insisted on uncompromising fidelity to recognizable detail, so that their works could not be accused of either obscurity or escapism. Their frankness in writing about sex evoked demands for censorship which eventuated a decade later in the obscenity trials of publishers who issued naturalistic novels.

The effect of the Pre-Raphaelite impact can be gauged by comparing the three great Oxford critics who determined the century's attitudes toward the arts. Ruskin, though he provided the young poets with their gospel of the primacy of beauty, was distressed by their emotionalism and candor. Arnold, who remained aloof from committing himself to any critical pronouncement on their work, presumably lumped them with his condemnation of the Romantic poets for being too much absorbed in their own emotions. Pater, however, who was only twenty years younger than Ruskin, was the totally committed apostle of aestheticism and initiated the whole next generation of poets and critics into the faith.

In another respect, too, the Pre-Raphaelite poets inaugurated a new era: their preoccupation with foreign literatures put an end to the parochialism that was stultifying English authorship. Here again a few of their immediate predecessors led the way. Coleridge and Carlyle introduced German romantic narrative and idealist philosophy; Byron imitated Pulci. In the mid-Victorian period Arnold inveighed against the provincialism of the English mind; but his actual contribution of knowledge about recent foreign writers was not extensive: Heine and Joubert, Sainte-Beuve and Sénancour were scarcely dynamic specimens of what the Continent could offer. The Pre-Raphaelites, on the other hand, widened the horizon in many directions. Rossetti made available the lyric elegance of Dante's contemporaries and the impudence of Villon; Swinburne dedicated himself to Hugo, Baudelaire, and Gautier; Morris discovered the Icelandic sagas for himself and transmitted them to the English public; all the group were proponents of the new American poets, Poe and Whitman. With regard to their own compatriots, too, their critical judgments were independent and decisive. They rescued Blake from obscurity; they promoted the ascendancy of Keats; they magnified Browning, theretofore little known to the public; and they launched FitzGerald's translation of the *Rubáiyát* on its fantastic renown.

The inherent ambiguity of the Pre-Raphaelite movement is well illustrated by the divers outcomes. Though one basic tenet was the depiction of contemporary subjects with saturated detail, the other was decorative design, using color and composition in a picture, meter and melody in a poem, to produce an aesthetically delightful effect. From the latter principle developed not only the symbolism and aestheticism of the nineties but also the whole present-day concept of the alienated artist, socially isolated and psychologically introverted, producing nonrepresentational pictures or incomprehensible poems of private self-expression. The principle of current relevance, on the other hand, anticipated the naturalistic fiction of the eighties (which was supposedly imported intact from France); Rossetti's "Jenny" and Meredith's *Modern Love* are as much forerunners of George Moore as are Zola and Maupassant. More remarkably, from the same principle, through Swinburne's diatribes against autocrats and prelates, and Morris's crusade for the practical application of art and its function in social amelioration, came the modern doctrine of total commitment. There is an obviously direct line of descent from Carlyle through Ruskin and Morris to Bernard Shaw, the Fabian Society, the English Labour party, the American New Deal, and all the writers and college dons who have concerned themselves with the Spanish civil war or the eradication of imperialism. (pp. 3-6)

[The Pre-Raphaelite element is also] obvious in the large group of poets who came to be classified as the Aesthetes and the Decadents. Every discussion of their work has indicated how faithfully they accepted and exaggerated the doctrines of Pater.

Several of them—Oscar Wilde, Ernest Dowson, Lionel Johnson—had come directly within his orbit at Oxford, and others caught their enthusiasm at the Rhymers' Club. Yeats had a direct affiliation with the original Pre-Raphaelites through his father's artistic activities; he says in his *Autobiographies* that in his early London days he was "in all things Pre-Raphaelite." His devotion to Blake was another manifestation of the Rossetti-Swinburne influence. Of the whole fin-de-siècle group he declared, "we were all Pre-Raphaelites then," and more specifically in "The Tragic Generation" he explained, "If Rossetti was a subconscious influence, and perhaps the most powerful of all, we looked consciously to Pater for our philosophy."

To this indigenous source was joined the kindred influence of the French symbolists, promoted particularly by Arthur Symons. The concept of the alienated poet, writing solely to express his inward vision of beauty and despising the philistine standards of the everyday world, was carried over into the writers' personal behavior, as they indulged in alcohol or narcotics or sexual aberrations and usually declined into an early and miserable death. For this stereotype, Rossetti and Swinburne were models as conspicuous as Verlaine and Rimbaud. Even nonmembers of the Aesthetic group, such as Francis Thompson, conformed to the pattern. Not only in attitude, in subject matter, and in conduct, but also in the techniques of imagery, vocabulary, and versification, the poets of the eighties and nineties were the heirs of their Pre-Raphaelite predecessors.

In all essentials, then, the movement initiated by Rossetti proved to be the most potent force in mid-Victorian poetry. Shaping themselves on the great Romantics—Coleridge, Byron, Shelley, and Keats—they flouted the Victorian compromise with gentility and social consciousness. They revitalized English poetry by an injection of foreign hormones, and they determined not only the whole theory and practice of the so-called Last Romantics of the next generation but also to a large extent the poetic assumptions of such twentieth-century writers as the imagists. The dynamic energy of Pre-Raphaelite poetry had been generated by the electrical interplay among a half-dozen highly individual personalities during the crucial years from 1850 to 1870. Their stubborn rejection of materialistic values and a mechanistic society remains vitally important a century later. (pp. 304-05)

> *Lionel Stevenson, in his* The Pre-Raphaelite Poets,
> *The University of North Carolina Press, 1972, 330 p.*

ADDITIONAL BIBLIOGRAPHY

PRIMARY SOURCES

Buckley, Jerome H., ed. *The Pre-Raphaelites*. Modern Library College Editions. New York: Random House, The Modern Library, 1968, 514 p.

Lang, Cecil Y., ed. *The Pre-Raphaelites and Their Circle*. 2d ed. Chicago: University of Chicago Press, 1975, 541 p.

Merritt, James D., ed. *The Pre-Raphaelite Poem*. New York: E. P. Dutton & Co., 1966, 224 p.

Stanford, Derek, ed. *Pre-Raphaelite Writing: An Anthology*. London: Dent, 1973, 207 p.

Welland, D.S.R., ed. *The Pre-Raphaelites in Literature and Art*. Life, Literature and Thought Library. London: George C. Harrap & Co., 1953, 215 p.

SECONDARY SOURCES

Beerbom, Max. *Rossetti and His Circle*. London: Heinemann, 1922, 22 p.
  A collection of twenty-three caricatures of the Pre-Raphaelites.

Beers, Henry A. "The Pre-Raphaelites." In his *A History of English Romanticism in the Nineteenth Century*, pp. 282-351. New York: Henry Holt and Co., 1918.
  A discussion of romantic and medieval elements in the poetry of Dante Gabriel Rossetti, William Morris, and Algernon Charles Swinburne.

Bell, Clive. "The Pre-Raphaelites." In his *Landmarks in Nineteenth-Century Painting*, pp. 107-17. London: Chatto and Windus, 1927.
  A consideration of the Pre-Raphaelites in the context of nineteenth-century art history.

Bickley, Francis. *The Pre-Raphaelite Comedy*. New York: Henry Holt & Co., 1932, 276 p.
  A popularized history of the Pre-Raphaelite Brotherhood.

Bloom, Harold, ed. *Pre-Raphaelite Poets*. Modern Critical Views. New York: Chelsea House Publishers, 1986, 309 p.
  A collection of essays on the poetry of Dante Gabriel Rossetti, George Meredith, Christina Rossetti, William Morris, Algernon Charles Swinburne, and Coventry Patmore.

Buckley, Jerome Hamilton. "The Fear of Art." In his *The Victorian Temper: A Study in Literary Culture*, pp. 161-84. Cambridge: Harvard University Press, 1951.
  A study of the importance of Pre-Raphaelitism to Victorian aesthetics. Buckley focuses on the conflicting artistic ideals of Robert Buchanan and Dante Gabriel Rossetti.

De Armond, Anna Janney. "What Is Pre-Raphaelitism in Poetry?" *Delaware Notes* 19 (1946): 67-88.
  A consideration of the development and characteristics of Pre-Raphaelite poetry.

Dickens, Charles. "Old Lamps for New Ones." *Household Words* 1, No. 12 (15 June 1850): 265-67.
  A negative appraisal of the Pre-Raphaelites prompted by John Everett Millais's painting *Christ in the House of His Parents*. Dickens describes the painting as "the lowest depths of what is mean, odious, repulsive, and revolting."

Evans, Ifor. *English Poetry in the Later Nineteenth Century*. Rev. ed. London: Methuen & Co., 1966, 497 p.
  Includes several chapters devoted to poets of the Pre-Raphaelite movement.

Fleming, G. H. *Rossetti and the Pre-Raphaelite Brotherhood*. London: Rupert Hart-Davis, 1967, 233 p.
  A history of the Pre-Raphaelite Brotherhood emphasizing Dante Gabriel Rossetti's importance to the group.

———. *That Ne' er Shall Meet Again: Rossetti, Millais, Hunt*. London: Michael Joseph, 1971, 468 p.
  Concentrates on the careers of William Holman Hunt, John Everett Millais, and Dante Gabriel Rossetti after their association in the Pre-Raphaelite Brotherhood.

———. "The Pre-Raphaelities." In *The Victorian Poets: A Guide to Research*, 2d ed., edited by Frederic E. Faverty, pp. 251-316. Cambridge: Harvard University Press, 1968.
  A bibliographical overview of materials on Pre-Raphaelitism.

Gaunt, William. *The Pre-Raphaelite Tragedy*. Rev. ed. London: Jonathan Cape, 1975, 231 p.
  A popular account of the Pre-Raphaelite movement first published in 1942.

———. *The Aesthetic Adventure*. New York: Harcourt, Brace and Co., 1945, 269 p.
  A continuation of *The Pre-Raphaelite Tragedy* (see entry above).

Grigson, Geoffrey. "The Preraphaelite Myth." In his *The Harp of Aeolus and Other Essays on Art, Literature and Nature*, pp. 86-97. London: Routledge, 1947.
  Regards Pre-Raphaelitism as a cult joined by the magnetism of Dante Gabriel Rossetti's personality.

Hamilton, Walter. *The Aesthetic Movement in England*. 1882. Reprint. New York: AMS Press, 1971, 127 p.
  Examines the importance of Pre-Raphaelitism to the Aesthetic movement in England.

Hilton, Timothy. *The Pre-Raphaelites*. New York: Harry N. Abrams, 1970, 216 p.
  An illustrated history of Pre-Raphaelite art.

Hosmon, Robert Stahr. "*The Germ* (1850) and *The Oxford and Cambridge Magazine* (1856)." *The Victorian Periodicals Newsletter*, No. 4 (April 1969): 36-47.
  Lists the contents of the two periodicals as well as their contributors.

———. Introduction to "*The Germ*": *A Pre-Raphaelite Little Magazine*, edited by Robert Stahr Hosmon, pp. 9-23. Coral Gables, Fla.: University of Miami Press, 1970.
  An introduction to a reprint of the *Germ*. Hosmon provides a history of the periodical and summarizes nineteenth-century critical response to it.

Hough, Graham. *The Last Romantics*. London: Gerald Duckworth & Co., 1949, 284 p.
  A study of John Ruskin's influence on nineteenth- and early twentieth-century art and thought. Hough devotes chapters to Dante Gabriel Rossetti, William Morris, and Walter Pater.

Hueffer, Ford Madox. *The Pre-Raphaelite Brotherhood: A Critical Monograph*. The Popular Library of Art. 1906. Reprint. London: Duckworth & Co., 1920, 174 p.
  An account of the history and achievements of the Brotherhood.

Hunt, John Dixon. *The Pre-Raphaelite Imagination, 1848-1900*. Lincoln: University of Nebraska Press, 1968, 262 p.
  Explores the dominant characteristics of Pre-Raphaelite art.

Hunt, William Holman. *Pre-Raphaelitism and the Pre-Raphaelite Brotherhood*. 2d ed. 2 vols. London: Chapman & Hall, 1913.
  An account of the history and concerns of the movement by one of its founders.

Ironside, Robin, and Gere, John. *Pre-Raphaelite Painters*. British Artists. Edited by John Rothenstein. New York: Phaidon Publishing, 1948, 143 p.
  Includes a brief introduction to Pre-Raphaelite art, a catalogue of paintings, 94 plates, and an index of collections.

Jones, Howard Mumford. "The Pre-Raphaelites." In *The Victorian Poets: A Guide to Research*, edited by Frederic E. Faverty, pp. 161-95. Cambridge: Harvard University Press, 1956.
  A bibliographical survey.

Marsh, Jan. *Pre-Raphaelite Sisterhood*. London: Quartet Books, 1985, 408 p.
  Examines the lives and works of the women associated with the Pre-Raphaelite movement.

Meisel, Martin. "Pre-Raphaelite Drama." In his *Realizations: Narrative, Pictorial, and Theatrical Arts in Nineteenth-Century England*, pp. 351-72. Princeton: Princeton University Press, 1983.
  A discussion of the dramatic qualities of Pre-Raphaelite painting.

Sambrook, James, ed. *Pre-Raphaelitism: A Collection of Critical Essays*. Patterns of Literary Criticism, edited by R. J. Schoeck and Ernest Sirluck. Chicago: University of Chicago Press, 1974, 277 p.
  Reprints important essays, including both primary accounts by members of the Pre-Raphaelite movement and modern studies.

Spalding, Frances. *Magnificent Dreams: Burne-Jones and the Late Victorians*. New York: E. P. Dutton, 1978, 80 p.

An illustrated history of the careers of the later Pre-Raphaelite artists.

Staley, Allen. *The Pre-Raphaelite Landscape*. Oxford Studies in the History of Art and Architecture, edited by Anthony Blunt, Francis Haskell, and Charles Mitchell. Oxford: Clarendon Press, 1973, 193 p.
    Analyzes how Pre-Raphaelite artists treated nature in landscape painting.

Stansky, Peter. *Redesigning the World: William Morris, the 1880s, and the Arts and Crafts*. Princeton: Princeton University Press, 1985, 293 p.
    Considers Morris's widespread influence in relation to the contemporary political and aesthetic climate.

Symons, Arthur. "Dante Gabriel Rossetti." In his *Studies in Strange Souls*, pp. 7-49. London: Charles J. Sawyer, 1929.
    An anecdotal and critical discussion of several members of the Pre-Raphaelite movement.

Sypher, Wylie. "Neo-Mannerism: Nazarenes, Lyonnais, and Pre-Raphaelites." In his *Rococo to Cubism in Art and Literature*, pp. 197-215. New York: Random House, 1960.
    Discusses the place of what Sypher terms the "international Pre-Raphaelite movement" in art and literary history.

Watkinson, Raymond. *Pre-Raphaelite Art and Design*. Greenwich, Conn.: New York Graphic Society, 1970, 208 p.
    A history of the origins and growth of Pre-Raphaelite painting.

Waugh, Evelyn. *PRB: An Essay on the Pre-Raphaelite Brotherhood, 1847-54*. Westerham, England: Dalrymple Press, 1982, 44 p.

An appreciative pamphlet first published privately in 1926.

Welby, T. Earle. *The Victorian Romantics, 1850-70: The Early Work of Dante Gabriel Rossetti, William Morris, Burne-Jones, Swinburne, Simeon Solomon and Their Associates*. London: Gerald Howe, 1929, 161 p.
    An illustrated study of the works of several Pre-Raphaelite artists.

Williamson, Audrey. *Artists and Writers in Revolt: The Pre-Raphaelites*. Newton Abbot, England: David & Charles, 1976, 208 p.
    Explores the factors that led to the Pre-Raphaelites' rebellion against the conventions of nineteenth-century art and life.

Winwar, Frances. *Poor Splendid Wings: The Rossettis and Their Circle*. Boston: Little, Brown, and Co., 1933, 413 p.
    A semifictional history of the movement.

Wood, Christopher. *The Pre-Raphaelites*. New York: Viking Press, A Studio Book, 1981, 160 p.
    An illustrated study of Pre-Raphaelite painting.

Wood, Esther. *Dante Rossetti and the Pre-Raphaelite Movement*. London: Sampson Low, Marston and Co., 1894, 323 p.
    An early critical examination of the movement, including chapters on its forerunners, its history and development, the Pre-Raphaelites' use of religious and medieval themes, and the poetry of Dante Gabriel Rossetti.

Young, Vernon. "From Pre-Raphaelitism to Bloomsbury." Arts Yearbook 1 (1957): 101-16.
    A negative appraisal of the Pre-Raphaelite aesthetic. Young considers the movement a precursor to Decadence.

The Russian Civic Critics

INTRODUCTION

The Civic Critics were an influential group of mid-nineteenth-century Russian literary commentators who evaluated literature primarily on the basis of its social and political content. The critical approach of these writers was grounded in the cultural milieu of Russia during the first half of the nineteenth century, a period that saw the emergence of a publicly prominent intelligentsia, an educated class with progressive social ideals and a highly developed sense of social responsibility. Members of the intelligentsia served as critics of all aspects of Russian life, often demonstrating a tendency to view social, cultural, and political concerns as interrelated aspects of a moral mission to improve Russia's general welfare. Partly as a result of this tendency, and partly as a result of progressively harsher governmental censorship that restricted overt social and political commentary, literary criticism became the primary forum for the discussion of social and political issues.

The first prominent practitioner of socially committed literary criticism was Vissarion Belinsky, whose writings of the 1830s and 1840s made him the most influential Russian critic of the nineteenth century. Maintaining that society could only be educated through art, Belinsky combined aesthetic appreciation of literary works with the demand that literature also advance progressive philosophical, social, and political ideals. This utilitarian trend in literary criticism reached its peak in the late 1850s and the 1860s with the Civic Critics, Nikolay Chernyshevsky, Nikolay Dobrolyubov, and Dmitry Pisarev. While considering themselves Belinsky's ideological heirs, these writers dramatically narrowed the focus of literary criticism, subordinating all considerations of style, form, characterization, and theme to literature's educative function. The Civic Critics—who are also known as the radical, utilitarian, nihilist, and revolutionary democratic critics—often used criticism as a pretext for exposing social ills under the czarist regime, and their essays frequently took the form of partisan commentaries on issues of the day.

Chernyshevsky, the first of the Civic Critics, served as literary editor of *Sovremennik* (*The Contemporary*) from 1855 through 1858, using the journal as a forum to demand a literature with a specific social function: to represent reality, to instruct the reader about the nature of reality, and to judge reality against an ideal. In 1858 Dobrolyubov succeeded Chernyshevsky as literary editor of the *Contemporary* and added to civic criticism the study of "social types": discussion of literary characters as if they were actual people. Often his reviews analyzed the personalities portrayed in a literary work and the prevailing social forces that had shaped them, taking no account of the author's purpose in creating the characters. Pisarev, the most militant of the Civic Critics, first attained prominence by attacking Dobrolyubov in print. He criticized Dobrolyubov, and eventually Chernyshevsky and Belinsky, for not demanding that literary form be entirely disregarded in favor of socially useful content. Violently opposing pure art as "drivel" and "a waste of time," Pisarev argued that only instructive works of literature had a right to exist.

Despite their rejection of traditional aesthetic concerns, the Civic Critics are credited with important literary insights as well as advances in the methodology of criticism. Their work is particularly valued for initiating the study of literature's relationship to its social milieu, and for helping to evaluate and define the social orientation of nineteenth-century Russian literature. The most enduring influence of the Civic Critics on Russian literature is the widespread acceptance they won for instructive literature that possesses a clear-cut sociological function. Many commentators trace a line of descent from the "social tendency" of Belinsky's writings to the strict precepts of socialist realism, the official doctrine of Soviet art, which demands that literature affirm and uphold the Soviet way of life. In modern Soviet criticism, the Civic Critics are considered revolutionary heroes for their opposition to the czarist government, as well as for establishing the theoretical foundations for a socially engaged literature.

PRINCIPAL FIGURES AND HISTORICAL BACKGROUND

HERBERT E. BOWMAN

[*Bowman discusses the interrelationship of literature and society in nineteenth-century Russia.*]

The hazards of a conscious insistence upon the interdependence of art and society are perhaps nowhere more available to observation than in the literary history of modern Russia. Main currents in Russian cultural life during the nineteenth and twentieth centuries have constantly worked to direct Russian critical thought toward a sharp awareness of the social role of literature. In the first place, the intellectual elite in modern Russia has traditionally performed the combined tasks of social philosopher and literary critic. In important cases the two spheres of activity become identical. This feature of Russian intellectual life expresses a peculiar cultural situation, which crystallized with the emergence of a well-defined and publicly active "intelligentsia" in the first half of the nineteenth century.

It became the function of the Russian intelligentsia to maintain constant surveillance over national affairs generally by passing critical judgment—artistic, philosophical, political—upon the whole state of Russian social and cultural life. Collaboration in this critical function constituted the major criterion of membership in the intelligentsia, for in every other respect its members remained free to assume differing or antagonistic positions. The common cause remained the cause of Russia: her enlightenment, her general welfare. All workers in that cause belonged to a single spiritual community, in which the accidental differences of social origin and private life became irrelevant: whether their class alignments were aristocratic, plebeian, or mixed; whether they lived together as friends or enemies or in merely casual awareness of one another; whatever the differences in their formal education, intellectual compe-

402

tence, or moral character; indeed, whether or not they agreed in any important principle in the philosophies by which they passed judgment upon Russian national life or in their conceptions of the best methods to be employed in giving any social or political philosophy a practical expression.

The degree to which the attitudes of the intelligentsia tended to be radical is partly a measure of official oppression and social isolation. Precisely because they set themselves up as critics of the existing order, these self-appointed tribunes, whatever the character of their thought, were certain to embarrass the authorities, by whose lights the very attitude of criticism or freethinking was condemnation enough. The government's stupidity and ruthlessness in suppressing free thought naturally became in its turn an object of critical censure to its victims. By such a tragic or ridiculous evolution even the most harmless opinion could give a start to a career of radicalism. But even more important than official censure in making for radicalism among the intelligentsia is the fact that its members constituted an exceedingly small contingent within a multitude of inert or hostile humanity—a few bright candles in a dark night of popular ignorance or indifference. A sense of being few against desperately great odds helped in itself to cultivate the spirit of a militant minority predisposed toward extreme positions and extreme measures. Looking up to see an insensitive, arbitrary officialdom; looking down to see a vast herd of characterless subjects of the realm aimlessly at large; looking across at each other to see disagreement and disunity among a handful of potential collaborators—the members of the intelligentsia were from any point of view certain to be impressed by the hopelessness of their isolation and, as an inevitable consequence, to develop the moral and intellectual belligerence that inspired radical philosophic and political attitudes.

Inspired or irritated by his assignment to an almost single-handed critical attack against the total structure of Russian national life, the member of the intelligentsia was stimulated to direct his criticism against the entire foundation of Russian cultural existence. He thus inclined toward "radicalism" in the sense that he busied himself not merely with pruning the dead leaves of national culture but with a deliberate probing at its roots; not merely with specialization upon a selected pathological detail but with an examination of the total organism. Consciousness of an unresolvable social problem in national dimensions has constantly weighed upon the spirit of the Russian intellectual. Hardly elsewhere in the modern world has so much intellectual energy been expended in efforts to define the role, the mission, the needs, the destiny, of the national life. With whatever justification, this preoccupation with crisis in Russia has given continuing stimulation to the mentality of radicalism.

Thus reinforced by historical events, the tendency to take a critical attitude toward the national culture in its entirety led, among other consequences, to an inclusion of all cultural activities under a single judgment: to a sharpening of the sense that no single organ of the national life would function regularly until the total organism was regulated. Particularly in its origins in the nineteenth century, modern Russian literary criticism, carried forward at first by an intelligentsia of such "radical" or "totalitarian" mentality, moved toward a social criticism which judged any particular literary work or current at least partly by its contribution to Russian cultural identity and enlightenment, as the expression of the national society and also as the vehicle of cultural advance. To be sure, major currents in modern Russian literature run counter to this utilitarianism.

Indeed, part of the inspiration of such important movements as Russian Decadence, Symbolism, Acmeism, Formalism, can be found in their reaction against the confinements and distortions of the social interpretation of literature, and in their exuberant desire to restore to literary art its full freedom. But even such major attacks as these upon the "civic" conception of art did not work toward an absolution of the Russian artist from the responsibility of performing a civic function. Rather the broadening of the confines of art made for a broadening of the artist's responsibility. An eminent example is Alexander Blok (1880-1921), probably the foremost Russian poet of the twentieth century, whose sense of vocation as a voice of national prophecy was acute and tragic.

The tendency to take literature "seriously" finds its most deliberate expression, of course, among the critics. The gravity of his assumed obligations to his public so weighed upon the Russian critic that he typically adopted not only a grim but often also a grandiose sense of mission. A Russian literary historian [Ivan I. Ivanov] has defined this moral duty of the critic in explicit terms:

> The critic who is without a leading principle which has been rigorously thought out and which is religiously adhered to, is a negative quantity rather than a positive asset to any . . . literature. Over against the world of external reality, he should represent a rich inner world of personal morality, a soul of unbounded receptivity, and a mind occupied by serious reflection. Every fact should find in him an answering echo; both the trivial and the important phenomena of life should stimulate in him the activity of disinterested thought, concerned only with truth and justice.

Such a heavy pressure of obligation was bound to shape the very definition of literary criticism—which, in its more extreme "utilitarian" or "civic" forms, came to be primarily concerned with the public to which it was addressed and which it proposed to "enlighten" by means of the interpretation of literary works. This insistence that literary art perform a work of national enlightenment is by no means confined in Russia to the critic. The names of Gogol, Dostoevski, and Tolstoi alone may serve as dramatic reminders of the Russian artist's preoccupation with his moral mission within Russian society. Only in rare cases, however, did the Russian literary artist show himself ready to impose upon art the moral and ideological demands which leading Russian critics of the nineteenth century commonly made.

The conception of literature as an expression and guide of the national cultural life made a particularly effective appeal to the intelligentsia of the second quarter of the nineteenth century—a period marked by the conscious effort of a great nation to come of age. The dominant problem of the period is nothing less than to determine and to articulate a cultural identity. "All men the least bit wakened to thought set out around this time to seek, with the fervor and greediness of hungry minds, the foundations of a conscious rational existence in Russia" [Pavel V. Annenkov]. It would not be easy to find another example in similar dimensions of an entire national community turning in upon itself to resolve the riddle of its existence. The student of the period is sure to be impressed or amused by the gravity and extent of its deliberations. But the age is by no means a time of merely dilettante philosophizing about grandiose theoretical propositions. Not less notable than the extensiveness of the philosophic effort is the "fervor and greediness" with which it is made. Questions which strike us today as almost hopeless in their sweep stand at this time as the urgent problems of a vigorous national life. It is this uncommon combination of largeness and urgency in the philosophic quest which gives the period its tremendous adolescent overflow of intellectual intensity. (pp. 6-10)

> Herbert E. Bowman, "Introductory: Literature and Society" in his Vissarion Belinski, 1811-1848: A Study in the Origins of Social Criticism in Russia, Cambridge, Mass.: Harvard University Press, 1954, pp. 1-14.

RALPH E. MATLAW

[*Matlaw outlines the careers and literary views of the Civic Critics and their primary influence, Belinsky.*]

The Sense of social responsibility, political commitment, and moral vision that informs Russian literature is in large part the product of a critical tradition established in the middle third of the nineteenth century. Belinsky, Chernyshevsky, and Dobrolyubov, men of widely differing temperaments and abilities, created an empirical doctrine of vast importance to the progress of Russian letters. In emphasizing the political implications of literature, largely at the expense of aesthetic criteria, its practitioners have at various times been known as "civic," "utilitarian," "sociological," or "radical" critics. In the Soviet Union they have retrospectively been opted as forerunners of Marxist-Leninist criticism, and renamed "Revolutionary Democrats." In addition to their places in literary history, they therefore also figure as cultural phenomena, with a vitality and importance rarely accorded to literary figures in modern times.

Vissarion Grigor'evich Belinsky, the most gifted and formidable Russian critic in the nineteenth century, the fountainhead of this tradition and the prototype for the figure that permeates mid-century Russian literature and dominates its attitudes, can be compared in stature and influence not so much with other prolific and influential critics and theoreticians of the nineteenth century, men like Sainte-Beuve and Taine in France, Friedrich Schlegel in Germany, and Coleridge in England, but rather with those men like Dr. Johnson or Boileau who do not at all resemble him in literary tastes and theories but who, like him, determined the cultural temper of a whole age. He was born in 1811, the son of a poor provincial doctor. He entered Moscow University in 1829, but was expelled three years later, officially "because of unsound health and also because of limited capabilities," but more likely for a very bad and somewhat inflammatory play on the theme of serfdom. A liberal young professor of European literature who founded the periodical *The Telescope* offered him a post as reviewer. From 1833 until his death in 1848 from consumption aggravated by overwork, he poured out a stream of reviews, articles, theoretical analyses, and statements upon the appearance of every literary work of any importance, with ever-increasing popularity among, and adulation from, the liberal-minded youth of the day. In 1839 he moved from Moscow to St. Petersburg, reaching his most important formulations in his annual reviews of Russian literature, particularly those for 1846 and 1847, which appeared in the most influential of the liberal periodicals, *The Contemporary*.

Belinsky's career is associated with, and typifies, two important notions in Russian intellectual history. The first is the rise of the "intelligentsia," a term, apparently of Russian invention, that designates intellectuals of all persuasions dedicated in one form or another to the improvement of life in Russia, and so carries far greater ethical implications than the mere

word "intellectual." The second is that of the *raznochintsy,* literally "persons of various classes," a term applied to those members of classes other than the gentry, usually the clergy or the minor and provincial professional and bureaucratic classes, who sought to pursue a career other than the one their background would normally indicate. Frequently they became members of the intelligentsia, usually after considerable privation. Unlike members of the gentry such as Herzen or Turgenev, who could always turn to other sources if necessary, they were entirely dependent upon their intellectual labors, whether as tutors, journalists, or writers, and from their position derived no small part of their exaltation and indefatigability. While there were factions and enmities within the intelligentsia, all its members were in principle agreed on one point: opposition to the conditions of life around them. Clearly connected with these conditions is the intrusion of the *raznochintsy* into literature, until 1830 or so the exclusive purview of the gentry, who were all too eager to avoid the imputation of professionalism. In style and in tone a sharp shift may be observed, and no one better exemplifies this change than Belinsky himself. (pp. vii-viii)

He hated oppression and dogma more than anything else—ironically, he has become sanctified in the Soviet Union—and never shrank from the implications of his theories or from renouncing and correcting them when they proved unsatisfactory. Ultimately he was concerned with the dignity of man, and his criticism was directed to that final criterion. As a result of his passionate concern and of his temperament, his literary judgments frequently foisted upon works social criteria that, while commendable, do not correspond to their authors' intention or to the work at hand. Through his enormous influence on the reading public, he unmade as well as made reputations, doomed authors to oblivion, determined the interpretation (or misinterpretation) of writers until the present time. Belinsky always sought to distinguish the original from the merely imitative, the genuine response from the artificial one, the valid from the meretricious. He recognized, elucidated, and encouraged almost every literary talent as soon as it appeared in those remarkable years that saw so many of Russia's great novelists and poets first breaking into print: Gogol and Lermontov, Turgenev, Goncharov, Dal', Nekrasov, Herzen, Dostoevsky, and Grigorovich, not to mention a host of lesser figures. Belinsky's is an enviable record in comparison to Sainte-Beuve's lack of enthusiasm when first confronted with Balzac, Stendhal, Flaubert, and Baudelaire.

Yet it was essentially those articles that presented the broad outlines of literature, rather than his analyses of individual works, that give him his eminence as the greatest of Russia's literary historians, for he had to a remarkable degree the faculty for seeing things (whether correctly or not) in broad outlines, organized according to a unifying scheme. Thus his first important work, the "Literary Reveries" of 1834, despite its gaps of knowledge and its prejudices, is the first significant attempt to show the nature of Russian literature, its development, its historical logic, and its achievement. And his last significant critical article, "Russian Literature in 1847," turns on the relevance of literature to the current scene and the notion of progress.

Belinsky's career is usually treated in three stages, though his influence depends primarily on a small part of his work in the last five, or even two, years of his life, when he had reached the broadest and most forceful formulation of his views, when he began to turn literary criticism into discussions of social movements—conceived in moral rather than in political terms—and when, by his relentless and vehement opposition to metaphysics and theology, to roseate and sentimental views, he affected the whole course of literary and critical realism in Russia. Belinsky began his career under the profound influence of German romantic and idealistic philosophy, proclaiming that literature is "the expression of the national spirit, the symbol of the inner life of a nation, the physiognomy of a nation," that insight is gained through imagination and poetic discovery, that art is an organic whole, and that "the poet thinks in images." At this stage, as indeed throughout his career, Belinsky asserted that art had first to be art, and could only then serve or express other interests. He distinguished between the "real" and the "ideal" by the formula "Realism deals with life, idealism with ideas," differentiating works in the first group (Don Quixote, Onegin) from the second (Faust, Manfred). Art is connected with real life, rather than with abstract beauty or theory. As the "real" and "natural" gained ascendance in his scheme, as he came more and more to demand "the closest possible resemblance of the persons described to their models in life," he championed Gogol as a keen portrayer of Russian life, and praised Gogol's followers, the so-called "natural" school, who attempted to portray a character in his environment, for using proper methods to depict crying injustices. As time went on, he tended to place increasing emphasis on the real and its implications, and to minimize the "ideal" and the artistic. Thus after welcoming Dostoevsky's "realistic" Poor Folk (which he misread as a work in Gogol's tradition), he castigated Dostoevsky's first really original and important work, The Double, by writing, "The fantastic belongs only in lunatic asylums, not in literature. It is the business of doctors, not of poets."

Belinsky's middle phase, the two brief years 1840-1841, were a shock and embarrassment to his friends, and a source of infinite misery to himself. For with that peculiar Russian characteristic of carrying logical implications to impossible extremes even when these are demonstrably absurd or dangerous (which paradoxically is both the ultimate worship of reason and its absolute denial), Belinsky now adopted the Hegelian formula "All that is real is rational, all that is rational is real" literally. He accepted the social order he had so stanchly opposed before, and refused to fight its patent injustices. During these years he wrote about the universal, timeless themes, and on the fallacy of asking art to serve immediate ends. Finally he admitted his error and gratefully if painfully returned to the underlying and motivating impulse of his life and work: concern for the lives of human beings, whose misery could not be explained away or assuaged by any philosophical system or historical necessity. Thus in one of the early works of the final phase, "The Discourse on Criticism," he writes: "What is the art of our times? A judgment, an analysis of society, consequently criticism. . . . For our time a work of art is lifeless if it depicts life only in order to depict it, without a mighty subjective urge that springs from the prevailing thought of the epoch, if it is not a cry of suffering, or a dithyramb of rapture, if it is not a question, or an answer to a question."

He embarked at this time on a long series of articles on Pushkin, and was the first Russian critic to assess Pushkin's many-sided greatness. Belinsky keenly appreciated Pushkin's art, though he also had drastic blind spots about some of Pushkin's most perfect, but to Belinsky's mind trivial, works, such as the Tales of Belkin and the jocular narrative poems. (Belinsky and his followers were entirely devoid of humor.) While Belinsky greatly admires Pushkin's psychological and artistic skill, he now treats Pushkin as a purveyor of certain truths about Russian life and its development, particularly in the discussion of morality in Eugene Onegin. The correspondence between art and life has now become much closer. The next step is clear: Pushkin reflects a bygone era, and no longer adequately satisfies contemporary problems and readers, who find Lermontov's works more interesting, for they deal with current life. Gogol plays a central role in this shift, moving from "ideals" (in Belinsky's peculiar sense) to the copying of real life before him, introducing true Russian matter into literature. Belinsky praises Gogol for making the ugly and mean the subject of art, for introducing types from lower social levels, in short, for introducing life where previously only ideals reigned. Belinsky's wrath at what he considered Gogol's betrayal and apostasy, the wrath that he expressed in the famous "Letter," reached such proportions no doubt precisely because Gogol was the most gifted and important writer of the age. Parenthetically, it must be stated that only at the end of the nineteenth century did critics begin to question Belinsky's view of Gogol's realism.

Belinsky's education was spotty; he had no languages; his information and judgments were at times woefully deficient. But he loved literature profoundly. He also had critical genius, an immediate though far from infallible appreciation for excellence. He was able at once to penetrate to the essence of a work, to communicate it, to show its function and importance in the context of the times. He was, as has already been suggested, a man of complete honesty who never hesitated to say what he thought. His critical practice was to immerse himself in the work at hand until permeated by it, and then to expound the meaning as it appeared to him, largely through comments on extensive quotations. His work gives the impression of being improvised, written at white heat. It is prolix, ill organized, the style journalistic, obscure, confusing, and often grating, but remarkably vigorous and direct. It communicates the overwhelming excitement experienced by Belinsky himself, and lets the reader follow, as it were, the steps in Belinsky's contact with the text and the resulting view. Very frequently in his working articles he merely exclaims rapturously at the veracity and beauty of a passage, and lets the text speak for itself. When this has been done, he will frequently launch into a discussion of the underlying merits and implications, as, for example, in the articles on Lermontov, where he dissects the pose of Pechorin, notes that A Hero of Our Time mirrors current dissatisfaction with life, and observes a profound despair at life beneath the posturing and mask of Lermontov's verse.

His review articles and summaries differ in method and in impact. Here he moves, particularly in the later ones, to generalizations about literary requirements and achievements, about literature's reflection of the social scene. Historically they are his most important works, though critically such excathedra pronouncements do not show him to best advantage. He recognized, too, that his personality, his devotion and dedication to a moral vision, would ultimately be as influential as his written work. In fact the figure of Belinsky has become something of a legend, while his writings created a solid foundation for the "sociological" approach to literature, emphasizing that literature has a social function and that criticism's proper concern lies there rather than in the analysis of form.

The ten years that saw the flowering of German philosophical thought and the establishment of the intelligentsia have aptly been named "The Marvelous Decade" by one of its participants and its chief chronicler [P. V. Annenkov]. The decade from 1855-1865, when so many of the masterpieces of Russian literature appeared, can only be called something like the "Civic Decade" as far as criticism is concerned. It is dominated by two figures who saw themselves as the heirs of the tradition bequeathed by Belinsky but who used literary masterpieces as springboards for their own views. These were Nicolay Chernyshevsky and Nicolay Dobrolyubov. They were influenced by the English utilitarians Mill and Bentham; they were profoundly affected by the new materialism and scientific outlook; they were much more committed to a specific political platform of the far left, and actively campaigned for political reform under the guise of literary criticism. Aesthetic values went by the wayside. To these two may be added the most radical of all, Dmitri Pisarev, the incarnation of the nihilist in thought, campaigning ultimately for what in the title of one of his more militant pieces was "The Destruction of Aesthetics."

The period is ushered in by the disaster of the Crimean War, the death of the repressive autocrat Nicholas I (which was greeted as an occasion for great celebration by many), the promise of reforms that culminated in the abolition of serfdom in 1861 and a series of further reforms. Growing political consciousness created a background where social problems and theories and tendentious "civic" criticism could flourish.

The most important figure of the period was Nicolay Chernyshevsky (1828-1899). The son of a priest, he was educated at a theological school and attended the University of St. Petersburg, publishing his Master's dissertation on *The Aesthetic Relations of Art and Reality* (1855). In it he argues that art is merely an inferior reproduction of reality and that its only function is to spread knowledge about reality. No one, Chernyshevsky claims, would ever hesitate in choosing between a real apple and a painted one. Aesthetic achievement is dismissed as mere sensual pleasure, and infinitely inferior to beauty in real life. That same year he joined the staff of *The Contemporary,* the most liberal of the so-called "Thick Journals," monthly publications whose size engendered their name and which were devoted to economics, history, foreign affairs, philosophy, and literature. There he published his *Studies in the Gogol Period of Russian Literature,* patterned after Belinsky's longer attempts to convey the literary history of an era. The *Studies,* however, are far more documentary in scope, and less concerned with aesthetic values than with the correspondence of literature to life. Here, as in his long articles on Pushkin, Chernyshevsky "corrected" Belinsky's views by fitting the same literary works into his own theoretical frame. He wrote a number of critical articles before relinquishing the literary department to his brilliant protégé Dobrolyubov in order to devote himself to the economic and political sections. In 1862 he was arrested as the leader of the radicals. Before his exile to Siberia in 1863, an event that established him as the martyr of the radical cause, he wrote, in the Peter and Paul fortress, a work entitled *What Is To Be Done? (From Stories About the New Men),* a didactic novel conceived as an antidote to the unsuccessful revolutionary depicted in Turgenev's *Fathers and Children.* Here, in a work that can barely pretend to literary merit, he developed his ideas of science, reason, rationalism, man's acting for his own advantage, the doctrine of environment, of man's perfectibility and striving toward a harmonious, phalanstery-like community. The novel had an enormous vogue as a guide to radical youth, and has become a prototype for much Soviet fiction. Only in 1883 was Chernyshevsky allowed to return to Astrakhan, but he never came closer to the capital than Saratov, where he died in 1889.

Chernyshevsky had some keen insights into literature and into problems of language. His most perceptive criticism occurs in a short article on Tolstoy. In reviewing the *Sevastopol Sketches* (1856), he was the first to note that Tolstoy was a psychologist who describes "the psychic process itself, its forms, its laws, . . . the dialectics of the soul." Tolstoy is able to do more than communicate the mystery of the soul. He can dissect the movement of the soul, analyze it, explain it to the reader. Ironically, this man who had little use for literature first used the term "interior monologue" in an important passage of this review, applying it to that which passes in the mind of the dying soldier. Chernyshevsky also compares Tolstoy's descriptive art to that of the painter who catches the flicker of light on rustling leaves. Thus he grasped immediately two salient features of Tolstoy's art: his psychological finesse and his concern with fleeting states, that is, with change. But most of Chernyshevsky's articles can hardly be considered as literary criticism at all. His most famous article, "The Russian at the *Rendez-vous,*" ostensibly a review of Turgenev's elegiac story *Asya,* becomes an attack on the indecisiveness and weakness of Russian liberalism. The story develops into an instructive warning not to vacillate or hesitate, but to attain the goal. He dismisses Turgenev's poetic rendering of frustrated love with the typical and often quoted passage: "Forget about them, those erotic questions! They are not for a reader of our time, occupied with problems of administrative and judiciary improvements, of financial reforms, of the emancipation of the serfs."

Even in an English translation, the enormous differences between Belinsky and Chernyshevsky are manifest. Belinsky's vocabulary is heavily tinged with terms common to romantic and Hegelian philosophy; Chernyshevsky's, with scientific and sociological jargon of the mid-century. Belinsky's seriousness and excitement are communicated in the very inelegance of his prose; Chernyshevsky's turgid prose and heavy-handed irony convey pedantry and indifference to human problems. His meandering sentences frequently remain incomplete or incorrect, his logic specious. Belinsky repeats his central ideas in article after article; Chernyshevsky is incredibly repetitious even within so short a scope as the article on Tolstoy. Whatever the enormous significance of Chernyshevsky's dissertation in providing the philosophic basis for subsequent "radical" criticism, it clearly shows him to be a Philistine. His literary criticism reflects the discomfort of a man who would rather be dealing with ideas in a purer state than that possible in artistic garb.

Chernyshevsky did some pioneering work on Russian prosody in the process of defending Nekrasov's use of the rhythms and meters of folk poetry. He claimed that in Russian, trisyllabic feet are more natural (hence "nearer to prose" and "better") than bisyllabic, a concept that was later to play a considerable role in freeing Russian poetic forms. But his importance ultimately does not rest on these minor pieces within his voluminous production. He was, and remains, the central figure in Russian radical thought of that era, and its theoretician in many fields. In literature, too, he did yeoman service, by codifying and exemplifying the utilitarian function of literature.

The second figure, Nicolay Dobrolyubov (1836-1861), was, like Chernyshevsky, the son of a priest, and received his education at a theological seminary and pedagogical institute. He wrote much more extensively on literature than his predecessor and mentor had, but fundamentally had just as little concern for art, and in his capacity as literary critic he reviewed many works in the social sciences. In 1857 he assumed the post of critic for *The Contemporary,* thereby freeing Chernyshevsky for work in other fields. Again like Chernyshevsky, he felt that literature is merely words that can reflect but cannot change reality. At times, however, he felt that literature might be ''an auxiliary force, whose importance lies in propaganda.'' Dobrolyubov's important addition to the literary theories of his predecessors is that of ''social types.'' Dobrolyubov writes primarily about characters in literature, treating them as real beings when he does not use them for mere polemics. The rationale is that ''in these [living] images the poet may, imperceptibly even to himself, grasp and express an inner meaning long before his mind can define it. It is precisely the function of criticism to explain the meaning hidden in these images.'' In one of his last essays, on Dostoevsky's *Insulted and Injured*, an essay that shows greater concern for formal problems, he modified his view so far as to recognize that ''the poet creates a whole, finds a vital link, fuses and transforms the diverse aspects of living reality.''

Dobrolyubov's fame rests on four essays that deal with literary themes. Their titles are significant, for they indicate Dobrolyubov's polemical intention: ''What is Oblomovitis?'' (on Goncharov's *Oblomov*), ''When Will the Real Day Come?'' (on Turgenev's *On the Eve*), ''The Kingdom of Darkness'' (on Ostrovsky's plays about coarse bigotry and superstition among the old Moscow merchants), and an incredibly obtuse review of Ostrovsky's *The Storm* called ''A Ray of Light in the Kingdon of Darkness.''

The most important of these is clearly ''What is Oblomovitis?'' which in a sense creates, though it pretends to bury, ''the superfluous man.'' Looking over thirty years of Russian literature, Dobrolyubov claims a striking discovery about Russian literary heroes. Using Goncharov's Oblomov as his starting point, he generalizes about the pattern of vacillation, weakness, egotism, and inactivity ostensibly shared by such figures as Griboedov's Chatsky, Pushkin's Onegin, Lermontov's Pechorin, and Turgenev's Rudin. The literary character is judged for his failure in the real world—not the world of the novel—for literature, after all, is only a reflection of the real world. Oblomov thus becomes ''Oblomovitis,'' a disease common to Russians, whose roots lie in the moral and social corruption of society. Dobrolyubov uses the book as a springboard to the ''real'' world; and once he has explored the ills of that world, he projects them back onto the novel without, unfortunately, dealing with the novel itself or even analyzing its main character. Oblomov is merely a repellent nonentity, a symbol of the disease produced by the institution of serfdom.

The essay is important in the unfortunate practice of discussing literary characters as if they had real existence. Dobrolyubov is rigorous in this pursuit. He traces the literary ancestry of the heroine, primarily in order to elaborate on the development of Russian women in the past thirty years. He even denies Oblomov's foil, the efficient and active Stolz, a place as a figure in a novel of Russian life, for Stolz comes of a German family. Yet Dobrolyubov also notes that the portrait is abstract and not quite successful.

Similarly, Turgenev's *On the Eve* is the springboard for a discussion of Russian revolutionary possibilities. While it is perfectly obvious that Turgenev made Insarov a Bulgarian because the censor would never have passed a book depicting a Russian revolutionary, Dobrolyubov finds that this character can act because his cause is directed at a foreign oppressor, while a Russian would have to struggle against internal ills. Insarov is not a Russian, and hence is technically disqualified by Dobrolyubov, who nevertheless finds his ''indomitable loyalty to an idea'' interesting. The real point of the essay is

implied in the title: When will the day come when a Russian revolutionary can be depicted? Needless to say, for Dobrolyubov this clearly presupposes his existence in real life.

In no other article did Dobrolyubov stray so far from his text as in his analysis of Ostrovsky's *The Storm*. He read this gloomy play about a pitiful, ignorant, superstitious woman in an oppressive milieu as a kind of joyous glorification of the best in the Russian spirit. The heroine, Katerina, commits adultery, and later, in fear of the tortures of afterlife and in despair at her situation, commits suicide. Dobrolyubov saw in Katerina an ''instinctive consciousness of her inalienable right to love, happiness, and life,'' and in her death an inspiration to readers, an assertion that tyranny, as represented by the microcosm of the merchant family, would no longer be countenanced. It is a prime example of exalted feelings and laudable sentiments making for very poor criticism.

Had Dobrolyubov not died at so young an age, he might well have developed into a major critic. He was very gifted, and for all his concern with political implications had considerable sense of literature, in part evident in the verse he wrote. To be sure, it is ''civic verse,'' and not of striking quality, but it testifies to a deeper involvement with art than his theoretical formulations would lead one to expect.

In some ways a more interesting figure, and the most radical of all, is Dmitri Pisarev, who incarnates the mid-century realistic temperament in what Turgenev called its ''nihilistic'' phase. He drowned in 1868 at the age of twenty-eight (there is some suspicion that he committed suicide), after spending a number of years in prison for having published radical propaganda. A member of the gentry, with considerable sensitivity to language and form, he deliberately affected a crude and coarse approach. He campaigned for the ''Destruction of Aesthetics,'' asserting that a pair of shoes was better than a Shakespearean tragedy, for the former could be worn, while nothing could come of the latter. Even ''radical criticism'' was dismissed; in ''Pushkin and Belinsky,'' the most vicious of his articles, he disposes of Pushkin as a frivolous poet without an adequate sense of social consciousness, and just as crudely dismisses Belinsky for having wasted his time by taking Pushkin's work seriously and commenting on it.

Pisarev's is essentially an anarchical mind, expressed at the extreme of utilitarianism. He refused to grant value to any manifestation that has no social consequence, and rejoices at the decline of letters. His review of *Crime and Punishment* ignores the novel in order to discuss poverty as the cause of crime. *War and Peace* is for him a senseless glorification of the old aristocracy, a waste of time. But Pisarev's reputation began with a rebuttal to Dobrolyubov's views of Oblomov, and his best work deals with the definition of the ''new man'' adumbrated by Chernyshevsky. Pisarev's most solid work is his review (''The Realists'') of Turgenev's *Fathers and Children,* where he gave an acute analysis of Bazarov's character and significance. He saw, through what was more an act of insight into himself than an act of critical genius, the essence of his temperament and of the aspirations of his contemporaries, and he projected it clearly. In his iconoclasm, in his violent, independent, and sometimes imaginative sallies, he stands somewhat apart from the tradition of Belinsky, Chernyshevsky, and Dobrolyubov, though he clearly has many points in common with it.

The tradition begun by Belinsky was thus extended and codified by Chernyshevsky, Dobrolyubov and, to a far lesser extent,

Pisarev. It was by no means the only critical camp. It would be instructive to compile a collection of essays by such figures as Maykov, Druzhinin, Grigoryev, Strakhov, and others who are more interesting as critics and who have been unjustly neglected, indeed, who have not even been reprinted. Yet it is clear that the tradition discussed here was the more important one in the nineteenth century, affecting the attitudes and interests of a large portion of the reading public and of lesser writers. The most important determinant of this direction was the practice and perhaps even more the figure of Belinsky. For all his crudity and critical errors, he served as a reminder and an inspiration for the deep moral and social importance of art. His followers, men of smaller stature, committed to more immediate aims and more doctrinaire methods, played a more important political role. They emphasized the philosophical, ideological implication of art at the expense of the aesthetic, but in the process created a type of criticism that for the first time dealt systematically with the relation between literature and society. Such criticism, of course, has by now been extensively practiced, and underlies the work of critics as disparate in mind and sensitivity as V. L. Parrington and Edmund Wilson. In Russia the tradition itself was continued, adapted to changing needs and views, and modified by men like N. K. Mikhaylovsky, G. Plekhanov, Lunacharsky, and others. Its final, logical metamorphosis is "Socialist Realism," the prescriptive Soviet doctrine that literature and art must depict reality while simultaneously showing man in the progress toward a better, socialist life. (pp. ix-xx)

> Ralph E. Matlaw, in an introduction to Belinsky, Chernyshevsky, and Dobrolyubov: Selected Criticism, edited by Ralph E. Matlaw, E. P. Dutton & Co., Inc., 1962, pp. vii-xx.

MARC SLONIM

[Slonim was a Russian-born American critic who wrote extensively on Russian literature. In the following excerpt, Slonim places the Civic Critics in the historical context of the late 1850s and the 1860s, discussing their writings as an expression of and influence on the radical temper of the times.]

The reign of Nicholas I ended [in 1855] with the collapse of an illusion—the unhappy Crimean war of 1854-5 bared all the technical and political ills of a régime which had previously boasted of its strength. Slavophiles, as well as Westernizers, bitterly resented military defeat accompanied by a loss of prestige in Europe and in the Middle East. The new Czar Alexander II lacked firmness. He could not break away from his reactionary environment or destroy the wall erected by the court between the throne and the country; but he became aware of the necessity for reforms, and was ready to grant them, without, however, going too far. This ambivalence caused all the contradictions in his policy and had fateful consequences; but at the beginning of Alexander II's reign, his liberal tendencies prevailed, and under the pressure of public opinion the formidable problem of serfdom, the greatest issue in Russian life, was finally solved. In 1861 the Czar's decree announcing its abolition set free millions of peasants who were granted land allotments with the retention of mir, the collective rural community.... The peasants, however, had to pay the price of their freedom—indemnities to landowners on an instalment basis. By 1903, the sum paid by Russian peasants (with poll taxes and accrued interest) rose to over a billion gold dollars.

The liberation of the serfs released new economic forces and necessitated readjustments in the whole fabric of the State.

Measures taken by the government changed the face of the country, and the sixties were called the 'era of great reforms'. The introduction of Zemstwo, local self-government which, despite its limited functions and nondemocratic structure, played a great role in Russia's social development; the establishment of universal military training (with certain exemptions for privileged classes); the revision of the Judicial Code, followed by public hearings, trial by jury, and the abolition of corporal punishment (retained, however, for peasants and Siberian exiles); relaxation of censorship, expansion of education based on a new school system, widening of academic freedom in universities, annulment of restrictions in the Press and book trade—these and many other improvements stirred every social group. Even though the basic relationship between the ruling group and the rest of the country remained untouched, and autocracy maintained its absolute 'divine' rights, rejecting the idea of a parliamentary régime, still, the impact of the transformation was momentous, and it was within the social, economic, and political framework created in the sixties that Russia lived and grew until the first revolution of 1905.

The liberation of the serfs, the rise of the bourgeoisie and the economic progress of the lower middle class strongly affected educated society. The Romantic military nobleman of the twenties and the idealistic landowner or civil servant of the forties, were replaced by the intellectual who hailed practicality and action. The nobility kept losing its exclusive cultural position; and 'rasnochintsy', scions of various social groups, mostly of the lower classes, and all with new intellectual attitudes, rose to important positions in arts, letters, and science. The 'rasnochintsy' sustained the 'natural school' in literature and applauded Ostrovsky's plays; they promoted realism in painting and music and greatly contributed to the development of the natural sciences; in fact, they dominated the whole artistic and moral atmosphere of the period. Their rationalism and social radicalism found its expression in the works by Nicholas Chernyshevsky, son of a priest, economist, and literary critic. His articles in The Contemporary, a most influential monthly, attacked sentimentalism and Utopism, and interpreted current literary production, poetry and prose alike, as determined by social and material environment. The authorities, disturbed by the growing popularity of this socialist, and his influence on the youth, arrested Chernyshevsky, accused him of plotting against the security of the State, and, despite scanty legal evidence, sentenced him to hard labour. After twenty-one years of Siberian exile, he was allowed to return to Russia; but he died a few years later, a broken man. During his lifetime, his name was banned from the Russian Press; he was usually called the 'author of Essays on the Gogol Period in Russian Literature', the title of his important series of articles on Gogol, in which he analysed the salient features of the 'natural school' and announced the victory of realism in Russian letters. The radical youth, however, mentioned him in their songs as the author of What is to be Done? Chernyshevsky wrote this famous novel while imprisoned in the St. Peter and Paul Fortress in St. Petersburg, and his heroes such as Vera Pavlovna, the new emancipated woman, or Kirsanov, the rationalist physician, served as models for young nihilists and radicals. Even more popular and impressive seemed to them the third protagonist of this fictional social manifesto, the young nobleman Rakhmetov, who renounces all the pleasures of the earth in order to serve the cause. Even though he is utterly unbelievable and poorly depicted, he symbolized the dreams of the young and inflamed their imagination. They saw in his monastic severity and intransigent extremism a perfect counterpart to the 'superfluous man'. However curious it might seem, this bloodless figure initiated a series of equally artificial images which abounded in Soviet fiction between 1930 and 1955, when dozens of energetic and virtuous party secretaries were themselves moulded on Rakhmetov.

In the twentieth century Chernyshevsky was often considered as a forerunner of communist aesthetics. He not only affirmed the supremacy of life over art, considering literary works solely as reflections of social phenomena, but he also made an attempt at building a theoretical basis for the strictly sociological method he employs in his dry, pedestrian critical essays. His pupil, Nicholas Dobroliubov, also the son of a priest and former student in a theological seminary, was a much better writer. Even though he never departed from the strictures of sociological methods, his articles on Turgenev, Goncharov, and Ostrovsky, went beyond the analysis of ideas and social conditions. But the tone of his and Chernyshevsky's essays, in which art was interpreted as a direct representation of reality, determined Russian literary criticism for years to come. Dobroliubov identified literature with social service, and demanded from writers a conscientious effort at reforming society. The work of art was to him a source of energy and an expression of ideas. Its contents actually shaped its form. For a generation which was more interested in economics and natural science than in history and philosophy, such statements appeared very logical and attractive. Young men and women of the sixties always wanted to deal with 'facts' and looked with contempt at 'castles-in-the-air'. Their aspirations were formulated in a most challenging way by the 'enfant terrible' of the period, Dimitri Pisarev, a young nobleman who possessed the witty pen of a first-rate journalist and polemicist. Like Dobroliubov's, his life was short (he died at the age of twenty-eight, probably committing suicide), but he was already well known at twenty-two. Each of his articles made a sensation—he seemed to be the exact voice of his contemporaries, uttering what they thought and wished to say. First of all, he discarded sentimentalism, platonic love, idealism, and poetic dreams as 'sheer drivel', as a sign of weakness. 'Whatever detracts us from our main tasks—education, scientific development, material, and social progress—is useless and therefore obnoxious'—this statement by Pisarev became gospel to the young. They agreed heartily when he said that money spent on ballet, theatre and books of poetry should be used for building railroads, Pisarev attacked Pushkin's works as 'something that merely helped the drones to kill time'. While he enjoyed making such statements ('a pair of boots is more useful than a Shakespeare play') in order to 'tease the philistine', his readers took him most seriously. Thousands of them were rallying under the banner of 'positive thinking and no nonsense'.

Chernyshevsky and Dobroliubov were mainly concerned with large economic and social issues, and emphasized the problems of history and political change. Pisarev was chiefly interested in the individual and advised his followers to rely on experimental knowledge as the 'only safe ground for a truly rational outlook on nature, man, and society'. He denied all authority, moral or literary, and spoke of independence of judgement, freedom, and utility as the supreme guiding principles for every self-respecting person. The nihilists were particularly sensitive to these sermons. Their revolt began within their family—they questioned paternal authority, challenged social conventions and good manners, broke away from homes, and adopted brusque, often coarse ways of speech and behaviour. A great many of them came from the nobility, and their defiance of the accepted code was simply a reaction against the stuffiness of 'gentlefolk nests' and the idealistic aestheticism of their

elders. It was precisely among the upper classes that the term 'nihilism' acquired its derogatory meaning and became the symbol of anarchy and debauchery.

Horrified mothers and fathers saw girls cut their hair, smoke cigarettes and—the sign of utter perdition—treat males as equals, while boys wore peasant boots and Russian blouses, grew long whiskers, talked loudly without mincing their words and spoke of religion as 'a lot of trash'. The new fashion called for the strangest kind of attire ('we have no time for such trifles as coiffeurs, frills, and cosmetics'), and it certainly was the unusual exterior of the nihilists that struck the imagination of their less eccentric contemporaries. A bespectacled student with bobbed hair (if female) and with long hair (if male) represented the nihilist in the eyes of polite society; but for the authorities, nihilist meant 'an enemy of the established order'. In truth, nihilism was initially non-political—under its disguise of rudeness and exaggeration lay a desire for work and practical action. It was egotistical and secular. Thousands of its followers went into all sorts of professions, contributed to the building of railroads and schools or studied abroad; and the movement for feminine emancipation originated in nihilist circles, spread far and wide throughout Russia and forced the government to establish various institutions of higher learning for women.

In the early sixties, nihilism remained within the bounds of a purely intellectual fad. Its followers sympathized with the socialist and radical trend of their times, but were not politically-minded. The chance came when their attempts at practical activity clashed with police authority, and when they were confronted with the actual conditions of Russian life. The government looked at them with suspicion and hampered their efforts; and their discontent coincided with that in liberal and radical circles, when expectations of a basic change in Russia's régime and in a 'crowning of reforms' were not fulfilled. The Czar, swayed by members of the landed aristocracy and old bureaucrats, refused to yield to the idea of parliamentary monarchy and kept intact his autocratic rule. Besides, even after the reforms, the whole structure of Russian society was most discriminatory, and only classes privileged by birth (aristocracy and nobility), function (bureaucracy and clergy), wealth (landed proprietors and 'Merchants of the First Guild'), or education (university graduates), fully enjoyed civic rights. The peasants, the lower middle class, the artisans, the workers, the common folk at the base of the social pyramid, were treated as 'scum of the earth' and were subject to oppression, exploitation, and abuse. The young radicals did not hesitate to express their feelings in revolutionary action, and in 1866 Karakozov, a university student, fired at the Czar. After his execution, authorities adopted an iron-handed policy which, instead of inspiring fear, heightened the tension. The nihilists, who before were mainly interested in their personal rebellion, became involved in political conspiracy. Numerous underground circles in which the writings of Herzen and Chernyshevsky, as well as those of Western economists and sociologists were discussed, became sources of revolutionary propaganda.

By the beginning of the seventies, the transformation was complete. While the educated society, chiefly the youth, was seething with clandestine left-wing agitation, the influence of Dobroliubov, Psarev, and other 'men of the sixties' (such as Zaitsev and Tkachev), was supplanted by that of the exponents of socialism. (pp. 110-18)

Marc Slonim, "From Nihilists to Revolutionaries," in his An Outline of Russian Literature, *Oxford University Press, London, 1958, pp. 110-22.*

THE CIVIC CRITICS AND RUSSIAN NIHILISM

JAMES P. SCANLAN

[*In the following excerpt, the critic examines the emergence of Russian nihilism under the leadership of the Civic Critics, contrasting the nihilists' social and philosophical views with those of their intellectual forerunners, the "Westernizers" of the 1840s.*]

When Michael Bakunin closed his essay, "The Reaction in Germany," in 1842 with a celebration of "the passion for destruction," he was in effect anticipating the men of the 1860's—Russian thinkers who went much further in intellectual and social iconoclasm than the Westernizers of the 1840's. On a positive foundation of utilitarianism and materialism in philosophy, the men of this later generation mounted an all-out attack on prevailing Russian social institutions and habits of thought. They were the Russian "Nihilists," led by Nicholas Chernyshevsky (1828-1889), Nicholas Dobrolyubov (1836-1861), and Dmitry Pisarev (1840-1868).

Bakunin himself was a Westernizer whose long and active career as writer and revolutionary spanned both periods, and he accepted the later, Nihilist outlook almost as completely as the younger men did. But on the whole the Westernizers were an obsolete older generation in the eyes of the Nihilists—a situation forcefully dramatized in Ivan Turgenev's *Fathers and Sons* (1862), which gave the very word "Nihilist" to Russian literature and thence to the world. The "fathers" of the novel are full of humanitarian, progressive sentiments; like Belinsky and Herzen, they extol "personality" and individual dignity. But to the "sons," typified by the brusque, scientifically minded Bazarov, the "fathers" were concerned too much with generalities, not enough with the specific material evils of the day. They tended to look at things aesthetically and abstractly rather than scientifically and concretely. "Nature," Bazarov says, "is not a temple but a workshop." Science and its direct practical application alone will benefit man, and no accepted principles or moral rules, no established social institutions, no useless cultural frills like music or painting must be allowed to distract man from them. In one of their direct confrontations, an incredulous "father" questions the Nihilist "sons":

> "I do not understand how you can avoid recognizing principles, rules. What is the motive of your actions?"
>
> "I have already told you, uncle, that we don't recognize any authorities," Arkady intervened.
>
> "We act by the force of what we recognize as beneficial," Bazarov declared. "At the present time rejection is the most beneficial of all things, and so we reject."
>
> "Everything?"
>
> "Everything."
>
> "How? Not only art, poetry—but also—it is a terrible thing to say—"
>
> "Everything!" Bazarov repeated with complete imperturbability.

To the "fathers" they seemed a strange new breed.

The flesh and blood Nihilist leaders bore greater resemblance to human beings and were less alienated from their intellectual forebears than Turgenev suggests, but they *were* men of a somewhat different sort. For one thing, they came chiefly from a lower social stratum. Among the Westernizers only Belinsky was not a member of the gentry; the others were cultivated gentlemen who never completely lost the aura of aristocracy. Among the Nihilists, on the other hand, only Pisarev was of gentry origin. Both Chernyshevsky and Dobrolyubov were sons of provincial Russian Orthodox priests, and in general the Nihilists represented a new class on the Russian intellectual scene—the *raznochintsy*, or men of miscellaneous rank below the gentry: they came from the families of clerics, professional men, minor officials, merchants. Many of them supported themselves by writing for literary journals when they were not in prison or in Siberia. Deeply, even fanatically, dedicated to the cause of freedom and justice, they were the first true members of the non-aristocratic Russian *"intelligentsia"* (another word given to the world by these mid-nineteenth-century currents of Russian intellectual life).

Furthermore, the Nihilists of the 1860's and the Westernizers of the 1840's lived in different social climates. The men of the forties pleaded for reforms which could scarcely be anything but distant dreams at the height of Nicholas' absolutism. Both Herzen and Bakunin emigrated, and Belinsky died young in 1848. But even while they lived in Russia they were more spectators than hopeful activitists, always somewhat removed from the possibility of genuine change. The men of the sixties, on the other hand, had had their appetites whetted for reform. A liberal spirit swept over Russia with the accession of Alexander II in 1855. Restrictions on admittance to the universities were eased, control of the press was reduced, and broad social reforms were promised—above all the abolition of serfdom. When emancipation finally came in 1861, however, it was a bitter disappointment to the men of the sixties, for its terms gave the serfs little chance of economic self-sufficiency or genuine freedom. There were peasant uprisings and student disturbances. Nationalist disorders in Poland added to the agitation of both the government and the *intelligentsia*. Repressive measures against the universities and the press were reintroduced, and the upsurge of hope dating from 1855 began another decline. Chernyshevsky was arrested in 1862 and banished to Siberia in 1864. Pisarev was also arrested in 1862, was imprisoned in the Peter and Paul fortress in Saint Petersburg until 1866, and died near Riga, Latvia, in 1868. The Nihilists, closer to the immediate social evils of Russian life and to the possibility of reform, had greater reason to grow frustrated and take to extremes as this possibility was removed.

A final difference between the Westernizers and the Nihilists lay in their intellectual ancestry. The Westernizers were reared on German idealism, progressing from its romantic extremes to Hegel, who at least temporarily had a great attraction for them. The Nihilists were never enthusiastic idealists if they were idealists at all. Their intellectual pabulum was Feuerbach, the French socialists, and the German "vulgar materialists." Büchner, Moleschott, and Vogt were favorites. Comte's positivism appealed to them. John Stuart Mill came to have great influence among them: they detested his bourgeois liberalism but accepted wholeheartedly the utilitarian pleasure-principle and its ruthless application to hoary traditions and institutions. Later they read Darwin, who appealed to them because he brought man out of the clouds and into the mud of animal life—though Chernyshevsky preferred the Lamarckian version of the mechanics of evolution. Unlike the Westernizers, they never passed through a stage of spiritualizing man or advocating a "reconciliation with reality."

It is hardly surprising, then, that the Nihilists should surpass the Westernizers in debunking and rejecting. All these influences conspired to give them a naturalistic outlook in philosophy and a horror of the social *status quo*; their attention was directed to temporal man, encumbered by "irrational" institutions that had, they thought, no right to exist. No doubt they found it not only an intellectual duty but a pleasure to prick the balloons of pompous conventionalism and "aestheticism" in Russian thought and life. Not a little sheer perverse satisfaction is in evidence when Pisarev puts chefs and billiards players on an artistic level with Beethoven and Raphael, or enjoins writers to "hate with a great and holy hatred the enormous mass of petty and rotten stupidities" in Russian life. Among the Nihilist leaders' less scholarly disciples and among the Russian students who used the name "Nihilism" to dignify youthful rebelliousness, this rejection of traditional standards went still further, expressing itself in everything from harmless crudities of dress and behavior to the lethal fanaticism of a revolutionary like Sergey Nechayev. And it was a "Nihilist student," Dmitry Karakozov, whose attempt on the Tsar's life in 1866 completed the return of Russian society to the dark repression of the era of Nicholas I.

It would be a mistake, however, to regard the intellectual leaders of Nihilism as bomb-throwing negativists devoid of positive interests or ideals—a misinterpretation unfortunately fostered by the term "Nihilism" itself. Actually a coherent positive doctrine lay behind the harsh slogans; the rejections had a purpose. The "great and holy hatred" Pisarev recommended was needed, he maintained, because existing practices prevented "the ideas of the good, the true, and the beautiful from clothing themselves in flesh and blood and becoming living actuality." Indeed, the philosophical message of Nihilism suffered more from dogmatism than from negativism: the Nihilists were cocksure of their ideas, and they formulated them in a blunt, simplistic fashion foreign to the more measured reflections of the older generation of Westernizers. Chernyshevsky maintains, for example, that "the moral sciences already have theoretical answers to nearly all the problems that are important for life," and as he presents them these answers are by no means complex. Oversimplified and dogmatic, a philosophical system is nonetheless offered by the Nihilists which can be summarized briefly under traditional headings.

Metaphysically, the Nihilists adopted a broadly materialistic position. Both Chernyshevsky and Pisarev explicitly regarded themselves as materialists. To the philosophical critic of today, however, the materialism of the Nihilists, like that of the present-day Dialectical Materialists, may seem extremely capacious, if not vague. Pisarev, in "Nineteenth-Century Scholasticism," identifies materialism simply with the view that only what is perceptible exists, and a similar conception is adopted by Chernyshevsky in "The Anthropological Principle in Philosophy." Pisarev himself provided a revealing commentary on the broad use of "materialism" and related philosophical terms by Russian thinkers: "Since we ourselves," he writes, "have hitherto not been party to any philosophical school, we have contrived to give our own meaning to all the philosophical terms which have come to us in accordance with the level of our own intellectual processes. The results have been most unexpected: anyone who eats, drinks, and sleeps to excess we call a materialist, while to utter fools who cannot do anything practical we give the name of romantic or idealist." But under whatever name, the Nihilists were concerned to view man as a unitary animal organism, to deny the existence of "spirits" of any sort, embodied or disembodied—in short, to acknowledge the world of the natural sciences as the world of reality.

Vissarian Belinsky.

Man, says Chernyshevsky, is a complex chemical compound, governed strictly by the law of causality.

On this "scientific" basis, Chernyshevsky and Pisarev advanced a hedonistic ethics of "rational egoism" or egoistic utilitarianism in which man is viewed as acting, inevitably and properly, to promote his own self-interest. Their objection to what Pisarev called "moral twaddle" was, like Nietzsche's after them, not an objection to the realm of the ethical as such but to an unrealistic and sentimental emphasis on altruism and benevolence—impulses by which men are never really moved. In this connection, despite their exposure to the writing of John Stuart Mill, they more closely resembled the earlier British utilitarians, Jeremy Bentham and James Mill. But while the Nihilists emphasize man's selfishness they also insist that only in an ill-constructed society does egoism yield socially undesirable consequences. In a properly ordered society the most egoistic behavior will also be the behavior most prouctive of the public good. Fundamentally and naturally, the interests of society and the interests of the individual are identical.

As for the social philosophy in which this proper ordering of society is depicted, however, there is again considerable looseness in the Nihilists' doctrine—owing at least in part to the fact that censorship prevented the frank expression of radical convictions. They were, of course, democrats and socialists. In his famous novel, *What Is To Be Done?*, the most influential literary vehicle of Nihilism, Chernyshevsky addressed himself to the socialist order of the future in which cooperation rather than competition would prevail. But aside from idealized pictures of a seamstresses' cooperative, the book contains little specific discussion of how this order is to come about or precisely what it will consist of. In other writings Chernyshevsky took up the idea, first stated by Herzen, that the commune and the *artel* gave Russia a ''special path'' to socialism; but it was left to the Populists of the 1870's to construct a comprehensive social philosophy incorporating this idea.

In many respects the most significant area of Nihilist philosophical activity was the sphere of aesthetics, literary criticism, and art. Here again censorship played an important role: literary criticism was permissible where social or religious criticism was not. As a result, much of what is most interesting in the writings of these as well as of other nineteenth-century Russian thinkers comes in the guise of literary criticism or theory of art. But there was also a substantive reason for the Nihilists' attention to aesthetics: it was the stronghold of everything they opposed philosophically. Existing conceptions of aesthetics and art were the bulwark of sentimentalism, emotionalism, irrationalism, spiritualism, and, most of all, of the expenditure of valuable social resources on ''useless frills.'' When Pisarev calls for ''the annihilation of aesthetics'' it is these conceptions, survivals from the heyday of German romanticism and idealism, that he is attacking. For the Nihilists art *can* be justifiable and valuable, but only if it is *socially useful*. Literature, in particular, can perform an important function in awakening and educating men, stimulating them to improve themselves and ultimately to improve society; to do so it must be hortatory and didactic. On this ground the Russian tradition of ''civic criticism,'' inaugurated by Belinsky in his later years, flourished at the hands first of Dobrolyubov and then of Pisarev among the Nihilists.

But while the major Nihilists gave art a significant role in society, and devoted their own energies largely to the service of art in the form of literature, it was *science* that they saw as man's single most potent intellectual tool. More than anything else it is the worship of natural science that characterized Nihilism as a positive philosophical attitude in the Russia of the 1860's. The Nihilists rejected art when it lay completely outside the realm of science or did not serve science. They rejected history as a study because its content and methods were scientifically dubious. Pisarev observes somewhat petulantly in ''The Realists'' that if Belinsky had had a proper education in mathematics and the natural sciences, he would have done Russia ten times more good, given his enormous talent, than he did with the ''semi-literary, semi-philosophical'' education he received. Study the natural sciences and follow no authority but that of your own scientific intellect—such in brief was the positive message of Nihilism.

As a movement Nihilism did not outlast the sixties. By the end of that decade the major figures were either dead or banished, and most of the minor figures had emigrated, many to join the Bakuninist party of revolutionary anarchists. Never a numerous movement, Nihilism nonetheless spawned much discussion, not only among its supporters but also among its critics. Dostoevsky, for example, whose novel *The Possessed* portrays Nihilist leaders in a severly critical light, was strongly affected by Nihilism and returned to the subject repeatedly in other works. Through the Nihilist movement the secularization and radicalization of the Russian *intelligentsia* was completed and a major step was taken toward the more fully developed materialism and socialism of the Russian Marxists. As forerunners of Marxism-Leninism in Russia, the Nihilist leaders are highly regarded by present-day Soviet thinkers. (pp. 3-10)

James P. Scanlan, ''The Nihilists,'' in Russian Philosophy: The Nihilists, the Populists, Critics of Religion and Culture, Vol. II, *edited by James M. Edie and others, Quadrangle Books, 1965, pp. 1-10.*

NICOLAS BERDYAEV

[*Berdyaev was a Russian historian, critic, and philosopher best known for political and religious writings. He suffered imprisonment and exile under both the czarist and communist governments for his outspoken criticism of both regimes, and spent most of the latter part of his life in Paris. There he published his most important critical, historical, and philosophical works, including* The Bourgeois Mind, and Other Essays, Freedom and the Spirit, The Fate of Man in the Modern World, *and* The Destiny of Man. *In the following excerpt, Berdyaev discusses Russian nihilism as a religious phenomenon and outlines the views of the Civic Critics, stressing ascetic elements of their lives and thought.*]

Nihilism is a characteristically Russian phenomenon; in its Russian form it is unknown in Western Europe. In the narrower sense of the word, nihilism is the intellectual liberation movement of the 'sixties, and Pisarev is recognized as its chief exponent. The Russian nihilist was sketched by Turgeniev in Bazarov. But in actual fact nihilism is a much wider thing than that for which Pisarev stands. It is to be found in the subsoil of Russian social movements, although nihilism in itself is not a social movement. There is a nihilist basis in Lenin, although he lives in another epoch. ''We are all nihilists,'' says Dostoyevsky. Russian nihilism denied God, the soul, the spirit, ideas, standards and the highest values. And none the less nihilism must be recognized as a religious phenomenon. It grew up on the spiritual soil of Orthodoxy; it could appear only in a soul which was cast in an Orthodox mould. It is Orthodox asceticism turned inside out, an asceticism without Grace. At the base of Russian nihilism, when grasped in its purity and depth, lies the Orthodox rejection of the world, its sense of the truth that ''the whole world lieth in wickedness,'' the acknowledgement of the sinfulness of all riches and luxury, of all creative profusion in art and in thought. Like Orthodox asceticism, nihilism was an individualist movement, but it was also directed against the fulness and richness of life. Nihilism considers as sinful luxury, not only art, metaphysics and spiritual values, but religion also. All its strength must be devoted to the emancipation of earthly man, the emancipation of the labouring people from their excessive suffering, to establishing conditions of happy life, to the destruction of superstition and prejudice, conventional standards and lofty ideas, which enslave man and hinder his happiness. That is the one thing needful, all else is of the Devil. In the intellectual sphere, one must find an ascetic satisfaction in the natural sciences, which destroy the old beliefs, and overthrow prejudices, and in political economy which inculcates the organization of a more righteous social order.

Nihilism is the negative of Russian apocalyptic. It is a revolt against the injustices of history, against false civilization; it is a demand that history shall come to an end, and a new life, outside or above history, begin. Nihilism is a demand for nakedness, for the stripping from oneself of all the trappings of culture, for the annihilation of all historical traditions, for the setting free of the natural man, upon whom there will no longer be fetters of any sort. The intellectual asceticism of nihilism found expression in materialism; any more subtle philosophy was proclaimed a sin.

The Russian nihilists of the 'sixties—and I have in mind not only Pisarev but also Chernishevsky, Dobrolyubov and others—were Russian prophets of enlightenment. They declared war against all historical traditions; they opposed "reason," the existence of which as materialists they could not recognize, to all the beliefs and prejudices of the past. But the Russian prophets of enlightenment, in accord with the maximalist character of the Russian people, always became nihilists. Voltaire and Diderot were not nihilists. In Russia, materialism assumed an entirely different character from its Western form. Materialism was turned into a peculiar sort of dogmatic theology. This is a striking fact about the materialism of the communists. But already in the 'sixties materialism had assumed this theological tinge; it became a dogma of moral obligation and behind it was concealed a distinctive nihilist asceticism. A materialist catechism was framed, and was adopted by the fanatical circles of the left Russian intelligentsia. Not to be a materialist was to be taken as a moral suspect. If you were not a materialist, then you were in favour of the enslavement of man both intellectually and politically. The attitude of the Russian nihilists to science was idolatrous. Science, by which was to be understood principally the natural sciences, which at that time were presented in materialist colours, became an object of faith; it was turned into an idol. There were admirable scholars in Russia at that date who in themselves constituted a special phenomenon. But the nihilist prophets of enlightenment were not men of science. They were men of belief—and dogmatic belief. The methodical doubt of Descartes suits the nihilists, and indeed the Russian nature in general, but little. The typical Russian cannot go on doubting for very long; his inclination is to make a dogma for himself fairly quickly, and to surrender himself to that dogma whole-heartedly and entirely. A Russian sceptic is a Western type in Russia. There was nothing sceptical in Russian materialism; it was a faith.

In nihilism still another trait of the Russian Orthodox type was reflected in a distorted view, the lack of a solution of the problem of culture due to the Orthodox background of Russian mentality. Ascetic Orthodoxy was doubtful about the justifiability of culture; it was inclined to see sinfulness in cultural creativeness. This found expression in the painful doubt felt by the great Russian writers about the justifiability of their own literary work. Religious, moral and social doubt of the justification of culture is a most characteristically Russian theme. Doubt has been constantly expressed among us as to whether philosophical and artistic creativeness is justifiable. The problem of the cost at which culture is purchased will be dominant in the social thought of the 'seventies. Russian nihilism was a withdrawal from a world which "lieth in wickedness," a break with the family and with all settled and established life. Russians accepted this break more easily than Western peoples. They considered the State, law and traditional morals sinful, for these things had been used to justify the enslavement of man.

More remarkable than anything is the fact that Russians, when nihilism had shaped them, readily sacrificed themselves and went to penal servitude and the gallows. They were striving after a future, but for themselves they had no hope whatever, either in this earthly life or in the life everlasting which they denied. They did not understand the Mystery of the Cross, but they were in the highest degree capable of sacrifice and renunciation. In this respect they compared favourably with the Christians of their day, who displayed very little capacity for sacrifice, and so repelled men from Christianity. Chernishevsky, who was a genuine ascetic in life, said that he preached liberty, but for himself he would never avail himself of any sort of liberty whatever, lest it should be thought that he defended liberty with a selfish purpose. The wonderful capacity

for sacrifice in men of a materialist view of life is evidence of the fact that nihilism was a distinctively religious phenomenon.

It was not by chance that seminarists, children of priests and those who passed through the Orthodox school played a great part in Russian nihilism. Dobrolyubov and Chernishevsky were sons of arch-priests and had studied in a seminary. The ranks of the "left" intelligentsia among us were filled to a large extent by members of the clerical class. The significance of this fact is twofold. In the theological school the seminarist acquired a certain configuration of spirit in which ascetic denial of the world played a large part. At the same time, among the seminarists of the second half of the 'fifties and the beginning of the 'sixties, a violent protest against the decadent Orthodoxy of the nineteenth century was coming to a head, against the unseemliness of the lives of the clergy, and against the obscurantist atmosphere of the clerical schools. Seminarists were beginning to be permeated by the emancipating ideas of education, but permeated after the Russian fashion, that is to say, in an extremist, nihilist manner. No small part in this was played by the *ressentiment* of the seminarists to the culture of the nobility. At the same time a thirst for social justice was awakening in the young, and for them it meant the birth of Christianity in a new form. The seminarists and *raznochintsi* brought with them a new build of character, sterner, ethical, exacting and exclusive, formed by a severer and more painful school of life than that in which the cultured members of the nobility had grown up. This new young generation changed the type of Russian culture. The type of culture in the men of the 'sixties, Dobrolyubov, Chernishevsky, the nihilists, the growing revolutionary intelligentsia, was somewhat low in comparison with that of the cultured nobility of the 'thirties and 'forties, the culture of Chaadaev, Iv. Kireevsky, Khomyakov, Granovsky and Hertzen. Culture always develops and reaches more finished forms in aristocratic circles. When it becomes democratic and is diffused among other classes of society, its standard is lowered, and only later, as the human material is worked over, can culture rise higher again. That same process went on in Russia on a small scale among the intelligentsia of the 'sixties, and on a wide, national scale it took place at the Russian revolution. The change in the type of culture was expressed primarily in the different objects towards which it was directed. This had already been anticipated by Belinsky in the latest period of his development. The "idealists" of the 'forties were interested mainly in the humane sciences, philosophy, art, literature. The nihilists of the 'sixties were chiefly interested in the natural sciences and political economy, and thus these became the interests also of the communist generation of the Russian revolution.

In the understanding of the genesis of Russian nihilism in the wide sense of the word and the Russian revolutionary spirit of the 'sixties, the figure of Dobrolyubov is of great interest. In him is seen the sort of soul in which revolutionary and nihilist ideas were born. It was the kind of soul from which saints are made. That may be said of Dobrolyubov and of Chernishevsky alike. Dobrolyubov left behind him a Diary in which he describes his childhood and youth. He had a purely Orthodox religious upbringing. In his childhood and even in early youth he was very religious. The cast of his soul was ascetic. He had a strong sense of sin and was disposed to frequent confession. The most insignificant sins caused him pain. He could not forgive himself if he ate too much jam, slept too long and so on. He was very devout. He loved his parents tenderly, especially his mother, and he could not become reconciled to her death. Dobrolyubov was a pure, stern, serious man, without any of that lightness of touch which gave such a charm to the cultured nobility. And then this devout, ascetic soul, serious to the degree of harshness, lost his faith, appalled by the evil, the injustice, and the suffering of life. He could not reconcile himself to the fact that with so evil a world, full of injustice and suffering, there exists an all-good and all-powerful Creator. Here is the destructive Marcion theme at work. Dobrolyubov is stunned by the fact that his beloved mother dies.

Nor can he reconcile himself to the low level of life among the Russian clergy, its lack of spirituality, its obscurantism, its absence of any application of Christianity to life. He feels himself surrounded by "the kingdom of darkness." His principal essay, written *á propos* of Ostrovsky, is entitled "A Ray of Light in the Kingdom of Darkness." Man must himself bring light into the kingdom of darkness. What is needed is enlightenment, a revolutionary change in the whole order of life. Dobrolyubov was a critic; he wrote about literature. He did not go to such extremes as Pisarev in the repudiation of aesthetics, but even for him aesthetics were a luxury, and on ascetic grounds he rejected the superfluous luxury of aesthetics. He desired earthly happiness for man, and after he lost his faith he knew no other purpose in life. But he himself knew no happiness, his life was joyless, and he died of consumption almost in his youth. One can imagine Russian nihilism only as a youth movement; nihilism in the elderly has a repulsive character.

N. Chernishevsky dominated the thought not only of the radical intelligentsia of the 'sixties, but also of succeeding generations. The halo which surrounded his name in penal servitude contributed very greatly to his popularity. Chernishevsky was charged with drawing up proclamations to the peasantry, the charge against him being supported by forgery and false evidence. He was condemned to seven years' penal servitude, and after that spent twelve years in Eastern Siberia under extremely severe conditions. He bore Siberia and penal servitude as a genuine ascetic. Chernishevsky was a very gentle person; he had a Christian soul and there were marks of saintliness in his character. This harrying of Chernishevsky was one of the most shameful actions of the Russian government of the old régime. Chernishevsky, like Dobrolyubov, was the son of an archpriest. His earliest education was theological, and he was brought up in a seminary. He was a very learned person, a veritable encyclopaedist; he knew both theology and philosophy down to the philosophy of Hegel; he knew history and the natural sciences; but he was chiefly an economist. As an economist Marx ranked him very high. He had gifts which might have made him a specialist, and if they did not actually do so, it was simply because he was attracted by the conflict in the field of social ideas. But all the same he was a bookish man, and gave no impression of having a passionate nature. He wrote novels with a moral purpose, but he possessed no special talent for literature. Notwithstanding the breadth of his learning, Chernishevsky was not a man of high culture. His standard of culture was rather low compared with that of the people of the 'forties. There was a lack of taste in it, due to the influence of the seminarists and *raznochintsi.*

Chernishevsky was a rationalist, a disciple of Feuerbach and at the same time one who idealized the soil, like Dobrolyubov and like all the best representatives of the revolutionary and nihilist intelligentsia. He had a strong ascetic side to him also. It was a result of his asceticism that he professed his extreme materialism, which was, philosophically speaking, naïve and pitiful; and it was due to his moral sense and love of the good

that he affirmed a utilitarian ethic of rational egoism. The ethical motive was always very strong among the nihilists, though theoretically they repudiated all morals. Idealism, spiritual metaphysics, and religion were connected in their minds with practical materialism and social injustice. Christianity provided sufficient grounds for this. Those who professed to have an idealistic and spiritual outlook too often concealed the basest self-interest behind the expression of lofty ideas. And, therefore, on behalf of a vital idealism, for the sake of the realization of social justice, they began to assert a crude materialism and utilitarianism, and to reject all lofty ideas and rhetoric.

Chernishevsky wrote a utopian novel called *What is to be done?* which became a sort of catechism of Russian nihilism, a textbook of the Russian revolutionary intelligentsia. From an artistic point of view the novel was sufficiently weak and tasteless, but it is very interesting from the point of view of the history of the Russian intelligentsia. The attacks upon it on moral grounds from the right wing were monstrously unjust and libellously false. The notable Russian theologian, Bukharev, who recognized its Christian character, was right. *What is to be done?* is an ascetic book, a sort of manual of the devout life for Russian nihilists. Rakhmetov, the hero, sleeps on nails in order to harden his character and train himself to endure pain and suffering. The preaching of free love did not mean the preaching of dissoluteness, a thing which flourished precisely among the conservative governing classes, the guards officers and so on, but not among the nihilists, who were men of ideas. It meant a demand for sincerity in emotion, a liberation from all conventions, lies and oppression. Chernishevsky's ethics, of course, stood a great deal higher than the slave morality of "Domostroi." Vera Pavlovna's dream in the novel pictures a socialist Utopia in which co-operative workshops are organized. Chernishevsky's socialism, more than any other, still bore a partly *narodnik* and partly utopian character, but was already one of the predecessors of the Communism of the 'sixties. Plekhanov, the founder of Russian Marxism, recognizes this in his book on Chernishevsky. Not without reason did Marx study Russian in order to read Chernishevsky.

It was as an economist that the latter was most independent. He was not, like many other *narodniks,* an opponent of industrial development. But he poses the traditional problem for Russian nineteenth century thought: Can Russia escape capitalist development? and answers it by saying that Russia can shorten the capitalist period to nothing, and go straight on from the lower forms of economy to socialist economy. . . . Chernishevsky sets national wealth and popular well-being in opposition to each other, which was characteristic of *narodnik* socialism. In capitalist countries, national wealth increases and the people's welfare diminishes. Chernishevsky is a defender of the peasant Commune. He asserts that the third and highest socialist period of development will resemble the first and lowest. Chernishevsky, like Hertzen and later Mikhailovsky, identifies the interests of the people with the interests of human personality in general. Of all those who wrote books that the law allowed to be published, Chernishevsky was the most clearly expressed socialist, and this marks his significance for the Russian intelligentsia, which in its moral consciousness was most wholly socialist in the second half of the nineteenth century. Nihilism of the Pisarev type was a weakening of the socialist theme, but this was a temporary phenomenon. Chernishevsky's philosophical position was specially weak. Although he derived it from so admirable a thinker as Feuerbach, yet his materialism was vulgar, and coloured by the popular natural science books of that day, much more vulgar than the dialectic materialism of the Marxists.

Chernishevsky wrote on aesthetic questions too, and was a typical representative of Russian journalistic criticism. He defended the thesis that reality is higher than art and desired to construct a realist aesthetic. There was a strong ascetic motive in Chernishevsky's anti-aestheticism. He was already seeking that type of culture which triumphed in communism—frequently in caricature—the dominance of the natural and economic sciences, the rejection of religion and metaphysics, the subservience of literature and art to social aims, an ethic of social utilitarianism, the subjection of the internal life of the individual to the interests and requirements of society. Chernishevsky's asceticism and the practical Christian virtues of this "materialist" provided an immense endowment of moral capital on which the communists are living, although they themselves do not possess those virtues.

In contrast with Chernishevsky and Dobrolyubov, Pisarev, the principal exponent of Russian nihilism in the proper sense, was a scion of the nobility. He was an elegant and smart young man with gentle, by no means nihilist, manners. This "destroyer of aesthetics" had aesthetic taste. As a writer he was more gifted than Chernishevsky and Dobrolyubov. His fate was typically Russian. He was arrested on some trivial ground and spent four years in prison in solitary confinement, where he wrote most of his essays. Pisarev died soon after he was set free, and when he was quite a young man, being drowned as a result of an unfortunate accident. Coming from a generation of prophets of enlightenment in the 'sixties, he was very much of an individualist, and the social theme was weaker in him than in Chernishevsky. Pisarev was mainly interested in the emancipation of the individual person, in its liberation from superstition and prejudice, from the ties of family, from traditional morals, and the conventions of life. Intellectual freedom held a central position for him, and he hoped to attain it by popularizing natural science. He preached materialism, which he was naïvely convinced sets personality free, although at the same time materialism denies personality. If personality is entirely produced by environment, then it cannot possess freedom and independence of any sort.

Pisarev wanted to produce a new type of human being; this interested him more than the organization of society. This new human type he called "the thinking realist." The realist generation of "sons" is sharply opposed to the idealist generation of "fathers." In his type of "thinking realist" Pisarev anticipated to a large extent the type produced by Russian communism. A number of the traits of this "thinking realist" were sketched by Turgeniev in Bozarov (*Fathers and Sons*), though not with any particular success. Among the Russian intelligentsia, before the appearance of nihilism, the human type predominated which was known as the "idealist of the 'forties." It was the continuation of the type which belonged to the end of the eighteenth and beginning of the nineteenth centuries, and was connected with mystical masonry. It was the outcome of the working over by Russian thought of German romanticism and idealism. It grew up on the soil provided by cultured Russian gentry. This type of man, a very honourable type, was prone to the highest aspirations, to appreciation of taste and beauty. As later on Dostoyevsky loved to observe with irony, it was given to much day dreaming and had but a feeble capacity for action and putting into practice; there was no little of the Russian laziness to which the gentry were liable. From this type the "superfluous people" came. The type of

"thinking realist" preached by Pisarev produces completely different traits, which are often engendered in reaction against the idealist type. The "thinking realist" was alien from all day dreaming and romanticism; he was the foe of all lofty ideas which had no relation whatever to action and were not put into practice. He was inclined to be cynical when it came to unmasking illusions, whether religious, metaphysical or aesthetic. His cult was a cult of work and labour. He recognized only the natural sciences, and despised the humanities. He preached the ethic of reasoned egoism, not because he was more egoistic than the idealist type (on the contrary, the reverse was the case), but because he desired the merciless exposure of fraudulent lofty ideas which were made to subserve the basest interests.

But the level of philosophical culture of the "thinking realists" was low, much lower than that of the "idealists of the 'forties." Buchner and Moleshott—exponents of the most vulgar materialism based on the popularization of the natural science of the day—were taken to be notable philosophers and became teachers. This was a terrible fall from Feuerbach, not to speak of Hegel. The "thinking realists" set out to find the solution of the mystery of life and of existence in the dissection of a frog. It was precisely from the "thinking realists" of the 'sixties that there came that absurd argument, which became so popular among the radical Russian intelligentsia, that the dissection of a corpse did not reveal the existence of a soul in man. The reverse bearing of this argument escaped their notice; if they had brought the soul to light by the dissecting of a corpse, this would have been evidence on the side of materialism. There was a great contrast between the seriousness and significance of the human crisis which took place in the "thinking realists," and the pitifulness of their philosophy, their crude and vulgar materialism and utilitarianism.

The "thinking realist" was, of course, a foe of aesthetics, and denied the independent significance of art. In that respect he demanded a stern asceticism. Pisarev perpetrated a positive pogrom of aesthetics; he rejected the perfect achievement of Pushkin, and proposed that the Russian novelists should write popular tracts on natural science. In this respect the cultural programme of the communists is more reasonable; it proposes the study of Pushkin, and assigns some meaning to art. Dialectic materialism is less vulgar than the materialism of Buchner and Moleshott. But among the communists technical knowledge plays the same part as natural science, and especially the biological sciences, played in the 'sixties. Pisarev's nihilism announced that "boots are above Shakespeare." The idea of the subservience of art and literature to social aims was asserted in Pisarev's system in an even more extreme form than in communism. If the programme of Russian nihilism were actually realised to the full in Russian communism, the results for culture would have been more destructive than those we actually see in Soviet culture. The appearance of the "thinking realist" meant the appearance of a harsher type than the "idealist of the 'forties," and at the same time a more active type. But in the nihilism of Pisarev there was a healthy reaction against fruitless, romantic day dreaming, idleness and egoistic self-absorption; it was a wholesome summons to labour and knowledge, although a one-sided knowledge. There was a simple and active liberating force in nihilism. The movement had an immense and a positive significance for the emancipation of women. An analogous process recurred among us Russians in the change from the type of person who created the cultural renaissance of the beginning of the twentieth century—the "idealist" movement of that day—to the Russian communist.

The exponents of nihilism did not observe the radical contradiction which lay at the roots of their aspirations. They sought the liberation of personality; they proclaimed a revolt against all beliefs, all abstract ideas, for the sake of that liberation. On behalf of the liberation of personality, they emptied it of its qualitative content, devastated its inner life, and denied it its right to creativeness and spiritual enrichment. The principle of utilitarianism is in the highest degree unfavourable to the principle of personality; it subjects personality to utility, which holds sway tyrannically over personality. In its thought and creative activity nihilism displayed a violent asceticism intruded from without. Materialism was such an intruded asceticism and poverty of thought. The principle of personality can in no way stand and develop on the soil of materialism. Personality, as they conceived it, is found to be deprived of the right to creative fulness of life. If the talented Pisarev had lived to more mature years, he would perhaps have observed this fundamental contradiction; perhaps he would have understood that one cannot fight for personality on the ground of one's belief "in the frog." The tendencies of the 'seventies rubbed off the corners of the nihilism of the 'sixties. The chief influence on the thought of the radical intelligentsia of the 'seventies was not that of Buchner and Moleshott, but of Comte and Herbert Spencer. A change over took place from materialism to positivism, a reaction against the predominance of natural science. To some extent the rights of aesthetics were upheld, and art was not repudiated. But the idea of the subservience of art to social aims continued to dominate the minds of the intelligentsia. (pp. 48-63)

Nicolas Berdyaev, "Russian Socialism and Nihilism" in his The Origin of Russian Communism, *translated by R. M. French, Geoffrey Bles: The Centenary Press, 1937, pp. 38-63.*

AESTHETIC AND CRITICAL VIEWS

RENÉ WELLEK

[Wellek's A History of Modern Criticism *is a comprehensive study of the literary critics of the last three centuries. His critical method, as demonstrated in the* History *and outlined in his* Theory of Literature, *is one of describing, analyzing, and evaluating a work solely in terms of the problems it poses for itself and how the writer solves them. For Wellek, biographical, historical, and psychological information is incidental. In the following excerpt from* A History of Modern Criticism, *he surveys the principal critical writings of Chernyshevsky, Dobrolyubov, and Pisarev and assesses the strengths and weaknesses of their critical views.]*

After the death of Belinsky (1848) a vacuum seems to have existed in Russian criticism for a few years. But in the middle fifties a devoted follower of Belinsky, Nikolay Chernyshevsky, began writing on aesthetic theory and criticism. His critical activity lasted only a few years, as his interests were more and more absorbed in economics and politics. In 1862 he was arrested and later deported to Siberia. His young disciple, Nikolay Dobrolyubov, began writing criticism in 1857 but died four years later of tuberculosis. Just about the time the careers of Chernyshevsky and Dobrolyubov had come to an end, Dmitri Pisarev began his short writing life, of which four years were spent in a fortress: he committed suicide by drowning, aged only 28.

The continuity between these critics and their master, Belinsky, is obvious. Still, they differ sharply from him, however sincerely they may have thought that they were only developing the ideas and conceptions of Belinsky's last stage. The intellectual atmosphere had changed greatly in the short time since Belinsky's death. Belinsky had grown up in the shade of German idealism and had never abandoned its basic doctrines on art and history. Chernyshevsky, Dobrolyubov, and Pisarev had no understanding of the German romantic views. Their philosophy precluded this: it is frequently called Feuerbachian and considered identical with that of the latest stage of Belinsky. But I cannot see any evidence that these writers adopted the specific doctrines of Feuerbach, a highly sentimental, fervid theologian, imbued with Hegel's ways of thinking. They must rather be described as materialistic monists, most deeply influenced by such popularizers of the scientific outlook as Vogt, Moleschott, and especially Büchner, and by the English Utilitarians. They propounded a materialism substantially identical with that of Holbach and Cabanis: mental processes are physical processes, hence all action is completely determined by them. Religion is superstition. This deterministic materialism is paradoxically combined with great fervor for social reform: and even with a spirit of sacrifice, unexplainable by the hedonism, enlightened egoism, and utilitarianism of their theories.

But we must confine ourselves to their literary theory and criticism, and make sharp distinctions between them, on this point. Chernyshevsky, though a commanding figure in the Russian revolutionary movement, eminent also as an economist, must be ranked lowest among the group as a literary critic. He seems to have been a man with hardly any aesthetic sensibility: a crude, harsh thinker, preoccupied, even when speaking of literature, with immediate politics. Chernyshevsky does not even believe in the social role of art. It is apparently no mere smokescreen for the censor when he argues at length and with many examples that "not by books or periodicals or newspapers is the spirit of a nation awakened—but only by events." Rather, literature induces a peaceful and reasonable disposition in the mind aroused by events. Those who wish for the preservation of existing customs should not be afraid of literature. It cannot incite new demands and promote new tendencies. Though this might almost seem to be said with tongue in cheek, we must conclude from Chernyshevsky's other writings and his philosophical position that he actually thought of literature as a mere surrogate, *Ersatz* for life, a passive mirror of society.

Chernyshevsky's theoretical views are most fully stated in his dissertation *The Aesthetic Relations of Art to Reality* (1855). There he argues against Hegelian aesthetics, or rather against isolated Hegelian formulas in F. T. Vischer's volumes. His own position is then stated simply and clearly. Art is an inferior reproduction of reality. The only function of art is that of spreading knowledge about reality: to remind us of it or to inform those who have not experienced it. The purely aesthetic is dismissed as mere sensual pleasure, trivial at its best, reprehensible at its worst. Beauty is simply life, and not a quality distinguishable from it: thus almost all young women are beautiful.

His views of the individual arts are similarly crude. Sculpture is quite useless: any number of persons walking the streets of Petersburg are more beautiful than the most beautiful statue. Painting is even more inferior to reality: greenish and reddish colors on a picture cannot compare with the real color of a human body or face. Chernyshevsky recognizes music as the direct outpouring of feeling only in song: but then it is not art but nature itself, like the song of birds. All music that deviates from natural song, especially instrumental music, is a mere substitute for song and hence inferior. Poetry, as it does not affect the senses directly but appeals to imagination, fares even worse compared to reality. The strength and clarity of its impression is far below that of the other arts, as words are always general and hence pale and feeble. The poet's invention must not be overrated: the more we know about the poet, the more we have to conclude that he is a historian, an author of memoirs. Nor is plot-invention anything to boast of: any French or English crime gazette contains more interesting and more intricate real-life stories than any writer can devise. All the superiority of literature over an exact report can be reduced to a greater fullness of details supplied by literature, to a "rhetorical amplification" of the facts. Why then is art valued at all? asks Chernyshevsky, and he can answer only that man values what he has made himself, out of vanity, or because art satisfies his propensity for daydreaming, his innate sentimentality, or simply because art reinforces his memory. A portrait reminds us of an absent friend; a picture, of the sea. Imagination is weak: we need reminders. Art may acquaint us with what we could not experience ourselves. But basically art does no more than any reasonable discussion of a subject. Art is, at most, a "handbook" for those beginning to study life: it prepares us for the reading of the original sources and, from time to time, serves as reference. Here, surely, aesthetics has reached its nadir: or rather it has been asked to commit suicide.

Similar crude views are propounded on less general questions. What is tragic? asks Chernyshevsky and answer: simply any suffering or death; even a chance death. What is sublime? Anything that is larger in comparison to what we expect in a given context. Form and content are entirely separate. The content of art is all reality, however ugly by old standards; and who cares for form?

These views are matched by opinions about specific works of art: Homer is incoherent, offends by his cynicism and lacks all moral feeling. Aeschylus and Sophocles are rude and dry. Beethoven is often incomprehensible and wild; Mozart's *Don Giovanni* is boring.

In short this famous dissertation still admired in Soviet Russia and by Georg Lukács [see Additional Bibliography], which makes a show of scholarly rigor with its parade of definitions, is a crude act of defiance by a young provincial who wants to thumb his nose at what the world has hitherto considered great and beautiful, worth their time and supreme effort. But Chernyshevsky is deadly serious in exalting reality, worshiping fact and knowledge, rejecting everything sensual, artificial, and useless, and asserting the complete identity of art and life.

Some of the positions of the dissertation are elucidated, in their historical relationships and applications, by an early review of a Russian translation of Aristotle's *Poetics* (1854) and by the long series of articles called *Studies in the Age of Gogol* (1855). The review of Aristotle makes an appeal to Plato's rejection of art but finds something valuable in Aristotle's theory of imitation, though Aristotle is criticized for his dry formalism. Chernyshevsky violently rejects Plotinus' aesthetics as the source of contemporary (German) mystical aestheticism. Though Chernyshevsky's knowledge of the ancients is largely second-hand, the paper shows insight into the eternal relevance of the positions taken by the main Greek philosophers and a sense of the unity of theory and history. "Without history," says Chernyshevsky, "there is no theory, without theory no history." But as in the dissertation, Chernyshevsky constantly minimizes

and distributes the values of art. He recognizes that art causes pleasure but argues that "sitting and chatting on the bench in front of the house among peasants or around the samovar among the townspeople has done more to develop good humor and good feeling toward other people than all the paintings, from the bast pictures of peasants to the *Last Day of Pompeii*." A curious new argument is put forward for identifying novel and drama. "A dramatic work can just as well (or even better) be told in epic form." Yet he admits that the converse is not quite true, because a novel turned into a stage play would become even more tiresome. Boredom is multiplied a thousandfold by the presence of a thousand bored spectators.

Studies in the Age of Gogol shows that Chernyshevsky had the makings of an intellectual historian. He gives accurate and firsthand descriptions of the critics of the time, Polevoy, Senkovsky, Shevyrev, Nadezhdin, in order to introduce a full exposition of Belinsky's ideas. Much of the book is quotation: but one must realize that Belinsky's writings could not be collected at that time and that quoting them from the periodicals in which they had been printed was, in itself, a great service to his audience. One cannot expect a dispassionate attitude from Chernyshevsky: he was a publicist defending and promoting a cause. But his claims for Belinsky seem to me reasonable and even moderate. He emphasizes the fact that Belinsky was the first genuine historian of Russian literature who had clear conceptions about the nature of literary history. He defends the good sense and restraint of the reputedly "furious" Belinsky; he tries to demonstrate the logic and continuity of Belinsky's development; and he rightly asserts that criticism in Russia has a much wider function than in the West. In Germany there are special publics, for instance, for the novel. In England there are philosophers, jurists, economists read by the layman. "With us," says Chernyshevsky, "literature constitutes the whole intellectual life of the nation." In Russia, then, writers and poets should feel their obligations a thousand times more strongly than in the West.

It is sometimes difficult to distinguish what is exposition and what is commentary in Chernyshevsky's text: he wanted to shield himself behind the authority of Belinsky or, to put it more kindly, to fuse the master's authority with his own. But if we take into account long reviews of editions of Pushkin and Gogol and other scattered pronouncements, a picture of Chernyshevsky's views on the main Russian classics emerges.

Though Chernyshevsky wrote a laudatory *Life of Pushkin* for popular consumption and honored his work and name, he looks at him as a figure of the past, a pure artist who has only historical significance. Pushkin is praised as the founder of Russian literature, "as the first among us who raised literature to national significance. He was a man of extraordinary intellect and excellent education, though he was neither a thinker nor a scholar. Every page of his overflows with good sense and the life of an educated mind, though one must not seek deep meaning, clearly discerned or coherent ideas in his writings." Besides, Pushkin seems not original enough: he reminds one too much of Byron, Shakespeare, and Scott.

The main praise goes to Gogol as the founder of the "critical tendency" in Russian literature, the creator of a school, who made Russian literature independent of foreign influences and made it an organ of national self-knowledge. Chernyshevsky approaches Gogol's literary evolution in the spirit of a historian of ideas. Using the letters first collected at that time, he shows that one cannot speak of a betrayal of the liberal cause by Gogol, as his later views were prepared and anticipated from the first. Chernyshevsky analyzes the second volume of *Dead Souls,* stressing its continuity with the first. It seems to him as good as the first as long as Gogol moves in the old sphere. He shows some literary discernment in pointing out the passages and scenes where Gogol does this but strangely enough admires extravagantly the dreary concluding speech of the Governor General against corruption. While Chernyshevsky is right in seeing the continuity of Gogol's evolution, he is, as a liberal democrat, inclined to dismiss Gogol's ideas. For instance, he pays no attention to Gogol's early essays, which show a respectable knowledge of conservative, largely German romantic theories of history and art. Chernyshevsky ascribes Gogol's reactionary views to his poor education, the "narrow horizon" of his youth, his expatriation and isolation, and his association with writers such as Shevyrev and Zhukovsky during his later years. Still, within the limits of Chernyshevsky's incomprehension of the religious and conservative outlook on life, his view of Gogol even as a political writer shows considerable historical insight and psychological sympathy.

The exposition in *Studies in the Age of Gogol* of Belinsky's last writings allows Chernyshevsky to restate his views of the relation between literature and society. His attack on "pure art," art for art's sake, is, we see more clearly than in his dissertation, not a reasoned rejection of German theories of the autonomy of art or even a rejection of the flaming proclamations of French romantics, but an attack on the view that art is pleasure. Chernyshevsky cannot think of pure art as anything but drinking songs and erotic conversation; art, I should say, not for art's sake but for the sake of wine or sex. It is easy for him to argue that this Epicureanism lacks a vital link with the rational needs of the modern age, an age devoted to humanity, to the struggle for the betterment of human life. In obvious contradiction to his usual skepticism as to the social effect of art, Chernyshevsky says now that "poetry is life, action, struggle, passion," and that literature cannot help serving the tendencies of an age. He admires and recommends the social writers of his age: Béranger, George Sand, Heine, Dickens, Thackeray, without making much distinction between them.

Chernyshevsky's attitude toward his Russian contemporaries was defined in many reviews during the next years: one hesitates to call the bulk of these articles literary criticism. He shows, for instance, the detrimental influence of the Slavophiles on Ostrovsky, and he attacks the flabby liberalism of Turgenev in the guise of a review of the story of *Asya.* This article, "The Russian at a *Rendezvous*" (1858), is too characteristic of his method and the methods of the whole group not to merit description. Turgenev's protagonist (not hero surely), a weak man who retreats before the love of an ardent girl, is declared the representative of Russian society, a symbol of the decaying aristocracy. The scene of Asya's rejection is considered a "symptom of the disease that corrupts all our actions." This melancholy story of an abortive love is used as an allegory of Russian will-lessness, as a peg to hang on a warning to the aristocracy to heed the needs of the time. The general attitude is blatantly set forth in an often-quoted passage: "Goodbye erotic questions! A reader of our time, occupied with problems of administrative and judiciary institutions, of financial reforms, of the emancipation of the serfs, does not care for them." The reader is Chernyshevsky, and the public for which he spoke either rejected art as sensual pleasure or wanted to use it as an instrument of propaganda. Turgenev's delicate art did not interest them at all.

But it would be a mistake to deny to Chernyshevsky all literary sensibility and ability in analysis. His review of Tolstoy's

Childhood, Boyhood and *Sebastopol Stories* (1856) shows that there were the germs of a good critic in him. Tolstoy is praised as a psychologist who describes the "psychic process, its forms, its laws, its dialectics accurately." Chernyshevsky quotes a passage describing the feelings of a soldier waiting for the fall of a shell and calls it "interior monologue." He then compares Tolstoy's art with that of a painter who catches the sparkling reflection of light on quickly bouncing waves or the shimmer of a ray of light on rustling leaves. Something similar seems to him to have been achieved by Tolstoy in describing the mysterious movement of the life of the soul. Chernyshevsky points out what has been elaborated since: Tolstoy's technique has affinity with impressionism. But it is typical of Chernyshevsky and his audience that after praising Tolstoy's moral purity, Chernyshevsky suddenly turns to an embarrassed defense of Tolstoy's theme of childhood. *Childhood,* he says at length, is about a child and not about issues such as war or social reform, but it is still worth reading.

It is to Chernyshevsky's credit that he himself saw that literary criticism was not his strong point or main interest and that he ceded the literary department of the *Contemporary* to his young disciple, Nikolay Dobrolyubov, in 1857. After that he wrote hardly any literary criticism. The book *Lessing, His Time, His Life, His Work* (1857), though obviously devised to exalt the role of the critic in national life, is a disappointing compilation from Danzel and Guhrauer. It is preoccupied with history and biography and never gets to a proper discussion of Lessing's works or significance.

Dobrolyubov was, of course, just as little interested in art as his master, though he wrote much more exclusively about belles-lettres. But he applied more consistently, more systematically and consciously the point of view indicated by Chernyshevsky. He was the most important of these critics as a literary theorist, though he had as little literary taste and sensibility and was as diffuse and repetitious as Chernyshevsky. He is even more lumpish and stodgy, and lacks all literary grace and intellectual agility; he is strangely unctuous in his violently secular way.

Dobrolyubov never tires of repeating the view expounded by Chernyshevsky that literature is only a mirror of life which reflects but cannot change reality. This view expressed in an early discussion of Saltykov-Shchedrin's *Provincial Sketches* (1857) and just as emphatically in his last essay on Dostoevsky's *Insulted and Injured* (1861), runs through all of Dobrolyubov's writings. Sometimes he refutes absurdly inflated claims for the effect of literature on society: Virgil, he says, could not change Tiberius into Aeneas, Demosthenes could not save Athens from Philip of Macedon. Literature did not raise the question of the emancipation of the serfs: rather it was raised by life, and then literature brought about a "calm discussion, a cold-blooded survey of all the aspects of the problem." At times, Dobrolyubov points to a vague future, to social action for the solution of a problem posited by literature. Thus Ostrovsky's plays, he shows at great length, describe types of domestic tyrants and downtrodden women: they make us see this "realm of darkness" among the Russian merchant class. But the way out of it must be found by life itself: "Literature only reproduces life, it never portrays what does not exist in reality." Similarly Dostoevsky (Dobrolyubov, of course, knew only the early Dostoevsky, up to *Insulted and Injured*) shows us forgotten, oppressed people, whose human dignity has been humiliated and insulted, but offers no solution or way out. Dostoevsky needs supplementation and commentary, presumably of a kind Dobrolyubov was anxious to supply. The essay concludes with a call to follow the "uninterrupted, powerful, irresistible stream of life," the wave of the future in which all these critics believed.

But in spite of these many declarations of the humbleness of literature's role as a mere passive mirror of life, Dobrolyubov, almost as often, assigns it a slightly more active role. The influence of literature, he says early, is only indirect; it spreads slowly; but still it helps to clarify existing tendencies in society. Literature is "a way of knowing what is defeated and what is victorious, or what is beginning to permeate and predominate in the moral life of society." It may even be useful in "quickening and giving greater fullness to the conscious work of society." "Literature is an auxiliary force, the importance of which lies in propaganda, and the merit of which is determined by what it propagates and how it propagates it." Once he goes further: the very greatest writers have grasped the truths of philosophers and depicted them in action. Representing a higher stage of human consciousness in a given age, they rise above the auxiliary role of literature and enter the ranks of historical leaders who have helped mankind to become clearly conscious of its vital strength and natural inclinations. Shakespeare is Dobrolyubov's one example of such greatness; he considers Dante, Goethe, and Byron to be of lower rank: none of them so fully symbolizes an entire phase of human development as Shakespeare did. Occasionally, Dobrolyubov would even express a touching trust that the dissemination of ideas by literature might be easily "expressed in administrative activity"; that "at a certain point of evolution, literature becomes one of the powers moving society." Literature tells "society of honorable and useful activity. It chants always the same song: Get up! wake up! raise yourself! look at yourself!" Thus Dobrolyubov runs the gamut from complete pessimism to messianic hopes: from the view that literature is a passive mirror to the view that it incites to direct action, transforms society.

An early essay, "On the Share of the People in the Development of Russian Literature" (1858), ostensibly a review of A. Milyukov's *Studies in the History of Russian Poetry*, suggests a historical scheme according to which Russian literature moves toward becoming truly national, all-national, representative not only of one class but of the whole people. The ideal is phrased in terms of romantic nationalism, but its implications are much more concretely social. "Literature," he says, "cannot anticipate life, but it can anticipate the formal, official manifestations of the interests active in life. As long as an idea is only in the minds of people, as long as it is seen as realizable only in the future, literature should evaluate it from various sides and from the point of view of different interests. But as soon as the idea has become an act, has been formulated and solved definitely, literature has nothing more to do. It can at most only praise what has been done." This awkward passage well illustrates Dobrolyubov's pervasive dilemma: his theoretical conviction that literature is mere words which cannot affect reality, and the practical impossibility of the resignation implied, the need of demanding from literature a discussion of what he considered new and progressive ideas in the hope that they may prevail after all.

The same hesitation runs through the historical survey: on the one hand, the development of literature is said to reflect the changes of society passively and inertly; on the other, it seems to him shameful that literature has not expressed what he considers the real needs and character of the nation. Dobrolyubov wants an all-national literature, above parties and cliques, but recognizes that literature has "always expressed the interests

and opinions of those whose job was the writing of books or of those who supported them ever so little." In glancing at Old Russian literature he can see only a complete lack of poetry, deadness, abstractness. In discussing a religious tract, he complains that one could hardly have chosen anything more remote from the life of the nation than the theme of ritual. Lomonosov is chided for not "feeling for the class from which he has risen." Pushkin, though praised for his historical role and his artistry, is considered as lacking in true national spirit. His aristocratic prejudices, his epicurean tendencies, his French education, his dilettantism (he was a man to whom "strenuous activity of the mind was unknown")—all this prevented him from being permeated by the spirit of Russian nationality. He acquired only its form, not its substance. Gogol came nearer to Dobrolyubov's ideal but did not reach it. He achieved a truly national point of view but did so unconsciously. Thus the proper fusion of literature and nationality is still an ideal in the future.

Dobrolyubov wavers between a romantic conception of nationality as something uniquely Russian and a hope for a literature written for the peasant masses, representing them and comprehensible to them. He has a very real sense of the thinness and smallness of contemporary Russian literary culture; he says that there are only 20,000 subscribers to all Russian magazines and only 15,000 school teachers in the whole country. It is, he admits wryly, an illusion to think that Russian literature is truly national. "Our interests, our sufferings are incomprehensible to the mass: our enthusiasm seems to it even comic." Feeling his isolation as an intellectual, Dobrolyubov raises the question of popular art, which was to find such radical answer in Tolstoy and in Soviet policies.

But Dobrolyubov rarely turns to these problems. In his practical criticism he centers mainly on one problem: the trueness to life of the novels and plays he discusses. Often, he quite consciously applies the realistic standard of the "slice of life." He complains that Ostrovsky does not show us how a character in a play "grew and was brought up, what influenced him in his youth." He disparages strictly coordinated and logical plots and consistent characters such as Tartuffe, Richard III, and Shylock, because presenting them on the Russian stage would mean ascribing to Russian life something it does not contain. "Suppose," he asks, "that naturalness precludes consistency?" He never doubts that "naturalness" has precedence over unity and coherence. Dobrolyubov thus attacks the demands made on the drama by the French well-made play. Why should there not be subordinate figures if they help to explain the situation? There is no need of poetic justice, as there is no justice in real life. He defends Ostrovsky's *Storm* against critics who complain of a dispersion of interest in the conflict with the mother-in-law or of the parallel love affairs. All this may happen in life and thus can be represented on the stage.

The criterion of lifelikeness is equally applied to Dostoevsky: *The Double* is unfortunately fantastic; Natasha in *Insulted and Injured* sounds like the author; her love for the depraved Alyosha is unnatural; and the psychology of the narrator is obscure. Dobrolyubov would like to praise Dostoevsky for his pictures of downtrodden humanity but cannot bring himself to consider *Insulted and Injured* as a work of art at all. It cannot be studied from an aesthetic point of view; the result, he implies, would be entirely negative. He takes Dostoevsky's or rather the narrator's disparaging remarks about his novel writing very literally and is pleased by his lack of aesthetic pretensions. Besides, he argues, "as long as literature has the slightest possibility of even distantly serving social interests and of expressing even obscurely and feebly its sympathy with them, one cannot get excited even by the most brilliant of aesthetic studies.'' In the case of Ostrovsky, Dobrolyubov feels that aesthetic canons have happily been violated in favor of realism (and hence should be discarded). Confronted with Dostoevsky's art, he cannot approve its deviations from the canon of the realistic novel. He throws him easily to the aesthetic wolves.

For the most part, Dobrolyubov cheerfully admits his lack of interest in literary matters. He constantly repeats that subject matter alone decides: he condemns Fët for writing about babbling brooks and prefers Tyuchev for his interest in principles and social questions. Pushkin, we are told, would not attract any attention in the present day if he appeared with the same contents. Dobrolyubov says that he himself writes ''pathological studies of Russian society,'' that he looks for the moral in a fable. In a suppressed conclusion to the essay on Ostrovsky's ''Realm of Darkness'' Dobrolyubov boasts that he uses metaphorical expressions out of necessity: he is obliged to deal mainly with the products of an author's imagination and not directly with the phenomena of life. Censorship, he implied, prevents him from writing on society and politics: literature is only a pretext.

Still, Dobrolyubov made a contribution to the theory of the social study of literature. He, apparently for the first time, thought clearly of ''social types'' as revealing an author's world-view, independently of or even contrary to his conscious intentions. The actual world-view of a writer must be sought in the living images he creates. He concentrates the facts of real life into them. ''In these images the poet may, imperceptibly even to himself, grasp and express an inner meaning long before his mind can define it. Sometimes the artist may even fail to grasp the meaning of what he himself is depicting. It is precisely the function of criticism to explain the hidden meaning of these images.'' The contrast between the social import of Gogol's characters and the theories formulated later by the author is Dobrolyubov's stock example. The author's intention may remain forever unknown, and even if it be clearly expressed, it may not be in complete harmony with what his artistic nature has imbibed from the impressions of real life. The conscious intention of an author remains a secondary and personal question.

This method of studying social types, with its dismissal of what today is called the ''intentional fallacy,'' seems a valuable technique; it distinguished between an overt and a latent meaning of a work of art somewhat as, in different contexts, Freud, Pareto, or Mannheim distinguish them. It is a call to penetrate hidden assumptions, to identify the crystallizing points of social change. Social types—in the sense of general types like the gentleman, the intellectual, the peasant—had already begun to attract consideration in French literary discussions. The German romantic critics, especially A. W. Schlegel and Schelling, had discussed the great mythical types of humanity: Faust, Hamlet, Don Quixote, Sancho Panza. Schlegel and other German critics had dismissed conscious intention as a criterion of value. But these motifs had not, I believe, coalesced, as they did in Dobrolyubov.

Unfortunately, Dobrolyubov was unable to keep steadily to his central insight, either in theory or in critical practice. He thought of literary images, with his pat utilitarianism, as ''facilitating the formulation of correct ideas about things and the dissemination of these ideas among men.'' He conceived the truth of

Nikolay Chernyshevsky at sixty.

these images often very narrowly, blandly identifying truth with morality: voluptuous scenes and dissolute adventures or the glorification of war are simply ''untrue.'' The artist, he implies, should be a moralist, but at the same time apparently also a scientist. Science and poetry should merge, but science to Dobrolyubov means ''correct'' social and moral ideas. What seems to be a Platonic fusion of the true, the good, and the beautiful, in practice becomes simple didacticism, and even a crude allegorizing to serve immediate polemical purposes.

We can show Dobrolyubov's method at work by discussing his most famous critical papers. ''What is Oblomovism?'' (1859) takes Oblomov and abstracts from him one quality, indolence, and declares this to be the key to the riddle of many manifestations of Russian life. ''Oblomovka is our motherland: a large portion of Oblomov is within every one of us.'' Dobrolyubov sees the continuity between Oblomov and the type of ''superfluous man'' depicted in Onegin and Pechorin, yet he wants to dismiss these two fictional types as belonging to a dead past. ''They have lost their significance, they have ceased to mislead us with their enigmatic mystery.'' Instead of pursuing the theme and analyzing Oblomov, Dobrolyubov dismisses Goncharov's obvious sympathy for his hero and his psychological explanation of the growth of his weakness and declares him a ''disgusting nonentity.'' At the end he can only hold him up as a kind of warning example, a bogeyman, an allegory of Russian backwardness. He has lost sight of the book and the figure.

Next he uses his technique in analyzing Ostrovsky's early comedies in a very long piece, ''The Realm of Darkness'' (1859). Here Dobrolyubov does not have to deal with a complex character such as Oblomov: he is faced with a great variety of figures, which he can reduce to a few types and for which he then tries to define the social causes that created them. He can easily show that Ostrovsky depicts a type of domestic tyrant and bully *(samodur)* and the abject, ignorant wives and girls surrounding him. He is anxious to show that Ostrovsky—though in his political ideas affected and, in his opinion, corrupted by Slavophile views—actually exposes and ridicules tyranny and oppression at every point. Ostrovsky must be claimed as an unconscious liberal and ally. But when Dobrolyubov starts to give causal explanations of these conditions, he loses sight of the plays completely: he argues about a false respect for law and order and talks about the economic dependence of the victims on the merchant tyrants. He darkly hints that he could say more if censorship allowed it, and one must recognize that his description of tyranny and despotism (though ostensibly limited to the plays under discussion) could easily be and certainly *was* read as a general indictment of Russian autocracy. The plays are used to document tyranny, oppression, ignorance, superstition, downtrodden resignation, vices which Dobrolyubov with the Rousseauistic faith of his time ascribes to bad social conditions, since "baseness and crime are not inherent in human nature."

The later article on Ostrovsky's *Storm* (1869) shows the method at its insensitive worst. Dobrolyubov sets himself to see the heroine of the play, Katerina, as the "representative of a great national idea" and to glorify her suicide and her defiance of her tormentors as "the height to which our national life is rising in its development." Her drowning herself in the Volga is interpreted as a "challenge to the power of tyranny," and her character is seen as a "reflection of a new movement of national life." Dobrolyubov, conscious of the paradox of his interpretation, defies those who charge him with having made "art the instrument of an extraneous idea." He asks and expects affirmative answers: Does the interpretation follow from the play? Does living Russian nature find expression in Katerina? Are the demands of the nascent movement of Russian life truly reflected in the meaning of the play? Ostrovsky, he concludes triumphantly, "has challenged Russian life and Russian strength to take determined action." But if my own reading of the play is anywhere near the text, Katerina must rather be considered as a pitiful figure, dominated by dark instinct, who rushes into an adulterous adventure, trembles before the wrath of God, shudders at a thunderstorm and pictures of hell-fire, and finds refuge, from her sense of sin and guilt, in the waters of the Volga. The atmosphere of the play is that of a fairy tale. The evil mother-in-law, the stupid husband, the lover at the gate, the watchmaker who tries to discover the secret of perpetual motion, the gossipy pilgrim-woman, the half mad lady shouting "All of you will burn in unquenchable fire" give the play a tone of weird unreality like that of a story of E.T.A. Hoffmann. To make Katerina, an adultress and a suicide, a superstitious ignorant woman pursued and crushed by a sense of guilt and doom into the symbol of revolution seems the very height of what could be called "loss of contact" with the text. Anything must serve the cause, and if it does not it must be made over to fit.

The slightly earlier article, "When will the day come?" (1860), dealing with Turgenev's novel *On the Eve*, is somewhat subtler. Dobrolyubov has not quite surrendered his critical sense and sees that the Bulgarian hero is rather shadowy. No action of Insarov's is shown. The story cannot be considered a rebuke to the young Russian generation; it is impossible to hold up Insarov as a model of civic courage. Turgenev did not want

to write and could not write a heroic epic. Dobrolyubov admires the scenes in Venice preceding the sudden death of the hero and comments favorably on the love story as a story. His analysis of Yelena is quite sympathetic, but suddenly and in flat contradiction to what he has said just a few pages before, he goes off into his usual allegorizing. Why is Insarov a Bulgarian and not a Russian? The answer is, of course, that Turgenev has to import him from Bulgaria because there are no rebels and no need of rebels in Russia. With heavy irony, Dobrolyubov tells his readers and the censors how everything in Russia is peaceful, orderly, governed by law; that Russians would not dream of cutting the limb of the tree on which they are sitting. But this ironical disclaimer of a Russian Insarov is then openly revoked in the expression of the "hope that there will be soon an opportunity for actions." "We need a man like Insarov, but a Russian Insarov." The ominous phrase "The day will come" concludes the piece. The insight of the critic (shown also in his sympathetic analysis of Yelena) is lost; the lay figure Insarov serves as a pretext for a call to revolution.

One can discover some signs of growth in sensibility in Dobrolyubov's last article, called "Forgotten People" (1861), dealing with Dostoevsky's *Insulted and Injured*. Though Dobrolyubov disparages Dostoevsky as an artist, he shows some power of analysis and characterization, not only of the novel that is the ostensible subject of the review, but of the other writings of the early Dostoevsky. Even *The Double* is considered with some attention to the motivation of the split in Golyadkin's personality. There is one passage that displays a sudden recognition of the role of imagination in art. An artist, says Dobrolyubov, is not a "photographic plate." "He supplements the isolated moment with his artistic feeling. He creates a whole, finds a vital link, fuses and transforms the divers aspects of living reality." The poet's work is "something that must be so, and cannot be otherwise." The power of Dostoevsky's imagination, the personal tone, dark and diseased though it seemed to Dobrolyubov, had its effect. Dobrolyubov began to glimpse the nature of art as creation and to use ideas from Belinsky which might have led him to a deeper understanding. But, unfortunately, he died in the year of this article (1861), aged not yet 26.

Dmitri Pisarev first rose to prominence as a rival of Dobrolyubov. He established his critical reputation by contradicting and refuting the views and interpretations of Dobrolyubov. But this rivalry should not obscure the fact that Pisarev was also a pupil of Chernyshevsky and of Belinsky in his later stage, and that on matters of literary theory and general philosophical outlook there is little difference between Pisarev and Dobrolyubov. Pisarev in the Soviet Union today is not so highly valued or so widely studied and reprinted as Chernyshevsky or Dobrolyubov, mainly because he is suspected of radical individualism and even anarchism. Even Masaryk [see Additional Bibliography] compares him with Stirner and Nietzsche. But there seems to me very little justice in all this. Pisarev was a radical Utilitarian who believed in a rational egoism finally working toward the common good. He differs from Chernyshevsky in having little hope in the peasant. After four years in the Peter-and-Paul Fortress, he apparently became also much more skeptical as to the imminence of revolution; all his hopes were put into the dissemination of rational and scientific ideas, into the slow creation of a materialistic intelligentsia. He was distrustful of utopias in the style of Fourier's phalansteries, and kept up an early fear of the omnipotent state. But in his writings there is hardly any trace of romantic individualism or exaltation of genius. Pisarev shares the basic outlook of Chernyshevsky and Dobrolyubov. He is, like them, a rigid naturalistic monist. He devotes much of his writing to exposition and popularization of the writings of Vogt, Moleschott, Büchner, and, later, Huxley and Darwin. He has cut off all connections with the idealistic romantic past, and has done so more completely than they. He ridicules Heine's prophecy of the revolutionary importance of German philosophy as a bad jest and dismisses the German romantics as completely dead figures. When he discusses Belinsky, whom he reveres as the father of realism, he wants to take off the shell of Hegelianism. He rejects the idea of organic development as a mere delusion: Belinsky's attempt to show the inevitable evolution from Derzhavin through Batyushkov and Zhukovsky to Pushkin seems to him arrant nonsense. He is completely nonplussed by the idea of a parallel development of all the arts and activities of man expressing a common spirit of the time. He argues that you can never explain why, for instance, people wore full-bottomed wigs under Louis XIV and powdered their hair with starch under Louis XV. It was only individual caprice and not the expression or reflection of any world-view. Like his fellow critics, Pisarev has ceased to understand the role of imagination, the wholeness of a work of art, the distinction between life and fiction. He ridicules the inspiration theory and the whole idea of unconscious creation. A poet thinks up an idea and then fits it into a chosen form. That costs labor. He is like a tailor who cuts his cloth, adds to it, snips this bit off and another there, changes this or that. One can become a poet as one can become a lawyer, a professor, a journalist, a shoemaker or a watchmaker. A poet or artist is an artisan like any other.

Form and content are completely divorced in Pisarev's mind. Form is, at most, necessary in order not to obstruct content. Language is communication to be valued only as we value the telegraph wire. Thus Pisarev quite consciously brushes aside questions of artistic merit: to distinguish the manner of one writer from another would mean writing dreary stylistic investigations. What interests him is only what a writer did for our social awareness.

On aesthetic matters, Pisarev pushes the ideas of Chernyshevsky to even greater polemical extremes. His notorious paper "The Destruction of Aesthetics" (1865) is an enthusiastic endorsement of Chernyshevsky's dissertation. Pisarev draws its logical conclusions. If beauty is life, he says, then "every healthy and normal person is beautiful," and aesthetics dissolves, to Pisarev's apparent satisfaction, into physiology and hygiene. If art expresses everything that interests man, we must ask what interests man. Criticism will be an argument not about art but about natural science, history, politics, and moral philosophy. Chernyshevsky is right in showing that an aesthetician can judge only the form of a work of art and thus can have no opinion of its substance. The true critic is a thinking man who judges the contents, i.e., the phenomena of life represented in a work of literature.

Aesthetics to Pisarev thus means the view that form is more important than content; it means aestheticism, art for art's sake. By a sleight of hand, aesthetics can mean to him any theory of art. But such a theory is impossible because all art appeals to a purely subjective feeling of pleasure and thus is not and cannot be science. This "destruction of aesthetics," with Pisarev, easily widens into a destruction of art itself. First of all, he rejects what he considers the purely ornamental sensuous arts of music, painting, and sculpture, for which he sees no possible social use. In a famous *boutade* he finally concedes that drawing may be necessary for making plans for houses or

illustrations to works such as Brehm's *Tierleben*. Next, poetry as verse seems to him completely outmoded, and in his attack on Pushkin he purposely prints all verse as prose. Poetry is a dying art, and we should rejoice at it. "No man of our generation of real intelligence and talent can spend his life piercing sensitive hearts with killing iambs and anapaests."

What remains is only the novel and the drama with a social purpose. Even these, though they are the main topics of Pisarev's literary essays, are considered temporary expedients, makeshift instruments of propaganda useful to shape the world view of readers, but of no intrinsic value. The general decline in the status of belles-lettres is consistently hailed as a sign of social progress.

Some of Pisarev's statements against art and aesthetics were undoubtedly rhetorical flourishes, polemical extravagances designed to shock the reader (*épater le bourgeois*). But I think Pisarev is quite serious in his rejection of art: he must be grouped with a long line of thinkers that begins with Plato, goes through the Elizabethan puritans, the "geometrical" partisans of the Moderns under Louis XIV, to the Benthamite Utilitarians and men like Proudhon, who all wanted to banish the poets from the Republic. Pisarev was concerned with the economy of society and of the Russian intelligentsia in particular. He was shocked by the existence of a conservatory of music in a nation that lacked sufficient bread to prevent famine or by a "scientific expedition to the shores of the Tigris to decipher cuneiform inscriptions at a time when the ordinary Russian could not make out printed letters in his own language." Young men should be warned off the arts. They should revere Darwin, Liebig, Claude Bernard, rather than Bryulov (a painter), Glinka, and Mochalov (an actor). Today science and the spread of science is the one thing needful, at least in Russia. Pisarev's slogan, "realism," is simply analysis, criticism, intellectual progress. A realist is a "thinking worker." Literature and especially the art of the novel is, at most, recognized as a means of communicating and disseminating such ideas. "Literature raises psychological problems, shows the clash of passions, characters, and situations, leads the reader to thinking about these conflicts and the means of abolishing them." Literature, in short, helps in forming public opinion: novels change the morals and convictions of a society, though they do so very slowly, like drops wearing out a stone. In his general condemnation of art, Pisarev makes an exception in favor of writers who are "knights of the spirit." They need not be "imaginative writers." He is pleased to note that Belinsky and Dobrolyubov have become famous without writing poetry, novels, or dramas. He concedes even that Nekrasov may continue to write verse if he cannot express himself in any other manner; that Turgenev may continue to write novels if he cannot explain but only depict his Bazarov; that Chernyshevsky may put into fictional form what might have been a treatise on sociology. But his is only a temporary concession to the deplorable weaknesses of human nature. Pisarev sees art consistently as a past form of human endeavor that has been vanquished or should be vanquished shortly by science.

Pisarev's attitude toward history and literary history in particular is thus completely negative. All historical novels are useless. So is all literary history. He ridicules a man devoted to the study of Old Russian literature. What of it even if he were as great as Grimm? Grimm might have accomplished something if his study of German folk speech had induced him to write on science in popular language. But what is the use of antiquarianism? "I say with all sincerity that I would rather be a Russian shoemaker or baker than a Russian Raphael or Grimm.'' Pisarev was himself a student of history: he compiled a great number of articles on history, e.g., on Metternich, on the history of the press in France, on Erckmann-Chatrian's *Histoire d'un paysan*. But they all serve a purely practical purpose. The historical novel by Erckmann-Chatrian allows Pisarev to retell the story of the French Revolution for his starved readers.

Pisarev's extreme views on general questions—his blatant enmity toward art, his rejection of all the central insights achieved in the history of criticism—bode ill for the value for his practical criticism. But strangely enough, he has genuine critical insights and a considerable power of analysis. In spite of many doctrinaire aberrations and blind spots he seems to me a more sensitive practical critic and a far more lively writer than either Chernyshevsky or Dobrolyubov. He even has wit and polemical brilliance. One must, of course, make large allowances: the famous attack on Pushkin (in ''Pushkin and Belinsky,'' 1865) is often downright silly. It is the kind of brutal execution, the jeering verbal quibbling that defeats its own purpose. The picture of Onegin as a shallow, cowardly dandy whose boredom is not genuine dissatisfaction with life but simply *Katzenjammer* is an amusing tour de force, but is marred by a constant attempt to identify Pushkin and Onegin. It leads to the conclusion that ''we modern Russians have nothing in common with the type which Onegin represents.'' The insensitive mauling of Tatyana and Lensky is merely coarse. In the dissection of several poems Pisarev tears words and phrases out of context, ignores the fictional framework, and shows a literal-mindedness that seems to me only deplorable. The harmless poem ''October 19, 1825'' is pressed quite mercilessly as evidence for snobbery. Still, one understands why Pisarev disliked Pushkin's claims to supernatural inspiration, his contempt for the crowd, and his anti-Polish patriotism. The conclusion that Pushkin reveals his ''inner vacuity, his spiritual poverty, and intellectual impotence,'' that he was ''unable to analyze and to understand social and philosophical problems,'' does not differ very much from what had been said by Dobrolyubov and even by Chernyshevsky. But everything in Pisarev is said so bluntly and indiscriminately that the modicum of polemical truth becomes a falsehood.

The treatment of Pushkin is paralleled in the frequent references to Goethe, for whom Pisarev conceived a similar dislike and whom he also saw as the representative of a past aristocratic art. Pisarev simply adopts the views of Börne and never enters into a close discussion. His one essay on a foreign poet, that on Heine (1867), is by no means imperceptive of aesthetic values or obtuse in psychological insight, as are the essays on Pushkin. Pisarev gives a good description of the violent transitions in Heine's prose: ''Colors of extreme brightness are suddenly replaced by the face of a charming woman; then by the demoniac eyes of a hideous satyr; the turn into a bushy tree, and instead of a tree, there appears a porcelain tower and below it a Chinaman on a fantastic dragon; and then all this is obliterated and the author looks at us with a contemptuous and melancholy smile.'' Thus Pisarev can, on occasion, write evocative criticism, a kind totally inaccessible to his fellow critics. He can see Heine's inner division and see through his posturing about his innumerable mistresses. But the focus of the essay is on Heine's political and aesthetic opinions. Pisarev sees them both as ambiguous, undecided, wavering. Heine wants to be a ''courageous soldier in the war of humanity'' but at the same time wants to be a pure artist and even an irresponsible clown. He is horrified by the mob: he tells us

that he has to wash his hands everytime he has brushed against somebody in the crowd. Heine is a liberal tied to the decaying corpse of the *Gironde*. His attitude toward art is similarly vacillating. We find in him all answers, today this and tomorrow the opposite. ''When the poet sings like a nightingale without purpose, Heine feels the smell of fresh hay. If he puts himself under the banner of a definite idea, Heine shouts that the world is being flooded with Rumford's Utility Soup.'' Heine praises ''nightingales'' such as Uhland, Tieck, and Arnim, but also propagandists such as Laube and Gutzkow. Pisarev defends Heine's sincerity and tries to give a historical explanation of his confused position. Writers of the 18th century like Voltaire or Diderot passionately believed in political revolution. Writers of our time believe in ''economic regeneration,'' Pisarev's euphemism for socialism. But Heine lived in the in-between, dark zone filled with disillusionment, doubt, and vague aspirations. He has lost the old faith and has not acquired the new one. He lacks faith as he lacks a public and roots in his own nation. Voltaire and Diderot were whole men; Heine is divided, tragically torn apart. Today we have whole men again: Proudhon, Louis Blanc, Lassalle—and, we might add, Pisarev.

The definition of the new whole men in Russia is Pisarev's main concern in analyzing current Russian fiction. He begins his literary career by rejecting Dobrolyubov's analyses. Oblomov, he finds, cannot be considered a representative type: he is abnormal physically and temperamentally. Stolz is not a man but a puppet, and so is Olga. Goncharov is a man without ideas, an ironical skeptic who does not sympathize with any one of his figures, though he understands them all. He is a pure artist, of no relevance to the ''new men'' of Pisarev's persuasion.

Turgenev, before *Fathers and Sons,* is judged more sympathetically than Goncharov, but still severely. Pisarev likes his women, especially Asya, but disagrees wih Dobrolyubov about *On the Eve.* Insarov is entirely impossible, a mere synthetic figure of heroism who offers no hope that the day will come.

When Dobrolyubov died, literary criticism in the *Contemporary* was taken over by Maxim Antonovich (1835-1918), who reviewed *Fathers and Sons,* denouncing Bazarov as a monster, a caricature, a libel on the young generation. Pisarev saw further and better. He hailed Bazarov as the representative of the new man and analyzed him sympathetically and penetratingly. In the article ''Bazarov'' (1862) Pisarev recognizes Bazarov's brutality, ill manners, and cynicism, but praises his forthrightness, his scientific outlook, and his sturdy independence. He is even independent of what he professes; he is capable, as shown by his behavior at Mme Odyntsov's and his duel with Pavel, of making a fool of himself. His feelings of love on his deathbed are not a symptom of weakness; rather they show that he has become a man instead of being only the embodiment of the theory of nihilism. His rationality has been extreme, but it disappears in the time of approaching death. He has struggled against this love because he felt he might become unfaithful to his image of life. Bazarov's death is pure chance. The story is broken off, to be completed by the future, in reality. Pisarev sees that the author's attitude toward his hero is what we would call today ambivalent. Turgenev does not fully sympathize with any one of his figures; he is not content with either fathers or children. Turgenev cannot share Bazarov's ruthless negations, but he respects them. Though he himself inclines toward idealism, none of the idealists in the book is comparable even to Bazarov in strength of mind and character. In creating Bazarov,

Turgenev might have wanted to lower him, but his artistic integrity made him pay the tribute of just respect.

In a later development of this characterization, in "The Realists" (1864), Pisarev, on the whole, repeats the early analysis but elaborates on the relation between Bazarov and Mme. Odyntsov. He makes a wholehearted defense of Bazarov's high-mindedness and respect for the woman he loves, mostly because Bazarov has been attacked for immorality and cynicism. Pisarev shows that Turgenev depicts a strong and even sublime passion, but in the process he somehow deprives Bazarov of his original vigor and crudity; he makes him too much of a hero "without stain and reproach," even defending his courting of Fenichka. Whatever one may object to details of Pisarev's interpretation, his recognition of Bazarov's significance was important: it has its personal touch of pathos. In Bazarov, Pisarev discovered himself and his generation. His criticism was a genuine act of self-knowledge, a justification of a method that treats a fictional figure as a symbol quite apart from the overt intentions of the author. One could argue that Pisarev's interpretation influenced Turgenev's later attitude toward his own creation: it certainly made him look at it with greater sympathy and admiration.

That Pisarev identified himself fully with Bazarov can be seen also from the curious letter he wrote to Turgenev about *Smoke*. Turgenev was afraid that Pisarev would not like the scenes ridiculing the revolutionary emigrants and their leader Bubarev, a caricature of Ogarev. But Pisarev brushes them aside, recognizing that some balance was needed to make the blow at the reactionaries more effective. He is saddened, however, by the hero of the novel, Litvinov, who seems to him only another Arkady, the weak student-friend of Bazarov from *Fathers and Sons*. "What has happened to Bazarov?" he asks. "Do you think the first and last Bazarov actually died in 1859 of a cut on his finger?"

There is nothing so good as the discussion of Bazarov in all of Pisarev's later writings. The rivalry with the dead Dobrolyubov is still obvious when Pisarev attacks the early satires of Saltykov-Shchedrin. Saltykov seems to him a mere entertainer whose influence is based on a misunderstanding, and he gives him blunt advice to abandon fiction and do something useful, such as translating or writing on science for a popular audience. Pisarev is on firmer ground when he rejects Dobrolyubov's interpretation of Ostrovsky's *Storm* and its heoine Katerina. She is, rather, "a Russian Ophelia who, after committing several foolish acts, commits the last and most foolish and throws herself into the Volga." Pisarev becomes most satirical when he shoots at targets hardly worth aiming for: at a novel, *A Woman's Fate*, by Stanitsky, the pseudonym of Mme Paneva, at the bad novels of a lesser Tolstoy, Theophil, or at novels such as Leskov's *No Exit*, caricaturing the radicals. He waxes most enthusiastic, deliriously so, when he praises Chernyshevsky's *What Shall We Do?* He finds even artistic value in this dreary revolutionary tract.

His reviews of Dostoevsky and Leo Tolstoy are the most interesting to us. Pisarev reviews the *Memoirs from a Dead House* and contrasts them maliciously with *Sketches* by Pomyalovsky describing life in a priests' seminary. Pisarev shows or pretends to show that the life of the chained convicts in the Siberian stockade is, to judge from Dostoevsky's account, much freer and much more hopeful and less degraded than that of the cowed and oppressed seminarists. The title of the article, "The Dead and the Dying" (1865), reverses ordinary expec-

tations: the inhabitants of the House of the Dead have a chance of recovery; the seminarists have perished utterly.

When Pisarev came to review *Crime and Punishment* as "The Struggle for Life" (1867), he knew Dostoevsky's convictions and must have looked upon him as a political enemy. A letter shows that he was completely carried away by the book, but his review pays only very perfunctory compliments to Dostoevsky's psychological insight and announces that he will ignore the point of view of the author and discuss only the manifestations of social life depicted in the book. The method is Dobrolyubov's, the same that Pisarev had used on Bazarov. Pisarev assumes that the author, if he is a good writer, reflects life accurately, and that his attitudes and mere theories are irrelevant: intentions, logical schemes do not count. He has succeeded well with Bazarov, but he fails with Raskolnikov. His polemical purpose made him ignore the obvious fact that Dostoevsky does not merely impose his ideology upon his figure (he does little of that), but actually presents a drama of ideas in the actions and persons of the novel itself. Pisarev, sensing that Dostoevsky wants to show up the "new men," adopts the strategy of proving that Raskolnikov's crime was entirely due to poverty. His convictions had no influence on the action; the root of his illness was not in the brain but in the pocket. His share of freedom was exceedingly small. His views have nothing in common with those of the "new men." Pisarev takes Raskolnikov's article, discovered by the police, and demonstrates that Raskolnikov has illicitly expanded the term "criminal" to include every historical leader. In Pisarev's mind a great man who spills blood wantonly and commits crimes against humanity, ceases to be a great man. And the whole view that individuals can change the stream of history is mistaken. Raskolnikov's theory is not the cause of the crime, any more than hallucination is the cause of an illness. Raskolnikov, after the crime, goes to pieces and puts himself under the tutelage of a good-natured but uneducated girl. The implication is obvious. One need not take Raskolnikov's regeneration and final conversion seriously. All this is cleverly devised by Pisarev and is an effective argument against an interpretation of the novel as saying, "Look—these new ideas lead to crime." But it is not good literary criticism because it ignores the bulk of Dostoevsky's text. Dostoevsky ascribes the crime not to poverty but to a complex of motives which includes Raskolnikov's theories—not only romantic titanism, which Pisarev dislikes, but also Utilitarianism (or rather an extreme version in which anything is permissible if it leads to the ultimate good of society), a thing that Pisarev believes in. Dostoevsky did not and could not write a novel *á la* Zola, with the thesis "poverty leads to crime," because he believed in human self-determination, in moral freedom. Pisarev distorts the book because he ignores half of Raskolnikov's motivation and almost all that follows after the crime. There, after all, is the real emphasis of the book. Pisarev's method of discussing a situation as if it were one in real life, from the point of view of his own determinism, breaks down in face of a book that is a closely knit and complex drama of ideas.

He fails even worse with Tolstoy. "The Blunders of an Immature Mind" (1864) is a review of some of Tolstoy's early writings: *Childhood, Boyhood, Youth; A Landlord's Morning;* and *Lucerne*. The "immature mind" is Tolstoy's hero Nekhlyudov in the last two stories. Pisarev shows him to be a transitional type, less inactive and passive than Rudin, less active than Bazarov. He is trapped by his aristocratic education, incapable of sound and practical views of the world because he lacks scientific training. Nekhlyudov is given advice as if he were a real person: it was a foolish idea to stay on his estate; he should have liberated his peasants and moved away completely. His behavior in Lucerne, inviting a singer into the elegant hotel, was merely hysterical, impractical, and foolish. Though Pisarev sympathizes with Tolstoy's humanitarianism and professes admiration for his power as a writer, he has no comprehension of his mental struggles nor any perception of the Rousseauistic criticism of civilization that runs though all of Tolstoy's work. Still, the article has something to say: the placing of Irtenev-Nekhlyudov as a type in Russian social history is roughly correct.

The late review of *War and Peace* (1868), or rather of its first half then published, shows a definite decline of Pisarev's powers. "The Old Nobility" of Pisarev's title includes merely two characters of the novel: Boris Drubetskoy and Nikolay Rostov, who are used to show up the crudely scheming, ambitious, spoilt, and lazy old aristocracy. Again Pisarev professes to ignore the intentions of the author, but again, as in the review of *Crime and Punishment*, it is the bulk of the actual text which is ignored. The whole atmosphere of nostalgia for the past is completely missed. In Pisarev's defense, one must say that the article was only the first of a projected series which would have taken up Pierre, Andrey, and Natasha. But nothing came of it. During the last two years of his life Pisarev was obviously at a dead end. Most of his articles are mere compilations—for instance, from W. H. Dixon's *Spiritual Wives* and from Sismondi's *History of the Italian Republics*. An unfinished article, recently published, on "Diderot and his Time" is only an abstract from the book by Karl Rosenkranz. Pisarev found it difficult to publish after the suppression of the *Russian Word*, the periodical that had printed most of his work. He tried to get into the *Contemporary*. But he was, as he says in the letter to Turgenev, now quite alone, and he perished soon afterward, in despair.

Looking back at our three critics, we should admire their devotion to their cause. We must recognize that they were not primarily interested in literature at all. They were revolutionaries, and literature was only a weapon in the battle. They did not see and did not want to see that man is confronted with questions that surpass those of his own age; that the insight art provides into the full meaning of existence does not necessarily grow out of his immediate social preoccupations. As critics they constantly lose sight of the text, confuse (sometimes deliberately) life and fiction, treat figures in novels as if they were men or women on the street, or allegorize the fictional character, make it evaporate to represent some generalization: the decadent aristocrat, the desire for freedom, the new man, and so on. They constantly succumb to two not unrelated fallacies: naturalism and intellectualism. They lose hold on the concrete universal, the fusion of the particular and general in every work of art. Content and form are divorced: the unity of the work of art broken up, imagination reduced to a mere combinatory intellectual power. Art in short is denied as a value in itself. It is distributed between a despised sensual pleasure of form and a purely cognitive or hortatory content. Art, at bottom, is superfluous, and Pisarev spoke only the truth, like any *enfant terrible*.

But this tendency, destructive of the very nature of literary criticism and art in general, should not make us ignore the real contribution of Pisarev and his fellows to a social study of literature. Their analysis of social types was something new and important methodologically. One must, besides, recognize that Russia at that time was actually producing a social novel,

that poetry was then derivative, and the drama rather a reflex of the novel. Our critics helped to define and describe the nature of the social novel, the obligation of the writer toward social truth; his insight, conscious or unconscious, into the structure and typical characters of society. It seems a pity that they did so in narrow local terms shackled by their gross utilitarianism. The noise of the battle deafened them. (pp. 238-65)

René Wellek, "The Russian Radical Critics," in his A History of Modern Criticism, 1750-1950: The Later Nineteenth Century, *Yale University Press, 1965, pp. 238-65.*

VICTOR TERRAS

[Terras analyzes the Civic Critics' aesthetic theory.]

[Černyševskij's] aesthetics was, as he himself pointed out in a preface to the third edition of *The Aesthetic Relations of Art to Reality* (1888), an application of Feuerbach's materialistic philosophy to aesthetic theory.

Černyševskij had little inclination and no talent for literary criticism. His interests lay in the areas of political science, sociology, and economics. He became a part-time literary critic and one of Russia's most influential writers on aesthetic theory, mainly because he realized that in Russia literature constituted virtually the entire intellectual life of the nation. In his *Sketches of the Gogolian Period of Russian Literature*, Černyševskij observed quite correctly that in Russia fiction served as a medium for many ideas which in the West would have been discussed in works of nonfiction, by economists, jurists, publicists, and philosophers. This, Černyševskij adds with a measure of pride, accounts for the originality of Russian literature.

With all his revolutionary fervor and idealistic devotion to the cause of "the people," Černyševskij was a consistent materialist and determinist. He believed that so-called mental processes were physical processes not yet fully understood, but entirely determinate. Religion was the same as superstition. Scientific and technological progress, if rationally manipulated, would eventually take man out of history, time, and suffering.

Černyševskij also argued, in positivist terms, against any kind of aesthetic transcendence, rejecting the concepts of inner vision, inspiration, and genius as self-delusions of artists and poets overly convinced of their own importance:

> One cannot imagine a face that is more beautiful than those faces which one has happened to see in real life. Yet, on the other hand, one can *say* [italics added] all one wants to say. One can say: "iron gold," "warm ice," "sugary bitterness," and so forth. To be sure, our imagination cannot imagine "warm ice" . . . which is why these phrases remain completely empty for us, giving no meaning whatsoever to our imagination. Yet, having mixed some empty words with representations that are accessible to the imagination, one may delude oneself into believing that the dreams of fantasy are much richer, fuller, more luxurious than reality.
>
> *(The Aesthetic Relations of Art to Reality)*

Černyševskij's argument is that of a man who is not only uninterested in art, but who actually has never bothered to find out what art is. It is the argument of a man unfamiliar with aesthetic experience. Plexanov was quite right in calling Černyševskij an "enlightener" (*prosvetitel'*). In his aesthetic views,

Černyševskij returned to pre-Kantian eighteenth-century ideas, seeking to account for aesthetic phenomena entirely in terms of either rational intelligence or simple sense experience. Much like eighteenth-century enlighteners, Černyševskij considered excessive passion, excitability, and fantasy to be nothing but pathological conditions to be treated by medical therapists. His ideal was that of a "normal" and "rational" development of man's "natural" faculties. Černyševskij's anthropology, much as that of the eighteenth-century Enlightenment, was optimistic: man, though naturally an egoist, was a rational being, well capable of pursuing his self-interest intelligently in accordance with the laws of nature, and with some enlightened consideration for other human beings; he was therefore perfectly capable of progress, that is, of creating ever-improving conditions of life for himself and his fellowmen.

The key notion of Černyševskij's aesthetics proper is a total rejection of the Kantian doctrine of the autonomous and specific nature of the aesthetic fact. Černyševskij did everything to destroy all the barriers separating art from science, from politics, from publicism, and from ordinary practical activity. He made a point of showing that so-called aesthetic concepts were by no means applicable to art and poetry alone. In a way, this "abolition of aesthetics" (as Pisarev later called it) amounted to organicism in reverse: art and life were still one, though in a quite different sense than had been the case in idealist organic aesthetics.

Astaxov points out that Černyševskij's unqualified identification of art with its nonaesthetic social functions failed to take into account the concrete historical fact of art's autonomous power. As a result, Astaxov thinks, Černyševskij lost his grip on the power of art, which he would have liked to control for the benefit of society. Actually, Černyševskij's position was much more consistent and logical than that of Belinskij, Plexanov, or their contemporary Soviet followers, all of whom . . . want to have their cake and eat it, too. Černyševskij's combination of a frank and thorough utilitarianism with a low evaluation of the value of art makes a great deal of sense—provided, of course, one is not interested in art as such. If art is viewed exclusively as an educational, propaganda, and information medium (rather than as an end in itself), much is to be said for Černyševskij's aesthetics.

As just suggested, Černyševskij arrived at an organicist position of sorts, though it was organicism with an inverse relationship. In idealist organicism, "ordinary" life is aestheticized. In Černyševskij's materialist aesthetics, art is subjected to the norms of ordinary life. Belinskij had tried to let art grow autonomously, hoping that it would proceed in step with—or even a step ahead of—social life. Černyševskij integrated art into social life by simply letting art meet the practical demands of society.

To begin with, Černyševskij flatly rejected the doctrine which had been the pivot of all post-Kantian aesthetics, namely, the notion of the disinterestedness of true art. "The foremost and the universal purpose of all works of art," said Černyševskij, "is the reproduction of those phenomena of real life which are of interest to man" *(vosproizvedenie interesnyx dlja čeloveka javlenij dejstvitel'-noj žizni)*. Art, Černyševskij believed, was a kind of running commentary on life, designed largely for an audience not well enough educated to comprehend a serious and factual scientific commentary on the same subjects. Černyševskij saw no basic difference between poetry and history, though he followed Aristotle in asserting that "a learned work

tells you what precisely was or is, while a work of fiction tells you how things always, or usually, lean in this world."

Furthermore, Černyševskij's aesthetics is characterized by an uncompromising naturalism—again, a trait which links him to eighteenth-century thought. "An apology of reality against fantasy, an effort to prove that works of art definitely cannot stand comparison with living reality—that is the essence of this treatise," he says of his dissertation. To illustrate this thesis, Černyševskij points out that any French or English crime gazette contains many more interesting and far more intricate real-life stories than any writer of fiction could possibly conceive. The most beautiful landscape painting could not possibly serve as a substitute for a real landscape. And as for human portraits, "painting at its present level of technical proficiency cannot express well either the color of the human body in general, or the human face in particular: its colors, as compared to the natural hue of a human face and body are nothing but a crude, wretched imitation—instead of a delicate body, the painting shows something greenish or reddish. . . ." Černyševskij's naturalism reaches a *non plus ultra* when he asserts that instrumental music, being in effect a feeble imitation of vocal music, is much inferior to the vocal. Vocal music, in turn, is naturally a direct expression of human emotions. Both of these notions were also widely popular in the eighteenth century.

At any rate, with astounding casualness Černyševskij reduces art to a surrogate of reality and rejects the fantastic in art, *l'art pour l'art*, romantic art—in short, everything that does not fit his naturalist conception.

Černyševskij anticipated Tolstoj's rejection of Shakespeare, and on much the same grounds. He even anticipated Tolstoj's observation that romantic aesthetics was created *ad hoc* to fit Shakespeare's art. Consistent with his uncompromising naturalism, Černyševskij systematically debunked all "aesthetic categories" (the Beautiful, the Sublime, the Tragic), reducing them to nonaesthetic terms. Again, he arrived at a kind of organicism in reverse, as he defined Beauty as follows: "Beauty is life; beautiful is that being in which we see life as it ought to be according to our concepts; beautiful is that object which is expressive of life or reminiscent of life." This definition almost coincides with Belinskij's, or Hegel's, for that matter. In its practical application, however, Černyševskij's definition was an absurd reversal of Hegel's conception. Honest materialist and positivist that he was, he developed his aesthetic theory from his empirical observations of the pleasures and satisfactions of "ordinary" and "natural" life rather than from any observation, ideal or empirical, of either art, concrete works of art, or the creative process as conceived by artists or critics: "For people who have not reached your dispassionate heights, a young housewife who, like a child, rejoices at having neatly furnished her modest apartment, consisting of three or four rooms, is more poetic than any Venus of either Medici or Louvre could possibly be" ("A Critical View of Contemporary Aesthetic Concepts").

Černyševskij decreed that only the honest representation of the simple good life and of things that were a part of it was truly beautiful, and he arrived at a model of "true art" (where "beauty" equals "life") by excluding from art everything that did not satisfy his demand for "naturalness," simplicity, wholesomeness, and rational, robust realism. Like Tolstoj in *What Is Art?* Černyševskij felt obliged to reject as "nonart" or "inferior art" much of what most educated men would consider truly great art. Without being aware of it, Černyševskij had lapsed into eighteenth-century classicist thinking, for what he postulated in lieu of the romantic conception of Beauty as the perfect fusion of the ideal and the real in effect coincided with Batteux's "imitation of beautiful nature."

Černyševskij's objectivism led to some outright absurd positions. Seeking to demonstrate that the artist depended entirely on objective reality and could not depart from it with impunity, he asserted, for example, that no painter would ever paint a tree "without atmosphere, without a piece of land on which it grows, without a landscape a part of which it represents, without an animal or a human figure." This is an amazing factual blunder in view of Černyševskij's otherwise impressive scholarship.

In refuting the Hegelian notion that "that object is beautiful in which an idea finds its full expression," Černyševskij brings up Gogol's description of a mudhole in "The Tale of How Ivan Ivanovič Quarreled with Ivan Nikiforovič," pointing out that the idea of a mudhole has found its fullest expression in that passage—"yet you will agree with me that it was still a foul sight to see, and smelled even fouler." Here Černyševskij completely ignores what Aristotle and Plutarch had already taken care to point out, namely, that in art it is not the "what" that matters, but the "how." In effect, Černyševskij's example proves Hegel right. Hegel himself, in defending Flemish genre painting, had said precisely that a low and ungainly subject could be elevated by the *idea* imparted to it by art. Černyševskij had completely forgotten that Gogol's story had an *idea,* too.

Černyševskij similarly reduced the other "aesthetic categories" to ordinary sense experience. He defined the Sublime as simply "that which is much larger than anything near it or similar to it," and the Tragic as something strikingly sad or terrible. Likewise, Černyševskij rejected the whole theory of genres, seeing no inherent difference between them, except in the external circumstances of the presentation of a work—a matter of convenience and economy, no more.

Černyševskij's naïve objectivism led him into many difficulties. He knew, of course, that some works of art which did not at all correspond to his notion of what true art was supposed to be like gave some people a great deal of pleasure. Černyševskij's explanation of this fact was the one later given by Tolstoj, by Marxist aestheticians (Plexanov, in particular), and by Soviet critics of "modernism" today. In these instances, Černyševskij believed, we are dealing with the decadent art of an idle and parasitic upper class:

> An artificially educated man has many artificial needs, distorted to the point of complete falseness and fantastic dimensions, needs which can never be completely satisfied because they are really not natural needs, but mere daydreams of a corrupt imagination; to satisfy a man's whims does not mean to meet his needs.
>
> *(Aesthetic Relations)*

Without noticing it, Černyševskij has fallen from extreme objectivism into extreme subjectivism: the quality of art is now determined by a moral evaluation of its consumer.

Černyševskij's naïve view which made him assume that objective reality was both rational and relatively simple to grasp led him to the extraordinary opinion that a clever and well-educated man, possessed of the right ideas and a sufficient number of correct empirical observations could very well create worthwhile works of art. This was possible because Černyševskij, in a way which was diametrically opposed to the organicist tradition, considered "form" merely an assemblage

of mechanical details of execution and a decidedly secondary criterion of artistic merit. Such separation of "content" and "form," or complete subordination of "form" to "content," had to lead to a crude didacticism and moralism in Černyševskij's practical criticism. As a corollary, it also had to lead to an equally crude formalism whenever "form" would come up in his discussions.

Černyševskij visualized the ideal poet as a man who, being himself possessed of rational, enlightened, and noble ideas, induces other people to share his humanitarian and progressive attitudes. He found the Governor-General's concluding speech in the second part of *Dead Souls* (an unctuous moral tirade) the best part of that work. Of course, he was guided by his attitude when he wrote his own fiction. On the other hand, Černyševskij observed that "for a single [formal] virtue of some kind, people are willing to forgive a work hundreds of faults," giving Horace and Vergil as examples of poets whose total lack of any other value is forgiven on account of their "elegant language." In this way, Černyševskij unwittingly reverted to a pre-Belinskian "critique of details" and outright "formalism."

However, as regards formalism, Černyševskij was inconsistent. More often than not he would stick to the Belinskian organicist position, asserting that even the most elegant form could not possibly save a work which was ideologically and factually false from being anything but shapeless and ugly. Like Belinskij—and Hegel, of course—he tended to believe that an immoral idea would destroy itself by its own falseness and, in the process, also destroy the form in which it was expressed. In fact, Černyševskij often denounced eclectic art and eclectic criticism, using the familiar organicist arguments in so doing:

> A human body is a whole; one cannot tear it into parts and say: this part is beautiful, while this is ugly. Here, too, as in so many other instances, selectivity, a mosaic structure, eclecticism result in incongruities: either accept all, or accept nothing—only then will you be right, at least from your particular point of view.
>
> *(Aesthetic Relations)*

The one corollary of this organic conception which Černyševskij failed to see was that a poor or inadequate form could very well destroy the soundest idea—a point on which Dostoevskij insisted with great vehemence. Černyševskij carried Belinskij's "contentualism" to its extreme consequences, namely, the notion that a sound "content" would somehow take care of its own expression, making "form," the proper domain of the artist, a mere luxury.

In spite of his low evaluation of art, Černyševskij was as eager as Belinskij—or Dostoevskij, for that matter—to integrate art, and especially literature, into the country's social life and to make it into a vehicle of progress. However, the role which Černyševskij assigned to literature was modest, as compared with Belinskij's confident and enthusiastic vision of Russian men of letters leading the country toward a better future. Černyševskij, who had a good knowledge of history and the history of world literature, assessed the social role of art and literature more soberly than Belinskij. In his essay on Lessing, Černyševskij stated quite explicitly that, while literature always played a certain role in the historical process, this role was nevertheless invariably a secondary one. As far as Černyševskij was concerned, literature merely "filled orders" which it received from society, for the public's judgment was far superior to that of most literary men (poets, critics, editors). Literature, said Černyševskij, responds to the public needs of the day. So long as it refuses to do that, pursuing its own intrinsic goals, it will remain not only ineffectual but also insignificant in its own terms.

Černyševskij's evaluation of Russian literature before Gogol' was even lower than Belinskij's. He assigned to Puškin the largely "historical" role of Russia's first genuine poet, who educated the Russian public to appreciate fine poetry. (Belinskij had said much the same thing.) But inasmuch as most of Puškin's works had "little live connection with society, they remained fruitless for society as well as for literature." One of the works so characterized in Černyševskij's Fourth essay on Puškin is "The Stone Guest," considered by many one of Puškin's finest works.

Černyševskij's notion of how literature could contribute to social progress was simple. In order to remedy the unsatisfactory condition of Russian society, one had to recognize the ills which plagued it. "The initiative for change will not come from the peasants," Černyševskij wrote in an essay, "The Beginning of Change, Perhaps?" (1861), "but still, one must know their character in order to know what stimuli must be applied to make our initiative have an effect on them." In the same essay, Černyševskij demanded a straightforward and unsentimental treatment of "the people" and their problems, instead of the sentimental humanism of Gogol's *Overcoat* or Grigorovič's *Village*. Russian muzhiks, he said, were simply people. They should not be either idealized or vilified, but educated and helped. Černyševskij's program for Russian literature was, accordingly, one of competent, positivistic "case studies." Therefore, he approved of Nikolaj Uspenskij's bleak, naturalistic stories, defending them against attacks by *počvenniki* and Slavophiles (who felt that Uspenskij had failed to bring out the godly side of the Russian peasant) as well as by liberals (who found fault with Uspenskij's stark, "unaesthetic" naturalism).

Thus, Černyševskij accepted the cognitive function of art, but on entirely different terms than had been the case in Belinskij's organic conception. The writer's intuition is replaced by fact-finding, inspiration by information, and creation by reportage. In a way, Černyševskij realized Balzac's metaphoric boast that a modern writer was a doctor of the social sciences.

What Belinskij had called the "ideal" in literature . . . , Černyševskij would rather see made explicit than presented in quintessential symbols: "The quintessence of a thing does not usually resemble the thing itself: theine is not tea, alcohol is not wine," he wrote in *The Aesthetic Relations of Art to Reality*. Černyševskij was frankly in favor of literature which made a point of "serving a distinct tendency of moral strivings" (*služenie opredelennomu napravleniju nravstvennyx stremlenij*). Gogol' was, in his opinion, the first Russian writer to have done this consciously and consistently. He was, in Černyševskij's opinion, the father not only of Russian prose, but also of the "critical tendency" *kritičeskoe napravlenie*) in Russian literature. To Černyševskij, as to Belinskij, Gogol' was Russia's "social poet" par excellence:

> No other Russian writer has expressed an awareness of his patriotic significance (*soznanie svoego patriotičeskogo značenija*) as vividly and clearly as Gogol'. He straightforwardly considered himself a man called upon to serve not art, but his country, thinking of himself: "I am not a poet, I am a citizen!"

Černyševskij approved of Gogol' even more wholeheartedly than did Belinskij. He had words of the highest praise for the extant sections of the second part of *Dead Souls*. As Andrej Belyj once put it: "Belinskij had chastised Gogol', Černyševskij rehabilitated him." In fact, Černyševskij quite unreservedly placed Gogol' above Puškin.

The discussion thus far shows that Černyševskij carried Belinskij's cautious deviations from a Hegelian organicist aesthetics to bold extremes. This pattern emerges most clearly in Černyševskij's version of historicism. Since Černyševskij believes in absolute historical progress and that the value of the work of art depends solely on its relevance to contemporary interests and to progress, this value is inevitably bound to decrease with the passage of time. The greatest poets of the past are "of historical importance only" (one of Černyševskij's favorite phrases).

Černyševskij was convinced that the literature and criticism of the future would far outstrip those of his own age, that a period would come, presumably soon, "when everything that has existed or exists now in Russian literature, even including Belinskij's criticism, will appear unsatisfactory." Often Černyševskij voices judgments which give evidence of a thoroughgoing aesthetic relativism. For example, he will call Gogol''s "Hans Küchelgarten" a poem which was "very weak even for that age." The poem appeared in 1829, when Russian poetry was at a peak it was never to reach again. Or he will compare the critic Polevoj (with whose ideas he disagreed) to a doctor who has not been following the progress of medicine and keeps prescribing pills in the efficacy of which no one believes any more.

To summarize, Černyševskij's aesthetics constituted, by and large, a relapse into some of the shallowest notions prevalent in the eighteenth century, the most fateful of which was probably his failure to distinguish "art" from "pleasure," on the one hand, and from "enlightenment," on the other. As a result of this notion, artists, critics, and all those who enjoyed art become either epicureans, hypocrites, and idlers (fiddling while Rome burned, hiding their selfish interests behind allegedly "disinterested" art, and wasting their time amusing themselves), or enlighteners, moralists, and socially "concerned" altruists. There could be nothing in between. Likewise, Černyševskij conceived of works of contemporary literature as either useful analytic descriptions of objective reality, or useless, even harmful, exercises in frivolity, nebulous mysticism, and idle daydreams. Again, there was nothing in between.

Černyševskij's aesthetics involves an honest, straightforward, and eloquent treatment of art by an otherwise educated man who completely lacks aesthetic sense. Černyševskij was acquainted with a considerable volume of Russian and world literature. He correctly observed many important things about it—except the "art" in it. His judgments of some of the world's great poets, artists, and composers are veritable examples of Tolstoian *ostranenie* ("making it strange" by viewing an object naïvely, through the eyes of a man who lacks the conventional frame of reference for it): Homer is incoherent, offends by his cynicism, and lacks all moral feeling, Beethoven is incomprehensible and wild, Mozart's *Don Giovanni* is boring. Quite inevitably, Černyševskij's aesthetics is attractive to critics who share his handicap, critics who, like Černyševskij, deal with literature professionally, but lack the gift to either appreciate or understand it as "art." There have been many such critics in Russia, and there still are. (pp. 236-45)

N. A. Dobroljubov is next in importance to Pisarev as the most talented and influential practicing critic who applied Černyševskij's principles to the Russian literature of his age. Dobroljubov's aesthetics ostensibly coincided with Černyševskij's. However, he was a genuine critic, not without some poetic talent and with more aesthetic sense than he would himself admit. Whenever he made aesthetic comments on the works under discussion in his articles, they were often sound and perceptive. Dobroljubov's literary essays (really "sermons," for which works of Russian literature served as texts, as D. S. Mirsky put it) bear a strong resemblance to Belinskij's. Needless to say, Dobroljubov's love and admiration for Belinskij were great. Ordinarily austere and reserved in his judgment, he becomes unreservedly enthusiastic and unabashedly lyrical when he greets the appearance of *The Works of V. Belinskij* (1859).

Dobroljubov shared Černyševskij's optimistic anthropology. If anything, his faith in the rational and altruistic qualities of "natural man," unspoiled by society, was even stronger than Černyševskij's. The many ills of Russian life he saw entirely in terms of the "abnormal relations" *(nenormal'nye otnošenija)* established by a perverted social order, as, for example, Dobroljubov's famous statement about crime:

> He committed his crimes without any difficult or extended struggle with himself, but simply "so," accidentally, without being himself quite aware of what he was doing. . . . Whence comes such a phenomenon? It comes from the fact that every crime, rather than being a consequence of human nature *(sledstvie natury čeloveka),* is in fact a consequence of those abnormal conditions into which he has been placed with regard to society. And, the stronger this abnormality, the more often crimes will be committed, even by naturally decent individuals.
>
> ("A Kingdom of Darkness")

It is this statement that Razumixin combats in Chapter 5 of Part 3 of *Crime and Punishment* (the scene at Porfirij Petrovič's flat).

Dobroljubov was as much of a fanatic of "enlightenment" as Černyševskij. Černyševskij had blamed Gogol''s ultimate failure to complete his life's work on the fact that Gogol', like all "half-educated" men, had no conscious conception of the world around him and could only go as far as his sound instincts took him. Dobroljubov used the same approach to Puškin (toward whom he was more disrespectful than Černyševskij, although not quite as disrespectful as Pisarev): "The direction taken by Puškin during his last years did not at all develop from the natural urgings of his soul, but was merely a consequence of his weakness of character, which lacked the inner support of serious convictions, independently developed."

To Dobroljubov, the fact (doubted by no one by then) that Puškin had been a great poet was insignificant compared with the fact that he had done little to promote the causes of social and scientific progress in Russia. Time and again, Dobroljubov stressed that the aesthetic aspect of contemporary literature was of secondary importance and that what really mattered was its social mission: "Aesthetic criticism has now become the domain of sentimental young ladies," he remarked in the introductory paragraph of his famous review of Turgenev's novel *On the Eve,* "When Will There Really Be Day?" (1860).

Like Černyševskij, Dobroljubov is often guilty of flagrant aesthetic intellectualism, as he assumes that a knowledge of the "correct facts" and possession of the "right ideas" can seriously help an artist:

> The free transformation of the highest intellections into living symbols . . . is an ideal which would mean the complete fusion of science and poetry and which no one has as yet attained. But an artist who, in his general concepts, is guided by the right principles still has an advantage over an uneducated or falsely educated writer, in that he can follow more freely the urgings of his artistic nature. His immediate feeling will always point out things to him correctly. But if the writer's general concepts are false, an inner struggle, doubts, and indecision will inevitably occur in his mind, and even if his work will not prove to be completely false as a result of this, it will still be weak, colorless, and misshapen.

And, quite concretely, Dobroljubov will give preference to a work which is "true to reality," though aesthetically imperfect, over a work which is aesthetically perfect, yet distorts life and the meaning of life ("The Stories and Short Stories of S. T. Slavutinskij"). Dobroljubov is quite unaware of the "formalism" which is implied in this assumption.

Dobroljubov's conception of "correct ideas" and "right convictions" as the fruits of a "sound education" involves materialism, positivism, and scientism unchecked by any traditionalist, teleological, or idealist "superstitions." His view of the heritage of Byzantine and Muscovite Russia is aggressively negative. He explicitly rejects all teleological thinking, making fun of people who think that the eye was miraculously made by God so that man could see, or that the Volga flowed toward the Caspian Sea because it had a striving for it. And he exclaims: "The time has come to free life from the oppressive tutelage imposed on it by the ideologues!" ("On the Degree of *narodnost'* in Russian Literature").

Dobroljubov's version of social organicism is simple and straightforward: Literature is to serve society and specifically social progress (by which he means "the revolution," although he cannot say it, of course). Also, he believes—and here he inadvertently lapses into teleological thinking—that Russian literature, as a body, will devote itself freely and enthusiastically to this cause, "considering service to the cause of social improvement its most sacred calling." Nevertheless, Dobroljubov has a more thoughtful view of what literature can do for society than Černyševskij and most of the other Nihilists. To be sure, exposing social ills and extolling all that is good and noble are still literature's main tasks, he thinks. And accordingly, he believes that it is the principal task of literary criticism "to explain those phenomena of reality which have called forth certain works of art" ("When Will There Really Be Day?"). In other words, he wants the literary critic to discuss social problems as reflected in works of art—which is what he practices himself.

In so doing, Dobroljubov is not ignoring his opponents' charge that he is not discussing works of literature; he is merely using these works as occasions for his extra-literary observations. He counters it by pointing out that the authors whose works he discusses—Turgenev, in particular—actually invite this kind of criticism, for they are obviously intent upon making their works true mirrors of Russian life and expressing definite views on its problems and its progress.

To be sure, Dobroljubov, like Černyševskij, favors an uncompromising naturalism in art: "Is it not a fact that man is incapable of inventing as much as a grain of sand which was not

Vilyuisk prison, where Chernyshevsky was incarcerated for twelve years.

already in existence in this world? Good or bad—all is equally taken from nature and from the reality of life.''

But then, Dobroljubov places a higher evaluation on the artist's contribution than Černyševskij did, and he gives it a much more specific content. To begin with, he observes that the artist can choose important and interesting subjects, rather than trivial and boring ones, like the proverbial roses and nightingales. Moreover, the artist can also see the reality of life truthfully, clearly, and broadly—or less so, or not at all. Here, Dobroljubov reverts to a Belinskian position, granting the artist a measure of cognitive power: Art can grasp intuitively what science learns analytically. Having made the shrewd observation that outside literature there is little opportunity to see people and society as they really are, since in virtually all of our contacts we meet people only in their ''official'' functions, Dobroljubov goes on to say:

> An artist-writer, even if he does not care about making any general conclusions regarding the conditions of public opinion and morality, always knows how to capture their essential traits, how to illuminate them brightly, and how to place them directly before the eyes of thinking people. . . . Here, then, a writer's talent will be measured by how broad a grasp he has of life, and by how solid and inclusive the symbols *(obrazy)* are which he has created.

The principal power of a talented writer lies, then, in his ability to create ''types'' which help an intelligent reader to recognize important facts of social life and of social change: ''Sometimes these very symbols will lead a thinking man to the formulation of a correct conception regarding certain phenomena of real life.'' Gončarov's Oblomov is precisely such a ''type.'' The story of Oblomov's sorry failure in life is a trivial one as such, says Dobroljubov, but it is a perfect reflection of an important aspect of Russian life which, Dobroljubov adds prophetically, will henceforth be called ''oblomovitis'' *(oblomovščina)*. The word, in turn, will serve as a key to the understanding of many phenomena of Russian life. And so, the appearance of Gončarov's novel is an event of social import.

Eventually, Dobroljubov develops a conception of the social role of literature which can be called ''dialectic.'' In an essay, ''Loyalty and Activity'' (1860), which deals with the contemporary Russian short story, he formulates a theory which is far more specific than anything that Belinskij had had to say about *social'nost'* and which comes close to the ideal of Soviet literature in Socialist Realist aesthetics. He points out that works of fiction can play a useful role in accelerating and intensifying society's conscious work at effecting certain necessary social changes. The more artistic plenitude and power is found in a work, the more effective it will be as a catalyst of such change.

Černyševskij had assigned an ancillary *(služebnyj)* historical role to literature, though he, too, had believed in its partial effectiveness as an instrument of social change, specifically in Russia. Dobroljubov does not accede to this without a reservation. There have been, he says, in the history of world literature, some geniuses, such as Shakespeare, whose gifts were so great that they could intuitively grasp and vividly express great truths which philosophers could merely guess at in their theories. Such geniuses were able ''to rise above the ancillary role of literature and join the ranks of active historical personages who helped mankind to grasp more clearly its own living powers and natural strivings'' (''A Ray of Light in the Kingdom of Darkness''). This is a return to a Belinskian, that is, Hegelian, position.

When it came to evaluating concrete examples of socially active literature in his own time, Dobroljubov did badly. The populist mystique of his age had a much stronger hold on him than on Belinskij. Also, his emotional involvement in the cause of the revolution, which by this time was beginning to shape up as a political reality, made him susceptible to overestimating works which he found ideologically congenial. Thus, unlike Belinskij, who almost always retained his critical sense, Dobroljubov spent a good deal of time pointing out the merits of some third-rate works. For example, he wholeheartedly defended Marko Vovčok's populist peasant stories, and specifically one of her characters, a freedom-loving peasant woman named Maša, against the anticipated charge (Dobroljubov had enough aesthetic sense to realize that something was wrong with these stories: the charges were actually raised by Dostoevskij and Družinin) that these peasants, and especially Maša, were idealized, abstract, manufactured, and completely untrue to life. Dobroljubov admitted that the form which Maša's love of freedom and resentment of serfdom took in Marko Vovčok's story might indeed be exceptional, but not the basic idea, or content, he felt. Dobroljubov was strongly convinced that what was obviously the projection of a Russian intellectual's (and thus, his own) feelings upon idealized peasant characters was, in fact, an objective reflection of Russian reality. In the end, he asserts that Marko Vovčok's tales ''are true to Russian reality, touch upon extremely important aspects of popular life,'' and that in them ''one meets, in spite of their easy touch, traits which reveal the hand of a skillful master as well as profound, serious study of the subject matter.'' Of course, Dobroljubov was wrong, and Dostoevskij, who exposed Marko Vovčok's stories as the sentimental fabrications which they were, was right—as a literary critic. However, Dobroljubov was right in another sense: the sentiments expressed by Marko Vovčok and innumerable other populist writers of that period ultimately seeped through to the people, and literature—inferior literature, for the most part—had a hand in it. *Uncle Tom's Cabin* was not a good novel, but as a historical and social event it outweighed some great novels. The same happened in Russia.

A characteristic antinomy vitiated Dobroljubov's thinking regarding ''the people.'' On the one hand, he agreed with Belinskij that the life of the plain Russian people was ''ahistorical'' in the sense that it was governed not by any rational ideas, but rather by the merest accidents of trivial everyday living. But on the other hand, Dobroljubov approved of a literature which was ideologically oriented and expressed "the natural strivings of the people" *(estestvennye stremlenija naroda)*. In fact, his essay "On the Degree of *narodnost'* in Russian Literature" (1858) presents a sketch of the history of all Russian literature from the organicist and historicist viewpoint of its growing identification with the "actual" interests of the Russian people as a whole rather than with those of a small segment of it. Thus, the teleological principle enters Dobroljubov's aesthetic theory through a back door, as it were, clothed in the assumption that, somehow, the literature of every age will meet the needs of its epoch:

> In their own day, not only Puškin and Lermontov but even Karamzin and Deržavin were useful to our society. If a poet with that very same content as Puškin were to appear today, we would not pay any attention to him; Lermontov—but even he is not what we need now. . . . But so long as no poet of comparable talent has appeared, we pay careful attention to everything which reveals a healthy living content, even though it be without particular power or talent.
>
> ("The Poetry of Ivan Nikitin")

The inner contradictions which had first developed in Belinskij's critical thought are thus dramatically enhanced in Dobroljubov's criticism. The conflict is between Dobroljubov the positivist and Dobroljubov the populist and revolutionary optimist. The positivist prevails when Dobroljubov discusses the objective—largely negative—phenomena of Russian life, the optimist when his mystic faith in the Russian people and Russia's bright future comes to the fore. Though Dobroljubov's revolutionary ideal is ostensibly a rational and presumably a realizable one, it is no less an abstract ideal than Dostoevskij's "spiritual regeneration." And if Dobroljubov believes that this ideal ("the natural strivings of the Russian people") is and ought to be expressed by Russian literature, he is, in effect, postulating a "realism in a higher sense" no less than his idealist predecessors and opponents. Thus, after all, Dobroljubov ends with an art which is a fusion of the "ideal" and the "real."

Dobroljubov's real differences with the *počvenniki* are political and ideological, not aesthetic or literary. Dobroljubov believes in creative intuition. Like Belinskij, he often speaks of "artistic instinct." His conception of the creative process clearly coincides with Belinskij's, being essentially that of an "inner vision" transforming the impressions of objective reality into an organic whole:

> [The artist must] create an artistic whole . . . give solid, typical life to the personages whom he presents. . . . To accomplish this, he needs a great deal more than only knowledge and a sure eye as well as narrative talent: He needs not only to know, but to have himself deeply and strongly refelt, relived that life; he needs to feel a strong living bond with these people; he needs to have thought with their heads, to have wished with their will; he must slip into their skin and into their soul. To do all this, a man who has not himself actually emerged from this milieu must possess a very substantial gift—a gift which belongs to artistic natures, a gift which cannot be replaced by any kind of knowledge.
>
> ("The Stories of Slavutinskij")

Dobroljubov believes that "artistic instinct" (or "artistic sense") will guard even an ideologically biased author against presenting an untruth. For example, Dobroljubov points out, Ostrovskij certainly sympathizes with all the beautiful ideas expressed by Žadov, a character in his play *A Profitable Job*

(Doxodnoe mesto). Yet his artistic instinct tells him that to make Žadov *do* these things (rather than just *say* them) would mean to distort actual Russian reality; "Here the demands of artistic truth stopped Ostrovskij from being carried away by an extraneous tendency and helped him to avoid the path taken by Messrs. Sollogub and L'vov." By the same token, Dobroljubov is inclined to dismiss as "artistically untrue" a work such as Pisemskij's famous novel *One Thousand Souls* (1858) by stating that "the whole social aspect of that novel was forcibly hitched to a preconceived idea."

Very definitely, too, Dobroljubov is a believer in the reality and importance of the creative imagination and its product, the poetic image. He uses the terms *obraz* ("image," "form," "symbol") and *izobraženie* ("image," "representation") in exactly the same meaning as Belinskij or Grigor'ev:

> If a man knows how to foster in his soul the image *(obraz)* of an object and eventually to present it vividly and fully, this means that he possesses both alert impressionability and depth of feeling. . . . He can, so it would seem, stop life in its tracks and crystallize, stand permanently before us even its most fleeting moment, so that we might look at it forever and ever, learning from it and enjoying it.
>
> ("What is Oblomovitis?")

Furthermore, Dobroljubov draws a strict line between impression and expression: "What is important for us is not so much what the author *wanted* to say, as what *was actually said* by him, even though this may have happened unintentionally, simply as a result of a truthful reproduction of the facts of life." [One meets] this particular conception in Belinskij. It is also met frequently in contemporary Soviet criticism. Balzac, the *légitimiste*, who, his political conservatism notwithstanding, exposed the ills of French post-Restoration society, is often cited as an example. Such understanding is tantamount to a recognition of "unconscious" creation and an admission of the notion, so important in romantic thought, that the work of art can outgrow and overwhelm its creator. Certainly, a positivist such as Dobroljubov will simply say that the truth of life surmounted the author's personal bias, while a mystic will assert that the "inner vision" of an inspired artist, being God-given, could not possibly be false. But the substance of the conception is the same in both instances, namely, that an organic bond, which is to some extent independent of the artist's conscious control, exists between "objective truth" and "poetic truth."

Dobroljubov believes in "talent" and "genius," using both terms in exactly the same sense as Belinskij or Grigor'ev. "Talent" is essentially "power":

> Talent is a property of human nature, and for this reason it undoubtedly guarantees the presence of a certain power *(sila)* and breadth of natural strivings in the individual whom we recognize as having talent. Consequently, his creations, too, must be created under the influence of these natural, regular needs of nature; his consciousness must be clear and vivid, his ideal simple and rational, nor will he ever consent to serve an untruth or nonsense—not because he would not want to do it, but simply because he could not do it, even if he would decide to do violence to his talent.
>
> ("A Ray of Light")

Thus, Dobroljubov fully shares Belinskij's—and Grigor'ev's as well as Dostoevskij's—belief in artistic "talent" (not to speak of "genius") as a reliable safeguard against the creation of "false" works and a sure guide to the "truth of life." Yet with a virtually identical aesthetic theory, Dobroljubov, on the one side, and Dostoevskij, on the other, arrive at diametrically opposed evaluations of "objective reality" and its representations in contemporary works of art. When Dobroljubov says that "poetry has to do with life, with living human activity, with man's eternal struggle and eternal striving for harmony with himself and with nature," he repeats what Belinskij and Grigor'ev had said before him. But when it comes to pointing out the nature and the cause of the dissonance which poetry expresses and seeks to resolve, Dobroljubov completely disagrees with his idealist opponents: while they see it in "the dualistic organization of the human creature" (*v dualističeskom ustrojstve čelovečeskogo suščestva*), Dobroljubov presupposes that the roots of this eternal conflict and alienation are social and economic.

With the same confidence with which Dostoevskij proclaims that true art will inevitably lead man to a metaphysical view of life, Dobroljubov asserts the contrary. Dobroljubov, like Belinskij before him and his opponent Dostoevskij, rejects the notion that the artist be a mere copyist of nature. As he upbraids Dostoevskij for having let the pure, noble, and strong-willed Nataša fall in love with the weak and worthless Aleša Valkovskij (in *The Insulted and Injured*), he uses precisely the same organicist arguments as found in Grigor'ev's or Dostoevskij's attacks on populist fiction:

> But we know, of course, that the artist is not a photographic plate which reflects only the present moment: if it were otherwise, there would be neither life nor sense in works of art. With his own artistic sense, the artist supplements the fragmentariness of a moment captured; in his soul, he generalizes particular phenomena; from uncoordinated traits he creates an organized whole; he finds a living tie and consistency between seemingly disconnected phenomena; the varied and contradictory aspects of living reality he fuses and transforms into the universals of his world view. Therefore, a true artist, as he creates his work, carries it in his soul, whole and complete, from beginning to end, with all its hidden springs and concealed corollaries, which are often incomprehensible to logical reasoning, yet reveal themselves to the artist's inspired gaze.
>
> ("Downtrodden People")

Dobroljubov's point is clear: while the romance between Nataša Ixmenev and young Valkovskij could very well happen in real life, as an isolated case, it is not "typical," not revealing of the universal truth of life. Dostoevskij strongly believed that the contrary was the case, for he insisted on presenting essentially the same "mismatch" over and over again. The argument between Dobroljubov and Dostoevskij obviously has to do with philosophical anthropology, not with aesthetic theory. To Dobroljubov, man is essentially a rational being with a natural striving toward the Good, the True, and the Beautiful. Dostoevskij's image of man is dualistic: man is inherently rational and irrational, good and evil, he "naturally" strives toward the True and the Beautiful, but equally so toward the Lie and toward the Perverse. But both Dobroljubov and Dostoevskij believe that "true art" is necessarily a faithful reflection of the human condition as they conceive of it.

Dobroljubov's real enemies, as far as aesthetic theory and literary criticism are concerned, are Kant, subjective idealism, and formalism. In essence, he has no real argument with Grigor'ev or Dostoevskij—not as far as aesthetic theory is concerned. Of course, neither he nor Dostoevskij realized this, as

they both projected their political differences into the aesthetic sphere. In summary, Dobroljubov's criticism is largely organicist, though with exceedingly strong emphasis on "social organicism."

Among the Nihilist critics, D. I Pisarev was by far the most talented. His theoretical position is one of singular clarity and consistency. Pisarev saw the antinomies in the aesthetic theories of his predecessors and sought to resolve them. In the process, he arrived at an explicit rejection of the organic tradition started by Belinskij. In his polemic essays on "Puškin and Belinskij," he cleverly debunked Belinskij's efforts "to see something organic and necessary in every versified prank of a Batjuškov, Žukovskij, or Puškin," and to give a deep historical meaning to sundry trivialities of life simply because they had been correctly captured in literature.

Even though he destroyed Belinskij's most cherished positions, Pisarev insisted that he did so "not to mock the sacred memory of our great teacher Belinskij, but to show to the reader how very dangerous and fatal an involvement with things aesthetic can become even to the strongest and most remarkable minds."

In his brilliant essay "The Abolition of Aesthetics," Pisarev drew some correct conclusions from Černyševskij's *Aesthetic Relations of Art to Reality:* the science of aesthetics, he said, had a *raison d'être* only if the concept of Beauty had any meaning at all that was independent of the infinite variety of individual tastes. Černyševskij had proved to Pisarev's satisfaction that this was not the case. Therefore, the whole science of aesthetics had been rendered superfluous.

Pisarev raised the question of the priority of values in connection with art and literature (a question raised in our own day by I. A. Richards, among others) and, puritan that he was, decided that moral and intellectual values were to be placed high above aesthetic values. The right to pass ultimate judgment on any serious work of literature should belong not to those who were inclined—and competent—to judge its form, but to "thinking men who would judge its content, that is, judge it by [its relationship to] the phenomena of life." Pisarev then decided that much of Russian literature, past and present, has aesthetic value only. He gladly ceded these works to his opponents of the so-called school of "pure art" which was then upholding the Puškinian tradition in Russian literature. They were, of course, hopeless and contemptible sensualists, as far as Pisarev was concerned.

Not surprisingly, Pisarev had a low opinion of Puškin—essentially on the same moral grounds that Tolstoj would later have in *What Is Art?* Pisarev also demonstrated, very deftly, how Belinskij, having implicitly condemned Puškin's aestheticism, had still avoided drawing the logical conclusion from Puškin's cycle "on the poet": that most, if not all, of Puškin's poetry was purely "imaginary," that it had none but aesthetic value, and that its relevance to the reality of Russian life was negligible.

Somewhat more surprisingly, Pisarev found Dobroljubov guilty of the same error which, in his opinion, had vitiated much of Belinskij's criticism: in Pisarev's opinion, Dobroljubov, too, construes "organic" ties between works of Russian literature and Russian life where there simply are none objectively. For example, in his essay "A Ray of Light in the Kingdom of Darkness," Dobroljubov had asserted that the rebellion of Katerina, heroine of Ostrovskij's drama *The Thunderstorm*, was symbolic of the imminent breakup of "the kingdom of darkness" of Russian backwardness, barbarity, and superstition. Pisarev disagrees with his optimistic interpretation. He finds

Katerina quite "untypical" in the first place. That this adulteress and suicide be a positive character, as Dobroljubov had
asserted, he finds questionable. And besides, her "rebellion"
is purely personal and has nothing to do with any breakup of
"the kingdom of darkness." And all together, Pisarev refuses
to see any "ray of light" in it.

Still more surprisingly, Pisarev found that even the satirical
works of Saltykov-Ščedrin were of rather dubious extra-aesthe-
tic value. In an article devoted to Saltykov-Ščedrin, "Flowers
of Innocent Humor" (1864), Pisarev exclaims:

> Yes, Ščedren, the leader of our exposé literature (*ob-
> ličitel'naja literatura*) can be called quite justifiably
> a perfectly pure exponent of our latest version of pure
> art. Ščedrin does not subject his writings either to a
> cherished idea or to the voice of wrought-up emotion;
> nor does he ask, as he seizes his pen, whom his
> accusing arrow will hit—friend or foe, "titular coun-
> cilor or nihilist." . . . Ščedrin's pointless and aimless
> laughter, as such, is as useless to our social con-
> sciousness as Fet's pointless and aimless cooing.
>
> ("Flowers of Innocent Humor")

Pisarev, like Černyševskij before him, took an uncompromisingly utilitarian view of art. His position was sounder than
Černyševskij's, however. Unlike Černyševskij, Pisarev was a
man of brilliant literary talent and keen aesthetic sense. He
knew very well that a work of art could have aesthetic value
quite regardless of its merits before society. In fact, he arrived
at the conclusion that most works of art that he knew were of
aesthetic value only. Like Černyševskij, Pisarev was more interested in economics, education, and politics than in art. Accordingly, he held aesthetic values in low esteem and considered it a waste of time to discuss aesthetic problems. Therefore,
he was perfectly willing to leave the "aesthetes" alone and
let them indulge in their childish games. In his essay "The
Realists" (1864), Pisarev thus defined his position:

> It is precisely the presence of a higher guiding idea
> in the mind of a consistent realist and the absence of
> such an idea in the aesthete's mind that make up the
> difference between these two groups of people. What
> is this idea? It is the idea of the common weal or of
> universal human solidarity. Like all people . . . both
> aesthetes and realists are perfect egoists. But the ego-
> ism of an aesthete resembles the senseless egoism of
> a child who is ready any moment to stuff himself
> with the cheapest candy or honey cake. Meanwhile,
> a realist's egoism is the conscious . . . egoism of a
> mature person who provides himself with a supply
> of ever-fresh delight for his whole life.

Pisarev thus wholly rejected Belinskij's aesthetic organicism.
His utilitarian view of art left the door wide open to sensualist
or Kantian subjective-idealist "aesthetic criticism," untram-
meled by any sociohistorical or moral determinism. By relinquishing much of art and literature as "socially irrelevant,"
Pisarev really invited the aesthetes to claim it as their sole
possession. No wonder, then, that Pisarev found more im-
placable enemies in the left-wing followers of a Hegelian "organic" aesthetics, such as Plexanov, than in right-wing believers in the autonomy of art. Dostoevskij rather liked Pisarev,
in spite of Pisarev's radical "nihilism." With his unerring
intuition, Dostoevskij must have sensed that Pisarev was really
a friend of Art in disguise. Needless to say, "official" Soviet
opinion of Pisarev has been consistently negative. (pp. 245-57)

Victor Terras, "Belinskij's Heritage," in his Belinskij and Russian Literary Criticism: The Heritage of
Organic Aesthetics, *The University of Wisconsin Press,
1974, pp. 206-86.*

THELWALL PROCTOR

*[Proctor examines the philosophical and aesthetic principles un-
derlying the critical writings of Chernyshevsky, Dobrolyubov, and
Pisarev.]*

Černyševskij was active as a literary critic principally between
1854-1858. After this his attention was devoted mainly to questions of history and economics. His aesthetic theorizing and
literary criticism occupy a position decidedly of secondary importance in the conspectus of his work. However, it is necessary
to devote attention to his views on aesthetics since they served
as the foundation of Dobroljubov's position as a critic and
exercised, both independently and through their development
by his successors, an enormous and continuing influence. Even
more conspicuously than in the case of Belinskij, the critical
ideas of the revolutionary democratic stream of thought find
expression in Černyševskij's work. Many of the ideas of Belinskij's final period were revived by Černyševskij, and an attempt was made to bring them into some coherent relationship;
an attempt, however, so unstable in its results that later critics,
taking one or another aspect of Černyševskij's ideas, attempted
to work them out more fully and satisfactorily. A study of
Černyševskij's dissertation is thus necessary in order to understand the aesthetic ideas of the whole movement. (pp. 66-7)

Černyševskij's dissertation, *Èstetičeskie otnošenija iskusstva k
dejstvitel'nosti,* has two aspects: an attack upon Hegelian aesthetics and an attempt to establish aesthetics upon a new basis.
Černyševskij's attack was launched from the materialist position of Feuerbach. A direct attack upon Hegel was tactically
impracticable since the very mention of his name in print was
at that time forbidden in Russia, so Černyševskij's fire was
directed at Hegel's disciple, F. T. Vischer. (p. 67)

In Černyševskij's opinion, Hegelian aesthetics as interpreted
by Vischer was rooted in philosophical idealism. Beauty was
conceived as an absolute, existing only in the world of ideals.
Art was an attempt to realize this ideal by creating in works
of art that perfection which cannot exist in the real world and
an expression of man's thirst for perfection. Against this position Černyševskij made a series of objections. In the first
place, Černyševskij argued that the real world was superior to
the world of ideals. This was the attitude of Feuerbach's materialism as Černyševskij interpreted it. In the second place,
the real world affords examples of beauty more satisfying than
any work of art and is, in respect to satisfying man's desire
for beauty, superior to art. In the third place, rather than having
a thirst for perfection, man is satisfied simply with the good,
of which a healthy man can find enough in the real world,
without having recourse to ideals.

In place of the aesthetics which he criticized and rejected,
Černyševskij proposed his own. Instead of defining beauty as
an absolute value, Černyševskij approached his definition of
beauty in terms of the effect which it produces. "The feeling
produced in man by the beautiful is a bright joy like that which
fills us in the presence of a creature dear to us." From the
effect, Černyševskij proceeds to the cause: "What is common
to that which is dear to man and the dearest thing in the world
to him is life." Thus Černyševskij arrives at his famous definition: "Beauty is life." This definition is, however, too general to be very useful, so Černyševskij expands it as follows:
"The definition of beauty, 'beauty is life', 'beautiful is that

being in which we see life as it should be, according to our understanding, beautiful is that object which manifests in itself life or reminds us of life'—it would seem that this definition satisfactorily explains all of the occasions arousing in us the sense of the beautiful."

As a result of Černyševskij's definition of beauty as life as it should be according to our understanding, one expects him to define the content of art as the depiction of life as it should be. For idealistic aestheticians, beauty had been an end in itself. Černyševskij, however, criticizes this attitude as unnecessarily and artificially limiting the content of art and specifically denies the beautiful as the sole object of art. (We shall see, later, why Černyševskij was forced to discard the beautiful as the content of art.) Instead, he proposes a different definition of the content of art: "All that variety of objects, events, questions, aspects of life which interests man forms the content of art." This point of view derives from Belinskij's late work and Černy- ševskij maintained it in his *Očerki gogolevskogo perioda*.

If reality is superior to art, as Černyševskij maintained, why should art exist at all? Černyševskij answers this question by asserting that reality is superior to art but that reality is not always readily accessible, whereas art may be. Thus art is superior to reality in that it is more accessible. Another problem is the difficulty of simultaneously experiencing and reflecting upon life. Reality presented by means of art affords opportunity for reflection. Further, art serves to call attention to beauties in reality which would otherwise be missed. Thus Černyševskij tends to regard art as a convenient substitute for life: "Let art be . . . in the absence of reality, a kind of equivalent for it." This idea Dobroljubov was to develop further.

Černyševskij attempted to differentiate between the "repro- duction" of life and the "imitation" of life, dear to the neo- classicists. As Černyševskij interpreted the doctrine, "Neo- classical theory really understood art as the imitation of reality to the end of deceiving the senses." In contradistinction, "Re- production has as its goal to aid the imagination and not to deceive the senses, as imitation wants to do." Lavreckij points out that Černyševskij was not always able to keep this dis- tinction clear.

In addition to "reproducing" reality so that art can serve as a convenient substitute for experience, art may have a second function, to explain experience. "Science and art (poetry) are a *Handbuch* for those beginning to study life; their significance is to prepare one for the study of sources and then, from time to time, to serve as a reference."

Further, in addition to "reproducing" and "explaining" life, art must also "judge" it. "A poet or artist cannot, even if he wanted to, refuse to pronounce his judgment on the phenomena depicted, and this judgment is expressed in his work. This is another significance of art by which art becomes one of the moral activities of man."

The ideas which have just been outlined were a consequence of Černyševskij's *Weltanschauung* and can best be appreciated in relation to it. Its main outlines are clear from what Černy- ševskij wrote in his dissertation, particularly as amplified by his auto-critique. Philosophically, the problem which lies at the heart of Černyševskij's thinking is the relationship of what *is* and what *ought to be*. Idealistic philosophy had taken the position that the real world was the world of ideas and ideals (what *ought to be*) and that the actual world in which we live (what *is*) could, at best, but approximate and never coincide with the ideal world. Černyševskij took the position that the

world of ideas and ideals could (and, in fact, sometimes did) coincide with the actual world. The idealists had seen the world as both imperfect and imperfectible. For Černyševskij the world was composed of elements both perfect (what *is* and *ought to be*) and imperfect (what *is* and *ought not to be*), and was at least partially perfectible by the transformation of the imperfect into the perfect.

When Černyševskij argues the superiority of reality to art, that a living girl is more beautiful than any possible representation of her in art, he is, fundamentally, arguing that, in some cases, what *is* and what *ought to be* do, in fact, coincide. He does not argue that *every* living girl is superior to *every* represen- tation of a girl in art. In other words, he does not argue that everything which *is, ought to be,* only that what *ought to be,* on occasion, *is*. It is true that when Černyševskij is arguing against the idealistic view of perfection as something that can- not exist in the actual world, in the attempt to persuade the reader that the perfect does exist in the actual world, he tends to exaggerate and to suggest that the actual world is perfect, that what *is, ought to be*. For example, he writes, "A man with uncorrupted aesthetic feeling delights in nature without reserve, finds no defects in its beauty." It is important to note Černyševskij's limitation, "uncorrupted." We shall examine later what this term meant to him. It has been pointed out that in addition to tending to over-emphasize the perfection of what *is,* Černyševskij also, when he is arguing the superiority of life to art, tends to exaggerate the artificiality of art.

For Černyševskij, reality was not only that which *is* and *ought to be,* but also that which *was, may be,* or *will be* and *ought to be.* "Reality includes not only dead nature but also human life, not only the present, but also the past, insofar as it has expressed itself in action, and the future, insofar as it has being prepared by the present." Further, reality, for Černyševskij, includes not only what ought to exist, actually or potentially, in the objective world but also what exists subjectively, in man's subjective world of thought, insofar as it contributes to the transformation of the actual world into the "real" world. "Thought is not something in opposition to reality, because thought is born of reality and tends toward realization, and for that reason constitutes an indivisible part of reality." This position is repeated and emphasized in Černyševskij's auto- critique.

Thus, to recapitulate, for Černyševskij, what was "real" was that which *ought to be.* What is real exists, in part, in the actual world, but more fully and completely in potentiality (in the actual world of the future, as transformed by man's ac- tivity), less fully and completely in the past (only insofar as the past has contributed to what is real in the present), also in whatever in the intellectual and moral life of man contributes to the transformation of what actually *is* and *ought not to be* into what *ought to be.*

Černyševskij's conception of the relationship of what *is* and what *ought to be* leads to apparently paradoxical results. Whereas, for the idealist, the opposition between what *is* and what *ought to be* had been absolute (what *is* could never be what *ought to be*), for Černyševskij, this opposition was relative, rather than absolute (what *is* may or may not be what *ought to be*), as Lavreckij emphasizes. Černyševskij's "rehabilitation of real- ity" was effected simply by insisting that what *is,* on occasion and in part, coincides with what *ought to be.* But by no means all of what *is* is also what *ought to be.* That portion of what *is* which *ought not to be* is condemned in the name of what *ought to be.* Thus we arrive at the apparent paradox that a body of thought at once "rehabilitates reality" and "condemns and denies" reality. The reality which is "rehabilitated" is that which *is* and *ought to be* (what *is* and *ought to be* is declared superior to what *ought to be* but never *is*); the reality which is "condemned and denied" is what *is* and *ought not to be* (what *is* and *ought not to be* is condemned in the name of what *ought to be* and *will* or *may be*). In both cases, the standard is what *ought to be* (either actually or potentially). As Plexanov justly observes: "Concern with what *ought to be* predominates in Černyševskij's dissertation over a theoretical interest in what *is*, at times, quite different." To the extent that Černyševskij's thinking is concerned with what *ought to be* (rather than what *is*), he is, in a sense, an idealist. But Černyševskij locates the ideal not exclusively in a world discontinuous with the world around us, but in the world around us, so far as it both *is, was, will* or *may be* and *ought to be*.

Faith in progress, implicit in Černyševskij's thinking, when combined with his concept of the relationship of what *is* to what *ought to be*, also produces curious results. For Černyševskij, in the actual world only what *is* and *ought to be* is "real." Much of the actual world *is* and *ought not to be*. But what *is* and *ought not to be* is capable of being transformed by man's action into what *is* and *ought to be*. Černyševskij hoped for this transformation and his thought is oriented toward the future (what both *will be* and *ought to be*). Thus we arrive at another paradox: to the "realist" Černyševskij the actual world is less "real" than the future, which, in terms of the present, does not exist at all. The "realist" is concerned not so much with the actual world (except insofar as it coincides with what *ought to be*) as with what *ought to be* (insofar as it exists in the present or will exist in the future. But how can we be sure of what will exist in the future? Černyševskij solved this question by faith in progress. Later, the Marxists were to solve it with a "scientific" theory of history. Thus the Marxists were able to accept and to incorporate into their aesthetics much of Černyševskij's thinking.

Man and his needs are central to Černyševskij's *Weltanschauung*, and it was Černyševskij's view that it was not for man to adjust himself to the world as he finds it but rather to mold the world to his requirements. In his auto-critique, Černyševskij writes: "Nature does not always correspond to his needs; therefore man, for the peace and happiness of his life, must change reality objectively in many respects in order to adapt it to his practical needs." In order to change the world so as to make it correspond more closely to man's requirements it is necessary to determine what those requirements are, and for this purpose, it is necessary to select a criterion, a standard by means of which man's needs can be recognized. This criterion, for Černyševskij, was the ideal of man as he *ought to be* as a kind of absolute. Černyševskij's idea of the nature of man clearly derives from that point of view popularized by Rousseau: that man is fundamentally good; if he is, in fact, bad, this condition is a result of his having been corrupted by circumstance. Černyševskij writes: "Intellectual and moral life (developing in a suitable way when the organism is healthy— that is, when the material side of man's life proceeds satisfactorily)—this is truly that life appropriate to man and most attractive to him." Thus, for Černyševskij, given proper circumstances (a satisfactory material level of existence) man's life will be what it *ought to be* and at the same time what he both desires and needs.

This proposition seems reasonable enough, in the abstract, but in its historical context, the proposition raises difficulties. In Russia at that time the only social class whose life proceeded under relatively satisfactory material conditions was the aristocracy. Logically, the life of that class, according to Černyševskij's definition, should have represented the most immediate approximation of what *ought to be* and was most desirable and necessary. But the material welfare of that class depended upon the institution of serfdom, an institution which Černyševskij, together with numbers of other people, felt to be an abomination deserving only prompt liquidation. Therefore, the life of the aristocracy could not be accepted as the criterion of what *ought to be*.

How, then, ignoring the most obvious concrete example, are we to know what man *ought to be*? Černyševskij, in his dissertation, gives no very satisfactory answer to this question. Man as he *is* cannot serve as a criterion, for he is the product of a mixture of what *ought to be* and what *ought not to be* (serfdom, for example). Man's desires furnish no criterion. True, when man is what he *ought to be*, his needs and desires coincide, but since man is not what he *ought to be*, his present desires furnish no dependable indication as to his needs. Since neither man as he *is* nor his present desires can furnish an indication as to his needs, how are we to discover them? Černyševskij answers the question in these terms: "In part, instinct, yet more science (knowledge, thought, experience) give man the means of understanding what manifestations of reality are good and beneficial to him and consequently should be supported and encouraged by his action and which manifestations of reality, on the other hand, are injurious and damaging to him and consequently should be destroyed or, at least, weakened in the interests of human life." But this is scarcely science as we understand the term now, for Černyševskij goes on to say: "Science is not abstract and cold: it approves and disapproves, discourages and encourages—it approves noble people who concern themselves with the moral needs of man and who grieve, seeing them so often unsatisfied, as it approves also those who concern themselves with the material needs of their brethren." (pp. 68-74)

The orientation of Černyševskij's thought toward the future, combined with a faith in progress and "science," justified the urge to transform the world as it was into the world as it *ought to be* and *would be*, an impulse strong in the whole revolutionary democratic stream of thought. This impulse was bound to affect the aesthetics of the movement. As Plexanov remarks, "Our enlighteners did not in the least disdain poesy, but they preferred the *poesy of action* to every other." As a result of this imperative urge to remake the world, the revolutionary democrats were tempted to consider art as a tool, a lever, an instrument, a means for effecting the hoped-for, necessary, and justified change. This tendency has been pointed out by numerous critics, and it was another element of revolutionary democratic thought which the Marxists were able to adopt.

What place does art have in such a *Weltanschauung*? Traditionally, aesthetics has been understood as the science of the beautiful and art as its embodiment. As we have seen, Černyševskij rejected beauty as the sole content of art and proposed rather the "interesting." What is Černyševskij's attitude toward beauty, if it is not to be considered as the principal content of art? As Ikov has forcefully pointed out, at times Černyševskij argues as if beauty were some sort of absolute value, at others as if it were simply a fundamentally irrelevant accident.

For example, when Černyševskij is arguing the superiority of real life as opposed to art, he maintains that a living girl may be more beautiful than any possible artistic representation of her. If this is a valid reason for valuing a real girl above a representation of her, life above art, then beauty must be a kind of absolute value, a relevant standard by which one thing can be measured against another. Here, however, Černyševskij is attacking idealistic aesthetics in terms of its own system of values. Elsewhere Černyševskij argues the dependence of a sense of beauty upon other conditions. He points out that a peasant has a notion of beauty, and standards in this respect, quite different from that of an aristocrat. What the one finds beautiful, the other finds ugly, and vice versa. Is beauty simply dependent upon a point of view? If so, how, then, can beauty be any kind of an absolute or standard? How is one to measure one thing against another in its terms, except to say that the one corresponds to the conception of beauty peculiar to one class and the other to that of another class? It would seem that we arrive at de gustibus non est disputandum, a position which, as we shall see, Pisarev was to adopt.

Černyševskij, however, was far from willing to leave the matter there. Though he is not explicit on this point, it is clear that for Černyševskij some sort of standard existed. He writes, "A passion for pale, sickly beauty is a sign of an artificial depravity of taste," so his standard would seem to be what is not artificially depraved, spoiled, and unnatural. But by what standard is one to determine what is natural, unspoiled, healthy?

This is another point on which Černyševskij is resolutely unexplicit. The assumption would seem to be that a healthy, unspoiled taste is superior to an unhealthy or spoiled taste. Thus what is beautiful is that which appeals to such a taste. This introduces a further modification in Černyševskij's definition of the beautiful. Instead of "The beautiful is that being in which we see life as it should be according to our understanding," we get something on the order of "The beautiful is that being in which we see life as it should be according to our understanding, provided we see life from a healthy point of view." Such a formulation brings us to a situation of this sort: in life we are surrounded by things which may be either what they ought to be or what they ought not to be; a sense of beauty is no safe criterion by which to choose between them since we may have an unhealthy or spoiled taste; the relevant standard is a healthy or unspoiled taste (whether or not it corresponds with our own). Thus aesthetic questions tend to shift ground. The question which must be answered is not "Is this beautiful?" (Does this satisfy my understanding of life as it ought to be?) but "Is this beautiful from a healthy point of view?" (Does this satisfy an understanding which is what it ought to be?)

The epithets, "unhealthy," "corrupt," etc., are usually applied by Černyševskij to the taste of the merchant class or the aristocracy. The implication is that the taste of the peasantry is healthy and unspoiled. But if this is so, then the life of the peasants must be what it ought to be since it has produced a taste which is what it ought to be. It is easy to see why Černyševskij does not develop this line of reasoning. His implied standard seems to be not so much the peasants as they are but as they ought to be.

Actually, the criterion seems to be reason. Černyševskij writes, "To gratify man's whims does not mean to satisfy man's needs. The greatest of these needs is truth." Thus an aesthetics which started out as one based upon the reality of aesthetic emotion ("a feeling like that which fills us in the presence of a being dear to us") ends as a rationalist aesthetics based not upon what is but upon what ought to be, judged by rational criteria. It is difficult not to agree with Plexanov when he writes of

Černyševskij's dissertation that "Its attention is concentrated not on what is and what was but on what ought to be and actually would be if people began to listen to the voice of 'reason'." Another aspect of Černyševskij's attitude toward beauty will be discussed later.

According to Černyševskij's scheme, the function of art is to produce not the beautiful but rather the interesting. As Nikolaj Solev'ev tartly observes, "Instead of aesthetics, a science of the beautiful, something on the order of a science of the interesting makes its appearance." And what is interesting? As we have already seen, Černyševskij was deliberately vague and ambiguous on this point. In Russian, as in English, the adjective interesting suggests principally something attractive and engaging, in other words, something arousing our desires. But the noun interest, in Russian as in English, may mean profit, gain, advantage, in other words, something answering our needs. It is perhaps permissible to suggest that as Černyševskij used the adjective, both ideas are involved. To Černyševskij as a rational egoist what was interesting to man was what brought him advantage, gain, good. Need and desire coincide. But, as we have seen, desire is not a safe criterion for determining man's needs, rather "science," a political ideology, reason, is the criterion.

Where the function of art is concerned, Černyševslij seems to be arguing from the point of view of things as they are, what is, rather than from the point of view of what ought to be. As we have seen, if man were what he ought to be, then his needs and desires would coincide, and art, which caters to man's desires, would serve also his needs. The beautiful and interesting coincide. But in the actual world, where man's desires are liable to corruption, his desires and needs may not coincide, and in this case the beautiful serves only man's desires to the possible detriment of his needs.

Černyševskij's distrust of man's desires is clear. In his dissertation we find, "Art strives to satisfy our inclinations, and reality cannot be subjected to our tendency to see everything in that light and in that order which pleases us or accords with our conceptions, often one-sided." On the other hand, Černyševskij does not maintain that aesthetic satisfaction necessarily runs counter to man's needs, for he writes, "Aesthetic satisfaction may be differentiated from material interest or a practical view of an object, but it is not opposed to it."

What, then, is the situation at which we arrive, according to Černyševskij's theory? Art is life as it ought to be, according to man's understanding. If man's understanding were what it ought to be, man's need and desires would coincide: but, due to the corrupting influence of a world which is only very partially what it ought to be, man is not what he ought to be. As a result, his understanding is not what it ought to be, and what he needs and what he desires may not necessarily coincide. Since this is the case, man's needs are to be served rather than his desires.

This situation puts the artist in an almost impossible position. The difficulty is that, in Černyševskij's system, the aesthetic effect of a work of art is dependent upon its serving man's desires. Man's desires, however, may be corrupt, and by serving them the artist may be sacrificing man's needs in order to achieve aesthetic effect, whereas man's needs should take precedence over his desires. If the artist serves man's needs rather than his desires, he runs the risk of failing to make the aesthetic effect at which he aims. Until man is what he ought to be, it seems impossible for art to be what it *ought to be*. This dilemma is never posed by Černyševskij, but it is implicit in his system.

One way out of this dilemma lies in improving man's understanding, for when man's understanding is what it *ought to be*, then man's needs and desires coincide. Thus it is in the interest of artists to help to transform man's understanding into what it *ought to be* by advancing the cause of "science." Through "science" man's understanding can be transformed into what it *ought to be*, and the problem of the artist is solved. (Not, it is true, in the present, where the artist's problem remains fundamentally insoluble, but in the future, which, since it is more fully what it *ought to be* than the present, is more real.)

Černyševskij wanted art to serve "science." He writes, for example, in his auto-critique, "Science is worthy of [filial love] because it serves man's good as art is worthy of it when it serves man's good. And art brings him very much good, because the work of an artist, particularly of a poet worthy of the name, is a 'textbook of life', . . . a text-book which everyone makes use of with pleasure, even those who know and love no other. Art should be proud of this lofty, beneficent significance." It is perhaps worth pointing out that here Černyševskij justifies art not on the grounds of its serving the aesthetic impulse (as he himself defined it) but on the grounds of its deserving respect as serving the needs (though not necessarily the desires) of man. That Černyševskij wanted art to serve what he called science is perfectly clear. *How* it was to do so is perfectly obscure. If art depends for its effect upon catering to man's desires, then it is impossible to see how it can effectively serve man's needs, unless desires and needs coincide.

Černyševskij's emphasis upon art as a handmaiden to science was seized upon both by his opponents and by his successors. That art should subordinate itself to science was disputed by his opponents. One of his successors, Pisarev, not only supported Černyševskij's position but went on to ask a further question: what is the function of art once the public becomes educated? His answer was that art, having fulfilled its function, would simply disappear, a conclusion with which it is difficult to believe that Černyševskij could have agreed, since, as we have seen, when man is what he *ought to be*, his needs and desires coincide and what satisfies his interests is also beautiful.

Černyševskij's system poses other thorny problems to the artist in addition to those already mentioned. It will be remembered that Černyševskij gives three functions to art: to "represent" life, to "explain" life, and to "judge" life. These three functions are not altogether compatible. In "representing" life, art presumably focuses its attention upon what *is;* in "explaining" and "judging" life, attention is focussed upon what *ought to be*. The problem posed for the artist is the difficult one of presenting life both as it *is* and as it *ought to be*, for life as it *ought to be* is only a part of life as it *is*. Art as an "explanation" of life also presents problems for the artist in a period of conflicting values. He can "explain" life only from one point of view. He must commit himself to the *Weltanschauung* of a party, and he thus becomes a committed partisan. He is in this position also when he "judges" life. Černyševskij, together with the other revolutionary democratic critics—not to mention the Marxists—emphasizes the bias of art.

Art, all art, comes to be regarded fundamentally as propaganda, more or less overt. In Russian critical literature, this quality of art, its propagandistic aspect, is often referred to as *tendencija*. A recent Soviet dictionary of literary terms defines *tendencija* as follows: "*Tendencija* in a work of art . . . is the idea, the conclusion toward which the author attempts to lead the reader by drawing pictures of life and characters in a work," and the writer goes on to comment: "In contrast to the sometimes hidden *tendencija* of bourgeois literature, attempting, by distorting the truth of life, to lead the reader to reconciliation with social injustice, to distract his thoughts from the necessity of struggle with capitalism, and to encourage in him a conviction in the hopelessness of that struggle, Soviet literature, correctly depicting life, not only does not hide its *tendencija*, its Communist direction, but attempts in every way that a work of art show an example of a real man, that it inspire the people to struggle for its happiness, that it help to build a Communist society." For the revolutionary democrats, as for the Marxists, every work of art had a *tendencija*, a bias. The problem is not whether or not a work of art is propaganda; all art is propaganda; the problem is propaganda for what? Those who did not share this point of view tended to use the adjective *tendencioznyj* to describe, pejoratively, only that literature which adhered to the revolutionary democratic bias.

Aničkov points out that this emphasis on the propagandistic aspect of art (its *tendencija*) derives from the views of Young Germany and that its demand that art "judge" life runs counter to the demands of realism, if realism is understood as the depiction of what *is*. Yet one aspect of *tendencija* does emphasize what *is*. The "condemnatory" aspect of Černyševskij's theory has already been mentioned. "Condemnatory" literature is the negative aspect of *tendencija*.

Let us see how "condemnatory" art fits into Černyševskij's system. If life as it *is* is composed both of elements which are what they *ought to be* and of others which are what they *ought not to be*, then when life is depicted as it *is*, some of it will be beautiful (since it corresponds to life as it should be according to our conceptions) and some of it will be ugly (since it does not so correspond). If art is concerned only with the beautiful, then it must ignore those elements of what *is* which are not what they *ought to be*. But these were precisely those elements in which Černyševskij was interested. Somehow he had to make room for the ugly as a suitable content for art. When he insists that the content of art should be the "interesting" rather than the "beautiful," he accomplishes this end. The depiction of the ugly is then justified, not because it brings aesthetic satisfaction, but because it does good by calling attention to what *ought not to be* (which must be ignored if the content of art is exclusively the beautiful), thus encouraging the person exposed to a work of art to attempt to eliminate or to transform the ugly (what *ought not to be*) into the beautiful (what *ought to be*). So long as the content of art remains exclusively the beautiful, art cannot be realistic (in the sense of depicting what *is*, insofar as it *ought not to be*). Černyševskij's theory encourages realism (the depiction of what *is*) in that he provides a justification for the inclusion in the content of art of what *is* and *ought not to be*. On the other hand, Černyševskij's idea that what *ought to be*, if only in potentiality, is "real," pulls in the opposite direction (toward the depiction of what *ought to be* but as yet *is not*.)

If all art is *tendencioznyj*, this fact, again, poses a difficult problem for the artist. It would seem that if the artist wished to serve man's needs surely, he must of necessity take care consciously to adopt the requisite *tendencija*. In his dissertation, Černyševskij specifically avoids committing himself on this issue. He writes: "Perhaps it is now more needful clearly to set forth the dependence of beauty on the conscious *ten-*

Nikolay Dobrolyubov at twenty-four.

the passage: ''. . . man, i.e., a creature by his nature inclined to honor and love truth and goodness and to abhor everything else,—a creature able to transgress the laws of goodness and truth only through ignorance, mistake, or the influence of conditions stronger than his character and reason, but never able, willingly and freely, to prefer evil to good.'' Thus the artist, if left alone, will arrive, of himself, at the suitable *tendencija.* But, as Dostoevskij was to emphasize in *Zapiski iz podpol'ja* (*Memoirs from Underground*), man may be so constituted that he knows what is good and still desires what is evil.

If Černyševskij does not insist that the artist consciously adopt a *tendencija,* on the other hand, it is difficult to take very seriously those critics who maintain that Černyševskij stood unequivocally for artistic freedom. It has been pointed out that when Černyševskij voiced a demand for freedom of the artist, he was apt to have in mind the artist's freedom from the demands of idealistic criticism, as in the case of his remarks about the poet Ščerbina. That the problem of the freedom of the artist still troubles Soviet critical theory is evident. For example, Lavreckij writes of *tendencija:* ''It cannot be imposed on an artist.'' But he goes on to say, ''The artist creates freely, but his creation attains highest value only when it is permeated freely from within by the truest understanding of life.'' If this is the case, then the canny artist, anxious to achieve work of the highest value, will take care to see that his work is suitably permeated. Even in this case, however, the artist's problems are not necessarily solved. A contemporary Soviet critic, Z. V. Smirnova, writes,

> Immediate tasks in the development of Marxist aesthetics and Soviet art focus, in our opinion, on two main questions. One of them is the problem of the possibility of a lack of correspondence between the objective ideational content of a work of art and the subjective ideational intent of the writer. . . . So far as the second question is concerned, it may be formulated as the problem of the role of a progressive, scientific *Weltanschauung,* i.e., the Marixst-Leninist *Weltanschauung,* in the development of contemporary progressive art and especially of Soviet art.

Neither in his dissertation nor in his auto-critique does Černyševskij say anything about the role and function of the critic. In a minor article, ''Ob iskrennosti v kritike'' (''On Sincerity in Criticism''), which answered objections raised by the *Otečestvennye zapiski,* Černyševskij protested against toothless criticism. He defines criticism rather conventionally: ''Criticism is a judgement as to the merits and defects of any literary work.'' He then immediately goes on to say, ''Its function is to serve as an expression of the opinion of the best section of the public and to cooperate in its further dissemination in the mass.'' Here we have a clear echo of Belinskij's concept of criticism as the mentor of society. Further, it seems clear that Černyševskij is trying to guide the writer in directions which he feels desirable: ''But the defects from which Mr. Avdeev's talent suffers can vanish, if he seriously wants this, since they lie not in the genuineness of his talents but in the absence of those qualities necessary to the fruitful development of talent which are not given (like talent) by nature, which are acquired by some through the difficult experience of life, by others through science, by others through the society in which they live; to these conditions the *Sovremennik* tried to direct Mr. Avdeev through the whole length of its review and expressed them as clearly as possible at the end.'' Lavreckij calls attention to a letter in which Černyševskij confesses that he is trying to influence Tolstoj. Thus the attempt, begun by Belinskij, to

dencija of the artist than to expatiate upon the fact that the works of a truly creative talent always have a great deal that is unpremeditated, instinctive. Be that as it may, both points of view are familiar, and it is unnecessary to dwell upon them here.'' Although Černyševskij admits the efficacy of unconscious creativity, he also writes, ''A poet worthy of the name usually wants to communicate to us in his work his ideas, his views, his feelings, and not exclusively only the beauty which he has created.'' He also betrays a certain distrust of the artistic instinct: ''How often artists are mistaken in their understanding of beauty! How often even the artistic instinct deceives them!''

Lunačarskij attributes Černyševskij's ambiguity on the issue of ''unconscious creativity'' versus *tendencioznost'* to Černyševskij's understanding of the difficulties involved. ''If the artist does not feel himself to be free and instead of producing that which has ripened within him, that truth which he sees, he tries to stifle his truth—This is very bad for art. This is a delicate problem: here it is very easy to make a mistake and begin crassly to insist that the artist produce what we demand. Černyševskij admirably understood this truth.'' Perhaps, but the understanding of the delicacy of this aspect of the problem may be more Lunačarskij's than Černyševskij's.

Protopopov explains Černyševskij's lack of dogmatism on this issue in a different, and possibly more convincing, way: he attributes it to Černyševskij's faith in man's goodness and quotes establish the critic as the mentor of the artist was continued by Černyševskij and, more particularly, by his successors.

As a practising critic, Černyševskij was bedevilled by the antithesis between what *is* and what *ought to be*, between the need to evaluate current literature and at the same time to legislate the literature of the future. . . . [*Tendencija*], conscious or unconscious, was the decisive criterion in Černyševskij's evaluation of any work of art. Though he approved conscious *tendencija*, in his critical practice he more often attributed the effectiveness of literary works to the operation of "unconscious creativity," for example, in his discussion of Pisemskij's work as Lavreckij points out. We shall find Dobroljubov and Pisarev . . . behaving in an identical fashion, theoretically proclaiming the necessity of a proper conscious *tendencija* in a work of art but falling back on the theory of "unconscious creativity" in the discussion of specific works and writers. The practical and immediate critical problem for Černyševskij (as it had been for Belinskij and would be for Černyševskij's successors) was a dearth of works written with a *tendencija* of which he approved.

[There can be] observed, in Belinskij's treatment of Dostoevskij's work, a disposition to treat beauty of form as a function of correct ideological content. It will be remembered that when Belinskij approved of the content of Dostoevskij's work, he also praised its form and that as he became disillusioned with its content, he became increasingly critical of its form. Černyševskij's attitude is similar. In his dissertation Černyševskij insists upon beauty of form, for he calls it "a necessary quality of every work of art." Elsewhere than in his dissertation, Černyševskij writes: "In order to determine the artistic worth of a work, it is necessary to investigate, as strictly as possible, whether or not the idea serving as the base of the work is true or not. If the idea is false, there can be no question of artistic quality because the form also will be false and full of incongruities. Only works in which a true idea is incarnated are artistic, if the form perfectly fits the idea." Obviously, for Černyševskij, more overtly than for Belinskij, form and content are not independent aspects of a work. Beauty of form is dependent upon correct ideological content and possible only when that content is acceptable. In determining artistic quality, content clearly takes precedence over form, and beauty is simply a function of content. This theoretical formulation Černyševskij applied in specific cases. Steklov calls attention to his treatment of the work of Ostrovskij. Černyševskij condemned Ostrovskij's play *Bednost' ne porok (Poverty is no Sin)* on both ideological and artistic grounds, but when a later play satisfied Černyševskij's ideological demands, he granted it both ideological and artistic merit.

Černyševskij has been accused by both friends and foes of being the "destroyer of aesthetics." How far does he deserve this dubious distinction? Russian critics give conflicting answers to this question. The crux of the matter seems to be what is understood by the term "aesthetics." Aesthetics had been understood as the study of the beautiful and the importance of art was its exemplification of the beautiful. In place of this definition, Černyševskij sought to substitute the idea of aesthetics as the study of art, of which the beautiful was but one aspect and by no means the most important. If the term "aesthetics" means the idealistic aesthetic system, then Černyševskij, insofar as his theory was successful, is its destroyer. Though his attitude toward art (specifically literature) is fundamentally the same as Belinskij's at the end of his career, in Belinskij's work one seeks in vain for so thorough and reasoned

a development of a theoretical position as inimicable to idealistic aesthetics as that to be found in Černyševskij. And if by "aesthetics" one has in mind the "art for art's sake" position, then, too, Černyševskij, like Belinskij before him, takes a position hostile to this point of view. In his *Očerki gogolevskogo perioda*, Černyševskij wrote: "History knows no works of art which were created exclusively by the idea of the beautiful; even if there are or were such works, then they attract no attention from contemporaries and are forgotten by history as too feeble, feeble even artistically. For Černyševskij, as for Belinskij, the "art for art's sake" position was identified with an ideological position which they considered reactionary. (pp. 74-84)

[The] romantic idealists gave a leading cultural role to art (specifically literature). In Černyševskij's scheme of ideas, this function was transferred from art to what he called science. With this transfer of primary importance, literature necessarily assumes a secondary, though by no means insignificant, role. The significance of art, while remaining great, consists of the services which it can render a greater interest: "science," or a political ideology.

Polemical considerations also complicate the question. When the successors of Černyševskij (Pisarev, in particular) were accused of being "destroyers of aesthetics," it was convenient for them to take refuge behind the authority of Černyševskij. Opponents who were unwary enough to take the bait faced the necessity of refuting Černyševskij before they could deal with their opponents, who had retired behind what might be called a defense in depth composed of red herrings. The result, as Aničkov remarks, was that "Both opponents and adherents look upon him as the destroyer of aesthetics and read into his book that aesthetics is utterly unnecessary, that neither true art nor a real understanding of it has anything to do with aesthetics."

Like Belinskij, Černyševskij was by no means indifferent to aesthetic values. Rather than to deny the validity and importance of aesthetic values, he sought to establish them on what seemed to him a broader foundation. When this aspect of his views is not ignored, Černyševskij is seen to deserve the title "the destroyer of aesthetics" no more than Belinskij, and, in general, critics writing after the polemics of the sixties refuse him the right to it. Ivanov-Razumnik remarks: "It is necessary to give Černyševskij his due: in all this he showed a great deal of patience and the soundest relationship to the question of art in the whole period of the sixties." Though Černyševskij seems not to deserve the title "the destroyer of aesthetics," at the same time, it cannot be denied that in Černyševskij's aesthetics the balance between ideological and aesthetic criteria shifts significantly, and with his successors, it shifted further. As Plexanov observes, "Critics who subscribed to Černyševskij's aesthetics were inclined to overlook the question of the aesthetic qualities of the works which they analyzed, focussing their principal attention on the ideas in these works." (pp. 84-5)

When the center of Černyševskij's activity shifted away from literature, his place as the principal literary critic of the *Sovremennik* was taken by his protégé, Nikolaj Aleksandrovič Dobroljubov. (p. 90)

Like Černyševskij, Dobroljubov was influenced by Feuerbach, with whose work he had become acquainted while yet a student through Belinskij's "Vzgljad na russkuju literaturu 1847 goda" ("Survey of Russian Literature for 1847"), and in 1855, before he met Černyševskij, Dobroljubov began a translation of Feuerbach's *Todesgedanken*. Most of those who have studied the two men agree as to the dependence of Dobroljubov's aesthetic theories upon those elaborated by Černyševskij and emphasize their similarity in critical procedure, polemical style, and literary personality. Bursov points out even close textual similarities, and goes on to say, "At times it was as if one of them continued and developed ideas expressed earlier by the other." If Dobroljubov's and Černyševskij's ideas were nearly identical in matters of aesthetics, they were equally close in socio-economic matters. On the staff of *Sovremennik,* the two men functioned as a united team, Černyševskij discussing socio-economic problems and Dobroljubov devoting himself to literature.

In full agreement with the ideas of Černyševskij as expressed in his dissertation, Dobroljubov placed life above art. Dobroljubov accepted Černyševskij's formula, "the beautiful is life," and the idea that "art reproduces whatever is interesting to man in life." Černyševskij had assigned three functions to art: to "reproduce" reality, to "explain" it, and to "judge" it. Of these three, Dobroljubov emphasized particularly the first. Dobroljubov's position, as interpreted by Pypin, was that "A genuine artist is truthful; his works reflect life truly and thus provide material for the study of life itself in its material and moral aspects." For Černyševskij, one of the principal virtues of art was its accessibility. Dobroljubov tended simply to equate art with life, the difference being that art was life made more accessible through the intervention of the artist.

As to the question of artistic method, . . . Černyševskij refused to choose between conscious *tendencija* and "unconscious creativity." In his dissertation, he simply remarked the existence of the two theories. Nor did Dobroljubov pronounce unequivocally in favor of one theory or the other. For the most part, in his critical practice, Dobroljubov relied on the theory of "unconscious creativity." On the other hand, he demanded that the artist "keep abreast of life," so that he be equipped to understand it aright, so that he not misinterpret phenomena as he observes them, so that in taking an informative "slice of life," he make the correct section.

The problem of artistic method involves the relationship of art to knowledge. Are art and science simply different and equally valid techniques for the apprehension of reality, or is one more valid than the other, and if so, which? In his attitude toward this problem, Dobroljubov harks back to Belinskij. The thinker (the scientist or philosopher) expresses his *Weltanschauung* in logical constructs; the artist (writer) expresses his in images. Both require an equally powerful intellect and creative ability. Their works are created in response to the environment surrounding them, but the artist, more liberally endowed with intuition, grasps significant facts before he comprehends them theoretically. According to this line of argument, employed earlier by both Belinskij and Černyševskij, it would appear that the artist has an advantage over the thinker, that he goes in advance as a roadbreaker for the systematic thinker. This line of argument supports "unconscious creativity" as an artistic method.

On the other hand, when it is desired to support *tendencija,* quite a different line of argument comes into play. The demand is made that the writer keep abreast of contemporary thought (rather than in advance of it) so that his work will correctly reflect the phenomena which strike his attention. As a consequence of this line of reasoning, knowledge ("science") is given the upper hand and becomes the standard guiding art. However, on occasion, Dobroljubov denied that he supported

tendencija. Charles Corbet, for one, points out the incompatibility of these two lines of reasoning.

In his critical practice, Dobroljubov was also inconsistent. As Aničkov points out, when dealing with the work of Marko-Vovčok (Mar'ja Aleksandrovna Markovič), for example, Dobroljubov seems to approve *tendencioznost',* but, on the other hand, in discussing Ostrovskij and Turgenev, he takes his more common stand on "unconscious creativity." Various attempts have been made to reconcile or explain this inconsistency. Lebedev-Poljanskij, for example, argues that, though Dobroljubov actually opposed *tendencija* in any narrow sense, at the same time, when he rejected *tendencija in toto,* he was carried away in the heat of argument with polemical opponents and misrepresented his real position. Skabičevskij sees in this inconsistency a reflection of the ambiguity of Belinskij's position at the end of his career (an inconsistency shared by Černyševskij). Aničkov detects an evolution of Dobroljubov's thought in the direction of *tendencija* (an evolution similar to that ocurring in Belinskij and Černyševskij). Perhaps we see here, rather, simply an alteration dependent upon the material discussed (a technique originated by Černyševskij and perfected by Pisarev). When material reflecting the requisite *tendencija* was available (in the case of Marko-Vovčok), it was invoked. When (as in the case of Ostrovskij) *tendencija* could not be invoked (a much more frequent situation), "unconscious creativity" was relied upon.

Černyševskij, in his dissertation, omitted discussion of the role of the critic. Dobroljubov was more explicit. Belinskij, at the end of his career, had seen the role of the critic as that of being not so much a critic of art as a critic of life. This position was adopted by Dobroljubov. As we have seen, he emphasized the idea that it was the function of art to reproduce life. The critic of art and the critic of life are one because art and life are one. Should it be necessary to make a choice between art and life, Dobroljubov left no doubt as to what his choice would be, for he wrote: "If one is to choose between art and reality, then let there be stories, not fulfilling the requirements of aesthetic theories but true to the meaning of reality rather than impeccable from the point of view of abstract art but distorting life and its true significance." However, Dobroljubov did not feel that art and life were necessarily in antithesis. (Nor, it will be remembered, did Černyševskij.) In Dobroljubov's view, if a choice of the sort indicated had to be made, then the artist was at fault. Dobroljubov, then, was interested first and foremost in life (that is to say, society), and he saw the function of literary criticism as being not to draw conclusions about works of art but to draw conclusions about society. In order to be able to do this, works which reproduced life were required.

It will be remembered that in Černyševskij's aesthetics, the second and third functions of art, in addition to "reproducing" life, were "explaining" and "judging" it. These functions Dobroljubov transferred, in the main, from art to criticism. It was the function of the artist to assemble the necessary raw materials for arriving at an explanation and a judgment of life, but it was the critic who "explained" and "judged" life, not the artist. In this fashion, the critic arrived at a position of superiority to the artist.

Again we may have to do here with the practical problem of a critic obliged to exercise his skills upon work which does not embody his ideals but which he wishes to use for his own purposes. When, as in the case of the stories of Marko-Vovčok, Dobroljubov encountered work whose *tendencija* he approved, he was willing to surrender to the artist the right to "explain" and to "judge" life (since that "explanation" and that "judgment" coincided with his own). When, on the other hand, he chose to discuss works whose *tendencija* was not his own, he reserved to himself the right of "explanation" and "judgment." In this case, Dobroljubov deliberately ignored the meaning which the author himself gave to his work, analyzed how far his "reproduction" of life corresponded to reality, and on the basis of this estimate, drew his own conclusions. In justification of this procedure, Dobroljubov writes, in his discussion of Ostrovskij, for example: "Sometimes the artist may even not understand the meaning of what he himself has depicted," an opinion endorsed, significantly, by Gončarov, whose novel *Oblomov* had served as the pretext for Dobroljubov's influential essay, "Čto takoe oblomovščina?" ("What is Oblomovism?"), when he wrote (in 1879), "The author himself often perceives the idea—with the help of an acute critical interpreter such as, for example, Belinskij or Dobroljubov."

Here the critic emerges as the intermediary between the artist and society. The artist functions as a sort of oracle, the meaning of whose pronouncements may be obscure to or mistakenly apprehended by the oracle himself. It is the critic who, as the interpreter of the oracle, plays the key role, interposes his interpretation of a work of art between it and the public, uses the work of art as a kind of raw material out of which the critic creates an expression of his own *Weltanschauung*. It has been asserted that Dobroljubov's criticism functions in this way, perhaps most frequently in the case of Ostrovskij's work, but also in the case of Gončarov's *Oblomov* and Turgenev's *Nakanune (On the Eve)*. Ždanov remarks that it is common to think of Katerina, the heroine of Ostrovskij's *Groza (The Storm)* as Dobroljubov's creation rather than Ostrovskij's (an opinion the origin of which he attributes to Pisarev). Šelgunov goes so far as to write, "it has justly been remarked that Dobroljubov created Ostrovskij."

Dobroljubov, however, does not confine himself to this one system of relationships between the critic, the artist, and the public. Lebedev-Poljanskij emphasizes Dobroljubov's concept of the artist as the leader of society. On the other hand, Ivanov-Razumnik and Vorovskij, for example, emphasize Dobroljubov's idea that the artist simply formulates the questions raised by society as it develops.

Several forces may be seen at work here. Like Belinskij, Dobroljubov saw both the artist and the critic as seeking the answers to social problems. The difficulty was this: Could the artist be trusted to find them? If he did, then he deserved the position of a leader of society. If not, then he must be content as a follower, and it was safer for society to follow the critic than the artist. It has been pointed out that Černyševskij suggested a class theory of literature. Lebedev-Poljanskij and Lavreckij find the same suggestion in Dobroljubov. This concept was useful to discredit the artist as a leader of the whole of society, and it was in accord with a materialist view of man as the product of his *milieu*. Presumably the critic had emancipated himself from this class limitation.

Why were Dobroljubov's aesthetic pronouncements so obviously contradictory, inconsistent, and piecemeal? In part, these inconsistencies were inherited from his predecessors, Belinskij and Černyševskij. Further, like Černyševskij, Dobroljubov's principal focus of attention centered on social problems, though Dobroljubov left the direct handling of such questions to his mentor. It is important not to forget that in addition to being students of Feuerbach, Černyševskij and Do-

broljubov were also influenced by the Utopian socialists, Saint-Simon, Louis Blanc, and Fourier, and politically they were revolutionary democrats, seeking to promote changes in the social order by such means as lay at their disposal. Like Belinskij at the end of his life, like his master Černyševskij, Dobroljubov was a socialist, but one in whom the revolutionary element was more pronounced than it was in Belinskij. This revolutionary element helps to explain the attractiveness to Dobroljubov and the other revolutionary democrats of the didactic aspect of literature. They saw in "education" a lever by means of which social change might be effected.

Here the theurgic motif, the desire to change reality . . . , expresses itself. This motif was reflected in Dobroljubov's attitude toward literature. As Lebedev-Poljanskij puts it, "He clearly acknowledged the organizing social function of ideology in general, of art and literature in particular. As an opponent of aesthetic criticism, as a social activist, he particularly emphasized this function." But Dobroljubov's attitude on this point, as on so many others, is not consistent, a fact which has been pointed out by a variety of critics.

Another influence which needs to be taken into account when considering Dobroljubov's literary criticism is the influence of the times. . . . As the Emancipation drew closer and closer, the need for a program of action became . . . imperative. Volynskij, a writer generally critical of the Belinskij school, writes: "There is no doubt that Dobroljubov's activity coincided with one of the most remarkable moments in Russian history, when all the forces of society, tense in the expectation of reform of the social order already set in movement by the first hints of a new epoch, endeavoured to solve the immediate historical problem." At such a moment it is not to be wondered at that the search for the answers to social problems took precedence over other considerations.

Like his master Černyševskij, Dobroljubov has been accused of being the "destroyer of aesthetics." But, as was the case with Černyševskij, most of those who have studied Dobroljubov's criticism deny him the right to this questionable distinction. But it is true that Dobroljubov was more interested in the content of a work of art than its form. As a result, aesthetic analysis plays a relatively unimportant and isolated role in Dobroljubov's criticism. He regarded form simply as an external matter and not as an integral principle controlling the very organization of content. Though he did not label the pursuit of beauty in itself as socially harmful, he did not consider it socially useful. Like Černyševskij, Dobroljubov did not theoretically deny the validity of "aesthetic" criticism; he simply tended to consider such questions essentially irrelevant.

This relative neglect of and indifference to the aesthetic aspects of literature is at least in part attributable to Dobroljubov's hostility to the champions of "pure art." This attitude, as we have seen, had been adopted by Belinskij and by Černyševskij and was simply continued by Dobroljubov, who treated "aesthetic criticism" with contempt. This contempt for "aestheticism" does not mean that Dobroljubov was himself devoid of aesthetic taste, but the general effect of his literary criticism was to increase the emphasis upon the social function of literature and literary criticism.

Dobroljubov's significance in emphasizing the "publicistic" element in Russian literary criticism is rather widely acknowledged. . . . Vengerov attributes to it the strong socio-political coloration of Russian literature from his time on and the tendency of Russian writers to assume (and to be granted) the role of socio-political leaders. Volynskij attributes to Dobroljubov's influence a neglect of the aesthetic aspects of literature on the part of literary critics and a consequent decay of literary criticism, although he is willing to admit that such criticism may have played a social role. Both phenomena are commonly acknowledged, but how much they are attributable specifically to Dobroljubov's influence, apart from the general influence of the school of literary criticism in which he, admittedly, played a conspicuous role, seems open to question. (pp. 91-8)

Biographers of Pisarev and students of his work, both foreign and Russian, pre-Soviet and Soviet, have claimed for him a position as a central figure in the intellectual life of Russia during the period when he was active. This claim has been seconded by scholars with a more general interest in the period, particularly pre-Soviet and emigré Russian scholars and foreigners. In general, Soviet scholars (except for those devoting themselves especially to the study of Pisarev's work) tend to ignore or minimize the significance of his contribution. As an ideological leader of the period, Pisarev shares honors with Černyševskij and Dobroljubov; indeed, his work is almost inconceivable without theirs as a foundation. Though Pisarev's attitude toward both men was customarily reserved and even, on occasion, hostile, he was very strongly influenced by them. As we study Pisarev's *Weltanschauung,* we shall find frequent echoes of Černyševskij's and Dobroljubov's ideas, reproduced sometimes faithfully and sometimes in distortion, as well as ideas and intellectual positions peculiar to Pisarev alone.

Pisarev's *Weltanschauung* was by no means coherent and consistent. Indeed, in Pisarev's thinking, dissonances and inconsistencies are, perhaps, more obvious than in the thinking of [Belinskij, Černyševskij, and Dobroljubov]. As with Belinskij and Dobroljubov, the excuse for this confusion of ideas is attributed by Pisarev's apologists in part to the times and in part to the conditions under which he was obliged to work. In part it was premeditated and conscious; Pisarev wrote: "There can be nothing more disastrous for the student of nature than to have a general outlook on the universe." Nevertheless, when Pisarev's work is reviewed as a whole, certain leading themes emerge, sometimes coalescing into coherent clusters and sometimes clashing. Even at the end of his life, after his release from prison when he was trying to find his way in a new political atmosphere, the ensemble of his ideas remained characteristic and recognizable.

What, then, are some of the leading themes of Pisarev's thought? In the first place, Pisarev was a socialist and a democrat, faiths which he shared with Černyševskij, Dobroljubov, and, in general, the whole westernizing wing of the Russian intelligentsia of his time. Pisarev's attitude toward socialism, however, had certain characteristics which distinguish it from that of his contemporaries. Pisarev shared neither Gercen's faith in a federal socialism based on the peasant nor Černyševskij's belief that in the *mir* lay seeds that could grow into a social order which would satisfy Russia's needs. Rather, he shared Blagosvetlov's view that the masses needed the leadership of an elité dedicated to the task of educating and rousing them. Perhaps more important was the fact that while Černyševskij and Dobroljubov were political revolutionaries, Pisarev was essentially, except for the unfortunate episode which led to his arrest and imprisonment, a believer in political evolution. Such an attitude is compatible with the determinism which marked Pisarev's thinking as well as with the political implications of the evolutionary theory of Darwin, whose convert and propagandist Pisarev became. Pisarev's political ideas also reflect

an impressively wide acquaintance with Western European political writers. Coquart detects in Pisarev's articles echoes of Humboldt, Fourier, Robert Owen, Lassalle, and Proudhon. He was rather less influenced by the ideas of Hegel and Feuerbach than Belinskij, Černyševskij, and Dobroljubov.

In the second place, Pisarev was a mechanistic materialist and a determinist, a follower of Büchner, Vogt, and Moleschott. The ideas of these men had influenced Černyševskij and Dobroljubov and the *Weltanschauung* of many others of Pisarev's generation. It is Coquart's thesis that Büchner's *Stoff und Kraft* was especially significant in the case of Pisarev. From Büchner Pisarev adopted a number of leading ideas: in the first place, materialism, with its attendant hostility to idealism in all of its manifestations; second, determinism and allied with it an absolute faith in science as the force which was capable of resolving all human problems together with a conviction of the necessity of propagating the physical and natural sciences; third, egoism; and fourth, a belief that morality is based on social needs. One of the contradictions which plagued Pisarev was inherited from Büchner: How is one to reconcile individual egoism with social utility? Reenforcing the influence of Büchner and the other German materialists was that of the English historian Buckle, an influence which Pisarev shared with many other Russians of his generation. The source of Buckle's attractiveness was his idea of linking history to the natural sciences, of coordinating the physical and moral worlds in a single system whose universal laws were yet to be discovered. Pisarev's faith in the natural sciences was inspired originally by Büchner, but it was reenforced by the influence of Auguste Comte. Pisarev's absolute faith in science finds expression as early as his articles in *Rassvet,* and his efforts in favor of the natural sciences were not only ardent and consistent but eminently successful. . . . A good deal of the intensity and effectiveness of Pisarev's campaign in favor of the natural sciences was the result of his linking a faith in science with his desire for social and political change. He declared that an increase in the number of individuals whose thought and action were firmly grounded in the natural sciences would inevitably lead to the expeditious amelioration of social and political institutions: thus a concentrated effort should be directed toward the creation of such an elite.

In third place and closely related to Pisarev's faith in the natural sciences and materialism was his advocacy of utilitarianism, a cast of thought which he was by no means unique in upholding in the Russia of his day, though he was, perhaps, readier than others to follow the doctrine to extreme conclusions and to accept it as a fundamental moral standard. Indubitably, Pisarev's utilitarianism is in line with the general shift in interest from philosophical idealism to materialism, and it owes a good deal, specifically, to Černyševskij. So far as non-Russian thinkers were concerned, Coquart believes that John Stuart Mill exercised a greater influence upon Russian thought at this period than Jeremy Bentham, and he detects in Pisarev's thought a strong influence deriving from Saint-Simon, especially in the case of Pisarev's ideas on the social organization of labor.

In the fourth place, Pisarev was an ardent believer in individualism, in self-development, in egoism, a faith which he shared with Blagosvetlov. Like his devotion to socialism, mechanistic materialism, and utilitarianism, his belief in individualism was widely shared. This faith in individualism was nurtured by Pisarev's early contacts with the Majkov Circle, in which the idea of individual self-development played an important role, and it is echoed in Pisarev's early articles for *Rassvet.* It was reenforced by Černyševskij's and Dobroljubov's "rational egoism," which owed a good deal to the English utilitarians. As developed by Pisarev, it became a powerful destructive tool, a vital weapon in the arsenal of his nihilism.

A fifth element in Pisarev's *Weltanschauung* is his nihilism, his relentless, adroit, persistent, and effective negative criticism. The beginnings of this sort of criticism are to be found in the work of Belinskij. Černyševskij and Dobroljubov made their contributions toward developing it, and another influence was that of Gercen. Curiously enough, an important influence upon Pisarev's nihilism is that of Turgenev, or rather that of the character of Bazarov in Turgenev's novel, *Otcy i deti (Fathers and Sons)*. Instead of interpreting Bazarov as a calumny on the younger generation, Pisarev rose to Bazarov's defense and adopted him as a personal ideal. Another important purely literary influence upon Pisarev was that of Raxmetov, the hero of Černyševskij's novel, *Čto delat'? (What is to be Done?)*. A component of Pisarev's nihilism, and one which it will be necessary to consider in some detail, was his notorious hostility to art. As we shall see, Pisarev's anti-aestheticism was complex in its sources and complex in its services to ideas which Pisarev held dear.

As a result of the preceding cursory summary of the principal themes in Pisarev's thinking, certain conflicts become obvious. As the most important of these, Coquart sees two: the conflict between mechanistic determinism and individualism and reconciliation of the interests of the individual with those of society. In neither case was Pisarev able to reach a satisfactory resolution.

Mechanistic determinism and individualism imply quite different interpretations of history. Mechanistic determinism holds that events succeed one another in a rigidly linked chain of cause and effect. In this case, since the present and the future are already determined by the unalterable past, such a system admits no possibility of altering the already predetermined course of history. But belief in individualism implies faith that man is not powerless to alter the course of history and the development of social institutions. At first Pisarev espoused an extreme and thoroughgoing determinism, but he soon saw the difficulties of such a position and vacillated. In his article, "Populjarizatory otricatel'nyx doktrin" ("Vulgarizers of Negative Doctrines"), he retreated considerably. He now took the position that progress was not automatic and that a significant role was played by the individual. He thus enunciated a relative rather than an absolute determinism, suggesting an interplay between determinism and human will. But Pisarev was unable to maintain this positon. In 1867, in two articles published almost simultaneously, he took almost perfectly opposed positions. In discussing Pope Gregory VII, he reached the conclusion that Gregory is an example of the intervention of an individual in the course of history. But in his articles on Dostoevskij's *Prestuplenie i nakazanie (Crime and Punishment)*, he reverted to strict determinism. . . . Thus Pisarev was never able to reconcile determinism and individualism. (pp. 120-24)

If Pisarev was unable to reconcile the claims of determinism and individualism, neither was he able to reconcile the claims of society with those of the individual. At the beginning of his career, Pisarev preached individualistic hedonism. It was in this sense that he understood Černyševskij's rational egoism. For Pisarev, the emancipation of the individual meant the freeing of the individual from social and moral restraints. In prison Pisarev discovered altruism. This revelation forced a re-evaluation of his ideas on individualism. As a result, it became the duty of the individual to serve the needs of society. This new attitude of Pisarev's toward the relationship of the individual to society is expounded in "Realisty" ("Realists"), written in June and July, 1864, and appearing in the *Russkoe slovo* under the title, "Nerazrešennyj vopros" ("An Unsettled Question") in September, October, and November of the same year. Did not this new position mean a surrender on the part of the individual, a submission of his own proper ends to those of society? By no means, according to Pisarev. He contended that the interest of the individual coincided with that of society and that, so far as individuals were concerned, "the more profound their egoism becomes, the stronger becomes their love of humanity." (pp. 124-25)

Glaring and obvious as the contradictions and unresolved conflicts of ideas in Pisarev's thinking are, they did not redound to his discredit nor serve to limit his influence. On the contrary, they were part and parcel of the confusions of his time, and the vigor with which he expressed them accounts, at least in part, for his popularity and influence. In this respect Pisarev is strongly reminiscent of Belinskij in his aspect as a mirror of the intellectual preoccupations of his time as well as an influential ideologue. (p. 125)

> *Thelwall Proctor, in his* Dostoevskij and the Belinskij School of Literary Criticism, *Mouton Publishers, 1969, 198 p.*

WILLIAM F. WOEHRLIN

[*Woehrlin summarizes the essential differences between the critical approaches of Chernyshevsky, Belinsky, Dobrolyubov, and Pisarev.*]

Chernyshevskii's writings on aesthetic theory and criticism formed a vital link in the tradition of civic or utilitarian art which extends, with many shifts of method and emphasis, from Belinskii to the present day. For several decades in the nineteenth century, long before the Soviet state established its own version of civic art as literary dogma, pressure for a socially useful art helped direct the work of Russia's writers and artists. Chernyshevskii's part in the development of this doctrine may be seen in a comparison of his views with those of Belinskii, Dobroliubov, and Pisarev. Chernyshevskii proudly recognized Belinskii as his teacher. In different ways, he might have recognized Dobroliubov and Pisarev as his pupils.

Paradoxically, the views of Belinskii in his later years and those of Chernyshevskii were similar, and yet widely disparate. Except for his own unique attempt to refashion the basic definitions and categories in aesthetics, there is no question that Chernyshevskii's views on the role of art and the artist relied heavily on earlier statements by Belinskii. The idea of art as the expression of national cultural life, the rejection of art as mere enjoyment, and even the ambiguous claim that the artist, though free to create, was under obligation to help mold national culture—all came from Belinskii's writings. Similarly, Chernyshevskii made extensive use of Belinskii's evaluations of earlier writers. But even this common core of doctrine and value judgment cannot justify an equation of the two men or unqualified acceptance of the statement that Chernyshevskii merely continued his teacher's work.

Unlike the critics who followed him, Belinskii experienced every phase of influence from German idealistic philosophy, and the experience left an indelible mark. René Wellek noted that, through the entire course of his career, Belinskii used the same categories, concepts, and procedures, the same basic theoretical idiom in his criticism, whatever his shifting emphasis and political convictions. Throughout his restless search to find the proper meaning of art, Belinskii kept a respect for the inviolability of the artist as a discoverer, as opposed to merely a conveyor, of truth. Chernyshevskii, for all his protestations, could not maintain this respect. Probably no man in nineteenth century Russia sensed the shortcomings of his native environment more profoundly than Belinskii, and surely his views of art were firmly joined to social protest and a rejection of idealism in the later years of his career. But when Belinskii turned the attention of literature to social questions, he did so with an unquestioned concern for the literature itself. Even in the face of social injustice, literature could not be simply a tool. In his final review of Russian literature for 1847, Belinskii wrote: "Without any doubt, art must first of all be art, and only then may it be an expression of the spirit and direction of society in a given epoch. Whatever the beautiful thoughts that fill a poem, however strongly it speaks about contemporary problems, if it has no poetry it can have neither beautiful thoughts, nor problems, and all one may note in it is good intention, badly fulfilled."

Chernyshevskii also possessed a concern for literature, as well as a desire to influence the course of society, but in him the two factors were weighted in a significantly different way. He had no legacy from earlier intellectual commitments that might act as a limit on the temptation to use literature, especially as the changing times held out more possibility that his hopes might in fact be realized. His primary interests were not artistic or literary. More important to him was the fact that aesthetics and criticism could serve as a convenient battleground to argue a total point of view and a program of change. This modification of emphasis by Chernyshevskii, who saw art more as a means of propagating truth than as an area of human experience in which truth might be found, was a necessary prelude to the crude exaggerations of utilitarian criticism in the decades following.

Dobroliubov, in turn, made his career as an effective advocate of Chernyshevskii's interpretation of Belinskii. He generally worked so closely with his teacher that it is difficult to tell where the influence of one man left off and the characteristics of the other began. Furthermore, Dobroliubov wrote the bulk of his criticism a few years later than Chernyshevskii, at a time when the radical wing of Russian public opinion had openly assumed on all fronts a more extreme or, indeed, revolutionary position. Yet some distinction between the men can be made. Dobroliubov, like Chernyshevskii, remained ambivalent on the question of whether literature could be an active influence on social change, but in his extensive and forcefully written reviews, he went beyond Chernyshevskii in openly mixing politics and literary criticism.

To accommodate his primary concern with social questions, Dobroliubov developed a type of critical review whose main function was to effect a rapid change of subject away from the literature under consideration to an analysis of society. The most explicit statement of this technique appeared in 1860 in the opening pages of "When Will the Real Day Come?" Dobroliubov's discussion of Turgenev's *On the Eve*. Dobroliubov rejected "aesthetic criticism" as having become the possession of sentimental young ladies. At the same time, he denied a desire to bind the author to his own ideas or to set up tasks for the author's talent. What the author wanted to say was not so important as what he in fact did say, even unintentionally,

in the process of reproducing facts from life. Dobroliubov thus variously described his method of criticism as an attempt to interpret the phenomena of life on the basis of a literary production, or to explain those phenomena of reality that called forth a given artistic work. Within this general approach, Dobroliubov's acceptance or rejection of literary characters, and his evaluations of the fidelity to life of a literary work, became direct comments on Russian society. In theory, his approach to criticism might have remained a tool of analysis to investigate the creative process and the relation of literature to society; in practice, it became a weapon in the hands of an angry social critic, who used it to underscore the weaknesses of the existing social order, to castigate his political opponents, and to demand that literature produce a hero, created in accordance with his own radical ideals.

In their different ways and in different degrees, Belinskii, Chernyshevskii, and Dobroliubov all maintained a considerable respect for the unique contribution of the artist. They also shared the dubious hope that a truly spontaneous literature could somehow be coaxed into serving their visions of progress. A theoretical position that demanded no more than a crude utility from literature was reached only by Pisarev in the middle of the 1860's. In his most extreme statements, which admittedly obscured the complexity and sophistication of his other writings, Pisarev reduced art to the communication of socially useful ideas, and the role of the critic to a judgment of those ideas. Thus concerned with content, Pisarev viewed form as a

Dmitri Pisarev in his early twenties.

mere vehicle of expression, totally separate from content and not worth considering for its own sake, as aestheticians were inclined to do. He declared himself completely indifferent to the traditional arts of music, sculpture, and painting, because they did not contribute directly to the moral and intellectual perfection of humanity. Such arts displayed only ornamental sensuousness, and in this regard, even poetry, seen as a dying art, was little better. Literature still had a social use, although its utility would diminish as mankind progressed to a higher age of science.

Although Pisarev frequently found himself at odds with Chernyshevskii's direct heirs on *The Contemporary,* he defended his general onslaught against aesthetics with specific references to Chernyshevskii's master's dissertation. Pisarev's article "The Destruction of Aesthetics" in 1865 claimed merely to continue a process that Chernyshevskii had begun. He argued that Chernyshevskii himself had wanted to destroy aesthetics, but that he had realized the need to speak to society in a familiar fashion that it could understand. Chernyshevskii had gone as far as he could at the time when he argued that there were no absolute standards of beauty, only the relative preference of each individual.

There is no evidence in Chernyshevskii's writings that he ever made direct comment on these views of a man who claimed to be his pupil. It would appear that Pisarev took the element of conscious didacticism, which belonged more to Chernyshevskii's practice of criticism than to his theory of aesthetics, and carried it to its logical and ridiculous conclusion. But even if Chernyshevskii had rejected Pisarev's most extreme ideas, he also would have recognized them as a part of the tradition he had done as much as any man to establish. (pp. 182-86)

> *William F. Woehrlin, "Aesthetics and Literary Criticism," in his* Chernyshevskii: The Man and the Journalist, *Cambridge, Mass.: Harvard University Press, 1971, pp. 144-86.*

ADDITIONAL BIBLIOGRAPHY

PRIMARY SOURCES

Chernyshevsky, Nikolay Gavrilovich. *What Is to Be Done? Tales about New People.* Translated by Ludmilla B. Turkevich. Boston: Tucker, 1883, 329 p.

————. *Selected Philosophical Essays.* Moscow: Foreign Languages Publishing House, 1953, 610 p.

Dobrolyubov, Nikolay Alexandrovich. *Selected Philosophical Essays.* Translated by J. Fineberg. Moscow: Foreign Languages Publishing House, 1948, 650 p.

Edie, James M., and others, eds. "Book Four: The Nihilists." In *Russian Philosophy.* Vol. II, *The Nihilists, the Populists, Critics of Religion and Culture,* pp. 3-108. Chicago: Quadrangle Books, 1965.

Matlaw, Ralph E., ed. *Belinsky, Chernyshevsky, and Dobrolyubov: Selected Criticism.* New York: E. P. Dutton & Co., 1962, 226 p.

Pisarev, Dmitry Ivanovich. *Selected Philosophical, Social, and Political Essays.* Moscow: Foreign Languages Publishing House, 1958, 711 p.

SECONDARY SOURCES

Annenkov, P. V. *The Extraordinary Decade: Literary Memoirs.* Edited by Arthur P. Mendel. Translated by Irwin R. Titunik. Ann Arbor: University of Michigan Press, 1968, 281 p.
   A reminiscence of a ten-year period beginning in 1839. Annenkov was the contemporary and acquaintance of many prominent figures who shaped literary, critical, and social thought in Russia, and his memoir includes references to the lives and careers of Belinsky and Herzen, among others.

Confino, Michael. "On Intellectuals and Intellectual Traditions in Eighteenth- and Nineteenth-Century Russia." *Daedalus* 101, No. 2 (Spring 1972): 117-49.
   Explores the factors that contributed to the development of a Russian intelligentsia. Confino disputes the common view of the "men of the sixties" as bitter ideological opponents of the "men of the forties."

Gleason, Abbott. "The New Era and Its Journalists: Herzen and Chernyshevsky." In his *Young Russia: The Genesis of Russian Radicalism in the 1860s,* pp. 77-113. New York: Viking Press, 1980.
   Examines the conflict between the radical ideology of Chernyshevsky and the moderate ideology of Herzen with respect to the social and political climate of mid-nineteenth-century Russia.

Herzen, Alexander. *My Past and Thoughts.* Edited by Dwight Macdonald. Translated by Constance Garnett and Humphrey Higgens. Berkeley and Los Angeles: University of California Press, 1982, 684 p.
   Contains Herzen's reminiscences of Belinsky and of nineteenth-century Russian literary circles.

Kropotkin, Prince. "Political Literature; Satire; Art Criticism; Contemporary Novelists." In his *Ideals and Realities in Russian Literature,* pp. 263-317. New York: Alfred A. Knopf, 1915.
   Surveys nineteenth-century Russian literature and literary criticism, including commentary on the Slavophile and Westerner critical circles and on the careers of Herzen, Belinsky, Chernyshevsky, Dobrolyubov, and Pisarev, among others.

Lampert, E. *Sons against Fathers: Studies in Russian Radicalism and Revolution.* Oxford: Oxford at the Clarendon Press, 1965, 405 p.
   A history of Russian radical and revolutionary thought in the 1860s, with sections devoted to early nineteenth-century Russian history, Chernyshevsky, Dobrolyubov, and Pisarev.

Lindstrom, Thaïs S. "New Ideologies: Trail Blazers to the Revolution." In her *A Concise History of Russian Literature.* Vol. I, *From the Beginning to Chekhov,* pp. 111-28. New York: New York University Press, 1966.
   Pronounces Chernyshevsky and Dobrolyubov the "codifiers of radical thought" in nineteenth-century Russian literature.

Lukács, George. "The International Significance of Russian Democratic Literary Criticism." In his *Studies in European Realism: A Sociological Survey of the Writings of Balzac, Stendhal, Zola, Tolstoy, Gorki, and Others,* translated by Edith Bone, pp. 97-125. London: Hillway Publishing Co., 1950.
   Contends that, because the writings of Chernyshevsky, Belinsky, and Dobrolyubov are little known outside Russia, Russian literary criticism has been misunderstood as exclusively concerned with the political significance of literature.

Masaryk, Thomas Garrigue. "Realism and Nihilism: Černyševskii and Dobroljubov. Pisarev." In his *The Spirit of Russia: Studies in History, Literature and Philosophy,* translated by Eden Paul and Cedar Paul, pp. 2-89. London: George Allen & Unwin, 1919.
   Studies the writings of Chernyshevsky, Belinsky, and Dobrolyubov in relationship to numerous ideologies, including utilitarianism, positivism, nihilism, and anarchism.

Mathewson, Rufus W., Jr. "Part One: The Divided Tradition." In his *The Positive Hero in Russian Literature,* 2d ed., pp. 13-112. Stanford: Stanford University Press, 1975.

> Examines the demand of the Civic Critics for literary characters who embody progressive ideology and for literary criticism that incites action.

Mirsky, D. S. "The Age of Realism: Journalists, Poets, and Playwrights." In his *A History of Russian Literature from Its Beginnings to 1900,* edited by Francis J. Whitfield, pp. 215-55. New York: Random House, Vintage Books, 1958.

> Briefly describes the roles of Chernyshevsky, Dobrolyubov, and Pisarev as leaders of the radical intelligentsia during the late 1850s and the 1860s.

Seduro, Vladimir. "The Early 'Radical' Critics." In his *Dostoyevsky in Russian Literary Criticism, 1846-1956,* pp. 3-38. New York: Columbia University Press, 1957.

> Examines Dostoevsky's reception among the Civic Critics.

Slonim, Marc. "The Critics and the Nihilists." In his *The Epic of Russian Literature: From Its Origins through Tolstoy,* pp. 203-18. New York: Oxford University Press, 1964.

> Discusses the social and political climate in Russia between 1854 and 1866 and provides an introduction to the lives and works of Chernyshevsky, Dobrolyubov, and Pisarev.

Stacy, R. H. "The Civic Critics." In his *Russian Literary Criticism: A Short History,* pp. 55-65. Syracuse: Syracuse University Press, 1974.

> Outlines the careers of Chernyshevsky, Dobrolyubov, and Pisarev.

Swiderski, Edward M. "The Sources and Origins of Marxist-Leninist Aesthetics." In his *The Philosophical Foundations of Soviet Aesthetics: Theories and Controversies in the Post-War Years,* pp. 47-67. London: D. Reidel Publishing Co., 1979.

> Discusses the Civic Critics as the "spiritual fathers" of Soviet aesthetics.

Venturi, Franco. *Roots of Revolution: A History of the Populist and Socialist Movements in Nineteenth Century Russia.* Translated by Francis Haskell. New York: Alfred A. Knopf, 1964, 850 p.

> A highly regarded study of Russian revolutionary history that includes a chapter on Chernyshevsky and numerous references to the other Civic Critics.

Weinstein, Fred. "The Origins of 'Nihilist' Criticism." *Canadian Slavic Studies* III, No. 2 (Summer 1969): 165-77.

> Examines the psychosocial basis of the rationalism expressed in writings by Dobrolyubov and Chernyshevsky, focusing on Dobrolyubov's analysis of the novel *Oblomov* by Ivan Goncharov.

Yarmolinsky, Avrahm. *Road to Revolution: A Century of Russian Radicalism.* London: Cassell & Co., 1957, 349 p.

> A history of the revolutionary tradition in Russia during the nineteenth century, containing many references to the contributions of Chernyshevsky, Dobrolyubov, and Pisarev.

Appendix

The following is a listing of all sources used in Volume 20 of *Nineteenth-Century Literature Criticism*. Included in this list are all copyright and reprint rights and acknowledgments for those essays for which permission was obtained. Every effort has been made to trace copyright, but if omissions have been made, please let us know.

THE EXCERPTS IN NCLC, VOLUME 20, WERE REPRINTED FROM THE FOLLOWING PERIODICALS:

THE EXCERPTS IN NCLC, VOLUME 20, WERE REPRINTED FROM THE FOLLOWING BOOKS:

Abrams, Meyer Howard. From *The Milk of Paradise: The Effect of Opium Visions on the Works of De Quincey, Crabbe, Francis Thompson, and Coleridge.* Cambridge, Mass.: Harvard University Press, 1934. Copyright 1934 by the President and Fellows of Harvard College. Renewed © 1962 by Meyer Howard Abrams. Excerpted by permission of the publishers.

Alexander, Jean. From "The Outlaw" and "The Poet," in *Affidavits of Genius: Edgar Allan Poe and the French Critics, 1847-1924.* Edited by Jean Alexander. Kennikat Press, 1971. Copyright © 1971 by Jean Alexander. All rights reserved. Reprinted by permission of the author.

Andrews, William L. From "The First Fifty Years of the Slave Narrative, 1760-1810," in *The Art of Slave Narrative: Original Essays in Criticism and Theory.* Edited by John Sekora and Darwin T. Turner. Western Illinois University, 1982. Copyright © 1982 by Western Illinois University. Reprinted by permission of the publisher.

Bakhtin, M. M. From *Speech Genres and Other Late Essays.* Edited by Caryl Emerson and Michael Holquist, translated by Vern W. McGee. University of Texas Press, 1986. Copyright © 1986 by the University of Texas Press. All rights reserved. Reprinted by permission of the publisher.

Balakian, Anna. From *The Symbolist Movement: A Critical Appraisal.* Random House, 1967. Copyright © 1967 by Random House, Inc. Reprinted by permission of the publisher.

Beddow, Michael. From *The Fiction of Humanity: Studies in the Bildungsroman from Wieland to Thomas Mann.* Cambridge University Press, 1982. © Cambridge University Press 1982. Reprinted with the permission of the publisher and the author.

Berdyaev, Nicolas. From *The Origin of Russian Communism.* Translated by R. M. French. Geoffrey Bles: The Centenary Press, 1937.

Berridge, Virginia, and Griffith Edwards. From *Opium and the People: Opiate Use in Nineteenth-Century England.* St. Martin's Press, 1981. Copyright © Virginia Berridge and Griffith Edwards, 1981. All rights reserved. Used with permission of St. Martin's Press, Inc.

Block, Haskell M. From *Mallarmé and the Symbolist Drama.* Wayne State University Press, 1963. Copyright © 1963 by Wayne State University Press, Detroit 2, Michigan. All rights reserved. Reprinted by permission of the publisher and the author.

Bowman, Herbert E. From *Vissarion Belinski, 1811-1848: A Study in the Origins of Social Criticism in Russia.* Cambridge, Mass.: Harvard University Press, 1954. Copyright 1954 by the President and Fellows of Harvard College. Renewed © 1982 by Herbert Eugene Bowman. Excerpted by permission of the publishers.

Buckley, Jerome Hamilton. From *Season of Youth: The Bildungsroman from Dickens to Golding.* Cambridge, Mass.: Harvard University Press, 1974. Copyright © 1974 by the President and Fellows of Harvard College. All rights reserved. Excerpted by permission of the publishers.

Burne-Jones, Edward. From a letter in *Memorials of Edward Burne-Jones.* By Georgina Burne-Jones. Macmillan & Co., Ltd., 1904.

Butterfield, Stephen. From *Black Autobiography in America.* University of Massachusetts Press, 1974. Copyright © 1974 by The University of Massachusetts Press. All rights reserved. Reprinted by permission of the publisher.

Byerman, Keith. From "We Wear the Mask: Deceit as Theme and Style in Slave Narratives," in *The Art of Slave Narrative: Original Essays in Criticism and Theory.* Edited by John Sekora and Darwin T. Turner. Western Illinois University, 1982. Copyright © 1982 by Western Illinois University. Reprinted by permission of the publisher.

Chadwick, Charles. From *Symbolism.* Methuen, 1971. © 1971 Charles Chadwick. Reprinted by permission of Methuen & Co. Ltd.

Christ, Carol T. From *The Finer Optic: The Aesthetic of Particularity in Victorian Poetry.* Yale University Press, 1975. Copyright © 1975 by Yale University. All rights reserved. Reprinted by permission of the publisher.

Coleridge, Samuel Taylor. From *Christabel. Kubla Khan: A Vision. The Pains of Sleep.* John Murray, 1816.

Coleridge, S. T. From *Letters of Samuel Taylor Coleridge, Vol. II.* Edited by Ernest Hartley Coleridge. William Heinemann, 1895.

Davis, Charles T., and Henry Louis Gates, Jr. From "Introduction: The Language of Slavery," in *The Slave's Narrative.* Edited by Charles T. Davis and Henry Louis Gates, Jr. Oxford University Press, 1985. Copyright © 1985 by Oxford University Press, Inc. All rights reserved. Reprinted by permission of the publisher.

Dickason, David Howard. From *The Daring Young Men: The Story of the American Pre-Raphaelites.* Indiana University Press, 1953. Copyright, 1953, by Indiana University Press. Renewed 1981 by Marjorie H. Dickason. Reprinted by permission of the publisher.

Dixon, Melvin. From "Singing Swords: The Literary Legacy of Slavery," in *The Slave's Narrative.* Edited by Charles T. Davis and Henry Louis Gates, Jr. Oxford University Press, 1985. Copyright © 1985 by Oxford University Press, Inc. All rights reserved. Reprinted by permission of the author.

Eliot, T. S. From a foreword to *Symbolisme from Poe to Mallarmé: The Growth of a Myth.* By Joseph Chiari. Rockliff, 1956.

Foster, Frances Smith. From *Witnessing Slavery: The Development of Ante-bellum Slave Narratives.* Greenwood Press, 1979. Copyright © 1979 by Frances Smith Foster. All rights reserved. Reprinted by permission of Greenwood Press, Inc., Westport, CT.

Fredeman, William E. From *Pre-Raphaelitism: A Bibliocritical Study.* Cambridge, Mass.: Harvard University Press, 1965. Copyright © 1965 by the author. All rights reserved. Reprinted by permission of the author.

Gilbert, William Schwenck. From *Patience; or, Bunthorne's Bride!* Chappell & Co., 1881.

Gourmont, Remy de. From *The Book of Masks.* Translated by Jack Lewis. J. W. Luce and Company, 1921.

Hayter, Alethea. From *Opium and the Romantic Imagination.* Faber, 1968. © 1968 by Alethea Hayter. Reprinted by permission of Faber & Faber Ltd.

Heath-Stubbs, John. From *The Darkling Plain: A Study of the Later Fortunes of Romanticism in English Poetry from George Darley to W. B. Yeats.* Eyre & Spottiswoode, 1950.

House, Humphry. From *All in Due Time: The Collected Essays and Broadcast Talks of Humphry House.* Rupert Hart-Davis, 1955.

Houston, John Porter, and Mona Tobin Houston. From an introduction to *French Symbolist Poetry: An Anthology.* Edited and translated by John Porter Houston and Mona Tobin Houston. Indiana University Press, 1980. Copyright © 1980 by John Porter Houston and Mona Tobin Houston. All rights reserved. Reprinted by permission of the publisher.

Howe, Susanne. From *Wilhelm Meister and His English Kinsmen: Apprentices to Life.* Columbia University Press, 1930.

Jones, L. E. From *À La Carte.* Secker & Warburg, 1951.

Jullian, Philippe. From *Dreamers of Decadence: Symbolist Painters of the 1890s.* Translated by Robert Baldick. Praeger Publishers, 1971. Translation copyright © 1971 by Pall Mall Press Limited. All rights reserved. Reprinted by permission of Henry Holt and Company, Inc.

Loggins, Vernon. From *The Negro Author: His Development in America to 1900.* Columbia University Press, 1931. Copyright 1931 Columbia University Press. Renewed 1959 by Vernon Loggins. Reprinted by permission of the Literary Estate of Vernon Loggins.

Lukács, Georg. From *The Theory of the Novel: A Historico-Philosophical Essay on the Forms of Great Epic Literature.* Translated by Anna Bostock. M.I.T. Press, 1971. Translation © The Merlin Press, 1971. Reprinted by permission of The MIT Press, Cambridge, MA.

Mallarmé, Stéphane. From *Mallarmé: Selected Prose, Poems, Essays, & Letters.* Translated by Bradford Cook. Johns Hopkins Press, 1956. © 1956, The Johns Hopkins Press. Renewed 1984 by Bradford Cook. Reprinted by permission of the publisher.

Mallock, William Hurrell. From *Every Man His Own Poet; or, the Inspired Singer's Recipe Book.* N.p., 1872.

Matlaw, Ralph E. From an introduction to *Belinsky, Chernyshevsky, and Dobrolyubov: Selected Criticism.* Edited by Ralph E. Matlaw. Dutton, 1962. Copyright, ©, 1962, by E. P. Dutton. All rights reserved. Reprinted by permission of the publisher, E. P. Dutton, a division of NAL Penguin Inc.

Mégroz, R. L. From *Modern English Poetry: 1882-1932.* Ivor Nicholson & Watson, Ltd., 1933.

Moréas, M. Jean. From "A Literary Manifesto," translated by Eugen Weber, in *Paths to the Present: Aspects of European Thought from Romanticism to Existentialism.* Edited by Eugen Weber. Dodd, Mead & Company, Inc., 1960. Copyright © 1960 by Harper & Row, Publishers, Inc. All rights reserved. Reprinted by permission of Harper & Row, Publishers, Inc.

Nordau, Max. From *Degeneration.* William Heinemann, 1895.

Olney, James. From "'I Was Born': Slave Narratives, Their Status as Autobiography and as Literature," in *The Slave's Narrative.* Edited by Charles T. Davis and Henry Louis Gates, Jr. Oxford University Press, 1985. Copyright © 1985 by Oxford University Press, Inc. All rights reserved. Reprinted by permission of the author.

Osofsky, Gilbert. From "Introduction: Puttin' On Ole Massa, the Significance of Slave Narratives," in *Puttin' On Ole Massa: The Slave Narratives of Henry Bibb, William Wells Brown, and Solomon Northup.* Edited by Gilbert Osofsky. Harper & Row, 1969. Copyright © 1969 by Gilbert Osofsky. All rights reserved. Reprinted by permission of the Literary Estate of Gilbert Osofsky.

Parssinen, Terry M. From *Secret Passions, Secret Remedies: Narcotic Drugs in British Society, 1820-1930.* Institute for the Study of Human Issues, 1983. Copyright © 1983 by ISHI, Institute for the Study of Human Issues, Inc. All rights reserved. Reprinted by permission of the publisher.

Pascal, Roy. From *The German Novel: Studies.* Manchester University Press, 1956.

Peyre, Henri. From *What Is Symbolism?* Translated by Emmett Parker. University of Alabama Press, 1980. English translation Copyright © 1980 by The University of Alabama Press. All rights reserved. Reprinted by permission of the publisher.

Pierrot, Jean. From *The Decadent Imagination: 1880-1900*. Translated by Derek Coltman. University of Chicago Press, 1981. © 1981 by The University of Chicago. All rights reserved. Reprinted by permission of the publisher.

Proctor, Thelwall. From *Dostoevskij and the Belinskij School of Literary Criticism*. Mouton, 1969. © copyright 1969 in The Netherlands, Mouton & Co. N.V., Publishers, The Hague. Reprinted by permission of the Literary Estate of Thelwall Proctor.

Reed, John R. From an introduction to *Decadent Style*. Ohio University Press, 1985. © 1985 by John R. Reed. All rights reserved. Reprinted by permission of the publisher.

Robson, W. W. From "Pre-Raphaelite Poetry," in *From Dickens to Hardy*. Edited by Boris Ford. Revised edition. The Pelican Guide to English Literature, Vol. 6. Penguin Books, 1960. Copyright © Penguin Books Ltd., 1958. Reproduced by permission of Penguin Books Ltd.

Rossetti, Christina. From *The Poetical Works of Christina Georgina Rossetti*. Edited by William Michael Rossetti. Macmillan and Co., Ltd., 1904.

Rossetti, William Michael. From *Dante Gabriel Rossetti: His Family-Letters, Vol. I*. Roberts Brothers, 1895.

Rossetti, William Michael. From an introduction to *The Germ: Thoughts towards Nature in Poetry, Literature and Art, Being a Facsimile Reprint of the Literary Organ of the Pre-Raphaelite Brotherhood*. Edited by William Michael Rossetti. E. Stock, 1901.

Ruskin, John. From *Pre-Raphaelitism*. J. Wiley, 1851.

Scanlan, James P. From "The Nihilists," in *Russian Philosophy: The Nihilists, the Populists, Critics of Religion and Culture, Vol. II*. Edited by James M. Edie and others. Quadrangle Books, 1965. Copyright © 1965 by Quadrangle Books, Inc. All rights reserved. Reprinted by permission of the author.

Schneider, Elisabeth. From *Coleridge, Opium and "Kubla Khan."* University of Chicago Press, 1953. Copyright 1953 by The University of Chicago. Renewed 1981 by Elisabeth Wintersteen Schneider. All rights reserved. Reprinted by permission of the publisher and the Literary Estate of Elisabeth Schneider.

Shaffner, Randolph P. From *The Apprenticeship Novel: A Study of the "Bildungsroman" as a Regulative Type in Western Literature with a Focus on Three Classic Representatives by Goethe, Maugham, and Mann*. Lang, 1984. © Peter Lang Publishing Inc., New York 1984. All rights reserved. Reprinted by permission of the publisher.

Slonim, Marc. From *An Outline of Russian Literature*. Oxford University Press, 1958. Copyright © 1958 by Marc Slonim. Renewed 1986 by Tatiana Slonim. Reprinted by permission of Oxford University Press, Inc.

Smith, Sidonie. From *Where I'm Bound: Patterns of Slavery and Freedom in Black American Autobiography*. Greenwood Press, 1974. Copyright © 1974 by Sidonie Smith. All rights reserved. Reprinted by permission of Greenwood Press, Inc., Westport, CT.

Smith, Tennyson Longfellow (pseudonym of John Burley Waring). From *Poems Inspired by Certain Pictures at the Art Treasures Exhibition*. N.p., 1857.

Starling, Marion Wilson. From *The Slave Narrative: Its Place in American History*. Hall, 1981. Copyright 1981 by G. K. Hall & Co. Reprinted with the permission of the publisher.

Stepto, Robert B. From *From Behind the Veil: A Study of Afro-American Narrative*. University of Illinois Press, 1979. © 1979 by the Board of Trustees of the University of Illinois. Reprinted by permission of the publisher and the author.

Stevenson, Lionel. From *The Pre-Raphaelite Poets*. University of North Carolina Press, 1972. Copyright © 1972 by The University of North Carolina Press. All rights reserved. Reprinted by permission of the publisher.

Sussman, Herbert L. From *Fact into Figure: Typology in Carlyle, Ruskin, and the Pre-Raphaelite Brotherhood*. Ohio State University Press, 1979. © 1979 by the Ohio State University Press. All rights reserved. Reprinted with permission of the publisher.

Swales, Martin. From *The German Bildungsroman from Wieland to Hesse*. Princeton University Press, 1978. Copyright © 1978 by Princeton University Press. All rights reserved. Reprinted with permission of the publisher.

Symons, Arthur. From *Days and Nights*. Macmillan & Co., 1889.

Symons, Arthur. From *The Symbolist Movement in Literature*. Revised edition. Dutton, 1919. Copyright, 1919 by E. P. Dutton. Renewed 1946 by Nona Hill. All rights reserved. Reprinted by permission of the publisher, E. P. Dutton, a division of NAL Penguin Inc.

Tennyson, G. B. From "The 'Bildungsroman' in Nineteenth-Century English Literature," in *Medieval Epic to the "Epic Theater" of Brecht: Essays in Comparative Literature*. Edited by Rosario P. Armato and John M. Spalek. University of Southern California Press, 1968. © Copyright 1968 by The University of Southern California. Reprinted by permission of the author.

Terras, Victor. From *Belinskij and Russian Literary Criticism: The Heritage of Organic Aesthetics*. The University of Wisconsin Press, 1974. Copyright © 1974 The Regents of the University of Wisconsin System. All rights reserved. Reprinted by permission of the publisher.

Nineteenth-Century
Literature Criticism

Archive Volume

Cumulative Indexes

This Index Includes References to Entries in These Gale Series

Contemporary Literary Criticism

Presents excerpts of criticism on the works of novelists, poets, dramatists, short story writers, scriptwriters, and other creative writers who are now living or who have died since 1960. Cumulative indexes to authors and nationalities are included, as well as an index to titles discussed in the individual volume. Volumes 1-51 are in print.

Twentieth-Century Literary Criticism

Contains critical excerpts by the most significant commentators on poets, novelists, short story writers, dramatists, and philosophers who died between 1900 and 1960. Cumulative indexes to authors, nationalities, and titles discussed are included in each new volume. Volumes 1-31 are in print.

Nineteenth-Century Literature Criticism

Offers significant passages from criticism on authors who died between 1800 and 1899. Cumulative indexes to authors, nationalities, and titles discussed are included in each new volume. Volumes 1-20 are in print.

Literature Criticism from 1400 to 1800

Compiles significant passages from the most noteworthy criticism on authors of the fifteenth through eighteenth centuries. Cumulative indexes to authors, nationalities, and titles discussed are included in each new volume. Volumes 1-9 are in print.

Classical and Medieval Literature Criticism

Offers excerpts of criticism on the works of world authors from classical antiquity through the fourteenth century. Cumulative indexes to authors, titles, and critics are included in each volume. Volumes 1-2 are in print.

Short Story Criticism

Compiles excerpts of criticism on short fiction by writers of all eras and nationalities. Cumulative indexes to authors, nationalities, and titles discussed are included in each new volume. Volumes 1-2 are in print.

Children's Literature Review

Includes excerpts from reviews, criticism, and commentary on works of authors and illustrators who create books for children. Cumulative indexes to authors, nationalities, and titles discussed are included in each new volume. Volumes 1-16 are in print.

Contemporary Authors Series

Encompasses five related series. *Contemporary Authors* provides biographical and bibliographical information on more than 90,000 writers of fiction, nonfiction, poetry, journalism, drama, motion pictures, and other fields. Each new volume contains sketches on authors not previously covered in the series. Volumes 1-124 are in print. *Contemporary Authors New Revision Series* provides completely updated information on active authors covered in previously published volumes of *CA*. Only entries requiring significant change are revised for *CA New Revision Series*. Volumes 1-24 are in print. *Contemporary Authors Permanent Series* consists of updated listings for deceased and inactive authors removed from the original volumes 9-36 when these volumes were revised. Volumes 1-2 are in print. *Contemporary Authors Autobiography Series* presents specially commissioned autobiographies by leading contemporary writers. Volumes 1-7 are in print. *Contemporary Authors Bibliographical Series* contains primary and secondary bibliographies as well as analytical bibliographical essays by authorities on major modern authors. Volumes 1-2 are in print.

Dictionary of Literary Biography

Encompasses three related series. *Dictionary of Literary Biography* furnishes illustrated overviews of authors' lives and works and places them in the larger perspective of literary history. Volumes 1-72 are in print. *Dictionary of Literary Biography Documentary Series* illuminates the careers of major figures through a selection of literary documents, including letters, notebook and diary entries, interviews, book reviews, and photographs. Volumes 1-5 are in print. *Dictionary of Literary Biography Yearbook* summarizes the past year's literary activity with articles on genres, major prizes, conferences, and other timely subjects and includes updated and new entries on individual authors. Yearbooks for 1980-1987 are in print. A cumulative index to authors and articles is included in each new volume.

Concise Dictionary of American Literary Biography

A six-volume series that collects revised and updated sketches on major American authors that were originally presented in *Dictionary of Literary Biography*. Volumes 1-3 are in print.

Something about the Author Series

Encompasses two related series. *Something about the Author* contains heavily illustrated biographical sketches on juvenile and young adult authors and illustrators from all eras. Volumes 1-53 are in print. *Something about the Author Autobiography Series* presents specially commissioned autobiographies by prominent authors and illustrators of books for children and young adults. Volumes 1-6 are in print.

Yesterday's Authors of Books for Children

Contains heavily illustrated entries on children's writers who died before 1961. Complete in two volumes. Volumes 1-2 are in print.

Literary Criticism Series
Cumulative Author Index

This index lists all author entries in the Gale Literary Criticism Series and includes cross-references to other Gale sources. For the convenience of the reader, references to the *Yearbook* in the *Contemporary Literary Criticism* series include the page number (in parentheses) after the volume number. References in the index are identified as follows:

AITN: *Authors in the News*, Volumes 1-2
CAAS: *Contemporary Authors Autobiography Series*, Volumes 1-7
CA: *Contemporary Authors* (original series), Volumes 1-124
CABS: *Contemporary Authors Bibliographical Series*, Volumes 1-2
CANR: *Contemporary Authors New Revision Series*, Volumes 1-24
CAP: *Contemporary Authors Permanent Series*, Volumes 1-2
CA-R: *Contemporary Authors* (revised editions), Volumes 1-44
CDALB: *Concise Dictionary of American Literary Biography*, Volumes 1-3
CLC: *Contemporary Literary Criticism*, Volumes 1-51
CLR: *Children's Literature Review*, Volumes 1-16
CMLC: *Classical and Medieval Literature Criticism*, Volumes 1-2
DLB: *Dictionary of Literary Biography*, Volumes 1-72
DLB-DS: *Dictionary of Literary Biography Documentary Series*, Volumes 1-5
DLB-Y: *Dictionary of Literary Biography Yearbook*, Volumes 1980-1987
LC: *Literature Criticism from 1400 to 1800*, Volumes 1-9
NCLC: *Nineteenth-Century Literature Criticism*, Volumes 1-20
SAAS: *Something about the Author Autobiography Series*, Volumes 1-6
SATA: *Something about the Author*, Volumes 1-53
SSC: *Short Story Criticism*, Volumes 1-2
TCLC: *Twentieth-Century Literary Criticism*, Volumes 1-31
YABC: *Yesterday's Authors of Books for Children*, Volumes 1-2

Author Index

Benavente (y Martinez), Jacinto
     1866-1954 . . . . TCLC 3
     See also CA 106

Benchley, Peter (Bradford)
     1940- . . . . CLC 4, 8
     See also CANR 12
     See also CA 17-20R
     See also SATA 3
     See also AITN 2

Benchley, Robert   1889-1945 . . . . . . TCLC 1
     See also CA 105
     See also DLB 11

Benedikt, Michael   1935- . . . . CLC 4, 14
     See also CANR 7
     See also CA 13-16R
     See also DLB 5

Benet, Juan   1927- . . . . CLC 28

Benét, Stephen Vincent
     1898-1943 . . . . TCLC 7
     See also CA 104
     See also YABC 1
     See also DLB 4, 48

Benét, William Rose
     1886-1950 . . . . TCLC 28
     See also CA 118
     See also DLB 45

Benn, Gottfried   1886-1956 . . . . TCLC 3
     See also CA 106
     See also DLB 56

Bennett, Alan   1934- . . . . CLC 45
     See also CA 103

Bennett, (Enoch) Arnold
     1867-1931 . . . . TCLC 5, 20
     See also CA 106
     See also DLB 10, 34

Bennett, George Harold   1930-
     See Bennett, Hal
     See also CA 97-100

Bennett, Hal   1930- . . . . CLC 5
     See also Bennett, George Harold
     See also DLB 33

Bennett, Jay   1912- . . . . CLC 35
     See also CANR 11
     See also CA 69-72
     See also SAAS 4
     See also SATA 27, 41

Bennett, Louise (Simone)
     1919- . . . . CLC 28
     See also Bennett-Coverly, Louise Simone

Bennett-Coverly, Louise Simone   1919-
     See Bennett, Louise (Simone)
     See also CA 97-100

Benson, E(dward) F(rederic)
     1867-1940 . . . . TCLC 27
     See also CA 114

Benson, Jackson J.
     1930- . . . . CLC 34 (404)
     See also CA 25-28R

Benson, Sally   1900-1972 . . . . CLC 17
     See also CAP 1
     See also CA 19-20
     See also obituary CA 37-40R
     See also SATA 1, 35
     See also obituary SATA 27

Benson, Stella   1892-1933 . . . . TCLC 17
     See also CA 117
     See also DLB 36

Bentley, E(dmund) C(lerihew)
     1875-1956 . . . . TCLC 12
     See also CA 108
     See also DLB 70

Bentley, Eric (Russell)   1916- . . . . . . CLC 24
     See also CANR 6
     See also CA 5-8R

Berger, John (Peter)   1926- . . . . . CLC 2, 19
     See also CA 81-84
     See also DLB 14

Berger, Melvin (H.)   1927- . . . . CLC 12
     See also CANR 4
     See also CA 5-8R
     See also SAAS 2
     See also SATA 5

Berger, Thomas (Louis)
     1924- . . . . CLC 3, 5, 8, 11, 18, 38
     See also CANR 5
     See also CA 1-4R
     See also DLB 2
     See also DLB-Y 80

Bergman, (Ernst) Ingmar
     1918- . . . . CLC 16
     See also CA 81-84

Bergstein, Eleanor   1938- . . . . CLC 4
     See also CANR 5
     See also CA 53-56

Bermant, Chaim   1929- . . . . CLC 40
     See also CANR 6
     See also CA 57-60

Bernanos, (Paul Louis) Georges
     1888-1948 . . . . TCLC 3
     See also CA 104
     See also DLB 72

Bernhard, Thomas   1931- . . . . CLC 3, 32
     See also CA 85-88

Berrigan, Daniel J.   1921- . . . . CLC 4
     See also CAAS 1
     See also CANR 11
     See also CA 33-36R
     See also DLB 5

Berrigan, Edmund Joseph Michael, Jr.
     1934-1983
     See Berrigan, Ted
     See also CANR 14
     See also CA 61-64
     See also obituary CA 110

Berrigan, Ted   1934-1983 . . . . CLC 37
     See also Berrigan, Edmund Joseph
       Michael, Jr.
     See also DLB 5

Berry, Chuck   1926- . . . . CLC 17

Berry, Wendell (Erdman)
     1934- . . . . CLC 4, 6, 8, 27, 46
     See also CA 73-76
     See also DLB 5, 6
     See also AITN 1

Berryman, Jerry
     1914-1972 . . . . CDALB 1941-1968

Berryman, John
     1914-1972 . . . . . CLC 1, 2, 3, 4, 6, 8, 10,
                                                      13, 25
     See also CAP 1
     See also CA 15-16
     See also obituary CA 33-36R
     See also CABS 2
     See also DLB 48
     See also CDALB 1941-1968

Bertolucci, Bernardo   1940- . . . . CLC 16
     See also CA 106

Besant, Annie (Wood)
     1847-1933 . . . . TCLC 9
     See also CA 105

Bessie, Alvah   1904-1985 . . . . CLC 23
     See also CANR 2
     See also CA 5-8R
     See also obituary CA 116
     See also DLB 26

Beti, Mongo   1932- . . . . CLC 27
     See also Beyidi, Alexandre

Betjeman, (Sir) John
     1906-1984 . . . . . . CLC 2, 6, 10, 34 (305),
                                                               43
     See also CA 9-12R
     See also obituary CA 112
     See also DLB 20
     See also DLB-Y 84

Betti, Ugo   1892-1953 . . . . TCLC 5
     See also CA 104

Betts, Doris (Waugh)
     1932- . . . . CLC 3, 6, 28
     See also CANR 9
     See also CA 13-16R
     See also DLB-Y 82

Bialik, Chaim Nachman
     1873-1934 . . . . TCLC 25

Bidart, Frank   19??- . . . . CLC 33

Bienek, Horst   1930- . . . . CLC 7, 11
     See also CA 73-76

Bierce, Ambrose (Gwinett)
     1842-1914? . . . . TCLC 1, 7
     See also CA 104
     See also DLB 11, 12, 23, 71
     See also CDALB 1865-1917

Billington, Rachel   1942- . . . . CLC 43
     See also CA 33-36R
     See also AITN 2

Binyon, T(imothy) J(ohn)
     1936- . . . . CLC 34 (32)
     See also CA 111

Bioy Casares, Adolfo
     1914- . . . . CLC 4, 8, 13
     See also CANR 19
     See also CA 29-32R

Bird, Robert Montgomery
     1806-1854 . . . . NCLC 1

Birdwell, Cleo   1936-
     See DeLillo, Don

Birney (Alfred) Earle
     1904- . . . . CLC 1, 4, 6, 11
     See also CANR 5, 20
     See also CA 1-4R

Bishop, Elizabeth
     1911-1979 . . . . . . CLC 1, 4, 9, 13, 15, 32
     See also CA 5-8R
     See also obituary CA 89-92
     See also CABS 2
     See also obituary SATA 24
     See also DLB 5

Bishop, John   1935- . . . . CLC 10
     See also CA 105

Bissett, Bill   1939- . . . . CLC 18
     See also CANR 15
     See also CA 69-72
     See also DLB 53

Author Index

Author Index

Cowper, William   1731-1800 ...... NCLC 8

Cox, William Trevor   1928-
    See Trevor, William
    See also CANR 4
    See also CA 9-12R

Cozzens, James Gould
    1903-1978.............. CLC 1, 4, 11
    See also CANR 19
    See also CA 9-12R
    See also obituary CA 81-84
    See also DLB 9
    See also DLB-Y 84
    See also DLB-DS 2
    See also CDALB 1941-1968

Crane, (Harold) Hart
    1899-1932................ TCLC 2, 5
    See also CA 104
    See also DLB 4, 48

Crane, R(onald) S(almon)
    1886-1967..................... CLC 27
    See also CA 85-88
    See also DLB 63

Crane, Stephen
    1871-1900.............. TCLC 11, 17
    See also CA 109
    See also YABC 2
    See also DLB 12, 54
    See also CDALB 1865-1917

Craven, Margaret   1901-1980...... CLC 17
    See also CA 103

Crawford, F(rancis) Marion
    1854-1909................. TCLC 10
    See also CA 107
    See also DLB 71

Crawford, Isabella Valancy
    1850-1887.................... NCLC 12

Crayencour, Marguerite de   1913-
    See Yourcenar, Marguerite

Creasey, John   1908-1973.......... CLC 11
    See also CANR 8
    See also CA 5-8R
    See also obituary CA 41-44R

Crébillon, Claude Prosper Jolyot de (fils)
    1707-1777...................... LC 1

Creeley, Robert (White)
    1926-........ CLC 1, 2, 4, 8, 11, 15, 36
    See also CA 1-4R
    See also DLB 5, 16

Crews, Harry (Eugene)
    1935-.................. CLC 6, 23, 49
    See also CANR 20
    See also CA 25-28R
    See also DLB 6
    See also AITN 1

Crichton, (John) Michael
    1942-....................... CLC 2, 6
    See also CANR 13
    See also CA 25-28R
    See also SATA 9
    See also DLB-Y 81
    See also AITN 2

Crispin, Edmund   1921-1978 .... CLC 22
    See also Montgomery, Robert Bruce

Cristofer, Michael   1946-........... CLC 28
    See also CA 110
    See also DLB 7

Crockett, David (Davy)
    1786-1836................. NCLC 8
    See also DLB 3, 11

Croker, John Wilson
    1780-1857................. NCLC 10

Cronin, A(rchibald) J(oseph)
    1896-1981................... CLC 32
    See also CANR 5
    See also CA 1-4R
    See also obituary CA 102
    See also obituary SATA 25, 47

Cross, Amanda   1926-
    See Heilbrun, Carolyn G(old)

Crothers, Rachel   1878-1953...... TCLC 19
    See also CA 113
    See also DLB 7

Crowley, Aleister   1875-1947 ...... TCLC 7
    See also CA 104

Crumb, Robert   1943-.............. CLC 17
    See also CA 106

Cryer, Gretchen   1936?- .... CLC 21
    See also CA 114

Csáth, Géza   1887-1919.......... TCLC 13
    See also CA 111

Cudlip, David   1933- .... CLC 34 (38)

Cullen, Countee   1903-1946 .... TCLC 4
    See also CA 108
    See also SATA 18
    See also DLB 4, 48, 51

Cummings, E(dward) E(stlin)
    1894-1962......... CLC 1, 3, 8, 12, 15
    See also CA 73-76
    See also DLB 4, 48

Cunha, Euclides (Rodrigues) da
    1866-1909.................... TCLC 24

Cunningham, J(ames) V(incent)
    1911-1985................. CLC 3, 31
    See also CANR 1
    See also CA 1-4R
    See also obituary CA 115
    See also DLB 5

Cunningham, Julia (Woolfolk)
    1916-........................ CLC 12
    See also CANR 4, 19
    See also CA 9-12R
    See also SAAS 2
    See also SATA 1, 26

Cunningham, Michael
    1952-.................... CLC 34 (40)

Currie, Ellen   19??- .... CLC 44 (39)

Dąbrowska, Maria (Szumska)
    1889-1965.................... CLC 15
    See also CA 106

Dabydeen, David   1956?-..... CLC 34 (147)

Dacey, Philip   1939-............ CLC 51
    See also CANR 14
    See also CA 37-40R

Dagerman, Stig (Halvard)
    1923-1954.................. TCLC 17
    See also CA 117

Dahl, Roald   1916- .... CLC 1, 6, 18
    See also CLR 1, 7
    See also CANR 6
    See also CA 1-4R
    See also SATA 1, 26

Dahlberg, Edward
    1900-1977.............. CLC 1, 7, 14
    See also CA 9-12R
    See also obituary CA 69-72
    See also DLB 48

Daly, Maureen   1921-.............. CLC 17
    See also McGivern, Maureen Daly
    See also SAAS 1
    See also SATA 2

Däniken, Erich von   1935-
    See Von Däniken, Erich

Dannay, Frederic   1905-1982
    See Queen, Ellery
    See also CANR 1
    See also CA 1-4R
    See also obituary CA 107

D'Annunzio, Gabriele
    1863-1938.................. TCLC 6
    See also CA 104

Danziger, Paula   1944-............. CLC 21
    See also CA 112, 115
    See also SATA 30, 36

Darío, Rubén   1867-1916.......... TCLC 4
    See also Sarmiento, Felix Ruben Garcia
    See also CA 104

Darley, George   1795-1846 .... NCLC 2

Daryush, Elizabeth
    1887-1977................. CLC 6, 19
    See also CANR 3
    See also CA 49-52
    See also DLB 20

Daudet, (Louis Marie) Alphonse
    1840-1897.................. NCLC 1

Daumal, René   1908-1944 .... TCLC 14
    See also CA 114

Davenport, Guy (Mattison, Jr.)
    1927-.................. CLC 6, 14, 38
    See also CA 33-36R

Davidson, Donald (Grady)
    1893-1968............. CLC 2, 13, 19
    See also CANR 4
    See also CA 5-8R
    See also obituary CA 25-28R
    See also DLB 45

Davidson, John   1857-1909 .... TCLC 24
    See also CA 118
    See also DLB 19

Davidson, Sara   1943- .... CLC 9
    See also CA 81-84

Davie, Donald (Alfred)
    1922-................... CLC 5, 8, 10, 31
    See also CAAS 3
    See also CANR 1
    See also CA 1-4R
    See also DLB 27

Davies, Ray(mond Douglas)
    1944-....................... CLC 21
    See also CA 116

Davies, Rhys   1903-1978 .... CLC 23
    See also CANR 4
    See also CA 9-12R
    See also obituary CA 81-84

Davies, (William) Robertson
    1913-............ CLC 2, 7, 13, 25, 42
    See also CANR 17
    See also CA 33-36R

Davies, W(illiam) H(enry)
1871-1940................... **TCLC 5**
See also CA 104
See also DLB 19

Davis, H(arold) L(enoir)
1896-1960.................... **CLC 49**
See also obituary CA 89-92
See also DLB 9

Davis, Rebecca (Blaine) Harding
1831-1910................ **TCLC 6**
See also CA 104

Davis, Richard Harding
1864-1916................ **TCLC 24**
See also CA 114
See also DLB 12, 23

Davison, Frank Dalby
1893-1970.................... **CLC 15**
See also obituary CA 116

Davison, Peter 1928-............ **CLC 28**
See also CAAS 4
See also CANR 3
See also CA 9-12R
See also DLB 5

Davys, Mary 1674-1732............ **LC 1**
See also DLB 39

Dawson, Fielding 1930-............ **CLC 6**
See also CA 85-88

Day, Clarence (Shepard, Jr.)
1874-1935................ **TCLC 25**
See also CA 108
See also DLB 11

Day Lewis, C(ecil)
1904-1972.............. **CLC 1, 6, 10**
See also CAP 1
See also CA 15-16
See also obituary CA 33-36R
See also DLB 15, 20

Day, Thomas 1748-1789............. **LC 1**
See also YABC 1
See also DLB 39

Dazai Osamu 1909-1948........ **TCLC 11**
See also Tsushima Shūji

De Crayencour, Marguerite 1903-
See Yourcenar, Marguerite

Deer, Sandra 1940-............... **CLC 45**

Defoe, Daniel 1660?-1731........... **LC 1**
See also SATA 22
See also DLB 39

De Hartog, Jan 1914-............. **CLC 19**
See also CANR 1
See also CA 1-4R

Deighton, Len 1929-......**CLC 4, 7, 22, 46**
See also Deighton, Leonard Cyril

Deighton, Leonard Cyril 1929-
See Deighton, Len
See also CANR 19
See also CA 9-12R

De la Mare, Walter (John)
1873-1956................. **TCLC 4**
See also CA 110
See also SATA 16
See also DLB 19

Delaney, Shelagh 1939-............ **CLC 29**
See also CA 17-20R
See also DLB 13

Delany, Samuel R(ay, Jr.)
1942-............... **CLC 8, 14, 38**
See also CA 81-84
See also DLB 8, 33

De la Roche, Mazo 1885-1961......**CLC 14**
See also CA 85-88

Delbanco, Nicholas (Franklin)
1942-................ **CLC 6, 13**
See also CAAS 2
See also CA 17-20R
See also DLB 6

Del Castillo, Michel 1933-........**CLC 38**
See also CA 109

Deledda, Grazia 1875-1936......**TCLC 23**

Delibes (Setien), Miguel
1920-................... **CLC 8, 18**
See also CANR 1
See also CA 45-48

DeLillo, Don
1936-...... **CLC 8, 10, 13, 27, 39** (115)
See also CANR 21
See also CA 81-84
See also DLB 6

De Lisser, H(erbert) G(eorge)
1878-1944................ **TCLC 12**
See also CA 109

Deloria, Vine (Victor), Jr.
1933-....................**CLC 21**
See also CANR 5, 20
See also CA 53-56
See also SATA 21

Del Vecchio, John M(ichael)
1947-....................**CLC 29**
See also CA 110

Denby, Edwin (Orr)
1903-1983....................**CLC 48**
See also obituary CA 110

Dennis, Nigel (Forbes) 1912-........**CLC 8**
See also CA 25-28R
See also DLB 13, 15

De Palma, Brian 1940-............**CLC 20**
See also CA 109

De Quincey, Thomas
1785-1859................. **NCLC 4**

Deren, Eleanora 1908-1961
See Deren, Maya
See also obituary CA 111

Deren, Maya 1908-1961 ....**CLC 16**
See also Deren, Eleanora

Derleth, August (William)
1909-1971....................**CLC 31**
See also CANR 4
See also CA 1-4R
See also obituary CA 29-32R
See also SATA 5
See also DLB 9

Derrida, Jacques 1930-............**CLC 24**

Desai, Anita 1937-............ **CLC 19, 37**
See also CA 81-84

De Saint-Luc, Jean 1909-1981
See Glassco, John

De Sica, Vittorio 1902-1974.......**CLC 20**
See also obituary CA 117

Desnos, Robert 1900-1945 ....**TCLC 22**
See also CA 121

Destouches, Louis-Ferdinand-Auguste
1894-1961
See Céline, Louis-Ferdinand
See also CA 85-88

Deutsch, Babette 1895-1982........**CLC 18**
See also CANR 4
See also CA 1-4R
See also obituary CA 108
See also DLB 45
See also SATA 1
See also obituary SATA 33

Devkota, Laxmiprasad
1909-1959................. **TCLC 23**

DeVoto, Bernard (Augustine)
1897-1955................. **TCLC 29**
See also CA 113
See also DLB 9

De Vries, Peter
1910-........**CLC 1, 2, 3, 7, 10, 28, 46**
See also CA 17-20R
See also DLB 6
See also DLB-Y 82

Dexter, Pete 1943-........... **CLC 34** (43)

Diamond, Neil (Leslie) 1941-.......**CLC 30**
See also CA 108

Dick, Philip K(indred)
1928-1982................ **CLC 10, 30**
See also CANR 2, 16
See also CA 49-52
See also obituary CA 106
See also DLB 8

Dickens, Charles
1812-1870.............**NCLC 3, 8, 18**
See also SATA 15
See also DLB 21, 55, 70

Dickey, James (Lafayette)
1923-........**CLC 1, 2, 4, 7, 10, 15, 47**
See also CANR 10
See also CA 9-12R
See also CABS 2
See also DLB 5
See also DLB-Y 82
See also AITN 1, 2

Dickey, William 1928-........ **CLC 3, 28**
See also CA 9-12R
See also DLB 5

Dickinson, Charles 1952-..........**CLC 49**

Dickinson, Peter (Malcolm de Brissac)
1927-.................... **CLC 12, 35**
See also CA 41-44R
See also SATA 5

Didion, Joan 1934- .... **CLC 1, 3, 8, 14, 32**
See also CANR 14
See also CA 5-8R
See also DLB 2
See also DLB-Y 81, 86
See also AITN 1

Dillard, Annie 1945- ....**CLC 9**
See also CANR 3
See also CA 49-52
See also SATA 10
See also DLB-Y 80

Dillard, R(ichard) H(enry) W(ilde)
1937-....................**CLC 5**
See also CAAS 7
See also CANR 10
See also CA 21-24R
See also DLB 5

Fauset, Jessie Redmon
1884?-1961....................CLC 19
See also CA 109
See also DLB 51

Faust, Irvin 1924-..................CLC 8
See also CA 33-36R
See also DLB 2, 28
See also DLB-Y 80

Fearing, Kenneth (Flexner)
1902-1961....................CLC 51
See also CA 93-96
See also DLB 9

Federman, Raymond 1928-.....CLC 6, 47
See also CANR 10
See also CA 17-20R
See also DLB-Y 80

Federspiel, J(ürg) F. 1931-........CLC 42

Feiffer, Jules 1929-............CLC 2, 8
See also CA 17-20R
See also SATA 8
See also DLB 7, 44

Feinstein, Elaine 1930-............CLC 36
See also CA 69-72
See also CAAS 1
See also DLB 14, 40

Feldman, Irving (Mordecai)
1928-........................CLC 7
See also CANR 1
See also CA 1-4R

Fellini, Federico 1920-............CLC 16
See also CA 65-68

Felsen, Gregor 1916-
See Felsen, Henry Gregor

Felsen, Henry Gregor 1916-.......CLC 17
See also CANR 1
See also CA 1-4R
See also SAAS 2
See also SATA 1

Fenton, James (Martin) 1949-......CLC 32
See also CA 102
See also DLB 40

Ferber, Edna 1887-1968...........CLC 18
See also CA 5-8R
See also obituary CA 25-28R
See also SATA 7
See also DLB 9, 28
See also AITN 1

Ferlinghetti, Lawrence (Monsanto)
1919?-...............CLC 2, 6, 10, 27
See also CANR 3
See also CA 5-8R
See also DLB 5, 16
See also CDALB 1941-1968

Ferrier, Susan (Edmonstone)
1782-1854................... NCLC 8

Feuchtwanger, Lion
1884-1958................... TCLC 3
See also CA 104

Feydeau, Georges 1862-1921..... TCLC 22
See also CA 113

Fiedler, Leslie A(aron)
1917-.............. CLC 4, 13, 24
See also CANR 7
See also CA 9-12R
See also DLB 28

Field, Andrew 1938-........ CLC 44 (463)
See also CA 97-100

Field, Eugene 1850-1895 .... NCLC 3
See also SATA 16
See also DLB 21, 23, 42

Fielding, Henry 1707-1754.......... LC 1
See also DLB 39

Fielding, Sarah 1710-1768 .... LC 1
See also DLB 39

Fierstein, Harvey 1954- ....CLC 33

Figes, Eva 1932-..................CLC 31
See also CANR 4
See also CA 53-56
See also DLB 14

Finch, Robert (Duer Claydon)
1900-........................CLC 18
See also CANR 9
See also CA 57-60

Findley, Timothy 1930-...........CLC 27
See also CANR 12
See also CA 25-28R
See also DLB 53

Fink, Janis 1951-
See Ian, Janis

Firbank, (Arthur Annesley) Ronald
1886-1926................... TCLC 1
See also CA 104
See also DLB 36

Firbank, Louis 1944-
See Reed, Lou

Fisher, Roy 1930-.................CLC 25
See also CANR 16
See also CA 81-84
See also DLB 40

Fisher, Rudolph 1897-1934 ...... TCLC 11
See also CA 107
See also DLB 51

Fisher, Vardis (Alvero)
1895-1968....................CLC 7
See also CA 5-8R
See also obituary CA 25-28R
See also DLB 9

FitzGerald, Edward
1809-1883................... NCLC 9
See also DLB 32

Fitzgerald, F(rancis) Scott (Key)
1896-1940.......... TCLC 1, 6, 14, 28
See also CA 110
See also DLB 4, 9
See also DLB-Y 81
See also DLB-DS 1
See also AITN 1

Fitzgerald, Penelope 1916-..... CLC 19, 51
See also CA 85-88
See also DLB 14

Fitzgerald, Robert (Stuart)
1910-1985.......... CLC 39 (318; 470)
See also CANR 1
See also CA 2R
See also obituary CA 114
See also DLB-Y 80

FitzGerald, Robert D(avid)
1902-........................CLC 19
See also CA 17-20R

Flanagan, Thomas (James Bonner)
1923-........................CLC 25
See also CA 108
See also DLB-Y 80

Flaubert, Gustave
1821-1880............NCLC 2, 10, 19

Fleming, Ian (Lancaster)
1908-1964............... CLC 3, 30
See also CA 5-8R
See also SATA 9

Fleming, Thomas J(ames)
1927-........................CLC 37
See also CANR 10
See also CA 5-8R
See also SATA 8

Flieg, Hellmuth
See also Heym, Stefan

Flying Officer X 1905-1974
See Bates, H(erbert) E(rnest)

Fo, Dario 1929-..................CLC 32
See also CA 116

Follett, Ken(neth Martin)
1949-........................CLC 18
See also CANR 13
See also CA 81-84
See also DLB-Y 81

Foote, Horton 1916- ....CLC 51
See also CA 73-76
See also DLB 26

Forbes, Esther 1891-1967.........CLC 12
See also CAP 1
See also CA 13-14
See also obituary CA 25-28R
See also DLB 22
See also SATA 2

Forché, Carolyn 1950-............CLC 25
See also CA 109, 117
See also DLB 5

Ford, Ford Madox
1873-1939............... TCLC 1, 15
See also CA 104
See also DLB 34

Ford, John 1895-1973.............CLC 16
See also obituary CA 45-48

Ford, Richard 1944-..............CLC 46
See also CANR 11
See also CA 69-72

Foreman, Richard 1937-..... CLC 50 (159)
See also CA 65-68

Forester, C(ecil) S(cott)
1899-1966....................CLC 35
See also CA 73-76
See also obituary CA 25-28R
See also SATA 13

Forman, James D(ouglas)
1932-........................CLC 21
See also CANR 4, 19
See also CA 9-12R
See also SATA 8, 21

Fornes, Maria Irene
1930-................. CLC 39 (135)
See also CA 25-28R
See also DLB 7

Forrest, Leon 1937-................CLC 4
See also CAAS 7
See also CA 89-92
See also DLB 33

Author Index

Kennedy, Joseph Charles 1929-
See Kennedy, X. J.
See also CANR 4
See also CA 1-4R
See also SATA 14

Kennedy, William
1928-.............CLC 6, 28, 34 (205)
See also CANR 14
See also CA 85-88
See also DLB-Y 85

Kennedy, X. J. 1929- .... CLC 8, 42
See also Kennedy, Joseph Charles
See also DLB 5

Kerouac, Jack
1922-1969...... CLC 1, 2, 3, 5, 14, 29
See also Kerouac, Jean-Louis Lebrid de
See also DLB 2, 16
See also DLB-DS 3
See also CDALB 1941-1968

Kerouac, Jean-Louis Lebrid de 1922-1969
See Kerouac, Jack
See also CA 5-8R
See also obituary CA 25-28R
See also CDALB 1941-1968
See also AITN 1

Kerr, Jean 1923-.................CLC 22
See also CANR 7
See also CA 5-8R

Kerr, M. E. 1927-............ CLC 12, 35
See also Meaker, Marijane
See also SAAS 1

Kerrigan, (Thomas) Anthony
1918-..................... CLC 4, 6
See also CANR 4
See also CA 49-52

Kesey, Ken (Elton)
1935-............ CLC 1, 3, 6, 11, 46
See also CANR 22
See also CA 1-4R
See also DLB 2, 16

Kesselring, Joseph (Otto)
1902-1967...................CLC 45

Kessler, Jascha (Frederick)
1929-.......................CLC 4
See also CANR 8
See also CA 17-20R

Kettelkamp, Larry 1933-..........CLC 12
See also CANR 16
See also CA 29-32R
See also SAAS 3
See also SATA 2

Kherdian, David 1931-.......... CLC 6, 9
See also CAAS 2
See also CA 21-24R
See also SATA 16

Khlebnikov, Velimir (Vladimirovich)
1885-1922.................. TCLC 20
See also CA 117

Khodasevich, Vladislav (Felitsianovich)
1886-1939.................. TCLC 15
See also CA 115

Kielland, Alexander (Lange)
1849-1906.................. TCLC 5
See also CA 104

Kiely, Benedict 1919- .... CLC 23, 43
See also CANR 2
See also CA 1-4R
See also DLB 15

Kienzle, William X(avier)
1928-.......................CLC 25
See also CAAS 1
See also CANR 9
See also CA 93-96

Killens, John Oliver 1916-.........CLC 10
See also CAAS 2
See also CA 77-80
See also DLB 33

Killigrew, Anne 1660-1685.......... LC 4

Kincaid, Jamaica 1949?- ....CLC 43

King, Francis (Henry) 1923- ....CLC 8
See also CANR 1
See also CA 1-4R
See also DLB 15

King, Stephen (Edwin)
1947-................... CLC 12, 26, 37
See also CANR 1
See also CA 61-64
See also SATA 9
See also DLB-Y 80

Kingman, (Mary) Lee 1919- ....CLC 17
See also Natti, (Mary) Lee
See also CA 5-8R
See also SATA 1

Kingsley, Sidney 1906- ...... CLC 44 (229)
See also CA 85-88
See also DLB 7

Kingston, Maxine Hong
1940-.................... CLC 12, 19
See also CANR 13
See also CA 69-72
See also SATA 53
See also DLB-Y 80

Kinnell, Galway
1927-........... CLC 1, 2, 3, 5, 13, 29
See also CANR 10
See also CA 9-12R
See also DLB 5

Kinsella, Thomas 1928- ..... CLC 4, 19, 43
See also CANR 15
See also CA 17-20R
See also DLB 27

Kinsella, W(illiam) P(atrick)
1935-................... CLC 27, 43
See also CAAS 7
See also CANR 21
See also CA 97-100

Kipling, (Joseph) Rudyard
1865-1936............. TCLC 8, 17
See also CA 20, 105
See also YABC 2
See also DLB 19, 34

Kirkup, James 1918-...............CLC 1
See also CAAS 4
See also CANR 2
See also CA 1-4R
See also SATA 12
See also DLB 27

Kirkwood, James 1930- ....CLC 9
See also CANR 6
See also CA 1-4R
See also AITN 2

Kizer, Carolyn (Ashley)
1925-................. CLC 15, 39 (168)
See also CAAS 5
See also CA 65-68
See also DLB 5

Klausner, Amos 1939-
See Oz, Amos

Klein, A(braham) M(oses)
1909-1972...................CLC 19
See also CA 101
See also obituary CA 37-40R

Klein, Norma 1938-...............CLC 30
See also CLR 2
See also CANR 15
See also CA 41-44R
See also SAAS 1
See also SATA 7

Klein, T.E.D. 19??-.......... CLC 34 (70)
See also CA 119

Kleist, Heinrich von
1777-1811................... NCLC 2

Klimentev, Andrei Platonovich 1899-1951
See Platonov, Andrei (Platonovich)
See also CA 108

Klinger, Friedrich Maximilian von
1752-1831................... NCLC 1

Klopstock, Friedrich Gottlieb
1724-1803................. NCLC 11

Knebel, Fletcher 1911-............CLC 14
See also CAAS 3
See also CANR 1
See also CA 1-4R
See also SATA 36
See also AITN 1

Knight, Etheridge 1931-...........CLC 40
See also CA 21-24R
See also DLB 41

Knight, Sarah Kemble 1666-1727..... LC 7
See also DLB 24

Knowles, John 1926-......CLC 1, 4, 10, 26
See also CA 17-20R
See also SATA 8
See also DLB 6

Koch, C(hristopher) J(ohn)
1932-.......................CLC 42

Koch, Kenneth
1925-.............CLC 5, 8, 44 (239)
See also CANR 6
See also CA 1-4R
See also DLB 5

Kock, Charles Paul de
1794-1871................. NCLC 16

Koestler, Arthur
1905-1983....... CLC 1, 3, 6, 8, 15, 33
See also CANR 1
See also CA 1-4R
See also obituary CA 109
See also DLB-Y 83

Kohout, Pavel 1928-..............CLC 13
See also CANR 3
See also CA 45-48

Konrád, György 1933- .... CLC 4, 10
See also CA 85-88

Konwicki, Tadeusz 1926-....... CLC 8, 28
See also CA 101

Kopit, Arthur (Lee)
1937-................. CLC 1, 18, 33
See also CA 81-84
See also DLB 7
See also AITN 1

Nelligan, Émile 1879-1941 .... **TCLC 14**
See also CA 114

Nelson, Willie 1933- .... **CLC 17**
See also CA 107

Nemerov, Howard
1920- .... **CLC 2, 6, 9, 36**
See also CANR 1
See also CA 1-4R
See also CABS 2
See also DLB 5, 6
See also DLB-Y 83

Neruda, Pablo
1904-1973 .... **CLC 1, 2, 5, 7, 9, 28**
See also CAP 2
See also CA 19-20
See also obituary CA 45-48

Nerval, Gérard de 1808-1855 ..... **NCLC 1**

Nervo, (José) Amado (Ruiz de)
1870-1919 .... **TCLC 11**
See also CA 109

Neufeld, John (Arthur) 1938- ...... **CLC 17**
See also CANR 11
See also CA 25-28R
See also SAAS 3
See also SATA 6

Neville, Emily Cheney 1919- .... **CLC 12**
See also CANR 3
See also CA 5-8R
See also SAAS 2
See also SATA 1

Newbound, Bernard Slade 1930-
See Slade, Bernard
See also CA 81-84

Newby, P(ercy) H(oward)
1918- .... **CLC 2, 13**
See also CA 5-8R
See also DLB 15

Newlove, Donald 1928- .... **CLC 6**
See also CA 29-32R

Newlove, John (Herbert) 1938- ..... **CLC 14**
See also CANR 9
See also CA 21-24R

Newman, Charles 1938- .... **CLC 2, 8**
See also CA 21-24R

Newman, Edwin (Harold)
1919- .... **CLC 14**
See also CANR 5
See also CA 69-72
See also AITN 1

Newton, Suzanne 1936- .... **CLC 35**
See also CANR 14
See also CA 41-44R
See also SATA 5

Ngugi, James (Thiong'o)
1938- .... **CLC 3, 7, 13, 36**
See also Ngugi wa Thiong'o
See also Wa Thiong'o, Ngugi
See also CA 81-84

Ngugi wa Thiong'o
1938- .... **CLC 3, 7, 13, 36**
See also Ngugi, James (Thiong'o)
See also Wa Thiong'o, Ngugi

Nichol, B(arrie) P(hillip) 1944- ..... **CLC 18**
See also CA 53-56
See also DLB 53

Nichols, John (Treadwell)
1940- .... **CLC 38**
See also CAAS 2
See also CANR 6
See also CA 9-12R
See also DLB-Y 82

Nichols, Peter (Richard)
1927- .... **CLC 5, 36**
See also CA 104
See also DLB 13

Nicolas, F.R.E. 1927-
See Freeling, Nicolas

Niedecker, Lorine
1903-1970 .... **CLC 10, 42**
See also CAP 2
See also CA 25-28
See also DLB 48

Nietzsche, Friedrich (Wilhelm)
1844-1900 .... **TCLC 10, 18**
See also CA 107

Nightingale, Anne Redmon 1943-
See Redmon (Nightingale), Anne
See also CA 103

Nin, Anaïs
1903-1977 .... **CLC 1, 4, 8, 11, 14**
See also CANR 22
See also CA 13-16R
See also obituary CA 69-72
See also DLB 2, 4
See also AITN 2

Nissenson, Hugh 1933- .... **CLC 4, 9**
See also CA 17-20R
See also DLB 28

Niven, Larry 1938- .... **CLC 8**
See also Niven, Laurence Van Cott
See also DLB 8

Niven, Laurence Van Cott 1938-
See Niven, Larry
See also CANR 14
See also CA 21-24R

Nixon, Agnes Eckhardt 1927- ...... **CLC 21**
See also CA 110

Nkosi, Lewis 1936- .... **CLC 45**
See also CA 65-68

Nodier, (Jean) Charles (Emmanuel)
1780-1844 .... **NCLC 19**

Nordhoff, Charles 1887-1947 ..... **TCLC 23**
See also CA 108
See also SATA 23
See also DLB 9

Norman, Marsha 1947- .... **CLC 28**
See also CA 105
See also DLB-Y 84

Norris, (Benjamin) Frank(lin)
1870-1902 .... **TCLC 24**
See also CA 110
See also DLB 12, 71
See also CDALB 1865-1917

Norris, Leslie 1921- .... **CLC 14**
See also CANR 14
See also CAP 1
See also CA 11-12
See also DLB 27

North, Andrew 1912-
See Norton, Andre

North, Christopher 1785-1854
See Wilson, John

Norton, Alice Mary 1912-
See Norton, Andre
See also CANR 2
See also CA 1-4R
See also SATA 1, 43

Norton, Andre 1912- .... **CLC 12**
See also Norton, Mary Alice
See also DLB 8, 52

Norway, Nevil Shute 1899-1960
See Shute (Norway), Nevil
See also CA 102
See also obituary CA 93-96

Norwid, Cyprian Kamil
1821-1883 .... **NCLC 17**

Nossack, Hans Erich 1901-1978 ..... **CLC 6**
See also CA 93-96
See also obituary CA 85-88
See also DLB 69

Nova, Craig 1945- .... **CLC 7, 31**
See also CANR 2
See also CA 45-48

Novalis 1772-1801 .... **NCLC 13**

Nowlan, Alden (Albert) 1933- ...... **CLC 15**
See also CANR 5
See also CA 9-12R
See also DLB 53

Noyes, Alfred 1880-1958 .... **TCLC 7**
See also CA 104
See also DLB 20

Nunn, Kem 19??- .... **CLC 34 (94)**

Nye, Robert 1939- .... **CLC 13, 42**
See also CA 33-36R
See also SATA 6
See also DLB 14

Nyro, Laura 1947- .... **CLC 17**

Oates, Joyce Carol
1938- ..... **CLC 1, 2, 3, 6, 9, 11, 15, 19, 33**
See also CA 5-8R
See also DLB 2, 5
See also DLB-Y 81
See also AITN 1

O'Brien, Darcy 1939- .... **CLC 11**
See also CANR 8
See also CA 21-24R

O'Brien, Edna
1932- .... **CLC 3, 5, 8, 13, 36**
See also CANR 6
See also CA 1-4R
See also DLB 14

O'Brien, Flann
1911-1966 ...... **CLC 1, 4, 5, 7, 10, 47**
See also O Nuallain, Brian

O'Brien, Richard 19??- .... **CLC 17**

O'Brien, (William) Tim(othy)
1946- .... **CLC 7, 19, 40**
See also CA 85-88
See also DLB-Y 80

Obstfelder, Sigbjørn
1866-1900 .... **TCLC 23**

O'Casey, Sean
1880-1964 .... **CLC 1, 5, 9, 11, 15**
See also CA 89-92
See also DLB 10

Ochs, Phil 1940-1976 .... **CLC 17**
See also obituary CA 65-68

Author Index

Robbe-Grillet, Alain
1922- ..... **CLC 1, 2, 4, 6, 8, 10, 14, 43**
See also CA 9-12R

Robbins, Harold 1916- ....**CLC 5**
See also CA 73-76

Robbins, Thomas Eugene 1936-
See Robbins, Tom
See also CA 81-84

Robbins, Tom 1936- ....**CLC 9, 32**
See also Robbins, Thomas Eugene
See also DLB-Y 80

Robbins, Trina 1938- ....**CLC 21**

Roberts, (Sir) Charles G(eorge) D(ouglas)
1860-1943.................**TCLC 8**
See also CA 105
See also SATA 29

Roberts, Kate 1891-1985 ....**CLC 15**
See also CA 107
See also obituary CA 116

Roberts, Keith (John Kingston)
1935-.......................**CLC 14**
See also CA 25-28R

Roberts, Kenneth 1885-1957 .....**TCLC 23**
See also CA 109
See also DLB 9

Roberts, Michèle (B.) 1949-........**CLC 48**
See also CA 115

Robinson, Edwin Arlington
1869-1935................**TCLC 5**
See also CA 104
See also DLB 54
See also CDALB 1865-1917

Robinson, Henry Crabb
1775-1867.................**NCLC 15**

Robinson, Jill 1936-...............**CLC 10**
See also CA 102

Robinson, Kim Stanley
19??- ....**CLC 34** (105)

Robinson, Marilynne 1944- ....**CLC 25**
See also CA 116

Robinson, Smokey 1940- ....**CLC 21**

Robinson, William 1940-
See Robinson, Smokey
See also CA 116

Robison, Mary 1949-..............**CLC 42**
See also CA 113, 116

Roddenberry, Gene 1921- ....**CLC 17**

Rodgers, Mary 1931- ....**CLC 12**
See also CANR 8
See also CA 49-52
See also SATA 8

Rodgers, W(illiam) R(obert)
1909-1969.....................**CLC 7**
See also CA 85-88
See also DLB 20

Rodríguez, Claudio 1934-..........**CLC 10**

Roethke, Theodore (Huebner)
1908-1963...... **CLC 1, 3, 8, 11, 19, 46**
See also CA 81-84
See also CABS 2
See also SAAS 1
See also DLB 5
See also CDALB 1941-1968

Rogers, Sam 1943-
See Shepard, Sam

Rogers, Will(iam Penn Adair)
1879-1935..................**TCLC 8**
See also CA 105
See also DLB 11

Rogin, Gilbert 1929-..............**CLC 18**
See also CANR 15
See also CA 65-68

Rohan, Kōda 1867-1947........**TCLC 22**

Rohmer, Eric 1920-................**CLC 16**
See also Scherer, Jean-Marie Maurice

Rohmer, Sax 1883-1959 ....**TCLC 28**
See also Ward, Arthur Henry Sarsfield
See also DLB 70

Roiphe, Anne (Richardson)
1935-.......................**CLC 3, 9**
See also CA 89-92
See also DLB-Y 80

Rolfe, Frederick (William Serafino Austin
Lewis Mary) 1860-1913.....**TCLC 12**
See also CA 107
See also DLB 34

Rolland, Romain 1866-1944......**TCLC 23**
See also CA 118

Rölvaag, O(le) E(dvart)
1876-1931.................**TCLC 17**
See also CA 117
See also DLB 9

Romains, Jules 1885-1972 ....**CLC 7**
See also CA 85-88

Romero, José Rubén
1890-1952................**TCLC 14**
See also CA 114

Ronsard, Pierre de 1524-1585.......**LC 6**

Rooke, Leon 1934-....... **CLC 25, 34** (250)
See also CA 25-28R

Rosa, João Guimarães
1908-1967....................**CLC 23**
See also obituary CA 89-92

Rosen, Richard (Dean)
1949-.................. **CLC 39** (194)
See also CA 77-80

Rosenberg, Isaac 1890-1918......**TCLC 12**
See also CA 107
See also DLB 20

Rosenblatt, Joe 1933- ....**CLC 15**
See also Rosenblatt, Joseph
See also AITN 2

Rosenblatt, Joseph 1933-
See Rosenblatt, Joe
See also CA 89-92

Rosenfeld, Samuel 1896-1963
See Tzara, Tristan
See also obituary CA 89-92

Rosenthal, M(acha) L(ouis)
1917-.......................**CLC 28**
See also CAAS 6
See also CANR 4
See also CA 1-4R
See also DLB 5

Ross, (James) Sinclair 1908- ....**CLC 13**
See also CA 73-76

Rossetti, Christina Georgina
1830-1894..................**NCLC 2**
See also SATA 20
See also DLB 35

Rossetti, Dante Gabriel
1828-1882..................**NCLC 4**
See also DLB 35

Rossetti, Gabriel Charles Dante 1828-1882
See Rossetti, Dante Gabriel

Rossner, Judith (Perelman)
1935-...................**CLC 6, 9, 29**
See also CANR 18
See also CA 17-20R
See also DLB 6
See also AITN 2

Rostand, Edmond (Eugène Alexis)
1868-1918..................**TCLC 6**
See also CA 104

Roth, Henry 1906-...........**CLC 2, 6, 11**
See also CAP 1
See also CA 11-12
See also DLB 28

Roth, Philip (Milton)
1933-......**CLC 1, 2, 3, 4, 6, 9, 15, 22,**
31, 47
See also CANR 1, 22
See also CA 1-4R
See also DLB 2, 28
See also DLB-Y 82

Rothenberg, Jerome 1931-..........**CLC 6**
See also CANR 1
See also CA 45-48
See also DLB 5

Roumain, Jacques 1907-1944 ....**TCLC 19**
See also CA 117

Rourke, Constance (Mayfield)
1885-1941..................**TCLC 12**
See also CA 107
See also YABC 1

Rousseau, Jean-Baptiste
1671-1741......................**LC 9**

Roussel, Raymond 1877-1933 ....**TCLC 20**
See also CA 117

Rovit, Earl (Herbert) 1927-.........**CLC 7**
See also CA 5-8R
See also CANR 12

Rowe, Nicholas 1674-1718..........**LC 8**

Rowson, Susanna Haswell
1762-1824..................**NCLC 5**
See also DLB 37

Roy, Gabrielle 1909-1983......**CLC 10, 14**
See also CANR 5
See also CA 53-56
See also obituary CA 110

Różewicz, Tadeusz 1921- ....**CLC 9, 23**
See also CA 108

Ruark, Gibbons 1941-..............**CLC 3**
See also CANR 14
See also CA 33-36R

Rubens, Bernice 192?- .... **CLC 19, 31**
See also CA 25-28R
See also DLB 14

Rudkin, (James) David 1936- ......**CLC 14**
See also CA 89-92
See also DLB 13

Rudnik, Raphael 1933-.............**CLC 7**
See also CA 29-32R

Ruiz, José Martínez 1874-1967
See Azorín

Sartre, Jean-Paul
  1905-1980...... **CLC 1, 4, 7, 9, 13, 18, 24, 44** (493), **50** (369)
  See also CANR 21
  See also CA 9-12R
  See also obituary CA 97-100
  See also DLB 72

Sassoon, Siegfried (Lorraine)
  1886-1967....................**CLC 36**
  See also CA 104
  See also Obituary CA 25-28R
  See also DLB 20

Saul, John (W. III) 1942-.........**CLC 46**
  See also CANR 16
  See also CA 81-84

Saura, Carlos 1932-..............**CLC 20**
  See also CA 114

Sauser-Hall, Frédéric-Louis 1887-1961
  See Cendrars, Blaise
  See also CA 102
  See also obituary CA 93-96

Savage, Thomas 1915- ....**CLC 40**

Savan, Glenn 19??- .... **CLC 50** (77)

Sayers, Dorothy L(eigh)
  1893-1957................ **TCLC 2, 15**
  See also CA 104, 119
  See also DLB 10, 36

Sayers, Valerie 19??-........ **CLC 50** (82)

Sayles, John (Thomas)
  1950-..................**CLC 7, 10, 14**
  See also CA 57-60
  See also DLB 44

Scammell, Michael 19??- .... **CLC 34** (480)

Scannell, Vernon 1922-............**CLC 49**
  See also CANR 8
  See also CA 5-8R
  See also DLB 27

Schaeffer, Susan Fromberg
  1941-.................. **CLC 6, 11, 22**
  See also CANR 18
  See also CA 49-52
  See also SATA 22
  See also DLB 28

Schell, Jonathan 1943- ....**CLC 35**
  See also CANR 12
  See also CA 73-76

Scherer, Jean-Marie Maurice 1920-
  See Rohmer, Eric
  See also CA 110

Schevill, James (Erwin) 1920-.......**CLC 7**
  See also CA 5-8R

Schisgal, Murray (Joseph)
  1926-.........................**CLC 6**
  See also CA 21-24R

Schlee, Ann 1934- ....**CLC 35**
  See also CA 101
  See also SATA 36, 44

Schlegel, August Wilhelm von
  1767-1845..................**NCLC 15**

Schlegel, Johann Elias (von)
  1719?-1749....................**LC 5**

Schmitz, Ettore 1861-1928
  See Svevo, Italo
  See also CA 104

Schnackenberg, Gjertrud
  1953-......................**CLC 40**
  See also CA 116

Schneider, Leonard Alfred 1925-1966
  See Bruce, Lenny
  See also CA 89-92

Schnitzler, Arthur 1862-1931 ..... **TCLC 4**
  See also CA 104

Schorer, Mark 1908-1977 ....**CLC 9**
  See also CANR 7
  See also CA 5-8R
  See also obituary CA 73-76

Schrader, Paul (Joseph) 1946-......**CLC 26**
  See also CA 37-40R
  See also DLB 44

Schreiner (Cronwright), Olive (Emilie Albertina) 1855-1920 .... **TCLC 9**
  See also CA 105
  See also DLB 18

Schulberg, Budd (Wilson)
  1914-...................... **CLC 7, 48**
  See also CANR 19
  See also CA 25-28R
  See also DLB 6, 26, 28
  See also DLB-Y 81

Schulz, Bruno 1892-1942 .... **TCLC 5**
  See also CA 115

Schulz, Charles M(onroe)
  1922-......................**CLC 12**
  See also CANR 6
  See also CA 9-12R
  See also SATA 10

Schuyler, James (Marcus)
  1923-...................... **CLC 5, 23**
  See also CA 101
  See also DLB 5

Schwartz, Delmore
  1913-1966............**CLC 2, 4, 10, 45**
  See also CAP 2
  See also CA 17-18
  See also obituary CA 25-28R
  See also DLB 28, 48

Schwartz, Lynne Sharon 1939-.....**CLC 31**
  See also CA 103

Schwarz-Bart, André 1928-...... **CLC 2, 4**
  See also CA 89-92

Schwarz-Bart, Simone 1938-........**CLC 7**
  See also CA 97-100

Schwob, (Mayer Andre) Marcel
  1867-1905.................. **TCLC 20**
  See also CA 117

Sciascia, Leonardo 1921- ..... **CLC 8, 9, 41**
  See also CA 85-88

Scoppettone, Sandra 1936-........**CLC 26**
  See also CA 5-8R
  See also SATA 9

Scorsese, Martin 1942-............**CLC 20**
  See also CA 110, 114

Scotland, Jay 1932-
  See Jakes, John (William)

Scott, Duncan Campbell
  1862-1947.................. **TCLC 6**
  See also CA 104

Scott, Evelyn 1893-1963 ....**CLC 43**
  See also CA 104
  See also obituary CA 112
  See also DLB 9, 48

Scott, F(rancis) R(eginald)
  1899-1985...................**CLC 22**
  See also CA 101
  See also obituary CA 114

Scott, Joanna 19??-.......... **CLC 50** (88)

Scott, Paul (Mark) 1920-1978.......**CLC 9**
  See also CA 81-84
  See also obituary CA 77-80
  See also DLB 14

Scott, Sir Walter 1771-1832...... **NCLC 15**
  See also YABC 2

Scribe, (Augustin) Eugène
  1791-1861 .... **NCLC 16**

Scudéry, Madeleine de 1607-1701..... **LC 2**

Seare, Nicholas 1925-
  See Trevanian
  See also Whitaker, Rodney

Sebestyen, Igen 1924-
  See Sebestyen, Ouida

Sebestyen, Ouida 1924-............**CLC 30**
  See also CA 107
  See also SATA 39

Sedgwick, Catharine Maria
  1789-1867................. **NCLC 19**
  See also DLB 1

Seelye, John 1931-.................**CLC 7**
  See also CA 97-100

Seferiades, Giorgos Stylianou 1900-1971
  See Seferis, George
  See also CANR 5
  See also CA 5-8R
  See also obituary CA 33-36R

Seferis, George 1900-1971 ...... **CLC 5, 11**
  See also Seferiades, Giorgos Stylianou

Segal, Erich (Wolf) 1937-....... **CLC 3, 10**
  See also CANR 20
  See also CA 25-28R
  See also DLB-Y 86

Seger, Bob 1945- ....**CLC 35**

Seger, Robert Clark 1945-
  See Seger, Bob

Seghers, Anna 1900-1983...........**CLC 7**
  See Radvanyi, Netty Reiling
  See also DLB 69

Seidel, Frederick (Lewis) 1936-.....**CLC 18**
  See also CANR 8
  See also CA 13-16R
  See also DLB-Y 84

Seifert, Jaroslav
  1901-1986......**CLC 34** (255), **44** (421)

Selby, Hubert, Jr.
  1928-..................**CLC 1, 2, 4, 8**
  See also CA 13-16R
  See also DLB 2

Sénacour, Étienne Pivert de
  1770-1846................. **NCLC 16**

Sender, Ramón (José)
  1902-1982....................**CLC 8**
  See also CANR 8
  See also CA 5-8R
  See also obituary CA 105

Serling, (Edward) Rod(man)
  1924-1975....................**CLC 30**
  See also CA 65-68
  See also obituary CA 57-60
  See also DLB 26
  See also AITN 1

Serpières 1907-
See Guillevic, (Eugène)

Service, Robert W(illiam)
1874-1958................. **TCLC 15**
See also CA 115
See also SATA 20

Seth, Vikram 1952-...............**CLC 43**

Seton, Cynthia Propper
1926-1982....................**CLC 27**
See also CANR-7
See also CA 5-8R
See also obituary CA 108

Seton, Ernest (Evan) Thompson
1860-1946.................. **TCLC 31**
See also CA 109
See also SATA 18

Settle, Mary Lee 1918-............**CLC 19**
See also CAAS 1
See also CA 89-92
See also DLB 6

Sexton, Anne (Harvey)
1928-1974....... **CLC 2, 4, 6, 8, 10, 15**
See also CANR 3
See also CA 1-4R
See also obituary CA 53-56
See also CABS 2
See also SATA 10
See also DLB 5
See also CDALB 1941-1968

Shaara, Michael (Joseph)
1929-.......................**CLC 15**
See also CA 102
See also DLB-Y 83
See also AITN 1

Shackleton, C. C. 1925-
See Aldiss, Brian W(ilson)

Shacochis, Bob 1951- .... **CLC 39** (198)
See also CA 119

Shaffer, Anthony 1926-...........**CLC 19**
See also CA 110
See also CA 116
See also DLB 13

Shaffer, Peter (Levin)
1926-..............**CLC 5, 14, 18, 37**
See also CA 25-28R
See also DLB 13

Shalamov, Varlam (Tikhonovich)
1907?-1982...................**CLC 18**
See also obituary CA 105

Shamlu, Ahmad 1925- ....**CLC 10**

Shange, Ntozake 1948-......**CLC 8, 25, 38**
See also CA 85-88
See also DLB 38

Shapcott, Thomas W(illiam)
1935-.......................**CLC 38**
See also CA 69-72

Shapiro, Karl (Jay) 1913-..... **CLC 4, 8, 15**
See also CAAS 6
See also CANR 1
See also CA 1-4R
See also DLB 48

Sharpe, Tom 1928-..............**CLC 36**
See also CA 114
See also DLB 14

Shaw, (George) Bernard
1856-1950.............**TCLC 3, 9, 21**
See also CA 104, 109
See also DLB 10, 57

Shaw, Henry Wheeler
1818-1885................ **NCLC 15**
See also DLB 11

Shaw, Irwin
1913-1984........**CLC 7, 23, 34** (368)
See also CANR 21
See also CA 13-16R
See also obituary CA 112
See also DLB 6
See also DLB-Y 84
See also CDALB 1941-1968
See also AITN 1

Shaw, Robert 1927-1978 ....**CLC 5**
See also CANR 4
See also CA 1-4R
See also obituary CA 81-84
See also DLB 13, 14
See also AITN 1

Shawn, Wallace 1943-.............**CLC 41**
See also CA 112

Sheed, Wilfrid (John Joseph)
1930-.................. **CLC 2, 4, 10**
See also CA 65-68
See also DLB 6

Sheffey, Asa 1913-1980
See Hayden, Robert (Earl)

Sheldon, Alice (Hastings) B(radley)
1915-1987
See Tiptree, James, Jr.
See also CA 108
See also obituary CA 122

Shelley, Mary Wollstonecraft Godwin
1797-1851.................. **NCLC 14**
See also SATA 29

Shelley, Percy Bysshe
1792-1822.................. **NCLC 18**

Shepard, Jim 19??-................**CLC 36**

Shepard, Lucius 19??-....... **CLC 34** (108)

Shepard, Sam
1943-...... **CLC 4, 6, 17, 34** (264), **41,**
44 (263)
See also CANR 22
See also CA 69-72
See also DLB 7

Shepherd, Michael 1927-
See Ludlum, Robert

Sherburne, Zoa (Morin) 1912- .....**CLC 30**
See also CANR 3
See also CA 1-4R
See also SATA 3

Sheridan, Frances 1724-1766........ **LC 7**
See also DLB 39

Sheridan, Richard Brinsley
1751-1816................. **NCLC 5**

Sherman, Martin 19??-.............**CLC 19**
See also CA 116

Sherwin, Judith Johnson
1936-.................... **CLC 7, 15**
See also CA 25-28R

Sherwood, Robert E(mmet)
1896-1955................... **TCLC 3**
See also CA 104
See also DLB 7, 26

Shiel, M(atthew) P(hipps)
1865-1947.................. **TCLC 8**
See also CA 106

Shiga, Naoya 1883-1971..........**CLC 33**
See also CA 101
See also obituary CA 33-36R

Shimazaki, Haruki 1872-1943
See Shimazaki, Tōson
See also CA 105

Shimazaki, Tōson 1872-1943...... **TCLC 5**
See also Shimazaki, Haruki

Sholokhov, Mikhail (Aleksandrovich)
1905-1984................. **CLC 7, 15**
See also CA 101
See also obituary CA 112
See also SATA 36

Shreve, Susan Richards 1939-......**CLC 23**
See also CAAS 5
See also CANR 5
See also CA 49-52
See also SATA 41, 46

Shulman, Alix Kates 1932-...... **CLC 2, 10**
See also CA 29-32R
See also SATA 7

Shuster, Joe 1914-
See Siegel, Jerome and Shuster, Joe

Shute (Norway), Nevil
1899-1960....................**CLC 30**
See also Norway, Nevil Shute

Shuttle, Penelope (Diane) 1947-......**CLC 7**
See also CA 93-96
See also DLB 14, 40

Siegel, Jerome 1914-
See Siegel, Jerome and Shuster, Joe
See also CA 116

Siegel, Jerome 1914- and
Shuster, Joe 1914- ....**CLC 21**

Sienkiewicz, Henryk (Adam Aleksander Pius)
1846-1916................. **TCLC 3**
See also CA 104

Sigal, Clancy 1926- ....**CLC 7**
See also CA 1-4R

Sigüenza y Góngora, Carlos de
1645-1700.................... **LC 8**

Sigurjónsson, Jóhann
1880-1919................. **TCLC 27**

Silkin, Jon 1930- .... **CLC 2, 6, 43**
See also CAAS 5
See also CA 5-8R
See also DLB 27

Silko, Leslie Marmon 1948-........**CLC 23**
See also CA 115, 122

Sillanpää, Franz Eemil
1888-1964....................**CLC 19**
See also obituary CA 93-96

Sillitoe, Alan 1928- .... **CLC 1, 3, 6, 10, 19**
See also CAAS 2
See also CANR 8
See also CA 9-12R
See also DLB 14
See also AITN 1

Silone, Ignazio 1900-1978..........**CLC 4**
See also CAP 2
See also CA 25-28
See also obituary CA 81-84

Silver, Joan Micklin 1935-.........**CLC 20**
See also CA 114

Author Index

Author Index

NCLC Cumulative Nationality Index

Nationality Index

AMERICAN
Alcott, Amos Bronson 1
Alcott, Louisa May 6
Alger, Jr., Horatio 8
Allston, Washington 2
Bellamy, Edward 4
Bird, Robert Montgomery 1
Brackenridge, Hugh Henry 7
Brown, William Wells 2
Bryant, William Cullen 6
Calhoun, John Caldwell 15
Channing, William Ellery 17
Child, Lydia Maria 6
Cooke, John Esten 5
Cooper, James Fenimore 1
Crockett, David 8
Douglass, Frederick 7
Dunlap, William 2
Dwight, Timothy 13
Emerson, Ralph Waldo 1
Field, Eugene 3
Frederic, Harold 10
Freneau, Philip Morin 1
Fuller, Margaret 5
Hammon, Jupiter 5
Hawthorne, Nathaniel 2, 10, 17
Holmes, Oliver Wendell 14
Irving, Washington 2, 19
Jefferson, Thomas 11
Kennedy, John Pendleton 2
Lanier, Sidney 6
Lazarus, Emma 8
Lincoln, Abraham 18
Longfellow, Henry Wadsworth 2
Lowell, James Russell 2
Melville, Herman 3, 12
Parkman, Francis 12

Paulding, James Kirke 2
Poe, Edgar Allan 1, 16
Rowson, Susanna Haswell 5
Sedgwick, Catharine Maria 19
Shaw, Henry Wheeler 15
Simms, William Gilmore 3
Stowe, Harriet Beecher 3
Thoreau, Henry David 7
Tyler, Royall 3
Very, Jones 9
Warren, Mercy Otis 13
Whitman, Sarah Helen 19
Whitman, Walt 4
Whittier, John Greenleaf 8

ARGENTINE
Echeverría, Esteban 18
Hernández, José 17

AUSTRALIAN
Clarke, Marcus 19
Kendall, Henry 12

AUSTRIAN
Grillparzer, Franz 1
Lenau, Nikolaus 16

CANADIAN
Crawford, Isabella Valancy 12
Haliburton, Thomas Chandler 15
Moodie, Susanna 14

DANISH
Andersen, Hans Christian 7
Grundtvig, Nicolai Frederik Severin 1

ENGLISH
Ainsworth, William Harrison 13
Arnold, Matthew 6
Arnold, Thomas 18
Austen, Jane 1, 13, 19
Bagehot, Walter 10
Beardsley, Aubrey 6
Beckford, William 16
Beddoes, Thomas Lovell 3
Blake, William 13
Borrow, George 9
Brontë, Anne 4
Brontë, Charlotte 3, 8
Brontë, Emily 16
Browning, Elizabeth Barrett 1, 16
Browning, Robert 19
Bulwer-Lytton, Edward 1
Burney, Fanny 12
Byron, George Gordon, Lord Byron 2, 12
Carroll, Lewis 2
Clare, John 9
Coleridge, Samuel Taylor 9
Collins, Wilkie 1, 18
Cowper, William 8
De Quincey, Thomas 4
Dickens, Charles 3, 8, 18
Disraeli, Benjamin 2
Eden, Emily 10
Eliot, George 4, 13
FitzGerald, Edward 9
Forster, John 11
Gaskell, Elizabeth Cleghorn 5
Godwin, William 14
Hood, Thomas 16
Hopkins, Gerard Manley 17
Hunt, Leigh 1

Jerrold, Douglas 2
Keats, John 8
Kemble, Fanny 18
Lamb, Charles 10
Landon, Letitia Elizabeth 15
Landor, Walter Savage 14
Lear, Edward 3
Lewis, Matthew Gregory 11
Marryat, Frederick 3
Mill, John Stuart 11
Mitford, Mary Russell 4
Montagu, Elizabeth 7
Morris, William 4
Pater, Walter 7
Patmore, Coventry Kersey Dighton 9
Radcliffe, Ann 6
Reade, Charles 2
Reeve, Clara 19
Robinson, Henry Crabb 15
Rossetti, Christina Georgina 2
Rossetti, Dante Gabriel 4
Shelley, Mary Wollstonecraft Godwin 14
Shelley, Percy Bysshe 18
Southey, Robert 8
Surtees, Robert Smith 14
Thackeray, William Makepeace 5, 14
Trollope, Anthony 6
Wordsworth, William 12

FRENCH
Balzac, Honoré de 5
Banville, Théodore de 9
Barbey d'Aurevilly, Jules Amédée 1
Baudelaire, Charles 6
Becque, Henri 3

517

Chateaubriand, François René
de 3
Constant, Benjamin 6
Daudet, Alphonse 1
Dumas, Alexandre (*père*) 11
Dumas, Alexandre (*fils*) 9
Flaubert, Gustave 2, 10, 19
Fromentin, Eugène 10
Gaboriau, Émile 14
Gautier, Théophile 1
Gobineau, Joseph Arthur
de 17
Goncourt, Edmond de 7
Goncourt, Jules de 7
Hugo, Victor Marie 3, 10
Joubert, Joseph 9
Kock, Charles Paul de 16
Laclos, Pierre Ambroise
François Choderlos de 4
Laforgue, Jules 5
Lamartine, Alphonse de 11
Lautréamont, Comte de 12
Mallarmé, Stéphane 4
Maupassant, Guy de 1
Mérimée, Prosper 6
Musset, Alfred de 7
Nerval, Gérard de 1
Nodier, Charles 19
Rimbaud, Arthur 4
Sade, Donatien Alphonse
François, Comte de 3
Sainte-Beuve, Charles
Augustin 5
Sand, George 2
Scribe, Eugène 16
Sénancour, Étienne Pivert
de 16
Staël-Holstein, Anne Louise
Germaine Necker, Baronne
de 3
Sue, Eugène 1
Taine, Hippolyte Adolphe 15
Tocqueville, Alexis de 7
Verlaine, Paul 2
Vigny, Alfred de 7

Villiers de l'Isle Adam, Jean
Marie Mathias Philippe
Auguste, Comte de 3

GERMAN
Arnim, Achim von 5
Brentano, Clemens 1
Droste-Hülshoff, Annette Freiin
von 3
Eichendorff, Joseph Freiherr
von 8
Fouqué, Friedrich de La
Motte 2
Goethe, Johann Wolfgang
von 4
Grabbe, Christian Dietrich 2
Grimm, Jakob Ludwig Karl 3
Grimm, Wilhelm Karl 3
Heine, Heinrich 4
Herder, Johann Gottfried
von 8
Hoffmann, Ernst Theodor
Amadeus 2
Hölderlin, Friedrich 16
Immermann, Karl 4
Jean Paul 7
Kleist, Heinrich von 2
Klinger, Friedrich Maximilian
von 1
Klopstock, Friedrich 11
Ludwig, Otto 4
Marx, Karl 17
Mörike, Eduard 10
Novalis 13
Schlegel, August Wilhelm
von 15
Storm, Theodor 1
Tieck, Ludwig 5
Wagner, Richard 9
Wieland, Christoph Martin 17

GREEK
Solomos, Dionysios 15

HUNGARIAN
Madách, Imre 19

INDIAN
Chatterji, Bankim Chandra 19

IRISH
Banim, John 13
Banim, Michael 13
Carleton, William 3
Croker, John Wilson 10
Darley, George 2
Edgeworth, Maria 1
Griffin, Gerald 7
Le Fanu, Joseph Sheridan 9
Maginn, William 8
Maturin, Charles Robert 6
Moore, Thomas 6
Sheridan, Richard Brinsley 5

ITALIAN
Foscolo, Ugo 8

LITHUANIAN
Mapu, Abraham 18

NORWEGIAN
Wergeland, Henrik Arnold 5

POLISH
Fredro, Aleksander 8
Krasicki, Ignacy 8
Krasiński, Zygmunt 4
Mickiewicz, Adam 3
Norwid, Cyprian Kamil 17
Słowacki, Juliusz 15

RUSSIAN
Aksakov, Sergei
Timofeyvich 2
Belinski, Vissarion
Grigoryevich 5
Chernyshevsky, Nikolay
Gavrilovich 1
Dobrolyubov, Nikolai
Alexandrovich 5
Dostoevski, Fedor
Mikhailovich 2, 7

Gogol, Nikolai 5, 15
Goncharov, Ivan
Alexandrovich 1
Herzen, Aleksandr
Ivanovich 10
Karamzin, Nikolai
Mikhailovich 3
Krylov, Ivan Andreevich 1
Lermontov, Mikhail
Yuryevich 5
Nekrasov, Nikolai 11
Pushkin, Alexander 3
Saltykov, Mikhail
Evgrafovich 16

SCOTTISH
Baillie, Joanna 2
Campbell, Thomas 19
Ferrier, Susan 8
Galt, John 1
Hogg, James 4
Lockhart, John Gibson 6
Oliphant, Margaret 11
Scott, Sir Walter 15
Stevenson, Robert Louis 5, 14
Thomson, James 18
Wilson, John 5

SPANISH
Alarcón, Pedro Antonio de 1
Caballero, Fernán 10
Castro, Rosalía de 3
Larra, Mariano José de 17
Tamayo y Baus, Manuel 1
Zorrilla y Moral, José 6

SWEDISH
Bremer, Fredrika 11
Tegnér, Esias 2

SWISS
Amiel, Henri Frédéric 4
Keller, Gottfried 2
Wyss, Johann David 10